Current Issues in Monetary Theory and Policy

Current Issues in Monetary Theory and Policy

Second Edition

Edited by

Thomas M. Havrilesky
Duke University

John T. Boorman
International Monetary Fund

AHM Publishing Corporation
Arlington Heights, Illinois 60004

ISBN: 0-88295-406-7
Library of Congress Card Number: 79-55733
PRINTED IN THE UNITED STATES OF AMERICA
7119

Contents

Preface to the Second Edition

Controversy regarding monetary theory and policy has changed considerably in recent years. The debate concerning at least two of the several issues that were the focus of the first edition—the role of the money supply versus interest rates in monetary stabilization policy and the relative merits of Keynesian versus Monetarist macroeconometric models of the economy—has shifted to anterior, more fundamental questions. Instead of arguing about whether various monetary aggregates or interest rates are the appropriate variables upon which policymakers should focus, many question whether the politicization of monetary policy makes an optimal choice possible on purely economic grounds. To reflect this development, a new section entitled "The Political Economy of Monetary Policymaking" replaces numerous readings on the money versus interest rates issue. Moreover, the section entitled "The Implementation of Monetary Policy" now contains a reading regarding the difficulty of measuring monetary aggregates in a rapidly changing regulatory environment.

Controversy over Keynesian versus Monetarist macroeconometric models has yielded to a questioning of whether stabilization policy, using *any* model, is feasible. The rational expectations hypothesis (in conjunction with the expectations-augmented Phillips curve) suggests that policy-induced changes in aggregate output and employment may be possible only when policymakers behave in an unanticipated manner. A regime of unanticipated policy surprises can hardly be labeled "stabilization policy."

In order to reflect this new development much of the material on macro-econometric models has been displaced by a new section entitled "The Phillips Curve, Rational Expectations, and Policy Stabilization." The two new sections together with new articles (on portfolio theory, the term structure of interest rates, and the derivation of the monetary base) that complement older material make this a truly current collection of readings.

We are grateful to Ralph Byrnes, Joseph Crews, Richard Froyen, Edward Kane, George Kaufman, Herbert Kaufman, Raymond Lombra, Thomas Mayer, Robert Rasche, Robert Schweitzer, and William Yohe for their guidance during the selection of readings; Maureen Trobec for her assistance in the production process; and our editors, Roger Williams and Harlan Davidson, for their encouragement and help during all stages of this preparation. Finally, we congratulate all contributors to this volume for their contribution to scholarship.

THOMAS M. HAVRILESKY
Durham, North Carolina

JOHN T. BOORMAN
Washington, D.C.

April 1979

Preface to the First Edition

Monetary theory and policy have been among the more controversial areas in economics in recent years. The continuing debate between Keynesians and Monetarists rages not only in scholarly journals but also in the financial press and increasingly in the political sphere.

As the struggle goes on, it becomes more difficult to identify the ever-shifting lines of battle: the latest Monetarist thrust or Keynesian parry. Perhaps confusion in the din of combat is characteristic of all wars—even intellectual ones. Nevertheless, many economists earn at least part of their living off the intellectual battlefield—by explaining the issues to others. Thus, such difficulty makes life especially trying for the teacher of money and banking, macroeconomic theory, or monetary economics. As the Monetarist versus Keynesian debate takes on new dimensions (as theoretical refinement and empirical work uncover new perspectives), it is no easy task for teachers to illuminate the issues. In the classroom, where one once could simply focus on disagreement over the stability of the demand for money and the implications of flexible money wages and prices, the instructor must now address crucial new questions.

This book of readings focuses on those questions. The articles have been selected to guide the student through recent developments in monetary theory and policy. We have chosen works on the basis of their lucidity, representativeness, relevance, ability to stimulate discussion and debate, and complementarity with other readings. We have tried to sustain balance between theoretical and empirical work and to avoid exceedingly complex formulations that would be beyond the ken of most students. We have attempted in each subject area to choose articles that present the issues most cogently, regardless of the Monetarist or Keynesian leanings of the author or his or her place of employment.

In our selection process we were not bound by traditional formulas for books of readings in monetary economics and money and banking. There are, for instance, no readings on debt management, the incidence of monetary policy, rules versus discretion, or incomes policy. Nor are there lengthy critiques of the "tools" of monetary policy. These subjects were more important at one time and may very well come into prominence again, but they are topics that most current textbooks cover in timely detail. In an effort to keep the book reasonably sized (and reasonably priced), we have not emphasized topics that are adequately developed in textbooks, nor have we concentrated on topical areas that, command an entire volume of readings by themselves, such as recent developments in commercial banking.

We are grateful to Ralph Byrnes, Joseph Crews, Richard Froyen, Edward Kane, Raymond Lombra, Robert Schweitzer, and William Yohe for their guidance during the selection of readings. We acknowledge Paul Funk, James Johnson, Maxine McGee, Katie Frye, and Jean Peek in Durham, Annie Sarino and Ziska Lalamentik in Jakarta and Maureen Trobec in Arlington Heights for their assistance in the production process. A note of thanks is due our editors, Harry Metzger and Harlan Davidson, for their encouragement and help during all stages of this preparation. Finally, we congratulate all contributors to this volume for their contribution to scholarship.

THOMAS M. HAVRILESKY
Durham, North Carolina

JOHN T. BOORMAN
Jakarta, Indonesia

October, 1975

Analytical Models and Descriptive Overview

In the opening article of this section, Warren L. Smith presents the seminal exposition of the Keynesian version of the aggregate demand (*LM-IS* analysis) and aggregate supply sectors of a global model of the macroeconomy. The underemployment equilibrium of Keynes is shown fundamentally to be a result of rigidity of money wages, and the neoclassical (often called Monetarist) propositions are shown to be a result of money wage and price flexibility. Robert H. Rasche's sketch of the Monetarist analytical framework is in accord with the main implications of Smith's article. Rasche's analysis, however, appends to the basic aggregate demand–aggregate supply model two key Monetarist features: (1) explicit treatment of the price (and money wage) perceptions that lie behind the underemployment-creating "rigidities" (discussed by Smith) and (2) inclusion of a government sector and an outstanding stock of government debt to allow for fuller examination of the effects of fiscal and monetary policy. The material in these two selections, read together, is an important supplement to treatments found in standard textbooks in the fields of macroeconomics, money and banking, and monetary theory. In addition, many of the issues introduced in these opening readings are explored in greater detail later in the book.

The standard paradigms of economic theory have received a new challenge from the work of Axel Leijonhufvud, Robert Clower, and others who have reexamined Keynesian models (represented here by Warren L. Smith's reading) and Monetarist models (represented here by Robert H. Rasche's contribution) and contrasted them with the original work of John Maynard Keynes. Is Keynes's work a special (e.g., rigid nominal wage) case of a more general neoclassical theory, or does it represent a rather unique world view? In a brilliant exposition featured as the third essay in this section, A. J. Hines represents the growing number of economists who opt for the latter position. Hines succinctly reveals the exciting perspective on macroeconomic theory expounded by the new students of Keynes's system. A stimulating fourth selection is Hyman P. Minsky's incisive exploration of a theory of investment expenditures that is consistent with the economics of Keynes as outlined by Hines. Minsky lucidly shows how the financing of investment expenditures is sensitive to cyclical swings of creditor and debtor enthusiasm.

"There is but one macroeconomics (or monetary theory), and it has been around for over two hundred years." This statement characterizes the brisk and provocative final essay in the section. John H. Wood argues that there is fundamentally no paradigmatic conflict between the world views of Keynes and Monetarist Milton Friedman. Wood contends that Keynes and Friedman would both agree that it is an unstable monetary environment that produces the general uncertainty of future prices that allows changes in aggregate demand to have short-run effects on output and employment.

A Graphical Exposition of the Complete Keynesian System

Warren L. Smith*

The purpose of this paper is chiefly expository. A simple graphical technique is employed to exhibit the working of several variants of the Keynesian model. Many of the issues discussed have been dealt with elsewhere,[1] but it is hoped that the analysis presented here will clarify some of the issues and be useful for pedagogical purposes.

Reprinted from the *Southern Economic Journal,* Vol. 23, No. 3 (October, 1956), pp. 115-125, by permission of the Southern Economic Association and the estate of Warren L. Smith.

* The development of the technique employed in this paper is a result of discussions with many persons, particularly Professor Daniel B. Suits of the University of Michigan, to whom the writer wishes to express his thanks.

[1]See particularly L. R. Klein, "Theories of Effective Demand and Employment," *Journal of Political Economy,* Vol. LV (April 1947), pp. 108-31, reprinted in R. V. Clemence (ed.), *Readings in Economic Analysis,* Vol. I (Cambridge, Mass.: Addison-Wesley Press, 1950), pp. 260-83, and *The Keynesian Revolution* (New York: Macmillan Co., 1950), esp. Technical Appendix; F. Modigliani, "Liquidity Preference and the Theory of Interest and Money," *Econometrica,* Vol. XII (Jan. 1944), pp. 45-88, reprinted in F. A. Lutz and L. W. Mints (eds.), *Readings in Monetary Theory* (Homewood, Ill.: Richard D. Irwin, Inc., 1951), pp. 186-239; also V. Lutz, "Real and Monetary Factors in the Determination of Employment Levels," *Quarterly Journal of Economics,* Vol. LXVI (May 1952), pp. 251-72; L. Hough, "The Price Level in Macroeconomic Models," *American Economic Review,* Vol. LXIV (June 1954), pp. 269-86.

I. The Keynesian System with Flexible Wages

This system can be represented symbolically by the following five equations:

$$y = c(y,r) + i(y,r) \tag{1}$$

$$\frac{M}{p} = L(y,r) \tag{2}$$

$$y = f(N) \tag{3}$$

$$\frac{w}{p} = f'(N) \tag{4}$$

$$N = \phi\left(\frac{w}{p}\right) \tag{5}$$

Here y = real GNP (at constant prices), r = an index of interest rates, M = money supply (in current dollars), p = index of the price level applicable to GNP, N = the volume of employment (in equivalent full-time workers), w = the money wage. The model represents a theory of short-run income determination with capital stock fixed and labor the only variable factor of production.

The working of this model is illustrated in Figure I. Figure I should be studied in clockwise fashion, beginning with Chart I(a) in the lower lefthand corner. In I(a), *DD* represents the demand for labor [equation (4)] and *SS* represents the supply of labor [equation (5)]. The level of employment and the real wage are determined at the full employment levels, N_f and $(w/p)_f$. Proceeding to I(b), the curve *OP* represents the aggregate production function [equation (3)], its shape reflecting diminishing returns.[2] With employment of N_f, y would be at the level y_f, indicated in I(b).

Chart I(c) is the type of diagram developed by Hicks and utilized by others to depict the condition of monetary equilibrium in the Keynesian system.[3] The *IS* curve in I(c) depicts equation (1) and indicates for each possible level of the interest rate (r) the equilibrium level of income (y) which would prevail after the multiplier had

[2]According to the mathematical formulation of our model in equations (1)-(5), the curve *DD* in I(a) is the derivative of curve *OP* in I(b), the relation reflecting the operation of the marginal productivity law under competitive conditions. This precise condition is not important, however, and we shall make no attempt to draw the curves in such a way as to fulfill it. For one thing, the presence of monopoly in the economy or failure of entrepreneurs to seek maximum profits would destroy the precision of the equations, but relations of the type depicted in Figure I would in all probability continue to hold.

[3]For a detailed discussion of this diagram, see J. R. Hicks, "Mr. Keynes and the 'Classics': A Suggested Interpretation," *Econometrica*, Vol. V (April 1937), pp. 147-59; also A. H. Hansen, *Monetary Theory and Fiscal Policy* (New York: McGraw-Hill, 1949), chap. 5. The reader's attention is directed to the fact that we have reversed the axes of the Hicks diagram; we measure the interest rate on the horizontal axis and income on the vertical axis.

worked itself out fully.[4] We treat the stock of money as an exogenous variable determined by the monetary authority. Given M, the LM curves in I(c), of which there would be one for each possible price level (p) which might prevail, represent equation (2) in our model. For example, if the price level were held constant at p_o, the curve $LM(p_o)$ depicts the different interest rates that would be required to preserve equilibrium in the money market at different income levels. The fact that rising income levels are associated with higher interest rates reflects the presumption that as income rises, transactions cash requirements are larger, leaving less of the fixed (in real terms) quantity of money to satisfy demands for idle balances, thus pushing up the interest rate.

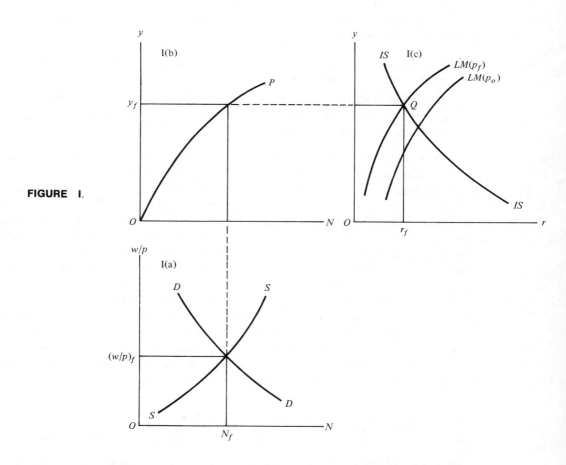

FIGURE I.

If prices and wages are flexible and the situation is as depicted in Figure I, full employment will automatically be maintained, since the price level will adjust to the level p_f, establishing the *LM* curve in the position $LM(p_f)$ where it will intersect the *IS* curve at point *Q* which corresponds to the full employment level of income (y_f). If, for example, the real wage is initially above $(w/p)_f$, money wages will fall due to the excess of supply of labor. This will reduce costs, resulting in increased output and employment and lower prices. Falling prices shift the *LM* curve upward by increasing the real value of cash balances (M/p), thus lowering the interest rates and expanding aggregate demand to the point where the market will absorb the output corresponding to full employment.[5]

Two important and related propositions can be set down concerning interest and money in the above model:

1. The rate of interest is determined solely by saving and investment and is independent of the quantity of money and liquidity preference.

2. The quantity theory of money holds for this model—that is, a change in the quantity of money will bring about an equal proportional change in the price level and will have no effect on real income or employment.

In other words, the quantity of money and liquidity preference serve not to determine the interest rate, as alleged by Keynes, but the price level. As can readily be seen from Figure I, income is established at the full employment level [I(a) and I(b)], the interest rate adjusts to equate savings and investment [on the *IS* curve in I(c)] at this income level, and the price level adjusts so as to satisfy liquidity requirements at this interest rate [establishing the *LM* curve at the appropriate position in I(c)].

It is a comparatively simple matter to modify the analysis of Figure I to take account of the possible effect of changes in the real value of liquid assets on consumption (the Pigou effect).[6] The real value of the stock of liquid assets would be included in equation (1), and falling prices would then shift the *IS* curve to the right, thus strengthening the tendency toward full employment equilibrium. This suggests the question: Does the introduction of the Pigou effect give the quantity of money the power to change the rate of interest when prices and wages are flexible? The answer to this question cannot be deduced from the curves of Figure I, but it is not difficult to find the answer with the aid of the following simple model:

---

[5]We abstract from the possibility of dynamic instability which may arise due to falling prices if the public has elastic expectations. See D. Patinkin, "Price Flexibility and Full Employment," *American Economic Review,* Vol. XXXVII (September 1948), pp. 543-64, reprinted with slight modification in Lutz and Mints, *op. cit.,* pp. 252-83.

[6]On the Pigou effect, see A. C. Pigou, "Economic Progress in a Stable Environment," *Economica,* New Series, Vol. XIV (August 1947), pp. 180-88, reprinted in Lutz and Mints, *op. cit.,* pp. 241-51; Patinkin, *op. cit.,* G. Ackley, "The Wealth-Saving Relationship," *Journal of Political Economy,* Vol. LIX (April 1951), pp. 154-61; M. Cohen, "Liquid Assets and the Consumption Function," *Review of Economics and Statistics,* Vol. XXXVI (May 1954), pp. 202-11; and bibliography in the latter two articles.

$$\bar{y} = c(\bar{y}, r, a) + i(\bar{y}, r)$$

$$\frac{M}{p} = L(\bar{y}, r)$$

$$a = \frac{A}{p}$$

Here a = the real value of liquid assets which is included in the consumption function and A = their money value. The last three equations of our original model are assumed to determine the real wage, employment, and real income. These equations are dropped and y is treated as a constant (having value $\bar{y}$) determined by those equations. We can now treat M and A as parameters and r, a, and p as variables, differentiate these three equations with respect to M, and solve for dr/dM. This gives the following expression:

$$\frac{dr}{dM} = \frac{\dfrac{c_a}{i_r} \dfrac{A}{M}(1 - \eta_{AM})}{p\left(1 + \dfrac{c_r}{i_r} + \dfrac{A}{M}\dfrac{L_r c_a}{i_r}\right)} \tag{6}$$

In this expression, the subscripts refer to partial derivates, e.g., $c_a = \delta c/\delta a$. Normally, the following conditions would be satisfied: $c_a > 0$, $i_r < 0$, $L_r < 0$. We cannot be sure about the sign of c_r, but it is likely to be small in any case. The coefficient η_{AM} has the following meaning:

$$\eta_{AM} = \frac{M}{A}\frac{dA}{dM} = \frac{\dfrac{dA}{A}}{\dfrac{dM}{M}}$$

For example, if a change in M is brought about in such a way as to produce an exactly proportionate change in A, η_{AM} will be unity. Or if the change in M is not accompanied by any change in A, η_{AM} will be zero. It is apparent from the above expression that a change in the quantity of money will not affect the rate of interest if $\eta_{AM} = 1$, while an increase (decrease) in the quantity of money will lower (raise) the rate of interest if $\eta_{AM} < 1$.[7] Thus, the way in which changes in the quantity of

---

[7]We assume that $c_r < 0$, or if $c_r > 0$,

$$1 + \frac{A}{M}\frac{L_r c_a}{i_r} > \frac{c_r}{i_r}$$

so that the denominator of (6) is positive.

money affect the rate of interest depends upon what asset concept is included in the consumption function (i.e., what is included in A) and how the volume of these assets is affected by monetary change. If M itself is the appropriate asset concept to include in the consumption function (i.e., if $A = M$), changes in M will not affect the interest rate, since in this case η_{AM} is equal to unity. However, the consensus of opinion seems to be that some other aggregate, such as currency, deposits, and government securities held by the nonbank public minus the public's indebtedness to the banks, is more appropriate.[8] If this concept is employed, most of the usual methods of increasing the money supply will ordinarily either leave A unchanged ($\eta_{AM} = 0$) or cause it to increase less than in proportion to the increase in M ($0 < \eta_{AM} < 1$).[9] We may conclude that the Pigou effect gives monetary changes power to influence the rate of interest, even if wages and prices are fully flexible. An increase (decrease) in the quantity of money will ordinarily lower (raise) the rate of interest and also increase (decrease) investment and decrease (increase) consumption, but will not change income and employment which are determined by real forces (the last three equations of our complete model).[10,11]

II. Possibilities of Underemployment Disequilibrium

There are several possible circumstances arising from the shapes of the various schedules which might produce a situation in which, even though the relations in the above model held true, it might be impossible, at least temporarily, for equilibrium (full employment or otherwise) to be reached. The most widely discussed of these possibilities is depicted in Figure II.

[8]The question of what asset concept is appropriate is discussed in Patinkin, *op. cit.*, Cohen, *op. cit.*, and J. Tobin, "Asset Holdings and Spending Decisions," *American Economic Review Papers and Proceedings*, Vol. XLII (May 1952), pp. 109-23.

[9]Open market purchases of government securities by the central bank from the nonbank public will leave A unchanged, since the initial purchase transaction will result in a decline in the public's security holdings and an equal increase in M, while any induced expansion of loans and investments by the banks will result in an increase in M offset by an equal increase in the public's indebtedness to the banks. On the other hand, if the Treasury prints currency and gives it to the public, A will be increased by the same absolute amount as M but the increase in A will be proportionately smaller than the increase in M (provided the public's holdings of government securities exceed its indebtedness to the banks so that $A > M$).

[10]The fact that the existence of a wealth effect on savings may confer upon the quantity of money the power to affect the rate of interest even with flexible wages is demonstrated in L. A. Metzler, "Wealth, Saving, and the Rate of Interest," *Journal of Political Economy*, Vol. LIX (April 1951), pp. 93-116. Metzler's conclusions, which differ from those given here, can be attributed to assumptions that he makes, particularly the assumption that the only assets are money and common stock.

[11]If the supply of labor is affected by the real value of wealth held by workers, changes in the quantity of money may affect output and employment by shifting the SS curve in Figure I(a). Also, even though monetary change does not affect the *current* level of income and employment, if, due to the operation of the Pigou effect, it changes the interest rate and thereby investment, it may affect the *future* level of employment, since the change in capital stock will ordinarily shift the demand for labor [DD curve in Figure I(a)] at a future date. Both these points are mentioned in V. Lutz, *op. cit.*

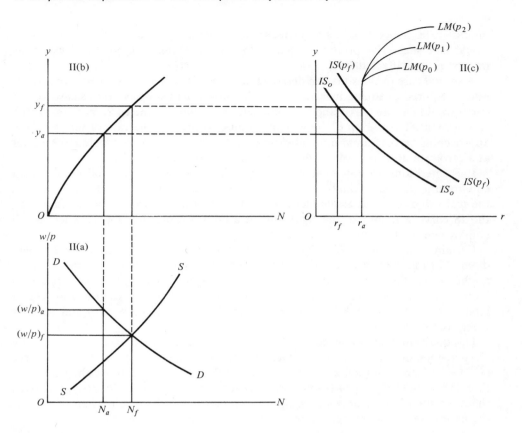

FIGURE II.

II(a) and II(b) are similar to I(a) and I(b). However, the *LM* curves in II(c) are drawn to reflect the much-discussed possibility mentioned by Keynes[12] that the liquidity preference schedule might become infinitely elastic at some low level of interest rates [r_a in II(c)], due either to the unanimous expectations of investors that interest rates would rise when they reached this extremely low level relative to future expectations or to the cost of investments. In the case depicted, full employment (N_f) would involve a level of income of y_f. If the *IS* curve were at the level IS_0, the interest rate required to make investment equal to saving at income y_f would be r_f. But the infinite elasticity of the *LM* schedule prevents the interest rate from falling below r_a. The result would be that employment and income would be prevented from rising above the level N_a and y_a by inadequate effective demand. The real wage would hold at the level $(w/p)_a$ which is above the full employment level $(w/p)_f$. Competition for employment would reduce money wages, costs, and prices. But the falling price level, although it would increase the quantity of money in real terms, would not affect the

[12]J. M. Keynes, *General Theory of Employment, Interest, and Money* (New York: Harcourt, Brace and Co., 1936), pp. 201-4.

interest rate, hence would not increase investment. As prices fell, the *LM* curve would take successive positions, such as $LM(p_0)$, $LM(p_1)$, $LM(p_2)$, etc., leaving the interest rate unaffected.[13]

A special case of the situation depicted in Figure II may arise if a negative interest rate is required to equate investment to full employment savings. In this case, the *IS* curve would cut the *y*-axis and lie to the left of it at an income corresponding to full employment. Then, even if there were nothing to prevent the rate of interest from approaching zero, it could not go below zero,[14] and the *LM* curve would have a floor at a zero rate, thus preventing full employment from being attained.

It is interesting to note that if the Pigou effect is operative, a full employment equilibrium may be attainable even in the case illustrated in Figure II. As prices fall, the real value of liquid assets increases. If this increases consumption expenditures, the *IS* curve will shift to the right until it attains the position $IS(p_f)$, where a full employment equilibrium is reached.

Certain other conceivable situations which might lead to an underemployment disequilibrium are worthy of brief mention. One possibility is that the supply of labor might exceed the demand at all levels of real wages. Such a situation seems very improbable, however, since there is reason to believe that the short-run aggregate labor supply is quite inelastic over a considerable range of wage rates and declines when wage rates become very low.[15]

Disequilibrium situations could also arise if (*a*) the demand curve for labor had a steeper slope than the supply curve at their point of intersection, or (*b*) the *IS* curve cut the *LM* curve in such a way that *IS* lay to the right of *LM* above their intersection and to the left of *LM* below their intersection in Figure I(c) or II(c). Actually, these are situations of unstable equilibrium rather than of disequilibrium. However, in these cases, a slight departure from equilibrium would produce a cumulative movement away from it, and the effect would be similar to a situation of disequilibrium.

III. Underemployment Equilibrium Due to Wage Rigidity

Next we may consider the case in which the supply of and demand for labor are essentially the same as in Figures I and II, but for institutional or other reasons the

---

[13]Equations (1)-(5) above apply to the situations covered in both Figure I and Figure II. In the latter case, however, the equations are mathematically inconsistent and do not possess a solution. Mathematics does not tell us what will happen in this case (although the additional conditions necessary to describe the results could be expressed mathematically). The statements made above concerning the results (i.e., that income will be y_a, prices and wages will fall together, etc.) are propositions in economics.

[14]Since the money rate of interest cannot be negative, as long as it costs nothing to hold money. In fact, a zero rate of interest would be impossible, since in this case property value would be infinite; however, the rate might *approach* zero. The *real* rate of interest, *ex post,* may be negative due to inflation, but this is not relevant to our problem. On this, see I. Fisher, *The Theory of Interest* (New York: Macmillan Co., 1930), chaps. ii, xix, and pp. 282-86.

[15]On the probable shape of the short-run aggregative supply of labor, see G. F. Bloom and H. R. Northrup, *Economics of Labor Relations* (Homewood, Ill.: Richard D. Irwin, Inc., 1954), pp. 250-53.

money wage does not fall when there is an excess supply of labor.[16] This rigidity of money wages may be due to various factors, including (a) powerful trade unions which are able to prevent money wages from falling, at least temporarily, (b) statutory provisions, such as minimum wage laws, (c) failure of employers to reduce wages due to a desire to retain loyal and experienced employees and to maintain morale,[17] or (d) unwillingness of unemployed workers to accept reduced money wages even though they would be willing to work at lower real wages brought about by a rise in prices.[18]

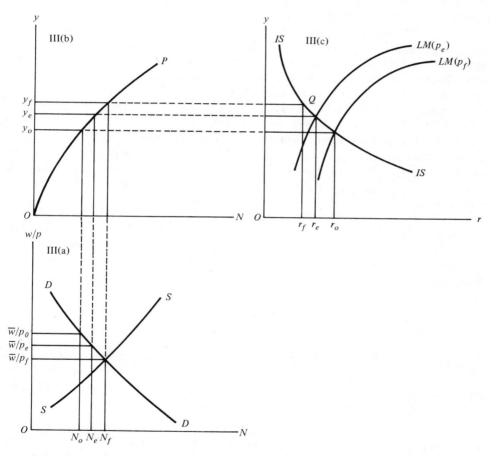

FIGURE III.

[16]We will assume that this rigidity does not prevail in an upward direction—i.e., money wages will rise when there is an excess demand for labor.

[17]See A. Rees, "Wage Determination and Involuntary Unemployment, *Journal of Political Economy,* Vol. LIX (April 1951), pp. 143-53.

[18]Keynes, *op. cit.,* chap. 2; J. Tobin, "Money Wage Rates and Employment," in S. E. Harris (ed.), *The New Economics* (New York: Knopf, 1947), pp. 572-87.

A situation of this kind is depicted in Figure III. The fixed money wage is designated by $\bar{w}$. In order for full employment (N_f) to be attained, the price level must be at p_f (such as to make $\bar{w}/p_f$ equal to the real wage corresponding to full employment), income will be y_f, and the interest rate must reach r_f. However, in the case shown in Figure III, the quantity of money, M, is such that when p is at the level p_f, the LM curve [$LM(p_f)$] intersects the IS curve at an income (y_0) below the full employment level and an interest rate (r_0) above the full employment level. Hence, full employment cannot be sustained due to inadequate effective demand. On the other hand, if production and employment are at y_0 and N_0, with a price level such (at p_0) as to establish a real wage appropriate to this volume of employment, the LM curve will be at a level above $LM(p_f)$. This is because p_0 must be less than p_f in order to make $\bar{w}/p_0$ higher than $\bar{w}/p_f$. In this case, production and employment will tend to rise because aggregate demand exceeds current output. Therefore, income must be between y_f and y_0, employment between N_f and N_0, the interest rate between r_f and r_0, the price level between p_f and p_0. An equilibrium will be reached somewhere between these limits, say at N_e, y_e, p_e, and r_e.[19]

This is a case of underemployment equilibrium. It should be noted that full employment can be attained by an increase in the quantity of money (M) sufficient to shift the $LM(p_f)$ curve to the position where it will intersect the IS curve at point Q. Two propositions can be set down here to be contrasted with the two stated in connection with Figure I:[20]

1. Changes in the quantity of money cause changes in both the price level and the level of output and employment, and the quantity theory of money does not hold true.[21]

2. An increase (decrease) in the quantity of money causes a decrease (increase) in the rate of interest. In this case, the interest rate is determined by the interaction of all the relations in the model. Saving, investment, liquidity preference, and the quantity of money all have a hand in its determination.

Introduction of the Pigou effect into Figure III would not prevent the occurrence of an underemployment equilibrium, although it would somewhat complicate the process of adjustment since changes in p or M would cause changes in the IS curve as well as the LM curve.

---

[19]In the case depicted in Figure III, an additional equation $\bar{w} = w$ is added to equations (1)-(5) above. This gives six equations and only five unknowns (y, N, p, w, and r). Such a system of equations is *overdetermined* and does not, in general, possess a solution. If the quantity of money is treated as a variable which is adjusted so as to maintain full employment, we have six equations and six unknowns and there will be a solution (unless the equations are inconsistent).

[20]See p. 5, *supra*.

[21]In the limiting case in which the *DD* curve has a horizontal stage which includes the current level of employment, the entire effect of an increase in M is on y, with no change in p. A considerable part of Keynes' *General Theory* (prior to the discussion of wages and prices in Book V) has reference primarily to this situation.

To summarize, our analysis of Figures I and III indicates that rigidity of money wages is, in general, a necessary condition for (a) the occurrence of an underemployment equilibrium, (b) the quantity of money to have an effect on the level of real income and employment. The rate of interest will not be affected by the quantity of money and liquidity preference unless (a) there is rigidity of money wages or (b) the Pigou effect is operative with $\eta_{AM} \neq 1$. Monetary theories of the rate of interest, whether of the loanable funds or liquidity preference variety, ordinarily assume rigidity (or at least stickiness) in the structure of money wages.[22]

IV. Concluding Comments

In conclusion, we would like to call the reader's attention to further uses to which our graphical technique can be put. With appropriate modifications to suit the occasion, it can be used to analyze other variations of the Keynesian model.[23] Additional factors affecting the income, employment, and price levels, such as those suggested by Hough[24] and by Lutz[25] can be quite easily introduced into the analysis through appropriate shifts in the schedules shown in our system of graphs. Fiscal policy and its relation to monetary policy can be dealt with, since fiscal policy influences the level and shape of the *IS* curve. Finally, it provides a useful starting point for the study of economic growth. Factors affecting the rate of growth, such as capital accumulation, population growth, technological change, etc., can be brought in by allowing for their effects on the various schedules.

[22]The relative merits of loanable funds and liquidity preference types of monetary interest theories we do not consider, except to say that when appropriately formulated, the two are equivalent.

[23]For example, the models with which Modigliani begins his analysis (*op. cit.,* pp. 46–48 in original, pp. 187–90 in *Readings in Monetary Theory*). Analysis of these models requires some alteration in the graphical technique, since he assumes that consumption, investment, and the demand for money, all in current dollars, depend upon money income and the rate of interest, thus introducing "money illusions" into his scheme at several points.

[24]L. Hough, "The Price Level in Macroeconomic Models," *American Economic Review*, Vol. LXIV (June 1954), pp. 269–86.

[25]V. Lutz, "Real and Monetary Factors in the Determination of Employment Levels," *Quarterly Journal of Economics*, Vol. LXVI (May 1952), pp. 251–72.

A Comparative Static Analysis of Some Monetarist Propositions

Robert H. Rasche

The typical textbook approach to macroeconomic analysis is almost completely barren with respect to what has become characterized as the "monetarist position" on the effects of monetary and fiscal policy actions. These propositions might be summarized as follows:

(1) the long-run impact of monetary actions is on nominal variables, such as nominal GNP, the general price level, and nominal interest rates;

(2) long-run movements in real economic variables, such as output and employment, are little influenced, if at all, by monetary actions;

(3) in the short run, actions of the central bank exert an impact on both real and nominal variables;

(4) fiscal actions have little lasting influence on nominal GNP but can affect short-run movements in output and employment; and

(5) government expenditures financed by taxes or borrowing from the public tend to crowd out, over a fairly short period of time, an equal amount of private expenditures.[1]

Reprinted from the Federal Reserve Bank of St. Louis, *Review* (December, 1973), pp. 15–23, by permission of the publisher and the author.
[1]These propositions have been gleaned from Leonall C. Andersen, "A Monetarist View of Demand Management: The United States Experience," this *Review* (September 1971), pp. 3–11.

It would seem that a static analytic framework could be developed which could shed some light on the theoretical underpinnings of monetarism, although the mode of analysis is obviously insufficient to cope with the dynamic propositions which are associated with this school. Unfortunately, the literature is extremely scarce. Milton Friedman has set forth a static framework, and alleges that the differences between monetarists and post-Keynesians have to do with assumptions about price (and wage) behavior. Monetarism, he alleges, assumes that the aggregate price level is determined in such a way as to clear all markets in the long run. For the short run, he alleges that neither the monetarist nor the fiscalist has a satisfactory theory of the response of real output and the general price level to monetary shocks. Unfortunately, Friedman's excursion into dynamics and differential equations is difficult, if not impossible, to relate to individual market forces.[2]

Thus, the issue remains unsettled. On the one hand, we are left without a clearly specified analytical framework for the monetarist approach which can be contrasted with the well-developed static income determination model. On the other hand, and even more importantly, there is no general model which can produce the post-Keynesian model as a particular case and the monetarist and classical models as alternative cases. Such a framework is useful in order to discriminate between alternative hypotheses and to construct empirical tests which have the potential to refute one or both positions.

This study attempts to develop a general model by examining equilibria which differ by the length of the "run." This Marshallian tool should be clearly defined as applying to the behavior which is assumed to be embodied in the *ceteris paribus* assumptions: the more behavior which is embodied in *ceteris paribus*, the shorter the "run." Traditional macrostatics has been of the Marshallian "short-run" variety; that is, the real capital stock has been held constant. This leads to some unfortunately confusing terminology. Most of the traditional analysis from which the "long-run" monetarist propositions can be gleaned is not long-run analysis in the Marshallian sense. At the risk of adding further confusion to the discussion we shall stay with the traditional short-run definition as the "short run," and compare the results of this model with those of an even shorter run, or "monetary-run" model.

It is well established that a Patinkin-type four market model (labor services, commodities, bonds, and money), under assumptions of complete price flexibility, absence of money illusion, unitary elasticity of price expectations, and perfect information on market prices, will exhibit propositions (1), (2), and (5) above, in comparison of "short-run" equilibria which differ because of a shock to some policy variable.[3]

---

[2]Milton Friedman, "A Theoretical Framework for Monetary Analysis," *Journal of Political Economy* (March/April 1970), pp. 193-238.

[3]For a derivation of these propositions and a discussion of the effects of the presence or absence of government bonds in the model, see Don Patinkin, *Money, Interest, and Prices: An Integration of Monetary and Value Theory*, 2nd ed. (New York: Harper & Row, 1965), chap. 10; Robert L. Crouch, *Macroeconomics* (New York: Harcourt Brace Jovanovich, 1972), chaps. 6-9; and Franco Modigliani, "The Monetary Mechanism and Its Interaction with Real Phenomena," *Review of Economics and Statistics, Supplement* (February 1963), pp. 79-107.

However, these analyses have nothing to contribute to the discussion of propositions (3) and (4).

Basic Elements of Model

More than a decade ago, it appears that the assumption of perfect information on prices was implicitly relaxed in some of the research work of leading monetarists. Friedman, in his work on the demand for money, distinguished between the current commodity price index and a longer-run concept which he called the "permanent price level." He argued that:

> . . . holders of money presumably judge the "real" amount of cash balances in terms of the quantity of goods and services to which the balances are equivalent, not at any given moment of time, but over a sizable and indefinite period; that is, they evaluate them in terms of "expected" or "permanent" prices, not in terms of the current price level. This consideration does not, of course, rule out some adjustment to temporary movements in prices.[4]

Recently, following the pioneering work of George Stigler and Armen A. Alchian, considerable theoretical and empirical work on labor market behavior and the Phillips curve has been produced.[5] These studies assume that workers do not possess perfect information on the wages available to them in return for their labor services, and it is costly for workers to search out information on the opportunities available to them. Within this framework it is necessary to distinguish between the nominal wage rate which is actually offered for labor services at a point in time, W, and the wage rate which is perceived by suppliers of labor services, W_e. In this paper we employ a wage rate information parameter, λ_1, to relate the perceived wage rate to the currently offered rate and an exogenous, or predetermined, component, W_o.

The relationship we postulate is:

$$W_e = W^{\lambda_1} (W_o)^{1 - \lambda_1}$$

so the perceived nominal wage rate is a geometric average of the current wage rate and a predetermined wage rate, presumably based on the history of previous wage experience. If the wage information parameter, λ_1, is set equal to 1.0, there is costless information and the perceived wage rate is the current nominal wage. At the other

[4]Milton Friedman, "The Demand for Money: Some Theoretical and Empirical Results," *Journal of Political Economy* (August 1959), pp. 327-351.

[5]George J. Stigler, "Information in the Labor Market," *Journal of Political Economy, Supplement* (October 1962), pp. 94-105, and Armen A. Alchian, "Information Costs, Pricing, and Resource Unemployment," Edmund Phelps et al., *Microeconomic Foundations of Employment and Inflation Theory* (New York: Norton, 1970), pp. 27-52.

extreme, if λ_1 is set equal to zero, information about the current wage rate has an infinite price and there is total ignorance of current market conditions.

This cost of information approach can be extended to the commodity market. We assume that households make their consumption and portfolio decisions on the basis of their perceived commodity price index, P_e, which can differ from the actual commodity price index if information on commodity prices is imperfect and costly to gather.[6] Analogous to the case of the wage rate, we postulate a price information parameter, λ_2, which relates the perceived price index to the current price index as follows:

$$P_e = P^{\lambda_2}(P_o)^{1 - \lambda_2}$$

Again the perceived commodity price index is a geometric average of the current price index and an exogenously determined price level. When λ_2 equals one, information on the commodity price is free, and all information on current prices can be incorporated into decision making. When λ_2 is equal to zero, the cost of information is infinite, and no current market behavior is incorporated into decision making.

Once we allow the perceived price level and perceived wage rate to differ from the respective current market value, we must explicitly introduce P_e and W_e into the model. This is indicated in Table 1, where the labor supply function of households is expressed as a function of the perceived real wage rate (W_e/P_e), real consumption demand is a function of perceived real net worth (V/P_e) and perceived real disposable income, as are real bond demand and the demand for real cash balances. If we interpret P_e as equivalent to Friedman's "permanent" price index concept, the money demand equation (equation XII in Table 1) is the money demand function used by Friedman with the exception of his use of a per capita specification and an explicit functional form.[7] All other functions are specified exactly as in the Patinkin model. In particular it should be noted that the interest elasticity of the demand for real cash balances has not been constrained to zero.

First, the behavior of the labor market has to be considered. As indicated in Figure 1, there is a single labor demand curve plotted as a function of the prevailing real wage (W/P). We have to analyze how the labor supply curve interacts with this labor demand curve. Consider a situation in which the movement from one equilibrium to another involves a rise in the commodity price index, P. If, under these circumstances, the labor supply function shifts to the right, from N^s_1 to N^s_2, then the new equilibrium of the system is characterized by higher employment and a lower real wage rate than the initial equilibrium. Since employment is higher, real output is also higher in the new equilibrium relative to the initial equilibrium.

---

[6]For simplicity, we assume firms have zero information costs with respect to wages and prices.
[7]Friedman, "The Demand for Money," pp. 327-351.

It can be shown that a sufficient condition for the labor supply curve to shift to the right in the real wage-employment plane in response to increases in the commodity price index is that λ_1, the information parameter for the perceived nominal wage rate, be greater than λ_2, the information parameter for the perceived commodity price

Table 1. Equations for the Complete Macroeconomic Model
(excluding a Government Sector)

	Equation	Name	Market
(I)	$N^d = N^d\left(\dfrac{W}{P}, \bar{K}\right)$	Labor demand function	
(II)	$N^s = N^s\left(\dfrac{W_e}{P_e}\right)$	Labor supply function	Labor market
(III)	$N^d = N^s = N$	Labor market equilibrium condition	
(IV)	$X^s = X^s\,(N, \bar{K})$	Production (or commodity supply) function	
(V)	$C = C\left(X_d, \dfrac{V}{P_e}\right)$	Commodity demand function for consumption (the consumption function)	
(VI)	$I = I\,(X, r)$	Commodity demand function for investment (the investment function)	Commodity market
(VII)	$X = C + I$	Total (or aggregate) commodity demand function	
(VIII)	$X = X^s$	Commodity market equilibrium condition	
(IX)	$\dfrac{B^d}{rP_e} = B^d\left(X_d, \dfrac{1}{r}, \dfrac{V}{P_e}\right)$	Bond demand function	
(X)	$\dfrac{B^s}{rP} = B^s\left(X^s, \dfrac{1}{r}, \dfrac{V}{P}\right)$	Bond supply function	Bond market
(XI)	$B^d = B^s$	Bond market equilibrium condition	
(XII)	$\dfrac{M^d}{P_e} = L\left(X_{d,}\, r, \dfrac{V}{P_e}\right)$	Money demand function	
(XIII)	$M^d = \overline{M^s}$	Money market equilibrium condition and (exogenous) money supply function	Money market

Table 1. *(continued)*

Equation	Name	Market
(XIV) $\quad S = X^s - C$	Definition of saving	
(XV) $\quad Y = PX^s$	Definition of money income	
(XVI) $\quad V = P\overline{K} + \overline{M^s}$	Definition of money wealth (net assets or net worth)	Definitions of supplementary variables
(XVII) $\quad X_d = \dfrac{Y}{P_e}$	Definition of real perceived disposable income	
(XVIII) $\quad W_e = W^{\lambda_1} W_0^{(1-\lambda_1)}$	Definition of perceived wage rate	
(XIX) $\quad P_e = P^{\lambda_2} P_0^{(1-\lambda_2)}$	Definition of perceived price level	

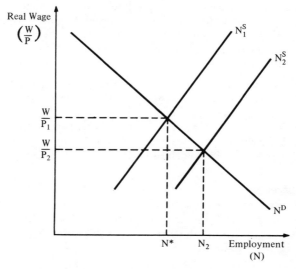

index.[8] In the analysis which follows, we shall characterize the "momentary" equilibrium as one in which information on both wages and prices is not free—that is, $0 < \lambda_2 < \lambda_1 < 1$. The short-run equilibrium will be characterized by perfect information on both wages and prices—that is, $\lambda_1 = \lambda_2 = 1$. In the short run, there are no shifts

[8]For a proof of this proposition see Appendix A, which is available only in the reprint [no. 82, Spring 1974] to this article.[At the time of this printing, copies of this Reprint were available from the Research Department of the Federal Reserve Bank of St. Louis, St. Louis, Missouri.—Ed.]

of the labor supply curve in response to changes in commodity prices and the equilibrium level of employment remains at N*, the initial equilibrium level. This phenomenon appears to be identical to that conceived by Friedman in his discussion of the natural unemployment rate.[9] N* could be termed the "natural level of employment" in this static model.

Changes in the Money Stock

It remains to be seen how the model reacts in a momentary equilibrium after the money stock has changed. A monetarist scenario has been provided by Friedman:

> . . . suppose . . . that the "natural" [unemployment] rate is higher than 3 percent. Suppose also that we start out at a time when prices have been stable and when unemployment is higher than 3 percent. Accordingly, the [monetary] authority increases the rate of monetary growth. This will be expansionary. By making nominal cash balances higher than people desire, it will tend initially to lower interest rates and in this and other ways to stimulate spending. Income and spending will start to rise.
>
> To begin with, much or most of the rise in income will take the form of an increase in output and employment rather than in prices. People have been expecting prices to be stable, and prices and wages have been set for some time in the future on that basis. It takes time for people to adjust to a new state of demand. Producers will tend to react to the initial expansion in aggregate demand by increasing output, employees by working longer hours, and the unemployed, by taking jobs now offered at former nominal wages. This much is pretty standard doctrine.
>
> But it describes only the initial effects. Because selling prices of products typically respond to an unanticipated rise in nominal demand faster than prices of factors of production, real wages received have gone down—though real wages anticipated by employees went up, since employees implicitly evaluated the wages offered at the earlier price level. Indeed, the simultaneous fall *ex post* in real wages to employers and rise *ex ante* in real wages to employees is what enabled employment to increase.[10]

This is precisely the behavior implicit in our four-market model. The increase in the money stock initially causes an excess supply in the "money market," an excess demand for bonds, and an excess demand for commodities through increased consumption demand, since both (V/P_e) and (V/P) are larger. In the momentary equilibrium, real output, commodity prices, and money wages are all higher than their initial equilibrium values.[11] However, the change in W, the money wage rate, is less than proportional to the change in P, and the actual real wage rate declines. The real wage perceived by suppliers of labor services (W_e/P_e) increases as long as the cost of

[9]Milton Friedman, "The Role of Monetary Policy," *American Economic Review* (March 1968), p. 8.
[10]Friedman, "The Role of Monetary Policy," pp. 9–10.
[11]The mathematical proof of these propositions, with a statement of sufficiency conditions, can be found in Appendix B, which appears only in the [original 1974] reprint to this article. [See footnote 8.]

obtaining information about prices is greater than the cost of obtaining information about wages ($\lambda_2 < \lambda_1$). Thus, the labor supply curve shifts to the right. The momentary equilibrium results correspond quite closely to the monetarist scenario outlined by Friedman and to the third proposition taken from Andersen.

An interesting question remains on the extent to which prices respond to a change in the money stock in this momentary equilibrium. In particular, we wish to consider the percentage change in the commodity price index generated by a one percent change in the money stock. In Appendix B (included only in reprint)* it is shown that when (1) a set of sufficient conditions for a positive change in real output in response to a positive change in the money stock is satisfied and (2) the money

Table 2. Notation

I. Endogenous Variables
   A. Flow variables
      1. N^d, demand for labor (labor services per time period)
      2. N^s, supply of labor (labor services per time period)
      3. X^s, real income (total output of commodities per time period)
      4. C, real consumption (commodities consumed per time period)
      5. I, real investment (commodities invested, added to the capital stock, per time period)
      6. X, real aggregate demand (total demand for commodities per time period)
      7. S, real saving (output of commodities not consumed per time period)
      8. Y, money income (money value of total output of commodities per time period)
      9. X_d, perceived real disposable income
   B. Stock variables
      1. B^d, demand for bonds (number of bonds demanded to hold)
      2. B^s, supply of bonds (number of bonds planned to be outstanding)
      3. M^d, demand for nominal money (number of dollars demanded to hold)
      4. V, nominal wealth, or net worth (dollar value of real assets and money)
   C. Price variables
      1. P, the absolute, or nominal, price level (the price of commodities)
      2. W, the absolute, or nominal, wage level (the price of labor or wage rate)
      3. $1/r$, the absolute, or nominal, price of bonds
II. Exogenous Variables
   A. Flow variables
      1. G, government demand for commodities (commodities per time period)
      2. $\$B^g$, interest cost of the outstanding government debt (equals B^g times one dollar per time period)
      3. T, real tax receipts (per time period)
   B. Stock variables
      1. $\bar{K}$, the real capital stock (the number of commodities that have been accumulated up to the beginning of the present time period)
      2. $\bar{M}^s$, the supply of nominal money (the number of dollars available to be held)
      3. B^g, supply of government bonds (number of government bonds outstanding)
   C. Price variables
      1. P_0, predetermined component of the perceived price level
      2. W_0, predetermined component of the perceived wage rate

* See footnote 8.

demand function is elastic with respect to perceived real disposable income, then the elasticity of the price level with respect to the money stock is less than one. Hence, the change in the price level between the two equilibrium states is less than proportional to the change in the money stock.

This result allows some interesting comparative static results to be obtained between the momentary equilibrium and the short-run equilibrium in which perceptions have been allowed to adjust fully to the change in the actual price level. In this state money can be shown to be neutral. Therefore, in comparison to the initial equilibrium, the percentage change in the commodity price index must be equal to the percentage change in the money stock. Thus, P must be higher in the short-run equilibrium than it is in the momentary equilibrium for a given change in the money stock. On the other hand, in the short-run equilibrium real output and employment must be unchanged from the initial equilibrium and, therefore, employment must be *lower* than in the momentary equilibrium.

This simultaneous increase in the price level and reduction in employment is a close analog to the dynamic phenomena of increasing inflation and increasing unemployment which perplexed economists and policymakers during 1970-1971. In the model, the cause of this type of behavior is not price rigidity or monopolistic market power, but rather the correction of false perceptions.

Open Market Operations in Existing Government Debt

The analysis of the previous section applies to an economy in which there is no government debt, and money has to be created by some artificial construct such as throwing it out of airplanes. This is frequently the convention with textbook models. More realistically, the model should be expanded to include a government sector and an outstanding stock of government debt. In such an economy, open market operations can be conducted with the monetary authorities purchasing or selling government debt in exchange for cash balances. The modifications to the equations of Table 1, necessary to incorporate the government sector, are given in Table 3.

There are three basic additions to the model of Table 1. First, the commodity demand equation has to be expanded to incorporate the government demand for goods and services, G. Second, we assume that the public does not discount future tax liabilities which will be required to pay the interest on the outstanding debt, so that the value of the stock of government debt is a component of private wealth. Third, the definition of perceived real disposable income must be modified to allow for the taxing of income by the government, T, and the payment of interest on the outstanding debt.

The remaining problem is to define what is meant by a pure open market operation. Open market operations are defined as exchanges of government debt and cash balances of equal value between the monetary authorities and the private sector of

Table 3. Modified Equations to Incorporate a Government Sector in the Macroeconomic Model

VIIa	$X = C + I + G$	Aggregate commodity demand function
XIa	$B^d = B^s + B^g$	Bond market equilibrium condition
XVIa	$V = P\bar{K} + \bar{M}^s + \dfrac{B^g}{r}$	Definition of money wealth
XVIIa	$X_d = \dfrac{P}{P_e}(X - T) + \dfrac{\$B^g}{P_e}$	Definition of real perceived disposable income

Government financing constraint:

$$P(G - T) + \$B^g = \frac{dB^g}{r} + dM$$

the economy. Unfortunately, we cannot leave the definition at this point. It is now well established that macroeconomic models frequently have been careless in the treatment of the relationships between government fiscal and monetary operations which are implicit in a financing constraint on the government sector.[12] In the model developed here, the government must finance the difference between its tax receipts and the value of its purchases of goods and services plus the interest payments on the outstanding debt either by issuing new debt or by printing new money. This relationship is indicated as the government financing constraint in Table 3.

Consider an initial equilibrium of the economy where the right-hand side of the equation for the financing constraint is zero; that is, tax receipts just cover government expenditures and interest cost. Now consider an open market operation which changes the amount of government debt held by the public. Since debt and cash balances of equal value are exchanged in the transactions, if the right-hand side of the financing constraint was zero initially, it remains zero. Since the stock of debt held by the private sector has changed, the left-hand side of the equation can no longer sum to zero without some changes in either G or T, to offset the direct effect on the financing constraint of the change in the interest cost, and the indirect effect of the change in value of government purchases and taxes through induced changes in commodity prices. We shall define a *pure open market operation* as an exchange of government debt and cash balances between the monetary authorities and the private sector, which is *simultaneously* accompanied by whatever change in T is necessary to maintain the government financing constraint, with G remaining unchanged.

The effects of a pure open market operation in the momentary equilibrium are analyzed in Appendix C (included only in reprint).* The sufficiency conditions for positive responses of real output, employment, and commodity prices to an open market operation which increases the stock of money held by the public are the same

[12]Carl Christ, "A Simple Macroeconomic Model with a Government Budget Restraint," *Journal of Political Economy* (January/February 1968), pp. 53-67.
* See footnote 8.

as those for the situation where the stock of money was increased in the absence of government debt.

It is well known that in the Patinkin-type model with which we are working money will not be neutral in the short run in the presence of interest-bearing government debt. Therefore, the response of prices to open market operations in the short run must be analyzed before we can determine that all of the results of the first model carry over to this case.[13] There are no real output or employment responses relative to the initial equilibrium in this case, since the classical labor market behavior without any money illusion is present.

It can be shown that the conditions which are sufficient for a positive output response to an open market operation which increases the stock of money in the momentary equilibrium are also sufficient to insure that the elasticity of the price index to the increase in the money stock is greater in the short run than in the momentary run. Thus, the result of the first model that prices are higher in the short run relative to the momentary equilibrium, even though employment is lower between the two equilibria, carries over to the model including government debt in the presence of a pure open market operation.

Fiscal Policy: Tax-Financed Changes in Real Government Expenditures

The conclusions for the comparative static impacts of fiscal policy in the momentary equilibrium are quite similar to those of monetary policy. A tax-financed increase in real government purchases of goods and services generates an initial excess demand in the commodity market which causes commodity prices to rise. The increased commodity price causes a shift of the labor supply function as in Figure 1, since the same type of money illusion prevails here as in the monetary policy case. In the momentary equilibrium real output, employment, prices, and money wages are higher than in the initial equilibrium, but real wages are lower. In this case, since the stock of money has not changed, we can conclude unambiguously that the interest rate, r, must be higher for the "money" and bond markets to be restored to equilibrium.

It is well known that in the short-run equilibrium the increases in real government purchases and taxes do not have any impact on real output and employment. Hence, output and employment must be lower relative to the momentary equilibrium. Real government purchases, in the short run, "crowd out" an equal amount of real private expenditures. This "crowding out" comes about through increases in P and r which reduce both private consumption demand and private investment demand. Since in

---

[13]This analysis is carried out in Appendix D, which is available only as part of the [original 1974] reprint to this article. See footnote 8.

the short-run equilibrium, as compared to the initial equilibrium, P is higher and X remains unchanged, "crowding out" does not in general occur in nominal terms.[14]

In this model, crowding out occurs in nominal terms only if P remains unchanged, and all the adjustment of private demand comes about through interest rate changes. This occurs only if additional assumptions are made about the nature of the demand for real cash balances. In particular, complete nominal "crowding out" of tax-financed changes in government purchases of goods and services occurs in this model only if both the interest elasticity of the demand for real cash balances and the real wealth elasticity of the demand for real cash balances are equal to zero. In addition, the demand for real cash balances must be specified as a function of real output, and not real disposable income, to the extent that there exists a current real income elasticity of this function. Under these circumstances, if P were to rise (fall), the supply of real cash balances would decline (rise), but the demand for real cash balances would remain unchanged. Hence, any P other than the initial P would be inconsistent with equilibrium in the "money" market.

Fiscal Policy: Changes in Real Government Expenditures Financed by Selling Debt or Printing Money

The impacts of changes in government expenditures financed by debt issue or money creation are similar to those of the tax financing case, but the magnitudes are different. In the debt financing case, there exists a problem of definition similar to that encountered in the open market operation discussed above. Changes in outstanding debt imply changes in interest costs. Also, to the extent that there are induced effects on the commodity price level, the value of government purchases of goods and services and the value of tax receipts are changed, upsetting the financing constraint. We have assumed that a debt-financed change in government expenditures is accompanied by changes in real taxes which leaves real disposable income in the short-run equilibrium unchanged from the initial equilibrium value. Using this convention, a situation of financing by printing money, which can be thought of as a debt financing situation simultaneously accompanied by a pure open market purchase of government debt, requires no change in taxes.

---

[14]Nominal "crowding out" is implied by Andersen's fourth proposition. It is not clear how generally this proposition is accepted among "monetarists." The implication of the St. Louis model (Leonall C. Andersen and Keith M. Carlson, "A Monetarist Model for Economic Stabilization," this *Review* (April 1970), pp. 7-25), is that changes in nominal *high employment* government expenditures, if unaccompanied by changes in the money stock, will ultimately leave nominal GNP unchanged. Since high employment government expenditures differ from actual government expenditures only by some adjustments to unemployment compensation, this equation might be interpreted as implying complete "nominal crowding out." For a further defense of the nominal crowding out position, see Roger W. Spencer and William P. Yohe, "The 'Crowding Out' of Private Expenditures by Fiscal Policy Actions," this *Review* (October 1970), pp. 12-24.

As noted above, the effects of changes in government expenditures on the commodity price level in the short-run equilibrium differ depending on the financing mode. In particular, debt financing has a smaller impact on the price level than printing money. Further, the impact of a debt-financed change in government expenditures on the price level is not zero, unless both the interest elasticity and the wealth elasticity of the demand for real cash balances are zero. Again, complete nominal crowding out of real government expenditures requires extreme assumptions in this model.

The Relation of This Model to the Textbook
Post-Keynesian Model

The model presented in Tables 1 and 3 has been discussed in terms of the monetarist propositions stated in the introduction. It has been shown that comparison of a momentary run, in which information costs are positive, with a short run, in which information is perfect, can produce conclusions similar to those alleged by the proponents of monetarism.

Consider a situation in which, no matter what the length of the run, households remain perfectly ignorant with respect to commodity prices ($\lambda_2 = 0$). In contrast, assume households possess perfect information on money wages ($\lambda_1 = 1$). The perceived real wage rate in all runs is then $(W_e/P_e) = (W/P_o)$, and the labor supply function states that the quantity of labor services supplied is a function solely of the nominal wage rate, regardless of the length of the run. This, however, is just the usual post-Keynesian assumption about the labor supply function.

Theoretical consistency suggests that these assumptions about the information parameters be carried over to the other household behavior functions. This implies that the consumption function and asset demand functions should not be homogenous of degree zero in money income, nominal wealth, and commodity prices. The post-Keynesian literature on these functions is not completely consistent on this interpretation. Modigliani states that the homogeneity restrictions should be applied to both the consumption functions and asset demand equations, even though the labor supply function depends only on the nominal wage rate.[15]

In empirical studies, the approach has been mixed. At least one study of the consumption function has taken the approach that the specification should allow for the existence of money illusion in the consumption function and the data should be allowed to indicate the result.[16] More frequently, the homogeneity restrictions have been applied *a priori*. In the empirical literature on the money demand function, the approach has been less one sided, with both homogeneous and nonhomogeneous functions prevalent in the literature.[17]

[15]Modigliani, "The Monetary Mechanism," pp. 79–107.

[16]William H. Branson and Alvin K. Klevorick, "Money Illusion and the Aggregate Consumption Function," *American Economic Review* (December 1969), pp. 832–849.

[17]See David Laidler, "The Rate of Interest and the Demand for Money: Some Empirical Evidence," *Journal of Political Economy* (December 1966), pp. 543–555.

The assumption that $\lambda_2 = 0$ and $\lambda_1 = 1$ is of course just a particular case of the general case of $\lambda_2 < \lambda_1 \leq 1$, which we use to characterize the momentary equilibrium case above. Thus, all of the results which were discussed for the momentary equilibrium are characteristic of the post-Keynesian case. Within this framework, the main difference between the post-Keynesians and the monetarists appears to be how rapidly households develop correct perceptions of price and wage developments.

The Relation of This Model to Other Monetarist Issues

It was noted at the beginning of this analysis that the results which were generated from this framework would satisfy many of the monetarist propositions about the working of the macroeconomy. However, it was emphasized that this should not be considered as "the" monetarist model. In particular, there are many aspects of it which monetarists would allege are incomplete. Since the analysis is confined to comparative statics, nothing has been said, nor can anything be said, about real versus nominal interest rates.

In addition, the analysis is restricted to the four-market model which is usually presented, implicitly or explicitly, in the commonly used macroeconomics texts. This has been done purposefully in the attempt to maintain comparability. On the other hand, the model definitely will appear deficient to many monetarists because of this restriction. In particular, no banking sector has been explicitly developed, so all cash balances in the economy are high-powered money. Thus, all problems associated with the relationship between money and a monetary base concept are swept aside.

Recently, Karl Brunner and Allan Meltzer have alleged that the four-market model is an inadequate framework within which to discuss the working of the macroeconomy because it omits an essential market, the market for existing real capital.[18] The analysis presented above could be extended to include an additional market and an additional price, that of existing assets. Obviously, such a model can have different implications on the results of various policy actions, and it is possible that a thorough analysis of such a model along the lines presented here would produce considerably more optimistic results for those who are persuaded that "nominal crowding out" of real government expenditures, in the absence of monetary financing, is an important feature of the economic picture.

Conclusions

All of the "monetarist" propositions about the results of monetary policy actions, and all but one of the propositions about the results of fiscal policy actions (the

[18]Karl Brunner and Allan Meltzer, "Money, Debt, and Economic Activity," *Journal of Political Economy* (September/October 1972), pp. 951-977.

exception being nominal "crowding out"), have been derived without any explicit restrictions on the interest elasticity of the demand function for real cash balances. In particular, the results *do not* require that this elasticity be zero, either at momentary equilibrium or at short-run equilibrium. Rather, the propositions are derived from explicit and differing assumptions about price perceptions. Furthermore, the original model, with the labor supply curve replaced by the assumption of a permanently rigid money wage rate, is easily recognizable as the textbook "complete" Keynesian model.

The rather pessimistic conclusion suggested by this analysis is that a decade of academic debate on the relative stability of monetary velocity and the autonomous expenditure multiplier has been totally extraneous to the basic problem. On balance, the debate has probably been harmful to our understanding of the impact of alternative stabilization policies. The issues involved in these debates just do not discriminate between alternative hypotheses of macroeconomic behavior.

The (Neo)-Classical Resurgence and the Reappraisal of Keynes' Theory of Employment

A. G. Hines

The (Neo)-Classical Resurgence

Within the past five years the work of Clower, Leijonhufvud and others has re-awakened interest in the question of what constitutes the theoretical basis of the "Keynesian" revolution.

Before this there had been a consensus among the majority and perhaps dominant school in the profession as to the nature of Keynes' contribution to economics. That consensus was not very flattering to Keynes' claim to have produced a general theory which provided a synthesis between the theory of value and the theory of money. For the consensus asserted that Keynes had really taken the then current model, and had arbitrarily imposed certain restrictions upon it—converting certain functions into constraints, setting certain price elasticities equal to infinity or to zero—and then had claimed not only to have refuted the Classical model but also to have provided a more general theory. As was pointed out during the great debate, to make that kind of claim and to make it stick, one has to take on a theory on its own grounds. According to the consensus, this is precisely what Keynes had failed to do. It would not be overstating the position to say that the prevailing view was that so far as pure theory was concerned Keynes would have been well advised not to have written the

Reprinted with deletion of footnotes from *On the Reappraisal of Keynesian Economics* (London: Martin Robertson, 1971), pp. 7-22, by permission of the publisher and the author.

General Theory at all. He should have written a note in the Economic Journal (or perhaps more appropriately written a letter to *The Times*) making the rather obvious observation that in modern capitalist economies money wages are rigid in a downward direction. It would also have helped if he had not clouded the issue by making incantatory noises about the "dark forces, of time and ignorance, which envelop our times," and by introducing funny mechanical toys such as the multiplier.

If proof were required that this was in fact the dominant view of the Keynesian revolution, one has only to look at the Neo-Classical resurgence, the revival of the Quantity Theory or the work of Patinkin and the character of the debate which surrounded it. True, there still existed in various corners of England some followers of Keynes. But then the English are well known for their love and reverence for ancient monuments and relics.

The standard models in terms of which the debate was conducted are well known and it is not necessary to write them down. The usual argument is familiar. Given wage and price flexibility, the equations of the labour market determine a market clearing real wage rate at full employment of labour. Since the historically given capital stock is thrown on to the market in perfectly inelastic supply, the production function determines the maximum obtainable level of output. Given output, the equilibrium condition in the market for commodities simultaneously determines the rate of interest and the proportion of its income which the community wishes to consume currently, and the proportion which it wishes to use to add to the man-made means of production. With real income and the rate of interest determined, the equilibrium condition in the money market determines the price level for a given stock of money. This result is not vitiated by adding to the model an asset demand for money and by setting its partial derivative with respect to the rate of interest equal to infinity. Nor is it affected by setting the elasticities of the expenditure sector with respect to the rate of interest close to, or equal to, zero. So long as there is a stock of outside government debt, which is assumed to be the net worth of the private sector, under a regime of wage and price flexibility, the solution state of the model exhibits full employment, i.e., it lies on the physical transformation frontier of society.

Naturally, if one assumes that one price, the money price of labour, is rigid because workers are organised in trade unions and/or suffer from money illusion, then it follows trivially that for a given stock of money the model no longer necessarily yields a unique full-employment solution. In this context the introduction of a speculative demand for money together with the money illusion which is allegedly built into it does not matter. It simply weakens the strong version of the quantity theory of money.

It had to be admitted that the logical validity of the Classical model depended ultimately on the existence of a stock of outside money and the indifference of the public sector to the size of its liabilities. It was agreed that this was a slender reed on which to lean in a situation in which the real wage rate was too high. Consideration of time lags, the relevant magnitudes of the response of aggregate expenditure to changes in net worth, possible perverse expectations and so on indicated that both social justice and efficiency in the choice of instruments required the use of fiscal and monetary policies to correct any chance departure from the equilibrium state. As Leijonhufvud points out, it was this admission which was responsible for the recent truce and the burial of the Keynes vs. Classics debate. For the theorists were prepared to concede to those with a more practical turn of mind that the so called "Keynes special case" is the one which is empirically relevant for short-run policy. The Classics won the intellectual battle; Keynes won the policy war. Again the victorious theorists were too polite to point out that "Keynesian" policies were being advocated by a varied assortment of men long before the General Theory appeared.

This state of affairs has been rudely shattered by the work of Clower and Leijonhufvud. For, if they are correct—as indeed they are correct—Keynes' claim is substantiated or, at the very least, is still on the agenda. A major revision and abandonment of certain well-entrenched views is in order, and the theoretical questions which Keynes posed still stand at the frontier of on-going research in our subject. For their thesis is that Keynes' under-employment state (it is a matter of semantics whether we call it an equilibrium state, since equilibrium is nothing more than a short-hand term for the set of values of the variables that satisfies the equations of a given model) can be shown to exist independently of liquidity traps, the equality of savings and investment requiring a non-feasible negative price vector, money illusion, rigid wages, etc.

Let me summarise, or rather give my own interpretation of, the core of their contention.

The Reappraisal of Keynes' Theory of Employment

Keynes was well aware that if he was to show that he had a theory which was more general than that of his predecessors, he had to take on their theory on its own grounds. Consequently, he accepted the following (Neo)-Classical assumptions.

(a) Households are rational in the sense that they maximise well-ordered utility functions irrespective of whether the arguments of these functions are contemporaneously available commodities or present and future commodities.

(b) Firms maximise profits.

(c) Well-behaved physical transformation functions exist.

(d) There is a "large" number of traders on each side of each market.

(e) Price incentives are effective.

(f) Transactors do not suffer from money illusion.

His challenge went to the very heart of Neo-Classical theory, for as Leijonhufvud points out: "in a large system where decision making is decentralised, the efficient working of the price mechanism requires that it fulfils two functions simultaneously: (a) prices should *disseminate the information* necessary to co-ordinate the economic activities and plans of the independent transactors and (b) prices should *provide the incentives* for transactors to adjust their activities in such manner that they become consistent in the aggregate." In other words, if the market clearing vector of relative prices (which is assumed to exist) is known by all transactors, and if each transactor adjusts to these parameters, the system simultaneously generates an optimal allocation of resources and ensures that they are fully employed. To demonstrate his thesis Keynes was willing to accept the proposition that price incentives are effective. What he denied was that the price system disseminates the appropriate information with sufficient efficiency to guarantee the full employment of the economy's resources, at any rate in the short run.

The question of the dissemination of information concerning the market clearing price vector has worried the truly great minds of our profession. Adam Smith thought that it was all done by "the invisible hand"; Edgeworth allowed his traders to "re-contract"; Walras had an auctioneer who, without cost to the system, called out the prices. Walras made the proviso, which is very apposite in this context, that contracts were not binding and no trade was to take place until the market clearing vector of prices was finally announced. Moreover, if the system was subjected to some exogenous disturbance, say a change in tastes or in technology, the auctioneer would immediately announce the new market clearing price vector and, given the implied infinite velocity of price adjustments, the system would immediately adjust to its new optimal position. If we extend the argument to an economy in which accumulation is taking place and in which expenditure plans extend over n time periods, the optimal operation of such an economy requires that the Walrasian auctioneer should disseminate the information concerning the vector of inter-temporal relative prices which would simultaneously clear all present and future markets.

But what is the situation if, as Keynes insisted, there is no such auctioneer? We immediately face a dilemma. For, as Arrow points out, if each transactor is a price taker, who is left over to make the price? Let us imagine that the going price vector is somehow correct; then everything is satisfactory. But now let the system be subject to some exogenous disturbance such that it requires a new market clearing vector if plans are to mesh in the aggregate. What then? It is clear that we are no longer in a state of perfect competition. Perfect competition requires that each transactor be able to buy and sell as much as he wishes at going prices and this clearly cannot happen at a wrong set of relative prices. As long as disequilibrium exists, each optimising transactor must behave like a monopolist, since he faces downward sloping demand and upward sloping supply curves along which he must search for the correct combination of prices and/or quantities. And we are immediately faced with the probability that trade may take place at false prices.

In an attempt to be more realistic than Walras and Edgeworth, Hicks wished to generalise his analysis of the determination of relative prices to markets in which there is no auctioneer and/or in which re-contracting is not permitted. He therefore had to admit the possibility of false trading at disequilibrium prices. However, he wished to show that the same equilibrium price set is attainable as in the case in which all trade takes place at equilibrium prices. Consequently, he assumed that the only effect of false trading would be a re-distribution of income between buyers and sellers and that the income effects of such re-distribution would be small, because the volume of false trading would be small and would occur at prices which did not deviate much from the set of equilibrium prices and would in any case tend to cancel out on both sides of the market "if any intelligence is shown in price fixing." Hicks observed "that a certain degree of indeterminateness is nearly always imparted by income effects to the laws of economic theory" and that false trading intensifies this indeterminateness. However, he did not really offer a solution to the question of how the system behaves when there is false trading. For this theoretical issue cannot be settled by the introduction of an empirical assumption which amounts to saying no more than "that income effects can be ignored if they are sufficiently unimportant to be neglected."

What then are we to assume about the behaviour of the typical transactor who holds stocks of assets such as labour, money, bonds, capital goods, etc., and who must in a disequilibrium situation make some assumption about expected market prices and/or quantities? The assumption made by Keynes' predecessors and by the majority of post-Keynesians is that the elasticity of price expectations is unity. Each transactor regards the first set of prices that emerge in the wake of a disturbance as correct. If each transactor acts immediately upon this belief, then unemployed resources cannot emerge even though the resulting situation may not be Pareto optimal. But is this the most reasonable assumption to make? Why, as this argument implies, should transactors regard the present value of their assets as being perfectly variable? Why is it rational for transactors who have some memory and who make plans for the future to regard passively such changes in their net worth as normal?

Imagine a worker who, because of some change which results in a reduction in the demand for his labour, is made unemployed or can only keep his present job by accepting a substantial cut in his money wages. He must decide whether to accept this cut or choose to become unemployed. To make a decision, he has to form a view as to whether the new situation is local or is generalised, is permanent or is temporary. If he regards the situation as localised and temporary, so that the previous wage rate will presently be restored, then this implies that he regards that previous wage as normal. He will, therefore, choose to become unemployed (or more likely to be laid off by his employers without being offered the alternative of accepting a lower wage). He must then begin a search for employment at the expected wage, balancing the cost of search against the probability of obtaining a better offer. At each stage he must compare the present value of the income streams which will emerge if he accepts the next offer against that which he would obtain at his expected best offer, the expected wage itself being a decreasing function of the length of search. Several writers have shown that the inescapable consequence of such phenomena is the emergence of unemployed resources which can be regarded at the *micro* level as a reservation demand on the part of the owner for the services of his own assets.

Or again, consider the position of a bond holder. The typical ultimate asset holder in Keynes' theory is an individual in the middle of his life cycle who owns a share in the system's physical capital. Given the assumption that more roundabout processes are physically more productive than less roundabout ones—a Cassellian proposition which begs the index number question—the economy is tempted by the profitability of "long" processes to carry a stock of illiquid assets. But this stock will turn over more slowly than households want. Our typical asset holder from some future date onwards plans to consume in excess of current gross incomes, the amounts and dates of the necessary encashments being presently uncertain. But the maturity structure of his representative share in the system's capital stock is assumed to be too long to match this encashment schedule. He is subject to capital uncertainty since assets may have to be sold at a loss to meet planned encashments. The representative transactor who is presumed to be a risk averter must be offered some compensation for the risk which this speculative position entails, just as a bank must be offered a yield differential between deposits and earning assets in order to borrow short and lend long. Now suppose that there is a fall in bond prices. The bond holder (who like the worker is assumed to have inelastic price expectations) will, as a risk-averting optimiser, buy bonds on the expectation of a capital gain if he regards the previous price as normal, i.e., he will re-arrange his portfolio so that on balance it moves towards the less liquid end of the maturity spectrum. (The argument is symmetrical for a fall in the interest rate.) This is, of course, the basis of the doctrine of liquidity preference.

Exactly the same analysis holds for the owner of any other asset, including entrepreneurs who invest directly in capital goods. Thus in Keynes' short-run model *every* transactor is assumed to have inelastic price expectations; it is not an assumption which applies exclusively to the holders of bonds.

We are, therefore, in a world whose differences from its classical predecessors flow from the failure of the price mechanism to disseminate the information which is required to co-ordinate the plans of transactors both now and in the future. It is a world of inelastic expectations, reservation demands and adjustment costs. Instead of a known vector of relative prices of currently produced commodities, prices are the outcome of a non-*tâtonnement* search procedure. Moreover, whereas one can conceive of changes in institutional arrangements which would improve the dissemination of information concerning the market clearing vector of current relative prices, *in principle* the provision of adequate information concerning the appropriate intertemporal price vector of an uncertain future appears to be impossible. Instead of a known vector of inter-temporal prices we, therefore, have two phenomena: (a) the long-term state of expectations, alias the marginal efficiency of capital which summarises entrepreneurial conjectures about the prospective income streams to be obtained from outlays on physical capital; (b) liquidity preference which determines the composition of portfolios with respect to the continuum of assets with varying dates to maturity. Hence, if plans are to be consistent in the aggregate in the absence of the appropriate forward markets, both the marginal efficiency of capital and the structure of asset prices—"the rate of interest"—must correctly anticipate and reflect future prices and quantities in commodity and financial markets.

Now there is a forward market of sorts in the economy. It is the stock exchange. But this market does not transmit the information that would be provided by the Walrasian auctioneer. For, as Keynes pointed out, although there is the activity of "enterprise" in this market—the genuine attempt, on imperfect information, to forecast the future yields from sources of income and to act upon such forecasts—there is also the activity of "speculation." And in times of disequilibrium the latter easily dominate the former. But it is just at such times that the activity of enterprise should dominate if the effects of the workings of this market are to be stabilising rather than de-stabilising.

Keynes' problem then was to analyse "the economic behaviour of the present under the influence of changing ideas about the future," noting that "it is by reason of the existence of durable equipment that the future is linked to the present." What triggers off a cumulative contraction in the General Theory is a failure in the co-ordination of production, trading and consumption plans in the future. The exogenous disturbances with which Keynes was concerned were either a change in the long-run state of expectations or a change in tastes which altered the propensity to save or the form in which wealth holders chose to hold their assets.

We must now investigate the system-wide implications with respect to the level of aggregate output and employment of any such disturbance.

In a barter system, where all commodities are directly tradeable against each other, the system-wide consequences of such disturbances are not clear. But the Keynesian system is a monetary economy, i.e., it is a system in which money is the only commodity which is directly tradeable in all markets. Here the system-wide implications are abundantly clear.

In a money economy it is necessary to distinguish between *desire* (which may be based on feasible transformation possibilities) and effective demand—desires backed by the ability to pay in *cash*. In such an economy it is money offers to buy and to sell which take over the role of the system of relative prices and act as the mechanism which transmits the relevant market signals to transactors. But this means, as Clower has pointed out, that we must now distinguish between *notional* excess *demands*—excess demands which reflect the underlying real transformation possibilities of the system—and actual or *effective* excess demands—those which are backed by the ability to pay in money and which, therefore, constitute relevant market signals. These two sets of excess demands are only equal when the system is in a full equilibrium. What this means is that except in a full equilibrium in which each excess demand is zero, Walras' Law does not hold as between notional and effective excess demands.

Walras' Law is the proposition that the sum of the value of all excess demands is zero, i.e.,

$$\sum_{i=1}^{n} P_i q_i = 0, \; q_i \equiv D_i - S_i.$$

In a barter economy with a *tâtonnement* mechanism such that trade never takes place at 'false' prices, all excess demand functions hold simultaneously and "the offer of any commodity is an exercise of effective purchasing power over any other commodity." Hence, Walras' Law follows by logical necessity. This is not the case in a money economy since every act of exchange between two non-monetary commodities is necessarily indirect. All this does not matter in full equilibrium when all excess demands are zero. Then Walras' Law does hold. However, in a state of transactor disequilibrium, Walras' Law as usually defined does not hold. Thus, consider an equilibrium which is disturbed by the decision of some transactor to increase his consumption (or holdings) or some commodity i by supplying some other commodity j to the market. In a barter economy with all other excess demand functions equal to zero, we would simply write $X_i = -X_j$ where X_i and X_j are the value of the excess demand for the ith and jth good, respectively. But in a monetary economy, this procedure is not appropriate unless the jth commodity is money. If it is not money, then in order to make his plans effective the individual must first exchange the jth commodity for money and, *if he is successful,* he then exchanges money for the ith commodity. And, since in a non-*tâtonnement* system the actual vector of prices might be such that plans to demand money (plans to supply goods, bonds or factor services) may not be achieved, i.e., actual sales may fall short of or exceed planned sales, the contingent plans to demand goods, bonds and money to hold as an asset stand subject to revision. Clower has analysed what this involves for the optimising transactor as a *"dual decision hypothesis."* Transactors maximise their utility subject to the constraint of their notional income. If their realised and notional incomes are equal, the system is in a full equilibrium and the excess demand functions generated by the solution to the familiar constrained maximisation problem yield relevant market signals. But if actual incomes are not equal to notional incomes, a second round of decision making is in order: the transactor must maximise utility subject to the constraint of realised income, which is the money value of the receipts from the sale of factor services. It is the resulting income-constrained excess demand functions which provide relevant market signals.

Now suppose that, starting from a position of equilibrium, there is an exogenous change in the state of long-term expectations such that entrepreneurs re-evaluate in a downward direction the prospective yields from the services of capital goods and that this results in a reduction in planned investment expenditures at each level of the rate of interest. In the classical full information system, there is a fall in the interest rate which increases the consumption income ratio at an unchanged level of output and employment. In Keynes' theory there is an implication for the level of output and employment. The rate of interest does fall: but its fall is insufficient to equate savings and investment at an unchanged level of income. The limitation in the fall of the interest rate is due to the existence of liquidity preference. Speculators who consider that the rise in bond prices will be reversed offer savers existing bonds from their portfolios (equal in value to the reduced supply of the investors in capital goods) in exchange for money and hoard the proceeds of sale. In these circumstances, there is a fall in expenditure on new capital goods and, given the assumptions which we have already made, unemployed resources emerge in this sector before any countervailing effects of the possible unwinding of the speculative position taken up by the "bears" can make itself felt.

Unemployed resources emerge because of the sequence of trades which is assumed to take place in a production economy in which contracts are made in terms of money. In the absence of a market clearing vector of prices which is known, entrepreneurs plan their output on the basis of the level of demand which they expect to rule in the future and which depends in part upon a weighted average of past levels of sales. Given planned output, firms enter into price contracts, fixed for a stated period, for the services of productive resources. Faced with an unexpected fall in demand, entrepreneurs who are assumed to have inelastic price expectations do not reduce the price of their output within the unit period by an amount which is sufficient to dispose of their current output. They are, therefore, faced with an unintended accumulation of inventories at the end of the period. Even if they plan to make some reduction in the price of output in the next period, they will now reduce the amount of factor services for which they will contract at the end of the current period, especially since the assumption of inelastic price expectations also applies to the owners of these productive services so that they would not accept a reduction in rates of remuneration sufficient to keep their factors employed in the same establishment.

Now consider an unemployed worker in this sector who now begins a search for a wage rate which is consistent with his current estimate of the present value of his labour services. His notional excess supply of labour does not provide him with the means to transmit relevant information concerning his corresponding excess demand for goods. How is he to maintain his desired levels of expenditure? He could run down any accumulated non-labour assets. But then he must do this in a situation in which uncertainty about their realisable value has increased. He could try to borrow, offering as collateral his human and/or non-human wealth. But, in addition to his uncertain but inelastic expectations about their present values, lending institutions themselves have no hard knowledge but must conjecture about the value of the collateral which is being offered. Moreover, in the postulated situation, lending institutions are also attempting to increase the liquidity of their portfolios. The costs of being unemployed are high and we may expect downward revisions in the worker's reservation price as the unemployment state persists. But so long as the elasticity of expectations is less than unity in Keynes' short period, the worker in the sector in which the disturbance first occurs will have an actual income which is less than his notional income and, since actual income now constitutes a binding constraint on actual behaviour, effective demands are now reduced in markets in which the initial shock may have had no impact. Unemployed resources now emerge in these markets and "the search instituted by unemployed workers and producers with excess capacity will yield information on 'effective' demands not on 'notional' demands. The 'multiplier' repercussions thus set in motion make the information acquired 'dated' even while it is being gathered." To each set of trades which takes place there corresponds a set of wrong relative prices which are themselves unknown to all transactors. There is no reason to assume (at any rate without further specification) that in the short run the system is converging to the correct vector of relative prices.

Rather, as Keynes' theory implies, the observed price and quantity changes are *deviation amplifying* and the system probably contracts to a floor which is set by the given stock of money.

The same analysis holds if there is an increase in the propensity to save which is the result of a change in tastes such that households wish to alter the time profile of their consumption stream in favour of future consumption. In the Classical system the rate of interest now falls so that the increased demand for bonds which is assumed to be the analogue of the increase in savings is met by new issues by investors. Savings and investment are equated at a higher investment to income ratio and full employment is maintained. In Keynes' theory the level of output and employment falls. An act of saving is a plan to increase the transactor's future command over *purchasing power in general.* Unlike money expenditure on currently produced goods and services, it does not transmit relevant information to producers concerning the specific goods and the combination thereof which will be demanded in the future. In the absence of this information, the relevant inter-temporal price vector is unknown. Consequently, entrepreneurs do not have the same incentive as in the Classical system to shift the composition of their portfolios towards the less liquid end of the maturity spectrum. The rate of interest does fall, but because of liquidity preference its fall is partially stabilised. Just as in the case of the fall in the marginal efficiency of capital, "bear" speculators offer those who wish to increase their current savings existing bonds from their portfolios and hoard the proceeds of sale. Thus, only a fraction of the increased demand for bonds is met by new issues. In these circumstances there is a fall in expenditure on consumer goods which is not offset by the increased expenditure on investment goods. Unemployed resources emerge; the process which we have already described is under way, and when the equality of savings and investment does come about, it is the result of a cumulative contraction in incomes and employment.

Thus, contrary to what has become standard doctrine, liquidity preference—or rather the hypothesis of inelastic price expectations which underlies the notion of liquidity preference—can explain under-employment equilibrium. The multiplier does amplify initial disturbances. For we have been analysing the consequences of false trading in a situation in which the actual vector of relative prices is not only wrong but is unknown. To generate Keynes' under-employment state, we simply relinquish the strong, but in the context inappropriate, Classical assumption of infinite velocity of prices and zero velocity of quantities within the unit period. A reversal of the ranking of price and quantity velocities is sufficient. Specifically, the assumption of an absolute rigidity in the money wage rate is not necessary to explain under-employment. Indeed the Keynesian analysis leads to the distinctly non-Classical conclusion that in a general equilibrium model unemployed resources may emerge in the ith market at a correct money price in that market because the money price is wrong in the jth market. In this case, the ith market is the labour market: the jth market is the market for "bonds." Moreover, contrary to Walras' Law, the system can attain a (temporary) equilibrium with an excess supply of labour which is not matched by an equivalent value of *effective* excess demand for goods. The unemployed workers may be said to have an excess demand for money. However, it is notional rather than effective inasmuch as it cannot work "directly on the price system to offset prevailing elements of excess supply." The contingent excess demand for goods is also notional since it cannot be communicated to producers unless and until labour is successfully exchanged for money.

In such a situation a policy of cutting money wages is a faulty prescription based on a wrong diagnosis. For in Keynes' analysis of advanced capitalist economies, a disequilibrium is usually assumed to originate in a change in long-run expectations or in liquidity preference, which generates a rate of interest too high for a general equilibrium. A sufficient cut in money wages would, *ceteris paribus,* restore a correct relative price between "bonds" and labour services. But since we are in a general equilibrium model, this would clearly not achieve the appropriate price ratios between "bonds" and the other commodities of the model. Moreover, the Pigou effect—the direct effect on aggregate expenditure of a change in the value of the nominal money stock—is irrelevant in this setting. For, as we have seen, Keynes' diagnosis of the malady is that relative prices are "wrong"; and, if this is the case, an all-round deflation will not help. A priori it could only work if it affected relative prices, i.e., if it lowers the rate of interest relative to the money wage rate. This is possible since the rate of interest has the highest ranking in terms of velocity among the set of prices in Keynes' short-period model. But now we are really talking about the Keynes' wealth effect, i.e., the effect on aggregate consumption of changes in the rate of interest. Leijonhufvud's dismissal of the Pigou effect is very neat.

Liability Structures and the Pace of a Unit's Investment

Hyman P. Minsky

4

Although Keynes did not go into the details of how finance affected system behavior, he emphasized that in an economy with borrowing and lending, finance took on a special importance:

> Two types of risk affect the volume of investment which have not commonly been distinguished, but which it is important to distinguish. The first is the entrepreneur's or borrower's risk and arises out of doubts in his own mind as to the probability of his actually earning the prospective yield for which he hopes. If a man is venturing his own money, this is the only risk which is relevant.
>
> But where a system of borrowing and lending exists, by which I mean the granting of loans with a margin of real or personal security, a second type of risk is relevant which we may call the lender's risk. This may be due to either a moral hazard i.e. voluntary default or other means of escape, possibly lawful, from the fulfillment of the obligation, or the possible insufficiency of the margin of security i.e. involuntary default due to the disappointment of expectation. [*GT,* p. 144]

Loans, mortgages, bonds, and shares are the currency business firms use, either directly or indirectly after first exchanging them for money, to buy capital assets from the market, or from new production (i.e., investment). As against the prospec-

Reprinted from Hyman P. Minsky, *John Maynard Keynes* (New York: Columbia University Press, 1975), pp. 106–114, by permission of the publisher and the author.

tive yield, Q, on additions to their capital assets, firms which finance in this manner pledge to pay, by contract CC on additions to their liabilities. Except when it involves shares this pledge is contractual, with penalties for default; for shares any deviation of dividends from the expected will affect equity prices.

Each acquisition of a capital asset, either from the market or from new production of capital assets, when financed in this way involves a margin of security. Typically, additional capital assets are acquired partially by own funds and partially by borrowed or outside funds, new-share capital being one class of outside funds. As was emphasized earlier, the fundamental speculative decision by a firm is how to finance control over its needed capital assets: how much by the firm's own resources and how much by borrowed resources. This decision is a determinant of both the firm's size, as measured by capital assets or sales, and the rate of growth of the firm's capital assets and sales.

Let us examine the financing behavior of a representative investing firm.

Such a firm expects this coming period's gross profits after taxes, and after its required payments on its debts and its dividends to stockholders, to be $\hat{Q}_i$; $\hat{Q}_i$ is independent of the level of the firm's own investment, although aggregate investment, by affecting income, affects the aggregate $\hat{Q}$. $\hat{Q}_i$ is the internal financing that the firm expects will be available this coming period.

We also assume that the supply price of the capital asset it expects to purchase, P_{I_i}, determined by the producers of capital assets, is independent of the amount purchased by this firm; the firm is not so large a buyer of capital assets that its own demand affects the price. Therefore, the amount of investment which can be financed internally is $\hat{I}_i = \hat{Q}_i/P_i$; that is, $P_{I_i}\hat{I}_i = \hat{Q}_i$; the internal financing constraint is a rectangular hyperbola in the (P_I, I) plane $(\hat{Q}_i-Q_i$ in Diagram 1).

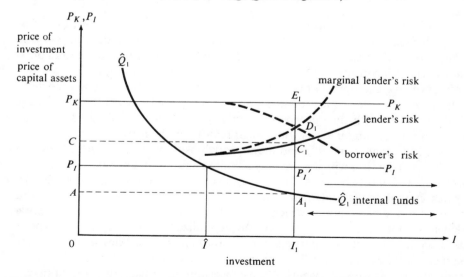

DIAGRAM 1. THE FINANCING BEHAVIOR OF A REPRESENTATIVE FIRM

In Diagram 1, if the firm would buy $\hat{I}$ of investment at P_I it could finance the entire amount internally. If the firm purchases $I_1 > I$ of investment at P_I, then $P_I I_1 - \hat{Q}$ will be debt financed: the firm will promise to pay future cash, in the form of various flows, CC, in exchange for $P_I I_1 - \hat{Q}$ of current cash. There is an exception. The firm may have excess current cash or marketable securities, which it uses to finance these purchases. There are valid reasons in a world of uncertainty why a firm or household with debts will also own idle money and other financial assets, i.e., other unit's debts. In part, this cash and financial-asset position insulates the normal operations of the firm from market vicissitudes. When such cash assets are drawn down, the firm decreases this protection. Analytically, the decrease in such cash buffers is equivalent to a rise in debts; both changes imply that the set of events in nature which can seriously affect the firm's ability to meet commitments or carry out plans has increased—the margin of security has decreased.

The firm capitalizes its prospective yields, Q_i—which include dividends, interest, and other cash payments on debt but exclude taxes—at a rate $\hat{K}$. This places a value on the firm's stock of capital assets, $\hat{P}_{K_i} \cdot K_i = \hat{K}(Q_i)$, which is independent of the firm's financial structure. The firm also capitalizes its cash-flow commitments, CC, due to debts, dividends, etc. We assume, in this argument, that the capitalization rate on debts is also $\hat{K}$, although we really expect the capitalization rate on CC, debts, to be higher than on Q, prospective yields. This is so because to a borrower the cash flows on debts, the CCs, are viewed as being certain, whereas the cash flows from capital assets, the Qs, are uncertain.

For investment to take place it is necessary that $P_{K_i} > K(Q_i)/K_i \geq P_I$, that the price of a unit of capital be greater than or equal to the price of a unit of investment. In the absence of debt-financing we have $\hat{I} = \hat{Q}_{io}/P_I$. This is the $\hat{I}$ of investment in Diagram 1.

For capital-asset acquisition to be financed either by retained earnngs, $\hat{Q}_i$, or by debt, it is necessary that $\hat{K}(Q_i - CC_i) > 0$. In an abstract, hypothetical world in which the supply of finance to a firm is infinitely elastic, in which all prices and prospective yields are independent of the firm's own scale of operation, and into which the realities of risk and uncertainty never intrude, if the cash flows CC on the debts necessary to finance the acquisition of a unit of capital are less than the prospective yields, then a firm, with such prospects, would want to buy an unlimited—nay, an infinite—amount of capital assets. But vulgar realities in the form of borrower's and lender's risk, let alone monopoly and monopsony positions, intrude, so that even if $\hat{K}(Q - CC) > 0$ the firm will acquire only a limited amount of capital assets.

Borrower's risk has two facets. First, in a world with uncertainty, where the fates of various capital assets and firms can differ, a risk averter will diversify. This means that beyond some point, which for the individual wealth owner or corporation depends upon the size of his wealth, the capitalization rate for any one type of capital asset to be used in a particular line of commerce declines as the amount owned increases. Second, since the borrower sees the cash flows due to debts (CCs) as certain and the prospective yields (Qs) as uncertain, increasing the ratio of investment that is debt-financed decreases the margin of security and thus lowers the capitalization rate the borrower applies to the Qs.

Because of borrower's risk, therefore, the demand price for capital assets "falls away" from P_K, and this falling away can be expected to become more precipitous the greater the commitment to this particular type of capital asset and the greater the ratio of borrowed funds. The falling away will normally take place at some point to the right of $\hat{I}$, the amount of investment that can be internally financed, but it may take place to the left of $\hat{I}$. The latter will happen if the view develops that either the inherited commitment to this particular type of capital asset is too great, so that a desire to diversify or to disinvest becomes dominant, or that the inherited balance sheet contains too much debt. These "new" views can arise as a result of events. Symmetrical views can develop favoring more specialization and more debt.

Borrower's risk is subjective; it never appears on signed contracts. It is a focal point for the "quivers and quavers" of uncertainty and the "surprise" of high animal spirits.

Lender's risk does appear on signed contracts. For any set of market conditions, lender's risk, as it applies to a particular firm, takes the form of increased cash-flow requirements in debt contracts, as the ratio of debt to total assets increases. Lender's risk shows up in financial contracts in various forms: higher interest rates, shorter terms to maturity, a requirement to pledge specific assets as collateral, and restrictions on dividend payouts and further borrowing are some of them. Lender's risk rises with an increase in the ratio of debt to equity financing or the ratio of committed cash flows to total prospective cash flows.

In a significant sense, the current supply price of a capital asset to a particular prospective purchaser is not the price per unit at which it is purchased. The supply price is the price at which a producer—or an owner—offers to sell the capital asset plus a capitalized value of the excess of the cash-flow commitments in the financial contract over the commitments which would have been implicit if the investment were internally financed. This "add on" is the capitalized value of the inverse of insurance. The greater the leverage an investing unit uses, i.e., the greater the ratio of debt to internal financing, the greater are such excess contractual cash-flow commitments. Thus the effective P_I curve has a discontinuity at the amount of investment that can be internally financed, $\hat{I}$. After some positive amount of debt-financing the P_I curve can be expected to begin to rise and then to rise at an increasing rate. Furthermore, as the contractual debt ratio rises, all debt issued by the unit will, upon refinancing, have to conform to the marginal contract; thus with a lag a curve marginal to the rising supply curve, the equivalent of a "monopsony" curve, becomes the relevant decision-determining relation which embodies lender's risk.

The fundamental fact about both borrower's and lender's risks is that they reflect subjective valuations. Two entrepreneurs facing identical objective circumstances but having different temperaments would view the borrower's risk quite differently: where one decision-maker will invest, say, I_1, another will extend himself to invest more or be satisfied with less. Lender's risks do lead to observable patterns of borrowing rates, such as those that appear in the "ratings" put on municipal and corporate debt by various services or the premiums over the prime rate that firms have to pay at banks. At any one time, "the market" seems to operate with a consensus about the extent to which operations can be debt-financed for a particular rating, but this consensus can be both stretched and changed: both the acceptable and the actual debt-equity ratios vary in a systematic way over the longer business-cycle swings.

The intersection of the demand curve, allowing for borrower's risk, and the supply curve, adjusted for lender's risk, determines the scale of investment. In Diagram 1, with the intersection of these supply and demand curves incorporating borrower's and lender's risk at D_1, investment will be I_1, at a price, per unit of capital assets, of P_I. Of the total investment spending of $0P_IP_I'I_1$, $0A\ A_1I_1$ will be internally financed and $A\ P_IP_I'A_1$ will be debt-financed.

Of the prospective yields per unit of capital, the borrowing results in pledged cash flows proportional to A_1C_1/I_1E_1, and the equity owners expect to receive cash flows proportional to $(IA_1 + C_1E_1)/I_1E_1$.

After the capital assets are integrated into the firm's production process, and if these capital assets yield the anticipated Qs, then at the capitalization rate $\hat{K}$, the capital assets $0I_1$ will be valued at P_K. Their total value will be $0P_KE_1I_1$; the investor will have a capital gain. The debts, now more secure, will be generating a cash flow proportional to A_1C_1, but will be capitalized at a lower interest rate than they were initially, for the lender's risk premium will have proven to be excessive. As a result the bondholders will also have a capital gain. The value to the equity owners of their

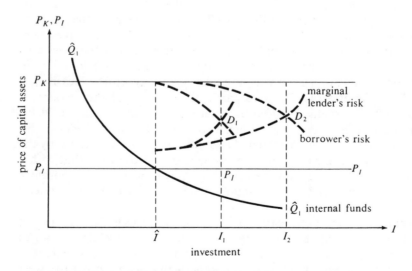

DIAGRAM 2. SENSITIVITY OF INVESTMENT TO RISK ESTIMATES

initial investment $\hat{Q}_1$, (equal to $0AA_1I_1$) will be $0AA_1I_1$ plus $CP_KE_1C_1$. This should be reflected in the showing on the exchange of the price of these shares. The existence of lender's risk and borrower's risk as factors limiting investment assures that the successful operation of capital assets will lead to capital appreciation for both the borrower and lender. The Shakespearean dictum "Neither a borrower nor a lender be" fails to take into account the capital gains both parties can enjoy.

The pace of investment is most sensitive to these borrower's and lender's risks. If the curves fall away sharply from the capitalized value of the Qs and rise sharply from the price of investment goods, then investment will be mainly internally financed; if they are shallow rather than steep, the financing of investment will be more heavily levered.

Each period inherits both a liability structure and a set of capital assets from the past. If the repercussions of experience upon preferences and expectations are such that the borrower's and lender's risks are lowered, so that $I_2 > I_1$ of investment is undertaken for a given $\hat{Q}$, (as is illustrated in Diagram 2), then a comparable shift will have to take place in the acceptable debt-equity ratio for the stock of capital assets owned by the unit. This will uncover a great deal of ability to finance investment by borrowing on the basis of ownership of the inherited stock of capital assets. That is, for the stock of capital assets owned by firms, the ratio of CC, cash due on debts, to Q, the gross cash flows after taxes, will be low by the new standards. The leverage of investment financing on expected earnings can be very high during a period of decreasing risk aversion, because capital appreciation uncovers borrowing power.

If a decrease in risk aversion affects households that own shares in the same way that it affects managers and bankers, who effect the shifts in acceptable debt ratios for investment and capital holdings, then households will become more willing to use more debt to own shares, and bankers will be more willing to finance such "margin" purchases of shares. This will lead to a rise in share prices. Such a rise in the market price of equities was interpreted by Keynes as involving "an increase in the marginal efficiency of the corresponding type of capital" (*GT*, p. 151, footnote 1), which in the terminology used here raises P_K for given Qs.

Keynes noted that "During a boom the popular estimation of both of these risks, both borrower's risk and lender's risk, is apt to become unusually and imprudently low" (*GT*, p. 145). This implies that during a boom the ratio of debt-financing to investment increases: this is borne out by the available data on corporate debt.

Aggregate Investment

The above argument has been for a hypothetical firm or household. We need to aggregate to extend the argument to the economy. We carry over from the earlier analysis the proposition that for a given stock of capital assets, portfolio preferences yield a market price–money supply relation for capital assets in general which is such that the market price of a capital asset is positively related to the quantity of money.

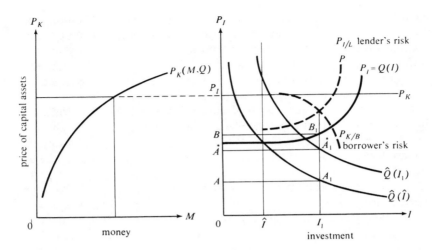

DIAGRAM 3. AGGREGATE INVESTMENT AND FINANCE

This $P_K = P_K(M,Q)$ function has embodied in it the three "slips" identified by Keynes; between money and the interest rate on debts; between the debt interest rate and the marginal efficiency of capital, i.e., the capitalization factors for capital assets; and between the marginal efficiency of capital and the prospective yield on capital assets. Given the quantity of money, this relation determines a demand price for investment goods. The demand curve for capital assets is positively sloped with respect to the supply of money.

Diagram 3 illustrates the relation between aggregate investment and finance. The supply curve of investment goods is a rising function of the quantity of investment. The anticipated internal funds are given by $\hat{Q}(\hat{I})$. The intersection of $P_{I,L}$ and $P_{K,B}$—the supply price of investment goods conditional upon the lender's risk of bankers and the demand price of investment goods conditional upon the borrower's risk of firms—determines the actual pace of investment. Of the total amount spent on investment $0BB_1I_1$, $0AA_1I_1$ are anticipated internal funds and ABB_1A_1 are anticipated borrowed funds.

Let us assume that the financing plan, for the investment of I_1, was based upon the profits firms anticipated they would earn if aggregate income were sufficient to finance an aggregate investment of $\hat{I}$. In fact aggregate investment is I_1, and as this excess investment leads to a higher than anticipated aggregate income, it will also lead to a flow of internal funds of $\hat{Q}(I_1)$, which is greater than anticipated. As a result, after the event, the internal cash flows are such that $0*A *A_1I_1$ of the investment is financed internally and $*ABB_1*A_1$ is financed externally. In the case illustrated the improvement of realized profits partially frustrates the planned debt-financing of investments of firms and simultaneously reinforces the willingness of firms and bankers to debt-finance further increases in investment. The unused leverage carries over and is available for financing future investment. In addition, as debt charges are lower than anticipated, the share earnings are greater. Equity prices will respond favorably to such increases in the flow of internal funds.

We have constructed a way of looking at investment in which the "popular estimation" of lender's and borrower's risk, which is admittedly influenced by the past performance of the economy, acts as the immediate governor of the pace of investment and thus of the economy. Whenever the willingness to debt-finance increases and is carried through, as is illustrated in Diagram 2, then the objective ratio of the *CC*s to the *Q*s increases. As the *CC*s rise relative to the *Q*s, the gross profits after taxes and after the cash commitment due to liabilities will begin to grow less rapidly than the pace of investment and of debt. As lenders and borrowers seek new ways to finance investment, borrowers increasingly, on the margin, will tap sources of funds that value liquidity ever more highly—that is, contract terms on debts will rise. This implies that short-run cash needs due to debts can outrun the cash being generated by the *Q*s. This is due mainly to the short-term nature of many boom debts, which require the repayment of principal at a faster pace than the cash generated by the underlying operation permits. Units which use this type of debt need to refinance their debt as contracts fall due.

A boom once started lives a precarious life. It depends upon realization of optimistic expectations about yields, so that capital gains accrue to investors in debts and shares as well as to investors in capital assets. From a multitude of possible causes—rising wages or production costs, feedbacks from rising interest rates to the value of older long-term debt, the high cost of refunding previous debt—a large number of units can be forced to try to raise cash at the same time by taking advantage of the liquidity that some of their assets are presumed to have, i.e., by attempting to sell "liquid" assets. Furthermore, for some units the burden of debt in the form of cash commitments can become so large that they are forced to sell or pledge capital assets to acquire cash to meet debt commitments.

This can happen to ordinary firms and to financial organizations.

Assets are liquid so long as there is no preponderance of sellers over buyers. Whenever the need to make position by selling assets becomes quite general, then, unless there is a large standby market supporter, such as a conscientious central bank, asset prices can fall precipitously. When prices of assets—including shares— fall, the corresponding marginal efficiency, or the corresponding demand price of the capital assets, falls too.

In Diagram 4 the situation after a "crisis," or a reconsideration of the desirable debt structure, is portrayed. With $P_{K_i}(M,Q)$ and M_0 of money the market price of capital assets is high enough so that positive debt-financing could result. However, recent experience has made the potential borrowers view their risk in such a way that only $0I_1$ of investment is desired. This will occur if management begins to view liability structures as being too daring. A conservative restructuring of the balance sheet is then desired; for example, of anticipated internal funds, Q, some $0BB_1I_1$ is to be spent on investment and $I_1B_1B_2X_2$ is to be used to retire debt or acquire financial assets. In this situation, if the income which would generate anticipated internal

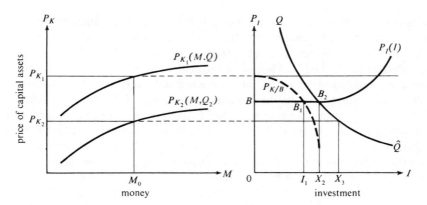

DIAGRAM 4. EFFECT OF A SHIFT IN THE P_K (M) FUNCTION

funds of Q required aggregate investment in excess of I_1, then realized internal funds would be lower than anticipated. The desired improvement in balance sheets will not be realized, and a recursive debt-income deflationary process could be triggered.

If P_{K_2} is the pricing-of-capital-assets relation, all the anticipated internal funds will be used to retire debt or acquire financial assets. As drawn, the maximum $P_{K_2}(M,Q)$ is less than the minimum P_I. Within the set of diagrams used to illustrate the investment relation, this is an illustration of the liquidity trap. The impotence of monetary policy illustrated here does not require that the interest rate on government debt remain constant when the money supply is increased. As illustrated, even if the interest rate on financial assets continues to fall as the supply of money is increased, the capitalization rate applied to investment assets may not rise by enough to induce investment.

Money and Output: Keynes and Friedman in Historical Perspective

J. H. Wood*

It's not quite the Montagues and the Capulets, even the Hatfields and the McCoys, again, but a long-time feud has been raging between two prominent "families" of economists.

Money—its quantity, importance, and efficacy—is the root of the squabble. Each camp, armed with logic, statistics, and other essential academic trappings, has dug in for a long and running battle—or debate—over the effectiveness of governmental monetary and fiscal policies as means of influencing economic activity.

One clan—the Keynesians, self-styled followers (or disciples) of John Maynard Keynes—argues that money and monetary policy have little or no impact on income and employment, particularly during severe economic downturns; and that government taxation and spending are the most effective remedies for inflation and unemployment, especially the latter.

The other group—the Monetarists, largely rallying around Milton Friedman of the University of Chicago—emphasizes money's role in the economic process. Spurning the notion that fiscal policy is paramount, they argue that a rule which requires the

Reprinted with deletions, from the Federal Reserve Bank of Philadelphia, *Business Review* (September, 1972), pp. 3-12, by permission of the publisher and the author.

* This article is adapted from an inaugural lecture delivered at the University of Birmingham, March 21, 1972. The author wishes to express his deep appreciation to the Esmée Fairbairn Charitable Trust, whose generosity made possible the research leading to this lecture, and to Douglas Vickers for encouragement and helpful discussions in the early stages of that research.

monetary authorities to cause the stock of money to increase at some constant rate, say 3 percent annually, would effectively reduce fluctuations in prices, output, and employment.

It is curious that when the dust settles on this debate, the problems that have interested Keynes and Friedman, the policy tools each has used, and the principal results each has obtained resemble not only each other but those of eighteenth-century British economists as well. In short—and this may jolt some economists and noneconomists—*there are no fundamental theoretical differences between Keynes and Friedman.* As with such controversies, the differences between Keynes and Friedman on the employment of fiscal and monetary policies to achieve economic stability hinge on differences in economic conditions existing at the times that each economist wrote and from dissimilar political philosophies rather than from any theoretical differences over money's influence on output. Moreover, the genesis of most of these "differences" can be found in the positions taken by many British economists of previous centuries.

Enter Keynes

In his *Tract on Monetary Reform* (1923), Keynes was highly critical of the pre-1914 theory of Ricardo, Mill, and others.

> Now "in the long run" this theory is probably true. If, after the American Civil War, the dollar had been stabilized and defined by law at 10 percent below its present value, it would be safe to assume that M [money] and P [prices] would now be just 10 percent greater than they actually are and that the present values of V [velocity] and T [volume of transactions] would be entirely unaffected. But this *long run* is a misleading guide to current affairs. *In the long run* we are all dead. Economists set themselves too easy, too useless a task if in tempestuous seasons they can only tell us that when the storm is long past the ocean is flat again.[1]

But things were different after 1914. Keynes began his *Tract* in the same way that he had begun the *Economic Consequences of the Peace* (1919), discussing what he believed had been the extremely delicate, short-lived, and essentially unstable economic system existing before 1914:

> For a hundred years the system worked throughout Europe with an extraordinary success and facilitated the growth of wealth on an unprecedented scale. To save and to invest became at once the duty and the delight of a large class.[2]

Keynes wrote during a time of extraordinary upheaval. Between 1914 and 1920 prices tripled, then dropped by nearly one-half by 1922. He pointed out that the

---

[1]John Maynard Keynes, *The Collected Writings of Keynes* (London: Macmillan Ltd., 1971), p. 6.
[2]Ibid., p. xiv.

arrangements of the nineteenth century could not work properly if money, the assumed standard, is not dependable.

> Unemployment, the precarious life of the worker, the disappointment of expectation, the sudden loss of savings, the excessive windfalls to individuals, the speculator, the profiteer—all proceed, in large measure, from the instability of the standard of value.[3]

If businessmen are to develop their productive capacity and if the savings of households are to be converted into investment projects, then businessmen must be able to foresee with a reasonable degree of assurance the prices of the products coming out of their new plants and the costs of the inputs from which those products will be made.

To Keynes, the overriding determinant of investment is price expectations. Expectations of price increases encourage investment; expected deflation discourages investment. Uncertainty is the worst offender. If rapid monetary changes have occurred in the past and are expected to be repeated in the future—in which direction no one knows—businessmen will refuse to bear the risk of investment.

The problems that Keynes considered as well as the remedies proposed in his *Treatise on Money* (1930) were the same as those analyzed and advanced in the *Tract*. Only his methodology had changed; it had become more sophisticated. He traced in detail the effects of changes in the quantity of money on the level and composition of output. Some passages in the *Treatise* echo Cantillon. Like the latter, Keynes always carefully specified the source of an assumed monetary disturbance before discussing its effects. For him, most increases in money resulted from increases in bank loans to businessmen. He stressed that the failure of different prices to move together is the essence of short-period fluctuations and that an easier monetary policy that leads to low interest rates and rising prices results in higher profits and increases investment.

The processes through which monetary disturbances lead to variations in output in the first instance are the same in the *General Theory of Employment, Interest and Money* as in the *Tract* and the *Treatise:* namely, through price changes and their influence on expectations of future prices. He argued that the relation between current and future prices influences investment decisions most.

Keynes came to the conclusion that in a world of rapidly fluctuating prices uncertainty on the part of businessmen would be so great that the state would have to undertake the investment necessary for growth and economic stability. Since 1924 he had advocated public works in a supporting role to monetary policy as an antideflationary device. But, from the behavior of the Bank of England—from its determination to accept and enforce whatever price fluctuations were consistent, first with the return to gold at the prewar par and then with the maintenance of the gold standard at a fixed rate—Keynes became convinced that the nation would have to rely on means other than monetary policy to stabilize prices and output.

[3]Ibid.

. . . Then Friedman

Reading Milton Friedman and Anna Jacobson Schwartz's *A Monetary History of the United States* (1963) is a frustrating experience. On the one hand, the authors present a wealth of highly suggestive and expertly handled historical data. But, on the other hand, just as they seem to be on the verge of explaining causal relationships (that is, of giving an explicit statement of the processes through which, in their view, money affects economic activity), they descend into a quagmire of algebraic manipulations. But, if we carefully examine the way in which Friedman handles the data in this and other historical discussions, we can get an inkling of how, in his view, money matters.

In comparing the two periods 1865–1879 and 1879–1897 as well as other lengthy intervals, Friedman and Schwartz conclude that over long periods "generally declining or generally rising prices had little impact on the rate of growth [of output], but the period of great monetary uncertainty in the early nineties produced sharp deviations from the long-term trend."

They make this point again and again, concluding:

> Apparently, the forces determining the long-run rate of growth of real income are largely independent of the long-run rate of growth of the stock of money, so long as both proceed fairly smoothly. But marked instability of money is accompanied by instability of economic growth.[4]

Surprise is the key word in all this. To the extent that changes in money and prices proceed smoothly and are foreseen, money does not influence economic activity. But sudden and unforeseen monetary disturbances produce fluctuations in output.

There is a close connection here and elsewhere between Friedman's descriptions of historical periods and Mill's argument that changes in the money supply that people expect and upon which they can plan allow employment, output, and other economic variables to be determined by nonmonetary forces.

Parallel in Theory but Parting in Prescription

Both Keynes and Friedman, therefore, fear monetary instability. They both desire a stable growth rate in the money supply as a way of minimizing fluctuations in prices, output, and employment. But they part ways in approach and emphasis on how to achieve the benefits of monetary stability.

Keynes, on the one hand, was pragmatic. He was a man of a thousand plans. If one was impractical, he would try another. To him monetary policy was important

---

[4]Milton Friedman and Anna Jacobson Schwartz, *A Monetary History of the United States, 1867–1960* (Princeton: Princeton University Press, 1963), p. 678.

but not the "be-all and end-all." And so he moved from a reliance on monetary to fiscal policy when he thought it unrealistic on political or other grounds to expect a stable growth in the money supply.

Friedman, on the other hand, has less confidence than Keynes in the willingness or ability of the authorities—monetary or fiscal—to make the economy work smoothly. That is why Friedman wants to tie both the monetary and fiscal authorities to certain specific rules—not because the people who would make the rules are more intelligent than those who formulate and implement discretionary policies, but because, whatever the rule, it will be known. People can formulate plans on the basis of what they can expect the future money supply and price level to be. In such a way, Friedman hopes, as Keynes did with fiscal policy, that money *CAN BE MADE* not to matter.

The Transmission Process
and Policy Implications

The contrasting models presented in the previous section provide clues to the challenging and fascinating world of monetary theory. The readings in this section, without requiring an extensive use of mathematical and graphical analysis, will survey slightly more sophisticated views of the monetary economy.

An important subject in monetary analysis is the various ways (through short-term interest rates, long-term interest rates, wealth, etc.) in which monetary impulses may be transmitted to spending, production, employment, and prices. The first three essays will examine the major contributions regarding the channels through the relative price and wealth affects work.

The opening reading by Yung Chul Park is a most interesting survey of this "transmission" mechanism. Park's analysis is invaluable because of its fairly intensive examination of the views of Boris Pesek and Thomas Saving (and their critics) on the contribution of bank deposits to private wealth. Park's article is further unique because it offers a specific model representing Milton Friedman's theoretical conceptualization of the transmission mechanism. The essay ends with an examination of the "reduced-form" versus the "structural" approach to the effect of monetary and fiscal impulses on the economy.

Roger W. Spencer's article on the transmission process, the second in this section, complements that of Park. Spencer provides an interesting historical background by surveying the work of Knut Wicksell, Irving Fisher, and John Maynard Keynes on this problem. Like Park, Spencer compares and contrasts the views of Milton Friedman, James Tobin, Karl Brunner, and Allan Meltzer. His article ends with an appendix containing helpful numerical examples of how the relative price and wealth affects work.

What is the effect of fiscal policy on economic activity? In recent years the work of Carl Christ and others has demonstrated that neither fiscal nor monetary policy can be viewed independently of one another. The stimulatory effect of increases in government expenditures on aggregate demand should not be analyzed without regard to their concomitants of either raising taxes, increasing the stock of money, or expanding the supply of interest-bearing government debt. In the third essay, Roger W. Spencer and Keith M. Carlson survey recent theoretical and empirical literature pertaining to the influence of fiscal actions on economic activity.

Some Current Issues on the Transmission Process of Monetary Policy

Yung Chul Park

6

There is widespread agreement that money is of some importance in determining the course of economic events. There is, however, substantial disagreement concerning the extent to which money matters (that is, the size of the money multiplier). Monetarists argue that changes in the stock of money are a primary determinant of changes in total spending. On the other hand, nonmonetarists, although they may readily admit that money matters, also regard changes in the various components of aggregate demand as having an important influence on the level of economic activity; they, therefore, place as much emphasis on fiscal policy as on monetary controls. In fact, a spectrum of views on the importance of money ranges from "money matters little" at one extreme to "money alone matters" at the other extreme. An important question is the extent to which these differences in opinion may be traced to differences in models of the monetary process (that is, the transmission mechanism explaining how monetary influences affect real output, employment, and the price level). The objective of this paper is to examine this question by reviewing critically

Reprinted, with deletions, from the *Staff Papers,* International Monetary Fund (March 1972), pp. 1–43 by permission of the publisher and the author.

the analytical bases for the different views among monetarists and nonmonetarists;[1] only casual reference will be made to the vast and growing empirical literature. Since the transmission process is an integral part of the entire operational structure of the economy, the survey cannot be carried out without discussing divergent views on how the economy in general operates. While this may lengthen the paper, it will help us to analyze the mechanism in a proper context. The review begins in Section I with a discussion of post-Keynesian developments, followed in Section II by an analysis of the nonmonetarist views of the neo-Keynesians and the neo-Fisherians. The monetarist view is elaborated in Section III, and a summary and concluding remarks comprise Section IV.

I. Post-Keynesian Analysis: The Wealth Effect, Credit Rationing, and Portfolio Balance

The Cost-of-Capital Channel

The main process by which monetary forces influence the real economy in Keynesian income/expenditure models is through the cost-of-capital channel. In a simple Keynesian framework, monetary policy operates through changes in the rate of interest. The change in the volume of money alters "the" rate of interest—a rate of interest usually approximated by the long-term government bond rate—so as to equate the demand for money with the supply. The change in the rate of interest affects investment and possibly consumption; the change in aggregate demand, in turn, has a multiple effect on equilibrium income. Thus, the rate of interest is viewed as a measure of the cost of capital, as the indicator of the stance of monetary policy, and as the key linkage variable between the real and financial sectors.

In addition to the cost-of-capital channel, post-Keynesians also recognized two other channels, namely, the wealth effect on consumption expenditure and the credit rationing linkage between the financial and real sectors.

The Wealth Effect

THE POST-KEYNESIAN VIEW

One of the most significant post-Keynesian developments has been the emphasis on net private wealth as well as income as a factor influencing real flows of expendi-

---

[1]Readers are also referred to other excellent reviews on this topic and on recent developments in monetary economics: Maurice Mann, "How Does Monetary Policy Affect the Economy?" *Federal Reserve Bulletin*, Vol. 54 (1968), pp. 803–14; Allan H. Meltzer, "Money, Intermediation, and Growth," *The Journal of Economic Literature*, Vol. VII (1969), pp. 27–56; Harry G. Johnson, "Recent Developments in Monetary Theory—A Commentary," in *Money in Britain, 1959–1969*, ed. by David R. Croome and Harry G. Johnson (Oxford University Press, 1970), pp. 83–114; Warren L. Smith, "On Some Current Issues in Monetary Economics: An Interpretation," *The Journal of Economic Literature*, Vol. VIII (1970), pp. 767–82; Harry G. Johnson, "The Keynesian Revolution and the Monetarist Counter-Revolution," American Economic Association, *Papers and Proceedings of the Eighty-third Annual Meeting* (*The American Economic Review*, Vol. LXI, May 1971), pp. 1–14.

tures. The connection between net wealth of the private sector and consumption was first pointed out by Pigou[2] and Haberler,[3] and in a more rigorous manner by Patinkin,[4] in the form of real cash balance effect: changes in the real quantity of money could affect real aggregate demand even if they did not alter the rate of interest. The central feature of the real cash balance effect is the assumption that the stock of money is a component of the net wealth of the economy. However, the stock of money that these economists considered as part of net wealth was not the usually defined concept of narrow money (currency outside banks *plus* demand deposits) but rather the monetary base, or, in Gurley and Shaw's terminology, outside money alone.[5] The justification for excluding demand deposits (inside money) as part of wealth is that these deposits are claims of the public on the banking system that are counterbalanced by the debts of the public to the banking sector. Therefore, when the balance sheets of all economic units are consolidated, inside money disappears and, hence, should not be considered as part of wealth.

This justification, however, brings out immediately the question of why the same logic should not be applied to outside money, which is, after all, the noninterest-bearing debt of the government. If, indeed, outside money is government debt, as it has been treated in the post-Keynesian literature,[6] a consolidation of the balance sheet of the private and government sectors must result in the cancellation of outside money as an item of net wealth. It then follows that a change in outside money cannot exert a wealth effect, since the change cannot cause a simultaneous change in net wealth. To establish that the change in outside money does indeed have economic consequences, one has to provide an explanation other than that outside money is part of wealth. The explanation that has had widest support has been that the government, unlike other debtors, is unconcerned about the size of its debt and makes its economic decisions accordingly.[7] Thus, the only effect of the change in

---

[2]A. C. Pigou, "Economic Progress in a Stable Environment," *Economica,* New Series, Vol. XIV (1947), pp. 180–88.

[3]Gottfried Haberler, *Prosperity and Depression* (New York, Third Edition, 1946), pp. 242, 403, and 491–503.

[4]Don Patinkin, "Price Flexibility and Full Employment," in *Readings in Monetary Theory,* ed. by Friedrich A. Lutz and Lloyd W. Mints (New York, 1951), pp. 252–83.

[5]Outside money is defined as the money that is backed by foreign or government securities or gold, or fiat money issued by the government, whereas inside money—commercial bank demand deposits—is based on private domestic securities. See John G. Gurley and Edward S. Shaw, *Money in a Theory of Finance,* The Brookings Institution (Washington, 1960), pp. 363-64.

[6]See James Tobin, "Money, Capital, and Other Stores of Value," American Economic Association, *Papers and Proceedings of the Seventy-third Annual Meeting (The American Economic Review,* Vol. LI, May 1961), pp. 26–37; James Tobin, "Commercial Banks as Creators of 'Money'," Chapter 1 in *Financial Markets and Economic Activity,* ed. by Donald D. Hester and James Tobin, Cowles Foundation, Monograph 21 (New York, 1967), pp. 1–11, also included in *Banking and Monetary Studies,* ed. by Deane Carson (Homewood, Illinois, 1963); James Tobin, "Money and Economic Growth," *Econometrica,* Vol. 33 (1965), pp. 671–84; Gurley and Shaw, *Money in a Theory of Finance* (cited in footnote 5); Don Patinkin, *Money, Interest, and Prices: An Integration of Monetary and Value Theory* (New York, Second Edition, 1965).

[7]The government, the argument claims, ignores the real value of its debt because it can pay its debts by issuing new debts; the government is able to do so since (1) it controls the supply of money and (2) it possesses the taxing power. See Harry G. Johnson, "Monetary Theory and Policy," in his *Essays in Monetary Economics* (Harvard University Press, 1967), p. 24.

outside money is the effect of the increase in assets of the private sector. This explanation reduces the wealth effect of changes in outside money to a distribution effect of a wealth transfer between the private and government sectors. This explanation also suggests that the traditional distinction between inside and outside money is based not on a measure of wealth applicable to all types of assets but rather on asymmetric responses of various economic decision-making units to changes in assets and debts.[8]

Later developments have extended this wealth effect beyond money to other forms of wealth, such as the real market values of equities and interest-bearing government debt. It is fairly easy to appreciate the wealth effect or distribution effect associated with outside money. However, it is not evident whether the same argument could be applied to interest-bearing government debt. There is an important difference between the two assets. Unlike outside money, the interest burden on interest-bearing government debt must be financed by future taxes. Hence, if the private sector discounts its future tax liabilities in the same way in which it discounts future interest receipts, the existence of government bonds represents an asset as well as a liability to the public and will, therefore, not generate any net wealth effect.[9] However, if the public considers only a constant fraction of total interest-bearing government debt as a liability, then an open market purchase of government bonds will increase net private wealth and thereby directly affect aggregate demand.

At the theoretical level, the link between the net wealth of consumers and real consumption has been refined as in the life cycle hypothesis of Ando, Brumberg, and Modigliani, which holds that consumers allocate consumption over their lifetime, given initial net worth, a rate of time preference, and expectations regarding labor income.[10]

The Keynesian approach uses the rate of interest on long-term bonds as the representative rate on all types of earning asset. "This implicitly assumes that equities, government bonds, and private debt are all perfect substitutes for one another."[11] As a result, the Keynesian analysis considers only substitution between money and bonds important but ignores entirely the substitutability between money and real assets or real expenditures. The intellectual importance of the real cash balance effect lies in the fact that it allowed the possibility of substitution between money, on the one hand, and real expenditures, on the other hand, in macroeconomic analysis.[12]

[8]For a further elaboration on this point, see the following section.

[9]Patinkin, *Money, Interest, and Prices* (cited in footnote 6), p. 289.

[10]Albert Ando and Franco Modigliani, "The 'Life Cycle' Hypothesis of Saving: Aggregate Implications and Tests," *The American Economic Review,* Vol. LIII (March 1963), pp. 55–84; Franco Modigliani and Richard Brumberg, "Utility Analysis and the Consumption Function: An Interpretation of Cross-Section Data," in *Post Keynesian Economics,* ed. by Kenneth K. Kurihara (Rutgers University Press, 1954), pp. 388–436; Franco Modigliani and Albert Ando, "The 'Permanent Income' and the 'Life Cycle' Hypothesis of Saving Behavior: Comparison and Tests," in *Consumption and Saving,* Vol. II, ed. by Irwin Friend and Robert Jones (Wharton School, University of Pennsylvania, 1960), pp. 49–174.

[11]Tobin, "Money, Capital, and Other Stores of Value" (cited in footnote 6), p. 30.

[12]Milton Friedman, "Postwar Trends in Monetary Theory and Policy," in *Money and Finance: Readings in Theory, Policy, and Institutions,* ed. by Deane Carson (New York, 1966), p. 187.

This fact has, to a great extent, contributed to the explicit treatment of real capital goods in portfolio analysis and to a reemphasis on the role of money.

THE PESEK AND SAVING THESIS

In a recent book by Pesek and Saving,[13] the authors argue that commercial bank demand deposits (inside money) should also be treated as part of the net wealth of the economy, because demand deposits are an asset produced by banks and sold by them to the public in exchange for the latter's statements of indebtedness.[14] Demand deposits, unlike outside money, carry an "instant repurchase clause"—an obligation by the banks to repurchase them with outside money. But this characteristic, Pesek and Saving argue, does not affect the basic fact that demand deposits are part of net wealth.

If Pesek and Saving's thesis is valid, then their analysis will have important implications for the effects of monetary policy. Their analysis literally means that monetary authorities can directly create or destroy nominal private wealth at will through monetary policy. This, in turn, implies that monetary policy can affect aggregate demand *directly* and in theory can have strong effects on the level of economic activity. For instance, a central bank's open market purchase of government bills, given the money supply multiplier, will generate a multiple expansion of the initial increase in outside money. The increase in money supply should be considered an increase in nominal private wealth, which will, in turn, increase consumption expenditure. This means that the open market operation has a direct wealth effect in addition to the conventional liquidity effect[15] and the interest-rate-induced wealth effects (capital gains or losses on government bonds and equities) on total spending. For this reason, Pesek and Saving's argument deserves careful examination.

Pesek and Saving's view is based on the principle that the economically relevant measure of wealth is the capitalized value of a stream of net income. When this measure of wealth is applied to outside money, it is shown that outside money is a component of net wealth because it yields a net flow of services to the user—not because the government is unconcerned with its outstanding debt. The flow of services of outside money is the saving of time in barter transactions, which stems from the role of money as a medium of exchange. The saving of time may be used either for leisure or for the production of capital goods. Hence, outside money generates a positive stream of income; the capitalized value of this income is then an addition to the net wealth of the economy. The same reasoning applies to demand deposits, the basic difference between government fiat money and demand deposits being one of institutional arrangements. The arrangement is that government fiat money is produced by the government, whereas demand deposits are produced by the government agents, namely, commercial banks that have received the monopoly right of producing money. From this point of view, there is no difference between outside money

[13]Boris P. Pesek and Thomas R. Saving, *Money, Wealth, and Economic Theory* (New York, 1967).
[14]*Ibid.,* Chapter 4, "Bank Money as Wealth," pp. 79–102.
[15]The liquidity effect, or the substitution effect, refers to changes in interest rates that are brought about by changes in money supply via a liquidity preference relation.

and demand deposits. To put it differently, inside money also represents a stream of net income, since demand deposits, as a medium of exchange, yield a flow of services that banks have agreed to provide. For inside money, however, the net income takes the form of the earnings of the banks through the process of money creation or intermediation. The capitalized value of the earnings is then an increase in the net wealth of the economy.[16]

To elaborate further on this point, let us assume that a commercial bank receives $5,000 of demand deposits and that the bank is subject to a reserve requirement of 20 percent. The bank then retains $1,000 in cash reserves and creates demand deposits amounting to $4,000 by lending this amount to the private nonfinancial sector of the economy. Suppose that there is a single rate of interest, say, 5 percent, in this economy. This means that, *ceteris paribus,* the bank is earning an additional $200. The present value of this interest earning, given the 5 percent interest rate, is $4,000, which is exactly equal to the increase in demand deposits held by the public. This present value represents an increase in the net worth of the bank. Since the bank is a private one, the increase should be reflected also in the balance sheets of its stockholders; *ceteris paribus,* the increase in the net worth of the bank will be reflected in an increase in the market value of the bank's stocks, which is equivalent to an increase in the public's wealth.

The argument so far is based on the assumption that the costs of producing (or servicing) demand deposits are negligible. However, in reality the commercial banking industry has operating costs just like any other industry and is fairly competitive. To the extent that there are operating costs connected with demand deposits (or outside money, for that matter), the whole value of demand deposits is not necessarily part of the net wealth of the economy. In the extreme case where the banking industry is fully competitive and is not subject to government controls and regulations, Patinkin shows that the capitalized value of the banks' operating costs (the sum of the present values of the current operating costs and of the imputed annual interest charge on the fixed assets) is equal to the value of demand deposits and that, consequently, demand deposits should be excluded from net national wealth.[17] The implication of the perfect competition case is, of course, that the true origin of the net worth of the banking sector is in its monopoly right of creating demand deposits.

However, if the assumption of zero costs of managing demand deposits is unrealistic, so is the assumption of perfect competition in the banking sector. A reasonable assumption would then be that, since entry into the banking industry is restricted by the necessity of obtaining a license, the present value of the income from creating demand deposits should be regarded, in part, as a component of net private wealth.

---

[16]Reviewing the book by Pesek and Saving, Patinkin points out that the true origin of the net worth of the banking sector lies not in the production of demand deposits per se but in the monopoly right of producing demand deposits, which this sector has received from the government. See Don Patinkin, "Money and Wealth: A Review Article," *The Journal of Economic Literature,* Vol. VII (1969), pp. 1140-60. See also the reviews by Meltzer, "Money, Intermediation, and Growth" (cited in footnote 1), pp. 32-36, and Smith, "On Some Current Issues in Monetary Economics: An Interpretation" (cited in footnote 1), pp. 769-70.

[17]Patinkin, "Money and Wealth" (cited in footnote 16), pp. 1147-54.

This conclusion, in turn, raises an important question as to whether the conventional specification of the economically relevant wealth equation for theoretical as well as empirical studies is a proper one, and if it is not, how it should be modified.[18]

Net private (nonhuman) wealth (W) is generally defined as the sum of outside money and the market values of interest-bearing government debt and of the existing stock of physical capital:

$$W = PK + M_0 + B,$$

where P = price level; K = real stock of capital; M_0 = outside money; B = supply of government bonds.[19]

The market value of real assets or equities (V) has been defined, for instance, as

$$V = 100 \left(\frac{Y_{cd}}{R_d} \right),$$

where Y_{cd} = corporate dividend payments; R_d = dividend/price ratio on common stock (percentage).[20]

On the other hand, Pesek and Saving define real nonhuman wealth for the purpose of general analysis as

$$W = \frac{M}{P} + \frac{y_n}{r_n} + \frac{g}{r_g},$$

where M = nominal quantity of money (narrow definition of currency *plus* demand deposits); P = price level; y_n = real nonhuman income; g = real nonhuman income yielded by government securities; r_n = capitalization rate applicable to real nonhuman income; r_g = capitalization rate applicable to real government interest payments.[21]

Brunner and Meltzer, following Pesek and Saving's reasoning, also explicitly introduce the net worth of the commercial banking sector into their definition of nonhuman wealth:

$$W = PK + B + (1 + \sigma)M_0,$$

where σ = the banking system's net worth multiplier; σM_0 = the net worth contri-

---

[18]Once the monopoly is broken and perfect competition is restored in the banking sector, the monopoly profits (earnings) of banks will be transferred to the owners of demand deposits in the form of nonpecuniary services. See Meltzer, "Money, Intermediation, and Growth" (cited in footnote 1), p. 34.

[19]See, for example, Franco Modigliani, "The Monetary Mechanisn and Its Interaction with Real Phenomena," *The Review of Economics and Statistics,* Vol. XLV (Supplement, February 1963), p. 80.

[20]Frank de Leeuw and Edward M. Gramlich, "The Channels of Monetary Policy," *Federal Reserve Bulletin,* Vol. 55 (1969), p. 481.

[21]Pesek and Saving, *Money, Wealth, and Economic Theory* (cited in footnote 13), pp. 289–90.

bution of the banking sector, or the capitalized value of net earnings of the banking system.[22]

The basic difference between the definition of Pesek and Saving (or of Brunner and Meltzer) and the conventional one is, of course, that the former includes demand deposits (in whole or in part) as a component of net private wealth whereas the latter does not. At first sight, it may appear that the appropriate definition of wealth is the specification of either Pesek and Saving or Brunner and Meltzer. But that is not so. It was pointed out that any increase in the net worth of the banking sector would, *ceteris paribus,* lead to a corresponding increase in the net worth of the nonbanking private sector in the form of an increase in the market value of bank stocks. This means that the value of demand deposits in Pesek and Saving's definition, or the net worth contribution of the banking sector (σM_0) in Brunner and Meltzer's, is already included in the market value of equities (PK, V, or Y_n/r_n) to the extent that demand deposits (in whole or in part) are part of net wealth; adding the net worth of the banking sector to the market value of equities amounts to a double counting of the market value of commercial bank stocks. For this reason, the wealth definitions of Pesek and Saving and of Brunner and Meltzer should probably be rejected. One might then conclude that the conventional definition of net wealth is economically appropriate regardless of the validity of Pesek and Saving's thesis and that the direct wealth effect of monetary policy implied by their analysis has been accounted for in traditional analysis without being explicitly recognized.

Credit Rationing

Keynesian income/expenditure models assume a well-functioning competitive capital market in which desired investments are equilibrated to desired savings through the mechanism of the interest rate. In these models there exists a single short-run equilibrium rate of interest that simultaneously measures the rate of return to lenders, the cost of borrowings, the internal marginal rate of return from investments, and the opportunity cost of holding money. No one would question that the assumption of perfectly competitive capital markets is unrealistic; in reality, capital markets are not well functioning, and the price allocation mechanism may not work. It is, however, the proposition of the credit rationing channel that the Keynesian view of the transmission process of monetary policy and its consequences may have to be modified when market imperfections in capital markets are properly taken into consideration.

The most widely accepted view of the credit rationing channel appears to be the following proposition: under imperfect capital markets interest rates charged to borrowers by financial intermediaries, including commercial banks, are controlled by institutional forces, not by market forces, and tend not to change even when there is a change in the demand for funds, so that lenders ration the available supply of

---

[22]Karl Brunner and Allan H. Meltzer, "Fiscal and Monetary Policy in a Non-Keynesian World" (unpublished paper, 1970).

credit (by various nonprice terms). Accordingly, the demand for credit is limited "not by the borrowers' willingness to borrow at the given rate but by the lenders' willingness to lend—or, more precisely, by the funds available to them to be rationed out among the would-be borrowers."[23] Under these circumstances the single short-run equilibrium rate of interest in the perfect capital market framework is replaced by a plurality of rates—one for the lending units (depositors) and another for the rationed borrowers. This proposition implies that monetary policy could affect total expenditures directly by changing the degree of credit rationing and consequently the volume of lending, even if monetary controls did not change interest rates appreciably or if aggregate demand was interest inelastic. It also implies that insofar as "sticky" lending rates prevail, monetary policy would be less effective if it were geared to control the power of banks to create money rather than the actual money supply.[24]

While the credit rationing phenomenon has been well known, it has proved to be rather difficult to deal with effectively in macroeconomic analyses. One difficulty is that what is observed as credit availability is actually only a temporary disequilibrium situation in the capital market, one that may cause changes in interest rates in other parts of the capital market to levels that will eventually clear the market. Another difficulty is the empirical problem of measuring and identifying the degree of credit rationing. In most cases the specific details of credit rationing are not observable or recorded, so that indirect—often unsatisfactory—means must be used to represent credit rationing.

Portfolio Balance Approach

A more fundamental and basic development in monetary theory subsequent to Keynes' liquidity preference theory has been the capital theoretic formulation of the demand for money. This analysis emphasizes money as an asset that can be compared with other real as well as financial assets; its emphasis is on what is called portfolio balance. The analysis of portfolio and balance sheet adjustments has been extended beyond the Keynesian two-asset (money and bonds) models to include various financial and real assets other than bonds and has been integrated with varying degrees of complexity into the Keynesian income/expenditure framework.

The portfolio approach to monetary theory involves a new view of how the influence of monetary policy is transmitted to the real economy. The general view that has been emerging from the writings of both neo-Keynesians and monetarists stresses the impact of monetary policy changes on the composition of assets held by the public and the influence of these changes on interest rates on these assets and ultimately on the rate of return from investing in the production of new physical assets. In the portfolio view the impact on the real sector of an initial monetary disturbance is the result of changing relative prices among a wide array of financial and real

[23]Modigliani, "The Monetary Mechanism and Its Interaction with Real Phenomena" (cited in footnote 19), p. 98.
[24]*Ibid.,* p. 100.

assets. An increase in the supply of money, following an open market purchase of government securities, results in excessive holdings of money relative to other forms of wealth. Holders of wealth will be induced to exchange these excessive balances for other assets, which will in turn raise asset prices and lower rates of return across the board. As a result, an increase in the supply of money may eventually stimulate new investment in many directions.

This broad description of the transmission mechanism appears to be acceptable to both monetarists and nonmonetarists. There is, however, considerable disagreement as to the major variables and interest rates that must be defined in order to take account of all the ways in which monetary policy works out its effects. In what follows, focusing on this aspect, we will review and compare the views of nonmonetarists and monetarists on the transmission process of monetary policy.

II. The Nonmonetarist View

Neo-Keynesian Analysis: The Yale School View

It is always misleading to classify economists, who do not necessarily have common views about the subject matter concerned, under a single label as we do in this paper. It should be understood that the nomenclature is introduced solely for the convenience and clarity of exposition. Some economists whom we consider neo-Keynesians could take substantially different positions on particular issues. With this risk in mind, we summarize what appear to be the major arguments and findings of neo-Keynesians, or the Yale school.

(1) Neo-Keynesians consider that the stock of money, conventionally defined, is not an exogenous variable completely controlled by the monetary authorities but is partly an endogenous quantity that reflects the economic behavior of financial intermediaries and nonfinancial private economic units.[25]

(2) The sharp traditional distinctions between money and other assets and between commercial banks and other financial intermediaries are not warranted. Instead, monetary analysis should

> focus on demands for supplies of the whole spectrum of assets rather than on the quantity and velocity of "money"; and to regard the structure of interest rates, asset yields, and credit availability rather than the quantity of money [or the rate of interest] as the linkage between monetary and financial institutions and policies on the one hand and the real economy on the other.[26]

[25]*Financial Markets and Economic Activity* (cited in footnote 6), "Foreword," p. viii. See also Lyle E. Gramley and Samuel B. Chase, Jr., "Time Deposits in Monetary Analysis," *Federal Reserve Bulletin,* Vol. 51 (1965), pp. 1380-1406; John H. Kareken, "Commercial Banks and the Supply of Money: A Market-Determined Demand Deposit Rate," *Federal Reserve Bulletin,* Vol. 53 (1967), pp. 1699-1712; J. A. Cacy, "Alternative Approaches to the Analysis of the Financial Structure," Federal Reserve Bank of Kansas City, *Monthly Review* (March 1968), pp. 3-9; Richard G. Davis, "The Role of the Money Supply in Business Cycles," Federal Reserve Bank of New York, *Monthly Review* (April 1968), pp. 63-73.

[26]Tobin, "Commercial Banks as Creators of 'Money' " (cited in footnote 6), p. 3.

This argument has been known as the New View, a view that clearly is related to, if not similar to, the Radcliffe Committee's position some years ago. In fact, Johnson claims that the Yale school has provided the intellectual foundations of the Radcliffe position on monetary theory and policy.[27]

(3) Proposition (2) implies that the crucial distinction in a neo-Keynesian framework is between the financial sector and the real sector rather than between the banking system and the rest of the economy or between liquid and illiquid assets. The construction of the financial sector reflects the theory of portfolio management by economic units. The theory takes as its subject matter stocks of assets and debts, and their framework is the balance sheet; the decision variables in this sector are stocks.[28] The real sector deals with flows of income, saving, expenditures, and the production of goods and services. Its accounting framework is the income statement, and the decision variables are flows. The two sectors are linked by "accounting identities—e.g., increase in net worth equals saving plus capital appreciation—and by technological and financial stock-flow relations."[29] This, together with proposition (2), implies a rather complicated relationship between the two sectors in the linkage sequence. Some attempts have been made to synthesize the two sectors with varying degrees of simplification, but none of them seems satisfactory. Considering the emphasis on and the amount of attention paid to the building and analyzing of the interactions within the financial sector, it is indeed surprising to find that there has been no satisfactory attempt to bridge the gap. In our discussion we will consider perhaps the most widely accepted of these attempts, the synthesis developed by Brainard and Tobin.[30]

(4) While there is still considerable debate on the link between the real and financial sectors, there appears to be a consensus among neo-Keynesians that monetary policy operates through changes in the market price of equities that represent claims on existing real assets, such as plant and equipment.[31] The prime indicator of stance and the proper target of monetary policy is thus "the required rate of return on capital," or the equity yield. "Nothing else, whether it is the quantity of 'money' or some financial interest rate, can be more than an imperfect and derivative indicator of the effective thrust of monetary events and policies."[32] In a neo-Keynesian framework an expansionary monetary policy, for example, raises the price of equities (that is, reduces the yield on equities), thereby generating a positive discrepancy between the valuation of real assets on these markets (the price of equities) and their costs of production. The discrepancy provides an incentive to expand production of these

---

[27]Johnson, "Recent Developments in Monetary Theory—A Commentary" (cited in footnote 1), p. 101.

[28]*Financial Markets and Economic Activity* (cited in footnote 6), "Foreword," pp. v–vi.

[29]Tobin, "Money, Capital, and Other Stores of Value" (cited in footnote 6), p. 28.

[30]William C. Brainard and James Tobin, "Pitfalls in Financial Model Building," American Economic Association, *Papers and Proceedings of the Eightieth Annual Meeting* (*The American Economic Review*, Vol. LVIII, May 1968), pp. 99–122.

[31]Neo-Keynesians assume that capital goods have two separate market prices: the prices of existing (secondhand) capital goods represented by the price of equities and the output prices of these goods (or the prices of newly produced capital goods).

[32]Brainard and Tobin, "Pitfalls in Financial Model Building" (cited in footnote 30), p. 104.

capital goods. Suppose that the existing plant and equipment of a corporation that could be reproduced for $1 million is valued at $2 million in the stock market. This margin between the market valuation and the cost of reproducing the existing capital goods will then stimulate new investment in these goods.[33] On this reasoning, the stock market plays a significant role in influencing economic activity, and indeed changes in the Dow-Jones averages give some measure of the stance of monetary policy.[34]

The most serious criticism that may be made of the neo-Keynesian analysis is that despite the very complex financial sector, incorporating detailed specifications of asset preferences, its transmission mechanism remains naïve and simple. The synthesis by Brainard and Tobin assumes that the equity rate is the major link between money and the level of economic activity. Compared with the Keynesian transmission process, this simply involves replacing the rates of interest on financial assets by the equity yield—a yield that is now taken to represent the influence of monetary forces. Also, neo-Keynesians appear to ignore the relative importance of borrowing costs and, hence, the importance of debt financing in business firms.

The Neo-Fisherian View

All of the major empirical studies have found that the demand for money and velocity are responsive to interest rates, although the choice of rates between short-term and long-term is not clear cut. However, neither Keynes' speculative motive of holding money nor Tobin's portfolio selection theory provides a rational explanation of the nonzero interest elasticity of the demand for money in an economy where there exist short-term securities—such as time deposits, savings and loan shares, treasury bills, high-grade commercial paper, and negotiable certificates of deposit for large investors—that dominate money. When these assets are readily available, the public—faced, for example, with a low current rate of interest and an expectation of capital losses owing to an expected rise in the current rate of interest—will be induced to shift from long-term to short-term securities, but not to money. This is so because these short-term assets possess the same properties as money—near perfect liquidity and no risk of default—while yielding a positive rate of return.[35]

Given these short-term securities, changes in the current rate of interest and expec-

---

[33]For further discussion on this investment behavior, see Brainard and Tobin, "Pitfalls in Financial Model Building" (cited in footnote 30), p. 112; Hyman P. Minsky, "Private Sector Asset Management and the Effectiveness of Monetary Policy: Theory and Practice," *The Journal of Finance*, Vol. XXIV (1969), p. 229; W. L. Smith, "A Neo-Keynesian View of Monetary Policy," in *Controlling Monetary Aggregates* (Proceedings of a monetary conference in Massachusetts), Federal Reserve Bank of Boston (June 1969), p. 106; Ralph Turvey, *Interest Rates and Asset Prices* (London, 1960); James Tobin, "An Essay on Principles of Debt Management," in *Fiscal and Debt Management Policies*, Commission on Money and Credit (Englewood Cliffs, New Jersey, 1963), p. 150; James Tobin, "Monetary Semantics," in *Targets and Indicators of Monetary Policy*, ed. by Karl Brunner (San Francisco, 1969), pp. 173–74.

[34]Tobin, "Monetary Semantics" (cited in footnote 33), p. 174. See the Appendix for a systematic discussion on the neo-Keynesian transmission process of monetary policy.

[35]See Smith, "On Some Current Issues in Monetary Economics: An Interpretation" (cited in footnote 1), pp. 774–75.

tation of capital gains or losses no longer explain the substitution between long-term securities and money but the substitution between long-term and short-term securities.[36] Therefore, the only plausible theory of the demand for money that is consistent with the existing empirical evidence seems to be the transactions cost approach of the demand for money, developed by Baumol and Tobin.[37] The basic hypothesis of this approach, which has been labeled as neo-Fisherian, is that "the demand for money is basically related to the flow of transactions and arises from a lack of synchronization between receipts and payments, coupled with the transactions costs involved in exchanging money for short-term assets."[38] This hypothesis implies that (i) the wealth variable does not appear in the demand for money function, since money is held primarily to facilitate transactions and that (ii) the demand for money is sensitive to short-term interest rates.

The financial sector of the Federal Reserve–MIT econometric model embodies the neo-Fisherian hypothesis.[39] In the financial sector of the model the reciprocal of velocity (the Cambridge k) is related to the rates of interest on short-term assets relative to transactions costs. Assuming no significant variation in transactions costs, the demand for money is then expressed as $M^d = k(i)Y$, where i = a set of available rates of return on short-term assets, Y = nominal gross national product (GNP), and M is narrow money.[40]

Within the neo-Fisherian framework, changes in the quantity of money have their direct impact on short-term interest rates.[41] Through the process of portfolio substitutions, changes in short-term interest rates affect, in turn, the long-term interest rates, equity yields, and possibly other rates of return on real assets.[42] Changes in these variables then influence aggregate demand for goods and services. This transmission process indicates that the full effect of monetary policy is subject to a considerable

[36]The Keynesian speculative demand for money ceases to be an explanation of holding money but becomes the basis for an expectational theory of the term structure of interest rates.

[37]William J. Baumol, "The Transactions Demand for Cash: An Inventory Theoretic Approach," *The Quarterly Journal of Economics,* Vol. LXVI (1952), pp. 545-56; James Tobin, "The Interest-Elasticity of Transactions Demand for Cash," *The Review of Economics and Statistics,* Vol. XXXVIII (1956), pp. 241-47.

[38]Franco Modigliani, Robert Rasche, and J. Philip Cooper, "Central Bank Policy, the Money Supply, and the Short-Term Rate of Interest," *Journal of Money, Credit and Banking,* Vol. II (1970), p. 167. The neo-Fisherian model of the demand for money developed by these authors is basically the one in the Federal Reserve–MIT econometric model.

[39]Robert H. Rasche and Harold T. Shapiro, "The F.R.B.–M.I.T. Econometric Model: Its Special Features," American Economic Association, *Papers and Proceedings of the Eightieth Annual Meeting (The American Economic Review,* Vol. LVIII, May 1968), pp. 123-49.

[40]*Ibid.,* p. 137.

[41]However, if the monetary authorities dealt in the long-term bond market, changes in the quantity of money resulting from open market operations would affect the long-term interest rate directly.

[42]The process through which changes in short-term interest rates affect long-term interest rates may be explained directly by an equation from the term structure of interest rates based on the expectations hypothesis. This approach allows us to omit the equations of supply and demand for many financial assets. The Federal Reserve–MIT model follows this approach, relying on the term structure hypothesis developed by Franco Modigliani and Richard Sutch, "Innovations in Interest Rate Policy," American Economic Association, *Papers and Proceedings of the Seventy-eighth Annual Meeting (The American Economic Review,* Vol. LVI, May 1966), pp. 178-97.

lag, because it takes time for changes in monetary policy to be reflected in long-term interest rates and equity yields and also requires additional delay for this rate change to be reflected in various components of aggregate demand.[43]

III. The Monetarist View

The theoretical framework used by nonmonetarists to explain how monetary and fiscal policies affect economic activity is a variant of the Keynesian income/expenditure model. While nonmonetarists are rather explicit in their theoretical argument, monetarists have not been very precise in providing a convincing explanation of how money affects the economy and how changes in the supply of money could have markedly more potent and direct effects than changes in fiscal variables. Instead, their argument seems to be based on several kinds of empirical evidence, the most widely publicized being the findings of the reduced form equation studies. These studies relate changes in GNP to the simultaneous and lagged changes in the supply of money and a budget variable or autonomous expenditures.

In this section we will discuss the views of Friedman, Brunner and Meltzer, and other monetarists. The general view that emerges from the writings of these monetarists is that "changes in the money stock are a primary determinant of changes in total spending, and should thereby be given major emphasis in economic stabilization programs."[44] In addition to this, monetarists emphasize the following three points: (1) The monetary authorities can dominate movements in the stock of money over time and over business cycles. (2) Movements in the quantity of money are the most reliable measure of the thrust of monetary impulses. (3) Monetary impulses are transmitted to the real economy through a relative price process (portfolio adjustment process), which operates on a vast array of financial and real assets.[45]

---

[43]In the Federal Reserve-MIT model the costs of capital are defined to be linear combinations of various long-term interest rates and the dividend/price ratio. The effect of monetary policy is felt immediately in the short-term interest rates. Through the term structure equation, changes in short-term rates affect the long-term rates with a time lag. The long-term rate in turn affects the cost of capital directly as one of its components and indirectly through the dividend/price ratio. The cost of capital influences the demand functions for final output with an additional time lag. See Rasche and Shapiro, "The F. R. B.-M. I. T. Econometric Model" (cited in footnote 39), p. 146. See also de Leeuw and Gramlich, "The Channels of Monetary Policy" (cited in footnote 20), pp. 485-90.

[44]Leonall C. Andersen and Keith M. Carlson, "A Monetarist Model for Economic Stabilization," Federal Reserve Bank of St. Louis, *Review*, Vol. 52 (April 1970), p. 7. An important qualification of this is Friedman's view that, notwithstanding the importance of money, monetary policy—because it operates with a long and variable lag—should not be used for short-run stabilization. Instead, money should be allowed to grow at a constant rate over time.

On the general view of monetarists, see Milton Friedman, *The Counter-Revolution in Monetary Theory*, first Wincott Memorial Lecture, delivered at the Senate House, University of London, September 16, 1970, Occasional Paper 33, Institute of Economic Affairs (London, 1970); Karl Brunner, "The 'Monetarist Revolution' in Monetary Theory," *Weltwirtschaftliches Archiv*, Band 105, Heft 1 (1970), pp. 1-30.

[45]Karl Brunner, "The Role of Money and Monetary Policy," Federal Reserve Bank of St. Louis, *Review*, Vol. 50 (July 1968), pp. 9, 18, and 24.

Friedman: The Monetary Theory of
Nominal Income

Professor Milton Friedman, as the chief architect of the monetarist view, is responsible for the intellectual revival of the quantity theory in the postwar period—a revival that has for some years provoked a good deal of commentary and critical interpretation. Much of this controversy has been attributed to his failure to make explicit the theoretical framework that encompasses his views on the role of money. In two recent articles,[46] he has responded to this criticism, but it is not clear to what extent he has succeeded in answering his critics.[47]

Friedman's theoretical framework in the most recent expression of his views is a Keynesian income/expenditure model, which, he claims, is acceptable to both monetarists and nonmonetarists.[48]

The model is given as follows:

$$\frac{C}{P} = f\left(\frac{Y}{P}, r\right) \tag{1}$$

$$\frac{I}{P} = g(r) \tag{2}$$

$$\frac{Y}{P} = \frac{C}{P} + \frac{I}{P} \tag{3}$$

$$M^d = P L\left(\frac{Y}{P}, r\right) \tag{4}$$

$$M^s = h(r) \tag{5}$$

$$M^d = M^s, \tag{6}$$

where Y = money income; C = consumption; I = investment; r = the rate of interest; P = the price level; M^s = supply of money; M^d = demand for money.

Equations (1)-(3) describe the real sector of the economy, while equations (4)-(6) outline the monetary sector. In this model, real consumption expenditure is ex-

---

[46]Milton Friedman, "A Theoretical Framework for Monetary Analysis," *Journal of Political Economy,* Vol. 78 (March/April 1970), pp. 193-238; "A Monetary Theory of Nominal Income," *Journal of Political Economy,* Vol. 79 (March/April 1971), pp. 323-37.

[47]Prior to this, Patinkin had shown conclusively that Friedman's reformulation of the quantity theory was an elegant exposition of the modern portfolio approach to the demand for money, which can be seen as a continuation of the Keynesian liquidity preference theory. (See Don Patinkin, "The Chicago Tradition, the Quantity Theory, and Friedman," *Journal of Money, Credit and Banking,* Vol. I 1969, pp. 46-70.) In recent writings, Friedman himself has acknowledged that his reformulation was much influenced by the Keynesian liquidity analysis. (See Friedman, "Postwar Trends in Monetary Theory and Policy" (cited in footnote 12) p. 188. See also Milton Friedman, "Money: Quantity Theory," *International Encyclopedia of the Social Sciences,* Vol. 10 (New York, 1968), pp. 432-47.

[48]See Friedman, "A Theoretical Framework for Monetary Analysis" (cited in footnote 46), pp. 217-18.

plained by real income and the interest rate (equation 1) and real investment is explained by the interest rate (equation 2). Equation (3) is the equilibrium condition in the commodity market, or the income identity. Real money balances are a function of real income and the rate of interest (equation 4), while the nominal supply of money is assumed to be an increasing function of the interest rate (equation 5). The equilibrium condition in the money market is given by equation (6).

The model consists of six independent equations with seven endogenous variables (C, I, Y, P, M^d, M^s, r), so that the system of equations cannot determine simultaneously the solution values of these variables. One of these variables must be determined exogenously by relationships outside the system. Friedman discusses three different ways of solving the system that correspond to three different macroeconomic theories. The first two methods are well known in the literature; they are the income/expenditure theory and the quantity theory approach. The difference between the two theories is the condition that is added to make the model determine the solution values of the seven endogenous variables. The Keynesian income/expenditure theory assumes that the general level of prices is determined outside the system—the Keynesian assumption of price or wage rigidity ($P = P_0$). Given this assumption, the system of equations determines simultaneously the solution for the level of income and the rate of interest, as usually described in the familiar Hicksian *IS/LM* apparatus.[49] The quantity theory approach, on the other hand, assumes that real income is determined outside the system—the classical assumption of full employment. This assumption allows a dichotomy of the system into the real and monetary sectors, with the result that the demand for and supply of money functions determine the price level.[50] Friedman takes the view that the quantity theory model is valid for long-run equilibrium, so that, in the long run, variations in the rate of change in the quantity of money will change only the rate of inflation and not growth of real output.[51]

According to Friedman, neither the quantity theory nor the income/expenditure theory model is satisfactory as a framework for short-run analysis. This is so, Fried-

---

[49]The price rigidity assumption, $P = P_0$, allows equations (1)-(3) to define one relation between r and real income (*IS* curve) and equations (4)-(6) to define a second such relation (*LM* curve). Their simultaneous solution gives the rate of interest and real income.

[50]Given the level of real income, $Y/P = y$, equations (1)-(3) determine the rate of interest. Equations (4)-(6) then yield an equation relating the price level to the quantity of money.

[51]In conditions where the rate of growth of real output is determined independently by real forces in the economy, conditions that are assumed to prevail in the long run, changes in the money supply will dominate only changes in the price level, notwithstanding the fact that the demand for money is interest sensitive. Specifically, Friedman argues that in the long run monetary policy cannot control real variables—the real rate of interest, the level of unemployment, and real income—but can control only nominal quantities—the price level, money rate of interest, and nominal income. See Milton Friedman, "The Role of Monetary Policy," in his *The Optimum Quantity of Money and Other Essays* (Chicago, 1969), p. 105.

Critics of Friedman have frequently pointed out that his extreme view of the role of money is valid only if the demand for money is insensitive to interest rates, implying a close linkage between the stock of money and income. In the light of the above discussion and his recent reformulation on the demand for money, this kind of criticism seems no longer valid. See also Milton Friedman, "Interest Rates and the Demand for Money" in his *The Optimum Quantity of Money and Other Essays*, pp. 141-55.

man claims, mainly because neither theory can explain "(*a*) the short-run division of a change in nominal income between prices and output, (*b*) the short-run adjustment of nominal income to a change in autonomous variables, and (*c*) the transition between this short-run situation and a long-run equilibrium described essentially by the quantity-theory model."[52]

The third alternative way to determine the system of equations is given by the monetary theory of nominal income—a theory that, Friedman claims, is superior to either the income/expenditure or the quantity theory as an approach to closing the system for the purpose of analyzing short-period changes. This third approach synthesizes Irving Fisher's ideas on the nominal and real interest rates and Keynes' view that the current market rate of interest (long-term) is determined largely by the rate that is expected to prevail over a long period. The Keynes and Fisher synthesis is then integrated into a quantity theory model together with the empirical assumption (i) that the real income elasticity of the demand for money is unity and (ii) that a difference between the anticipated real interest rate and the anticipated growth rate of real income is determined outside the system.[53] The result is a monetary model in which current income is related to current and prior nominal quantities of money.

The monetary model may be described as follows:[54]

THE MONETARY SECTOR
Given the assumption of unitary real income elasticity of the demand for money, equation (4) can be rewritten as

$$M^d = F(r)Y \tag{4$'$}$$

In order to simplify the exposition of the model, let us assume that the supply of money is determined exogenously:

$$M^s = M \tag{5$'$}$$

Then equations (4)', (5)', and equilibrium conditions (6) yield

$$M = F(r)Y \tag{7}$$

Equation (7) can be written as

$$Y = \frac{1}{F(r)} M = H(r)M \tag{8}$$

[52]Friedman, "A Theoretical Framework for Monetary Analysis" (cited in footnote 46), p. 223. Both theories analyze short-run adjustments in terms of shifts from one static equilibrium position to another without explaining a dynamic adjustment process involved in such a change in equilibrium positions.

[53]This assumption is the counterpart of the third approach of the full employment and rigid-price assumptions of the quantity theory and income/expenditure theory.

[54]See Friedman, "A Monetary Theory of Nominal Income" (cited in footnote 46), pp. 325–32.

The Fisherian distinction between the nominal and real rate of interest is given by the following identity:

$$r = q + \left(\frac{1}{P}\frac{dP}{dt}\right),$$ (9)[55]

where q = the real rate of interest; $(1/P\ dP/dt)$ = the rate of change of the price level.

From equation (9), it also follows that

$$r^* = q^* + \left(\frac{1}{P}\frac{dP}{dt}\right)^*,$$ (10)

where the variables with an asterisk refer to anticipated (or expected) values.

Following Keynes' argument that market rates of interest are determined largely by speculators with firmly held expectations, Friedman assumes that

$$r = r^*$$ (11)[56]

From the identity, $Y = yP$, it follows that

$$\left(\frac{1}{P}\frac{dP}{dt}\right)^* = \left(\frac{1}{Y}\frac{dY}{dt}\right)^* - \left(\frac{1}{y}\frac{dy}{dt}\right)^*$$ (12)

Combining equations (10), (11), and (12) we obtain

$$r = q^* - g^* + \left(\frac{1}{Y}\frac{dY}{dt}\right)^*,$$ (13)

where $g^* = (1/y\ dy/dt)^*$ = the anticipated rate of growth of real income.

Substitution of equation (13) into (8) yields

$$Y = H\left[q^* - g^* + \left(\frac{1}{Y}\frac{dY}{dt}\right)^*\right]M$$ (14)

Equation (14) states that the level of income Y is determined by q^*, g^*, $(1/Y\ dY/dt)^*$, and M. Friedman assumes that the difference between q^* and g^* is a constant. In a static framework, the expected rate of growth of nominal income

[55]Notice that both the simple quantity and income/expenditure theories assume a stable price level; hence, real and nominal rates of interest are the same.

[56]Suppose that a substantial number of asset owners have the same expectation on the future rate of interest and hold the expectation firmly, then the demand for money will become perfectly elastic at the current rate of interest that is equal to the expected rate of interest, namely, when $r = r^*$. Money and other earning assets (bonds in the Keynesian analysis) would become perfect substitutes; the demand for money has a liquidity trap at $r = r^*$. In this situation, the monetary authorities would not be able to change the rate of interest by changing the quantity of money; no matter what the monetary authorities do with the supply of money, asset owners will force the current rate of interest into conformity with their expectations on the future rate of interest. Friedman argues that this is the basic idea behind the Keynes' short-run liquidity trap. See Friedman, "A Theoretical Framework for Monetary Analysis" (cited in footnote 46), p. 214.

$(1/Y\,dY/dt)^*$ may be treated as a predetermined variable. Then equation (14) determines the level of nominal income for a given supply of money without any reference to the real sector of the model.[57] In a dynamic framework, however, it would be natural to regard $(1/Y\,dY/dt)^*$ as determined by the past history of nominal income. Since the past history of nominal income is in turn a function of the past history of money as implied by equation (8) for earlier dates, equation (14) becomes a relation between the level of nominal income at each point in time and the past history of the quantity of money.

This dynamic character of the model may be better understood by analyzing an example given by Friedman. Take the logarithm of equation (14) and differentiate with respect to time.

This gives

$$\frac{1}{Y}\frac{dY}{dt} = s \cdot \frac{d}{dt}\left(\frac{1}{Y}\frac{dY}{dt}\right)^* + \frac{1}{M}\frac{dM}{dt}, \tag{15}$$

where $s = 1/H\,dH/dr = $ the slope of the regression of log H on the rate of interest.

Suppose that the expected rate of growth of nominal income is determined by an adaptive expectation process:

$$\frac{d}{dt}\left(\frac{1}{Y}\frac{dY}{dt}\right)^* = \beta\left[\frac{1}{Y}\frac{dY}{dt} - \left(\frac{1}{Y}\frac{dY}{dt}\right)^*\right] \tag{16}[58]$$

[57]Once we make the distinction between the nominal and real rate of interest, the rate of interest relevant to the consumption and investment functions is the real rate of interest, q. Hence, the equations describing the real sector of the model are modified as

$$\frac{C}{P} = f\left(\frac{Y}{P}, q\right) \tag{1}'$$

$$\frac{I}{P} = g(q) \tag{2}'$$

$$\frac{Y}{P} = \frac{c}{P} + \frac{I}{P} \tag{3}$$

Assume that the realized real rate of interest q is constant,

$$q = q^* = q_o \tag{15}$$

Then equations (1)'-(3) become a self-contained system of three equations with three unknowns: C/P, I/P, and Y/P. The price level would then be determined by substituting Y/P obtained from the real sector and Y from the monetary sector into the following identity, $Y = y \cdot P$.

Friedman considers this way of combining the monetary and real sectors as highly unsatisfactory for two reasons: the assumption of a constant real rate of interest is likely to introduce serious errors, particularly through the real sector, and the consumption function (1) ignores several important arguments, such as wealth and expected rate of inflation. See Friedman, "A Monetary Theory of Nominal Income" (cited in footnote 46), p. 330.

[58]Equation (16) is analogous to

$$\left(\frac{1}{Y}\frac{dY}{dt}\right)^*_T = \int_{-\infty}^{T} e^{\beta(t-T)}\left(\frac{1}{Y}\frac{dY}{dt}\right)_t dt,$$

Substituting equation (16) into equation (15) and solving for $(1/Y \, dY/dt)$, we have

$$\frac{1}{Y}\frac{dY}{dt} = \left(\frac{1}{Y}\frac{dY}{dt}\right)* + \frac{1}{(1 - \beta s)}\left[\frac{1}{M}\frac{dM}{dt} - \left(\frac{1}{Y}\frac{dY}{dt}\right)*\right] \qquad (17)$$

When
$(1/Y \, dY/dt)* = 1/M \, dM/dt$, equation (17) gives the quantity theory result that nominal income changes at the same rate as money supply.

Friedman states that his monetary model of nominal income corresponds to the broader framework implicit in much of the theoretical and empirical work that he and others have done in analyzing monetary experience in the short run and is consistent with many of their empirical findings.[59]

However, Friedman's model sheds little light on his view concerning the precise mechanism through which changes in the quantity of money affect income. This is so because the model is designed primarily for empirical analysis of the relation between money and income. What this model reflects is rather his view on the appropriate empirical approach to evaluating the role of money—a view that is in sharp contrast to the more common one held by nonmonetarists. Contrary to the impression that one might gather from his model—possibly a rigid and mechanical connection between money and income—his view on the transmission mechanism in a conceptual framework is a complicated portfolio adjustment process that involves many uncertain channels and impinges on a wide array of assets and expenditures. The process[60] following an exogenous change in the supply of money begins with changes in the prices and yields of financial assets and spreads to nonfinancial assets. These changes in the prices of financial and nonfinancial assets influence spending to produce new assets and spending on current services. At the same time, these changes alter real wealth of the public relative to income and thereby affect consumption. This is, in a simple fashion, the way in which the initial impulse is diffused from the financial markets to the markets for goods and services. The exposition stresses portfolio adjustment and is strikingly similar to that described by many economists.

The transmission process is also essentially consistent with the Keynesian liquidity

---

which means that the expected rate of growth of nominal income at T is a weighted average of past growth rates of nominal income, the weights ($e^{\beta(t-T)}$) declining exponentially where t is the time of the observation weighted. See Edgar L. Feige, "Expectations and Adjustments in the Monetary Sector," American Economic Association, *Papers and Proceedings of the Seventy-ninth Annual Meeting* (*The American Economic Review*, Vol. LVII, May 1967), pp. 463–67.

[59]Friedman, "A Monetary Theory of Nominal Income" (cited in footnote 46), pp. 324 and 334.

[60]Milton Friedman and Anna J. Schwartz, "Money and Business Cycles," *The Review of Economics and Statistics*, Vol. XLV (Supplement, February 1963), pp. 59–63; Milton Friedman and David Meiselman, "The Relative Stability of Monetary Velocity and the Investment Multiplier in the United States, 1877-1958," *Stabilization Policies*, Commission on Money and Credit (Englewood Cliffs, New Jersey, 1963), pp. 217–22; Milton Friedman, "The Role of Monetary Policy," in his *The Optimum Quantity of Money and Other Essays* (cited in footnote 51), p. 100, and *The Counter-Revolution in Monetary Theory* (cited in footnote 44), pp. 24–25.

preference doctrine as to how money affects income. As in the income/expenditure theory, interest rates play a key role. This being so, it has been pointed out that Friedman cannot be saying anything different from Keynes[61] and that there is no clear reason why one should look at money supply as a target as Friedman insists rather than at interest rates directly.[62] However, these criticisms miss the fundamental points of Friedman's view. The difference between Friedman and the non-monetarists concerning the transmission process is not whether changes in the supply of money operate through interest rates but rather (i) the range of interest rates considered and (ii) the empirical approach to estimating the actual influence of monetary policy. Friedman argues that the impact of monetary policy is likely to be understated in magnitude and narrowed in scope in the Keynesian income/expenditure theory. One reason is that, since monetary policy impinges on a broad range of capital assets and a correspondingly broad range of associated expenditures, the Keynesian practice of looking only at recorded market interest rates, which are only part of a much broader spectrum of rates, makes one underestimate the actual impact of monetary policy. The rates of interest that influence investment decisions are for the most part implicit yields and hence not observable, so that one cannot hope to obtain useful results by looking at relations between market interest rates and the categories of spending associated with these rates. Also, recorded market interest rates may not provide an appropriate measure of the cost of capital, since these interest rates are not real rates of interest that reflect the basic forces of productivity but nominal rates that are influenced by the expected rate of inflation. Moreover, monetary influences may work through channels that we have not been able to identify. In fact, it may not be possible to trace through any particular channel, as monetary policy operates through an extremely complicated process of portfolio adjustments.

For all these reasons, Friedman considers that even the most complex structure of a general equilibrium model cannot be expected to capture actual monetary influences adequately. A more reliable empirical approach would be to pursue the methodology of positive economies, the essence of which is to select the crucial and simple theoretical relationships that allow one to predict something large (such as GNP) from something small (for instance, the supply of money), regardless of the intervening chain of causation. One such relationship is claimed to be the velocity function relating income to money, which is the essence of the quantity theory; another is the multiplier relationship relating income to autonomous expenditure, which is the essence of the income/expenditure theory.[63]

[61]Nicholas Kaldor, "The New Monetarism," *Lloyd's Bank Review* (July 1970), p. 9.

[62]H. C. Wallich, "Quality Theory and Quantity Policy," Chapter 10 in *Ten Economic Studies in the Tradition of Irving Fisher* (New York, 1967), p. 260.

[63]This is Johnson's interpretation of Friedman's view. See Johnson, "Recent Developments in Monetary Theory—A Commentary" (cited in footnote 1), pp. 86–87; see also Johnson, "The Keynesian Revolution and the Monetarist Counter-Revolution" (cited in footnote 1), p. 9.

Friedman argues that the velocity function (that is, the relationship between money and nominal income) has been shown, on average, to be more stable and less affected by institutional and historical change than the multiplier relationship and that, consequently, the velocity function may be the key relationship in understanding macroeconomic developments.[64] It then follows that a much more promising approach to the question of evaluating the affects of monetary policy on the economy is to try to relate changes in income directly to changes in the quantity of money. Friedman's monetary model of nominal income seems to reflect this point of view.

Friedman's view, however, raises two important issues. One issue is concerned with the conditions under which one could derive a simple relationship between income and money. It has been argued frequently that Friedman's view is valid only if the demand for money is not significantly influenced by the rate of interest. As indicated earlier, Friedman now states clearly and repeatedly that the rate of interest is an important determinant of the demand for money. If indeed the demand for money depends on the rate of interest, then one cannot—critics of Friedman argue— hope to find such a simple relationship between money and income, unless one specifies an independent theory of the determination of the rate of interest.

The Keynes and Fisher synthesis that Friedman incorporates into his monetary model appears to be one such independent theory. It is an independent theory in the sense that the determination of the nominal rate of interest depends on relationships outside the system of six equations. According to Friedman's monetary model, the rate of interest is determined solely by the anticipated rate of growth of money income $(1/Y \, dY/dt)^*$, given the assumptions that $r = r^*$ and that $q^* - g^* = k_0$. While these assumptions are crucial to a model that allows one to relate current money income directly to current and prior quantities of money, it should be realized that they are also responsible for several defects of the model. One serious defect is that the model rules out liquidity or substitution effects of a change in the quantity of money on the interest rate.

In Friedman's monetary model, a change in the rate of change of money supply $(1/M \, dM/dt)$ directly affects the rate of growth of nominal income $(1/Y \, dY/dt)$ (see equation 17) with little direct effect on change in the interest rates, that is, the change does not initially produce the liquidity effect but immediately produces an income effect. The change in $(1/Y \, dY/dt)$ then causes a change in the expected rate of growth of nominal income $(1/Y \, dY/dt)^*$ (equation 16), which, in turn, influences the nominal rate of interest (equation 13). In other words, the change in the rate of change in money supply affects market rates of interest only as it influences the courses of current and expected nominal income and, in consequence, the expected rate of inflation. This process does not appear to be supported by the existing empirical evidence on the effects of changes in money supply on the interest rates and

---

[64]See Friedman and Meiselman, "The Relative Stability of Monetary Velocity and the Investment Multiplier in the United States, 1877-1958" (cited in footnote 60).

income.[65] Nor does it seem to be consistent with Friedman's own earlier exposition on the transmission mechanism of monetary policy, in which he argues that a change in the supply of money has its first impact on the financial markets and much later on the market for goods and services.[66]

However, the failure of the model to explain the liquidity effect is clearly not a point of disagreement with Friedman, for he admits that the model neglects the effects of changes in the nominal quantity of money on interest rates.[67] Yet, it is not clear to what extent he appreciates the analytical significance of relaxing either of his two critical assumptions to permit a strong liquidity effect in the model. Relaxation of these assumptions would mean that Friedman's model would be modified in such a way that the rate of interest is determined within the model through the interaction of demand for and supply of money together with other behavioral relationships in the real sector of the economy. Such a modification would then suggest that one may not utilize velocity to derive a simple relation between money income and the quantity of money.

The other issue that Friedman's monetary model raises is whether the methodology of positive economics embodied in the model is a scientifically acceptable method. The general consensus seems to be that the methodology is seriously inadequate. We shall return to this topic in some detail in the final section of this paper.

Brunner and Meltzer

The transmission process described by Brunner and Meltzer is basically a process of portfolio (balance sheet) adjustment, which is, on a general level of discussion, shared by both neo-Keynesians and other monetarists.[68] The difference between

[65]In examining the relationship between changes in the rate of change in money supply and changes in the commercial paper rates, Cagan found that an increase in the monetary growth rate initially exerts a negative liquidity effect on the interest rate. The negative effect is then offset by positive income and price effects within about one year, following the increase in the monetary growth rate. See Phillip Cagan, "The Channels of Monetary Effects on Interest Rates" (mimeographed, National Bureau of Economic Research, 1966).

Friedman himself acknowledges that change in the rate of change in the quantity of money will have no appreciable effect on the rate of change in money income for six months to nine months, on average, in the United States. See Friedman, "A Monetary Theory of Nominal Income" (cited in footnote 46), p. 335.

In a recent study by Gibson, however, the initial liquidity effects are shown to be fully offset by positive effects only after a period of three or five months, depending on which definition of money one uses. See William E. Gibson, "Interest Rates and Monetary Policy," *Journal of Political Economy,* Vol. 78 (May/June, 1970), pp. 431-55.

[66]See footnote 60.

[67]See Friedman, "A Monetary Theory of Nominal Income" (cited in footnote 46), p. 333. He also states that the model cannot explain satisfactorily the movements of interests and velocity in the first nine months or so after a distinct change in the rate of monetary growth. (*Ibid.,* p. 335.)

[68]For a more detailed discussion, see Karl Brunner, "The Report of the Commission on Money and Credit," *The Journal of Political Economy,* Vol. LXIX (December 1961), pp. 605-20; Karl Brunner, "Some Major Problems in Monetary Theory," American Economic Association, *Papers and Proceedings of the Seventy-third Annual Meeting* (*The American Economic Review,* Vol. LI, May 1961), pp. 47-56; Karl Brunner and Allan H. Meltzer, "The Place of Financial Intermediaries in the Transmission of Monetary

Brunner and Meltzer and other economists, if any, may be found in the different degrees of emphasis on the importance of real capital in the mechanism. Brunner and Meltzer point out that the analysis of portfolio balance reveals that changes in the level of output emerge fundamentally from this balance sheet adjustment, particularly in response to the public's decision to adjust its real capital holdings. In order, then, to capture the total effects of monetary policy changes, it is necessary to specify the appropriate stock-flow relationship centered on real capital goods, since changes in the asset price of real capital relative to its output price form a crucial linkage in the transmission process. Accordingly, they distinguish four classes of output—output for real consumption and for Types I, II, and III of capital goods—and also consider various financial assets together with the stocks of real capital disaggregated into the three types.

Type I capital goods are those that have separate market prices for equity claims on existing stock and for new output. (Examples under this category would be machinery, plant, and equipment.)[69] Type II capital goods have a single price for existing assets and new output of comparable quality (housing and automobiles); Type III has a price for new output only, and there is no market for existing assets or claims to them (consumer durables, such as washing machines). Corresponding to these different types of capital goods are different paths through which monetary policy can affect the real economy. An increase in the supply of money, for example, will, through portfolio substitutions, lead to an overall increase in the asset prices of all these types of real capital goods. The increase in the equity price for Type I real capital relative to its output price accelerates the actual rate of accumulation of this type of capital goods.[70] The increase in the asset price of Type II capital, *ceteris paribus,* stimulates the production of Type II capital goods. Furthermore, the rise in the asset prices of real capital and the fall in the rates of return on financial assets result in an increase in the market value of public wealth, which, in turn, raises the desired stock of Type III capital and consumption expenditure. The total effects of the expansionary monetary policy will then be the sum of these influences.[71]

The income/expenditure theory as represented by the conventional *IS/LM* framework, in Brunner and Meltzer's view, fails to accommodate the public's stock-flow behavior bearing on its real capital position, which they consider crucial in the transmission process. Because of this failure, Brunner and Meltzer argue that the Keynesian approach of relating investment expenditure to interest rates in some financial assets as a measure of the costs of borrowing—supplemented by the wealth

Policy," American Economic Association, *Papers and Proceedings of the Seventy-fifth Annual Meeting* (*The American Economic Review,* Vol. LIII, May 1963), pp. 372–82; Karl Brunner, "The Relative Price Theory of Money, Output, and Employment" (unpublished, based on a paper presented at the Midwestern Economic Association Meetings, April 1967); Brunner and Meltzer, "Fiscal and Monetary Policy in a Non-Keynesian World" (cited in footnote 22).

[69]The transmission mechanism identified in the analysis of the neo-Keynesian portion centers around Type I capital goods.

[70]This process is analogous to the one described and emphasized by neo-Keynesians.

[71]Brunner and Meltzer, "The Place of Financial Intermediaries in the Transmission of Monetary Policy" (cited in footnote 68), pp. 374–77. Brunner and Meltzer do not emphasize the interest rate effect on the desired stock of Type II capital but only the wealth effect.

effect—can hardly capture the actual impact of monetary policy and that, thus, the Keynesian approach should be rejected.

A more satisfactory approach that would be consistent with Brunner and Meltzer's view would require a structural model of general equilibrium—a model that specifies the whole spectrum of real and financial assets and the explicit relations between the production of new real capital goods and the existing ones. In a recent unpublished paper,[72] Brunner and Meltzer attempt to construct such a model. However, in formulating the model they choose to ignore entirely the markets for Types II and III of real capital goods and focus on the market for Type I real capital, the equity market. The result of this modification, or simplification, of their view is a model that is, in all important aspects, analogous to the neo-Keynesian model discussed in the Appendix.[*]

Therefore, the model suggests that Brunner and Meltzer—contrary to their claim—accept the Keynesian view on the nature of the transmission process; what they seem to reject is the heuristic simplification of reality with regard to the range of assets considered in the Keynesian income/expenditure theory . . .

IV. Concluding Remarks

The main purpose of this paper has been to review divergent views on the transmission process of monetary policy. The review indicates that at the level of general description there appear to be no significant differences in the transmission process of monetary influences among a variety of monetary economists. Both monetarists and nonmonetarists appear to support some version of the portfolio adjustment process as a framework to describe the effects of monetary policy on the real economy. The disagreement between them on this process centers on the range of assets and interest rates that should be considered and the technical relationships involving the stocks of real assets and the flows of real expenditure corresponding to these assets. The range of assets and interest rates considered by nonmonetarists is rather limited, whereas monetarists stress a broad range of assets and the expenditures associated with these assets. Also, both monetarists and nonmonetarists emphasize the wealth effect channel and, in various forms, the credit rationing channel.

From these observations one might conclude that the question of the relative effectiveness of monetary and fiscal policy is essentially an empirical issue, not a theoretical one. Although the issue has evoked a great deal of empirical study in recent years, the controversy still is far from being settled. The evidence from several of the large-scale econometric models—the estimation method favored by nonmonetarists—is that monetary variables are, in general, less important than fiscal variables in influencing aggregate expenditures.[73]

[72]Brunner and Meltzer, "Fiscal and Monetary Policy in a Non-Keynesian World" (cited in footnote 22).

[73]A notable exception is the Federal Reserve-MIT quarterly econometric model for the United States. It shows that monetary policy has a powerful effect, although less powerful than suggested by monetarists. See de Leeuw and Gramlich, "The Channels of Monetary Policy" (cited in footnote 20).

[*] The Appendix to this article is not reprinted here.—Ed.

On the other hand, monetarists have produced an imposing volume of empirical evidence of several kinds in support of their central proposition. One kind of evidence draws on historical case studies, such as the one by Friedman and Schwartz,[74] and the experience of a number of countries with easy-money policies that led to inflation after World War II. A second type of evidence is the "statistical stability" of the demand function for money in several industrial countries, notably in the United States. Some monetarists view the demand function for money as the crucial relationship in the understanding of macroeconomic developments. The stability of this function is then presented as evidence in favor of the traditional quantity theory as opposed to the income/expenditure theory, and the function is then used to explain and to predict the level of money income.[75] The demand function for money may well be of central importance to economic activity. However, insofar as the money demand is sensitive to interest rates, evidence for which has been demonstrated beyond any reasonable doubt in all of the major empirical studies on the demand function for money, one has to provide a theory of the determination of interest rates along with its interrelationship with a theory of income determination to prove that money indeed matters. A third type of empirical evidence bearing on this question is the reduced form equation studies, which invariably show that the quantity of money is far more significant than various exogenous components of aggregate demand in explaining the movements in money income.

The debate on the reduced form approach, or the direct estimation method, also reflects a sharp disagreement between nonmonetarists and monetarists on the methodological questions of how best to estimate the effects of monetary and fiscal actions on the level of economic activity. As noted above, nonmonetarists favor estimation through large-scale econometric models. Monetarists, however, argue that the channels through which monetary policy operates are so diverse and complicated that it is inherently impossible to identify and to measure them with structural equation models, no matter how detailed they may be. Basically, for this reason, they contend that a more reliable method would be the direct estimation technique whereby final demand variables, such as money GNP, are regressed upon monetary and fiscal variables.

No one would deny the complexity involved in the channels of monetary policy; however, the important questions are whether this complexity justifies the use of the reduced form approach and, if it does, whether the approach is a scientifically acceptable method. Judging by the prevailing standards of academic economics, indeed, the direct estimation approach is seriously inadequate as an empirical methodology.[76]

One of the most serious weaknesses of the approach is that the structural model

[74]Milton Friedman and Anna Jacobson Schwartz, *Monetary History of the United States, 1867-1960,* National Bureau of Economic Research, Studies in Business Cycles, No. 12 (Princeton University Press, 1963).

[75]See Karl Brunner and Allan H. Meltzer, "Predicting Velocity: Implications for Theory and Policy," *The Journal of Finance,* Vol. XVIII (1963), pp. 319-54.

[76]Johnson, "The Keynesian Revolution and the Monetarist Counter-Revolution" (cited in footnote 1), p. 12.

from which a reduced form equation is derived may not be consistent internally. The direct estimation approach completely ignores a priori restrictions on the coefficients of the independent variables of the equation, for example, the restrictions that are built into general equilibrium models through identities, lags, omitting variables, etc. Because of the absence of these restrictions, there is no way of knowing whether the structural model is consistent internally.[77] If it is not, the reduced form equation is no more than a linear equation relating an "alleged" endogenous variable, such as money GNP, to a set of "alleged" exogenous variables with no meaningful economic causations between the endogenous and exogenous variables.

Another equally damaging weakness is the problem of selecting exogenous monetary and fiscal variables. Depending upon which variable one assumes to be exogenous—monetary base, free reserves, narrow money, or broad money on the monetary side and the various definitions of autonomous expenditures on the fiscal side—one can take a "money mostly" stance, a "fiscal policy mostly" stance, or a "both matter" stance.[78]

In response to the first defect, some monetarists have begun to extend their efforts in specifying the details of the structural models that underlie the various reduced form equations that they estimate. These models are invariably some version of Keynesian income/expenditure models.[79] Therefore, the response may be an open admission that monetarists are increasingly compromising with the Keynesian income/expenditure theory, which they had set out to question. The response also suggests that monetarists are, in compromising with nonmonetarists, burdening themselves with another difficult task, namely, giving a convincing explanation as to why such a great divergence exists in empirical evidence between the reduced form and structural model approaches. A satisfactory answer has yet to come.

In view of these assessments of the monetarist view, it appears that one cannot read too much into the results of various reduced form equation studies. These assessments also suggest that a more promising road toward the settlement of the controversy concerning the relative strengths of fiscal and monetary actions lies in further development and refinement of existing econometric models. In this regard, the monetarist view suggests a number of factors that have been inadequately treated

[77]A good example of the internal inconsistency of a reduced form equation may be found in the recent study by Leonall C. Andersen and J. Jordan, "Monetary and Fiscal Actions: A Test of Their Relative Importance in Economic Stabilization," Federal Reserve Bank of St. Louis Review, Vol. L (November 1968), pp. 11-24. They show that the impact coefficient of government expenditure on the level of money income is less than unity. Given that money income should rise by at least the same amount as the increase in government expenditure, Andersen and Jordan's finding means that some private endogenous spending is falling by a larger amount as a consequence of the government expenditure. Since they do not specify the structural model of their reduced form equation, one cannot determine what expenditure is falling and why. One possible reason for such a low impact coefficient may be that the structural model is not consistent internally. See Edward M. Gramlich, "The Usefulness of Monetary and Fiscal Policy as Discretionary Stabilization Tools," Journal of Money, Credit and Banking, Vol. III (1971), p. 514.

[78]Ibid., pp. 523-24.

[79]This type of response can be found in a series of unpublished articles by Andersen in which he develops a Keynesian income/expenditure model and then derives from the model a reduced form equation. See Leonall C. Andersen, "Influence of Monetary and Fiscal Actions in a Financially Constrained Economy" (unpublished paper, May 1971).

in existing models and that may account partly for the sluggish response of monetary influences in these models.

We may point out two such factors relevant to our subject matter. One possible factor is the failure of existing econometric models to include implicit rates of return on real capital and consumer durables. The other is the failure to distinguish between nominal and real interest rates in some of these models. The rates of interest used in these models are nominal rates that are affected by the expectation on future prices. However, interest rates that are relevant to the consumption and investment functions are clearly the real rates of interest that are relatively unaffected by changes in the level of prices. It has been shown empirically that high nominal interest rates are accompanied by a high rate of increase in money supply—an easy stance of monetary policy—and vice versa.[80] This is so because a high growth rate of money supply causes a rise in current prices and then the expectation of future inflation, which ultimately leads to a higher nominal rate of interest. It is, therefore, questionable whether nominal interest rates are meaningful indicators of the monetary posture, except perhaps in the very short run.

When these and other factors[81] are properly taken into consideration, it is quite possible that econometric models may turn up a much sharper and more rapid response of monetary influence than has been shown in the past.

[80]See, for example, William P. Yohe and Denis S. Karnosky, "Interest Rates and Price Level Changes, 1952-69," Federal Reserve Bank of St. Louis, *Review,* Vol. 51 (December 1969), pp. 18-38; William E. Gibson, "Price Expectations Effects on Interest Rates," *The Journal of Finance,* Vol. XXV (1970), pp. 19-34; Gibson, "Interest Rates and Monetary Policy" (cited in footnote 65).

[81]For other factors, see David I. Fand, "The Monetary Theory of Nine Recent Quarterly Econometric Models of the United States: A Comment," *Journal of Money, Credit and Banking,* Vol. III (1971), pp. 450-60.

Channels of Monetary Influence: A Survey

Roger W. Spencer*

Among the numerous controversies surrounding "money," few are further from resolution than the issue of how money affects the economy. Compounding the controversy is the fact that the arguments advanced are not divided neatly along so-called monetarist and nonmonetarist lines, but are separated by other criteria.

To be sure, monetarists have long taken exception to the intellectual strait jacket of the Keynesian framework which limited the influence of monetary actions to the response of investment to interest rate changes. However, the monetarist alternatives offered have been far from uniform. Certainly, monetary actions result in the change of more than one relative price—the interest rate—and one type of spending—investment. However, substantial disagreement among monetarists (as well as other economists) persists beyond this point.

There is basic agreement that at less than full employment changes in the rate of growth of the money supply affect output and employment before prices, a proposition which may be traced back at least two hundred years (Hume [48]), but this tells nothing about how total spending and its components react to monetary actions. It is

Reprinted from the Federal Reserve Bank of St. Louis, *Review* (November, 1974), pp. 8-26, by permission of the publisher.

* The author acknowledges the helpful comments on earlier drafts of George Kaufman, Thomas Mayer, John Pippinger, Robert Rasche, William Rawson, Clark Warburton, and William Yohe. They are blameless for remaining errors.

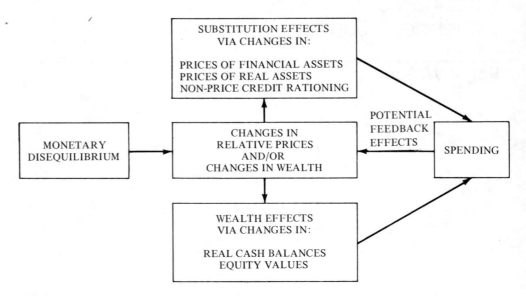

FIGURE 1. The Monetary Transmission Process

necessary to examine the changes in relative prices and wealth associated with monetary impulses to gain insight into the money-spending relation.

When the existing money stock (however defined) either exceeds or falls short of the quantity demanded, wealth and/or relative prices change and this sets off both substitution and wealth effects, as indicated in Figure 1.[1] The changes in relative prices typically involve changes in the rates of return on real capital and financial assets as well as changes in the prices of goods and services. Ways in which changes in wealth may influence spending include movements in real cash balances and changes in the market value of equities.

There remains considerable disagreement about the relative importance of these factors in the transmission of monetary inpulses. This is not surprising, given the history of the relative price and wealth relations. Keynes, as well as prominent economists who preceded him, was ambiguous on the subject. This article first traces the early development of these two factors and then analyzes more recent work in each area.

---

[1]The "correct" definition of money and the determinants of money demand and supply functions are matters closely related to, but beyond the scope of the present article. Another limitation is that because of the large number of authors surveyed, only the briefest of summaries can be given here. In some cases, this results in considerable oversimplification of complex analyses.

Substitution and wealth effects are treated here as essentially equivalent to substitution and income effects of generally-accepted price theory. Although monetary-induced changes in relative prices or changes in wealth may generate both substitution and wealth effects, the relative price change has often been associated more with substitution effects and the wealth change more with wealth effects; we will follow that practice.

Historical Background

Among the better early efforts to explain the money-spending linkages were those of Irving Fisher and Knut Wicksell. Writing around the turn of the century, they both maintained a short-run view of the transmission process which was dominated by interest rate movements and a long-run view in which the key role was played by changes in real cash balances (Money/Price Level).

Fisher and Wicksell

Fisher, like other neoclassical writers, determined that output was at its full-employment level in the long run. In the short (or transitional) run, however, business cycles occurred in Fisher's time, as well as in other periods before and since. Consequently, macroeconomic analysts have continued to attempt explanations of this phenomenon. Fisher's view of the business cycle depended strongly on "sticky" interest rates.[2]

This relative price effect (via interest rates) was set off by an increase in the money stock relative to the quantity of money demanded. The nominal money supply may be assumed to have increased due to a rise in the gold stock and, consequently, bank reserves. With the additional assumption that output and velocity were fixed initially, a rise in the commodity price level was expected to be associated with the money supply increase. Because Fisher assumed that the commodity price rise preceded the increase in interest rates, with interest costs being viewed as a significant component of firms' operating costs, the rise in the price level produced an increase in firms' profits.

A continued increase in demand deposits (through business investment loan demand) relative to currency resulted in yet further increases in prices and profits. Eventually, however, excess reserves would run out; the interest rate would become "unstuck" and would rise even faster than commodity prices. With the rise in firms' costs of operation, there would occur a decline in profits and investment and a sharp increase in bankruptcies. The downward phase of the cycle was reversed when excess reserves again rose and the interest rate had fallen accordingly.

Wicksell's well-known "cumulative process" also captured cyclical movements of the economy largely through interest rate changes. Some initial disturbance, such as an innovation or technological breakthrough would foster an increase in the desire to invest at the prevailing interest rate. The demand for loanable funds would then rise as would the "normal" or "natural" rate of interest, the rate "at which *the demand for loan capital and the supply of savings* exactly agree" (Wicksell [89], p. 193). If, however, the banking community failed to realize that investment demand had risen, they would maintain the same *market* rate of interest through increases in the money

---

[2]See especially Fisher's Chapter 4, "Disturbance of Equation and of Purchasing Power During Transition Periods," in Fisher [25]. In later years, Fisher [24] associated severe swings of the business cycle with changes in debt activity.

supply which, given the usual classical assumptions, would result in commodity price rises.

Note that at this point the money supply has risen, observed interest rates have been kept low in relation to the normal rate, and business spending has been the component of aggregate demand which has increased. After some period of time, the banks' reserve position deteriorates and monetary growth is curbed. The market rate of interest rises to the level of the natural rate, an action which leads to the elimination of excess aggregate demand and price level increases.

In the above short-run dynamic analyses, both Fisher and Wicksell relied on the relative price mechanism inherent in a money-interest rates-investment framework. However, in their approach to the determination of long-run equilibrium, interest rates and investment were replaced by a treatment of the role of real cash balances.

Fisher's real balance explanation began with an assumed doubling of the money supply:

> Suppose, for a moment, that a doubling in the currency in circulation should not at once raise prices, but should halve the velocities instead; such a result would evidently upset for each individual the adjustment which he had made of cash on hand. Prices being unchanged, he now has double the amount of money and deposits which his convenience had taught him to keep on hand.[3]

With the apparent increase in wealth, everyone tries to reduce their cash balances by purchasing goods and services, according to Fisher. Because velocity (V) and output (Q) in the equation of exchange MV = PQ are determined to be fixed in the long run, a doubling of the money supply (M) cannot generate any increased holdings of goods and services, but must result in a doubling of the price level (P).

Wicksell also saw real balances as the adjusting variable on the return path to restoring long-run equilibrium after the economy had been disturbed by an exogenous shock.

> Now let us suppose that for some reason or other commodity prices rise while the stock of money remains unchanged, or that the stock of money is diminished while prices remain temporarily unchanged. The cash balances will gradually appear to be *too small in relation to the new level of prices.* . . . I therefore seek to enlarge my balance. This can only be done—neglecting for the present the possibility of borrowing, etc.—through a *reduction* in my *demand* for goods and services, or through an *increase* in the *supply* of my own commodity . . . or through both together.[4]

The reduction in demand and/or increase in supply will cause commodity prices to fall until they have reached their equilibrium level. Neither Wicksell nor Fisher mentioned the money-interest rates-investment spending channel of monetary influ-

[3]Fisher [25], p. 153.
[4]Wicksell, [90], pp. 39-40. Wicksell's treatment of the real balance effect is considered superior to Fisher's because the former avoided the trap of dichotomizing the determination of relative prices and the absolute price level. See Patinkin [63].

ence in their analyses of movements to long-run equilibrium. Both focused on changes in real cash balances without explaining in detail the substitution and wealth processes involved. Although their long-run vs. short-run analyses were similar in many respects, Fisher was probably more noted for his long-run quantity theory views and Wicksell more for his short-run cumulative process.

Keynes

Like Wicksell and Fisher, Keynes' position on the monetary transmission mechanism was somewhat ambiguous. Some critics have contended that he found little or no role for either wealth or relative price effects while others have credited Keynes with having advanced a significant role for both.

Keynes' substitution effect, which was a part of a relatively early portfolio choice model, stressed the money-interest rates-investment spending channel. Did Keynes think changes in the rate of growth of the money supply affected interest rates? There seems to be little doubt that he did. The principal evidence to the contrary may be found in the following passage from *The General Theory of Employment, Interest and Money:*

> There is the possibility, for the reasons discussed above, that, after the rate of interest has fallen to a certain level, liquidity-preference may become virtually absolute in the sense that almost everyone prefers cash to holding a debt which yields so low a rate of interest. In this event the monetary authority would have lost effective control over the rate of interest. But whilst this limiting case might become practically important in future, I know of no example of it hitherto. Indeed, owing to the unwillingness of most monetary authorities to deal boldly in debts of long term, there has not been much opportunity for a test. Moreover, if such a situation were to arise, it would mean that the public authority itself could borrow through the banking system on an unlimited scale at a nominal [very low] rate of interest.[5]

Note that after raising the possibility that a "liquidity trap" situation could conceivably arise in the future, Keynes immediately disavowed its existence under conditions (the low-employment, low-interest rate period of the 1930s) in which Keynesian analysis suggested it would likely occur.

Regarding the second part of the money-interest rates-investment channel, there is considerable evidence that Keynes thought investment to be quite responsive to interest rate changes (Leijonhufvud [53], pp. 157–185). However, the interest sensitivity of investment was restricted in the main to long-term rates, which changed only slowly.

There are a number of wealth effects to be found in *The General Theory* which relate to either price-induced changes in wealth (changes in wealth associated with changes in the absolute price level) or interest-induced movements in wealth (changes in wealth associated with changes in yields). Of the basic price-induced and interest-induced wealth effects, it has been alleged that "Keynes stated both parts of

---

[5]Keynes [51], p. 207. Bracketed expression supplied.

the wealth effect, emphasized their importance, and then let wealth slip through his fingers by his failure to build it into his analysis." (Pesek and Saving [64], p. 21). This criticism is unjustified to the extent that those parts of Keynes' analyses which subsequently enjoyed sustained popularity are not necessarily those parts favored by Keynes. For example, the "liquidity trap" was not an intrinsic part of Keynes' analysis (he denied its occurrence); yet it became closely associated with his name as one of his major contributions.

It is easy to see how Keynes' wealth effects were overlooked by those analysts quick to interpret and popularize his basic theory. Keynes brought up the price-induced wealth effect and minimized its significance in the same passage: "It is, therefore, on the effect of a falling wage- and price-level on the demand for money that those who believe in the self-adjusting quality of the economic system must rest the weight of their argument; though I am not aware that they have done so. If the quantity of money is itself a function of the wage- and price-level [a variant of the real bills doctrine], there is indeed, nothing to hope in this direction."[6]

Keynes endorsed interest-induced wealth effects more vigorously, but made it clear that even these were of secondary importance. As a man well acquainted with the stock market and windfall gains and losses, he thought interest-induced "windfall effects" had only a minor influence on spending habits.

> For if a man is enjoying a windfall increment in the value of his capital, it is natural that his motives towards current spending should be strengthened, even though in terms of income his capital is worth no more than before; . . . Apart from this, the main conclusion suggested by experience is, I think, that the short-period influence of the rate of interest . . . is secondary and relatively unimportant, except, perhaps, where unusually large changes are in question.[7]

There is, however, sufficient question about Keynes' view of wealth effects, which appear frequently in *The General Theory*, to spark a continuing debate.[8] What Keynes actually meant is less significant than his failure to give either monetary-induced substitution or wealth effects a leading part in his attack against orthodox, classical theory. By vacillating on the importance of the two major channels of monetary influence, Keynes in effect was inviting his interpreters to close off the channels completely.

The Relative Price Relation

The most frequently cited of the relative price relations, money-interest rates-investment, obviously consists of a money-interest rates channel and an interest rates-

---

[6]Keynes [51], p. 206. Bracketed expression supplied.

[7]Keynes [51], p. 94.

[8]See Keynes [51], pp. 92-93, 319. Among the participants in the Keynes wealth effect debate have been Ackley [1], Patinkin [63], Pesek and Saving [64] and Leijonhufvud [53].

investment channel. Closure of either of these channels would eliminate a basic route through which money is presumed to affect spending. This route was virtually sealed off by early interpreters of Keynes (among others) and not reopened for about a quarter of a century.

Closed and Reopened

The initial part of the money-interest rates-investment channel was attacked indirectly through innuendo rather than directly either by overpowering theory or evidence. Although Keynes repeatedly stressed the importance of the money-interest rates linkage, J. R. Hicks, the chief architect of the IS–LM "Keynesian" framework, failed to pass along Keynes' emphasis. In Hicks' [44] relatively brief article which became the most popular condensed version of Keynes, Hicks focused on the liquidity trap as one of Keynes' major contributions upsetting neoclassical theory. Nowhere did he indicate that Keynes was unaware of any such situation actually having occurred. The adoption of such slogans as "you can't push on a string" or "you can lead a horse to water, but you can't make him drink" provided popular support for Hicks' interpretation of Keynes' view of the money-interest rates channel in periods of economic slack.

Empirical studies of the late 1930s were the main instrument employed to seal off the interest rates-investment channel. Researchers in England and the United States published results of surveys in which businessmen were questioned about the importance of the interest rate in their investment decisions.[9] A vast majority indicated that interest rates had little or no effect on their decisions to invest. These studies were cited prominently by Alvin Hansen [39] in his 1938 American Economic Association presidential address as evidence of the impotence of monetary policy. Moreover, as Samuelson recently noted, ". . . people like Sir John Hicks said that as far as short-term investment is concerned, interest is of no consequence as a cost; and as far as long-term investment is concerned, uncertainty is so great that it completely swamps interest, which leaves you with only a miniscule of intermediate investment that is interest elastic."[10]

The eventual rebirth of the relative price channel did not occur until well into the 1950s, although the seeds were planted long before. The emergence of portfolio choice models in the 1950s and 1960s ushered in, among other channels, the old money-interest rates-investment route.

Much of the literature dealing with portfolio choice models has been associated with money demand studies. Portfolio choice theory, however, provides the rationale for the holding of any asset in one's portfolio, including money. Instead of focusing on the individual's or firm's income statement which deals with flows, portfolio

---

[9]See Henderson [42], Meade and Andrews [57], and Ebersole [21]. For a humorous criticism of the survey approach, see Eisner [22], pp. 29–40. A more recent example of the survey approach is found in Crockett, Friend, and Shavell [18].

[10]Samuelson [70], p. 41.

choice analysis stresses the stock relationships which are found on the asset and liability sides of the balance sheet. The basic assumptions are that: (1) other things equal, everyone equates the marginal rate of return on each asset in the portfolio— allowing for risk (in terms of variance of return and *exclusive* of price level movements), costs of acquiring information and of conducting transactions; and (2) an increase in the supply of any asset (on a macro level) will lower the price of that asset relative to all others. The increased supply of the asset leads to diminishing marginal returns per unit of the asset, thereby motivating the wealth holder to attempt to substitute or exchange some of the asset whose price has fallen for some of those whose price has not.

Changes in relative prices are a consequence of wealth holders' efforts to restore equilibrium to their portfolio—that is, equate all marginal rates of return. The initial disturbance, a change in the stock of any asset, may produce a chain of substitution effects as wealth holders react to changing asset yields.

Although certain types of money have a zero nominal rate of return by law, money continues to be held in the portfolio for at least two reasons. First, as opposed to equities, for example (which may carry substantial risk along with a relatively high mean rate of return), money holding is less risky. Second, money economizes on the use of real resources in the gathering of information and in the conduct of transactions. An implication of this latter characteristic is that money is held to bridge the gap between income receipts and expenditures.[11]

Which assets, besides money, are included in the portfolio? Much of the controversy surrounding the portfolio choice framework has centered on the answer to this question. The early portfolio choice models greatly limited the range of assets and rates of return. Pigou [65] sketched a rough money-capital model, while Keynes [51] added government and private debt to the menu. By assuming perfect substitutability between capital and bonds, Keynes had only the yield differential between money and one other asset (he chose bonds) to explain. Patinkin's model [63] was similar to Keynes' in terms of assets included and yields explained.

A major change in the approach to the number of assets and yields to be examined occurred in the early 1960s. Tobin [77], Brunner and Meltzer [9], and Friedman [28] all expanded the portfolio menu, but in varying degrees.[12] The differing approaches of these contemporary monetary economists will be examined in some detail.

---

[11]To pursue further these distinctions would require a detailed analysis of money demand, a project much beyond the scope of this article. The interested reader may wish to consult Pigou [65], Hicks [43], Tobin [77] and Brunner-Meltzer [10].

[12]Cagan [13] also introduced a sketchy portfolio choice scenario. More recently, he focused on money-interest rate influences [14].

The relative price mechanism was also employed by Warburton as early as 1946 to explain the transmission process. "In practice the effects of a change in demand or in supply, either of a specific commodity or of money (circulating medium), are felt, first in some particular part of the economy and spread from that part to the rest of the economy through the medium of price differentials created at each stage of adjustment." Warburton [88], p. 85.

Three Views on the Relative Price Relation

Tobin ([77], p. 36) suggested that "a minimal program for a theory of the capital account" should include six assets—all of which, except the capital stock, are financial assets—and six yields. The number of assets is only slightly greater than the earlier models, but a substantial step toward reality is taken with the elimination of Keynes' perfect substitutability assumption. The choice of assets is closely restricted to facilitate "purchasing definiteness in results at the risk of errors of aggregation" (Tobin [77], p. 28). If increases in the money supply happen to reduce the supply price of capital—the rate which wealth holders require in order to hold in their portfolios the current capital stock—below its marginal productivity, the capital stock will rise. This is the sole linkage between the financial and real sectors. The "if" is necessary because the increase in the supply of money—which lowers the price of money relative to other assets—may simply result in an increased demand for financial assets, rather than for the capital stock (real assets).

One infers from Tobin that an increase in the stock of *any* of the financial assets in the macro portfolio is about as likely to stimulate investment expenditures as is money.[13] In this view it is unclear as to whether an increase in the money stock can lower the supply price of capital *directly* without setting off a chain of substitution effects ranging all through the spectrum of assets with different shades of risk-return characteristics. It is apparent from Tobin's comparative static framework, however, that no feedback from the real to the financial sector occurs.

The types of real capital which are affected by portfolio shuffling are delineated closely by Brunner-Meltzer [9], although the number of assets and relevant yields in the macro portfolio are not. They classify three types of capital according to the relation between asset prices and output prices—language somewhat comparable with Tobin's supply price of capital and marginal productivity.[14]

Increases in real capital occur as (not "if") a rise in the stock of base money lowers the relative price of base money and that of its close substitutes, resulting in an increased demand for other assets, those assets being dominated by real capital. "The increase in the price of financial assets simultaneously raises real capital's market value relative to the capital stock's replacement costs and increases the desired stock relative to the actual stock." (Brunner [5], p. 612.) Real capital is defined to exclude consumer nondurable goods and services.[15] Unlike Tobin (with regard to his comparative static models), Brunner-Meltzer ([19], p. 379) view the monetary transmission mechanism as having important feedback effects.

[13]The view that financial or liquid assets other than money (M_1) can about as likely affect the real sector, is advocated more strongly by the Radcliffe Committee [17], Gurley and Shaw [37], and Gramley and Chase [35], in what became known as the "New View" (from Tobin [78]).

[14]Friedman's [28] terminology is prices of services and prices of sources as explained in the excerpt from Friedman on page 90. A parallel semantic issue is Tobin's preference for the term "demand debt," Friedman for "high-powered money," and Brunner-Meltzer for "base money."

[15]Brunner added the general thought that "The wealth, income, and relative price effects involved in the whole transmission process also tend to raise demand for nondurable goods." Brunner [5], p. 612.

Friedman [28], in his portfolio choice-relative price analysis, is less formal than either Tobin or Brunner-Meltzer in that he attempts no classification of types of real capital, portfolio assets, or relevant yields. Friedman acknowledges that an increase in the money supply affects the portfolio of the financial sector first, but the subsequent increase in demand may be as likely reflected next in consumer nondurables as in any areas of real capital. Possible scenarios are outlined by Friedman in several places.[16] Initially, the prices of sources are raised relative to the prices of services, thereby inducing investment and consumer expenditures.

> The key feature of this process is that it tends to raise the prices of sources of both producer and consumer services relative to the prices of the services themselves; for example, to raise the prices of houses relative to the rents of dwelling units, or the cost of purchasing a car relative to the cost of renting one. It therefore encourages the production of such sources (this is the stimulus to "investment" conceived broadly as including a much wider range of items than are ordinarily included in that term) and, at the same time, the direct acquisition of services rather than of the source (this is the stimulus to "consumption" relative to "savings"). But these reactions in their turn tend to raise the prices of services relative to the prices of sources, that is, to undo the initial effects on interest rates [broadly defined]. The final result may be a rise in expenditures in all directions without any change in interest at all.[17]

A Comparison of Three Views

The Friedman, Tobin, and Brunner-Meltzer views of the monetary substitution effect are distinguished by a number of points of agreement and disagreement. The three views are coincident in the following: (1) the total response of the financial sector to a change in the money supply occurs *before* the total response of the real sector; (2) money as a medium of exchange is of less significance than money as an asset with regard to the portfolio choice transmission mechanism; (3) changes in rates of return or yields on real or financial assets are the key elements in the transmission process.

To a large extent, the differences in the three views are due not so much to contradictory theories, but rather to shades of emphasis among similar approaches. Because Tobin insists on a formal separation of the capital account (stocks) from the production and income account (flows), he is led to highlight different aspects of the portfolio choice process than Friedman and Brunner-Meltzer.[18]

Tobin gives the impression that portfolio choice analysis adds little to the Keynesian (not Keynes') view of money-interest rates-investment. Given a consumption

---

[16]Friedman [28], Friedman-Meiselman [33], Friedman-Schwartz [34]. Other attempts at pinning down the open market purchase-bank reserves-interest rates, etc., channels can be found in Cagan [13], Davis [19], and Ettin [23].

[17]Friedman [28], p. 462. Bracketed expression supplied. The latter part of this quote represents one of Friedman's interpretations of the feedback effect.

[18]"Treatment of the capital account separately from the production and income account of the economy is only a first step, a simplification to be justified by convenience rather than realism" (Tobin [81], p. 15). It appears, however, that Tobin's efforts at moving toward greater realism (Tobin [84]) are inhibited by the "General Equilibrium Approach" (Tobin [81]).

function dependent on income, but not wealth or relative prices, consumption can be affected by monetary actions only *after* investment via the standard Keynesian multiplier. In his portfolio choice analysis, the potential end result of the shuffling of portfolios is a change in real capital;[19] feedback effects from the real to the financial sector do not fit into Tobin's capital account approach. Tobin specifically draws attention to the insignificance of money's medium of exchange property *vis a vis* its zero nominal rate of return in his portfolio analysis and generally denigrates money's "uniqueness." Changes in money may set off a chain of portfolio reverberations which results in a change in desired real capital, or it may not.

Friedman's avoidance of formal, structural models which specify any unique monetary transmission process has probably contributed significantly to the charge that monetarists' views of how money works are locked in a "black box."[20] Friedman's informal tracing of possible monetary channels stresses the point that consumer spending is as likely to be the real sector component first to respond to monetary actions as is investment spending. Although changes in yields are the key to portfolio adjustments, "These effects can be described as operating on 'interest rates,' if a more cosmopolitan interpretation of 'interest rates' is adopted than the usual one which refers to a small range of marketable securities" (Friedman [28], p. 462).

Brunner-Meltzer tread a path between Tobin and Friedman in their methodological approach to portfolio analysis. Like Tobin, they attempt to organize the pattern of response of the real sector to monetary impulses and eventually construct a formal model (Brunner-Meltzer [12]). They also emphasize the significance of real capital in the process with only minor references to such spending components as consumer nondurable goods and services.

Like Friedman, Brunner-Meltzer do not attach "if" considerations to the money-real sector linkage, nor do they stress long substitution chains relating money and other financial assets. Their view is also similar to Friedman's in that they: (1) emphasize financial sector-real sector feedbacks; (2) do not denigrate money as an indicator of monetary actions; and (3) stress relative prices, of which yields on securities are only a part. Brunner points out that "every change in relative prices of assets (that is, durables) with different temporal yield streams involves also a change in suitably defined interest rates."[21]

In their money demand theory, Brunner-Meltzer [10] dwell on the medium of exchange property of money, but this property does not appear specifically in their formal model [12] of the *transmission* mechanism. Relative prices in the 1972 model take the form of asset (including securities) prices and output prices, but no distinction is made between investment and consumer goods prices. Finally, in spite of their

---

[19]In an informal analysis, Tobin added consumer durables to the list of "storable and durable" goods—or real capital—influenced in the monetary transmission process. See Tobin [80].

[20]Friedman's formal model [30], [31] sheds little light on specific monetary transmission linkages.

[21]Brunner [8], p. 27. He adds, "The general role of interest rates does not distinguish therefore between the Keynesian and non-Keynesian positions. The crucial difference occurs in the range of the interest rates recognized to operate in the process. The Keynesian position restricts this range to a narrow class of financial assets, whereas the relative price theory includes interest rates over the whole spectrum of assets and liabilities occurring in balance-sheets of households and firms" (Brunner [8], p. 27).

criticism of IS–LM models which reflect a "Keynesian" approach to the transmission mechanism, they grant that if changes in the stock of government debt were presumed to have no effect on wealth, "our model could be pressed into the standard, IS–LM framework" (Brunner-Meltzer [11], p. 953).

In summation, these three approaches to tracing monetary impulses are probably not as different as they at first appear. Once the semantic issues are put aside and the preferences for formal vs. informal models are understood, the Tobin, Brunner-Meltzer, Friedman approaches to the relative price channels of monetary influence are quite similar. It remains to be resolved, however, if more is to be gained by Tobin's admittedly heroic abstractions from reality, Friedman's apparent presumption that the channels are too complex to be captured in any economic model, or Brunner-Meltzer's approach somewhere between these two in terms of answering the questions of the academic fraternity and the general public of how money works.

Other Developments in the Relative Price Relation

Two extensions of the relative price relation which, although out of the mainstream of monetary transmission research, merit elaboration are (1) credit rationing and (2) the overshoot, or feedback, phenomenon. The former involves the allocation of resources by price *and* nonprice criteria, and the latter is a consequence of the dynamic adjustment of the economy to a monetary shock.

CREDIT RATIONING

So long as the price mechanism functions in an open market with complete factor and product homogeneity, resources (including credit) are rationed by price. In so-called "imperfect" markets, however, nonprice discriminatory practices abound. Among borrowers who are the same in every respect but one, net worth for example, lenders may advance one borrower credit at an X percent rate and another borrower zero credit at any interest rate. At least, that is one implication of the term "credit rationing." As used here, "global" credit rationing is defined to indicate a reduction in (the rate of) total spending due to a rise in the non-observed interest price of loans.

Traditionally, "local" credit rationing has been associated with the behavior of commercial banks in extending loans in a period of "tight credit." Arguments for commercial bank credit rationing were advanced in 1951 by Robert Roosa [68]. He asserted that in periods of falling security prices (rising interest rates), bankers prefer to pass over relatively more lucrative commercial loans and continue to hold on to their securities in order to avoid a recorded capital loss. Moreover, Roosa contended that banks preferred to hold securities as a means of countering the uncertainty fostered by the monetary authorities during critical, high-interest rate periods.

Paul Samuelson [69] objected to this analysis on the grounds that it did not conform to the usual tenets of profit-maximizing behavior of the firm. He argued that the usual way of rationing anything in "short supply" was to allow a higher price to do the rationing. Samuelson would not agree that over any other than a very brief period, bankers would hold their assets in relatively low-yielding securities, while rationing a set volume of loans at a fixed interest rate.

Subsequently, additional arguments were employed to buttress the credit rationing view.[22] One of these was that default risk increased relatively more for loans than for securities in tight credit periods. Another was that the banking industry is oligopolistic and is better off to restrict the volume of loans rather than lend out to the point required by the competitive market solution.

Legal interest ceilings have been invoked more recently in explanations of the working of credit rationing. The basic idea is that a financial institution might be perfectly willing to lend to a borrower at X percent in accord with such criteria as size of loan, default risk, and compensating balance requirements, but if usury or other laws set a ceiling at Y percent which happens to be below X percent, the prospective borrower will not obtain the loan. He may be able to obtain funds from some other source, such as from a lending facility in a state whose ceiling is higher, or from an effectively unregulated private individual. There are, however, considerable costs of information involved in addition to the higher interest costs which may cause the potential borrower to drop out (that is, be rationed out) of the funds market.

Interest ceilings also affect the flows of funds into financial and nonfinancial institutions. When market interest rates rise above rates payable (considering liquidity, risk, maturity, and tax factors) by savings institutions and state and local governments, many savers put their funds into less regulated securities markets. The bypassed institutions accordingly cut back their lending activities. Whether the rechanneling of credit results in a reduction of total spending, however, is another matter—one which is rarely treated in the credit rationing literature.

One study, for example, found that Regulation Q ceilings encouraged savers to bypass commercial banks in certain tight credit situations, allegedly forcing commercial banks to curtail credit extensions.[23] Since bank credit is only one component of total credit, it cannot be assumed that a reduction in total credit or total spending could be attributed to the workings of Regulation Q. According to the authors of the study, the reduction of credit available to commercial bank customers "would presumably occur to the benefit of customers of other intermediaries and/or of those firms able to raise funds directly in the market."[24]

If it is presumed that credit rationing at one institution is *not* offset by increased loan activity elsewhere, then "global" credit rationing, which is accompanied by a slowing in the rate of total spending, occurs. Because all observed interest rates do

---

[22]Lindbeck [55], Hodgman [47], and Kane [50] are among those who have substantially advanced the credit rationing literature.

[23]Federal Reserve Regulation Q places a ceiling on interest rates payable by member banks on time and savings accounts.

[24]Jaffee and Modigliani [49], pp. 871-72. Although Jaffee and Modigliani suggest that credit rationing of commercial banks is offset by increased loan activity in other areas, the reverse does not necessarily hold. The FRB-MIT model, with which Modigliani has been closely associated, finds a credit rationing effect through noncommercial bank savings institutions *not* offset by increased commercial bank activity. See deLeeuw and Gramlich [20].

not necessarily capture a rise in the relative price of credit as represented by greater information and transactions costs (which are assumed to include such costs as increased compensating balances), interest rate changes alone would not give a complete picture of the effectiveness of monetary actions. In certain tight credit situations, interest rates rise to slow down spending. But after some point at which interest yields are confronted by legal rate ceilings, interest rates would not give a correct picture of the true cost of credit. An important implication of this analysis is that interest rates likely emit inconsistent signals with respect to monetary influences on spending via relative price changes.

OVERSHOOT EFFECT

The "overshoot effect" is analogous to the previously-mentioned feedback effect, in which the real sector reacts back upon the financial sector, with the original disturbance having come from the financial sector. Although the overshoot may occur by way of relative price or wealth influences, the vast majority of the literature on this topic is couched in a relative price framework. The term "overshoot' is indicative of the tendency of the initial adjustment of such economic variables as interest rates and income to exceed the steady-state levels. Friedman is often identified as the current leading advocate of this thesis, but the argument has its roots in studies by Fisher, Wicksell, Keynes, and Tooke.[25]

Friedman [28], [29], [33] pointed out in several places that changes in the money supply and interest rates are inversely related for only a short period. A rise in the money supply, for example, is associated with a fall in interest rates initially. After some period of time, the fall in interest rates will have stimulated spending and the demand for credit. The rise in the demand for credit will tend to reverse the initial fall in interest rates. If spending is continually stimulated, demand pressures will force up the price level and price anticipations which, in turn, add upward pressures to interest yields.

The extent to which interest rates overshoot their equilibrium value is dependent on many factors, including initial conditions and the duration and degree of monetary stimulus. It should be noted that the rise in the price level lowers the real value of monetary assets. At the higher price level, the quantity of money demanded is less in real terms. Also, the rate of increase of the money supply tends to slow automatically due to "feedback effects through the monetary mechanism" (Friedman and Schwartz [34], p. 562). Thus, prices, interest rates, money, and general economic activity are all subject to the overshoot phenomenon.

Similar dynamic analysis has been offered by Brunner-Meltzer. Through changes in wealth and relative prices, they postulate that monetary impulses alter the magnitude of and rate of return on the capital stock. "Variations in the stock of real capital, of income expected from human wealth, or the yield expected from real capital affect the allocation pattern of financial assets, trigger the interest mechanism,

---

[25]See Fisher [25], Wicksell [89] (natural interest rate vs. market interest rate), Keynes [51] (the Gibson paradox), and Tooke [86] (the Ricardo-Tooke Conundrum).

and generate a feedback to the asset prices of real capital." Thus, "monetary impulses not only affect the real processes but real impulses feed back to financial processes."[26] Brunner also noted the role of price anticipations in the feedback process and postulated that without continuing money growth acceleration, initial output and employment gains would be offset over time.[27]

Tobin's basic comparative static framework revealed no role for the overshoot effect. On at least two occasions (Tobin [82], [84]), however, he engaged in dynamic analysis. On both occasions he pointed out that initial disturbances in the real sector which affect the money supply (endogeneity of money) are a plausible explanation of observed money-income relationships. In one instance (Tobin and Brainard [84], p. 119), he noted that an exogenous change in bank reserves would produce an adjustment path of the yield on real capital which overshoots and oscillates.

Even the standard IS-LM framework can be altered so as to give interest rate and income overshoots.[28] It can be shown that differences in the adjustment pattern of investment to interest rates and money demand to interest rates are capable of producing interest rate and income overshoots. If investment is dependent at all on the current interest rate, a sharp drop in interest rates can cause investment to expand and income to rise; if money demand is a function of income, there ensues a rise in money demand which reacts back on interest rates.

It is possible to conjecture fairly complicated reaction patterns to relative price changes, even without such complications as an accelerator effect, or changes in the absolute price level. Even working within a simple analytical framework, it would be difficult for policymakers to attempt to stabilize incomes or interest rates if they did not know whether the adjustment paths were monotonic or cyclical. Considerable empirical verification of the overshoot or cyclical process in the "real" economy has been provided.[29]

The Wealth Relation

The monetary channel of influence which operates through changes in wealth is best approached by examination of the linkages between wealth and consumption. Although the substitution effect, in some versions, is seen to work through consumer spending as well as investment, the wealth effect has been typically limited to the consumer sector. One definition of nonhuman money wealth is

$$W_{NH} = PK + D + \frac{G}{r}$$

[26]Brunner-Meltzer [9], p. 379.

[27]Brunner [7], p. 13. Friedman ([29], p. 10) made the same point regarding monetary acceleration via a comparison of the market unemployment rate-natural unemployment rate with the market interest rate-natural interest rate.

The feedback effects noted in the formal Brunner-Meltzer model [12] are started by an initial disturbance in the *output* market, and thus are not quite comparable to earlier analysis.

[28]See Laidler [52], Smith [73], Tanner [74], and Tucker [87].

[29]See Silber [72] and Christ's ([16], pp. 444-45) review of large econometric models.

where

P = price of real capital
K = stock of capital (PK = market value of equity)
D = monetary base plus fraction of bank debt not counted in PK
G = government debt (one dollar multiplied by the number of securities outstanding, each of which is assumed to be a consol)
r = market interest rate (G/r = market value of outstanding debt).

Monetary factors affect each of these components of nonhuman money wealth in varying degrees.

Real human wealth, w_H, is determined by the present value of one's expected lifetime income, a concept related to permanent income or even disposable income (with the appropriate lags), but not directly related to monetary actions. Real consumption (c) is assumed to be a function of both types of wealth as described by

$$c = c(w_H, \frac{W_{NH}}{P}).$$

The human wealth concept forms the typical Keynesian element in the consumption function. The relation between nonhuman wealth (divided by the price level) and consumption is probably less well accepted.

Because the arguments for the D and G/r elements of the wealth effect are closely intertwined, they will be discussed together as "Real Balance Effects." The PK section follows under the heading "Equity Effects."

Real Balance Effects

As mentioned earlier, Keynes discussed several different real balance effects, but made little use of them in his general framework. Ironically, it was the work of a prominent Keynesian interpreter which sparked renewed interest in real cash balances. Pigou, who generally receives the lion's share of the credit for reviving real cash balances,[30] was disturbed by Alvin Hansen's stagnation thesis.

Hansen [40] charged that even *with* flexible prices and wages a perpetual state of less than full employment could well be the natural resting place for the economy. Such neoclassical economists as Pigou were willing to concede that an assumption of inflexible prices and wages could be consistent with the thesis of a less than full-employment state, but only given this important assumption. Pigou demonstrated that the rise in real cash balances associated with a falling price level and unchanged money stock would increase consumer spending, reduce saving, and thereby permit the rate of interest to rise above some assumed "liquidity trap" level.

[30]Pigou [66]. See also Haberler [38] and Scitovszky [71].

By associating consumption with real cash balances, Pigou drove a wedge into the small opening left for monetary policy by the Keynesians of the late 1930s. Because consumption comprises a much larger percentage of total spending than business fixed investment, the potential for monetary policy to affect total spending was greatly expanded. Pigou and others who formulated real cash balance theories in the early 1940s did not claim much empirical significance for this effect. Their concern was only to show that it was theoretically plausible for the economy to return to full employment under the assumption of price and wage flexibility. They did not take up Keynes' windfall effect or any other aspect of the monetary wealth effect. Thus, their concern was limited to the "D" portion of the nonhuman wealth definition, with the relevant debt typically taken to be the government's demand debt (or monetary base).

Don Patinkin took up the discussion of real cash balances in the postwar period.[31] He also ignored the interest-induced wealth effects and focused on theoretical rather than empirical considerations. Patinkin's chief contribution to the channels of influence controversy was to spell out the interplay between the positive real cash balance effect and the negative real cash balance effect which combine to produce proportionality between money and prices (the "quantity theory") between periods of short-run equilibrium.[32]

Prominent among those disputing the usefulness of the real cash balance approach have been Hicks and Hansen, who also downgraded the monetary relative price channel. Hansen's [41] criticism of the real balance effect was limited to a short note in which he agreed that the effect could theoretically bring a halt to a downturn, but could not generate the spending required to attain full employment.

Hicks devoted more effort to wealth considerations, as demonstrated by the important role of wealth in his landmark book, *Value and Capital* [45]. However, neither in *Value and Capital* nor subsequently did he attach much significance to a monetary wealth effect. Hicks omitted real balance effects in *Value and Capital* and only thirty years later did he find any use for the concept at all.[33] The dominant channel of

---

[31]Patinkin [63]. Patinkin's first articles on real cash balances appeared in the late 1940s.

[32]The positive real balance effect associates the demand for real balances (positively) with money and the negative real balance effect associates the demand for real balances (inversely) with prices. The demand for goods is related to one's holding of real cash balances.

[33]Leijonhufvud noted Hicks' lack of consideration for either price-induced or interest-induced wealth effects in *Value and Capital*. "It is interesting to note that the first edition of *Value and Capital* did not take the real balance effect into account. In the second edition, Hicks responded to the criticisms of Lange and Mosak on that issue by admitting: 'I was too much in love with the simplification which comes from assuming that income-effects [Pigou effects] cancel out when they appear on both sides of the market' (p. 334). While this did not lead him to reconsider also the assumption that the wealth effects of interest changes cancel, it may well be that the same remark applies also to this problem." (Leijonhufvud [53], p. 275.)

Hicks eventually took note of the real cash balance version of the wealth effect in a review of the first edition of Patinkin's book. Hicks missed the point initially that a rise in real cash balances stimulates spending, as he later admitted in his *Critical Essays* ([46], p. 52). In 1967 he recognized the existence of a 'liquidity pressure effect'—but thought it had merit only in restraining an expanding economy. This concept, of course, is a variation on the monetary policy "can't push on a string" thesis.

monetary influence, so long as no liquidity trap exists, was through his portfolio choice-relative price route.

Exactly what should be included in the "D" portion of the real balance wealth definition has been the subject of debate in more recent years. In most cases, private debt typically is assumed to cancel out. However, Pesek and Saving [64] maintained that because no interest is paid for demand deposits, wealth (which accrues to bank stockholders) increases in proportion to demand deposits. Thus, they would count both inside money (demand deposits) and outside money (monetary base) in net private wealth, contrary to the traditional view which counts only outside money. To include all inside money as wealth, however, would likely result in some double counting.

If the inside money benefits to banks are capitalized in the value of the banks' stock, as are the typical gains to nonbank firms, the same inside money would be found in the "D" portion and the "PK" portion of the wealth equation. To the extent that demand deposit gains are *not* capitalized instantaneously, there should be some allowance made for the addition of inside money to net wealth. The effect on spending would be through additional outlays by bank stockholders.

What about government securities (G) held by the public? Do these represent private wealth? They only represent private wealth to the extent that the public does not anticipate offsetting future tax increases to eliminate such debt. The G/r term in the wealth equation may have some effect on spending through: (1) changes in the magnitude of G; (2) changes in the composition of G; and (3) changes in r.

One source of controversy concerning changes in wealth has been the relation between G and D. The two have frequently been summed (interest-bearing debt plus noninterest-bearing debt) in empirical and theoretical investigations of the effects of "liquidity" on the economy. If it can be assumed that G and D are good substitutes, their composition is of less concern than their sum.[34] Early empirical investigations of wealth effects published shortly after the accumulation of much government debt in World War II often tested the real balance effect as the sum of G and D.[35] Many found a strong relation between liquid wealth and consumption. If this can be called a direct channel, a more indirect route, via interest rates, has been envisioned by others.

---

[34]Proponents of the "New View" also add nongovernment, nonbank liabilities, such as savings and loan shares, to the total. See Brunner [6].

The Radcliffe Committee [17] found a role for money to affect spending *if* it added to total liquidity, to include funds made available by nonbank financial institutions. John Gurley noted that the Committee "believes that changes in these [interest] rates have had little direct effect on spending; and it does not think that there is any direct, close connection between the money supply and spending. But while money is shoved out of the house through the front door, for all to see, it does make its reappearance surreptitiously through the back door as a part of general liquidity: and the most important source of liquidity is the large group of financial institutions." (Gurley [36], p. 685. Bracketed expression supplied.)

[35]See Patinkin's empirical chapter [63]. Lerner [54] theorized that continued growth of government debt, as in World War II, would eventually induce sufficient consumer expenditures as to eliminate any excess of savings over investment at full-employment income. He did not attempt an empirical test, however.

Tobin [79] emphasized aggregate monetary wealth and its composition with respect to the effect on interest rates. Not only does an increase in monetary wealth relative to real assets lower the supply price of capital and thereby induce investment, but an increase in short-term government debt relative to long-term debt (no change in aggregate debt) may achieve the same result. These actions are closer to fiscal policy or debt management policy than to what is normally labeled monetary policy.

To the extent that monetary actions affect the yields on government debt, there is an interest-induced monetary wealth effect on consumption. If expansive monetary actions lower the "r" component of G/r proportionately more than "G" in the wealth definition, nonhuman money wealth rises, as does (under typical assumptions) consumption. Of course, a monetary overshoot effect would reverse the fall in interest rates and subsequently work in the opposite direction on consumer expenditures. Also, if the rise in the price of securities (fall in interest rates), induces those wealth holders who have not yet purchased securities to pay a higher price for their securities, this particular group may *curtail* their outlays for consumer goods.[36]

As far as the real balance effect, especially that part which pertains to "D" is concerned, there is little indication that Tobin, Brunner-Meltzer, or Friedman envision monetary influences as having much impact through this channel.[37] In at least two cases, however, these leading monetary economists have found a strong role for the money-equity channel. Their views on the money-equity route will be discussed after mention of some of the earlier proponents of this channel.

Equity Effect

How can monetary actions affect the market value of equity, "PK"? One answer was provided by Lloyd Metzler, who reopened the equity channel in 1951 which had been described earlier by Keynes. Metzler [58] was probably the first economist whose formal model included the investment-borrowing costs channel and both aspects of the wealth channel—real cash balances and private equities.[38] Metzler, however, made the unusual assumption that the Federal Reserve increases the money stock through purchases of privately held common stock.

An increase in the money stock (in the Metzler model), given full employment,

[36]See Leijonhufvud ([53], pp. 241–42) for a discussion of this effect. Lawrence Klein, who recognized the potential of interest-induced changes in wealth to affect consumption inversely, related to the author recently that an inverse relation is more likely in the depression state, such as the 1930s, than today.

[37]"Like Friedman (1970, pp. 206–7) we believe that the real-balance effect is one of several explanations of long-run changes in the IS curve. We agree, also, that the short-run importance of the real-balance effect is small enough to neglect in most developed economies where real balances are a small part of wealth. In our analysis the size of the traditional real-balance effect depends on the proportion of money to total nonhuman wealth, a factor that is less than .05 for the United States." (Brunner and Meltzer [11], p. 847.)

[38]Tinbergen provided the first empirical test of an equities-consumption relation. Dividing consumption into that by income earners and nonworkers, he found that "a fall in capital gains had already caused a decline in consumption between 1928 and 1929" (Tinbergen [75], p. 78).

results in a proportional increase in prices and thus no change in consumption with real balances remaining constant. The Federal Reserve's purchase of common stock *lowers* net private wealth (the volume of securities in private hands falls) and consequently, consumer spending. The fall in consumer expenditures is accompanied by a rise in saving, a fall in the rate of interest, and the consequent increase in capital intensity. Criticism of Metzler's model centered on his unusual assumptions, which, among other results, gave a negative association between monetary growth and consumer spending.

The more orthodox conjecture, that monetary growth, the market valuation of equities, and consumer spending are all positively related, has been given theoretical and empirical support by Franco Modigliani. Modigliani [59], [60] advanced formal theoretical models in 1944 and 1963. He recognized a role for wealth-consumption influences in his revised model of the economy (called the "mid-50s" model) which he acknowledged had been omitted from the 1944 model. His new consumption equation was

$$C = C(X, \frac{NW}{p}, r, \left[\frac{Vo}{p}\right])$$

where

$$X = \text{real income}$$
$$\frac{NW}{p} = \text{Modigliani's life-cycle aggregate labor income variable[39]}$$
$$r = \text{the rate of return on (or cost of) capital}$$
$$\frac{Vo}{p} = \text{the net worth of the private sector.}$$

The two latter monetary-related terms, the borrowing cost variable and the wealth variable, appeared in much the same form in the FRB–MIT model of the later 1960s, a model with which Modigliani has been closely identified.

The money-equities-consumption channel in the FRB–MIT model hinges on the substitutability of bonds and stocks. If an increase in demand for, say, Treasury securities, by the Federal Reserve results in lower yields and higher prices for these securities, other investors could well be discouraged from purchasing the now higher-priced Treasury securities, but securities whose price was not initially affected by the Federal Reserve action. To the extent that demand is shifted to equities from Treasury securities because of their higher price, there is a rise in common stock prices, which is reflected in a rise in PK.

The higher equity prices represent capital gains to equity owners. The wealth effect

---

[39]Modigliani-Brumberg [62] in 1954 related consumption to one's expected income over his life span. The discounted value of "permanent" income is human wealth, or $Y/r = W$.

Neither Modigliani-Brumberg nor Friedman [27] related monetary-induced nonhuman wealth to consumption at this early stage.

portion of this process is the inducement to spend on the part of equity owners because of their increased net worth. Over a sixteen-quarter period, the equity channel represents 45 percent of the entire monetary influence on total spending in the FRB–MIT model.[40]

It is not likely that Friedman would credit any sort of *monetary-induced* nonhuman wealth effect as having that much influence on spending. The relative price channel dominates his discussion of the channels of monetary influence in numerous articles (Friedman [28], [33], [34]). In more recent studies in which Friedman developed a formal economic model, he omitted wealth from the consumption function, using only $C/p = f(Y/p, r)$.[41] One indication that nonhuman wealth is of some significance in his view of the transmission process emerged in a recent article in which he attempted to delineate initial and subsequent shifts in the IS-LM apparatus.[42]

Until recently, Tobin apparently shared Friedman's lack of enthusiasm for monetary-induced wealth effects on consumption. His omission of wealth influences on consumption may be found in his informal models of the early 1960s as well as his more detailed models of the late 1960s.[43] It is not so much that Tobin denied a wealth effect, rather that he preferred to keep stock and flow variables separate. Thus, consumption (and saving) were functions of flow variables—specifically income—and not wealth, a stock concept. "The propensity to consume may depend upon interest rates, but it does not depend *directly* on the existing mix of asset supplies or on the rates at which these supplies are growing."[44]

In a significant departure from most of his previous studies, Tobin [85] stressed the importance of wealth effects in an article co-authored with Dolde in 1971. They considered the "two major recognized channels of monetary influence on consumption: (A) changes in wealth and in interest rates, (B) changes in liquidity constraints."[45] They recognized the historical significance of the Pigou effect, but wealth

---

[40]deLeeuw and Gramlich [20], p. 487. Other simulations by Modigliani of the FRB–MIT model indicate an even stronger equities effect when alternate forms of the money-equities-consumption equations are run. Modigliani [61], however, did not accept these as realistic.

[41]Friedman recognized the inadequacy of the above consumption function ([30], p. 223) and ([31], p. 331) "in a full statement" ([30], p. 223), because it excluded wealth, but he stated he was attempting to stick to Keynesian short-period analysis. In a much earlier study, Friedman [26] endorsed the real balance effect more vigorously.

[42]Friedman ([32], p. 916) discussed shifts in IS-LM curves (first-round effects vs. subsequent effects) in a manner consistent with the view that wealth influences subsequent shifts. Friedman did not mention "wealth," but Blinder-Solow [2] interpreted his discussion in that context.

[43]See Tobin's early models [77], [78] and later models [81], [84]. He did mention monetary influences on saving/consumption in "Money, Capital, and Other Stores of Value" [77], and gave the relation somewhat more prominence in the earlier "Relative Income, Absolute Income, and Saving" [76].

[44]Tobin [81], p. 16.

[45]Tobin-Dolde [85], p. 100. Tobin's comments concerning the volatility of the marginal propensity to consume, especially with respect to the 1968 tax surcharge, provide a clue as to why he chose to include wealth in the consumption function. "Now if it had been true that the income-flow theory of consumption was a resounding success, and that its indications were being borne out all the time, then we wouldn't need to go into the wealth theory or the life-cycle theory and all that. We wouldn't need to seek a fundamental theory about why savings ratios are what they are and how they relate to various parameters. But we all know that the cash income theory is not a resounding success." (Tobin [83], p. 159.)

changes in their study were associated with capital gains (equity effect). Their liquidity effect referred to the cost of converting nonliquid assets to liquid form in a world of imperfect capital markets. The level of the penalty rate of interest (a relative price) inhibits or encourages conversion of nonliquid to liquid assets.

Using a Modigliani-Brumberg life-cycle model, they concluded that wealth (equity values), interest rates, and the liquidity constraint all have important influences on consumer spending. Their model was basically a reduced form, in that they did not provide the linkages between monetary policy actions and monetary effects.

Brunner-Meltzer have long included a prominent role for wealth effects in their view of the monetary transmission process. "PK" is the component of nonhuman wealth mentioned most favorably in their analysis. For example, in discussing the chain of events following an injection of base money, Brunner-Meltzer noted that "the resulting rise in the market value of the public's (nonhuman) wealth raises the desired stock of capital III and the desired rate of real consumption."[46] They further stated that relative price effects also operate to increase real consumption following the expansive monetary action.

At a later date Brunner again stressed the importance of "PK" relative to the real balance effect in the transmission process. "The dominant portion of the wealth adjustment induced by a monetary impulse occurs beyond a real balance effect and depends on the relative price change of existing real capital. The monetarist analysis of the transmission mechanism determines that this portion of the total wealth effect thoroughly swamps the real balance or even the financial asset effects."[47]

Real balances are included, however, in Brunner-Meltzer's [12] formal model. Total spending (which includes consumer spending) in that model is influenced by, among other factors, nonhuman wealth. Their nonhuman wealth variables include real capital, the monetary base, the stock of government debt, and the value of commercial banks' monopoly position excluded from real capital (Pesek and Saving effect).

Formal economic models now routinely include wealth and/or substitution effects on consumption.[48] Few, if any, of the empirically-oriented, structural models permit all the wealth effects on consumption described above. For example, the FRB-MIT model (Board of Governors [3]) has an equities effect but no real balance effect; the Wharton Mark III model (McCarthy [56]) has a real balance effect but no equities effect. Only when model builders make allowance for all possible monetary effects are so-called structurally rich models as likely to reflect as significant a money-spending impact as reduced form models. There is, of course, a good possibility that yet undiscovered wealth, relative price, and even monetary income effects will be found in the monetary channels of the future.

---

[46]Brunner and Meltzer [9], p. 377. Capital III refers primarily to certain types of consumer durable goods. Examples of the other two types of capital delineated by Brunner and Meltzer are machinery and equipment (Type I) and houses (Type II).

[47]Brunner [7], p. 5.

[48]See, for example, Christ [15] and Rasche [67].

Summary

This article surveyed the relative price and wealth changes set in motion when the quantity of money supplied changes relative to money demanded. Relative price and wealth changes were viewed as major elements of the monetary transmission mechanism around the turn of the century (in rudimentary fashion) and in recent years, but in much of the intervening period their role was subjected to considerable question.

Fisher and Wicksell favored one approach in which wealth was the dominant monetary force and another in which relative prices were of more significance. Keynes amplified both views, but his major interpreters were not so inclined. It is, in fact, ironic that J. R. Hicks, who formulated the IS-LM interpretation of Keynes, downgraded both monetary wealth and relative price influences, despite his pioneering research into basic wealth [45] and portfolio choice fields [43].

Real balance wealth effects were revived by Pigou, Patinkin, and others while Metzler reformulated the equity wealth effect. Tobin, Brunner-Meltzer, and Friedman advanced the portfolio choice-relative price effect in the early 1960s, and with the exception of Friedman, have also highlighted the equity wealth effect.

These hardly exhaust all the ways in which monetary impulses affect spending. For example, an income effect occurs when the Treasury draws down its bank balances to purchase goods and services. A decline in Treasury deposits relative to demand deposits increases the money supply (other things equal) and income.

Alternatively, a rise in the money supply may be associated with a change in relative prices and no change in wealth. For example, a fall in currency relative to demand deposits increases the money supply and lowers bank loan rates, but there is no rise in real balances—if defined only as outside money—and no change in government debt.

Thus, depending on how the money supply is caused to change relative to money demand, some effects on spending are set in motion, but not necessarily all. Moreover, the fact that initial conditions, to include all relative prices, are never the same suggests that under one set of circumstances initial monetary effects may be on, say, consumer durable goods expenditures and under another set, state and local government purchases. To follow explicitly the channels of monetary influence whenever there occurs a change in the quantity of money supplied relative to the quantity demanded, one would have to know as a minimum the cause of the change in the money supply, all relevant relative prices, and the impact of other exogenous events on spending units. Add to this the effect of feedback forces, both relative price and wealth, and it becomes less surprising that the contents of the monetary black box have been difficult to unravel.

The complexity of the forces at work, however, does not mean that one should despair of *forecasting* the effect of monetary influences on total spending and rely on (presumably) more elementary tools to guide economic activity. The effects of other policy actions are also difficult to trace with certainty.[49]

---

[49]It has become clear in recent years that simply *forecasting* the result of fiscal policy effects on total

The likelihood is that all possible channels of monetary or other policy actions have not been spelled out completely in any one model. There remains much room for research which would narrow the gap between economic reality and economic models.

Examples of How Money Works

The following is an oversimplified description of monetary impulses working through the relative price and wealth channels. The numbers are chosen entirely for illustrative purposes and bear no relation to current actual magnitudes. This hypothesized scenario represents some of the possible ways in which spending might respond to a monetary injection. To begin, assume a sale of government bonds by the Treasury to bond dealers, the bonds being subsequently purchased by the Federal Reserve.

Relative Price Channel

The purchase of government debt by the Federal Reserve (Fed) increases bank reserves and lowers the yield (raises the price) on Treasury securities. The banks lend out (increase demand deposits) some multiple of the higher level of reserves by lowering bank loan rates; the higher price of Treasury securities encourages investors to purchase securities whose prices have not yet risen.

At this point the money supply has risen and interest rates have declined. Borrowers obtained money balances in order to purchase real assets (cars, houses, machinery) and/or financial assets (stocks, bonds), depending on the current and expected relative prices of the assets. If real assets are purchased through either consumer or investment expenditures, the price of existing real capital rises. If financial assets are purchased, the price of existing real capital rises via capitalization of the assets. The rise in the price of existing real capital encourages the production of additional capital. Observed declines in interest rates also represent lower borrowing costs, an additional stimulus to the production of goods and services. The lower costs may be interpreted as a fall in the rental price for the services rendered by an asset. More-

---

spending requires more than reliance on some variation of the deceptively simple relations $Y = C + I + G$ and $C = C(Y - T)$. These relations imply a direct link between government spending (G) and total spending (Y), and between disposable income $(Y - T)$, which includes tax changes, and consumption (C). What does not appear in these simple relations are the vector of relative prices, the type of government spending involved, how the government spending is to be financed, and whether the tax changes are presumed to be temporary or permanent.

Fiscal policy actions may also influence wealth and interest rates in addition to income, the income effect presumably being what is referred to as the *direct* effect of fiscal actions on spending. Although monetary and fiscal channels of influence are both complex, only monetary actions have typically been viewed as operating within a black box.

over, a fall in interest rates could eliminate the effects of credit rationing, which are presumed to occur at high levels of interest rates.

In other terms, if both consumption (c) and investment (i) depend on interest rates (r) and the price of existing real capital (P) relative to the price level (p), then c = f (r, P/p) and i = g (r, P/p). Both c and i are stimulated if r falls from say, 0.04 to 0.02 and P/p rises from 1/1 to 2/1.

As the money supply rises, however, and new recipients of money balances hire more workers, buy more equipment, pay out larger dividends, or pay higher wages, the price level begins to rise. The closer the economy is to capacity operations, the more rapid the increase in the price level. Moreover, demand for credit expands, and this, together with the price-level rise, puts upward pressure on market interest rates. The result may be a return of the interest rate and price variables to their earlier relations; that is

$$\bar{c} = f\,(.04, \frac{2}{2}) \text{ and } \bar{i} = g\,(.04, \frac{2}{2}).$$

Wealth Channel

The issuance of government debt by the Treasury results in a transfer of assets from transactor A (who purchased the debt) to transactor B (paid by the government with the proceeds from A). A holds an asset, interest and principal on which can be paid off by the government through, among other means, an increase in taxes. To the extent that the public does *not* anticipate the government raising taxes to pay off its outstanding debt, government debt represents wealth to the private sector. Whether taxes are anticipated or not, the value of a unit of government debt falls with the rise in interest rates caused by the issuance of new debt.

Federal Reserve purchase of government debt, however, unambiguously increases wealth because the Fed cannot raise taxes, and its purchase of government debt initially lowers interest rates. In other words, if monetary nonhuman wealth consists of outside money (D), government bonds (G) divided by the market rate of interest (r), and the price of capital (P) times the capital stock (K), then $W = D + \beta G/r + PK$. $\beta < 1$ indicates that wealth holders believe some portion of the government debt will be paid off by increased future taxes. Real nonhuman wealth, w, is obtained by deflating the above by the price level, p, or $w = D/p + \beta G/pr + PK/p$. Given initial values of D = 100, G = 200, K = 10,000, r = .04, β = .5, p = 1 and P = 1, then w = 100/1 + (.5)(200)/1(.04) + 1(10,000)/1, and therefore, w = 100 + 2500 + 10,000. It is assumed that c = c(w) where c' > o; that is, wealth positively influences consumption expenditures.

Issuance of new government debt by the Treasury of 5 bonds is assumed to raise interest rates to 0.041, such that this component of wealth remains unchanged: $\beta G/pr = 0.5(205)/1(.041) = 2500$. If the Fed purchases the government debt, however, the change in the first two wealth components is: $D/p + \beta G/pr = 105/1 + 0.5(200)/1(0.04) = 105 + 2500$.

A number of other wealth effects may be distinguished, some of which are not related to a Fed purchase of Treasury debt:

1) The Pigou effect normally associates a fall in the price level with a constant level of D. Example:
   Value of D/p rises from $100/1 = 100$ to $100/0.5 = 200$.

2) The real financial effect associates a fall in the price level with a constant level of G. Example:
   Value of $\beta G/pr$ rises from $0.5(200)/1(0.04) = 2500$ to $0.5(200)/0.5(0.04) = 5000$. There is also a Keynes effect which goes beyond the Pigou effect by assuming the rise in real cash balances lowers interest rates and stimulates investment.

3) Keynes' windfall effect may apply to either the government bonds or the capital stock portion of nonhuman wealth:

   A. a fall in interest rates. Example: Value of $\beta G/pr$ rises from $0.5(200)/1(0.04) = 2500$ to $0.5(200)/1(0.02) = 5000$.

   B. a rise in the price of real capital. Example: Value of PK/p rises from $1(10,000)/1 = 10,000$ to $2(10,000)/1 = 20,000$.*

4) The Pesek-Saving effect takes into account the possibility that some commercial bank debt (demand deposits) is not adequately capitalized in the PK/p term and should be included as a part of D. Example: Assume $\alpha = 0.5$ is the fraction of demand deposits (dd) to be included in the wealth term, such that if there is a rise in demand deposits, the value of the $D + \alpha(dd)/p$ term rises from $100 + 0.5 (150)/1 = 175$ to $100 + 0.5 (160)/1 = 180$.

5) It should be noted that just as a rising price level tends to offset the initially expansive effects of monetary actions through the relative price effect, a rising price level also tends to counter a monetary-induced wealth effect. Example: An increase of the (outside) money stock (D) initially increased the value of nonhuman wealth from $w = D/p + \beta G/pr + PK/p = 100/1 + 0.5(200)/1(0.04) + 1(10,000)/1 = 12,600$ to $200/1 + 0.5(200)/$

---

* Leijonhufvud ([53], pp. 324–25) provides a more detailed description of effects 1–3 in the context of Keynes' views on wealth-consumption influences.

1(0.02) + 2(10,000)/1 = 25,200. But if the price level also increases, w = 200/2 + 0.5(200)/2(0.04) + 2(10,000)/2 = 11,350, which is a decline from the initial value of wealth due to the effect of the price rise on government debt.

REFERENCES

1. ACKLEY, GARDNER. "The Wealth-Saving Relationship." *The Journal of Political Economy* 59 (1951).
2. BLINDER, ALAN S., and SOLOW, ROBERT M. "Does Fiscal Policy Matter?" *Journal of Public Economics* 2 (1973).
3. Board of Governors of the Federal Reserve System. *Equations In The MIT-PENN-SSRC Econometric Model Of The United States.* (1973).
4. BROWN, A. J. "The Liquidity-Preference Schedules of the London Clearing Banks." *Oxford Economic Papers* 1 (1938).
5. BRUNNER, KARL. "The Report of The Commission On Money and Credit." *The Journal of Political Economy* 69 (1961).
6. ———. "The Role of Money and Monetary Policy." this *Review* 50 (1968).
7. ———. "The 'Monetarist Revolution' in Monetary Theory." *Weltwirtshaftliches Archiv* 105 (1970).
8. ———. "A Survey of Selected Issues in Monetary Theory." *Schweizerische Zeitschrift für Volkswirtschaft und Statistik* 107 (1971).
9. BRUNNER, KARL, and MELTZER, ALLEN H. "The Place of Financial Intermediaries In The Transmission of Monetary Policy." *The American Economic Review* 53 (1963).
10. ———. "The Uses of Money: Money in the Theory of an Exchange Economy." *The American Economic Review* 61 (1971).
11. ———. "Friedman's Monetary Theory." *The Journal of Political Economy* 80 (1972).
12. ———. "Money, Debt, and Economic Activity." *The Journal of Political Economy* 80 (1972).
13. CAGAN, PHILLIP. "Why Do We Use Money In Open Market Operations?" *The Journal of Political Economy* 66 (1958).
14. ———. *The Channels of Monetary Effects on Interest Rates.* New York: National Bureau of Economic Research, 1972.
15. CHRIST, CARL F. "A Model of Monetary and Fiscal Policy Effects on the Money Stock, Price Level, and Real Output." *Journal of Money, Credit and Banking* 1 (1969).
16. ———. "Econometric Models of the Financial Sector." *Journal of Money, Credit and Banking* 3 (1971).
17. Committee on the Working of the Monetary System. *Report.* London: Her Majesty's Stationary Office, 1959.
18. CROCKETT, JEAN; FRIEND, IRWIN; and SHAVELL, HENRY. "The Impact of Monetary Stringency on Business Investment." *Survey of Current Business* 47 (1967).
19. DAVIS, RICHARD G. "The Role of the Money Supply in Business Cycles." Federal Reserve Bank of New York *Monthly Review* 50 (1968).
20. DELEEUW, FRANK, and GRAMLICH, EDWARD M. "The Channels of Monetary Policy." Federal Reserve *Bulletin* 55 (1969).

21. EBERSOLE, J. FRANKLIN. "The Influence of Interest Rates Upon Enterpreneurial Decisions In Business—A Case Study." *Harvard Business Review* 17 (1939).

22. EISNER, ROBERT. "Factors Affecting The Level of Interest Rates: Part II." United States Savings and Loan League. *Savings and Residential Financing:* 1968 *Conference Proceedings,* 1968.

23. ETTIN, EDWARD C. "A Qualitative Analysis of the Relationships Between Money and Income." *Weltwirtschaftliches Archiv* 96 (1966).

24. FISHER, IRVING. *Booms and Depressions: Some First Principles.* New York: Adelphi Company, 1932.

25. ———. *The Purchasing Power of Money: Its Determination And Relation To Credit Interest And Crises.* rev. ed. New York: Reprints of Economic Classics, 1963.

26. FRIEDMAN, MILTON. "A Monetary and Fiscal Framework for Economic Stability." *The American Economic Review* 38 (1948).

27. ———. *A Theory of the Consumption Function.* New York: The National Bureau of Economic Research, 1957.

28. ———. "The Lag in Effect of Monetary Policy." *The Journal of Political Economy* 69 (1961).

29. ———. "The Role of Monetary Policy." *The American Economic Review* 58 (1968).

30. ———. "A Theoretical Framework for Monetary Analysis." *The Journal of Political Economy* 78 (1970).

31. ———. "A Monetary Theory of Nominal Income." *The Journal of Political Economy* 79 (1971).

32. ———. "Comments on the Critics." *The Journal of Political Economy* 80 (1972).

33. FRIEDMAN, MILTON, and MEISELMAN, DAVID. "The Relative Stability of Monetary Velocity and the Investment Multiplier In The United States." In *Stabilization Policies,* Commission on Money and Credit. Englewood Cliffs, New Jersey: Prentice-Hall, Inc., 1963.

34. FRIEDMAN, MILTON, and SCHWARTZ, ANNA J. "Money And Business Cycles." *The Review of Economics and Statistics* 45 (1963).

35. GRAMLEY LYLE E., and CHASE, SAMUEL B., JR. "Time Deposits in Monetary Analysis." Federal Reserve *Bulletin* 51 (1965).

36. GURLEY, JOHN G. "The Radcliffe Report and Evidence: A Review Article." *The American Economic Review* 50 (1960).

37. GURLEY, JOHN G. and SHAW, EDWARD S. *Money in a Theory of Finance.* Washington, D.C.: The Brookings Institution, 1960.

38. HABERLER, GOTTFRIED. *Prosperity and Depression: A Theoretical Analysis of Cyclical Movements.* 3d ed. Geneva: League of Nations, 1941.

39. HANSEN, ALVIN H. "Economic Progress and Declining Population Growth." *The American Economic Review* 29 (1939).

40. ———. *Fiscal Policy and Business Cycles.* New York: W. W. Norton & Company, Inc., 1941.

41. ———. "The Pigouvian Effect." *The Journal of Political Economy* 59 (1951).

42. HENDERSON, H. D. "The Significance of the Rate of Interest." *Oxford Economic Papers* 1 (1938).

43. HICKS, J(OHN) R. "A Suggestion for Simplifying The Theory of Money." *Economica* 2 (1935).

44. ———. "Mr. Keynes and the 'Classics'; A Suggested Interpretation." *Econometrica* 5 (1937).

45. ———. *Value and Capital: An Inquiry into Some Fundamental Principles of Economic Theory.* 2d ed. Oxford: The Clarendon Press, 1946.

46. ———. *Critical Essays in Monetary Theory.* Oxford: The Clarendon Press, 1967.

47. HODGMAN, DONALD R. *Commercial Bank Loan and Investment Policy.* Champaign, Illinois: Bureau of Economic And Business Research, 1963.

48. HUME, DAVID. *Writings on Economics.* Edited by Eugene Rotwein. Madison: The University of Wisconsin Press, 1970.

49. JAFFEE, DWIGHT M., and MODIGLIANI, FRANCO. "A Theory and Test of Credit Rationing." *The American Economic Review* 59 (1969).

50. KANE, EDWARD J. "Is There a Predilected Lock-In Effect?" *National Tax Journal* 21 (1968).

51. KEYNES, JOHN MAYNARD. *The General Theory of Employment, Interest and Money.* New York: Harcourt, Brace and Company, 1936.

52. LAIDLER, DAVID. "Expectations, Adjustment, and the Dynamic Response of Income to Policy Changes." *Journal of Money, Credit and Banking* 5 (1973).

53. LEIJONHUFVUD, AXEL. *On Keynesian Economics and the Economics of Keynes: A Study in Monetary Theory.* New York: Oxford University Press, 1968.

54. LERNER, A. P. "The Burden of the National Debt." *Income, Employment and Public Policy: Essays in Honor of Alvin H. Hansen.* New York: W. W. Norton & Company, Inc., 1948.

55. LINDBECK, ASSAR. "The 'New' Theory Of Credit Control In The United States." 2d ed. Stockholm Economic Studies Pamphlet Series I. Stockholm: Almqvist & Wiksell, 1962.

56. MCCARTHY, MICHAEL D. *The Wharton Quarterly Econometric Forecasting Model: Mark III.* Philadelphia: University of Pennsylvania, 1972.

57. MEADE, J. E., and ANDREWS, P. W. S. "Summary of Replies to Questions on Effects of Interest Rates." *Oxford Economic Papers* 1 (1938).

58. METZLER, LLOYD A. "Wealth, Saving, And The Rate Of Interest." *The Journal of Political Economy* 59 (1951).

59. MODIGLIANI, FRANCO. "Liquidity Preference and the Theory of Interest and Money." *Econometrica* 12 (1944).

60. ———. "The Monetary Mechanism and Its Interaction with Real Phenomena." *The Review of Economics and Statistics* 45 (1963).

61. ———. "Monetary Policy and Consumption: Linkages via Interest Rate and Wealth Effects in the FMP Model." Federal Reserve Bank of Boston. *Consumer Spending and Monetary Policy: The Linkages,* 1971.

62. MODIGLIANI, FRANCO, and BRUMBURG, RICHARD. "Utility Analysis and the Consumption Function: An Interpretation of Cross-Section Data." *Post Keynesian Economics.* Edited by Kenneth K. Kurihara. New Brunswick, New Jersey: Rutgers University Press, 1954.

63. PATINKIN, DON. *Money, Interest, and Prices: An Integration of Monetary and Value Theory.* 2d ed. New York: Harper & Row, 1965.

64. PESEK, BORIS P., and SAVING, THOMAS R. *Money, Wealth, and Economic Theory.* New York: The Macmillan Company, 1967.

65. PIGOU, A. C. "The Value of Money." *The Quarterly Journal of Economics* 32 (1917-1918).

66. ———. "The Classical Stationary State." *Economic Journal* 1943.

67. RASCHE, ROBERT H. "A Comparative Static Analysis of Some Monetarist Propositions." this *Review* 55 (1973).

68. ROOSA, ROBERT V. "Interest Rates and the Central Bank." *Money, Trade, and Economic Growth: In Honor of John Henry Williams.* New York: The Macmillan Company, 1951.

69. SAMUELSON, PAUL A. U.S., Congress, Joint Economic Committee. *Monetary Policy and the Management of The Public Debt: Their Role in Achieving Price Stability And High-Level Employment.* 82nd Congress, 2nd session, 1952.

70. ———. "Money, Interest Rates and Economic Activity: Their Interrelationship in a Market Economy." The American Bankers Association. *A Symposium on Money, Interest Rates and Economic Activity,* 1967.

71. SCITOVSZKY, T. DE. "Capital Accumulation, Employment and Price Rigidity." *The Review of Economic Studies* 8 (1940-1941).

72. SILBER, WILLIAM L. "The St. Louis Equation: 'Democratic' and 'Republican' Version And Other Experiments." *The Review of Economics and Statistics* 53 (1971).

73. SMITH, PAUL E. "Lags in the Effects of Monetary Policy: Comment." *The American Economic Review* 62 (1972).

74. TANNER, ERNEST J. "Lag in the Effects of Monetary Policy: A Statistical Investigation." *The American Economic Review* 59 (1969).

75. TINBERGEN, JAN. *Statistical Testing of Business-Cycle Theories.* Geneva: League of Nations, 1938.

76. TOBIN, JAMES. "Relative Income, Absolute Income and Saving." *Money, Trade and Economic Growth: In Honor of John Henry Williams.* New York: The Macmillan Company, 1951.

77. ———. "Money, Capital, and Other Stores of Value." *The American Economic Review* 51 (1961).

78. ———. "Commercial Banks as Creators of 'Money'." *Banking and Monetary Studies.* Edited by Deane Carson. Homewood, Illinois: R. D. Irwin, Inc., 1963.

79. ———. "An Essay on Principles of Debt Management." In *Fiscal and Debt Management Policies,* Commission on Money and Credit. Englewood Cliffs, New Jersey: Prentice-Hall, Inc., 1963.

80. ———. "Monetary Semantics." *Targets and Indicators of Monetary Policy.* Edited by Karl Brunner. San Francisco: Chandler Publishing Company, 1969.

81. ———. "A General Equilibrium Approach to Monetary Theory." *Journal of Money, Credit and Banking* 1 (1969).

82. ———. "Money and Income: Post Hoc Ergo Propter Hoc?" *The Quarterly Journal of Economics* 84 (1970).

83. ———. "Rebuttal." Federal Reserve Bank of Boston. *Consumer Spending and Monetary Policy: The Linkages,* 1971.

84. TOBIN, JAMES, and BRAINARD, WILLIAM C. "Pitfalls in Financial Model Building." *The American Economic Review* 58 (1968).

85. TOBIN, JAMES, and DOLDE, WALTER. "Wealth, Liquidity and Consumption." Federal Reserve Bank of Boston. *Consumer Spending and Monetary Policy: The Linkages,* 1971.

86. TOOKE, THOMAS. *A History of Prices and of the State of the Circulation from 1792 to 1856.* London: P. S. King and Son, Ltd., 1928.

87. TUCKER, DONALD P. "Dynamic Income Adjustment to Money-Supply Changes." *The American Economic Review* 56 (1966).

88. WARBURTON, CLARK. *Depression, Inflation, and Monetary Policy: Selected Papers, 1945-1953*. Baltimore: The John Hopkins Press, 1966.
89. WICKSELL, KNUT. *Lectures on Political Economy: Money*. Vol. 2. Edited by Lionel Robbins. London: Routledge & Kegan Paul Ltd., 1950.
90. ———. *Interest and Prices: A Study of the Causes Regulating the Value of Money*. Translated by R. F. Kahn. New York: Reprints of Economic Classics, 1962.

Crowding Out and Its Critics

Keith M. Carlson
Roger W. Spencer*

8

Does Government spending displace a near-equal amount of private spending? This notion, popularly known as the "crowding-out" effect of government expenditures, has recently gained widespread attention at two levels. First, at the policy level, public officials have expressed concern that massive current and projected federal deficits will have a deleterious effect on private capital expenditures for some time to come. Second, at the academic level, "crowding out" is at least one of the issues which helps to distinguish between followers of the two major macroeconomic schools of thought—Keynesians and monetarists.

This article focuses on "crowding out" from more of an academic than a practical policy point of view. Policy implications can be drawn from this discussion, but, for the most part, the abstract economic models used in academic circles are not easily adaptable to observable phenomena. Yet the origins of the recent crowding-out controversy at the academic level are traceable to certain empirical results based on U.S. experience.

New research has been conducted in this area and some old arguments have been

Reprinted from the Federal Reserve Bank of St. Louis *Review,* (December 1975), by permission of the publisher.

* The authors acknowledge the helpful comments of James Barth, William Dewald, Dean Dutton, Thomas Havrilesky, Robert Rasche, Paul Smith, Frank Steindl, and William Yohe, none of whom should be held responsible for remaining errors.

revived.[1] Many of the developments in the crowding-out controversy can be described in the context of the standard IS-LM analytic framework. In this framework, which is the cornerstone of most macroeconomics courses taught throughout the Western world, the IS curve represents the locus of points (pairs of interest rates and real income) in which the real sector of the economy is in equilibrium and the LM curve represents a similar locus of points for which the demand for money equals the supply.* The IS-LM apparatus has distinct limitations, but because of its widespread use as a pedagogical device, it serves a useful function in highlighting the issues in the crowding-out controversy.[2]

The subject of crowding out is approached by first investigating a number of separate "cases" which provide various explanations of how crowding out might occur. Next, the role of stability considerations in the controversy is assessed. Finally, several econometric models are examined to determine what empirical implications they have for the crowding-out issue.

Some Preliminaries

To set the stage for the discussion, two matters of a preliminary nature are taken up in this section. First, crowding out is defined for the purposes at hand. Much of the recent discussion of crowding out has been confusing simply because the term has not been carefully defined. Second, since the controversy has moved through several stages in recent years and has oftentimes involved complex and subtle arguments, an overview is provided as a guide to the reader.

What Is Crowding Out?

Crowding out generally refers to the economic effects of expansionary fiscal actions. If an increase in government demand, financed by either taxes or debt issuance to the public, fails to stimulate total economic activity, the private sector is said to have been "crowded out" by the government action. The presumption of a constant money supply insures that the policy action accompanying the increase in government demand is fiscal and not monetary.

The analysis may be conducted in either real or nominal terms. The crowding-out hypothesis maintains that if prices are held constant, as in typical IS-LM fashion, an increase in real government demand financed by real taxes or debt has no lasting

---

[1]For a survey that includes a discussion of the views of the classical economists on crowding out, see Roger W. Spencer and William P. Yohe, "The 'Crowding Out' of Private Expenditures by Fiscal Policy Actions," Federal Reserve Bank of St. Louis *Review* (October 1970), pp. 12-24.

[2]For discussion of the limitations of the IS-LM framework, see Karl Brunner and Allan Meltzer, "Monetarism: The Principal Issues, Areas of Agreement and the Work Remaining," Jerome L. Stein, ed., *Monetarism* (Amsterdam: North Holland Publishing Co., forthcoming), and "Mr. Hicks and the 'Monetarists'," *Economica* (February 1973), pp. 44-59.

*The LM-IS model is developed in the article by Warren Smith in Section I of this book.

effect on real income. Alternatively, crowding out implies that an increase in government spending, given flexible prices and a constant money supply, has no lasting effect on nominal income. In other words, the steady-state government spending multiplier, under the above conditions, is approximately zero.[3]

By approximately zero, we mean that increased government demand may crowd out exactly the same amount of private demand, or slightly less, or slightly more. There is complete crowding out if $1 of government demand displaces $1 of private demand, partial crowding out if $1 of government demand displaces less than $1 of private demand, and over crowding out if $1 of government demand displaces more than $1 of private demand. The increased government demand may increase aggregate demand temporarily, permanently, or not at all, as will be explained below.

Overview

The origins of the recent controversy are traceable primarily to the empirical results published by Andersen and Jordan in 1968 and supporting studies by Keran in 1969 and 1970.[4] These results indicated that nominal crowding out occurs, that is, a change in federal spending financed by either borrowing or taxes has only a negligible effect on GNP over a period of about a year. These studies did not suggest that fiscal actions have no effect, but showed instead that the initial effect of an expansionary fiscal action is positive, and this positive effect is followed in later quarters by an approximately offsetting negative effect.

The response to these empirical results took place at two levels—statistical and theoretical. At the statistical level the validity of the results was questioned.[5] Were proper statistical procedures followed in their derivation? On the theoretical level the question was whether or not the results were consistent with what seemed to be the accumulated evidence on certain theoretical propositions.[6]

Although all the returns regarding the validity of the Andersen-Jordan empirical procedures are not yet in, this article focuses on the theoretical arguments that have

---

[3]These definitional issues are explored in more detail in the Appendix.

[4]Leonall C. Andersen and Jerry L. Jordan, "Monetary and Fiscal Actions: A Test of Their Relative Importance in Economic Stabilization," Federal Reserve Bank of St. Louis, *Review* (November 1968), pp. 11–24; Michael W. Keran, "Monetary and Fiscal Influences on Economic Activity—The Historical Evidence," Federal Reserve Bank of St. Louis *Review* (November 1969), pp. 5–24, and "Monetary and Fiscal Influences on Economic Activity: The Foreign Experience," Federal Reserve Bank of St. Louis *Review* (February 1970), pp. 16–28.

[5]See E. Gerald Corrigan, "The Measurement and Importance of Fiscal Policy Changes," Federal Reserve Bank of New York, *Monthly Review* (June 1970), pp. 133–45: Richard G. Davis, "How Much Does Money Matter? A Look at Some Recent Evidence," Federal Reserve Bank of New York, *Monthly Review* (June 1969), pp. 119–31; and Edward M. Gramlich, "The Usefulness of Monetary and Fiscal Policy as Discretionary Stabilization Tools," *Journal of Money, Credit and Banking* (May 1971), pp. 506–32.

[6]James Tobin, "Friedman's Theoretical Framework," *Journal of Political Economy* (September/October 1972), pp. 852–63; Warren L. Smith, "A Neo-Keynesian View of Monetary Policy," in Federal Reserve Bank of Boston, *Controlling Monetary Aggregates* (June 1969), pp. 105–26; and Ronald L. Teigen, "A Critical Look at Monetarist Economics," Federal Reserve Bank of St. Louis *Review* (January 1972), pp. 10–25.

since evolved. The first theoretical argument offered in response to the crowding-out concept was an alleged inconsistency between such results and the prevailing estimates of the interest elasticity of the demand for money.[7] The critics charged, on the basis of the IS-LM framework, that in order for crowding out to occur, the proponents of these results must be assuming that the demand for money is nearly perfectly interest-inelastic. This allegation meant acceptance of the proposition that the LM curve is vertical. According to the critics, most empirical estimates do not support an interest elasticity of money demand of zero.

In answer to this charge of inconsistency, Milton Friedman and others argued that the slope of the LM curve was largely irrelevant to the crowding-out discussion.[8] In particular, Friedman pointed out the necessity of distinguishing between initial and subsequent effects of fiscal actions. According to Friedman, an "expansionary" fiscal action might first be reflected in a rise in output, but the financing of the deficit would set in motion contractionary forces which would eventually offset the initial stimulative effect.[9]

In response to the Friedman explanation, the critics developed still another argument, again pointing out an alleged inconsistency. This time the critics attempted to demonstrate that the Friedman argument, which stemmed from explicit consideration of the government's financing requirements, is not consistent with generally accepted assumptions concerning stability of the economic system (as represented by the IS-LM apparatus).[10] In particular, a debt-financed increase in government spending in a world where crowding out occurs does not set in motion a set of forces that will drive the IS-LM model to a new equilibrium once it is disturbed from an initial equilibrium.

All of these arguments are reviewed in some detail in this article. Several alternative explanations are offered as to how crowding out might occur regardless of the slope of the LM curve. A number of shortcomings of the recently advanced arguments based on stability analysis are introduced. Finally, returning to the empirical level, the results of some well-known econometric models are examined to see what light they shed on the crowding-out controversy.

---

[7]Tobin, "Friedman's Theoretical Framework."

[8]Milton Friedman, "Comments on the Critics," *Journal of Political Economy* (September/October 1972), pp. 906–50; and Karl Brunner and Allan H. Meltzer, "Money, Debt, and Economic Activity," *Journal of Political Economy* (September/October 1972), pp. 951–77.

[9]For further discussion of the role of the Government financing constraint, see Spencer and Yohe, "The 'Crowding Out' of Private Expenditures"; Carl F. Christ, "A Short-Run Aggregate-Demand Model of the Interdependence and Effects of Monetary and Fiscal Policies with Keynesian and Classical Interest Elasticities," *The American Economic Review* (May 1967), pp. 434–43, and "A Simple Macroeconomic Model with a Government Budget Restraint," *The Journal of Political Economy* (January/February 1968), pp. 53–67; and William L. Silber, "Fiscal Policy in IS-LM Analysis: A Correction," *Journal of Money, Credit and Banking* (November 1970), pp. 461–72.

[10]Alan S. Blinder and Robert M. Solow, "Does Fiscal Policy Matter?" *Journal of Public Economics* (November 1973), pp. 319–37; and James Tobin and Willem Buiter, "Long-Run Effects of Fiscal and Monetary Policy on Aggregate Demand," Cowles Foundation Discussion Paper No. 384 (December 13, 1974).

Crowding Out and the Slope of the LM Curve

Until recently, it was suggested by a number of analysts that contemporary monetarists view the vertical LM curve as a requirement for the existence of crowding out. James Tobin, for example, observed that a vertical LM curve leads to the "characteristic monetarist" proposition that "a shift of the *IS* locus, whether due to fiscal policy or to exogenous change in consumption and investment behavior, cannot alter Y."[11] William Branson, in his popular macroeconomics textbook, noted that

> The monetarist position is that the interest elasticities of the demand for and supply of money are zero, so that the *LM* curve is vertical. In this case fiscal policy changes the composition, but not the level of national output, while monetary policy, shifting a vertical *LM* curve, can change the level of output.[12]

Similar statements can be found in other texts.

This classical case of crowding out is examined in some detail because of its presumed importance in the crowding-out discussion. Following discussion of this classical case, several alternative explanations are offered as to how crowding can occur in the IS-LM framework, even if the interest elasticity of money demand is not zero.

The Classical Case: A Vertical LM Curve

In order for government spending to stimulate economic activity, it must either foster increases in the money stock (however defined) or increases in the rate at which the existing money stock turns over. Because the former possibility does not involve net debt purchases by the private sector or increases in taxes, there is no reason to think that private spending would be crowded out. However, if the money stock does not increase, government spending must be financed by debt issuance or increased tax revenue, either of which could result in a reduction in private spending. If private spending is not curbed by such actions, total spending rises, which implies a rise in velocity—the rate at which the money stock turns over.

It is an axiom of classical economics that velocity is virtually constant and cannot be increased by government actions. In particular, the rise in interest rates, which is associated with the issuance of government debt, does not induce the private sector to attempt to hold less money balances because the demand for money is not sensitive to interest rate changes. This idea can be illustrated graphically with the Hicksian IS-LM apparatus in Figure 1.

[11]Tobin, "Friedman's Theoretical Framework," p. 853.

[12]William H. Branson, *Macroeconomic Theory and Policy* (New York: Harper & Row, Publishers, 1972), p. 281. It is of interest to note that Tobin labels the case in which only monetary policy can affect income as characteristically monetarist and the situation in which *both* monetary and fiscal policies can alter income as characteristically neo-Keynesian. Branson symmetrically views the vertical LM case as "extreme" monetarist, and the vertical IS case as "extreme" neo-Keynesian (or "fiscalist").

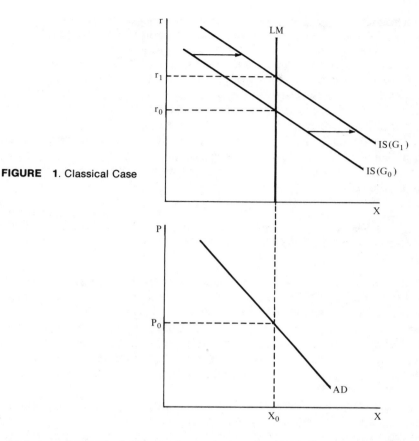

FIGURE 1. Classical Case

The LM curve is vertical (drawn for a given price level, P_0) in the classical case, reflecting a zero interest elasticity of the demand for (and supply of) money. Thus, an increase in government spending which shifts the IS curve to the right can only increase the interest rate, but does not stimulate velocity. Consequently, aggregate demand, as shown in the bottom half of Figure 1, does not shift.* One or more components of private spending are crowded out by an amount equal to the amount of the government spending increase. As a result, with aggregate demand failing to shift in response to the increase in government spending, crowding out occurs in both real and nominal terms.

Alternative Cases: Crowding Out Without a Vertical LM Curve

Five cases are presented which represent economic situations conducive to government displacement of private spending *without* the requirement of a vertical LM

* Although shown as a straight line, the true spirit of the classical case would be better preserved if aggregate demand were drawn as a rectangular hyperbola.

curve. The architects of these frameworks range from such disparate figures as the Chicago economists, Frank Knight and Milton Friedman, to John Maynard Keynes.

THE KEYNES CASE: EXPECTATIONS EFFECTS

John Maynard Keynes in 1936 provided the thrust for the proposition that government spending does *not* crowd out private spending in his landmark book, *The General Theory of Employment, Interest and Money*.[13] It is ironic that certain passages in that book provide strong support for the opposite contention.

Keynes, throughout his *General Theory*, was much concerned with expectations and confidence. He did not overlook the possibility, even in those times of relatively small budget deficits, that government spending could adversely affect the confidence of the private sector in its economic future.

> With the confused psychology which often prevails, the Government programme may, through its effect on "confidence," increase liquidity-preference or diminish the marginal efficiency of capital, which, again, may retard other investment unless measures are taken to offset it.[14]

An increase in liquidity preference is depicted in the IS-LM framework (see Figure 2) by a leftward shift of the LM curve, and a diminished marginal efficiency of investment schedule is reflected by the subsequent backward shift of the IS curve to the position denoted as IS (G_1).[15] If these shifts in the IS and LM curves result in no change in aggregate demand at the given price level P_o, both nominal and real crowding out will occur. However, the actual shift in aggregate demand could be positive, negative, or negligible, depending on the relative shifts of the IS and LM curves.

A number of analysts have recently invoked the Keynes case to explain the sluggishness of capital expenditures in recent years. They, however, are not the first since Keynes to attribute lackluster investment plans to stepped-up government spending. Describing a situation with some similarities to the present, Daniel Throop Smith observed (in 1939) that

> A continued experience with deficits which do not produce sustained recovery, as in this country, or a recent inflation and collapse, as in continental European countries, is likely to make a deficit matter for concern and anxiety. And if there is disbelief in the benefits of a deficit, then the new money spent by the government may well be more than offset by additional withdrawals of private money which would otherwise be spent. Likewise, if consumer incomes do increase immediately as a result of the deficit, business may anticipate that the increase is temporary and refrain from long-term commitments.[16]

[13]John Maynard Keynes, *The General Theory of Employment, Interest and Money* (New York: Harcourt, Brace and Company, 1936), pp. 119-20.

[14]Ibid., p. 120.

[15]For an algebraic analysis that takes into account some of the relevant aspects of this Keynes case, see Richard J. Cebula, "Deficit Spending, Expectations, and Fiscal Policy Effectiveness," *Public Finance* (3-4/1973), pp. 362-70.

[16]Daniel Throop Smith, "Is Deficit Spending Practical?" *Harvard Business Review* (Autumn 1939), p. 38.

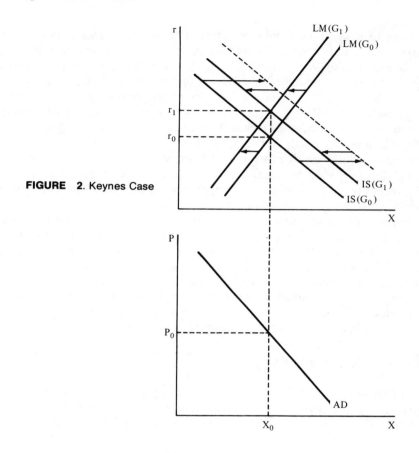

FIGURE 2. Keynes Case

THE KNIGHT CASE: A HORIZONTAL IS CURVE

This case is constructed on the basis of the writings of Frank Knight.[17] The analysis does not do justice to the complex theories of Knight but is offered as being roughly consistent with the spirit of his theory of capital and interest.[18] Though Knight certainly did not conduct his analysis within an IS-LM framework, an attempt is made to translate his ideas into such terms.

[17]No attempt is made to cite all of Knight's articles on interest and capital, but a summary is contained in Frank H. Knight, "Capital and Interest," in *Readings in the Theory of Income Distribution,* American Economic Association (Philadelphia: The Blakiston Company, 1949), pp. 384-417. The Knight case was suggested to the authors by William Dewald of Ohio State University, but he is absolved of any responsibility for the particular analysis here.

[18]The difficulty of interpreting Knight's writing is illustrated by Friedrich A. Lutz, *The Theory of Interest* (Chicago: Aldine Publishing Company, 1968), p. 104, where he introduces his chapter on Knight as follows:

> It is not easy to give an exposition of Knight's theory of capital and interest. Over a number of years Knight devoted many papers to the subject; and, as anyone who ever attempted to work his way through Knight's theory knows, these writings have passages which are very difficult to understand and also, either apparently or really, contradictory.

According to Knight, we should expect no diminishing returns from investment. One reason for a nearly perfectly interest-elastic investment function is that the quantity of capital is so large relative to the additions to it that these additions should not be expected to have much of an effect on the yield of capital.[19] Another reason, according to Knight, is that investment carries with it an investment in knowledge, including research and development. As a result, a declining marginal product of capital is approximately offset by technological advances so that an aggregate investment curve is drawn as nearly horizontal with respect to the yield on capital.

When translated into an IS-LM frame of reference, the Knight case introduces an interesting element to the crowding-out controversy. A perfectly flat IS curve (see Figure 3) means that fiscal actions are incapable of shifting the IS curve. An increase in government spending, for example, absorbs saving and reduces the amount available for private investment (any increase in government spending shows up as a one for one displacement of private investment). Combining the flat IS curve with the LM curve provides a case where monetary policy dominates the determination of output. Fiscal actions have no effect on either output or the interest rate.[20] It is of interest to note that monetary policy has no effect on the interest rate either, an implication which runs counter to some statements by Knight.[21] But because fiscal actions do not shift aggregate demand for this so-called Knight case, the implication is that both nominal and real crowding out occur.[22]

THE ULTRARATIONAL CASE: DIRECT SUBSTITUTION EFFECTS

Recently, Professors Paul David and John Scadding developed some arguments for crowding out that are derived from an assumption of ultrarationality on the part of households.[23] The notion of ultrarationality is based on the assumption that house-

---

[19]For a discussion of the relationship between stocks and flows in the market for capital goods, see James G. Witte, Jr., "The Micro Foundations of the Social Investment Function," *The Journal of Political Economy* (October 1963), pp. 441-56.

To add to the confusion relating to the interpretation of Knight's writings, it should be noted that Knight did not accept the three-part division of resources into land, labor, and capital. His interpretation, rather, was that anyone who has control over productive capacity will employ any or all sources in such a way as to maximize the return for their use. For an analysis that preserves this broad definition of capital, see Milton Friedman, *Price Theory: A Provisional Text* (Chicago: Aldine Publishing Company, 1962), pp. 244-63.

[20]It is surprising that this case has not received more attention in the literature because it is every bit as monetarist as the vertical LM case. For an example of one writer who does mention this case, see Martin Bronfenbrenner, *Income Distribution Theory* (Chicago: Aldine-Atherton, 1971), pp. 339-40. However, Bronfenbrenner dismisses it as a long-run case with little short-run significance.

[21]See Knight, "Capital and Interest," p. 406.

[22]Though the Knight case has not been empirically tested, it has implications which are consistent with the results of a number of empirical studies. The Andersen-Jordan results relating changes in GNP to monetary and fiscal actions are consistent with such a case. The inability to find a stable relationship between interest rates and various measures of fiscal action is also consistent. And finally, the stability of real interest rates over time—at least to the extent real rates have been measured—provides indirect evidence in support of the Knight model.

[23]Paul A. David and John L. Scadding, "Private Savings; Ultrarationality, Aggregation, and 'Denison's Law,'" *Journal of Political Economy* (March/April 1974), pp. 225-50.

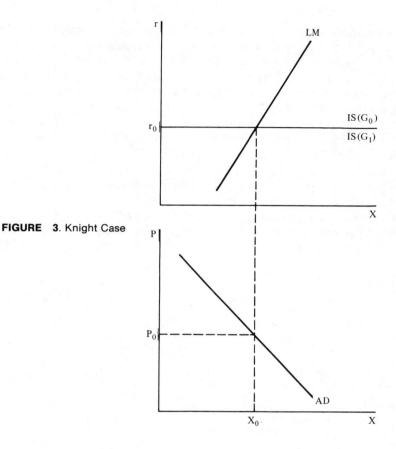

FIGURE 3. Knight Case

holds regard the corporate and government sectors as extensions of themselves—as instruments of their private interests. This fundamental behavioral assumption is offered as an explanation for Denison's Law—the observed stability of the ratio of gross private saving to GNP in the United States.[24]

The David-Scadding article is of relevance to the crowding-out controversy be- cause of its fiscal policy implications. The assumption of ultrarationality implies displacement effects of government spending which the authors call "*ex ante* crowd- ing out." They argue that stability of the gross private saving ratio in the face of substantial variation in the government deficit suggests that private debt and public debt are close substitutes. An extra dollar of government deficit displaces a dollar of

[24]Edward F. Denison, "A Note on Private Saving," *The Review of Economics and Statistics* (August 1958), pp. 261–67. David and Scadding suggest that if government and corporate activity simply substitute for, rather than augment, household activity, there should be virtually no change in such broad aggregates as the ratio of gross private saving to GNP.

private investment expenditure because deficit financing is viewed as public investment and substitutes for private investment, in that households tend to classify both
in terms of future consumption benefits. This case is shown in Figure 4, where an
increase in government spending financed by borrowing induces an offsetting change
in private investment so that the IS curve does not shift on balance.

Similarly, government consumption has a displacement effect on private consumption. Tax-financed expenditures are viewed in terms of their present consumption
benefits and substitute perfectly for private consumption. With an increase in government spending for consumption financed by increased taxes, the increase in taxes
reduces private consumption with no effect on private saving. As a result, there is a
shift in the composition of output from the private sector to the government, but
there is no shift in aggregate demand.

Consequently, with tax-financed government expenditures displacing private consumption and government bond issues (deficit financing) displacing private debt
issues, there is no way that fiscal actions can affect total demand for goods and

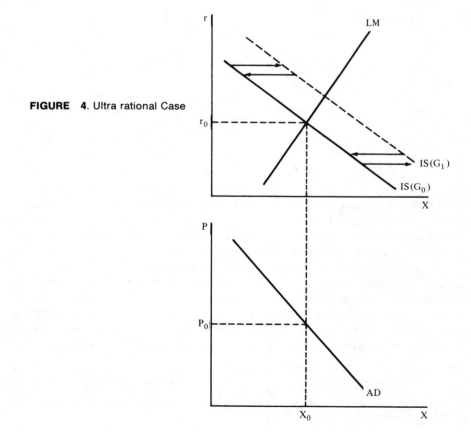

FIGURE 4. Ultra rational Case

services. In the parlance of the IS-LM framework, fiscal actions (defined as either tax- or debt-financed government expenditures) have no net effect on the IS curve or on aggregate demand, which implies both nominal and real crowding out. Also, for this case, fiscal actions have no influence on interest rates.

Whether the David-Scadding ultrarational case is to be taken as a serious explanation of crowding out is an open question. Yet it is important to note the implications of this model because it represents a departure from the severe restrictions implicit in the IS-LM model. In particular, the IS-LM model allows for no substitution between private spending and public spending, and David-Scadding have shown that moving away from these restrictive assumptions acts in the direction of reducing the fiscal policy multipliers. Furthermore, by way of Denison's Law, they conclude that the evidence leans more toward the extreme of ultrarationality than the extreme of the IS-LM model.

THE EXTENDED IS-LM CASE: PRICE FLEXIBILITY

All cases discussed thus far have not presented any conflicts with respect to the nominal versus real crowding-out issue because aggregate demand typically does not shift. There is, however, another way in which crowding out might occur, reflecting a response of the price level to a step-up in government spending. This case argues that crowding out is possible even without the assumption that aggregate demand does not shift. The implication for nominal versus real crowding out is ambiguous for this case, however.

Robert Rasche constructed a sophisticated version of the IS-LM apparatus, which was based primarily on the textbook presentation of Robert Crouch.[25] The model included wealth in the consumption and money demand functions, a government budget constraint, and a labor sector, as well as an endogenous price level. According to Rasche's analysis, an increase in real government purchases, financed either by taxes or debt issuance, increases aggregate demand and, consequently, the commodity price level. Although there may also be a rise in consumption owing to a presumed positive effect of debt issuance on wealth, there is an offsetting increase in the demand for money associated with such wealth gains (see Figure 5). The rise in the price level reduces private consumption as well as the real supply of money. Together with a decline in the amount of private investment owing to an increase in interest rates, these factors tend to crowd out an amount of real private expenditures equivalent to the increase in government purchases. Crowding out occurs in this model in real terms, but with a higher price level; crowding out is not likely to occur in nominal terms.

These results lead Rasche to conclude that nominal crowding out requires "extreme" assumptions about the interest elasticity and the wealth elasticity of the demand for real cash balances. It should be pointed out, however, that Rasche, in his

[25]Robert H. Rasche, "A Comparative Static Analysis of Some Monetarist Propositions," *Federal Reserve Bank of St. Louis Review* (December 1973), pp. 15–23; and Robert L. Crouch, *Macroeconomics* (New York: Harcourt Brace Jovanovich, Inc., 1972). *Editors' Note: The Rasche article is found in Section 1 of this book.

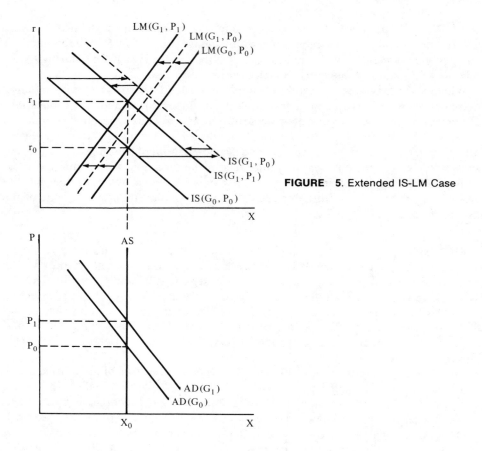

FIGURE 5. Extended IS-LM Case

manipulation of the model, did not allow for a Keynes expectation effect, an ultrarational direct substitution effect, or a Knight effect, all of which leave the aggregate demand curve unmoved in response to an initial increase in government spending.

THE FRIEDMAN CASE: INITIAL VS. SUBSEQUENT EFFECTS

Milton Friedman's role in the crowding-out controversy was established in a series of articles published in the *Journal of Political Economy* over the period 1970 to 1972.[26] Friedman did not rely solely on the IS-LM model as a framework for his analysis, but most of his ideas can be summarized in such a context. Friedman denied emphatically that the monetarist propositions rested on the shape of the LM locus.

[26]Friedman, "Comments on the Critics"; "A Theoretical Framework for Monetary Analysis," *Journal of Political Economy* (March/April 1970), pp. 193-238; and "A Monetary Theory of Nominal Income," *Journal of Political Economy* (March/April 1971), pp. 323-37.

Instead, Friedman stressed the continuing effects of deficit finance and a fundamental distinction between stocks and flows.

Friedman dealt with a large number of complex issues in his reply to the critics, and it is difficult to determine to what extent he supported the notion of fiscal crowding out. His chief point seems to have been that the power of monetary actions far surpasses that of fiscal actions, which is not the same thing as declaring a belief in crowding out. Nevertheless, he concluded that the expansionary effect of an increase in government spending by borrowing is likely to be minor.

To show the Friedman case, consider Figure 6. The IS curve is drawn quite flat, reflecting Friedman's statement that " 'saving' and 'investment' have to be interpreted much more broadly than neo-Keynesians tend to interpret it. . . ."[27] Though Friedman does not emphasize it, this interpretation puts him close to the Knight case because the implication of more inclusive investment tends to flatten the IS curve

[27]Friedman, "Comments on the Critics," pp. 915.

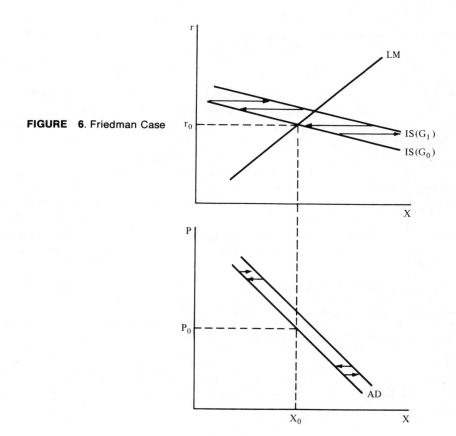

FIGURE **6**. Friedman Case

and dampen the power of fiscal actions.[28] In addition, Friedman indicates that the wealth effects of increased bond holdings on spending will be minimal because increases in debt would tend to be offset by an increase in expected tax liabilities.

Perhaps an even more important reason to doubt the long-run expansive capacity of increased government spending is its effect on the future production of goods and services. Friedman notes that debt-supported government spending leads to a "reduction in the physical volume of assets created because of lowered private productive investment."[29] In other words, potential output in the future will be lowered relative to what it would otherwise be with the transfer of resources from private investment, which generates the future capital stock, to government spending, which absorbs it.

Apart from these objections to the idea of stimulative government actions, an initial shift of the IS curve (see Figure 6) may still be consistent with crowding out over the longer term. For a given LM curve, the relatively flat IS curve, which Friedman apparently envisions, yields a shift of aggregate demand which is very small. In addition, Friedman notes that "the evidences of government debt are largely in place of evidences of private debt—people hold Treasury bills instead of bills issued by, for example, U.S. Steel."[30] If this statement is given the ultrarational interpretation discussed earlier, private expenditure is cut back, offsetting the initial increase in government spending. Whether such an effect is a partial or complete offset is not made clear, but if it exists, the IS and aggregate demand curves move back toward their original positions.

These are the initial effects of a debt-financed increase in government spending, but Friedman goes on to emphasize that subsequent effects will continue as long as a deficit exists. In later periods the IS curve will continue shifting back to the left because private expenditures continue to be cut back as government debt is substituted for private debt. Eventually, the stock of private wealth will be reduced relative to what it otherwise would be because of reduced investment, thereby reinforcing the leftward movement of the IS curve.[31]

Because Friedman is not clear with regard to the role of commodity prices in his analysis, it is difficult to assess his view of real versus nominal crowding out. It is perhaps best simply to conclude that the impact of an increase in debt-financed government spending is very small and that there is little difference between the

---

[28]Norman Van Cott and Gary Santoni, "Friedman versus Tobin: A Comment," *Journal of Political Economy* (July/August 1974), pp. 883-85. In this article the authors show that the effect of broadening the interpretation of saving and investment is to make the IS schedule flatter. They demonstrate this by adding the interest rate as an argument in the consumption function and then showing that the extent to which the IS curve is shifted is unaffected by fiscal actions; only the slope is changed.

[29]Friedman, "Comments on the Critics," p. 917.

[30]Ibid.

[31]For a recent paper that works out a numerical example of the first-round and subsequent effects of a fiscal action in an IS-LM framework, see Laurence H. Meyer, "The Balance Sheet Identity, the Government Financing Constraint, and the Crowding-Out Effect," *Journal of Monetary Economics* (January 1975), pp. 65-78.

effects of debt versus tax-financed expenditure. A relatively flat IS curve yields these results, and any ultrarational effects would reinforce them.

Crowding Out and Stability Considerations

The Friedman emphasis on the longer-run effects of monetary and fiscal actions prompted two major papers (one by Alan Blinder and Robert Solow and the other by James Tobin and Willem Buiter) that attempted to demonstrate that the crowding-out effect of fiscal actions is not consistent with the assumption of stability of the economic system, as represented by the IS-LM model.[32] Both of these papers are discussed in this section along with a third—by Karl Brunner and Allan Meltzer—which actually antedates the other two.[33] All three models essentially employ comparative static tools to examine a dynamic phenomenon.

The Long-Run Balanced Budget Models

BLINDER AND SOLOW
Recently, Blinder and Solow developed a rigorous theoretical attack on the crowding-out thesis.[34] They envisioned three possible levels of crowding out:

1. The government undertakes activities which would otherwise be provided, on a one-for-one basis, by the private sector. They point out that this sort of crowding out (to the extent it exists) would occur regardless of how the government spending was financed;

2. Debt issues floated by the government to finance its spending drive up interest rates and crowd out private borrowing;

3. Increases in wealth, derived from the issuance of government bonds, increase money demand, that is, shift the LM curve leftward sufficiently to negate the rightward shifts of the IS curve.

Blinder-Solow constructed an extended version of the IS-LM framework which incorporated consumption and money demand as functions of wealth, and a government budget constraint providing for government debt interest payments. They ad-

---

[32]Blinder and Solow, "Does Fiscal Policy Matter?" and Tobin and Buiter, "Long-Run Effects."

[33]Brunner and Meltzer, "Money, Debt, and Economic Activity."

[34]Many of the ideas in the Blinder-Solow article did not originate with them. See Frank G. Steindl, "Wealth, Fiscal Policy and the Government Budget Restraint," unpublished (April 1973). For papers criticizing the Blinder-Solow analysis, see Albert Ando, "Some Aspects of Stabilization Policies, The Monetarist Controversy, and the MPS Model," *International Economic Review* (October 1974), pp. 541-71; Paul E. Smith, "The Government Budget Constraint, Crowding Out, and Stability of Equilibrium," unpublished (May 1975); and James R. Barth, James T. Bennett, and Richard H. Sines, "Fiscal Policy and Macroeconomic Activity," paper presented at the meetings of the Southern Economic Association, New Orleans, Louisiana, November 14, 1975.

hered to the usual IS-LM customs of treating the price level as fixed and of ignoring the existence of a banking system.

Blinder-Solow then attempted to discern the likelihood of crowding-out phenomena occurring by investigating the stability properties of the model. They arrived at the following theoretical implications:

1. If government spending financed by bond issuance is contractionary, as (according to Blinder-Solow) monetarists claim, the IS-LM model is unstable;

2. If government spending is expansive, as neo-Keynesians claim, but *less* expansive than government spending financed by money creation, the model is unstable;

3. If government spending financed by bond issuance is *more* expansive than government spending financed by money creation, the model is stable.

The unusual result that theoretical stability conditions imply that bond-financed government spending is more stimulative than money-financed government spending comes about because of the inclusion of interest payments on outstanding debt in the government budget constraint. For the model to be stable, the budget must be in balance in the long run to insure unchanging stocks of money and debt. In order for the budget gap to close after the initial shock of fiscal stimulus, income must rise by a larger amount in the bond-financed case than in the money-financed case. This result follows because higher tax receipts must be induced to offset the increased interest payments on the government debt.

TOBIN AND BUITER
Recently Tobin and Buiter also formulated an IS-LM model for the purpose of examining the crowding-out thesis. Although some of the equations differ from those employed by Blinder-Solow, the basic assumptions, such as a constant price level, and the methodology, which is marked by the stability requirement of a balanced budget process, are virtually the same.[35] Their analysis is also marked by the stability requirement of a balanced budget process. Like Blinder-Solow, Tobin-Buiter utilized more than one variation of the basic IS-LM model, and, like Blinder-Solow, they arrived at the conclusion that the stability considerations inherent in the balanced budget requirement generate a positive government spending multiplier. Tobin-Buiter emphasized that the analysis is conducted for periods in which the economy is less than fully employed.

BRUNNER AND MELTZER
Another model has recently been developed which is adaptable to analysis of the crowding-out question. Brunner and Meltzer constructed a model of the economy along IS-LM lines, but with a number of significant differences. The Brunner-Meltzer model contains markets for real assets, financial assets, and current ouput and

---

[35]Although the bulk of their analysis assumes a constant price level, as does an earlier model on which their paper was based, Tobin-Buiter present one version of the model which employs a variable price level.

permits wealth owners to choose among money, bonds, real capital, and current expenditures. In contrast with the Blinder-Solow and basic Tobin-Buiter models, the Brunner-Meltzer model permits the price level to be determined endogenously and includes a banking sector. The analysis also features, as do the other models, stability considerations and a government sector which issues interest-bearing debt.

Apparently, these common elements of the models are the elements which lead to the unusual results already noted in the Blinder-Solow model and which also emerge in the Brunner-Meltzer model. In particular, Brunner-Meltzer find that government spending financed by debt issuance is more stimulative than government spending accompanied by expansionary monetary actions. Such a result is again dictated by the requirement of a balanced budget. Once disturbed by, say, an increase in government spending, the budget is required to return to balance, and the presence of interest payments in the budget constraint means that a larger increase in income is required for bond financing than for money financing.

Brunner-Meltzer recognized this obvious discrepancy between their model's results and the historical evidence, particularly as interpreted by monetarists. They note that their model results imply "that inflation or deflation can occur without any change in B [the monetary base, which is the prime determinant of the money supply]."[36] Brunner-Meltzer take a markedly different view of the causes of inflation *outside* their model construct and in the context of observable phenomena: "Our analysis of inflation, presented at the Universities–National Bureau Conference on Secular Inflation, analyzes the issue in more detail and explains why most inflations or deflations have resulted from changes in money."[37]

One must bear in mind that the results of the Brunner-Meltzer model are predicated on: (1) the absence of money illusion (in the usual sense), but the existence of a possible wealth illusion by way of incomplete discounting of future tax liabilities; (2) the requirement of a balanced budget; (3) a fixed capital stock (Blinder-Solow, in contrast, present a variation of their model in which the capital stock is permitted to grow); (4) no labor sector (to facilitate changes in output in lieu of the absence of a changing capital stock); and (5) the presumption that asset prices respond more strongly to an increase in government debt than to an increase in the monetary base.[38]

Shortcomings of the Stability Models

The recent attack on the crowding-out thesis by way of stability analysis introduces a new element into the controversy. There are several reasons to question the impli-

[36]Brunner and Meltzer, "Money, Debt, and Economic Activity," p. 973 (bracketed words supplied).
[37]Ibid.
[38]The last-mentioned item is particularly critical for the Brunner-Meltzer results. Whereas asset prices can be expected to respond in a positive manner to increases in the monetary base, there is ambiguity in the response of asset prices to the issuance of government debt. A positive wealth effect (given incomplete discounting of a future tax liabilities) must outweigh a negative substitution effect (caused by government debt competing in asset markets with private debt) for the Brunner-Meltzer results to hold.

cations of these models of the economy which indicate that crowding out is not consistent with model stability.

Treatment of Price Level Changes

The Blinder-Solow model and the basic Tobin-Buiter model, which are somewhat sophisticated versions of the basic IS-LM apparatus, permit no rule for price level changes.[39] Considering world-wide economic developments over the past decade, one must question the relevance of so-called "structural" models which omit the existence of inflationary pressures and inflationary expectations. Moreover, an important channel through which crowding out might occur is closed off when price level changes are forbidden to emerge.

Blinder-Solow recognized this deficiency of their model to some extent, as indicated by their acknowledgment that the fiscal policy multiplier would be lowered in several ways by the inclusion of an endogenously determined price level: (1) higher prices lower the real value of the money stock and shift the LM curve to the left; (2) higher prices reduce real wealth, and thus consumption, shifting the IS curve to the left; (3) progressive taxes combined with inflation increase the real yield of the tax system, which also tends to shift the IS curve leftward; (4) a rising price level depresses exports and induces imports in an open economy, which again pushes the IS curve to the left.[40]

Blinder-Solow maintained that although the fiscal multiplier will be less than before with the inclusion of price level changes, the sign of the multiplier will remain positive. Because it is their view that the crowding-out hypothesis requires the fiscal multiplier to be negative, the authors considered only the sign of the coefficient to be at issue. This, however, is a gross exaggeration. To our knowledge, there have been no claims that the crowding-out hypothesis requires that a dollar of government spending, unsupported by monetary expansion, *must* reduce private spending by *more* than a dollar, which is the implication of a negative fiscal policy multiplier.[41] Crowding out of the private sector occurs not only when $1 of government spending reduces private spending by $1 (a multiplier of zero), but when $1 of government spending reduces private spending by 50 cents (a multiplier of 0.50). Crowding out, then, is a matter of degree rather than of absolute magnitudes. A negative multiplier is not a necessary condition for crowding out. And the omission of changing price levels in various IS-LM models contributes to the likelihood that crowding-out tendencies will not emerge.

[39]The Brunner-Meltzer model permits price level flexibility but excludes a labor sector, which presumably plays an important part in realistic attempts to capture the economic structure.

[40]Blinder-Solow added this final price effect in "Analytical Foundations of Fiscal Policy," in *The Economics of Public Finance* (Washington, D.C.: The Brookings Institution, 1974), p. 47.

[41]It should be pointed out that various econometric models indeed have uncovered negative fiscal multipliers.

BALANCED BUDGET EQUILIBRIUM

The three models under consideration show that in order for the budget to be balanced, and for the model to be in long-run equilibrium, the fiscal policy multiplier must be positive. A full equilibrium requires that the levels of stocks and flows be unchanging. But the question remains, How does such a formal analysis contribute to an explanation of the empirical results that imply crowding out occurs?

Tobin-Buiter made two significant points in this connection. First, they questioned the ability of economic analysis—presumably, as incorporated in abstract models— to track changing economic variables to some logical end. "The trouble with such discussions, including this one, is that a long run constructed to track the ultimate consequences of anything is a never-never land. For that abstraction we apologize in advance."[42] If one is really interested in tracking changes in economic variables over time, the better approach would be to construct dynamic models rather than comparative static models.

Second, Tobin-Buiter questioned the stability requirements (including a balanced budget) associated with the IS-LM investigations into the crowding-out controversy. Their concluding remarks were:

Finally, we observe again that it is disturbing that the qualitative properties of models—the signs of important system-wide multipliers, the stability of equilibria—can turn on relatively small changes of specifications or on small differences in values of coefficients. We do not feel entitled to use the "correspondence principle" assumption of stability to derive restrictions on structural equations and parameters. *There is no divine guarantee that the economic system is stable.*[43]

The economic system may be stable in the sense that the U.S. economy has not exploded, but it is a long jump from that sort of stability to one which requires stock-flow equilibrium including a balanced budget. Indeed, the budget of the U.S. government has been in deficit in eleven of the past fifteen years.

Stock-flow equilibrium models, then, are basically empty of empirical content. Although there may have been periods in which some of the relevant flows were approximately in balance, one would be hard pressed to uncover data points corresponding to periods of unchanging stocks. Without the necessary data, it is impossible to confirm or refute the hypotheses associated with stock-flow equilibrium models.

FISCAL VS. MONETARY STIMULUS

The underlying assumptions and stability requirements of the models in question combine to produce a most curious result: government spending financed by debt issuance is more expansionary than government spending accompanied by money

[42]Tobin-Buiter, "Long-Run Effects," p. 1.
[43]Ibid., p. 42 (italics supplied).

creation. The expansionary effect is summarized in terms of real output in the Blinder-Solow model and in terms of prices in the Brunner-Meltzer model.

These theoretical implications run contrary to virtually every investigation conducted into the impacts of fiscal and monetary policy actions on economic activity. None of the architects of these models attempted to reconcile the model implications with the mass of empirical studies contradicting them.

Brunner-Meltzer acknowledged this discrepancy. However, they offered no explanation for the fact that even though their model implies that bond-financed government spending is more inflationary than money-financed spending, their own empirical studies indicate just the opposite.[44] One is led to conclude that manipulation of these theoretical models constitutes an interesting academic exercise but contributes little of practical significance to the crowding out controversy. With empirical considerations coming to the fore, the discussion now turns to the econometric literature to determine what evidence that approach has brought to bear on the issue of crowding out.

Econometric Models and Crowding Out

In a recent study of a number of econometric models, Gary Fromm and Lawrence Klein published simulation results showing the implied government expenditure and tax multipliers for these models.[45] The results showed long-run government spending multipliers ranging from about 1 to 5 when measured in terms of impact on current dollar GNP.[46] However, the majority of the large models surveyed revealed that crowding out did occur in real terms over time. Some indicated $1 of government spending for goods and services crowded out even more than $1 of private spending.

For example, the Wharton Mark III Model yielded a multiplier of minus 3 after forty quarters, and the Bureau of Economic Analysis (U.S. Department of Commerce) Model gave a real government spending multiplier over the same time period of minus 23. These results go well beyond monetarists' contentions that complete crowding out gives a multiplier of approximately zero, though these results are less than clear on the issue of nominal crowding out.

Fromm and Klein's survey of the empirical results suggested that crowding out typically occurred because of a rising price level, capacity constraints, and rising

---

[44]Karl Brunner, Michele Fratianni, Jerry L. Jordan, Alan H. Meltzer, and Manfred J. Neumann, "Fiscal and Monetary Policies in Moderate Inflation," *Journal of Money, Credit and Banking* (February 1973), pp. 313–53.

[45]Gary Fromm and Lawrence R. Klein, "A Comparison of Eleven Econometric Models of the United States," *The American Economic Review* (May 1973), pp. 385–93. These models, unlike the IS-LM abstractions discussed earlier, were not forced to a full stock-flow equilibrium.

[46]Blinder and Solow cited these results as attesting to the absence of crowding out in large income-expenditure models. Acknowledging the nonexistence of government budget constraints in the models, they added that despite this deficiency, "All we can do now is render a verdict on the basis of the evidence already in." They ignored the real crowding out results implied by the econometric models, which is surprising, in that their own model emphasized the crowding out issue in real terms. Blinder and Solow, "Analytical Foundations of Fiscal Policy," p. 47.

nominal interest rates. These results are consistent with those implied by the extended IS-LM case described above, and they do not necessarily corroborate crowding out of the nonshifting aggregate demand variety, that is, those cases which imply that crowding out occurs because fiscal actions are offset by other components of aggregate demand.

However, Fromm and Klein recognized that the model simulations produced evidence not in accord with the usual standard Keynesian presumption of positive government spending multipliers:

> Conventional textbook expositions generally depict real expenditure multipliers approaching positive asymptotes. In fact, most of the models here show such multipliers reaching a peak in two or three years and then declining thereafter in fluctuating paths. At the end of five to ten years, some of the models show that continued sustained fiscal stimulus has ever-increasing *perverse* impacts.[47]

Klein suggested elsewhere that perhaps these new estimates of the fiscal multiplier are not as damaging to the Keynesian position as they initially appear.[48] After all, it takes a considerable length of time in some of the models for the government spending multiplier to approach zero or turn negative, and policymakers historically have shown little concern for the long run. We would only add that this argument reflects the progression of the debate on crowding out from "Does it exist?" to "What is the time period?"

As far as small models are concerned, the monetarist model of the Federal Reserve Bank of St. Louis set off much of the current controversy. Fiscal crowding out emerges in the reduced-form equations published in the St. Louis *Review* only after a period of time, even though it is a much shorter period of time than that of the large income-expenditure models, and it occurs in nominal terms rather than in just real terms. Government spending, as measured by high-employment expenditures, exercises a relatively strong influence on GNP (assuming a constant change in the money supply) in the current quarter and the next quarter, but it is approximately offset within a year's time.

These results, which are confirmed by regression analysis employing data through mid-1975, should not be interpreted to suggest that "government spending doesn't matter"; it matters very much over a certain period. Moreover, if government spending were to accelerate or decelerate rapidly rather than be held to a steady rate of change, the impact on GNP would be considerable.

The chief reason that these reduced-form results are of interest is that they do not follow from a structural model that constrains the channels of transmission from fiscal actions to economic activity. Government expenditures cover a wide range of activities, some of which substitute for private consumption and investment and

[47]Fromm and Klein, "A Comparison," p. 393 (italics supplied).
[48]See Lawrence R. Klein, "Commentary on 'The State of the Monetarist Debate,' " Federal Reserve Bank of St. Louis, *Review* (September 1973), pp. 9–12.

others which serve as substitutes or complements to private factors of production.[49] With such diverse effects, any model which restricts the transmission of fiscal actions to income and/or interest rate channels runs the risk of missing the full effects of government interaction with the private sector.[50] The St. Louis results certainly do not do justice to the measurement of the effects of the complexities of the government-spending process, but they serve the function of questioning the results from models which restrict the operation of fiscal actions via fixed channels.

Summary and Conclusions

This article has surveyed the recent literature on the subject of the crowding-out effect of fiscal actions. Crowding out was defined as a steady-state government spending multiplier of near zero, a definition which was extended to differentiate the terms "nominal" and "real" crowding out.

This survey indicates that the controversy has taken place on two fronts—theoretical and empirical. First, the theoretical literature has developed primarily with reference to the IS-LM model or modifications thereof. Several cases were examined which serve as candidates providing theoretical support for the crowding-out hypothesis. In addition, the role of stability conditions in the crowding-out controversy was examined. In general, the conclusion was that stability considerations are of limited relevance with respect to the acceptance or rejection of the crowding-out hypothesis.

The empirical literature, on the other hand, has taken the form of simulations of government actions and has yielded results that show signs of being consistent with the crowding-out hypothesis. This crowding out tends to be very slow in developing, however, and occurs in real rather than nominal terms. The St. Louis results still stand out relative to the large econometric models in that crowding out occurs more quickly and also in nominal terms.

As a result of this survey, it is clear that the crowding-out controversy continues to exist. Apparently these issues will not approach resolution until additional structural models are developed and tested. The Keynesians have developed many models, but

[49]We, like most other analysts, have had little to say about the effect of fiscal actions on aggregate supply. For an attempt to enrich standard macroeconomic analysis with such considerations, see Kenneth J. Arrow and Mordecai M. Kurz, *Public Investment, the Rate of Return, and Optimal Fiscal Policy* (Baltimore: Johns Hopkins Press, 1970), and Lowell E. Gallaway and Paul E. Smith, "The Government Budget Constraint and Aggregate Supply," paper presented at the meetings of the Southern Economic Association, New Orleans, Louisiana, November 14, 1975.

[50]See R. L. Basmann, "Remarks Concerning the Application of Exact Finite Sample Distribution Functions for GCL Estimates in Econometric Statistical Inference," *Journal of the American Statistical Association* (December 1963), p. 944, where he says:

". . . the entire burden of statistical inference in econometric simultaneous equations models falls on the unconstrained estimates and test statistics associated with the reduced-form, at least, if empirical confirmation of the underlying economic postulates is the goal aimed at. Whenever the unconstrained reduced-form statistics are judged to be in good agreement with the propositions (theorems) deduced from the underlying economic postulates, then do the structural estimates emerge as sound and convenient summaries of that part of the sample statistical information which is relevant to the numerical values of structural parameters, but generally not otherwise."

these models have not been tested as interdependent units.[51] Monetarists, on the other hand, have not offered structural models to go along with their reduced-form results.[52] Such a turn toward hypothesis testing could lead toward a resolution of the issues in the crowding-out controversy. Although the controversy has been explored in this article primarily on a theoretical level, the implications of these issues for practical matters of stabilization policy are of great significance.

Appendix

For purposes of definition consider Figure 7, Panel (A) which is a representation of the market for total output of goods and services. The intersection of aggregate supply (AS_0) and demand (AD_0) determine the equilibrium level of output, X_0, and the price, P_0, at which it will be sold. Label this intersection as point A and interpret it as an initial equilibrium. Now, introduce an expansionary fiscal action like increased government demand for goods and services financed by sales of government debt to the public.

Assume that the net effect of increased government demand and the issuance of debt is an increased demand for goods and services, as indicated by the shift of the demand curve to AD_1. Further, suppose that the expanded government sector adversely affects efficiency and productive capacity, resulting in a shift of the supply curve to AS_1. If the new equilibrium occurs anywhere on the vertical line through point A, say at point B, we say that *real* crowding out has occurred, that is, increased real government demand has been completely offset by a decline in real private demand.

Consider now Panel (B) in Figure 7. The curved line drawn through point A is a rectangular hyperbola indicating that P times X, which is defined as the nominal value of total output (that is, GNP), is constant and equal to $P_0 X_0$. In other words, there is an infinite number of combinations of P and X, besides P_0 and X_0, which would give the same dollar value of total output as at point A. Suppose that in response to an expansionary fiscal action, aggregate demand and aggregate supply shift in various directions (depending on the assumptions made) and the new equilibrium settles on the curved line, say at point B or C. Under these conditions, *nominal* crowding out is said to occur. That is, an increase in government spending has been offset by a decline in the dollar amount of spending by the private sector.

This distinction between nominal and real crowding out is important because clearly one does not imply the other. This is shown in Panel (C), which combines the

[51]See Keith M. Carlson, "Monetary and Fiscal Actions in Macroeconomic Models," this *Review* (January 1974), pp. 8–18. A suggested testing of models as interdependent units requires that the model be specified in structural form but that the testing of the model focuses on the reduced form. For further discussion of this approach, see James L. Murphy, *Introductory Econometrics* (Homewood, Ill.: Richard D. Irwin, Inc., 1974).

[52]For recent efforts in this direction, however, see Leonall C. Andersen, "A Monetary Model of Nominal Income Determination," this *Review* (June 1975), pp. 9–19.

definitions of real and nominal crowding out from Panels (A) and (B). The lines are not demand and supply curves; they are the loci of points defining real and nominal crowding out.

Note that the lines are now drawn as the midpoint of a shaded band. This is done to reflect the crowding-out hypothesis, that is, an increase in government demand, not supported by monetary expansion, results in a steady-state income multiplier of *approximately* zero. The middle of these bands represents those points at which $1 of government demand crowds out exactly $1 of private demand. The shading to the right of either line describes that area in which partial crowding out (a multiplier between 0 and $+1$) occurs; the shading to the left of either line describes that area in

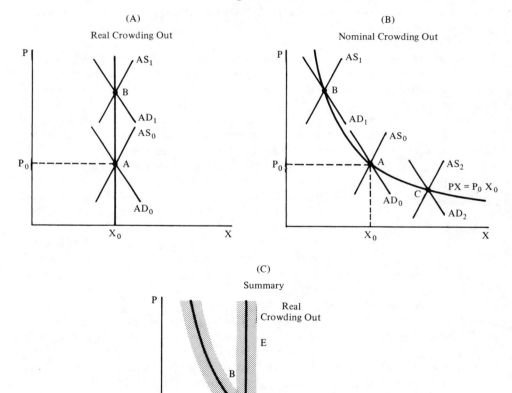

FIGURE 7.

which over crowding out (a multiplier between 0 and -1) occurs. Of course, it is possible that $1 of government spending might crowd out more than $2 of private spending, resulting in a multiplier of less than -1 and an equilibrium point to the left of either of the bands.

Various combinations of real and nominal crowding out are possible, given an expansionary fiscal action. For example, at point A there is partial nominal and partial real crowding out. At point B there is partial nominal, but over real, crowding out and so on around the intersection of the two bands through point D. At some point outside this area such as point E, there is partial real crowding out, but a complete absence of any sort of nominal crowding out. It is clear that a complete analysis of the fiscal process requires an assessment of both the demand and supply factors involved in order to describe accurately the extent to which nominal and real crowding out might occur.

The Phillips Curve, Rational Expectations, and Stabilization Policy

In recent years no area of monetary theory has received as much attention as the rational expectations hypothesis. The seminal research in this area was done by Thomas Sargent and Neil Wallace and by Robert Lucas. (These seminal articles and other important sources are included in several of the bibliographies in the selections that follow.) The rational expectations hypothesis simply conjectures that individual economic agents (households, labor suppliers, etc.) will exploit *all* pertinent information when making forecasts, including price and wage forecasts. Of itself, this argument hardly seems earth-shaking, but when included in certain macroeconomic models it has powerful implications.

These implications are most forcefully apparent in the case of the expectations-augmented Phillips curve. The first article in this section is Thomas M. Humphrey's analysis of the accelerationist views (often identified with the Monetarists) and the nonaccelerationist views (often identified with the Keynesians) of the notion that lower unemployment can be attained if added price inflation is acceptable. Humphrey shows that such a tradeoff is plausible if and only if inflation is not completely anticipated and that inflation will not be completely anticipated as long as expectations are based solely on historical experience. In the second article in this section, Humphrey labels the latter the adaptive expectations view and juxtaposes it to a rational expectations view, in which the public will utilize all sources of information, including the behavior of the policymaker, in order to better anticipate inflation. Under the rational expectations view, only "surprise" stabilization policy actions can generate unanticipated inflation and hence a reduction in unemployment; otherwise government "stabilization" policy can have no effect on employment and production and is not needed.

The real world implications of disagreement over the nature of the inflation-unemployment (Phillips curve) tradeoff are forcefully driven home in the third selection in this section, by Keith M. Carlson. Carlson brilliantly shows how the policy program and predictions of the 1978 Council of Economic Advisers seems to have been predicated on a belief in a negative tradeoff between inflation and unemployment. Carlson contrasts this program and its predictions with those that would be generated by a rational expectations view of the Phillips curve, which he calls "the monetary view." After reading this article, one can more easily understand monetarist consternation with: (1) the pronouncements of Keynesians regarding "the great sacrifice of unemployment required to root out inflation," (2) use of Phillips curve–type models to make projections of nominal income upon which monetary aggregate target growth rates are based (as described in the essay by Lombra and Torto in Section VIII), and (3) the lack of concern among Keynesians when growth rates of the monetary aggregates exceed those targets (often because of concern for sustaining lower nominal rates of interest, as indicated by the readings by Davis, Pierce, and Lombra and Torto in Section VIII).

In the final selection in this section, Franco Modigliani makes a case against the monetarist rational expectations assertion that stabilization policy is not needed. He argues that, in the last decade, the most serious shocks to employment and production have not been surprise stabilization policy actions but rather supply shocks, such as the Arab oil embargo. He suggests that an active stabilization policy should be used to compensate for such supply shocks.

The appropriateness of the policymaker's response to actual and potential "shocks" to the economy is fundamentally a political problem. If, out of political necessity, strong macroeconomic policy responses are made to fairly weak shocks, then the policy "cure" may be worse than the shock "affliction." The readings in Section X explore further some of the aspects of this issue—the fundamentally political nature of monetary policy.

Changing Views of the Phillips Curve*

Thomas M. Humphrey

9

One of the more fashionable tools of contemporary macroeconomic analysis is the so-called "Phillips curve," named after its originator, British economist A. W. Phillips. An empirical relation between the rate of wage-price change and the rate of unemployment, the Phillips curve purportedly shows the set of inflation-unemployment "trade-offs," or feasible policy choices, available to the economic stabilization authorities. First introduced in 1958, the Phillips curve gained swift acceptance by economists who used it to analyze the persistent problems plaguing economic policy-makers attempting to achieve simultaneously society's apparently conflicting goals of high employment and stable prices.

Over the past fifteen years the Phillips curve has played a prominent role in policy discussion and formulation. For example, Phillips curve analysis provided a rationale for the incomes (wage-price) and labor-market (manpower) policies implemented during the past decade. The recent Phase I and II programs, as well as the earlier wage-price guidepost, job-training, and retraining programs, were designed within a framework that can be described in terms of the Phillips curve.

. . . The rapid penetration and assimilation of early Phillips curve analysis in the non-technical economic literature has been matched by equally rapid recent shifts in

Reprinted with deletions from the Federal Reserve Bank of Richmond, *Monthly Review* (July, 1973), pp. 2–13, by permission of the publisher and the author.

* *Editor's Note:* This selection can most profitably be read in conjunction with its companion piece, reading 10.

economists' understanding and interpretation of the Phillips curve. Initially, the Phillips curve was interpreted as a simple, stable, and permanent empirical relationship between wage-price changes and unemployment. Subsequent research and experience, however, have revealed that the relation was neither as simple nor as stable as originally thought. Instead of a unique, invariant relation, economists have found a variety of shifting short-run Phillips curves, each corresponding to different underlying conditions and expectations in the labor and product markets. Economists now acknowledge the importance of a host of other variables ("shift parameters") influencing the position of the Phillips curve. Changes in these shift parameters have rendered the curve quite unstable.

The findings of the short-run instability of the inflation-unemployment trade-off have served to provoke a lively controversy over the usefulness and validity of the Phillips curve concept. Some economists have even gone so far as to deny the existence of a permanent trade-off between inflation and unemployment. Other economists, however, contend that a long-run trade-off exists and that, given a more sophisticated interpretation, the Phillips curve remains a valid and useful concept. Consequently, much ingenuity and a large proportion of recent research in the field of macroeconomics have been devoted to establishing theoretical and empirical support for a reformulated Phillips curve that may have relevancy in long-run economic analysis.

. . . This article traces, with the aid of a sequence of charts, the development of the Phillips curve concept from its origins in 1958 to its current interpretation in policy analysis.

The Original Phillips Curve (Chart 1)

The first Phillips curve appeared in a 1958 study investigating the influence of the rate of unemployment (taken as an index of the degree of excess demand or "labor shortage" in the labor market) on the rate of change of wages. In that study, Professor A. W. Phillips of the London School of Economics fitted an empirical curve to a statistical scatter diagram of time series data for annual percentage rates of money wage changes (w) and unemployment (u) for the British economy over the interval 1861–1913. The resulting curve was downward-sloping, indicating an inverse relation between the two variables. Thus, Phillips' data showed that in years when the labor market was tight and unemployment low, money wages tended to rise at a rapid clip. But when the labor market was slack and unemployment high, wage changes tended to be very slight.

The chief novelty of the Phillips curve, however, was its apparent demonstration that inflation could coexist with unemployment. This finding had important policy implications. In the 1940's and 1950's, the policymakers' mission was viewed as one of achieving full employment without inflation. Price stability and full employment would indeed be attainable, compatible goals if inflation and unemployment were

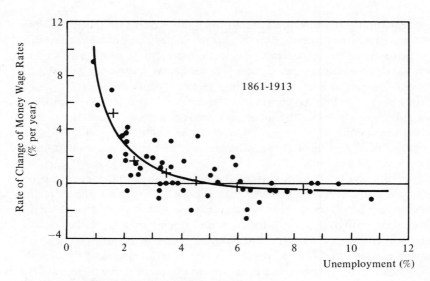

CHART 1   THE ORIGINAL PHILLIPS CURVE.

Source: A. W. Phillips. "The Relation Between Unemployment and the Rate of Change of Money Wage Rates in the United Kingdom, 1861-1957," *Economica,* 25, No. 100 (November 1958) 285.

mutually exclusive phenomena. In this ideal case one could eradicate unemployment without generating inflation. According to the Phillips curve, however, wage-price increases in the United Kingdom actually would start to occur long before absolute full employment was reached. Wages would begin to rise at an unemployment rate of just under 5½ percent, the point at which the Phillips curve crossed the horizontal axis. And to the left of this intersection, progressively lower rates of unemployment would provoke faster wage inflation. The policy implications were unmistakable: it would be impossible for the authorities to hit the twin targets of zero inflation and full capacity. Price stability and full employment were incompatible, conflicting goals. More of one objective could be obtained only at the cost of less of the other, but it would be impossible to attain both. Thus, the hope of simultaneous achievement of stable prices and full employment gave way to the notion of trade-offs between these goals.

Demand-Pull and Cost-Push Cases
(Chart 2)

Phillips himself contended that wages tend to be pulled up by rising demand. As numerous economists have since pointed out, however, the rising segment of the Phillips curve is consistent with the operation of supply-oriented cost-push, as well as demand-pull, forces. In conditions of excess demand for labor, money wages can be advanced by sellers, forced up by frictional or structural impediments ("bottle-necks") to labor mobility, and bid up by buyers. More generally, wage escalation is now viewed as partly stemming from a variety of market imperfections including labor-capital immobilities, job-information deficiencies, and employer-union monopoly power. Because of these imperfections or rigidities on the supply side, rising

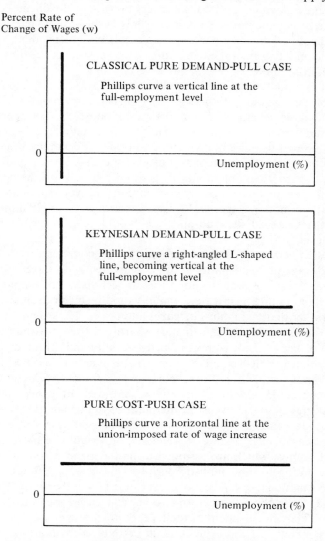

CHART 2 PHILLIPS CURVES FOR CRUDE DEMAND-PULL AND COST-PUSH CASES.

demand can exert upward pressure on wages even when sizable numbers of workers are still unemployed.

Although both cost-push and demand-pull elements can be used to explain the rising portion of the Phillips schedule, there is more to the Phillips curve interpretation of inflation than just simple demand-pull and cost-push conceptions. The essence of the Phillips curve approach is that it expresses an interdependent *relationship* between unemployment and wage changes that yields the dilemma of conflicting policy goals: less unemployment is attainable only at the cost of faster wage inflation. By contrast, these variables were treated as completely independent, unrelated, and therefore non-conflicting in crude demand-pull and cost-push theories that predated the Phillips interpretation.

Prior to Phillips' analysis, the chief explanations of wage-level determination were two versions of the demand-pull theory. The *Classical* version of this theory assumed that full employment would be maintained continuously by the operation of complete and instantaneous wage-price flexibility. Production and labor utilization would always be tied to full employment, and prices and money wages would float with the level of aggregate demand. In this extreme Classical case, the only magnitudes that could vary would be money wages and prices. With the economy always at full capacity, any increases or decreases in demand would be matched solely by rises or declines in money wages and prices. Consequently, the Phillips curve corresponding to the Classical demand-pull case would be a vertical line at the full-employment level.

The *Keynesian* version of the demand-pull theory combined the Classical postulate of upward wage-price flexibility at full employment with the assumption of rigid downward inflexibility of wages and prices at less than full employment. In the Keynesian system, falling aggregate demand would result in declines in output and employment rather than reductions in wages and prices. Thus, as shown by the right-angled Phillips curve, one could distinguish sharply between two mutually exclusive situations: (1) unemployment with wage-price stability and (2) full employment with inflation. No policy conflicts could develop in the Keynesian case because wage-price increases could not occur before full employment was reached. Consequently, macroeconomic policy could eliminate unemployment without provoking inflation by maintaining aggregate demand just at the point of full capacity.

At the opposite extreme of the Classical demand-pull case was the hypothetical pure cost-push case. Here the rate of wage inflation would be determined solely by union wage demands, which are assumed to be independent of the level of unemployment. According to the simplistic pure cost-push theory, unions would adhere tenaciously to inflationary wage claims regardless of whether the labor market was brisk or slack. As in the Classical and Keynesian cases, the rate of wage change would be completely independent of the level of unemployment. Again, there would be no policy conflicts: unemployment could be reduced without causing additional inflation. The Phillips curve in this case would be a horizontal line at the union-determined rate of wage increase.

Derivation of the Inflation-Unemployment Trade-Off Via Conversion from Wages to Prices (Chart 3)

The original Phillips curve related unemployment to wage changes. Other economists, however, soon transformed the wage-unemployment relation into a price-unemployment relation by assuming that the rate of change of prices (p) was simply the difference between the rate of change of wages (w) and the constant trend rate of increase of man-hour productivity (q), i.e., $p = w - q$. On the Phillips chart this

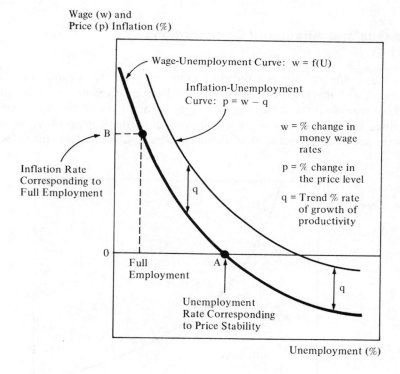

CHART 3 DERIVATION OF THE INFLATION-UNEMPLOYMENT TRADE-OFF VIA CONVERSION FROM WAGES TO PRICES. The inflation-unemployment curve (heavy line) is derived from the wage-unemployment curve by subtracting the trend rate of growth of productivity (q) from the latter. Note that point A shows the unemployment rate at which prices would be stable, while point B shows the rate of price inflation corresponding to full employment.

conversion was accomplished via a vertical downward shift of the schedule in such a way that the new price-unemployment curve was located q percentage points below the old wage-unemployment curve.

The transformed Phillips curve, it was thought, would be more useful to the policymakers since policy goals tend to be specified in terms of target rates of change of prices rather than of wages. From the inflation-unemployment curve, the authorities could determine how much unemployment would be associated with any given target rate of inflation and vice versa. For example, the curve would permit the policymakers to calculate both the rate of unemployment required to achieve complete price stability (point A) and the rate of inflation that would have to be tolerated as the price for maintaining a specified full-employment target (point B).

Trade-Offs and Attainable Combinations (Chart 4)

Phillips curve analysis stresses the distinction between the *location* (i.e., distance from origin) and the *slope* of the curve. The location fixes the inner boundary, or frontier, of feasible (attainable) combinations of inflation and unemployment rates. Determined by the structure of labor and product markets, the position of the curve defines the set of all coordinates of inflation rates and unemployment rates the au-

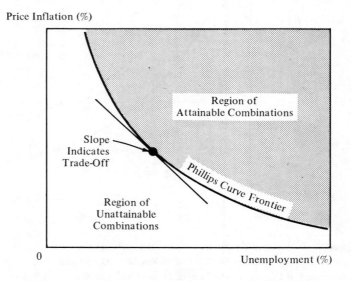

CHART 4 TRADE-OFFS AND ATTAINABLE COMBINATIONS.
The location of the curve fixes the inner boundary of attainable combinations. The slope of the curve shows the trade-offs or rates of exchange between policy goals.

thorities could achieve via implementation of monetary and fiscal policies. Using these macroeconomic policies, the authorities could put the economy anywhere on or to the right of the curve. But, according to the Phillips curve analysis of the early 1960's, the authorities would reject all combinations to the right of the curve because superior positions involving less unemployment and/or inflation would be available on the curve. Moreover, whereas the policymakers *would not* operate to the right of the curve, they *could not* operate to the left of it. The Phillips curve could be viewed as a constraint preventing the authorities from achieving still lower levels of both inflation and unemployment. Given the structure of labor and product markets, it would be impossible for monetary-fiscal policy alone to reach combinations in the region to the left of the curve.

The *slope* of the curve was thought to be of critical importance since it shows the relevant policy trade-offs (rates of exchange between policy goals) available to the authorities. As explained by early advocates of the Phillips curve approach to policy problems, these trade-offs arise because of the existence of irreconcilable conflicts among policy objectives. When the goals of full employment and price stability are not simultaneously achievable, then attempts to move the economy closer to one will necessarily move it further away from the other. The rate at which one objective must be given up to obtain a little bit more of the other is measured by the slope of the Phillips curve. For example, when the Phillips curve is steeply sloped, it means that a small reduction in unemployment would be purchased at the cost of a large increase in the rate of inflation. Conversely, when the curve is flat, considerably lower unemployment could be obtained at a relatively cheap sacrifice of inflation objectives. Knowledge of these trade-offs would enable the authorities to determine the price-stability sacrifice necessary to buy any given reduction in the unemployment rate.

The Best Selection on the Phillips Frontier (Chart 5)

In the 1960's it was frequently said that the Phillips curve offered policymakers a menu of feasible policy choices between the two evils, unemployment and inflation. If so, the policymakers had to select from the menu the particular inflation-unemployment mix resulting in the smallest social cost. To do this, they would have to assign relative weights to the twin evils in accordance with society's views of the comparative harm caused by each. Then the authorities could move along the Phillips curve, trading off unemployment for inflation (or vice versa) until they arrived at the optimum, or least undesirable, combination. At this point on the Phillips constraint, they would have reached the lowest attainable social disutility contour (shown as the convex or bowed-out curves radiating outward from the origin of Chart 5). Here the unemployment-inflation combination chosen would be the one that minimized social harm.

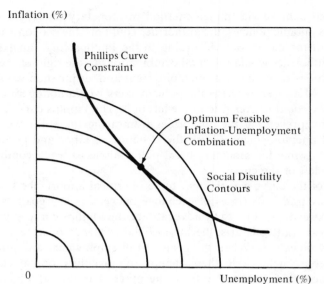

Inflation (%)

CHART 5 THE BEST SELECTION ON THE MENU OF CHOICES. The bowed-out curves are social disutility contours. Each contour shows all the combinations of inflation and unemployment resulting in a given level of social disutility. The closer to the origin the lower will be the level of disutility. The slopes of these contours reflect the relative weights that society (or the policymakers) assigns to the evils of inflation and unemployment. The best combination of inflation and unemployment that the policymakers can reach, given the Phillips curve constraint, is the mix appearing on the lowest attainable social disutility contour.

Different Preferences, Different Outcomes (Chart 6)

It was recognized, of course, that policymakers would differ in their assessment of the comparative social disutility of inflation vs. unemployment. Thus, different policymakers might assign different weights to the two evils depending on their evaluation of the relative harmfulness of each. Policymakers who considered joblessness to be more undesirable than rising prices would assign a much higher relative weight to the former than would policymakers who judged inflation to be the worse evil. Hence, those with a marked aversion to unemployment would prefer a point much higher up on the Phillips curve than would those more anxious to avoid inflation, as shown in Chart 6. Whereas one administration might try to run a high-pressure economy because it thought the social benefits of low unemployment exceeded the harm done

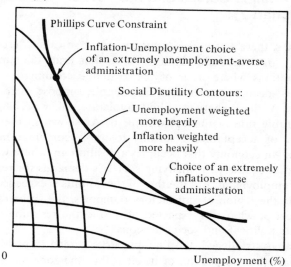

Inflation (%)

Phillips Curve Constraint

Inflation-Unemployment choice
of an extremely unemployment-averse
administration

Social Disutility Contours:

Unemployment weighted
more heavily

Inflation weighted
more heavily

Choice of an extremely
inflation-averse
administration

0   Unemployment (%)

**CHART 6 DIFFERENT PREFERENCES, DIFFERENT POL-
ICY CHOICES.** Successive political administrations may differ
in their evaluations of the social harmfulness of inflation relative to that of unemployment. Thus, in their policy deliberations they will attach different relative weights to the two evils
of inflation and unemployment. These weights will be reflected in the slopes of the social disutility contours (as those
contours are interpreted by the policymakers). The flat contours reflect the views of those attaching higher relative
weight to the evils of inflation; the steep contours to those
assigning higher weight to unemployment. The unemployment-averse administration will choose a point on the Phillips
curve involving more inflation and less unemployment than
would the combination selected by the inflation-averse administration.

by inflation, another administration might deliberately shoot for a low-pressure economy because it believed that some economic slack was a relatively painless means of
eradicating harmful inflation. Both groups of policymakers of course would prefer
combinations to the southwest of the Phillips constraint, down closer to the diagram's origin (the ideal point of zero inflation and zero unemployment). But this
would be impossible, however, given the structure of the economy, which determines
the position or location of the Phillips frontier. Thus, as previously mentioned, the
policymakers would be constrained to combinations lying on (or to the right of) this
boundary, unless they were prepared to alter the economy's structure.

Pessimistic Phillips Curves and the "Cruel Dilemma" (Chart 7)

In the mid-1960's, there was much discussion of the so-called "cruel-dilemma" problem imposed by an unfavorable Phillips curve. The cruel dilemma refers to certain pessimistic situations where *none* of the available combinations on the menu of policy choices is socially acceptable. For example, suppose there is some maximum rate of inflation, A, that society is willing to tolerate. Likewise, suppose there is some maximum tolerable rate of unemployment, B. As shown in the chart, these limits define the zone of acceptable or socially tolerable combinations of inflation and unemployment. An economy that occupies a position anywhere within this zone will have performed adequately in satisfying society's demands for reasonable price stability and high employment. But if either of these limits is exceeded and the economy ends up outside the region of satisfactory outcomes, the system's performance will have fallen short of what was expected of it, and the resulting discontent may severely aggravate political and social tensions.

If, as some analysts alleged, the Phillips curve tended to be located so far to the right in the chart that no portion of it fell within the zone of acceptable combina-

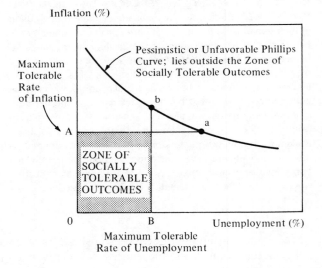

CHART 7 PESSIMISTIC PHILLIPS CURVE AND THE "CRUEL DILEMMA". Given the unfavorable Phillips curve, policymakers are confronted with a cruel choice. They can achieve acceptable rates of inflation (point a) or unemployment (point b) but not both. The rationale for the wage-price guideposts and manpower policies, implemented in the 1960's, was to shift the Phillips curve down into the zone of acceptable outcomes.

tions, then the policymakers would indeed be confronted with a painful dilemma. At best they could hold *either* inflation or unemployment down to acceptable levels. But they could not hold both simultaneously within the limits of toleration. Faced with such a pessimistic Phillips curve, policymakers would find it impossible to achieve combinations of inflation and unemployment acceptable to society.

It was this concern and frustration over the seeming inability of monetary-fiscal policy to resolve the unemployment-inflation dilemma that induced some economists in the 1960's to urge the adoption of incomes (wage-price) and labor-market (man-power) policies. Monetary-fiscal policies alone were thought to be insufficient to resolve the cruel dilemma. The most these policies could do, it was feared, was enable the economy to occupy alternative positions on the pessimistic Phillips curve. That is, monetary-fiscal policies could move the economy *along* the given curve, but they could not move the curve itself into the zone of tolerable outcomes. What was needed, it was argued, were new policies that would shift the Phillips frontier toward the origin of the diagram. Thus, the rationale for such measures as wage-price guide-posts, job-training, and retraining programs was to shift the Phillips frontier down into the zone of toleration so that the economy could choose more socially acceptable inflation-unemployment combinations.

Doubts about the Phillips Curve

Up until the late 1960's, the Phillips curve had received widespread and largely uncritical acceptance. Despite a lack of convincing statistical evidence of a significant inverse inflation-unemployment relation for the United States, few questioned the usefulness, let alone the existence, of this construct. In policy discussion as well as economic textbooks, the Phillips schedule was treated as a unique, consistent, and stable relation. In fact, so influential was this concept of a unique and stable trade-off, that it was instrumental in shaping several basic tenets of economic stabilization policy in the 1960's including (1) the idea that permanently lower unemployment could be preserved at the price of some constant rate of inflation and (2) the notion that guidepost and/or manpower policies should be used to shift the Phillips curve down and to the left.

In the late 1960's, however, doubts about the Phillips curve began to develop. Contributing to the mounting skepticism were two major factors. The first of these was the inflationary experience in the closing years of the decade, when events consistently went counter to the predictions of the conventional trade-off view. According to the standard Phillips curve analysis of the 1960's, one would expect rising rates of inflation to be accompanied by falling unemployment; or, conversely, one should expect to observe an unchanged rate of unemployment maintained at a constant rate of inflation. Neither of these things happened, however. Instead, the record for 1967-1969 shows that although inflation accelerated sharply, the unemployment rate remained unchanged. Far from purchasing lower unemployment, escalating inflation evidently was required just to keep the unemployment rate fixed in place. In short,

Phillips curve forecasts parted company with experience. And the forecasting errors were even worse in 1970 when *both* inflation and unemployment increased.

A second source of skepticism was the steady accumulation of statistical findings that indicated that the Phillips relation might not be as stable or as consistent as was commonly believed. In numerous empirical studies conducted during the 1960's, Phillips curves had been statistically fitted to inflation-unemployment data for the United States. These efforts, however, had not been entirely successful. The trouble was that there was usually a large degree of dispersion, or variance, of the actual inflation-unemployment observations about the fitted Phillips curves. In other words, the simple, two-variable Phillips relationship was shown to be very loose and inexact. Additional variables—including, among others, corporate profits, the rate of change of unemployment, lagged changes in the cost of living, indexes of the dispersion of unemployment across separate labor markets, trade union membership, vacancy rates—had to be introduced to explain this variance and improve the statistical fit. Unfortunately, these studies proved that numerous, different Phillips curves could be fitted to the same set of inflation-unemployment observations, depending on which specific additional variables were used in the curve-fitting procedure. This discovery, of course, made it difficult to determine which, if any, was *the* true Phillips curve.

These findings ultimately led an increasing number of economists to question the consistency, uniqueness, and stability of short-run Phillips curves. Apparently, there was not one Phillips curve but rather numerous families of short-run Phillips curves corresponding to the host of other variables (shift parameters) influencing the infla-tion-unemployment relation. Because of these influences, a given observed short-run Phillips curve did not stand still but, instead, shifted over time as the values of the other variables changed. But which of these underlying variables exercised the domi-nant influence? In his 1967 Presidential address to the American Economic Associ-ation, Milton Friedman suggested the answer: inflation expectations. He argued that expectation-induced shifts in the Phillips curve would, in every case, render trade-off policy ineffective. Thus, in the hands of Friedman and others, the expectations hy-pothesis emerged as the main challenge to the validity of the Phillips curve. By the late 1960's many other observers also had begun to suspect that price expectations might be the most important factor causing the short-run Phillips curve to shift.

Accelerationists, the Expectations Hypothesis, and the Vertical Phillips Curve (Chart 8)

In its most extreme version, the expectations hypothesis denies the existence of a permanent trade-off between inflation and unemployment and asserts the accelera-tionist view that policymakers' attempts to preserve low unemployment will provoke explosive, ever-accelerating inflation. Led by Milton Friedman of the University of Chicago and Edmund Phelps of the University of Pennsylvania, accelerationists ar-gue that in the long run the Phillips curve is a vertical line at the natural rate of

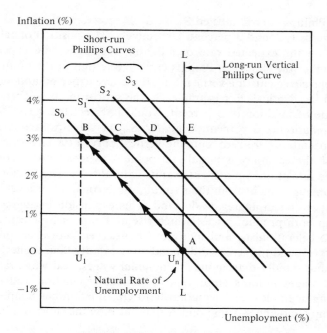

CHART 8 THE EXPECTATIONS HYPOTHESIS AND THE VERTICAL PHILLIPS CURVE. Attempts to lower unemployment from the natural rate, U_n, to U_1 via movement along short-run trade-off curve S_0 will evoke wage bargaining and other adaptations to inflationary expectations. The economy will travel the path ABCDE to the new equilibrium, point E, where unemployment is the same but inflation is higher than it was originally.

unemployment, i.e., the rate of unemployment at which the rate of change of prices is steady (neither accelerating nor decelerating) and *real* wages are in equilibrium (money wages having been fully adjusted to allow for correctly-anticipated inflation).

Accelerationists, of course, do not deny the existence of short-run trade-offs. But they think those trade-offs are transitory phenomena that arise from *unexpected* inflation and vanish as soon as expectations adapt to inflationary experience. Accordingly, accelerationists argue that movements along a short-run Phillips curve would alter expectations, thereby inducing *shifts* in the schedule in the direction of the vertical zero-trade-off line.

The sequence envisioned by accelerationists can be illuminated with the aid of Chart 8. On the chart is shown the vertical long-run Phillips curve (labeled L) passing through the natural rate of unemployment. The natural rate of unemployment is that particular rate of unemployment at which expected inflation equals actual inflation and where the real wage rate is at its equilibrium level. Also shown on the chart are four short-run Phillips curves, labeled S_0, S_1, S_2, S_3, corresponding to expected rates of inflation of zero, 1, 2, and 3 percent, respectively. The position of each short-run curve depends on the expected rate of inflation; the higher the expected rate of inflation, the higher the short-run Phillips curve. Note that at the point where each short-run Phillips curve cuts the vertical long-run curve expected and actual rates of inflation would be identical. For example, S_3, the short-run curve corresponding to an expected rate of inflation of 3 percent, would intersect the vertical curve at an actual rate of inflation of 3 percent. Similarly, S_0, the short-run curve along which inflationary expectations are zero, cuts the vertical curve at a zero rate of inflation.

Now suppose the economy is initially at point A, where there is complete price stability and the rate of unemployment is at its natural level. The authorities, intending to reduce unemployment from the natural rate to some lower level like U_1, then engineer an expansion in aggregate demand. This expansion in aggregate demand initially bids up both product prices (which rise at a rate of 3 percent) and wages. According to accelerationists, and many other observers, however, product prices initially tend to respond to increased demand more rapidly than money wages. With prices rising more rapidly than money or nominal wages, real wage rates fall.[1] The decline in real wages induces employers to expand production and employment, thereby lowering unemployment temporarily to U_1. Inflation has temporarily stimulated the economy, moving it from point A to point B on the short-run Phillips curve, S_0.

In the accelerationist model, however, such an inflationary stimulus would be short-lived. The stimulus will start to weaken almost immediately as price expectations are revised in light of actual inflationary experience. At first workers were fooled by the 3 percent inflation; they did not anticipate that rising prices would erode their real wages. But workers cannot be fooled for long. Over time, as inflation persists at the 3 percent rate, workers learn to adjust their expectations to the actual rate of inflation and to incorporate these price anticipations in their wage bargains. Thus, as the gap between anticipated and actual inflation narrows, so too does the discrepancy between the rates of increase of prices and money wages. Money wage increases begin to catch up with price increases, thereby tending to lift the real wage rate back to its pre-inflation level. This rise in the real wage induces employers to cut back employment, thus reversing the initial downward movement of unemployment. As the unemployment rate rises back to its original natural level, the economy moves along the path BCDE to long-run equilibrium. In the long run, (1) price changes will be fully anticipated, i.e., the 3 percent expected rate of inflation will equal the actual rate of inflation; (2) the expected rate of inflation will be completely incorporated in wage demands, i.e., money wages will be rising at the same rate as prices; (3) the original real wage will be reestablished and the old natural rate of unemployment restored; but (4) the steady-state rates of wage and price inflation will be higher than originally.

---

[1]For simplicity, productivity growth is assumed to be zero in this example. Thus the percentage change in real wage rates is just the difference between the percentage changes in nominal wages (w) and the price level (p), that is, $w - p$.

Policy Implications of the Accelerationist View (Chart 9)

Several important policy implications arise from the accelerationist analysis. The first is that attempts to hold unemployment below the natural rate will result in explosive, ever-accelerating inflation. Maintenance of unemployment at some target level U_1 (Chart 9) requires that real wage rates be kept low enough to induce employers to add sufficient numbers of jobseekers to their work forces. But the required permanent reduction in real wage rates can be achieved only if rising prices continually outstrip money wage increases. Since past rates of price increase (a proxy for expected inflation) tend to feed back into current money wage increases, however, the rate of price increase must be ever escalating to stay a step ahead of money wage increases. Alternatively stated, actual inflation must be kept running continually ahead of expected inflation, which workers incorporate in their wage demands. But since expected inflation is always rising in an attempt to catch up with actual inflation, the latter must be continually accelerated, from P_1 to P_2 to P_3, etc., in order to keep the gap open and continually frustrate workers' attempts to close it.

A second policy implication is that a stable rate of inflation purchases little in the way of lower unemployment. Since any steady rate of inflation would eventually be

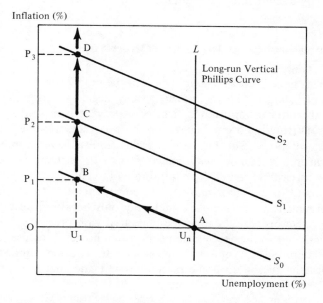

CHART 9 THE ACCELERATIONIST HYPOTHESIS. Attempts to maintain unemployment at some lower than natural rate, u_1, will provoke explosive, ever-accelerating inflation. The economy will travel the path ABCD with the rate of inflation rising from P_1 to P_2 to P_3, etc.

fully anticipated, inflation could have no lasting impact on unemployment. This conclusion is in direct conflict with the Phillips trade-off view that a permanently low rate of unemployment could be achieved at the price of some constant rate of inflation. Accelerationists claim that the trade-off view offers a treacherous guide to policy. For if the policymakers follow it, they will find that in the long run, they will have institutionalized inflation without permanently lowering unemployment.

A third policy implication is that since the natural rate of unemployment is consistent with *any* stable rate of inflation, the best thing the policymakers could do would be to choose the zero rate of inflation. But this means that the authorities should never try to reduce unemployment below the natural rate, since attempts to do so inevitably lead, via shifting expectations, to positive steady-state rates of inflation.

Finally, accelerationists also argue that the best path the economy can take in returning to its long-run, natural rate equilibrium is the path that leads to the zero rate of inflation. Since an economy in disequilibrium can return to equilibrium at *any* rate of steady, permanent inflation along the vertical Phillips curve, it might as well be the zero rate. Thus, accelerationists are willing to tolerate a deflationary policy that keeps unemployment high for as long as it takes to eliminate inflationary expectations and bring the economy to long-run equilibrium at the zero permanent rate of inflation. But they argue that inflationary expectations would vanish quickly, thereby necessitating only a short interval of high unemployment.[2]

The Non-Accelerationist Rebuttal (Chart 10)

Many economists have been unwilling to accept the policy conclusions flowing from the accelerationist model. They acknowledge that accelerationists have successfully demonstrated the crucial importance of price expectations in shifting the short-run Phillips curves. (Virtually no one believes in the existence of naive, stable short-run Phillips curves any more.) But they think accelerationists have adopted too extreme a position regarding price and employment policy. In particular, they dispute the accelerationists' interpretation of the natural rate of unemployment as corresponding to full employment in the labor market. Moreover, they point out that the natural rate of unemployment is a poor policy guide, not only because it results in too much joblessness, but also because it cannot be measured with precision.

The main challenge to the accelerationist position, however, focuses on the issue of the long-run Phillips curve. Anti-accelerationists point out that, contrary to the natural rate hypothesis, recent econometric studies indicate that a long-run trade-off

---

[2]When the economy is in the high-unemployment region to the right of the long-run vertical Phillips curve, actual inflation will always fall *below* anticipated inflation, thus inducing people to revise expectations downward. But how *fast* will these expectations be adjusted? Some accelerationists contend that the speed of adjustment is directly proportional to the discrepancy between expected and experienced inflation. Since this disparity tends to vary systematically with the rate of unemployment, high unemployment may be required for the swift dampening of inflationary expectations.

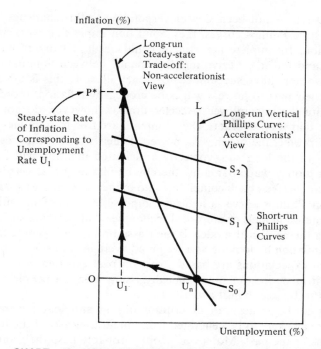

Inflation (%)

Long-run
Steady-state
Trade-off:
Non-accelerationist
View

P*

Steady-state Rate
of Inflation
Corresponding to
Unemployment
Rate U_1

L

Long-run Vertical
Phillips Curve:
Accelerationists'
View

S_2

S_1

Short-run
Phillips
Curves

O

U_1

U_n

S_0

Unemployment (%)

CHART 10 NON-ACCELERATIONIST VIEW OF LONG-RUN STEADY-STATE TRADE-OFF. Non-accelerationists argue that a downward sloping steady-state Phillips curve does exist to prevent ever-accelerating inflation. Hence, unemployment can be maintained permanently at U_1, yet inflation will never exceed its stable, steady-state rate p*

curve *does* exist. This curve, while steeper than short-run Phillips curves, is not completely vertical. Instead, it is negatively sloped, still providing trade-off opportunities for the policymakers.

These findings, if correct, would be extremely damaging to the accelerationist position. If a steady-state trade-off does exist, then permanent reductions in the level of unemployment will not require ever-accelerating inflation. Instead, for each level of unemployment, including *low* levels, there will be some stable, constant, permanently sustainable rate of inflation. Thus, when unemployment is lowered, inflation will start to climb and will continue to rise until it reaches the long-run, steady-state Phillips curve, at which point it stops rising. Chart 10 illustrates this case. As indicated in the chart, when unemployment is lowered from U_N to U_1, price expectations are set in motion, causing inflation to rise until it reaches its steady-state rate of p*. Thereafter, unemployment can be maintained permanently at U_1 without the rate of price increase exceeding p*.

Accelerationists have not been slow in responding to this challenge. Downward-sloping, steady-state Phillips curves, they point out, imply that workers never fully adjust to inflation. Incomplete adjustment could occur if workers have irrational *money illusion* and fail to perceive the discrepancy between nominal (money) and real wages. If workers have succumbed to money illusion, this is tantamount to a willingness on their part to let real wages be eroded by inflation in order to induce employers to hire the unemployed. Accelerationists, however, do not believe that workers behave that way. Workers, they contend, are free from money illusion and actively seek to *protect* the purchasing power of their wages from erosion by inflation. Therefore, in the long run, correctly anticipated inflation will be completely incorporated in money wage bargains, thereby maintaining real wages. And if expected price increases feed back completely into money wage increases, a downward-sloping long-run Phillips curve is logically impossible. Something must be wrong with the econometric models or empirical techniques that generate such curves. Perhaps the flaw in the empirical models is their assumption that people form expectations of future inflation by looking at a weighted average of past rates of inflation. If it were true that expectations are based solely on *past* experience and are adjusted with a lag, then in periods of monotonically rising inflation people would always expect inflation to be less than it actually is.

But this may not be an accurate description of how anticipations are formulated. Expectations are as likely to be generated from direct forecasts of the future as from mere projections of the past. Moreover, people probably base their anticipations at least as much on new information about a variety of current developments as on old data pertaining to past price changes only. Accelerationists contend that if the expectations formation process were correctly specified, then empirical models would not show systematic underestimation of inflation by workers.

Non-accelerationists acknowledge this latter shortcoming in their models, but they point out that accelerationists likewise have been unsuccessful in formulating satisfactory models of the formation of expectations. Moreover, Phillips curve advocates even concede that given sufficient time, e.g., several decades, steady inflation might conceivably cause the curve to become vertical. But they maintain that this very long run is of little practical importance. They still insist that over the policymakers' time horizon the trade-off does exist.[3] Finally, trade-off adherents argue that workers *are* willing to accept reductions in real wages if accomplished by inflation. Yet this does not necessarily signify irrational behavior or money illusion. Why? Because, it is claimed, workers care more about *relative* (comparative) real wages than about the absolute level of their wages. And inflation, which supposedly hits all wage earners alike, is a means of reducing absolute real wages without altering relative wage relationships. Debate on these issues continues, and the controversy over the existence of the long-run Phillips curve remains unresolved.

---

[3]Frequent disturbances, triggered by exogenous events, may prevent the economy from ever reaching long-run equilibrium. If so, then the intermediate-run Phillips curve may be most appropriate for policy purposes—and this curve could be negatively sloped.

Optimal Paths Off the Phillips Curve (Chart 11)

Even if long-run trade-offs do exist, however, there still remains the very real problem of what to do if the curve is unfavorable, i.e., if it falls outside the zone of socially acceptable inflation-unemployment combinations. Several possible strategies have been suggested to deal with this likely situation. The simplest calls for the policymakers to pick a point on the bad Phillips curve and then stay there. This strategy, however, would probably be rejected by most policymakers.

A better alternative, perhaps, would be for the policymakers to chart a course *off* the curve. Instead of choosing the best *point* on a bad long-run Phillips curve, the authorities can select the optimum *path* around the Phillips curve, deliberately abandoning the long-run equilibrium policy solution for a dynamic sequence of short-run disequilibrium positions.

For example, the authorities might opt for the vertical path lying completely to the left of the steady-state Phillips curve. This path corresponds to a policy decision to adhere to a low-unemployment target, fully accepting the accompanying risks of

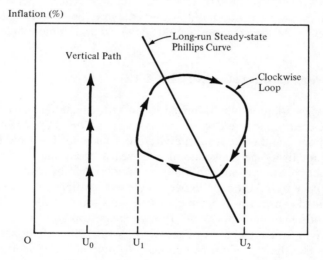

CHART 11 ALTERNATIVE DYNAMIC DISEQUILIBRIUM PATHS. Policymakers may elect to travel a path off the long-run Phillips curve instead of occupying a point on the curve. If they choose the vertical path at the left, they will hold unemployment at U_0 and hope that inflation will not accelerate too rapidly. If they choose the clockwise loop, they will be willing to let unemployment fluctuate within the range U_1 to U_2. Unemployment will be raised when inflationary expectations develop and lowered when they subside.

inflation. These risks, advocates argue, might not be as great as commonly believed. It all depends on how fast the path would unfold in the direction of higher inflation. If acceleration proved to be slow, then significant output and employment gains could be obtained before inflation began to approach socially intolerable levels. Moreover, future leftward shifts in the steady-state Phillips curve, owing to structural improvements in labor and product markets, might further reduce the danger of runaway inflation by lowering the ceiling toward which the path ultimately tends. Less sanguine observers, however, contend that the vertical path is too risky to be a practical alternative.

Another type of path the policymakers might consider takes the form of a dynamic loop or cycle around the steady-state curve. This type of path results when policy-makers permit fluctuations to occur in the economy. Instead of maintaining a con-tinually high-pressure economy with its attendant risks of accelerating inflation, the authorities would rely on periodic, controlled variations in economic activity and employment to contain inflation and keep expectations in check. Growth would be slowed and unemployment raised via contractive monetary-fiscal policy when infla-tionary expectations needed to be subdued. Later, with inflation quelled and price expectations dormant, fast growth could be resumed. After a period of slack the economy could move to a position of low unemployment with low inflation. Over the complete policy cycle the economy would move around dynamic clockwise loops.

Inflexible Price Expectations (Chart 12)

The stop-go policy solution would indeed be an attractive alternative if inflationary expectations tended to fade quickly in downswings and build up slowly in upswings. Then, contractions could be kept short and expansions long. The trouble is, however, that things do not always go that smoothly. As we learned in the late 1960's and early 1970's, inflationary expectations can build up rapidly, thereby leading to swift accel-eration in the pace of inflation. Moreover, these expectations may become so firmly entrenched and downwardly inflexible as to be resistant to all but the most pro-tracted sieges of severe unemployment. In such cases stop-go could become a night-mare of long, painful contractions punctuated by brief but inflationary expansions.

In situations like these it might be necessary to supplement monetary-fiscal policy with wage-price freezes, guideposts, and similar controls. The purpose of such con-trols is two-fold: first, to break and quickly dispel price expectations, thereby short-ening the period of slack needed for inflation to decline to acceptable levels; second, to stabilize (deactivate) inflationary expectations so that they will not intervene early to check a vigorous recovery.

The reversal and stabilization of inflationary expectations was a principal rationale for the wage-price controls imposed after mid-1971. In the preceding year, policy-makers had thought that the high inflation rates built up in the late 1960's could be brought down to acceptable levels via a temporary period of slack. By 1971, how-ever, inflation had declined only slightly even though unemployment had increased

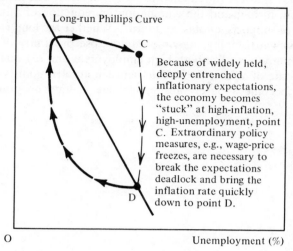

Inflation (%)

Long-run Phillips Curve

Because of widely held, deeply entrenched inflationary expectations, the economy becomes "stuck" at high-inflation, high-unemployment, point C. Extraordinary policy measures, e.g., wage-price freezes, are necessary to break the expectations deadlock and bring the inflation rate quickly down to point D.

O   Unemployment (%)

CHART 12 INFLEXIBLE PRICE EXPECTATIONS. If inflationary expectations are deeply entrenched and downwardly inflexible, inflation may be resistant to all but the most protracted sieges of severe unemployment. In such cases the economy may be trapped in a deadlock like point C, where both high inflation and high unemployment persist interminably. Here wage-price freezes and similar controls may be used to break up and dispel the inflationary expectations, thereby shortening the period of high unemployment needed for inflation to decline to acceptable levels like point D.

by almost a full percentage point to a level of roughly 6 percent. Moreover, computer forecasts were indicating that it might take as long as four or five years—with unemployment maintained at 6 percent—to bring the inflation rate down to acceptable levels. This contraction would have been too long. So the initial plan of de-escalating inflation via the unemployment route was scrapped, and wage-price controls were instituted.

The preceding discussion has described three alternative strategies for policymakers confronted with an unfavorable long-run trade-off: namely, (1) stay on the curve, (2) hold unemployment down and let inflation go, and (3) follow a path of controlled loops around the curve. None of these solutions, however, is ideal. Perhaps the best solution, most analysts agree, would be to engineer a leftward shift of the curve by adopting policies to improve the structure and performance of labor and product markets. A host of measures could be used to this end, including job-retraining programs; job-information and job-counseling services; vocational training and similar policies that would improve the coordination of labor force skill characteristics with the economy's skill requirements; provision of relocation subsidies; reduction of discrimination in hiring; and the elimination or reduction of minimum wage laws, agricultural price supports, quotas, and tariffs. Whether the long-run Phillips curve is vertical or downward-sloping, moving it into close proximity of the origin would enable the economy to realize both high employment and reasonable price stability. In this happy state of affairs, the debate between accelerationists and non-accelerationists would become a purely academic issue, having no practical importance.

Some Recent Developments in Phillips Curve Analysis

Thomas M. Humphrey

Economists' views of the Phillips curve concept have changed drastically in recent years. The original interpretation of the Phillips curve as a stable trade-off relationship between inflation and unemployment has given way to the view that no such trade-off exists for policymakers to exploit. As a result, some economists now argue that economic stabilization policies are incapable of influencing output and employment, even in the short-run.

Instrumental to this change were several key developments in Phillips curve analysis, most notably the so-called *natural rate* and *rational expectations* hypotheses. The purpose of this article is to explain these developments and their policy implications and to show how they altered economists' perceptions of the Phillips curve. Accordingly, the first half of the article traces the evolution of Phillips curve analysis focusing particularly on the natural rate hypothesis. The second half concentrates on the rational expectations idea, currently the most hotly-debated aspect of Phillips curve analysis.

Early Versions of the Phillips Curve

Phillips curve analysis has evolved through at least five major stages since its inception in 1958. The first stage involved the formulation of a simple, stable trade-off

Reprinted from *Economic Review,* January/February 1978, pp. 15–23, by permission of the Federal Reserve Bank of Richmond and the author.

relation between inflation and unemployment. The initial Phillips curve depicted a relationship between money wage changes and unemployment. But the assumption that product prices are set by applying a constant mark-up to unit labor costs permitted the Phillips relationship to be transformed into a price-change equation of the form[1]

$$p = ax \qquad (1)$$

where p is the percentage rate of price inflation, x is overall excess demand in labor and hence product markets—this excess demand being proxied by the inverse of the unemployment rate—and a is a coefficient expressing the numerical value of the trade-off between inflation and excess demand.

This equation expresses the early view of the Phillips curve as a stable, enduring trade-off permitting the authorities to obtain permanently lower rates of unemployment in exchange for permanently higher rates of inflation or vice versa. Put differently, the equation was popularly interpreted as offering a menu of alternative inflation-unemployment combinations from which the authorities could choose. Being stable, the menu never changed.

Economists soon discovered, however, that the menu was not as stable as originally thought and that the Phillips curve had a tendency to shift over time.[2] Accordingly, the equation was augmented with additional variables to account for such movements.

Introduction of Shift Variables

The addition of shift variables to the trade-off equation marked the second stage of Phillips curve analysis. The inclusion of these variables meant that the Phillips equation could now be written as

$$p = ax + z \qquad (2)$$

where z is a vector of variables—productivity, profits, trade union effects, unemployment dispersion and the like—capable of shifting the inflation-excess demand trade-off. Absent at this stage were variables representing price expectations. Although the past rate of price change was sometimes used as a shift variable, it was rarely interpreted as a proxy for anticipated inflation. Not until the late 1960s were expectational variables fully incorporated into Phillips curve equations. By then, of course, inflationary expectations had become too prominent to ignore and many analysts were perceiving them as the dominant cause of observed shifts in the Phillips curve.

---

[1]For simplicity, the additive constant term contained in most empirical Phillips curve equations is disregarded in Equation 1.

[2]Indeed, Phillips himself in his 1958 article had recognized the possibility of such shifts.

The Expectations-Augmented Phillips Curve and the Adaptive-Expectations Mechanism

Three innovations ushered in the next stage of Phillips curve analysis. The first was the respecification of the excess demand variable. Originally defined as the inverse of the unemployment rate, excess demand was redefined as the discrepancy between actual and normal capacity real output or, equivalently, as the gap between the actual and the natural rates of unemployment. The natural rate of unemployment itself was defined as the rate that, given the frictions and structural characteristics of the economy, is just consistent with demand-supply equilibrium in labor and product markets. This innovation effectively identified full-employment equilibrium (i.e., zero excess demand) with normal capacity output and the natural rate of unemployment.

The second innovation was the introduction of price anticipations into Phillips curve analysis resulting in the expectations-augmented equation

$$p = ax + p^e \qquad (3)$$

where p^e is the price expectations variable representing the anticipated rate of inflation. This expectations variable entered the equation with a coefficient of unity, reflecting the assumption that price expectations are completely incorporated in actual price changes. The unit expectations coefficient implies the absence of money illusion, i.e., it implies that sellers are concerned with the expected real purchasing power of the prices they receive and so take anticipated inflation into account. As will be shown later, the unit expectations coefficient also implies the complete absence of a trade-off between inflation and unemployment in the long run when expectations are fully realized. Note also that the expectations variable is the sole shift variable in the equation. All other shift variables have been omitted, reflecting the view, prevalent in the early 1970s, that changing price expectations were the predominant cause of observed shifts in the Phillips curve.

The third innovation was the incorporation of an expectations-generating mechanism into Phillips curve analysis to explain how the price expectations variable itself is determined. Generally a simple *adaptive expectations* or *error-learning* mechanism was used. According to this mechanism, expectations are adjusted (adapted) by some fraction of the error that occurs when inflation turns out to be different than expected. In symbols

$$\dot{p}^e = B(p - p^e) \qquad (4)$$

where the dot over the expectations variable indicates the rate of change (time derivative) of that variable, $p - p^e$ is the expectations error (i.e., the difference between actual and expected price inflation), and b is the adjustment fraction. Assuming, for example, an adjustment fraction of ½, Equation 4 says that if the actual and expected rates of inflation are 10 percent and 4 percent, respectively—i.e., the expectational error is 6 percent—then the expected rate of inflation will be revised upward by an amount equal to half the error, or 3 percent. Such revision will continue until the expectational error is eliminated. It can also be shown that Equation 4 is equivalent to the proposition that expected inflation is a geometrically-weighted average of all past rates of inflation with the weights summing to one. Therefore, the error-learning mechanism can also be expressed as

$$p^e = \Sigma \, w_i \, p_{-i} \qquad\qquad\qquad (5)$$

where Σ indicates the operation of summing the weighted past rates of inflation, i represents past time periods, and w_i stands for the weights attached to past rates of inflation. These weights decline geometrically as time recedes, i.e., people are assumed to give more attention to recent than to older price experience when forming expectations. How fast the weights fall depends on the strength of people's memories of inflationary history. Rapidly declining weights indicate that people have short memories so that price expectations depend primarily on recent price experience. By contrast, slowly declining weights imply long memories so that expectations are influenced significantly by inflation rates of the more distant past. Both versions of the adaptive expectations mechanism (i.e., Equations 4 and 5) were combined with the expectations-augmented Phillips equation to explain the mutual interaction of actual inflation, expected inflation, and excess demand.

The Natural Rate Hypothesis

These three innovations—the redefined excess demand variable, the expectations-augmented trade-off, and the adaptive-expectations mechanism—formed the basis of the so-called natural rate and accelerationist hypotheses that radically altered economists' views of the Phillips curve. According to the natural rate hypothesis, there exists no permanent trade-off between unemployment and inflation since real economic variables tend to be independent of nominal ones in long-run equilibrium. To be sure, trade-offs may exist in the short run. But they are inherently transitory phenomena that stem from unexpected inflation and that vanish when expectations adjust to inflationary experience. In the long run, when inflationary surprises disappear and expectations are realized, unemployment returns to its natural (equilibrium) rate. This rate is consistent with all fully-anticipated steady-state rates of inflation, implying that the long-run Phillips curve is a vertical line at the natural rate of unemployment.

Equation 3 embodies these conclusions. That equation, when rearranged to read $p - p^e = ax$, states that the trade-off is between *unexpected* inflation (the difference between actual and expected inflation $p - p^e$) and excess demand. The equation also says that the trade-off disappears when inflation is fully anticipated, i.e., when $p - p^e$ is zero. Moreover, if the equation is correct, excess demand must also be zero at this point, which implies that unemployment is at its natural rate. Zero excess demand and the natural rate of unemployment are therefore compatible with *any* rate of inflation provided it is fully anticipated. In short, Equation 3 asserts that if inflation is fully anticipated there will be no relationship between inflation and unemployment, contrary to the original Phillips hypothesis.

The Accelerationist Hypothesis

Equation 3, when combined with Equation 4, also yields the accelerationist hypothesis. The latter, a corollary of the natural rate hypothesis, states that since there exists no long-run trade-off between unemployment and inflation, attempts to peg the former variable below its natural (equilibrium) level must produce ever-accelerating inflation. Such acceleration will keep actual inflation always running ahead of expected inflation, thereby perpetuating the inflationary surprises that prevent unemployment from returning to its equilibrium level.

These conclusions are easily demonstrated. As previously mentioned, Equation 3 states that excess demand can differ from zero only as long as actual inflation deviates from expected inflation. But Equation 4 says that, by the very nature of the error-learning mechanism, such deviations cannot persist unless inflation is continually accelerated so that it always stays ahead of expected inflation. If inflation is not accelerated, but instead stays constant, then the gap between actual and expected inflation will eventually be closed. Therefore acceleration is required to keep the gap open if excess demand is to be maintained above its natural equilibrium level of zero. In other words, the long-run trade-off implied by the accelerationist hypothesis is between excess demand and the rate of acceleration of the inflation rate, in contrast to the conventional trade-off between excess demand and the inflation rate itself as implied by the original Phillips curve.[3]

Policy Implications of the Natural Rate and Accelerationist Hypotheses

Two policy implications stem from the natural rate and accelerationist propositions. First, the authorities can either peg unemployment or stabilize inflation but not both. If they peg unemployment, they will ultimately lose control of inflation since the latter eventually accelerates when unemployment is held below its natural level. Alternatively, if they stabilize the inflation rate, they will lose control of unem-

[3]The proof is simple. Equation 3 states a relationship among actual inflation, expected inflation, and excess demand. From that equation it follows that the relationship among the rates of change of those variables is given by the expression $\dot{p} = a\dot{x} + \dot{p}^e$ where the dots indicate rates of change (time derivatives) of the attached variables. Substituting Equation 4 into this expression yields $\dot{p} = a\dot{x} + b(p - p^e)$, which, by Equation 3's assertion that the expectational error $p - p^e$ is equal to ax, further simplifies to $\dot{p} = a\dot{x} + bax$. Finally, if excess demand is unchanging so that $\dot{x}$ is zero—as would be the case if the authorities were pegging x at some desired level—this last expression reduces to $\dot{p} = bax$ showing a trade-off relation between the rate of acceleration of inflation $\dot{p}$ and excess demand x.

ployment since the latter will return to its natural level at any steady rate of inflation. Thus, contrary to the original Phillips hypothesis, they cannot peg unemployment at any constant rate of inflation.

A second policy implication stemming from Equations 3 and 4 is that the authorities can choose from among alternative transitional adjustment paths to the desired steady-state rate of inflation. Suppose the authorities wish to move to a lower target inflation rate. To do so they must lower inflationary expectations, a major component of the inflation rate. But Equations 3 and 4 state that the only way to do this is to create slack capacity (excess supply) in the economy, thus causing the actual rate of inflation to fall below the expected rate, inducing a downward revision of the latter. The equations also indicate that the speed of adjustment depends on the amount of slack created. Much slack means fast adjustment and a relatively rapid attainment of the inflation target. Conversely, little slack means sluggish adjustment and relatively slow attainment of the inflation target. Thus the policy choice is between adjustment paths offering high unemployment for a short time or lower unemployment for a long time.

Statistical Tests of the Natural Rate Hypothesis

The fourth stage of Phillips curve analysis involved statistical testing of the natural rate hypothesis. These tests led to criticisms of the adaptive-expectations or error-learning model of inflationary expectations and thus helped prepare the way for the introduction of the alternative rational-expectations idea into Phillips curve analysis.

The tests themselves were mainly concerned with estimating the numerical value of the coefficient on the price-expectations variable in the expectations-augmented Phillips curve equation. If the coefficient is one, as in Equation 3, then the natural rate hypothesis is valid and no long-run inflation-unemployment trade-off exists for the policymakers to exploit. But if the coefficient is less than one, the natural rate hypothesis is refuted and a long-run trade-off exists. This can be seen by writing the expectations-augmented equation as

$$p = ax + \phi p^e \tag{6}$$

where ϕ is the coefficient attached to the price expectations variable. In long-run equilibrium, of course, expected inflation equals actual inflation, i.e., $p^e = p$. Setting expected inflation equal to actual inflation as required for long-run equilibrium and solving for the actual rate of inflation yields

$$p(1 - \phi) = ax. \tag{7}$$

This shows that a long-run trade-off exists only if the expectations coefficient is less than one. If the coefficient is one, however, the trade-off vanishes.

Many of the empirical tests estimated the coefficient to be less than unity and concluded that the natural rate hypothesis was invalid. But this conclusion was sharply challenged by economists who contended that the tests contained statistical bias that tended to work against the natural rate hypothesis. These critics pointed out that the tests invariably used adaptive-expectations schemes as empirical proxies for the unobservable price expectations variable. They further showed that if these proxies were inappropriate measures of expectations then estimates of the expectations coefficient could well be biased downward. If so, then estimated coefficients of less than one constituted no disproof of the natural rate hypothesis.

Finally, the critics argued that the adaptive-expectations scheme is a grossly inaccurate representation of how people formulate price expectations. They pointed out that it postulates naive expectational behavior, holding as it does that people form anticipations solely from a weighted average of past price experience with weights that are fixed and independent of economic conditions and policy actions. This implies that people look only at past price changes and ignore all other pertinent information—e.g., money growth rate changes, exchange rate movements, announced policy intentions and the like—that could be used to reduce expectational errors. It seems implausible that people would fail to exploit information that would improve expectational accuracy. In short, the critics contended that adaptive expectations are not wholly rational if other information besides past price changes can improve predictions.

Many economists have since pointed out that it is hard to accept the notion that individuals would form price anticipations from *any* scheme that is inconsistent with the way inflation is actually generated in the economy. Being different from the true inflation-generating mechanism, such schemes will produce expectations that are systematically wrong. If so, rational agents will cease to use them. For example, suppose inflation were actually accelerating or decelerating. According to Equation 4, the adaptive expectations model would systematically underestimate the inflation rate in the former case and overestimate it in the latter. Perceiving these persistent expectational mistakes, rational agents would quickly abandon the error-learning model for more accurate expectations-generating schemes. Once again, the adaptive-expectations mechanism is implausible because of its incompatibility with rational behavior.

From Adaptive Expectations to Rational Expectations

The shortcomings of the adaptive expectations approach to the modeling of expectations led to the incorporation of the so-called rational expectations approach into Phillips curve analysis. According to the rational expectations hypothesis, individuals will tend to exploit *all* the pertinent information about the inflationary process when making their price forecasts. If true, this means that forecasting errors ultimately could arise only from random (unforeseen) shocks occurring to the economy. At first, of course, forecasting errors could also arise because individuals initially possess limited or incomplete information about the inflationary mechanism. But it is unlikely that this latter condition would persist. For if the public is truly rational, it will quickly learn from these inflationary surprises and incorporate the new information into its forecasting procedures, i.e., the sources of forecasting mistakes will be swiftly perceived and systematically eradicated. As knowledge of the inflationary process improves, forecasting models will be continually revised to produce more accurate predictions. Eventually all systematic (predictable) elements influencing the rate of inflation will become known and fully understood, and individuals' price expectations will constitute the most accurate (unbiased) forecast consistent with that knowledge.[4] When this happens people's price expectations will be the same as those implied by the actual inflation-generating mechanism. As incorporated in natural-rate Phillips curve models, the rational-expectations hypothesis implies that thereafter, except for unavoidable surprises due to purely random shocks, price expectations will always be correct and the economy will always be at its long-run steady-state equilibrium.

Policy Implications of Rational Expectations

The strict rational-expectations approach has some radical policy implications. It implies that systematic policies—i.e., those based on feedback control rules defining the authorities' response to changes in the economy—cannot influence real variables even in the short run, since people would have already anticipated what the policies are going to be and acted upon those anticipations. To have an impact on output and employment the authorities must be able to create a divergence between actual and expected inflation. This follows from the proposition that inflation influences real variables only when it is unanticipated. The authorities must be able to alter the actual rate of inflation without simultaneously causing an identical change in the expected future rate. This may be impossible if the public can predict policy actions.

Policy actions, to the extent they are systematic, are predictable. Systematic policies are simple rules or response functions relating policy variables to lagged values of other variables. These policy response functions can be estimated and incorporated into forecasters' price predictions. In other words, rational agents can use past observations on the behavior of the authorities to predict future policy moves. Then, on the basis of these predictions, they can correct for the effect of anticipated policies beforehand by making appropriate adjustments to nominal wages and prices. Consequently, when stabilization actions do occur, they will have no impact on real variables since they will have been discounted and neutralized in advance. The only conceivable way that policy can have even a short-run influence on real variables is for it to be unexpected, i.e., the policymakers must either act in an unpredictable random fashion or secretly change the policy reaction function. Apart from such tactics, which are incompatible with most notions of the proper conduct

---

[4]Put differently, rationality implies that current expectational errors are uncorrelated with past errors and all other known information, such correlations already having been perceived and eliminated in the process of improving price forecasts.

of public policy, there is no way the authorities can influence real variables. They can, however, influence a nominal variable, namely the inflation rate, and should concentrate their efforts on doing so if some particular rate is desired.

To summarize, the rationality hypothesis denies the existence of exploitable Phillips curve trade-offs in the short run as well as the long. In so doing it differs from the adaptive expectations version of natural-rate Phillips curve models. Under adaptive expectations, short-run trade-offs exist because expectations do not adjust instantaneously to policy-engineered changes in the inflation rate. With expectations adapting to actual inflation with a lag, monetary policy can generate unexpected inflation and consequently influence real variables in the short-run. This cannot happen under rational expectations where both actual and expected inflation adjust identically and instantaneously to anticipated policy changes. In short, under rational expectations, systematic policy cannot induce the expectational errors that generate short-run Phillips curves.

A Simple Illustrative Model

The preceding arguments can be clarified with the aid of a simple illustrative model. The model contains five relationships including an expectations-augmented Phillips curve equation, an inflation-generating mechanism, a policy reaction function, a rational price expectations equation, and finally a rational money-growth expectations equation. Taken together, these equations show that deterministic policies, by virtue of their very predictability, cannot induce the expectational errors that generate short-run Phillips curves. Phillips curves may exist, to be sure. But they are entirely the result of unpredictable random shocks and cannot be exploited by policies based on rules. In sum, the model shows that, given expectational rationality and the natural rate hypothesis, systematic trade-offs are impossible in the short run as well as the long.[5]

Phillips Curve Equation

The first component of the model is the expectations-augmented Phillips curve equation

$$p - p^e = ax \qquad (8)$$

that expresses a trade-off relationship between unexpected inflation and real excess demand. In the rational expectations literature this equation is often treated as an

---

[5]Note that the rational expectations hypothesis also rules out the accelerationist notion of a stable trade-off between excess demand and the rate of acceleration of the inflation rate. If expectations are formed consistent with the way inflation is actually generated, the authorities will not be able to fool people by accelerating inflation or by accelerating the rate of acceleration, etc. Indeed, no systematic policy will work if expectations are formed consistently with the way inflation is actually generated in the economy.

aggregate supply function stating that firms produce the normal capacity level of output when actual and expected inflation are equal but produce in excess of that level when fooled by unexpected inflation. This view holds that firms mistake unanticipated general price increases for rises in the particular (relative) price of their own products. Surprised by inflation, they treat the price increase as special to themselves and so expand output.

An alternative interpretation of the equation treats it as a price-setting relation according to which businessmen raise their prices at the rate at which they expect other businessmen to be raising theirs and then adjust that rate upward if excess demand appears. Either interpretation yields the same result. Expectational errors cause real economic activity to deviate from its normal capacity level. The deviations disappear when the errors vanish.

Inflation-Generating Mechanism

The next relationship describes how inflation is generated in the model. Written as follows

$$p = m + \epsilon \tag{9}$$

it expresses the rate of inflation as the sum of the growth rate of money m per unit of capacity real output and a random shock variable ϵ, the latter assumed to have a mean (expected) value of zero. The capacity-adjusted money growth rate is simply the difference between the respective growth rates of the nominal money stock and capacity real output, the latter variable serving as a proxy for the trend rate of growth of the real demand for money. In essence, Equation 9 says that while the rate of inflation is determined basically by the growth rate of money per unit of capacity output, it is also influenced by transitory disturbances unrelated to money growth. For convenience, it is assumed in what follows that the growth rate of capacity output is zero so that the capacity-adjusted money growth rate is identical to the growth of the nominal money stock itself.

Policy Reaction Function

The third ingredient of the model is a policy-reaction function stating how the monetary authorities respond to changes in the level of economic activity. Written as follows

$$m = m(x_{-1}) + u \tag{10}$$

it states that the current rate of money growth is a function of last period's excess demand x_{-1} and a random disturbance term u, the latter assumed to have a mean value of zero. The interpretation of the equation is straightforward. The authorities attempt to adjust money growth in the current period to correct real excess demand or supply occurring in the preceding period according to the feedback control rule $m = m(x_{-1})$. Money growth cannot be controlled perfectly by the feedback rule, however, and the slippage is represented by the random term u that causes money growth to deviate unpredictably from the path intended by the authorities. Note that the disturbance term u can also represent deliberate monetary surprises engineered by the policy authorities.

Price Expectations Equation

The fourth element of the model is a price-expectations equation describing how rational inflationary anticipations are formed. By definition, rational expectations are the same as the predictions yielded by the actual inflation-generating process, represented in the model by Equation 9. And since that equation states that the actual rate of inflation is equal to the actual money growth rate plus a random variable, it follows that the expected rate of inflation predicted by the equation is equal to the expected money growth rate plus the expected value of the random term. The latter, however, is zero and thus drops out, leaving anticipated inflation equal to expected money growth. In symbols

$$p^e = m^e. \tag{11}$$

Note that these symbols now have a dual interpretation. They represent anticipations formulated by the public. They also represent mathematical expectations—i.e., expected (mean) values of the stochastic inflation and money growth variables—calculated from a model that, in principle at least, is a true representation of the inflationary process. Here is the essence of the notion that people's expectations are rational when they are the same as those implied by the relevant economic model.[6]

Anticipated Money Growth Equation

Finally, rational expectations are employed to determine the anticipated rate of monetary growth. Here rational expectations are the same as the predictions of the actual money growth generating mechanism, represented in the model by Equation

---

[6]Analysts often stress this point by expressing anticipated inflation formally as the mathematical expected value of the actual inflation rate, conditional on information available when the expectation was formed. Symbolically, $p^e = E(p/I)$ where E is the mathematical expectation and I is known information. Since this information includes the inflation-generating mechanism summarized by Equation 9, it follows that anticipated inflation will be equal to the mathematical expectation of that mechanism, i.e., to the sum of the expected values of the money growth rate and the random term, respectively.

10 (the policy-reaction function). Put differently, the expected value of the reaction function constitutes the rational expectation of money growth. And since the function contains a systematic (predictable) component whose expected value is simply itself and a random term with an expected value of zero, that expectation is

$$m^e = m(x_{-1}).$$ (12)

In short, the anticipated rate of monetary growth is given by the predictable component of the policy-reaction function. Rational agents know everything in the policy-reaction function except the random element. They know the constant terms, the coefficients, and the predetermined variable. They use all this information in formulating expectations of the rate of monetary growth, expectations which are given by Equation 12.

The Reduced Form Equation

Equations 8–12 constitute the fundamental relationships of the rational-expectations model. The model can be condensed to a single reduced-form expression by substituting Equations 9–12 into Equation 8 to yield

$$\epsilon + u = ax$$ (13)

which states that Phillips curve trade-offs result solely from inflationary surprises caused by random shocks. Note in particular that only that part of monetary growth arising from unpredictable random disturbances enters Equation 13. The systematic component is absent. This means that systematic monetary policy cannot affect real economic activity (as represented by excess demand x). Only unexpected money growth matters.

The foregoing implies that the authorities can influence economic activity in only two ways. First, they can pursue a random policy, altering monetary growth in a haphazard unpredictable manner. That is to say they can manipulate the disturbance term u in the policy reaction function in a totally unpredictable way. Second, they can secretly change the feedback control rule, thereby affecting output and employment during the time people are learning about the new rule. It is unlikely, however, that this latter policy would prove effective for very long since rational agents would learn to predict rule *changes* just as they predict the rule. This leaves random policy as the only way to affect economic activity. But randomness seems hardly a proper basis for public policy.

To summarize, the strict rational-expectations approach implies that expectational errors are the only source of departure from steady-state equilibrium, that such errors are short-lived and random, and that systematic policy rules will have no impact on real variables since those rules will already be fully embodied in rational price expectations. Thus, except for unpredictable random shocks, steady-state equilibrium always prevails and systematic monetary changes produce no surprises, no disappointed expectations, no transitory impacts on real economic activity. Trade-offs are totally adventitious phenomena that cannot be exploited by systematic policy even in the short run. In short, no role remains for counter-cyclical stabilization policy. The only thing such policy can influence is the rate of inflation, which adjusts immediately to expected changes in money growth. The full effect of anticipated policy actions will be on the inflation rate. It follows that the authorities should concentrate their efforts on controlling this variable if it is desirable to do so since they cannot systematically influence real variables.

Evaluation of Rational Expectations

The preceding paragraphs have shown what happens when rational expectations are incorporated into a model containing feedback policy rules, an inflation-generating mechanism, and an expectations-augmented Phillips curve or aggregate supply function embodying the natural rate hypothesis. An evaluation of the rational-expectations approach is now in order.

One advantage of the rational-expectations hypothesis is that it treats expectations formation as a part of optimizing behavior. By so doing, it brings the theory of price anticipations into accord with the rest of economic analysis. The latter assumes that people behave as rational optimizers in the production and purchase of goods, in the choice of jobs, and in making investment decisions. For consistency, it should assume the same regarding expectational behavior.

In this sense, the rational-expectations theory is superior to rival explanations, all of which imply that expectations are always consistently wrong. It is the only theory that denies that people make systematic expectation errors. Note that it does not claim that people possess perfect foresight or that their expectations are always accurate. What it does claim is that they perceive and eliminate *regularities* in their forecasting mistakes. In this way they discover the actual inflation-generating process and use it in forming price expectations. And with rational expectations the same as the mean value of the inflation-generating process, those expectations cannot be wrong on *average*. Any errors will be random, not systematic. The same cannot be said for other expectations schemes, however. Not being identical to the expected value of true inflation-generating process, those schemes will produce biased expectations that are systematically wrong.

Biased expectations schemes are difficult to justify theoretically. Systematic mistakes are harder to explain than is rational behavior. True, nobody really knows how expectations are actually formed. But a theory that says that forecasters don't continually make the same mistakes seems intuitively more plausible than theories that imply the opposite. Considering the profits to be made from improved forecasts, it seems inconceivable that systematic expectational errors would persist.

Somebody would surely note the errors, correct them, and profit by the correction. Other forecasters would make similar corrections. Together, the profit motive and competition would reduce forecasting errors to randomness.

Criticism of the Rational-Expectations Approach

Despite its logic, the rational-expectations approach has many critics. Some still maintain that expectations are basically nonrational, i.e., that people are too stupid, naive, or uninformed to formulate unbiased price expectations. A variant of this argument is that expectational rationality will be attained only after a long learning period during which expectations will be nonrational.

Most of the criticism, however, is directed not at the rationality assumption per se but rather at three other assumptions underlying the rational-expectations approach, namely the assumptions of (1) costless information, (2) no policymaker information advantage, and (3) price flexibility. The first states that information used to form rational expectations can be obtained and processed costlessly. The second holds that private forecasters possess exactly the same information as the authorities regarding the inflationary process. The third assumption states that prices and the rate of inflation respond fully and immediately to anticipated changes in monetary growth and other events. In effect, this last assumption denies that prices are sticky and costly to adjust.

Critics maintain that all of these assumptions are implausible and that if any are violated then the strong conclusions of the rational-expectations approach cease to hold. In particular, if the assumptions are violated then activist policies can have systematic effects on real variables. Indeed, the critics have demonstrated as much by incorporating constraints representing information costs, policymaker informational advantages, and sluggish price adjustment into rational-expectations models similar to the one outlined above.

Proponents of the rational-expectations approach readily admit that such constraints can restore the potency of activist policies. But they still insist that such policies are inappropriate and that the proper role for policy is not to systematically influence real activity but rather to neutralize the constraints. Thus if people form biased price forecasts, then the policymakers should publish unbiased forecasts. If information is costly to collect and process, then a central authority should gather it and make it available. If the policy authorities have informational advantages over private individuals, they should make that information public rather than attempting to exploit the advantage. Finally, if prices are sticky and costly to adjust, then the authorities should minimize these price adjustment costs by following policies that stabilize the general price level.

In short, advocates of the rational expectations approach argue that feasibility alone constitutes insufficient justification for activist policies. Policies should also be *desirable*. Activist policies hardly satisfy this latter criterion since their effectiveness is based on deceiving people into making expectational errors. The proper role for policy is not to influence real activity via deception but rather to reduce information deficiencies and perhaps also to minimize the costs of adjusting prices.

Conclusion

This article has examined some recent developments in Phillips curve analysis. The chief conclusions can be stated succinctly. The Phillips curve concept has changed radically over the past 20 years as the notion of a stable enduring trade-off has given way to the view that no such trade-off exists for the policymakers to exploit. Instrumental to this change were the natural-rate and rational-expectations hypotheses, respectively. The former attributes trade-offs solely to expectational errors while the latter holds that systematic policies, by virtue of their very predictability, cannot possibly generate such errors. Taken together, the two hypotheses imply that systematic policies are incapable of influencing output and employment, contrary to the claims of policy activists. True, critics of the rational-expectations model have shown that relaxation of its more stringent assumptions restores the short-run potency of stabilization policy. But members of the rational-expectations school reply that activist policies are undesirable in any case since those policies must rely on deception. Whatever the verdict on the rational expectations approach, one must at least agree that it has posed a provocative challenge to proponents of activist stabilization policies.

BIBLIOGRAPHY

1. ARAK, M. "Rational Price Expectations: A Survey of the Evidence and Implications." Federal Reserve Bank of New York. Research Paper No. 7716, March 1977.
2. BARRO, R. J., and S. FISCHER. "Recent Developments in Monetary Theory." *Journal of Monetary Economics* 2 (April 1976), pp. 155–64.
3. FRIEDMAN, M. "Unemployment versus Inflation: An Evaluation of the Phillips Curve." I. E. A. Occasional Paper 44, pp. 11–30. London: The Institute of Economic Affairs, 1976.
4. FRISCH, H. "Inflation Theory 1963–1975: A Second Generation Survey." *Journal of Economic Literature* 15 (December 1977), pp. 1290–97, 1301–1302.
5. GORDON, R. J. "Recent Developments in the Theory of Inflation and Unemployment." *Journal of Monetary Economics* 2 (April 1976), pp. 185–219.
6. ———. "The Theory of Domestic Inflation." *American Economic Review* 67 (February 1977), pp. 128–34.
7. "How Expectations Defeat Economic Policy." *Business Week,* November 8, 1976, pp. 74, 76.
8. LAIDLER, D. "Expectations and the Phillips Trade Off: A Commentary." *Scottish Journal of Political Economy* 23 (February 1976), pp. 55–72.
9. LEMGRUBER, A. C. *A Study of the Accelerationist Theory of Inflation.* Unpublished Ph.D. dissertation. University of Virginia, May 1974.

10. MCCALLUM, B. T. "Rational Expectations and the Theory of Macroeconomic Stabilization Policy." The Thomas Jefferson Center for Political Economy at the University of Virginia. Non-Technical Report No. 107, June 6, 1977.

11. MILLER, P. "Epilogue." In *A Prescription for Monetary Policy: Proceedings from a Seminar Series,* pp. 99–103. Minneapolis: Federal Reserve Bank of Minneapolis, December 1976.

12. ———, C. W. NELSON, and T. M. SUPEL. "The Rational Expectations Challenge To Policy Activism." In *A Prescription for Monetary Policy: Proceedings from a Seminar Series,* pp. 51–63. Minneapolis: Federal Reserve Bank of Minneapolis, December 1976.

13. MULLINEAUX, D. J. "Money Growth, Jobs, and Expectations: Does a Little Learning Ruin Everything?" Federal Reserve Bank of Philadelphia. *Business Review,* November/December 1976, pp. 3–10.

14. ———. "Inflation Expectations in the U. S.: A Brief Anatomy." Federal Reserve Bank of Philadelphia. *Business Review,* July/August 1977, pp. 3–12.

15. POOLE, W. "Rational Expectations in the Macro Model." *Brookings Papers on Economic Activity,* No. 2, 1976, pp. 436–505.

16. SANTOMERO, A. M. and SEATER, J. J. "The Inflation-Unemployment Trade-Off: A Critique of The Literature." Federal Reserve Bank of Philadelphia. Research Paper No. 21, March 1977.

17. SARGENT, T. J. "Testing for Neutrality and Rationality. In *A Prescription for Monetary Policy: Proceedings from a Seminar Series,* pp. 65–85. Minneapolis: Federal Reserve Bank of Minneapolis, December 1976.

18. ———, and N. WALLACE. "Rational Expectations and the Theory of Economic Policy." *Journal of Monetary Economics* 2 (April 1976), pp. 169–84.

Inflation, Unemployment, and Money: Comparing the Evidence from Two Simple Models

Keith M. Carlson

Two years ago, Professors Barro and Fischer introduced their survey of monetary theory with the following statement:

> Perhaps the most striking contrast between current views of money and those of thirty years ago is the rediscovery of the endogeneity of the price level and inflation and their relation to the behavior of money.[1]

This assessment contrasts sharply with that of the Council of Economic Advisers in their 1978 *Annual Report*.[2] In a forty-one page chapter on inflation and unemployment, there are only two oblique references to monetary policy as a contributing factor to the inflationary process.

The theory of inflation that underlies the Council's discussion is conventional— inflation is usually initiated by excess demand, but once the momentum builds up, "the rate of wage and price increase reacts very slowly to idle resources and excess supply."[3] The Council believes there is a trade-off between inflation and unemployment, but rejects the terms of the trade-off as too costly. They argue that

Reprinted from *Review*, September 1978, pp. 2–6, by permission of the Federal Reserve Bank of St. Louis and the author.

[1]Robert J. Barro and Stanley Fischer, "Recent Developments in Monetary Theory," *Journal of Monetary Economics*, April 1976, p. 133.

[2]*Economic Report of the President*, 1978, pp. 138–78.

[3]Ibid., p. 150.

. . . it would take at least 6 years of the current degree of economic slack (an unemployment rate near 6½ percent) to cut the inflation rate from 6 to 3 percent.[4]

Consequently, the Council's recommended strategy for inflation control is one of "voluntarism," jawboning, and structural improvements. Implicit in this strategy is a stabilization policy stimulative enough to propel the economy to high employment and full utilization of capacity.[5]

The Council's strategy for economic policy rests on a belief in the inflation-unemployment trade-off and a neglect of money. In particular, the apparent current policy strategy is reminiscent of that applied in August 1971 when the price-wage freeze was introduced. At that time the same thinking prevailed—hold prices down directly and reduce unemployment via expansionary monetary and fiscal policy.[6]

The purpose of this article is to demonstrate that the apparent trade-off between inflation and unemployment is in fact the result of variable monetary growth. The approach draws heavily on recent work by Professor Stein of Brown University.[7] The appearance of a trade-off results from differences in the timing of the response of inflation and unemployment to changes in monetary growth. However, the trade-off is an illusion. Unemployment responds to monetary growth in the short run, but tends towards a steady-state value in the long run. Effects of monetary growth on inflation are just the opposite; there is little effect in the short run, with the full and permanent effect coming in the long run. These processes have implications that are strongly at variance with those advocated by the Council of Economic Advisers.

The Relation between Inflation and Unemployment: The Conventional View and Modifications

The relation between inflation and unemployment is usually depicted by the Phillips curve.[8] According to this relationship, high rates of inflation are associated with low rates of unemployment; likewise, low inflation rates are associated with high unemployment rates. Within recent years, however, experience in the United States and other countries has run counter to the prediction of the original relation. In particular, there have been times that inflation and unemployment have moved in the same direction, a phenomenon that has been labeled "stagflation." Economists have reacted to this experience by augmenting Phillips curve theory with consideration of the effects of inflationary expectations.[9]

[4]Ibid.
[5]Ibid., pp. 73–75, 152–56.
[6]*Economic Report of the President,* 1972, pp. 22–27.
[7]Jerome L. Stein, "Inflation and Stagflation," forthcoming in *Journal of Banking and Finance,* and "Inflation, Employment and Stagflation," *Journal of Monetary Economics,* April 1978, pp. 193–228.
[8]The original analysis is found in A. W. Phillips, "The Relation between Unemployment and the Rate of Change of Money Wage Rates in the United Kingdom, 1861–1957," *Economica,* November 1958, pp. 283–99.
[9]For a survey of the Phillips curve literature, see Robert J. Gordon, "Recent Developments in the Theory of Inflation and Unemployment," *Journal of Monetary Economics,* April 1976, pp. 185–220.

Lately, the Phillips curve discussion has taken yet another twist. Some economists have suggested that accelerations and decelerations of inflation are related to the level of unemployment. For example, according to Modigliani and Papademos,

> . . . historical experience clearly supports the proposition that there exists some *critical* rate of unemployment such that, as long as unemployment does not fall below it, inflation can be expected to decline. . . .[10]

They go on to refer to this critical unemployment rate as the noninflationary rate of unemployment (NIRU). In this case, "noninflationary" is defined to mean that the rate of inflation, at whatever level, is not increasing.

The value of NIRU can be derived from an estimate of the following simple relation:[11]

$$p_t - p_{t-1} = \alpha_0 + \alpha_1 U_{t-1}$$

The symbol p is the year-to-year percent change in the GNP deflator and U is the unemployment rate. Using annual data from 1952 to 1976, this equation is estimated as

$$p_t - p_{t-1} = 2.463 - .453 \, U_{t-1} \qquad R^2 = .15$$
$$(1.970) \; (-1.894) \qquad\qquad SE = 1.41 \quad (1)$$
$$DW = 1.79$$

Since the dependent variable is a second difference, there is considerable variation in it. The unemployment rate explains only a small portion of this variation, although both the coefficients in the equation are significant at the ten percent level (t statistics are shown in parentheses).

Since NIRU is defined as that rate of unemployment which is consistent with nonaccelerating inflation, its value can be found by setting $p_t - p_{t-1} = 0$ in Equation 1 and solving for U. The value of NIRU for this estimated equation is 5.44 percent.

This estimate of Equation 1 is consistent with the Council of Economic Advisers' assessment of the terms of the inflation-unemployment trade-off in their 1978 *Annual Report*. A 6.5 percent unemployment rate was used as an example of sufficient slack in the economy such that a deceleration of inflation of 0.5 percent per year would be generated. Substituting 6.5 into Equation 1 yields a decline in p of 0.48 percentage points per year.

By way of comment, it should be noted that this model does not indicate how a particular rate of inflation or rate of unemployment is attained. Rather, the equation simply shows how inflation will change, given the degree of slack in the

---

[10]Franco Modigliani and Lucas Papademos, "Monetary Policy for the Coming Quarters: The Conflicting Views," *New England Economic Review*, March/April 1976, p. 4.

[11]The Modigliani-Papademos approach to estimating NIRU is much more convoluted. For a critique of the Modigliani-Papademos results, see Stein, "Inflation, Employment and Stagflation."

economy as measured by the unemployment rate. To complete the model, an equation specifying the determination of the unemployment rate would have to be added. In this way the effect of monetary and fiscal policy could be captured via the effect on the unemployment rate.

The Relation between Inflation and Unemployment: A Monetary View

An alternate view of the relation between inflation and unemployment is that both variables are responding to the movements of a third variable. To the extent that there appears to be a relationship between movements in prices and unemployment, it is in fact a reflection of differential time responses to changes in the third variable. This is the monetary view, which stresses the long-run relation between money and prices, but also takes into account transitory effects of money on real product growth and unemployment.

According to the monetary view, shifts in the short-run Phillips curve are associated with changes in the growth rate of money. The hypothesis is that the *fundamental* determinant of the inflation rate is the rate of monetary expansion. Regardless of the initial conditions, the inflation rate will tend to converge to the rate of monetary growth, and the unemployment rate will tend toward its steady state value. This steady state value is not, however, related to the NIRU concept mentioned above. In fact, the monetary interpretation denies the validity of the NIRU argument.

In an attempt to keep the analysis simple, another single equation is specified as representative of the monetary view. Like Equation 1 the focus is on accelerations and decelerations of inflation. According to the monetary view, inflation will accelerate if money growth exceeds the ongoing inflation rate for an extended period of time (approximately one year). This simple representation of the monetary view appears as follows:

$$p_t - p_{t-1} = \beta_0 + \beta_1(m_{t-1} - p_{t-1})$$

Symbols are as defined above, with the addition of m, the year-to-year percent change in the narrowly defined money stock (M1).

Estimating this equation for the period 1954 to 1976, using annual data, yields the following:[12]

$$p_t - p_{t-1} = \quad .449\,(m_{t-1} - p_{t-1}) \qquad\qquad R^2 = .43$$
$$(4.106) \qquad\qquad\qquad\qquad SE = 1.13 \quad (2)$$
$$DW = 1.93$$

These results indicate that inflation will accelerate by 0.45 of a percentage point in each year following that in which money growth exceeds the inflation rate by one

---

[12]β_0 was not significant, so the equation was reestimated without the constant.

percentage point. Based on the specification of this equation, inflation will not accelerate or decelerate if the money growth rate equals the inflation rate. Comparing the monetary equation with the conventional equation indicates that the monetary equation explains a larger proportion of the variation in $p_t - p_{t-1}$, and the standard error of the equation is reduced by 20 percent.

Suppose now that both views have merit. Can the rate of monetary expansion and the unemployment rate be used to explain accelerations and decelerations of inflation? To investigate this possibility, the following version was estimated:

$$p_t - p_{t-1} = \gamma_0 + \gamma_1(U_{t-1} - U_E) + \gamma_2(m_{t-1} - p_{t-1})$$

The value of the critical unemployment rate, as calculated from Equation 1, was inserted into the equation as U_E. Again, using annual data from 1952 through 1976, the following results were obtained:

$$
\begin{aligned}
p_t - p_{t-1} = \;\; &.001 - \quad .177\,(U_{t-1} - 5.44) \qquad\qquad\quad (3)\\
&(.004) \quad (-.826)\\
+ \;\; &.406\,(m_{t-1} - p_{t-1}) \qquad\qquad\quad R^2 = \;.45\\
&(3.301) \qquad\qquad\qquad\qquad\quad SE = 1.16\\
&\qquad\qquad\qquad\qquad\qquad\qquad\quad DW = 1.99
\end{aligned}
$$

For this specification of the equation, supposedly allowing for both conventional and monetary effects, neither the unemployment rate nor the constant are significant. However, the monetary variable remains significant, although the value of the coefficient is slightly less than in (2). The R^2 and standard error are only slightly changed from (2).

The implication of these results is that accelerations and decelerations of inflation are not systematically related to the degree of resource utilization as measured by the unemployment rate. Restricting the analysis to very simple models, changes in the rate of inflation are much more closely associated with monetary growth, with no independent effect coming from the unemployment rate.

What does the monetary view say about the determination of the unemployment rate? The monetary view recognizes short-run impacts of money on output and employment. This relationship can be specified as:

$$U_t - U_{t-1} = \delta_0 + \delta_1 U_{t-1} + \delta_2(m_{t-1} - p_{t-1})$$

This equation is simply a distributed lag response of the unemployment rate, U, to monetary growth. There is a transitory effect of money on unemployment when monetary growth is greater or less than the inflation rate. Over the long run, however, steady monetary growth has no effect on unemployment because, according to Equation 2, monetary growth and inflation are the same in equilibrium. As a result, the $m_{t-1} - p_{t-1}$ term goes to zero and the equilibrium unemployment rate is determined by δ_0 and δ_1.

The estimated unemployment equation for the period 1954–76 is as follows:

$$U_t - U_{t-1} = 3.958 - \quad .721\, U_{t-1} \tag{4}$$
$$(5.079) \quad (-4.862)$$
$$- \quad .380\,(m_{t-1} - p_{t-1}) \qquad R^2 = .61$$
$$(-4.466) \qquad\qquad\qquad SE = .80$$
$$DW = 1.57$$

The implied steady state value for the unemployment rate, found by setting $U_t = U_{t-1}$, is 5.49 (that is, 3.958 ÷ .721), essentially the same result as in Equation 1. The interpretation of this equation is that money growth in excess of the inflation rate has a temporary effect on unemployment, but this effect disappears as the inflation rate converges to the growth rate of money in the long run. The steady state unemployment rate for the monetary view differs from NIRU in that inflation can accelerate even if the unemployment rate is in excess of its critical value.

Policy Implications

The policy implications of these two views of the relation between inflation and unemployment differ substantially. The concept of NIRU suggests that policy-makers need not consider inflation a problem until unemployment approaches this critical value. On the other hand, the monetary view stresses the effect of excessive monetary growth on inflation, independent of the prevailing unemployment rate. The lesson of the monetary view is that, in the long run, a steady growth of money will eventually result in a rate of inflation equal to that of monetary growth, and a rate of unemployment that will go to its steady state value. Only by constantly accelerating monetary growth is it possible to use monetary actions to reduce unemployment.

Consider the two views in terms of conditions as they exist in 1978. The inflation rate for 1977 over 1976 was 5.9 percent, and the unemployment rate in 1977 averaged 7 percent. The conventional view argues that inflation will not accelerate as long as unemployment stays above 5.44 percent. Consequently, it appears that output can be stimulated until the critical unemployment rate is reached. Then the stimulus can be reduced to a rate commensurate with long-term growth. The monetary view, on the other hand, indicates that money growth in excess of the ongoing inflation rate can lead to an acceleration in inflation even if the unemployment rate is above its critical value.

Two different policy paths for the conventional model are shown in Tables 1 and 2. Table 1 summarizes a policy directed toward a gradual return to full employment (NIRU) by 1980, and Table 2 shows an attempt to reach full employment quickly—in 1978. These cases were constructed by selecting a target path for unemployment and then calculating the effect of unemployment on inflation using Equation 1. An Okun's Law[13] equation (See Equation 2, Table 1) was added to the model to find the

---

[13]Arthur M. Okun, "Potential GNP: Its Measurement and Significance," *The Political Economy of Prosperity* (Washington, D.C.: The Brookings Institution, 1970), pp. 132–45.

Table 1. Hypothetical Case A: Conventional View (Attempted Gradual Return to Full Employment)

(1) $p_t - p_{t-1} = 2.463 - .453\,U_{t-1}$
(2) $U_t - U_{t-1} = -.412\,(x_t - 3.5)$

	x	U	p	y	m
1977 (Act.)	4.9%	7.0%	5.9%	11.0%	7.2%
1978	4.7	6.5	5.2	10.1	6.6
1979	4.7	6.0	4.7	9.6	6.1
1980	4.7	5.5	4.5	9.4	5.9
1981	3.7	5.4	4.4	8.2	4.7
1982	3.5	5.4	4.4	8.0	4.5
1983	3.5	5.4	4.4	8.0	4.5
1984	3.5	5.4	4.4	8.0	4.5
1985	3.5	5.4	4.4	8.0	4.5

Note: A path for U was selected and then the path of p was calculated using Equation 1. The U path was used to derive the implied x (the growth rate of output), assuming potential output grows at 3.5 percent per year. The x and p paths were then used to derive y (the growth rate of nominal GNP), and then assuming velocity growth of 3.5 percent per year, the path of m was derived.

Table 2. Hypothetical Case B: Conventional View (Attempted Rapid Return to Full Employment)

(1) $p_t - p_{t-1} = 2.463 - .453\,U_{t-1}$
(2) $U_t - U_{t-1} = -.412\,(x_t - 3.5)$

	x	U	p	y	m
1977 (Act.)	4.9%	7.0%	5.9%	11.0%	7.2%
1978	7.4	5.4	5.2	13.0	9.5
1979	3.5	5.4	5.2	8.9	5.4
1980	3.5	5.4	5.2	8.9	5.4
1981	3.5	5.4	5.2	8.9	5.4
1982	3.5	5.4	5.2	8.9	5.4
1983	3.5	5.4	5.2	8.9	5.4
1984	3.5	5.4	5.2	8.9	5.4
1985	3.5	5.4	5.2	8.9	5.4

Note: See Table 1.

growth of output consistent with the unemployment path. By adding together the rates of increase in output and the price level the implied growth of nominal GNP was calculated as a step towards deriving the growth rate of money consistent with the path of the other variables. [14]*

[14]This is based on the following:

$$m + v = p + x$$

where m: rate of increase in money
    v: rate of increase in velocity
    p: rate of increase in the price level
    x: rate of increase in output.

*Editor's Note: For a description of how nominal income growth projections are used to generate growth projections for the monetary aggregates, see the selection by Lombra and Torto in Section VIII.

According to Table 1, based on a gradual return to full employment, inflation and unemployment decline simultaneously until 1980, and then stabilize. By adding an assumption of constant velocity growth of 3.5 percent to the conventional model, steady state rates of monetary growth and inflation are also derived. These steady state rates appear little different than those for the monetary model. However, the path to this equilibrium differs substantially.

According to Table 2, also based on the concept of NIRU, there appears to be no obstacle to returning to full employment quickly. The difference between the results in Tables 1 and 2 is that a quick return to full employment "locks" the model in at a higher growth rate of money and inflation than does the gradual approach. The reason for this disparity of results for the conventional model is that the attempted

Table 3. Hypothetical Case A: Monetary View (Attempted Gradual Return to Full Employment)

(1) $p_t - p_{t-1} = .449\,(m_{t-1} - p_{t-1})$
(2) $U_t - U_{t-1} = 3.958 - .721\,U_{t-1} - .380\,(m_{t-1} - p_{t-1})$

	x	U	p	y	m
1977 (Act.)	4.9%	7.0%	5.9%	11.0%	7.2%
1978	3.4	5.4	6.5	10.1	6.6
1979	2.9	5.4	6.5	9.6	6.1
1980	2.9	5.6	6.3	9.4	5.9
1981	2.0	5.7	6.1	8.2	4.7
1982	2.4	6.1	5.5	8.0	4.5
1983	2.8	6.0	5.0	8.0	4.5
1984	3.1	5.8	4.8	8.0	4.5
1985	3.2	5.7	4.7	8.0	4.5

Note: The path of m was taken from Table 1 and the path of p was calculated from Equation 1. Given m and p, the U path was then calculated from Equation 2. The y path from Table 1 and the p path were used to calculate an implied x.

Table 4. Hypothetical Case B: Monetary View (Attempted Rapid Return to Full Employment)

(1) $p_t - p_{t-1} = .449\,(m_{t-1} - p_{t-1})$
(2) $U_t - U_{t-1} = 3.958 - .721\,U_{t-1} - .380\,(m_{t-1} - p_{t-1})$

	x	U	p	y	m
1977 (Act.)	4.9%	7.0%	5.9%	11.0%	7.2%
1978	6.1	5.4	6.5	13.0	9.5
1979	1.0	4.3	7.8	8.9	5.4
1980	2.1	6.1	6.7	8.9	5.4
1981	2.6	6.1	6.1	8.9	5.4
1982	2.9	6.0	5.8	8.9	5.4
1983	3.1	5.8	5.6	8.9	5.4
1984	3.2	5.6	5.5	8.9	5.4
1985	3.2	5.6	5.5	8.9	5.4

Note: See Table 3 except that the paths for m and y are taken from Table 2.

Table 5. Alternative Cases: Monetary View (Rapid Return to Steady Money Growth)

(1) $p_t - p_{t-1} = .449 (m_{t-1} - p_{t-1})$

(2) $U_t - U_{t-1} = 3.958 - .721 U_{t-1} - .380 (m_{t-1} - p_{t-1})$

	2% Money Growth		4% Money Growth		6% Money Growth		8% Money Growth	
	p	U	p	U	p	U	p	U
1977 (Act.)	5.9%	7.0%	5.9%	7.0%	5.9%	7.0%	5.9%	7.0%
1978	6.5	5.4	6.5	5.4	6.5	5.4	6.5	5.4
1979	4.5	7.2	5.4	6.4	5.9	5.7	7.2	4.9
1980	3.4	6.9	4.8	6.3	5.9	5.5	7.5	5.0
1981	2.8	6.4	4.4	6.0	5.9	5.5	7.7	5.2
1982	2.4	6.1	4.2	5.8	6.0	5.4	7.9	5.3
1983	2.2	5.8	4.1	5.6	6.0	5.5	7.9	5.4
1984	2.1	5.7	4.1	5.6	6.0	5.5	7.9	5.4
1985	2.1	5.6	4.0	5.6	6.0	5.5	7.9	5.4

quick return to full employment allows the effect of unemployment on inflation to operate for only one year.

Compare these results with those implied by the monetary model of inflation and unemployment. Using the growth rates of money derived for the conventional model in Tables 1 and 2, the paths for inflation and unemployment for the monetary model are traced out in Tables 3 and 4. According to Table 3, attempting a gradual return to full employment can be accomplished, but in the early stages there is an acceleration of inflation rather than the deceleration predicted by the conventional model. In 1980, inflation decelerates in response to the slowing in the growth rate of money. However, unemployment also rises again before the steady state is finally approached in 1984 and 1985.

Examination of the other case (Table 4)—an attempted quick return to full employment—indicates severe oscillations in inflation and unemployment before the steady state is approached. The unemployment target is overshot, and the rapid growth in money in 1978 has its effect on the inflation rate for several years.

To explore in greater depth the implications of the monetary view, alternative simulations of steady growth rates of money are shown in Table 5. In each case, the steady-state rate of monetary growth is begun in 1978. According to these simulations, there appears to be little prospect for reducing the inflation rate from its 1977 value without incurring a period of rising unemployment during the interim. However, the policies of inflation control (2 and 4 percent money growth) show that once the period of rising unemployment is weathered, both inflation and unemployment decline from their 1977 values toward their steady-state values.

Conclusions

The Administration has taken an approach to controlling inflation that is predicated on the assumption that economic slack is a factor in determining the inflation rate.

In particular, the direct approach to inflation control has been chosen by the Administration because the terms of the trade-off between inflation and unemployment are deemed unacceptable.

Policy based on this type of reasoning is potentially disruptive. According to the simple monetary model used here, attempts to stimulate output with expansionary monetary policy will have accompanying effects on inflation, despite apparent slack in the economy. Even though there is a similarity in long-run targets, substantially different paths to this equilibrium are derived, depending on which model is used and how fast the policymakers hope to achieve their targets.

The Monetarist Controversy, or Should We Forsake Stabilization Policies?

Franco Modigliani

In recent years and especially since the onset of the current depression, the economics profession and the lay public have heard a great deal about the sharp conflict between "monetarists and Keynesians" or between "monetarists and fiscalists." The difference between the two "schools" is generally held to center on whether the money supply or fiscal variables are the major determinants of aggregate economic activity, and hence the most appropriate tool of stabilization policies.

My central theme is that this view is quite far from the truth, and that the issues involved are of far greater practical import. There are in reality no serious analytical disagreements between leading monetarists and leading nonmonetarists. Milton Friedman was once quoted as saying, "We are all Keynesians, now," and I am quite prepared to reciprocate that "we are all monetarists"—if by monetarism is meant assigning to the stock of money a major role in determining output and prices. Indeed, the list of those who have long been monetarists in this sense is quite extensive, including among other John Maynard Keynes as well as myself, as is attested by my 1944 and 1963 articles.

In reality the distinguishing feature of the monetarist school and the real issues of disagreement with nonmonetarists are not monetarism, but rather the role that should probably be assigned to stabilization policies. Nonmonetarists accept what I

Reprinted from *American Economic Review*, March 1977, pp. 1–19, by permission of the American Economic Association and the author.

regard to be the fundamental practical message of *The General Theory:* that a private enterprise economy using an intangible money *needs* to be stabilized, *can* be stabilized, and therefore *should* be stabilized by appropriate monetary and fiscal policies. Monetarists by contrast take the view that there is no serious need to stabilize the economy; that even if there were a need, it could not be done, for stabilization policies would be more likely to increase than to decrease instability; and, at least some monetarists would, I believe, go so far as to hold that, even in the unlikely event that stabilization policies could on balance prove beneficial, the government should not be trusted with the necessary power.

What has led me to address this controversy is the recent spread of monetarism, both in a simplistic, superficial form and in the form of growing influence on the practical conduct of economic policy, which influence, I shall argue presently, has played at least some role in the economic upheavals of the last three years.

In what follows then, I propose first to review the main arguments bearing on the *need* for stabilization policies, that is, on the likely extent of instability in the absence of such policies, and then to examine the issue of the supposed destabilizing effect of pursuing stabilization policies. My main concern will be with instability generated by the traditional type of disturbances—demand shocks. But before I am through, I will give some consideration to the difficult problems raised by the newer type of disturbance—supply shocks.

The Keynesian Case for Stabilization Policies

The General Theory

Keynes' novel conclusion about the need for stabilization policies, as was brought out by the early interpreters of *The General Theory* (for example, John Hicks, the author, 1944), resulted from the interaction of a basic contribution to traditional monetary theory—liquidity preference—and an unorthodox hypothesis about the working of the labor market—complete downward rigidity of wages.

Because of liquidity preference, a change in aggregate demand, which may be broadly defined as any event that results in a change in the market clearing or equilibrium rate of interest, will produce a corresponding change in the real demand for money or velocity of circulation, and hence in the real stock of money needed at full employment. As long as wages are perfectly flexible, even with a constant nominal supply, full employment could and would be maintained by a change of wages and prices as needed to produce the required change in the real money supply—though even in this case, stability of the price level would require a countercyclical monetary policy. But, under the Keynesian wage assumption the classical adjustment through prices can occur only in the case of an increased demand. In the case of a decline, instead, wage rigidity prevents the necessary increase in the real money supply and the concomitant required fall in interest rates. Hence, if the nominal money supply is constant, the initial equilibrium must give way to a new stable one, characterized by lower output and by an involuntary reduction in employment, so labeled because it does not result from a shift in notional demand and supply schedules in terms of real wages, but only from an insufficient real money supply. The nature of this equilibrium is elegantly captured by the Hicksian *IS-LM* paradigm, which to our generation of economists has become almost as familiar as the demand-supply paradigm was to earlier ones.

This analysis implied that a fixed money supply far from insuring approximate stability of prices and output, as held by the traditional view, would result in a rather unstable economy, alternating between periods of protracted unemployment and stagnation, and bursts of inflation. The extent of downward instability would depend in part on the size of the exogenous shocks to demand and in part on the strength of what may be called the Hicksian mechanism. By this I mean the extent to which a shift in *IS,* through its interaction with *LM,* results in some decline in interest rates and thus in a change in income which is smaller than the original shift. The stabilizing power of this mechanism is controlled by various parameters of the system. In particular, the economy will be more unstable the greater the interest elasticity of demand for money, and the smaller the interest responsiveness of aggregate demand. Finally, a large multiplier is also destabilizing in that it implies a larger shift in *IS* for a given shock.

However, the instability could be readily counteracted by appropriate stabilization policies. Monetary policy could change the nominal supply of money so as to *accommodate* the change in real demand resulting from shocks in aggregate demand. Fiscal policy, through expenditure and taxes, could *offset* these shocks, making full employment consistent with the initial nominal money stock. In general, both monetary and fiscal policies could be used in combination. But because of a perceived uncertainty in the response of demand to changes in interest rates, and because changes in interest rates through monetary policy could meet difficulties and substantial delays related to expectations (so-called liquidity traps), fiscal policy was regarded as having some advantages.

The Early Keynesians

The early disciples of the new Keynesian gospel, still haunted by memories of the Great Depression, frequently tended to outdo Keynes' pessimism about potential instability. Concern with liquidity traps fostered the view that the demand for money was highly interest elastic; failure to distinguish between the short- and long-run marginal propensity to save led to overestimating the long-run saving rate, thereby fostering concern with stagnation, and to underestimating the short-run propensity, thereby exaggerating the short-run multiplier. Interest rates were supposed to affect, at best, the demand for long-lived fixed investments, and the interest elasticity was deemed to be low. Thus, shocks were believed to produce a large response. Finally, investment demand was seen as capriciously controlled by "animal spirits," thus providing an important source of shocks. All this justified calling for very active stabilization policies. Furthermore, since the very circumstances which produce a large response to demand shocks also produce a large response to *fiscal* and a small response to *monetary* actions, there was a tendency to focus on fiscal policy as the main tool to keep the economy at near full employment.

The Phillips Curve

In the two decades following *The General Theory,* there were a number of developments of the Keynesian system including dynamization of the model, the stress on taxes versus expenditures and the balanced budget multiplier, and the first attempts at estimating the critical parameters through econometric techniques and models. But for present purposes, the most important one was the uncovering of a "stable" statistical relation between the rate of change of wages and the rate of unemployment, which has since come to be known as the Phillips curve. This relation, and its generalization by Richard Lipsey to allow for the effect of recent inflation, won wide acceptance even before an analytical underpinning could be provided for it, in part because it could account for the "puzzling" experience of 1954 and 1958, when wages kept rising despite the substantial rise in unemployment. It also served to dispose of the rather sterile "cost push"–"demand pull" controversy.

In the following years, a good deal of attention went into developing theoretical foundations for the Phillips curve, in particular along the lines of search models (for example, Edmund Phelps et al.). This approach served to shed a new light on the nature of unemployment by tracing it in the first place to labor turnover and search time rather than to lack of jobs as such: in a sense unemployment is all frictional—at least in developed countries. At the same time it clarified how the availability of more jobs tends to reduce unemployment by increasing vacancies and thus reducing search time.

Acceptance of the Phillips curve relation implied some significant changes in the Keynesian framework which partly escaped notice until the subsequent monetarists' attacks. Since the rate of change of wages decreased smoothly with the rate of unemployment, there was no longer a unique Full Employment but rather a whole family of possible equilibrium rates, each associated with a different rate of inflation (and requiring, presumably, a different long-run growth of money). It also impaired the notion of a stable underemployment equilibrium. A fall in demand could still cause an initial rise in unemployment but this rise, by reducing the growth of wages, would eventually raise the real money supply, tending to return unemployment to the equilibrium rate consistent with the given long-run growth of money.

But at the practical level it did not lessen the case for counteracting lasting demand disturbances through stabilization policies rather than by relying on the slow process of wage adjustment to do the job, at the cost of protracted unemployment and instability of prices. Indeed, the realm of stabilization policies appeared to expand in the sense that the stabilization authority had the power of choosing the unemployment rate around which employment was to be stabilized, though it then had to accept the associated inflation. Finally, the dependence of wage changes also on past inflation forced recognition of a distinction between the short- and the long-run Phillips curve, the latter exhibiting the long-run equilibrium rate of inflation implied by a *maintained* unemployment rate. The fact that the long-run tradeoff between unemployment and inflation was necessarily less favorable than the short-run one, opened up new vistas of "enjoy-it-now, pay-later" policies, and even resulted in an entertaining literature on the political business cycle and how to stay in the saddle by riding the Phillips curve (see for example, Ray Fair, William Nordhaus).

The Monetarists' Attack

The Stabilizing Power of the Hicksian Mechanism

The monetarists' attack on Keynesianism was directed from the very beginning not at the Keynesian framework as such, but at whether it really implied a need for stabilization. It rested on a radically different empirical assessment of the value of the parameters controlling the stabilizing power of the Hicksian mechanism and of the magnitude and duration of response to shocks, given a stable money supply. And this different assessment in turn was felt to justify a radical downgrading of the *practical relevance* of the Keynesian framework as distinguished from its *analytical validity*.

Liquidity preference was a fine contribution to monetary theory but in practice the responsiveness of the demand for money, and hence of velocity, to interest rates, far from being unmanageably large, was so small that according to a well-known paper by Milton Friedman (1969), it could not even be detected empirically. On the other hand, the effect of interest rates on aggregate demand was large and by no means limited to the traditional fixed investments but quite pervasive. The difficulty of detecting it empirically resulted from focusing on a narrow range of measured market rates and from the fact that while the aggregate could be counted on to respond, the response of individual components might not be stable. Finally, Friedman's celebrated contribution to the theory of the consumption function (1957) (and my own work on the life cycle hypothesis with Richard Brumberg and others, reviewed by the author, 1975) implied a very high short-run marginal propensity to save in response to transient disturbances to income and hence a small short-run multiplier.

All this justified the conclusion that (i) though demand shocks might qualitatively work along the lines described by Keynes, quantitatively the Hicks mechanism is so strong that their impact would be *small* and *transient,* provided the stock of money was kept on a steady growth path; (ii) fiscal policy actions, like other demand shocks, would have *minor* and *transitory* effects on demand, while changes in money would produce *large* and *permanent* effects on money income; and, therefore, (iii) the observed instability of the economy, which was anyway proving moderate as the postwar period unfolded, was most likely the result of the unstable growth of money, be it due to misguided endeavors to stabilize income or to the pursuit of other targets, which were either irrelevant or, in the case of balance of payments goals, should have been made irrelevant by abandoning fixed exchanges.

The Demise of Wage Rigidity and the
Vertical Phillips Curve

But the most serious challenge came in Friedman's 1968 presidential address, building on ideas independently put forth also by Phelps (1968). Its basic message was that, despite appearances, wages were in reality perfectly flexible and there was accordingly *no* involuntary unemployment. The evidence to the contrary, including the Phillips curve, was but a statistical illusion resulting from failure to differentiate between price changes and *unexpected* price changes.

Friedman starts out by reviving the Keynesian notion that, at any point of time, there exists a unique full-employment rate which he labels the "natural rate." An unanticipated fall in demand in Friedman's competitive world leads firms to reduce prices and also output and employment along the short-run marginal cost curve—unless the nominal wage declines together with prices. But workers, failing to judge correctly the current and prospective fall in prices, misinterpret the reduction of nominal wages as a cut in *real* wages. Hence, assuming a positively sloped supply function, they reduce the supply of labor. As a result, the effective real wage rises to the point where the resulting decline in the demand for labor matches the reduced supply. Thus, output falls not because of the decline in demand, but because of the entirely voluntary reduction in the supply of labor, in response to erroneous perceptions. Furthermore, the fall in employment can only be temporary, as expectations must soon catch up with the facts, at least in the absence of new shocks. The very same mechanism works in the case of an increase in demand, so that the responsiveness of wages and prices is the same on either side of the natural rate.

The upshot is that Friedman's model also implies a Phillips-type relation between inflation, employment or unemployment, and past inflation,—provided the latter variable is interpreted as a reasonable proxy for expected inflation. But it turns the standard explanation on its head: instead of (excess) employment causing inflation, it is (the unexpected component of) the rate of inflation that causes excess employment.

One very basic implication of Friedman's model is that the coefficient of price expectations should be precisely unity. This specification implies that whatever the shape of the short-run Phillips curve—a shape determined by the relation between expected and actual price changes, and by the elasticity of labor supply with respect to the perceived real wage—the long-run curve *must be vertical.*

Friedman's novel twist provided a fresh prop for the claim that stabilization policies are not really needed, for, with wages flexible, except possibly for transient distortions, the Hicksian mechanism receives powerful reinforcement from changes in the real money supply. Similarly, the fact that full employment was a razor edge provided new suport for the claim that stabilization policies were bound to prove destabilizing.

The Macro Rational Expectations Revolution

But the death blow to the already badly battered Keynesian position was to come only shortly thereafter by incorporating into Friedman's model the so-called rational expectation hypothesis, or REH. Put very roughly, this hypothesis, originally due to John Muth, states that rational economic agents will endeavor to form expectations of relevant future variables by making the most efficient use of all information provided by past history. It is a fundamental and fruitful contribution that has already found many important applications, for example, in connection with speculative markets, and as a basis for some thoughtful criticism by Robert Lucas (1976) of certain features of econometric models. What I am concerned with here is only its application to macro-economics, or MREH, associated with such authors as Lucas (1972), Thomas Sargent (1976), and Sargent and Neil Wallace (1976).

The basic ingredient of MREH is the postulate that the workers of Friedman's model hold rational expectations, which turns out to have a number of remarkable implications: (i) errors of price expectations, which are the only source of departure from the natural state, cannot be avoided but they can only be short-lived and random. In particular, there cannot be persistent unemployment above the natural rate for this would imply high serial correlation between the successive errors of expectation, which is inconsistent with rational expectations; (ii) any attempts to stabilize the economy by means of stated monetary or fiscal rules are bound to be totally ineffective because their effect will be fully discounted in rational expectations; (iii) nor can the government successfully pursue *ad hoc* measures to offset shocks. The private sector is already taking care of any anticipated shock; therefore government policy could conceivably help only if the government information was better than that of the public, which is impossible, by the very definition of rational expectations. Under these conditions, *ad hoc* stabilization policies are most likely to produce instead further destabilizing shocks.

These are clearly remarkable conclusions, and a major *re*discovery—for it had all been said 40 years ago by Keynes in a well-known passage of *The General Theory:*

> If, indeed, labour were always in a position to take action (and were to do so), whenever there was less than full employment, to reduce its money demands by concerted action to whatever point was required to make money so abundant relatively to the wage-unit that the rate of interest would fall to a level compatible with full employment, we should, in effect, have monetary management by the Trade Unions, aimed at full employment, instead of by the banking systems. [p. 267]

The only novelty is that MREH replaces Keynes' opening "if" with a "since."

If one accepts this little amendment, the case against stabilization policies is complete. The economy is inherently pretty stable—except possibly for the effect of government messing around. And to the extent that there is a small residual instability, it is beyond the power of human beings, let alone the government, to alleviate it.

How Valid Is the Monetarist Case?

The Monetarist Model of Wage Price Behavior

In setting out the counterattack it is convenient to start with the monetarists' model of price and wage behavior. Here one must distinguish between the model as such and a specific implication of that model, namely that the long-run Phillips curve is vertical, or, in substance, that, in the long run, money is neutral. That conclusion, by now, does not meet serious objection from nonmonetarists, at least as a first approximation.

But the proposition that other things equal, and given time enough, the economy will eventually adjust to any indefinitely maintained stock of money, or nth derivative thereof, can be derived from a variety of models and, in any event, is of very little practical relevance, as I will argue below. What is unacceptable, because inconsistent with both micro and macro evidence, is the specific monetarist model set out above and its implication that all unemployment is a voluntary, fleeting response to transitory misperceptions.

One may usefully begin with a criticism of the Macro Rational Expectations model and why Keynes' "if" should not be replaced by "since." At the logical level, Benjamin Friedman has called attention to the omission from MREH of an explicit learning model, and has suggested that, as a result, it can only be interpreted as a description not of short-run but of long-run equilibrium in which no agent would wish to recontract. But then the implications of MREH are clearly far from startling, and their policy relevance is almost nil. At the institutional level, Stanley Fischer has shown that the mere recognition of long-term contracts is sufficient to generate wage rigidity and a substantial scope for stabilization policies. But the most glaring flaw of MREH is its inconsistency with the evidence: if it were valid, deviations of unemployment from the natural rate would be small and transitory—in which case *The General Theory* would not have been written and neither would this paper. Sargent (1976) has attempted to remedy this fatal flaw by hypothesizing that the persistent and large fluctuations in unemployment reflect merely corresponding swings in the natural rate itself. In other words, what happened to the United States in the 1930s was a severe attack of contagious laziness! I can only say that, despite Sargent's ingenuity, neither I nor, I expect, most others at least of the nonmonetarists' persuasion are quite ready yet to turn over the field of economic fluctuations to the social psychologist!

Equally serious objections apply to Friedman's modeling of the commodity market as a perfectly competitive one—so that the real wage rate is continuously equated to the *short*-run marginal product of labor—and to his treatment of labor as a homogenous commodity traded in an auction market, so that, at the going wage, there never is any excess demand by firms or excess supply by workers. The inadequacies of this model as a useful formalization of present day Western economies are so numerous that only a few of the major ones can be mentioned here.

Friedman's view of unemployment as a voluntary reduction in labor supply could at best provide an explanation of variations in labor force—and then only under the questionable assumption that the supply function has a significantly positive slope—but cannot readily account for changes in unemployment. Furthermore, it cannot be reconciled with the well-known fact that *rising* unemployment is accompanied by a fall, not by a *rise* in quits, nor with the role played by temporary layoffs to which Martin Feldstein has recently called attention. Again, his competitive model of the commodity market, accepted also in *The General Theory,* implies that changes in real wages, adjusted for long-run productivity trend, should be significantly negatively correlated with cyclical changes in employment and output and with changes in money wages. But as early as 1938, John Dunlop showed that this conclusion was rejected by some eighty years of British experience and his results have received some support in more recent tests of Ronald Bodkin for the United States and Canada. Similar tests of my own, using quarterly data, provide striking confirmation that for the last two decades from the end of the Korean War until 1973, the association of trend adjusted real compensations of the private nonfarm sector with either employment or the change in nominal compensation is prevailingly positive and very significantly so.[1]

This evidence can, instead, be accounted for by the oligopolistic pricing model—according to which price is determined by *long-run* minimum average cost up to a mark-up reflecting entry-preventing considerations (see the author, 1958)—coupled with some lags in the adjustment of prices to costs. This model implies that firms respond to a change in demand by endeavoring to adjust output and employment, without significant changes in prices relative to wages; and the resulting changes in available jobs have their initial impact not on wages but rather on unemployment by way of layoffs and recalls and through changes in the level of vacancies, and hence on the length of average search time.

If, in the process, vacancies rise above a critical level, or "natural rate," firms will endeavor to reduce them by outbidding each other, thereby raising the rate of change of wages. Thus, as long as jobs and vacancies remain above, and unemployment remains below, some critical level which might be labeled the "noninflationary rate" (see the author and Lucas Papademos, 1975), wages and prices will tend to accelerate. If, on the other hand, jobs fall below, and unemployment rises above, the noninflationary rate, firms finding that vacancies are less than optimal—in the limit the unemployed queuing outside the gate will fill them instantly—will have an incentive to reduce their relative wage offer. But in this case, in which too much labor is looking for too few jobs, the trend toward a sustained decline in the rate of growth of wages is likely to be even weaker than the corresponding acceleration when too many jobs are bidding for too few people. The main reason is the nonhomogeneity of labor. By far the largest and more valuable source of labor supply to a firm consists of those already employed who are not readily interchangeable with the unemployed and, in contrast with them, are concerned with protecting their earnings and not with reestablishing full employment. For these reasons, and because the first to quit are likely to be the best workers, a reduction of the labor force can, within limits, be accomplished more economically, not by reducing wages to generate enough quits, but by firing, or, when possible, by layoffs which insure access to a trained labor force when demand recovers. More generally, the inducement to reduce relative wages to eliminate the excess supply is moderated by the effect

[1] Thus, in a logarithmic regression of private nonfarm hourly compensation deflated by the private nonfarm deflator on output per man-hour, time, and private nonfarm employment, after correcting for first-order serial correlation, the latter variable has a coefficient of .17 and a *t*-ratio of 5. Similar though less significant results were found for manufacturing. If employment is replaced by the change in nominal compensation, its coefficient is .40 with a *t*-ratio of 6.5. Finally, if the change in compensation is replaced by the change in price, despite the negative bias from error of measurement of price, the coefficient of this variable is only — .09 with an entirely insignificant *t*-ratio of .7. The period after 1973 has been omitted from the tests as irrelevant for our purposes, since the inflation was driven primarily by an exogenous price shock rather than by excess demand. As a result of the shock, prices, and to some extent wages, rose rapidly while employment and real wages fell. Thus, the addition of the last two years tends to increase spuriously the positive association between real wages and employment, and to decrease that between real wages and the change in nominal wages or prices.

that such a reduction would have on quits and costly turnover, even when the resulting vacancies can be readily filled from the ranks of the unemployed. Equally relevant are the consequences in terms of loss of morale and good will, in part for reasons which have been elaborated by the literature on implicit contracts (see Robert Gordon). Thus, while there will be some tendency for the rate of change of wages to fall, the more so the larger the unemployment—at least in an economy like the United States where there are no overpowering centralized unions—that tendency is severely damped.

And whether, given an unemployment rate significantly and persistently above the noninflationary level, the rate of change of wages would, eventually, tend to turn negative and decline without bound or whether it would tend to an asymptote is a question that I doubt the empirical evidence will ever answer. The one experiment we have had—the Great Depression—suggests the answer is negative, and while I admit that, for a variety of reasons, that evidence is muddied, I hope that we will never have the opportunity for a second, clean experiment.

In any event, what is really important for practical purposes is not the long-run equilibrium relation as such, but the speed with which it is approached. Both the model sketched out and the empirical evidence suggest that the process of acceleration or deceleration of wages when unemployment differs from the noninflationary rate will have more nearly the character of a crawl than of a gallop. It will suffice to recall in this connection that there was excess demand pressure in the United States at least from 1965 to mid-1970, and during that period the growth of inflation was from some 1.5 to only about 5.5 percent per year. And the response to the excess supply pressure from mid-1970 to early 1973, and from late 1974 to date was equally sluggish.

The Power of Self-Stabilizing Mechanisms: The Evidence from Econometric Models

There remains to consider the monetarists' initial criticism of Keynesianism, to wit, that even without high wage flexibility, the system's response to demand shocks is small and short-lived, thanks to the power of the Hicksian mechanism. Here it must be acknowledged that every one of the monetarists' criticisms of early, simpleminded Keynesianism has proved in considerable measure correct.

With regard to the interest elasticity of demand for money, post-Keynesian developments in the theory of money, and in particular, the theoretical contributions of William Baumol, James Tobin, Merton Miller, and Daniel Orr, point to a modest value of around one-half to one-third, and empirical studies (see for example, Stephen Goldfeld) are largely consistent with this prediction (at least until 1975!). Similarly, the dependence of consumption on long-run, or life cycle, income and on wealth, together with the high marginal tax rates of the postwar period, especially the corporate tax, and leakages through imports, lead to a rather low estimate of the multiplier.

Last but not least, both theoretical and empirical work, reflected in part in econometric models, have largely vindicated the monetarist contention that interest effects on demand are pervasive and substantial. Thus, in the construction and estimation of the MIT-Penn-Social Science Research Council (MPS) econometric model of the United States, we found evidence of effects, at least modest, on nearly every component of aggregate demand. One response to money supply changes that is especially important in the MPS, if somewhat controversial, is via interest rates on the market value of all assets and thus on consumption.

There is, therefore, substantial agreement that in the United States the Hicksian mechanism is fairly effective in limiting the effect of shocks, and that the response of wages and prices to excess demand or supply will also work *gradually* toward eliminating largely, if not totally, any effect on employment. But in the view of nonmonetarists, the evidence overwhelmingly supports the conclusion that the *interim* response is still of significant magnitude and of considerable duration, basically because the wheels of the offsetting mechanism grind slowly. To be sure, the first link of the mechanism, the rise in short-term rates, gets promptly into play and heftily, given the low money demand elasticity; but most expenditures depend on long-term rates, which generally respond but gradually, and the demand response is generally also gradual. Furthermore, while this response is building up, multiplier and accelerator mechanisms work toward amplifying the shock. Finally, the classical mechanism—the change in real money supply through prices—has an even longer lag because of the sluggish response of wages to excess demand.

These interferences are supported by simulations with econometric models like the MPS. Isolating, first, the working of the Hicksian mechanism by holding prices constant, we find that a 1 percent demand shock, say a rise in real exports, produces an impact effect on aggregate output which is barely more than 1 percent, rises to a peak of only about 2 percent a year later, and then declines slowly toward a level somewhat over 1.5 percent.

Taking into account the wage price mechanism hardly changes the picture for the first year because of its inertia. Thereafter, however, it becomes increasingly effective so that a year later the real response is back at the impact level, and by the end of the third year the shock has been fully offset (thereafter output oscillates around zero in a damped fashion). Money income, on the other hand, reaches a peak of over 2.5, and then only by the middle of the second year. It declines thereafter, and tends eventually to oscillate around a *positive* value because normally, a demand shock requires eventually a change in interest rates and hence in velocity and money income.

These results, which are broadly confirmed by other econometric models, certainly do not support the view of a highly unstable economy in which fiscal policy has powerful and everlasting effects. But neither do they support the monetarist view of a highly stable economy in which shocks hardly make a ripple and the effects of fiscal policy are puny and fast vanishing.

The Monetarist Evidence and the
St. Louis Quandary

Monetarists, however, have generally been inclined to question this evidence. They countered at first with tests bearing on the stability of velocity and the insignificance of the multiplier, which, however, as indicated in my criticism with Albert Ando (1965), must be regarded as close to worthless. More recently, several authors at the Federal Reserve Bank of St. Louis (Leonall Andersen, Keith Carlson, Jerry Lee Jordan) have suggested that instead of deriving multipliers from the analytical or numerical solution of an econometric model involving a large number of equations, any one of which may be questioned, they should be estimated directly through "reduced form" equations by relating the change in income to current and lagged changes in some appropriate measure of the money supply and of fiscal impulses.

The results of the original test, using the current and but four lagged values of *M1* and of high Employment Federal Expenditure as measures of monetary and fiscal impulses, turned out to be such as to fill a monetarist's heart with joy. The contribution of money, not only current but also lagged, was large and the coefficients implied a not unreasonable effect of the order of magnitude of the velocity of circulation, though somewhat higher. On the other hand, the estimated coefficients of the fiscal variables seemed to support fully the monetarists' claim that their impact was both small and fleeting: the effect peaked in but two quarters and was only around one, and disappeared totally by the fourth quarter following the change.

These results were immediately attacked on the ground that the authors had used the wrong measure of monetary and fiscal actions, and it was shown that the outcome was somewhat sensitive to alternative measures; however, the basic nature of the results did not change, at least qualitatively. In particular, the outcome does not differ materially, at least for the original period up to 1969, if one replaces high employment outlays with a variable that might be deemed more suitable, like government expenditure on goods and services, plus exports.

These results must be acknowledged as disturbing for nonmonetarists, for there is little question that movements in government purchases and exports are a major source of demand disturbances; if econometric model estimates of the response to demand disturbances are roughly valid, how can they be so grossly inconsistent with the reduced form estimates?

Attempts at reconciling the two have taken several directions, which are reviewed in an article coauthored with Ando (1976). Our main conclusion, based on simulation techniques, is that when income is subject to substantial shocks from many sources other than monetary and fiscal, so that these variables account for only a moderate portion of the variations in income (in the United States, it has been of the order of one-half to two-thirds), then the St. Louis reduced form method yields highly unstable and unreliable estimates of the true structure of the system generating the data.

The crucial role of unreliability and instability has since been confirmed in more recent work of Daniel O'Neill in his forthcoming thesis. He shows in the first place that different methods of estimation yield widely different estimates, including many which clearly overstate the expenditure and understate the money multipliers. He further points out that, given the unreliability of the estimates resulting from multicollinearity and large residual variance, the relevant question to ask is not whether these estimates differ from those obtained by structural estimation, but whether the *difference is statistically significant;* that is, larger than could be reasonably accounted for by sampling fluctuations.

I have carried out this standard statistical test using as true response coefficients those generated by the MPS model quoted earlier.[2] I find that, at least when the test is based on the largest possible sample—the entire post-Korean period up to the last two very disturbed years—the difference is totally insignificant when estimation is in level form (F is less than one) and is still not significant at the 5 percent level, when in first differences.

This test resolves the puzzle by showing that there really is no puzzle: the two alternative estimates of the expenditure multipliers are not inconsistent, given the margin of error of the estimates. It implies that one should accept whichever of the two estimates is produced by a more reliable and stable method, and is generally more sensible. To me, those criteria call, without question, for adopting the econometric model estimates. But should there be still some lingering doubt about this choice, I am happy to be able to report the results of one final test which I believe should dispose of the reduced form estimates—at least for a while. Suppose the St. Louis estimates of the expenditure multiplier are closer to God's truth than the estimates derived through econometric models. Then it should be the case that if one uses their coefficients to forecast income beyond the period of fit, these forecasts should be appreciably better than those obtained from a forecasting equation in which the coefficients of the expenditure variable are set equal to those obtained from econometric models.

I have carried out this test, comparing a reduced form equation fitted to the period originally used at St. Louis, terminating in 1969 (but reestimated with the latest revised data) with an equation in which the coefficients of government expenditure plus exports were constrained to be those estimated from the MPS, used in the above F-test. The results are clear cut: the errors using the reduced form coefficient are not smaller but on the average substantially *larger* than those using MPS multipliers. For the first four years, terminating at the end of 1973, the St. Louis equation produces errors which are distinctly larger in eight quarters, and smaller in but three, and its squared error is one-third larger. For the last two years of turmoil, both equations perform miserably, though even here the MPS coefficients perform just a bit better. I have repeated this test with

---

[2]For the purpose of the test, coefficients were scaled down by one-third to allow for certain major biases in measured government expenditure for present purposes (mainly the treatment of military procurement on a delivery rather than work progress basis, and the inclusion of direct military expenditure abroad).

equations estimated through the first half of the postwar period, and the results are, if anything, even more one-sided.

The moral of the story is pretty clear. First, reduced form equations relying on just two exogenous variables are very unreliable for the purpose of estimating structure, nor are they particularly accurate for forecasting, though per dollar of research expenditure they are surprisingly good. Second, if the St. Louis people want to go on using this method and wish to secure the best possible forecast, then they should ask the MPS or any other large econometric model what coefficients they should use for government expenditure, rather than trying to estimate them by their unreliable method.

From the theory and evidence reviewed, we must then conclude that opting for a constant rate of growth of the nominal money supply can result in a stable economy only in the absence of significant exogenous shocks. But obviously the economy has been and will continue to be exposed to many significant shocks, coming from such things as war and peace, and other large changes in government expenditure, foreign trade, agriculture, technological progress, population shifts, and what not. The clearest evidence on the importance of such shocks is provided by our postwar record with its six recessions.

The Record of Stabilization Policies: Stabilizing or Destabilizing

Was Postwar Instability due to Unstable Money Growth?

At this point, of course, monetarists will object that, over the postwar period, we have *not* had a constant money growth policy and will hint that the observed instability can largely be traced to the instability of money. The only way of meeting this objection squarely would be, of course, to rerun history with a good computer capable of calculating 3 percent at the helm of the Fed.

A more feasible, if less conclusive approach might be to look for some extended periods in which the money supply grew fairly smoothly and see how the economy fared. Combing through our post-Korean War history, I have been able to find just two stretches of several years in which the growth of the money stock was relatively stable, whether one chooses to measure stability in terms of percentage deviations from a constant growth or of dispersion of four-quarter changes. It may surprise some that one such stretch occurred quite recently and consists of the period of nearly four years beginning in the first quarter of 1971 (see the author and Papademos, 1976). During this period, the average growth was quite large, some 7 percent, but it was relatively smooth, generally well within the 6 to 8 percent band. The average deviation from the mean is about .75 percent. The other such period lasted from the beginning of 1953 to the first half of 1957, again a stretch of roughly four years. In sharp contrast to the most recent period, the average growth here is quite modest, only about 2 percent; but again, most four-quarter changes fell well within a band of two percentage points, and the average deviation is again .7. By contrast, during the remaining 13-year stretch from mid-1957 to the end of 1970, the variability of money growth was roughly twice as large if measured by the average deviation of four quarter changes, and some five times larger if measured by the percentage deviation of the money stock from a constant growth trend.

How did the economy fare in the two periods of relatively stable money growth? It is common knowledge that the period from 1971 to 1974, or from 1972 to 1975 if we want to allow a one-year lag for money to do its trick, was distinctly the most unstable in our recent history, marked by sharp fluctuations in output and wild gyrations of the rate of change of prices. As a result, the average deviation of the four-quarter changes in output was 3.3 percent, more than twice as large as in the period of less stable money growth. But the first stretch was also marked by well above average instability, with the contraction of 1954, the sharp recovery of 1955, and the new contraction in 1958, the sharpest in postwar history except for the present one. The variability of output is again 50 percent larger than in the middle period.

To be sure, in the recent episode serious exogenous shocks played a major role in the development of prices and possibly output, although the same is not so readily apparent for the period 1953 to 1958. But, in any event, such extenuating circumstances are quite irrelevant to my point; for I am not suggesting that the stability of money was the major cause of economic instability—or at any rate, not yet! All I am arguing is that (i) there is no basis for the monetarists' suggestion that our postwar instability can be traced to monetary instability—our most unstable periods have coincided with periods of relative monetary stability; and (ii) stability of the money supply is not enough to give us a stable economy, precisely because there are exogenous disturbances.

Finally, let me mention that I have actually made an attempt at rerunning history to see whether a stable money supply would stabilize the economy, though in a way that I readily acknowledge is much inferior to the real thing, namely through a simulation with the MPS. The experiment, carried out in cooperation with Papademos, covered the relatively quiet period from the beginning of 1959 to the introduction of price-wage controls in the middle of 1971. If one eliminates all major sources of shocks, for example, by smoothing federal government expenditures, we found, as did Otto Eckstein in an earlier experiment, that a stable money growth of 3 percent per year does stabilize the economy, as expected. But when we allowed for all the historical shocks, the result was that with a constant money growth the economy was far from stable—in fact, it was distinctly less stable than actual experience, by a factor of 50 percent.

The Overall Effectiveness of Postwar Stabilization Policies

But even granted that a smooth money supply will not produce a very stable world and that there is therefore room for stabilization policies, monetarists will still argue that we should nonetheless eschew such policies. They claim, first, that allowing for unpredictably variable lags and unforeseeable future shocks, we do not know enough to successfully design stabilization policies, and second, that the government would surely be incapable of choosing the appropriate policies or be politically willing to provide timely enforcement. Thus, in practice, stabilization policies will result in destabilizing the economy much of the time.

This view is supported by two arguments, one logical and one empirical. The logical argument is the one developed in Friedman's Presidential Address (1968). An attempt at stabilizing the economy at full employment is bound to be destabilizing because the full employment or natural rate is not known with certainty and is subject to shifts in time; and if we aim for the incorrect rate, the result must perforce be explosive inflation or deflation. By contrast, with a constant money supply policy, the economy will automatically hunt for, and eventually discover, that shifty natural rate, wherever it may be hiding.

This argument, I submit, is nothing but a debating ploy. It rests on the preposterous assumption that the only alternative to a constant money growth is the pursuit of a very precise unemployment target which will be adhered to indefinitely no matter what, and that if the target is off in the second decimal place, galloping inflation is around the corner. In reality, all that is necessary to pursue stabilization policies is a rough target range that includes the warranted rate, itself a range and not a razor edge; and, of course, responsible supporters of stabilization policies have long been aware of the fact that the target range needs to be adjusted in time on the basis of foreseeable shifts in the warranted range, as well as in the light of emerging evidence that the current target is not consistent with price stability. It is precisely for this reason that I, as well as many other nonmonetarists, would side with monetarists in strenuous opposition to recent proposals for a target unemployment rate rigidly fixed by statute (although there is nothing wrong with Congress committing itself and the country to work toward the eventual achievement of some target unemployment rate through *structural* changes rather than aggregate demand policies).

Clearly, even the continuous updating of targets cannot guarantee that errors can be avoided altogether or even that they will be promptly recognized; and while errors persist, they will result in some inflationary (or deflationary) pressures. But the growing inflation to which Friedman refers is, to repeat, a crawl not a gallop. One may usefully recall in this connection the experience of 1965–70 referred to earlier, with the further remark that the existence of excess employment was quite generally recognized at the time, and failure to eliminate it resulted overwhelmingly from political considerations and not from a wrong diagnosis.[3]

[3]Friedman's logical argument against stabilization policies and in favor of a constant money growth rule is, I submit, much like arguing to a man from St. Paul wishing to go to New Orleans on important business that he would be a fool to drive and should instead get himself a tub and drift down the Mississippi: that way he can be pretty sure that the current will eventually get him to his destination; whereas, if he drives, he might make a wrong turn and, before he notices he will be going further and further away from his destination and pretty soon he may end up in Alaska, where he will surely catch pneumonia and he may never get to New Orleans!

There remains then only the empirical issue: have stabilization policies worked in the past and will they work in the future? Monetarists think the answer is negative and suggest, as we have seen, that misguided attempts at stabilization, especially through monetary policies, are responsible for much of the observed instability. The main piece of evidence in support of this contention is the Great Depression, an episode well documented through the painstaking work of Friedman and Anna Schwartz, although still the object of dispute (see, for example, Peter Temin). But in any event, that episode while it may attest to the power of money, is irrelevant for present purposes since the contraction of the money supply was certainly not part of a comprehensive stabilization program in the post-Keynesian sense.

When we come to the relevant postwar period, the problem of establishing the success or failure of stabilization policies is an extremely taxing one. Many attempts have been made at developing precise objective tests, but in my view, none of these is of much value, even though I am guilty of having contributed to them in one of my worst papers (1964). Even the most ingenious test, that suggested by Victor Argy, and relying on a comparison of the variability of income with that of the velocity of circulation, turns out to be valid only under highly unrealistic restrictive assumptions.

Dennis Starleaf and Richard Floyd have proposed testing the effectiveness of stabilization by comparing the stability of money growth with that of income growth, much as I have done above for the United States, except that they apply their test to a cross section of industrialized countries. They found that for a sample of 13 countries, the association was distinctly positive. But this test is again of little value. For while a negative association for a given country, such as suggested by my U.S. test, does provide some weak indication that monetary activism helped rather than hindered, the finding of a positive association across countries proves absolutely nothing. It can be readily shown, in fact, that, to the extent that differential variability of income reflects differences in the character of the shocks—a most likely circumstance for their sample—successful stabilization also implies a positive correlation between the variability of income and that of money.

But though the search for unambiguous quantitative tests has so far yielded a meager crop, there exists a different kind of evidence in favor of Keynesian stabilization policies which is impressive, even if hard to quantify. To quote one of the founding fathers of business cycle analysis, Arthur Burns, writing in 1959, "Since 1937 we have had five recessions, the longest of which lasted only 13 months. There is no parallel for such a sequence of mild—or such a sequence of brief—contractions, at least during the past hundred years in our country" (p. 2). By now we can add to that list the recessions of 1961 and 1970.

There is, furthermore, evidence that very similar conclusions hold for other industrialized countries which have made use of stabilization policies; at any rate that was the prevailing view among participants to an international conference held in 1967 on the subject, "Is the business cycle obsolete?" (see Martin

Bronfenbrenner, editor). No one seemed to question the greater postwar stability of all Western economies—nor is this surprising when one recalls that around that time business cycle specialists felt so threatened by the new-found stability that they were arguing for redefining business cycles as fluctuations in the *rate of growth* rather than in the *level* of output.

It was recognized that the reduced severity of fluctuations might in part reflect structural changes in the economy and the effect of stronger built-in stabilizers, inspired, of course, by the Keynesian analysis. Furthermore, the greater stability in the United States, and in other industrialized countries, are obviously not independent events. Still, at least as of the time of that conference, there seemed to be little question and some evidence that part of the credit for the greater stability should go to the conscious and on balance, successful endeavor at stabilizing the economy.

The Case of Supply Shocks and the 1974–76 Episode

Was the 1974 Depression due to Errors of Commission or Omission?

In pointing out our relative postwar stability and the qualified success of stabilization policies, I have carefully defined the postwar period as ending somewhere in 1973. What has happened since that has so tarnished the reputation of economists? In facing this problem, the first question that needs to be raised is whether the recent combination of unprecedented rates of inflation as well as unemployment must be traced to crimes of commission or omission. Did our monetary and fiscal stabilization policies misfire, or did we instead fail to use them?

We may begin by establishing one point that has been blurred by monetarists' blanket indictments of recent monetary policy: the virulent explosion that raised the four-quarter rate of inflation from about 4 percent in 1972 to 6.5 percent by the third quarter of 1973, to 11.5 percent in 1974 with a peak quarterly rate of 13.5, can in no way be traced to an excessive, or to a disorderly, growth of the money supply. As already mentioned, the average rate of money growth from the beginning of 1970 to the second half of 1974 was close to 7 percent. To be sure, this was a high rate and could be expected sooner or later to generate an undesirably high inflation—but how high? Under any reasonable assumption one cannot arrive at a figure much above 6 percent. This might explain what happened up to the fall of 1973, but not from the third quarter of 1973 to the end of 1974, which is the really troublesome period. Similarly, as was indicated above, the growth of money was reasonably smooth over this period, smoother than at any other time in the postwar period, staying within a 2 percent band. Hence, the debacle of 1974 can just not be traced to an erratic behavior of money resulting from a misguided attempt at stabilization.

Should one then conclude that the catastrophe resulted from too slavish an adherence to a stable growth rate, forsaking the opportunity to use monetary policy to stabilize the economy? In one sense, the answer to this question must in my view be in the affirmative. There is ample ground for holding that the rapid contraction that set in toward the end of 1974, on the heels of a slow decline in the previous three quarters, and which drove unemployment to its 9 percent peak, was largely the result of the astronomic rise in interest rates around the middle of the year. That rise in turn was the unavoidable result of the Fed's stubborn refusal to accommodate, to an adequate extent, the exogenous inflationary shock due to oil, by letting the money supply growth exceed the 6 percent rate announced at the beginning of the year. And this despite repeated warnings about that unavoidable result (see, for example, the author 1974).

Monetarists have suggested that the sharp recession was not the result of too slow a monetary growth throughout the year, but instead of the deceleration that took place in the last half of 1974, and early 1975. But this explanation just does not stand up to the facts. The fall in the quarterly growth of money in the third and fourth quarters was puny, especially on the basis of revised figures now available; from 5.7 percent in the second to 4.3 and 4.1—hardly much larger than the error of estimate for quarterly rates! To be sure, in the first quarter of 1975 the growth fell to .6 percent. But, by then, the violent contraction was well on its way—between September 1974 and February 1975, industrial production fell at an annual rate of 25 percent. Furthermore, by the next quarter, monetary growth had resumed heftily. There is thus no way the monetarist proposition can square with these facts unless their long and variable lags are so variable that they sometimes turn into substantial leads. But even then, by anybody's model, a one-quarter dip in the growth of money could not have had a perceptible effect.

What Macro Stabilization Policies Can Accomplish, and How

But recognizing that the adherence to a stable money growth path through much of 1974 bears a major responsibility for the sharp contraction does not per se establish that the policy was mistaken. The reason is that the shock that hit the system in 1973–74 was not the usual type of demand shock which we have gradually learned to cope with, more or less adequately. It was, instead, a supply or price shock, coming from a cumulation of causes, largely external. This poses an altogether different stabilization problem. In particular, in the case of demand shocks, there exists in principle an ideal policy which avoids all social costs, namely to offset completely the shock thus, at the same time, stabilizing employment and the price level. There may be disagreement as to whether this target can be achieved and how, but not about the target itself.

But in the case of supply shocks, there is no miracle cure—there is no macro policy which can both maintain a stable price level and keep employment at its natural rate. To maintain stable prices in the face of the exogenous price shock, say a rise in import prices, would require a fall in all domestic output prices; but we know of no macro policy by which domestic prices can be made to fall except by creating enough slack, thus putting downward pressure on wages. And the amount of slack would have to be substantial in view of the sluggishness of wages in the face of unemployment. If we do not offset the exogenous shock completely, then the initial burst, even if activated by an entirely transient rise in some prices, such as a once and for all deterioration in the terms of trade, will give rise to further increases, as nominal wages rise in a vain attempt at preserving real wages; this secondary reaction too can only be cut short by creating slack. In short, once a price shock hits, there is no way of returning to the initial equilibrium except after a painful period of both above equilibrium unemployment and inflation.

There are, of course, in principle, policies other than aggregate demand management to which we might turn, and which are enticing in view of the unpleasant alternatives offered by demand management. But so far such policies, at least those of the wage-price control variety, have proved disappointing. The design of better alternatives is probably the greatest challenge presently confronting those interested in stabilization. However, these policies fall outside my present concern. Within the realm of aggregate demand management, the only choice open to society is the cruel one between alternative feasible paths of inflation and associated paths of unemployment, and the best the macroeconomist can offer is policies designed to approximate the chosen path.

In light of the above, we may ask: is it conceivable that a constant rate of growth of the money supply will provide a satisfactory response to price shocks in the sense of giving rise to an unemployment-inflation path to which the country would object least?

The Monetarist Prescription: Or, Constant Money Growth Once More

The monetarists are inclined to answer this question affirmatively, if not in terms of the country's preferences, at least in terms of the preferences they think it should have. This is evidenced by their staunch support of a continuation of the 6 percent or so rate of growth through 1974, 1975, and 1976.

Their reasoning seems to go along the following lines. The natural rate hypothesis implies that the rate of inflation can change only when employment deviates from the natural rate. Now suppose we start from the natural rate and some corresponding steady rate of inflation, which without loss of generality can be assumed as zero. Let there be an exogenous shock which initially lifts the rate of inflation, say, to 10 percent. If the Central Bank, by accommodating this price rise, keeps employment at the natural rate, the new rate of 10 percent will also be maintained and will in fact continue forever, as long as the money supply accommodates it. The only way to eliminate inflation is to increase unemployment enough, above the natural rate and for a long enough time, so that the cumulated reduction of inflation takes us back to zero. There will of course be many possible unemployment paths that will accomplish this. So the next question is: Which is the least undesirable?

The monetarist answer seems to be—and here I confess that attribution becomes difficult—that it does not make much difference because, to a first approximation, the cumulated amount of unemployment needed to unwind inflation is independent of the path. If we take more unemployment early, we need to take less later, and conversely. But then it follows immediately that the specific path of unemployment that would be generated by a constant money growth is, if not better, at least as good as any other. Corollary: a constant growth of money is a satisfactory answer to supply shocks just as it is to demand shocks—as well as, one may suspect, to any other conceivable illness, indisposition, or disorder.

Why Constant Money Growth Cannot
Be the Answer

This reasoning is admirably simple and elegant, but it suffers from several flaws. The first one is a confusion between the price level and its rate of change. With an unchanged constant growth of the nominal money stock, the system will settle back into equilibrium not when the rate of inflation is back to zero but only when, in addition, the price level itself is back to its initial level. This means that when inflation has finally returned back to the desired original rate, unemployment cannot also be back to the original level but will instead remain above it as long as is necessary to generate enough deflation to offset the earlier cumulated inflation. I doubt that this solution would find many supporters and for a good reason; it amounts to requiring that none of the burden of the price shock should fall on the holder of long-term money fixed contracts—such as debts—and that all other sectors of society should shoulder entirely whatever cost is necessary to insure this result. But if, as seems to be fairly universally agreed, the social target is instead to return the system to the original rate of inflation—zero in our example—then the growth of the money supply cannot be kept constant. Between the time the shock hits and the time inflation has returned to the long-run level, there must be an additional increase in money supply by as much as the price level or by the cumulant of inflation over the path.

A second problem with the monetarists' argument is that it implies a rather special preference function that depends only on cumulated unemployment. And, last but not least, it requires the heroic assumption that the Phillips curve be not only vertical in the long run but also linear in the short run, an assumption that does not seem consistent with empirically estimated curves. Dropping this last assumption has the effect that, for any given social preference, there will be in general a unique optimal path. Clearly, for this path to be precisely that generated by a constant money growth, would require a miracle—or some sleight of the invisible hand!

Actually, there are grounds for holding that the unemployment path generated by a constant money growth, even if temporarily raised to take care of the first flaw, could not possibly be close to an optimal. This conclusion is based on an analysis of optimal paths, relying on the type of linear welfare function that appears to underlie the monetarists' argument, and which is also a straightforward generalization of Okun's famous "economic discomfort index." That index (which according to Michael Lovell appears to have some empirical support) is the sum of unemployment and inflation. The index used in my analysis is a weighted average of the cumulated unemployment and cumulated inflation over the path. The weights express the relative social concern for inflation versus unemployment.

Using this index, it has been shown in a forthcoming thesis of Papademos that, in general, the optimum policy calls for raising unemployment at once to a certain critical level and keeping it there until inflation has substantially abated. The critical level depends on the nature of the Phillips curve and the relative weights, but does not depend significantly on the initial shock—as long as it is appreciable. To provide an idea of the order of magnitudes involved, if one relies on the estimate of the Phillips curve reported in my joint paper with Papademos (1975), which is fairly close to vertical and uses Okun's weights, one finds that (i) at the present time, the noninflationary rate of unemployment corresponding to a 2 percent rate of inflation can be estimated at 5.6 percent, and (ii) the optimal response to a large exogenous price shock consists in increasing unemployment from 5.6 to only about 7 percent. That level is to be maintained until inflation falls somewhat below 4 percent; it should then be reduced slowly until inflation gets to 2.5 (which is estimated to take a couple of years), and rapidly thereafter. If, on the other hand, society were to rate inflation twice as costly as unemployment, the initial unemployment rate becomes just over 8 percent, though the path to final equilibrium is then shorter. These results seem intuitively sensible and quantitatively reasonable, providing further justification for the assumed welfare function, with its appealing property of summarizing preferences into a single readily understandable number.

One important implication of the nature of the optimum path described above is that a constant money growth could not possible be optimal while inflation is being squeezed out of the system, regardless of the relative weights attached to unemployment and inflation. It would tend to be prevailingly too small for some initial period and too large thereafter.

One must thus conclude that the case for a constant money growth is no more tenable in the case of supply shocks than it is in the case of demand shocks.

Conclusion

To summarize, the monetarists have made a valid and most valuable contribution in establishing that our economy is far less unstable than the early Keynesians pictured it and in rehabilitating the role of money as a determinant of aggregate demand. They are wrong, however, in going as far as asserting that the economy is sufficiently shockproof that stabilization policies are not needed. They have also made an important contribution in pointing out that such policies might in fact prove destabilizing. This criticism has had a salutary effect on reassessing what stabilization policies can and should do, and on trimming down fine-tuning ambitions. But their contention that postwar fluctuations resulted from an unstable money growth or that stabilization policies decreased rather than increased stability just does not stand up to an impartial examination of the postwar record of the United States and other industrialized countries. Up to 1974, these policies have helped to keep the economy reasonably stable by historical standards, even though one can certainly point to some occasional failures.

The serious deterioration in economic stability since 1973 must be attributed in the first place to the novel nature of the shocks that hit us, namely, supply shocks. Even the best possible aggregate demand management cannot offset such shocks without a lot of unemployment together with a lot of inflation. But, in addition, demand management was far from the best. This failure must be attributed in good measure to the fact that we had little experience or even an adequate conceptual framework to deal with such shocks; but at least from my reading of the record, it was also the result of failure to use stabilization policies, including too slavish adherence to the monetarists' constant money growth prescription.

We must, therefore, categorically reject the monetarist appeal to turn back the clock forty years by discarding the basic message of *The General Theory*. We should instead concentrate our efforts in an endeavor to make stabilization policies even more effective in the future than they have been in the past.

BIBLIOGRAPHY

ANDERSEN, L. C., and K. M. CARLSON. "A Monetarist Model for Economic Stabilization." Federal Reserve Bank St. Louis. *Review* 52 (April 1970), pp. 7–25.

———, and J. L. JORDAN. "Monetary and Fiscal Action: A Test of Their Relative Importance in Economic Stabilization." Federal Reserve Bank St. Louis. *Review* 50 (November 1968), pp. 11–23.

ARGY, V. "Rules, Discretion in Monetary Management, and Short-Term Stability." *Journal of Money, Credit and Banking* 3 (February 1971), pp. 102–22.

BAUMOL, W. J. "The Transactions Demand for Cash: An Inventory Theoretic Approach." *Quarterly Journal of Economics* 66 (November 1952), pp. 545–56.

BODKIN, R. G. "Real Wages and Cyclical Variations in Employment: A. Reexamination of the Evidence." *Canadian Journal of Economics* (August 1969), pp. 353–74.

BRONFENBRENNER, MARTIN. *Is the Business Cycle Obsolete?* New York, 1969.

BURNS, A. F. "Progress Towards Economic Stability." *American Economic Review* 50 (March 1960), pp. 1–19.

DUNLOP, J. T. "The Movement of Real and Money Wage Rates." *Economic Journal* 48 (September 1938), pp. 413–34.

ECKSTEIN, O., and R. BRINNER. "The Inflation Process in the United States." In Otto Eckstein, ed., *Parameters and Policies in the U.S. Economy*. Amsterdam, 1976.

FAIR, R. C. "On Controlling the Economy to Win Elections." Unpub. paper. Cowles Foundation, 1975.

FELDSTEIN, M. S. "Temporary Layoffs in the Theory of Unemployment." *Journal of Political Economy* 84 (October 1976), pp. 937–57.

FISCHER, S. "Long-term Contracts, Rational Expectations and the Optimal Money Supply Rule." *Journal of Political Economy,* forthcoming.

FRIEDMAN, B. M. "Rational Expectations Are Really Adaptive After All." Unpub. paper. Harvard University, 1975.

FRIEDMAN, MILTON. *A Theory of the Consumption Function.* Princeton, 1957.

———. "The Role of Monetary Policy." *American Economic Review* 58 (March 1968), pp. 1–17.

———. "The Demand for Money: Some Theoretical and Empirical Results." In his *The Optimum Quantity of Money, and Other Essays.* Chicago, 1969.

———, and A. SCHWARTZ. *A Monetary History of the United States 1867–1960.* Princeton, 1963.

GOLDFELD, S. "The Demand for Money Revisited." *Brookings Papers 3,* pp. 577–646. Washington 1973.

GORDON, R. J. "Recent Developments in the Theory of Inflation and Unemployment." *Journal of Monetary Economics* 2 (April 1976), pp. 185–219.

HICKS, J. R. "Mr. Keynes and the 'Classics'; A Suggested Interpretation," *Econometrica* 5 (April 1937), pp. 147–59.

KEYNES, JOHN MAYNARD. *The General Theory of Employment, Interest and Money.* New York, 1935.

LIPSEY, R. G. "The Relation Between Unemployment and the Rate of Change of Money Wage Rates in the United Kingdom, 1862–1957: A Further Analysis." *Economica* 27 (February 1960), pp. 1–31.

LOVELL, M. "Why Was the Consumer Feeling So Sad?" *Brookings Papers 2,* pp. 473–79. Washington, 1975.

LUCAS, R. E., JR. "Econometric Policy Evaluation. A Critique." *Journal of Monetary Economics* 1 (supplemental series, 1976), pp. 19–46.

———. "Expectations and the Neutrality of Money." *Journal of Economic Theory* 4 (April 1972), pp. 103–24.

MILLER, M., and D. ORR. "A Model of the Demand for Money by Firms." *Quarterly Journal of Economics* 80 (August 1966), pp. 413–35.

MODIGLIANI, F. "Liquidity Preference and the Theory of Interest and Money." *Econometrica* 12 (January 1944), pp. 45–88.

———. "New Development on the Oligopoly Front." *Journal of Political Economics* 66 (June 1958), pp. 215–33.

———. "The Monetary Mechanism and Its Interaction with Real Phenomena." *Review of Economic Statistics* (February 1963), pp. 79–107.

———. "Some Empirical Tests of Monetary Management and of Rules versus Discretion." *Journal of Political Economics* 72 (June 1964), pp. 211–45.

———. "The 1974 Report of the President's Council of Economic Advisers: A Critique of Past and Prospective Policies." *American Economic Review* 64 (September 1974), pp. 544–77.

———. "The Life Cycle Hypothesis of Saving Twenty Years Later." In Michael Parkin, ed., *Contemporary Issues in Economics.* Manchester, 1975.

———, and A. ANDO. "The Relative Stability of Monetary Velocity and the Investment Multiplier." *American Economic Review* 55 (September 1965), pp. 693–728.

————, and ————. "Impacts of Fiscal Actions on Aggregate Income and the Monetarist Controversy: Theory and Evidence." In Jerome L. Stein, ed., *Monetarism*. Amsterdam, 1976.

————, and R. BRUMBERG. "Utility Analysis and the Consumption Function: Interpretation of Cross-Section Data." In Kenneth Kurihara, ed., *Post-Keynesian Economics*. New Brunswick, 1954.

————, and L. PAPADEMOS. "Targets for Monetary Policy in the Coming Years." *Brookings Papers 1*, pp. 141–65. Washington, 1975.

————, and ————. "Monetary Policy for the Coming Quarters: The Conflicting Views." *New England Economic Review* (March/April 1976), pp. 2–35.

MUTH, J. F. "Rational Expectations and the Theory of Price Movements." *Econometrica* 29 (July 1961), pp. 315–35.

NORDHAUS, W. D. "The Political Business Cycle." *Review of Economic Studies* 42 (April 1975), pp. 169–90.

OKUN, A. M. "Inflation: Its Mechanics and Welfare Costs." *Brookings Papers 2*, pp. 351–90. Washington, 1975.

O'NEILL, D. "Directly Estimated Multipliers of Monetary and Fiscal Policy." Doctoral thesis in progress. M.I.T.

PAPADEMOS, L. "Optimal Aggregate Employment Policy and Other Essays." Doctoral thesis in progress. M.I.T.

PHELPS, EDMOND S. "Money-Wage Dynamics and Labor-Market Equilibrium." *Journal of Political Economics* (July/August 1968), pp. 678–711.

———— et al. *Microeconomic Foundations of Employment and Inflation Theory*. New York, 1970.

PHILLIPS, A. W. "The Relation between Unemployment and the Rate of Change of Money Wage Rates in the United Kingdom, 1861–1957." *Economica* 25 (November 1958), pp. 283–99.

SARGENT, T. J. "A Classical Macroeconomic Model for the United States." *Journal of Political Economics* 84 (April 1976), pp. 207–37.

————, and N. WALLACE. " 'Rational' Expectations, the Optimal Monetary Instrument, and the Optimal Money Supply Rule." *Journal of Political Economics* 83 (April 1975), pp. 241–57.

STARLEAF, D., and R. FLOYD. "Some Evidence with Respect to the Efficiency of Friedman's Monetary Policy Proposals." *Journal of Money, Credit, and Banking* 4 (August 1972), pp. 713–22.

TEMIN, PETER. *Did Monetary Forces Cause the Great Depression?* New York, 1976.

TOBIN, JAMES. *Essays in Economics: Vol. 1, Macroeconomics*. Chicago, 1971.

Empirical Evidence

IV

Most economists would contend that theoretical analysis can find useful application only when it is enriched by empirical measurement. Monetary economics has provided a major avenue for quantitative research. In recent years, both Keynesians and Monetarists have engaged in efforts to estimate the structural relations and implications of their models. The first article in this section, by Joseph M. Crews, focuses on two models that are somewhat representative of Keynesian and Monetarist views—the Federal Reserve Board–MIT econometric model and the econometric model of the Federal Reserve Bank of St. Louis. Crews chooses these two models because each features a well-developed monetary sector, each is fairly well seasoned as econometric models go, each has been widely debated, tested, and applied, particularly in the policy arena, and each is representative of a particular view of the transmission mechanism (discussed in detail in the Park and Spencer articles in a preceding section).

The second reading in this section, by Michael J. Hamburger, surveys recent opinion and evidence on the lag in the effect of monetary policy on the economy. Of the three factors considered that might account for the lag, Hamburger concludes that the most important is the specification of the explanatory monetary variable; the other two factors, the type of statistical model employed and the seasonal adjustment procedure, are less important.

VI

Empirical Evidence

Econometric Models: The Monetarist and Non-Monetarist Views Compared

Joseph M. Crews

The Non-Monetarist View

Two fundamentally different views of the role of money in economic activity underlie current econometric models. The Monetarist view is formulated as an econometric model by the Federal Reserve Bank of St. Louis. The non-Monetarist view, based largely on a disaggregated Keynesian approach to monetary analysis, has given rise to several large-scale econometric models containing up to several hundred equations. The approach is illustrated in this article by the so-called FRB-MIT model.[1]

The Historical Setting

Prior to the Depression of the 1930's, conventional economic theory considered the economy basically stable over the long run and tending toward full employment. The main theme of theoretical analysis was toward long-run equilibrium relationships,

Reprinted with deletions from the Federal Reserve Bank of Richmond, *Monthly Review* (February, 1973), pp. 3-12, by permission of the publisher and the author. The footnotes have been renumbered to follow the abridged article.

[1]Frank de Leeuw and Edward M. Gramlich, "The Channels of Monetary Policy: A Further Report on the Federal Reserve-MIT Model," *Journal of Finance,* 24 (May 1969), 265-90; and Leonall C. Andersen and Keith M. Carlson, "A Monetarist Model for Economic Stabilization," *Review,* Federal Reserve Bank of St. Louis, 52 (April 1970), 7-25.[The De Leeuw-Gramlich article and a more recent update of the Anderson-Carlson article are reprinted in this book.—Ed.]

with little attention devoted to the short-run process through which long-run equilibrium was attained. In this context, the quantity of money, together with the level of output, was viewed as determining the level of prices, but having little to do with long-run real productive growth. This *quantity theory* was brought into serious question as a result of the Depression. The development of an alternative theory of money, interest, and output was initiated by the British economist John Maynard Keynes.

Neo-Keynesian Theory

The approach to macroeconomics developed by Keynes and those who refined his work is known as the income-expenditure approach. Its basic characteristics may be summarized briefly. First, the economy is viewed as consisting of a number of sectors, e.g., the consumption, investment, and government sectors. Demand in each sector is determined by factors peculiar to the sector. Then, all sectoral demands are added together to determine aggregate demand, measured by gross national product, GNP. This process is illustrated in Exhibit 1, where equations 1 and 2 determine consumption and investment demand; government demand is exogenous. Aggregate demand is added together in equation 4. With larger, more complex models, each of these major components of aggregate demand is disaggregated. Consumption may be divided into expenditures for durables, nondurables, and services; in some cases, automobile demand is explained separately. Investment may be broken down into expenditures for producers' equipment, producers' structures, residential construction, and inventory changes. Government spending may be classified as Federal or state and local, with Federal expenditures further subdivided as defense or nondefense. This disaggregation procedure can be carried to any practical degree of detail, limited, of course, by the availability of appropriate data.

A second characteristic of neo-Keynesian models is a built-in policy transmission mechanism that deemphasizes the role of money. For the most part, this mechanism involves the *indirect* linkage of money with aggregate demand *via* interest rates. In its simplest form, it may be stated symbolically as:

$$OMO \rightarrow R \rightarrow M \rightarrow i \rightarrow I \rightarrow GNP.$$

An open market purchase of Government securities by the Federal Reserve, OMO, increases commercial bank reserves, R, and raises the banks' reserves-earning assets ratio. Banks operate to restore their desired ratios by extending new loans or by expanding bank credit in other ways. New loans create new demand deposits, thereby increasing the money supply, M. Given the public's liquidity preferences, a rising money supply causes the general level of interest rates, i, to decline. Given businessmen's "expected profits," expressed by Keynes as the *marginal efficiency of investment,* falling interest rates, i.e., reduced capital costs, induce expanded investment expenditures, I. Finally, increased investment spending causes successive

$$(1) \quad C_t = a_0 + a_1 Y_t + a_2 C_{t-1}$$

$$(2) \quad I_t = b_0 + b_1 P_t + b_2 K_{t-1}$$

$$(3) \quad W_t = c_0 + c_1 Y_t + c_2 t$$

$$(4) \quad Y_t = C_t + I_t + G_t$$

$$(5) \quad P_t = Y_t - W_t$$

$$(6) \quad K_t = K_{t-1} + I_t$$

where C = consumption

Y = income

W = wage income

P = nonwage income

I = net investment

K = capital stock at end of period

G = government expenditures on goods and services

t = time

EXHIBIT 1 AN ILLUSTRATIVE MODEL

Source: Adapted from a similar model presented in M. Liebenberg, A. Hirsch, and J. Popkin, "A Quarterly Econometric Model of the United States: A Progress Report," *Survey of Current Business,* 46 (May 1966), 13–16.

rounds of new final demand spending, causing GNP to rise by a multiple of the initial change in investment.[2]

A number of refinements to this process have been made by later economists. For example, this transmission process involves Keynes's liquidity preference trade-off of money and financial assets. In more sophisticated versions, this trade-off is generalized to better approximate a real world of "numerous financial assets, hence numerous interest rates on . . . different securities. Different types of investment spending are most sensitive to particular interest rates, e.g., plant and equipment investment to the corporate bond rate, residential construction to the mortgage rate, and inventory investment to the bankloan rate."[3] Policy-induced changes in bank reserves cause portfolio adjustments over a wide range of financial and real assets, eventually influencing the components of final demand spending.

In further refinement of the Keynesian theory, a number of writers now argue that

[2]William L. Silber, "Monetary Channels and the Relative Importance of Money Supply and Bank Portfolios," *Journal of Finance,* 24 (March 1969), 81–82.

[3]*Ibid.,* pp. 84–85.

changes in the money supply have direct wealth effects on consumption spending, in addition to the indirect wealth effects operating via interest rate changes, described above.

Two other characteristics of neo-Keynesian models are important as points of comparison with Monetarist models. First, the money supply, in the process described above, is an endogenous variable, whereas Monetarists consider it exogenous. Second, the basic Keynesian model treats the price level as independent of monetary forces. Large-scale neo-Keynesian econometric models, which generally encompass nonmonetary theories of price level determination, are consistent with this treatment. These two points will be clarified at appropriate points in the discussion below.

The FRB–MIT Model

The generalized neo-Keynesian approach to model building may be illustrated by the FRB-MIT model, which is a large-scale model of the U.S. economy constructed by the Board of Governors of the Federal Reserve System and the Economics Department of the Massachusetts Institute of Technology. Its stated purpose is to quantify the monetary policy process and its impact on the economy.[4] The model consists of 10 sectors, the most important of which are the financial, investment, and consumption/inventory sectors. The financial sector is displayed in Exhibit 2 and the real sector in Exhibit 3.

THE FINANCIAL SECTOR

The purpose of the financial sector is to establish the linkage between the instruments of monetary policy and the financial variables that are important in the real sector of the economy. Several types of variables appear in this sector. First, the instruments of monetary policy are nonborrowed reserves and the Federal Reserve discount rate. Nonborrowed reserves serve as a proxy for open market operations. Second, demands for short-term financial assets are explained. These assets include free reserves, demand deposits, currency, commercial loans, and time deposits held by banks, savings and loan associations, and mutual savings banks. Supply, i.e., rate-setting, equations explain interest rates on Treasury bills, commercial loans, commercial paper, mortgages, industrial bonds, and state and local bonds. Other rate-setting equations determine the stock market yield and rates on time deposits held by banks, savings and loan associations, and mutual savings banks. A term-structure equation relates the corporate bond rate to the commercial paper rate.

The workings of the financial sector may be illustrated by tracing the effects of a Federal Reserve purchase of Government securities, represented in the model as an increase in nonborrowed reserves, RU. As shown in Exhibit 2, this purchase causes a rise in free reserves, RF, and a rise in the price of Treasury bills, represented by a fall in the bill rate, RTB. Commercial banks are assumed to have, under given market conditions, a desired proportion of earning to nonearning assets (reserves). An in-

---

[4]See de Leeuw and Gramlich, *op cit.,* p. 266.

crease in nonborrowed reserves lowers the proportion of earning assets in the banks' portfolios below the desired level. In attempting to restore this ratio, banks attempt to purchase similar fixed coupon, short-term financial assets, increase their loan offerings, and increase their demands for commercial paper. The declining Treasury bill rate represents not only a decline in the yield on short-term Government securities but also a decline in short rates generally, for which RTB is a proxy. Other short rates, the commercial paper rate, RCP, and the rate on commercial loans, RCL, follow RTB downward. There follows a complex adjustment process serving to re-

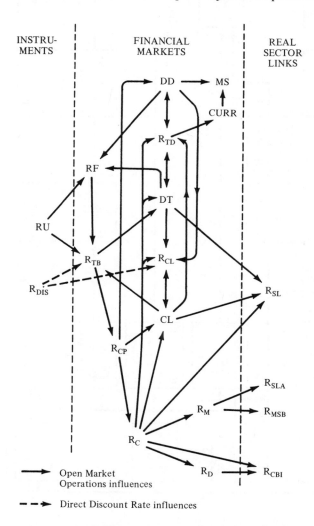

EXHIBIT 2 THE MONETARY POLICY PROCESS OF THE FRB–MIT MODEL

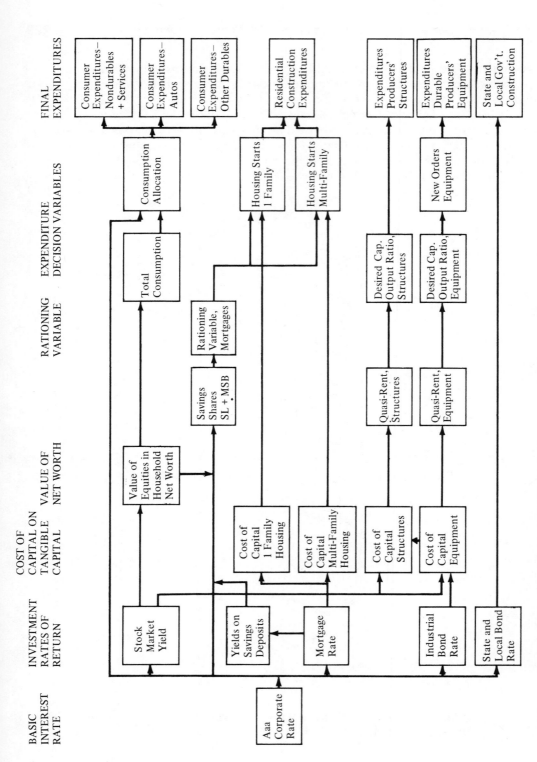

EXHIBIT 3 FIRST-ROUND EFFECTS OF MONETARY POLICY IN THE FRB-MIT MODEL

Source: Frank de Leeuw and Edward M. Gramlich, "The Channels of Monetary Policy," *Journal of Finance*, 24 (May 1969), 281.

store portfolio balance to the commercial banking market. This process is expressed primarily in the equations that determine the time deposit rate and the commercial loan rate.[5]

Part of the adjustment involves acquisition of longer-term financial assets, represented by a term-structure relationship linking the commercial paper rate and the corporate bond rate, RC. The corporate bond rate influences other long-term rates, the mortgage rate, RM, and the stock market yield, RD. These rates pass the monetary stimulus to the real sector by way of the industrial bond rate, RCBI; the state and local government bond rate, RSL; and the deposit rates of nonbank savings institutions, RSLA and RMSB.

THE FINANCIAL-REAL SECTOR LINKAGE

Monetary effects spread through the economy by way of three separate channels: the cost of capital, the net worth of households, and the availability of credit to the household sector. Continuing the above illustration, the impact of lower interest rates may be traced in Exhibit 3. The cost-of-capital channel captures the effect of three long-term interest rates—the corporate bond rate, the mortgage rate, and the stock market yield—on investment expenditures for plant and equipment, expenditures for consumer durables, expenditures for single-and multiple-family housing, and state and local Government construction spending.[6]

The net worth channel passes the effect of changing rates of return on bonds to the stock yield, to equity values in the net worth of households, and to consumption expenditures.

Finally, credit rationing, the third channel, is found to be important in the housing sector. Savings institutions experience large fluctuations in their deposit flows, because of the sluggishness of their lending and deposit rates. In addition, their portfolios usually include a high proportion of long-term, low turnover mortgages. In times of rising interest rates, these institutions are forced to restrict mortgage lending. This nonprice rationing of credit influences the residential construction component of final demand.

The FRB-MIT model thus illustrates two basic characteristics of neo-Keynesian models: (1) a highly detailed sector-by-sector buildup of aggregate demand and (2) a detailed specification of the portfolio adjustment process that attaches a central role to interest rates as an indirect link between monetary policy and final demand.

[5]This process is simplified in two ways for presentation in Exhibit 2. First, the portfolio balance terms are commercial loan-to-deposit ratios, which serve as measures of portfolio composition in determining each financial institution's desired deposit or loan rate. The actual market rate is a function of the discrepancy between the lagged actual rate and the desired rate. For simplicity, in Exhibit 2 each separate component of these ratios is shown rather than the full ratio. For example, rather than showing the ratio: CL/DD + DT, each component—commercial loans, CL; demand deposits, DD; and time deposits, DT—is shown separately. Second, in order to simplify the chart and to emphasize financial market interaction, no real sector feedback variables appear. These variables, such as GNP or net worth, enter the several asset demand equations as transactions or scaling variables. For further discussion of these points, see de Leeuw and Gramlich, *op. cit.,* pp. 267-80.

[6]For a more detailed description of the cost-of-capital channel, see de Leeuw and Gramlich, *loc cit.*

As a point of comparison with Monetarist models, one further characteristic of the FRB–MIT model should be mentioned. Prices are determined in this model by real sector forces, that is, by a variable markup over wage costs.[7] Factors influencing the size of this markup include a productivity trend variable, which allows producers to maintain profit shares even though wages rise faster than prices. Demand shifts and nonlabor cost-push forces are other factors involved in this essentially nonmonetary theory of the price level.

The Monetarist View

Although the quantity theory was in eclipse during the period of neo-Keynesian preeminence, a group of economists, led by Professor Milton Friedman at the University of Chicago, continued to develop the Monetarist approach, restructuring the theory and gathering supporting statistical evidence. With the problems of increasing inflation in the late 1960's and the questionable effectiveness of the 1968 tax surcharge in dampening inflationary pressures, the policy prescriptions and forecasts of neo-Keynesian economists became increasingly subject to question.[8] The Monetarist view gained increased respect among academic economists and policymakers.

Monetarist Theory

Modern Monetarists consider the economy basically stable, with most elements of instability the product of faulty monetary arrangements or improper policy. The reasoning behind this may be briefly summarized. First, there is a stable, but not precise, relationship between the growth rates of money and nominal, i.e., current dollar, national income or GNP. If money balances grow more rapidly in relation to income than people wish, they will attempt to spend the excess, causing prices to rise. On the other hand, if money grows too slowly in relation to income, people will try to build up their cash balances by reducing spending, which would result in a slowing of income growth and rising unemployment.[9] Changes in money and income do not occur simultaneously. On the average, a change in monetary growth will result in a change in real output growth six to nine months later, followed by changes in prices in another six to nine months, according to Friedman's estimates.[10]

[7]See de Leeuw and Gramlich, *op cit.*, Appendix, pp. A15–16.

[8]There is some debate concerning the effectiveness of the 1968 tax surcharge. See, for example, Robert Eisner, "Fiscal and Monetary Policy Reconsidered," *American Economic Review*, 59 (December 1969), 897–905; and the subsequent comments and reply in *American Economic Review*, 61 (June 1971), 444–61. See also, Milton Friedman, "The Counter-Revolution in Monetary Theory." *Occasional Paper No. 33* (London: The Institute of Economic Affairs, 1970), pp. 19–20, and Arthur M. Okun, "The Personal Tax Surcharge and Consumer Demand, 1968–70." *Brookings Papers on Economic Activity* (January 1971), pp. 167–213.

[9]William N. Cox, III, "The Money Supply Controversy," *Monthly Review*, Federal Reserve Bank of Atlanta, 54 (June 1969), 73.

[10]Friedman, *op. cit.*, p. 22.

Carrying this logic further, the Monetarists consider fiscal policy, when not accompanied by changes in the money supply, to be an unlikely source of economic change. For example, increased Government spending, if not accompanied by monetary expansion, will tend to "crowd out" some private spending and have minimal impact on aggregate demand.[11] Fiscal policy distributes income between the private and public sectors but has little impact on price level changes.[12] Thus, short-run variations in prices, output, and employment are thought to be dominated by movements in a policy-determined money supply.[13]

Long-run real economic growth, on the other hand, is thought to be independent of monetary change, being determined by basic growth factors such as expanding productive capacity, population growth, advancing technology, and natural resources. In the long run, monetary change affects only the price level. Accordingly, the basic objective of monetary policy is to "prevent money itself from being a major source of economic disturbance."[14] It follows that stabilization policy should seek a growth rate of money that closely approximates the long-term rate of growth of real productive capacity.

The Monetarist view of the role of interest rates in the policy transmission process may be summarized in the following way:

> . . . Monetary impulses are . . . transmitted by the play of interest rates over a vast array of assets. Variations in interest rates change relative prices of existing assets, relative to both yields and the supply prices of new production. Acceleration or deceleration of monetary impulses are thus converted by the variation of relative prices, or interest rates, into increased or reduced production, and subsequent revisions in supply prices of current output.[15]

Further, while interest rates serve to facilitate real and financial asset adjustments, "the impact of changes in money on any specific interest rate is both too brief and too weak to be either captured statistically or identified as a strategic variable in the transmission process."[16] Therefore, the Monetarists view the *money supply as the strategic variable,* affecting income directly. This view may be represented schematically as:

$$\text{OMO} \rightarrow \text{M} \rightarrow \text{SPENDING} \rightarrow \text{GNP.}$$

A comparison of this description with the generalized neo-Keynesian portfolio

[11]Andersen and Carlson, *op. cit.,* p. 8.

[12]Friedman, *op. cit.,* p. 24.

[13]Ronald L. Teigen, "A Critical Look at Monetarist Economics," *Review,* Federal Reserve Bank of St. Louis, 54 (January 1972), 13.

[14]Milton Friedman, "The Role of Monetary Policy," *American Economic Review,* 58 (March 1968), 12.

[15]Karl Brunner, "The Role of Money and Monetary Policy," *Review,* Federal Reserve Bank of St. Louis, 50 (July 1969), 18.

[16]W. E. Gibson and G. C. Kaufman, "The Relative Impact of Money and Income on Interest Rates: An Empirical Investigation," *Staff Economic Studies* (Washington, D. C. : Board of Governors of the Federal Reserve System, 1966), p. 3.

adjustment process, as illustrated by the FRB–MIT model, focuses on two crucial points at issue: the range of assets involved in the adjustment process and the response patterns of interest rates and prices. Concerning the former, Friedman argues that the spectrum of assets and rates of return influenced by monetary action is extremely broad, including many implicit rates, which are not recorded.[17]

Friedman further argues that recorded rates do not reflect the real cost of capital but rather include anticipated rates of inflation. Moreover, monetary policy may be routed through as yet undiscovered channels. In short, the transmission process is too complicated to be captured by statistical models. The standard practice of using recorded interest rates both underestimates the full impact of monetary actions and narrows the scope of the transmission process to only a relatively few channels. Therefore, Friedman concludes, even the most complex econometric model cannot adequately represent the monetary process.[18]

Monetarists also question the response patterns of interest rates and prices in neo-Keynesian models. They regard the fall in interest rates in response to monetary expansion as a temporary effect. In a longer view, monetary expansion, whether via interest rate effects or direct spending effects, causes rising income and expenditures. The Monetarists are careful to distinguish nominal from real changes. When the economy is operating below the full-employment level, changes in nominal money may significantly affect real economic variables—output and employment—rather than rising prices. As the economy approaches full employment, however, quantities become less responsive, and prices begin to rise. The real value of money balances grows more slowly, or declines, causing a reversal of the initial interest rate effect.[19] Thus, changes in interest rates may be only a result of the adjustment process, rather than a crucial link; and may be directly, rather than inversely, related to changes in money.

Prices, in this process, are a function of "demand pressure"—determined by how close to full employment the economy is operating. In addition, an accumulation of price changes over time tends to generate "price expectations," which serve as a separate influence in future price movements. Thus, the long-run insensitivity of real variables to changes in the money supply and the predominant short-run influence of money on real output and employment are consistent.

The St. Louis Model

The process described above has recently been incorporated into an econometric model by the Federal Reserve Bank of St. Louis.[20] The model makes no attempt to

[17]Friedman, *Occasional Paper No. 33*, p. 25.

[18]Yung C. Park, "Some Current Issues on the Transmission Process of Monetary Policy," *IMF Staff Papers,* 19 (March 1972), 24-26.

[19]For similar, but more detailed, expositions see Friedman, "The Role of Monetary Policy," *American Economic Review,* 58 (March 1968), 6; and David I. Fand, "A Monetarist Model of the Monetary Process," *Journal of Finance,* 25 (May 1970), 279-83.

[20]For a more detailed development, see Andersen and Carlson, *op. cit.,* pp. 8-11.

specify the structure of the economy; rather, it explains such broad measures as total spending, prices, and unemployment in terms of changes in money, Government expenditures, potential output, and price expectations.

The process by which monetary action predominates short-run changes in total spending can be seen by tracing through the flow chart, Exhibit 4. The responses in the actual model accumulate over a number of periods, but no lags except price changes appear in the chart. Total spending, measured by GNP, responds more strongly to money supply changes than to changes in the full-employment budget. The latter actually has a negative impact after three quarters, reflecting the Monetarists' "crowding-out" hypothesis.

Potential output is determined by underlying factors such as growth of natural resources, technology, labor force, and productive capacity. Total spending and potential output together determine the amount of "demand pressure" existing in the economy in the short-run. Demand pressure, a measure of short-run market conditions, combines with long-run price expectations to determine the current change in the price level. Price expectations, measured by a five-quarter weighted average of past price level changes, enter price determination as a separate influence.

The model thus determines changes in total spending and prices separately. Short-run changes in real output are then calculated as a residual by subtracting the price factor from changes in total spending.

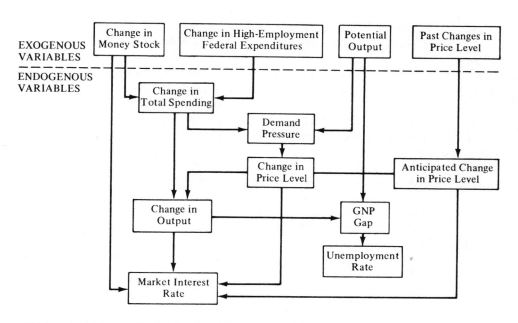

EXHIBIT 4 FLOW DIAGRAM OF THE ST. LOUIS MODEL

Source: Leonall G. Andersen and Keith M. Carlson, "A Monetarist Model for Economic Stabilization," *Review*, Federal Reserve Bank of St. Louis, 52 (April 1970), 10.

Changes in output are subtracted from changes in potential output to determine the GNP gap, a measure of productive slack in the economy. The unemployment rate is directly related to current and past levels of the GNP gap. Changes in output combine with changes in money supply, current and past changes in price levels, and price expectations to determine the level of interest rates. Market interest rates are a result of market interaction, not a crucial link in the transmission process as in the Keynesian view.

In sum, the St. Louis model is a direct formulation of the Monetarist view that monetary changes predominate short-run changes in the real economy, while in the long run money affects only nominal quantities. The model also reflects the contention that the full transmission mechanism cannot be captured by econometric models. The stable relationship found between money and total spending becomes the basis for a small, simple model that explains changes in broad economic aggregates in terms of changes in the money supply.

Summary

This article has examined the econometric implications of two alternative theories of the monetary process. Both the neo-Keynesians and the Monetarists see a general portfolio balance mechanism at work in the economy, but agreement seems to stop there. Their divergent views concerning the importance of interest rates, the direction of effect of money on interest rates, the nature of price determination, and the feasibility of representing the adjustment process econometrically have been discussed above.

Although the two models presented here are representative of current thinking, some preliminary movement toward synthesis is evident. Recent analytical work has introduced prices into Keynesian models as endogenous variables.[21] Later unpublished versions of the FRB–MIT model are structured so that either the money supply or reserves may be used as a policy variable.[22] Recent unpublished Monetarist work specifies structural detail more than in the past.[23] The problem of implicit interest rates remains unresolved. The resolution of this problem and the thrust of current research point in the direction of larger, more detailed econometric models.

[21]Arthur Benavie, "Prices and Wages in the Complete Keynesian Model," *Southern Economic Journal*, 38 (April 1972), 468–77; Teigen, *op. cit.*, p. 15 and footnote 27.

[22]"FRB–MIT–PENN Econometric Model," unpublished staff paper, Federal Reserve Board of Governors, July 13, 1971.

[23]Leonall C. Andersen, "Influence of Monetary and Financial Actions in a Financially Constrained Economy," unpublished paper, May 1971, p. 40.

The Lag in the Effect of Monetary Policy: A Survey of Recent Literature

Michael J. Hamburger*

14

During the last ten years the views of economists—both monetarists and nonmonetarists—on the lag in the effect of monetary policy on the economy have changed considerably. This article examines some of the recent evidence which has served as the basis for these changes.

Prior to 1960, quantitative estimates of the lag in the effect of monetary policy were rare. While there had always been disagreement on the effectiveness of monetary policy, a substantial number of economists seemed to accept the proposition that there was sufficient impact in the reasonably short run for monetary policy to be used as a device for economic stabilization. Although this view did not go unquestioned— see, for example, Mayer [26] and Smith [29][1]—the main challenge to the conventional thinking came from Milton Friedman. He argued that monetary policy acts with so long and variable a lag that attempts to pursue a contracyclical monetary policy might aggrevate, rather than ameliorate, economic fluctuations. In summarizing work done in collaboration with Anna Schwartz, he wrote [16]: "We have found

Reprinted from the Federal Reserve Bank of New York, *Monetary Aggregates and Monetary Policy* (1974), pp. 104-113, by permission of the publisher.

* The author wishes to acknowledge the helpful comments of Richard G. Davis, David H. Kopf, Robert G. Link, and other colleagues at the Federal Reserve Bank of New York. In addition, the excellent research assistance of Susan Skinner and Rona Stein is gratefully acknowledged. The views expressed in this paper are the author's alone and do not necessarily reflect those of the individuals noted above or the Federal Reserve Bank of New York.

[1]The numbers in brackets refer to the works cited at the end of this article.

that, on the average of 18 cycles, peaks in the rate of change in the stock of money tend to precede peaks in general business by about 16 months and troughs in the rate of change in the stock of money precede troughs in general business by about 12 months. . . . For individual cycles, the recorded lead has varied between 6 and 29 months at peaks and between 4 and 22 months at troughs."

Many economists were simply not prepared to believe Friedman's estimates of either the length or the variability of the lag. As Culbertson [11] put it, "if we assume that government stabilization policies . . . act with so long and variable a lag, how do we set about explaining the surprising moderateness of the economic fluctuations that we have suffered in the past decade?" Culbertson's own conclusion was that "the broad record of experience support[s] the view that [contracyclical] monetary, debt-management, and fiscal adjustments can be counted on to have their predominant direct effects within three to six months, soon enough that if they are undertaken moderately early in a cyclical phase they will not be destabilizing."

Kareken and Solow [5] also appear to have been unwilling to accept Friedman's estimates. They summarized their results as follows: "Monetary policy works neither so slowly as Friedman thinks, nor as quickly and surely as the Federal Reserve itself seems to believe. . . . Though the *full* results of policy changes on the flow of expenditures may be a long time coming, nevertheless the chain of effects is spread out over a fairly wide interval. This means that *some* effect comes reasonably quickly, and that the effects build up over time so that some substantial stabilizing power results after a lapse of time of the order of six or nine months."

However, as Mayer [27] pointed out, this statement is inconsistent with the evidence presented by Kareken and Solow. They reported estimates of the complete lag in the effect of monetary policy on the flow of expenditures for only one component of gross national product (GNP), namely, inventory investment, and this lag is much longer than Friedman's lag. For another sector—producers' durable equipment—they provided data for only part of the lag, but even this is longer than Friedman's lag. Thus, Mayer noted that Kareken and Solow "should have criticized Friedman, not for overestimating, but for underestimating the lag."

More recently, it is the *monetarists* who have taken the view that the lag in the effect of monetary policy is relatively short and the nonmonetarists who seem to be claiming longer lags. This showed up in the reaction to the St. Louis (Andersen and Jordan) equation [4]. According to this equation, the total response of GNP to changes in the money supply is completed within a year.

In his review of the Andersen and Jordan article, Davis [12] wrote "the most surprising thing about the world of the St. Louis equation is not so much the force, but rather the speed with which money begins to act on the economy." If the level of the money supply undergoes a $1 billion once-and-for-all rise in a given quarter, it will (according to the St. Louis equation) raise GNP by $1.6 billion in that quarter and by $6.6 billion during four quarters. In contrast, Davis found that in the Federal Reserve Board–Massachusetts Institute of Technology model—which was estimated by assuming nonborrowed reserves to be the basic monetary policy variable—a once-and-for-all increase in the money supply of $1 billion in a given quarter has almost no effect on GNP in that quarter and, even after four quarters, the level of GNP is only about $400 million higher than it otherwise would be. Thus, he concluded, "what is at stake in the case of the St. Louis equation is not merely a 'shade of difference' but a strikingly contrasting view of the world—at least relative to what is normally taken as the orthodox view roughly replicated and confirmed both in methods and in result by the Board-MIT model."[2]

The Federal Reserve Board-MIT model (henceforth called the FRB-MIT model) is not the only econometric model suggesting that monetary policy operates with a long distributed lag. Indeed, practically every *structural* model of the United States economy which has been addressed to this question has arrived at essentially the same answer.[3]

The most recent advocates of short lags are Arthur Laffer and R. David Ranson [25]. They have argued that: "Monetary policy, as represented by changes in the conventionally defined money supply [demand deposits plus currency], has an immediate and permanent impact on the level of GNP. For every dollar increase in the money supply, GNP will rise by about $4.00 or $5.00 in the current quarter, and not fall back [or rise any further] in the future. Alternatively, every 1 percent change in the money supply is associated with a 1 percent change in GNP."

This article reviews some of the recent professional literature on the lag in the effect of monetary policy, with the objective of examining the factors which account for differences in the results. Among the factors considered are: (1) the type of statistical estimating model, i.e., structural versus reduced-form equations; (2) the specification of the monetary policy variable; and (3) the influence of the seasonal adjustment procedure. For the most part, the analysis is confined to the results obtained by others. New estimation is undertaken only in those instances where it is considered necessary to reconcile different sets of results.

Structural versus Reduced-Form Models

We turn first to the question of whether it is more appropriate to use structural or reduced-form models to estimate the effects of stabilization policy on the economy. A structural model of the economy attempts to set forth in equation form what are considered to be the underlying or basic economic relationships in the economy. Although many mathematical and statistical complications may arise such a set of equations can, in principle, be "reduced" (solved). In this way key economic vari-

---

[2]The properties of the Federal Reserve-MIT model are discussed by de Leeuw and Gramlich [13, 14] and by Ando and Modigliani [6].

[3]See Hamburger [21] and Mayer [27]. For a recent discussion of why the lag should be long, see Davis [12], Gramlich [19], and Pierce [28]. The alternative view is presented by White [31], who also gives reasons for believing that the procedures used to estimate the parameters of large-scale econometric models, particularly the FRB-MIT model, may yield "greatly exaggerated" estimates of the length of the lag.

ables, such as GNP, can be expressed directly as functions of policy variables and other forces exogenous to the economy. While the difference between a structural model and a reduced-form model is largely mathematical and does not necessarily involve different assumptions about the workings of the economy, a lively debate has developed over the advantages and disadvantages of these two approaches.

Users of structural models stress the importance of tracing the paths by which changes in monetary policy are assumed to influence the economy. Another advantage often claimed for the structural approach is that it permits one to incorporate *a priori* knowledge about the economy, for example, knowledge about identities, lags, the mathematical forms of relationships, and what variables should or should not be included in various equations (Gramlich [20]).

On the other hand those who prefer the reduced-form approach contend that, if one is primarily interested in explaining the behavior of a few key variables, such as GNP, prices, and unemployment, it is unnecessary to estimate all the parameters of a large-scale model. In addition it is argued that, if the economy is very complicated, it may be too difficult to study even with a very complicated model. Hence, it may be useful simply to examine the relationship between inputs such as monetary and fiscal policy and outputs such as GNP.

Considering the heat of the debate, it is surprising that very little evidence has been presented to support either position. The only studies of which I am aware come from two sources: simulations with the FRB-MIT model, reported by de Leeuw and Gramlich [13, 14], and the separate work of de Leeuw and Kalchbrenner [15]. The latter study reported the estimates of a reduced form equation for GNP, using monetary and fiscal policy variables similar to those in the FRB-MIT model. The form of the equation is:

Equation 1

$$\Delta Y_t = a + \sum_{i=0}^{7} b_i \Delta NBR_{t-i} + \sum_{i=0}^{7} c_i \Delta E_{t-i} + \sum_{i=0}^{7} d_i \Delta RA_{t-i} + u_t$$

where

ΔY = Quarterly change in GNP, current dollars.
ΔNBR = Quarterly change in nonborrowed reserves adjusted for reserve requirement changes.
ΔE = Quarterly change in high-employment expenditures of the Federal Government, current dollars.
ΔRA = Quarterly change in high-employment receipts of the Federal Government in current-period prices.
u = Random error term.

All variables are adjusted for seasonal variation, and the lag structures are estimated by using the Almon distributed lag technique.[4]

Chart 1 illustrates the lag distributions of the effect on GNP of nonborrowed reserves—the principal monetary variable used in the studies just mentioned. The chart shows the cumulative effects of a one-dollar change in nonborrowed reserves on the level of GNP as illustrated by four experiments, the reduced-form equation of de Leeuw and Kalchbrenner, and three versions of the FRB–MIT model. The heavy broken line traces the sum of the regression coefficients for the current and lagged values of nonborrowed reserves in the de Leeuw-Kalchbrenner equation (i.e., the sum of the b_i's). The other lines show the results obtained from simulations of the FRB–MIT model; FRB–MIT 1969(a) and FRB–MIT 1969(b) represent simulations of the 1969 version of the model, with two different sets of initial conditions.[5] FRB–MIT 1968 gives the simulation results for an earlier version of the model.

Although there are some large short-run differences in the simulation results, these three experiments suggest similar long-run effects of nonborrowed reserves on income. Such a finding is not very surprising; what is significant, in view of the debate between those who prefer structural models and those who prefer reduced forms, is that after the first three or four quarters the de Leeuw-Kalchbrenner results lie well within the range of the simulation results.[6]

Thus, we find that when nonborrowed reserves are chosen as the exogenous monetary policy variable, i.e., the variable used in *estimating* the parameters of the model, it makes very little difference whether the lag in the effect of policy is determined by a structural or a reduced-form model. There is, to be sure, no assurance that similar results would be obtained with other monetary variables or with other structural models (including more recent versions of the FRB–MIT model). In the present case,

[4]Use of the Almon [1] procedure has become quite popular in recent years as it imposes very little *a priori* restriction on the shape of the lag structure, requiring merely that it can be approximated by a polynomial. In the applications discussed in this article, it is generally assumed that a second- or a fourth-degree polynomial is sufficiently flexible to reproduce closely the true lag structure.

[5]For the FRB–MIT 1969(a) simulation, the values of all exogenous variables in the model, except nonborrowed reserves, are set equal to their actual values starting in the first quarter of 1964. For the FRB–MIT 1969(b) simulation, the starting values for these variables are their actual values in the second quarter of 1958. The obvious difference between these two sets of initial conditions is the difference in inflationary potential. The quarters during and after 1964 were ones of high resource utilization, and an expansion of reserves at such a time might be expected to stimulate price increases promptly. On the other hand, there was substantial excess capacity in 1958 and a change in reserves under such conditions would be expected to have a minimal short-run effect on prices. The difference in these price effects is significant since it is movements in *current*-dollar GNP which are being explained.

[6]De Leeuw and Kalchbrenner do not estimate lags longer than seven quarters. While it is conceivable that the curve representing their results could flatten out (or decline) after period t-7, the shape of the curve up to that point and the results obtained by others, such as those shown in Chart 2, make this possibility seem highly unlikely. The initial negative values for the de Leeuw-Kalchbrenner curve arise because of the large negative estimate of b_0 in equation 1; the estimates for all other b's are positive. As de Leeuw and Kalchbrenner pointed out, it is difficult to provide an economic explanation for changes in nonborrowed reserves having a negative effect on GNP in the current quarter. It seems more reasonable, therefore, that the result reflects "reverse causation," running from GNP to nonborrowed reserves—that is, the Federal Reserve's attempt to pursue a contracyclical monetary policy. This point is discussed at greater length in Hamburger [22].

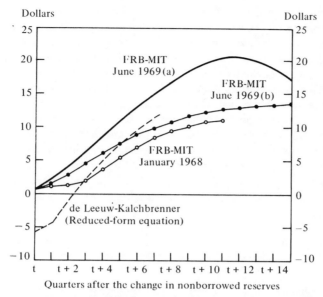

CHART 1 CUMULATIVE EFFECTS OF A ONE-DOLLAR CHANGE IN NONBORROWED RESERVES ON GNP

Note: FRB-MIT = Federal Reserve Board-Massachusetts Institute of Technology econometric model.

however, the use of reduced-form equations does not lead to estimates of the effects of monetary policy on the economy that differ from those obtained from a structural model. For the purposes of our analysis, this finding implies that the type of statistical model employed to estimate the lag in the effect of monetary policy may be less important than other factors in explaining the differences in the results that have been reported in the literature.

Specification of the Monetary Policy Variable

Another important difference among the various studies of the lag is the variable used to represent monetary policy. The aim of this section is not to contribute to the controversy about the most appropriate variable, but rather to summarize the arguments and spell out the implications of the choice for the estimate of the lag in the effect of policy.

In recent years three of the most popular indicators of the thrust of monetary policy have been the money supply, the monetary base, and effective nonborrowed reserves.[7] Monetarists prefer the first two variables on the grounds that they provide the most appropriate measures of the impact of monetary policy on the economy. Critics of the monetarist approach contend that these variables are deficient because they reflect the effects of both policy and nonpolicy influences and hence do not provide reliable (i.e., statistically unbiased) measures of Federal Reserve actions. The variable most often suggested by these economists is effective nonborrowed reserves.[8] In reply the monetarists have argued that, since the Federal Reserve has the power to offset the effects of all nonpolicy influences on the money supply (or the monetary base), it is the movements in the money variable and not the reasons for the movements which are important (Brunner [7] and Brunner and Meltzer [8]). However, this sidesteps the statistical question of whether the money supply or the monetary base qualify as exogenous variables to be included on the right-hand side of a reduced-form equation. (For a further discussion, see Ġramlich [20] and Hamburger[22].)*

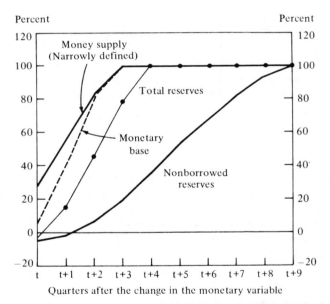

CHART 2 CUMULATIVE PERCENTAGE DISTRIBUTIONS OF THE EFFECTS OF VARIOUS MONETARY AGGREGATES ON GNP

Sources: See footnote 9.

[7]Nonborrowed reserves adjusted for changes in reserve requirements. A similar adjustment is made in computing the monetary base, which is defined as total member bank reserves plus the currency holdings of nonmember banks and the nonbank public. The reserve figure included in the base is also adjusted to neutralize the effects of changes in the ratio of demand deposits to time deposits and changes in the distribution of deposits among banks subject to different reserve requirements.

[8]Among others, see de Leeuw and Kalchbrenner [15], Gramely [18], and Hendershott [23].

* See the preceding article by Lombra and Torto for an interesting attempt to resolve this issue.—Ed.

Chart 2 presents the cumulative percentage distributions of the effects of various monetary variables on nominal GNP, as implied by the parameter estimates for equations similar to equation 1, that is, reduced-form equations relating quarterly changes in GNP to quarterly changes in monetary and fiscal policy variables. The monetary variables are effective nonborrowed reserves, the monetary base, the narrowly defined money supply (private holdings of currency and demand deposits), and total reserves. The latter is defined as effective nonborrowed reserves plus member bank borrowings from the Federal Reserve. It is also approximately equal to the monetary base less the currency holdings of nonmember banks and of the nonbank public. Once again, the lag structures for the monetary and fiscal policy variables are estimated using the Almon distributed lag technique. In all cases, with the possible exception of the monetary base, the lags chosen are those which maximize the $\bar{R}^2$ (coefficient of determination adjusted for degrees of freedom) of the equation. Percentage distributions are used to highlight the distribution of the effects over time as opposed to their dollar magnitudes.[9]

The results indicate that the choice of the exogenous monetary policy variable has a significant effect on the estimate of the lag in the effect of policy. If the money supply, the monetary base, or total reserves are taken as the monetary variable, the results suggest that the total response of GNP to a change in policy is completed within four or five quarters. On the other hand, those who consider nonborrowed reserves to be the appropriate variable would conclude that less than 40 percent of the effect occurs in five quarters and that the full effect is distributed over two and a half years.[10]

Thus, the evidence suggests that the relatively short lags that have been found by the monetarists in recent years depend more on their specification of the monetary policy variable than on the use of a reduced-form equation. Whether or not these estimates understate the true length of the lag, they seem roughly consistent with the prevailing view among economists in the early 1960's. They are, for example, essentially identical with Mayer's [26] results which suggested that most of the effect of a change in policy occurs within five quarters. As indicated above, wide acceptance of the proposition that monetary policy operates with a long lag—i.e., a substantial portion of the impact of a policy change does not take place until a year or more later—is of relatively recent vintage and appears to have been heavily influenced by

---

[9]The estimates shown in Chart 2 are derived from the equations reported by Corrigan [10] and by Andersen and Jordan [4]. Corrigan's results are used for the nonborrowed reserves, total reserves, and money supply curves (the nonborrowed reserves equation is not shown in his article but is available on request). He did not estimate an equation for the monetary base. The fiscal policies variables used in all three equations are the changes in the Government spending and tax components of the "initial stimulus" measure of fiscal policy. The monetary base curve is derived from the Andersen and Jordan results. The fiscal measures used in this study are the Government expenditure and receipt components of the high-employment budget. The criterion used by Andersen and Jordan to select their lag structures is described by Keran [24].

[10]A similar conclusion was reached by Andersen [2], who found even longer lags when nonborrowed reserves are used as the monetary policy variable.

the results of those who do not consider the money supply to be an appropriate measure of monetary policy impulses.

The Seasonal Adjustment Problem

One of the most recent investigations of the effects of monetary and fiscal policy on the economy is that conducted by Laffer and Ranson for the Office of Management and Budget [25]. Perhaps the most striking finding of this study is that every change in the money supply has virtually all its effect on the level of GNP in the quarter in which it occurs. Or, to put this differently, there is little evidence of a lag in the effect of monetary policy. This finding which stands at odds with most other evidence, both theoretical and empirical, is attributed by Laffer and Ranson largely to their use of data that are *not* adjusted for seasonal variation.[11] They contend that the averaging (or smoothing) properties of most seasonal adjustment procedures tend to distort the timing of statistical relationships. Hence, specious lag structures may be introduced into the results.

As shown below, however, the results reported by Laffer and Ranson are much more dependent on their choice of time period (1948-69) than on the use of seasonally unadjusted data. For, if their nominal GNP equation is reestimated for the period 1953-1969 (the period employed in the current version of the St. Louis model [3] and in most other recent investigations), it makes very little difference whether one uses seasonally adjusted or unadjusted data. They both indicate that a significant portion of the effect of a change in money does not occur for at least two quarters.

The equation selected by Laffer and Ranson to explain the percentage change in nominal GNP is:[12]

Equation 2

$$\%\Delta Y = 3.21 + 1.10\%\Delta M_1 + .136\%\Delta G - .069\%\Delta G_{-1}$$
$$(4.9) \quad (5.5) \quad\quad (6.9) \quad\quad (3.3)$$

$$- .039\%\Delta G_{-2} - .024\%\Delta G_{-3} - .046\Delta SH$$
$$(1.9) \quad\quad (1.2) \quad\quad (3.7)$$

$$+ .068\%\Delta S\&P_{-1} - 9.8\ D_1 + 2.5\ D_2 - 3.0\ D_3$$
$$(2.2) \quad\quad (12.1) \quad (2.6) \quad (4.1)$$

$$\bar{R}^2 = .958 \quad\quad SE = 1.31 \quad\quad Interval:\ 1948\text{-}I\ to\ 1969\text{-}IV$$

[11]Other studies which find very short lags in the effect of monetary policy are cited by Laffer and Ranson [25].

[12]The numbers in parentheses are t-statistics for the regression coefficients. SE is the standard error of estimate of the regression. A subscript preceded by a minus sign indicates that the variable is lagged that many quarters. In estimating their model, Laffer and Ranson use quarterly changes in the natural logarithms of the variables. This is roughly equivalent to using quarter-to-quarter percentage changes.

where

%ΔY	=	Quarterly percentage change in nominal GNP.
%ΔM₁	=	Quarterly percentage change in M_1 (the narrowly defined money supply).
%ΔG	=	Quarterly percentage change in Federal Government purchases of goods and services.
ΔSH	=	Quarterly change in a measure of industrial man-hours lost due to strikes.
%ΔS&P	=	Quarterly percentage change in Standard and Poor's Composite Index of Common Stock Prices (the "S&P 500").
D₁	=	Seasonal dummy variable for the first quarter.
D₂	=	Seasonal dummy variable for the second quarter.
D₃	=	Seasonal dummy variable for the third quarter.

All data used in the calculations are unadjusted for seasonal variation. The three dummy variables (D_1, D_2, and D_3) are introduced to allow for such variation and to permit estimation of the seasonal factors. In principle, joint estimation of the seasonal factors and the economic parameters of a model is preferable to the use of data generated by the standard type of seasonal adjustment procedure. However, in having only three dummy variables, Laffer and Ransom assume that the seasonal pattern in income is constant over the entire sample period. If this assumption is not correct, it becomes a purely empirical question as to whether their procedure is any better or worse than the use of seasonally adjusted data.

Stock market prices are included in the equation on the assumption that the current market value of equities provides an efficient forecast of future income. The variable representing the percentage of manhours lost due to strikes (SH) is included for institutional reasons.

Aside from these factors, the Laffer-Ranson equation is quite similar to the St. Louis equation. The most important difference is that the former contains only the current-quarter value of money. This implies that a change in the money supply has a once-and-for-all effect on the level of income. Equation 3 shows the results obtained when four lagged values of the percentage change in M_1 are included in the model. Only the coefficients of the money variables are shown below; the rest of the results for this equation as well as those for equation 2 are reproduced in the first portion of Table 1.

Equation 3

$$\%\Delta Y = 3.36 + 1.03\%\Delta M_1 - .41\%\Delta M_{1-1} + .49\%\Delta M_{1-2}$$
$$\quad (3.9) \quad (4.4) \quad\quad (1.7) \quad\quad\quad (2.1)$$

$$\quad\quad - .31\%\Delta M_{1-3} + .30\%\Delta M_{1-4} \ldots.$$
$$\quad\quad\quad (1.3) \quad\quad\quad (1.3)$$

$$\bar{R}^{-2} = .961 \quad\quad SE = 1.26 \quad\quad \text{Interval: 1948-I to 1969-IV}$$

Table 1. Regressions Explaining the Percentage Change in Gross National Product (Quarterly seasonally unadjusted data)

Equation	Constant	$\%\Delta M_1$	$\%\Delta M_{1-1}$	$\%\Delta M_{1-2}$	$\%\Delta M_{1-3}$	$\%\Delta M_{1-4}$	$\%\Delta G$	$\%\Delta G_{-1}$	$\%\Delta G_{-2}$	$\%\Delta G_{-3}$	ΔSH	$\%\Delta S\&P_{-1}$	D_1	D_2	D_3	$\bar{R}^2$ / SE
1948–I to 1969–IV																
2	3.21 (4.9)	1.10 (5.5)					.136 (6.9)	−.069 (3.3)	−.039 (1.9)	−.024 (1.2)	−.046 (3.7)	.068 (2.2)	−9.8 (12.1)	2.5 (2.6)	−3.0 (4.1)	.958 / 1.31
3	3.36 (3.9)	1.03 (4.4)	−.41 (1.7)	.49 (2.1)	−.31 (1.3)	.30 (1.3)	.136 (7.1)	−.073 (3.7)	−.034 (1.7)	−.024 (1.3)	−.045 (3.6)	.095 (2.9)	−9.5 (7.6)	1.3 (0.9)	−2.9 (2.4)	.961 / 1.26
1948–I to 1952–IV																
2a	5.05 (4.8)	.61 (1.6)					.125 (5.7)	−.119 (5.6)	−.022 (1.2)	−.015 (0.6)	−.050 (3.3)	.221 (3.2)	−11.0 (8.8)	−1.5 (0.8)	−2.7 (2.3)	.983 / 0.86
3a	2.38 (1.06)	1.11 (2.0)	−.29 (.5)	−.18 (.2)	−.24 (.3)	.66 (1.4)	.121 (3.7)	−.122 (4.0)	−.024 (.9)	−.030 (.9)	−.036 (1.9)	.171 (2.0)	−7.2 (2.3)	3.7 (.8)	1.0 (.3)	.983 / 0.86
1953–I to 1969–IV																
2b	4.16 (5.1)	.73 (3.1)					.143 (3.8)	−.008 (0.2)	−.042 (1.1)	−.048 (1.3)	−.022 (1.4)	.061 (1.8)	−11.2 (10.2)	1.8 (1.6)	−4.2 (4.2)	.964 / 1.20
3b	5.18 (5.1)	.64 (2.4)	−.40 (1.3)	.88 (3.1)	−.07 (.3)	−.05 (.2)	.160 (4.4)	.002 (.1)	−.044 (1.2)	−.068 (1.9)	−.026 (1.7)	.079 (2.1)	−11.6 (7.8)	−1.8 (1.0)	−5.2 (3.6)	.968 / 1.13

Note: Values of "t" statistics are indicated in parentheses. For explanation of the symbols other than those shown below, see equation 2 above.

$\bar{R}^2$ = Coefficient of determination (adjusted for degrees of freedom).

SE = Standard error of estimate of the regression.

Following Laffer and Ranson, the coefficients of this equation are estimated without the use of the Almon distributed lag technique. Although some of the lagged money coefficients approach statistical significance, equation 3—like equation 2— implies that the current and long-run effects of money on income are, for all practical purposes, the same. An increase of 1 percent in M_1 is associated with a roughly 1 percent rise in income in the current quarter and a 1.1 percent rise in the long run.

To test the hypothesis, suggested above, that it is the time interval used by Laffer and Ranson which is largely responsible for this result equations 2 and 3 were reestimated for the subperiods 1948-I to 1952-IV and 1953-I to 1969-IV. The results (see the two lower sections of Table 1) show that (a) the relationship between money and income in the 1948–1952 period is not statistically significant (equations 2a and 3a)[13] and (b) there is a significant lag in the effect of money on income during the

[13]The contribution of the five money variables to the explanatory power of equation 3a may be evaluated by using the statistical procedure known as the F-test. When this is done, we find that the relationship between money and income is not significant even at the .20 confidence level. It should also be noted that the poor showing of the money variables in the 1948–1952 period cannot be attributed simply to the shortness of the period and hence the limited number of degrees of freedom. These conditions do not prevent us from finding statistically significant relationships for most of the other variables included in equations 2a and 3a.

more recent period. Indeed, the largest single change in income as a result of a change in money during this period occurs after a lag of two quarters (equation 3b).[14]

Perhaps the most interesting feature of the results is the similarity between the "money coefficients" for the period 1953-1969 (equation 3b) and those which have been obtained by other researchers using seasonally adjusted data for the same period. To demonstrate this, equation 3b was reestimated with seasonally adjusted data for M_1, GNP, and G. The coefficients for the current and lagged money variables for this equation (3b′) and for equations 3 and 3b are reported in Table 2. Once again the equations are estimated *without* the use of the Almon distributed lag technique. Chart 3 shows the cumulative percentage distribution of the effects of money on income as implied by these equations. It is clear from the chart that it is the time

Table 2. Selected Regression Results for Equations Explaining the Percentage Change in Gross National Product

(Quarterly data)

| Equation | Time Period | Data | Regression Coefficients | | | | | $\bar{R}^2$ |
			$\%\Delta M_1$	$\%\Delta M_{1-1}$	$\%\Delta M_{1-2}$	$\%\Delta M_{1-3}$	$\%\Delta M_{1-4}$	SE
3	1948-I to 1969-IV	NSA	1.03 (4.4)	− .41 (1.7)	.49 (2.1)	− .31 (1.3)	− .30 (1.3)	.961 1.26
3b	1953-I to 1969-IV	NSA	.64 (2.4)	− .40 (1.3)	.88 (3.1)	− .07 (0.3)	− .05 (0.2)	.968 1.13
3b′	1953-I to 1969-IV	SA	.37 (1.8)	− .08 (0.3)	.53 (1.9)	.32 (1.2)	− .21 (1.1)	.541 0.71

Note: Values of "t" statistics are indicated in parenthesis. For explanation of the symbols other than those shown below, see equation 2.

$\bar{R}^2$ = Coefficient of determination (adjusted for degrees of freedom).
SE = Standard error of estimate of the regression.
NSA = Not seasonally adjusted.
SA = Seasonally adjusted data are used for M_1, GNP, and G.

[14]In fairness to Laffer and Ranson, it should be noted that even for equation 3b we are unable to reject the hypothesis (at the .05 confidence level) that the current-quarter money coefficient is less than 1.0. However, there appears to be no necessary reason why the current-quarter effect should be singled out for special consideration. Thus, equation 3b also implies that after six months the cumulative effect of money on income is not significantly different from zero.

The hypothesis that the same regression model fits the entire Laffer-Ranson sample period (1948-1969) may be evaluated by means of a procedure developed by Chow [9]. Doing this, we find that the hypothesis may be rejected at the .01 confidence level, that is, the differences in the parameter estimates of equations 2a and 2b and equations 3a and 3b are statistically significant.

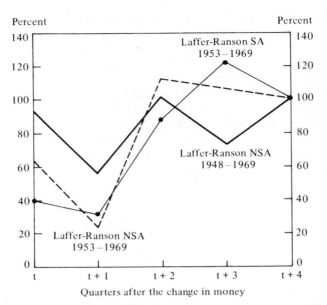

CHART 3 CUMULATIVE EFFECTS OF A ONE PERCENT CHANGE IN MONEY ON GNP

Note: NSA = not seasonally adjusted; SA = seasonally adjusted.

period chosen by Laffer and Ranson which is largely responsible for their controversial result rather than the use of seasonally unadjusted data. This shows up even more dramatically when the equations are estimated with the Almon procedure. When this is done, there is very little difference between the distributed lag implied by the Laffer-Ranson equations (using seasonally unadjusted data but fitted to the 1953-1969 period) and that implied by the St. Louis equation [3], see Chart 4.[15] Thus, once the period through the Korean war is eliminated from the analysis, it makes no difference at all whether the relationship between money and income is estimated with seasonally adjusted data or unadjusted data and dummy variables. Both procedures yield a relatively short, but nevertheless positive, lag in the effect of monetary policy.[16]

[15]For comparative purposes, the constraints imposed in estimating the Laffer-Ranson equations with the Almon procedure are the same as those used in the St. Louis equation, i.e., a fourth-degree polynomial with the $t + 1$ and $t - 5$ values of the money coefficients set equal to zero.

[16]An almost identical conclusion is reached in a paper by Johnson [23a]. Laffer and Ranson provide an alternative explanation of the difference between their own lag results—shown in equation 3—and the St. Louis results. However, there is no mention in their article that the time period employed to estimate their equations is considerably different from that used in the St. Louis model and most other recent studies.

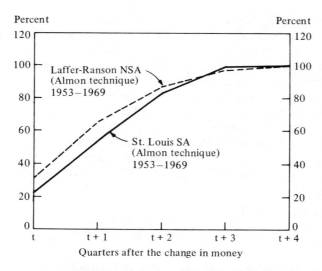

CHART 4 CUMULATIVE PERCENTAGE DISTRIBUTION OF THE EFFECTS OF MONEY ON GNP

Note: NSA = not seasonally adjusted; SA = seasonally adjusted.

The Almon Lag Technique

Finally, it seems worthwhile to say a few words about the use of the Almon technique and its effect on the estimates of the structure (or distribution) of the lag. As noted earlier, this procedure has become quite popular in recent years. It tends to smooth out the pattern of the lag coefficients and makes them easier to rationalize. However, the extent of the differences in the estimates obtained for individual lag coefficients, with and without the use of the technique, provides some reason for concern.

For example, in his experiments with the St. Louis equation, Davis found that either 29 percent or 46 percent of the ultimate effect of money on income could be attributed to the current quarter. The lower number was obtained when the equation was estimated using the Almon technique, while the higher value occurred when the Almon constraint was not imposed on the equation. The explanatory power of the equation was essentially the same in both cases.[17] In the Laffer-Ranson model as well, substantially different estimates of the lag structure are consistent with about the same $\bar{R}^2$. In this model the estimates of the current-quarter effect of money on income are 31 percent with the Almon technique and 64 percent with unconstrained

---

[17]See Davis [12]. The estimates of $\bar{R}^2$ are .46 and .47, respectively. The period used to estimate the equation was 1952-I to 1968-II.

lags (compare the Laffer-Ranson NSA curves for the 1953–1969 period in Charts 3 and 4). On the other hand, over the first six months it is the *Almon* technique which yields a faster response of income to money, for both the Davis experiments and the Laffer-Ranson model, than is obtained with unconstrained lags.

The wide divergence in these estimates of the impact of monetary variables over short periods, depending on the nature of the estimating procedure employed, suggests that existing estimates of the underlying lag structure are not very precise. One reason for this may be that the pattern of the lag varies over time.[18] In any event, the uncertainties surrounding the structure (distribution) of the lag are not eliminated by the Almon technique. Thus, use of any existing estimates of the lag structure as a firm basis for short-run policy making would seem rather hazardous at this time.

Concluding Comments

One finding stands out from the results presented above, namely, that there is a lag in the effect of monetary policy. Nevertheless, estimates of the length of the lag differ considerably. Of the three factors considered in this paper that might account for these differences, the most important is the specification of the appropriate monetary policy variable (or variables) in the construction of econometric models. Use of nonborrowed reserves as the exogenous monetary variable suggests that less than 40 percent of the impact of a monetary action occurs within five quarters and that the full effect is distributed over two and a half years. On the other hand, use of the money supply, the monetary base, or total reserves suggests that most of the effect occurs within four or five quarters. The latter estimate of the lag may appear to be relatively short. However, it does not seem to be grossly out of line with the view held by the majority of economists in the early 1960's.

The two other factors considered and found to be less important in explaining the differences in the estimates of the length of the lag are (1) the type of statistical estimating model (structural versus reduced-form equations) and (2) the seasonal adjustment procedure. In both of these instances, though, there is not enough evidence available to draw very firm conclusions; hence further work might prove fruitful.

Finally, more work is also needed to help refine estimates of the distribution of the lag. Existing estimates of the lag structure do not appear to be sufficiently precise to justify large or frequent short-run adjustments in the growth rates of monetary aggregates.

REFERENCES

1. ALMON, S. "The Distributed Lag between Capital Appropriations and Expenditures." *Econometrica* (January 1965), pp. 178–96.

[18]Some support for this hypothesis is provided by the simulation results for the FRB–MIT model shown in Chart 1 as well as the results obtained by Warburton [30] and Friedman and Schwartz [17] in their analyses of the timing relations between the upswings and downswings in money and economic activity.

2. ANDERSEN, L. C. "An Evaluation of the Impacts of Monetary and Fiscal Policy on Economic Activity." In *1969 Proceedings of the Business and Economic Statistics Section* (Washington, D.C.: American Statistical Association, 1969), pp. 233-40.

3. ANDERSEN, L. C., and CARLSON, K. M. "A Monetarist Model for Economic Stabilization." *Review* (Federal Reserve Bank of St. Louis, April 1970), pp. 7-27 (especially p. 11).

4. ANDERSEN, L. C., and JORDAN, J. "Monetary and Fiscal Actions: A Test of Their Relative Importance in Economic Stabilization." *Review* (Federal Reserve Bank of St. Louis, November 1968), pp. 11-24.

5. ANDO, A., BROWN, E. C., SOLOW, R., and KAREKEN J. "Lags in Fiscal and Monetary Policy." In Commission on Money and Credit, *Stabilization Policies* (Englewood Cliffs, N.J.: Prentice Hall, Inc., 1963), pp. 1-163 (especially p. 2).

6. ANDO, A., and MODIGLIANI, F. "Econometric Analysis of Stabilization Policies." *American Economic Review* (May 1968), pp. 296-314.

7. BRUNNER, K. "The Role of Money and Monetary Policy." *Review* (Federal Reserve Bank of St. Louis, July 1968), pp. 8-24.

8. BRUNNER, K., and MELTZER, A. H. "Money, Debt, and Economic Activity." *Journal of Political Economy,* (September/October 1972), pp. 951-77.

9. CHOW, G. "Tests of Equality between Two Sets of Coefficients in Two Linear Regressions." *Econometrica* (July 160), pp. 591-605.

10. CORRIGAN, E. G. "The Measurement and Importance of Fiscal Policy Changes." *Monthly Review* (Federal Reserve Bank of New York, June 1970), pp. 133-45.

11. CULBERTSON, J. M. "Friedman on the Lag in Effect of Monetary Policy." *Journal of Political Economy* (December 1960), pp. 617-21 (especially p. 621).

12. DAVIS, R. G. "How Much Does Money Matter? A Look at Some Recent Evidence." *Monthly Review* (Federal Reserve Bank of New York, June 1969), pp. 119-31 (especially pp. 122-24).

13. DE LEEUW, F., and GRAMLICH, E. M. "The Channels of Monetary Policy." *Federal Reserve Bulletin* (June 1969), pp. 472-91.

14. DE LEEUW, F., and GRAMLICH, E. M. "The Federal Reserve-MIT Econometric Model." *Federal Reserve Bulletin* (January 1968), pp. 11-40.

15. DE LEEUW, F., and KALCHBRENNER, J. "Monetary and Fiscal Actions: A Test of Their Relative Importance in Economic Stabilization—Comment." *Review* (Federal Reserve Bank of St. Louis, April 1969), pp. 6-11.

16. FRIEDMAN, M. *A Program for Monetary Stability* (New York: Fordham University Press, 1960), especially p. 87.

17. FRIEDMAN, M., and SCHWARTZ, A. J. *A Monetary History of the United States, 1867-1960* (Princeton: Princeton University Press, 1963).

18. GRAMLEY, L. E. "Guidelines for Monetary Policy—The Case Against Simple Rules." A paper presented at the Financial Conference of the National Industrial Conference Board, New York, February 21, 1969. Reprinted in W. L. Smith and R. L. Teigen (eds.) *Readings in Money, National Income, and Stabilization Policy* (Homewood, Ill.: Richard D. Irwin, Inc., 1970), pp. 488-95.

19. GRAMLICH, E. M. "The Role of Money in Economic Activity: Complicated or Simple?" *Business Economics* (September 1969), pp. 21-26.

20. GRAMLICH, E. M. "The Usefulness of Monetary and Fiscal Policy as Discretionary Stabilization Tools." *Journal of Money, Credit and Banking* (May 1971, Part 2), pp. 20, 506-32 (especially p. 514).

21. HAMBURGER, M. J. "The Impact of Monetary Variables: A Survey of Recent Econometric Literature." In *Essays in Domestic and International Finance* (New York: Federal Reserve Bank of New York, 1969), pp 37–49.

22. HAMBURGER, M. J. "Indicators of Monetary Policy: The Arguments and the Evidence." *American Economic Review* (May 1970), pp. 32–39.

23. HENDERSHOTT, P. H. "A Quality Theory of Money." *Nebraska Journal of Economics and Business* (Autumn 1969), pp. 28–37.

23a. JOHNSON, D. D. "Properties of Alternative Seasonal Adjustment Techniques, A Comment on the OMB Model." *Journal of Business* (April 1973), pp. 284–303.

24. KERAN, M. W. "Monetary and Fiscal Influences on Economic Activity—The Historical Evidence." *Review* (Federal Reserve Bank of St. Louis, November 1968), pp. 5–24 (especially p. 18, footnote 22).

25. LAFFER, A. B., and RANSON, R.D. "A Formal Model of the Economy." *Journal of Business* (July 1971), pp. 247–70 (especially pp. 257–59).

26. MAYER, T. "The Inflexibility of Monetary Policy." *Review of Economics and Statistics* (November 1958), pp. 358–74.

27. MAYER, T. "The Lag in Effect of Monetary Policy: Some Criticisms." *Western Economic Journal* (September 1967), pp. 324–42 (especially pp. 326 and 328).

28. PIERCE, J. L. "Critique of 'A Formal Model of the Economy for the Office of Management and Budget' by Arthur B. Laffer and R. David Ranson." In United States Congress, Joint Economic Committee, *The 1971 Economic Report of the President, Hearings,* Part I (February 1971), pp. 300–12.

29. SMITH, W. L. "On the Effectiveness of Monetary Policy." *American Economic Review* (September 1956), pp. 588–606.

30. WARBURTON, C. "Variability of the Lag in the Effect of Monetary Policy, 1919–1965." *Western Economic Journal* (June 1971), pp. 115–33.

31. WHITE, W. H. "The Timeliness of the Effects of Monetary Policy: The New Evidence from Econometric Models." *Banca Nazionale del Lavoro Quarterly Review* (September 1968), pp. 276–303.

Money Supply

V

The articles in Section II indicate that monetary aggregates have an effect on the performance of the economy. The articles in this section consider the relationships among these aggregates. The first article, by Anatol Balbach and Albert Burger, explains the derivation of the monetary base—the set of assets held by banks and the public that constrains the money supply. Because the money supply is not immediately controllable by the central bank and is sensitive to regulatory and institutional changes, as discussed in several of the readings in Section VIII, the monetary base, being much more controllable and stable, has gained importance in recent years.

The second piece, by Jerry L. Jordan, is a simple exposition of a linear framework for the determination of the money supply. Jordan shows how the money supply depends on the monetary base as well as the behavioral parameters of the "money multiplier."

Next, David I. Fand extends the Jordan framework by outlining, in general rather than linear notation, more sophisticated money supply theories. Some empirical estimation of the implication of these theories has taken place, and an impressive amount of it is reviewed in the final article in this section, by Robert H. Rasche. Rasche compares and contrasts different empirical estimates of the effect of various interest rates on the money stock.

Derivation of the Monetary Base

Anatol B. Balbach
Albert E. Burger

15

Although the monetary base has been a key concept in monetary analysis for two decades, its use has been primarily restricted to the monetary systems of industrial nations.[1] Specifically, the base as constructed and measured in the United States has tended to be applied with some modifications to other economies. This article is an attempt to establish a general definition of a monetary base applicable to all relevant institutional structures and to provide guidelines for the identification and measurement of the base.

Given a set of institutional arrangements and predictable behavior on the part of market participants, changes in the monetary base produce predictable changes in the money stock. Under these conditions the base can be used as a predictor of the money stock and as a variable whose control implies the control of changes in the quantity of money. Thus the practical use of the base encompasses only those in-

Reprinted from *Review*, November 1976, pp. 2-8, by permission of the Federal Reserve Bank of St. Louis and the author.

[1]For further discussion of the concepts of monetary base and high-powered money, see Karl Brunner and Allan H. Meltzer, "An Alternative Approach to the Monetary Mechanism," U.S. Congress, House of Representatives, Committee on Banking and Currency, Subcommittee on Domestic Finance, 88th Cong., 2nd sess., August 17, 1964, pp. 9-20; Milton Friedman and Anna Jacobson Schwartz, *A Monetary History of the United States 1867-1960* (Princeton: Princeton University Press, 1963); Phillip Cagan, *Determinants and Effects of Changes in the Stock of Money 1875-1960* (New York: National Bureau of Economic Research, 1965). Also see Leonall C. Andersen and Jerry L. Jordan, "The Monetary Base—Explanation and Analytical Use," Federal Reserve Bank of St. Louis, *Review,* August 1968, pp. 7-11.

stitutional structures where the money stock cannot be predicted and controlled *directly* by monetary authorities, but where the base can be measured and affected.

Where it is the case that every unit of the money stock can be directly created or destroyed by monetary authorities, or that economic forces or policy actions affect the base and the money stock by exactly the same magnitudes, there is no reason to resort to the use of the base concept. Alternatively, if the constraint on money creation consists solely of a single money-creator's decisions as to how much money to create in order to have it acceptable as money to all users, the base, while it exists in principle, is not obectively measurable and cannot be used either as a predictor or as a control variable. This leaves the monetary base as a useful concept in monetary systems which are characterized by the existence of fiat money, more than one money-creating institution, and fractional reserve banking.

The Concept

In a system which exhibits these features, the money stock in the hands of the public will potentially consist of commodity money (such as gold and silver coins), liabilities of monetary authorities (currency) and liabilities of private institutions (bank notes and/or bank deposits). These assets of the nonbanking public will be used as money only if transactions costs associated with other assets are higher. In other words, since the productivity of any asset used as money lies in its ability to facilitate transactions, it must be an instrument which minimizes the costs of conducting transactions. Apart from such features as divisibility, convenience and safety it must also reasonably maintain its purchasing power vis-a-vis other assets. Any asset that is convenient in every respect but whose purchasing power fluctuates widely and unpredictably will impose high risks on its holders and, in effect, high transaction costs.

The stability of purchasing power, as used here, refers to its exchange value against the bundle of all other available assets, goods, and services. One of the main requisites of this stability is a relatively stable supply of this asset called money. If money is created without restraint or if its production fluctuates widely, its purchasing power will fluctuate accordingly, and the costs imposed on its holders will encourage them to use some other asset to facilitate transactions. Thus, for any asset to function as money, its users must be convinced that its supply is constrained either by some institution they trust or by some set of other assets that are deemed to be relatively fixed in quantity or adequately controlled by market or institutional forces. The monetary base is this set of assets that constrains the growth of the money stock.

Commodity money is accepted because of the belief that market forces are such as to assure a relatively stable supply. Government liabilities—currency—are accepted so long as it is believed that the monetary authorities will maintain a relatively stable growth of these liabilities. But what induces the nonbanking public to accept liabilities of private, profit-making institutions such as banks? Obviously, it is because something limits the growth of these deposits and hence insures that there will remain a fairly stable rate of exchange of these deposits for other assets.

In a banking system where there exists more than one bank and where the money stock is comprised solely of bank liabilities (deposits, currency, and coin issued by the banks), the users of these liabilities will frequently deposit liabilities of one bank at another bank. If the banks were to use assets which were each others' liabilities as a basis for issuing new money, there would be no effective constraint on the expansion of money and, consequently, banks could find that their liabilities cease to be accepted as money. Knowing this, they will not accept each others' liabilities without being able to convert them into some asset which is not dominated by actions of banks themselves. The asset that will emerge will also have the lowest transactions cost. This asset, whatever it is, will then constitute part of the monetary base.

Each bank, knowing that its liabilities will be presented to it by other banks for conversion into this acceptable asset, will have to hold a stock of this asset as a reserve for conversion. In the absence of legal constraints, the size of this cushion or reserve, relative to the amount of monetary liabilities it creates, will depend upon the probability with which the bank's monetary liabilities are deposited at other banks. Thus, the total amount of this reserve asset will constrain the amount of money that can be produced by the system.

If the money stock includes commodity money or currency issued by monetary authorities in addition to private bank liabilities, then the banks will have to be ready to convert their monetary liabilities into forms acceptable not only to other banks but also to the nonbanking public. Thus they will have to hold a reserve of those assets that may be demanded by both. The monetary base will then consist not only of those assets that banks use to settle monetary liabilities among themselves but also those assets that are used to satisfy the conversion demands of the public. This does not preclude the possibility that the interbank settlement asset is the same as the one that is used in settling with the public.

To sum up, in a system where the money stock consists of commodity money, governmental liabilities, and bank liabilities, the base will consist of commodity money, governmental monetary liabilities, and whatever assets the banks use to settle interbank debts. The assets that constrain the growth of money stock (the monetary base) can therefore be identified in any monetary system by ascertaining and summing the following:

1. those assets which the consolidated banking sector uses to settle interbank debt;[2] and

2. those items, aside from bank liabilities, which are used as money.

---

[2]We look at the assets of the consolidated banking sector in order to eliminate correspondent balances which are used as instruments of settlement among respondent banks. These deposits are acceptable to respondent banks only because they represent a claim on the reserves of correspondent banks. Thus, the constraint is still exercised by the availability of assets which are not dominated by actions of individual banks.

Measurement and Control

Once the monetary base is identified and measured, and the behavior of the banks and the public described and estimated, changes in the base can be used to predict changes in the money stock. What remains is the task of finding what causes the base to change and how to control these changes, since control of the size of the base, given the behavior of banks and the public, implies the control of the money stock.

If the base were to consist solely of commodity money or real assets, then one would have to analyze the forces which affect the supply of these assets; attempts at control of these forces would constitute the exercise of monetary policy. For example, if gold coin were the sole constituent of the base, then the control of production and importation of gold coin would allow for the control of the money stock. Under such circumstances, factors affecting the supply of gold coin could be identified and measured in the balance sheets of domestic gold producers and in the balance of payments.

Suppose that the base consists of currency issued by the government. If we were to assume that government maintains a complete balance sheet and that its creation of currency depends upon changes in the configuration of its assets and liabilities, then the factors affecting the monetary base would be found in and could be analyzed from the balance sheet of the government. It is usually the case, however, that governments cannot and do not maintain complete balance sheets. Furthermore, the issuance of currency may be based on arbitrary or political decisions that cannot be quantified. Under such circumstances the base or its currency component has to be taken as given at any time and the control of the base rests solely with governmental authorities who, in their desire to have their liabilities acceptable as money, will presumably limit currency growth.

When, in addition to the above-mentioned components, the banking system uses central bank liabilities as reserves necessary for conversion of their own monetary liabilities, the factors affecting changes in this component of the base are summarized in the balance sheet of the central bank. Central banks do maintain balance sheets and any changes in their "reserve liabilities" reflect changes in their assets and/or other liabilities. By definition, a balance sheet implies that any subset of liabilities must equal the algebraic sum of all assets and remaining liabilities and capital in that balance sheet. Thus the central bank component of the base can be alternatively measured as the algebraic sum of all entries in the central balance sheet other than its reserve liabilities. This measure is frequently referred to as the "sources of the monetary base." Since factors supplying the central bank component of the base are represented in the sources, the analysis, prediction, and control of the monetary base must begin with the identification and measurement of its sources.

At present, in virtually all modern monetary systems the base consists of either central bank liabilities, government liabilities, or both. These items are the ones used to settle interbank debt and some circulate as money. Government liabilities must be taken as given since decisions as to their supply are determined by factors which cannot be quantified. In the case of central bank liabilities, it is necessary to derive the sources of the base component, which consist of the algebraic sum of all other assets and liabilities in the central bank balance sheet. These sources permit the identification of causes of changes in the monetary base and, consequently, of policy actions which control these changes.

Examples of Derivation and Usefulness of the Sources of Monetary Base

Case I: Base Consists Solely of Central Bank Liabilities

Suppose there exists a monetary system where the money stock consists of the public's deposits at banks and currency issued by the central bank and held by the public. Suppose that we observe further that the asset of the consolidated banking sector which is used to settle interbank debts consists of deposits at the central bank. Conversion of monetary liabilities of banks to the public is in the form of currency. This implies that the monetary base consists of banks' deposits at the central bank and currency issued by the central bank, which is thus the sole producer of the base. Since all changes in the base result in corresponding changes in all other entries of the central bank balance sheet, the sources of the base can be identified.

A hypothetical balance sheet of the central bank is given below.

Central Bank

Assets	Liabilities
Gold (G)	Demand Deposits of Banks (DB)
Foreign Assets (FA)	Currency Held by Banks (CB)
Government Securities (BC)	Currency Held by Public (CP)
Loans and Discounts (LD)	Demand Deposits of Treasury (DT)
Other Assets (OA)	Demand Deposits of Foreign Central Banks (DF)
	Currency Held by Treasury (CT)
	Other Liabilites and Capital (OL)

The monetary base is comprised of demand deposits of banks at the central bank (DB) and currency, issued by the central bank, that is held by banks (CB) and by the public (CP). Thus the sources of the base, as derived from the central bank's balance sheet, are the algebraic sum of all other balance sheet entries:

$$G + FA + BC + LD + OA - OL - DT - DF - CT$$

Measures of these items are readily available from central bank accounts and can be used to trace the impact of any transaction in the economy on the monetary base.

The process is simple—one must merely ascertain whether a transaction affects any of the items in the sources of the base and sum the effects. Suppose that the Treasury collects taxes and deposits the proceeds in its account at the central bank. The transactions involved are:

Central Bank		Banks	
DB − 100		DB − 100	DP − 100
DT + 100			

The only entry that appears in the sources statement of the base and is affected is demand deposits of the Treasury (DT), which is a negative item and rises by 100. Thus, the base declines by 100. It is immediately apparent what has happened with the base and what has caused the change.

Another example could be a central bank purchase of government securities from banks (BB).

Central Bank		Banks	
BC + 100	DB + 100	DB + 100	
		BB − 100	

Again, the only entry affected in the sources statement is government securities held by the central bank, an item which affects the base positively. It has risen by 100; thus the base has increased by 100.

Suppose this country engages in attempts to peg the exchange rate. A deficit in its international balance of payments will cause the central bank to enter the exchange market as a seller of foreign currencies (its holdings of these currencies are represented by the item foreign assets). A representative net transaction would be as follows:

Central Bank		Banks	
FA − 100	DB − 100	DB − 100	DP − 100

Foreign assets (FA) is the only item in the sources statement that has been affected. Its decline of 100 implies the same change in the base.

Case II: Base Consists of Central Bank and Government Liabilities

Another type of monetary system has a money stock that is made up of the public's deposits at private banks, currency issued by the government or by both the government and the central bank. If central bank deposit liabilities function as an instrument of interbank settlement and the public periodically converts some of its deposits into currency, the monetary base includes bank deposits at the central bank and currency issued by the central bank and by the Treasury.

In principle, this would mean that the sources statement of the base would have to be derived from the consolidation of Treasury and central bank balance sheets. But, as was discussed earlier, complete Treasury balance sheets are universally unavailable. In this case, the base and its sources must be modified by simply adding

Treasury currency in the hands of banks and the public to both the base and the sources of the base. The monetary base would then become demand deposits of banks at the central bank (DB) plus central bank currency held by banks (CB) plus Treasury currency held by banks (TCB) plus central bank currency held by the public (CP) plus Treasury currency held by the public (TCP). And the sources statement is:

$$G + FA + BC + LD + OA + TCB + TCP$$
$$- OL - DT - DF - CT$$

The analysis uses the new statement in exactly the same way that previous transaction examples used the preceding one. Suppose that the Treasury prints and sells new currency to commercial banks and deposits the receipts in the central bank.

Treasury		Central Bank		Banks	
DT + 100	TCB + 100		DB − 100	TCB + 100	
			DT + 100	DB − 100	

Treasury currency held by the banks increases and so do Treasury deposits at the central bank. Since they enter into the sources statement with opposite signs, there is no change in the monetary base. Commercial banks have simply changed the form of their reserves without changing the total amount.

Another illustrative transaction is the sale of Treasury currency to the central bank.

Treasury		Central Bank	
DT + 100	TCC + 100	OA + 100	DT + 100

Since Treasury currency at the central bank has not been specifically included in the central bank balance sheet, it must appear in other assets of the central bank (OA), which rises by 100 together with deposits of the Treasury at the central bank (DT). Since these items enter the sources statement with opposite signs there is, again, no change in the monetary base.

But if the Treasury prints new currency and buys services from the public, the transaction is recorded as follows:

Treasury		Central Bank	
Services + 100	TCP + 100	No Change	No Change

Banks		Public	
No Change	No Change	TCP + 100	
		Services − 100	

While the central bank balance sheet is unaffected, the sources statement indicates that the base rises by 100 because TCP has increased.

While the vast majority of relevant monetary systems are represented by the two cases discussed above, there are occasionally some institutional or market arrangements which require additional refinements.

It may be that the consolidated banking system, due perhaps to regulations imposed upon it, uses government securities as well as central bank deposits to settle interbank liabilities. As is the case with Treasury currency, there is no government balance sheet which allows us to identify the sources of this base component; therefore, holdings of government securities by banks and the public must be added to the base and its sources as derived from the central bank balance sheet. Similarly, if any other asset is used for interbank clearing or as part of the money stock, it must be accounted for in the sources of the monetary base. The general rule for inclusion is as follows:

1. If the asset is the liability of an entity that maintains a balance sheet, the balance sheets of that entity and the central bank are to be consolidated and the sources of the base derived in a similar manner as in Case I.

2. If the asset is a liability of an entity which does not have a balance sheet, or is a real asset, then the quantities of that asset that are held by commercial banks and the public must be added to the sources and the monetary base which were constructed from the central bank balance sheet.

Obviously, analysis and control are enhanced by the ability to identify as many factors as possible that may affect monetary base. Consequently, when balance sheets are available, they should be used in the derivation of base statements. The simple addition of other assets included in the base to the sources statement assumes that these assets are predetermined and not subject to control by the central bank.

Summary

In most general terms the monetary base is that set of assets held by the banks and the public which constrains the money stock. The items that constitute the base in any country can be identified by determining those assets which the consolidated banking sector uses to settle interbank debt, and those items, aside from bank liabilities, which are used as money. The factors that cause the amount of base to change can be determined by consolidating the balance sheets of the producers of the base. In the case where the central bank is the sole producer of base, this process can proceed from the balance sheet of the central bank. Any change in the base will appear as a change in one or more other entries in the central bank's balance sheet. When there are other producers of base, such as the Treasury, this article showed how the base could be constructed to take this into account.

The sources statement of the base is most important to the monetary authorities. This statement serves as a scheme for analyzing how actions taken by the monetary authorities, such as purchases or sales of securities, or lending to banks, influences the base and, hence, the money stock. It also permits them to analyze how other factors influence the base and, consequently, permits them to identify the type of offsetting actions that must be taken to counter these outside influences.

Appendix

The purpose of this Appendix is to demonstrate how the principles of monetary base construction can be applied to the U.S. monetary system and to show how a base construct can be reconciled with data which is regularly published in the Federal Reserve *Bulletin*.

The U.S. monetary system is characterized by the existence of three sets of money-creating institutions: (1) the U.S. Treasury which issues coin and which has some Treasury notes and silver certificates outstanding, (2) the Federal Reserve System, which issues Federal Reserve notes and demand deposits, and (3) commercial banks which issue demand deposits. Commercial banks, which constitute the private money-creating sector, can use as instruments of settlement currency (Federal Reserve notes and Treasury currency and coin) and demand deposits at the Federal Reserve Banks. Therefore, the base consists of monetary assets of the consolidated domestic private sector (currency and coin held by banks and the public, and demand deposits of member banks at Federal Reserve Banks). These are the monetary liabilities of the government sector to the private domestic sector. Consequently, the base and the sources of the base, as derived from the Federal Reserve balance sheet, must be supplemented by the addition of Treasury currency and coin held by commercial banks and the public.

It should also be noted that certain monetary relationships between the central bank and the government are unique to U.S. monetary institutions. For example, gold is held by the Treasury, which issues gold certificates to the Federal Reserve System, and coin is issued by the Treasury while almost all of the currency is issued by the Federal Reserve Banks. These unique features, however, present no difficulty in the development of base statements and perhaps demonstrate even more forcefully that such construction is applicable to all institutional arrangements.

A simplified balance sheet for the Federal Reserve System is given below:

Federal Reserve System

Assets	Liabilities
Gold Certificates (GC)	FR Notes Held by:
Special Drawing Rights (SDR)	Treasury (CT)
Coin Held by the FR (TCC)	Commercial Banks (CB)
Loans and Discounts (LD)	Public (CP)
Government Securities Held by FR (BC)	Demand Deposits:
	Treasury (DT)
Other Assets (OA)	Commercial Banks (DB)
	Foreign (DF)
	Other Liabilities and Capital of the FR (OL)

The base, as defined and identified in the Federal Reserve's balance sheet, consists of demand deposits of banks at the Federal Reserve Banks (DB), Federal Reserve notes held by banks and the public (CB + CP) and Treasury currency held by banks (TCB) and the public (TCP):

$$DB + CB + CP + TCB + TCP \qquad (1)$$

The sources statement consists of the algebraic sum of all the remaining assets and liabilities in the Federal Reserve balance sheet plus monetary liabilities of the Treasury held by banks and the public (TCB + TCP). Therefore, the sources of the base consist of the following balance sheet entries:

$$LD + BC + OA + GC + SDR + TCC - CT \qquad (2)$$
$$- DT - DF - OL + TCB + TCP$$

Data for derivation of sources of the base is published monthly in the Federal Reserve *Bulletin* in a table entitled "Member Bank Reserves, Reserve Bank Credit, and Related Items." This table is divided into two parts:

Factors supplying reserve funds:
Reserve Bank Credit Outstanding (RBC)
Gold Stock (G)
Special Drawing Rights (SDR)
Treasury Currency Outstanding (TCO), and

Factors absorbing reserve funds:
Currency in Circulation (CC)
Treasury Cash Holdings (TK)
Deposits, other than Member Bank Reserves with FR (d)
Other Federal Reserve Liabilities and Capital (OL)
Member Bank Reserves with FR Banks (DB)
Currency and Coin held by Member Banks (CMB)

In terms of this statement, the base consists of member bank deposits at Federal Reserve Banks (DB) plus currency and coin in circulation issued by the Federal Reserve Banks (CB + CP) and issued by the Treasury (TCB + TCP). Thus, in terms of our balance sheet notation, it consists of DB + CB + CP + TCB + TCP which is identical to Statement 1 from the balance sheet of the Federal Reserve.

For the sources statement we have to define the published entities in terms of balance sheet notation.

RBC = LD + BC + OA (where Federal Reserve float[1] is included in OA)
G   = Gold
SDR = Special Drawing Rights
TCO = TCB + TCP + TCC + TCT (where TCT refers to Treasury currency held
       by the Treasury)
TK = (G − GC) + TCT + CT
d   = DT + DF
OL = Other Liabilities

---

[1]Federal Reserve float is computed from the balance sheets and is cash items in process of collection minus deferred availability cash items. See Federal Reserve Bank of New York, Glossary: "Factors Affecting Bank Reserves, *Weekly Federal Reserve Statements,* October 1975, pp. 17–18.

The sources statement, which is derivable from factors supplying and absorbing reserve funds, is:

$$RBC + G + SDR + TCO - TK - d - OL. \tag{3}$$

When balance sheet notation is substituted for published notation, and addition and subtraction are completed, statement (3) becomes,

$$LD + BC + OA + GC + SDR + TCC - CT \tag{4}$$
$$- DT - DF - OL + TCB + TCP$$

This statement is an identical statement to (2) which implies that the data published in the form of factors supplying and absorbing reserve funds is consistent with the sources statement as derived from the Federal Reserve balance sheet.

As an example of this procedure the following numerical example is presented. The balance sheet for the Federal Reserve System is for September 29, 1976, as reported on page A10 of the October 1976 Federal Reserve *Bulletin*.

**Consolidated Statement of Condition of
All Federal Reserve Banks**
(Millions of Dollars)

Assets		Liabilities	
Gold Certificates	$ 11,598	FR Notes	$ 79,802
SDR	700	Demand Deposits:	
Cash Held by FR	365	Treasury	12,212
Loans and Discounts	324	Member Bank	
Government Securities		Reserves	29,807
Held by FR	99,224	Foreign	245
Other Assets	19,694	Other Liabilities[2]	
	$131,905	and Capital	9,839
			$131,905

In the notation used in this appendix, the base consists of demand deposits of commercial banks held at Federal Reserve Banks (DB) which equal $29,807 plus currency held by commercial banks and the public (CP + CB + TCP + TCB). This currency consists of FR notes ($79,802) plus Treasury currency outstanding ($10,757) which comes from the Treasury accounts, less the currency and coin held by Treasury ($425), called "Treasury cash," less Federal Reserve holdings of coin, called "cash held by FR" ($365).[3] The total currency component of the base consists of $89,769 million. Therefore, the base amounts to $29,807 plus $89,769, and equals $119,576.

[2]Includes $920 million of other deposits.
[3]FR notes held by FR banks are excluded from the entry. "FR notes" in the consolidated balance sheet.

The sources of the base consist of Treasury currency and coin held by commercial banks and the public, and all the items in the Federal Reserve's balance sheet except the two entries demand deposits of commercial banks (member bank reserves) and Federal Reserve notes. In other words, if one consolidates all the entries in the Federal Reserve balance sheet for the week of September 29, 1976, excluding Federal Reserve notes ($79,802) and demand deposits of member banks ($29,807), the total amount is $109,609 million. As was shown previously the amount of Treasury currency and coin held by commercial banks and the public was $9,967 million for the same date.[4] Hence, the total base is $109,609 plus $9,967 equals $119,576 million.

Using the notation presented in this appendix, the sources of the base may also be constructed from the entries that appear in the table "Member Bank Reserves, Federal Reserve Bank Credit, and Related Items" that appears on pages A2-A3 of the October 1976 Federal Reserve *Bulletin*. For September 29, 1976, the data are as follows:

Reserve Bank Credit (RBC)	$113,972 million
Gold (G)	11,598
SDR	700
Treasury Currency Outstanding (TCO)	10,757
Treasury Cash (TK)	425
Demand Deposits of Treasury (DT)	12,212
Foreign Demand Deposits (DF)	245
Other Liabilities[5] (OL)	4,569

Using the previous formula for the sources of the base given in Equation 3:

$$RBC + G + SDRs + TCO - TK - DT - DF - OL$$

we find that the summation of the sources stated in this manner, and applying the appropriate sign, equals $119,576 which is exactly equal to the base as derived from the Federal Reserve's balance sheet with the addition of Treasury currency held by commercial banks and the public.

[4]Treasury currency and coin held by banks and the public is the sum of silver certificates, United States notes and total coin. These amounts are available for the end of the month in Table MS-1, "Currency and Coin in Circulation," U.S. Department of the Treasury, Treasury *Bulletin*.

[5]Includes $920 million of other deposits.

Elements of Money Stock Determination

Jerry L. Jordan

16

Recent discussion of the role of money in stabilization policy has culminated in two central issues. The first involves the strength and reliability of the relation between changes in money and changes in total spending. If this relation is sufficiently strong and reliable, changes in the money stock can be used as an indicator of the influence of monetary stabilization actions on the economy.[1] The second issue centers on whether or not the monetary authorities can determine the growth of the money stock with sufficient precision, if it is deemed desirable to do so.

This article is concerned primarily with the second issue—determination of the money stock.[2] A framework describing the factors which influence the monetary authorities' ability to determine the money stock is presented, and the behavior of these factors in recent years is illustrated. In addition, examples of ways in which these factors influence the money stock are discussed.

Factors Influencing the Money Stock

The following sections present essential elements and concepts which are used to construct a "money supply model" for the U.S. economy. First, the necessary infor-

Reprinted from the Reserve Bank of St. Louis, *Review* (October, 1969), pp. 10-19, by permission of the publisher.
[1]Leonall C. Andersen and Jerry L. Jordan, "Monetary and Fiscal Actions: A Test of Their Relative Importance in Economic Stabilization," this *Review,* November 1968.
[2]Private demand deposits plus currency in the hands of the public.

mation regarding institutional aspects of the U.S. banking system are summarized. Then, the main elements of the model—the monetary base, the member bank reserve-to-deposit ratio, the currency-to-demand deposit ratio, the time deposit-to-demand deposit ratio, and the U.S. Government deposit-to-demand deposit ratio—are discussed.

Institutional Aspects of the U.S. Banking System

Students of money and banking are taught that if commercial bank reserve requirements are less than 100 percent, the reserves of the banking system can support a "multiple" of deposits. In fact it is often said that under a fractional reserve system the banking system "creates" deposits. The familiar textbook exposition tells us that the amount of deposits (D) in the system is equal to the reciprocal of the reserve requirement ratio (r) times the amount of reserves (R):

$$D = \frac{1}{r} \times R.$$

Thus if the banking system has $100 of reserves, and the reserve requirement ratio is 20 percent (.2), deposits will be $100/.2 or $500. If the banks acquire an additional $1 in reserves (for instance from the Federal Reserve), deposits will increase by $5.

There are many simplifying assumptions underlying this elementary deposit-expansion relation. First, it is assumed that all bank deposits are subject to the same reserve requirement. Second, all banks are subject to the same regulations; in other words, all banks are members of the Federal Reserve System, and the Federal Reserve does not differentiate among classes of banks. Third, banks do not hold excess reserves; they are always "loaned up." And finally, there is no "cash drain." The public desires to hold a fixed quantity of currency, and their desires for currency are not influenced by the existence of more or less deposits.

Since the above assumptions are not true, the accuracy with which a monetary analyst can estimate how many deposits will be "created" by an addition of $1 in reserves to the banking system, depends on his ability to determine:

1. how the deposits will be distributed between member and nonmember banks;
2. how the deposits will be distributed between reserve city and country banks, which are subject to different reserve requirements;
3. how the deposits will be distributed among private demand deposits, Government demand deposits, and the subclasses of time deposits, all of which are subject to different reserve requirements;
4. how the change in deposits will affect banks' desired ratio of excess reserves to total deposits; and
5. how a change in deposits will affect the public's desired ratio of currency to demand deposits.

These questions can be answered best within the context of a "money supply model" which is constructed to include the institutional realities of the U.S. banking system, and which does not require the special assumptions of the simple deposit expansion equation. A thoroughly developed and tested money supply model has been advanced by Professors Brunner and Meltzer.[3] The following sections present the general form and essential features of this model.

The Monetary Base

A useful concept for monetary analysis is provided by the "monetary base" or "high-powered money."[4] The monetary base is defined as the net monetary liabilities of the Government (U.S. Treasury and Federal Reserve System) held by the public (commercial banks and nonbank public). More specifically, the monetary base is derived from a consolidated balance sheet of the Treasury and Federal Reserve "monetary" accounts. This consolidated monetary base balance sheet is illustrated in Table 1, and monthly data for the monetary base (B) are shown in Chart 1.

The growth of the monetary base, that is, "base money," is determined primarily by Federal Reserve holdings of U.S. Government securities, the dominant asset or source component of the base.[5] In recent decades changes in other sources either have been small or have been offset by changes in security holdings. A change in the Treasury's gold holdings is potentially an important source of increase or decrease in the base. However, since March 1968 the size of the gold stock has been changing only by small increments. In the postwar period the influence of changes in the gold stock were generally offset by compensating changes in Federal Reserve holdings of U.S. Government securities.

The liabilities or uses of the monetary base, or net monetary liabilities of the Federal Reserve and Treasury, are shown in Table 1 to be currency in circulation plus member bank deposits at the Federal Reserve. Part of the currency in circulation is held by the public, part is held as legal reserves by member banks, and another part is held as desired contingency reserves by nonmember commercial banks. In order to relate the uses of the base to the money stock, the uses are regrouped from the *uses* side of Table 1 as currency held by the nonbank public plus reserves of all commercial banks, shown in Table 2.

[3]Karl Brunner and Allan Meltzer, "Liquidity Traps for Money, Bank Credit, and Interest Rates," *Journal of Political Economy*, Vol. 76, January/February 1968. Also see Albert E. Burger, *An Analysis of the Brunner-Meltzer Non-Linear Money Supply Hypothesis,* Working Paper No. 7, Federal Reserve Bank of St. Louis, May 1969.

[4]For further discussion of this concept, see Leonall C. Andersen and Jerry L. Jordan, "The Monetary Base: Explanation and Analytical Use," this *Review,* August 1968.

[5]For a discussion of the statistical relation among source components of the base, see Michael W. Keran and Christopher Babb, "An Explanation of Federal Reserve Actions (1933-68)," this *Review,* July 1969.

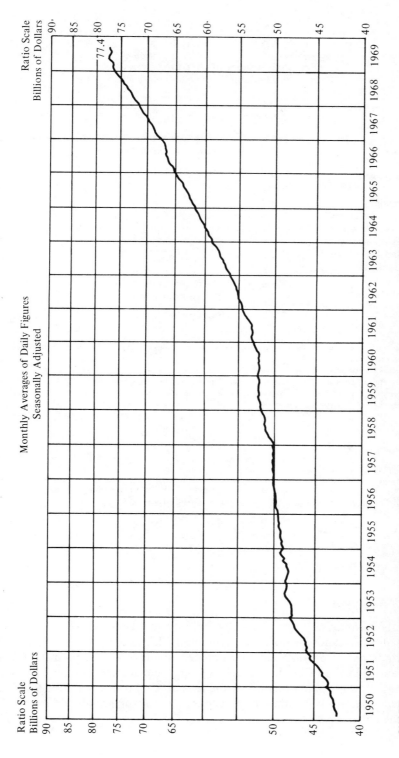

Ratio Scale
Billions of Dollars

Monthly Averages of Daily Figures
Seasonally Adjusted

Ratio Scale
Billions of Dollars

CHART 1 MONETARY BASE* MONTHLY AVERAGES OF DAILY FIGURES SEASONALLY ADJUSTED

*Uses of the monetary base are member bank reserves and currency held by the public and nonmember banks. Adjustments are made for reserve requirement changes and shifts in deposits among classes of banks.
Data are compiled by this bank.
Latest data plotted, September [1969]

Table 1. Monetary Base
(July 1969—billions of dollars)
Consolidated Treasury and Federal Reserve Monetary Accounts

Sources of the Base		Uses of the Base	
Federal Reserve Credit:			
Holdings of securities[a]	$54.3	Member bank deposits at Federal Reserve	$22.3
Discounts and advances	1.2	Currency in circulation	51.3
Float	2.7		
Other Federal Reserve assets	2.7		
Gold stock	10.4		
Treasury currency outstanding	6.7		
Treasury cash holdings	− .7		
Treasury deposits at Federal Reserve	− 1.1		
Foreign deposits at Federal Reserve	− .1		
Other liabilities and capital accounts	− 2.0		
Other Federal Reserve deposits	− .5		
Sources of the base	$73.6	Uses of the base	$73.6
Reserve adjustment[b]	3.9	Reserve Adjustment[b]	3.9
Monetary base	$77.5	Monetary base	$77.5

Note: Data are not seasonally adjusted. Member bank deposits at Federal Reserve plus currency held by member banks equals total reserves (required reserves plus excess reserves).

[a]Includes acceptances not shown separately.

[b]Leonall C. Andersen and Jerry L. Jordan, "The Monetary Base: Explanation and Analytical Use," this *Review*, August 1968.

Source: "Member Bank Reserves, Federal Reserve Bank Credit, and Related Items," the first table appearing in the Financial and Business Statistics section of the Federal Reserve *Bulletin*.

Table 2. Uses of Monetary Base
(July 1969—billions of dollars)

Currency in circulation	$51.3	Currency held by the nonbank public	$45.1
Member bank deposits at Federal Reserve	22.3	Commercial bank reserves*	28.5
Uses of the base	$73.6	Uses of the base	$73.6

Note: Not seasonally adjusted data.

*Includes vault cash of nonmember banks.

Uses of Reserves

As noted above, analysis of the U.S. monetary system is complicated by the existence of both member and nonmember banks, different classes of member banks, different reserve requirements on different types of deposits (private demand, Government demand, and time), and graduated reserve requirements for different amounts of deposits. It is thus necessary to allocate the uses of bank reserves among the different types of deposits. This is illustrated by an equation showing total bank reserves (R) in terms of their uses:

$$R = RR_m + ER_m + VC_n,$$

where

RR_m = required reserves of member banks,
ER_m = excess reserves of member banks,
VC_n = vault cash of nonmember banks.

In turn, required reserves of member banks are decomposed as:

$$RR_m = R^d + R^t,$$

where

R^d = required reserves behind demand deposits at member banks,
R^t = required reserves behind time deposits at member banks.

In turn, required reserves behind demand deposits at member banks are the sum of the amount of reserves required behind demand deposits over and under $5 million at each reserve city and country bank, and similarly for time and savings deposits.[6] Present required reserve ratios for each deposit category are shown in Table 3.

Table 3. Reserve Requirements of Member Banks
(In effect September 30, 1969)

Type of Deposit	Percentage Requirement
Net Demand deposits:*	
Reserve city banks:	
Under $5 million	17.0%
Over $5 million	17.5
Country banks:	
Under $5 million	12.5
Over $5 million	13.0
Time deposits (all classes of banks):	
Savings deposits	3.0
Other Time Deposits:	
Under $5 million	3.0
Over $5 million	6.0

*Demand deposits subject to reserve requirements are gross demand deposits minus cash items in the process of collection and demand balances due from domestic banks.

Source: Federal Reserve *Bulletin.*

[6]Expanding the equation for total bank reserves,

$$R = R^d + R^t + ER_m + VC_n.$$

And since R^d, for instance, is the appropriate required reserve ratio times the amount of deposits in each reserve requirement classification, the above expression is rewritten in terms of weighted average reserve ratios and deposits. See footnote 7.

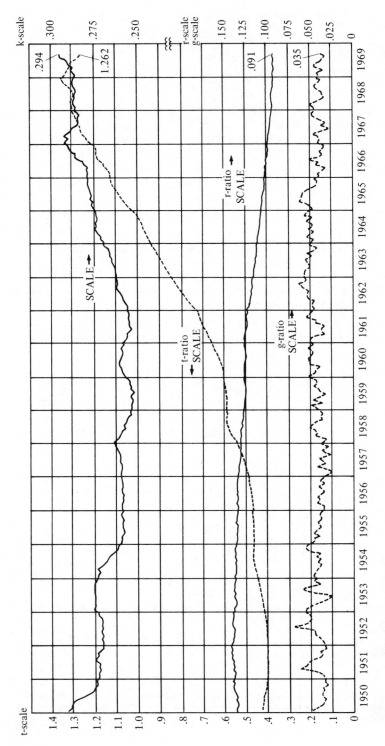

CHART 2 MONETARY MULTIPLIER RATIOS

Latest data plotted: September, 1969

Alternatively, the total amount of commercial bank reserves can be expressed as a proportion (r) of total bank deposits:

$$R = r (D + T + G).$$

where

> D = private demand deposits,
> T = time deposits,
> G = U.S. Government (Treasury) deposits at commercial banks.

The "r-ratio" is defined to be a weighted-average reserve ratio against all bank deposits, but is computed directly by dividing total reserves by total deposits.[7] The trend of the r-ratio in the postwar period is shown in Chart 2. An important factor contributing to the gradual downward trend of the r-ratio is the relatively more rapid growth of time deposits (which are subject to lower reserve requirements) than demand deposits.

Currency Held by the Public

One of the important factors influencing the amount of money the banking system can create, given an increase in monetary base, is the proportion of currency to demand deposits the public desires to hold. For example, if the public held a fixed total *amount* of currency, all changes in the supply of base money by the Federal Reserve would remain in the banking system as reserves and would be reflected entirely in changes in deposits, the amount depending on the reserve requirement ratios for different classes and types of deposit. On the other hand, if the public always desired to hold a fixed *ratio* of currency to demand deposits (for example exactly \$.25 in currency for every \$.75 of demand deposits), the deposit creating potential of the banking system would be substantially less. Clearly the "currency drain" associated with an increase in the base must be taken into account in deter-

---

[7]For the interested reader,

$$r = a \, \delta r^d + (1 - a) \, \tau \, r^t + e + v,$$

where

> a = the proportion of member bank demand deposits to total deposits,
> δ = the proportion of net demand deposits of member banks to total demand deposits,
> r^d = a weighted-average reserve requirement ratio for member bank demand deposits,
> τ = the proportion of net time deposits of member banks to total time deposits,
> r^t = a weighted average reserve requirement ratio for member bank time deposits,
> e = ratio of excess reserves to total bank deposits,
> v = ratio of nonmember bank vault cash to total bank deposits.

This definition is altered somewhat by the recently instituted lagged-reserve-requirement provisions of the Federal Reserve. It is worth emphasizing that some of the above ratios are determined by the behavior of commercial banks and the public, and others are determined primarily by the Federal Reserve. The fact that these ratios are not fixed does not impair the usefulness of the analysis.

mining how much base money must be supplied to achieve a desired increase in the money stock. Currency (C) can be expressed as a proportion (k) of demand deposits (D), that is:

$$C = k D,$$
$$\text{or}$$
$$k = C/D.$$

Changes in the level of the "k-ratio" over time are influenced by such factors as income levels, utilization of credit cards, and uncertainties regarding general economic stability. The trend of the k-ratio is shown in Chart 2.[8]

Time Deposits

Time deposits are not included in the definition of the money stock discussed in this article. Nevertheless, since member banks are required to hold reserves behind time deposits, information regarding the public's desired holdings of time to demand deposits is necessary in order to determine how much the stock of money will change following a change in the stock of monetary base.

Reserve requirements are much lower against time deposits than against demand deposits as shown in Table 3; consequently a given amount of reserves would allow more time deposits to be supported than demand deposits. Time deposits (T) can be expressed as a proportion (t) of demand deposits (D), that is:

$$T = t D,$$
$$\text{or}$$
$$t = T/D.$$

The trend of the "t-ratio" is shown in Chart 2.

The factors influencing the t-ratio are more complex to analyze than those affecting the k-ratio. Commercial banks are permitted to pay interest on time deposits up to ceiling rates set by the Federal Reserve and the Federal Deposit Insurance Corporation (see Table 4). Consequently, the growth of time deposits over time is influenced by competition among banks for individual and business savings within the limits permitted by the legal interest rate ceilings.

The interest rates which banks are willing to offer on time deposits (below the ceilings) are determined primarily by opportunities that are available for profitable investment of the funds in loans or securities. Similarly, the decisions by individuals and businesses to deposit their funds in banks are influenced by the interest rates available from alternative earning assets such as savings and loan shares, mutual

---

[8]For a detailed examination of the behavior of the currency to demand deposit ratio, see Phillip Cagan, *Determinants and Effects of Changes in the U.S. Money Stock, 1875–1960* (New York: National Bureau of Economic Research, 1965), chapter 4.

Table 4. Maximum Interest Rates Payable on Time and Savings Deposits
(Effective April 19, 1968)

Type of Deposit	Percent Per Annum
Savings deposits	4.00%
Other time deposits:	
Multiple maturity*:	
90 days or more	5.00
Less than 90 days (30–89 days)	4.00
Single maturity:	
Less than $100,000	5.00
$100,000 or more:	
30–59 days	5.50
60–89 days	5.75
90–179 days	6.00
180 days and over	6.25

*Multiple maturity time deposits include deposits that are automatically renewable at maturity without action by the depositor and deposits that are payable after written notice of withdrawal.
Source: Federal Reserve *Bulletin.*

savings bank deposits, bonds, stocks, commercial paper, and direct investments in real assets.[9] If the interest returns from these other assets are sufficiently high that the interest rate ceilings on time deposits prevent banks from effectively competing for the public's savings, then time deposits may not grow (or may even decline) and all increases in commercial bank reserves can be used to support demand deposits. This point will be discussed in more detail below.

U.S. Government Deposits

Commercial banks are required to hold the same proportion of reserves against Federal Government demand deposits as against private demand deposits. Therefore, even though Government deposits are *not* included in the definition of the money stock, changes in the amount of Government deposits influence the amount of private deposits the banking system can support with a given amount of base money or reserves. Government deposits (G) can be expressed as a proportion (g) of private demand deposits (D), that is:

$$G = g\,D,$$
$$\text{or}$$
$$g = G/D.$$

[9]Jerry L. Jordan, *The Market for Deposit-Type Financial Assets,* Working Paper No. 8, Federal Reserve Bank of St. Louis, March 1969.

The amount of Government deposits in commercial banks is determined by the flow of Treasury receipts (primarily from taxes) relative to Treasury expenditures and by the Treasury's discretion about what proportion of its balances to keep with commercial banks rather than at the Federal Reserve. Thus, short-run fluctuations in the "g-ratio" are primarily the result of actions by the U.S. Treasury. The Federal Reserve must assess, from past experience and information available from the Treasury, what will happen to Treasury balances in an impending period in order to determine the influence of changes in Treasury balances in the money stock. The monthly pattern of the g-ratio is shown in Chart 2.

The Monetary Multiplier

All of the essential elements for determination of the money stock have now been discussed. The definitional relations are as follows:

$$M = D + C \tag{1}$$

$$B = R + C \tag{2}$$

$$R = r(D + T + G) \tag{3}$$

$$C = kD \tag{4}$$

$$T = tD \tag{5}$$

$$G = gD \tag{6}$$

By substituting (3) and (4) into (2), we get:

$$B = r(D + T + G) + kD, \tag{7}$$

that is, we express the monetary base solely in terms of the various deposits. Substituting (5) and (6) into (7), we get:

$$B = r(D + tD + gD) + kD, \tag{8}$$

that is, we express the base solely in terms of private demand deposits to reduce the number of variables. Simplifying, we write (8) as:

$$B = [r(1 + t + g) + k] \times D, \tag{8'}$$

from which, by simple manipulation, we can express deposits in terms of the base as follows:

$$D = \frac{1}{r(1 + t + g) + k} \times B. \tag{9}$$

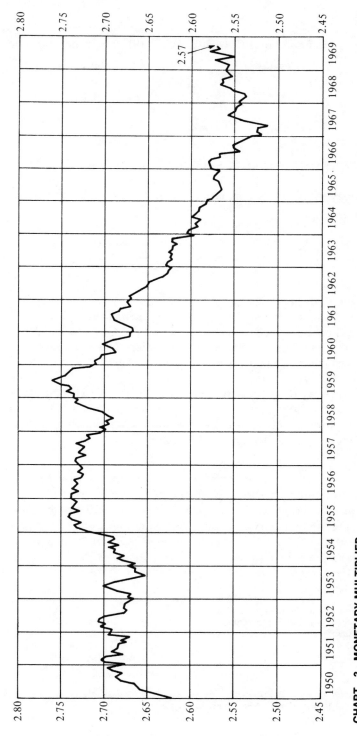

CHART 3 MONETARY MULTIPLIER

Latest data plotted: September.

Since we want to find D plus C, we use (4) and (9) to redefine C in terms of the base:

$$C = \frac{k}{r (1 + t + g) + k} \times B. \tag{10}$$

Substituting (9) and (10) into (1) gives:

$$M = \frac{1 + k}{r (1 + t + g) + k} \times B, \tag{1'}$$

or the money stock defined in terms of the monetary base.[10] We can denote the quotient as:

$$m = \frac{1 + k}{r (1 + t + g) + k},$$

where m is called the "monetary multiplier."[11]

The factors that can cause changes in the monetary multiplier are all of the factors which influence the currency (k), time deposit (t), Government deposit (g), and reserve (r) ratios, that is, the "behavioral parameters." The observed monthly values of these ratios in the past twenty years are shown in Chart 2, and the monthly values for the monetary multiplier (m) are shown in Chart 3. Quite obviously, if the monetary multiplier were perfectly constant, at say 2.5, then every $1 increase in the monetary base would result in a $2.50 increase in the money stock. On the other hand, if the monetary multiplier were subject to substantial unpredictable variation, the Federal Reserve would have difficulty in determining the money stock by controlling the base.

Since the monetary multiplier is not constant, the Federal Reserve must predict the value of the multiplier for the impending month in order to know how much to increase the monetary base to achieve a desired level of the money stock. Techniques for predicting the monetary multiplier go beyond the scope of this paper.[12] However, examples of how changes in time deposits and Government deposits influence the stock of money will be discussed.

---

[10]Since the monetary base is adjusted for the effect of changes in reserve requirements, a corresponding adjustment is made to the reserve ratio (r).

[11]The reader should be able to demonstrate that if money is defined to include time deposits ($M_2 = D + C + T$), then

$$m_2 = \frac{1 + k + t}{r (1 + t + g) + k}.$$

[12]For one straight-forward approach, see Lyle Kalish, *A Study of Money Stock Control,* Working Paper No. 11, Federal Reserve Bank of St. Louis, July 1969.

The Influence of Two Factors on the Money Stock

The following sections present examples of the ways changes in the growth of time deposits and U.S. Government deposits influence the money creation process. The effects are illustrated both by changes in the ratios in the monetary multiplier and with the use of commercial bank balance sheet "T-Accounts."

Changes in Time Deposits

The growth of time deposits relative to demand deposits is determined by many factors, including those which influence the interest rates offered by commercial banks on such deposits and those which influence the quantity of time deposits demanded by the public at each interest rate. Both the banks' supply of time deposits and the public's demand for them are a function of relative costs and returns of alternative sources of funds and earning assets. Thus, accuracy of predictions of the t-ratio (time deposits to demand deposits) for a future period is influenced by the ability of the forecasters to anticipate the banks' and public's behavior. Experience has shown that changes in this ratio tend to be dominated by rather long-run trends, with exceptions occurring at those times when interest rate ceilings imposed by the monetary authorities prevent banks from effectively competing for deposits. It is these special cases that will be discussed.

When market interest rates rise above the ceiling rates banks are permitted to offer on time deposits, some individuals and businesses who might otherwise hold time deposits decide to buy bonds or other earning assets instead. This effect has been most pronounced on the banks' class of time deposits called "large negotiable certificates of deposit" (CD's). To depositors, these are highly liquid assets which are considered by the purchasers to be close substitutes for Treasury bills and commercial paper.[13] On at least four occasions since 1965 the yields on these substitute assets have risen above the rates banks were permitted to offer on CD's, causing the growth of CD's to slow sharply or even become negative.

To illustrate the effect on the money stock of a rise in market interest rates above Regulation Q ceilings, assume that the growth of time deposits ceases, and banks hold the same total amount of time deposits while demand deposits continue to grow. In the money supply model this is reflected in a decline in the t-ratio (time deposits divided by demand deposits), and since the t-ratio appears in the denominator of the multiplier, the multiplier would get larger as the t-ratio gets smaller.

For example, assume the following initial values for the monetary base and the parameters of the multiplier:

$$B = \$75 \text{ billion}$$
$$t = 1.3$$

---

[13]Jordan, *Deposit-Type Financial Assets*, chapter 4.

$$g = .04$$
$$k = .3$$
$$r = .1$$

since

$$M = \frac{1 + k}{r(1 + t + g) + k} \times B,$$

we can solve to find $M = \$182.6$ billion.

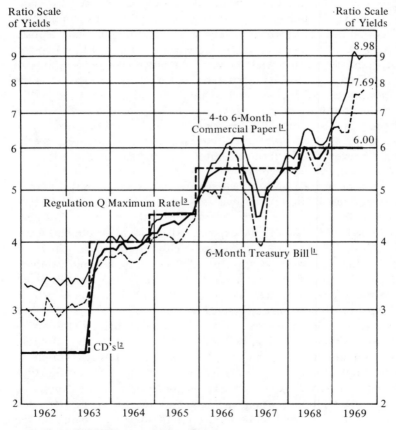

SHORT-TERM MONEY MARKET RATES

[1]Market yields converted from discount to bond equivalent basis.

[2]Average new issue rates on six month certificates of deposit of $100,000 or more. Data are estimated by the Federal Reserve Bank of St. Louis from guide rates published in the Bond Buyer and are monthly averages of Wednesday figures.

[3]Rate on deposits in amounts of $100,000 or more maturing in 90-179 days.

Latest data plotted: September.

Now suppose that in the course of several months the base increases by $1 billion, but time deposits do not grow at all as a result of the high market rates of interest relative to Regulation Q ceilings. If all of the ratios in the multiplier (including the t-ratio) had remained unchanged in this period, the money stock would have increased by about $2.4 billion to $185 billion. But since time deposits did not change while demand deposits continued to grow, the t-ratio would fall, to 1.28, for example, which causes the multiplier to increase (still assuming the other behavioral parameters remain the same).[14]

The reader should be careful not to interpret this greater increase in money (especially demand deposits) to mean that the banks can extend more credit than otherwise. Since the reserve requirements on demand deposits are greater than on time deposits, the $1 billion increase in monetary base would have supported a greater amount of *total* deposits (demand plus time) if time deposits grew proportionally to demand deposits, rather than only demand deposits increasing. With the assumed initial values for the parameters of the multiplier and the postulated $1 billion increase in the monetary base, money plus time deposits would have increased by almost $4.8 billion, almost twice as much as money.

To interpret the effects of this increase in money on the economy, it is necessary to analyze the increase in the supply of money compared to the demand for money to hold, and the supplies of and demands for other assets. We postulated above that market interest rates rose above the ceiling rates banks are permitted to pay on time deposits (especially CD's). In such a situation the volume of CD's (quantity *supplied*) is any amount depositors wish at the ceiling rates. Since the yields on good substitutes become more attractive than CD's, the *demand* for CD's declines, resulting in a decline in the outstanding volume of CD's or a slowing in the growth rate. In other words, a change in the relative yields on substitute assets causes a shift in the demand for CD's (negative), which causes a decline in the volume.

Disintermediation

We noted above that *total* deposits of banks may decline as a result of this "disintermediation" of time deposits. This means that banks must contract their assets, either loans or security holdings, as deposits decline. An understanding of the actions of banks in the face of a deposit drain and actions of those who withdraw their deposits is important information in assessing the effects of the disintermediation caused by the interest rate ceilings.

To illustrate two possible effects of disintermediation, we will use highly simplified examples and T-accounts (commercial bank balance sheets). Account 1 shows the banking system in its initial condition having total reserves (TR) = $25, required reserves (RR) = $25 and excess reserves (ER) = 0, security holdings (S) = $100 and loans outstanding (L) = $175. Bank liabilities are demand deposits (DD) = $100

---

[14]In practice, as the t-ratio falls from 1.3 to 1.28, demand deposits grow and time deposits do not, and the average reserve requirement ratio (r) will rise. This will slightly attenuate the increase in the multiplier and the money stock.

Account 1. Banking System

Assets				Liabilities	
TR			$ 25	DD	$100
	RR	$25		TD	200
	ER	0			
S			100		
L			175		
Total			$300	Total	$300

Account 2. Banking System

Assets				Liabilities	
TR			$ 25	DD	$100
	RR	$24		TD	180
	ER	1			
S			80		
L			175		
Total			$280	Total	$280

and time deposits (TD) = $200. We have assumed that reserve requirements against demand deposits are 15 percent and reserve requirements against time deposits are 5 percent.

Account 2 shows the effect of a corporation reducing its holdings of time deposits by $20 and buying $20 in securities from the banks because of the higher return available on the latter. The immediate effect is that the ownership of the securities is changed—the corporation directly holds the securities instead of having a deposit in a bank which owns the securities, hence the term "disintermediation"—and the banks are left with $1 of excess reserves. The banking system can create loans (or buy some securities), based on the dollar of excess reserves, and increase demand deposits by a multiple of $1. In this simplified example, the effect of disintermediation resulting from relatively low interest rate ceilings is potentially expansionary on total loans, even though total deposits decrease.

For the second example, a bank, in its usual role as an intermediary, sells CD's to a corporation which wishes to invest short-term funds. With the proceeds of the sale of the CD's, the bank lends to another corporation (less the amount the bank must hold as required reserves, of course). Another simplified example of the potential effects of disintermediation on the banking system and total credit is illustrated in Account 3. For exposition, assume that the one-bank holding companies of commercial banks establish subsidiaries for the purpose of buying and selling commercial paper.

Account 3. Banking System

Assets				Liabilities	
TR			$ 25	DD	$100
	RR	$24		TD	180
	ER	1			
S			100		
L			155		
Total			$280	Total	$280

Account 4. Subsidiary of One-Bank Holding Company

Assets		Liabilities	
Commercial paper held	$20	Commercial paper outstanding	$20

For our example, assume the first corporation does not wish to renew $20 of its CD holdings when they reach maturity, but rather, because of generally rising short-term market interest rates, seeks a yield greater than the bank is permitted to pay. Our hypothetical subsidiary of the one-bank holding company can offer to sell its own commercial paper (I.O.U.) to the first corporation at competitive market interest rates (Account 4).

We assume the corporation buys the subsidiary's commercial paper. As a result of their reduced deposits, the banks are forced to contract assets proportionately (as a first step in a partial analysis). Instead of selling securities, as in our previous example, the banks can contract loans outstanding by $20, as shown in Account 3 (as compared to Account 1). The subsidiary can in turn use the proceeds of its sale of commercial paper to purchase the paper of another corporation which seeks to borrow short-term money, possibly a corporation which was having difficulty getting a bank loan since bank assets and liabilities were contracting.

We find that the initial effect of the disintermediation is that the total of bank loans plus commercial paper debts of borrowing corporations is the same as the initial amount of bank loans outstanding and that the total of time deposits plus commercial paper assets of lending corporations is the same as the initial amount of time deposits at banks. However, we also find that banks have acquired an additional $1 of excess reserves which they can lend and thereby increase demand deposits.

In summary, both of the examples of the disintermediation of time deposits caused by the interest rate ceilings show that the same initial amount of reserves in the banking system can, under certain circumstances, support a larger amount of demand deposits (and therefore money stock). In other words, if the disintermediation means only that some funds flow through channels which are not subject to reserve requirements and interest rate ceilings, the effects of the relatively low interest rate ceilings on commercial bank time deposits are potentially expansionary on total loans.

U.S. Government Deposits and Money

As previously discussed, the monetary base summarizes all of the actions of the Federal Reserve which influence the money stock. However, the Treasury cannot be overlooked as an agency which can influence the money stock over at least short periods. In the money supply model, the influence of changes in the amount of Government deposits is reflected in movements in the g-ratio (Government deposits divided by private demand deposits) in the monetary multiplier.

In recent years the Government's balances at commercial banks have fluctuated from $3 billion to $9 billion within a few months time. Private demand deposits averaged about $150 billion in mid-1969. The g-ratio is therefore quite small, ranging from about .02 to about .06, but frequently doubles or falls by half over the course of a month or two.

Similar to the effect of changes in the t-ratio, increases in the g-ratio result in a fall in the multiplier since the ratio appears in the denominator. Using again the initial values we assumed for the base and multiplier, we have:

$$M = \frac{1 + .3}{.1\,(1 + 1.3 + .04) + .3} \times \$75 \text{ billion} = \$182.6 \text{ billion,}$$

where .04 is the value of the g-ratio. These values imply that demand deposits (D) are about $140.5 billion and Government deposits (G) are $5.6 billion. Now suppose that individuals and businesses pay taxes of $1 billion by writing checks which draw down (D) to $139.5 billion and Government balances rise to $6.6 billion. Assuming no change in time deposits or currency held by the public and no change in the base, we would find that the g-ratio rises to .047 (and the k- and t-ratios rise slightly) to give us:

$$M = \frac{1 + .302}{.1\,(1 + 1.309 + .047) + .302} \times \$75 \text{ billion} = \$181.6 \text{ billion.}$$

A similar example of the effects on the money stock of an increase in Government deposits at commercial banks which is associated with a change in time deposits (people pay taxes by reducing their savings or holdings of CD's) would be somewhat more complicated. In the above example, taxes were paid out of demand deposits, and the reserve ratio (r) was not changed, which implies that the distribution of the increment in Government deposits among reserve city, country, and nonmember banks was the same as the distribution of the $1 billion reduction in private demand deposits.

When taxes are paid out of time deposits, the r-ratio rises, since reserve requirements against Government deposits are approximately three times the reserve requirements against time deposits. These movements are very small, and any accompanying reduction in the excess reserve ratio would attenuate the effect. Nonetheless, the effect on money is a combination of small changes in the k-, r-, t-, and g-ratios.

Summary

The behavioral parameters of the money supply framework presented here are the currency (k), reserve (r), time deposit (t), and Government deposit (g) ratios. The changes in these ratios reflect the actions of the Treasury, banks, and nonbank public which influence the money stock. The k-ratio is determined by the public's preferences for currency versus demand deposits; the t-ratio reflects the interaction of the banks' supply of and the public's demand for time deposits as compared to the supply of and demand for demand deposits; and the g-ratio is dominated by changes in Government balances at commercial banks. The r-ratio is the least volatile of the behavioral parameters, although it is influenced by the banks' desired holdings of excess reserves and the distribution of total deposits among all the subclasses of deposits in the various classes of banks, which are subject to a large array of reserve requirements.

The main policy actions of the monetary authorities—open market operations, changes in reserve requirements, and administration of the discount window—are summarized by the monetary base. The growth of the base summarizes the *influence* of the monetary authorities' defensive and dynamic *actions* on the growth of the money stock, regardless of the *intent* of these actions. The degree of accuracy that can be achieved by the monetary authorities in controlling the money stock is a function of their ability to determine the monetary base, and to predict the net influence of the public's and banks' behavior as summarized by changes in the money supply multiplier.

Can the Central Bank Control the Money Stock?

David I. Fand

17

The money stock at any moment in time is the result of portfolio decisions by the central bank, by the commercial banks, and by the public (including the nonbank intermediaries):[1] the central bank determines the amount of high-powered money or monetary base, that is, currency plus bank reserves, that it will supply;[2] the commercial banks determine the volume of loans and other assets that they will acquire and the quantity of reserves they will hold as excess (and free) reserves; and the public determines how to allocate their holdings of monetary wealth among currency, de-

Reprinted from the Federal Reserve Bank of St. Louis *Review* (January, 1970), pp. 12-16, by permission of the publisher and the author.

[1]For a discussion of the determinants of the money stock see M. Friedman and A. Schwartz, *A Monetary History of the U.S. 1867-1960* (Princeton, 1963), Appendix B on "Proximate Determinants of the Nominal Stock of Money"; P. Cagan, *Determinants and Effects of Changes in the Stock of Money 1875-1960* (Columbia, 1965), Chapter I on "The Money Stock and Its Three Determinants"; K. Brunner, "A Schema for the Supply Theory of Money," *International Economic Review,* January 1961; D. Fand, "Some Implications of Money Supply Analysis," *American Economic Review,* May 1967.

[2]The high-powered money concept used by M. Friedman, A. Schwartz, and P. Cagan is essentially the monetary base concept used by K. Brunner, A. Meltzer, and others. The monetary base may be defined either in terms of the sources (Federal Reserve credit, gold stock, Treasury items, etc.) or *uses* (member bank reserves and currency). To compare movements in the monetary base over time, we need to make a correction for changes in reserve requirements. As used here, the monetary base includes a reserve adjustment; that is, it is equal to the source base plus the reserve adjustment.

For a very clear exposition see L. Andersen and J. Jordan, "The Monetary Base—Explanations and Analytical Use" in the August 1968 issue of the St. Louis Federal Reserve Bank *Review.*

mand, time and savings deposits, CD's, intermediary claims, and other financial assets. The money stock that emerges reflects all these decisions.

It is a natural question to consider whether the central bank, by controlling the monetary base, can actually achieve fairly precise control over the money stock. This depends on whether the link between the monetary base and bank reserves, and between bank reserves and the money stock (the *monetary base-bank reserves-money stock* linkage) is fairly tight and therefore predictable. If there is a tight linkage the monetary authorities can formulate their policies and achieve any particular target for the money stock; on the other hand, if there is significant and unpredictable slippage, and the central bank control over the money stock is not sufficiently precise to achieve a given target, it will necessarily have to formulate its policies in terms of other variables that it can control. The variable used to express (or define) the central bank's objective, or to implement its policy decisions, must therefore be one that it can control within reasonable limits.[3]

The recently recurring idea that the money stock is perhaps best viewed as an endogenous variable, although not a new idea (it would have been acceptable to "real bill" theorists), has received new and powerful support from those who follow the "New View" approach in monetary economics.[4] New View theorists have questioned the validity of much of classical monetary theory concerning the importance of money relative to other liquid assets, the uniqueness of commercial banks relative to other intermediaries, and the extent to which the central bank can control the nominal money stock.[5] They argue that the central bank can control its instruments (open market operations, reserve requirements, discount rate) and some money mar-

[3]It is presumably for this reason that some models treat unborrowed reserves as the policy variable (the practice followed in the FRB-MIT model and other econometric models). These model builders believe that some components of the monetary base, and perhaps the entire base, behave as endogenous variables—as the variables that respond to income changes, and are not directly (or completely) under the control of the central bank. They do believe that the Federal Reserve can control the volume of unborrowed reserves.

[4]For the development of the New View, see J. Gurley and E. Shaw, *Money in a Theory of Finance* (Brookings, 1959); D. Fand, "Intermediary Claims and the Adequacy of Our Monetary Controls," and J. Tobin, "Commercial Banks as Creators of 'Money,'" in D. Carson (ed), *Banking and Monetary Studies* (Irwin, 1963); H. Johnson, *Essays in Monetary Economics* (Allen and Unwin, 1967), Chapters 1 and 2; W. Brainard, "Financial Intermediaries and a Theory of Monetary Control," in D. Hester and J. Tobin (eds.), *Financial Markets and Economic Activity* (Wiley, 1967); and K. Brunner, "The Role of Money and Monetary Policy," in the July 1968 issue of the St. Louis Federal Reserve Bank *Review*.

[5]Tobin offers the following description of the New View: "A more recent development in monetary economics tends to blur the sharp traditional distinctions between money and other assets and between commercial banks and other financial intermediaries; to focus on demands for and supplies of the whole spectrum of assets rather than on the quantity and velocity of 'money'; and to regard the structure of interest rates, asset yields, and credit availabilities rather than the quantity of money as the linkage between monetary and financial institutions and policies on the one hand and the real economy on the other."

He also suggests that this general equilibrium approach to the financial sector tends to question the presumed uniqueness of commercial banks: "Neither individually nor collectively do commercial banks possess a widow's cruse. Quite apart from legal reserve requirements, commercial banks are limited in scale by the same kinds of economic processes that determine the aggregate size of other intermediaries."

J. Tobin, "Commercial Banks as Creators of 'Money,'" *op. cit.*, pp. 410-412.

ket variables (free reserves, Treasury bill rate); that the commercial banks supply deposits at a fixed rate; and that the stock of money and liquid assets which emerge—at least in the short run—largely reflect the public's preference for demand and time deposits, intermediary claims, and other financial assets.[6]

Two schools of monetary economics differ on the use of the money stock as an indicator or target variable and on the extent to which it is an endogenous variable and therefore not available to the monetary authorities as a stabilization instrument. The *nonmonetarists* believe that the central bank should formulate its policies in terms of money market variables and implement them through operations on the instrument variables. They view the money stock as (in part) an endogenous variable, and do not conceive of it as a proper instrument or target variable. The *monetarists* believe that the central bank can, and should, define its objectives and implement its policies in terms of the money stock. Indeed, these two conceptions of the money stock and its role in monetary policy decisions summarize some important substantive differences that have emerged in monetary economics:

1. between the *monetarist* view that changes in the nominal money stock may be a causal, active, and independent factor in influencing aggregate demand and the price level and the *nonmonetarist* views ranging from (a) the older "real bills" doctrine that the money stock responds primarily to changes in the real economy; (b) the Income-Expenditure theories (associated with the 45° diagram) which view money as an accommodating factor; and (c) the more recent New View doctrine that the money stock is best viewed as one of several endogenous liquidity aggregates;

2. between the monetarist view that the money stock—using either the conventional or the broader definition—is a reasonably well-behaved quantity and the Radcliffe-type view that rejects these measures as narrow and inappropriate and argues for a broader liquidity aggregate; and

3. between the monetarist view that the monetary policy posture should be gauged by the behavior of a monetary aggregate and the Income-Expenditure theories viewing market interest rates as the proper indicator variable.

Many who question the advisability of operating monetary policy in terms of money stock guidelines also question whether the central bank control is precise enough to comply with the guideline requirements. The extent of this control is therefore a key question. Is the money stock best viewed as an endogenous variable—determined by the interaction of the financial and real sectors—and outside the direct control of the central bank? Or is it more nearly correct to view it as an exogenous variable—as a policy instrument—that the authorities can control and whose behavior can be made to conform to the stabilization guidelines?

---

[6]Some monetary theorists have argued that while a skillfull central bank can manipulate its controls to keep the nominal money stock (M) on target, it is preferable nevertheless to think of (M) as an endogenous variable. They argue that a "theory which takes as data the instruments of control rather than M, will not break down if and when there are changes in the targets or the marksmanship of the authorities." See J. Tobin, "Money, Capital and Other Stores of Value," *American Economic Review,* May 1961.

This issue is essentially an empirical one: Does control over the monetary base and other instruments provide the central bank with sufficient powers to fit the behavior of the money stock into a given stabilization program? The *monetarists*, in assigning an important role for the money stock in stabilization policy, assume that the central bank can engineer the desired behavior of the money stock. The substantive issue can be reformulated in terms of an empirically refutable hypothesis, as follows: Do changes in commercial bank free reserve behavior, and do portfolio shifts by the public involving currency, demand and time deposits, and other financial assets introduce enough variability and enough "noise" to break the *monetary base-bank reserves-money stock* linkage and justify treating the money stock as an endogenous variable—and essentially outside the control of the central bank?

The empirical examination of this issue fits in naturally to a framework of money supply analysis which I have described in an earlier article.[7] The analysis developed there defines four money supply functions which incorporate alternative assumptions concerning portfolio adjustments.

If we let

M = the nominal money stock

X = a vector of Federal Reserve (monetary policy) instruments variables (the monetary base, reserve requirements, discount rate, Regulation Q)

r_b = a vector of endogenous financial variables (e.g., the Treasury bill rate, the Federal funds rate, the Eurodollar rate, the rate on time deposits and other intermediary claims)

T, C = time deposits, currency, shares, and other financial assets that are close substitutes for demand deposits

Y = a vector of real sector variables (*GNP*, business investment, durables, etc.)

a money supply (*M.S.*) function may be written as:

$$M = f(X, r_b; T, C: Y).$$

The four *M.S.* functions that follow reflect alternative *ceteris paribus* conditions changing the portfolio adjustments that we permit for both the banks and the public:

1. *M.S.*(I) is a short-run supply concept. It gives the money supply response to a change in reserves on the assumption that while banks may choose to adjust their free reserves, the public can only carry out a limited adjustment with respect to currency, time deposits, and other financial assets. There are several

[7]See D. Fand, "Some Implications of Money Supply Analysis," *American Economic Review*, May 1967.

ways to impose *certeris paribus* conditions on the public's holdings of currency, time deposits, and other financial assets. Some investigators hold *levels* of these assets constant, others hold *ratios* constant, and different investigators impose this *ceteris paribus* condition in a manner most compatible with their model. *M.S.*(I) is of the form $M = f(X, r_b; T, C: Y)$, where T and C specify our assumptions for currency, time deposits, and other close substitutes. To use it as a short-run concept, we assume that all variables in the real sector of the economy, including stocks of real assets and flows such as consumption and investment, are held constant, so that it is primarily a function of the monetary policy instrument variables. Accordingly, if *M.S.*(I) is fairly stable, it provides some support for the view that the monetary authorities can achieve fairly precise control over the money stock.

2. To construct *M.S.*(II), we remove some of these portfolio restrictions by permitting the public to adjust their holdings of currency and time deposits, and the terms on which banks supply time deposits to reflect the underlying preferences. This function is of the form $f(X, r_b: Y)$, and does not contain any arbitrary assumptions about currency, time deposits, or the rate paid on time deposits. It is derived by assuming (a) that the banks may adjust their free reserves and the rate paid on time deposits and (b) that the public's holdings of currency and time deposits will be determined by their demand function for these assets. Although *M.S.*(II) does permit a greater degree of portfolio adjustment, it still is a short-run and restricted function because it assumes that the real sector variables and all other financial assets are held constant.

3. To construct *M.S.*(III), we permit portfolio adjustments throughout the entire financial sector and solve all the equations in the financial sector simultaneously. The Treasury bill rate and other rates which are endogenous variables in the financial sector will therefore be determined and no longer enter as independent arguments in the money supply function. *M.S.*(III) is a reduced-form equation of the form $M = g(X: Y)$, where all endogenous financial variables will have values determined by the simultaneous solution of the behavior equations in the financial sector. This function measures the supply response due to a change in the monetary base or some other policy instrument, assuming that all the variables in the financial sector adjust simultaneously.

4. Finally, we define *M.S.*(IV) in the form of $M = g(X)$, a reduced-form equation which measures the movements in the money stock in response to adjustments in both the real and the financial sector. To derive this money supply, we must solve all the structural equations in the financial and real sectors simultaneously to obtain the reduced form. The real sector variables are no longer treated as exogenous variables, but are now determined simultaneously with all the endogenous financial sector variables. This reduced-form *M.S.* gives the equilibrium stocks of money as a function of the monetary base and other monetary policy instrument variables. This is the natural *M.S.* function to construct for those who view the money stock as passive and responding to real

sector developments and for those who view the money stock as an accommodating variable, whose changes may be necessary in order to validate changes in the real economy.[8]

This brief review of the four money supply functions suggests that it is possible to test some of the substantive points that have come up in the recent "control over the money stock" discussions. For example, *M.S.*(I) postulates that we can predict the effect of changes in the monetary base (and other instruments) on the money stock, assuming that the public's portfolio adjustments are restricted; *M.S.*(II) postulates that we can predict the effect of a change in the monetary base (and other instruments) on the money stock, even allowing the public to adjust their currency and holdings of demand and time deposits; while *M.S.*(III) postulates that we can predict the money stock response, even allowing the public to adjust their entire portfolios. These three *M.S.* functions assume that commercial bank free reserve behavior and the public's behavior with respect to currency and demand and time deposits are stable; and that the substitution of intermediary claims and liquid assets for money conforms to behavior that can be incorporated into a stable *M.S.* function. Econometric estimates of these three functions provide some evidence for testing the reliability of the *monetary base-bank reserve-money stock* linkage.[9]

Those who follow the "real bills" view—that the money stock is determined by the real sector variables—or the view in many income-expenditure models—that the money stock is an accommodating or permissive variable—presumably deny the possibility of constructing such functions. In their view these three *M.S.* functions do not allow any changes in fiscal policy or in the real sector variables; they permit only restricted changes in the financial sector variables, and they emphasize the monetary base and the central bank's instrument variables. Accordingly, they should predict that the first three *M.S.* functions highlighting the instrument variables are unstable and lack content; indeed, their approach to monetary theory implies that only *M.S.*(IV), which incorporates changes in the real sector, contains the relevant independent variables.

An analysis of these four money supply functions has implications for the use of the money stock as an independent and major instrument in stabilization. Those who argue that money is, at least in part, an endogenous variable, and who question the precision with which it can be controlled, assume (implicitly perhaps) that no statis-

---

[8]The *M.S.*(IV) function as written implies that an increase in the monetary base will affect the money supply if it induces some real sector changes. A "real bills" proponent might therefore prefer to write it as follows:

$$M = f(Y) \text{ and } X = g(Y),$$

where M and X are both determined by the real sector variables in Y.

[9]A comparison of the three *M.S.* functions enables us to evaluate the quantitative effects of these portfolio shifts on the money stock. Consider a given change in the monetary base, or any other instrument variable, and compare the money stock response in these three functions. The calculated differences reflect the portfolio adjustments that we introduce as we move from *M.S.*(I) to *M.S.*(III)—i.e., shifts among currency, demand and time deposits, and the substitution of intermediary claims for money—and thus provide a measure of these effects on the money stock.

tically significant supply function can be estimated relating the money stock to the monetary base and other instrument variables. Moreover, if such a function is estimated, it would have to be a reduced-form function and a variant of the *M.S.*(IV) concept, incorporating feedbacks from the real sector.

In an earlier study, we compared estimates of the *M.S.* functions calculated from different econometric models. We found that the elasticities and multipliers for the first three *M.S.* functions based primarily on financial variables appear to be stable enough to justify further effort toward their refinement and improvement. We also found that: "There are at present too few studies available to calculate reliable *M.S.*(IV) elasticities. But the available evidence, meager though it may be, does not point to any superiority of *M.S.*(IV) over *M.S.*(I), and does not appear to favor a real view over a monetary view. Those who take the view that money is passive, responding primarily to the real economy, have to recognize that this is an assumption rather than a proposition derived from empirical evidence."[10]

While this research is far from conclusive, it is consistent with a number of other findings.[11] It is difficult to maintain the view that the money stock is sufficiently endogenous so that it is outside the *direct* control of the authorities, without getting dangerously close to a "real bills" position. Accordingly, the focus of the "control over the money stock" discussion will shift, in my opinion, to the more interesting question—and the more relevant and less ideological question—concerning the length of the period needed to give the Federal Reserve System sufficient control to achieve a given money stock guideline. Assuming that a "reasonable" degree of precision has been defined, can the particular guideline requirements be achieved in a week? a month? a quarter? Or must we extend the period in order to overcome false signals, "noise," forecasting errors and other disturbances?"[12] It would appear that the degree of precision desired is not independent of the time period required for the execution of policy, and it is reassuring to note that recent discussions have been directed increasingly at these points.

[10]See D. Fand, "Some Implications of Money Supply Analysis," *op. cit.,* p. 392. The calculated elasticities and multipliers suggest that the short-run *M.S.* functions—such as the *M.S.*(I) and *M.S.*(II)—are reasonably stable. These are preliminary findings, derived by using the steady-state solutions to simplify the analysis; they are subject to revision and require the construction of significance tests.

[11]See the references to Andersen, Brunner, Cagan, Friedman and Schwartz, and Meltzer in footnotes 1, 2 and 4.

[12]This formulation of the problem has come up in several recent papers. Governor Maisel emphasizes this point as follows: "This growth of money supply in any period is the result of actions taken by the Federal Reserve, the Treasury, the commercial banks, and the public. Over a longer period, the Fed may play a paramount role, but this is definitely not the case in the short run. To the best of my knowledge, the Fed has not and probably would have great difficulties controlling within rather wide limits the growth of the narrowly defined money supply in any week or month."

See Sherman J. Maisel, "Controlling Monetary Aggregates," in *Controlling Monetary Aggregates* (Boston: Federal Reserve Bank of Boston, 1969). For some other discussions of this issue, see A. J. Meigs, "The Case for Simple Rules," *op. cit.;* L. Gramley, "Guidelines for Monetary Policy—The Case Against Simple Rules," *op. cit.;* the Hearings on Standards for Guiding Monetary Action, *op. cit.;* A. Meltzer, "Controlling Money," *Controlling Monetary Aggregates* (Boston: Federal Reserve Bank, 1969). See also L. Kallish, "A Study of Money Stock Control," *Working Paper No. 11,* Federal Reserve Bank of St. Louis, for an interesting attempt to develop confidence limits for measuring the money managers' success in controlling the money stock.

A Review of Empirical Studies of the Money Supply Mechanism

Robert H. Rasche

In recent years there has been considerable discussion concerning techniques for conducting monetary policy. The traditional practitioners of the art of policymaking have argued for the use of operating procedures which focus on "money market conditions." At various times this has been construed to mean free reserves, the Treasury bill rate, the Federal funds rate, or a combination of these.[1] Alternatively, it has been argued that the target of monetary policy actions should be a monetary aggregate and that this target can be achieved by control of some reserve aggregate concept such as the monetary base.[2]

This article surveys the accumulated empirical evidence on the interest sensitivity of some reserve multipliers. If these multipliers are highly sensitive to interest rate changes, then it may be difficult to implement monetary control through the control of reserve aggregates. The available evidence consistently indicates, however, that

Reprinted from the Federal Reserve Bank of St. Louis, *Review* (July, 1972), pp. 11-19, by permission of the publisher and the author.

[1]Stephen H. Axilrod, "The FOMC Directive as Structured in the Late 1960's: Theory and Appraisal," in *Open Market Policies and Operating Procedures—Staff Studies* (Washington, D.C.: Board of Governors of the Federal Reserve System, 1971), pp. 1-36.

[2]For example, see Albert E. Burger, Lionel Kalish III, and Christopher T. Babb, "Money Stock Control and Its Implications for Monetary Policy," this *Review* (October 1971), pp. 6-22.

the interest sensitivity of various multiplier concepts is extremely low. This suggests that control of monetary aggregates through reserve control should not be very difficult to implement.[3]

Conditions Inhibiting Control of the Money Stock

The issue examined here is the feasibility of control of a monetary aggregate such as the narrowly defined money stock (M_1), given control of some reserve aggregate concept. The problem can be illustrated by the equation

$$M = mR$$

where "M" is the money stock, "R" is some reserve aggregate concept, and "m" is the appropriate reserve multiplier.[4] Two sources of difficulty can arise in such a control procedure.

First, there can be systematic feedbacks on "m" through market forces which tend to offset the expected effect of a change in the reserve aggregate on the money stock. This influence of the behavior of reserves on the value of the multiplier can be stated as

$$m = f(R).$$

The sources of feedback from changes in "R" to changes in "m" will vary depending on the choice of a reserve aggregate concept. If the net source base concept is used for "R", the associated multiplier (m) is

$$m = \frac{1 + k}{(r - b)(1 + t + d) + k}$$

where "r" and "b" are the ratios of bank reserves and member bank borrowings to commercial bank deposits, respectively, "t", "k" and "d", respectively, are the ratios of time deposits, currency held by the public, and U.S. Government deposits at commercial banks to the demand deposit component of the money supply. Therefore, the important behavioral relationships influencing the stability of the multiplier

---

[3] If, however, these multipliers *are* highly sensitive to interest rate changes, then accurate monetary control through a reserve control procedure requires a precise estimate of the impact of reserve changes on interest rates, in addition to a precise estimate of the interest elasticity of the reserve multiplier.

[4] A number of candidates have been proposed for "R" including the monetary base, unborrowed reserves plus currency, total reserves, unborrowed reserves, and reserves available to support private deposits. For a discussion of the relative virtues of many of these, see Richard Davis, "Short-Run Targets for Open Market Operations," in *Open Market Policies and Operating Procedures—Staff Studies* (Washington, D.C.: Board of Governors of the Federal Reserve System, 1971), pp. 37-45.

in the presence of reserve changes are the public's demand for currency and time deposits, banks' demand for excess reserves and borrowings, and the supply of time deposits.[5]

An example of a feedback effect on "m" would be where there exists a sizable short-run interest elasticity of demand for excess reserves by commercial banks. In order to force additional reserves into the banking system to expand the money stock, the Federal Reserve would have to buy Government securities, thus pushing short-term interest rates down. If the amount of excess reserves demanded by banks is very sensitive to changes in short-term interest rates, this interest rate movement would induce banks to hold larger quantities of excess reserves. This portfolio shift then offsets the policy to increase the money stock.

The existence of strong feedback effects on the reserve multiplier does not mean that monetary control through reserve aggregates is impossible. The stronger the feedback, the larger the necessary magnitude of the open market operation required to achieve a given change in the money stock and the larger the associated variance in short-term interest rates.

The second source of difficulty in this type of monetary control procedure is that the relationship between the reserve aggregate and the money stock is subject to random fluctuation. Specifically, we can write

$$m_t = f(R_t) + \varepsilon_t$$

where "ε_t" is an unknown random disturbance to "m_t". If such fluctuations are truly random, then in the long run policymakers should be able to hit the desired average stock of money quite closely. If this random component is large, then in a short time period, such as one or two months, the average "m" could deviate considerably from the forecast "m" and cause a large average error around the desired path of the money stock.

It can be shown that for a given variance of "ε_t", under a control procedure such as that recently proposed by Burger, Kalish, and Babb, the variance of the actual path of the money stock around the desired path will depend on the sensitivity of the reserve multiplier (m) to changes in the reserve aggregate.[6] The smaller the sensitivity of the multiplier, the smaller will be the variance of the actual money stock around the desired money stock.

---

[5]For a detailed discussion of the functional relationship of the multiplier expression to asset holdings of the nonbank public, the banking system, and the Treasury, see Albert E. Burger, *The Money Supply Process* (Belmont, California: Wadsworth, 1971), especially chaps. 4-5, and Karl Brunner and Allan H. Meltzer, "Liquidity Traps for Money, Bank Credit, and Interest Rates, *Journal of Political Economy* (January/February 1968), pp. 1-37.

[6]Burger, Kalish, and Babb, "Money Stock Control."

The Nature of Available Evidence on Multiplier Sensitivity

Over the past decade there has been considerable empirical research directed at measuring the relationship between the money stock and various reserve aggregates. This work has evolved primarily from attempts to construct econometric models of basic financial relationships in the U.S. economy. As a by-product, these studies provide information on the interest elasticities of the behavioral parameters of the reserve multiplier, the existence of which cause feedbacks against policy actions as discussed above.

Most of the more detailed studies have worked with quarterly data, which may be too highly aggregated in time to provide information that policymakers desire if the reactions of the banking system and the public are distributed over time. However, studies using shorter time horizons do exist for some components of the money supply mechanism, and these can be used to obtain information on how the estimated elasticities are likely to change as the horizon becomes shorter.

There are several potential sources of feedback which will offset the expected impact of a change in reserve aggregates on the change in the money stock. Some of the feedback, such as a change in the demand for currency and time deposits by the nonbank public as a result of increased economic activity, has been shown to occur only slowly, and does not cause difficulties for short-run control.[7]

The troublesome source of changes in the multiplier relationship is the impact of changes in interest rates on the behavioral parameters in the multiplier. Changes in market interest rates and changes in reserves available to the banking system cannot be controlled simultaneously by the Federal Reserve System. When the Federal Reserve follows a reserve aggregate operating procedure, interest rates are affected by changes in reserves. Under a money market conditions operating strategy, changes in reserve aggregates come about as a result of the attempt to achieve certain levels of interest rates. Hence, if the goal is to control money through changes in reserve aggregates, the major issue is the interest elasticity of the relationship between the money stock and reserve aggregates.

It will be necessary to distinguish between short-run, or impact, elasticities of the reserve multiplier and long-run, or equilibrium, elasticities. The former include only the impact which comes from the adjustment of economic units to a change in interest rates within one period of time. Many studies, however, have indicated that economic units respond to such changes with a distributed lag; that is, part of the response takes place in the same period, and the remainder of the response takes place over several periods following a change in interest rates. The impact, or short-run, interest elasticity is the percentage change in the reserve multiplier with respect to a percentage change in interest rates within the time period in which the interest

[7]See David I. Fand, "Some Implications of Money Supply Analysis," *American Economic Review* (May 1967), pp. 380–400.

rate changes. The equilibrium, or long-run, elasticity is the total response of the reserve multiplier after economic units have had sufficient time to adjust to a new portfolio equilibrium.[8]

In the studies cited below, estimates have been obtained for the interest elasticity of the money stock for given values of various reserve aggregates. Thus, the money stock elasticities computed are the interest elasticities of the reserve multiplier.

Interest Elasticity Estimates from Data Prior to 1965

Teigen I

An early econometric investigation of the money supply relationship was that of Ronald Teigen.[9] His study does not develop the detailed specifications which are characteristic of more recent studies. In particular, the stocks of currency in the hands of the public and demand deposits at nonmember banks are assumed exogenous.[10] In addition, Teigen takes the quantity of time deposits at member banks and government deposits at member banks as exogenous variables.[11]

Teigen tests the hypothesis that the banking system takes more than one period to respond to changes in interest rates, but this hypothesis is rejected for the post-war data. Thus his impact and equilibrium interest elasticities of the money supply relationship are equal. His estimated coefficients of elasticity are 0.1950 for the commercial paper rate and −0.1695 for the discount rate.[12]

---

[8]For a discussion of impact versus long-run responses, see Arthur S. Goldberger, *Impact Multipliers and Dynamic Properties of the Klein-Goldberger Model* (Amsterdam: North-Holland, 1959).

[9]Ronald L. Teigen, "Demand and Supply Functions for Money in the United States: Some Structural Estimates," *Econometrica* (October 1964), pp. 476–509.

[10]It is necessary to distinguish here between the construction of the model from historical data and the use of the model to determine interest elasticities. In the construction of the model, the ratio of currency to demand deposits at member banks and the ratio of demand deposits at nonmember banks to those at member banks are, in fact, exogenous variables which vary from one observation to the next. In determining the value of the elasticity of the relationship, these exogenous variables are kept fixed at some point, conventionally their mean value for the sample period. Hence, the computations implicitly assume positive interest rate responses for the public's currency demand and the supply of demand deposits by nonmember banks, which are equal to the interest rate response of demand deposits supplied by member banks. For nonmember banks, the assumption probably does not seriously affect the analysis. On the other hand, the public's currency demand is usually found to have a zero, or slightly negative, interest elasticity, at least in the long run. If the true interest elasticity of currency demand is zero, then the bias introduced by the constant ratio of currency to money stock is indeterminate. On the one hand, the *direct* effect of increased currency in the hands of the public as demand deposits supplied by banks increase biases the interest elasticity of the money supply upward. On the other hand, the *indirect* effect that the assumed increase in currency withdraws reserves from the banking system causes the model to understate the desired amount of deposit expansion. Since the magnitudes involved are small, the net bias should not be substantial.

[11]These variables do not explicitly appear in his model. However, the reserve aggregate which he uses is unborrowed reserves available to support private demand deposits. Later studies use more broadly defined aggregates such as unborrowed reserves, or unborrowed reserves plus currency. To make the studies comparable, the model must be reformulated with time deposits at member banks and government deposits at member banks explicitly appearing as exogenous variables.

[12]Teigen, "Demand and Supply Functions," p. 502.

De Leeuw I

Frank de Leeuw attempted to obtain more detailed numerical estimates of behavior in important financial markets than did Teigen.[13] In particular, de Leeuw separates bank borrowing and excess reserve behavior, and explicity estimates functions for currency demand and time deposit demand at commercial banks by the nonbank public.

The interest elasticity estimates from this study are summarized in Table 1. In all cases the absolute value of the long-run elasticities are less than one, and the short-run elasticities never exceed 0.2 in absolute value. The available data do not permit reconstruction of the interest elasticities of excess reserves. However, de Leeuw did publish the results of a computation of the implicit interest elasticities of the money-reserve relationship derived from the estimated borrowings and excess reserves functions. In this computation, he takes the ratios of currency, time deposits, U.S. Government deposits, and nonmember bank demand deposits to money stock as constant. Thus the biases which were introduced into Teigen's computations are again present here. De Leeuw's reserve aggregate is nonborrowed reserves plus currency in the hands of the public. His estimated long-run elasticities, valued at the sample means, are 0.172 and −0.214 for the Treasury bill rate and the discount rate, respec-

Table 1. Interest Elasticities of Various Functions in de Leeuw's Original Brookings Model

Specification	Impact*	Equilibrium*
Currency Demand		
Private Securities Rate	− 0.032	− 0.364
Time Deposit Rate	− 0.012	− 0.136
Time Deposit Demand		
Treasury Bill Rate	− 0.038	− 0.374
Time Deposit Rate	0.070	0.683
Bank Borrowings		
Treasury Bill Rate	0.134	0.50
Discount Rate	− 0.186	− 0.70
Excess Reserves		
Treasury Bill Rate	n.a.	n.a.
Discount Rate	n.a.	n.a.

*Impact elasticities are calculated by using the respective equilibrium elasticities and regression coefficients of the lagged dependent variables from various tables in the source cited below. The equilibrium elasticities for currency and time deposit demand are from p. 493, and for bank borrowings from p. 512. The respective regression coefficients used in calculating the impact elasticities can be found in Tables 13.2, 13.4, and 13.12.

Source: Frank de Leeuw, "A Model of Financial Behavior," in *The Brookings Quarterly Econometric Model of the United States*, ed. James S. Duesenberry et al. (Chicago: Rand McNally, 1965), chap. 13.

[13]Frank de Leeuw, "A Model of Financial Behavior," in *The Brookings Quarterly Econometric Model of the United States*, ed. James S. Duesenberry et al. (Chicago: Rand McNally, 1965), chap. 13.

tively. When valued in 1962 (the end of his sample period) these elasticities are 0.245 and −0.348, respectively.[14]

These numbers seem quite compatible with those obtained by Teigen for approximately the same sample period. However, de Leeuw finds that the entire adjustment of banks to portfolio changes takes place only gradually over time, and his impact elasticities for borrowings are only about one-fourth of the equilibrium values. This suggests that if the data were available to compute the short-run elasticity for the money supply relationship, the estimates over a one-quarter period would be considerably lower than those obtained by Teigen.

The currency and time deposit demand equations which de Leeuw incorporates into the above computations are almost completely insensitive to interest rate changes over a one-quarter horizon. This implies that over a one-quarter horizon changes in reserves available to support private demand deposits, which are caused by interest induced changes in currency and time deposit demand, are negligible. Thus, it is highly probable that the assumptions of constant currency/money stock or time deposit/money stock ratios result in a net upward bias in the computed interest elasticity of the money supply relationship.

De Leeuw II

In a subsequent study for the Brookings model de Leeuw produced a condensed model of financial behavior in which the excess reserve and borrowings equations were aggregated into a single function to explain free reserves.[15] In that study estimates of the interest elasticity of the money supply relationship are not provided. However, using the free reserve-interest rate coefficient estimates and information given in the earlier study it is possible to replicate the computations of the larger model.[16]

The estimated impact elasticities at the sample means are 0.037 for the Treasury bill rate, and −0.046 for the discount rate.[17] The corresponding long-run elasticities are 0.096 and −0.118 respectively. The absolute values are lower by a factor of almost fifty percent from the values obtained in the earlier study, even though the data and the sample period have remained essentially unchanged.

It is likely that some downward bias has been introduced into these estimates by aggregating excess reserves and borrowings into free reserves in the estimation of the model. From the information presented in the first study, it is not possible to aggregate the interest elasticities of these two components. However, the early work suggests that the response of banks to a disequilibrium in borrowings from the Federal Reserve is much faster than the response to a similar situation with respect to excess reserves.

---

[14]Ibid., p. 518.

[15]Frank de Leeuw, "A Condensed Model of Financial Behavior," in *The Brookings Model: Some Further Results*, ed. James S. Duesenberry et al. (Chicago: Rand McNally, 1969), pp. 270–315.

[16]De Leeuw, "A Model of Financial Behavior."

[17]Unless otherwise stated, data cited have been computed by this author.

Goldfeld

The most detailed study of financial markets is found in the work of Stephen Goldfeld.[18] In this study, equations are specified for both the demand for excess reserves and the demand for borrowings from the Federal Reserve System. Separate equations are estimated for country banks and city banks.

The Goldfeld results suggest very large (in absolute value) interest elasticities for the borrowings equations relative to those found by de Leeuw. There do not appear to be large differences in the impact elasticities of borrowings across the bank classes, but the speed of adjustment to interest rate changes is much slower for borrowings by country banks than for city banks. This is reflected in the lower impact elasticities and the higher equilibrium elasticities for the country banks than the corresponding numbers for the city banks.

The excess reserve interest elasticities reported by Goldfeld are negligible, particularly when compared with the borrowings elasticities. In addition, he finds that banks respond quite quickly to disequilibrium in excess reserve holdings. Thus, the long-run elasticities for excess reserve demand are not much different from the impact elasticities, particularly for city banks. This result is similar to that of the Teigen study where no evidence of a distributed lag in bank response was found.

Goldfeld reports interest elasticities of a money supply relationship comparable to that derived by both Teigen and de Leeuw. The impact elasticities, with respect to the Treasury bill rate and the discount rate in this function, 0.042 and −0.029, respectively, are derived from the elasticities reported in Table 2. The corresponding long-run elasticities are 0.222 and −0.076.[19] These results are quite close to the values reported by both Teigen and de Leeuw for the Treasury bill rate, but considerably below the estimates for the discount rate in the other studies.

The sources of the differences are fairly conspicuous. In Teigen's study, where there is no disaggregation of excess reserves from borrowings, the Treasury bill rate and the discount rate appear only as the differential between the two rates. Hence the regression coefficient of the discount rate is constrained to have the same absolute value, but with the opposite sign from that of the bill rate. Since the mean of the discount rate for the sample period is slightly larger than that of the bill rate, the computed coefficient of elasticity of the discount rate is, in effect, constrained to be slightly smaller in absolute value than that of the bill rate. De Leeuw constrains this excess reserve specification to include only the differential between the bill rate and the discount rate. With the constraints that are imposed in the estimation of the Teigen and de Leeuw studies, it would seem reasonable to conclude that the Goldfeld estimate of the response of the money supply relationship to discount rate changes is more reliable for this period.

There seem to be no major discrepancies in the estimated long-run responsiveness of the money supply to changes in the bill rate, but considerable variance exists

[18]Stephen M. Goldfeld, *Commercial Bank Behavior and Economic Activity* (Amsterdam: North-Holland, 1966).
[19]Ibid., p. 191.

Table 2. Interest Elasticities of Various Functions in the Goldfeld Model

Specification	Impact*	Equilibrium*
Currency Demand		
Treasury Bill Rate	− 0.008	− 0.07
Time Deposit Rate	− 0.015	− 0.14
Time Deposit Demand		
Time Deposit Rate	0.028	0.37
Long-Term Government Rate	− 0.125	− 1.62
Bank Borrowings		
City Banks		
Discount Rate	− 0.98	− 2.382
Treasury Bill Rate	0.88	2.134
Country Banks		
Discount Rate	− 0.88	− 2.926
Treasury Bill Rate	0.79	2.625
Excess Reserves		
City Banks		
Treasury Bill Rate	− 0.38	− 0.35
Country Banks		
Treasury Bill Rate	− 0.15	− 0.25

*The equilibrium elasticities for currency and time deposit demand are found on p. 160 of the source cited below. The corresponding impact elasticities are calculated by using the equilibrium elasticities and regression coefficients of the lagged dependent variables from Tables 5.7 and 5.9, respectively. Both equilibrium and impact elasticities for bank borrowings and excess reserves are found on pp. 150 and 149, respectively.

Source: Stephen M. Goldfeld, *Commercial Bank Behavior and Economic Activity* (Amsterdam: North-Holland, 1966).

among the short-run elasticity estimates. The most uncertain issue, on the basis of the evidence reviewed so far, is the source of the interest elasticity. Goldfeld suggests that the source is bank borrowing behavior, de Leeuw suggests that it is bank behavior with respect to excess reserves, and Teigen does not attempt to discriminate between the two.

Goldfeld and Kane

There exists an additional study by Goldfeld and Kane which provides some independent information on the question of the interest elasticity of bank borrowings from the Federal Reserve.[20] This study is based on weekly data from the period July 1953 to December 1963 and disaggregates banks into four classes—New York City, Chicago, Other Reserve City, and Country banks. They find that the estimated short-run (one week) Treasury bill rate elasticities range from a high of 0.56 for New York

[20]Stephen M. Goldfeld and Edward J. Kane, "The Determinants of Member-Bank Borrowing: An Econometric Study," *Journal of Finance* (September 1966), pp. 499-514, and Stephen M. Goldfeld, "An Extension of the Monetary Sector," in *The Brookings Model: Some Further Results*, ed. James S. Duesenberry et al. (Chicago: Rand McNally, 1969), pp. 317-360.

City banks to a low of 0.08 for Chicago banks. When aggregated over all classes of banks, the short-run interest elasticity for the banking system as a whole is found to be 0.21. Their reported long-run interest elasticities of borrowings range from 2.8 to 3.9.[21]

These estimates seem consistent with the results of the quarterly study by Goldfeld and tend to add to the uncertainty of the high excess reserve and low borrowings elasticities reported by de Leeuw. The only difficulty in reconciling the weekly estimates with the quarterly work of Goldfeld is the implied definition of long run. In the quarterly study, the long run is achieved only after several quarters have elapsed. In the weekly study, the implied long run is a period of several weeks. The possibility remains that long run in the two studies has two different meanings. However, it seems safe to conclude that borrowing behavior of banks is an important source of interest elasticity of the money supply relationship when the Treasury bill rate changes and the discount rate remains constant.

Teigen II

A quarterly study which deals with the period of the 1950s through the early 1960s is that of Teigen.[22] The study contains supply elasticities only for the demand deposit component of the money supply. The results for the elasticity of the discount rate are not very different from those reported by Goldfeld, but the elasticity of the Treasury bill rate is considerably lower than the results obtained by Goldfeld, de Leeuw, and Teigen's earlier results.

Brunner and Meltzer

Karl Brunner and Allan Meltzer have estimated the interest elasticity of the money supply relationship using annual data over a sample period including the interwar and postwar periods.[23] In the two-stage least-squares estimates of their "nonlinear" money supply hypothesis, they find that the elasticity of the money supply function with respect to the adjusted monetary base is insignificantly different from one. Therefore, the interest elasticities of this function can be interpreted as interest elasticities of the reserve multiplier. Their estimate of the Treasury bill rate elasticity is 0.66 and the estimate of the discount rate elasticity is -0.31.[24] Since there are no lagged variables in the equation, these estimates can be compared with the equilibrium elasticities derived from the studies which used shorter time intervals. Both

[21]Goldfeld and Kane, "The Determinants of Member-Bank Borrowing: An Econometric Study," p. 512.

[22]Ronald L. Teigen, "An Aggregated Quarterly Model of the U.S. Monetary Sector, 1953–1964," in *Targets and Indicators of Monetary Policy,* ed. Karl Brunner (San Francisco: Chandler Publishing Company, 1969), pp. 175–218.

[23]Karl Brunner and Allan H. Meltzer, "Some Further Investigations of Demand and Supply Functions for Money," *Journal of Finance* (May 1964), pp. 240–283.

[24]Ibid., p. 277.

elasticities appear to differ from the implied equilibrium values of the quarterly studies by a factor of over two. Given the many difficulties in estimating distributed lag effects from time series data, such inconsistencies are not surprising.

Estimates from Data Including Post-1965 Period

The shortcoming of the studies discussed so far is that they are based on data generated in the 1950s and early 1960s. During the 1960s there were many changes in the environment in which the banking system operated which could have significantly altered (and presumably increased) the interest elasticity of the money supply relationship. These changes included the evolution of an active market for large negotiable certificates of deposit, the involvement of large banks in the Eurodollar market through borrowings from (or lending to) their foreign subsidiaries, and the entrance of banks into the commercial paper market through parent one-bank holding companies.

Unfortunately, it is difficult to obtain empirical evidence on many of these innovations since they were effectively legislated out of existence before enough data were generated to assess their effects. The impact of the CD market can be assessed, along with the responsiveness of the banking system in terms of free reserves in the 1960s, through the quarterly financial model in the MPS model.[25] In addition, estimates of the interest elasticity of the money supply-reserve relationship on a monthly basis can be obtained from a financial market model developed by Thomas Thomson and James Pierce.[26]

Evaluation of Quarterly Money Supply Elasticities

The quarterly MPS model contains a financial sector which includes detail specifications of the commercial loan market and the mortgage market, as well as specifications dealing with bank and nonbank behavior with respect to holdings of currency, time deposits and free reserves. The estimated elasticities for the latter set of functions are tabulated in Table 3. Both the CD demand and supply functions, which did not exist in the earlier studies, assume that the full response to an interest rate change takes place within one quarter. Thus the impact and equilibrium elasticities are equal.

The CD demand function, in particular, indicates a highly sensitive response to interest rate changes, which is consistent with casual impressions of the nature of the

[25]This model is the publicly available version which developed out of the Federal Reserve-MIT-Pennsylvania econometric model project.

[26]Thomas D. Thomson and James L. Pierce, "A Monthly Econometric Model of the Financial Sector" (a paper presented at the May 1971 meeting of the Federal Reserve System Committee on Financial Analysis).

Table 3. Interest Elasticities of Various Functions in the M.P.S. Model

Specification	Impact Elasticity	Equilibrium Elasticity
Currency Demand		
Treasury Bill Rate	0.0037	0.026
Non-CD Time Deposit Demand		
Time Deposit Rate	0.3	2.9
S&L—Mut. Sav. Bk. Rate	− 0.2	− 2.0
Treasury Bill Rate	− 0.15	− 1.4
CD Demand [1969 Values]		
Treasury Bill Rate	− 6.14	− 6.14
Commercial Paper Rate	− 4.28	− 4.28
CD Rate	11.46	11.46
Free Reserves		
Treasury Bill Rate		
1965 Values	− 2.99	− 6.42
1969 Values	− 3.95	− 8.47
Discount Rate		
1965 Values	3.23	6.93
1969 Values	3.48	7.46
Supply of CDs by Banks [1969 Values]		
CD Rate	− 1.06	− 1.06
Treasury Bill Rate	0.98	0.98

CD market. However, these estimates are drawn from a considerably smaller sample than that for the rest of the specifications, and therefore there is less certainty about the stability of the functions over time.

The estimates for the currency demand equation and the demand equation for non-CD time deposits tend to confirm the de Leeuw and Goldfeld results of extremely low impact elasticities. The time deposit function does suggest higher long-run elasticities than had been previously estimated. This appears attributable, in part, to the evolution of special forms of time deposit accounts, such as small consumer-type CDs, during the late 1960s.[27]

The MPS model does not distinguish between excess reserves and borrowings of member banks, but does estimate a relationship between the Treasury bill rate, the discount rate, and free reserves. No constraints are applied to the coefficients of the two rates. In Table 3 both the impact and the equilibrium elasticities of this function are considerably higher than those estimated in the earlier studies. This is partially due to the fact that the estimated function is linear and therefore the value of the elasticity coefficient is not constant at all points along the function. Evaluation of the

[27]The estimated function allows for a change in structure during the early 1960s, which indicates that the interest elasticities in the latter part of the sample period are about fifty percent higher than those estimated for the first part of the sample period.

elasticity coefficient at the very high values of interest rates in 1969 gives estimates of the impact and equilibrium Treasury bill rate elasticities which are 50 and 25 percent higher, respectively, than the values at 1965 interest rate levels. Even after accounting for the higher levels of interest rates in the late 1960s, it appears that differences in specifications and/or differences in sample periods have produced higher interest rate elasticity estimates for the free reserve relationship than had previously been found.

Simulation experiments were performed with the MPS model which permitted relaxation of restrictions under which interest elasticities of the money supply relationship were computed in the studies discussed above. First, in addition to the impact elasticities, the pattern of response of the money stock over time to a maintained change in the Treasury bill rate was computed. The simulations were continued for eight quarters, after which the computed elasticities settled down at close to the equilibrium values.

Second, the response of the demand for currency and the demand for time deposits to the changes in interest rates can be included or excluded from the computation of the elasticities. Time deposit demand is split into large negotiable certificates of deposit and other time deposits. The inclusion of the currency and time deposit responses in the simulation is analogous to a controlled experiment in which the nonbank private sector demand for bank demand deposits is shifted once and maintained in its new position. This shift is allowed to occur without any effect on the demand functions for time deposits or currency. This shift generates an initial change in interest rates. The changes in the money stock, which are observed over time, are the result of the interest rate induced portfolio shifts by banks and the nonbank public, and they trace out the interest elasticity of the money supply relationship over various time intervals. Finally, elasticities are computed for both demand deposits and the M_1 money stock concept.

The estimated elasticities from three sets of simulations are presented in Table 4. These computations are generated under the assumption that the Federal Reserve would not impose a Regulation Q constraint which would prevent banks from offering new CDs at competitive rates.

If such constraints were effective, increases in the Treasury bill rate would cause a shift in the demand for CDs. At the constrained new issue rate for CDs the public would not renew outstanding certificates as they matured. Over time the stock of CDs would decline, and there could be a sizable reduction in the ratio of time deposits to demand deposits. The change in this ratio would, in turn, cause a fluctuation in the reserve multiplier. The observed result would also be highly sensitive to the initial conditions of the Treasury bill rate relative to the Regulation Q ceiling, and the historical pattern of Regulation Q restraint.

In the first section of Table 4, the interest elasticities include the interest rate induced reactions in the public's demand for currency, large certificates of deposit as well as other time deposits, and the interest elasticity of the commercial banking sector's supply function for large certificates of deposit. The interest elasticity of M_1

is consistently smaller than the interest elasticity of the demand deposit component. This is because the model indicates a small negative response of the demand for currency to changes in interest rates. Hence, as interest rates increase and the amount of bank deposits available to the economy expands, there is an offsetting movement in currency balances outstanding.

The exclusion of the nonbank private sector's demand for currency and time deposits other than large certificates of deposit lowers the interest elasticity of the money supply relationship.[28] This is because a rise (fall) in interest rates decreases (increases) the quantity demanded of both of these assets. This relationship is straightforward in the case of currency. For time deposits the expected equilibrium response would be for a large quantity of time deposits to be demanded with higher levels of all interest rates. The model postulates, however, that the rate which banks offer on non-CD time deposits responds quite sluggishly to changes in market interest rates. Thus the short-run effect is for disintermediation away from commercial bank time deposits. If the elasticity patterns were computed over a longer time horizon, the elasticities in the first experiment would eventually become smaller than those for the second experiment. In all cases the impact elasticities are essentially the same size.

These results can be compared with those from earlier empirical studies which do not include the CD market. It appears from section C of Table 4 that when the CD market is operating freely, the estimated interest elasticity of the money supply relationship differs little from the results drawn from studies of earlier periods. If anything, the elasticities reported in this section of the table are generally lower than those discussed above. On the other hand, sections A and B of Table 4 suggest that the net bias involved in computing the interest elasticities with a constant currency/deposit ratio and a constant level of time deposits tends toward zero. That is, the estimates obtained under these assumptions give estimates of elasticities which are too low.

Evaluation of Monthly Money Supply Elasticities

The same type of analysis of the money stock-reserve relationship as that performed with the MPS quarterly econometric model can be carried out on a monthly basis using the financial market model of Pierce and Thompson. The results over an eighteen month period are presented in Table 5. In this model, demand for currency by the public is specified to be completely interest inelastic, so the assumptions underlying the calculations of sections B and C of Table 4 are identical to the assumptions made for the right-hand column of Table 5. The analogy to section A of Table 4 is presented in the left-hand column of Table 5.

---

[28]This exclusion of currency and time deposit demand allows these demand functions to shift in such a way that the quantity demanded at the new Treasury bill rate is exactly equal to the quantity demanded at the original level of the Treasury bill rate.

Table 4.   Money Supply Elasticity Computations—MPS Model

A. Currency, Time Deposits, and CDs Included

Quarter	Demand Deposits	M_1
1	0.106	0.083
2	0.175	0.137
3	0.214	0.167
4	0.240	0.188
First-Year Average	0.184	0.144
5	0.279	0.218
6	0.309	0.240
7	0.317	0.247
8	0.337	0.250
Second-Year Average	0.311	0.239

B. Currency, CDs Included; Time Deposits Excluded

Quarter	Demand Deposits	M_1
1	0.099	0.078
2	0.157	0.123
3	0.185	0.145
4	0.204	0.159
First-Year Average	0.161	0.126
5	0.233	0.181
6	0.254	0.196
7	0.256	0.198
8	0.259	0.200
Second-Year Average	0.251	0.194

C. CDs Included; Time Deposits, Currency Excluded

Quarter	Demand Deposits	M_1
1	0.094	0.074
2	0.149	0.118
3	0.173	0.136
4	0.186	0.147
First-Year Average	0.151	0.119
5	0.202	0.159
6	0.211	0.166
7	0.220	0.173
8	0.226	0.177
Second-Year Average	0.215	0.169

Table 5. Money Supply Elasticity Computations
(Monthly Financial Market Model)

Month	Time Deposits Included	Time Deposits Excluded
1	0.138	0.137
2	0.195	0.192
3	0.231	0.226
4	0.250	0.243
5	0.252	0.244
6	0.250	0.243
First 6-Month Average	0.219	0.214
7	0.266	0.256
8	0.272	0.262
9	0.275	0.262
10	0.279	0.269
11	0.284	0.272
12	0.292	0.281
Second 6-Month Average	0.278	0.267
13	0.303	0.290
14	0.311	0.296
15	0.236	0.222
16	0.220	0.202
17	0.233	0.216
18	0.246	0.230
Third 6-Month Average	0.258	0.243

The implication of the monthly model is that the money stock-reserve relationship is slightly more elastic in the short run than the various quarterly estimates imply. The implied impact elasticity (over a one-month period in this case) is about 0.15. The average elasticity over this first twelve months is estimated at about 0.25, or about one-third more than the estimate over the corresponding four-quarter horizon from the MPS model. After eighteen months have elapsed the elasticity values reflect the long-run, or equilibrium, values. This horizon agrees reasonably well with the horizon of the MPS model.

Conclusions

It is difficult to draw a finely defined set of conclusions from the set of studies which have been examined. There exists a range of elasticity estimates among these studies which cannot be reconciled with the information which is readily available at the present time.

However, while a single point cannot be established as the most probable value for the interest elasticity of the money supply, it appears that the studies do provide information which can be of value in policy discussions concerning the control of the money stock. A broad, but valuable conclusion is that the interest elasticity of the money supply during the sample period of these studies appears to be extremely low, It seems appropriate to conclude with almost complete certainty that the long-run elasticity during this period was less than 0.5 and that the impact elasticity (one quarter) was probably no greater than 0.10 to 0.15. All these elasticities are relevant for policy actions which result in changes in the Treasury bill rate, while leaving the discount rate unchanged.

For the class of policy actions which simultaneously alters the Treasury bill rate and the discount rate by the same amount from an initial position where the two are approximately equal, it is the sum of the interest elasticities of the money supply which is relevant. Two of the studies suggest that the elasticity with respect to the discount rate is slightly smaller than that with respect to the bill rate. The estimation of these relationships involves constraints on parameters, and hence, is not a valid test of the hypothesis that the two elasticities are significantly different. In the Goldfeld study, where there are no constraints imposed on the estimated parameters, the estimated coefficient of elasticity for the discount rate is considerably smaller in absolute value than that of the bill rate. Therefore, it would appear that while the interest elasticity of the money supply relationship is likely to be smaller when both rates are changed simultaneously, it is almost certain that the coefficient of elasticity will remain positive. Furthermore, the elasticity under such a policy probably does not exceed one-half to two-thirds of the interest elasticity under a policy of keeping the discount rate fixed.

The available evidence suggests quite conclusively that the short-run feedbacks through interest rate changes, which would be generated by policy changes in reserve aggregates, are very weak and should cause little, if any, difficulty for the implementation of policy actions aimed at controlling the money stock through the control of a reserve aggregate. Of course, the size of random fluctuations in the reserve multiplier remains a major factor in determining the size of deviations of the money stock from its targeted value. An issue which remains to be investigated is the size of the variance of the multipliers associated with various reserve concepts.

Money Demand

In Section I most of the articles indicated that one's view of the way monetary impulses affected the economy had important implications for the specification of the monetary demand relation.

In the first reading in this section, John T. Boorman reviews the major formulations of the money demand function. He compares the results of alternative tests of these relations that have been presented in the literature. His survey provides a summary treatment of the current consensus that has been achieved on the elements deemed most important in the determination of the public's demand for money. The second article in the section, by Thomas M. Havrilesky and John T. Boorman, provides a survey of portfolio theory. Since even moderately complete discussions of portfolio theory are seldom found in intermediate textbooks and since this topic is closely related to the theory of the demand for money, this selection makes an important addition to the student's kit of economic tools.

The Evidence on the Demand for Money: Theoretical Formulations and Empirical Results

John T. Boorman

19

Introduction

Numerous theories have been proposed to explain the public's demand for money. Though the range of hypotheses implicit in these theories is extremely broad, there are certain important elements common to all of them. Most significantly, almost all of these theories can be generalized into a proposition about the existence of a stable relationship between a few important economic variables and the stock of money demanded.

While diverse theories often posit similar variables to explain the demand for money, they frequently differ in the specific role assigned to each. For example, in the simplest version of the transactions theory of the demand for money, the stock of money demanded is hypothesized to be strictly proportional to a single variable—the volume of transactions to be facilitated by that money stock. In comparison, the inventory theoretic view, which recognizes the interest rate as an opportunity cost of holding money balances and introduces brokerage fees and other charges as explicit costs of switching wealth between interest-bearing assets and money, denies this proportionality between money and income. In this model the minimization of the

This article was revised especially for this volume. The original article appeared in John T. Boorman and Thomas M. Havrilesky, *Money Supply, Money Demand, and Macroeconomic Models* (Arlington Heights, Ill.: AHM Publishing Corporation, 1972). The author thanks Thomas Havrilesky for helpful comments.

total cost of managing money balances leads to a solution that suggests the possibility of substantial economies of scale in the demand for money.

As another example, in the liquidity preference theories of John Maynard Keynes and James Tobin the role of money as an asset is stressed and the motives for holding money examined. An analysis of the costs (income foregone) and benefits (risks avoided) of holding wealth in the form of money balances suggests a hypothesis in which income and the interest rate on alternative financial assets are suggested as the primary determinants of desired money balances. In comparison, Milton Friedman's "Restatement" of the quantity theory eschews a specific focus on the "roles" of money or on the "motives" of individuals in holding money balances.[1] Instead, Friedman emphasizes the services yielded by money in individual and business portfolios. In this view money is simply one among the many assets—including physical and human assets—held by the public. This leads to the hypothesis that all of the alternatives available to the wealth holder may influence his desired money balances.

These examples of alternative money demand hypotheses suggest some of the major questions that have been the focus of empirical investigation. A more complete list would include the following specific problems:

1. What empirical measure should be used to represent the theoretical concept of "money"?

2. How are empirically testable money demand functions conventionally specified? In this connection it is useful to examine some of the more common formulations that have included either a role for expectations in the determination of desired money balances or a distinction between the long-run equilibrium level and the short-run adjustment pattern by which equilibrium is approached.

3. What is the role of the interest rate in the money demand function? This issue raises several related questions:

   a. If the interest rate is statistically important in the determination of the demand for money, what is the interest elasticity of money balances?

   b. Which one of the alternative interest rate measures available is most relevant to the determination of the demand for money?

   c. Given that the interest rate is important in the money demand function, has evidence been presented that would support the existence (historical or potential) of a "liquidity trap"?

4. What is the relative significance of income, wealth, and other economic variables that have been suggested along with the interest rate as determinants of the demand for money?

[1]M. Friedman, "The Quantity Theory of Money, A Restatement," in Milton Friedman (ed.), *Studies in the Quantity Theory of Money* (Chicago, 1956). See D. Patinkin, "The Chicago Tradition, the Quantity Theory, and Friedman," *Journal of Money, Credit, and Banking,* 1 (February 1969), pp. 46–70.

5. Do money demand functions that include the essential arguments suggested by alternative theories appear to be stable over the postwar period?

These are the major issues raised in the empirical literature on the demand for money. Each of these will be considered in turn.[2]

The Empirical Definition of Money

What assets ought to be included in our measure of "the money stock"? If we focus on those theories that emphasize the transactions motive for holding money, the proper definition of money is not a profound problem. Money should be defined to consist only of those assets that serve as generally acceptable media of exchange. It is widely agreed that only commercial bank demand deposits and currency in circulation provide this service. However, if the public's demand for money is viewed as arising from a speculative motive, the list of assets in the definition of money may be expanded to include at least some assets that are stable in nominal value, i.e., fixed dollar assets whose value is independent of variations in the interest rate. Finally, if the demand for money is approached as part of the general theory of demand, all assets that are close substitutes for the media of exchange (and respond to the same yields in the demand function) should be included in the definition. This approach clearly indicates that the proper definition of money is largely an empirical question.

Allan H. Meltzer has enunciated one possible criterion for selecting the appropriate definition of money.

> The problem is one of defining money so that a stable demand function can be shown to have existed under differing institutional arrangements, changes in social and political environment, and changes in economic conditions, or to explain the effects of such changes on the function.[3]

This criterion focuses on the implications of the definition of money for the degree of control that the monetary authority has over crucial macroeconomic variables.[4] The money stock and interest rates are thought to have a strong effect upon aggregate demand, employment, and the price level in the economy. If the demand for money is unstable (shifts unpredictably), the effect of monetary policy actions on the equilibrium money stock and interest rates will be uncertain. In short, stability of the money demand function and a capability on the part of the monetary authority to influence closely the stock of assets corresponding to the theoretical concept of money employed in that function would seem to be necessary conditions for the successful

---

[2]More general issues, particularly those dealing with econometric problems in the estimation of money demand functions, will be discussed—often in footnotes—at various points of the text.

[3]A. H. Meltzer, "The Demand for Money: The Evidence from the Time Series," *Journal of Political Economy,* 71 (June 1963), p. 222.

[4]There are, of course, additional criteria by which to define a measure of the money stock. George

implementation of monetary policy.[5] These conditions will allow the authorities to exert a predictable influence over the equilibrium stock of money, the interest rate, and other variables in the money demand equation.

Economists traditionally have defined money in the "narrow" sense as the sum of demand deposit liabilities of commercial banks and currency held by the public. However, a number of analysts include time deposits at commercial banks within their measure of the money stock. Milton Friedman, for example, views time deposits as "a temporary abode of purchasing power" and includes them in the "broad" measure of money that he employs in his empirical work. A few researchers go beyond even this "broad" concept to include such things as savings and loan shares, mutual savings bank deposits, and claims against other financial intermediaries in their measure of "money." Conceptually, of course, it is possible to go even further and include still other financial assets (or even some measure of credit availability, such as commercial bank "lines of credit") in a measure of money.[6]

In this survey, evidence on the question of the best definition of money must be satisfied in accord with the Meltzer criterion. David Laidler has suggested an explicit set of conditions by which to evaluate the relative stability of alternative empirical functions. As he expresses it:

> A "more stable demand for money function" may be taken to be one that requires knowledge of fewer variables and their parameters in order to predict the demand for money with a given degree of accuracy or, which amounts to the same thing, one that yields parameter estimates that are less subject to variation when the same arguments are included in the function and hence enable more accurate prediction of the demand for money to be made.[7]

Kaufman, following Milton Friedman and David Meiselman, defines money according to its correlation with income (taking into consideration the possible lead-lag relationship between money and income). In selecting the set of financial assets to be included in the money supply, he employs two criteria originally specified by Friedman and Meiselman: choose that set that (1) has the highest correlation with income and (2) has a higher correlation with income than any of the components separately. This alternative operational approach, unlike the Meltzer criterion, derives from the proposition that the equilibrium nominal money stock can be controlled by the monetary authority and suggests a rather specific theoretical model on which to base monetary policy. The Meltzer criterion is preferred here since it is compatible with a more broadly defined set of money demand functions. See G. G. Kaufman, "More on an Empirical Definition of Money," *American Economic Review,* 59 (March 1969), pp. 78-87, M. Friedman and D. Meiselman, "Relative Stability of Monetary Velocity and the Investment Multiplier in the United States 1897-1957," Commission on Money and Credit, *Stabilization Policies* (Englewood Cliffs, N.J. 1963).

Frederick C. Schadrack, in "An Empirical Approach to the Definition of Money," *Monetary Aggregates and Monetary Policy.* Federal Reserve Bank of New York (1974) pp. 28-34 extends these empirical criteria to include goodness of fit, stability over time and predictive accuracy in regression equations with GNP as a dependent variable and six different monetary aggregates as alternative explanatory variables.

[5]See S. J. Maisel, "Controlling Monetary Aggregates," in *Controlling Monetary Aggregates: Proceedings of the Monetary Conference of the Federal Reserve Bank of Boston* (June 1969), pp. 152-174, and M. J. Hamburger, "The Demand for Money in 1971: Was There a Shift? A Comment," *Journal of Money, Credit and Banking,* 5 (May 1973), pp. 720-725.

[6]See A. B. Laffer, "Trade Credit and the Money Market," *Journal of Political Economy,* 78 (March/April 1970), pp. 239-267.

[7]D. Laidler, "The Definition of Money: Theoretical and Empirical Problems," *The Journal of Money, Credit and Banking,* 1 (August 1968), p. 516.

In an empirical study Laidler (40) contends that the most stable money demand function he has been able to isolate is one employing Friedman's broad definition of money (*M2*). This contrasts with earlier results presented by Karl Brunner and Allan Meltzer (5), in which they found that the narrow measure (*M1*)—demand deposits plus currency—yielded the most satisfactory money demand relation.

What accounts for these contrasting conclusions? First, these two studies specify different explanatory variables in their money demand equations. Second, they use data from different time periods to estimate the parameters of these relations. Finally, they employ different procedures to test their hypotheses. Since the relative performance of alternative measures of the money stock in empirical money demand functions is likely to be highly sensitive to all of these considerations, it is impossible to choose the better measure of money on the basis of these studies alone.

However, an alternative empirical approach is available. The stability of the money demand function is closely linked to the degree of substitutability that exists between money, as it is defined in that function, and other financial assets. For example, if the secular and cyclical changes in the competitive position of financial intermediaries make available substitutes for currency in circulation and demand deposits held by the nonbank public (the narrowly defined money stock), the demand for money, so defined, may shift as these substitutes appear. In such a case a demand function for some broader measure of money, one that includes these close substitutes, would be more stable, i.e., would shift less over time, than a function defined on a narrow money measure.[8] Under these conditions monetary policy actions that concentrate on the narrower measure of money would be focusing on an unstable, shifting target. Policy actions that focus on broader measures of money would be more appropriate.

A substantial body of evidence has now been presented on this issue. Specifically, the question that has been addressed is the following: Are assets such as commercial bank time deposits, savings and loan shares, mutual savings bank deposits, and others that have been suggested for inclusion in a measure of "money" sufficiently close substitutes for commercial bank demand deposits to warrant treating them in a single measure?

In a study on the demand for liquid assets by the public, Edgar Feige (15) mea-

---

[8]Gurley and Shaw, for example, emphasize the substitutability between claims on certain financial intermediaries and demand deposits at commercial banks, and they argue that "money" must be defined so as to include these substitutes. Evidence supporting this position is presented below. See J. G. Gurley and E. S. Shaw, *Money in a Theory of Finance* (Washington, D.C., 1960).

This view is also embodied in the report of the Radcliffe Committee, which views "liquidity" and "the stock of liquid assets" held by the public as the relevant concept on which to focus in monetary theory and policy. In this view only policy actions that change the *total liquidity* of the public—and not simply the composition of the public's stock of liquid assets—are likely to lead to predictable results. This is so because of the high degree of substitutability that exists between the narrowly defined money stock and near-monies. See *The Radcliffe Report,* Committee on the Working of the Monetary System (London, 1959).

sured the cross elasticities of demand between various assets.[9] Using data on the volume of liquid assets held by households in each state of the United States for each year during the period from 1949 to 1959, Feige found that the yields on nonbank intermediary liabilities (savings and loan shares, etc.) did not affect the demand for money. Ownership of each of these assets was found to be highly sensitive only to its "own rate" of interest. In Feige's results there appears to be little substitutability between demand deposits, time deposits, savings and loan shares, or mutual savings bank deposits. In fact, demand deposits were found to be mildly *complementary* with savings and loan shares and mutual savings bank deposits; demand and time deposits at commercial banks were only very weak substitutes for each other. From this and other evidence Feige concludes that the narrow definition of money is the preferred definition when estimating money demand functions and that analysts need not concern themselves with the effects of the activities of other intermediaries on the public's demand for money.[10]

Feige's conclusions are disputed by T. H. Lee (46) and V. K. Chetty (10). Lee's work will be described in detail in connection with our survey of the relevance of alternative interest rate measures in the money demand function. Briefly, Lee suggests that the liabilities of financial intermediaries, particularly savings and loan shares, are indeed very good *substitutes* for money. Rather than supporting Friedman's "broad" definition of money, however, he claims that the definition should be extended to encompass an even broader collection of assets, including as a minimum, shares in savings and loan associations.

Chetty makes a similar proposal. In his work a technique originally developed in production theory to measure the substitutability between capital and labor in the production process is employed to measure the substitutability among assets in the consumer's utility function.[11] Chetty assumes that consumers attempt to maximize

---

[9]The cross elasticity of demand is the most frequently used measure of substitutability. If we consider two assets X and Y, and the returns on each, i_x and i_y, the cross elasticity of X with respect to Y equals the percentage change in the quantity of X demanded, divided by the percentage change in the return of Y.

$$\eta_{x.y} = \frac{\Delta x/x}{\Delta i_y/i_y}$$

If an increase in the return on asset Y (Δi_y positive) causes a switch in holdings from X to Y, Δx will be negative and the cross elasticity will be negative. In this case the assets X and Y are said to be "substitutes." If $\eta_{x,y}$ is positive, indicating a *direct* relationship between the return on Y and holdings of asset X, these assets are said to be "complements."

[10]Feige's methods in deriving these results are subject to several criticisms. First, there are serious questions as to whether the way in which he measures the rate of return on commercial bank demand deposits reflects the relevant return considered by asset holders in allocating their portfolios. Second, his data measure the assets owned in a state by residents of all states when, in fact, the relevant measure for his purposes should have been the assets owned by the residents of each state. His data probably require the inclusion of rates on out-of-state assets in order to capture the effects of ownership that crosses state lines. These problems detract from Feige's results.

[11]See K. J. Arrow, H. B. Chenery, B. S. Minhas, and R. M. Solow, "Capital-Labor Substitution and Economic Efficiency," *Review of Economics and Statistics,* 63 (August 1961), pp. 225-250.

their utility (subject to the budget constraint) by combining money (demand deposits plus currency in circulation), time deposits, and other assets to produce desired levels of liquidity at the lowest cost. By combining the conditions required for utility maximization with the budget constraint, he derives an equation that contains parameters that, when estimated, yield measures of the partial elasticities of substitution between money and other assets.

On the basis of his estimates, Chetty concludes that while savings and loan shares and mutual savings bank deposits are rather good substitutes for money, time deposits appear to be virtually perfect substitutes. This last finding supports Friedman's use of the "broad" definition of money. Nevertheless, as did Lee, Chetty suggests that an even broader measure of money may be more appropriate and shows how such a measure may be calculated. Employing weights that measure the "moneyness' of assets as implied by their substitutability with demand deposits and currency, he constructs a weighted average of demand deposits and currency (with weights constrained to unity), time deposits (*TD*), saving and loan shares (*SL*), and mutual savings bank deposits (*MS*). The final form of the equation defining this average "money" stock is

$$M_a = DD + C + TD + 0.615SL + 0.88 \, MS.$$

Note that the coefficient (unity) on the time deposit variable reflects Chetty's conclusion of perfect substitutability between these deposits and narrowly defined money.[12]

While these findings by Lee and Chetty clearly favor a broader measure of money, an important recent study by Stephen Goldfeld (24), which provides consistent and comparable data on several of the questions addressed in this survey, contains persuasive evidence that focusing on narrow measures of money will yield demand functions with significantly superior predictive capabilities to those that define money in some broader fashion. Goldfeld does not concentrate explicitly on the substitutability of various potential components of "money." Rather, his procedure is to confront various hypotheses with the same set of data and very closely related functional specifications. This has the advantage of limiting the number of factors that can be introduced to explain differing statistical results—the major problem in making comparative judgements on the diverse evidence presented by the authors cited above.

Goldfeld begins by noting that the inclusion of time deposits in the definition of money seems questionable on theoretical grounds "since it constrains the specification . . . of *M*1 (narrow money) and time deposits to be the same" and potentially distorts the influence of interest rates on the component measures. However, he recognizes that these weaknesses could be offset if an empirically more stable de-

---

[12]This evidence also lends support to the broad measure of money used by Lydall in his empirical study of the demand for money in Britain and increases the importance of Lydall's conclusions on the issues discussed below. See H. Lydall, "Income, Assets, and the Demand for Money," *Review of Economics and Statistics,* 40 (February 1958), pp. 1–14.

mand function resulted from this formulation. His results, however, suggest that this "is definitely not the case."[13]

The alternative equations Goldfeld estimated with broad money include a lagged dependent variable, income, and interest rates as arguments. His estimates are such as to make one suspicious of the use of the broad money measure as the dependent variable. First, the time deposit rate appears to have a negligible influence on holdings of broad money. This may be an empirical reflection of the offsetting effects of this rate on demand deposits and time deposits and the loss of information involved in aggregating over those components. Second, the long-run elasticity of broad money is extremely high, exceeding the elasticities estimated separately for each of the components. Both of these results suggest serious problems with a function specified on the broad money measure. Goldfeld's additional statistical tests strengthen the initial suspicion engendered by those results. While the traditional criterion statistics—R^2 and the standard error of the estimate—provide little help choosing between the broad money or narrow money formulation, dynamic simulations and stability tests provide persuasive evidence of the superiority of the narrow money form. The broad money equation yields "ludicrously" large errors in long-run forecasting tests and is easily rejected on the basis of formal stability tests.[14]

Additional tests on the forecasting performance and stability of equations estimated for each of the components of $M2$ (broad money), suggest his general conclusion that

> the simple specification used for $M1$ will not work for time deposits, and . . . even given the questionable time deposit equation, the ex post forecasts of $M2$ obtained from the aggregate equation are inferior to those obtained from adding together the separate component forecasts, thus suggesting that *aggregation is inflicting some positive harm*[15] (emphasis added).

In short, Goldfeld's results suggest that in model building and other work *more* rather than *less* disaggregation of the money demand equation seems to be desirable.[16]

[13]S. M. Goldfeld, "The Demand for Money Revisited," *Brookings Papers on Economic Activity* (3:1973), p. 593.

[14]Goldfeld's primary test consists of dynamically simulating his estimated equations. This involves forecasting both within-sample and out-of-sample values for the dependent variable and evaluating the quality of those forecasts by a measure such as the root mean square error. His tests take two general forms: (1) four quarter ex post forecasts made by taking sequentially longer subperiods within the sample from which to derive coefficient estimates and evaluating forecasts for four quarters beyond each successive estimating period and (2) splitting the sample period in half, deriving estimates from the first half data and evaluating the long-run forecasting ability of the equation over the second half of the sample period. In both cases the broad money equation performed substantially worse than the narrow money form. These results were formerly confirmed through the use of the Chow test of stability. See Goldfeld, *op. cit.*, pp. 592–595.

[15]*Ibid.*, p. 595.

[16]Dickson and Starleaf suggest a similar conclusion. Their estimates of various functions that include distributed lags on all arguments suggest that "the Demand Functions for $M1$ and TD (time deposits) appear to be so different as to dictate their separate, rather than combined, analysis." H. D. Dickson and D. R. Starleaf, "Polynomial Distributed Lag Structures in the Demand Function for Money," *Journal of Finance*, 27 (December 1972), p. 1042.

Because of these conflicting results, many economists feel that this issue is still unresolved, and further evidence is sought. In the remainder of this survey, therefore, whenever we are reporting on empirical work, we shall cite the specific definition of money used by a particular author. In several instances, work reported on in connection with other issues will have direct implications for the appropriate empirical definition of money. Let us now turn to an examination of the general form of the money demand functions specified in empirical work and to a review of the evidence on the role of the interest rate in determining the public's demand for money. This latter issue has critical implications for national economic policy.

Conventional Formulations of the Demand for Money Function

In most formulations of the money demand function real money balances are related to "the" interest rate on relevant substitute assets and some scale variable related to economic activity, such as income or wealth. The equation specified is sometimes linear but more often exponential in form. These alternative forms may be specified as follows:

$$\frac{M_d}{P} = m_d = a_1 + a_2 i + a_3 X \tag{1}$$

$$\frac{M_d}{P} = m_d = \alpha i^{\beta_1} X^{\beta_2}, \tag{2}$$

where M_d/P is the stock of real money balances demanded, i is an interest rate, and X represents other variables such as wealth, permanent income, or current income.[17]

[17]Money demand functions are generally cast in real terms on the assumption that the price elasticity of nominal money balances is unity. The implication of this assumption is that price-level changes alone will cause no change in the demand for *real* money balances or, alternatively, that the demand for nominal balances is proportional to the price level. This assumption implies that the public is free of money illusion in its demand for real money balances. Let us examine this assumption further. Let X in equation (2) above be a measure of real wealth, W. Then;

$$\frac{M_d}{P} = \alpha \times i^{\beta_1} \cdot W^{\beta_2}.$$

If *nominal* money balances were specified as a function of *nominal* wealth, this equation would be

$$M_d = \alpha \times i^{\beta_1} \times (P \cdot W)^{\beta_2'}.$$

But these two equations are quite different. The first equation implies that the price-level elasticity is unity—the exponent of P equals one—and β_2 is the wealth elasticity of *real* money balances. But in the latter form β_2' is some *average* of the price level and wealth elasticities of nominal money balances. Consequently, if the price level elasticity is really unity, but the true wealth elasticity is not equal to one,

When equation (2) is employed, a logarithmic transformation is made so that the equation is *linear* in the logarithms of the variables and, more importantly, linear in the parameters to be estimated. Taking natural logs of both sides of the equation;

$$ln \frac{M_d}{P} = ln\ m_d = ln\ \alpha + \beta_1\ ln\ i + \beta_2\ ln\ X.^{18} \tag{3}$$

These simple linear (in the coefficients) models may be fitted to empirical observations of variables if, and only if, two additional assumptions are made. First, we must assume that the money market is always in equilibrium so that desired money balances, M_d, equal the actual money stock reported in the statistical series, M. Second, we must assume that there exist exact empirical counterparts to the theoretical variables specified; for example, the average of daily rates quoted by the New York Federal Reserve Bank on U.S. Treasury Bills may be chosen as the empirical measure of "the interest rate." With data on each of the variables specified in the equa-

---

β_2' will be *biased* toward that value and will not be a good estimate of the true wealth elasticity. To avoid that bias, investigators have generally chosen to work with functions cast in real terms.

The validity of this procedure is supported by evidence presented by Allan Meltzer (49). His work indicates that when the price variable is included as a separate argument in a log-linear equation, its coefficient is very close to unity. Furthermore, if nominal wealth is employed in an equation with nominal balances specified as the dependent variable, the wealth elasticity is closer to unity than if these measures are cast in real terms.

Additional evidence on this point has been presented by Harold D. Dickson and Dennis R. Starleaf (13). Employing an equation similar in form to (3) but with distributed lag functions defined on the independent variables, including GNP, they found that the estimated price elasticity of the narrowly defined money stock, $M1$, was not significantly different from unity. On this evidence they concluded that the demand for real money balances is homogeneous of degree zero in the price level; therefore, the demand for money is free of money illusion. On this and other evidence the assumed proportionality of nominal money balances to the price level would appear to have a firm basis in empirical analysis.

[18]In this form the coefficients β_1, and β_2 can be directly estimated by linear regression techniques, and those coefficients will be elasticities. This may be shown as follows: Let $\eta_{m \cdot i}$ denote the interest elasticity of money demand (let m in this instance represent real money balances demanded); then,

$$\eta_{m \cdot i} = \frac{\partial m/m}{\partial i/i} = \frac{\partial m}{\partial i} \cdot \frac{i}{m};$$

but, from equation (2),

$$\partial M/\partial i = \beta_1\ (\alpha X^{\beta_2}) \cdot i^{(\beta_1 - 1)};$$

therefore,

$$\eta_{M \cdot i} = \beta_1\ (\alpha X^{\beta_2}) \cdot i^{(\beta_1 - 1)} \cdot \frac{i}{\alpha X^{\beta_2} \cdot i^{\beta_1}} = \frac{\beta_1 \cdot i^{\beta_1}}{i^{\beta_1}} = \beta_1.$$

Consequently, elasticities may be estimated directly by employing the log-linear form of equation (2) in the regression procedure.

tion, multiple regression methods may be employed to derive estimates of the coefficients in these single equation models.[19]

Several modifications can be made to this basic equation to introduce significant additional flexibility into the hypotheses. One of the most important of these is the introduction of the concept of "desired," as opposed to "actual," money balances and the specification of a "partial adjustment" mechanism by which actual holdings adjust to desired levels.

For example, desired real money balances, $m_T{}^*$, may be postulated to depend upon the same variables specified in equation (3)

$$ln\ m_T{}^* = ln\ \alpha + \beta_1\ ln\ i_T + \beta_2\ ln\ X_T \qquad (4)$$

and the adjustment process of actual to desired levels of money demand may be specified as follows:

$$(ln\ m_T - ln\ m_{T-1}) = \lambda\ (ln\ m_T{}^* - ln\ m_{T-1}). \qquad (5)$$

In this form λ, the adjustment coefficient, measures the rate at which adjustments are made to bring *actual* money holdings in line with the current *desired* level. Generally, λ is specified to be between zero and one, indicating that any such process of adjustment is only partially successful during one period. (The magnitude of λ will often be explained in empirical literature as reflecting the cost of adjusting portfolios relative to the cost of not adjusting them).

While $m_T{}^*$, the current desired level of real money holdings, is not directly observable or measurable, postulation of the above adjustment process allows derivation of an estimating equation with solely observable quantities. Substituting equation (4) into the adjustment equation (5) and rearranging yields

$$ln\ m_T = \lambda\ ln\ \alpha + \lambda\beta_1\ ln\ i_T + \lambda\beta_2\ ln\ X_T + (1-\lambda)\ ln\ m_{T-1}. \qquad (6)$$

In this form λ can be calculated from the coefficient estimate of the lagged dependent variable, m_{T-1}, and α, β_1, and β_2 can be calculated from this value and the coefficients estimated for the other terms. If, for example, a coefficient of 0.60 is estimated

---

[19]Least-squares regression analysis may be defined as a procedure whereby an hypothesized relationship may be confronted with actual data in order to derive numerical estimates of the parameters specified in that relationship. Under specified conditions concerning the nature of the hypothesized relationship and the characteristics of the data employed, these techniques will yield estimates with certain desirable statistical properties. In the models above, for example, data on the size of the money stock, the value of the interest rate, and, say, national wealth may be employed in regression analysis to derive estimates of β_1, the interest elasticity of money demand, and β_2, the wealth elasticity of money demand. For a discussion of the mechanics of least-squares regression and the properties of least-squares estimators, see S. Hymans, *Probability Theory* (Englewood Cliffs, N.J., 1966) Chapter 8, and J. Kmenta, *Elements of Econometrics* (New York, 1971), Chapters 7 and 10.

on the lagged term, then $\lambda = (1 - 0.60) = 0.40$, suggesting that in each period 40 percent of the gap between actual and desired money balances will be closed by the public's actions.[20]

While this form has proved useful in many applications, it has the unfortunate characteristic of restricting the adjustment pattern in the dependent variable to be the same regardless of the source of the initial disturbance. Whether an interest rate change or an income (or wealth) change disturbs the initial (long-run) equilibrium, the adjustment path to a new equilibrium must be the same. There are several plausible theoretical reasons why this is not likely to be the case. In addition, empirical results often suggest implausibly long lags for the adjustment process. These long lags are difficult to explain on the basis of probable costs involved in adjusting financial portfolios.

An alternative, and perhaps superior, rationale for the presence of a significant lagged term in the money demand function derives from the "adaptive expectations" model. In this formulation it is assumed that the public is actually holding its desired level of money balances but that level itself is assumed to depend upon expected values of one or more of the independent variables rather than on current actual values. Thus,

$$ln\ m_T = ln\ \alpha + \beta_1\ ln\ i_T + \beta_2\ ln\ X_T^e, \tag{7}$$

where X_T^e is the value of X expected to prevail in period t. Since X_T^e is not observable some hypothesis must be specified on how expectations are formulated. It may be postulated, for example, that current expectations are formed by modifying previous expectations in the light of current experience. For example:

$$ln\ X_T^e - ln\ X_{T-1}^e = (1 - \lambda)\ (ln\ X_T - ln\ X_{T-1}^e) \tag{8}$$

or equivalently,

$$ln\ X_T^e = (1 - \lambda)\ ln\ X_T + \lambda\ ln\ X_{T-1}^e \qquad 0 \leq \lambda < 1.$$

This formulation depends upon knowledge of X_T in period t. An alternative formulation, which avoids this implicit assumption that X_T be known in advance of formu-

---

[20]In this formulation, the long run interest and income (or wealth) elasticities are β_1 and β_2, respectively. The short run elasticities are given by $\lambda\beta_1$ and $\lambda\beta_2$. For example, in steady-state equilibrium, $M_T = M_{T-1} = M_{T-2} \ldots$
Then, from equation (6),

$$ln\ M_T - (1 - \lambda)\ ln\ M_{T-1} = \lambda\ ln\ \alpha + \lambda\ \beta_1\ ln\ i_T + \lambda\ \beta_2\ ln\ X_T$$
$$ln\ M_T [1 - 1 + \lambda] = \lambda\ ln\ \alpha + \lambda\ \beta_1\ ln\ i_T + \lambda\ \beta_2\ ln\ X_T$$
$$ln\ M_T = ln\ \alpha + \beta_1\ ln\ i_T + \beta_2\ ln\ X_T$$

as in equation (4). Because of the assumed constraint on λ, short run elasticities will be smaller (in absolute terms) than longer run elasticities.

lating the expectation, makes the revision of expectations dependent upon the most recent error in expectations, assuming data on current period values are not available, i.e.,

$$ln\ X_T^e - ln\ X_{T-1}^e = (1 - \lambda)\ (ln\ X_{T-1} - ln\ X_{T-1}^e). \tag{9}$$

In this form expectations are revised by some fraction of the discrepency between last period's expectations and the actual value of X_{T-1}.

Either of these forms can be employed to derive an estimating equation specified solely in terms of observable values. For example, substituting the basic demand relation (4) into the first of the adaptive expectations models specified above (8) and applying a Koyck transformation yields,[21]

$$ln\ m_T = (1-\lambda)\ ln\ \alpha + (1-\lambda)\ \beta_1\ ln\ X_T + (1-\lambda)\ \beta_2\ ln\ i_T + \lambda\ ln\ m_{T-1}. \tag{10}$$

In this formulation the adaptive expectations model is formally the same as the partial adjustment model although the interpretation of the estimated coefficient on the lagged dependent variable and other variables is very different in the two equations. The adaptive expectations model, however, is the starting point for a whole family of models that allow the introduction of a great many alternative hypotheses into the basic structure. In particular, different expectational patterns may be specified for each of the independent variables in the equation or expectations on one or more of the variables may be allowed to adjust in different proportions to two or more of the previous expectations (forecasting) errors.[22] For example,

$$ln\ X_T^e - ln\ X_{T-1}^e = (1 - \lambda_1)\ (ln\ X_T - ln\ X_T^e)$$
$$+ (1 - \lambda_2)\ (ln\ X_{T-1} - ln\ X_{T-1}^e), \tag{11}$$

where λ_1 is not restricted to equal λ_2. In addition, the adaptive expectations model may be combined with the partial adjustment model to capture the potential lagged effects generated by each. An example of this will be seen below.

Unfortunately, the capacity to specify new and richer lag structures rather quickly surpasses the econometric ability to derive useful statistical estimates of the included parameters.[23] Because of this limitation, a far more general lag model has gained wide popularity. The Almon distributed lag technique allows estimation of a rather general lag pattern that can be rationalized in any number of ways. Only the length of the lag and the degree of the polynominal along which the weights lie must be

[21]See Kmenta, *op. cit.*, pp. 474 ff.
[22]See Goldfeld, *op. cit.*, p. 600.
[23]See Z. Griliches, "Distributed Lags: A Survey," *Econometrica*, 35 (January 1967).

specified in advance.[24] Perhaps the major advantage of this form over the models specified above is the elimination of the somewhat restrictive assumption that the weights describing the assumed adjustment path lie along a monotonically declining simple geometric lag structure. On the other hand, the method requires less care in the formulation of detailed hypotheses to rationalize the introduction of any lag structure.

Some form of one of the basic models specified above underlies most of the empirical work on the money demand function. We shall now turn to an examination of the results of that work for one of the most important issues in this area—the importance of the interest rate in determining the public's money demand.

The Role of Interest Rate in the Money Demand Function

Single-Equation Estimates

The stimulus for much of the econometric work on the demand for money and for the primary focus of that work on the importance of the interest rate as an argument in the money demand function derives from Keynes' presentation of the liquidity preference theory in *The General Theory of Employment, Interest, and Money* (1936). Although Pigou as early as 1917 had suggested that the interest rate was a potentially important factor determining the public's money holding behavior, it was Keynes full explication of the "speculative" motive for holding "idle" money balances that provided the major impetus for testing this hypothesis. Research has been further encouraged by the work of Milton Friedman (19). Contrary to the findings of most other investigators, he finds little basis for assigning a significant role for the interest rate in determining the demand for money.

One of the earliest studies to address this issue was done by Henry Latané (45). Latané specified and tested three alternative models of the demand for money. In his first test he proposed a constant ratio of total money balances to nominal national income, $M/Y = k$. This hypothesis represented a crude form of the quantity theory. By showing graphically that this ratio was highly variable, fluctuating between a low of 0.26 to a high of 0.50 in the period from 1919 to 1952, Latané rejected this hypothesis.

In his second test Latané proposed a Keynesian-type money demand function, in which the total demand for money balances was specified to be the sum of a transactions component dependent on the level of income and an asset or speculative component dependent on the rate of interest:

$$M = a \left(\frac{1}{i}\right) + bY + c. \tag{12}$$

[24]See S. Almon, "The Distributed Lag Between Capital Appropriations and Expenditures," *Econometrica*, 33 (January 1965).

Latané showed that this form implies a continually declining ratio of money balances to income as income increases (and the interest rate remains constant).[25] Since empirical evidence indicated that this was not the case, Latané also rejected this form.

Latané's last model proposed that the ratio of nominal money balances to (nominal) aggregate income was dependent upon the rate of interest:

$$\frac{M}{Y} = f(i). \tag{13}$$

In testing this model, he specified a simple linear form, and derived the following regression estimates:

$$\frac{M}{Y} = 0.0074 \left(\frac{1}{i}\right) + 0.1088.$$

This equation was then used to predict values of the dependent variable for dates not included in the original data. The success of these predictions prompted Latané to conclude that he had identified a stable behavioral relation between cash balances, income, and the long-term rate of interest. Specifically, "In the past thirty years, each 1.0 percent change in $(1/i)$ has tended to be associated with a change of 0.8 percent in gross national product held as currency and demand deposits."[26]

One characteristic of Latané's last model, shared by the money demand functions tested by several other authors, should be mentioned. The equation form chosen by Latané to test the interest sensitivity of the cash balance ratio constrains the income elasticity of the demand for money to equal unity.[27] The effects of this arbitrary

[25]This may be seen by dividing both sides of equation (12) by Y:

$$\frac{M}{Y} = \frac{a}{i \cdot Y} + b + \frac{c}{Y}$$

If Y increases, a/Y and c/Y will decline. Thus, with the interest rate constant, the proportion of income held in the form of money balances would decline as income increased.

[26]H. A. Latané, "Cash Balances and the Interest Rate—A Pragmatic Approach," *Review of Economics and Statistics*, 36 (November 1954), p. 460.

[27]This may be shown as follows: Let $\eta_{M \cdot Y}$ denote the income elasticity of money balances. Then,

$$\eta_{M \cdot Y} = \frac{\Delta M/M}{\Delta Y/Y} = \frac{\Delta M}{\Delta Y} \cdot \frac{Y}{M}.$$

But from Latané's basic model (13), we may write

$$\Delta M = f(i) \cdot \Delta Y.$$

Therefore,

$$\eta_{M \cdot Y} = f(i) \cdot \frac{Y}{M} = \frac{f(i) \cdot Y}{f(i) \cdot Y} = 1.$$

restriction on the value of the income elasticity of money balances can only be judged by comparing the results of this model with those derived from models that are not so constrained.

Several investigators, in testing the liquidity preference theory, have attempted to isolate the "asset" or "idle" balance component of the public's total money holdings from money balances held strictly for transactions purposes and to estimate the influence of the interest rate on the former component alone. James Tobin (64), in an early study, and Martin Bronfenbrenner and Thomas Mayer (4), in subsequent work, employed this approach.

In calculating the idle balance component of total money balances, Tobin (like Latané) assumed that desired *transactions* balances are proportional to the level of income. To determine the exact factor of proportionality between transaction balances and income, Tobin further assumed that during periods of very high interest rates and high economic activity, when the ratio of total money holdings to income is at its lowest level, idle balances are zero and the total money stock is held solely for transactions purposes. The minimum value for this ratio was found to occur in 1929. Therefore, Tobin asserted that this 1929 ratio actually measures the constant factor of proportionality between transactions balances and income. This may be seen symbolically. Let

$$M_{\text{total}} = M_{\text{idle}} + M_{\text{trans}} = f(i) + kY,$$

where

$$M_{\text{idle}} = f(i) \text{ and } M_{\text{trans}} = kY.$$

If $M_{idle} = f(i) = O$, as Tobin asserts for 1929, then in 1929

$$M_{\text{total}} = kY \text{ and } \frac{M_{\text{total}}}{Y} = k$$

One alternative but equally restrictive approach to the demand for transactions balances is represented by the inventory theoretic model of the Baumol-Tobin type. In this model the demand for money is shown to conform to the familiar "square root law" of inventory analysis, i.e.,

$$M_d = \frac{1}{2}\sqrt{\frac{2bT}{i}} = \frac{1}{2} \cdot \sqrt{2b} \cdot T^{\frac{1}{2}} \cdot i^{-\frac{1}{2}},$$

where T is the volume of expenditures financed in a given period, b is the cost of switching between income earning assets and money, and i is the interest rate. In this case

$$\eta_{M \cdot T} = \frac{\partial M}{\partial T} \cdot \frac{T}{M} = \frac{\frac{1}{2} \cdot \frac{1}{2} \cdot \sqrt{2b} \cdot T^{-\frac{1}{2}} i^{-\frac{1}{2}}}{1} \cdot \frac{T}{\frac{1}{2} \cdot \sqrt{2b} \cdot T^{\frac{1}{2}} \cdot i^{-\frac{1}{2}}} = \frac{1}{2}$$

i.e., the transactions (or income) elasticity of the demand for money balances is one half. In this framework one would expect to find substantial economies of scale in the holding of money balances. These are ruled out in Latané's formulation as they are in the crude form of the quantity theory. See W. Baumol, "The Transactions Demand for Cash: An Inventory Theoretic Approach," *Quarterly Journal of Economics*, 66 (November 1952).

Since k (the reciprocal of the transactions velocity of circulation of money, V_t) was assumed to be a constant, this allowed a calculation of idle balances for other years as

$$(M_{idle})_t = (M_{total})_t - (M_{trans})_t = (M_{total})_t - k_{1929}(Y_t)$$

Tobin plotted idle balances calculated in this manner for each year against interest rates. For the period ending in 1945 he obtained excellent representations of what appeared to be Keynesian liquidity preference functions—the roughly hyperbolic functions generally depicted in the discussion of Keynesian theory. Although the scatter diagrams did not appear to yield such well-behaved relations for subsequent years, it did appear that Tobin had isolated a statistical liquidity preference function.

In their work Bronfenbrenner and Mayer (4) estimated regression coefficients in equations that contained a wealth measure and lagged money balances as explanatory variables, in addition to the interest rate. As the dependent variable, they alternately used total money balances and a measure of idle balances, similar to the one originally defined by Tobin. The equation they estimated in log-linear form was

$$\log (M/P)_t = \alpha_1 + \alpha_2 \log i + \alpha_3 \log W + \alpha_4 \log (M/P)_{t-1}. \tag{14}$$

This is virtually identical to the basic form derived in the previous section. In the equations employing idle balances as well as in those specifying total money balances as the dependent variable, the coefficient of the interest rate had a negative sign attached to it and was statistically significantly different from zero at the 1 percent level.[28]

In further tests based on equations similar to the one above Bronfenbrenner and Mayer concluded that the liquidity preference hypothesis did a better job of predicting the movement of money balances from year to year than did a "naive" model that assumed that there would be no relation (or a random relation) between movements in the interest rate and money balances. This again appeared as evidence favorable to the liquidity preference hypothesis.

Virtually all work presented since the Bronfenbrenner and Mayer study has wisely avoided the arbitrary classification of money balances into active and idle components. Even earlier authors, such as Latané, felt that such a distinction did not allow for the possible effect of the interest rate on "active balances."[29] Many economists believe that such a dichotomy is unreasonable since total money balances are simply

---

[28]To say that a coefficient is "statistically significantly different from zero" at the 1 percent level is to imply that there is less than one chance in a hundred that the estimated coefficient differs from zero solely because of random (chance) factors affecting the data from which the estimate was derived. If we cannot judge a coefficient to be significantly different from zero at the 1 percent level or 5 percent level of significance, we generally have little confidence in the hypothesized relation which that coefficient represents.

[29]Latané, *op. cit.*, pp. 456-457.

one of many assets held for the services they provide and cannot be separated into unique components.[30]

Among studies specifying total money balances as the dependent variable are those by Meltzer (49), Brunner and Meltzer (5, 6), Laidler (40, 41), Heller (30), Chow (11) and Goldfeld (24). These studies use different time periods to test their basic hypotheses; they include variables other then the interest rate in the money demand equation; and often they differ in the empirical measure chosen to represent "the interest rate," some specifying the rate on U.S. Treasury Bills or short-term commercial paper, while others employ the rate on long-term government bonds or corporate securities. Yet, in spite of these many differences, these studies, like the ones above, show that the interest rate measure is an important factor in explaining variations in the demand for money. Some of the more important characteristics of these studies are summarized in Table 1.

In addition to the unanimous conclusion that the interest rate is an important determinant of the demand for money, these studies demonstrate a strong consistency in their estimates of the interest elasticity of money balances. (As discussed below, such consistency over different periods of time suggests a rather stable demand for money function.) Those studies employing a long-term rate of interest report elasticities in the range of − 0.4 to − 0.9. However, the estimates in the lower half of this range occur only when money is defined in a "broad" sense (inclusive of commercial bank time deposits). Considering only those studies that use the narrow measure of money we find that the range of elasticity estimates narrows to − 0.7 to − 0.9.

When the short-term rate of interest is employed, the estimated elasticities range from − 0.07 to − 0.50. However, the estimates in the upper part of this range derive from those studies that specify "idle" balances as the dependent variable. If we exclude these results and consider only total money balances as the dependent variable, the elasticity of money balances with respect to the short-term interest rate lies in the range from − 0.07 to − 0.20. This result holds whether money is defined in the "narrow" or "broad" sense. The difference between the long-rate and the short-rate elasticities may be an indication of the different rates of adjustment by the public to what they consider to be temporary versus long-term movements in financial variables. Statistically, it also reflects the fact that the long-term rate fluctuates far less than the short-term rate. We shall consider this point again below.

Simultaneous-Equation Models

All of the studies reported in Table 1 have one basic characteristic in common: the estimates of interest elasticities are derived from single-equation models. Elementary statistics teaches that in order for estimated coefficients derived by least-squares regression methods to have certain desirable characteristics (unbiasedness, efficiency, etc.), there must be a one-way causation from the independent to the dependent variable, with no direct feedback. Thus, in the single-equation models specified

[30]M. Friedman, "The Demand for Money—Some Theoretical and Empirical Results," *Journal of Political Economy*, 67 (June 1959), pp. 327-351.

above, the interest rate and other explanatory variables must be assumed to influence the stock of money, the dependent variable, but the stock of money must not, in turn, influence these variables.

In contrast, if the conventional aggregate economic model is considered, it is obvious that the causation between interest rates, real factors, and the money stock is not unidirectional. There are simultaneous interrelations between both the supply of and demand for money as well as between monetary and real factors. This leads to what is commonly referred to as an "identification" problem.[31]

[31]The source and nature of "simultaneous-equation bias" may be illustrated as follows. Consider the usual supply-demand relationship as drawn in Figure A.

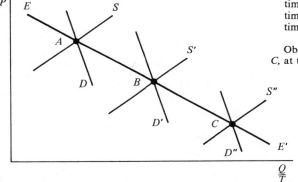

time (t)—supply S, demand D
time ($t+1$)—supply S', demand D'
time ($t+2$)—supply S'', demand D''

Observed price-quantity figures are A, B, C, at times t, $t+1$, and $t+2$, respectively.

An attempt to fit a statistical demand or supply curve to empirical observations will not, in fact, yield the desired relationship except in very special circumstances. The usual time series observations of price (P) and quantity (Q) do not correspond to either any one demand curve or any one supply curve. Rather, they are intersection points of various supply and demand curves that are almost continuously shifting either randomly or systematically due to the influence of outside factors.

Attempts to derive single-equation estimates of these curves on the basis of observed data will result in a statistical construct that is neither a supply curve nor a demand curve. For example, the least-squares regression line that could be fit to the data in Figure A would be EE'. This line would have a negative slope in the situation drawn here only because of the tendency for the supply curve to shift relatively more than the demand curve. Yet a statistical study of the data involved could easily be misunderstood by the unwary to represent the true demand relation. This would lead one to accept a meaningless estimate of the

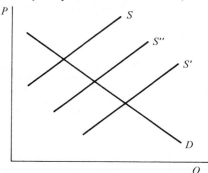

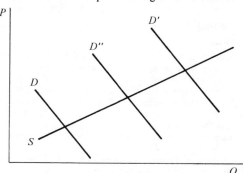

Table 1. The Demand for Money in Single-Equation Studies

Study		Interest Rate Elasticity of M			Interest Rate Measure Employed	Other Variables in M_D Function	Data and Time Period
1. Latané (45)			-0.7	$(M1)$	R_B	GNP	1919–1952 (A)
2. Bronfenbrenner and	a) -0.3	$-$	-0.5	(M_{Idle})	R_{4-6}	GNP, Wealth	1919–1956 (A)
Mayer (4)	b)	approx.	-0.1	$(M1)$	R_{4-6}	GNP, Wealth	1919–1956 (A)
3. Meltzer (49)	a) -0.7	$-$	-0.9	$(M1)$	R_{20} yr	Net Nonhuman Wealth	1900–1958 (A)
	b) -0.5	$-$	-0.6	$(M2)$	R_{20} yr	Net Nonhuman Wealth	1900–1958 (A)
	c)		-0.4	$(M3)$	R_{20} yr	Net Nonhuman Wealth	1900–1949 (A)
4. Heller (30)	a)		-0.1	$(M1)$	R_{60-80}	GNP	1947–1958 (Q)
	b)		-0.1	$(M2)$	R_{60-80}	Private Nonhuman Wealth	1947–1958 (Q)
5. Laidler (40)	a)	not available		$(M1)$	R_{4-6}	Permanent Income	1920–1960 (A)
	b)	not available		$(M2)$	R_{4-6}	Permanent Income	1892–1960 (A)
6. Laidler (41)	a) -0.18	$-$	-0.20	$(M1)$	R_{4-6}	Permanent Income	1919–1960 and subperiods (A)
	b) -0.5	$-$	-0.8	$(M1)$	R_{20} yr	Permanent Income	1919–1960 and subperiods (A)
	c)	approx. -0.15		$(M2)$	R_{4-6}	Permanent Income	1892–1960 and subperiods (A)
	d) -0.3	$-$	-0.5	$(M2)$	R_{20} yr	Permanent Income	1892–1960 and subperiods (A)
7. Chow (11)	a)	approx. -0.75		$(M1)$	R_{20} yr	Permanent Income	1897–1958 (excl. war years) (A)
	b)	approx. -0.79		$(M1)$	R_{20} yr	Current Income and Lagged Money Stock	1897–1958 (excl. war years) (A)
8. Goldfeld (25)	a)		-0.07 -0.16	$(M1)$	R_{4-6} R_{TD}	GNP	1952–1972 (Q)
	b)		-0.07 -0.15	$(M1)$	R_{4-6} R_{TD}	GNP (Almon lags)	1952–1972 (Q)

Notes: $M1 = DD + C$; $M2 = M1 + TD$; $M3 = M2 +$ Deposits at Mutual Savings Banks and the Postal Savings System; $R_B =$ interest rate on high-grade corporate bonds; $R_{20\,yr} =$ rate on 20-year corporate bonds; $R_{4-6} =$ rate on 4-6 month prime commercial paper; $R_{60-80} =$ rate on 60-80 day commercial paper; $R_{TD} =$ commercial bank time deposit rate; $A =$ annual; $Q =$ quarterly.

Fortunately, a substantial body of empirical work does assume simultaneity either between money supply and money demand or, more generally, between the monetary and the (real) expenditure sectors of the economy. These studies employ statistical techniques designed to correct for the interaction among "dependent" and "independent" variables specified within a single equation and to derive estimates which have certain desirable statistical properties. In these studies the money demand function is estimated as one element in a multiequation model. Some examples of the results of these studies are presented in Table 2.[32]

---

slope and, thus, of the elasticity of the demand curve.

The only way in which such time series data could readily yield true structural estimates of the parameters of either the supply curve or the demand curve would be in the very special circumstances where one of the curves is stable and the shifting of the other curve traces out points along the desired curve. This is pictured in Figure B. To get around this problem, the true interaction of supply-demand relations in determining price-quantity figures must be considered. This may be done by specifying a simultaneous-equation model including both a supply equation and a demand equation and by taking care to observe well defined rules for "identification." See G. Tintner, *Econometrics* (New York, 1962), Chapter 6.

[32]All of the studies reported in Table 2 employ two-stage least squares in the estimating process. For a discussion of the mechanics of this technique and the characteristics of the estimates derived from it, see J. Johnston, *Econometric Methods* (New York, 1963), Chapter 9, or Kmenta, *op. cit.*, Chapter 13.

Table 2. Money and Deposit Demand in Simultaneous-Equation Models

Study	Representative Equation (seasonal dummies omitted where appropriate)	Interest Elasticity	Interest Rate Measure	Data
1. Brunner and Meltzer (6)	$M1 = -18.994\ r^* + 0.201\ W/Pa - 54.72\ Y/Y_p + 0.347P_y$ W/Pa = real public wealth P_y = price index Y/Y_p = ratio of current to permanent income	-0.75	r = bond yield	1930–1959 (A)
	$M2 = -16.806\ r^* + 0.340\ W/Pa - 44.81\ Y/Y_p + 0.290P_y$	-0.42	r = bond yield	1930–1959 (A)
2. Teigen (62)	$\Delta D = 3.101 + 0.0719Y^* - 0.0018r_b^* Y^* - 0.0066r_p Y^*$ $- 0.1895\ D_{T-1}$ D = demand deposits adjusted at commercial banks Y = gross national product	-0.10 -0.43	r_b = Treas. bill rate r_p = rate on bank time deposits	1953–1964 (Q)
3. de Leeuw (47)	$\dfrac{\Delta D}{W} = 0.0067 - 0.158\left(\dfrac{D}{W}\right)_{r-1} - 0.00355r_s^*$ $- 0.0451r_p^* - 0.140\ \dfrac{Inv}{W_{r-1}} + $ other terms W = wealth measure $Inv.$ = bus. investment	-0.35 -0.17	r_s = yield on private securities r_p = rate on bank time deposits	1948–1962 (Q)
4. Goldfeld (24)	$\Delta D = -0.270 - 0.127D_{T-1} + 0.140Y^*$ $- 0.0066r_b^* Y^* - 0.012r_p Y^*$ Y = gross national product	-0.11 -0.18	r_b = Treas. bill rate r_p = rate on bank time deposits	1950–1962 (Q)
5. Dickson and Starleaf (13)	$M1 = \ln a_o + 0.660\ \ln Y^a - 0.077\ \ln R_{4-6}^a - 0.182\ \ln R_{TD}^a$ $+ 1.037\ \ln P^a$	-0.08 -0.18	R_{4-6} = comm. paper rate R_{TD} = comm. bank time deposit rate	1952–1969 (Q)

Where ^{a} indicates weighted average of current and past values; estimated using Almon distributed lags.

*An asterisk is used to denote an independent variable used in the money (or D) demand function, which is treated as endogenously determined within the multiequation model as a whole. A = annual; Q = quarterly

The results derived from simultaneous-equation models generally confirm the single-equation results reported above. Those studies employing a short-term market rate of interest in the money or demand deposit demand equation, report elasticities in the range of -0.08 to -0.18. This compares with the -0.7 to -0.2 range reported in the single equation studies in Table 1. The elasticity estimates with respect to the rate on commercial bank time deposits is generally -0.17 or -0.18.[33] The elasticity measures based on long-term rates are again substantially higher than the short-term rate elasticities. They range from -0.35 in de Leeuw's work to -0.75 in Brunner and Meltzer's model. Since de Leeuw's measure is a weighted average of rates on private securities of different maturities, and not a long-term rate comparable to the corporate bond yields used in the other studies, these results are not inconsistent with the evidence presented in Table 1.

Most of the equations reported in Table 2 are estimated within an explicitly specified structural model either of the monetary sector or of the monetary and expenditures sectors combined. Several authors, interested primarily in the money demand

[33]This is virtually identical to the result obtained by Goldfeld in his single-equation study. See Table 1.

relation outside the framework of a fully specified multiequation model but cognizant of the potential estimation problems implicit in the single-equation approach, have employed the method of instrumental variables in deriving their estimates of the parameters in the money demand equation. Essentially, this method allows one to act as if he is operating within a fully specified structural model by postulating the exogenous variables that would appear in the model were it to be fully defined. In this way those exogenous variables can be employed as "instruments" in the first stage of a two-stage least-squares estimation process with the predicted values of the "endogenous" or jointly dependent variables from this first-stage estimation being employed in the money demand function in the second stage.

One interesting example of this approach is contained in a recent paper by Harold D. Dickson and Dennis R. Starleaf (13). Their work is all the more interesting because it applies this technique to an equation that contains Almon-estimated distributed lag terms on each of the independent variables—income, the interest rate and the price level. Their results, reported in Table 2, are broadly consistent both with the results of simultaneous-equation models and with the single-equation results presented by Goldfeld, which employ a similar equation form. Using quarterly data for 1952-I through 1969-IV, they obtain estimated interest elasticities of -0.077 and -0.182 for the 4-6 month commercial paper rate and the rate on commercial bank time deposit, respectively.

In summary, it should be emphasized that both those studies based on single-equation models as well as those that employ multiequation estimation techniques appear to support the hypothesis that the interest rate is an important determinant of the demand for money. Furthermore, since the multiequation estimates are less likely to be biased because they take explicit consideration of the simultaneous nature of the relations involved, the similarity of results from those studies with those in single-equation work lends strong support to the single-equation estimates and indicates that, in this case, the identification problem may not be particularly serious.

Alternative Interest Rate Measures in the Money Demand Function

The studies cited in the previous section contain virtually overwhelming evidence that some interest rate should appear in the demand for money function. However, there is still disagreement as to which empirical measure should be used to represent the theoretical argument. Much of the available evidence that attempts to determine which rate best explains the demand for money is inconsistent. Furthermore, tests by different analysts often employ data from different time periods, specify different dependent variables, and include dissimilar constraints within the function, making comparisons among these empirical studies rather tenuous.

The problem may stem partly from the fact that theory provides little guidance on this issue. Some writers, like Brunner and Meltzer, argue that the demand for money should be treated within the broad theory of portfolio selection and suggest that this demand depends on the yield on equities as well as that on bonds. Others, like

Bronfenbrenner and Mayer (4), Laidler (40, 41), and Heller (30), argue that some short-term interest rate is the more relevant argument since it measures the opportunity cost of holding money as the rate of return on what they consider to be money's closest substitutes. Still others, including Gurley and Shaw (26) emphasize the liquidity of money and the minimal risks associated with changes in its nominal value. They argue that the closest substitutes for money are assets with similar characteristics, such as the liabilities of financial intermediaries (e.g., savings and loan associations), and that it is the rates on these assets that are most relevant to the money demand function.[34]

One attempt to present direct evidence on this issue was made by Heller in 1965. In alternative money demand equations Heller compared the performance of the long-term rate of interest as measured by the rate on U.S. government bonds with that of a short-term rate, measured as the yield on 60–90-day commercial paper. Regression coefficients were estimated for equations in log-linear form using quarterly observations for the period 1947–1958. Both $M1$ and $M2$ were tried as dependent variables with the interest rate and current income or nonhuman wealth specified as alternative constraints. In these regressions the long-term rate of interest *never* appeared as a statistically important explanatory variable,[35] while the short-term rate was important in all equations but one. Consequently, Heller concluded,

> The short-term rate is of greater importance (than the long-term rate) in the money function. The closest substitute for money available, a 60 to 90 day commercial paper, is most influential in deciding whether to hold assets in the form of money or not. Long-term interest rates do not influence the quantity of money demanded. . . .[36]

Results presented by Laidler (41) generally support Heller's conclusions. Laidler examines evidence derived from equations fit to annual data for the period 1892–1960 and for subperiods therein. He bases his analysis on the following proposition:

> Given that the interest rate is an important variable in the demand for money, and that movements of various interest rates are related to one another, one would expect almost any rate chosen at random to show some relationship to cash balances . . . however, though all interest rates are interrelated, there is no reason to suppose that the nature of their interrelationship remains unchanged for all time. Thus, if the demand function for money is stable, one would expect the "right" interest rate to show the same relationship to the demand for money in different time periods while the "wrong" one need not.[37]

[34]See the first section of this survey for some implications of this view.

[35]The long-term rate was never significant at the 5 percent level, and in some of the equations it appeared with the wrong sign.

[36]H. R. Heller, "The Demand for Money—The Evidence from the Short-Run Data," *Quarterly Journal of Economics,* 79 (May 1965), p. 297.

[37]D. Laidler, "The Rate of Interest and the Demand for Money—Some Empirical Evidence," *Journal of Political Economy,* 74 (December 1966), p. 547.

Laidler uses the rate on 4–6-month commercial paper and the yield on 20-year bonds as his alternative interest rate measures. His equations are in log-linear form and include only permanent income as an additional explanatory variable. When his dependent variable is $M2$, he claims that "there is little question of the superior explanatory power of the shorter interest rate."[38] When the dependent variable is specified as $M1$ his results are somewhat contradictory. When he employs levels of the logarithms of the variables, the long-term rate explains more of the variation in $M1$ for most periods than does the short rate. Nonetheless, he maintains his original conclusion that a short-term rate is the relevant rate measure in the money demand function arguing that "the contradictory conclusions obtained with the narrower definition reflect only the fact that that definition is an unsatisfactory one."[39] The basis for his conclusion on this matter is to be found in our comments on his previous work (40), reported in the first section of this survey.

The conclusions derived from this work by Heller and Laidler are challenged by Michael Hamburger. In his study of the demand for money by households Hamburger (27) concludes that long-term interest rates are the relevant determinants of the demand for money. Employing a model that includes distributed lags to measure the rate of adjustment of households to changed market conditions, he finds that in the household demand for money function "for short-run analysis . . . , it is useful to include two yields—one on debts and one equities—and that the elasticities of the demand for money are approximately the same with respect to both of these rates."[40] His findings show that government bills (short-term securities) may be poorer substitutes for money for the household sector than longer-term securities. Commenting on previous work, Hamburger claims that Heller's conclusions depend on the choice of time period. During the period 1947–1951 the Federal Reserve pegged interest rates distorting more normal market relationships. When Hamburger reruns Heller's regressions excluding these years, he finds that the long-term rate and the short-term rate appear equally important.

Additional evidence has been reported by T. H. Lee (46). Lee criticizes the previous work done by the cited authors because they restrict their comparisons to only two alternative rate measures. Furthermore, he argues that the *differentials* between interest rates and the yield on money, rather than simply interest rate *levels,* are the relevant measures that should appear in money demand functions.

Like Laidler, Lee specifies a Friedman-type permanent income money demand model as the basic framework for his tests. He tries both $M1$ and $M2$ as dependent variables and, in addition to his alternative interest rate measures, either permanent income or permanent income and lagged money balances as explanatory variables. His regression estimates show that "the yield on nonbank intermediary liabilities is the most significant interest rate variable in affirming the demand for money." Spe-

[38] *Ibid.,* p. 547.
[39] *Ibid.,* p. 553.
[40] The rates Hamburger used were Moody's Aaa rate on long-term corporate bonds and Moody's dividend yield. M. J. Hamburger, "The Demand for Money by Households . . . ," *Journal of Political Economy,* 74 (December 1966), p. 608.

cifically, "the yield on savings and loan shares performs the best in terms of R^2 among respective regressions of static or dynamic formulations."[41]

With the exception of Lee's work, the interest rate measure included in the other money demand functions cited was the absolute level of the rate on some asset alternative to money.[42] One implication of this formulation is that the (marginal) rate of return on money is assumed to be zero. Robert S. Barro and Anthony M. Santomero (2) have argued that "at least one component of (narrowly defined) money, demand deposits, bears a form of interest which should be taken into account in determining the opportunity cost of holding money."[43] Their argument rests on the assumption that the provision of services or the remission of charges by banks in accordance with the size of a customer's deposit balance represents an effective interest return on those deposits.

To test this proposition, Barro and Santomero surveyed the largest one hundred commercial banks in the United States to determine "the rates at which they have remitted service charges as a function of demand deposit balances."[44] From the survey results an annual series measuring the imputed marginal rate of return on demand deposits was constructed for 1950-1968. This measure was then employed within the framework of a Baumol-Tobin inventory theoretic model of the demand for money by households.[45] Relating real per capita money balances, (M/PN), real per capita consumption expenditure, (Y/PN), and the differential between the rate on an alternative asset—the dividend rate on savings and loan shares—and the imputed demand deposit rate, the following estimates are derived:

$$\log \left(\frac{M}{PN}\right)_T = -3.96 + 1.044 \log \left(\frac{Y}{PN}\right)_T - 0.549 \log (r_S - r_D)_T.$$

These results support the basic hypothesis: There is a substantial interest elasticity of household money demand with respect to the rate differential $(r_S - r_D)$.

[41]T. H. Lee, "Alternative Interest Rates and the Demand for Money: The Empirical Evidence," *American Economic Review,* 57 (December 1967), p. 1171.

[42]Hamburger later criticized Lee's evidence because his "findings depend critically on the use of interest rate differentials. Once this procedure is abandoned and the yield on money is introduced as a separate variable, there is little evidence that S + L shares are closer substitutes for money (narrowly defined) than other assets. In addition, the demand for money appears to adjust more slowly to changes in yields on S + L shares than to changes in other rates." Hamburger, "Alternative Interest Rates . . . ," *op. cit.,* p. 407.

[43]R. J. Barro and A. M. Santomero, "Household Money Holdings and the Demand Deposit Rate," *Journal of Money, Credit and Banking,* 4 (May 1972), p. 397.

[44]*Ibid.,* p. 399.

[45]An interesting implication of their formulation of the inventory model is that the income elasticity need not be less than one. This contradicts the conventional view that inventory models are necessarily associated with economies of scale as shown on page 330. As they argue; "The key element which is typically neglected is transactions costs. As transaction volume increases, economies of scale are realized only to the extent that transactions costs rise less than transactions volume. Since transaction costs depend largely on value of time, and since value of time may increase even faster than transactions volume, diseconomies of scale (money being a "luxury") is quite compatible with the inventory approach." Barro and Santomero, *op. cit.,* p. 408.

It is important to note that the estimated interest elasticity applies solely to the rate differential. Since that differential (as measured by Barro and Santomero) has been fairly constant over the postwar period, the elasticity with respect to the level of rates may be quite small. The coefficient of real per capita expenditure indicates the expenditure elasticity of money demand is close to unity, suggesting an absence of economies of scale in household demand for money.

The highly tentative nature of these results should now be evident. While Heller and Laidler argue that the short-term rate is the relevant measure in the money demand function, this conclusion is challenged by both Hamburger and Lee. Lee's results further indicate that it may be the differential between the yield on money and the yield on the liabilities of some financial intermediary rather than a market interest rate that is the most appropriate constraint on desired money balances. But this contention is disputed by Hamburger. Barro and Santomero's results suggest the addition of some measure of the return on demand deposits to the equation. Additional work in which a serious attempt is made to make new results comparable to the results of previous investigators will be required before any firm conclusions are possible on this critical empirical issue.

Interest Elasticity and the Liquidity Trap

The evidence reviewed above clearly supports the Keynesian notion of an interest sensitive demand for money or liquidity preference function.[46] However, Keynes went further than merely to posit the interest rate as a determinant of the public's demand for money. In *The General Theory* he also speculated briefly about the shape of the liquidity preference function. Specifically, he noted,

> There is the possibility . . . , that, after the rate of interest has fallen to a certain level, liquidity preference may become virtually absolute in the sense that almost everyone prefers cash to holding a debt which yields so low a rate of interest. In this event the monetary authority would have lost effective control over the rate of interest. But while this limiting case might become practically important in the future, I know of no example of it hitherto.[47]

In spite of Keynes' disclaimer, his suggestion that the liquidity preference curve *may* become perfectly interest elastic at some low level of the interest rate attracted much attention and stimulated a substantial amount of "searching" for this phenomenon. His suggestion is responsible for the shape given the liquidity preference curve in most texts (as shown in Figure 1).

The implication of this hypothesis, is that the interest elasticity of the liquidity

[46]All of the studies cited above employ data from the United States. The evidence employing data from the United Kingdom is somewhat less conclusive on this issue. See, for example, A. A. Walters, "The Radcliffe Report—Ten Years After: A Survey of Empirical Evidence" in O. R. Croome and H. G. Johnson (eds.), *Money in Britain 1959-1969* (Oxford, 1969).

[47]J. M. Keynes, *The General Theory of Employment, Interest, and Money* (London and New York, 1936), p. 207.

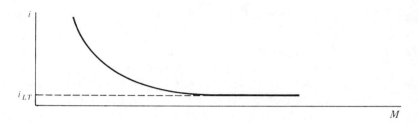

preference function should increase as the interest rate declines. This proposition has been tested by Bronfenbrenner and Mayer (4), by Meltzer (49), by Laidler (41), by Konstas and Khouja (38) and by others.

Bronfenbrenner and Mayer, after examining the relation between the short-term interest rate and the Cambridge k, (M/Y), tested to see if the elasticity of their estimated liquidity functions increased as the interest rate fell. Specifically, they calculated the "rank" correlation coefficient between elasticities and the level of interest rates. This involves ordering the level of interest rates from highest to lowest and comparing the ordering of the elasticities associated with those rates. If the highest rate were associated with the lowest elasticity, the lowest rate with the highest elasticity, and so on for all rates in between, there would be perfect negative rank correlation between these two measures. However, Bronfenbrenner and Mayer calculate a ranks correlation coefficient of $+ 0.16$, which not only is not statistically significant, but is of the wrong sign. They concluded that "the absence of a negative correlation in a period when interest rates were at times quite low, casts doubt on, if not the truth, then at least the relevance of the liquidity trap proposition. . . ."[48]

Other investigators have supported these conclusions. In 1963 Allan Meltzer (49) fit velocity functions for the six decades from 1900 to 1958. As he interprets his results, "The data deny that the interest elasticity of the demand for money or velocity became exceptionally large during that decade (the 1930's). Indeed, the interest elasticity of V_1 was slightly below the average for the (entire) fifty-nine years."[49] This evidence of a lower than average interest elasticity during periods of low interest rates is consistent with Bronfenbrenner and Mayer's positive rank-correlation coefficient.

Meltzer's work with Karl Brunner (5) adds additional support to this position. Using estimates derived from data for the 1930's, they were able to predict the velocity of circulation for the 1950's with sufficiently small mean errors to conclude that the velocity function remained highly stable over these periods of differing inter-

[48]M. Bronfenbrenner and T. Mayer, "Liquidity Functions in the American Economy," *Econometrica*, 28 (October 1960), p. 831.

[49]For the purpose of these tests, Meltzer defines income as the return on wealth, i.e., the interest rate or rate of return, r, times the wealth stock, W. The wealth measure used to calculate income in this formula is net nonhuman wealth of the public—the same variable employed in his money demand functions. The measure of money he employs is narrow money $(DD + C)$. Meltzer, *op. cit.*, p. 243.

est rate levels. They conclude that "the liquidity trap proposition is denied by the evidence."[50]

[50]Brunner and Meltzer, *op. cit.*, p. 350.

David Laidler (41) has reported evidence from a test somewhat similar to Bronfenbrenner and Mayer's. Employing both the narrow (*M*1) and the broad (*M*2) definitions of money and testing both the long-rate and the short-rate of interest in separate regressions, Laidler divided the observations for the period 1892–1960 into two subsets: those years in which the relevant interest rate was above the mean and those in which it was below the mean. The general equation tested was

$$ln\ M = a + b_1\ ln\ Y_p + b_2\ ln\ i,$$

where Y_p is permanent income. Laidler's results, using both logarithms and first differences of logarithms of the variables defined above, demonstrated very little tendency for the interest elasticity (b_2) to be higher (in absolute value) for the low interest rate observations than it was in the equations fitted to the high interest rate observations. As he notes, "the elasticity with respect to the short rate seems to fall a little at low rates of interest, though the elasticity with respect to the long rate rises slightly at low interest rates. . . . Thus, the hypothesis of the liquidity trap, as it is usually presented, appears to be refuted."[51]

An interesting article by Konstas and Khouja reports on statistical tests relevant to this issue. In their study the authors attempt to specify a functional form for the demand for money relation which accurately portrays the characteristics originally suggested by Keynes. In their model,

In regard to the speculative part of the demand for money, . . . the function which is consistent with Keynesian requirements must be stated in the following manner:

$$M2 = \frac{\beta}{r - \alpha};\ \beta > 0,\ \alpha > 0.\ [52]$$

This formulation quite accurately reflects the properties of the function shown in Figure 1. It allows for a minimum interest rate level, α, and for increasing interest elasticity of money balances as interest rates decline toward α. The authors estimate the parameters of this model using annual observations for the period 1919–1965. In general, the data seem to fit this relationship rather closely.

[50]Brunner and Meltzer, *op. cit.*, p. 350.
[51]Laidler, "The Rate of Interest . . .", *op. cit.*, p. 550.
[52]Konstas and Khouja, *op. cit.*, p. 767. For another study that claims to formulate and test Keynes' original liquidity preference hypothesis more accurately than is done in some of the literature cited above, see D. R. Starleaf and R. Reimer, "The Keynesian Demand Function for Money: Some Statistical Tests," *Journal of Finance,* 22 (March 1967), pp. 71–76. Their work relates primarily to the Keynesian proposition that it is not necessarily the absolute level of the rate of interest that is important in determining the demand for money but the relationship of that current rate to a conceptual "normal" rate. Starleaf and Reimer found no evidence to suggest that the normal rate, as they calculated it, was an important variable in the demand for money.

Konstas and Khouja use their estimated relation to examine the claim that the United States economy was in a liquidity trap in the 1930's. Specifically, they calculate an estimate of the speculative component of total money balances by subtracting estimated transactions balances from (actual) total money balances for each of the years 1919–1965. The pattern indicated in the relation between the long-term interest rate and calculated idle balances fails to confirm the claim that monetary policy was impotent in the 1930's because of the very high interest elasticity of the demand for money. They conclude that their test "does not seem to offer much evidence in support of this claim."[53] These results add to the weight of the evidence reported above.

Most of the individual tests cited in this section approach the question of the liquidity trap indirectly. Furthermore, some of the results of Laidler's tests with the long-term rate of interest could be taken as very weak support for the existence of the low level trap. However, the weight of all these studies together seems sufficient to allow a rather firm judgment against the historical existence of the liquidity trap. In addition, work by Brunner and Meltzer has shown that the necessary and sufficient conditions for the occurrence of a liquidity trap in the demand function for money are extremely restrictive.[54] Consequently, the conclusion on the absence of a liquidity trap would seem warranted by the lack of any falsifying evidence.

An Alternative View: Interest Rates, Permanent Income and Variations in Velocity

One implication of the work surveyed above is that cyclical variations in interest rates are important determinants of the evident cyclical variations in the demand for money and the velocity of circulation of money. This view has been disputed by at least one important analyst, Milton Friedman. Although in his "Restatement" of the quantity theory of money Friedman develops a theoretical money demand function that includes several interest rate terms as explanatory variables, his statistical work leads him to question the empirical significance of the interest rate in determining actual money holdings.

Friedman's empirical work begins with an observation on the behavior of the income velocity of money. He notes that from 1870 to 1954, over long periods of time, the income velocity of circulation (Y/M) moved in a direction opposite to that of real income, but over shorter periods of time, during business cycles, these variables moved in the same direction.[55] He attempts to reconcile these observations by explaining the public's behavior regarding the demand for real money balances.

[53]Konstas and Khouja, *op. cit.,* p. 774.

[54]K. Brunner and A. H. Meltzer, "Liquidity Traps for Money, Bank Credit, and Interest Rates," *Journal of Political Economy,* 76 (February 1968), 1–37.

[55]The inverse long-term relation between income and velocity implies more than simply a direct relation between income and money. It implies that as income increases, money increases more than proportionately, so that money may be viewed as a "luxury" good. This long-term relationship has not prevailed in the postwar period, however, as velocity has trended upward rather strongly.

Friedman argues that the *nominal* stock of money in the economy is determined in the first instance on the supply side of the market by the monetary authorities and that "holders of money cannot alter this amount directly." In contrast, however, the holders of money "can make the *real* amount of money anything in the aggregate they want to."[56] For, if individuals find themselves holding too large a stock of nominal money balances, their attempt to decrease these balances by increasing expenditures will reduce the real quantity of money to the desired level by raising money income and prices. Conversely, lowering expenditures to increase money holdings will lower money income and prices, thereby raising the real quantity of money to the desired equilibrium level.

This analysis suggests that since the *nominal* stock of money is predetermined by the monetary authorities, an explanation of the observed behavior of the *real* volume of money balances and the income velocity of money requires an examination of the demand for money.[57] It may be possible to explain the patterns exhibited by velocity through an analysis of the historical behavior of the explanatory variables that enter a stable demand for money function. However, Friedman's attempt to find variables in addition to income that enter the money demand function and that "exert an influence opposite to that of income . . . sufficiently potent to dominate the [cyclical] movement of velocity"[58] is unsuccessful. As he reports,

> . . . the other variables that come first to mind are interest rates, and these display cyclical patterns that seem most unlikely to account for the sizable, highly consistent, and roughly synchronous cyclical pattern in velocity.[59]

As an alternative approach, suggested by his work on the consumption function, Friedman employs the concept of permanent income in the money demand function to reconcile the cyclical and secular behavior of velocity. This attempt starts by viewing "the statistical magnitude called 'real income' as corresponding to a different theoretical construct in the cyclical than in the secular analysis."[60] This reconciliation depends on the relation between measured and permanent income. If permanent income rises less than measured income during cyclical expansions and falls less than measured income in contractions, and if money balances are adapted to permanent income, "they might rise and fall more than in proportion to permanent income, as is required by our secular results, yet less than in proportion to measured income, as is required by our cyclical results."[61]

[56]M. Friedman, "The Demand for Money . . . ," *op. cit.,* p. 330.
[57]Following Fisher in employing the equation of exchange, Friedman often couches his analytical discussion in terms of the velocity of circulation of money rather than the demand function for money balances. But since $V = (Y/M)$, an increase in the demand for nominal balances relative to nominal income will be reflected in a decrease in the income velocity of circulation of money and, conversely, a decrease in the demand for money will be reflected as an increase in velocity.
[58]Friedman, "The Demand for Money . . . ," *op. cit.,* p. 332.
[59]*Ibid.*
[60]*Ibid.*
[61]*Ibid.,* p. 334.

On the basis of this theoretical reconciliation of the conflicting behavior of observed velocity, Friedman turns to an empirical examination of this phenomenon. As he notes, "An interpretation in terms of interest rates can also rationalize the qualitative results; [but] we reject it because it appears likely to be contradicted on a more detailed quantitative level."[62]

In his empirical tests Friedman measures both money balances and permanent income in real (i.e., deflated) per capita form and specifies the following exponential money demand function:

$$\frac{M}{NP} = \alpha \left(\frac{Y_P}{NP}\right)^{\delta}$$

or, in logarithmic form,

$$ln \; \frac{M}{NP} = ln \; \alpha + \delta \; ln \left(\frac{Y_P}{NP}\right), \tag{15}$$

where P is an index of (permanent) prices, N is population, and Y_p is permanent income.[63]

Friedman fits this function to cycle-average data for the period 1869–1957. His estimate of δ, the permanent income elasticity of real money balances, is 1.8. Using this relationship, he calculates annual within-cycle projections of the velocity of circulation of money and finds that his formulation predicts actual velocity figures fairly well. Most importantly, however, he also finds that *the errors that are evident in these predictions are almost completely unrelated to the level of interest rates.* Thus, he concludes that there is little role for the interest rate, in addition to permanent income, in explaining variations in the velocity of circulation of money or the variation in money balances.[64]

Friedman achieves these results by using some statistical techniques not generally

[62]*Ibid.,* p. 335.

[63]Friedman originally derived his permanent income concept in connection with his studies on the consumption function. Permanent income is calculated as a weighted average of past income levels with the weights attached to the income levels of the more distant past declining geometrically. See M. Friedman, *A Theory of the Consumption Function* (Princeton, N.J., 1957), pp. 142–147.

[64]Friedman's conclusion would seem to be supported for the postwar period in evidence presented by Sam Peltzman. Challenging the conventional conclusion, Peltzman argues that his "results do imply strongly that interest rate movements cannot explain the postwar rise in velocity" (p. 134). In Peltzman's work this increase is associated with a secular trend in (unspecified) factors other than income and interest rates. See S. Peltzman, "The Structure of the Money-Expenditure Relationship," *American Economic Review,* 59 (March 1969), pp. 129–137. For a critique of Peltzman's methodology, see D. M. Jaffee, "The Structure of the Money Expenditure Relationship: Comment," *American Economic Review,* 60 (March 1970), pp. 216–219. In view of the serious econometric problems that arise in interpreting Peltzman's use of second differences and Jaffee's use of first differences, the uncertainty surrounding Peltzman's assumption about the public's behavior as regards the formulation of expectations about changes in the money stock, and the fact that Jaffee found some role for the interest rate in Peltzman's "reformulated" model, the overwhelming evidence on this issue from other sources would seem to stand.

used by other investigators. His use of cycle-average data,[65] for example, contrasts with the more common practice of using chronologically determined, annual or quarterly data in regression studies. Also, his use of the broad definition of money is claimed by many to bias his results against finding any role for the interest rate in the determination of money demand.[66] This latter contention may be explained as follows: if demand deposit balances are negatively related to interest rates, but time deposits are positively related to the rate paid on such deposits, a general increase in interest rates will decrease the demand for demand deposits and increase the demand for time deposits. If these two assets are added together in a single measure, these movements will tend to cancel out and the sum, $DD + TD$, may appear to be completely interest-insensitive.

In addition, Laidler (41) has pointed out that over the period covered by Friedman's study there was a slight downward trend in interest rates and that by omitting an interest rate term from his regression equation some of the (trend) influence of the interest rate on money balances was attributed to the trend in the permanent income variable. Since the decline in rates over this period would be expected to cause a relative increase in money balances, the absence of an interest rate term in the equation may help to explain the rather high (1.8) income elasticity estimated in Friedman's tests.

Friedman's results have been even more seriously challenged in the work of other analysts. Several of the studies reported in Table 1 include interest rates along with Friedman's measure of permanent income in log linear money demand functions. For example, Meltzer (49) showed that the long-term rate of interest generally appears as a highly significant variable in his regressions. He suggests that Friedman's use of the permanent income measure combines the influence of income, wealth, and interest rates into a single measure and obscures the separate impact of each on money demand. In addition to demonstrating the significant role of the interest rate when explicitly included in the function, Meltzer derives an estimate of the (permanent) income elasticity that is closer to unity than to Friedman's estimate of 1.8. This would appear to confirm Laidler's contention mentioned above.

Other works by Brunner and Meltzer (5) and by Chow (11) confirm the important role of the interest rate in alternative money demand or velocity functions. However, one important point with respect to these studies must be mentioned in defense of Friedman. These studies employ annual time series data, and these data are not strictly comparable to Friedman's (perhaps more subtle) cycle-average data. Consequently, their results do not represent a satisfactory refutation of his findings. However, Laidler (41), employing cycle-average data for the period 1891-1957, refitted

[65]An annual time series of observations on a given variable, X, represents a list of values for that variable for each year over a specified period of time. Cycle-average data on the other hand rely not on calendar years to generate observations, but rather on the cyclical swings in economic activity as defined by the National Bureau of Economic Research. Those who use cycle-average data argue that such a choice of values is economically more meaningful than the arbitrary designation of the calendar (or fiscal) year as the standard measure of time used to generate statistical data.

[66]See the discussion of this problem in connection with some results reported by Goldfeld (25).

Friedman's original equation and compared the results with those obtained when an interest rate term was included in the equation. His results are as follows:

$$\log \frac{M}{NP} = -2.017 + 1.618 \log \left(\frac{Y_p}{NP}\right)$$

$$\log \frac{M}{NP} = -1.403 + 1.430 \log \left(\frac{Y_p}{NP}\right) - 0.158 \log i_e$$

where i_e is the rate on 4-6-month commercial paper.

Laidler used these estimates to predict annual levels of per capita real money balances—a procedure very similar to Friedman's use of his equation to predict annual within-cycle values for the velocity of circulation of money. The mean error of prediction[67] for the equation that includes the interest rate is less than half that for the equation that contains only permanent income. Since the interest rate equation explains the data significantly better than Friedman's original equation, Laidler concludes that "the difference in the intercept and coefficient of the logarithm of permanent income that results from the omission of the interest rate is sufficient to produce misleading results (about the relation between prediction errors and the level of the rate of interest)." It appears that there was indeed "some secular (long-term) correlation between permanent income and [the] interest rate which caused permanent income to pick up part of the effect of interest rates in the regression from which the latter variable was omitted."[68]

As Laidler points out, then, the evidence coming from so many different sources is so persuasive that "it is probably safe to conclude that the rate of interest must be included in the demand function for money."[69] Friedman's results may be attributed in large part to his rather special statistical techniques.

The Scale Factor in Money Demand Functions: Current Income, Permanent Income, or Wealth

The results surveyed above suggest that the performance of any given interest rate measure in an empirical money demand function depends both on the way in which the dependent variable is defined and on the choice of other explanatory variables included in the equation. As already indicated, the other factors most commonly specified as determinants of the demand for money are income and wealth. The use of income—or some other measure of the volume of transactions—as a constraint on the level of money demand is generally related to the role of money as a medium of

[67]The mean error of prediction is the arithmetic average of the absolute value of the difference between the actual and predicted values of a given variable for all points for which a prediction is obtained.
[68]D. Laidler, "The Rate of Interest . . . ," *op. cit.,* p. 546.
[69]*Ibid.*

exchange. This is stated explicitly in Keynesian demand function, $M_d = L_1(Y) + L_2(i)$, in the Cambridge equation, $M = k \cdot Y$, and in the inventory theoretic model of money demand, $M_d = 1/2 \sqrt{2bT/i}$, where Y is the level of income and T is a measure of the volume of transactions.

On the other hand, when the role of money as a productive asset or a durable consumer good is stressed, a wealth measure is generally proposed as the relevant explanatory variable in the demand for money function. Attention is focused on "the equilibrium of the balance sheet, the allocation of assets, and the services that money provides." In this view "effecting a volume of transactions is but one of these services."[70]

In statistical work three measures have most frequently been employed as empirical counterparts to these theoretical constraints: current income, proposed as a proxy for the volume of transactions to be effected by the money stock; nonhuman wealth, measured as consolidated net worth in the balance sheet of the public; and Friedman's "permanent income," proposed as a proxy for a wealth concept that includes the present value of future labor income as well as the value of real physical assets. This last measure includes the value of both human and nonhuman wealth.[71]

Meltzer (49) tests all three of these variables in loglinear equations that specify both $M1$ and $M2$ as dependent variables and which include the yield on corporate bonds as the measure of the interest rate. Meltzer's basic model proposes nonhuman wealth (W) as the relevant constraint on money demand. He finds the elasticity of "narrow" money ($M1$) with respect to this measure of wealth to be close to unity. This contrasts with Friedman's finding (reported above) of an elasticity of "broad" money balances with respect to permanent income ("total" wealth) of 1.8.

Meltzer attempts to reconcile these results. His findings, which are confirmed by those of Laidler, suggest that Friedman's use of "broad" money as the dependent variable in his equation and the absence of an interest rate term from that equation are responsible for his very high estimate of this parameter. Meltzer contends that it is time deposits which are highly elastic with respect to wealth and that by including these deposits in his measure of "money" Friedman has overstated the wealth elasticity of money defined as ($DD + C$). More importantly, Meltzer claims that his measure of nonhuman wealth produces an empirical money demand function which explains a slightly higher proportion of the variance of money balances defined either as $M1$ or $M2$ than does Friedman's permanent income measure.[72]

[70]Meltzer, *op. cit.*, p. 232.

[71]Permanent income may be interpreted as "reflecting the effect of those factors that the unit regards as determining its capital value or wealth: the nonhuman wealth it owns; the personal attributes of the earners in the unit, such as their training, ability, personality; the attributes of the economic activity of the earners, such as the occupation followed, the location of the economic activity, and so on. It is analogous to the "expected" value of a probability distribution." M. Friedman, *A Theory of the Consumption Function*, *op. cit.*, p. 21.

[72]Meltzer's basic "wealth" definition includes "total wealth" as estimated by Goldsmith, adjusted to exclude government securities, inventories, public land, and the monetary gold and silver stock and to include the monetary and nonmonetary debt of state, local, and federal governments. R. W. Goldsmith, *A Study of Savings in the United States* (Princeton, N.J., 1956).

Meltzer also finds his wealth measure "superior" to current income in the empirical demand for money function; for when both wealth and income are included in the equation, the income variable appears to play no significant role in explaining the variation in money balances, whereas the wealth variable maintains approximately the same size coefficient (and significance) in all tests. Thus, Meltzer concludes that a nonhuman wealth measure is slightly superior to Friedman's permanent income variable and far more important than current, measured income in explaining variations in the demand for money.

These results are supported in further tests carried out by Brunner and Meltzer (5). Their experiments involved comparisons of the predictions of measured velocity made from various formulations of the money demand function. In their words,

> ... the tests sharply discriminate between the effects of income and wealth on the demand for money. ... income appears to play a much smaller role than wealth as a determinant of desired money balances. The evidence from a number of Keynesian-type equations that take income as a constraint and ignore the effect of wealth suggests that, in general, such equations will not predict velocity or desired money balances as well as a "naive" model.[73]

Their tests on human versus nonhuman wealth measures as explanatory variables in the money demand function yield less certain results. They conclude that the relative importance of these two measures remains an "open question" in their work.

Further evidence has been put forward by Heller (30), Laidler (40), Chow (11), and Goldfeld (24). Employing quarterly data for the postwar period, Heller calculates regression coefficients for six alternative relations. Both $M1$ and $M2$ are specified as dependent variables in equations that include income and the short-term rate of interest, wealth and the short-term rate, or both income and wealth and the short-term rate as explanatory variables. The coefficients of both GNP and wealth are statistically significant in all equations in which only one of these variables appears with the short-term interest rate. However, when both of these constraints are included in the same equation, only one of them retains its significance: GNP in the $M1$ equation and wealth in the $M2$ equation.

Heller attributes this result to the fact that time deposits (included in the $M2$ measure) are related positively to wealth and negatively to income. A negative income coefficient results when time deposits are regressed against both income and wealth in a single equation. This indicates a substitution effect between time deposits and demand deposits: i.e., with wealth constant an increase in GNP will cause a fall in the volume of time deposits and a rise in the quantity of currency and demand deposits. Heller interprets this evidence as showing that time deposits and demand deposits are demanded for different reasons: "the transactions motives for cash and demand deposits and the speculative or precautionary motive for time deposits."[74]

---

[73]Brunner and Meltzer, *op. cit.*, p. 350. The "naive" model referred to by the authors is a model that assumes that velocity in any one year will be the same as actual velocity in the previous period.

[74]Heller, *op. cit.*, p. 300.

The results of tests such as those conducted by Heller appear to be quite sensitive to the quarterly time frame in which the data are measured. Sharply contrasting results are derived from annual data. For example, Laidler set out to compare the explanatory power of four alternative money demand hypotheses. These include (1) the textbook equation with current income and an interest rate as constraints, (2) a Friedman-type permanent income formulation, (3) a model that includes permanent income as a proxy for the volume of transactions and a measure of accumulated transitory income and negative transitory consumption to account for the allocation of funds from these sources to money balances, and (4) a model that includes the last factor specified above and a nonhuman wealth measure defined as accumulated savings out of permanent income.

Implicit in Laidler's tests of these hypotheses is a comparison of the explanatory power of current income, permanent income, and his indirect measure of nonhuman wealth (accumulated savings out of Y_p) as explanatory variables in the money demand function. From his regressions, which employ first differences of annual observations, Laidler finds that "though the results are not absolutely decisive, they strongly suggest that permanent income provides a better theory of the demand for money than does either nonhuman wealth or any other set of variables tested."[75]

Laidler's third hypothesis, which includes a measure of transitory income in the money demand equation, performs the least satisfactorily over the period covered by his data. Although both the nonhuman wealth (4) and the permanent income (2) hypotheses explain the variation in the dependent variable quite satisfactorily, Laidler judges the results with permanent income to be marginally superior. More importantly, both wealth and permanent income explain more of the variation in the dependent variable than does current income (1) hypothesis. Furthermore, this last finding obtains regardless of the definition of money employed. Thus, using annual data rather than quarterly figures, Laidler challengers Heller's assertion that current income is the relevant constraint on narrow money balances.

An interesting set of experiments performed by Gregory Chow may shed some light on the apparent inconsistencies in these results. Chow attempts to isolate two different sets of factors influencing money holdings: those that determine the long-run equilibrium demand for money and those that influence the rate at which people will make short-run adjustments to restore equilibrium. These adjustments take place when a discrepancy exists between the long-run desired level of money balances and actual money holdings.

Chow reasons that money may be treated as a consumer durable good. He applies to the analysis of the demand for money a model originally developed to explain the demand for automobiles. In this model the long-run demand for money is posited to depend on some measure of the individual's total assets (a wealth measure) and the opportunity cost of holding those balances, the interest rate. The short-run demand for money, however, will depend on the rate at which individuals try to adjust their

[75]D. Laidler, "Some Evidence on the Demand for Money," *Journal of Political Economy,* 74 (February 1966), p. 63.

actual money balances to this long-run desired level. This speed of adjustment in turn depends on the actual size of any discrepancy between actual and desired balances and the rate of change of the individual's total assets (or the rate of savings)— the source from which money balances may be accumulated. Chow summarizes these factors as follows:

> Three sets of factors govern the demand for money. The first set is derived from considering the demand for services from holding money in the long-run. The second is due to time lags in the adjustment of demand to equilibrium. The third is from treating the change in the money stock as a part of saving.[76]

This model reflects both the expectational factors and partial adjustment mechanism described in the second section of this survey.

Like Laidler, Chow tests his hypothesis on annual data. The period covered is 1897-1958. In the long-run equilibrium demand function permanent income always performs far better than current income but, as in Laidler's work, only marginally better than a wealth measure.[77] However, in the short-run functions that attempt to measure the speed of adjustment to equilibrium current income is preferable to either wealth or permanent income.

A word of caution is in order in interpreting these estimates. The use of permanent income as the constraint variable determining the long-run desired level of money balances muddies the results. Permanent income is calculated as a weighted average of past levels of measured income. Consequently, the long-run demand for money function that employs this variable may be written as follows (ignoring interest rates):

$$\left(\frac{M_d}{P}\right)_T = f(Y_p) = b(Y_p)_T = b[\beta_0 \ Y_T + \beta_1 \ Y_{T-1} \ldots \beta_n \ Y_{T-n}].$$

Assuming the weights, β_i, follow a geometrically declining lag function (following Friedman), we may write

$$\left(\frac{M_d}{P}\right)_T = b[\beta_0 \ Y_T + \beta_0 \ (1 - \beta_0) \ Y_{T-1}$$
$$+ \ \beta_0 \ (1 - \beta_0)^2 \ Y_{T-2} \ldots \beta_0 \ (1 - \beta_0)^n \ Y_{T-n}).$$

But if $(1 - \beta_0)^j \to 0$ as $j \to n$, by a Koyck transformation,[78] this can be shown equivalent to

$$\left(\frac{M_d}{P}\right)_T = (1 - \beta_0) \left(\frac{M_d}{P}\right)_{T-1} + b\beta_0 Y_T. \tag{16}$$

[76]Gregory Chow, "On the Short-Run and Long-Run Demand for Money," *Journal of Political Economy,* 74 (April 1966), p. 115.

[77]Chow uses the same measure of net nonhuman wealth as was employed by Meltzer.

[78]The third section of this article explains the Koyck transformation. See also R. J. Wonnacott and T. H. Wonnacot, *Econometrics* (New York; 1970), pp. 145-146.

On the other hand, if the public only partially adjusts its current money holdings to the long-run desired level and this desired level depends on *current measured income*, the following may be specified to describe this behavior:

$$\left(\frac{M}{P}\right)_T - \left(\frac{M}{P}\right)_{T-1} = \lambda \left[\left(\frac{M}{P}\right)_T^* - \left(\frac{M}{P}\right)_{T-1} \right]$$

where $(M/P)_T^*$ is the desired level of money balances and

$$\left(\frac{M}{P}\right)_T^* = a\, Y_r$$

Substituting:

$$\left(\frac{M}{P}\right)_T - \left(\frac{M}{P}\right)_{T-1} = \lambda \left[a\, Y_T - \left(\frac{M}{P}\right)_{T-1} \right]$$

$$\left(\frac{M}{P}\right)_T = (1 - \lambda)\left(\frac{M}{P}\right)_{T-1} + \lambda a\, Y_T. \tag{17}$$

But this form (17), derived from a partial adjustment model in which desired money balances depend on current measured income, is indistinguishable from equation (16), which postulates that the demand for money depends on permanent income.

These relationships make unique interpretation of Chow's results impossible. They suggest that in his short-run adjustment relation, from which he concludes that current income is the appropriate explanatory variable in the demand for money function, he may simply have been measuring an equilibrium relation between desired money balances and permanent income. In short, this test is not sufficient to distinguish between a permanent income hypothesis and the hypothesis that the demand for money balances depends on current measured income but that the public is slow to adjust to its long-run desired level.

However, if there is any validity to Chow's results, they suggest a possible reconciliation of the conflict between those obtained by Heller using quarterly data and those presented by Laidler based on annual data. Heller's method may have picked up the influence of short-run adjustment factors which dominate the quarterly figures, but are less important in the longer-run annual observations.

Additional evidence using quarterly data is presented by Goldfeld (25). Within the framework of his basic log-linear model—which includes a lagged dependent variable (derived from a partial adjustment hypothesis) and both the commercial paper rate and the rate on bank time deposits—he compares the relative power of income, net worth, and changes in net worth in explaining holdings of narrow money. His results show that the absence of an income variable reduces the estimated speed of adjustment to an unreasonably low figure. When income and wealth are both included, the latter is insignificant while the former remains important. When the change in wealth is added as a third constraint, "the level effect of net worth is obliterated."[79]

The comparative predictive ability of Goldfeld's wealth equation in dynamic simulations is far inferior to that of his original income-only equation. In addition, though the inclusion of the change in net worth variable "improves the explanatory power of the equation, [it] slightly worsens its predictive ability."[80]

In summary, the bulk of the evidence available from studies employing annual data indicates rather clearly that some measure of wealth rather than measured income is the most relevant constraint on the equilibrium level of the demand for money balances. Whether this constraint is best represented by a permanent income measure that purports to include a human wealth component or by a nonhuman wealth measure, such as those employed by Chow or Meltzer, is much less apparent. At the same time, other evidence certainly suggests that current income may be related to the demand for money through short-run adjustments made to bring *actual* money balances in line with *desired* money holdings. Unfortunately, measurement difficulties with quarterly wealth data make the results of tests employing these measures difficult to interpret. However, this in turn suggests that for pragmatic policy purposes one may wish to choose that variable that performs best when the criteria chosen is predictive and forecasting accuracy. On these grounds, current income, as suggested by Goldfeld's results, is probably the most useful scale factor to employ in short-run money demand functions.

The Stability of the Money Demand Function

Harry Johnson, in his 1962 survey of monetary theory (32), listed three unsettled issues related to the demand for money. These issues included the appropriate empirical definition of money, the choice of arguments to be included in the money demand function, and the stability of the empirical relationship between those arguments and the monetary aggregate. These are not, of course, separable issues. The stability of any empirical function will depend upon the variables included in that function. Likewise, the criteria for choosing the appropriate definition of money has most often been defined in terms of the stability of the demand function for that monetary measure. However, for heuristic purposes, we have attempted to separate these issues in the empirical literature. It is hoped that by this point in the survey the major areas of agreement and of continuing contention on the first two issues have become evident.

[79]Goldfeld, *op. cit.,* p. 614
[80]*Ibid.,* p. 615.

It should be clear, however, that there has been an underlying assumption throughout this discussion that we were in fact dealing with stable relationships. While the diversity of functional forms and data periods employed by the various authors cited has made more difficult the task of reconciling divergent results, the similarity of elasticity estimates over these wide ranging studies would seem to support the essential validity of this assumption. It is worthwhile, however, briefly to consider this stability issue more explicitly.

One serious attack on the apparent stability of postwar money demand functions was presented by William Poole (54). Employing a log-linear money demand function similar to equation (3) above, Poole estimated interest elasticities of real money balances by constraining the values of the income elasticities within a range 0.5 to 3.0. Employing quarterly data for 1947–1969, his results demonstrate a *direct* relation between the constrained income elasticity and the estimated interest elasticity. More importantly, he finds that "the goodness of fit is practically unchanged over an extremely wide range of income elasticities," implying that there is insufficient information in the statistics to permit a choice among these results. On this evidence he makes the very strong assertion that "using postwar data alone, it is impossible to obtain a satisfactory estimate of the demand for money function."[81]

Goldfeld (24) has taken up this issue and persuasively countered Poole's critique. Employing an equation similar to the one specified by Poole but including a lagged dependent variable, he finds that "the interest elasticities display a clear tendency to increase with [the constrained income elasticity] but the rise is not nearly as pronounced as Poole found."[82] While Goldfeld also finds uniformly high R^2's for the various forms of the equations, he claims that this is misleading and convincingly demonstrates this by additional testing on these equations.

Though the R^2's are uniformly high for all equations, they tend to rise slightly with the constrained value of the income elasticity. However, this statistic is not strictly comparable across equations and cannot be used alone as a selection criterion. Goldfeld demonstrates this by constraining the income elasticity to the value first derived in an unconstrained form of the same equation. The constrained form reproduces the results of the unconstrained form except for the R^2, indicating the noncomparability of the R^2's resulting from the use of different dependent variables.[83]

However, there may still be a statistical means by which to choose among these equations. Goldfeld first examines the standard error of the regression and finds it lowest, as it must be, for the value derived from the unconstrained form. He then evaluates the equations by examining the root mean-square error derived from two

---

[81]W. Poole, "Whither Money Demand?" *Brookings Papers on Economic Activity* (3: 1970), pp. 489. Poole's final conclusion is not that we must give up on money demand functions, but rather that since postwar data are unreliable, additional weight must be given to long-run estimates.

[82]Goldfeld, *op. cit.,* p. 585.

[83]The dependent variable is ($ln\ M_T - e\ ln\ Y_T$), where e is the constrained income elasticity. This variable will differ, of course, for each assumed value of the elasticity constraint.

different types of dynamic simulations on the estimated equations. As he notes, this is a more stringent test of the estimation results and is likely to be more relevant from a forecasting point of view. His results show clearly that the root mean-square errors deteriorate even more rapidly than the standard error of the regression as elasticity values diverge further from the value estimated in the unconstrained equation. He concludes, then, that Poole's rejection of estimates derived from postwar data is unwarranted and that the "income elasticity can be pinned down within a reasonable range of accuracy."[84] The estimate that he derives is 0.68, significantly less than unity and consistent with the proposition that there are economics of scale in holding money balances.

Additional dynamic simulations on his basic equation convince Goldfeld that the relationship underlying his empirical estimates has remained rather stable in the postwar period. Both short-term (out of sample) forecasts four quarters ahead of various defined subsamples of the data period and longer-term simulations over a later part of the sample period based on estimates for an earlier subperiod, suggest reasonable stability. A formal Chow test of stability, carried out by splitting the data sample into two subperiods suggested by the major institutional change brought about by the introduction of certificates of deposits (CD's) in 1961, also fails to deliver evidence upon which to reject the hypothesis of stability.[85]

The evidence on the postwar stability of the money demand relation generally conforms to the results of work that has examined the issue over longer periods with annual data. The work by Brunner and Meltzer (9), Meltzer (49), Laidler (44), and other authors cited directly supports this long-run stability. Recent work by Moshin S. Khan, using a new and more flexible technique to determine whether a regression estimate is stable over a full sample period, adds to the weight of evidence in favor of this conclusion. Using either current income or permanent income along with a long-term rate of interest, his tests over the period 1901–1965 fail to offer any support for the hypothesis that there were significant structural shifts in the money demand relations over that period.[86]

One final piece of evidence is worth citing on this issue. In 1971, both within and outside of the Federal Reserve, it was fairly widely held that, regardless of the historical stability of the money demand function, a substantial shift had occurred in the early part of that year. Even the Council of Economic Advisers in the *Economic Report to the President* in 1972 expressed this view: "In the first half of 1971, the public apparently wanted to hold more money balances at the prevailing level of

---

[84]Goldfeld, *op. cit.*, p. 589.

[85]For an alternative view of the effect of the creation of the CD market see M. B. Slovin and M. E. Sushka, *"A Financial Market Approach to the Demand for Money and the Implications for Monetary Policy,"* Board of Governors of the Federal Reserve System (1972), manuscript.

[86]Kahn's tests with the short-term rate suggest some instability in the relationship around 1948. This instability appears whether money is defined narrowly or broadly. In this respect Kahn's results conflict with Laidler's conclusion that the most stable demand function is one that includes the short-term rate as an explanatory variable. See M. S. Khan, "The Stability of the Demand for Money Function in the United States, 1901-1965," International Monetary Fund (July 1974).

interest rates and income than past relations among income, interest rates, and money balances suggested."[87]

Hamburger (29) has examined this view in the light of more recent evidence. Fortunately for the conclusions reached in the studies cited above, but unfortunately for our judgment on the ability of monetary economists to recognize short-run fluctuations in money demand, this recent evidence fails to confirm the instability widely assumed over that period.

In the second quarter of 1971 in the face of an increase in interest rates and a decline in the rate of growth of income, contrary to what conventional theory would predict, there was a sharp *increase* in the growth of the narrow money stock. But there is a certain weakness in conventional theory in its simplest form in that it fails to consider delayed reactions ("adjustments") to previous income and interest rate changes. Hamburger suggests that within the framework of the FRB-MIT-PENN Model, once allowance is made for such lagged adjustments even "the evidence that was available in 1971 provided only marginal support for the hypothesis that there was an upward shift in the demand for money" at that time.[88] On the basis of results obtained with more recent versions of the model that incorporate the influence of inflation on money demand, even that marginal support disappears. Perhaps more disturbing, equations developed since that time to explain month-to-month changes in *M*1 have no difficulty "explaining the rapid growth of *M*1 during the second quarter of 1971 *with relationships derived from earlier periods*" (emphasis added).[89]

This episode is reviewed here to point out a continuing dilemma facing policy makers. While it can be shown that the existence of a stable demand for money function is necessary for the conduct of effective monetary policy and while it is widely accepted, on the basis of the evidence surveyed here, that this condition has been met over a long period in the United States, it is another matter entirely for policy makers and their advisers "to make reasonably accurate on-the-spot judgments as to whether changes in the demand for money are occurring at particular points in time."[90] At this point the science of the economist becomes partner to the artistry of the policy maker.

Concluding Comment

The first and most important result of this survey is that the evidence supporting the existence of a reasonably stable demand for money function would seem to be overwhelming. This is true both of long-term evidence covering the last seventy years or so and of the evidence from the postwar period. Second, and perhaps next in importance for the conduct of monetary policy, the vast majority of this same evidence

[87]Council of Economic Advisers, *Economic Report to the President* (January 1972), p. 58.
[88]M. J. Hamburger, "The Demand for Money in 1971 . . . ," *op. cit.*, p. 721.
[89]*Ibid.*, p. 723.
[90]*Ibid.*, p. 724.

supports the hypothesis that the interest rate plays a significant role in the determination of the public's desired money holdings. Furthermore, the range of estimates for the interest elasticity of money balances has been fairly narrowly circumscribed, with the best results suggesting an elasticity of about − 0.2 for the short rate and approximately − 0.7 for the long rate. Unfortunately, it is not yet possible to state confidently which particular interest rate measure yields the most stable money demand relationship. Moreover, this question is so intimately connected with the problem of the "correct" definition of money that judgment must be suspended on this issue pending additional work, including work on the term structure of interest rates.

Third, there appears to be almost no support for the liquidity-trap hypothesis.

Finally, the best evidence to date suggests that, in addition to an interest rate measure, some measure of wealth—either a direct balance sheet measure or a proxy variable such as permanent income—would seem to be most relevant to the public's long-run decision to hold money balances. However, there is a growing body of evidence that short-run movements in money balances, determined by the speed at which people adjust their actual money holdings to a long-run equilibrium level, may be dependent upon the flow of income in this period and in the recent past.

These conclusions rest primarily on the evidence cited in this study. Other important works, many of which are included in the References, could also have been used to support some of these conclusions. The studies reviewed were selected because of their historical importance in the debate on the issues to which we have directed our attention or because they represent the best starting point for students of these problems. In short, no claim is made that this survey, in spite of its length, represents an exhaustive review of all of the literature in this field.

REFERENCES

1. BARRO, ROBERT J., "Inflation, the Payments Period, and the Demand for Money," *Journal of Political Economy,* 78 (November/December 1970), pp. 1228-1263.
2. ———, and ANTHONY M. SANTOMERO, "Household Money Holdings and the Demand Deposit Rate," *Journal of Money, Credit, and Banking,* 4 (May 1972), pp. 397-413.
3. BAUMOL, W., "The Transactions Demand for Cash: An Inventory Theoretic Approach," *Quarterly Journal of Economics, 66* (November 1952), pp. 545-556.
4. BRONFENBRENNER, MARTIN, and THOMAS MAYER, "Liquidity Functions in the American Economy," *Econometrica,* 28 (October 1960), pp. 810-834.
5. BRUNNER, KARL, and ALLAN H. MELTZER, "Predicting Velocity: Implications for Theory and Policy," *Journal of Finance,* 18 (May 1963), pp. 319-354.
6. ———, "Some Further Evidence on Supply and Demand Functions for Money," *Journal of Finance,* 19 (May 1964), pp. 240-283.
7. ———, "Economics of Scale in Cash Balances Reconsidered," *Quarterly Journal of Economics,* 81 (August 1967), pp. 422-436.
8. ———, "Liquidity Traps for Money, Bank Credit, and Interest Rates," *Journal of Political Economy,* 76 (February 1968), pp. 1-37.

9. ———, "Comment on the Long-Run and Short-Run Demand for Money," *Journal of Political Economy,* 76 (November/December 1968), pp. 1234–1239.

10. CHETTY, V. K., "On Measuring the Nearness of Near-Moneys," *American Economic Review,* 59 (June 1969), pp. 270–281.

11. CHOW, GREGORY, "On the Short-Run and Long-Run Demand for Money," *Journal of Political Economy,* 74 (April 1966), pp. 111–131.

12. ———, "Long-Run and Short-Run Demand for Money: Reply and Further Notes," *Journal of Political Economy,* 76 (November/December 1968), pp. 1240–1243.

13. DICKSON, HAROLD D., and DENNIS R. STARLEAF, "Polynomial Distributed Lag Structures in the Demand Function for Money," *Journal of Finance,* 27 (December 1972), pp. 1035–1043.

14. EISNER, ROBERT, "Another Look at Liquidity Preference," *Econometrica,* 31 (July 1963), pp. 531–538.

15. FEIGE, EDGAR, *The Demand for Liquid Assets: A Temporal Cross Section Analysis.* Englewood Cliffs Company, 1964.

16. ———, "Expectations and Adjustments in the Monetary Sector," *American Economic Review,* 57 (May 1967), pp. 462–473.

17. FRIEDMAN, MILTON, *A Theory of the Consumption Function.* Princeton: Princeton University Press, 1957.

18. ———, "The Quantity Theory of Money, A Restatement," in Milton Friedman (ed.), *Studies in the Quantity Theory of Money.* Chicago: University of Chicago Press, 1956.

19. ———, "The Demand for Money—Some Theoretical and Empirical Results," *Journal of Political Economy,* 67 (June 1959), pp. 327–351.

20. ———, and ANNA J. SCHWARTZ, *A Monetary History of the United States, 1867–1960.* Princeton: National Bureau of Economic Research, 1963.

21. ———, and DAVID MEISELMAN, "Relative Stability of Monetary Velocity and the Investment Multiplier in the United States 1897–1957," in Commission on Money and Credit, *Stabilization Policies,* Englewood Cliffs, N.J., Prentice-Hall, 1963.

22. GALPER, HARVEY, "Alternative Interest Rates and the Demand for Money: Comment," *American Economic Review,* 59 (June 1969), pp. 401–407.

23. GOLDFELD, STEPHEN, *Commercial Bank Behavior and Economic Activity.* Amsterdam: North-Holland Publishing Company, 1966.

24. ———, "The Demand for Money Revisited," *Brookings Papers on Economic Activity* (3:1973), pp. 577–638.

25. GRILICHES, ZVI., "Distributed Lags: A Survey," *Econometrica,* 35 (January 1967), pp. 16–49.

26. GURLEY, JOHN G., and EDWARD S. SHAW, *Money in a Theory of Finance.* Washington, D.C.: The Brookings Institution, 1960.

27. HAMBURGER, MICHAEL J., "The Demand for Money by Households, Money Substitutes, and Monetary Policy," *Journal of Political Economy,* 74 (December 1966), pp. 600–623.

28. ———, "Alternative Interest Rates and the Demand for Money: Comment," *American Economic Review,* 59 (June 1969), pp. 407–412.

29. ———, "The Demand for Money in 1971: Was There a Shift? A Comment," *Journal of Money, Credit, and Banking,* 5 (May 1973), pp. 720–725.

30. HELLER, H. R., "The Demand for Money—The Evidence from the Short-Run Data," *Quarterly Journal of Economics,* 79 (June 1965), pp. 291-303.

31. JAFFEE, DWIGHT M., "The Structure of the Money-Expenditure Relationship: Comment," *American Economic Review,* 60 (March 1970), pp. 216-219.

32. JOHNSON, HARRY G., "Monetary Theory and Policy," *American Economic Review,* 52 (June 1962), pp. 335-384.

33. JONES, DAVID, "The Demand for Money: A Review of the Empirical Literature," Staff Economic Studies of the Federal Reserve System, paper presented to the Federal Reserve System Committee on Financial Analysis in St. Louis (October 1965).

34. KAMINOW, I. P., "The Household Demand for Money: An Empirical Study," *Journal of Finance,* 24 (September 1969), pp. 679-696.

35. KARNI, EDI, "The Value of Time and the Demand for Money," *Journal of Money, Credit, and Banking,* 6 (February 1974), pp. 45-64.

36. KAUFMAN, GEORGE G., "More on an Empirical Definition of Money," *American Economic Review,* 59 (March 1969), pp. 78-87.

37. KEYNES, JOHN MAYNARD, *The General Theory of Employment, Interest, and Money.* London and New York: Harcourt, Brace and Company, 1936.

38. KONSTAS, PANOS, and MOHAMAD W. KHOUJA, "The Keynesian Demand-for-Money Function: Another Look and Some Additional Evidence," *Journal of Money, Credit and Banking,* 1 (November 1969), pp. 765-777.

39. LAFFER, ARTHUR B., "Trade Credit and the Money Market," *Journal of Political Economy,* 78 (March/April 1970), pp. 239-267.

40. LAIDLER, DAVID, "Some Evidence on the Demand for Money," *Journal of Political Economy,* 74 (February 1966), pp. 55-68.

41. ———, "The Rate of Interest and the Demand for Money—Some Empirical Evidence," *Journal of Political Economy,* 74 (December 1966), pp. 545-555.

42. ———, *The Demand for Money: Theories and Evidence.* Scranton: International Textbook Company, 1969.

43. ———, "The Definition of Money: Theoretical and Empirical Problems," *Journal of Money, Credit and Banking,* 1 (August 1969), pp. 509-525.

44. ———, "A Survey of Some Current Problems," in G. Clayton, J. C. Gilbert, and R. Sidgewick (eds.), *Monetary Theory and Monetary Policy in the 1970's.* New York: Oxford University Press, 1971.

45. LATANÉ, HENRY A., "Cash Balances and the Interest Rate—A Pragmatic Approach," *Review of Economics and Statistics,* 36 (November 1954), pp. 456-460.

46. LEE, T. H., "Alternative Interest Rates and the Demand for Money: The Empirical Evidence," *American Economic Review,* 57 (December 1967), pp. 1168-1181.

47. DE LEEUW, FRANK, "A Model of Financial Behavior," in James Duesenberry, Gary Fromm, Lawrence Klein, and Edwin Kuh (eds.), *The Brookings Quarterly Econometric Model of the United States.* Chicago: Rand McNally and Company, 1965, pp. 464-530.

48. LYDALL, HAROLD, "Income, Assets, and the Demand for Money," *Review of Economics and Statistics,* 40 (February 1958), pp. 1-14.

49. MELTZER, ALLAN H., "The Demand for Money: The Evidence from the Time Series," *Journal of Political Economy,* 71 (June 1963), pp. 219-246.

50. ———, "The Demand for Money: A Cross Section Study of Business Firms," *Quarterly Journal of Economics,* 77 (August 1963), pp. 405-422.

51. OCHS, J., "The Transaction Demand for Money and Choices Involving Risk," *Journal of Political Economy,* 76 (March/April 1968), pp. 289-291.

52. PATINKIN, DON, "The Chicago Tradition, The Quantity Theory and Friedman," *Journal of Money, Credit and Banking,* 1 (February 1969), pp. 46-70.

53. PELTZMAN, SAM, "The Structure of the Money Expenditure Relationship," *American Economic Review,* 59 (March 1969), pp. 129-137.

54. POOLE, WILLIAM, "Whither Money Demand?" *Brookings Papers on Economic Activity* (3:1970), pp. 485-500.

55. SANTOMERO, ANTHONY M., "A Model of the Demand for Money By Households," *Journal of Finance,* 29 (March, 1974), pp. 89-102.

56. SCHADRACK, FREDERICK C., An Empirical Approach to the Definition of Money," *Monetary Aggregates and Monetary Policy,* Federal Reserve Bank of New York, (1974), pp. 28-34.

57. SHAPIRO, A. A., "Inflation, Lags, and the Demand for Money," *International Economic Review,* 16 (February 1975), pp. 81-96.

58. SHAPIRO, HAROLD, "Distributed Lags, Interest Rate Expectations and the Impact of Monetary Policy: An Econometric Analysis of a Canadian Experience," *American Economic Review,* 57 (May 1967), pp. 444-461.

59. SLOVIN, M. B., and M. E. SUSHKA, "A Financial Market Approach to the Demand for Money and the Implications for Monetary Policy," Board of Governors, Federal Reserve (1972), manuscript.

60. STARLEAF, DENNIS R., and RICHARD REIMER, "The Keynesian Demand Function for Money: Some Statistical Tests," *Journal of Finance,* 22 (March 1967), pp. 71-76.

61. TEIGEN, RONALD, "Demand and Supply Functions for Money in the United States, Some Structural Estimates," *Econometrica,* 32 (October 1964), pp. 477-509.

62. ———, "An Aggregated Quarterly Model of the U.S. Monetary Sector, 1953-1964," unpublished manuscript presented to the Conference on Targets and Indicators of Monetary Policy, University of California at Los Angeles (April 1966).

63. TOBIN, JAMES, "Liquidity Preference and Monetary Policy," *Review of Economics and Statistics,* 29 (May 1947), pp. 124-131.

64. ———, "The Interest Elasticity of Transaction Demand for Cash," *Review of Economics and Statistics,* 38 (August 1956), pp. 241-247.

65. ———, "Liquidity Preference as Behavior Towards Risk," *Review of Economic Studies,* 25 (February 1958), pp. 65-86.

66. TAYLOR, L. D., and J. P. NEWHOUSE, "On the Long-Run and Short-Run Demand for Money: A Comment," *Journal of Political Economy,* 77 (September/October 1969), pp. 851-856.

67. TSIANG, S. C., "The Precautionary Demand for Money: An Inventory Theoretical Analysis," *Journal of Political Economy,* 77 (January/February 1969), pp. 99-117.

68. TURNOVSKY, STEPHEN J., "The Demand for Money and the Determination of the Rate of Interest Under Uncertainty," *Journal of Money, Credit and Banking,* 3 (May 1971), pp. 183-204.

69. WALTERS, ALAN A., "The Demand for Money-The Dynamic Properties of the Multiplier," *Journal of Political Economy,* 75 (June 1967), pp. 293-298.

70. WHALEN, EDWARD L., "A Cross-Section Study of Business Demand for Cash," *Journal of Finance,* 20 (September 1965), pp. 423-443.

71. ZAREMBKA, P., "Functional Form in the Demand for Money," *Journal of the American Statistical Association,* 63 (June 1968), pp. 502-511.

Portfolio Theory

Thomas M. Havrilesky
John T. Boorman

. . . The basic premise in all portfolio theory is that the return or yield from an asset (or liability) in a portfolio cannot be known in advance with certainty. The best one can expect is that various possible outcomes from holding specific assets can be delineated and that a likelihood or probability can be associated with each of these outcomes. This, again, is simply to say that the yield cannot be predicted with certainty. Rather the yield itself is a random variable and the outcome of the investment process can be described only in terms of probability distributions.

One can gain considerable insight into empirical and theoretical work in portfolio analysis with knowledge of only a few fundamental concepts. Basically these are the statistical properties of a distribution of random outcomes: (1) the expected return of the portfolio and its components, (2) the variability of the expected return of a portfolio—an indicator of risk, and (3) the extent to which the expected returns to the component assets of a portfolio move together. A minimum knowledge of these concepts is necessary for further work in this area. Three standard statistical measures are used extensively to reflect these concepts. These are (1) the arithmetic mean or *expected value,* (2) the *variance* or the square root of the variance, the standard deviation, and (3) the *covariance* and the *coefficient of correlation* between two series. Let us begin by defining these concepts more precisely.

Reprinted, with deletions, from *Monetary Macroeconomics* (Arlington Heights, Ill.: AHM Publishing Corp., 1978), pp. 129–145, by permission of the publisher.

When an experiment is performed in which the result, represented by a numerical quantity, will depend upon chance, the experiment may be referred to as a *random* experiment and the result a random quantity. The throwing of a six-sided die is an obvious example of such an experiment. A *random variable* may then be defined as a function which relates some numerical quantity to each possible event or outcome that could occur in a random experiment. In the case of investment in a financial asset in which the possible outcomes of the investment experiment (holding the asset for a particular period of time) are themselves numerical (percentage yields or dollar returns) the random variable may be viewed as the listing of all possible numerical outcomes of that experiment.

The random variable may by its very nature assume many different values. However, for investment purposes we often need to compare the potential results of holding different assets, each of whose yield is random. Consequently, we need some means of comparing random variables. We can do this through the associated *probability distributions*. The (probability) distribution of a random variable is simply a listing of all possible values that the random variable may assume and the associated probability of each of the outcomes which generate those values in the performance of the random experiment.[1] For example, in the die throwing experiment cited above, each of the integer values from 1 to 6 associated with the outcome of the experiment may have a probability of $1/6$ associated with it.

In order to compare random variables, it is useful to be able to compare the properties of their probability distributions, most importantly, the means and variances of those distributions.

The *expected* (or *mean*) *value* of a (discrete) probability distribution is the sum of all values the random variable may assume, each weighted by its associated probability. If X is a random variable which can assume the values $x_1, x_2, \cdots, x_n$, each with an associated probability of $P(x_1), P(x_2), \cdots, P(x_n)$, then the expected value of X is

$$E(X) = \sum_{i=1}^{n} x_i \cdot P(x_i). \qquad (1)$$

While the expected value is a useful measure and serves, in one sense, to locate the "center" of a probability distribution, it tells us nothing about the spread of the values which the random variable may assume around that center. For example, if the age of a person picked at random from a "group" is the random variable, the expected value of the probability distribution of that random variable may be 20 years. However, the spread of the probability distribution or the variance of the values which may occur from picking a person at random will be very much different if we are picking from a "group" comprised of the entire population of the United States or from a group comprised solely of university students. The smaller the spread of a probability distribution around its central tendency or expected

---

[1]This definition is modified in the case of a continuous random variable which may theoretically assume any one of an infinite number of values. We assume here that the random variables describing the outcome of an investment "experiment" are discrete random variables, that is, random variables that may assume only a finite number of values.

value, the more confident one can be that, in the performance of a random experiment characterized by that probability distribution, the result will, in some sense, be "close to" that central tendency. In the case of financial investment, for example, if the probability distribution of the holding period yield on an asset has a relatively small dispersion, one can predict with greater confidence that the actual yield will differ from the expected yield by less than some given amount than he could in the case of an asset whose random yield had a larger dispersion. For this reason, some measure of the spread or dispersion of the probability distribution of asset yields has been used extensively as a measure of risk.

The most commonly used measure of dispersion is the variance. The *variance σ^2* of a probability distribution is measured as the sum of the squared deviation between each value the random variable may assume and the mean of that random variable weighted by the associated probability of that value; that is,

$$\sigma^2 = \sum_{i=1}^{n} (x_i - E(X))^2 \cdot P(x_i). \tag{2}$$

An additional useful measure is the square root of the variance, referred to as the standard deviation.

Probability distributions, such as those characterizing the return on investment in specific assets, may be compared by use of the expected value and the variance. However, the relation between the outcome of two random experiments may also be of interest. For example, an expected acceleration in the rate of inflation which would cause the outcome of the holding of a particular asset, such as land, to be relatively high may also lead to a relatively high yield on some other asset, such as agricultural commodities. In such a case, repeated experiments over time may indicate that *relatively* high (above expected value) values of one random variable tend to occur at the same time as *relatively* high values of some other random variable. In this case, the random variables would be said to be positively correlated or to have a positive covariance. The *covariance* between two random variables may be defined as the sum of the products of the deviation of each possible outcome of each of the random variables from their respective means, weighted by the (joint) probability of each pair of those values occurring together; that is, where x and y are random variables:

$$\text{cov}(X, Y) = \sum_{i=1}^{n} \sum_{j=1}^{n} [x_i - (Ex)][y_i - (Ey)] \cdot P(x_i y_j). \tag{3}$$

The *coefficient of correlation* is a related measure of similarity or dissimilarity in the behavior of two random variables,

$$\varrho_{zy} = \frac{\text{cov}_{xy}}{\sigma_x \sigma_y}. \tag{4}$$

This measures the covariance between two random variables, not as an absolute value but relative to the product of the standard deviations of the individual variables.

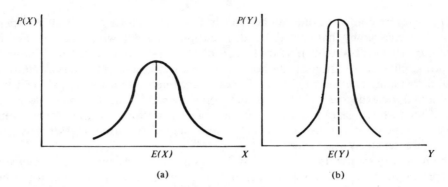

FIGURE 1. PROBABILITY DISTRIBUTIONS OF RANDOM VARIABLES *X* AND *Y*

These concepts can be illustrated graphically. Assume that there are two random variables *X* and *Y*. Their (probability) distributions are shown in Figure 1.[2] When the distribution is bell-shaped, as in Figure 1, it is often referred to as a *normal distribution*. This means, among other things, that the expected value and variance of the random variable are mathematically sufficient to completely specify the distribution. Assuming that *X* and *Y* are measured in the same units and that the same scale is depicted on the horizontal axes, in Figure 1 the expected value of *X*, *E(X)*, is greater than the expected value of *Y*, *E(Y)*. At the same time, the variance of *X* is considerably greater than the variance of *Y*. Finally, if it happens that relatively high values of *X* tend to be associated with relatively high (above mean) values of *Y* and relatively low values of *X* are associated with relatively low (below mean) values of *Y*, they are said to be positively correlated.

If one is working with *normal distributions*, then expected return and variance are the only statistical measures one need deal with. Unfortunately, few random variables in monetary and financial economics are going to have the smooth symmetry of the curves in Figure 1; today's sophisticated portfolio analysis does indeed consider abnormal distributions and their associated statistical measures.[3] However, the starting point of all work in portfolio theory confines the analysis to expected value as a measure of return and variance as a measure of risk.

The Expected Risk-Return Locus

One is generally concerned not solely with the return on any one particular asset, but rather with the return, and the variability of that return, on an entire portfolio consisting of more than one asset. The return on the portfolio will be denoted as the

[2]These random variables are pictured as having continuous distributions for simplicity's sake.
[3]See, for example, Bernell L. Stone, *Risk, Return and Equilibrium* (Cambridge: M.I.T. Press, 1970).

weighted sum of the returns on individual assets. The expected return on a portfolio consisting of two assets is[4]

$$E = x_1 E_1 + x_2 E_2 = x_1 E_1 + (1 - x_1)E_2 \qquad (5)$$

where x_1 is the (nonrandom) proportion of one's financial wealth held in the form of asset 1; x_2 is the (nonrandom) proportion of one's financial wealth held in the form of asset 2; and $x_1 + x_2 = 1$. E_1 is the expected return from asset 1 and E_2 is the expected return from asset 2. E_1 and E_2 are expressed as percentages.

The formula for the variance of the return on the portfolio is given as follows:[5]

$$\text{var } E = x_1^2 \text{ var } E_1 + 2x_1 x_2 \text{ cov}(E_1, E_2) + x_2^2 \text{ var } E_2$$

$$\sigma^2 = x_1^2 \sigma_1^2 + 2x_1 x_2 \, \varrho_{12} \, \sigma_1 \sigma_2 + x_2^2 \sigma_2^2$$

$$= x_1^2 \sigma_1^2 + 2x_1(1 - x_1) \, \varrho_{12} \sigma_1 \sigma_2 + (1 - x_1)^2 \sigma_2^2 \qquad (6)$$

where σ_1^2 is the variance of the return on asset 1 and σ_2^2 is the variance of the return on asset 2. The covariance must be included to reflect how variations in the return to asset 1 are offset or accentuated by variations in the return to asset 2 and vice versa. Equation 4 is substituted for $\text{cov}(E_1, E_2)$ in Equation 6.

Now in the case where the coefficient of correlation between the two returns is unity, $\varrho_{12} = 1$, Equation 6 yields

$$\sigma^2 = x_1^2 \sigma_1^2 + 2x_1(1 - x_1)\sigma_1 \sigma_2 + (1 - x_1)^2 \sigma_2^2$$

$$= [x_1 \sigma_1 + (1 - x_1)\sigma_2]^2. \qquad (7)$$

The square root of Equation 7 gives the standard deviation of the return on the portfolio:

$$\sigma = x_1 \sigma_1 + \sigma_2 - x_1 \sigma_2$$

$$= \sigma_2 + x_1(\sigma_1 - \sigma_2). \qquad (8)$$

Solving Equation 8 for x_1,

$$x_1 = \frac{\sigma - \sigma_2}{\sigma_1 - \sigma_2}$$

---

[4]This result derives from the fact that the expected value of a random variable (the return on the portfolio) defined as the sum of two or more random variables (the returns on individual assets) is equal to the sum of the expected values of those random variables.

[5]If a random variable is defined as a linear combination of two other random variables, for example, $Z = aX + bY$, where X and Y are random variables and a and b are constants, the variance of that random variable is given by the following:

$$\text{var } Z = a^2 \text{ var } X + b^2 \text{ var } Y + 2ab \text{ cov } (X, Y).$$

and substituting the result into Equation 5 yields

$$E = \left(\frac{\sigma - \sigma_2}{\sigma_1 - \sigma_2} \right)E_1 + E_2 - \left(\frac{\sigma - \sigma_2}{\sigma_1 - \sigma_2} \right)E_2$$

$$= E_2 - \sigma_2\left(\frac{E_1 - E_2}{\sigma_1 - \sigma_2}\right) + \left(\frac{E_1 - E_2}{\sigma_1 - \sigma_2}\right)\sigma, \qquad (9)$$

a linear function in (E, σ) space with constant term $E_2 - \sigma_2\left(\frac{E_1 - E_2}{\sigma_1 - \sigma_2}\right)$

and slope $\left(\frac{E_1 - E_2}{\sigma_1 - \sigma_2}\right)$.

The risk–expected return locus for this case is graphed in Figure 2. In common-sense terms, this line describes the tradeoff between risk and expected return when the expected returns on the two assets being considered always vary together in the same direction such that the correlation coefficient between them is positive and equal to unity. That is, whenever asset 1's return is below its average by a given number of standard deviations, the return on asset 2 is below its average by the same number of standard deviations; and whenever asset 1's return is above its average by a given number of standard deviations, the return on asset 2 is above its average by the same number of standard deviations.

If $\sigma_1 < \sigma_2$, it is seen from Equation 8 that minimum risk can be established where $x_1 = 1$ at point W. At this point by Equation 5 total expected return consists entirely of the expected return on asset 1, E_1, that is, if $x_1 = 1$, then $E = E_1 + E_2 - E_2 = E_1$. Total risk in Equation 8 consists entirely of the variation in the return of that asset, σ_1 (that is, if $x_1 = 1$, then $\sigma = \sigma_2 + \sigma_1 - \sigma_2 = \sigma_1$). (The extreme case of the least risky asset having a zero expected return and a zero risk is graphed in Figure 4.) As one diversifies the portfolio, that is, holds less of the less risky asset 1, the overall expected return rises because the more risky asset 2 will have a higher expected

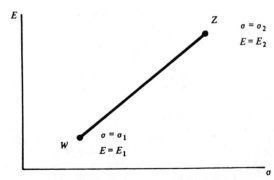

FIGURE 2. RISK-RETURN LOCUS WHERE TWO ASSETS ARE PERFECTLY CORRELATED

return in the market than the less risky one. At point Z the portfolio can become no riskier as it is exclusively devoted to the riskier asset 2, $x_2 = 1$.

$$E = 0 \cdot E_1 + E_2 - 0 \cdot E_1 = E_2 \qquad \text{and} \qquad \sigma = \sigma_2 + 0 \cdot (\sigma_1 - \sigma_2) = \sigma_2.$$

The preceding analysis may be clarified by an example of two assets with highly positively correlated returns. Two such assets might be long-term U.S. Treasury bonds and the long-term bonds of a typical highly rated industrial corporation. Their actual returns may move together (positively) very closely; the long-term government bond, however, has less risk, a lower variance, and, consequently, a lower expected return. If an investor confined his choice set to these two assets, a risk minimum could be realized by holding all financial wealth in long-term government bonds. A desire for higher expected return would require holding a larger proportion of riskier long-term industrial bonds.

This analysis suggests that if there existed a perfectly riskless asset that has a positive expected return (such as an FDIC-insured savings account), abstracting

Table 1. Relation between the Proportion Invested in Asset 1 and the Risk and Return of the Portfolio

Proportion of Portfolio Invested in Asset 1 X_1	Risk σ	Expected Return (in Percentages) E
1.0	10.0	30
.9	7.5	33
.8	5.0	36
.7	2.5	39
.6	0.0	42
.5	$(-)2.5$	45
.4	$(-)5.0$	48
.3	$(-)7.5$	51
.2	$(-)10.0$	54
.1	$(-)12.5$	57
0	$(-)15.0$	60

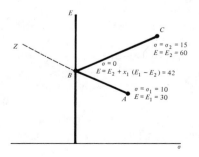

FIGURE 3. RISK-RETURN LOCUS FOR A TWO-ASSET PORTFOLIO WITH PERFECTLY NEGATIVELY CORRELATED RETURNS

from the various transactions and information costs . . . an investor would never hold money, narrowly defined. The risk-return locus for that asset and another risky asset with which its return was positively correlated would be a positively sloped straight line with a positive intercept. Even if the investor were completely risk averse, he could always attain zero risk and still have an expected return by holding all of his wealth in the insured savings account.

In the case where the correlation between the two returns is negative unity, $\varrho_{12} = -1$, Equation 4 can be substituted into Equation 6 to yield

$$\sigma^2 = x_1^2\sigma_1^2 - 2x_1(1 - x_1)\sigma_1\sigma_2 + (1 - x_1)^2\sigma_2^2$$
$$= [x_1\sigma_1 - (1 - x_1)\sigma_2]^2. \tag{10}$$

The square root of Equation 10 gives the standard deviation of the portfolio

$$\sigma = x_1\sigma_1 - \sigma_2 + x_1\sigma_2$$
$$= \sigma_2(-1 + x_1) + x_1\sigma_1. \tag{11}$$

In order to represent the risk-expected return locus graphically using Equations 11 and 5, let us now let x_1 vary over the range $0 < x_1 < 1$ to find the ordered triples (x_1,σ,E) where we assign the following values: $E_1 = 30\%$, $E_2 = 60\%$, $\sigma_1 = 10$, and $\sigma_2 = 15$. The results are given in Table 1. These values will satisfy Equations 11 and 5 and are graphed in Figure 3 as the (dashed) locus AZ. However, σ can never be negative and an absolute value restriction must be imposed on Equation 11, $\sigma \geq 0$. This restriction yields the (solid) discontinuous locus ABC in Figure 3.

In common sense terms Figure 3 describes the tradeoff that is possible between risk and expected return when the expected returns on the two assets always vary together in opposite directions. Whenever asset 1's return is above its average, the return on asset 2 is *below* its average by the same number of standard deviations; whenever the return on asset 1 is *below* its average, the return on asset 2 is *above* its average by the same number of standard deviations.

Table 1 and Equation 11 show that if the portfolio is devoted to the less risky asset ($x_1 = 1$), portfolio risk consists entirely of the risk associated with that asset, $\sigma = -\sigma_2 + \sigma_2 + \sigma_1 = 10$. At this point (point A in Figure 3), Table 1 and Equation 5 indicate that the overall expected return for the portfolio consists entirely of the expected return on the less risky asset, $E = E_2 + E_1 - E_2 = 30$.

Nevertheless, even though asset 1 is the less risky asset, by decreasing the proportion of the portfolio held in asset 1, that is, by diversifying the portfolio, we can, up to a point, actually *reduce* risk and *increase* expected return. This may be seen from Table 1 and Equation 11. Upward and to the left of A, as x_1 is reduced from unity, total risk declines because the negative term $\sigma_2 (-1 + x_1)$ increasingly offsets the positive term $x_1\sigma_1$.

Because the less risky asset has the lower expected return, as we hold less of it and more of the riskier asset with the higher return, total expected return increases.

Equation 11 indicates that this offsetting can proceed to the point where risk can be completely eradicated. This occurs where x_1 is set equal to $\sigma_2/(\sigma_1 + \sigma_2)$, because at that point

$$\sigma = 0 = \sigma_2(-1+x) + x_1\sigma_1 = -\sigma_2 + x_1\sigma_2 + x_1\sigma_1$$

$$= -\sigma_2\left(\frac{\sigma_1+\sigma_2}{\sigma_1+\sigma_2}\right) + \sigma_2\left(\frac{\sigma_2}{\sigma_1+\sigma_2}\right) + \sigma_1\left(\frac{\sigma_2}{\sigma_1+\sigma_1}\right)$$

$$= \frac{-\sigma^2_2 - \sigma_1\sigma_2 + \sigma_1\sigma_2 + \sigma^2_2}{\sigma_1+\sigma_2} = 0. \tag{12}$$

Substituting $x = \sigma_2/(\sigma_1 + \sigma_2)$ into Equation (5) gives a total expected return at that point of

$$E = x_1E_1 + (1 - x_1)E_2$$

$$= \frac{\sigma_2}{\sigma_1+\sigma_2}E_1 + \left(1 - \frac{\sigma_2}{\sigma_1+\sigma_2}\right)E_2$$

$$= E_2 + \left(\frac{E_1-E_2}{\sigma_1+\sigma_2}\right)\sigma_2$$

$$= E_2 + (E_1 - E_2)\left(\frac{\sigma_2}{\sigma_1+\sigma_2}\right) > E_1.$$

Since $E_2 > E_1$, the second term will be negative and equal to the difference between E_1 and E_2 but weighted by $\sigma_2/(\sigma_1 + \sigma_2)$ which is less than 1. Therefore, the second term reduces total return, but not as much as the difference between E_1 and E_2. As a result, the total return at point B in Figure 3 exceeds the total expected return at point A.

In summary, because of the negative correlation between returns, it is possible to reduce overall risk by holding some of the riskier asset. At the same time, because the riskier asset has a higher expected return, such *diversification* actually increases the overall expected return. Thus the rational investor would never consider a portfolio on the locus AB when he could always find a higher expected return for the same level of risk on the locus BC. Being on AB is inefficient; being on BC is efficient.

Upward from B in Figure 3, as x_1 is further decreased, the negative term in Equation 11, $\sigma_2(-1 + x_1)$, is increasingly less offset by the positive term, $x_1\sigma_1$). Algebraically σ becomes negative. However, because Equation 11 is subject to an absolute value restriction, total portfolio risk actually increases from zero upward and to the right of B. As portfolio risk increases, total portfolio return also increases. At point C in Figure 3 the entire portfolio is fully invested in asset 2, $x_2 = 1$. Here risk and expected return consist entirely of the risk and expected return associated with the riskier asset, $\sigma = -\sigma_2$ and $E = E_2$. For example, by Equation 11, $\sigma = -\sigma_2 + 0 \cdot \sigma_2 + 0 \cdot \sigma_1$ subject to $\sigma > 0$, and by Equation 5 $E = E_2 + 0 \cdot E_1 - 0 \cdot E_1$.

This analysis may also be illuminated by an example from the real world. Consider a portfolio consisting of two very highly, but not perfectly, negatively correlated assets. Such a situation may exist, for example, during certain stages of the business cycle. For instance, imagine a period in which the investor anticipates an acceleration of the rate of inflation. During such a period, if he were to purchase commodities to sell in the future at prices expected to prevail then, he would anticipate a higher return. During the same period, if he were to purchase long-term government bonds, he would expect a lower return. This occurs because if price inflation accelerates as he expects, as long as the acceleration had not been fully anticipated by other participants in the government bond market, the nominal yield on government bonds must rise (bond prices must fall) as other investors come to require higher yields to match the rate of inflation. The expected drop in bond prices would produce a capital loss for the bondholder.

The opposite of this pattern would occur during periods when the investor anticipates a deceleration of inflation ahead of other investors. Holding commodities would incur a lower return. Holding long-term bonds would result in a higher return because of likely capital gains to bondholders. Thus the expected returns on these two assets move in opposite directions.

Now let us assume that the rate of price inflation is never steady; it is either accelerating or decelerating. Let us further assume that commodities over the entire business or inflation cycle have higher risk but offer a higher return than long-term bonds.

If the investor confined his choice set to these two assets, he could never realize a risk minimum by holding all of his wealth in the form of bonds. Because returns always move in opposite directions, he could reduce risk *and* increase overall return by holding some proportion of his wealth in commodities.

Now in the real world expected returns are neither perfectly negatively nor perfectly positively correlated. In general the risk-return locus will fall between these two extreme cases. In fact, if we solved Equation 5 for x_1 and substituted the result into Equation 6, the risk-return locus would be a hyperbola such as that shown in Figure 4.

The riskiest portfolio, and the one with the highest expected return, is found at point C'. The least risky portfolio is found at the leftmost point, B'. However, without perfect negative correlation the locus will not reach the vertical axis; there will be no completely riskless portfolio. The closer the correlation coefficient is to

**FIGURE 4. PORTFOLIO WITH INTER-
MEDIATE CORRELATION OF RETURNS**

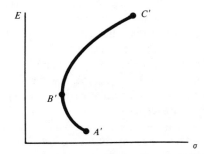

FIGURE 5A.4. Portfolio with intermediate correlation of returns.

+ 1, the more it will resemble the locus in Figure 2; the closer the correlation coefficient is to − 1, the more it will resemble the locus in Figure 3.

Finally, as in the preceding analysis, we can always find a frontier of efficient combinations of risk and expected return, $B'C'$, with no rational investor choosing to stay on the inefficient locus $A'B'$.

Investor Indifference Curves

. . . Our purpose now will be to present a . . . general formulation of investor attitudes toward risk and return. By making explicit the expected utility function, attitudes toward risk other than risk aversion can be shown. In addition, we can easily show that risk aversion reflects diminishing marginal utility of income.

Assume that an individual's total utility from income y is measurable. In a quadratic utility function

$$U = ay + by^2$$

where $a > 0$, marginal utility will be positive over a range of income beginning at zero, $dU/dy = a + 2by$. The range of b will indicate whether there is decreasing or increasing marginal utility of income; $d^2U/dy^2 = 2b < 0$ if $b < 0$, and $d^2U/dy^2 > 0$ if $b > 0$.

If we consider y a random variable, we should not talk about utility but must refer to *expected* utility. The assumption of a quadratic expected utility function is a convenient way of introducing a risk measure into the analysis. At the same time the assumption of a quadratic expected utility function has the advantage of limiting our approach to consideration of only two parameters, risk and expected return.[6]

In other words, where y is randomly, but not necessarily normally, distributed, the expected utility function

$$E(U) = E(ay) + E(by^2) \tag{13}$$

may be written

$$E(U) = aEy + b(Ey)^2 + b\sigma^2_y. \tag{14}$$

This follows because the expected value of a random variable times a constant is equal to the constant times the expected value of the random variable.[7] In addition,

---

[6]Earlier we mentioned that the assumption of a normally distributed random variable would *also* allow us to limit analysis to these two parameters.

[7]Assuming y is a discrete random variable,

$$E(ay) = \frac{1}{n} \sum_i ay_i = a \cdot \frac{1}{n} \sum_i y_i = a \cdot Ey.$$

the expected value of a random variable squared is equal to the variance of that random variable plus the square of its expected value.[8]

Now in order to derive the indifference curve, we must take the total differential of Equation 14 and set it equal to zero:

$$dE(U) = \frac{\partial E(U)}{\partial(Ey)} \, d(Ey) + \frac{\partial E(U)}{\partial \sigma_y} \, d\sigma_y = 0$$

$$= (a + 2bEy)dEy + (2b\sigma_y)d\sigma_y = 0. \tag{15}$$

The marginal rate of substitution,

$$\frac{dEy}{d\sigma_y} = \frac{-2b\sigma_y}{a + 2bEy}, \tag{16}$$

is positive where the marginal expected utility of expected return is positive,

$$\frac{\partial E(U)}{\partial Ey} = a + 2bEy > 0 \tag{17}$$

and where $b < 0$. Where the marginal rate of substitution is positive, it can easily be shown that there will be an *increasing* marginal rate of substitution. The upward-sloping indifference curve will be *convex* to the origin if the marginal expected utility of expected return is decreasing (that is, if b in Equation 16 is negative).[9] These properties generate the risk averse behavior depicted in Figure 5A. An intuitive explanation of why the risk averter's indifference curve is upward sloping and convex to the origin is simply that risk is a "bad" and return is a "good" and that consecutive *equal* increments of risk can preserve a constant level of expected utility only if they are compensated for it by consecutive *larger* increments of expected earnings because of the diminishing marginal expected utility of expected returns.

The marginal rate of substitution, Equation 16, is negative where the marginal expected utility of expected return and b have the same signs. If b is positive, the marginal expected utility of expected return is positive and increasing. There will be a decreasing marginal rate of substitution and the indifference curves will be concave to the origin. This depicts "risk loving" behavior. The indifference curves for a risk lover are drawn in Figure 5B.

For the risk lover, risk is not a "bad." Therefore, in order to stay at the same level of expected utility as an increment to risk is acquired, there must be a decrease in expected return. Thus the risk lover's indifference curves are downward sloping.

---

[8] $Ey^2 = \sigma_y^2 + (Ey)^2$
   $= E(y - Ey)^2 + (Ey)^2$
   $= E[(y^2 - 2y \cdot Ey + (Ey)^2] + (Ey)^2$
   $= Ey^2 - 2Ey \cdot Ey + (Ey)^2 + (Ey)^2$
   $= Ey^2 - 2(Ey)^2 + 2(EY)^2$
   $= Ey^2$

[9] $\dfrac{d^2Ey}{d\sigma_y^2} = \dfrac{d}{d\sigma_y}\left(\dfrac{-2b\sigma_y}{a + 2bEy}\right) = -2b \ \dfrac{a + 2bEy - \sigma_y\left(2b\dfrac{dEy}{d\sigma}\right)}{(a + 2bEy)^2} \quad 0, \text{ if } b < 0.$

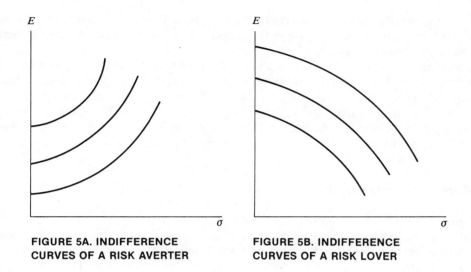

**FIGURE 5A. INDIFFERENCE
CURVES OF A RISK AVERTER**

**FIGURE 5B. INDIFFERENCE
CURVES OF A RISK LOVER**

Moreover, consecutive *equal* increments to risk, a "good," can preserve a constant level of total expected utility only if they are compensated for by consecutive *increasing* reductions in expected return, because of an increasing marginal expected utility of expected return.

Risk Aversion, Risk Loving, and the Efficient Risk-Return Locus

Combining the notion of an efficient risk-return locus and two classes of behavior toward risk, we see in Figure 6 contrasting modes of behavior. The risk averter chooses a point of tangency X between the risk-return locus and his indifference

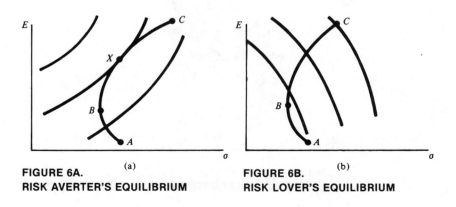

**FIGURE 6A.
RISK AVERTER'S EQUILIBRIUM**

**FIGURE 6B.
RISK LOVER'S EQUILIBRIUM**

map. It generally pays him to diversify. An increase in the rate of expected return on an asset will result in an increase in the proportion of the portfolio devoted to that asset if that asset is a normal good. . . .

The optimal position for the risk lover in Figure 6 will always be the upper end of the risk-return locus, *C*. His indifference curves can never be tangent to the efficient (upward sloping) part of the risk-return locus. The risk lover simply devotes his entire portfolio to the riskiest asset. Diversification has no advantage for the risk lover. However, in the real world even risk lovers may diversify; they may carry an inventory of a less risky asset, in order to save on transactions and information costs. . . .

More than Two Assets

Figure 7 shows the risk-return locus for a portfolio of more than two assets. In a world of three assets, there will be an additional risk-return locus in (σ, E) space representing some fixed proportion of asset 1 and asset 2 (*D* on the *AC* locus in Figure 7) and a third asset. The locus *DF* in Figure 7 represents combinations of the fixed proportion of asset 1 and asset 2 with asset 3. At point *D* all of the portfolio is in the fixed 2-asset combination; at point *F* all of the portfolio is in the third asset.

In general, every point on the *AC* locus represents the starting point of a three-asset portfolio. The shaded area in Figure 7 represents the domain of all such loci. The external boundary *AF* is the relevant risk-return locus in a three-asset world. As was the case in the 2-asset world, *GF* represents the efficient part of this locus. One can always obtain more expected return for any given level of risk in the 3-asset world than in the 2-asset world. The efficient *GF* locus is everywhere upward from the *BC* locus. The 3-asset portfolio presents the risk averter with the ability to move to a higher level of total expected utility. There are obvious gains here to the risk averter from further diversification as long as transaction costs are ignored.

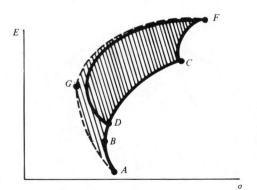

FIGURE 7. RISK-RETURN LOCUS FOR THE THREE-ASSET PORTFOLIO

The pure risk lover will never hold more than one asset, the riskiest one. In Figure 7 he, too, will be at a higher level of total expected utility at endpoint F than at C, his optimum in the 2-asset case. This analysis can easily be extended to more than three assets.[10]

[10]Obviously, in the real world of many assets an enormous number of computations would be required to identify the efficient locus because of the number of covariances involved for each pair of assets. To expedite security analysis, computational programs must be devised. The professional finance literature in this area considers a number of ways to perform the necessary calculations. See, for example, Harry Markowitz, *Portfolio Selection,* Cowles Foundation Monograph 16 (New York: Wiley, 1959). By relating return to an overall index of the performance of many assets, the burden of calculation can be reduced considerably. This line of reasoning led to the development and widespread use of the *beta* coefficient which relates the fluctuations in the price of a security to the fluctuations in the Dow-Jones Industrial Average. See William F. Sharpe, "A Simplified Model for Portfolio Analysis," *Management Science,* January 1963, pp. 277–93.

Interest Rates

The two essays in this section discuss the major factors determining the structure of interest rates in the economy. The implications of the quantity theory formulation of the demand for money for theories of the determination of the price level and interest rates are explored in a seminal article by Milton Friedman. Friedman's explanation is consistent with the notion discussed in the readings in Section II that money affects the economy through a wide spectrum of portfolio adjustments, wherein short-run effects on interest rates, especially long-term rates, may be quite small. Burton Malkiels's article views the term-to-maturity structure of interest rates as it is theoretically influenced by risk-liquidity, supply and demand, and expectational factors. Malkiel's treatment is an exhilarating practical perspective for students of money and capital markets.

Factors Affecting the Level of Interest Rates

Milton Friedman

21

There is a problem in terminology that is worth commenting on at the outset. In all sorts of monetary discussions, there is a tendency to use the word "money" in three different senses. We speak of a man making money when we mean that he is earning income. We speak of a man borrowing money when we mean that he is engaging in a credit transaction. Similarly, we speak of the money market in the sense of a credit market. Finally, we talk about money when we mean those green pieces of paper we carry in our pocket or the deposits to our credit at banks.

Confusion of Credit with Money

Much of the misunderstanding about the relationship between money and interest rates comes from a failure to keep those three senses of the term "money" distinct, in particular to keep "credit" distinct from "quantity of money." In discussing credit, it is natural and correct to say that the interest rate is the price of credit. General price theory tells us that the price of anything will be lowered by an increase in supply and will be raised by a reduction in supply. Therefore, it is natural to say that an increase in credit will reduce the rate of interest. That is correct. A shift to the right of the

Reprinted from the *Proceedings* of the 1968 Conference on Savings and Residential Financing, sponsored by the United States Savings and Loan League (Chicago: The League, 1969), pp. 11-27, by permission of the publisher and the author.

supply curve of loanable funds—that is, an increase in the supply of loanable funds at each interest rate—will, other things being the same, tend to reduce the interest rate. A decrease in supply will tend to raise it.

The tendency to confuse credit with money leads to the further belief that an increase in the quantity of money will tend to reduce interest rates and a reduction in the quantity of money will tend to increase interest rates.

Because of this confusion, there is also a tendency to regard the term "monetary ease" as unambiguous, as meaning either a more rapid increase in the quantity of money or lower interest rates and, similarly, monetary tightness as meaning either a reduction in the quantity of money or higher interest rates.

Interest Rate Price of Credit, Not Money

My main thesis is that this is wrong, that the relation between the quantity of money and the level and movement of interest is much more complicated than the relation that is suggested by the identification of money with credit. It is more complicated because the interest rate is not the price of money. The interest rate is the price of credit. The price level or the inverse of the price level is the price of money. What is to be expected from general price theory is what the quantity theory says, namely, that a rapid increase in the quantity of money means an increase in prices of goods and services, and that a decrease in the quantity of money means a decrease in the price of goods and services. Therefore, to see what effect changes in the quantity of money have on interest rates, it is necessary to look more deeply beneath the surface.

Before going into the detailed analysis, let me prepare the groundwork by discussing some facts. If you ask most economists, or most noneconomists for that matter, certainly if you ask most people at savings and loan institutions or in banks, whether an increased quantity of money will mean higher or lower interest rates, everybody will say lower interest rates; but looking at broad facts shows the reverse.

If I ask in what countries in the world are interest rates high, there will be widespread agreement that they are high in Brazil, Argentina, and Chile. If I say, "I take it that in those countries there are very low rates of increase in the quantity of money and that interest rates are high because money has been tight," you will laugh at me. Those are countries which have had very rapid increase in the quantity of money and inflation.

If I ask in what countries of the world are interest rates low, you will tell me in countries like Switzerland. On the usual view, this would imply that they have been having rapid increased in the quantity of money. Yet we all know that the situation is precisely the reverse. Switzerland is a country which has held down the quantity of money.

Let us turn to the United States. Suppose I said, "What is the period in the United States when interest rates fell most rapidly?" There is not the slightest doubt when that was. It was the period from about 1929 to the mid-1930s. Would you then say, "That must have been the period when the quantity of money was increasing."

Obviously not. We all know that it is the opposite. From 1929 to 1933, the quantity of money fell by one-third and, as I shall proceed later to say, therefore interest rates fell, although in terms of the usual presumptions that economists have and which are enshrined in our elementary textbooks, one would say precisely the opposite.

Similarly, interest rates are high now in the United States in nominal terms. Nominal interest rates are far higher than they were in the mid-'30s, far higher than they were just after the war. Yet, in the past five or six years, the quantity of money has been increasing relatively rapidly.

The point of this crude and rough survey of experience is to bring home that the broadest factual evidence runs precisely contrary to what most of us teach our students and what is accepted almost without question by the Federal Reserve System, by bankers, by the savings and loan business.

So far I have mentioned one set of broad facts, namely, the relation between the level of interest rates and the rate of change in the quantity of money. When the quantity of money has been increasing very rapidly, there is a tendency to have high interest rates; when it has been decreasing very rapidly or increasing slowly, there is a tendency to have low interest rates.

Gibson Paradox: Prices, Interest Rates Move Together

Another empirical regularity, which was pointed out many years ago, exists not between money and interest rates but between prices and interest rates. The Gibson paradox is the observed empirical tendency for prices and interest rates to move together. When prices are rising, interest rates tend to be rising; when prices are falling, interest rates tend to be falling.

This was regarded as a paradox because of the orthodox view I have been questioning. Ordinarily, prices would be expected to be rising because the quantity of money is increasing. If the quantity of money is increasing, the orthodox view is that interest rates should be falling. Yet we find that when prices are rising, interest rates are rising, and when prices are falling, interest rates are falling.

That is another piece of empirical evidence which needs to be interpreted by any theory which tries to explain the relationship between the changes in the quantity of money, on the one hand, and the level or direction of movement in interest rates, on the other hand.

Let me turn from this background to a theoretical analysis of the relationship between money and interest rates. This analysis is one which has been developed over the past few years, and in that period three different empirical pieces of work have been done which I am going to summarize for you. To the best of my knowledge, none is yet published.

The first is some work that Anna Schwartz and I have done in studying the relationships between longer term movements in the quantity of money and in interest rates. The second is some work that Phillip Cagan has done at the National

Bureau on shorter term movements in interest rates within the cycle. Anna's and my work uses as the basic unit a half-cycle, so it has to do with the intercycle movement. Phil Cagan's work has to do with the intracycle movement.

The third is a doctoral dissertation just recently completed at the University of Chicago by William Gibson, who is now at the University of California in Los Angeles, which also deals with the shorter period relationships between money and interest rates.

The new work in this area is an interesting phenomenon because it reflects a very long cycle. Irving Fisher worked on this problem back in the '20s and '30s. What the three of us have done is to redo Fisher and find that he was right after all. While there has been considerable work done in these past three years, it owes a great deal to the much earlier work done by Fisher. This is particularly true of the analysis of the Gibson paradox.

Analysis of Changes in Money, Interest Rates

I should like to present to you what seems to me now to be the correct theoretical analysis of the relationship between changes in the quantity of money and interest rates. I shall argue that there are three sets of effects which have to be distinguished. The first is the liquidity effect. The second is what I shall call the income effect. The third is the price anticipations effect. I shall argue that, of these three effects, the first one works in the direction which has been generally expected, but the second and the third work in the opposite direction. If the effect of monetary change on interest rates is to be understood, all three have to be taken into account.

The liquidity effect in its simplest form is the usual textbook relationship between the quantity of money and the interest rate which says that the larger the quantity of money, the lower the interest rate will have to be to induce people to hold it. I have drawn it in that form in Figure 1, but no one who is careful writes it in that form and this is one of the slips in the analysis. What really should be measured on the

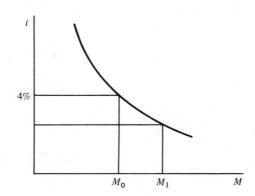

horizontal axis is not *M,* the nominal quantity of money, but *M/P,* the real quantity of money.

Part of the story of tracing the effect of a change in money is going from a change in the nominal quantity of money to what happens to the real quantity of money. For the moment, however, let us waive that. We shall come back to it because it is in the second set of effects—the income effect or income-and-price effect. Let us stay here for the moment with the liquidity effect.

Consider now Figure 2, in which time is measured on the horizontal axis. Let us suppose that up to some moment of time, t_0, there has been a constant rate of increase in the quantity of money, say 3 percent per year. At a certain time it suddenly starts increasing at 5 percent a year. Let us suppose that interest rates prior to t_0 have been 4 percent, as shown on Figure 2. What should we expect to be the pattern of behavior of interest rates as a result of this one-shot change in monetary growth as it works itself out through time? That is the central theoretical problem.

The first tendency of any economist, in terms of our present literature, is to stress the fact that in order to get people to hold the large quantity of money, interest rates will have to go down. As shown in Figure 1, people were willing to hold M_0 at a rate of interest of 4 percent. To get them to hold more, there will have to be a movement along the curve to lower interest rates. There is an implicit assumption in that analysis that needs to be brought to the surface. The implicit assumption is that prices are not in the first instance affected by the change in the quantity of money.

Let us suppose that prior to this time, prices were stable. Let us suppose for a moment that 3 percent corresponds to the rate of output increase in the economy and that velocity is constant, just to keep matters simple. None of these assumptions really affects the essence of what I am saying. If, when the quantity of money started increasing at 5 percent per year instead of 3 percent, prices suddenly started increasing at 2 percent per year, you would stay exactly in the same place on the curve in Figure 1 (if the horizontal axis is interpreted as *M/P*), and there would be no tendency for interest rates to go down. The implicit assumption that, in the first instance, the effect is not likely to be on prices, is consistent with much empirical evidence. I should qualify this statement. The implicit assumption seems correct *if* this jump from 3 percent to 5 percent is an unanticipated jump. If it were announced

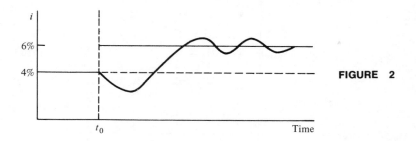

FIGURE 2

that the jump was going to occur, it would be more plausible that it would have an immediate effect on prices.

Liquidity Effect: Price of Securities Up, Interest Rate Down

If this is an unanticipated jump in the rate of monetary increase, it is reasonable to suppose that its first impact will be that people will find the composition of their portfolios disturbed. Holders of cash will find that they have more cash than they planned to have. Their first impulse will be to attempt to readjust the portfolios by replacing cash with other securities. This will bid up the price of other securities and lower the rate of interest. This would be the liquidity effect.

This is the effect which explains why academic economists, in general, will say offhand that an increase in the quantity of money will lower interest rates. In economic terminology, we would call this an effect through stocks. The financial economist or Federal Reserve economist will argue a little differently. He would expect an immediate effect through flows. He would say, "How is the rate of increase in the quantity of money stepped up?" He would say that in our kind of financial system ordinarily it will be stepped up by an increased rate of purchase of securities by the central banks, which in turn will add to the reserves of commercial banks which will expand by making additional loans. He would say that the very process of stepping up the quantity of money in our kind of financial system operates to raise the supply of loanable funds. That is entirely true of our kind of financial system.

It is interesting to note that discussions of the problem in earlier literature, for example, in John Stuart Mill's *Principles of Political Economy,* written over a century ago, very clearly stated that the first-round effect which was to be expected from a change in the quantity of money would be different as it occurred through the credit market or as it occurred through a change in gold production. It was argued that if it occurred through gold production, its first-order effect would be not on interest rates but on the wages of gold miners and the prices of commodities they bought and that it would spread from there. On the other hand, if the increase in the quantity of money occurred through the credit market, its first-round effect would be on interest rates.

These two factors—the effect on stocks and the effect through flows—would work in the same direction. However, the title "liquidity effect" under which I have included both is not an entirely descriptive term. Both factors tend to make for an initial decline in the rate of interest—the stock effect because of a movement along the liquidity curve and the flow effect because of a movement to the right in the supply of loanable funds. There is a difference. The flow effect would produce a decline in the interest rate which might be expected to happen immediately. As long as prices do not react, the effect through stocks will exert a continuing downward pressure on the interest rate. So it is not clear whether the liquidity effect would produce simply a sudden drop to a new level or a period during which interest rates fall, as I have shown it on Figure 2. That is the first effect—a liquidity effect.

Income-and-Price Level Effect

The next effect is the income-and-price level effect. As cash balances are built up, people's attempts to acquire other assets raise the prices of assets and drive down the interest rate. That will tend to produce an increase in spending. Along standard income and expenditure lines, it will tend to increase business investment. Alternatively, to look at it more broadly, the prices of sources of services will be raised relative to the prices of the service flows themselves. This leads to an increase in spending on the service flow and, therefore, to an increase in current income. In addition, it leads to an increase in spending on producing sources of services in response to the higher price which can now be obtained for them.

The existence and character of this effect does not depend on any doctrinal position about the way in which monetary forces affect the economy. Whether monetary forces are considered as affecting the economy through the interest rate and thence through investment spending or whether, as I believe, reported interest rates are only a few of a large set of rates of interest and the effect of monetary change is exerted much more broadly, in either case the effect of the more rapid rate of monetary growth will tend to be a rise in nominal income.

For the moment, let us hold prices constant and suppose that the rise in nominal income is entirely a result of rising output. What effect will that have? It will raise the demand curve for loanable funds. A business expansion is in process and the increasing level of income will raise the demand for loanable funds. This will exert a force tending to raise interest rates, or at least to counteract the downward pressure from the increasing stock of money. In addition, the rising incomes will tend to shift to the right the liquidity preference curve of Figure 1, since the higher the income, the larger the quantity of money demanded at each interest rate. (Strictly speaking, under our assumptions that the initial position was one of a 3 percent per year rate of growth in real income, the effect will be a still more rapid shift of the liquidity preference curve. Alternatively, we can interpret Figure 1 as representing a trend-corrected curve.)

Suppose the expansion in income takes the form in part of rising prices. This will not alter the tendency for the demand for loanable funds, expressed in nominal terms, to rise. But, if we measure the real quantity of money (M/P) on the horizontal axis of Figure 1, this tendency will affect that figure. Suppose prices go up as rapidly as the increased rate of monetary growth, in our assumed case, 2 percent. The real quantity of money will remain constant. If prices go up more rapidly than that, you will tend to move back along the curve. As income rises, whether or not prices rise, interest rates will turn around and go up, as a result of the rising demand for loanable funds, the shift of the liquidity preference curve, and the possible movement along it.

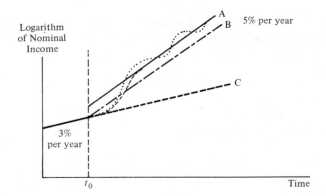

There are many reasons to believe that this rise in interest rates will go too far. It will overshoot. I cannot cover this point in full here, but let me suggest some reasons to expect even this short-run effect to overshoot.

In the first place, we started out by saying that prices will be slow to react and that the initial effect is the disturbance of portfolios. That means that there is some catching up to do. We can see what is involved most readily by looking at the ultimate long-run position.

If the rate of monetary growth stayed at 5 percent, the long-run equilibrium position would involve nominal income rising at 2 percent per year more than it did prior to the increase in the monetary growth rate. In Figure 3, Line C is a continuation of the orginal trend of rising income, let us say, at 3 percent a year. Line B shows a trend linked to the initial trend but with a rate of rise of 5 percent. If at first income proceeds along C but ultimately has to proceed along B, then for some period income will have risen more rapidly in order to catch up. That is one reason for a tendency to overshoot.

A second reason is a little more complicated. The true long-run equilibrium position of income will not be Line B but a higher line, say Line A. It will be a higher line because the amount of real balances that people want to hold will be smaller when prices are rising at 2 percent per year than when they are stable.

Price Anticipation Effect

This brings us to our third effect, the price anticipation effect. When prices are rising at 2 percent a year and people come to anticipate that they will continue to, this raises the cost of holding cash. Consequently, they will want to hold smaller balances relative to income. This is clearly the case and has been well-documented for hyper-inflation and substantial inflation. Phil Cagan's study on hyperinflation, which is by now a classic, documents very clearly that in such episodes, the higher the rate of change of prices, the higher is monetary velocity or the lower are real balances.

Studies for countries like Argentina and Brazil and Chile, countries that have had very substantial inflation, show the same phenomenon. For the United States, it has been much harder to pin down that phenomenon because our price movements have been mild.

In the study by Anna Schwartz and me, using averages for half-cycles, referred to earlier, we have been able for the first time to extract from the American data the same kind of response to the rate of change in prices as had been extracted for the more extreme inflationary episodes.

As a theoretical matter, the higher the rate of change of prices, the higher the velocity expected. This shows up as an empirical phenomenon. This is why the long period equilibrium will be a path like A in Figure 3 rather than like B. Therefore, even if there were no lag in the initial adjustment, at some time or other income or prices have to rise faster than the ultimate equilibrium rate of 2 percent per year in order to get up to this higher level. To digress for a moment, the phenomenon I have been describing is, in my opinion, the fundamental reason why a shift in the quantity of money tends to produce cyclical reaction patterns and not smooth movements. The dotted lines show two possible paths, one involving damped oscillations, the other a direct approach to equilibrium. But note that even the latter involves a cyclical reaction in the rate of change of income.

The price anticipation effect is the one that is most closely linked to Irving Fisher, that he investigated statistically, and that he introduced to explain the Gibson paradox.

If I may go back a moment, I am sliding over one point that I ought to make explicit. For simplicity, I have been talking as if the initial position we started from was one where there was reasonably full employment, so that while in the interim there can be a period with income increasing and prices stable, sooner or later the higher rate of rise in income will be translated into a higher rate of price increase. That really is not essential for my story at all.

It may be that part of the effect will be taken up in output rather than in prices. All that is essential is that there be some tendency for prices to rise somewhat more than they otherwise would, although I may say that, as an empirical matter, I would expect a shift from one fairly steady rate of monetary growth to another to be reflected fully, sooner or later, in prices.

Distinguish between Nominal, Real Rate of Interest

As long as there is some tendency for part of the increase in the rate of growth of the quantity of money to end up in a higher rate of price rise, sooner or later people will come to anticipate it. As people come to anticipate it, we introduce a distinction that I have so far kept out of the picture, namely, the distinction between the nominal rate of interest and the real rate of interest.

We are all very much aware of the distinction right now. It is also a distinction that goes back in our literature, at least to Irving Fisher who analyzed it most exhaustively. If the nominal interest rate is 4 percent per year and if prices over any period rise at the rate of 2 percent per year, then the realized real yield will be 2 percent, not 4 percent.

However, what matters for the market is not the *ex post* yield which is realized after the event but what people anticipate in advance. People today are buying bonds or other securities or making loans for the long-term future on the basis of what they anticipate will happen.

Let us designate the nominal interest rate by R_B (the B for bonds) and the real rate by R_E (E for equity). Now $1\ dP/P\ dt$ is the percentage rate at which prices are changing at time t. Let an asterisk attached to it stand for an anticipated rate, so $(1\ dP/P\ dt)^*$ is the anticipated rate of change in prices. Then, the relation Fisher developed is $R_B = R_E + (1\ dP/P\ dt)^*$. In other words, the nominal rate of interest on the market will be equal to the real rate of interest plus the anticipated rate of price change. Therefore, if R_E stays the same but the anticipated rate of price change goes up, the nominal interest rate will also go up. That is the third effect.

Returning to Figure 2, we see that if the whole of this 2 percent higher rate of monetary growth goes into prices, and if the initial equilibrium interest rate was 4 percent, then the new long-run equilibrium rate will be 6 percent. The interest rate pattern then will be something like that shown in Figure 2 and will ultimately get up to 6 percent.

What Theoretical Analysis Determines

That is the whole of the theoretical analysis that leads to tracing out a path of reaction in interest rates. I have exaggerated somewhat what can be traced out from the theoretical analysis alone since the fluctuations I have put in are not well determined. What is really determined by the theoretical analysis is an initial decline, a subsequent rise, and an ultimate attainment of a level about 2 percent higher than the initial one.

Let me give this theoretical analysis some empirical content. How long are these periods? What is their duration? Of the three studies that I have described, the one that Anna and I have done traces out the time pattern at the end, while Cagan's and Gibson's studies trace out the time pattern at the beginning. So far we have a missing link in between. The empirical work all three of us have done is entirely consistent with the pattern traced out in Figure 2. Empirically, there is a tendency for a rapid rate of monetary growth to be followed by a decline in interest rates and, after a lag, by a rise and then a final ultimate movement to a level higher than the starting point. The major patterns are recorded in the empirical evidence and do come out very clearly.

I have been talking about an increase in the rate of monetary expansion. Obviously, everything is reversed for a decrease, and our empirical studies, of course, cover both increases and decreases.

It turns out that the initial decline in interest rates after an acceleration of monetary growth lasts about six months. Clearly, there is variation but the average period is about six months. The time it takes to get back to the initial level is something like 18 months.

Long Period to Final Equilibrium Level

The period it takes to get to the final equilibrium level is very long. Fisher came out with a period of something like 20 years. He did a number of different studies which gave him estimates of 20 or 30 years. Our own estimates are about the same. They make a distinction which Fisher's did not. They suggest that the period is different for short rates than it is for long rates. Fisher did his studies for long rates and did not make that distinction.

As a purely theoretical matter, one would expect that it would take longer for long rates than for short rates. When you are buying a security with a short life, you are really interested in extrapolating price movements over a shorter future period of time than when you are buying a very long-term security. It seems not unreasonable that if you are extrapolating for a short period, you will look back for a shorter period than when you are extrapolating for a longer period.

I regard it as very strong empirical confirmation of this interpretation of the evidence that it does turn out that the period it takes to get full adjustment tends to be much longer for long rates than it does for short rates.

In Figure 2, the time it takes to get to the final equilibrium level depends on how long it takes for a change in the rate of monetary change to produce general anticipation of further price rises. That implicitly means that it depends on how far back people look in forming their anticipations. The mean period of price anticipation turns out to be something like 10 years for short rates and 20 years for long rates. Since these are the average periods, they imply that people take an even longer period of past history into account. These results are wholly consistent with Fisher's.

One more interesting point—and here I am much more tentative—such evidence as I have seen suggests what is to be expected, namely, that the period it takes is much longer in a country which has experienced mild price movements than in a country which has experienced rapid price movements. In one of the South American countries where prices have moved much more rapidly, the period it takes appears to be much shorter. That is what is to be expected in a more variable world where anticipations would be formed over a briefer period of time.

Relationship between Analysis and Gibson Paradox

Let me tie this in to the Gibson paradox and show how this analysis is related to that. The explanation that Fisher offered for the Gibson paradox was the same as what I

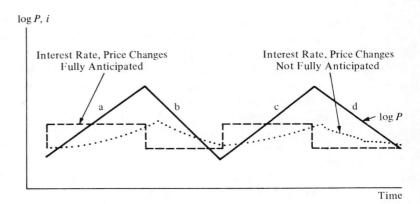

have called the third effect, but it hinges very much on how long it takes for people to form their anticipations. If price change were perfectly anticipated, if people instantaneously anticipated what was actually going to happen, high interest rates would be associated with rapid rates of price rise and low interest rates would be associated with low rates of price rise or with price declines, but there would be no reason to expect a connection between rising prices and rising interest rates.

Let me see if I can make this clear. Suppose that the historical record of prices was like that plotted in Figure 4, where the ordinate is the logarithm of the price, so that straight lines correspond to constant rates of price increase or decrease. If people fully anticipated this, the result would be that for periods a and c the interest rate would be high, for periods b and d the interest rate would be low—as shown by the dashed steps. There is no reason why rising prices should be associated with rising interest rates. Rising prices would be associated with high interest rates; falling prices with low interest rates. Yet the Gibson paradox is that rising prices are associated with rising interest rates and falling prices with falling interest rates.

In order to explain the Gibson paradox on this basis, Fisher says that if prices start to rise, people do not really believe it. It takes a long time before they accept the idea that prices are rising. Therefore, if we plot on Figure 4 not what the actual rate of change of prices is but what the anticipated rate of change of prices is, we find that it behaves like the wavy dotted line; the anticipated rate of change of prices starts being low, and only gradually rises, and keeps on rising for a time after actual prices start declining. Only after a lag will it start to decline, and then it will decline only gradually.

So, said Fisher, let prices start to rise when those prices have been stable. As prices rise, people gradually come to anticipate the rise. Only after prices have been rising for a long time will people take full account of the actual rate of rise.

Price Savings and Anticipation Time

In order for this delayed formation of anticipations to explain Gibson's paradox empirically, it is clear that there has to be a particular relation between the length of the period that it takes for people to form their anticipations and the actual long swings in prices. If people formed their anticipations very rapidly—much more rapidly than the length of a price rise or fall—then interest rates would rise for only a short period along with prices and soon would be high but constant. When prices started declining, interest rates would be low but constant. They would look more like the steps in Figure 4 than like the wavy dotted line. In order to have a close correlation between rising prices and rising interest rates, there must be a particular relation among the periods. It must be that the period of the long swings in prices is roughly comparable to the period of time which it takes for people to form anticipations.

That is what Fisher found. Indeed, that is the way in which he estimates the period it takes to form anticipation, and it is the way we have done it as well.

Fisher's conclusions as he presented them in the 1920s tended to be disregarded by almost all economists. Very few people paid any attention to him. The explanation is simple. People said, "That's silly theory, why should it take people 20 to 30 years to form anticipations about price changes? Surely, a theory which requires such a long period must be wrong."

What Anna Schwartz and I did was to recalculate the correlations for an additional 40 years or so beyond the period for which Fisher had data. The correlations are just as good for the additional 40 years as they were for the period before. This is a rare event in applied economics. All of us have had problems with spurious results. We try a dozen different correlations and finally get one that is satisfactory. How do we know it will hold for the future? It usually does not. But in this case, it so happens that Fisher studied this up through the '20s and we have about 40 more years of experience. Nobody since has paid any attention to this particular aspect of the data. Yet they show exactly the same thing for the period since then that they showed before, namely, a high correlation between the rate of change of prices and the rate of change of interest rates. The correlation is higher than the correlation between the level of interest rates and the rate of change of prices. That is to say, it is not the step relation in Figure 4 that dominates but the wavy one.

It is interesting to ask the question, "Why is it that it should take people so long to form anticipations?" I think another feature of the work that Anna and I did gives a very important clue to the answer and has importance beyond this particular problem. You will recall that I mentioned the repeated failure in former work to find a relationship between the rate of price change and velocity in the United States. In the study we made, we found it for the first time. The reason we did, I believe, is that we used as our unit of analysis the half-cycle. Ordinarily, in most such work when we introduce lags we tend to introduce constant chronological lags—one year, two years, three years.

When we started to work on this problem, we found ourselves introducing variable lags without intending to do so because if economic series are averaged over half-cycles, some half-cycles are short, some are long. Consequently, when we related velocity today to price change in a prior cycle phase, we implicitly had a lag that was long when the cycle phases were long and short when the cycle phases were short.

Distinction between Psychological, Chronological Time

What led me to continue along this line was the work that Maurice Allais described in his "A Restatement of the Quantity Theory of Money," recently published in the *American Economic Review* and in which he made a very basic and important distinction between psychological time and chronological time.

Let me translate this idea without going into Allais' particular way of putting it— though I believe his paper is one of the most important and original that has been written for a long time, not particularly because of its treatment of the demand for money but for its consideration of the problem of the formation of expectations.

People who are trying to form anticipations have some understanding of the nature of the society. They know that the economy goes in cycles and has its ups and downs. Suppose you are trying to form an anticipation about what is going to happen to prices. You will say, "I had better average out over these cycles. I had better look back to what was happening in a corresponding phase of the last cycle." If you are examining past history with the idea that there is some kind of cyclical pattern, it is perfectly reasonable for you to go back a roughly fixed number of cycles, not years.

That is exactly what our results suggested. Better results were obtained by taking as a unit of measurement the cycle and not the year. Let us apply this idea to the present problem. Let us say that you are going to buy a 40- or 50-year bond. You want to make a prediction for a long period on the basis of the past. It is reasonable for you to form your anticipation not on the basis of short-period data of the last few years but of a period that will encompass, as it were, full economic episodes.

Because of limitations of time, I am proceeding very dogmatically and sketchily, but this establishes a theoretical reason why it is not surprising to find that the period over which the anticipation is formed bears a relationship to the observed period of long swings in prices.

Correlation between Anticipation Period, Fluctuations

You might say that Fisher's result is a pure coincidence. His result depends on the periods of formation of anticipations being roughly as long as the periods of sustained price movements. Why should they be? If people are intelligently forming anticipations about the future on the basis of an analysis of the past, it is not a foolish thing for them to behave that way. That is why I believe that you will find that this period of anticipation is shorter in those countries which have sharper and more rapid fluctuations than in those which have slower and longer fluctuations.

I was very much struck with this point the other day when I was in New York acting as a representative of many of you at a College Retirement Equity Fund lunch. Some financial people started talking about the difference between the behavior of young people today and of their own behavior with respect to borrowing on credit. These people's behavior today was being very much influenced by what had happened in the 1930s. This was over a 30-year lag in their behavior.

Now of course the actual lag for the society is an average over all age classes and this is the longest lag, but once you start to look at it in that way, it does not seem to me too surprising that the lag should be so long.

Let me give you another empirical illustration. There is little doubt in my mind that the widespread expectation that prevailed in the United States after World War II that there would be a price fall involved using data going back roughly 150 years.

You ask yourself, "How shall I form an anticipation about what happens after a major war?" There is no use looking at what happened during peace time. It is better to look at what happened after earlier major wars. People who were forming these anticipations after World War II looked back at what happened after World War I, what happened after the Civil War, what happened after the War of 1812, and they found that in each of these cases, within about 10 or 15 years after the end of the war, prices were half what they had been at the end of the war. So it was not at all absurd for people to form their anticipations on the basis of a period stretching back over 100 years.

Recent Experience Illustrates Analysis

Let me conclude simply by applying this analysis to recent experience because it applies beautifully. When I say this analysis, I really am talking mostly about the short period analysis, not Fisher's long period analysis. Consider what happened in 1966 and 1967 because it was almost a perfect representation of the relationship I have shown in Figure 2.

There was a rapid rate of growth in money until April 1966. (The exact rate depends on whether you use a narrow or a broad definition of money but nothing I say will be affected by that because the patterns of behavior of the different rates are the same although the quantitative rates of change are different.) From April 1966 to about December 1966 there was a brief but sharp decline in the rate of monetary change.

From December 1966 or January 1967 through most of 1967, to something like October or November of 1967, there was an even more rapid rate of increase than before April 1966. Since about November 1967 there has been a tapering off in the rate of growth.

Delayed Impact of Earlier Monetary Growth

What happened to interest rates during that period? Prior to April 1966 interest rates were rising. Why were they rising? This was the delayed impact of the earlier high rate of monetary growth.

Suddenly there was a tightening of money—a sharp decrease in the rate of growth of the quantity of money. What does our theory say? Turn Figure 2 upside down. It says a rapid increase in interest rates would be expected because the delayed effect of earlier monetary ease is reinforced by the impact effect of monetary tightness. That, of course, is what happened. There was a very sharp rise in interest rates culminating in the so-called credit crunch.

The interesting thing is when did that culminate? In September or October 1966, several months before the reversal in monetary growth. That is exactly what our analysis would lead you to expect—a turnaround about six months after the shift in monetary growth.

At this point the tight money was having a depressing effect on interest rates. The liquidity effect had shot its bolt; the income effect was beginning to take over. That income effect resulted in a slowdown in the economy in the first half of 1967 which reduced the demand for loanable funds and so interest rates fell.

Then what happened? After monetary growth accelerated in January 1967, the short-term effects of easy money reinforced the delayed effect of the tighter money and so interest rates continued to fall. But this time the short-term effect was abnormally short—less than six months. Interest rates turned around some time in March or April that year and started to go up. These delayed effects of easy money were then reinforced in November 1967 by the tapering off of monetary growth.

Many Factors Affect Interest Rates

Obviously, I am not trying to say for a moment that monetary change is the only thing that affects interest rates. Do not misunderstand me. I am trying to isolate that part of the interest rate movement which is determined by monetary change. Many, many other things affect interest rates.

In particular, I have no reason to doubt that the sharp increase in the federal government's deficit, which meant an increase in the demand for borrowing by the federal government, was a factor which was raising interest rates through most of 1967. It may be that is why there was an abnormally short delay before the initial impact of easy money was reversed.

I should have made this qualification about other factors earlier. Our squared correlations are perhaps on the order of about 0.5 which means they account for half of the fluctuations in nominal interest rates. I do not for a moment want to suggest that if you understand the effect of monetary change on interest rates, you therefore have a theory of interest rates. In the first place, there are other forces which will change real interest rates. In the second place, there are undoubtedly other forces changing nominal interest rates, but it so happens that the major movements of nominal interest rates in 1966 and 1967 seem to have been dominated by the monetary effects so they serve to bring out very clearly the relations I have described.

One more word about the longer term relations. If this analysis is right, our present interest rates of 6 percent or 6.5 percent are still on the way up because they are still reflecting the building up of anticipations of price increases. Our present interest rates are extremely low—if you subtract the rate of price change, you have very low real interest rates. Therefore, if this analysis is right, the long-term trend of interest rates ought still to be up.

The Term Structure of Interest Rates: Theory, Empirical Evidence, and Applications

Burton G. Malkiel

22

Market rates of interest for the various types of debt securities differ for a variety of reasons. Perhaps the major cause of differences is the credit risk of the instruments, that is, the risk of default of the promised interest and principal payments. In addition, significant differences result from differences in the provisions of various sorts of bonds: whether they are tax-exempt, whether they can be converted into common stocks, whether they can be redeemed at the option of the company, and so forth. Indeed, the major reasons for differences in bond yields may be unrelated to the maturity of the securities involved. Nevertheless, one of the most intriguing differences among market interest rates concerns the relationship among the yields of high-grade securities that differ *only* in their term to maturity, that is, in the length of time until the principal amount of the loan becomes due and payable. This relationship is called the "term structure of interest rates," or, more popularly, "the shape of the yield curve."

In this essay, we shall first explain the algebra of bond yields and the method of construction of the yield curve, and then review the patterns that have occurred in the past. Next will be a discussion of three alternative explanations of the shape of the yield curve and of the empirical evidence that has been marshaled in their support. Then the implications of the analysis for monetary policy will be presented. Finally, we shall consider how investors interested in improving bond-portfolio per-

Reprinted from Malkiel, Burton G., *The Term Structure of Interest Rates: Theory, Empirical Evidence, and Applications* (1970). Reprinted by permission of Silver Burdett Company.

formance and corporate issuers interested in minimizing borrowing costs may benefit from an understanding of the determinants of the shape of the yield curve and a study of its historical patterns.

The Algebra of Bond Yields and Bond Prices

The market value of a bond is determined by four factors: (1) the face value of the bond, i.e., the principal amount to be paid at maturity, which we denote by F; (2) the coupon or interest paid periodically to the bondholder, denoted by C; (3) the effective interest rate per period, R, which is referred to as the bond's yield to maturity or, more simply, the yield of the security; and (4) N, the number of years to maturity. The market price, P, is simply the sum of the present values of all the coupons to be received as interest and the principal amount to be paid at maturity.[1]

$$P = \frac{C}{(1+R)} + \frac{C}{(1+R)^2} + \cdots + \frac{C}{(1+R)^N} + \frac{F}{(1+R)^N}. \tag{1}$$

Given the values of the promised coupon interest payments, face value, and length of time to maturity we may solve Equation 1 for R, the annual yield of the bond.[2]

An Illustration of the Bond-Pricing Equation

To illustrate the use of the bond-pricing equation, suppose a bond has a market price of $104, an annual coupon of $9, a term to maturity of five years, and a face value of $100. In fact, most bond prices are stated in terms of $100 of face or par value.[3] We may then calculate the annual yield to maturity from the bond-pricing formula:

$$104 = \frac{9}{1+R} + \frac{9}{(1+R)^2} + \frac{9}{(1+R)^3} + \frac{9}{(1+R)^4} + \frac{9}{(1+R)^5} + \frac{100}{(1+R)^5}. \tag{1a}$$

Equation 1a may be solved for R, which turns out to be 8 per cent.

[1] The present value of an amount S_1 to be paid one year from now, is defined as a present amount P, which when invested now at a given interest rate, R, will accumulate to the amount S_1 next year. Since a present amount invested at rate R will accumulate to an amount $S_1 = P(1 + R)$ next year, the present value, P, of that future amount S_1, is given by the expression $P = S_1/(1 + R)$. If the present amount P is left to accumulate at interest for two years, the relevant future amount $S_2 = P(1 + R)(1 + R) = P(1 + R)^2$. Hence the present value of S_2 is simply $S_2/(1 + R)^2$. In general, the present value of a future amount to be paid N years from now is $S_N/(1 + R)^N$.

[2] R is also referred to as the bond's internal rate of return. C, the periodic interest to be paid, is referred to as the bond's coupon because, in fact, coupons are usually attached to each bond indicating the amount of interest due at each payment date. These coupons may be "clipped" from the bond and surrendered for cash on the appropriate payment dates. In this study we shall use the words "interest rate" and "bond yield" interchangeably.

[3] Nevertheless, it is not possible to buy a $100 government or corporate bond. A single bond has traditionally consisted of $1,000 of face, or par, value. When one speaks then of buying ten bonds, one

We have assumed that coupon interest payments are made once a year. In fact, interest payments are typically made semiannually, with half the annual coupon paid each six months. This requires only a small change in the pricing formula:

$$P = \frac{C/2}{(1+R/2)} + \frac{C/2}{(1+R/2)^2} + \frac{C/2}{(1+R/2)^3} + \cdots + \frac{C/2}{(1+R/2)^{2N}} + \frac{F}{(1+R/2)^{2N}}. \quad (2)$$

For example, suppose a bond has an annual coupon of $6, a term of maturity of twenty years, and sells at a market price of 85½. The yield to maturity (expressed as an annual rate) may be calculated as follows:

$$85.50 = \frac{3}{(1+R/2)} + \frac{3}{(1+R/2)^2} + \cdots + \frac{3}{(1+R/2)^{40}} + \frac{100}{(1+R/2)^{40}}. \quad (2a)$$

The yield to maturity, R, is 7.40 percent. The present value of the stream of $3 coupons to be received each six months and of the $100 face value to be paid at maturity is $85.50 when discounted at a 7.40 percent rate.[4]

The Use of Bond Tables

Fortunately, there are handy books of tables, called "bond tables," that make laborious calculations unnecessary. Bond tables are available to cover most of the coupons and maturities that arise in practice. The tables show, for a given market price, coupon rate, and maturity, the appropriate yield to maturity. A sample page from a book of bond tables is shown in Table 1. Term to maturity is designated along the columns, yield to maturity is listed down the rows, while the numbers within the table are bond prices. The coupon, expressed as a percentage of the face value, is shown on the top right-hand corner. With this table we can see how easy it is to solve for R in a case such as that given in Equation 2a. By reading down the twenty-year column until we come to a bond price of 85½ (three rows up from the bottom) we find the corresponding yield in the left-hand column. For prices (or

means a purchase of bonds with a face value of $10,000. The coupon on a bond is of course adjusted for the particular face value. Thus, in our example above of a $9 coupon (per $100 of face value), the actual coupon on a $1,000 bond would be $90, or $45 semiannually.

[4]A simplified rule of thumb for the calculation of bond yields may aid in the interpretation of the concept. The yield to maturity is approximately equal to the average annual interest payment and capital-gain return expressed as a percentage of the investor's average investment. Looking at the return side first, we see that the purchaser of a twenty-year $100 bond at $85.50 will receive $6 annual interest and an average annual capital gain of $.725 (i.e., $1/20$ of $14.50, the difference between the $100 maturity value of the bond and the $85.50 current market price). Thus the average annual overall return is $6.725 per bond. The average investment over the life of the bond may be approximated by averaging the current value $85.50 and the maturity value $100, to obtain $92.75. On this approach

$$\text{Yield to maturity} \approx \frac{\text{average yearly returns}}{\text{average investment}} = \frac{6.725}{92.75} = 7.25\%$$

which is not too far from the correct yield of 7.40 percent.

Table 1. Sample Page from a Book of Bond Tables

6%

Mat. Yield	19 Y M	19½ Y M	20 Y M	20½ Y M	21 Y M	21½ Y M	22 Y M
4.40	120.46	120.80	121.14	121.45	121.78	122.10	122.41
4.45	119.74	120.07	120.39	120.70	121.01	121.31	121.60
4.50	119.02	119.34	119.65	119.95	120.24	120.53	120.81
4.55	118.31	118.61	118.91	119.20	119.48	119.75	120.02
4.60	117.61	117.90	118.18	118.45	118.72	118.99	119.24
4.65	116.91	117.19	117.45	117.72	117.98	118.23	118.47
4.70	116.22	116.48	116.74	116.99	117.23	117.47	117.71
4.75	115.53	115.78	116.02	116.26	116.50	116.72	116.95
4.80	114.85	115.09	115.32	115.55	115.77	115.98	116.19
4.85	114.17	114.40	114.62	114.83	115.04	115.25	115.45
4.90	113.50	113.71	113.92	114.13	114.33	114.52	114.71
4.95	112.83	113.04	113.23	113.43	113.62	113.80	113.98
5.00	112.17	112.37	112.55	112.73	112.91	113.08	113.25
5.05	111.52	111.70	111.87	112.04	112.21	112.37	112.53
5.10	110.87	111.04	111.20	111.36	111.52	111.67	111.82
5.15	110.22	110.38	110.54	110.69	110.83	110.97	111.11
5.20	109.58	109.73	109.87	110.01	110.15	110.28	110.41
5.25	108.95	109.09	109.22	109.35	109.47	109.60	109.72
5.30	108.32	108.45	108.57	108.69	108.80	108.92	109.03
5.35	107.69	107.81	107.92	108.03	108.14	108.24	108.35
5.40	107.07	107.18	107.28	107.38	107.48	107.58	107.67
5.45	106.46	106.56	106.65	106.74	106.83	106.92	107.00
5.50	105.85	105.94	106.02	106.10	106.18	106.26	106.34
5.55	105.24	105.32	105.40	105.47	105.54	105.61	105.68
5.60	104.64	104.71	104.78	104.84	104.91	104.96	105.02
5.65	104.05	104.10	104.16	104.22	104.27	104.32	104.38
5.70	103.45	103.50	103.55	103.60	103.65	103.69	103.73
5.75	102.87	102.91	102.95	102.99	103.03	103.06	103.10
5.80	102.28	102.32	102.35	102.38	102.41	102.44	102.47
5.85	101.71	101.73	101.75	101.78	101.80	101.82	101.84
5.90	101.13	101.15	101.17	101.18	101.20	101.21	101.22
5.95	100.56	100.57	100.58	100.59	100.60	100.60	100.61
6.00	100.00	100.00	100.00	100.00	100.00	100.00	100.00
6.05	99.44	99.43	99.42	99.42	99.41	99.40	99.40
6.10	98.88	98.87	98.85	98.84	98.82	98.81	98.80
6.15	98.33	98.31	98.29	98.27	98.24	98.22	98.20
6.20	97.79	97.75	97.73	97.70	97.67	97.64	97.62
6.25	97.24	97.20	97.17	97.13	97.10	97.07	97.03
6.30	96.70	96.66	96.62	96.57	96.53	96.49	96.45
6.35	96.17	96.12	96.07	96.02	95.97	95.93	95.88
6.40	95.64	95.58	95.52	95.47	95.41	95.36	95.31
6.45	95.11	95.05	94.98	94.92	94.86	94.81	94.75
6.50	94.59	94.52	94.45	94.38	94.32	94.25	94.19
6.55	94.07	93.99	93.92	93.84	93.77	93.70	93.64
6.60	93.56	93.47	93.39	93.31	93.23	93.16	93.09
6.65	93.05	92.96	92.87	92.78	92.70	92.62	92.54
6.70	92.54	92.44	92.35	92.26	92.17	92.09	92.00
6.75	92.04	91.93	91.83	91.74	91.65	91.56	91.47
6.80	91.54	91.43	91.32	91.22	91.12	91.03	90.94
6.85	91.04	90.93	90.82	90.71	90.61	90.51	90.41
6.90	90.55	90.43	90.32	90.20	90.09	89.99	89.89
6.95	90.06	89.94	89.82	89.70	89.59	89.48	89.37
7.00	89.58	89.45	89.32	89.20	89.08	88.97	88.86
7.10	88.62	88.48	88.35	88.21	88.09	87.96	87.85
7.20	87.68	87.53	87.38	87.24	87.11	86.98	86.85
7.25	87.21	87.06	86.91	86.76	86.62	86.49	86.36
7.30	86.75	86.59	86.44	86.29	86.14	86.00	85.87
7.40	85.84	85.67	85.50	85.35	85.19	85.05	84.91
7.50	84.94	84.76	84.59	84.42	84.26	84.11	83.96
8.00	80.63	80.42	80.21	80.01	79.81	79.63	79.45

1369

Source: *Comprehensive Bond Values Tables* (Financial Publishing, 1958).

Table 2.　Relationships between Bond-Price Movements and Yield Changes[a]

Years to Maturity (N)	Price (P) to Yield 7% (R) to Maturity	Loss Incurred If Market Yields Rise from 6% to 7%	Price (P) to Yield 5% (R) to Maturity	Gain Realized If Market Yields Fall from 6% to 5%
1	99.05	0.95	100.96	0.96
2	98.16	1.84	101.88	1.88
3	97.34	2.66	102.75	2.75
4	96.56	3.44	103.59	3.59
5	95.84	4.16	104.38	4.38
10	92.89	7.11	107.79	7.79
20	89.32	10.68	112.55	12.55
30	87.53	12.47	115.45	15.45
Consol (Perpetual Bond)	85.71	14.29	120.00	20.00

[a]All examples assume semiannual compounding.

maturities) between the ones listed in the table, the appropriate yields can be found by interpolation.

Bond Yields and Bond Prices

Economists have typically formulated theories of the structure of interest rates in terms of bond yields rather than bond prices. Bonds are traded in terms of price, however, not yield. They are bought and sold by speculators, long-term investors, and financial institutions who are vitally concerned with price movements. An examination of the connection between bond yields and bond prices will be very helpful in understanding the actual structure of yields in the bond markets.

First, it should be noted from (1) that an increase in yield, R, implies a lower present value and thus a lower bond price. Moreover, for a given change in yield the corresponding change in bond prices is greater the longer the term to maturity. For example, if the yields of bonds of all maturities rose from 6 percent to 7 percent, the prices of long-term bonds would fall more than short-term issues. In Table 2, the greater price volatility of long-term issues, for a given change in interest rates, is illustrated. Bond prices are calculated for cases where yields for all maturities either rise to 7 percent or fall to 5 percent. The table assumes that initially all bonds are selling at face value (100) and have $6 coupons.[5]

The Yield Curve: Method of Construction and Historical Patterns

The yield curve is the most widely used graphic device for examining the relationship between yield and term to maturity of comparable debt securities. It refers simply to

[5]By the formula shown in 1, it will be seen that for $P = F = 100$ and $C = 6$, the initial yield to maturity, R, of each bond must be 6 percent.

a chart depicting the general shape of the relationship among bond yields of varying maturities. Along the horizontal scale is measured years to maturity and along the vertical axis, yield to maturity. A point is plotted on the chart for each security whose yield is to be used in constructing the curve. Then a relatively smooth curve is drawn, which describes the indicated relationship. Only issues similar in all characteristics should be plotted together, since, as was indicated above, special features of particular issues may alter their yields significantly. It is important, for example, to avoid plotting low- and high-coupon issues together, since low-coupon issues give more of their total yield in favorably taxed capital gains and hence tend to sell at relatively low yields.

Illustration of the Construction of a Yield Curve

The construction of a yield curve may be illustrated by using the actual yields of U.S. Treasury bonds on a specific date. Table 3 presents the actual price and yield

Table 3.   Prices of Selected Treasury Bonds[a]

Government, Agency and Miscellaneous Securities

Tuesday, March 31, 1970
Over-the-Counter Quotations: Source on request.
Decimals in bid-and-asked and bid change represent
32nds (101.1 means 101 1-32).

Treasury Bonds		Bid	Asked	Bid Chg.	Yld.
4s,	1970 Aug.	99.0	99.4	....	6.37
2½s,	1966-71 Mar.	96.8	96.12	....	6.49
4s,	1971 Aug.	96.4	96.12	+ .2	6.81
3⅞s,	1971 Nov.	95.8	95.16	....	6.86
4s,	1972 Feb.	94.19	94.27	+ .1	6.98
2½s,	1967-72 June	91.2	91.10	....	6.81
4s,	1972 Aug.	93.14	93.22	....	6.93
2½s,	1967-72 Sept.	90.2	90.10	....	6.86
2½s,	1967-72 Dec.	89.3	89.11	....	6.88
4s,	1973 Aug.	90.16	90.24	− .2	7.13
4⅛s,	1973 Nov.	90.6	90.14	....	7.17
4⅛s,	1974 Feb.	89.16	89.24	....	7.20
4¼s,	1974 May	89.16	89.24	....	7.17
3⅞s,	1974 Nov.	86.28	87.4	− .2	7.20
4s,	1980 Feb.	78.24	79.8	− .8	6.94
3½s,	1980 Nov.	73.24	74.8	− .8	6.97
3¼s,	1978-83 June	69.4	69.20	− .2	6.76
3¼s,	1985 May	68.14	68.30	− .2	6.57
4¼s,	1975-85 May	74.14	74.30	− .6	6.95
3½s,	1990 Feb.	68.8	68.24	− .4	6.27
4¼s,	1987-92 Aug.	72.8	72.24	− .4	6.59
4s,	1988-93 Feb.	70.2	70.18	....	6.48
4⅛s,	1989-94 May	70.8	70.24	− .4	6.56
3s,	1995 Feb.	68.10	68.26	− .2	5.26
3½s,	1998 Nov.	68.8	68.24	− .4	5.74

[a]Bonds for which a range of maturity dates are given (such as the 4s, 1988–93 Feb.) mature on the final date listed, February 1993, but may be redeemed as early as February 1988 at the option of the government. The yield to maturity has been calculated on the basis of the final maturity date, since the government is unlikely to wish to exercise its early call privilege when the general level of market yields is higher than the coupons on existing bonds. If the general level of market yields were lower than existing coupons, however, the yield to maturity would have been figured to the earliest call date (February 1988).

Source: *Wall Street Journal,* April 1, 1970.

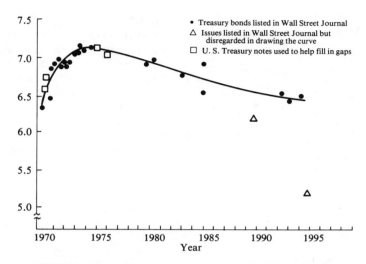

FIGURE 1. YIELD CURVE FOR U.S. TREASURY SECURITIES, MARCH 31, 1970

quotations for selected Treasury bonds as of March 31, 1970. Reading across the last row of the table we find first the description of the bond. "3½s, 1998 Nov." refers to the U.S. Treasury bonds maturing in November 1998 and carrying a 3½ percent coupon. Next we find the bid-price, $68^8/_{32}$, the price at which government-bond dealers stood ready to buy these bonds from sellers, and then the asked price, $68^{24}/_{32}$, the price at which dealers were willing to sell bonds to buyers. The next column shows that the bid price of a bond fell $^4/_{32}$ from the previous day's quotation. Finally, the yield to maturity (based on the asked price) is calculated. The term to maturity of the bond is simply the number of years from the date of the quotation to the maturity date of the bond, or slightly more than twenty-eight and a half years.

In Figure 1, the yields of the bonds quoted in Table 3 and their corresponding maturities are indicated on the chart. In addition, the yields of a few additional Treasury issues (not listed in the table) were plotted to help fill in some of the maturity gaps.[6] Then a relatively smooth free-hand curve was fitted by eye to the scatter of points to present the general relationship between yields and term to maturity. Care was taken in fitting the yield curve to avoid using those issues whose yields were significantly affected by special features. Three Treasury securities so affected by extraneous factors are indicated by a triangle in the figure.[7] These three issues, when part of the estate of a decedent, are redeemable at par (100) in payment of estate taxes. Since these issues were selling at just over 68, the potential tax benefit for certain investors was substantial. Consequently, we would expect that these se-

---

[6]In selecting these additional issues care was taken to avoid using Treasury securities with very low coupons (e.g., 1½ percent) or very high coupons (e.g., 8 percent) for the reasons mentioned in the text.

[7]The issues are the 3½s of 1990, the 3s of 1995, and the 3½s of 1998.

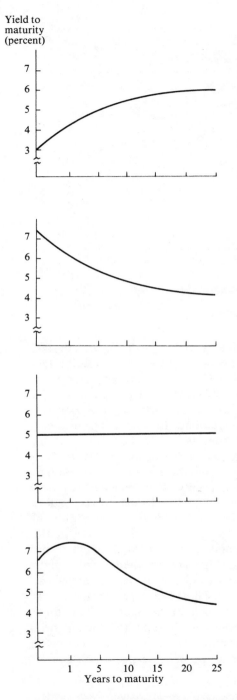

Ascending Curve

An ascending yield curve is formed when interest rates are lowest on short-term issues and then rise at a diminishing rate until they level out in the longest maturities. From 1930 through the middle 1960s ascending yield curves have been the most common curves for bond yields in the United States. Such curves appear to be characteristic of periods when relatively low interest rates prevailed for both maturity groups.

Descending Curve

A descending (or reverse) yield curve is formed when yields are highest on short-term securities and then decrease at a diminishing rate until they level out in the longest maturities. Descending yield curves were most common for high-grade corporate bonds during the period from 1906 to 1929 and during the late 1960s and early 1970s. Such curves have been characteristic of periods when relatively high interest rates prevailed for both long- and short-term securities.

Flat Curve

At times, yields on short- and long-term securities are approximately equal, thus forming a horizontal line or flat yield curve. In the United States, level curves characterized the period 1901–1905 when yields were necessarily measured on corporate securities. Level curves have appeared most frequently when short- and long-term rates have been near or somewhat above the middle of the range between the historical highs and lows.

Humped Curve

A humped yield curve is formed when yields rise in the early maturities, reach a peak, and then decline until they finally level out in later maturities. Conspicuously humped curves of the yields of U.S. Treasury securities existed through many months of 1957, 1959, 1960, and 1966–1970. Like descending curves, humped yield curves have usually appeared when the general level of interest rates is relatively high.

FIGURE 2. ALTERNATING SHAPES OF THE YIELD CURVE

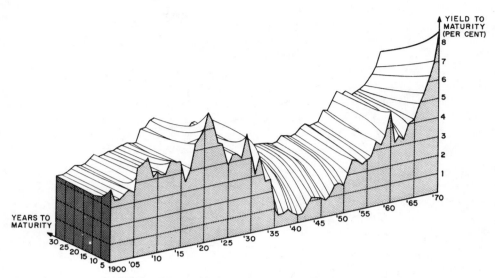

FIGURE 3. YIELD CURVES FOR PRIME U.S. CORPORATE BONDS

curities should sell at considerably lower yields than would issues of the same maturity similar in all respects except for the estate-tax advantage. It would be highly misleading to use such issues in the construction of the yield curve.

Historical Yield-Curve Patterns

Generally, the yield curve approximates one of four shapes illustrated in Figure 2. The curve may display the lowest yields on short-term issues and then rise at a diminishing rate until it becomes relatively flat in the longest maturities, thus forming an ascending curve. Alternatively, but somewhat less frequently, yields may be highest on short-term securities and then decrease at a diminishing rate until they level out, thus forming a descending (or reverse) yield curve. Still less frequently, yields are the same for all maturities, thus forming a flat yield curve. Finally, yields may rise in the early maturities, reach a peak, and then decline until they finally level out in the later maturities, as they did on March 31, 1970.

In Figure 3 yield curves for the highest-quality U.S. corporate bonds (free from all extraneous influences) during the twentieth century are depicted in three dimensions.[8] It will be noted that short-term yields have been considerably more volatile

[8]These yield curves were estimated by David Durand from 1900 through 1958. Yields for the period 1959 through 1970 were estimated by methods similar to those employed by Durand. Yields until 1942 were estimated from averages of yields recorded during the first three months of the year; yields after 1942 were calculated using January and February prices; and since 1951 yields have been based on February 15 prices. Since Durand was attempting to estimate the yields of the highest-quality corporate bonds outstanding, his curves were fitted to the lowest yields plotted. Also, it should be noted that

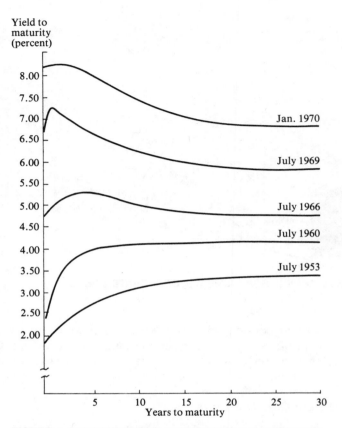

FIGURE 4. SELECTED YIELD CURVES FOR U.S. TREASURY SECURITIES

than long-term yields. In periods of restricted credit conditions short rates tend to rise more than long rates, while in periods of easy money they fall farther. Furthermore, the data indicate that descending yield curves (or curves with descending segments) are apt to occur when both long- and short-term rates are relatively high. Conversely, ascending yield curves have always been formed when relatively low rates prevailed for all maturities. On average, however, over the present century short rates have been considerably lower than long rates. . . . It is worth noting that conspicuously humped yield curves existed through many months of 1957, 1959, 1960, and 1966 through 1970,[9] when relatively high interest rates prevailed. For

Durand limited himself to fitting only the top three of the basic yield-curve shapes depicted in Figure 2. Finally, the freehand curves were smoothed to make successive differences between maturities sufficiently regular. I am grateful to Sidney Homer of the investment firm of Salomon Bros. & Hutzler for making the yield curves since 1958 available to me.

[9]The method employed by Durand for estimating the yields of corporate bonds precludes the identification of humped yield curves for these securities.

selected dates, some representative yield curves are displayed in Figure 4. As was true in the case of the corporate securities, the "average" yield curve for U.S. Treasury securities is an ascending one. Similar yield-curve patterns have been observed for Canadian and British securities, as well as for the securities of those few other nations whose capital markets are sufficiently developed to generate data covering a wide range of securities.

Usefulness of the Yield Curve

Before turning to an explanation of the various yield-curve patterns we observe in the market, it is possible to point out immediately one potential benefit that bond investors can derive from the construction of a yield curve. Once the individual yields are plotted and the yield curve is drawn, one can immediately identify those particular issues that are "out of line" with comparable bonds of the same maturity. Such a procedure may aid the investor in bond selection. Bonds whose yields are substantially lower than other securities of comparable maturity may be regarded as "overpriced" and should not be purchased. On the other hand, issues whose yields are well above the average for that maturity, as indicated by the yield curve, may be regarded as "underpriced" and may offer particularly good value, given the investor's circumstances. For example, it is quite clear that unless an investor can use the particular potential estate-tax advantage offered by the 3s of February 1995, this issue should be avoided. Similarly, from time to time issues may offer very good value. This might occur, for example, at a time when a large new issue is being "digested" by the market. The very construction of the curve may be useful in isolating such temporary pricing anomalies or market imperfections that may be exploited for profit by bond investors.[10]

Alternative Explanations of the Slope of the Yield Curve

What determines the slope of the yield curve? Why are short-term rates of interest sometimes higher and at other times lower than long-term yields? Despite the considerable study that has been devoted to these questions, much controversy remains. Among economists, three competing theories have attracted the widest attention.

---

[10]Of course, some bonds may offer particularly high yields because they have relatively large coupons and thus their returns tend to be taxed at ordinary income tax rates. On the other hand, deep-discount bonds with low coupons may offer relatively low yields because they tend to give a substantial part of their return in favorably taxed capital gains. Whether or not the higher-yielding bond with the larger coupon is in fact a good buy depends on the tax bracket of the investor. Clearly, for tax-exempt investors, only the yield to maturity matters. For an investor who pays taxes, the yields to maturity of the various bonds available for purchase may be calcuated on an after-tax basis in order to isolate particularly good values for that particular investor. Depending on the investor's tax bracket, different issues will better suit his objectives.

These are known as the expectations, liquidity-preference, and institutional or hedging-pressure theories of yield curve.

The Expectations Theory

According to the expectations theory, the shape of the yield curve can be explained by investors' expectations of future interest rates. Suppose, for example, investors believe that the prevailing level of bond yields is unusually high relative to historical precedent and that lower rates in the future are more probable than higher ones. In fact, a survey [see Kane and Malkiel, 1967] of interest-rate expectations (of the major institutional investors in the United States) during 1966 revealed that just such expectations were held then. Under such circumstances, long-term bonds will appear to many investors relatively more attractive than short-term ones if both maturities sell at equal yields. This is so for two reasons: First, long-term bonds will afford an investor an option of earning a high rate relative to the historical level of rates for a longer time period than will shorter issues. Investors who buy short-term bonds will subject themselves to the risk of having to reinvest their funds later at the lower yields that are expected. Second, if the investor sells prior to maturity, the longer the maturity of the bond he buys, the larger will be the potential capital appreciation he gains should his expectations prove correct. For example, the magnitude of the differential gains from a fall in all yields from 6 to 5 percent was illustrated in Table 2.

If investors act in accordance with these expectations, they will tend to bid up the prices (force down the yields) of long-term bonds and sell off short-term securities, causing their prices to fall (yields to rise). These operations will produce a descending yield curve with short-term issues yielding more than long-term bonds. . . .

In a similar manner, the expectations theory predicts that the yield curve will be upward sloping at a time when investors expect interest rates to rise. If yields were the same on all securities, investors would sell intermediate- and long-term bonds (where possibilities of substantial capital loss exist) and buy short-term securities. Such purchases and sales would tend to raise long rates relative to short rates.

The relationship of long and short rates under the expectations theory The expectations theory implies a formal relationship between long- and short-term rates of interest. Specifically, the analysis leads to the conclusion that the long rate is an average of current and expected short-term rates. To see why this is so, consider the following very simple example. Let us suppose that there are only two securities, a one-year bond and a two-year bond, and that all investors have funds at their disposal for either one or two years. Assume further that the current one-year market rate of interest is 7 percent, today's actual two-year rate is 7½ percent, and the one-year rate expected next year is 8 percent. The standard (but, unfortunately, necessarily complicated) notation, which can serve as a reference for the rest of the study, uses the following conventions:

• Let capital *R*s stand for actual market rates (yields).

- Let lower-case *r*s stand for expected rates.
- The pre-subscript represents the time period for which the rates are applicable.
- The post-subscript stands for the maturity of the bonds.

- For example, in the expression $_tR_5$
  pre-subscript t = period for which rate is applicable
  capital R = actual rate
  post-subscript 5 = maturity of bond for which rate applies.

- Specifically, $_tR_5$ stands for the actual five-year market rate of interest (the yield to maturity on a five-year bond) today, i.e., in period t.
- $_{t+1}r_5$ stands for the *expected* five-year market rate of interest that investors anticipate for the next year (period $t + 1$).

- $_{t+2}r_1$ indicates the one-year rate of interest that investors anticipate will prevail in the market two years from now, i.e., in period $t + 2$.

Thus, in our simple example above, $_tR_1$ = 7 percent, $_tR_2$ = 7½ percent, and $_{t+1}r_1$ = 8 percent.

Under the assumptions of the pure expectations theory, there are no transactions costs and all investors make identical forecasts of future interest rates. Moreover, there is perfect certainty and accurate forecasting. If investors are profit maximizers, it follows that *each investor will choose that security (or combination of securities) that maximizes his return for the period during which his funds are available.*

Let us consider the alternatives open to the investor who has funds at his disposal for two years. He may buy a two-year bond from which he obtains an annual yield of 7½ percent. Alternatively, he may buy a one-year bond, from which he receives a 7 percent return, and next year he may reinvest the proceeds in another one-year bond expected to yield 8 percent. In either case his average annual return is (approximately) 7½ percent.

The comparison is only slightly more complicated in the case of the investor with funds at his disposal for one year. If he buys a one-year bond, the return over his investment period (i.e., his holding-period yield) is 7 percent. Why can't he do better by buying a two-year bond yielding 7½ percent and then selling it after holding it for one year? The answer is that if one-year rates do indeed rise to 8 percent next year, the buyer of the two-year security will suffer a half-point capital loss.[11] Thus, the

---

[11]Assume that the two-year security bears a 7½ percent coupon and is currently selling at par (100). The price next year may be found by the bond-pricing formula, Equation 1.

$$\text{Price} = \frac{\text{coupon payment} + \text{face value at maturity}}{1 + \text{yield}}$$

In our example, next year's price = $(7½ + 100)/108 \approx 99½$, so the investor has a half-point capital loss.

realized return from the two-year bond over his investment period will be only 7 percent, as is shown below:

$$\text{Return over investment period} =$$

$$\frac{\text{coupon payment + capital gain (loss)}}{\text{purchase price}} = \frac{7\frac{1}{2} - \frac{1}{2}}{100} = 7\%. \qquad (3)$$

Correspondingly, we find that the investor with funds available for one year also receives the same return whichever maturity he buys. Again the holding-period return is the same on both maturities.

From this simple example, the determination of an equilibrium rate structure can be made clear. Suppose that expected returns on one-year and two-year securities were *not* equal. For example, let the two-year rate be 8 percent rather than 7½ percent, but let the future rate on one-year securities still be expected to equal 8 percent next year. It would turn out that all investors would prefer to hold the two-year security because it would promise a larger holding-period yield irrespective of the investment period of the buyer.[12] Consequently, investors would tend to sell one-year securities and buy two-year bonds. This process would continue until any differential in expected returns over the two investment periods was eliminated. On the assumptions of the theory, the long rate must turn out to be an average of present and future short-term rates of interest. Only when this is true can the pattern of short and long rates in the market be sustained. The long-term investor, for example, must expect to earn through successive investment in short-term securities the same return over his investment period that he would earn by holding a long-term bond to maturity.

The equilibrium relationship between long and short rates may be shown formally as follows. The two-year investor will have no incentive to move from one bond to another when he can make the same investment return from buying a combination of short issues or holding one long issue to maturity. If such an investor invests one dollar in a one-year security and then reinvests the proceeds at maturity [i.e., $(1 + {}_tR_1)$] in a one-year issue next year, his total capital will grow to $(1 + {}_tR_1)(1 + {}_{t+1}r_1)$ at the end of the two-year period.[13] Alternatively, if he invests his dollar in a two-year issue (and leaves all interest to be reinvested until the final maturity date in two years) he will have at maturity $(1 + {}_tR_2)^2$. In equilibrium, where the investor has no

---

[12]The two-year investor would earn an 8 percent annual yield by buying the longer security, whereas an average yield of only 7½ percent would be earned by buying one-year bonds now yielding 7 percent and reinvesting the proceeds in 8 percent issues next year. Similarly, the one-year investor would earn 8 percent by buying two-year bonds and selling them after one year, whereas only 7 percent would be earned by holding one-year bonds to maturity.

[13]For example, if an investor invested $1.00 in an investment that paid interest at the rate of 5 percent, paid annually, he would have at the end of the year his original investment of $1.00 plus interest of .05 × 1.00 or $.05, for a total of $1.05 = $1.00 (1.05). If he then reinvested the proceeds of $1.05 at a 6 percent interest rate, he would have at the end of the next year $1.05(1.06) = $1.113 = $1.00(1.05)(1.06).

incentive to switch from security to security, the two alternatives must offer the same overall yield, i.e.,

$$(1 + {_t}R_2)^2 = (1 + {_t}R_1)(1 + {_{t+1}}r_1). \tag{4}$$

Thus, the two-year rate can be expressed as a geometric average involving today's one-year rate and the one-year rate of interest anticipated next year.

$$(1 + {_t}R_2) = \sqrt{(1 + {_t}R_1)(1 + {_{t+1}}r_1)}. \tag{5}$$

In similar fashion, the rate on longer-term issues can be expressed in terms of a whole series of expected short rates. In general,

$$(1 + {_t}R_N) = [(1 + {_t}R_1)(1 + {_{t+1}}R_1) \ldots (1 + {_{t+N-1}}r_1)]^{1/N}. \tag{6}$$

How the theory accounts for the different shapes of the yield curve The expectations theory can account for every sort of yield curve. If short-term rates are expected to be lower in the future, then the long rate, which we have seen must be an average of those rates and the current short rate, will lie below the short rate. Similarly, long rates will exceed the current short if rates are expected to be higher in the future. It is even possible to account for humped yield curves (of the type that existed in the United States during many periods of the 1960s) by assuming that investors expect rates first to rise and then to fall later to much lower levels.

A simple numerical example will be useful both to clarify the averaging mechanism and to show the conditions under which a humped yield curve may be generated. Suppose the current one-year rate, ${_t}R_1$, is 7 percent. Further assume that the market expects next year's one-year rate, ${_{t+1}}r_1$, to be 8 percent, and that future anticipated (one-year) rates are as listed in the right-hand side of the table below:

Actual Market Rates	Anticipated Market Rates
${_t}R_1 = 7\%$	
${_t}R_2 =$	${_{t+1}}r_1 = 8\%$
${_t}R_3 =$	${_{t+2}}r_1 = 6\%$
${_t}R_4 =$	${_{t+3}}r_1 = 5\%$

Using the averaging formula in Equation 5, we find that the equilibrium two-year rate, ${_t}R_2$, is, according to the expectations theory, approximately 7½ percent.[14] The three-year rate, ${_t}R_3$, is an average of the one-year rate, ${_t}R_1$, 7 percent; the one-year rate expected next year, ${_{t+1}}r_1$, 8 percent; and the one-year rate expected two years from now, ${_{t+2}}r_1$, 6 percent. The equilibrium three-year rate is then approximately 7

---

[14]For simplicity, one can use arithmetic rather than geometric averaging to get an approximate answer. Thus, Equation 5 becomes

$${_t}R_2 = \frac{{_t}R_1 + {_{t+1}}r_1}{2}. \tag{5a}$$

percent. The reader may verify that the equilibrium four-year rate is approximately 6½ percent. Notice that the yield curve, which can be plotted from the market rates for the different maturities, will first rise and then fall to lower levels, giving a humped appearance.

In all this analysis, relative supplies of securities of different maturities have not even been mentioned. The previous argument shows that, in the model of the expectations theory, changes in the maturity composition of the total outstanding debt are irrelevant for the determination of the rate structure. Unless they alter expectations, changes in relative supplies can have no long-run effect on the term structure, which is determined fully by expectations of future short-term interest rates in the manner shown by Equation 6. The reason is that in equilibrium all investors (no matter how long their investment period) are indifferent concerning which maturities they hold. The investor with funds for one year, for example, will earn the same return over his investment period whether he holds one-year bonds and lets them mature or long-term issues, which he sells after one year. Consequently, if the maturity distribution of the outstanding debt changes so that the relative supply of one-year issues decreases while the relative supply of long-term bonds increases, investors will be happy to rearrange their portfolios with no change in the relative yields of short- and long-term issues.

Notice that the expectations theory is consistent with the historical patterns of yield curves depicted in Figures 3 and 4. When the general level of rates was low relative to the historical "normal" level, so that investors may plausibly have expected a rise in rates, we can see that ascending curves were the rule. On the other hand, yield curves (or segments of curves) that descend have been recorded when the general level of rates was very high relative to historical precedent. Thus, the expectations theory can explain the shape of the yield curve in a manner consistent with the historical evidence under an assumption of "return-to-normality" forecasting of interest rates. As will be indicated below, formal statistical tests confirm this finding.

Expected interest rates and the rate of inflation Before leaving our discussion of the expectations theory it will be helpful to examine the relationship between the yield curve and expected rates of inflation. Inflation influences the yield curve through its effect on expected interest rates. Irving Fisher argued that the stated (nominal) rate of interest in the market may be decomposed into two constituent parts: first, a "real rate of interest" paid to investors as a reward for foregoing present consumption, and, second, a compensation for the expected loss of purchasing power the investors will suffer from inflation. Thus, if the stated interest rate is, say, 8 percent, perhaps 5 percent represents the real rate of interest with the remaining 3 percent a compensation for the anticipated rate of inflation.

Suppose we know that the real rate of interest for both the current year and expected for next year is 5 percent and that a 3 percent inflation is expected this year while a 4 percent inflation is anticipated next year. In such a case the current stated one-year rate ($_tR_1$) will be 8 percent (equal to the sum of the real rate plus the compensation for inflation), while the expected market rate next year ($_{t+1}r_1$) will rise to 9 percent because of the increase in the anticipated rate of inflation. Thus, the two-year market rate, $_rR_2$, will be 8½ percent, higher than the one-year rate because the market expects an increase in the rate of inflation. Other things being the same, an increase in the expected rate of inflation in the future will tend to raise long rates relative to short ones, while a decrease in the expected rate of inflation will have the opposite effect.

Summary We may now summarize our discussion by noting that the expectations theory explains the shape of the yield curve by investors' anticipations about future interest rates. If the market expects higher rates in the future, the yield curve will tend to be upward sloping. Bond investors would favor short-term over longer securities if both sold at the same yield. Short-term issues will soon be paid off at face value, allowing investors to reinvest the proceeds at the coming higher interest rates. On the other hand, long-term bonds will decline in value if interest rates do indeed rise as forecast. The result is that the prices of short issues would be bid up (their yields would fall) and long-term bonds would fall in price (their yields would rise). Similar sorts of incentives exist for would-be borrowers as well. At a time when the general level of rates was expected to rise, borrowers in need of funds over a long period would be particularly anxious to convert short-term indebtedness into long-term bonds. Such switches would insure that long-run needs of the firm can be financed at the current advantageously low rates. Of course, the simultaneous retirement of short-term debt and issuance of long-term bonds will also tend to raise long rates relative to short ones. The larger the rise in rates that is expected, the steeper will be the slope of the yield curve. The theory explains the shapes of other types of yield curves with the same logic.

The Liquidity-Preference Theory

An important line of criticism against the expectations theory has been directed at the naive extension of the perfect-certainty variant of the theory (where forecasting is presumed to be accurate) to a world of uncertainty (where forecasting errors will be the rule rather than the exception). It is argued that in a world of uncertainty short-term issues are more desirable than longer securities because the former are more "liquid." By the liquidity of an asset we generally refer to the characteristic of its convertibility into cash on short notice without appreciable loss of principal value. The basic argument can best be understood in the context of a situation where short rates were expected to remain unchanged in the future. In such a case, liquidity theorists would argue, the long-term bonds ought to yield more than shorts by the amount of a risk premium. The holder of a long-term bond must be given a yield in excess of that obtainable on short-term issues in order to compensate him for assuming the risks of greater potential price fluctuations, should there be an unexpected change in the level of rates. As was indicated in Table 2, if the general level of rates does change, long-term bonds can be expected to fluctuate in price to a far greater extent than short-term issues. The expectations theory, on the other hand, holds that short- and long-term bonds ought to sell at equal yields whenever no change is expected in future rates. This is so because, neglecting transactions costs, the investor's expected return from buying longs or shorts will be the same no matter how long he has funds to invest.

A numerical example will help clarify the disagreement between the two theories. Suppose that the current short (one-year) rate is 6 percent and that the short rate for the following year and for all succeeding years is also expected to be 6 percent. The expectations theory holds there should be a flat yield curve and that a one-year investment will earn 6 percent whether a security maturing in one, two, or twenty years is bought.

According to the liquidity theory, however, an investor with short-term funds for investment will prefer the shorter security. If interest rates do not stay at the 6 percent level as expected, but instead unexpectedly rise to 7 percent, an investor who bought the one-year security will be unaffected by the change—his security will mature and be paid off at par. Indeed, even if he has to sell his bond prior to maturity he will be little affected by the change in rates since the prices of short-term issues are relatively unresponsive to changes in market interest rates. Consequently, the investor in short-term bonds takes little or no risk—he is assured of earning his 6 percent for the year he has funds available for investment. On the other hand, the investor who buys the twenty-year, 6 percent coupon bond in the expectation of selling it at par the next year will find that its price has fallen to approximately 89½ with the change in interest rates. Thus, instead of receiving a 6 percent return, he will lose 4½ percent (equal to 6 percent interest minus 10½ percent capital loss) on his investment. The longer the security he buys, the larger will be the investor's risk of price decline should the general level of interest rates rise unexpectedly. This is so because long-term bonds fluctuate more in price than shorts, for a given change in rates.

Of course, if all interest rates fall, the prices of long-term bonds will rise more than the price of shorter issues, as we showed in Table 2.[15] Nevertheless, if an investor has funds to invest for only a short time and does not wish to take a chance of losing some of his principal, he will prefer to invest in short-term issues and will accept a somewhat lower yield thereon as the price of gaining added safety.

The crux of the liquidity-preference theory is that long-term bonds, because of their greater potential price volatility, ought to offer the investor a larger return than short-term securities. If no premium were offered for holding long-term bonds, it is argued, most individuals and institutions would prefer to hold short-term issues to minimize the variability of the money value of their portfolios.[16] On the borrowing

---

[15]In practice, long yields do not usually change by as much as short yields and therefore Table 2 overstates the probable extra volatility of longer-term issues. As was mentioned earlier, long yields are conceived as being a complicated geometric average of current and future short-term rates of interest. Even if investors raise their forecasts of short-term rates for a few periods ahead, long-term rates need not rise by the same amount if the forecasted short ranges many years in the future remain unchanged. Nevertheless, empirical evidence indicates that when expectations are revised in an uncertain world, investors usually change a whole series of expected short-term rates and not just those rates for the years immediately ahead. Thus, long rates do tend to be quite volatile and investors in long-term bonds subject themselves to considerably more price variability than to purchasers of shorter issues.

[16]For an alternative explanation of liquidity premiums, see Stiglitz.

side, however, there is assumed to be an opposite propensity. Borrowers can be expected to prefer to borrow at long term to assure themselves of a steady source of funds. This leaves an imbalance in the pattern of supply and demand for the different maturities—one which speculators might be expected to offset. Hence, the final step in the argument is the assertion that speculators are also averse to risk and must be paid a liquidity premium to induce them to hold long-term securities. Thus, even if interest rates are expected to remain unchanged, the yield curve should be upward sloping, since the yields of long-term bonds will be augmented by risk premiums necessary to induce investors to hold them. While it is conceivable that short rates could exceed long rates if investors thought that rates would fall sharply in the future, the "normal relationship" is assumed to be an ascending yield curve. This is consistent with the historical evidence reported above that, on average, long-term rates have exceeded short rates over the present century.

Formally, the liquidity premium is typically expressed as an amount that is to be added to the expected future rate in arriving at the equilibrium-yield relationships described in Equations 4 through 6. If we let L_2 stand for the liquidity premium that should be added to next year's forecasted one-year rate, we have

$$(1 + {_t}R_2)^2 = (1 + {_t}R_1)(1 + {_{t+1}}r_1 + L_2), \tag{7}$$

and

$$(1 + {_t}R_2) = \sqrt{(1 + {_t}R_1)(1 + {_{t+1}}r_1 + L_2)}. \tag{8}$$

Thus, if L_2 is positive (i.e., if there is a liquidity premium), the two-year rate will be greater than the one-year rate even when no change in rates is expected. It has also been customary to assume that L_3, the premium to be added to the one-year rate forecasted for two years hence (i.e., for period $t + 2$) is even greater than L_2, so that the three-year rate will exceed the two-year rate when no change is expected in short-term rates over the next three years. In general, the liquidity-premium model may be written as

$$(1 + {_t}R_N) = [(1 + {_t}R_1)(1 + {_{t+1}}r_1 + L_2)(1 + {_{t+N-1}}r_1 + L_N)]^{1/N}. \tag{9}$$

Assuming that $L_N > L_{N-1} > \cdots > L_2 > 0$, the yield curve will be positively sloped even when no changes in rates are anticipated.

The Institutional or Hedging-Pressure Theory

Another group of critics of the expectations theory argues that liquidity considerations are far from the only additional influence on bond investors. While liquidity may be a critical consideration for a commercial banker looking for an investment outlet for a temporary influx of deposits, it is not important for a life insurance company seeking to invest an influx of funds from the sale of annuity contracts. Indeed, if the life insurance company wants to hedge against the risk of interest-rate fluctuations, it will prefer long maturities. This is because an annuity contract, in essence, guarantees to the annuitant a specified earnings rate over a long period. Therefore, the risk-averting insurance company will base its contracts on currently available long-term yields to maturity and immediately invest the proceeds from the sale of such contracts in the long market. Such long-term investments will guarantee the insurance company a profit regardless of what happens to interest rates over the life of the contract.

Many pension funds and retirement savers find themselves in a wholly analogous situation. While investment in short-term issues insures that the principal of the fund will be kept intact, such investments leave uncertain the fund's future income. Since such investors are concerned with guaranteeing themselves *certainty of income* (rather than *certainty of principal*) over the long run, risk aversion on their part should lead to a preference for long-term rather than short-term securities.

The institutional critics freely admit that other financial institutions such as commercial banks and corporate investors are interested primarily in liquidity and hedge against risk by the purchase of short-term issues. But that is precisely the thrust of the hedging-pressure argument. The institutionalists believe that different groups of investors have different maturity needs that lead them to confine their security purchases to restricted segments of the maturity spectrum. Similarly, many bond issuers are believed to tailor the maturity of their offerings to the type of asset to be financed or the length of time over which they need the funds. Thus, there are severe impediments to substitutability over maturity ranges of the yield curve for the various participants on both sides of the market. Under an extreme form of this argument, the short and long markets are effectively segmented. Financial institutions are presumed to select a maturity structure of assets suited to their needs and hold to that structure regardless of expected future interest-rate changes. The prices and yields in the short and long sectors of the market are set solely by the particular supply-and-demand relationships existing within it, since allegedly neither borrowers nor lenders shift between markets in response to rate differentials.

An institutional view of the determination of the term structure has been advanced by economists such as Culbertson but has perhaps been most vigorously argued by some market practitioners. For example, Homer and Johannesen (members of a large Wall Street firm specializing in bonds) do not regard short- and long-term issues as two ends of the same moustache, but rather ". . . as different from each other as stocks are from bonds, or more so . . . the [yield] curve should not be expected to behave traditionally or logically, as though the rates were linked together by a mathematical formula."

An important implication of the institutional theory is that the relative supplies of debt instruments play a central role in the determination of the equilibrium-yield structure. If, for example, the government retired $10 billion of short-term debt and increased the supply of long-term issues by the same amount, institutionalists would expect such an operation to raise the long rate relative to the short. In contrast, according to the expectations theory, such changes in the maturity composition of the outstanding bonds should, by themselves, have no effect on market-yield relationships.

Summary Comments

To summarize the discussion to this point, three theories have been advanced to explain the shape of the yield curve. The expectations theory argues that the term structure of interest rates can be fully explained by the market's anticipations regarding the course of future interest rates. According to this theory, an upward-sloping yield curve is formed when the market expects rates to rise in the future; a descending curve is formed when rates are expected to fall. The liquidity-preference theory, while not denying the importance of expectations, insists that an important additional factor must be considered. Specifically, liquidity theorists have argued that a yield premium must be offered to the buyers of long-term bonds to compensate bondholders for greater potential price volatility of such issues compared with short-term securities. Consequently, even when no change in future rates is expected, long-term bonds ought to yield more than shorts by the amount of risk (or illiquidity) premium. The institutional or hedging-pressure theory recognizes the risk-aversion argument advanced by the liquidity theorists and agrees that it is a good description of the behavior of many investors with fairly short horizons, such as commercial banks. Nevertheless, for certain investors with long-term obligations such as insurance companies, hedging behavior would indicate a preference for long-term bonds, which promise certainty of income payments over a long period, rather than short issues. Thus, different types of institutions have different maturity preferences. In the extreme form of the argument, the maturity preferences of different investors and borrowers are so strong that they never purchase securities outside their preferred maturity ranges to take advantage of yield differentials. As a result, it is argued that the short and long markets are effectively segmented and yields are determined by supply and demand in each market. . . .

Summary of Empirical Work

Empirical studies . . . have found considerable evidence concerning the importance of expectational elements in determining the shape of the yield curve. Unfortunately, little evidence is available on the actual expectations held by investors at different periods in the past. Nevertheless, empirical investigators have developed indirect methods of estimating how expectations might have been formed that have enabled us to make reasonable judgments that expectations play a central role in the determination of the rate structure. The shapes of actual yield curves have consistently been related to these fabricated expectations in precisely the manner suggested by the expectations theory.

There is also evidence, however, that expectations are not the unique determinant of the term structure. It would appear that the yield curve has an upward bias. For example, the normal average yield curve, calculated over long periods of bond-market history, has been an ascending one. This evidence is consistent with the liquidity-preference view that investors in long-term bonds must be paid a yield in excess of that obtainable on short-term securities for accepting the risks of greater potential price fluctuations. The institutional or hedging-pressure theory has generally been tested by examining a major implication of the theory—that non-expectations-induced changes in the maturity structure of the outstanding debt should alter the shape of the yield curve. Various problems associated with these tests suggest, however, that the evidence assembled thus far is inconclusive. . . .

We have seen that it is possible to marshal strong empirical evidence in support of both the expectations and the liquidity-preference theories of the yield curve. Evidence supporting the importance of institutional factors is rather weak, but, as noted above, the tests performed suffer from several drawbacks. In any case, all three theories should really be viewed as complementary rather than competitive. For example, the liquidity-preference explanation does not deny the importance of expectations; it only suggests that expectations *alone* are insufficient to determine the shape of the yield curve. Thus, those two theories together may be viewed as offering a more complete explanation of the term structure of interest rates than either theory alone. . . .

BIBLIOGRAPHY

ALMON, SHIRLEY. "The Distributed Lag between Capital Appropriations and Expenditures." *Econometrica* 33 (January 1965), pp. 78–96.

BAUMOL, WILLIAM J., BURTON G. MALKIEL, and RICHARD E. QUANDT. "The Valuation of Convertible Securities." *Quarterly Journal of Economics* 80 (February 1966), pp. 48–59.

BIERWAG, G. O., and M. A. GROVE. "A Model of the Term Structure of Interest Rates." *Review of Economics and Statistics* 49 (February 1967), pp. 60–62.

BUSE, A. "Interest Rates, the Meiselman Model and Random Numbers." *Journal of Political Economy* 75 (February 1967), pp. 49–62.

CAGAN, PHILLIP. "A Study of Liquidity Premiums on Federal and Municipal Government Securities." In Jack M. Guttentag and Phillip Cagan, eds. *Essays on Interest Rates.* Columbia University Press for the National Bureau of Economic Research, 1969.

CONARD, JOSEPH W. *The Behavior of Interest Rates.* Columbia University Press for the National Bureau of Economic Research, 1966.

CULBERTSON, JOHN M. "The Term Structure of Interest Rates." *Quarterly Journal of Economics* 71 (November 1957), pp. 485–517.

DE LEEUW, FRANK. "A Model of Financial Behavior." In James Duesenberry et al., eds. *The Brookings Quarterly Econometric Model of the United States.* Rand McNally, 1965.

DILLER, STANLEY. "Expectations in the Term Structure of Interest Rates." In Jacob Mincer, ed. *Economic Forecasts and Expectations.* Columbia University Press for the National Bureau of Economic Research, 1967.

DURAND, DAVID. *Basic Yields of Corporate Bonds, 1900–1942*. Technical Paper 3, National Bureau of Economic Research, 1942.

FAIR, RAY C., and BURTON G. MALKIEL. *The Determination of Yield Differentials between Debt Instruments of the Same Maturity*. Research Memorandum No. 5, Financial Research Center, 1970.

FISHER, LAWRENCE. "Determinants of Risk Premiums on Corporate Bonds." *Journal of Political Economy* 67 (June 1959), pp. 217–37.

GRANT, J. A. G. "Meiselman on the Structure of Interest Rates: A British Test." *Economica* 31 (February 1964), pp. 51–71.

HICKMAN, W. BRADDOCK. "The Interest Structure and War Financing." Unpublished manuscript. National Bureau of Economic Research, 1943.

HOMER, SIDNEY, and RICHARD I. JOHANNESEN. *The Price of Money, 1946 to 1969*. Rutgers University Press, 1969.

KANE, EDWARD J. "The Term Structure of Interest Rates: An Attempt to Reconcile Teaching with Practice." *Journal of Finance* 25 (May 1970), pp. 361–74.

KANE, EDWARD J., and BURTON G. MALKIEL. "The Term Structure of Interest Rates: An Analysis of a Survey of Interest-Rate Expectations." *Review of Economics and Statistics* 49 (August 1967), pp. 343–55.

KESSEL, REUBEN A. *The Cyclical Behavior of the Term Structure of Interest Rates*. Occasional Paper 91, National Bureau of Economic Research, 1965.

MACAULAY, FREDERICK R. *The Movements of Interest Rates, Bond Yields, and Stock Prices in the United States since 1856*. National Bureau of Economic Research, 1938.

MALKIEL, BURTON G. *The Term Structure of Interest Rates: Expectations and Behavior Patterns*. Princeton University Press, 1966.

———. "How Yield Curve Analysis Can Help Bond Portfolio Managers." *The Institutional Investor,* 1 May 1967.

———, and EDWARD J. KANE. "Expectations and Interest Rates: A Cross-Sectional Test of the Error-Learning Hypothesis." *Journal of Political Economy* 76 (July–August 1968), pp. 453–70.

MEISELMAN, DAVID. *The Term Structure of Interest Rates*. Prentice-Hall, 1962.

MODIGLIANI, FRANCO, and RICHARD SUTCH. "Innovations in Interest Rate Policy." *American Economic Review: Papers and Proceedings* 56 (May 1966), pp. 178–97.

———. "Debt Management and the Term Structure of Interest Rates: An Empirical Analysis." *Journal of Political Economy* 75 (August 1967), pp. 569–89.

———. "The Term Structure of Interest Rates: A Reexamination of the Evidence." *Journal of Money, Credit and Banking* 1 (February 1969), pp. 112–20.

NELSON, C. R. "Time Series Methods for Testing a Model of the Term Structure of Interest Rates." Unpublished manuscript. 1969.

ROSS, MYRON H. " 'Operation Twist': A Mistaken Policy?" *Journal of Political Economy* 74 (April 1966), pp. 195–99.

SLOANE, PETER E. "Determinants of Bond Yield Differentials." *Yale Economic Essays* 3 (Spring 1963), pp. 3–55.

STIGLITZ, JOSEPH E. "The Term Structure of Interest Rates and Portfolio Management." Unpublished manuscript, 1968.

TELSER, LESTER G. "A Critique of Some Recent Empirical Research on the Explanation of the Term Structure of Interest Rates." *Journal of Political Economy* 75 (August 1967), pp. 546–61.

THEIL, HENRI. *Economic Forecasts and Policy,* 2nd ed. North Holland, Amsterdam, 1961.

VAN HORNE, JAMES. "Interest Rate Risk and the Term Structure of Interest Rates." *Journal of Political Economy* 73 (August 1965), pp. 344–51.

WALLACE, NEIL. "Buse on Meiselman—A Comment." *Journal of Political Economy* 71 (July–August 1969), pp. 524–27.

WHITE, WILLIAM H. "The Structure of the Bond Market and the Cyclical Variability of Interest Rates." *International Monetary Fund Staff Papers,* March 1962.

WOOD, JOHN H. "Expectations, Errors, and the Term Structure of Interest Rates." *Journal of Political Economy* 31 (April 1963), pp. 160–71.

The Implementation
of Monetary Policy

For over a decade many economists have argued that the official policy procedures described in the first reading in this section are not enough to ensure economic stability. They have insisted that the Federal Reserve needs to specify a "strategy"—outlining its conception of the structure of the economy, its objectives for the performance of the economy, and the information constraints within which it must operate. The second article in this section, by Raymond E. Lombra and Raymond G. Torto, is an important step in this direction. Lombra and Torto provide an analytical view of Federal Reserve "strategy." They show that an interest rate, the Federal funds rate, was, until 1979, still the central instrument of monetary policy in that strategy. They also show that despite the formal role of monetary aggregates as intermediate target-variables in that pre-1979 strategy, the Federal Reserve's concern over interest rate volatility prohibited their use as such. As discussed in the Editors' Appendix to the article, in 1979 the Federal Reserve shifted to a strategy wherein the focus of policy was on the supply of bank reserves and the monetary base.

Richard G. Davis's survey article begins with a review of some technical problems in choosing the best definition of the money supply. Then he goes on to examine the costs of not controlling money as well as an operational program for its control over various periods of time. In attempting to influence the money stock, as an intermediate target-variable, the policymaker can choose either an interest rate or a monetary aggregate as his policy instrument. Davis debates the problem of which instrument should be controlled and which one allowed to fluctuate. A key to his considerations is an empirical test of how closely the money stock can be controlled using various instruments. Davis closes his survey with an examination of the optimum period of time over which to attempt to control the money supply, as an intermediate target-variable.

James Cacy's article carefully considers the theory of the optimal instrument for monetary policy—the money supply or the interest rate. This theory has become popular in the lecture hall but is not yet found in many textbooks.

Even if the money supply or some monetary aggregate were an optimal instrument, in the sense outlined by Cacy, and if the conceptual problems outlined by Davis were overcome, there still would be difficulties in controlling it. The next article, by James Pierce, argues forcefully that some of the difficulties are political. Back in 1975 Congress assumed responsibility for overseeing monetary policy; Pierce shows that between 1975 and 1978 money-stock control actually deteriorated, because during that time the Federal Reserve, in a fashion outlined in the article by Richard Davis in this section, opted for close control of the interest rate. Nevertheless, Pierce contends, Congressional oversight has caused more attention to be paid to the technical problems of controlling monetary aggregates. Indeed, since the Federal Reserve switched in 1979, as indicated in the Lombra and Torto article, to a strategy that places more emphasis on the monetary aggregates and less on interest rates, these technical problems have assumed great importance.

The closing selection in this section, by several members of the staff of the Board of Governors of the Federal Reserve System, focuses on these technical problems by discussing how recent regulatory and institutional changes have distorted the conceptual meaning of many monetary aggregates. The article closes with a far-reacing proposal to redefine many of the monetary aggregates, by grouping together deposits at financial institutions that have grown increasingly similar because of these regulatory and institutional changes.

The Strategy of
Monetary Policy

Raymond E. Lombra
Raymond G. Torto*

23

I. Introduction

While much has been written over the years concerning monetary policy, there is apparently a discontinuity in the flow of information between policymakers, on the one hand, and academic researchers and participants in financial markets, on the other. Much of this lack of communication centers specifically on the formulation and implementation of monetary policy.** As a result, much of the research into the policy process is based on incorrect assumptions concerning how policy is managed. Sherman Maisel, a former member of the Federal Reserve Board of Governors, argues that the Fed itself is a source of this communications gap: "The Fed has always resisted being too specific about [its] methods and its goals, clothing its operations in a kind of mystique that left it more freedom to maneuver" [18, p. 26].

Reprinted from the Federal Reserve Bank of Richmond, *Monthly Review* (September/October, 1975), pp. 3–14, by permission of the publisher and the authors.

* The authors express gratitude to Charles Cathcart, Lauren Dillard, Cathy Gaffney, Gary Gillum, Herbert Kaufman, Donald Kohn, Thomas Mayer, John Pippenger, William Poole, Richard Puckett, Steven Roberts, and the staff of the Federal Reserve Bank of Richmond, particularly Alfred Broaddus and Joseph Crews, for very helpful comments that have materially improved the paper.

** In the next three articles different words are applied to the same concepts. "Operating targets" here is synonymous with "instruments" used elsewhere, e.g. article 25. "Intermediate target variables" used here is synonymous with "Objectives" used elsewhere (article 24).—Ed.

In the opinion of many policy observers, this communications failure has real costs, both in terms of public understanding and the effectiveness of policy. While the Fed is reluctant to specify its procedures too explicitly in order to protect its freedom of action, "its attempt to protect itself from both outside critics and internal disappointment . . . weakens its ability to improve its performance" [18, p. 311].

Recently a number of papers have been directed toward unraveling the mystique that surrounds monetary policy.[1] The purpose of this article is to synthesize and extend the recent literature on this subject and thereby provide an interpretation of the monetary policy process and a model of current open market strategy. Hopefully, this article will contribute to a better understanding of current policy procedures and will help to identify problem areas toward which further research should be directed.[2]

This article consists of seven sections. Section II presents the background to the current strategy. The following three sections describe long-run aspects of current policy formulation, the linkages between the long- and short-run policy process, and short-term open market strategy, respectively. An analysis of the effect of the constraint on interest rate volatility on short-run policy actions is presented in Section VI, followed by some final remarks in Section VII.

II. The Evolution of the Current Strategy

An important paper by Jack Guttentag, published in 1966, described the Federal Reserve's policy procedures of the 1950's and early 1960's as the money market strategy [10]. Under the money market strategy, the Federal Reserve's proximate focus was on the "condition of the money market"—generally understood to include the value of a constellation of interest rates, free reserves, and the inventory positions and financing costs of securities dealers. With such national economic goals as full employment and price stability remote in time and causal connection from conditions in the money market, the use of money market conditions as a proximate target tended to focus policy too narrowly. As a result, Guttentag argued:

> The main weakness of the [money market] strategy is its incompleteness, i.e., the fact that the Federal Open Market Committee (FOMC) does not set specific quantitative target values for which it would hold itself accountable for the money supply, long-term interest rates, or any other "strategic variable" that could serve as a connecting link between open market operations and system objectives; rather it tends to rationalize the behavior of these variables after the fact [10, p. 1].

---

[1]See, for example, the important articles by Axilrod and Beck [1], Brimmer [3], Kane [12], Maisel [17], Pierce [22, 23], Pierce and Thomson [25], Poole [26], and Tschinkel [29].

[2]This discussion is not meant to imply that all monetary research has been useless or that no one understands the essence of current policy procedures. With regard to the latter, it is clear that many financial market analysts have considerable expertise in assessing the implications of day-to-day Federal Reserve actions.

To correct the deficiencies in the money market strategy, Guttentag suggested that the Fed adopt a complete strategy—consisting of quantifiable targets specified over given control periods, with the sequence of targets linked empirically to the ultimate price and output goals of the economy. Targets are defined as strategic variables that policymakers can affect by manipulating policy instruments.[3] Included in the set of targets are both intermediate targets such as interest rates, bank reserves, and monetary aggregates, and longer-term final targets (or goal variables) such as output, employment, and prices. Instruments are the magnitudes under direct policy control and include open market operations, the discount rate, reserve requirements, and interest rate ceilings.

A control period is the time interval over which the attainment of targets is planned. A complete policy strategy involves a number of control periods, each giving primary emphasis to different target variables. For example, over a weekly control period, an operating target such as the Federal funds rate or nonborrowed reserves might receive emphasis; over a monthly or quarterly control period, an intermediate target such as the growth rate of M_1 might receive emphasis. In control periods as long as six months or a year, long-term target variables such as output and employment would be the major policy goals.

A strategy is complete if its intermediate target is a strategic variable, linked empirically to the economy's long-term output, price, and employment goals. This implies that the policymaker is cognizant of the linkages among the various elements of the strategy. In a more formal sense, a model of the monetary policy transmission mechanism such as: instrument→intermediate target→long-term target must be developed.[4]

Guttentag was careful to distinguish between policy strategy, which involves the selection of the target variables to be explicitly considered by policymakers, and policy formulation, which involves the setting of specific values, or *dial settings,* for the target variables. In selecting these values, the policymaker examines a set of policy determinants such as relevant financial and economic data and forecasts. Clearly the development of an overall policy strategy is logically prior to policy formulation, since the particular policy determinants that the policymaker considers are dependent upon the strategy being pursued and the transmission mechanism it embraces [7, pp. 6–11].

The thrust of the Guttentag critique was reinforced by a number of events that increased public awareness of monetary policy. In the late 1960's the economic stimulus provided by the Vietnam war and the delay of the 1968 tax surcharge and the intellectual stimulus of the monetarist counterrevolution served to focus increasing public attention on monetary policy. During the same period, the development of

---

[3]Discussions of monetary policy have long been plagued by semantic difficulties with such words as targets, indicators, guides, objectives, etc., with the same words having different meanings to different writers. Such problems have played a major role in several major controversies in monetary economics [20].

[4]The arrows indicate the direction of causation. See [7] for a clear discussion of the transmission mechanism in monetarist and nonmonetarist models. [See article 6 of this book.—Ed.]

large-scale econometric models reflected the substantial impact of monetary policy on economic activity and tended to emphasize quantification of policy targets. In view of these developments, it is perhaps not surprising that the Federal Reserve moved toward the development of a more complete strategy. In 1966 the FOMC added a "proviso clause" to its Directive, giving explicit weight to movements in bank credit in determining policy actions. In 1970 the FOMC first began to include explicit references to monetary aggregates in its instructions to the Trading Desk. An important step in this ongoing process was probably the appointment of Arthur Burns as Chairman of the Federal Reserve Board in early 1970. In this regard Maisel states: "From the first day in office [Burns] put the weight of his office behind greater quantification" [18, p. 70].

The result of this evolutionary process can be stated simply—monetary aggregates (e.g., M_1, M_2, M_3, and bank credit) now receive more weight in policy deliberations and actions. The Directive—the FOMC's instructions to the Manager of the Trading Desk—now includes *specific* values for various strategic target variables, such as the Federal funds rate, bank reserves, and the monetary aggregates.[5] It is useful for expository purposes to divide the discussion of current policy procedures and strategy into its long- and short-term aspects. A description of these components and their interrelationship begins in the next section.

III. A View of Long-Run Strategy

The policy process begins at the Federal Reserve Board with the development of staff forecasts for GNP, prices, unemployment, and other long-run targets four quarters into the future.[6] These basic forecasts are undertaken three or four times each year and are updated each month. The projections are referred to as consensus forecasts, since judgmental and econometric inputs are combined into a single forecast.

The econometric forecast is made using the Board's version of the SSRC-MIT-PENN (SMP) econometric model.[7] Initially, model simulations are conducted using expected values of exogenous variables not under Federal Reserve control, such as Federal Government outlays, and a trajectory for an intermediate target variable under potential Federal Reserve control, such as the growth rate of the money stock. The same money stock trajectory, for example a 5 percent annual

[5]The more specific the instructions contained in the Directive, the less discretion or latitude the Manager has in executing policy actions. One of Guttentag's criticisms of the Fed's operating procedures in the 1950's and 1960's was the ambiguity in the Directive. He stated: "It is natural and a type of poetic justice that the words used by the Committee in giving instructions to the Manager are thrown back to the Committee. If the Committee instructs him to follow an 'even keel tipped on the side of ease', for example, he can report back that he 'maintained an even keel . . .' and the Committee is not in a position to complain that it does not understand what these words mean" [10, p. 18].

[6]This discussion draws heavily from the work of former members of the Board staff: Pierce [23], Pierce and Thomson [25]; and the work of former Governors Brimmer [2, 3] and Maisel [17, 18].

[7]See [5], [7], and [9] for discussions of the policy transmission mechanism of the SMP model. *Editors' Note:* [7] is reprinted in section II of this book.

growth rate, is also assumed by the judgmental forecasters. The judgmental forecast, prepared by staff economists in various sections of the Federal Reserve Board, is often more accurate in the near term than the model forecast [23, p. 12]. Differences in the econometric and judgmental forecasts are reconciled, and the consensus forecast is prepared.

One should not infer that the econometric projections are "pure" in the sense of a mechanical application of an existing model; as is true in most econometric work, a considerable degree of judgment is involved. This notion has been summarized by Hymans:

> No [model] operator—at least, one with much success as a forecaster—lets the computer center run his model. Rather, the operator considers the model to be nothing better than the best statement of the internal logic of the economy which he happens to have available. While he rarely tampers with the model's interactive logic, he recognizes that there are relevant factors which he thinks he knows, and which he is sure the model does not know, about current realities in the economy. In some way, he attempts to communicate this information to the model. . . . And what is most important, much of the relevant information which has to be communicated to the model is simply not contained in the values of the exogenous variables [11, p. 537].

For the sake of completeness, it should also be noted that the judgmental forecast is not independent of the econometric projections. The various forecasters interact continually and therefore a judgment about the path of economic activity (especially over a long time horizon) is no doubt influenced by the model simulations.

Following the development of the consensus forecast, the Board staff usually produces a number of alternative long-run scenarios of economic activity for evaluation by the FOMC. First, the consensus forecast is reproduced quarter-by-quarter, variable-by-variable with the econometric model by adjusting the constant terms in selected equations. Alternative trajectories of monetary growth are then fed into the model to produce a consistent set of monetary, GNP, price, and unemployment estimates.[8] The FOMC then evaluates these alternative scenarios and selects an explicit monetary growth path for the forthcoming six- or twelve-month period.

It is important to note that the implicit dial settings for the final targets embedded in the staff forecast may not, for a variety of reasons, be accepted by members of the FOMC. For instance, an individual member of the FOMC may not believe the staff forecast and may therefore foresee a different real sector outcome. Each Reserve Bank President has his own staff's view of the economic and financial outlook to consider, and it is possible that his staff has a forecast quite different from that of the

---

[8]As Pierce has discussed [23], a less extensive forecasting effort is made each month just prior to a FOMC meeting. This effort involves the updating of earlier forecasts through an extensive examination of incoming data and how they agree with, or have tended to modify, the projections presented in previous months. See also [2].

Board staff. More generally, there is no reason to assume that each member of the FOMC will embrace the estimates developed by the Board staff with regard to the impact of monetary policy on economic activity.[9]

Alternatively, an FOMC member may have a longer planning horizon for policy than the four- to six-quarter projection horizon and, therefore, might not believe that such a short-term projection should be a major determinant of current policy actions. In the current setting, for example, a policymaker may desire to drive unemployment down to 4 percent by mid-1976 but might feel that existing economic constraints, as well as structural relationships, make the risk of intensifying inflationary pressures under such a policy high. Hence, the return to full employment should be, in this member's view, more gradual and occur over a two- to three-year period.

Another possibility is that an FOMC member may have little faith in any of the assorted projections and instead may be strongly influenced by current economic and financial conditions. This view implies a shorter planning horizon than four to six quarters. Pierce has summarized some reasons why this last possibility may prevail from time to time:

> It is very difficult to convince a policymaker to move an instrument in what he views to be the wrong direction. That is to say, if income is expanding very rapidly and the models are predicting that it is going to fall in the future unless he eases up, it is very difficult to get him to ease up because that sort of policy recommendation is contrary to what is going on currently. I must say that until our models do a lot better, his wariness may be justified. Again, the problem is one of how to handle risk: what if the model were wrong? What if the economy were expanding very rapidly, the policymaker eases up, but economic expansion becomes more rapid? The cost of the error to the policymaker would be very large [23, p. 18].[10]

A Model of the Long-Run Strategy

The longer-term policy process described above conforms to a general class of constrained optimum problems. That is, policymakers may be viewed as maximizing a utility or preference function subject to the constraints imposed by the economic structure or by other considerations. Equation (1) states that the utility of the policymaker is a function of the deviation of the final targets from their desired levels, with

---

[9]In recent testimony by Chairman Burns before the Senate Banking Committee (July 24, 1975), members of the Senate Committee requested the release of the staff economic forecast conditional on a particular growth rate in the money stock. Chairman Burns did not appear to favor this suggestion, and his response emphasized some of the same points discussed in this and following paragraphs.

[10]The issue here is quite complex. The policymaker must act in the face of uncertainty over structural parameters and with the knowledge that there is a lag between actions and effects. In addition, there is the distinct possibility that incoming data may be revised substantially and thereby alter the appropriate policy response. Against this background, it is often difficult for policymakers to be convinced to move an instrument now to affect a final target one year in the future. Perhaps some of the recent applications of control theory to stabilization policy will prove helpful in educating both policy advisers and policymakers.

greater utility being associated with smaller deviations.[11] Let U represent the policy-maker's utility. Then:

$$\text{maximize} \quad U = f_1\,(Y^A - Y^*) \tag{1}$$

$$\text{subject to} \quad Y^A = f_2\,(M_L, X_L) \tag{2}$$

$$\text{and} \quad \sigma_R^2 \leq \alpha \tag{2a}$$

where Y is a vector of final target variables such as GNP and prices. The superscript A denotes the actual value of the variable, and the asterisk denotes a desired value. The symbol σ_R^2 represents the variance of some interest rate R, α is a constant, M is the money stock, X represents other determinants of the final targets, and the subscript L is a distributed lag operator. The side constraints represented by equations (2) and (2a) reflect the limitations imposed on policymakers by the structure of the economy and by the volatility of interest rates.

The expected values of the final targets will generally depend upon the structure of the economy, the particular dial settings for the intermediate target variable selected by the central bank, dial settings for fiscal policy selected by Congress and the President, and the values of other determinants such as the level of consumer and business confidence, price expectations, the degree of capacity utilization, and international developments. The forecast of final targets by the staff assumes specific dial settings for the intermediate target variables, e.g., the money stock, and also involves assumptions concerning all of the above determinants of economic activity not under the direct control of the Federal Reserve.[12] This process is summarized by equation (2), which condenses the SMP model and the consensus forecast for the final targets into a simple expression.[13] It is presumed that the policymaker believes that changes in the money stock lead in a systematic fashion, albeit with a lag, to changes in prices, output, and employment.[14]

Equation (2a) is included as a constraint to account for the Fed's ongoing desire to avoid disorderly conditions in financial markets that, in turn, might frustrate the

[11]To be more precise, (f_1) is an inverse function; that is, the policymaker is minimizing disutility (or "losses") by minimizing the deviations of the actual target values from desired levels.

[12]This being the case, the forecast may be wrong because the fiscal policy assumption is wrong, the Federal Reserve does not achieve the dial setting for the intermediate target, the structural parameters underlying the forecast are incorrect, or there is a stochastic shift in a behavioral relationship. One point relevant to this problem, which has received all too little attention in the literature, is the interdependence of stabilization policy actions. For example, if a restrictive monetary policy leads to a response by the Congress or the President to ease fiscal policy, the forecaster must anticipate this reaction.

[13]As noted above, each member of the FOMC might, in effect, have a different specification for equation (2) because of an alternative view of structural relationships. In this regard, equation (2), despite its simplicity, should not be mistaken for so-called reduced form models purporting to link the money stock or the monetary base to economic activity.

[14]Throughout this article error terms are generally ignored. Clearly, the staff should express the confidence intervals and standard errors around a particular forecast for the final targets.

achievement of the final targets. A discussion of the constraint on interest rate volatility is the subject of Section VI.

Before closing the discussion of the long-term strategy, it is important to emphasize that many members of the FOMC might object to the casual sequence that seems to underlie equation (2): open market operations→money stock→economic activity. More specifically, some might prefer:

$$Y^A = f_2(R_L, X_L)$$

where R is a short- or long-term interest rate, and the implied causal sequence is more like the transmission mechanism of the SMP model [7, pp. 7-9].

$$\begin{bmatrix} \text{Open} \\ \text{Market} \\ \text{Operations} \end{bmatrix} \rightarrow \begin{bmatrix} \text{Interest} \\ \text{Rates} \end{bmatrix} \rightarrow \begin{bmatrix} \text{Cost of Capital,} \\ \text{Household Net Worth,} \\ \text{Credit Availability} \end{bmatrix} \rightarrow \begin{bmatrix} \text{Economic} \\ \text{Activity} \end{bmatrix}$$

In part the issue involved here concerns the endogeneity or exogeneity of R and M and which variable ought to be the intermediate policy target [27]. For purposes of this article, this complex issue is sidestepped for two reasons. First, if one ignores the error term in the demand for money function, it may be solved in terms of the interest rate or the money stock, and either may be treated exogenously for forecasting purposes.[15] That is, a large macroeconometric model may contain a correctly estimated money demand function:

$$M = a_0 + a_1 y + a_2 R$$

where a_0, a_1, and a_2 are estimated parameters, M is money demand, y is nominal income, and R is the interest rate. The forecast for the final targets is independent of whether the money demand equation is solved for M or for R:

$$R = \frac{M - a_0 - a_1 y}{a_2}$$

Second, M is the assumed intermediate target variable in equation (2) because the FOMC has chosen to index its policy stance publicly in terms of M_1 and other monetary aggregates.[16] The use of the word "index" is meant to imply that even though members of the FOMC may have different views of the policy transmission mechanism in general, and the causal role of changes in the money stock in particular, the FOMC has been able to reach an agreement to express its policy in terms of growth rates in the monetary aggregates.

---

[15]Such a procedure would not be legitimate for estimation purposes because of the bias that would be introduced by treating a variable exogenously if in fact it were endogenous. See [16] for a discussion of this latter point and how it is related to models of money stock determination.

[16]See the "Record of Policy Actions" appearing each month in the *Federal Reserve Bulletin*.

IV. The Linkage between the Long- and
Short-Run Strategy

Having selected a long-run dial setting for money stock growth, perhaps 5 percent over the next twelve months, the FOMC must now guide its open market operations monthly so as to achieve the desired long-run monetary growth path. It is important to recognize that there are an infinite number of monthly and quarterly patterns of monetary growth for the money stock that could turn out to *average* 5 percent over a full year. As will be shown, the monthly pattern desired by the FOMC will generally depend upon interest rate considerations and the current position of the money stock vis-à-vis the long-run target.

The relationship between the short- and long-run dial settings for M_1 is illustrated in Figure 1. It is assumed that a 5 percent long-run growth path for M_1 was adopted in December, and by the January FOMC meeting M_1 is well below its targeted long-run path. Under these circumstances the staff would normally prepare three (or more) alternative short-run money stock paths for FOMC consideration, each designed to return M_1 to the long-term path but each requiring successively longer adjustment periods.[17] With reference to Figure 1, a rapid return to the long-run path

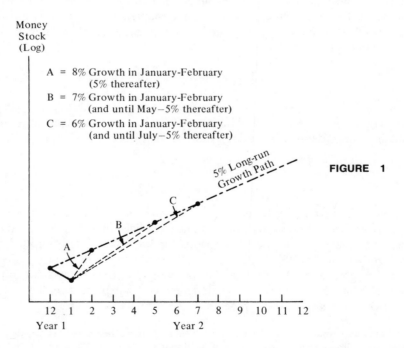

FIGURE 1

[17]Currently the control period for the FOMC's short-run strategy is two months—in December the control period is December-January, in January it is January-February, etc.

may require an 8 percent growth rate for M_1 in the January-February control period (A). Alternatively, slower growth rates of 7 and 6 percent in the January-February control period and in several successive periods would return M_1 to the long-run path in May (B) and July (C), respectively. The process underlying the selection of these alternative paths—i.e., the short-run formulation of policy and the actual short-run alternative selected by the FOMC—are discussed in the following sections.

V. A View of the Short-Run Strategy

The short-run strategy of the FOMC involves the selection of a short-run dial setting for the money stock and the development of an operating procedure for achieving the desired monetary growth path. The process begins with the staff presenting to the FOMC each month a set of alternative short-run (two-month) growth rates for the money stock. Associated with each alternative short-run path for the money stock will be a growth rate of bank reserves and a level of the Federal funds rate.

In formulating the short-run strategy, income movements are taken as given; that is, income for the coming two-month control period is interpolated from the quarterly projection of economic activity described earlier. The important assumptions underlying this procedure are that the quarterly projection and the monthly interpolation are correct and that there is no significant simultaneity problem over a one- or two-month period. To illustrate, again consider the example used in Figure 1. Assume that it is the end of January, that the consensus forecast specifies 5 percent monetary growth from December to July, and that the money stock actually declines in January. Normally, in the face of this one-month shortfall in the money stock, the staff would not revise its income projection for the coming months. This, in effect, assumes the policy lag is greater than one or two months and that subsequent policy actions will result in growth in the money stock that will overshoot the target by enough to offset the miss in the first month.

Given income and the current position of the money stock vis-à-vis the long-run target path as depicted in Figure 1, the staff might present at the January FOMC meeting a set of short-run alternatives, as in Table 1.[18]

The first row contains alternative short-run growth rates that will return the money stock to its long-run path. Alternative (A) and the staff discussion accompanying it would indicate that to achieve an 8 percent growth rate in M_1 and to return to the long-run path by February, the growth in reserves over the January-February period

---

[18]The alternatives, along with a discussion of the situation that might develop in financial markets under each option, appear in the "Bluebook," which is prepared monthly for the FOMC. See [2, p. 285]. The actual alternative selected by the FOMC is now published with a 45-day lag as part of the policy record. The alternatives contained in the Record of Policy Actions for the January 1974 FOMC meeting are the first available. In the discussion that follows we will, for simplicity, ignore M_2, even though it appears with M_1 under each alternative the FOMC considers.

Table 1. Alternative Short-Run Dial Settings
(Percent)

Target	Alternative		
	(A)	(B)	(C)
Money stock growth	8	7	6
Federal funds rate	6	7	8
Reserve growth	8	7	6

Note: The growth in reserves and the money stock are expressed at seasonally adjusted annual rates, while the funds rate is expressed as a level.

would have to be 8 percent and the level of the Federal funds rate required is 6 percent.[19]

The Federal funds rates, shown in row 2 of the table, are derived in two steps. First, assuming income given, a money demand function is solved for the short-term interest rate necessary to achieve the alternative short-run money path. The required Federal funds rate is then determined using a term structure equation relating it to the short-term interest rate. As was true in the forecast of economic activity, each alternative represents a staff consensus based on econometric models and judgmental considerations.[20]

The third row of the table could in theory be derived by solving a money supply function for the rate of growth in reserves necessary to achieve each money stock alternative. That is, if one viewed the money supply as the product of a reserve aggregate, such as reserves available to support private deposits RPD,[21] and a multiplier m, then the necessary growth in reserves could be obtained by estimating the multiplier, calculating the different February levels of the money supply M consistent with each money stock alternative, and dividing one by the other (RPD = M/m).[22]*

[19]It is worth noting that the FOMC has from time to time selected an alternative that has included, for example, the money stock under (A) and the funds rate under (B). In this case, the FOMC decided the staff had misspecified the relationship between the funds rate and monetary growth and has constructed a new alternative thought to be internally consistent. Thus, the FOMC is free to evaluate and to accept or reject the trade-offs among interest rates, reserves, and money stock growth implied by the staff estimates. See also n. 27.

[20]Monthly financial models developed at the Federal Reserve Board and the Federal Reserve Bank of New York are major inputs in this process. For a discussion of these models, see the papers by Pierce and Thomson [24, 25] and Davis and Shadrack [8].

[21]The reserve aggregate currently employed by the FOMC in its deliberations is called "reserves available to support private deposits" RPD. This magnitude is defined as total reserves minus required reserves against government and interbank deposits. It should be noted here that there is little objective evidence that RPD's have received much weight in the formulation or implementation of policy. Speaking of the 1973 period, Tschinkel said: "The Manager [reflecting the desires of the FOMC] found RPD of lesser importance in the determination of his response to the emerging patterns of monetary growth" [29, p. 105]. See also the recent evaluation of Kane [12, pp. 841-43] and the discussion that follows.

[22]The particular reserve aggregate one chooses (e.g., total reserves, nonborrowed reserves, the monetary base, RPD, etc.) is not a critical issue here.

* Here the Federal funds rate and reserve aggregates play the role of what most literature refers to as "instruments" of monetary policy.—Ed.

In practice, as discussed by Axilrod and Beck [1], the approach is demand oriented. After projecting the interest rates consistent with the short-run money stock growth rate for each alternative, these rates are used to estimate bank demand for required and excess reserves [1, p. 89]. An important characteristic of this approach is that it results in the supply of reserves and money being perfectly elastic at the targeted level of the interest rate R and the volume of reserves and money, therefore, being demand determined. This is illustrated in Figure 2, where the demand for reserves is expressed as a function of the interest rate.[23] Assume the position and slope of the demand schedule for reserves TR_D have been estimated by the staff and that TR_1 is the level of total reserves in February that is derived from deposit demand consistent with a 6 percent growth rate in the money stock. Under the demand approach discussed above, the required interest rate is R_1, and the System will supply reserves elastically at that rate. Thus the supply function TR_S is horizontal. This means that stochastic shifts in the reserve demand (or money demand) function, an error in the income projection, or any other disturbance on the demand side will, in the first instance, alter the position of TR_D to TR'_D and lead to changes in the quantity of reserves to TR_2.[24]

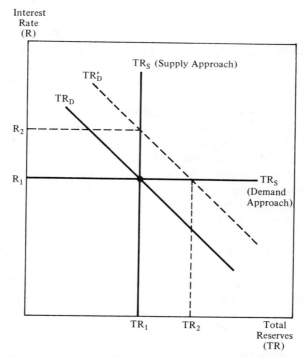

[23]While the following diagram relates the interest rate to reserves, one could just as easily substitute the money stock for reserves.

[24]While income is a shift parameter in this two-dimensional diagram, an increase in income would actually result in a movement along the demand function for demand deposits, time deposits, and reserves in three-dimensional space.

Table 2. Short-Run Dial Settings for 1974*

Date of Meeting	2-Month Control Period	Money Stock Range (SAAR)	Actual Money Stock (SAAR)	RPD Range (SAAR)	Actual RPD (SAAR)	Federal Funds Rate Range (Percent)	Actual Federal Funds Rate (Percent)
Jan. 22, 1974	Jan.–Feb.	3.00 to 6.00	4.7	4.75 to 7.75	3.3	8.75 to 10.00	8.93 to 9.47
Feb. 20, 1974	Feb.–Mar.	6.50 to 9.50	11.8	3.50 to 6.50	5.8	8.25 to 9.50	8.81 to 9.33
Mar. 19, 1974	Mar.–Apr.	5.50 to 8.50	9.6	4.00 to 7.00	15.8	9.00 to 10.50	9.61 to 10.36
Apr. 16, 1974	Apr.–May	3.00 to 7.00	6.5	6.00 to 11.00	20.7	9.75 to 11.25[1]	10.78 to 11.46
May 21, 1974	May–Jun.	3.00 to 7.00	6.3	13.00 to 20.00	20.0	11.00 to 11.75[1]	11.45 to 11.85
Jun. 18, 1974	Jun.–Jul.	3.50 to 7.50	4.8	10.00 to 13.50	13.5	11.25 to 13.00[1]	11.97 to 13.55
Jul. 18, 1974	Jul.–Aug.	2.00 to 6.00	2.1	8.75 to 11.75	9.0	11.50 to 13.00	12.02 to 12.60
Aug. 20, 1974	Aug.–Sep.	4.75 to 6.75	1.5	7.75 to 9.75	7.7	11.50 to 12.50	11.48 to 11.84
Sep. 10, 1974	Sep.–Oct.	3.00 to 6.00	2.6	6.00 to 8.50	3.5	10.25 to 12.00[2]	10.11 to 11.41
Oct. 15, 1974	Oct.–Nov.	4.75 to 7.25	5.3	5.50 to 8.00	− 2.1	9.00 to 10.50	9.34 to 9.81
Nov. 19, 1974	Nov.–Dec.	6.50 to 9.50	4.5	2.50 to 5.50	3.2	8.50 to 10.00	8.72 to 9.46
Dec. 17, 1974	Dec.–Jan.	5.00 to 7.00	− 3.4	9.00 to 11.00	3.9	7.13 to 9.00[2]	7.17 to 8.45

*Short-run dial settings for the money stock and RPD are expressed as seasonally adjusted annual rates of growth (SAAR) averaged over two-month target period. The range for the Federal funds rate and the actual outcome apply to statement week averages during intermeeting period. Actuals for the money stock and RPD do not reflect benchmark revisions or revisions in the seasonal factors made following the period to which data relate.

[1] Upper limit of range raised between meetings to figure shown.

[2] Lower limit of range lowered between meetings to figure shown.

This can be contrasted with a supply approach to money stock control, which would lead to the interest rate being demand determined. Again with reference to Figure 2, the level of total reserves thought necessary to achieve the 6 percent growth in the money stock remains TR_1. Accordingly, the System would supply the volume of reserves represented by the vertical TR_S function. Any disturbance on the demand side will alter the interest rate to R_2 and leave the quantity of reserves (and money) unaffected. In the absence of any disturbance (i.e., in a deterministic system) both approaches yield the same result (R_1 and TR_1).*

The point that must be emphasized is that one should not infer from the appearance of a reserve aggregate in Table 1 that the FOMC has adopted a supply approach to money stock control.[25] Evidence that the growth in reserves has had a low weight in the System's reaction function (i.e., in the formulation and implementation of policy) is easily obtained. Simply compare the specifications voted for reserves RPD, the money stock, and the funds rate in 1974 with the actual outcomes, shown in Table 2.[26] This exercise in revealed preference shows that the Federal Reserve rarely missed the funds rate range but allowed reserves and the money stock to move away from the specified range in about one-half of the two-month control periods. Assuming the initial specifications were internally consistent, the conclusion must be that in the short run disturbances were allowed to affect quantity and not price.

*Editors' note: The supply approach to money stock control has recently been adopted by the Federal Reserve. This approach, more appropriately called a reserve or monetary base approach, is discussed in the Appendix update that follows this article.

[25] Brunner and Meltzer, Friedman, and the St. Louis Federal Reserve Bank have long advocated such an approach.

[26] As detailed in Section VI, the short-run dial settings selected by the FOMC are actually expressed as ranges. The rationale for the ranges is explained in Section VI.

While this issue will be discussed in more detail in Section VI (of this article) the evidence in Table 2 suggests the System was not controlling reserves over the short run.[27]

A Model of the Short-Run Strategy

The following set of equations may be used to link the Federal funds rate to open market operations on the one hand and the money stock on the other:[28]

$$M_D = f_3 (y_L, R_L) \tag{3}$$

$$R = f_4 (RFF_L) \tag{4}$$

$$RFF = f_5 (TR_D, TR_S) \tag{5}$$

$$TR = NBR + MBB = ER + RR \tag{6a}$$

$$NBR = FR + RR \tag{6b}$$

where M_D is the demand for money, y is nominal income, R is a short-term interest rate such as the ninety-day commercial paper rate, RFF is the Federal funds rate, NBR is nonborrowed reserves, MBB is member bank borrowings, ER is excess reserves, FR is free reserves (ER − MBB), RR is required reserves, and TR_D is the demand for and TR_S the supply of total reserves. The first three relations are straightforward. Equation (3) is a standard money demand function; equation (4) is a term structure relation, where the short-term rate (e.g., the ninety-day commercial paper rate) is a function of a distributed lag on the funds rate (single-day maturity).[29] Equation (5) specifies the funds rate as a function of the demand for and supply of total reserves. In (6a) total reserves are divided into familiar components—required reserves and excess reserves—which, by definition, must equal reserves borrowed from the System and all other reserves (nonborrowed reserves). By rearranging terms, a convenient identity (6b) can be formed. This latter identity may be transformed into an equation with behavioral content by considering the right-hand side as reflecting the behavior of the public and the banks and the left-hand side as reflecting the behavior of the Fed. That is, the banks' demand for required reserves is derived from the public's demand for deposits. This, together with the banks' demand for free reserves, must equal the total of nonborrowed reserves supplied by the

[27]An interesting feature of this approach to policymaking is that a member of the FOMC might vote for alternative (A) in Table 1 even though he viewed monetary policy as operating primarily through interest rates and thus really preferred the interest rate under alternative (B). In other words, members of the FOMC may vote for individual elements in the table rather than columns. Support for this interpretation is provided by Maisel: "A possible side advantage of this strategy is that it can be followed even though it might be impossible to get agreement among the members of the FOMC either as to ultimate goals, or the form or level of an intermediate monetary variable, or as to how to define what strategy is being followed" [17, p. 154].

[28]For simplicity we will continue to ignore time deposits and therefore M_2.

[29]See [14] for evidence that a major portion of the variance in short-term rates can be explained by current and lagged movements in the Federal funds rate.

Federal Reserve open market operations.[30] Other factors, such as the gold stock, float, and Treasury deposits at the Federal Reserve, also affect the supply of nonborrowed reserves. However, holding these other factors constant or assuming that the System engages in so-called "defensive" open market operations to offset movements in these factors, NBR is controllable by policymakers. For present purposes, these other factors are held constant, and the change in nonborrowed reserves is assumed equal to the change in the System's holdings of securities. Therefore, the change in nonborrowed reserves directly reflects open market operations (i.e., $\Delta NBR = OMO$). In summary, the funds rate is determined by the supply of nonborrowed reserves relative to the demand for required reserves and free reserves.[31]

To close the model, the System's short-run reaction function relating OMO to RFF must be specified. Ignoring for the moment the constraint on interest rate volatility, the desired level of the funds rate RFF* can be determined by solving equations (1) to (4) recursively for a relationship between long-run target values of the money stock and RFF:

$$RFF^* = f_6(M^*) \tag{7}$$

In practice it is the short-run target value for the money stock, rather than the long-run target value that would usually appear in equation (7). The reason, as discussed in Sections IV and VI, is that the change in the funds rate required to get the money stock back on the long-run path (assuming it is significantly off the path), is usually deemed too large and disruptive by the policymaker.

Once equations (1) to (4) have been solved for RFF*, equation (8) follows from equation (5) and the supporting identities:

$$\Delta NBR = OMO = f_7(RFF^* - RFF^A) \tag{8}$$

Simply put, the System will absorb (inject) reserves by selling (buying) securities when the funds rate is below (above) the desired level. This policy approach ensures that the supply of reserves is perfectly elastic at the desired funds rate and the quantity of reserves is demand determined. In the first instance, deviations in the demand for reserves from the FOMC specifications lead to an equivalent change in the stock of reserves but to no change in the funds rate.[32]

---

[30]See [5, Chapter 1] for a discussion of the key role of the free reserves equation in the financial sector of the SMP model.

[31]It should be emphasized that the set of equations presented is intended to be very general and should not be construed as a complete model of the financial sector and its interaction with Federal Reserve policy. This is a task beyond the scope of the present paper. As it stands the set of equations is underidentified, and no attempt is made to account for various aspects of simultaneity.

[32]A point worth mentioning in this context is that a change in reserve requirements has virtually no impact on reserves or the money stock unless accompanied by a change in the funds rate target. If, for example, the System lowers the reserve requirement on demand deposits, other things equal, this will push down the funds rate. However, as depicted in equation (8), this will result in the System selling securities and, therefore, absorbing the free reserves.

There is in theory a mechanism that limits the procyclical movement in reserves. The dynamics of the intermeeting phase of the short-run policy process are embedded in a feedback control loop that can be summarized by:

$$\Delta RFF^* = f_8(M^* - M^A) \qquad (9)$$

That is, movements in the funds rate depend upon deviations of the money stock from its desired value. To illustrate, assume incoming data on the money stock suggest that monetary growth over the short-run two-month target period will exceed the short-run dial setting selected at the last FOMC meeting. In response the Manager of the Trading Desk would be expected to increase the dial setting for the funds rate. In practice, however, the timing and magnitude of the Manager's initial response to apparent deviations of monetary growth from desired levels are often not so straightforward. If the tone of the securities markets is weak, for example, the FOMC might decide not to change the funds rate for the time being, even though the money stock is growing above the desired rate.[33]

A more difficult problem contributing to cautious adjustments of the funds rate is the uncertainty concerning the money stock forecasts. This uncertainty results from the fact that forecasts of the money stock over the short run (e.g., one to three months ahead) have not been very accurate [29]. This being the case, the FOMC often may delay its response to an apparent deviation of actual from desired monetary growth until more data are available to confirm the error. The rationale is that the policymaker prefers to avoid "whipsawing" the market—i.e., raising the Federal funds rate now if money growth appears to be exceeding desires and lowering it later if the money stock projections prove incorrect and actual money growth is found to be close to that desired. This, of course, is another facet of the System's desire to minimize short-run interest rate volatility and is discussed in the next section.

VI. The Constraint on Interest Rate Volatility and Its Interaction with Policy Targets

Within the FOMC's current strategy, the target values for the Federal funds rate, reserves, and the money stock are actually expressed as ranges. Referring back to Table 1, under alternative (A) for example, the entry for the money stock might be 7 to 9 percent and the entry for the Federal funds rate might be 5.5 to 6.5 percent. From the viewpoint of the staff, the ranges presented to the FOMC generally represent a standard error around a point estimate at the midpoint of the range. From the viewpoint of the FOMC, however, the ranges may have a somewhat different meaning. The range for the money stock is typically viewed as a range of tolerance. If the

[33]Thus, the Federal funds rate *is* the Federal Reserve's policy "instrument" and reacts to changes in the state of the economy reflected here in the "intermediate target variable" (M^*-M^A). Note that the Federal Reserve's structural hypothesis is ambiguous and thus prevents any suggestion that this (or any) instrument is an *optimal* one.—Ed.

money stock is expanding at a rate within its range, then the desired level of the Federal funds rate will probably not be altered to any significant degree.[34] Thus, in terms of equation (9), M* is a range and ΔRFF* equals zero unless M^A is outside the range.

The following quotations suggest there are at least two interpretations attached to the reasoning behind any given range for the money stock adopted by the FOMC: (1) "The inherent short-run volatility of the monetary aggregates is one reason why Committee expresses its short-run guides in terms of ranges of tolerance" [21, p. 334]. In this view the range implies a standard error around a point estimate. (2) "The Committee chose tolerance ranges for M_1 . . . that were at least as restrictive as the alternatives presented by the staff and reduced the lower ends of these ranges to indicate its willingness to accept substantially slower growth in the near term" [29, p. 108]. In this view the Committee skews its preferences, perhaps in response to previous deviations of actual from desired levels. Suppose the staff presents an alternative such as (C), which implies that an 8 percent Federal funds rate will translate into a 5–7 percent growth in the money stock, the point estimate being 6 percent growth. The FOMC, responding to past shortfalls in money stock growth, might then modify this alternative by changing the range to 5–8 percent, indicating its willingness to err on the side of more, rather than less, monetary growth relative to projected levels. Operationally, this means that if the money stock actually should grow at an 8 percent rate, this will not result in a raising of the desired Federal funds rate.

The significance of the Federal funds range is that it specifically limits the degree of response by the Manager to a deviation of monetary growth from the desired range. As shown in Table 2, this range in 1974 was typically 100–150 basis points. If the midpoint of the range selected is equal to the Federal funds rate prevailing just prior to the FOMC meeting, then the FOMC has typically been willing to tolerate a maximum change in the funds rate of 50–75 basis points in one direction over any given intermeeting period.[35] Against this background, it is interesting to note that the money demand functions that underlie the specifications presented to the FOMC exhibit very low interest elasticities [4; 8; 24; 25]. The monthly model discussed by Pierce and Thomson [25, p. 351], for example, indicates that, other things equal, a 100 basis point change in the Federal funds rate will lead to only about a 0.3 percentage point change in the annual growth rate of the money stock over a one-month period and only about a one percentage point change over a six-month period. Assuming the interest elasticities embedded in the monthly models are reasonably accurate, the constraint on the monthly movement in the Federal funds rate, as explicitly revealed by the range in the Policy Record for the funds rate, suggests that

[34]This discussion assumes that incoming data and forecasts of nonfinancial developments are consistent with the projections set out when the long-run trajectory for the money stock was first selected; as a result, the FOMC has not modified the long-run money stock target.

[35]From time to time the FOMC has been willing to change the upper or lower end of the range on the funds rate and thus permit a larger intermeeting movement in the funds rate. For a recent example, see the "Record of Policy Actions" of the FOMC in the *Federal Reserve Bulletin,* (February 1975), p. 88. In addition, if the funds rate prevailing at the time of the meeting is at the upper or lower end of the adopted range, it is possible that the full 100–150 basis point range could be used during the intermeeting period.

the FOMC is willing to tolerate relatively large short-run deviations of monetary growth from desired levels.[36]

Whether or not the constraint on month-to-month movements in interest rates has significant destabilizing effects on output and prices depends on the narrowness of the short-run constraint and whether or not it frustrates achievement of the long-run money stock target.[37]

With regard to the narrowness of interest rate tolerance bands, Pierce conducted some experiments with the SMP model and concluded: "The results indicate that the placement of sufficiently narrow bounds on the change in the bill rate can have a large impact on the simulated value of GNP" [22, p. 101]. It is worth emphasizing that *if the band on interest rate movements is fairly narrow and inflexible, it is reasonable to question whether or not the money stock is being "controlled" at all.**

In theory, at least, the current FOMC approach to the formulation of policy is designed to guard against short-run deviations of money stock growth affecting the achievement of the long-run money stock target. This is illustrated in Figure 3. Assume the FOMC selected a 4-6 percent long-run growth path for the money stock in month 1 of year 1, growth in the money stock in months 5 and 6 of year 1 has been 8 percent, and the FOMC is meeting at the beginning of month 7. Further, assume the prevailing Federal funds rate is 5 percent. As discussed in Section IV, the short-run alternatives for the money stock presented to the FOMC by the staff will typically be tied to a specific time path for returning the growth of the money stock to the desired range. For example, alternative (A) would envision only 2 percent growth in the money stock over the next two months and thus an early return to the range. This might require a sharp rise in the Federal funds rate to perhaps 7 percent. Alternative (B), however, would envision a slower return to the upper end of the desired range; the money stock might be expected to grow at a 5 percent rate for five months and return to the range by month 11. This alternative would require a smaller current rise in the Federal funds rate to perhaps 6 percent, possibly followed by further rises in subsequent months.[38] An examination of month-to-month movements in the funds rate and in monetary growth over the past several years suggests that the FOMC has in practice more often preferred to pursue an alternative such as (B).[39]

[36]In other words, short-run monetary control is considered too "costly" because of the volatility of interest rates that seems to be required. For a critical review of this issue see [15]. For some evidence that short-run deviations of monetary growth from the desired trajectory might not be "costly" in terms of missing price and output targets, see [6, p. 24].

[37]It also depends, of course, on the willingness of the FOMC to modify the constraint over time. In this regard, the FOMC has clearly been willing to tolerate larger swings in interest rates over the first half of the 1970's than it did over most of the 1960's.

* This raises questions as to whether money is actually serving as an intermediate target-variable despite lip-service given to its strategic role.—Ed.

[38]It should be noted that one alternative may envision an immediate return to the desired range without any significant change in the funds rate. The explanation accompanying such an alternative may be that the monthly pattern of income growth suggests smaller increases in coming months and thus less strength in money demand. Another possible explanation is that the current spurt in monetary growth is a random occurrence not likely to persist.

[39]The revealed tendency to view short-run deviations of monetary growth (and their mirror image, the short-run smoothing of interest rates) as costless is controversial. Within the Hicks-Hansen IS-LM framework, the presumption is that there are stochastic shifts in the LM curve that are larger than the random shifts of the IS curve. See Poole [27] and the pathbreaking report of Weintraub [30, especially pp. 63-66].

Editors' Note: See article 25 in this section.

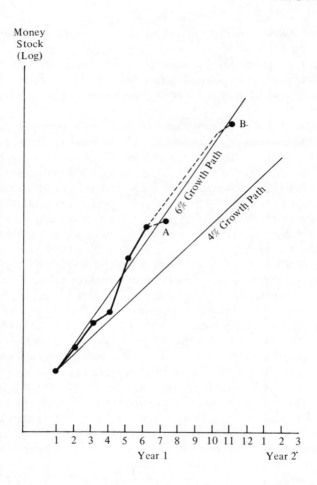

One significant area of concern with regard to this policy approach is the possible existence, from time to time, of a serially correlated error in the income projection. Suppose the staff is underestimating the strength in aggregate demand and the money stock is expanding more rapidly than desired. Since the growth of the money stock appears to be inconsistent with the income projection and the associated estimate of the demand for money, the initial tendency may be for the policymaker to discount the jump in monetary growth and wait for further data that would confirm greater strength in economic activity and money demand. The incorrect presumption is that the spurt in monetary growth is the result of a stochastic shift in money demand. The long-run implications of accommodating this growth are a more procyclical policy than desired and, given the lags in the effect of policy, the need later on for a very sharp tightening in policy to offset past excesses.

An important problem for monetary control that can result from a series of short-run deviations of monetary growth is that the FOMC might give up on the long-run

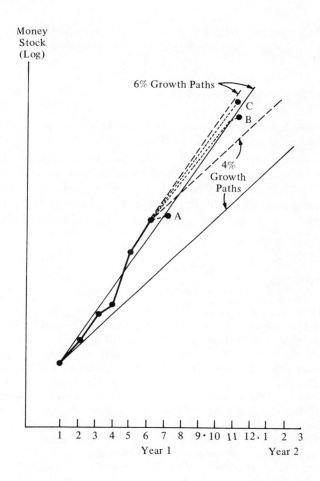

money stock target *de facto* by continually resetting the starting (or base) date of the control period over which the target value is to be attained. This might happen, for example, if the policymakers find it impossible to tolerate the large increases in interest rates necessary to offset past excesses in monetary growth. This is illustrated in Figure 4, which is similar to Figure 3 except that the FOMC is presumed to adopt alternative (C) at its meeting early in month 7. The long-run target remains 4-6 percent but is calculated from month 6 rather than from month 1.[40] Unfortunately,

[40]The FOMC recently made such a shift in the base of its current long-run money stock target. On May 1, 1975, Chairman Burns announced before the Senate Banking Committee that the FOMC planned money stock growth of 5 to 7.5 percent over the period March 1975-March 1976. On July 24, 1975, the Chairman announced before the House Banking Committee that the targeted growth rate was the same, but the period over which it was to be obtained was the second quarter of 1975 to the second quarter of 1976. Since the money stock grew at nearly a 9 percent rate in the second quarter of 1975, this change in the base, in effect, accepts much of the intervening monetary expansion.

this subtle ratcheting-up (or down) of the long-run monetary growth rate could exacerbate the cyclical swings in output and prices.[41]

VII. Some Final Remarks

This article has presented a view of the Federal Reserve's current approach to the formulation and implementation of monetary policy. It is hoped the general interpretation presented will be critically examined, the discussion of particular phases of the strategy carefully scrutinized, and the models that underlie the strategy empirically tested. This should result in a clearer understanding of current monetary policy procedures, more carefully developed advice for policymakers on how to improve their performance, and greater success in achieving the goals of monetary policy.

REFERENCES

1. AXILROD, STEPHEN and DARWIN BECK. "Role of Projections with Monetary Aggregates as Policy Targets," in *Controlling Monetary Aggregates II: The Implementation.* Federal Reserve Bank of Boston, 1973, pp. 81-102.
2. BRIMMER, ANDREW. "Tradition and Innovation in Monetary Management," in *Monetary Economics: Readings.* Ed. Alan Entine, Belmont, California: Wadsworth, 1968, pp. 273-89.
3. ———. "The Political Economy of Money: Evolution and Impact of Monetarism in the Federal Reserve System," *American Economic Review,* (May 1972), 344-52.
4. CICCOLO, JOHN H. "Is Short-Run Monetary Control Feasible?" in *Monetary Aggregates and Monetary Policy.* Federal Reserve Bank of New York, 1974, pp. 82-91.
5. COOPER, J. PHILLIP. *Development of the Monetary Sector, Prediction and Policy Analysis in the FRB-MIT-PENN Model.* Lexington: D. C. Heath, 1974.
6. CORRIGAN, E. GERALD. "Income Stabilization and Short-Run Variability in Money," in *Monetary Aggregates and Monetary Policy.* Federal Reserve Bank of New York, 1974, pp. 92-103.
7. CREWS, JOSEPH M. "Econometric Models: The Monetarist and Non-Monetarists Views Compared," *Monthly Review,* Federal Reserve Bank of Richmond, (February 1973), 3-12.
8. DAVIS, RICHARD and FREDERICK C. SCHADRACK. "Forecasting the Monetary Aggregates with Reduced-Form Equations," in *Monetary Aggregates and Monetary Policy.* Federal Reserve Bank of New York, 1974, pp. 60-71.
9. DE LEEUW, FRANK and EDWARD GRAMLICH. "The Federal Reserve-MIT Econometric Model," *Federal Reserve Bulletin,* (January 1968), 11-40.
10. GUTTENTAG, JACK. "The Strategy of Open Market Operations," *Quarterly Journal of Economics,* (February 1966), 1-30.

---

[41]See Poole's recent paper [26, pp. 25-30] for some further possible pitfalls within the current strategy.

11. HYMANS, SAUL. "Comment" in *Econometric Models of Cyclical Behavior.* Ed. Bert Hickman, New York: National Bureau of Economic Research.

12. KANE, EDWARD. "All for the Best: The Federal Reserve Board's 60th Annual Report," *American Economic Review,* (December 1974), 835-50.

13. ———. "The Re-Politicization of the Fed," *Journal of Financial and Quantitative Analysis,* (November 1974), 743-52.

14. LOMBRA, RAYMOND and LEIGH RIBBLE. "The Linkages Among Short-Term Interest Rates." Paper presented at the Eastern Economic Association Meetings. October 1974.

15. ——— and FREDERICK STRUBLE. "Monetary Aggregate Targets and the Volatility of Interest Rates." Unpublished manuscript, August 1975.

16. ——— and RAYMOND G. TORTO. "An Endogenous Central Bank and Its Implications for Supply and Demand Approaches to Money Stock Determination," *Quarterly Review of Economics & Business,* (Summer 1975), 71-79.

17. MAISEL, SHERMAN. "Controlling Monetary Aggregates," in *Controlling Monetary Aggregates.* Federal Reserve Bank of Boston, 1968, pp. 152-74.

18. ———. *Managing the Dollar.* New York: W. W. Norton, 1973.

19. ———. "The Economic and Finance Literature and Decision Making," *Journal of Finance,* (May 1974), 313-22.

20. MASON, WILL E. *Clarification of the Monetary Standard.* University Park: Penn State University Press, 1963.

21. "Numerical Specifications of Financial Variables and Their Role in Monetary Policy," *Federal Reserve Bulletin,* (May 1974), 333-37.

22. PIERCE, JAMES. "The Trade-off Between Short- and Long-term Policy Goals," in *Open Market Policies and Operating Procedures—Staff Studies.* Washington, D.C.: Board of Governors of the Federal Reserve System, 1971, pp. 97-105.

23. ———. "Quantitative Analysis for Decisions at the Federal Reserve," *Annuals of Economic and Social Measurement,* (March 1974), 11-19.

24. ——— and THOMAS THOMSON. "Some Issues in Controlling the Stock of Money," in *Controlling Monetary Aggregates II: The Implementation.* Federal Reserve Bank of Boston, 1973, pp. 115-36.

25. ——— and ———. "Short-Term Financial Models at the Federal Reserve Board," *Journal of Finance,* (May 1974), 349-57.

26. POOLE, WILLIAM. "The Making of Monetary Policy: Description and Analysis," *New England Economic Review,* Federal Reserve Bank of Boston, (March-April 1974), 21-30.

27. ———. "Optimal Choice of Monetary Policy Instruments in a Simple Stochastic Macro Model," *Quarterly Journal of Economics,* (May 1970), 197-216.

28. SIMS, CHRISTOPHER. "Optimal Stable Policies for Unstable Instruments," *Annuals of Economic and Social Measurement,* (January 1974), 257-65.

29. TSCHINKEL, SHEILA. "Open Market Operations in 1973," *Monthly Review,* Federal Reserve Bank of New York, (May 1974), 103-16.

30. WEINTRAUB, ROBERT. "Report on Federal Reserve Policy and Inflation and High Interest Rates," *Reserve Policy and Inflation and High Interest Rates.* U.S. Congress. House Committee on Banking and Currency, 93rd Congress (July-August 1974), pp. 31-76.

Appendix: An Update for the 1980s,
by Thomas M. Havrilesky

As Lombra and Torto point out, if the Federal funds rate approach to monetary control is used, the Federal Reserve pegs the Federal funds rate at a level it believes to be consistent with its money supply target and supplies all the reserves that banks demand at this rate. However, as they show in Figure 2, the supply function for reserves is then horizontal, and any shift in demand leads to changes in the quantity of reserves. This has often led to the Federal Reserve's accommodating the banks and overshooting its money supply growth targets. When such overshooting persists over an extended period, the result is an increase in the rate of inflation.

An alternative, pointed out by Lombra and Torto, would be to focus on the level of bank reserves or the monetary base rather than on the Federal funds rate. In Section V the readings by Balbach and Burger and by Jordan reveal that the money supply is a product of bank reserves or the monetary base and the money multiplier. If the Federal Reserve has an estimate of the money multiplier, it can easily control the supply of money by controlling the level of reserves or the monetary base. Under this reserves or supply strategy, as shown in Figure 2 of the Lombra and Torto article, the supply of reserves is a vertical line, and if the demand for reserves shifts the Federal funds rate will change, as it is now demand-determined. Which is preferable, a volatile, demand-determined Federal funds rate or inadequate control of the supply of money?

In the decade and a half preceding 1979 it became increasingly apparent that the Federal Reserve's procedure of focusing on the Federal funds rate led to prolonged periods of procyclical monetary policy during which the Federal Reserve chronically missed its money supply targets, as discussed by Lombra and Torto. Then, in October, 1979, the new Chairman of the Board of Governors of the Federal Reserve, Paul Volcker, announced a change in Federal Reserve procedure from a funds rate approach to a reserves approach. How long will the Fed be able to stick to the new approach? Will the Federal Reserve have technical problems in controlling the monetary aggregates as described in the articles by Davis, Pierce, and the staff of the Board of Governors later in this section? Will political pressures on the Federal Reserve, arising from demand-determined volatility in interest rates, or temporary variations in unemployment, as discussed in the articles by Cobham, Lindbeck, and Brunner in Section X, cause an abandonment of the reserves-supply approach to monetary policy? Further reading of the remaining articles will provide insight into these questions.

Implementing Open Market Policy with Monetary Aggregate Objectives

Richard G. Davis*

24

The purpose of this paper is to survey recent research on some technical problems of implementing open market policy at a time when the proper intermediate policy objective is widely believed to be the behavior of the money supply and related monetary aggregates. The mere existence of a widely held preference for monetary aggregate targets in setting policy is a relatively recent development. Even five years ago, the notion that the money supply should be the primary target of monetary policy was a decidedly minority position. This was true not only of academic and business economists, but of policy makers and the interested general public as well. Ten to fifteen years ago, discussions of monetary policy were only rather rarely couched in terms of the money supply. Practical discussions of policy were framed mainly in terms of interest rates and credit market conditions.

Things are now quite different. If one asks the average bank or business economist what they think monetary policy should be over the coming months, most will eventually get around to saying that the money stock should grow at such and such a rate.

Reprinted, with deletions, from the Federal Reserve Bank of New York, *Monetary Aggregates and Monetary Policy* (New York: The Bank, 1974), pp. 7–14, by permission of the publisher and the author.

*This paper was prepared for Second District economics professors attending a central banking seminar at this Bank on April 23, 1973. The views expressed are the responsibility of the author alone and do not necessarily reflect the views of the bank or of the Federal Reserve System.

This article is reprinted, with minor revisions, from *Monthly Review* (Federal Reserve Bank of New York, July 1973), pages 170–82.

The ensuing elaboration will often owe more to the familiar equation of exchange than to the Keynesian "IS-LM" analysis.[1] Similar comments could be made of discussions of monetary policy in the Congress and in the business press.

There is, to be sure, a danger of overdrawing this picture. Views on these matters are not and never have been uniform or monolithic. Yet, it is really striking the extent to which the monetarists have succeeded in shifting the focus of commonly received opinion on the role of money. One could, of course, ask whether this shift has been justified by an equally clear shift in the weight of the evidence. And one may entertain reservations on this score. However, the subject matter of the present paper is limited to the problems of implementing the monetarist program as regards using monetary policy to control the money supply and related monetary aggregates.

The Changing Role of Money Supply Targets in The United States[2]

For better or worse, money supply targets have come to have a growing importance in policy making, as already indicated. Before turning to the technical problems raised by the attempt to implement such targets, however, it may be useful to sketch briefly how the role of money supply objectives in policy formulation has evolved in recent years. First, it should be noted that the very concept of a "money supply policy" is open to some ambiguities. The Federal Reserve, of course, does not control the money stock directly. The actual behavior of the money supply is the joint result of Federal Reserve actions with respect to its own instrument variables—its open market portfolio, discount rate, etc.—and the actions of the Treasury, of foreigners, of the banks, and of the nonbank public. Thus, both Federal Reserve and non-Reserve influences interact to make the money supply whatever it is at any given time. Under these circumstances, there can really only be a money supply "policy" if

---

[1]In this algebraic summary of a simplified version of the Keynesian system, often used in the classroom, the so-called "LM" equation represents alternative combinations of GNP and the level of interest rates at which the supply and demand for money are equal. Similarly, the "IS" equation represents alternative combinations of GNP and interest rates at which the supply and demand for current output, including consumption goods, capital goods, and Government purchases, are equal. This solution of these two equations, the equilibrium value of the system as a whole, is that particular combination of income and interest rates for which *both* the supply and demand for money *and* the supply and demand for currently produced output are equal. Algebraically, the equilibrium values of GNP and interest rates are determined by the simultaneous solution of the two equations, LM and IS, each of which contains two unknowns, GNP and the level of interest rates (treated for simplicity as a single, "representative" interest rate). Graphically, the equilibrium values of the unknowns are shown by the intersection of the LM and IS lines (see reading 25 by James Cacy in this section).

[2]Editors' Note: In this article the author uses the label "operating targets" to refer to what the literature and the next reading call "instruments." The confusion arises because of the implicit definition of the policy control period. For very short periods many variables cannot be controlled and hence cannot qualify as "instruments." The label "objectives" used by Davis refers to what most of the literature calls "intermediate target variables."

the Federal Reserve consciously seeks to achieve a certain path for money by using its instruments to offset the effects of actions taken by others

Prior to at least 1960, while there was much *"monetary policy,"* there can really not be said to have been much *"money supply policy."* The Federal Reserve, by and large, marched to a different drummer. The actual behavior of the money supply "fell out," for the most part an endogenous by-product of the System's actions with respect to whatever targets it *was* following and the actions of the public and the banks. To be sure, it can be argued—and has been by some—that whatever the System's *conscious* targets, the actual behavior of the money stock, or at least its broader and more significant movements, have been dominated all along by the behavior of the Federal Reserve's policy instruments rather than by the behavior of the public or the banks. But even if this were true, it would still imply only that the Federal Reserve *could* control the money stock if it chose to, not that it actually *did* so in any particular historical period.

As the 1960's wore on, the behavior of the money supply seemingly came to have increasing importance in the thinking of the policy makers, roughly paralleling developments in the economics profession and among the public generally. In the first instance, this meant that some individual members of the Federal Open Market Committee (FOMC) began to give more weight to money supply behavior in voting on specific policy alternatives. But despite this increased weight, it is probably fair to say that at no time in the 1960's did the recent and prospective behavior of the money stock become the dominant influence in the policy makers' thinking with regard to open market policy targets. Moreover, the FOMC continued to eschew any agreed-upon, formal money supply target. Actual policy alternatives continued to be stated in terms of money market conditions, as measured, for example, by free reserves and the levels of certain key money market interest rates.

Perhaps the earliest operational result, insofar as open market strategies were involved, of the increased concern over the behavior of the money supply and related monetary aggregates was the use by the FOMC, beginning in 1966, of the so-called "proviso clause." This was a clause included in the directive addressed by the FOMC at each of its monthly meetings to the Account Management at the Federal Reserve Bank of New York. It required the Account Management to shift money market targets from the levels initially directed by the Committee in an appropriately offsetting direction whenever growth in bank credit proved to be deviating significantly from the rates projected at the time of the previous meeting. The significance of this "proviso clause" as a step toward direct targeting of money supply and other aggregates was limited, however. First, it stopped short of committing the FOMC to an explicit target. Second, in practice it involved only quite gingerly and modest adjustments of "money market conditions" targets in response to unexpectedly rapid or slow growth in the bank credit proxy.

A more fundamental change took place in early 1970 when the Committee for the first time adopted explicit goals for the behavior of the narrow and broadly defined money supply (M_1 and M_2) and the bank credit proxy. At most of its meetings since early 1970 the Committee has continued to adopt explicit goals, covering varying time horizons, for the growth rates of one or more of these aggregates. At the same time, the Committee has experimented with various operational tactics to achieve these goals. However, this most emphatically does *not* mean that actual money supply behavior over the period since early 1970 can be interpreted as conforming to the FOMC's objectives in the short run. The bulk of the remainder of this paper is devoted to reasons why the money supply cannot, and perhaps even *should not,* be made to conform exactly to predetermined target values over short periods. Beyond this, however, goals for the growth rates of the monetary aggregates have seldom been the sole immediate objective of the FOMC even in the period since 1970. The Committee has generally retained concern for avoiding unstable conditions in the money markets and has also retained an interest in the behavior of short-term interest rates and money and capital market conditions generally.

The Choice of a Target among the Monetary Aggregates

Turning directly to some of the technical problems of implementing monetary policy where the intermediate objectives of policy are framed in terms of the monetary aggregates, several fairly basic questions come to mind immediately. The first might well be which monetary aggregate do you use: M_1, M_2, some measure of bank credit, total reserves, the monetary base (i.e., what is sometimes called "high-powered money," or total reserves plus currency in the hands of the nonbank public)? Without defending the point in detail, I would argue that, while measures of reserves and the monetary base may be useful in developing strategies to achieve goals for one of the other aggregates, these measures are not themselves the best choices for framing monetary policy goals. The basic point is that we are interested in influencing the economy at large, not the banking sector *per se.* Setting targets in terms of reserves would allow random developments within the banking sector—which might be summarized by movements in the reserve-deposit multiplier—to be transmitted to the overall economy, interfering with the achievement of the more basic goals for the gross national product (GNP) and similar variables.[3]

---

[3]In "Improving Monetary Control" (*Brookings Papers on Economic Activity,* 2-1972), William Poole extends his analysis cited earlier to examine the situation where the central bank's options are not M and r, but the monetary base (B) and r. The additional variance introduced by the banking sector via the supply equation for money may make B targets inferior to r targets even where M targets would be superior to r targets. The argument against B targets is simply that the authorities ought to permit themselves maximum flexibility in adjusting as needed to variations in the relationship between B and M. As Poole points out, arguments for a steady rate of growth in M simply cannot be extended to a steady rate of growth in B.

With regard to the remaining choices, between, say, M_1, M_2, and some measure of total bank credit, I would argue that this is essentially a second-order issue. It is, for example, very difficult to differentiate between these three aggregates in terms of the closeness of their relationship to GNP in the postwar period.[4] Real questions about which aggregate to use are, however, likely to develop during periods when Regulation Q ceilings are changed or when open market rates are rising above or falling below existing ceilings. Such "artificial" distortions in rate spreads induce marked decelerations or accelerations of time deposit growth and therefore distort the "normal" growth rate relationships among M_1, M_2, and bank credit.[5] For example, a rise in market rates above Regulation Q ceilings will cause the public to shift out of time deposits and into open market securities. The resulting slowdown in M_2 undoubtedly overstates the restrictiveness of monetary policy in such periods. The moral would seem to be that policy makers can, with reasonable safety, set goals either in terms of M_1, M_2, or bank credit during normal times (provided allowance is made for differences in trend growth rates), but careful interpretation of differential growth rates is imperative during periods when Regulation Q (or some other special disturbances that do arise from time to time) is a factor.[6]

How Large Are the Economic Costs of Failing to Hit Monetary Targets in the Short Run?

A second basic question with regard to implementing monetary aggregate targets for monetary policy is how long or short should the time horizon be for achieving these

[4]Michael Hamburger presents some results for changes in GNP regressed on current and lagged changes in various monetary aggregates in "Indicators of Monetary Policy: The Arguments and the Evidence," *American Economic Review* (May 1970). For the 1953–1968 period, the R^2's are 0.39 for M_1 and bank credit and 0.28 for M_2. However in the 1961–1968 subperiod, M_2 does much better than M_1 (0.43 versus 0.31) and only a little less well than bank credit (0.45). A paper by Frederick C. Schadrack, "An Empirical Approach to the Definition of Money" (June 1971), summarizes some previously published work of George Kaufman and Milton Friedman and Anna Schwartz and presents some new results using Almonized distributed lag techniques. For the period 1953–1968 there is very little to choose between M_1 and M_2, both including and excluding large CDs (all adjusted R^2's are around 0.55), though bank credit does a bit better at 0.61. Schadrack, however, expresses some preference for M_2 (excluding large CDs) on the grounds that its coefficients appear more stable over time.

[5]The view that Regulation Q provides the main reason for worrying about whether to use M_1 or M_2 was expressed as long ago as 1959 by Milton Friedman in *A Program for Monetary Stability*, page 91.

[6]Milton Friedman has recently expressed a preference for M_2 (excluding large CDs) over M_1 on the grounds that the income velocity of M_2 has shown essentially no trend since the early 1960's while the income velocity of M_1 has continued to show an uptrend of somewhat uncertain dimensions (see "How Much Monetary Growth" in the *Morgan Guaranty Survey*, February 1973). Friedman's argument is couched in terms of the substantially larger range of the *level* of the M_1 income velocity relative to the range of the *level* of the M_2 income velocity in the 1962–1972 period. The relevant issue, however, is the variance of the rates of growth of these two velocity measures—at least as far as setting intermediate-run or countercyclical monetary growth targets is concerned. To put it differently, what one cares about for these purposes is the closeness of fit of equations relating growth in nominal income to growth in money, not the size of the constant term in such equations.

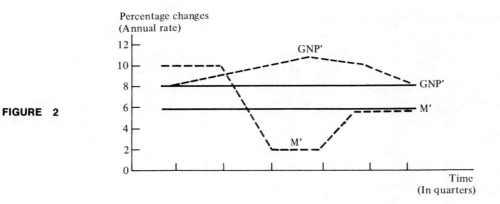

Percentage changes
(Annual rate)

FIGURE 2

Time
(In quarters)

targets: i.e., should you try to set and meet targets for monetary growth over a month, a quarter, six months, a year? The answer to this question seems to depend essentially on two factors: (1) the decreasing feasibility of controlling the aggregates over successively shorter periods and (2) the increasing costs in terms of economic stability of failing to hit them over successively longer periods. This second aspect is examined first.

Just how much difference does it make to aggregate demand objectives if the M_1 target is missed by 2 percentage points over one month, over three months, etc.? The key to this question lies in the lag structure relating money growth to the behavior of the economy at large. If, for example, the influence of M on GNP were essentially instantaneous, deviations from monetary targets lasting even for very short periods could have a marked impact. On the other hand, if the influence of money operates with a long distributed lag, the impact of deviations from M_1 targets may be greatly attenuated. Suppose, for example, the Federal Reserve wants to hit a 6 percent money growth rate target. Suppose, instead, it actually hits 10 percent for two quarters in a row (as illustrated in Figure 2) and then drops down to 2 percent for the next two quarters. If the influence of money operates with a distributed lag—i.e., the effective impact of money at any point reflects a weighted average of past money supply growth rates—the overshoot effect of the two 10 percent quarters will never register its full impact on GNP. Long before this can happen, the *over*shoot effects will begin to be offset by the *under*shoot effects of the two 2 percent quarters. If lags are sufficiently long, the course of events in the economy may turn out to differ little from what would have happened had the 6 percent money target been successfully reached in each and every quarter instead of just on average over the whole four-quarter period.

One way to arrive at quantitative estimates of the costs of permitting M to deviate from target values over periods of varying lengths is to use econometric model simulations. Such simulations can be used to compare the results of steady monetary

Table 1.   Simulations of Gross National Product

Period	Control Simulation (Steady 6% M_1 Growth)		Simulation II		Simulation III		Simulation IV	
	% Δ M	Level of GNP (billions of dollars)	% Δ M	GNP Minus Control Simulation (billions of dollars)	% Δ M	GNP Minus Control Simulation (billions of dollars)	% Δ M	GNP Minus Control Simulation (billions of dollars)
1972: I	6	1,092.9	10	2.4	10	2.4	10	2.4
II	6	1,108.5	2	3.3	10	8.3	10	8.3
III	6	1,125.8	6	2.6	2	12.0	10	17.1
IV	6	1,145.6	6	1.1	2	10.3	2	22.6
1973: I	6	1,166.3	6	− 0.3	6	5.4	2	21.1
II	6	1,187.3	6	− 0.4	6	0.9	2	13.5
III	6	1,208.4	6	− 0.4	6	− 0.8	6	5.3
IV	6	1,229.7	6	− 0.4	6	− 0.8	6	0.5

Note: Simulations were performed with the equation described in "A Monetarist Model for Economic Stabilization" by L. Andersen and K. Carlson (Federal Reserve Bank of St. Louis *Review,* April 1970). The simulations are reported in James Pierce and Thomas Thomson, "Some Issues in Controlling the Stock of Money."

growth at an x percent rate with uneven monetary growth that averages out to the same rate over the longer run. One such simulation has been performed on a version of the well-known Federal Reserve Bank of St. Louis econometric equation.[7] In this equation, nominal GNP is determined mainly by the behavior of the money supply in the current and three prior quarters. The control simulation assumes a steady 6 percent rate of growth in M_1 in each quarter. Other simulations assume M_1 growth rates of 10 percent for one, two, and three quarters, respectively, followed by growth rates of 2 percent for an offsetting number of quarters, with M_1 returning to a 6 percent growth rate thereafter.

The results of these simulations (see Table 1) suggest that a one-quarter deviation of M_1 growth from target amounting to 4 percentage points or less would have essentially negligible effects on GNP. Deviations from target lasting for *two* quarters would have only moderate effects. In this case, the resulting deviations of GNP from the path implied by steady 6 percent M_1 growth path would reach a maximum of only about 1 percent of the level of GNP. Deviations of M_1 from its target growth rate amounting to 4 percentage points and lasting for as long as three quarters do have more serious effects, however.

Of course, these results are only as valid as the lag structures embodied in the underlying model. Probably most large-scale structural models incorporate somewhat longer lags in the money-GNP relationship than do St. Louis-type "reduced-

[7]See James Pierce and Thomas Thomson, "Some Issues in Controlling the Stock of Money," in *Controlling Monetary Aggregates II: The Implementation* (Federal Reserve Bank of Boston, 1972), pages 115-36.

form" equations. As a result, simulations with these models would no doubt suggest that deviations from target growth rates could occur over somewhat longer periods without serious consequences for aggregate demand objectives. For what they are worth, however, the available simulation results suggest that the FOMC need not be too concerned about even fairly sizable deviations from M_1 target growth rates lasting up to around six months—providing there is some subsequent undershooting. Putting it somewhat differently, the policy makers should perhaps not be too disturbed by sizable intrayearly fluctuations in M_1 growth, provided the average growth rate for the year as a whole comes out about on target.[8]

Achieving Monetary Objectives: The Need for Short-Run Operating Targets*

Having tried to establish some notion of the costs of failing to hit money supply targets over varying lengths of time, we address the next question, What operational procedures are available to achieve these M targets and how well can such procedures be expected to work? One begins from the obvious fact, noted earlier, that the Federal Reserve has direct control only over certain instrument variables, most notably the size of its open market portfolio of Government securities. To hit targets for any monetary variable—be it the money supply, the monetary base, or even member bank nonborrowed reserves—forecasts of noncontrolled factors influencing these variables must first be made. Next, the Federal Reserve's instrument variables must be adjusted in such a way as to take account of the movements of these noncontrolled factors. The harder the movements of these noncontrolled factors are to predict, or the more complex are their interaction with movements in the Federal Reserve's own instrument variables, the more difficult will it be to hit any given target.

This is a complex matter, but the main points can be summarized as follows: to implement a money supply objective, defined, say, in terms of the desired M_1 growth rate over a month or period of months, an operationally meaningful strategy requires

---

[8]These conclusions are also supported by the results presented in "Income Stabilization and Short-run Variability in Money" by E. Gerald Corrigan, *Monthly Review* (Federal Reserve Bank of New York, April 1973), pages 87–98. In this paper, Corrigan first uses a "money-only" reduced-form equation to compare what GNP behavior would have been in 1970–1971 if M_1 had grown at a steady value equal to its average growth over the entire period relative to (a) the actual behavior of GNP over the period and (b) what the money-only equation would have projected for GNP given the actual behavior of M_1 over the period. Corrigan concludes that events would not have been very different with steady growth. In all but two quarters, GNP growth in the steady M_1 case would have differed by only 0.7 percent (annual rate) or less relative to the GNP growth indicated by the equation given the actual pattern of M_1 growth rates. The 1963–1965 period exhibits similar results. Simulations of the Board–MIT econometric model for 1970–1971 also indicate little difference between the results of smooth M_1 growth and the quite uneven quarterly pattern of M_1 growth rates that actually occurred—the largest difference for any quarter was a 0.6 percent annual rate of growth in GNP. Corrigan also runs simulations similar to the Pierce-Thomson simulations cited in Table 1 and the text, though using a money-only reduced-form equation. The results are essentially the same as the Pierce-Thomson results.

  *See editors' note on page 447.

that week-to-week open market operations be laid out in terms of target values for other variables, variables easier to hit than the money supply itself. The targeted levels of these other variables must then be adjusted so that their achievement maximizes the likelihood of achieving the money supply target itself. In other words, one has to project, for example, the week-by-week levels of nonborrowed reserves that appear to be consistent with the desired money supply growth rate. Once this is done, the day-to-day decisions as to whether to buy or sell in the open market can be made in terms of the nonborrowed reserve objectives.[9]

As a practical matter, what variables are open to the Federal Reserve as feasible day-to-day and week-to-week operating targets? In practice, the number of available options is really rather small. First, one would have to rule out all total reserve and related measures, such as the total monetary base and the recently developed concept of RPD (total reserves behind private nonbank deposits). In practice, the Federal Reserve does not have the power to fix the levels of any of these measures within a given week. The problem is that changes in borrowings at the discount window, a magnitude over which the System exerts only the most general influence, will offset the effects on total reserves of System actions taken to change nonborrowed reserves.[10] However, by the same token, the various measures of nonborrowed reserves, including the nonborrowed monetary base and nonborrowed RPD, *are* feasible weekly operating targets. This is not to say the weekly targets for these nonborrowed reserve measures are easy to hit with accuracy. Quite the contrary. The non-Federal Reserve-controlled factors affecting reserves, most notably float, are very difficult to predict accurately on a weekly basis.[11]

[9]The problem of laying out short-term tactics for achieving the goals set in a money supply strategy is discussed in Richard G. Davis, "Short-Run Targets for Open Market Operations," in *Open Market Policies and Operating Procedures—Staff Studies* (Board of Governors of the Federal Reserve System, July 1971).

[10]This problem is examined in more detail in Davis (as cited above). If the Federal Reserve supplies nonborrowed reserves in excess of required reserves, which are fixed for a given reserve period under lagged reserve accounting, the result is likely to be mostly a paydown of outstanding borrowings and little if any buildup of excess reserves—at least up to the point where borrowings are reduced to frictional minima. On the other hand, reductions in the amount of nonborrowed reserves supplied are likely to lead to an offsetting increase in borrowings rather than a reduction in excess reserves. The point is simply that, in a period where excess reserves are very low and are probably very insensitive to money market rates in the short run, total reserves are fixed by required reserves (determined on the basis of deposit levels two weeks earlier) plus the frictional minimum level of excess reserves. (A regression of weekly levels of excess reserves on the weekly average Federal funds rate for 1970 and 1971 had a—nonsignificant—R^2 of only 0.005; the coefficient indicated that a full 1 percentage point increase in the Federal funds rate would reduce excess reserves by only \$16 million.) Fluctuations in nonborrowed reserves lead to offsetting movements in the Federal funds rate and in borrowed reserves but not, to any significant extent, to fluctuations in total reserves. Precisely the same argument applies to the total reserve base and total RPD. Note that the situation under lagged reserve accounting, with the resulting fixity of required reserves in any given week, may not be much different from the situation where reserve requirements are determined by deposit levels in the same week if bank asset supplies are quite insensitive to money market interest rates over periods as short as one week.

[11]In 1971, the average error in projecting market factors affecting nonborrowed reserves (float, currency in circulation, and the effects of Treasury and international transactions) as of the beginning of statement weeks was \$275 million. See "Open Market Operations and the Monetary and Credit Aggregates—1971," *Monthly Review* (Federal Reserve Bank of New York, April 1972), pages 79-94.

A different sort of weekly operational target that could be used to achieve the more basic money supply objectives is represented by money market interest rates, perhaps most notably the Federal funds rate (the rate on interbank overnight lending). On the one hand, this would be an operationally feasible target since the Trading Desk could feed funds into and out of the market as the actual market rate fell below or rose above the target rate. Thus, on a weekly average basis, say, it is possible to operate so that the average Federal funds rate will, most of the time, approximate a target rate. At the same time, the required weekly interest rate objective can be related to the more fundamental money supply target through forecasts of the demand for money at various interest rates. This problem is discussed further below.

In summary, to implement a money supply objective, the Federal Reserve must lay out a week-to-week program for operationally feasible short-run targets. It must set values for these targets that are projected to be consistent with the underlying money supply objective. If the projections prove wrong, the weekly target values will have to be adjusted. In practice, the Federal Reserve can use either a nonborrowed reserves measure or an interest rate measure, perhaps most especially the Federal funds rate, as its weekly operational target.

Relationship of Reserve and Interest Rate Operating Targets to Money Supply Objectives: A Simple Model of the Supply and Demand for Money*

Given the feasibility of either nonborrowed reserves or some measure of short-term interest rates as a week-to-week operating target, what is entailed in using these targets for achieving somewhat longer-run objectives for the money supply? To examine this, it is useful to set up an illustrative skeleton model of the supply and demand for money—or, to simplify matters somewhat, for deposits (D) alone. The demand equation for deposits in this model is the standard liquidity preference schedule. It includes a short-term interest rate (r) and some measure of transactions demand (Y). This latter variable can be treated as exogenous, given the short period purposes of the model. The supply of deposits is assumed to depend upon the level of nonborrowed reserves (Ru) and on the short-term interest rate (r). This latter dependency reflects the dependency of the banks' demand for borrowed reserves on short-term interest rates, the (smaller) dependency of their demand for excess reserves on rates, and the dependency on interest rates of the time-demand deposit mix. The latter of course has attendant effects on the banks' demand for reserves as a result of the difference in reserve requirement ratios for the two types of deposits. Thus, the model (in linear form) consists of

*See editors' note on pages 422 and 447.

$$D = b_1 Y + b_2 r + u \qquad \text{(Demand)} \qquad (1)$$

$$D = c_1 Ru + c_2 r + e \qquad \text{(Supply)}, \qquad (2)$$

where u and e are random terms.

Now the choice of an interest rate operating target to achieve the broader money supply objectives is tantamount to treating the interest rate as an exogenous variable. In such a situation, nonborrowed reserves become *en*dogenous, that is, such reserves are allowed to come out at whatever level proves necessary to achieve the interest rate target. The resulting reduced-form equation of the model is the same as the demand equation, i.e.,

$$D = b_1 Y + b_2 r^* + u, \qquad (3)$$

where r^* is the weekly interest rate target used by the Federal Reserve.

On the other hand, if the FOMC decides to work with a nonborrowed reserves operating target, the short-term interest rate becomes endogenous. The relevant reduced form for the reserve-target case is derived from the solution of the demand and supply equations as follows:

$$D = \frac{b_1 c_2}{c_2 - b_2} Y - \frac{b_2 c_1}{c_2 - b_2} R_u^* + \frac{c_2}{c_2 - b_2} u - \frac{b_2}{c_2 - b_2} e. \qquad (4)$$

A great deal of work has been done within the Federal Reserve System on estimating structural models of the type represented by equations (1) and (2)—though of course any realistic model requires far more than two structural equations—and reduced-form equations of the type represented by equations (3) and (4). While the estimation of these equations has raised the usual quota of econometric conundrums, some useful insights have been obtained from this work. Three areas in particular should be mentioned: (1) the different sorts of risk one is exposed to in using a nonborrowed reserves operating target as against an interest rate target, (2) the approximate limits of our ability to forecast and achieve money supply objectives with, respectively, these two types of operating targets, and (3) the existence of lags and their implication for policy making.

Sources of Error in Hitting Money Supply Objectives

As equation (3) indicates, the use of a short-term interest rate target entails making a short-term forecast of the demand for deposits. The interest rate target can then be set at the level that is expected to give the desired deposit behavior. (Of course, a formal econometric equation need not be used, but a judgmental forecast would require making much the same calculations implicitly.) There are two possible sources of error in picking the interest rate target needed to achieve the money supply goals: (1) random errors (or shifts in the demand equation) and (2) errors in forecasting Y—which is taken as exogenous for the short-term purposes at hand. Note that both types of error tend to be accommodated when using an interest rate target. That is, if the demand for money is greater than expected, for example, holding to the interest rate target (r* in Figure 3-a) will mean automatically supplying enough reserves to accommodate the demand.

This tendency for interest rate targets—and money market conditions targets generally—automatically to accommodate changes in the demand for money has been the chief complaint of monetarists about this type of target over the years. However, the complaint should not be leveled against interest rate operating targets *per se.* Rather, the complaint should have been, as applied to the procedures in use prior to 1970, (1) that the FOMC did not formulate explicit monetary growth rate objectives and (2) that it would not have been willing to move money market targets often enough, quickly enough, and decisively enough to achieve monetary growth objectives even if it had formulated them. Given the willingness to move interest rate targets as needed to achieve money supply objectives, such targets are a perfectly feasible way of operating open market policy to achieve money supply objectives.

As equation (4) indicates, the use of a nonborrowed reserves operating target can also be expected to lead to errors in controlling the money stock. The new element here is errors stemming from the supply side—errors which might be summarized in terms of unforeseen movements in the ratio of nonborrowed reserves to private deposits, i.e., unforeseen movements in the "deposit multiplier". Such movements can result, in turn, from unforeseen shifts in the banks' demand for excess and borrowed reserves and from unforeseen movements in the average required reserve ratio. This ratio is, of course, affected by shifts among the various categories of deposits and by movements of deposits between banks with different reserve requirement ratios. Another important potential source of error on the supply side can originate from unforeseen movements into and out of Treasury deposits at the commercial banks. These deposits absorb required reserves but are not themselves included in the money supply as usually calculated.

Relative to an interest rate target, nonborrowed reserves have some advantages and some disadvantages as an operating target for achieving money supply goals. Nonborrowed reserves are superior to interest rates in the face of a change in the demand for money. Such a change tends to get fully accommodated under an interest rate target, as already noted.[12] Under a nonborrowed reserves target, however, an increase in the demand for money will be accommodated only to the extent that the

---

[12]It should also be noted, however, that short-term, random, and reversible shifts in the demand for money *should* be accommodated since such accommodation prevents them from having any impact on real activity.

resulting upward pressure on money market rates engenders some elasticity of supply—to the extent, for example, that the banks themselves are induced by rising interest rates to accommodate the increase in demand by increasing borrowings from the Federal Reserve Banks or by drawing down excess reserves. Such offsets may not be too large, however, and will, in any case, not be complete. Thus, the money supply is likely to stay closer to target in the face of a demand shift if the Federal Reserve uses a nonborrowed reserves operating target than with an interest rate target.

On the other hand, a nonborrowed reserves target does not perform as well as an interest rate target in the face of an unforeseen shift in the average required reserve ratio—whatever its cause—or a shift in the banks' demand for excess and borrowed reserves. Such shifts will lead to a change in the actual money supply as long as the supply of nonborrowed reserves is held on target (see Figure 3-b). With an interest

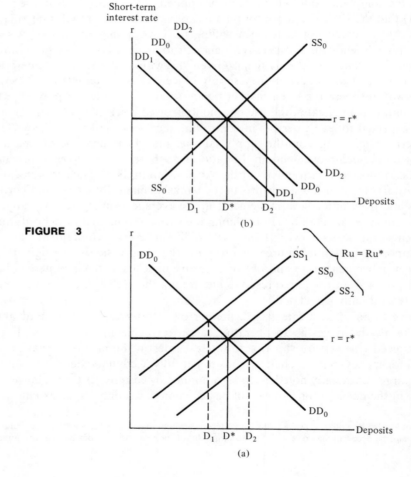

FIGURE 3

rate operating target, in contrast, the volume of nonborrowed reserves would automatically be adjusted to offset the impact on money of these changes in supply conditions. As a result, their distorting effects on the money supply would be neutralized.

Estimating Errors in Achieving Money Supply Objectives in the Short Run

In principle, then, either nonborrowed reserves or interest rates can be used as operating handles to achieve money supply goals; each has its own advantages and disadvantages.[13] Which can be expected to work better in practice, and how well each will work, are empirical questions. A fair amount of statistical work has been done in the Federal Reserve System on the probable size of errors in using these operating targets. Table 2 is fairly representative of the general thrust of the results—and it also gives some idea of the probable order of magnitude or errors in hitting money supply targets in the short run.

Three sets of forecasts are presented in Table 2.[14] The first two are based on reduced-form equations of the types suggested by equations (3) and (4) presented earlier. The first set uses changes in the Federal funds rate as the open market operating target: thus it is essentially a complex variant of equation (3) cited earlier.

[13]As a purely formal matter, the question of whether nonborrowed reserves or interest rates is the better instrument for controlling money can be treated with precisely the same analysis used by Poole to examine whether the money supply or the interest rate is the better handle to control GNP (see footnote 2). The question turns on the relative instability of demand (analogous to the IS curve in Poole's analysis) or supply (analogous to LM). The variance of deposits, using an interest rate target, depends on the variance in Y from forecast values and the variance of the error term u in equation (3) and on their covariances as well as on the income elasticity of demand. The variance of deposits, using a nonborrowed reserves target, depends on the variance of Y, the variances of the error terms in both supply and demand equations, their covariances, and the various income and interest rate elasticities in the supply and demand equations (see Pierce and Thomson, "Some Issues in Controlling the Money Stock"). Just as Poole's analysis has to be modified to allow for the possibility that M cannot be precisely controlled, however, the present analysis should really be modified for the possibility that nonborrowed reserves cannot be precisely controlled. In this case, nonborrowed reserves should be replaced in the supply equation with the sum of changes of Federal Reserve credit, the forecast value of operating factors affecting reserves, and a new random error term reflecting errors in forecasting operating factors. Some specialists object strongly to the proposition that nonborrowed reserves could be hit with any high degree of accuracy. They argue that under a pure nonborrowed reserves target, where the Federal funds rate could be expected to show much wider week-to-week movements than at present, the behavior of the Federal funds rate would no longer serve to assist the Open Market Account Management in warning when operating factors affecting reserves are going seriously off track. They argue that the margin of error in hitting the funds rate on average, week to week, would be much smaller. In that case, evidence purporting to compare nonborrowed reserves and the funds rate as competing targets for controlling money is seriously biased in assuming the two operating targets are themselves equally achievable

[14]These results represent an updating of material presented in a paper published in the November 1973 issue of the *Journal of Money, Credit, and Banking,* by Fred J. Levin, "Examination of the Money Stock Control Approach of Burger, Kalish, and Babb." See also A. E. Burger, L. Kalish III, and C. T. Babb, "Money Stock Control and Its Implications for Monetary Policy," *Review* (Federal Reserve Bank of St. Louis, October 1971).

Table 2. Errors in Forecasting M_1 Growth Rates, 1970–1972
(Seasonally adjusted annual rates; in percent)

Measure	Using Federal Funds Rate*	Using Nonborrowed Monetary Base†	FRB St. Louis Method‡
Mean absolute error of *ex post* monthly forecasts	2.91	3.47	6.33
Root mean square error of *ex post* monthly forecasts	3.60	4.22	8.61
Mean absolute error of *ex ante* monthly forecasts	3.36	3.61	§
Root mean square error of *ex ante* monthly forecasts	3.93	4.53	§
Mean absolute error of *ex ante* quarterly forecasts	2.10	2.13	§
Root mean square error of *ex ante* quarterly forecasts	2.34	3.08	§
Mean absolute error of *ex ante* six-month forecasts	1.19	2.10	§
Root mean square error of six-month *ex ante* forecasts	1.39	2.52	§

*Based on $\Delta M_1 = \sum_{i=0}^{7} b_i \Delta$ Federal funds rate $_{t-i} + \sum_{i=0}^{7} c_i \Delta$ business sales $_{t-i} + d \Delta$ Treasury deposits + constant. Estimated on 1965–69 data.

† Based on $\Delta M_i = \sum_{i=0}^{7} b_i \Delta$ nonborrowed monetary base $_{t-i} + \sum_{i=0}^{7} c_i \Delta$ business sales $_{t-i} + d \Delta$ Treasury deposits + constant. Estimated on 1965–69 data.

‡ See A. Burger, L. Kalish, and C. Babb, "Money Stock Control and Its Implications for Monetary Policy," *Review* (Federal Reserve Bank of St. Louis, October 1971).

§ Not available.

The second set of projections uses the nonborrowed monetary base as the operating target—i.e., it is a variant of equation (4). The third set is a method developed at the Federal Reserve Bank of St. Louis. It simply estimates the money-reserve base multiplier from a regression using a three-month moving average of past values of the multiplier, and adjustment for changes in legal reserve requirement ratios, seasonal dummies, and a measure of autocorrelation. The two reduced-form equations were estimated from 1965–1969 data, while the St. Louis method calls for updating the regression equation in each month. The forecasts were made for monthly changes in money supply (expressed as an annual rate of growth) over the 1970–1972 period. The forecasts labeled *ex ante* in the table are *ex ante* forecasts in the sense that all inputs were entered as of the estimates or projections that would have been available at the time.

Some interesting results emerge from Table 2. First, the forecasts using the nonborrowed monetary base and the Federal funds rate, respectively, do roughly equally well. Some other results (not presented in the table) which adjust nonborrowed reserves for required reserves against Treasury and interbank deposits (in other words, nonborrowed RPD) also seem to suggest a roughly comparable performance. This particular evidence, at least, does not provide a decisive case for or against any one of the potentially available operating targets.

A second point is that the two reduced-form equations forecast markedly better for this period than the St. Louis approach, which is essentially a purely autoregressive estimate of the money multiplier.

Finally, and most important, all three methods of projection do rather poorly in forecasting monetary growth rates for individual months. The same conclusion has to be drawn about attempts to forecast short-term growth rates judgmentally. Despite considerable investment of time and talent, all presently available techniques for making short-term projections of the monetary growth rate that would be associated with any particular setting of an operating target are subject to large errors on average and very large errors in many particular instances.

It is possible to be more optimistic when somewhat longer time horizons are considered, however. *Ex ante* forecasts for one quarter ahead have an average absolute error of 2.13 percent for the nonborrowed base equation and 2.10 percent for the Federal funds equation. Forecasts for six months ahead show corresponding average absolute errors of 2.10 percent and 1.19 percent, respectively. This means that for six-month periods, we seem to be able to get at least "ball park" estimates of the consequences for monetary growth rates of particular settings of open market operating targets. Even for these periods, however, the errors are clearly not negligible.

The Lags Between Federal Reserve Actions and Money Supply Response

Finally, with regard to the lags: All the econometric evidence available to us suggests that there is a lag between a change in operating targets and the full impact of that change on the money supply. Indeed both the Board staff's monthly money market model—a very complex version of structural equations (1) and (2)— and the reduced-form equations developed at this Bank—essentially complex versions of (3) and (4)—suggest that the effects may take on the order of six to eight months to work themselves out fully.[15] This means, for example, that a maintained step-up in the level of nonborrowed reserves will not have its full effect on the level of the money supply for several months. Similarly, a once-and-for-all increase in a Federal funds rate target will not have its full effect on the level of the money supply for several months.

Now it is of course true that the estimation of lag structures is a very uncertain business. The evidence that these lags are as long as six to eight months cannot be

[15]See "A Monthly Econometric Model of the Financial Sector" by Thomas Thomson and James Pierce, unpublished; and "Forecasting the Monetary Aggregates with Reduced-Form Equations" by Richard G. Davis and Frederick C. Schadrack.

considered at all firm. One possibility is that the use of monthly time units instead of shorter units may bias estimates of the lag upward; this sort of bias does seem to have turned up in some other areas of econometric work. However, the Board staff has also estimated a weekly model, and its lags, while not as long as those in the monthly model, are still substantial.[16] The point is that even if the true lags were, say, only one half the six- to eight-month range indicated by most of the econometric work, they would still have significant implications for policy.

The existence of these lags creates a potential control problem for the Federal Reserve in trying to hold monetary growth rates to any targeted rate. As indicated, these lags delay the ultimate impact on the money supply of a change in the operating target, be it nonborrowed reserves or short-term interest rates. By the same token, however, they also imply that an adjustment in the operating target large enough to produce a desired correction in the monetary growth rate *immediately* will ultimately overshoot this desired correction and will then have to be reversed (see Figure 4). For example, if M_1 is currently growing at 2 percent (January through March in Figure 4) and the Open Market Committee objective is 6 percent, the desired correction could be achieved by lowering a Federal funds rate target (labeled R_{ff} in the figure) or raising a nonborrowed reserves target (labeled Ru' in the figure). However, a reduction large enough to bring M_1 back to 6 percent within a month (April), would eventually (by June) push the monetary growth rate up to, say, 8 percent. At that point, a near-term correction back to 6 percent (in July) might require a drastic *increase* in the Federal funds rate target, one that might ultimately (in August and

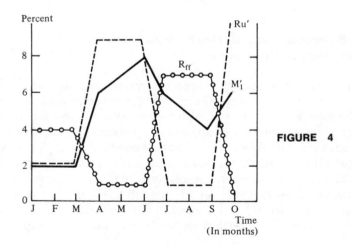

FIGURE 4

[16]Helen T. Farr, Steven M. Roberts, and Thomas D. Thomson, "A Weekly Money Market Model—A Progress Report" (June 1972, unpublished). The lags in the major structural equations of this model run from five to thirty-four weeks. Simulations performed by the authors indicate that an increase in nonborrowed reserves achieves its maximum effect on M_1 after about three months, while a decrease in the Federal funds rate produces its maximum impact after about six months.

September) push M_1 growth once more below the 6 percent target, and so on. Indeed, if the lag structure is sufficiently unfavorable, it would not be too difficult to imagine situations where explosive oscillations in the operational target would be required to hold the M_1 target, month by month, to a steady target growth rate.[17]

There appears to be a fairly clear moral to be derived from these implications of the existence of lags: policy makers should avoid taking too short a view in deciding where to set week-to-week operating targets. Even in a world where the money supply implications of a given target setting were known with certainty, operational targets should be set so as to achieve money supply goals *on average* over a period of time. Attempts to rejigger operating targets so as to hit the long-run money supply objectives in each and every month—assuming this to be possible at all—are likely to involve excessive volatility in the operating target. This volatility will mean excessive instability in money market rates. This will result directly, if the Federal funds rate is used as the operating target, and indirectly if some measure of nonborrowed reserves is used.

Similarly, when trying to speed up or slow down the monetary growth rate, the policy makers should keep in mind the fact that a movement in operating targets sharp enough to achieve this change rapidly will, because of lags, eventually overshoot. This overshooting will, in turn, require an eventual further adjustment of the instrumental target in the opposite direction. For this reason, it may well be desirable to take a somewhat gradualist approach to slowing down or speeding up monetary growth rates, aiming to accomplish the change over a period of months rather than immediately. Of course, in any particular situation, the right decision depends on for how long and by how much monetary growth has been deviating from what the

---

[17]In principle, at least, this proposition can be tested. First, reduced-form equations of the sort presented in Table 2, having been estimated statistically, can be solved for the current value of the instrument variable. Thus, for example, equation (1) in that table, where the Federal funds rate is the instrument variable, can be rewritten so that the current change in the Federal funds rate is the dependent variable and is a function of the current change in deposits, lagged changes in the Federal funds rate, and the current and lagged changes in the exogenous variables. If we assume the current change in deposits equal to some given target value in each and every month, we then have a seventh-order difference equation in the Federal funds rate plus some exogenous variables. This equation tells us the change in the instrument variable—the Federal funds rate in this case—that will be required to hold M on target given the current values of the exogenous variables and the past history of these variables and the funds rate. Some preliminary analysis of this equation suggests that, under a fairly wide range of assumptions about the lag coefficients on the Federal funds rate in the original reduced-form equation, the time path of monthly changes in the funds rate needed to maintain changes in M at the targeted rate in each and every month would be oscillatory and explosive. Moreover, if one uses some plausible values for the behavior of the exogenous variables and initial conditions as of early 1972, simulations of the difference equation for constant monthly changes in the money supply did generate explosive oscillations in the Federal funds rate. Indeed, the simulation after just a few months involved a negative funds rate to hold changes in deposits on target, clearly an impossibility. While one would hardly want to jump to the conclusion that these simulations accurately reflect the way the world is actually constructed, their results are not really so implausible. There may be literally *no* way of getting M to grow by more than x percent next month. At some point, injections of nonborrowed reserves may drive the funds rate and borrowed reserves to zero, with further injections merely having the effect of piling up excess reserves. Of course, as these reserves begin to be utilized, with a distributed lag, money supply growth could subsequently become explosive, forcing the authorities to jump the funds rate up by amounts that would rock the structure of the money market—and so on.

policy makers consider desirable and how serious the economic consequences of these deviations seem likely to be if not corrected promptly.

In thinking about these matters, it quickly becomes apparent that the use of a money supply strategy for monetary policy confronts the policy makers with a very interesting and complex problem in control theory—one that is only just now beginning to be appreciated and explored. The policy maker is confronted with two sets of distributed lags. One set of lags, the one just discussed, relates operationally feasible open market target variables, such as nonborrowed reserves and the Federal funds rate, to the money supply. The other set, mentioned earlier, relates the money supply to the variables that ultimately matter. *Shortening* the attempted time horizon of monetary control increases the technical problems of monetary management and the likelihood of an unacceptable degree of money market instability. *Lengthening* the period of control increases the probable deviations of aggregate demand and related variables from desired behavior.

No doubt there is an optimum control period here somewhere. It was mentioned earlier that some calculations seem to suggest that, if monetary growth rate targets are hit on average over a year, deviations of GNP from the path it would follow with absolutely steady monetary growth might well remain within acceptable limits. However, if monetary growth rates have drifted off target over the first half of the year, for example, the authorities then have only six months in which to get the yearly average back on track. Thus it seems fairly clear that the authorities will have to be prepared to move their instrument variables with sufficient vigor to control average monetary growth rates over periods shorter than one year. Clearly, there are some messy problems here in this whole area. Quite possibly they have not yet even been clearly formulated—let alone solved.[18]

Conclusion

The main points made in this paper can be summarized as follows. The Federal Reserve has moved with the shift in the general climate of ideas over the past few years, putting increasing emphasis on the money supply and other monetary aggregates as intermediate objectives of monetary policy. The Federal Open Market Committee now sets explicit goals for the growth of the money supply and bank credit and issues operating instructions to the Account Management in New York that are drawn up largely with a view to achieving these objectives. The qualification

---

[18]It might be noted that these problems would not disappear though they might be simplified, if one were to adopt a steady growth of the money supply at some fixed rate à la Milton Friedman. In the first place, the economy would not "start out" on its long-run trend path with full employment and a history of steady monetary growth, sustainable real growth, and an "acceptable" rate of inflation. Consequently, one might want to approach the long-run monetary growth rate target only gradually. Secondly, all the technical problems of short-run control over the money supply would remain. Consequently, the actual growth rate could expect to go off track much as it does now. Therefore, the problems of an optimum control period, how to compensate for past errors, and how sharply to adjust operating targets to get back on track would still exist.

"largely" is necessary since the behavior of money and capital market conditions, and international financial developments, have also continued as a source of explicit concern to the Committee. At times, this concern has dictated operating decisions different from those that might have been made if hitting money supply objectives had been the sole aim. In trying to improve its ability to achieve money supply goals, the FOMC has experimented with alternative approaches to operating tactics. It has also made a substantial investment of research resources in the problems of monetary control.

The results to date suggest that attempts to forecast and control the money supply over short periods, whatever operating targets are used, will normally be subject to quite large errors. A rough judgment might be that reasonably close forecasts, and control, can be achieved over periods down to six months if the Committee is prepared to move its operating targets sufficiently vigorously to achieve the desired results.

Fortunately, the tentative evidence also suggests that very short-term control over the money supply is not necessary for satisfactory economic performance. Evidently, fairly large deviations from target may not do any significant harm, provided they do not last longer than a quarter or two and provided monetary growth rates average out about on target over longer periods of perhaps a year. None of these estimates can be regarded as firmly established, however.

In controlling money, shorter term operating targets that are more readily achievable than the monetary targets themselves are needed as a guide to day-by-day and week-by-week decisions. Various measures of nonborrowed reserves and short-term interest rates are available for this purpose. Each has advantages and disadvantages. The available evidence does not establish any clear overall superiority for any one of them.

Finally, it is clear that a great deal has been learned about the problems and possibilities of implementing money supply targets in the past few years. Virtually all of the research drawn upon in this survey is less than three or four years old. Many of the topics discussed would have seemed quite novel only a relatively short time ago. The progress in this area has been rapid. Indeed, one may wonder if diminishing returns may not already have begun to set in in some respects. Perhaps the direction in which research efforts will now move is to deal with the implications of the lags and uncertainties—in short the "control theory" issues mentioned earlier. What should be the time horizon for monetary control? How should targets be adjusted in response to the past "misses" that will inevitably arise? Work in this area will have to be sufficiently grounded in reliable evidence and sufficiently "robust" to be useful to properly skeptical policy makers. Nevertheless, we can be hopeful that further progress in this area will be forthcoming over the period ahead.

The Choice of a Monetary Policy Instrument

James A. Cacy

25

Alternative methods of conducting monetary policy have been extensively debated in recent years. Much of the debate has centered around the question of whether the Federal Reserve should use interest rates or the money supply as the instrument variable in conducting monetary policy. This article analyzes some aspects of this question. The first section of the article defines an instrument variable and outlines the relationship between instrument and goal variables. . . . The second and third sections . . . analyze the choice of an instrument variable. The last section summarizes the article findings.

Instrument and Goal Variables

An instrument variable is one the Federal Reserve controls on a continuous basis. By controlling instrument variables, the Federal Reserve influences the behavior of goal variables, which measure conditions or processes related to the System's overall economic goals. The Federal Reserve's goals include, in general terms, reasonable price stability, high employment, satisfactory economic growth, and international balance. For example, a price index may be a goal variable because it measures the extent of inflation, a process related to the general goal of price stability. Thus, one

Reprinted, with deletions, from *Monthly Review,* November 1978, pp. 17–35, by permission of the Federal Reserve Bank of Kansas City and the author.

objective of the Federal Reserve in controlling instrument variables may be to influence the behavior of a price index.

Instrument variables have two characteristics. First, they are controllable—that is, they are closely related to Federal Reserve actions; and they can be observed continuously so that any imprecision in the relationship can be immediately compensated for by Federal Reserve actions. The other characteristic is that instrument variables are closely related to goal variables or to other variables related to goal variables; and information is available about these relationships.

Because a number of variables are potential instrument variables, the Federal Reserve must choose one or more to control. As mentioned earlier, this article deals with the choice between the interest rate and the money supply. The article also discusses the alternative of using both variables as instruments.[1] When only the interest rate is used, a "pure" interest rate policy is followed, defined as a policy of maintaining the interest rate at a specified level for a specified period. The period is referred to as the decision period. When only the money supply is used as an instrument variable, a pure money supply policy is followed, defined as a policy of maintaining the money supply at a specified level during the decision period. When both variables are used, a "combination" policy is followed, defined as moving the interest rate and the money supply during the decision period in response to certain developments.

National income is treated as the Federal Reserve System's goal variable in this article. It is assumed that policymakers want to achieve a specified level of income because income below that level is accompanied by unutilized resources, while income above that level is accompanied by inflationary pressure. . . .

Choosing the Instrument

The *IS-LM* model* may be used to analyze the choice of the best instrument to use in conducting monetary policy.[2] This section treats the choice between the interest rate and the money supply, while the following section discusses the possibility of using both variables. In general, the relative efficacy of the two variables as instruments

---

[1]The article assumes that there is only one interest rate and one measure of the money supply. Also, the article assumes that both the interest rate and the money supply can be continuously controlled. While these assumptions are unrealistic, they allow the analysis to focus on the important issue of the choice between interest rates and the money supply.

*Editors' note: For a review of the *IS-LM* model, see Reading 1, by Warren Smith.

[2]The *IS-LM* model was first used to rigorously analyze the problem of instrument choice in William Poole, "Optimal Choice of Monetary Policy in a Simple Stochastic Macro Model," *Quartery Journal of Economics* 84 (May 1970), pp. 197–216. Also see Stephen F. LeRoy and David E. Lindsey, "Determining the Monetary Instrument: A Diagrammatic Exposition," Board of Governors of the Federal Reserve System *Special Studies Paper No. 103* (1977); LeRoy and Roger N. Waud, "Applications of the Kalman Filter in Short-Run Monetary Control," *International Economic Review* 18 (February 1977), pp. 195–207; and Benjamin M. Friedman, "The Inefficiency of Short-Run Monetary Targets for Monetary Policy, Comments and Discussion," *Brookings Papers on Economic Activity,* Vol. 2 (Washington, D.C.: The Brookings Institution, 1977), pp. 293–346.

depends on the relative closeness of their relationship to the goal variable, national income. Relative closeness depends on the characteristics of the *IS* and *LM* functions, linking the interest rate, money supply, and income. In particular, relative closeness depends especially on whether and to what extent the two functions are stable.

In view of the importance of stability, this section's analysis of instrument choice is divided into four parts distinguished by the extent of stability. In the first part, both the real and the monetary sectors are assumed to be stable. In the second part, the real sector is stable, but the monetary sector is unstable. In the third part, the real sector is unstable, but the monetary sector is stable; and in the fourth part, both sectors are assumed to be unstable. The analysis of the better instrument is preceded by a brief discussion of the meaning of stability and instability.

Meaning of Stability and Instability

Stability in both the real and monetary sectors means that the *IS* and *LM* functions remain in the positions they are expected to occupy and do not fluctuate away from or around their expected positions. For the *IS* function to be stable, policymakers must know the precise levels of investment that investors plan at various interest rate levels, as well as the precise amounts of consumption and saving that consumers and savers plan to undertake at various income levels. For the *LM* function to be stable,

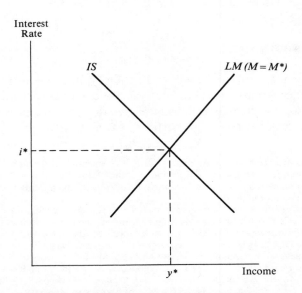

FIGURE 1. STABILITY IN REAL AND MONETARY SECTORS

policymakers must know the precise quantities of money demanded at various interest rate and income levels.

Instability in the monetary sector means that the *LM* function fluctuates around its expected position. That is, for various rates of interest, equilibrium income levels fluctuate above and below expected levels of income. Instability in the *LM* function arises when policymakers do not know the precise quantities of money balances that are demanded at various interest rate and income levels. Thus, they do not know, for various rates of interest, the precise levels of income that are consistent with equilibrium in the monetary sector of the economy. However, while policymakers are uncertain about the precise position of the *LM* function, they can estimate its expected position. That is, for various interest rate levels, they can estimate the levels of income that are expected to be consistent with monetary sector equilibrium.

Instability in the real sector means that the *IS* function fluctuates around its expected position. Instability in the *IS* function arises when policymakers do not know the precise amounts of investment that are planned at various interest rate levels or the precise amounts of consumption and saving that are planned at various income levels. Thus, policymakers do not know, for various interest rate levels, the precise levels of income that are consistent with equilibrium in the real sector of the economy. However, while policymakers are uncertain about the precise position of the *IS* function, they can estimate its expected position.

Instrument Choice under Stable Conditions

If both the monetary and real sectors are stable, neither an interest rate policy nor a money supply policy is preferred. Both policies are equally good because the target level of income is achieved by using either the interest rate or the money supply as an instrument variable.

Under stable conditions, an interest rate policy maintains the interest rate at that level associated with the target level of income, as indicated by the *IS* function. This is the interest rate that leads to a level of investment sufficient to generate the target level of income. The "maintained" interest rate level may be designated as i^* and the target level of income may be designated as y^*. (See Figure 1.) By maintaining the interest rate at i^*, the target level of income, y^*, is achieved. (Throughout this article, i^* designates the interest rate that is maintained under an interest rate policy, and y^* designates the target level of income.)

A money supply policy maintains the money supply at the level that causes the *LM* function to intersect the *IS* function at the target level of income. This is the money supply that equals the quantity of money demanded when income is at the target level. The maintained level of the money supply may be designated at M^*. As shown in Figure 1, by maintaining the money supply at M^*, the target level of income, y^*, is achieved. (Throughout this article, M^* designates the money supply that is maintained under a money supply policy.)

To summarize, if both the monetary and real sectors are stable, there is no difference between using the money supply and the interest rate as the instrument variable. Use of either variable achieves the target income level. Moreover, maintaining the interest rate at i^* under an interest rate policy results in a money supply of M^*—the maintained level under a money supply policy. Similarly, maintaining M^* results in i^*. In other words, i^* implies M^* and M^* implies i^*.

Instrument Choice under Instability in the Monetary Sector

If the real sector is stable but the monetary sector of the economy is unstable, an interest rate policy is better than a money supply policy. The interest rate policy is better because the target level of income is achieved when using the interest rate, but the target income may not be achieved when using the money supply.

Under these conditions of stability in the real and instability in the monetary sectors, an interest rate policy maintains the interest rate at the level associated with the target level of income, according to the *IS* function. As above, maintaining the interest rate at i^* achieves y^*.

A money supply policy maintains the money supply at that level that causes the expected *LM* function to intersect the *IS* function at the target level of income.

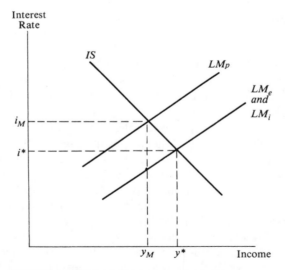

FIGURE 2. INSTABILITY IN THE MONETARY SECTOR

Note: LM_e represents the *LM* function that is expected when M^* is maintained, LM_p represents the function that may possibly result when M^* is maintained; and LM_i represents the function that results when i^* is maintained.

However, in this case, maintaining the money supply at M^* does not ensure the achievement of the target level of income because the *LM* function fluctuates and is unstable, as illustrated in Figure 2. In the figure, the expected *LM* function is labeled LM_e. The function may fluctuate, though, possibly shifting "leftward" to LM_p. (Throughout the remainder of the article, LM_e indicates the expected *LM* function when the money supply is maintained at M^*, while LM_p indicates the function that may possibly result when the money supply is maintained at M^*.) The leftward shift may be due to economic units temporarily demanding a greater than expected quantity of money balances. If the *LM* function shifts leftward to LM_p, the level of income achieved by maintaining the money supply at M^* is y_M, which is less than y^*. Alternatively, the *LM* function may shift "rightward" due to units demanding a smaller than expected quantity of money balances. In this case (not shown in Figure 2), the achieved level of income is greater than the target level.

In summary, if conditions are stable in the real sector but unstable in the monetary sector, the interest rate is better than the money supply as an instrument variable. Moreover, unlike the previous case, there is a difference between using the two variables. In this case, i^* does not necessarily imply M^*. Maintaining the interest rate at i^* may result in a money supply either above or below M^*, as the *LM* function fluctuates around its most likely position. In the case illustrated in Figure 2 of a leftward shift in the *LM* function to LM_p—due to a greater than expected demand for money—the money supply that results from maintaining i^* is higher than M^*. The higher level of money balances (which, under an interest rate policy, holds the *LM* function at the expected position) is needed to provide for the greater than expected demand for money. Similarly, maintaining the money supply at M^* may result in an interest rate above or below i^*. In the case of a leftward shift in the *LM* function, the level of the interest rate that results from maintaining M^* is higher than i^*. The higher interest rate (designated by i_M) is needed to reduce the greater than expected demand for money balances.

Instrument Choice under Instability in the Real Sector

If the monetary sector is stable but the real sector of the economy is unstable, a money supply policy is better than an interest rate policy. The money supply policy is better because, while the precise target level of income is not achieved by using either instrument, the divergence between the income level achieved and the target level will be less when using the money supply than when using the interest rate as an instrument variable.

Under conditions of monetary stability and real sector instability, an interest rate policy maintains the interest rate at that level associated with the target level of income as indicated by the *IS* function, assuming the function occupies its expected position. However, maintaining the interest rate at i^* does not ensure achievement of the target level of income. This is because the *IS* function fluctuates and is un-

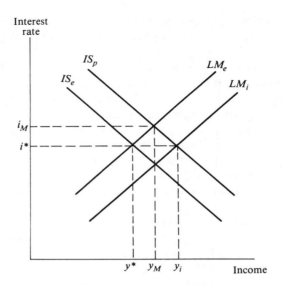

FIGURE 3. INSTABILITY IN THE REAL SECTOR

Note: LM_e represents the LM function that is expected when M^* is maintained, LM_p represents the function that may possibly result when M^* is maintained; and LM_i represents the function that results when i^* is maintained.

stable, as illustrated in Figure 3. In the figure, the expected IS function is labeled IS_e. The function may fluctuate, though, possibly shifting rightward to IS_p. (Through the remainder of the article, IS_e indicates the expected IS function, while IS_p indicates a possible function.) The rightward shift may be due to economic units temporarily investing more than expected. If the IS function shifts rightward to IS_p, the level of income achieved by setting the interest rate at i^* is y_i, which is more than y^*. Alternatively, the IS function may shift leftward due to units temporarily investing a smaller than expected amount. In this case (not shown in Figure 3) the achieved level of income is less than the target level.

A money supply policy maintains the money supply at that level that causes the LM function to intersect the expected IS function at the target level of income, assuming the IS function occupies its expected position. However, M^* does not ensure achievement of the target level of income because the IS function is unstable. In the case illustrated in Figure 3 of the rightward shift in the IS function to IS_p, the level of income achieved by maintaining the money supply at M^* is y_M, which is greater than y^*. In the case of a leftward shift in the IS function (not shown in Figure 3), the level of income achieved by maintaining the money supply at M^* is less than the target level.

In summary, if conditions are stable in the monetary sector but unstable in the real sector, the money supply is better than the interest rate as an instrument variable because the divergence between the achieved level of income and the target level is less when using the money supply than when using the interest rate. The smaller divergence is illustrated in Figure 3 which shows that the difference between y^* and y_M—the level of income achieved when using the money supply—is less than the difference between y^* and y—the level of income achieved using the interest rate. Moreover, there is a difference between the two policies, as i^* does not imply M^* and M^* does not imply i^*. Maintaining the interest rate at i^* may result in a money supply either above or below M^*, as the *IS* curve fluctuates around its most likely position. Similarly, maintaining the money supply at M^* may result in an interest rate either above or below i^*.

Instrument Choice under Instability in the Real and Monetary Sectors

If conditions are unstable in both the real and monetary sectors, either the interest rate or the money supply may be the best instrument variable, depending on certain factors. One factor is the relative instability of the *IS* and *LM* functions. As illustrated in Figure 4, a money supply policy is preferred if the *IS* function is less

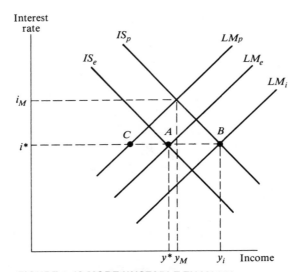

FIGURE 4. *IS* MORE UNSTABLE THAN *LM*

Note: LM_e represents the *LM* function that is expected when M^* is maintained, LM_p represents the function that may possibly result when M^* is maintained; and LM_i represents the function that results when i^* is maintained.

stable than the *LM* function. The figure assumes a rightward *IS* shift and a leftward *LM* shift, with the *IS* shift being more pronounced. The greater *IS* shift may be verified by noting that the distance between points *A* and *B* exceeds that between points *A* and *C*. Figure 4 shows that a money supply policy is preferred because the divergence between y^* and y_M is less than the divergence between y^* and y_i.

Since a money supply policy is preferred if the *IS* function is less stable than the *LM* function, the analyst might expect that an interest rate policy is preferred if the *LM* function is less stable. However, in the case of a less stable *LM* function, an interest rate policy is not necessarily preferred. The policy choice depends on the extent the *LM* function is less stable as well as on the slopes of the two functions. Ignoring the slopes, the money supply tends to be the better instrument if the instability of the *LM* function exceeds the *IS* function's instability by a small amount. If the excess instability of the *LM* function is large, however, the interest rate tends to be the better variable.

Figure 5 illustrates the impact on instrument choice of the degree of excess *LM* instability. The figure assumes a rightward *IS* shift and two alternative leftward *LM* shifts. Both *LM* shifts exceed the *IS* shift, with the shift labeled $LM_{p'}$, exceeding the *IS* shift by a larger amount than does the shift labeled LM_p. (Note that both line segments *AC* and *AD* exceed *AB*.) In the case of the relatively small shift to LM_p, a money supply policy is preferred even though the *LM* shift exceeds the *IS* shift. In the case of the relatively large *LM* shift to $LM_{p'}$, however, an interest rate policy is preferred.

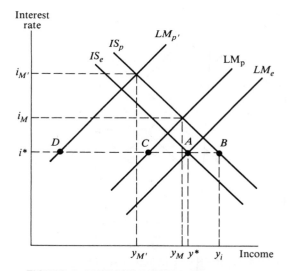

FIGURE 5. *LM* MORE UNSTABLE THAN *IS*

Note: LM_p and LM_p represent functions that may possibly result when M^* is maintained. The function labeled LM_i was not drawn; it would intersect IS_p at point *B*.

In addition to stability, the choice of an instrument depends on the slope of the *IS* and *LM* functions. The slope of a function refers to the relative changes in the interest rate and income that occur between equilibrium combinations of the two variables. The slope is "steep" if, for any given change in the interest rate, the change in income is small. The slope is "flat" if, for any given change in the interest rate, the change in income is large.

Ignoring the degree of excess instability of the *LM* function, if the *LM* function is relatively steep (flat), the interest rate (money supply) tends to be the better variable. The *LM* function is relatively steep (flat) if the demand for money is relatively insensitive (sensitive) to interest rate changes. Thus, an interest rate (money supply) policy tends to be preferred if the demand for money is relatively insensitive (sensitive) to changes in the rate of interest.

If the *IS* function is relatively steep (flat), the money supply (interest rate) tends to be the better instrument variable. The *IS* function is relatively steep (flat) if the demand for investment is relatively insensitive (sensitive) to interest rate changes. Thus, a money supply (interest rate) policy tends to be preferred if the demand for investment is relatively insensitive (sensitive) to changes in the rate of interest.[3]

Combination Policy

This section discusses the possibility that using both the interest rate and the money supply as instrument variables may be preferred to using either one or the other. The use of both instruments is referred to as a combination policy. Under a combination policy—instead of maintaining either the interest rate or the money supply at some specified level—policymakers move both variables in response to shifts in the *IS* and *LM* functions.

If precise information is available about shifts that occur in the functions, a combination policy is the preferred policy. For example, in the case illustrated in Figure 5, a combination policy would move the interest rate above i^*, and move the money supply above M^*. The policy would achieve the target income level, y^*, and would therefore be preferred to an interest rate or a money supply policy. While a

[3]The impact on instrument choice of the slope of the *LM* function can be illustrated by envisaging the impact on y_M of a progressive steepening of the *LM* function labeled LM_p in Figure 5. The steepening would be shown by a counterclockwise rotation of LM_p around an axis located at point *C*. As LM_p rotates and becomes steeper, y_M becomes progressively further from y^*. This increases the divergence between y_M and y^* and increases the likelihood that a money supply policy is inferior to an interest rate policy. (Note that the rotation in LM_p does not affect y_i.)

The impact on instrument choice of the slope of the *IS* function can be illustrated by envisaging the impact on y_M of a progressive steepening of the *IS* function labeled IS_p. The steepening would be shown by a clockwise rotation of IS_p around an axis at point *B*. As IS_p rotates and becomes steeper, y_M becomes progressively closer to y^*, increasing the likelihood that a money supply policy is preferred to an interest rate policy. (Note again that the rotation in IS_p does not affect y_i. Also note that at some point, the clockwise rotation is IS_p moves y_M above y^* and a further rotation beyond this point increases the divergence between y_M and y^*. However, the divergence cannot exceed the divergence between y^* and y_i. Thus, it cannot result in conditions whereby an interest rate policy is preferred.)

combination policy is preferred, its implementation may not be feasible because information about shifts in the *IS* and *LM* functions may not be available. An assumption that policymakers have precise information about the shifts is unrealistic and is equivalent to assuming that the functions are stable.

Some information, however, may be available that may possibly allow implementation of a combination policy. In general, three types of information may be available. First, some information is provided by observing the money supply and the interest rate. Thus, observed deviations of the interest rate away from i^*, when the money supply is maintained at M^*, indicate that the *IS* and *LM* functions have shifted. An observed tendency for the interest rate to move above i^* indicates a probable leftward shift in the *LM* function and a rightward shift in the *IS* function because leftward *LM* shifts and rightward *IS* shifts tend to place upward pressure on the interest rate. Similarly, a tendency for the interest rate to move below i^* indicates a leftward *IS* shift and a rightward *LM* shift.[4]

Information provided by observing the interest rate and the money supply, however, is not sufficient to support implementation of a combination policy. This is because the information indicates only the probable direction of *IS* and *LM* shifts and does not indicate their probable extent. For example, upward interest rate pressure may reflect either large *IS* and small *LM* shifts or small *IS* and large *LM* shifts. A large *IS* shift would call for a combination policy that moves the interest rate above i^* by a large amount, while a small *IS* shift would call for a policy that moves the interest rate above i^* by a small amount. Moreover, no basis would exist for determining the desirable course of action. Thus, information provided by observing the interest rate and the money supply is insufficient to allow the implementation of a combination policy.

A second type of available information may be about the relative stability of the *IS* and *LM* functions. For example, past experience may show that one of the functions tends to be more unstable than the other. Under these circumstances, it may be reasonable to assume that the more unstable function shifts more than the other one. This information about the relative stability of the *IS* and *LM* functions, along with information provided by observing the interest rate and money supply, may be sufficient to allow the implementation of a combination policy. The implementation may be based on two reasonable assumptions: (1) pressure on the interest rate to move away from i^*, when M^* is maintained, reflects counterdirectional shifts in the *IS* and *LM* functions; and (2) the extent of the shifts in the functions reflect their relative stability, as indicated by past experience. Im-

---

[4]The assumption that upward (downward) pressure on the interest rate is due to rightward (leftward) shifts in the *IS* function and to leftward (rightward) shifts in the *LM* function is based on the reasonable assumptions that some relationship exists between the magnitude of shifts and that small shifts are more likely to occur than large ones. In other words, any given degree of pressure on the interest rate most likely reflects the smallest possible shifts in each of the functions that would be consistent with the relationship and would produce the given degree of pressure. This implies, for example, that any given deviation of the interest rate above i^*, when M^* is maintained, is more likely to be caused by a small rightward *IS* shift and a small leftward *LM* shift than by, say, a large leftward *IS* shift and a large leftward *LM* shift.

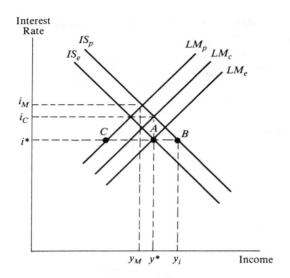

FIGURE 6. THE COMBINATION POLICY

Note: LM_c represents the LM function that results when the money supply is moved to M_c. LM_i is omitted.

plementing a combination policy is illustrated in Figure 6. In the figure, when M^* is maintained, the interest rate tends to move above i^* to i_M. It is assumed that the pressure on the interest rate reflects rightward IS and leftward LM shifts, and the LM shift is twice the IS shift. The greater LM shift may be verified by noting that the distance between points A and C on the chart is twice the distance between points A and B. If the functions shift as assumed, the combination policy achieves y^* by moving the interest rate to i_c and the money supply to M_c.[5] Thus, the policy would be preferred to either an interest rate policy or a money supply policy.

Of course, the combination policy would not always achieve y^*. The IS and LM functions would not always shift in accordance with past experience; that is, the two assumptions stated in the preceding paragraph would not always be realized. Nevertheless, the combination policy would be preferred because it would result, on average, in smaller divergencies between the achieved and target income levels than an interest rate or a money supply policy.

A third type of information may be about the behavior of income. While it is unrealistic to assume that the precise level of income is observed during the decision period, some information may be available about the extent that income is deviating from the target level. Suppose, for example, that information is available to indicate

[5]The combination policy assumes that the IS and LM functions shift in accordance with the ratio of the variances of the shifts. For a complete treatment of the combination policy, see LeRoy and Lindsey, "Determining the Monetary Instrument," cited earlier.

that income is falling below the target level. Also assume that the *LM* curve is known to be more unstable than the *IS* curve, and that the interest rate tends to move above *i** when *M** is maintained. Under these circumstances, as above, it is reasonable to assume that the *IS* curve has shifted rightward and the *LM* curve has shifted leftward, with the *LM* shift being more pronounced than the *IS* shift. In this case, though, the assumption of the leftward *LM* and the rightward *IS* shifts is solidified by the observation of a shortfall in income below the target level because these shifts tend to reduce income while opposite shifts tend to increase income. Thus, a combination policy may be implemented with increased confidence.

Conclusions

This analysis of the choice of a monetary instrument leads to several conclusions. One is that the choice depends importantly on the relative stability of the relationships among economic variables. The money supply tends to be better than the interest rate as a monetary instrument to the extent that the demand for money function is stable and the demand for investment and the saving functions are unstable. The interest rate is better to the extent that the demand for money function is unstable and the demand for investment and the saving functions are stable.

Another conclusion is that instrument choice also depends on the sensitivity of the demand for money and investment to changes in the rate of interest. The money supply is the better instrument variable to the extent that the demand for money is sensitive and the demand for investment is insensitive to changes in the rate of interest. The interest rate is better to the extent that the demand for money is insensitive and the demand for investment is sensitive to changes in the rate of interest.

A third conclusion is that a combination policy—using both variables as instruments—may be more effective than using either the money supply or the interest rate. The combination policy is better to the extent that information is available on the extent of stability in the relationships among economic variables and on the current behavior of economic variables.

The Myth of Congressional Supervision of Monetary Policy

James L. Pierce

26

For years, congressional committees have attempted in varying degrees to oversee monetary policy. Chairmen of the Federal Reserve Board have been interrogated intensively by some members of Congress attempting to learn what the Fed was doing and why it was doing it. These efforts were frustrated by the Federal Reserve's unwillingness to divulge its plans and objectives for monetary policy. The Fed was able to keep its intentions to itself. It apparently believed that to expose its policy decisions to public scrutiny would be detrimental to the Federal Reserve and to its policies. In effect, it told Congress not to ask too many questions; just "trust us." The Federal Reserve was able to defy requests and questions by these members of Congress in part because the general public and many members of Congress knew little about monetary policy. The Fed was also able to imbue its activities with a mystical quality, arguing in effect that secrecy was required for effective central banking. This ploy was successful because many potential critics of monetary policy were fearful that greater disclosure might result in some calamity for domestic or even international money markets. The lack of public interest and the mystical quality of American central banking could be combined with the Fed's considerable political power to withstand attacks by those who demanded greater disclosure of policy objectives and plans. The Federal Reserve's position was weakened in 1966 and 1969 when it subjected the economy to two highly visible credit crunches. In

Reprinted from *Journal of Monetary Economics,* Vol. 4, No. 2 (April 1978), pp. 363–70, by permission of the North Holland Publishing Co. and the author.

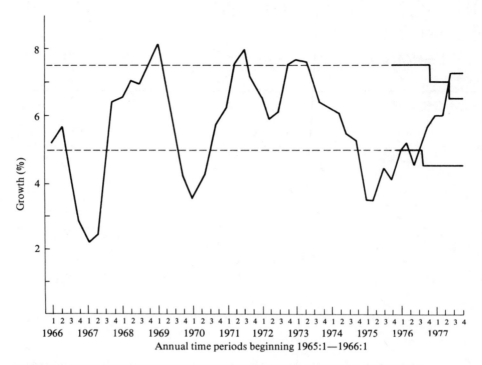

FIGURE 1. ANNUAL GROWTH OF THE MONEY STOCK (M1) AND LONG-TERM TARGET RANGES

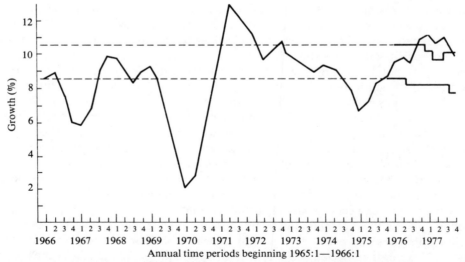

FIGURE 2. ANNUAL GROWTH OF THE MONEY STOCK (M2) AND LONG-TERM TARGET RANGES

1974, the Fed pursued a policy of such restrictiveness that Congress finally reacted by passing House Concurrent Resolution 133 in 1975. Major provisions of that resolution have recently become law.

The resolution of 1975 was historic for two reasons. First, it instructed the Federal Reserve to "pursue policies in the first half of 1975 so as to encourage lower long-term interest rates and expansion of the monetary and credit aggregates appropriate to facilitating prompt economic recovery." Congress had never given the Fed such strong and clear instructions. Second, the resolution required the Fed to appear regularly before the Senate and House Banking Committees to present its "objectives and plans with respect to the ranges of growth or diminution of monetary and credit aggregates in the upcoming 12 months." The Congress apparently decided that it could oversee the execution of monetary policy if it knew the Fed's plans for "the money and credit aggregates for the upcoming 12 months." The language concerning the monetary and credit aggregates has become the only operational feature of the recently passed law amending the Federal Reserve Act to provide for continuing Congressional review of monetary policy. With this amendment, monetarism passed from an interesting theoretical and philosophical proposition to a force immortalized in federal law.

It might appear that a revolution has occurred in Congressional oversight of monetary policy. Not only does Congress now actively oversee monetary policy, it does so using the tools of monetarism. This paper will argue that no revolution has occurred. Monetary policy continues to be pursued and executed in its customary fashion. Congress has seen fit to exert little or no influence on monetary policy and the Fed has not shifted its actual policies in a manner consistent with controlling the monetary aggregates. The Federal Reserve has succeeded in sidestepping the intent of Congressional resolution and public law alike and conducts its business in virtually the same ways it always has. Congress has salved its conscience by passing a resolution and then a law but it has showed little interest in providing meaningful oversight of monetary policy.

It is instructive to observe how the Fed responded to House Concurrent Resolution 133. It appeared before the banking committees armed with growth rate ranges for five different measures of money and credit aggregates. With this menu of aggregates it was able to create confusion and to direct attention away from policy objectives and toward the technical question of who has the best M. Furthermore, the growth rate ranges for each aggregate were sufficiently wide to be virtually assured of having at least one of the five aggregates within its range 12 months ahead. For example, in the second quarter of 1975 the Fed announced a 5.0–7.5 percent annual growth of M1 and an 8.5–10.5 percent annual growth of M2 as two of its objectives. As shown in figs. 1 and 2, for the period 1965 through the first quarter of 1975, the annual (quarter over quarter) growth in M1 was within the 5–7.5 percent range about 70 percent of the time and M2 growth was in the 8.5–10.5 percent range over 60 percent of the time. Furthermore, over that period, either M1 or M2 growth was within its growth range nearly 80 percent of the time. Thus, if the Fed continued to pursue policy after passage of House Concurrent Resolution 133 in the same way as it had in the past it ought to have been able to bat 700 or better. For reasons that will be described later, its record has been worse than what one might have expected.

As a further precaution, the Fed introduced a shifting base for its projections for the various Ms. By always stating its growth ranges for the aggregates on the basis of the *levels* of the aggregates in the quarter in which the Fed testified, it succeeded in making it difficult for its already confused Congressional supervisors to determine whether any target range had been hit. When some observers, including prominent monetarists, pointed out the implication of the shifting bases some members of the banking committees attempted to shorten the annual targets to quarterly ones arguing that at least for quarterly targets the Fed could not shift the base. The Fed countered by reminding these members that it was not required to either state or achieve quarterly targets and that quarterly movements in the Ms relative to longer-run paths should not be used to assess policy. The Federal Reserve discovered "catch 22"!

Some monetarists are willing to concede deficiencies in the current approach to Congressional oversight of the Federal Reserve, but point triumphantly to the requirement that the Fed announce its plan in terms of the monetary aggregates; rather than in terms of interest rates or other measures. One can understand their satisfaction over seeing the monetary aggregates singled out in a Congressional resolution and then a law. But it is difficult to understand how monetarists or any one else could conclude that any substantive changes have occurred in the execution of policy or in the supervision of that policy.

The evidence clearly points to the conclusion that the Federal Reserve has *not* placed greater emphasis on the monetary aggregates in its actual—as opposed to stated—policy-making. In fact the evidence suggests that the Fed has placed even greater reliance on stabilizing the money market, frequently at the cost of losing control over the monetary aggregates, since House Concurrent Resolution 133 was passed.

Beginning in 1974 the Federal Reserve has published quantitative targets in its "Record of Policy Actions of the Federal Open Market Committee." Three kinds of targets are presented: (1) a two-month target for the growth in the monetary aggregates with a shifting base; (2) a range over which the Federal funds rate will be permitted to fluctuate on a weekly average basis in the month that will elapse until the next FOMC meeting; and (3) since April 1975, 12-month growth ranges for the monetary aggregates (on a shifting base) in response to Congressional mandate. When the targets conflict, it is relevant to determine how the Fed responded. Upon examination, one finds that the range for the Federal funds rate is almost always hit and the targets for the monetary aggregates apparently left for later attention. That is to say, stabilizing the money market in terms of keeping the Federal funds rate within a predescribed range takes precedence.

For the policy actions in 47 FOMC meetings that have been published from January 1974 through November 1977, the last date available when this paper was prepared, the Fed managed to stay within its Federal funds rate band virtually 100

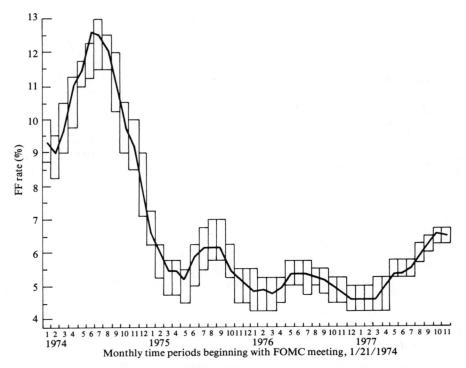

FIGURE 3. MEAN VALUES OF THE FEDERAL FUNDS RATE BETWEEN FOMC MEETINGS AND TARGET RANGES

percent of the time.[1] The target ranges and the monthly average values of the actual rate are shown in Figure 3. Over this same time interval the FOMC managed to hit its M1 growth targets only 40 percent of the time.[2] The target ranges and actual M1 growth are shown in Figure 4. This comparison might seem unfair; after all if the Federal funds rate range were wide and/or the M1 growth range narrow, the results would not be surprising. However, this was not the case. The mean Federal funds rate range over the period was approximately 100 basis points, e.g., a rate between 4 and 5 percent, but the mean absolute change in the monthly average rate from month to month was less than 40 basis points. The mean M1 growth range for the two-month horizons was 3.7 percent, e.g. growth in M1 over two months at an annual rate of 4 to 7.7 percent. The relatively narrow Federal funds rate band and the small changes in the actual rate are consistent with attempts to stabilize the

[1]Only during June 1974 did the Federal funds rate move outside its range. Two special meetings were required in 1974 to raise the band so that it could be achieved in a particular week. Even in these special cases, the old band was hit on a monthly basis.

[2]Data for October, November, and December 1977 are preliminary estimates.

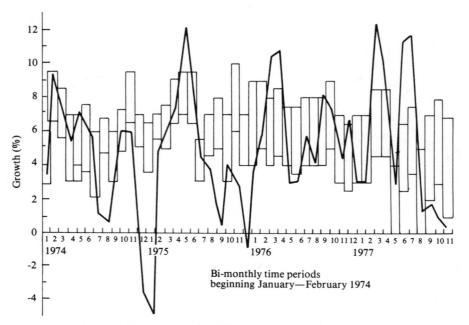

FIGURE 4. ANNUAL GROWTH OF THE MONEY STOCK (MI) AND BI-MONTHLY TARGET RANGES

money market. The result was a poor record in achieving short-term targets for the monetary aggregates despite wide target ranges for them.

Furthermore, it is interesting to note that the Fed tolerated larger changes in the Federal funds rate and had narrower bands for growth of the monetary aggregates in the period January 1974 through March 1975 than it adopted since March 1975 when House Concurrent Resolution 133 was passed. Over the period January 1974 through March 1975, the mean Federal funds rate range was 1.29 percentage points and the mean absolute monthly change in the Federal funds rate was 80 basis points. In the period since House Concurrent Resolution 133 was passed, the mean Federal funds rate range was 0.84 percentage points and the mean absolute change in the actual rate was 20 basis points. Thus, since House Concurrent Resolution 133 was passed the Federal funds rate band has been narrowed from 1.29 to 0.84 percentage points and the actual monthly absolute change in the rate has fallen from 0.80 to 0.20 percentage points. Since the passage of the Resolution, the mean width of the band for the two-month growth of M1 was raised from 3.0 percentage points to 3.9 percentage points. In the January 1974 through April 1975 period, M1 was in its two month growth range 47 percent of the time but since March 1975, M1 has been in its expended range only 37 percent of the time.

The record for hitting the annual targets is not better. Since the Fed has announced annual growth ranges for M1 and M2, it has kept both of these monetary aggregates within their ranges 50 percent of the time. This performance is truly remarkable since if these aggregates had simply grown since 1975 as they had in the past decade the Fed would have achieved 60 to 70 percent success.

Whatever can be said for Congressional supervision of monetary policy, it has not produced closer control over the monetary aggregates and it has not lessened the Fed's penchant for stabilizing movements in short-term interest rates. It appears safe to conclude that increased Congressional oversight has not altered the conduct of monetary policy. This oversight has heightened public awareness of monetary policy and it has helped produce some useful debate over that policy. Unfortunately, too much of the public discussion has focused on whose definition of money is best and what technical factors caused the Ms to be off target.

The various monetary aggregates can be useful indicators of the state of the economy and of Fed policy but there are many other useful indicators as well. Even if the Fed could be forced to improve its control over the monetary aggregates these aggregates would provide an incomplete story. The emphasis on the monetary aggregates has had the unfortunate effect of directing attention away from the real objectives of controlling inflation and encouraging employment, and national output. It is these objectives that are affected by monetary policy. It is these objectives that are of interest to Congress and the general public, not stories about the Ms.

It seems inescapable that Congress can only oversee monetary policy if it knows what that policy seeks to accomplish in terms of affecting the real economy and how the Fed intends to achieve its objectives. Implicit in House Concurrent Resolution 133 and the ensuing law is the simplistic notion that the Fed's objectives for the real sector can be inferred and assessed by determining its plans for the monetary aggregates. The monetary aggregates are important but they are not so important that they provide a basis for such heroic inferences. The linkages between the monetary aggregates and inflation, employment and production are far too weak to allow them to be used in the way implicit in House Concurrent Resolution 133. Furthermore, experience indicates that the relationship between what the Fed says are its objectives for the monetary aggregates and what actually materializes is weak indeed.

Such inferences are not necessary. Congress should direct the Federal Reserve to describe its objectives for the real economy for the upcoming 12–24 months and to defend its decision. The Fed should describe how it resolves conflicting goals for inflation, employment and production. The Federal Reserve should then describe how it would react if its objectives are not met. For example, if unemployment proves to be higher than anticipated, will the Fed ease monetary policy or will it keep policy unchanged for fear of increasing inflationary pressures? For the picture to be complete, the Fed must also describe how it intends to achieve its objectives. Objectives are useless if they cannot be achieved. It is here that "intermediate" variables such as the monetary aggregates come into play, but so do other intermediate variables and the actual instruments of monetary policy.

In contrast to its ineffective oversight of monetary policy, the Congress has made remarkable progress in analyzing the economic consequences of tax and expenditure programs. Here objectives are discussed and alternatives are analyzed. However, these activities are seriously deficient without a firm knowledge of the plans and consequences of monetary policy. One can only hope that Congress will wake up and take note of the importance of monetary policy and of the need to oversee it effectively.

Congress obviously cannot and should not attempt to actually execute monetary policy. That is the job of the Federal Reserve. But Congress must become more concerned with basic monetary policy decisions. These decisions are vital to national welfare and are too important to be left entirely to the Fed.

A Proposal for Redefining the Monetary Aggregates

Board of Governors of the Federal Reserve System

27

Regulatory changes and financial innovations in recent years have fundamentally altered the character of the public's monetary assets. These developments are responsible for growing similarities among certain kinds of deposits, and, at the same time, for disappearing resemblances among other kinds. Moreover, the distinctions between the deposit liabilities of commercial banks and those of thrift institutions have become blurred.

With the authorization of negotiable order of withdrawal (NOW) accounts and credit union share drafts, some savings balances at thrift institutions and commercial banks now provide the same transactions services as demand deposits. In ad-

Reprinted, with deletions, from Board of Governors of the Federal Reserve System, *Federal Reserve Bulletin,* Vol. 65, No. 1 (January, 1979), pp. 13–33. This *Bulletin* article presents proposals by the staff of the Board of Governors for redefining the monetary aggregates. They were formulated by a board staff group chaired by Stephen H. Axilrod, Staff Director for Monetary and Financial Policy. The proposals raise important issues regarding the payments system, the evolving role of depositary institutions, and the basis upon which the public chooses to hold various financial assets. To aid in further consideration of these proposals, comments are invited from the public. Please address comments to Office of the Staff Director for Monetary and Financial Policy, Board of Governors of the Federal Reserve System, Washington, D.C. 20551.

Thomas D. Simpson, Senior Economist in the Banking Section of the Division of Research and Statistics, had principal responsibility for the preparation of this article. Others making major contributions to the formulation and analysis of these proposals were Edward C. Ettin, John H. Kalchbrenner, David E. Lindsey, Richard D. Porter, Peter Tinsley, Darwin Beck, and William Barnett. Research assistance was provided by Daniel Rudolph and Juan Perea.

FIGURE 1. PRINCIPAL COMPONENTS OF M2

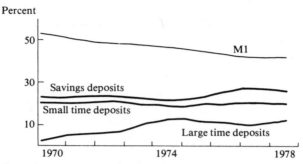

Quarterly averages, seasonally adjusted.

dition, preauthorization of bill payments and telephone transfer services have significantly increased the liquidity of savings deposits at both commercial banks and thrift institutions; and the automatic transfer from savings to demand accounts (ATS), recently authorized, has added substantially to the transactions-related character of savings deposits at commercial banks. [1]

Other developments have reduced similarities among various kinds of deposits, however. While savings balances at both commercial banks and thrift institutions have become more liquid in recent years, time deposits have generally become less liquid. Penalties for early withdrawal and the steady lengthening of maturities have reduced considerably the liquidity of small-denomination time deposits. As a consequence, the components of the M2 and M3 aggregates representing savings and small time deposits have become more dissimilar over time. Furthermore, a growing share of those time deposits included in M2—and in M3—is in large time deposits with denominations of $100,000 or more. Chart 1 shows that large time deposits currently make up a much larger proportion of M2 than they did in the early 1970s. Moreover, such deposits have behaved much like a managed liability, and their movements have tended to offset cyclical movements in savings and small time deposits, also shown in the chart. Over the cycle, large time deposits included in M2 have varied in much the same way as large negotiable time deposits (negotiable certificates of deposit) at large banks, which are excluded from the current M2 and M3 measures.

Commercial banks in recent years have also come to rely more heavily on some nondeposit liabilities, particularly security repurchase agreements (RPs). [2] From the

[1] Some thrift institutions—those with third-party-payment powers—are also permitted to offer automatic transfers. Moreover, the Federal Home Loan Bank Board has recently proposed that federally chartered savings and loan associations be authorized to offer a new kind of third-party-payment account—a payment order account—on which funds could be withdrawn by nonnegotiable, nontransferable orders.

[2] A security repurchase agreement is an arrangement whereby a bank "sells" a security in its portfolio—usually a treasury or federal agency security—to a customer and agrees to repurchase it at a specified price at some future date.

standpoint of the customer, RPs are a relatively safe and liquid alternative to holding deposits with commercial banks and other depositary institutions.

Because of these developments, the meaning of measures of the monetary aggregates has been changing, and a revision in existing definitions appears needed. The definitions proposed by the board staff in this article reflect recent developments by grouping together similar kinds of deposits at all depositary institutions. While the proposals seek to bring the monetary aggregates up to date, no one aggregate or group of aggregates can satisfy all purposes and, at times, it is necessary to deal with their principal components, which would be published separately.[3] Moreover, in view of the pace of regulatory and financial innovation, further redefinitions might well be needed as the character of the public's monetary assets continues to change.

The most important financial developments affecting the monetary aggregates in recent years are discussed in the next section. This is followed by a presentation of the proposed measures of the monetary aggregates. The next two sections discuss the empirical relationships among the proposed aggregates and other important economic variables, and the Federal Reserve's ability to control the various monetary aggregates. Important consolidation issues arise in the construction of measures of the public's monetary assets and some of these are discussed next. The last section contains a brief discussion of the timeliness of the data and data requirements. The appendix describes in some detail the procedures used in constructing the proposed monetary aggregates and the basic data sources.

Recent Developments Affecting the Public's Monetary Assets

Since 1970 a large number of regulatory changes and other financial developments have affected the nature of the public's monetary assets. The most significant of these are listed in Table 1. With the authorization of NOW accounts (Line 2), credit union share drafts (Line 6), and demand deposits at thrift institutions (Line 9), new accounts subject to withdrawal by draft or check have appeared. NOW balances at commercial banks had grown to about $2 billion by June 1978, while NOW accounts at thrift institutions had grown to over $1 billion (Table 2, last column). Balances in share draft accounts at credit unions (the third item in Table 2), plus demand deposits at thrift institutions (the fourth item) equaled almost $1½ billion, or about one-half of total NOW balances at that time.

Preauthorized transfers from savings accounts at commercial banks (Table 1, Line 1), government and business savings accounts (Line 7), telephone transfers (Line 8), and, most recently, automatic transfer services (ATS, Line 11) have

---

[3]In addition to the principal components of the proposed monetary aggregates, other pertinent deposit categories, such as U.S. Treasury deposits, interbank deposits, and deposits of foreign commercial banks and official institutions, would be published. Estimates of commercial bank repurchase agreements with the nonbank public would also be published.

Table 1.   Selected Developments Affecting the Nature of the Monetary Aggregates

Development	Date	Deposit Liability	Monetary Aggregate Containing Deposit Liability
1. Preauthorized transfers[a]	9/70, 4/75, 9/75	Savings balances at S&Ls and commercial banks	M-2, M-3
2. NOW accounts[b]	6/72, 9/72, 1/74, 2/76, 11/78	Savings balances at MSBs, S&Ls, and commercial banks	M-2, M-3[c]
3. 2½-year, 4-year, 6-year, and 8-year time deposits[d]	1/70, 7/73 12/74, 6/78	Time deposits at MSBs, S&Ls, and commercial banks	M-2, M-3
4. Substantial penalty on early withdrawal of time deposits	7/73	Time deposits at commercial banks, S&Ls, and MSBs	M-2, M-3
5. Point-of-sale terminals (POS) permitting remote withdrawals of deposits from savings	1/74	Savings balances at S&Ls	M-3
6. Credit union share drafts[e]	10/74, 3/78	Regular share accounts at federal credit unions	M-3
7. Savings accounts from domestic governments and businesses[f]	11/74, 11/75	Savings balances at commercial banks	M-2, M-3
8. Telephone transfers	4/75	Savings balances at commercial banks[g]	M-2, M-3
9. Demand deposits at thrifts[h]	5/76	Deposits of MSBs and S&Ls	M-3
10. 6-month money market certificates	6/78	Time deposits at S&Ls, MSBs, and commercial banks	M-2, M-3
11. Automatic transfer services (ATS)	11/78	Savings balances at commercial banks and thrifts having transactions balances	M-2, M-3
12. Payment order account (POA)	Proposed 11/78	Savings balances at S&Ls	M-3

[a]Savings and loans were permitted to make preauthorized nonnegotiable transfers from savings accounts for household-related expenditures in September 1970 and third-party nonnegotiable transfers from savings in April 1975. Commercial banks were authorized to make preauthorized third-party nonnegotiable transfers from savings in September 1975.

[b]State-chartered mutual savings banks began offering NOWs in Massachusetts in June 1972 and in New Hampshire in September 1972. In January 1974, depository institutions in Massachusetts and New Hampshire were authorized to offer NOWs. In March 1976, NOWs were authorized at depository institutions in Connecticut, Maine, Rhode Island, and Vermont; in November 1978, NOWs were authorized in New York State.

[c]NOWs at commercial banks appear in M2 (and M3), while NOWs at thrift institutions appear in M3.

[d]The increase in interest rate ceilings on the two-and-one-half year deposit was approved in January 1970, the increase on the four-year time deposit was approved in July 1973, the increase on the six-year deposit in December 1974, and the increase on the eight-year time deposit in June 1978.

[e]Temporary experimental share draft programs were first approved for federal credit unions in October 1974; final regulations for permanent programs became effective in March 1978.

[f]Savings accounts for domestic government units were permitted in November 1974, and for businesses (up to $150,000 per account per customer) in November 1975.

[g]Telephone transfers from savings balances at thrift institutions have been allowed since the 1960s.

[h]State-chartered mutual savings banks and savings and loans in New York State were authorized to offer demand deposits in May 1976. Prior to this time, these institutions were permitted to offer payment orders of withdrawal (POW) deposits. In addition, thrift institutions in some other states have been permitted to offer non-interest-earning transactions balances in households.

Table 2. Selected Deposit Balances at Commercial Banks and Thrift Institutions
(Millions of Dollars, Not Seasonally Adjusted)

Type of Deposit Balance	June 1974	June 1975	June 1976	June 1977	June 1978
NOW accounts					
At commercial banks	13	211	804	1,501	2,080
At thrift institutions	178	369	611	875	1,181
Share draft balances at credit unions	—	3	61	234	576
Demand deposits at thrift institutions	—	166	314	594	864
Savings at commercial banks					
By domestic governments	—	336	3,440	6,282	4,878
By businesses	—	—	6,013	10,123	10,757
Small-denomination time deposits with maturities over four years					
At commercial banks[a]	21,027	35,956	49,890	66,151	74,396
At thrift institutions[b]	40,600	82,100	117,500	158,400	196,800

[a]Measured as of July of each year.

[b]Estimated as of March of each year for savings and loans and April of each year for mutual savings banks.

substantially enhanced the liquidity and transactions character of commercial bank savings balances. Telephone transfers and ATS permit savings balances to be shifted readily into demand accounts, while preauthorized transfers permit direct payments from customers' savings. The authorization of savings accounts for businesses and domestic governments gives these depositors a highly liquid interest-earning alternative to holding funds in demand accounts. Funds in domestic government and business savings accounts (shown in Table 2) grew sharply just after being introduced but more recently have leveled off (business accounts) or declined (government accounts) in response to increases in market rates of interest. In late 1978, such balances amounted to about $15 billion.

Evidence on debits to savings accounts, available since July 1977, indicates that activity in these accounts has increased recently. As shown below, turnover rates,

Month	Debits to Savings Deposits (Billions of Dollars at Annual Rates)		Savings Deposit Turnover (Annual Rates)	
	Business	Other	Business	Other
1977				
July	40.8	307.8	4.0	1.5
October	41.9	313.2	4.0	1.5
December	49.1	304.9	4.6	1.5
1978				
March	48.3	333.5	4.6	1.6
July	55.6	376.5	5.1	1.8
October	67.2	394.2	5.8	1.9

defined as the annual dollar volume of debits divided by average balances, have risen since the summer of 1977. (These data do not include NOW accounts.) Turnover rates for business savings accounts advanced 45 percent from July 1977 to October 1978, while turnover rates for other savings accounts—mainly those of individuals and to a lesser degree domestic governments—rose about 25 percent.[4] To some extent, this increase in turnover rates might reflect higher market rates of interest, as some savings customers likely shifted their investment funds—relatively idle balances—to market instruments with higher yields. Nevertheless, savings balances of both businesses and others did expand between these dates, when turnover rates were rising, suggesting that any outflows of investment funds from savings were more than offset by inflows of more transactions-related funds.

Similarly, preauthorized and telephone transfers have enabled customers of thrift institutions to use their savings more effectively for transactions purposes. In addition, point-of-sale terminals (POS, Table 1, Line 5) have gone a step further by allowing these customers to make withdrawals and deposits from savings by using remote terminals placed at retailers. Most recently, the Federal Home Loan Bank Board has proposed that federally chartered savings and loan associations be permitted to offer a new "payment order account" (POA, Line 12), which could be used for making third-party payments.[5]

In contrast to these developments, the increase in regulatory ceiling rates on four-, six-, and eight-year time deposits (Line 3), which enabled depositary institutions to

FIGURE 2. LONG-TERM, SMALL-DENOMINATION TIME DEPOSITS

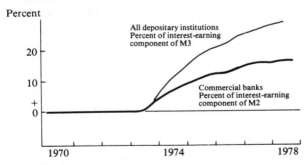

Original maturities of four years or longer. Commercial bank data are quarterly; observations for other depositary institutions are for March and September. Long-term time deposits at mutual savings banks and savings and loans have been estimated; those at credit unions, believed to be very small, are excluded.

[4]These turnover rates for savings deposits, however, are considerably smaller than turnover rates for demand deposits, which are about 100 per year for banks located outside New York City.

[5]The ceiling rate on POA accounts would, according to the proposal, be 5 percent, the same as that for all NOW accounts and ATS savings. The ceiling rate on share draft accounts at credit unions is 7 percent.

issue longer-term time deposits, has led to a significant reduction in the liquidity of time deposits by lengthening maturities at commercial banks, mutuals, and savings and loans. As Chart 2 shows, from the early 1970s to mid-1978, commercial bank time deposits with maturities of four years or more advanced from less than 1 percent of total time and savings deposits included in M2 to 15 percent; even more striking has been the trend in longer-term time deposits included in M3, also shown in the chart, which jumped from modest proportions in 1973 to an estimated 25 percent of total time and savings deposits included in this aggregate by the spring of 1978. Dollar amounts of longer-term time deposits at commercial banks and at savings and loans and mutual savings banks are given in the last two rows of Table 2. In mid-1978, such deposits accounted for about 45 percent of small-denomination time balances at commercial banks and about 70 percent of small time balances at savings and loans and mutual savings banks. The substantial penalty on early withdrawals of time deposits imposed in July 1973 has further reduced the liquidity of time deposits included in M2 and M3.[6]

The introduction in June 1978 of the six-month variable-ceiling money market certificate (Table 1, Line 10) has tended to offset the trend toward longer average maturities of time deposits. This new deposit has attracted a sizable volume of funds at both commercial banks and thrift institutions in just a few months. By late December, seven months after the introduction of money market certificates, such deposits at commercial banks had expanded to 4½ percent of total time and savings deposits included in M2; at both commercial banks and thrift institutions these certificates had risen by late December to about 6¾ percent of total time and savings deposits included in M3.

In addition to these developments, in the past decade the public began to use cash management techniques more intensively. With the application of such techniques as lock boxes, wire transfers, information-retrieval systems, and cash-concentration accounts, the public—particularly businesses—has been able to make transactions using relatively smaller amounts of demand deposits. In extensive interviews with board staff, cash managers and commercial bankers indicated that their reliance on cash management intensified around the mid-1970s. Much of the funds "released" from demand deposits was used to acquire highly liquid interest-earning investments, such as repurchase agreements, commercial paper, and treasury bills.[7]

---

[6]The depositor is required to forgo interest for 90 days and earns the passbook rate for the remaining time that the funds have been placed with the institution.

[7]In a recent econometric study of money demand, Tinsley, Garrett, and Friar conclude that the bulk of the shortfall in the public's demand for deposits during this period was mirrored by acquisitions of transactions-related RPs. See P. A. Tinsley, B. Garrett, with M. E. Friar, "The Measurement of Money Demand," Board of Governors of the Federal Reserve System, Division of Research and Statistics, Special Studies Section, November 1978; processed. An alternative interpretation of this period—one emphasizing the contribution of cash management services to reducing the variance of depositors' cash flow positions—can be found in Richard D. Porter and Eileen Mauskopf, "Cash Management and the Recent Shift in the Demand for Demand Deposits," Board of Governors of the Federal Reserve System, Division of Research and Statistics, Econometric and Computer Applications Section, October 1978; processed.

Proposed Monetary Aggregates

The four monetary aggregates being proposed by the board staff are presented in Table 3. The new measures are designed to replace the current monetary aggregates, M1 through M5, shown in Table 4. Proposed M1, by including new transactions accounts and by excluding selected foreign deposits, is a more comprehensive measure of transactions balances held for domestic expenditures than current M1. The next measure, M1+, adds to M1 all savings balances at commercial banks, which have become more transactions-related in recent years. Next, savings balances at thrift institutions, which have also become more liquid in recent years, are added to M1+ in deriving proposed M2. The fourth and broadest measure of the public's monetary assets, proposed M3, adds to proposed M2 time deposits at all depositary institutions, and has been designed to include all the deposit liabilities to the public of depositary institutions.

Two questions were asked in designing the proposed measures. First, do the assets

Table 3. Proposed Monetary Aggregates
(Dollar Amounts in Billions of Dollars, Not Seasonally Adjusted)

Proposed Aggregate	Components	Amount, June 1978
1. M-1	Current M-1	351.7
	Plus: NOW balances	3.3[a]
	Credit union share drafts	.6
	Demand deposits at thrifts	.9
	ATS savings	0[b]
	Less: Demand deposits of foreign commercial banks	
	and official institutions	11.3
	Total[c]	345.0
2. M-1+	Proposed M-1	345.0
	Plus: Savings balances at commercial banks[d]	221.6
	Total	566.6
3. M-2	Proposed M-1	345.0
	Plus: Savings balances at all depositary institutions[e]	495.3
	Total	840.3
4. M-3	Proposed M-1	345.0
	Plus: All time and savings deposits (including large time deposits)	
	at all depositary institutions[e]	1,154.6
	Total	1,499.7

[a]Consists of NOW balances in New England states. In November 1978, NOW accounts were authorized in New York State and by January 10, 1979, the stock of NOW balances at depositary institutions in New York is estimated to have been $0.6 billion.

[b]Would also include payment order accounts (POA) at savings and loans, if the current Federal Home Loan Bank Board proposal is adopted. ATS savings were first offered on November 1, 1978, and by January 10, 1979, estimated ATS balances were $4 billion.

[c]Total does not equal the sum of the components because of other miscellaneous adjustments to the total.

[d]Excludes NOW and ATS savings balances at commercial banks.

[e]Excludes all NOW, ATS, POA (if introduced), and credit union share draft balances.

Table 4. Current Monetary Aggregates
(Dollar Amounts in Billions of Dollars, Not Seasonally Adjusted)

Current Aggregate	Components	Amount, June 1978
1. M-1	Currency	92.9
	Plus: Demand deposits at commercial banks	258.8
	Total	351.7
2. M-2	M-1	351.7
	Plus: Saving balances at commercial banks	223.8
	Time deposits at commercial banks	352.8
	Less: Negotiable CDs at large banks	86.3
	Total	842.0
3. M-3	M-2	842.0
	Plus: Savings balances at thrift institutions	275.8
	Time deposits at thrift institutions	317.4
	Total	1,435.2
4. M-4	M-2	842.0
	Plus: Negotiable CDs at large banks	86.3
	Total	928.3
5. M-5	M-3	1,435.2
	Plus: Negotiable CDs at large banks	86.3
	Total	1,521.5

included serve as a transactions balance or a medium of exchange? Are they, that is, generally accepted in exchange for goods, services, and other assets? Traditionally, currency and demand deposits at commercial banks—which make up current M1—have been viewed as satisfying this condition. More recently, as noted earlier, other kinds of deposits, some of which are at other kinds of institutions, have come to meet this criterion. Thus, in defining the proposed M1 measure, transactions balances of various kinds have been aggregated across depositary institutions.

Second, is the asset readily convertible into a transactions balance? Does the public view it, that is, as a highly liquid alternative to transactions balances? Many believe that those assets that the public considers close substitutes for transactions balances should be included in broader measures of the monetary aggregates. The definition of the current M2 embodies this criterion by including savings and small time deposits at commercial banks along with conventional transactions media. This second criterion also implies limits to aggregation. Assets that are not viewed as close substitutes for media of exchange would be excluded from the monetary aggregates. In applying this criterion to the broader measures of the monetary aggregates, similar kinds of deposits at all depositary institutions have been combined.

Other considerations have influenced the design of the proposed monetary aggregates. One is data availability. For example, it can be argued that even though time deposits have generally become more illiquid over time, there are sizable amounts of short-term time deposits and they should be included with savings deposits in a measure of the money supply.[8] The problem with including time deposits is that data on remaining maturities are generally not available, and data on the original maturities of time deposits for some institutions, principally member banks, are available only for recent years.[9] The issue of data availability is discussed below and in the appendix.*

Another consideration in selecting measures of the monetary aggregates is their empirical relation to other economic variables, particularly the gross national product. Normally, a measure of money would be more desirable the closer its past relationship to GNP and other economic variables. By fundamentally altering the nature of the public's monetary assets, however, recent financial developments have diminished the usefulness of statistical relationships based on longer-term experience as guides to selecting aggregates. Indeed, in large part it is because of these developments that new measures of the monetary aggregates are being proposed. Empirical evidence on this issue is presented below. Finally, the ability of the Federal Reserve to control an aggregate is another important consideration in making a selection. This issue, too, is discussed later.

The remainder of this section examines each of the proposed monetary aggregates in some detail.

Proposed M1

The proposed M1 (Line 1 of Table 3) differs from the current M1 in that it includes new transactions-related savings deposits at commercial banks and thrift institutions—such as NOW balances. ATS balances, share draft balances at credit unions, and demand deposits at thrift institutions—while it excludes demand deposits of foreign commercial banks and official institutions.[10] The Advisory Committee on Monetary Statistics (the Bach Committee) recommended this exclusion because such balances are held primarily as clearing balances for international transactions and international reserves.[11] Thus, compared with the present M1, the proposed M1 is a more comprehensive measure of balances of

---

[8]While short-term time deposits tend to be liquid in the sense that the date of maturity is near, with current interest penalties such deposits tend to become less liquid as they approach maturity in the sense that the effective yield declines more the closer withdrawal is to maturity.

[9]Timely data on the original maturity of member bank time deposits for three maturity categories— under six months, six months to four years, and over four years—have been available weekly since late 1974. Less timely breakdowns by maturity—estimated for all commercial banks—are available as of the end of each quarter, beginning in 1968; however, maturity breakdowns have changed occasionally during this period in connection with actions affecting regulatory ceilings on different maturities of time deposits. Indirect data for savings and loans and mutual savings banks are available semiannually, beginning in 1973.

*Editors' note: The appendix is not reprinted in this volume.

[10]If the Federal Home Loan Bank Board proposal to create a new payment order account (POA) is adopted, these balances would be included in proposed M1.

[11]See Board of Governors of the Federal Reserve System, *Improving the Monetary Aggregates: Report of the Advisory Committee on Monetary Statistics* (June 1976), p. 4. See also Helen T. Farr, Lance W. Girton, Henry S. Terrell, and Thomas H. Turner, "Foreign Demand Deposits at Commercial Banks in the United States," in Board of Governors of the Federal Reserve System, *Improving the Monetary Aggregates: Staff Papers* (November 1978), pp. 35–54.

FIGURE 3. CURRENT AND PROPOSED M1

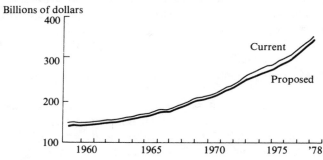

Quarterly averages, seasonally adjusted.

FIGURE 4. RATES OF GROWTH OF CURRENT AND PROPOSED M1

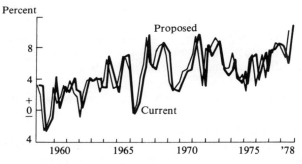

Seasonally adjusted at annual rates.

FIGURE 5. VELOCITIES OF CURRENT AND PROPOSED M1

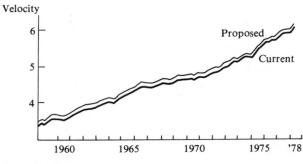

Seasonally adjusted.

domestically related transactions.[12] Proposed M1 satisfies the medium-of-exchange criterion, which calls for a narrow measure of money to represent funds available for immediate payment for goods, services, and other assets. Such a measure can be expected to be closely related to domestic transactions.

As Chart 3 reveals, proposed M1 is somewhat smaller than current M1, since the foreign-related demand deposits removed have exceeded the new transactions balances added. However, rates of growth (shown in Chart 4) are very similar for the two measures.

The public's demands for these measures of money relative to GNP move inversely with their velocities (Chart 5). The velocities for current and proposed M1 move in close parallel. While the demands for both current and proposed M1 relative to GNP appear to have decreased around 1975—at a time when market rates of interest were generally declining—econometric evidence indicates a slightly less pronounced decline for proposed M1.[13]

Although the more comprehensive measure of transactions balances, proposed M1, has behaved much like present M1, new developments are likely to cause the two to diverge. With ATS accounts growing in popularity, funds can be expected to shift from consumer demand balances to ATS savings, thereby depressing current M1 relative to total spending.[14] In addition, should the Congress and the various regulatory authorities continue to expand the opportunities of commercial banks and thrift institutions to offer new transactions accounts, further conversions from consumer demand deposits will reinforce the importance of broadening the coverage of M1.

Since NOW accounts, ATS savings accounts, and share draft accounts at credit unions can serve as both transactions balances and more permanent interest-earning savings balances, consumers are likely to hold larger amounts of funds in these kinds of accounts than they would otherwise have held in demand deposits, and growth in proposed M1 relative to GNP may be more rapid than historical growth of current M1. Also, since the interest-earning savings component of these new accounts is likely to be sensitive to spreads between market rates of interest and regulatory ceilings, proposed M1 may be more sensitive to changes in market interest rates than current M1.[15]

---

[12]Some transactions balances—such as traveler's checks and money market mutual funds—are excluded from proposed M1, primarily because data are unavailable.

[13]In simulations of money demand and reduced-form equations for both M1 measures over the period from mid-1974 to mid-1978, presented below, simulation errors were marginally smaller for proposed M1 than for current M1.

[14]While shifts of funds from consumer demand deposits to ATS savings (and POA savings, if offered) will not affect proposed M1, shifts of funds from other sources to ATS savings will cause this aggregate to rise relative to total spending. A break in the M1 series can be expected regardless of whether ATS savings are included. If they are excluded, M1 can be expected to decline relative to spending; if they are included, M1 can be expected to increase.

[15]Econometric evidence indicates that the demand for interest-earning savings balances is more responsive to changes in both income and interest rates than is the demand for demand deposits, and thus the demand for proposed M1, by including savings-related funds, might be more income elastic and interest elastic than the demand for current M1.

M1 +

The second proposed monetary aggregate shown in Table 3 (Line 2) is M1 + , which consists of proposed M1 plus savings balances at commercial banks.[16] As noted earlier, developments in recent years have significantly enhanced the liquidity of commercial bank savings accounts and have increased the similarities between such balances and demand deposits. Important among these developments have been the authorization of business and domestic government savings and preauthorized and telephone transfers, in addition to ATS and NOW accounts for individuals. The aggregation of savings at commercial banks and M1 into a new measure of money was a possibility suggested for consideration by the Advisory Committee on Monetary Statistics.[17] Moreover, some empirical evidence, based on the period before ATS, suggests that savings balances at commercial banks have had a higher degree of liquidity, or "moneyness," than those at other institutions.[18]

Depending on the direction of developments, the proposed M1 + aggregate may serve principally as a transitional measure. The importance of M1 + as a narrower monetary aggregate is tied very closely to the emerging role of automatic transfers. During the transition, when conversions to ATS savings are occurring, the relationships between M1 + on the one hand and GNP and interest rates on the other should resemble the historical pattern more than can be expected for either current or proposed M1. Although conversions from consumer demand balances to ATS savings will not disturb proposed M1, shifts from ordinary savings balances to ATS savings will result in an expansion of proposed M1 relative to GNP. Consequently, since shifts from ordinary savings to ATS savings would not affect the proposed M1 + during the transition, M1 + may serve as a useful supplement to proposed M1 for interpreting underlying growth in the public's demands for transactions balances.[19]

---

[16]The M1 + measure described in this section differs from the one currently published basically by excluding demand deposits of foreign commercial banks and official institutions.

[17]*Improving the Monetary Aggregates: Report,* p. 11.

[18]William A. Barnett, "A Fully Nested System of Monetary Quantity and Dual User Cost Price Aggregates." Board of Governors of the Federal Reserve System, Division of Research and Statistics, Econometric and Computer Applications Section, November 1978; processed. In this paper, the author constructs an ideal index under aggregation—which might be interpreted as a measure of "moneyness"— based on recent advances in the theory of index numbers and on newly developed econometric methods. The evidence suggests that a dollar's worth of savings balances at commercial banks makes a larger contribution to the "liquidity" of consumers' monetary assets than a dollar's worth of savings balances at thrift institutions, perhaps because of the convenience of having savings balances at the same location where one conducts other business. Nevertheless, the author also finds a very high degree of substitutability between savings deposits at commercial banks and savings at thrift institutions. When similar methods are applied to the measurement of substitutability between savings deposits and transactions balances, it is discovered that savings deposits and transactions balances are not viewed by the public as being as substitutable for each other as savings deposits at commercial banks and savings deposits at thrift institutions. See also W. E. Diewert, "Exact and Superlative Index Numbers," *Journal of Econometrics* 4 (May 1976), pp. 115–45.

[19]Shifts of funds to ATS savings from sources other than demand deposits and ordinary savings deposits will tend to disturb the relationships among M1 + , GNP, and interest rates. Available evidence

**FIGURE 6. RATES OF GROWTH OF PROPOSED M1
AND M1 +**

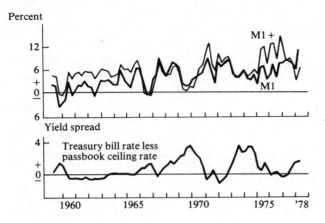

**FIGURE 7. VELOCITIES OF PROPOSED M1
AND M1 +**

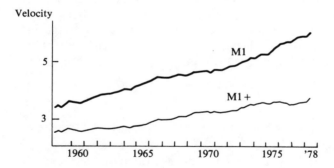

Since savings balances are more sensitive than demand deposits to interest rates—particularly to the difference between the rate paid by commercial banks and short-term market rates—growth in M1 + varies more over the course of the interest rate cycle than does growth in M1. This difference can be seen in Chart 6, which depicts the annualized rates of growth of proposed M1 and M1 + in the upper panel and the

indicates, however, that shifts of funds to ATS savings from these other sources have been relatively small.

If POA accounts are authorized for savings and loan associations and if these accounts become popular, the usefulness of M1 + as a supplemental aggregate will diminish. In this event, more attention could be given to proposed M2.

spread between the 90-day Treasury bill rate and the ceiling rate on commercial bank passbooks in the lower panel. When market yields were low relative to the ceiling rate—as in the early 1960s, 1971–72, and 1976–77—growth in M1 + was faster than growth in proposed M1. Conversely, when market rates rose substantially above ceiling rates—as in 1966, 1969–70, and 1973—growth in M1 + was slow relative to that of proposed M1.

Because movements in market interest rates have a discernible influence on M1 +, the velocity of that aggregate—shown in Chart 7—tends to vary directly with the interest rate cycle. The velocity of M1 + has tended to increase over time—along with the general level of interest rates—as has the velocity of proposed M1, also shown in the chart. In the period encompassing 1975 and 1976, however, the velocities of M1 + and M1 were somewhat disparate, with the M1 velocity rising sharply—at a time when market rates were generally declining—while the M1 + velocity was relatively steady. It appears that the expanding use of cash management techniques was largely responsible for the paring of transactions balances relative to GNP—particularly by large businesses—and for the corresponding jump in M1 velocity;[20] by contrast, relatively low market rates of interest at this time evidently swelled savings balances at commercial banks, thereby offsetting a similar rise in M1 + velocity.

M2

Proposed M2, shown in Table 3, adds savings deposits at all depositary institutions to proposed M1. In other words, similar deposits—savings balances—are combined across depositary institutions to obtain proposed M2; to obtain current M2 dissimilar deposits—savings and time deposits—at commercial banks are summed.[21] A comparison of Tables 3 and 4 indicates that proposed M2 and current M2 are of comparable size.

The discussion in an earlier section noted that many developments that have increased the liquidity of savings deposits at commercial banks have also enhanced the liquidity of savings deposits at thrift institutions. Because of these developments, the interest-earning savings balances of the public can now perform many of the functions previously reserved for demand deposits. Some empirical evidence suggests that, while the public may consider savings at commercial banks to be more liquid than savings at thrift institutions, a relatively high degree of substitutability exists between the two kinds of savings, and that savings at all depositary in-

---

[20]See Jared Enzler, Lewis Johnson, and John Paulus, "Some Problems of Money Demand," *Brookings Papers on Economic Activity* 1 (1976), pp. 261–80; Perry D. Quick and John Paulus, "Financial Innovations and the Transactions Demand for Money," Board of Governors of the Federal Reserve System, Division of Research and Statistics, Banking Section, February 1977; processed; Porter and Mauskopf, "Cash Management;" and Tinsley and others, "Measurement of Money Demand."

[21]Savings are distinct from time deposits on liquidity grounds. In practice, funds in savings accounts are usually available immediately while funds in time deposit accounts are available with a delay or are subject to a substantial early-withdrawal penalty.

FIGURE 8. RATES OF GROWTH OF PROPOSED M2 AND M1+

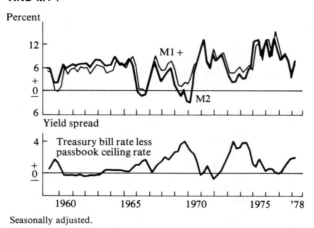

Seasonally adjusted.

FIGURE 9. VELOCITIES OF PROPOSED M2 AND M1+

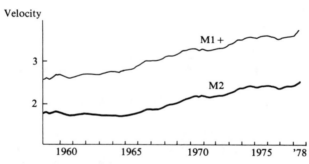

Quarterly, seasonally adjusted.

stitutions can be linearly combined in a monetary aggregate.[22] The combination of all savings balances with M1 was also a possibility suggested for consideration by the Advisory Committee on Monetary Statistics.[23]

As might be expected, the behavior of proposed M2 is very similar to that of M1+. Chart 8 shows this relation in the upper panel and also contains the spread

[22]Barnett, "A Fully Nested System of Monetary Quantity," concludes that, in such an aggregate, savings deposits at commercial banks would receive a higher weight than savings at thrift institutions. Indeed, the weight attached to a dollar's worth of savings at commercial banks would be roughly twice as large as the weight on a dollar's worth of savings at thrifts. Nevertheless, such a weighted series produces growth rates that have been very similar to a series that simply adds savings at commercial banks to savings at thrift institutions.

[23]*Improving the Monetary Aggregates: Report,* p. 11.

between the treasury bill rate and the ceiling rate on commercial bank passbooks in the lower panel. Growth in both measures tends to be sensitive to movements in the rate spread. The velocities of proposed M2 and M1+ —presented in chart 9—have both trended upward over time and have had synchronous movements over the interest rate cycle.

M3

Proposed M3 consists of proposed M2 along with all time deposits of all depositary institutions, regardless of denomination, maturity, or negotiability. Once again, similar deposits—in this instance, time deposits—have been aggregated across depositary institutions. Table 3 shows that proposed M3 is considerably larger than proposed M2 and also larger than current M3, shown in Table 4.

M3 is in effect a broad monetary aggregate that includes all liabilities of depositary institutions to the public. In principle, nondeposit liabilities of these institutions would be included along with their deposit liabilities. Among the most important nondeposit liabilities are security repurchase agreements (RPs).[24] As noted earlier, RP liabilities have become more important in recent years and tend to be viewed by the public as highly liquid alternatives to deposits. In practice, however, current data limitations militate against their inclusion in proposed M3. The board's staff has constructed an RP series using available information, and it would be published separately; but the estimates are inferior to those for other components of the monetary aggregates.[25] Once more complete data are collected. RPs could be added to M3 or perhaps to a narrower measure of money, if that is suggested by subsequent research.[26]

Chart 10 shows that rates of growth of proposed M3 tend to be higher and generally steadier than those of proposed M2. This relative stability reflects largely the actions of depositary institutions, mainly commercial banks, to offset over the

[24]Depositary institutions also attract nondeposit funds from other sources. However, much of the funds from such sources comes from other depositary institutions, domestic and foreign, and hence would be removed either by consolidation or by procedures that exclude those liabilities due to foreign banking offices. For example, commercial banks attract a sizable amount of federal funds from sources other than commercial banks, but the bulk comes from other depositary institutions—savings and loans and mutual savings banks. Also, commercial banks attract nondeposit funds in the form of Eurodollars, which are obtained from banking offices abroad.

[25]RP data are collected by the Reserve Banks on a regular basis from a sample of approximately 46 large banks that are estimated currently to have roughly 60 percent of all commercial bank RP liabilities to the nonbank public. However, unlike the data on commercial bank deposits that appear in the monetary aggregates, universe call report data are not available for RPs; commercial bank RPs with the nonbank public have not appeared as a separate item on the call report and indirect methods, subject to considerable error, must be used to estimate the universe. As a result, given the size and variability of commercial bank RPs, the dollar magnitude of estimation errors in the series for all commercial banks is probably very large. See also Tinsley, Garrett, and Friar, "Measurement of Money Demand," pp. A1–A10.

[26]Another candidate for inclusion in proposed M3 is Eurodollar deposits held by the U.S. nonbank public. Data on such holdings, however, are not available on a timely basis and are incomplete.

FIGURE 10. RATES OF GROWTH OF PROPOSED M2 AND M3

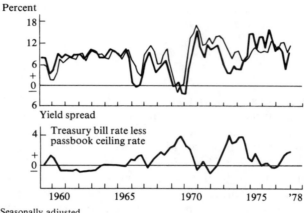

Seasonally adjusted.

FIGURE 11. VELOCITIES OF PROPOSED M2 AND M3

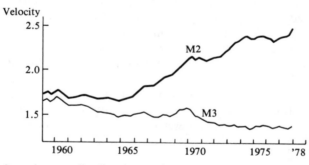

Quarterly, seasonally adjusted.

course of the interest rate cycle changes in inflows of savings and small time deposits—subject to interest rate ceilings—through the issuance of large time deposits that are free of such ceilings. When inflows of small time and savings deposits weaken because market rates rise considerably above regulatory ceilings, these institutions tend to step up the issuance of large time deposits; conversely, when inflows of other deposits strengthen, reliance on these managed liabilities is reduced. As a result, growth in this broader aggregate tends to be less variable than growth in aggregates that are strongly influenced by regulatory ceilings.[27]

[27]In this respect, proposed M3 is similar to the current M2 and M3 aggregates. As noted in the introduction, movements in those large time deposits currently included in M2, and in M3, tend to stabilize M2 growth by offsetting movements in savings and small time deposits.

The tendency for the growth of proposed M3 to be steadier than that of proposed M2 is also displayed in their respective velocities, presented in Chart 11. In contrast to the velocities of narrower measures of money, the velocity of proposed M3 has tended to decline over time and has shown less cyclical variability than that of proposed M2.

Empirical Evidence

A criterion that is frequently suggested for selecting among alternative measures of monetary aggregates is the degree to which each is linked to the ultimate targets, such as GNP. In a variety of theories of aggregate economic activity, the stock of money is related to GNP and to other economic variables, with changes in the stock of money causing changes in GNP and some other economic variables. Such theories, while not providing much a priori guidance to precise definitions of monetary aggregates, imply that the more stable and predictable is the public's demand for a monetary aggregate, the more predictable will be the impact of changes in the supply of this aggregate, other influences remaining the same, on GNP and these other economic variables.

Econometric techniques can be used to correlate changes in alternative measures of the money stock with changes in GNP, while removing the contribution of other influences, and to estimate demand functions for alternative measures of money. Normally, the definitions selected that use this approach would be those that had been most strongly correlated with GNP or had displayed the most stable demand relationship. The presumption would be that the aggregates selected according to these criteria would continue to have the strongest and most predictable relationship with GNP. However, since recent financial innovations have fundamentally altered the characteristics of the public's monetary assets, the usefulness of such econometric evidence is limited. In these cases, an important econometric postulate—that the public view the aggregate being demanded (in this case money) as having homogeneous properties over the sample period—may be violated. Moreover, given recent innovations and regulatory changes, a monetary aggregate selected for its desirable econometric properties based on past relationships may no longer be closely linked with the ultimate targets; while another, having weaker econometric properties in the past, may now be more tightly linked with the ultimate targets. Indeed, a reexamination of the definitions of the monetary aggregates is warranted precisely because the established relationships among the aggregates and other economic variables have been altered by recent developments.

Another empirical basis for selecting measures of the monetary aggregates is their usefulness as indicators of the underlying state of the economy. Information on the public's holdings of currency and deposit balances is generally available on a more timely basis than information about the behavior of the economy. As a consequence, incoming information on the monetary aggregates can be used to make inferences regarding developments in the economy before direct information is

Table 5. Representative Money Demand Equations for Proposed Monetary Aggregate[a]

Proposed Monetary Aggregate[b]	Independent Variable						Summary Statistic		
	Constant	GNP	Treasury Bill Rate	Commercial Bank Passbook Saving Rate	Commercial Bank Passbook Deposit Rate[c]	Lagged Dependent Variable	Adjusted R^2	Standard Error of Estimate (Annual Percentage Rate)	Root Mean-Square Error of Annualized Growth Rate[d] (Annual Percentage Rate)
M1[e]									
5.1a	−.791 (−2.439)	.042 (3.184)	−.010 (−2.709)	−.009 (−.696)	—	1.020 (34.842)	.9902	1.80	—
5.1b	1.359 (1.614)	.144 (3.632)	−.011 (−2.382)	−.024 (−1.359)	—	.733 (6.936)	.9934	1.66	3.29
M1+[e]									
5.2a	.208 (.624)	.067 (3.378)	−.021 (−3.956)	0.27 (1.398)	−.009 (−.627)	.912 (24.172)	.9945	1.91	—
5.2b	−.138 (−.339)	.072 (2.876)	−.020 (−3.715)	.032 (1.495)	−.019 (−1.045)	.934 (19.991)	.9954	1.64	2.81
M2[e]									
5.3a	−.042 (−.139)	.046 (2.681)	−.027 (−4.514)	.034 (1.540)	−.012 (−.824)	.957 (41.560)	.9943	1.99	—
5.3b	−.446 (−1.342)	.055 (2.723)	−.025 (−4.144)	.042 (1.776)	−.031 (−1.599)	.979 (39.100)	.9960	1.76	3.44
M3[f]									
5.4a	−.0009 (−.116)	.0005 (.012)	−.0007 (−3.049)	.004 (3.412)	−.0003 (−.463)	.961 (20.171)	.9974	1.86	—
5.4b	.0006 (.068)	−.054 (−1.225)	−.001 (−3.989)	.004 (2.732)	.0002 (.278)	1.035 (19.913)	.9960	1.90	3.96

[a] The numbers in parentheses are t-statistics.

[b] The a and b equations differ in sample period. The period for equation 5.1a, 5.2a, and so on, is 1960Q4 to 1978Q2; the period for the b equations is 1960Q4 to 1974Q2.

[c] The time deposit rate used is the one for the time deposit maturity having the highest yield, after adjusting for the prevailing term structure of interest rates.

[d] The root mean-square error for dynamic simulations over 1974Q3 to 1978Q2. Simulated levels of the money stock are converted to annual rates of growth and errors are computed on the basis of implicit simulated money growth and actual growth.

[e] The dependent variable and GNP are divided by the GNP deflator. The lagged dependent variable is divided by the GNP deflator in the current period. The specification of the equation is double logarithmic.

[f] The dependent variable, lagged dependent variable, and GNP variable are divided by current nominal wealth.

Table 6. Representative Money Demand Equations for Current Monetary Aggregate[a]

Current Monetary Aggregate[b]	Independent Variable						Summary Statistic		
	Constant	GNP	Treasury Bill Rate	Commercial Bank Passbook Saving Rate	Commercial Bank Passbook Deposit Rate[c]	Lagged Dependent Variable	Adjusted R^2	Standard Error of Estimate (Annual Percentage Rate)	Root Mean-Square Error of Annualized Growth Rate[d] (Annual Percentage Rate)
M1[e]									
6.1a	−.832 (−2.381)	.044 (3.151)	−.009 (−2.347)	−.015 (−1.089)		1.022 (29.795)	.9916	1.74	—
6.1b	1.530 (1.848)	.163 (3.987)	−.010 (−2.215)	−.031 (−1.865)		.699 (6.549)	.9946	3.39	3.39
M2+[e]									
6.2a	.405 (−1.991)	.166 (2.629)	−.025 (−4.944)	−.004 (−.187)	.023 (1.605)	.856 (13.625)	.9994	1.68	—
6.2b	−.699 (−2.759)	.190 (2.335)	−.028 (−5.145)	.009 (.395)	.014 (.790)	.853 (11.126)	.9993	1.65	2.35
M2'[f]									
6.3a	.004 (.643)	−.010 (−.307)	−.0009 (−5.184)	.003 (3.612)	.0004 (.861)	.964 (21.270)	.9972	1.54	—
6.3b	.002 (.340)	−.044 (−1.171)	−.001 (−5.521)	.003 (2.232)	.0009 (1.349)	1.033 (19.829)	.9966	1.47	2.01

[a]The numbers in parentheses are t-statistics.

[b]The a and b equations differ in sample periods. The period for the a equations is 1960Q4 to 1978Q2; the period for the b equations is 1960Q4 to 1974Q2.

[c]The time deposit rate used is the one for the time deposit maturity having the highest yield, after adjusting for the prevailing market term structure of interest rates.

[d]The root mean-square error for dynamic simulations over 1974Q3 to 1978Q2. Simulated levels of the money stock are converted to annual rates of growth and errors are computed on the basis of implicit simulated money growth and actual growth.

[e]The dependent variable and GNP are divided by the GNP deflator. The lagged dependent variable is divided by the GNP deflator in the current period. The specification of the equation is double logarithmic.

[f]The dependent variable, lagged dependent variable, and GNP variable are divided by current nominal wealth.

available.[28] For example, a slowing of monetary growth may be interpreted to mean that total spending or GNP is weakening. If the behavior of an indicator is believed to be highly reliable, monetary policymakers may wish to adjust the posture of policy in the light of this development—before direct information on the state of the economy is available—should they judge it unhealthy for the economy. Again, changes in the character of monetary assets may tend to undermine the value of some indicators selected on the basis of historical evidence.

In the remainder of this section, demand properties of the various measures of money are first examined. Next, reduced-form equations relating GNP to alternative definitions of money and selected other variables are presented. Finally, the usefulness of the various measures as indicators of economic activity is discussed.

Properties of Money Demand*

Properties of the demands for the proposed monetary aggregates are shown in Table 5 and those of the current aggregates are shown in Table 6.[29] Each money demand equation relates the public's demand for an aggregate, on a quarterly basis, to GNP, a market rate of interest, the rate on commercial bank passbook savings, and, in the case of the broader aggregates, a rate representing the yield on commercial bank time deposits.[30] In each instance, the public is assumed to adjust its actual money balances partially to a desired level—based on GNP and interest rates—and the coefficient of the lagged dependent variable can be used for inferring the speed of adjustment.[31] For each monetary aggregate, two demand equations are reported. Both are estimated using a sample period beginning in late 1960, but the first ends in

---

[28]The indicator criterion is very similar to the previous criterion relating to linkages with ultimate targets. In the case of the linkage criterion, causality running from money to the ultimate target is presumed. In the case of the indicator criterion, no causality is presumed. Changes in money may cause changes in economic activity, or changes in economic activity may cause changes in money, or both may be affected by some third factor.

*Editors' Note: For a survey of the empirical literature in the demand for money see the selection by John Boorman that appears in Section VI.

[29]More extensive evidence on the properties of money demand functions for current and proposed aggregates, over a variety of sample and postsample periods, is discussed in Richard D. Porter, Eileen Mauskopf, David E. Lindsey, and Richard Berner, "Current and Proposed Monetary Aggregates: Some Empirical Issues," Board of Governors of the Federal Reserve System, Division of Research and Statistics, Econometric and Computer Applications Section, January 1979; processed.

[30]For all of the monetary aggregates except proposed and current M3, the money stock and GNP are divided by the implicit GNP price deflator. Also, the lagged dependent variable in each case is divided by current, and not lagged, prices, in order to permit the equation to pick up potential lagged responses in the public's demands for money to changes in the price level. All of the variables in these equations are entered in logarithmic form and thus coefficient estimates are short-run elasticities. In the case of both the proposed and the current M3 measures, the money variable and GNP are divided by current wealth, as is the lagged dependent variable in these equations. In all cases, the Cochrane-Orcutt adjustment for serial correlation has been used.

[31]The coefficient of adjustment is equal to 1 minus the coefficient of the lagged dependent variable. For example, if the coefficient of the lagged dependent variable has a value of 0.9, the public removes 10 percent of the discrepancy between its actual and its desired money balances in any one quarter; thus, about one-half of the adjustment to desired money balances is completed in two years. Implied speeds of adjustment for the monetary aggregates are all apparently very slow.

mid-1978 while the second ends in mid-1974; as noted earlier, the pace of financial developments in recent years has been particularly rapid, and many believe that historical statistical relationships have changed since 1974, particularly the public's demand for demand deposits. In all but the M3 equations, coefficient estimates for the independent variables are short-run or impact elasticities; they indicate how the demand for money responds in the current period, in percentage terms, to a 1 percent change in GNP or interest rates.[32]

Summary statistics for each aggregate are presented in the last three columns of Tables 5 and 6. The R^2 statistic indicates the proportion of the variation in the demand for the monetary aggregate that is explained by GNP, interest rates, and the lagged dependent variable; and the standard error of estimate is a measure of the amount by which money demand estimated from the equation differs from the actual money stock. For example, the standard error of estimate for proposed M1 over the longer sample period (Equation 5.1a) is 1.8 percent, expressed at an annual rate, which suggests that about two-thirds of the estimation errors for proposed M1 are smaller than 1.8 percent. The final column provides an indication of how well the money demand equation has predicted the rate of growth of the money stock in the period from mid-1974 to mid-1978,[33] the smaller the root mean-square error for an aggregate, the better is that aggregate's forecasting record during this volatile period.[34]

Equations 5.1a, 5.1b, 6.1a, and 6.1b suggest that the demands for current and proposed M1 are similar. The impact of GNP and other explanatory variables is nearly the same for each narrow measure of money. Moreover, the coefficients of GNP in Equations 5.1a and 6.1a show a marked decline, respectively, from 5.1b and 6.1b in the impact of GNP on each aggregate, while the coefficient of the lagged dependent variable for both M1 measures rose substantially over the longer sample period. This contrast appears to reflect a decrease in the public's demand for demand deposits—which make up a considerable share of each M1 aggregate—and is believed to have been an outgrowth of the more intensive use of cash management around 1974, particularly by businesses. Although the prediction performance of each measure of transactions balances has been poor in the post-1974 period, proposed M1 has a slightly better record than current M1.

The second monetary aggregate presented in Table 5 is M1 +. As might be expected, the demand for this aggregate tends to increase with increases in the commercial bank passbook rate, while it declines in response to increases in the treasury bill rate and the yield on time deposits. In contrast to the demand for both M1

---

[32]Long-run elasticities are derived by multiplying each coefficient by the reciprocal of 1 minus the coefficient of the lagged dependent variable.

[33]Root mean-square errors are for dynamic simulations expressed in rates of growth; in other words, simulated levels of the money stock are converted to rates of growth and errors are computed on the basis of implicit simulated money growth and actual growth.

[34]The preduction performance of all the monetary aggregates is relatively weak. However, the 1974–78 period is believed to have seen substantial changes in the characteristics of many of the deposit liabilities appearing in these monetary aggregates.

Table 7. Reduced-Form Equations Relating Percentage Change in Nominal GNP to Percentage Changes in Proposed Monetary Aggregates, a Fiscal Variable, and a Strike Variable[a]

Proposed Monetary Aggregate[b]	Independent Variable				Summary Statistic		
	Constant	Sum of Money Coefficients	Sum of Fiscal Coefficients[c]	Strike Variable[d]	Adjusted R^2	Standard Error of Estimate (Annual Percentage Rate)	Root Mean-Square Error (Annual Percentage Rate)[e]
M1							
7.1a	2.197 (2.198)	1.175 (6.133)	1.138 (3.031)	−4.667 (−4.069)	.492	2.67	—
7.1b	2.508 (2.586)	1.067 (5.459)	.983 (2.363)	−3.666 (−2.611)	.432	2.50	3.77
M1+							
7.2a	3.317 (3.412)	.801 (5.244)	.900 (2.223)	−4.807 (−4.159)	.454	2.77	—
7.2b	2.455 (2.126)	.997 (4.637)	.503 (1.138)	−2.743 (−1.899)	.407	2.55	4.16
M2							
7.3a	4.945 (4.541)	.521 (3.149)	.838 (1.718)	−4.997 (−4.116)	.352	3.02	—
7.3b	5.400 (4.339)	.417 (1.937)	.473 (.813)	−3.857 (−2.646)	.256	2.86	3.94
M3							
7.4a	3.228 (2.020)	.540 (3.098)	.934 (1.945)	−5.076 (−4.182)	.357	3.01	—
7.4b	3.290 (2.205)	.494 (2.956)	.501 (.935)	−3.731 (−2.545)	.314	2.74	4.30

[a]The equations were estimated using a third-order polynomial distributed lag with money and fiscal variables lagged five quarters and the coefficients of the final lagged variables constrained to be zero. The number in parentheses are t-statistics.

[b]The a and b equations differ in sample periods. The period for the a equations is 1960Q4 to 1978Q2, the period for the b equations is 1960Q4 to 1974Q2.

[c]The fiscal variable is the change in the high-employment federal deficit as a percent of nominal potential GNP.

[d]The strike variable is the change in manhours lost due to strikes as a percentage of manhours worked.

[e]Root mean-square error for dynamic simulations over the period 1974Q3 to 1978Q2 are based on coefficient estimates for the sample period ending 1974Q2.

Table 8. Individual Lag Coefficients for Proposed Monetary Aggregates and a Fiscal Variable from Reduced-Form Equations[a]

Lag Length	Proposed M1				Proposed M1+				Proposed M2				Proposed M3			
	Equation 7.1a		Equation 7.1b		Equation 7.2a		Equation 7.2b		Equation 7.3a		Equation 7.3b		Equation 7.4a		Equation 7.4b	
	Money Variable	Fiscal Variable	Money Variable	Fiscal Variable	Money Variable	Fiscal Variable	Money Variable	Fiscal Variable	Money Variable	Fiscal Variable	Money Variable	Fiscal Variable	Money Variable	Fiscal Variable	Money Variable	Fiscal Variable
0	.444 (2.936)	.180 (1.481)	.370 (2.131)	.373 (2.362)	.259 (1.826)	.057 (.457)	.326 (1.953)	.186 (1.085)	.156 (1.024)	.050 (.367)	.120 (.659)	.105 (.553)	.011 (.064)	.088 (.653)	.060 (.365)	.169 (.922)
1	.231 (2.201)	.245 (2.135)	.076 (.528)	.225 (2.126)	.043 (.455)	.203 (1.678)	.099 (.922)	-.029 (-.199)	.049 (.501)	.176 (1.228)	.041 (.382)	-.077 (-.424)	.129 (1.263)	.235 (1.659)	.082 (.844)	-.006 (-.034)
2	.173 (1.807)	.278 (2.626)	.087 (.672)	.177 (1.782)	.078 (.897)	.259 (2.287)	.119 (1.252)	.012 (.088)	.066 (.729)	.236 (1.728)	.056 (.547)	.014 (.085)	.168 (1.737)	.269 (1.986)	.116 (1.238)	.030 (.188)
3	.177 (2.434)	.260 (2.14)	.208 (1.800)	.165 (2.385)	.195 (3.285)	.236 (2.194)	.219 (3.327)	.141 (1.133)	.121 (1.932)	.227 (1.777)	.098 (1.393)	.186 (1.164)	.147 (2.442)	.221 (1.716)	.132 (2.417)	.136 (.890)
4	.150 (1.561)	.174 (1.748)	.243 (1.910)	.127 (1.360)	.225 (2.514)	.146 (1.397)	.234 (2.383)	.193 (1.459)	.128 (1.322)	.149 (1.257)	.102 (.917)	.245 (1.560)	.085 (.875)	.121 (1.003)	.103 (1.122)	.173 (1.122)

[a]The numbers in parentheses are t-statistics. See Table 7 for regression results. The a and b equations differ in sample period. The sample period for the a equations in 1960Q4 to 1978Q2; the period for the b equations is 1960Q4 to 1974Q2.

Table 9. Reduced-Form Equations Relating Percentage Change In Nominal GNP to Percentage Changes in Current Monetary Aggregates, a Fiscal Variable, and a Strike Variable[a]

Current Monetary Aggregate[b]	Independent Variable				Summary Statistic		
	Constant	Sum of Money Coefficients	Sum of Fiscal Coefficients[c]	Strike Variable[d]	Adjusted R^2	Standard Error of Estimate (Annual Percentage Rate)	Root Mean-Square Error[e] (Annual Percentage Rate)
M1							
8.1a	2.382 (2.346)	1.129 (5.833)	1.184 (3.093)	−4.987 (−4.328)	.473	2.72	—
8.1b	2.656 (2.842)	1.016 (5.492)	1.047 (2.553)	−4.075 (−2.897)	.424	2.51	3.90
M2							
8.2a	.681 (.496)	.955 (5.504)	.997 (2.583)	−5.142 (−4.413)	.452	2.78	—
8.2b	1.090 (.820)	.877 (4.996)	.614 (1.466)	−3.454 (−2.405)	.413	2.54	4.03
M3							
8.3a	1.418 (1.015)	.769 (4.841)	.971 (2.368)	−5.239 (−4.451)	.431	2.83	—
8.3b	1.863 (1.203)	.699 (3.755)	.610 (1.288)	−3.633 (−2.479)	.361	2.65	3.88

[a]The equations were estimated using a third-order polynomial distributed lag with money and fiscal variables lagged five quarters and the coefficients of the final lagged variables constrained to be zero. The numbers in parentheses are *t*-statistics.

[b]The a and b equations differ in sample period. The period for the a equations is 1960Q4 to 1978Q2; the period for the b equations is 1960Q4 to 1974Q2.

[c]The fiscal variable is the change in the high-employment federal deficit as a percentage of nominal potential GNP.

[d]The strike variable is the change in manhours lost due to strikes as a percentage of manhours worked.

[e]Root mean-square errors for dynamic simulations over the period 1974Q3 to 1978Q2 are based on coefficient estimates for the sample period ending 1974Q2.

Table 10. Individual Lag Coefficients for Current Monetary Aggregates and Fiscal Variable from Reduced-Form Equations[a]

Lag Length	Current M1				Current M2				Current M3			
	Equation 8.1a		Equation 8.1b		Equation 8.2a		Equation 8.2b		Equation 8.3a		Equation 8.3b	
	Money	Fiscal Variable	Money	Fiscal Variable	Money	Fiscal Variable	Money	Fiscal Variable	Money	Fiscal Variable	Money	Fiscal Variable
0	.405 (2.626)	.178 (1.431)	.292 (1.869)	.375 (2.148)	.191 (1.309)	.107 (.863)	.205 (1.395)	.253 (1.477)	.030 (.184)	.114 (.875)	.078 (.437)	.184 (1.035)
1	.257 (2.400)	.263 (2.262)	.264 (2.494)	.109 (.773)	.163 (1.782)	.267 (2.330)	.131 (1.488)	.058 (.422)	.162 (1.575)	.260 (2.120)	.097 (.903)	.022 (.144)
2	.192 (1.962)	.297 (2.768)	.218 (2.214)	.114 (.903)	.196 (2.289)	.290 (2.701)	.159 (1.921)	.051 (.395)	.223 (2.294)	.279 (2.434)	.157 (1.525)	.059 (.419)
3	.161 (2.199)	.271 (2.672)	.157 (2.342)	.215 (1.890)	.224 (3.977)	.222 (2.129)	.204 (3.863)	.116 (.943)	.215 (3.599)	.213 (1.958)	.200 (3.256)	.160 (1.187)
4	.113 (1.143)	.175 (1.732)	.084 (.892)	.235 (1.856)	.181 (2.168)	.110 (1.059)	.179 (2.262)	.137 (1.040)	.140 (1.455)	.105 (.991)	.168 (1.672)	.186 (1.327)

[a] The numbers in parentheses are t-statistics. See Table 8 for the regression results. The a and b equations differ in sample period. The sample period for the a equations is 1960Q4 to 1978Q2, the period for the b equations is 1960Q4 to 1974Q2.

measures, the demand for M1 + has not demonstrated a noticeable tendency to shift in the period since mid-1974; coefficient estimates for each explanatory variable, with the possible exception of the time deposit rate, are very similar for the two sample periods. Moreover, the predictive power of the M1+ demand equation during this period, indicated by its root mean-square error, was better than that of both M1 measures.

The demand properties of the proposed M2 aggregate are similar to those of M1 + . Coefficient estimates indicate that the sensitivity of proposed M2 to interest rates and GNP is nearly the same as that of M1 + . While the coefficients of the two equations for proposed M2 shown in Table 5 are very similar, other results for the 1960s, on the one hand, and the 1970s, on the other, suggest that proposed M2 has become more transactions-related in the 1970s; in particular, the demand for proposed M2 appears to have become more responsive to GNP in the 1970s, and the speed of adjustment of actual to desired proposed M2 balances appears to have increased.[35] The prediction performance of proposed M2 in the post-1974 period is not so good as that of M1 + , and proposed M2 has a larger forecast error than current M2 (Table 6).

The demand for proposed M3 is shown in the last two equations of Table 5. As might be expected of any broad measure of money, the demand for this aggregate is not so strongly influenced by GNP as are the more narrow, transactions-related measures. In relative terms, the rate of interest and the wealth variables are more important determinants of the public's demand for this aggregate. The properties of the public's demand for current M3 and proposed M3 are in many respects similar, as shown in Tables 5 and 6.

Reduced-Form Equations

Reduced-form equations that relate the annualized percentage change in GNP, measured in current dollars, to current and lagged annualized percentage changes in monetary growth, current and lagged values of a fiscal variable, and a strike variable are presented in Tables 7 through 10.[36] Tables 7 and 8 contain reduced-form equations and corresponding lag coefficients using the proposed monetary aggregates, and Tables 9 and 10 contain results for the current measures. Reduced-form results are used by some to infer the impact of money growth on GNP, although considerable care must be used in interpreting such results.[37]

---

[35]See Porter et al., "Current and Proposed Monetary Aggregates," pp. 8, 17–18. The evidence presented in this paper also suggests that the demand for M1—both the current and the proposed measure—has become more sensitive to the passbook savings rate, implying that savings balances may have become more substitutable for transactions balances in the 1970s.

[36]More detailed evidence on the reduced-form equations for current and proposed aggregates over a variety of sample and postsample periods is discussed in Porter and others "Current and Proposed Monetary Aggregates."

[37]Reduced-form estimates of the contribution of changes in money to changes in GNP can be artificially strengthened by reverse causality, running from GNP to money. This is a problem primarily of interpreting the coefficient of the money variable for the current quarter, but also the R^2 and standard error of estimate. In addition, should changes in a particular measure of money tend to smooth growth in GNP, the estimated impact of this variable on GNP in a reduced-form equation would be understated.

The reduced-form results for proposed M1 are given in Equations 7.1a and 7.1b. As in the case of the money demand estimates, two equations are presented for each aggregate. Both sample periods begin in late 1960, but the first ends in mid-1978 while the second ends in mid-1974. In addition, the last column contains the root mean-square error for postsample forecasts over the period from mid-1974 to mid-1978, and indicates the recent forecasting record of the monetary aggregate.

The sum of the coefficients of proposed M1—shown in the second column—is near unity, the value suggested by some economic theories. Also, the results for proposed M1 are very similar to those for current M1, shown in Table 9.[38] For both proposed and current M1, about 40 percent of the estimated impact of the monetary aggregate on GNP is felt in the current quarter, but much of this may also reflect reverse causality running from GNP to money. A comparison of the root mean-square errors shows that predictions based on proposed M1 have been marginally better than those based on current M1.

The sum of the money supply coefficients for the broader proposed monetary aggregates is smaller than the sum for proposed M1. However, the con-temporaneous relationship between money and GNP is less strong for these broader aggregates than for M1, and a relatively large share of the overall measured contribution of money growth to GNP growth is attributed to prior changes in money. The predictive power of M1+ is somewhat weaker than that of proposed M1. Proposed M2 appears to predict GNP growth slightly better than does current M2, while the recent prediction record for proposed M3 is poorer than that of current M3.

Indicator Properties

Since measures of the monetary aggregates are available with a relatively short lag, they may serve as valuable indicators of the current state of the economy, before direct information is available, and thus permit more timely adjustments of policy.[39] Table 11 contains estimates of the various current and proposed measures of money as indicators of GNP growth for three periods—the period of the 1960s, the period of the 1970s, and the entire sample period.[40] In essence, the numbers show the extent to which deviations in the rate of growth of GNP from trend can be detected using deviations in the rates of growth of alternative measures of money from trend. A higher indicator value for a monetary aggregate means that more can be inferred

[38]In both instances, the sum of money coefficients does not differ much for the two sample periods. This result contrasts with those for the M1 demand equations, which suggest a shift in the relationship between money and GNP in the post-1974 period. This matter is discussed in more detail in Porter and others, "Current and Proposed Monetary Aggregates."

[39]Some nonfinancial variables, such as retail sales, are also available with a relatively short lag and can be used as indicators of movements in economic activity.

[40]See P. A. Tinsley, P. A. Spindt, with M. E. Friar, "Indicator and Filter Attributes of Monetary Aggregates: A Nit-Picking Case for Disaggregation," Board of Governors of the Federal Reserve System, Division of Research and Statistics, Special Studies Section, October 1978; processed. The authors conclude that more useful information about the state of the economy can be obtained by using the components of monetary aggregates jointly than by using the aggregates themselves.

Table 11.   Monetary Aggregates as Indicators of GNP Growth (Percent)

Monetary Aggregate	Indicator Value[a]		
	1960Q4–1978Q2	1960Q4–1969Q4	1970Q1–1978Q2
Proposed			
M1	33	18	36
M1 +	22	6	17
M2	13	*	18
M3	11	*	7
Current			
M1	29	15	30
M2	17	5	13
M3	14	*	11

Source: Based on P. A. Tinsley, P. A. Spindt, with M. E. Friar, "Indicator and Filter Attributes of Monetary Aggregates: A Nit-Picking Case for Disaggregation," Board of Governors of the Federal Reserve System, Division of Research and Statistics, Special Studies Section, October 1978; processed, pp. 31–32.

[a]The percentage by which the variance of the forecast error of the growth rate of nominal GNP can be reduced using current observations on the growth rate of the corresponding monetary aggregate. These values were obtained by regressing the percentage change in nominal GNP on the percentage change in the corresponding monetary aggregate. The R^2 statistic, adjusted for degrees of freedom, is then a measure of the percentage by which the variance of forecasted GNP can be reduced by observing the change in the monetary aggregate.

[b]Negligible.

from it about current growth in GNP. In the limit, with an indicator value of 100, variations in monetary growth would serve as perfect indicators of both the direction and the magnitude of variations in GNP growth.

In general, the narrower measures of money contain more useful information about underlying GNP growth than do the broader aggregates. For the proposed aggregates, indicator values generally decline with each successive level of aggregation. In addition, proposed M1 tends to be a better indicator of GNP growth than is current M1, particularly during the 1970s. While the indicator value of proposed M2 was very low for the 1960s, it increased considerably in the 1970s; indeed, for the period of the 1970s, proposed M2 had a higher indicator value than current M2. As an indicator of GNP growth, current M3 tends to outperform proposed M3.[41]

Controllability

Another important consideration in selecting monetary aggregates is how well the Federal Reserve can control their size and rate of growth. Some aggregates, while

[41]Note that the indicator results are for a highly simplified situation, one for which no specific model of the economy is utilized. Alternatively, econometric models of the economy, such as the board's quarterly model, can be used to relate forecast errors in money growth to forecast errors in GNP growth; in this way, the accuracy of GNP forecasts can be improved as information on money growth becomes available. Estimations of the indicator value of alternative measures of money using more sophisticated procedures yield results that are qualitatively similar to the ones discussed here.

Table 12. Proportion of Monetary Aggregates Subject to Reserve Requirements Set by the Federal Reserve, June 1978 (Figures are Percentages)

Aggregate	Total Aggregate[a]	Deposits
Proposed		
M1	75.8	66.9
M1 +	73.2	67.9
M2	49.3	43.0
M3	44.7	41.0
Current		
M1	76.4	67.9
M2	70.2	66.5
M3	41.8	37.1

[a]Currency is treated as subject to a 100 percent Federal Reserve reserve requirement.

closely linked to ultimate targets, many be difficult to control with the available instruments of monetary policy. To a considerable extent, the Federal Reserve's control over a monetary aggregate will depend on the system's operating procedures—whether its operating target is reserves or short-term interest rates.

Under a reserves operating target, a key factor in monetary control is the nature of the reserve requirements applied to the components of the monetary aggregate. Deposits that are subject to reserve requirements established by the Federal Reserve and for which required reserves must be held as vault cash or deposits with the Federal Reserve are generally those that can be controlled best through use of a reserves aggregate.[42] Although other deposits—those of nonmember institutions— may be backed indirectly by reserves at the Federal Reserve through deposit balances held with member bank correspondents, the slippage between the provision of reserves by the Federal Reserve and the volume of such deposits is typically more pronounced than the slippage for deposits directly subject to the system's reserve requirements.

Table 12 shows the proportions of each of the proposed (and current) measures of money that are subject to reserve requirements established by the Federal Reserve. Larger proportions of the proposed M1 and M1 + measures than of the proposed broader aggregates are subject to Federal Reserve reserve requirements. A comparison of the proposed aggregates with their current counterparts reveals that by and large smaller percentages of the proposed aggregates are subject to system reserve requirements. Thus, with a reserves operating target, control might be weaker over the proposed aggregates than over the current aggregates, unless

[42]Required reserve ratios are also important to monetary control. In general, with higher ratios the control over monetary aggregates is strengthened with a reserves operating target. Also, monetary control under a reserves operating target is enhanced when similar ratios are required for the various deposits included in the aggregate. See Kenneth J. Kopecky, "The Relationship between Reserve Ratios and the Monetary Aggregates under Reserves and Federal Funds Rate Operating Targets," Staff Economic Studies 100, Board of Governors of the Federal Reserve System, December 1978.

legislation were approved extending reserve requirements to the monetary liabilities of nonmember institutions.

With an interest rate operating target, control over a monetary aggregate depends on whether the demand for that aggregate is sensitive to changes in short-term interest rates.[43] A desired change in the quantity of a monetary aggregate is achieved by varying the attractiveness of holding the monetary aggregate through changes in short-term interest rates.

Although a change in interest rates will have a greater effect on those aggregates that are most interest sensitive, what is important from the standpoint of controlling money using interest rates is whether the particular aggregate under consideration is in fact sensitive to interest rates. Indeed, economic theory establishes that in achieving some desired monetary stimulus the quantities of monetary aggregates that are highly sensitive to changes in interest rates must be changed by more—in relative terms—than aggregates that are less sensitive to interest rates; hence, while a given change in interest rates will have a greater impact on the quantities of highly interest-sensitive monetary aggregates, a larger change in their quantities is needed to obtain an economic objective.

All of the proposed monetary aggregates move inversely to changes in the Treasury bill rate and thus can be controlled using an interest rate operating target (see Table 5, Column 3). Proposed M1 is less sensitive to current changes in interest rates than are M1 + and proposed M2. In addition, a comparison of Tables 5 and 6 suggests that the impact of changes in interest rates on the proposed monetary aggregates is about the same as that on their current counterparts. Thus, with an interest rate operating target, controlling the proposed monetary aggregates would likely be no more difficult than controlling the current measures.[44]

Consolidation

The monetary aggregates being proposed by the board staff have been constructed using principles of account consolidation to exclude those deposits held by depositary institutions with other depositary institutions that would otherwise lead to double counting. In particular, at each level of aggregation an attempt has been made to net out deposits maintained by depositary institutions for purposes of

[43]In addition, control over a monetary aggregate under an interest rate operating target is importantly influenced by the ability to forecast the impact of other factors, particularly GNP, on the public's demand for this aggregate. In other words, the stability of the relationship between the public's demand for an aggregate and the explanatory variables, such as GNP and interest rates, together with the accuracy of projections of explanatory variables other than interest rates, determines the potential controllability of this aggregate.

[44]Another consideration in controlling a monetary aggregate with an interest rate target is the influence of unpredictable factors on the demand for that aggregate. The greater the influence of unpredictable factors on money demand, the less precise is monetary control. Standard errors of estimate presented in Tables 5 and 6, which reflect the impact of factors other than explanatory variables on money demand, suggest that the effects of unpredictable influences have been roughly similar on the proposed monetary aggregates and on their current counterparts, particularly in the cases of the narrower aggregates.

servicing other deposits included in the measure.[45] This procedure yields a more accurate estimate of the public's monetary assets.

Consolidation involves primarily the appropriate netting out of some or all demand deposits at commercial banks owned by commercial banks and, for the broader measures, by other depositary institutions. A depositary institution can increase the liquidity, and thus the attractiveness, of its deposit liabilities by maintaining demand balances that can be used to meet the withdrawal requests of its customers; such demand balances may also serve as clearing balances. For example, commercial banks hold demand balances with other commercial banks, a large portion of which is used for conducting their own demand deposit business. Simply combining all demand deposits at all commercial banks would overstate the public's holdings of demand balances by the amount of such interbank demand balances, because demand balances held by commercial banks for use in their own demand deposit business would be counted once when they were deposited by the public and again when they were redeposited at other banks. Similarly, demand deposits maintained by commercial banks and thrift institutions for conducting their savings business would be netted out from proposed M2, and demand balances maintained by depositary institutions for conducting their time deposit business would be netted from proposed M3.

Consolidation similarly involves the netting out of some savings and time deposits in constructing the broader monetary aggregates. . . .

While in principle this kind of consolidation is straightforward, in practice data limitations necessitate some compromises. For example, although demand deposits between commercial banks can be estimated with some precision, the proportions held for conducting demand, savings, and time deposit business are unknown. As a consequence, the conventional practice of deducting all interbank demand deposits from gross demand deposits has been followed here, although it tends to understate somewhat the appropriate measure of the public's demand deposits. In addition, shortcomings in the data render it difficult to measure and to allocate by function all demand deposits owned by thrift institutions, although an effort was made to allocation by function demand deposits owned by mutual savings banks. . . .

Data Availability and Data Needs

All proposed monetary aggregates are available on a monthly basis from existing sources.[46] Data on total deposits for thrift institutions—the sum of savings and time

---

[45]This is in line with the recommendation of the Advisory Committee on Monetary Statistics. This recommendation served as a guide in consolidating accounts in the proposed monetary aggregates. See *Improving the Monetary Aggregates: Report,* pp. 12–17.

[46]Preliminary historical data on the proposed monetary aggregates and related series are available from the Board of Governors of the Federal Reserve System, Division of Research and Statistics, Banking Section.

deposits—are available as of the end of each month with a lag of about one week.[47] At that time, savings deposits at thrift institutions can be crudely estimated for inclusion in M2, until actual figures on savings are available about one month later. Breakdowns of total savings deposits at thrift institutions into transactions balances—for inclusion in proposed M1—and ordinary savings balances must be estimated until figures are available on NOW accounts and share draft balances at credit unions, which involves an additional two-month lag. The lack of timely data on the breakdown of savings and transactions balances at thrift institutions does not affect the estimation of proposed M3, since total deposits at these institutions are included in this aggregate.

In addition to monthly availability, commercial bank demand deposits, savings deposits, and time deposits are estimated weekly with a lag of one week. However, with existing data, any weekly estimations of thrift institution deposits would likely be subject to unusually large estimation errors.

Should the proposed monetary aggregates be adopted and current data flows used, the quality of initially published estimates of M1 and M2 is likely to deteriorate and such estimates are likely to be subject to greater revisions than is currently the case. In order to reduce the size and frequency of such revisions, publication of the monetary aggregates could be delayed from the current schedule or, alternatively, new data could be collected; in particular, timely data on ATS balances, NOW account and other transactions balances, and savings and time balances at thrift institutions would be needed.[48] The collection of such data from nonmember institutions would require the cooperation of the Federal Deposit Insurance Corporation, the Federal Home Loan Bank Board, and the National Credit Union Administration. Moreover, an accurate and comprehensive series on commercial bank repurchase agreements with the nonbank public would require the collection of new data.

[47]However, sample data on total deposits at thrift institutions are available more promptly and can be used to prepare early estimates of the monetary aggregates.

[48]Also, data on the deposit holdings of savings and loans and credit unions would be needed in order more accurately to consolidate accounts and improve measures of the public's money holdings. As noted in the previous section, only an incomplete consolidation can be done using existing data on the deposit holdings of thrift institutions.

Balance of Payments Theory and Monetary Policy in an Open Economy

One of the major themes in the recent development of both monetary theory and monetary policy has been the effect of growing economic interdependence between nations. Recent changes in the exchange rate system have greatly influenced the effectiveness of traditional policy instruments. The oil crisis and persistent deficits in the U.S. balance of payments, on the one hand, and surpluses in the Japanese and German accounts, on the other hand, have heightened general awareness of these issues.

The opening article in this section, by Harry Johnson, compares the monetary approach to balance of payments theory that has been reemerging in recent years with the other theories that have been in vogue in the postwar period. The next article, by Donald S. Kemp, presents a review of the basic propositions of the monetary approach to the balance of payments, develops a model in which these propositions are expressed as a set of equations, and applies this model to cases of both fixed and floating exchange rates. The important differences resulting from a monetary disturbance in the case of a reserve currency country are also examined.

In the last article in this section, by Michael Parkin, the results of tests of various hypotheses about the causes of inflation in a fixed exchange-rate world are surveyed. The author also reviews several postulates concerning the mechanism for the international transmission of world inflation. Though referenced solely on the period of fixed exchange rates, the results presented in this article are relevant to current conditions. This is so, first, since many countries still peg their currencies to one or more of the currencies of a few major industrial nations and, second, since even "floating" rates are sometimes managed and may not move solely according to market forces.

The Monetary Approach to Balance-of-Payments Theory

Harry G. Johnson

28

My purpose in this paper is to outline a new approach to the theory of the balance of payments and of balance-of-payments adjustment (including devaluation and revaluation) that has been emerging in recent years from several sources. Concretely, this new approach is found in the change in policy orientation adopted by the British government under pressure from the International Monetary Fund after the devaluation of 1967 failed to produce the expected improvement in the British balance of payments. The theoretical basis for the new orientation can be traced back to the work of the Dutch economist J. J. Koopmans. The new approach is also evident in the theoretical work of my colleagues at the University of Chicago and R. A. Mundell and his students, although it is only fair to note that economists elsewhere have been working along similar lines. The essence of this new approach is to put at the forefront of analysis the monetary rather than the relative price aspects of international adjustment.

To put the new approach in perspective, it is helpful to go back to the origins of balance-of-payments theory in the work of David Hume and specifically his contribution of the analysis of the price-specie-flow mechanism. Hume was concerned about refuting the concentration of the mercantilists on the objective of accumulating precious metals within the country and their consequent recommendation of

Reprinted from the *Journal of Financial and Quantitative Analysis,* 7, 2 (March, 1972), pp. 1555–1564, by permission of the publisher and the author.

policies designed to bring about a surplus on the balance of payments. His analysis, couched in terms relevent to the emerging new approach to balance-of-payments theory, showed that the amount of money in a country would be adjusted automatically to the demand for it (through surpluses or deficits in the balance of payments) induced by the effects on relative national money price levels of excess supplies of or excess demands for money. Hence, the mercantilist desire to accumulate "treasure" was in conflict with the basic mechanism of international monetary adjustment and could only be *ephemerally* successful.

Three points are worth noting about the price-specie-flow mechanism. First, in contemporary terminology, it assumes (in line with the stylized facts of that time) that all money is "outside" money (precious metals). That is, there is no commercial or central banking system capable of creating money not backed by international reserves with domestic money and international reserves being the same. Second, the mechanism of adjustment focuses on international transactions in goods, as distinguished from securities; this has remained dominant in balance-of-payments theory. Third, in the detailed analysis of the mechanism there is a rather awkward compromise between the assumption of a closed and an open economy in which it is assumed that domestic prices can vary from purchasing-power-parity under the influence of imbalances between money demand and money supply, but such variations give rise to changes in trade flows which alter the balance of payments and hence the domestic stock of money in the longer run. As we shall see, the new approach to balance-of-payments theory, while basically Humean in spirit, places the emphasis not on relative price changes but on the direct influence of excess demand for or supply of money on the balance between income and expenditure, or more generally between total acquisition and disposal of funds whether through production and consumption or through borrowing and lending, and therefore on the overall balance of payments.

Hume's analysis was in terms of an automatic mechanism of international adjustment motivated by money flows and consequential changes in national money price levels. The subsequent elaboration of the theory, up to and partly through the 1930s, retained the general notion of automaticity while adding in the complications required by the existence of credit money provided by commercial banks and the existence of central banking based on partial international reserve holdings, and the complications required by the possible attraction of international short-term capital movements through international interest-rate differentials. In addition, Cassel contributed the purchasing-power-parity theory of the equilibrium determination of the values of floating exchange rates.

In the 1930's, under the stimulus, on the one hand, of the collapse of the international regime of fixed exchange rates and the emergence of mass unemployment as a major economic problem and, on the other hand, of the Keynesian revolution—which altered the basic assumptions of theory from wage and price flexibility with full employment to wage rigidity with normal mass unemployment—a new approach to balance-of-payments theory emerged, one which viewed international adjustment not as an automatic process but as a policy problem for governments. The key problem examined in Joan Robinson's classic article on the foreign exchanges was the conditions under which a devaluation would improve a country's balance of payments. In Keynesian assumptions of wage rigidity, a devaluation would change the real prices of domestic goods relative to foreign goods in the foreign and domestic markets, thereby promoting substitutions in production and consumption. In Keynesian assumptions of mass unemployment, any repercussions of these substitutions on the demand for domestic output could be assumed to be met by variations in output and employment, and repercussions of such variations onto the balance of payments could be regarded as secondary. Finally, in the same assumption together with the general Keynesian denigration of the influence of money on the economy and concentration on the short run, the connections between the balance of payments and the money supply and between the money supply and aggregate demand could be disregarded. Attention was, therefore, concentrated on the "elasticity conditions" required for the impact effect of a devaluation—that is, of the associated change in relative real prices—to be an improvement in the balance of payments. These conditions were (1) for a simple model with perfectly elastic supplies and initially balanced trade, that the sum of the elasticities of home and foreign demand for imports should exceed unity (the so-called "Marshall-Lerner condition"), and (2) for more complex models assuming independent elasticities of demands for imports and supplies of exports, that a fearfully complex algebraic expression should be satisfied but challenging to derive and explore. (Much of the interest in this body of work was in the related questions of whether a devaluation that improved the balance of payments would necessarily turn a country's terms of trade against it and increase domestic employment.)

The so-called "elasticity approach" to devaluation proved demonstrably unsatisfactory in the immediate postwar period of full and over-full employment because of its implicit assumption of the existence of unemployed resources that could be mobilized to produce the additional exports and import substitutes required to satisfy a favorable impact effect. Recognition of this by the profession came in three versions. The first version involved carping at the irrelevance of "orthodox theory" (which the elasticity approach really was not) generally associated with the recommendation of exchange controls and quantitative import restrictions as an alternative to devaluation. The second was S. S. Alexander's "absorption approach," which argued essentially that a favorable effect from devaluation alone, in a fully employed economy, depends not on the elasticities but on the inflation resulting from the devaluation in these conditions, producing a reduction in aggregate absorption relative to aggregate productive capacity. Foreshadowing the new approach to be discussed below, part of the mechanism in Alexander's analysis that might bring this about is the "real balance effect" by which the rise in price consequent on the excess demand generated by devaluation deflates the real value of the domestic money supply and induces a reduction in spending out of income.

The presentation of the "absorption approach" as an alternative to the "elasticity approach" led to considerable controversy and extensive efforts to reconcile the two. However, the truth lies in recognition that a fully employed economy cannot use devaluation alone as a policy instrument for correcting a balance-of-payments deficit. It must use a combination of devaluation (to obtain an allocation of foreign and domestic demand among domestic and foreign output consistent with balance-of-payments equilibrium) and deflation (to match aggregate domestic demand with aggregate domestic supply). More generally, it must use a proper combination of what I have elsewhere called "expenditure-reducing" and "expenditure-switching" policies. This general principle is developed at length in James Meade's classic book, *The Theory of International Economic Policy: The Balance of Payments.* This principle constitutes the third, and most useful, version of recognition of the inadequacies of the "elasticity approach." In addition, it provides a synthesis, between that approach and the "absorption approach," that is logically satisfactory (though not economically satisfactory from the point of view of the new monetary approach). Unfortunately, Meade presented his analysis in terms of a short-run equilibrium analysis and based it on the assumption that the policy makers understood the theory as well as he did, thus making the book extremely inaccessible to policy makers. This may help to account for the bumbling of British demand-management policy after the devaluation of 1967. Also, following the tradition of British central banking and monetary theory, Meade identified monetary policy with fixing the level of interest rates, a procedure that automatically excludes consideration of the monetary consequences of devaluation by assuming them to be absorbed by the monetary authorities. (This is the reason for the economic objection to the Meade synthesis mentioned above.)

Subsequent to the work of Meade and others in the 1950's, the main development in conventional balance-of-payments theory has been the development of the theory of the fiscal-monetary policy mix, following the pioneering contributions of R. A. Mundell. In the general logic of the Meade system, a country has to have two policy instruments if it is to achieve simultaneously internal and external balance (full employment and balance-of-payments equilibrium). In Meade's system, the instruments are demand management by fiscal and/or monetary policy and the exchange rate (or controls or wage-price flexibility). What if wages are rigid, and controls and exchange rate changes are ruled out by national and international political considerations? A solution can still be found, at least in principle, if capital is internationally mobile in response to interest rate differentials. Fiscal expansion and monetary expansion then have the same effects on the current account, increasing imports and possibly decreasing exports, but opposite effects on the capital account. Fiscal expansion, increasing domestic interest rates and attracting a capital inflow, has the opposite effect on monetary expansion, which lowers interest rates and repels capital so that the two policies can be "mixed" in order to achieve a capital account surplus or deficit equal to the current account deficit or surplus at the level of full employment of the economy. This extension of the Meade approach has lent itself to almost infinite mathematical product differentiation, with little significant improvement in quality of economic product, and will not concern us further, except to remind us that theoretical investigation of the model has led naturally to the question of what would happen if capital were prefectly mobile and specifically to the implications of this assumption for the ability of the monetary authority to control the domestic money supply.

To recapitulate, the essential structure of what may be termed the standard model of balance-of-payments theory is a Keynesian model of income determination in which flows of consumption and investment expenditure are determined by aggregate income and demand-management policy variables (taxes and expenditures and interest rates) and in which the level of exports and the division of total expenditure between domestic and foreign goods (imports) are determined by the exchange rate which fixes the relative real prices of exports relative to foreign prices and of imports relative to domestic prices. By choosing a proper mix of demand-management policies and the exchange rate, the authorities can obtain full employment consistent with any current-account surplus or deficit. The net current-account surplus (or deficit) is equal to the excess (or deficiency) of the economy's flow of production over its flow of absorption, or to the excess (or deficiency) of its exports over its imports, or to its net excess (deficiency) of the flow of savings in relation to the flow of investment. By convention, but by no means necessarily, the current-account surplus or deficit is identified with the overall balance-of-payments position; it is easy enough to add in the determination of the balance-on-capital account by the differential between domestic and foreign interest rates, as is done in the theory of the fiscal-monetary policy mix.

The basic assumption, on which rests this system of balance-of-payments analysis and which forms the point of departure for the new "monetary" approach to balance-of-payments theory, is that the monetary consequences of balance-of-payments surpluses or deficits can be and are absorbed (sterilized) by the monetary authorities so that a surplus or deficit can be treated as a flow equilibrium. The new approach assumes—in some cases, asserts—that these monetary inflows or outflows associated with surpluses or deficits are not sterilized—or cannot be, within a period relevant to policy analysis—but instead influence the domestic money supply. And, since the demand for money is a demand for a stock and not a flow, variation of the supply of money relative to the demand for it associated with deficit or surplus must work toward an equilibrium between money demand and money supply with a corresponding equilibration of the balance of payments. Deficits and surpluses represent phases of stock adjustment in the money market and not equilibrium flows and should not be treated within an analytical framework that treats them as equilibrium phenomena.

It should be noted, however, that this criticism applies to the use of the standard model for the analysis and policy prescription of situations involving deficits or surpluses. The standard model, when used for the analysis of policies required to secure balance-of-payments equilibrium, is generally not subject to this criticism because by assumption the domestic money market will be in equilibrium. But even in this case, the fiscal-monetary mix version of it is open to criticism for confusing stock adjustment in the market for securities, in response to a change in interest-rate differentials between national capital markets, with a flow equilibrium.

In order to obtain flow-equilibrium deficits or surpluses on the basis of stock adjustments in the money market (and also possibly the securities market), it is necessary to construct a model in which the need for stock adjustments is being re-created continuously by economic change—in other words, it is necessary to analyze an economy, or an international economy, in which economic growth is in progress. This is one of the important technical differences between the new "monetary" models of the balance of payments and the standard Keynesian model—and a potential source of difficulty in comparing the results of the two types of analysis.

Another difference between the two types of models is that the "monetary" models almost invariably assume—in contrast to the emphasis of the standard model on the influence of relative prices of trade flows—that a country's price level is pegged to the world price level and must move rigidly in line with it. One justification for this assumption is that, at least among the advanced industrial countries, industrial competition is so pervasive that elasticities of substitution among the industrial products of the various countries approximate infinity more closely than the relatively low numbers implicit in the standard model. Another more sophisticated justification is derivable from the general framework of the monetarist approach, namely, that changes in relative national price levels can only be transitory concomitants of the process of stock adjustment to monetary disequilibrium and that in the longer-run analysis of balance-of-payments phenomena among growing economies attention should be focused on long-run equilibrium price relationships—which for simplicity can most easily be taken as constant.

This point has sometimes been put in terms of the positive charge that the standard model rests on "money illusion," in the sense that it assumes that workers will accept a reduction in their real standard of living brought about by a devaluation which they would not accept in the form of a forced reduction of domestic money wages. An alternative version of this charge is that the standard model assumes workers can be cheated out of their real marginal product by devaluation. However, the charge is incorrect. If rectification of a balance-of-payments deficit requires that the domestic marginal product of labor in terms of foreign goods falls, because the price of domestic goods relative to foreign goods must be reduced in the foreign and home markets to induce substitution between these goods favorable to the balance of payments, it requires no money illusion but only economic realism for the workers to accept this fact. Applications of the standard model to the case of devaluation, however, do require the assumption of money illusion if the elasticities of substitution between domestic and foreign goods are in fact high (approximately infinite) and it is, nevertheless, assumed that wages will remain unchanged in terms of domestic currency. In this case it is expected that workers will be content to accept wages below the international value of their marginal product and that employers will not be driven by competition for labor in the face of this disequilibrium to bid wages up to their marginal productivity levels. The issue, therefore, is not one of the standard model wrongly assuming the presence of money illusion on the part of the workers but of its possibly wrongly assuming low elasticities of substitution between domestic and foreign goods—which is an error in empirical assumptions rather than in model construction.

One further difference between the two types of model of balance-of-payments theory is worth noting. Whereas the Keynesian model assumes that employment and output are variable at (relatively) constant prices and wages, the monetary models assume that output and employment tend to full-employment levels, with reactions to changes taking the form of price and wage adjustments. This difference mirrors a broader difference between the Keynesian and quantity theory approaches to monetary theory for the closed economy. The assumption of full employment in the monetary balance-of-payments models can be defended on the grounds that these models are concerned with the longer run and that for this perspective the assumption of full employment is more appropriate than the assumption of general mass unemployment for the actual world economy since the end of the second World War.

I now turn from the discussion of theoretical issues in model construction to an exposition of some monetarist models of balance-of-payments behavior in a growing world economy. The models to be constructed are extremely simple, inasmuch as they concentrate on the overall balance of the balance of payments, i.e., on the trend of international reserve acquisition or loss, and ignore the composition of the balance of payments as between current account, capital account, and overall balance, as well as the question of changes in the structure of the balance-of-payments accounts that may occur as a country passes through various stages of economic growth. Nevertheless, they will, I hope, provide some interesting insights into balance-of-payments phenomena.

To begin with, it is useful to develop some general expressions relating the growth rates of economic aggregates to the growth rates of their components or of the independent variables to which they are functionally related. These can be established by elementary calculus and are merely stated here. In the formulas g is the growth rate per unit of time of a subscripted aggregate or variable; A and B are components of an aggregate; f(A,B) is a function of A and B and η denotes the elasticity of the aggregate defined by the function with respect to the subscripted variable. Then we have

$$g_{A+B} = \frac{A}{A + B} g_A + \frac{B}{A + B} g_B$$

$$g_{A-B} = \frac{A}{A - B} g_A - \frac{B}{A - B} g_B$$

$$g_{AB} = g_A + g_B$$

$$g_{A/B} = g_A - g_B$$

$$g_{f(A,B)} = \eta_A g_A + \eta_B g_B,$$

where η denotes an elasticity.

I begin with a discussion of monetary equilibrium in a single country maintaining a fixed exchange rate with the rest of the world, assumed to be growing over time, and small enough and diversified enough in relation to the world economy for its price level to be the world price level and its interest rate the world's interest rate. (Differentials between domestic and foreign price indices, or between domestic and foreign interest rates, could readily be allowed for, provided they are assumed fixed by economic conditions.) In addition, it is assumed that the supply of money is instantaneously adjusted to the demand for it because the residents of the country can get rid of or acquire money either through the international market for commodities or through the international securities market. Which mechanism of adjustment of money supply to money demand prevails will determine the way in which monetary policy affects the composition of the balance of payments, but that is a question not pursued in the present analysis.

The consequence of these assumptions is that domestic monetary policy does not determine the domestic money supply but instead determines only the division of the backing of the money supply the public demands, between international reserves and domestic credit. Monetary policy, in other words, controls the volume of domestic credit and not the money supply, and control over domestic credit controls the balance of payments and thus the behavior of the country's international reserves.

The demand for money may be simply specified as

$$M_d = p \cdot f(y \cdot i),$$

where M_d is the nominal quantity of domestic money demanded; y is real output; i is the interest rate or alternative opportunity cost of holding money; p is the foreign and therefore domestic price level; and multiplication of the demand for real balances $f(y,i)$ by p assumes the standard homogeneity postulate of monetary theory. The supply of money is

$$M_s = R + D,$$

where R is the international reserve and D the domestic credit or domestic assets backing of the money supply. Since by assumption M_s must be equal to M_d,

$$R = M_d - D$$

and

$$g_R = \frac{1}{R} B(t) = \frac{M_d}{R} g_{Md} - \frac{D}{R} g_D,$$

where $B(t) = dR/dt$ is the current overall balance of payments. Letting $r = R/M_s$ R/M_d, the initial international reserve ratio, and substituting for g_{Md},

$$g_R = \frac{1}{r}(g_p + \eta_y g_y + \eta_i g_i) - \frac{1-r}{r} g_D.$$

Simplifying by assuming constant world prices and interest rates,

$$g_R = \frac{1}{R} \eta_y g_y - \frac{1-r}{r} g_D,$$

that is, reserve growth and the balance of payments are positively related to domestic economic growth and the income elasticity of demand for money and are negatively related to the rate of domestic credit expansion. Simplifying still further by assuming no domestic growth ($g_y = 0$),

$$g_R = \frac{-1-r}{r} g_D,$$

that is, reserve growth and the balance of payments are inversely related to the rate of domestic credit expansion.

These results are contrasted with various Keynesian theories about the relation between economic growth and the balance of payments. According to one theory derived from the multiplier analysis, economic growth must worsen the balance of payments through increasing imports relative to exports. This theory neglects the influence of demand for money on export supply and import demand and on the international flow of securities. According to another more sophisticated theory, domestic credit expansion will tend to improve the balance of payments by stimulating investment and productivity increase, thus lowering domestic prices in relation to foreign prices and improving the current account through the resulting substitutions of domestic for foreign goods in the foreign and domestic markets. This theory begs a number of questions even in naive Keynesian terms; in terms of the present approach it errs in attempting to deduce the consequences of domestic credit expansion from its presumed relative price effects without reference to the monetary aspect of balance-of-payments surpluses and deficits.

A Monetary View of the Balance of Payments

Donald S. Kemp

29

In surveying the body of research dealing with the balance of payments, two major shortcomings are immediately apparent.[1] First, there are no widely accepted theories of the balance of payments which simultaneously incorporate both the current and capital account. The great majority of models used in payments theory consider either the capital account or the current account separately. Second, there have been very few attempts to include even the fundamentals of portfolio choice theory in balance-of-payments models. This is particularly surprising in view of the essentially monetary nature of payments theory.

This article presents an approach to payments theory which addresses both of these shortcomings. Since this essentially involves an extension of the rudiments of monetary theory to the area of the balance of payments, it is henceforth referred to as a monetary view of the balance of payments (MBOP).[2]

Reprinted from the Federal Reserve Bank of St. Louis, *Review* (April, 1975), pp. 14-22, by permission of the publisher and the author.

[1]For a lucid analysis of the current state of payments theory, see Anne O. Krueger, "Balance-of-Payments Theory," *The Journal of Economic Literature* (March 1969), pp. 1-26.

[2]The theoretical foundation of this approach to payments theory may be found in Robert A. Mundell, *Monetary Theory: Inflation, Interest, and Growth in the World Economy* (Pacific Palisades, California: Goodyear, 1971). The formal model, presented later in this article, draws extensively on work done at the University of Chicago Workshop in International Economics and the analysis presented in Harry G. Johnson, "The Monetary Approach to Balance-of-Payments Theory," *Further Essays in Monetary Economics* (Cambridge: Harvard University Press, 1973), pp. 229-49. This article is essentially a synthesis and extension of these previous works.

An Overview of the Theory

The MBOP may be summarized by the proposition that the transactions recorded in balance-of-payments (BOP) statistics reflect aggregate portfolio decisions by both foreign and domestic economic units. Under a system of fixed exchange rates, such as the gold standard or the type of arrangment set up in 1944 at Bretton Woods, overall net surpluses (deficits) in the trade and capital accounts are viewed as flows associated with either an excess demand for money on the part of domestic (foreign) economic units or an excess supply of money in foreign economies (the domestic economy). Consequently, in analyzing the rate of change of international reserves (the money account[3]) the monetary approach focuses on the determinants of the excess demand for or supply of money. According to this view, surpluses (deficits) in the money account measure the rate at which money balances are being accumulated (reduced) domestically. That is, a BOP flow is one of the mechanisms by which actual money balances are adjusted to their desired levels.

Suppose, for example, there is an autonomous increase in the money supply of country j, which leads to an increase in the demand for goods, services, and securities in that country. Under a system of fixed exchange rates, any such increase in domestic demand will result in a tendency for prices of domestic real and financial assets in country j to rise, in the short run, relative to those in foreign markets. Economic units in country j will react by decreasing their demands for domestic real and financial assets in favor of foreign assets while domestic suppliers of these assets will seek to sell more at home and less abroad. At the same time, foreign economic units will decrease their demands for the assets of country j, and foreign suppliers will attempt to sell more of their own assets in country j. All of these factors work in favor of an increase in imports and a decrease in exports in country j. The resultant deterioration of the BOP reflects the exchange of money balances for real and financial assets by economic units of country j. The foreign recipients of these money balances will convert them into their own currencies at their respective central banks. These foreign central banks will then present the balances to the central bank in country j in return for international reserves. Since international reserves are one of the components of a country's monetary base,[4] the effect of this transaction will be a decrease in the money supply of country j toward its level prior to the autonomous increase and an increase in the money supplies of its surplus trading partners.

Under a system of freely floating exchange rates, the required adjustment of mon-

---

[3]The overall net balance in the trade and capital accounts will henceforth be referred to as the money account. This reflects the fact that all transactions recorded below the line in this account have a direct impact on a nation's money supply. Under a pure gold standard, changes in official gold holdings are the only item below the line in this account. Under a Bretton Woods type system changes in official holdings of gold, SDRs, and foreign exchange and changes in the reserve position at the IMF are all included below the line in the money account.

[4]For a detailed discussion and analysis of the concept of the monetary base, see Leonall C. Andersen and Jerry L. Jordan, "The Monetary Base—Explanation and Analytical Use," this *Review* (August 1968), pp. 7-11.

ey balances is accomplished through movements in the exchange rate. Under such a system the BOP (on a money account basis) equals zero by definition, and there are no intercountry movements of international reserves. As such, required adjustments in money balances cannot be accommodated through balance-of-payments flows. In this case the adjustment of actual money balances to their desired levels is accomplished by changes in domestic prices and exchange rates (which change concomitantly with and accommodate the required movement in domestic price levels).

The above approach is in sharp contrast with what amounts to the current conventional wisdom of payments theory; namely, the elasticities and absorption approaches. Implicit in both of these approaches is the assumption that either there are no monetary consequences associated with the BOP or that, to the extent the potential for such consequences exists, they can be and are absorbed (sterilized) by domestic monetary authorities.[5]

The MBOP regards all BOP deficits and surpluses and movements in floating exchange rates as phases in a stock adjustment which are the result of a disparity between the demand for and supply of money. This approach asserts that, under a system of fixed exchange rates, there are inflows (outflows) of international reserves associated with BOP surpluses (deficits) and that these flows cannot be sterilized in the long run. Furthermore, because of the impact of these reserve flows on a country's monetary base, they will result in variations in the supply of money relative to the demand for it and thus have an equilibrating impact on the level of money balances and the BOP. According to this view, the only way to obtain persistent deficits or surpluses is to construct a model in which the need for stock adjustments is being continuously recreated.

The only solutions to these reserve flows are processes which facilitate the return of actual money balances to their desired levels. This adjustment can be accomplished either automatically, through inflows or outflows of international reserves, or through appropriate actions by the domestic monetary authorities which change some other component of the monetary base by the same amount. Under a system of freely floating exchange rates the adjustment is also accomplished either automatically by changes in domestic price levels and the concomitant changes in the exchange rate or again by the appropriate actions on the part of the monetary authorities. The only other potentially successful policy actions available are those which, in the end, have the same effect on money balances as those just mentioned.

---

[5]The elasticity and absorption approaches are theories of the trade account alone, and they neglect the issue of capital flows. For a discussion of the essentials of the elasticities approach, see Joan Robinson, "The Foreign Exchanges," *Readings in the Theory of International Trade,* Committee of the American Economic Association (Philadelphia: The Blakiston Company, 1949), pp. 83–103. For a discussion of the absorption approach, see Sidney S. Alexander, "Effects of a Devaluation on a Trade Balance," *Readings in International Economics,* Committee of the American Economic Association (Homewood, Illinois: Richard D. Irwin, Inc., 1968), pp. 359–73. For a discussion of the differences between the monetarists' approach and both the elasticities and absorption approaches to payments theory, see Johnson, "The Monetary Approach to Balance-of-Payments Theory," pp. 229–49.

Some Fundamental Propositions

In order to facilitate the development of a model later in this article, there are some fundamental propositions associated with the MBOP that should be discussed.

(1) The MBOP maintains that the transactions recorded in the balance of payments are essentially a reflection of monetary phenomena. As such, it places emphasis on the direct influence of an excess demand for or supply of money on the BOP.

Implicit in this approach is the assumption that the demand for and supply of money are stable functions of a limited number of variables. The MBOP does not imply that changes in the money supply are the only factors which affect the BOP. It, nevertheless, does say that the primary channel by which changes in any real variable affect the BOP is through their effects on the demand for or supply of money.[6] Thus, any analysis of the impact of a policy or other change must begin with an analysis of how this change generates a divergence between actual and desired money balances or affects such a divergence that already exists.

(2) In the analysis presented in this article, the crucial BOP concept is that which captures all transactions reflecting the adjustment of actual money balances to their desired levels. That is, the only transactions considered below the line are those which have an influence on domestic and foreign monetary bases and thus on domestic and foreign money supplies.[7]

The analysis presented here does not attempt to provide a theory of the individual subaccounts; it merely lumps the individual components (goods, services, transfers, short- and long-term capital) into a single category—"items above the line." This approach recognizes that an excess supply of or demand for money may be cleared through the markets for either goods, services, or securities.[8] Furthermore, if the BOP is viewed within this framework, the pitfalls of placing emphasis on any particular subaccount are obvious. For example, the effects on aggregate economic activity of a deficit in the merchandise trade account could be neutralized by a surplus in one of the capital accounts. In this case, any negative aggregate demand effects resulting from an increase in imports of goods would be offset by an inflow of capital and thus an increase in investment demand. The two effects would offset each other and aggregate money balances would be unchanged.

---

[6]For an analysis of the BOP effects of changes in a real variable (a change in tariff) within a monetarist's framework, see Michael Mussa, "A Monetary Approach to Balance-of-Payments Analysis," *Journal of Money, Credit and Banking* (August 1974), pp. 333–51.

[7]For a review of balance-of-payments concepts and their meaning, see John Pippenger, "Balance-of-Payments Deficits: Measurement and Interpretation," this *Review* (November 1973), pp. 6–14. For a discussion of which trasactions to include below the line, see footnote 3 of this article.

[8]This is not to say the MBOP framework would not be useful in analyzing individual subaccounts. However, such analysis would require a rigorous specification of the channels of monetary influence. For a survey and analysis of the literature pertaining to these channels, see Roger W. Spencer, "Channels of Monetary Influence: A Survey," this *Review* (November 1974), pp. 8–26. For an example of how this framework could be applied to the analysis of the capital account alone, see Pentti J. K. Kouri and Michael G. Porter. "International Capital Flows and Portfolio Equilibrium," *Journal of Political Economy* (May/June 1974), pp. 443–67.

(3) The MBOP relies on the assumption of an efficient world market for goods, services, and securities.[9] Under a system of fixed exchange rates, the price of any good or service in one country relative to its price in any other country can change only in the short run. Likewise, the rate of return on any asset can differ from the rate of return on assets of comparable risk and maturity in any other country only in the short run. It follows that in the long run price levels and interest rates in all countries must move rigidly in line with one another. In fact, in a fixed exchange rate regime it is the attempts to arbitrage intercountry price and interest rate differentials that are the driving force leading to the reduction or accumulation of money balances and a concomitant temporary BOP deficit or surplus.

Under a system of freely floating exchange rates, price levels may move at different rates between countries. However, the impact of these differential rates of change on individual relative prices between countries is offset by opposite movements in exchange rates. The same arbitrage opportunities that lead to reserve flows under fixed rates lead to exchange rate adjustments that exactly compensate for differential price level changes between countries.

(4) The MBOP is a theory of an automatic adjustment process. According to this theory, any BOP disequilibrium or exchange rate movement reflects a disparity between actual and desired money balances and will automatically correct itself. While the adjustment process is different under different exchange rate regimes, the implication is that the process is automatic and that its effects cannot be neutralized in the long run. Any BOP imbalance or exchange rate change is a phase in the automatic adjustment process and attempts to counter these processes merely increase the forces which give rise to the adjustment ultimately required for a return to equilibrium.

(5) The MBOP is concerned primarily with the long run. The approach recognizes that short run analysis is often complicated by the fact that the postulated adjustment behavior is incomplete in the short run. For example, the adjustment of actual money balances to their desired levels does not occur instantaneously, but rather requires the passage of time. As another example, it is possible that the monetary authorities may attempt to neutralize the impact of international reserve flows on their respective money supplies in the short run.[10] However, the MBOP asserts that governments cannot follow such policies in the long run. This seems reasonable because, in the long run, success in neutralizing the effects of international reserve flows implies that the governments of some (surplus) countries are willing to trade investment and consumption goods for foreign currency balances. The accumulation

---

[9]While it is acknowledged that there are some goods that are not traded internationally, there are limits to relative price changes between these nontraded goods and other (traded) goods. The higher the elasticities of substitution between these two classes of goods in both production and consumption, the smaller the scope for relative price changes and the more direct the international price interdependence.

[10]For an analysis of West German attempts to neutralize the effects of reserve flows, see Manfred Willms, "Controlling Money in an Open Economy: The German Case," this *Review* (April 1971), pp. 10-27.

of these balances by surplus country governments represents a nonmarket induced transfer of wealth away from domestic to foreign consumers. For whatever reason, it is unrealistic to suppose that a government would pursue such policies in the long run.

(6) An implication of this theory is that, under a system of fixed exchange rates, domestic monetary policy does not control a country's money supply. Excessive monetary expansion (contraction), via expansion (contraction) of some controllable component of the monetary base, will result in an outflow (inflow) of international reserves (an uncontrollable component of the monetary base) and a tendency for the money supply to return to its former level.[11] The resulting BOP deficit (surplus) is only a reflection of these uncontrollable international reserve outflows (inflows). Through this process, the inflationary or deflationary impact of domestic monetary policy is mitigated with respect to the domestic economy and is imposed on the rest of the world via intercountry flows of international reserves. At the same time, however, the domestic economy is subject to the influence of inflationary or deflationary monetary actions taken in other countries.

Under a system of freely floating exchange rates, the domestic monetary authorities retain dominant control over the money supply, while the interaction of domestic and foreign monetary policies determines the exchange rate rather than the BOP (which is now zero by definition). In this case, a country neither imports nor exports international reserves. As a result, the domestic economy is subjected to the full consequences of inflationary or deflationary domestic monetary policies and is insulated from the effects of monetary actions taken in other countries.

(7) Another feature of the MBOP is that it provides a framework within which one is able to assess the differential impact of monetary disturbances which occur in a world in which there is at least one reserve currency country (RCC) as opposed to those occurring in a world with no RCC's. An RCC is a country whose currency is held by others as a form of international reserves. It is this special status afforded to the currency of the RCC which leads to a slightly altered adjustment process for the world and the RCC itself.

The Special Case of a Reserve Currency Country

Because international reserves and reserve currencies exist only under a system of fixed exchange rates, the following analysis applies only to that case. For all non-RCCs, expansionary (contractionary) monetary policies are offset by a BOP deficit (surplus) and the resulting contraction (expansion) of the international reserve component of the monetary base. However, for an RCC this need not be the case. An expansionary (contractionary) monetary policy in the RCC may have no effect on its

---

[11]While this is true for most countries, it is not necessarily the case for a reserve currency country. The special case of a reserve currency country will be discussed in the next section.

BOP as defined in this article. However, the RCC's trading partners will always experience a BOP surplus (deficit) and an inflow (outflow) of international reserves as a result of such RCC policies.[12] The reason for this is that the RCC currency is held by foreign central banks as a form of international reserves. While non-RCC monetary authorities are not willing to accumulate large balances denominated in other non-RCC currencies, they are willing to accumulate large balances denominated in the RCC currency. Because these balances are themselves a type of international reserves, non-RCC monetary authorities may not be inclined to present them to the RCC authorities in exchange for other international reserves.

However, to the extent that the RCC loses no international reserves as a result of an increase in other components of its monetary base, it does experience an accumulation of liquid liabilities to foreign official holders.[13] As these liabilities of the RCC are regarded as assets by foreign official holders, their accumulation represents an inflow of international reserves and a BOP surplus for RCC trading partners.

The how and why of all of this can be brought out by reference to the balance sheets of the world's monetary authorities. While the following analysis applies to the case of expansionary monetary policy in the RCC, it is equally applicable to the analysis of contractionary monetary policy. In addition, in order to simplify the analysis, we will assume that foreign central banks invest *all* of their RCC currency holdings in government securities issued by the RCC. However, we fully recognize that this need not be the case. Non-RCC central banks can and frequently do invest their RCC currency holdings in other assets or simply allow them to accumulate as deposits at the RCC central bank. Whatever the non-RCC authorities decide to do, however, all that is crucial for our analysis to hold is that they do not accumulate deposits at the RCC central bank.

Illustration 1 indicates what happens to the monetary bases of all countries as a result of an attempt by the RCC monetary authorities to increase the domestic money supply in the face of a fixed demand for money. Tier (A) illustrates that the initial impact of such an undertaking is to increase the monetary base of the RCC only. Tier (B) illustrates what happens to the respective monetary bases as a result of the forthcoming intercountry reserve flows. Non-RCCs accumulate international reserves (R) in the form of deposits denominated in the RCC currency held at the RCC central bank. As long as these R are held in this form, the RCC monetary base decreases towards its initial level and the non-RCC monetary bases increase, just as in the case of a world in which there are no RCCs.

Since the non-RCCs view these reserve currency balances as R, they are willing to accumulate them in the same manner that they accumulate other R. However, these R differ from others in one significant aspect—namely, they can be invested in government securities issued by the RCC. When non-RCCs choose to do this, the effects

---

[12]Recall that the BOP concept used in this article is the balance in the money account. That is, the only items recorded below the line are those that affect the domestic money supply.

[13]While the accumulations or reductions of the holdings of liabilities do not affect the RCC balance of payments as defined in this article, they do affect some RCC balance-of-payments concepts. For example, such transactions would affect the Official Settlements Balance in the United States.

Illustration 1

Tier	RCC Monetary Authority's Balance Sheet		Collective Balance Sheet for All Non-RCC Monetary Authorities	
(A)	R(O) D(+) − OL(O)	DR(+) C(O)	R(O) D(O) − OL(O)	DR(O) C(O)
(B)	R(O) D(O) − OL(+)	DR(−) C(O)	R(+) D(O) − OL(O)	DR(+) C(O)
(C)	R(O) D(O) − OL(−)	DR(+) C(O)	R(O) D(O) − OL(O)	DR(O) C(O)
(NET)	R(O) D(+) − OL(O)	DR(+) C(O)	R(+) D(O) − OL(O)	DR(+) C(O)

where

    R = official holdings of international reserves

    D = domestic credit; this consists of central bank holdings of securities, discounts and advances, and float.

  − OL = other liabilities of the monetary authorities (including foreign deposits at Federal Reserve Banks). These items conventionally appear on the source side of the base as a negative item. They are subtracted from other items in calculating the source base.[1]

    C = currency held by the public

  DR = reserves of the domestic banking community

_____

[1] See Albert E. Burger, *The Money Supply Process* (Belmont, California: Wadsworth Publishing Company, 1971), p. 38.

are as illustrated in tier (C). When non-RCC monetary authorities purchase RCC government securities, the OL entry in the RCC balance sheet is drawn down. This has the effect of increasing the monetary base of the RCC without causing a decrease in the monetary bases of the non-RCCs. The net effect of all of this is that the monetary bases of all countries have increased (as shown in the NET tier).

In view of the above analysis, a world in which there exists at least one RCC differs significantly from a world in which there are no RCCs. In a world with RCCs, BOP deficits and surpluses may by themselves decrease and increase the level of R in the world and in individual countries. In a world with no RCCs, BOP deficits and surpluses result in a redistribution of an existing stock of R among countries, but produce no change in the overall level. As a result, in a world with RCCs, the world and each individual non-RCC will ordinarily experience much more difficulty in controlling its money supply. Thus, the existence of RCCs compounds the problems of money stock control which are already inherent in any system of fixed exchange rates.

In addition, this analysis implies that the inflationary or deflationary impact of RCC monetary policy is spread over the entire world. Unlike the case of a non-RCC, however, there may be no mitigation of the impact on the domestic economy since the RCC may neither gain nor lose reserves. As a result, prices in the RCC could change by the same amount as they would under a system of freely floating exchange rates. What's worse, however, is that the rest of the world will gain or lose international reserves and bear the same price level impact as the RCC. Thus, the potential for large BOP surpluses and deficits and for worldwide inflations and deflations are greater under a fixed exchange rate system with RCCs than under any other system considered in this article.

A Monetary Model of the Balance of Payments

Now that the essential features of the MBOP have been spelled out, let us turn to the derivation of a model in which these features are expressed by a set of equations.[14] First, the model is derived for a non-RCC under a system of fixed exchange rates. Second, the same model is applied to the case of an RCC under fixed exchange rates. Finally, the model is applied to the case of freely floating exchange rates.

The common elements in each of these models are stable money demand and money supply functions.[15] The money supply function for each country may be stated as

$$MS_j = a_j [R_j + D_j] \qquad (1)$$

where

MS_j = money supply in country j
a_j = money multiplier in country j
R_j = official holdings of international reserves in country j; hereafter referred to as the international component of the monetary base.
D_j = all other components of the monetary base in country j; hereafter referred to as the domestically controlled component of the monetary base.
$D_j + R_j = MB_j$ = monetary base in country j

[14]In order to simplify the presentation, many of the steps in the derivation of the model have been bypassed in the text. For the interested reader, a more thorough presentation of the model is provided in an appendix, which is available from this Bank upon request.

[15]For an analysis of the development of the money supply function employed in this article, see Jerry L. Jordan, "Elements of Money Stock Determination," this *Review* (October 1969), pp. 10-19.

The demand for money in each country is assumed to be a function of real income, the nominal rate of interest, and prices.

$$MD_j = f_j[y_j, r, P] \tag{2}$$

where

MD_j = demand for money in country j
P = price index in the world and thus in country j[16]
y_j = real income in country j
r = nominal rate of interest in the world and thus in country j.

In accordance with the general monetarist framework of the model, country j is in equilibrium if and only if the growth of the supply of money equals the growth of the demand for money. We are able to specify the conditions necessary for fulfilling this requirement by expressing equations (1) and (2) in terms of rates of change and then equating the resulting expressions. This procedure allows us to derive an expression for the rate of growth of international reserves in country j.[17]

$$\frac{R_j}{MB_j} g_{Rj} = g_p + \alpha_j g_{yj} + \beta_j g_r - \frac{D_j}{MB_j} g_{Dj} \tag{3}$$

where

α_j = income elasticity of demand for money in country j
β_j = interest rate elasticity of demand for money in country j.

We are able to derive an expression for the growth rate of world prices $[g_p]$ by summing the expressions for the growth rates of the demand for and supply of money over all countries and equating the resultant expressions.

$$g_p = \sum_{i=1}^{N} w_i g_{MSi} - \sum_{i=1}^{N} w_i [\alpha_i g_{yi} + \beta_i g_r] \tag{4}$$

where

$$w_i = \frac{MS_i}{\sum_{i=1}^{N} MS_i} = \text{weights calculated on the basis of money supplies converted by exchange rates to equivalent units of currency } j.$$

[16]This reflects the assumption that under a system of fixed exchange rates, a country's price level and interest rates move in line with the world price level and interest rates. However, in the case of freely floating exchange rates the assumption regarding the price level is no longer valid. As such, the money demand function must be specified somewhat differently in that case.

[17]Henceforth in this article $g_x = dlnx/dt$. That is, g_x is the expression for the continuous rate of growth of variable x.

Fixed Exchange Rates in A World with No RCCs

Recall that by definition $g_{Rj} = (1/R_j)(dR_j/dt)$. Under a system of fixed exchange rates in a world in which there are no reserve currency countries, dR_j/dt is the expression for the balance of payments in the money account. It represents the rate at which country j is either gaining or losing international reserves during a given time period (t). With this in mind, and upon making some simplifying assumptions regarding the interest and income elasticities of demand for money, we are able to substitute expression (4) into expression (3) and get an expression for the balance of payments in country j.[18]

$$\frac{1}{MB_j} BOP_j = \left[\sum_{i=1}^{N} w_i g_{MS_i} - \frac{D_j}{MB_j} g_{D_j} \right] + \left[g_{yj} - \sum_{i=1}^{N} w_i g_{yi} \right] \qquad (5)$$

Expression (5) is essentially an embodiment of the features of the price specie flow mechanism, which operates under a system of fixed exchange rates in a world in which there are no reserve currency countries.[19] That is, expression (5) states that the BOP is a function of:

1. the rate of growth of real income in country j relative to the average rate of growth of real income for all countries, and

2. the rate of growth of the domestically controlled component of the monetary base in country j relative to an average rate of money growth for the whole world.

Fixed Exchange Rates in a World with at Least One RCC

In a world in which there is at least one RCC, expression (5) is still an appropriate representation of the forces giving rise to BOP flows in non-RCCs. However, for an RCC there may be no international reserve flows associated with the BOP accounts; in which case $g_{Rj} = 0$. In the case of an RCC, excessive expansion (contraction) of

[18]We have assumed that $\alpha_i = 1$ for all i and that $(\beta_j = \sum_{i=1}^{N} w_i \beta_i)$.
Neither of these assumptions are crucial to the analysis at hand. They are invoked here mainly to simplify the presentation. The assumption that $\alpha_1 = 1$ is interpreted as assuming that the income elasticity of demand for money is unity in all countries. Assuming that $(\sum_{i=1}^{N} w_i \beta_i = \beta_j)$ means that the interest elasticity of demand for money in country j is equal to a weighted average of the interest elasticities of demand for money in all countries. A more restrictive implication of this assumption would be that the interest elasticities are equal in all countries.

[19]The price specie flow mechanism is an attempt to explain international gold flows under the gold standard. It is associated primarily with the work of David Hume in the eighteenth century. However, in our case the BOP includes more than just gold flows. It includes flows of all international reserves—gold, SDRs, foreign exchange, and reserve positions at the IMF.

the domestically controlled component of the monetary base need not lead to an offsetting contraction (expansion) of the international reserve component. At the same time, however, excessive expansion (contraction) of the domestically controlled component of the monetary base in the RCC will lead to an accumulation (reduction) of international reserves in all other countries. As mentioned previously, we will assume that these international reserves will be held in the form of securities issued by the RCC government to non-RCC official holders. For the RCC, it is the net accumulation or reduction of such liabilities that is determined by monetary actions in our model. This process can be captured in our model by setting $g_{RRCC} = 0$ (where the RCC is the jth country) and replacing the term $\sum_{i=1}^{N} w_i g_{MSi}$ in expression (5) with a more detailed formulation of the factors contributing to the growth of the money supply in all countries.

$$\frac{1}{MB_w} BOL_{RCC} = \left[\sum_{i=1}^{N} w_i \frac{D_i}{MB_i} g_{Di} - \frac{D_{RCC}}{MB_{RCC}} g_{DRCC} \right] + \left[g_{yRCC} - \sum_{i=1}^{N} w_i g_{yi} \right] \quad (6)$$

where

MB_w = the sum of the monetary bases of all countries in the world.
BOL_{RCC} = the net accumulation of claims against the RCC by foreign official institutions during time period (t).[20]

This expression states that the change in the level of the liabilities of the RCC to foreign official holders that results from domestic monetary policy in the RCC is determined by the following:

1. the rate of growth of the domestically controlled component of the monetary base in the RCC relative to a weighted average of its rate of growth in all countries.

2. the rate of growth of real income in the RCC relative to a weighted average of the rates of growth of real income in all countries.

Freely Floating Exchange Rates

For the case of freely floating exchange rates, two modifications of the model are necessary. First, the model must be adapted to reflect the fact that there are no international reserve flows, so that the growth rate of a country's money supply is determined solely by domestic monetary policy [g_{Dj}]. Second, the money demand

[20]For the United States this BOP concept closely resembles the balance on liabilities to foreign official holders. However, this account is distinctly different from the BOP concept utilized in (5). Expression (5) explains the balance in the money account, whereas the BOP concept used in expression (6) has no relation to the money supply.

function must be modified to reflect the fact that the rate of price level change in one country may differ from the rate prevailing in the rest of the world.

Upon incorporating both of these modifications into the model, we are able to derive an expression for the determination of movements in the exchange rate.

$$g_{E_j} = [g_{MS_{ROW}} - g_{MS_j}] + [g_{y_j} - g_{y_{ROW}}] \tag{7}$$

where

$$E_j = \frac{P_{ROW}}{P_j} = \text{the price of currency j in terms of foreign currencies}$$

$$P_{ROW} = \sum_{i=1}^{N-1} h_i P_i = \text{the price level in the rest of the world; that is, a weighted average of the price levels in all other countries.}$$

$$h_i = \frac{y_i}{\sum_{i=1}^{N-1} y_i} = \text{weights calculated on the basis of real GNP}$$

$$P_j = \text{price level in country j}$$

This expression states that the exchange value of currency j in terms of foreign currencies is determined by the rate of growth of the money supply and real income in country j relative to the rate of growth of the money supply and real income, respectively, in the rest of the world. As such, it implies that currency depreciations are the result of excessive monetary growth. It, therefore, supports the proposition that inflation causes depreciation of the domestic currency rather than vice versa.

Summary and Conclusions

The MBOP may be summarized by the proposition that the transactions recorded in balance-of-payments statistics reflect aggregate portfolio decisions by both foreign and domestic economic units. The framework presented in this article suggests some important policy considerations that cannot be addressed within the framework which characterizes most of the currently accepted body of payments theory.

The analysis presented here casts the balance of payments in the role of an automatic adjustment mechanism. Balance-of-payments deficits and surpluses, or movements in freely floating exchange rates, are viewed as being simultaneously both the result of a divergence between actual and desired money balances and a mechanism by which such a divergence is corrected. As such, persistent balance-of-payments deficits (surpluses) or depreciation (appreciations) of the foreign exchange value of a currency reflect a continual re-creation of a situation in which excessive monetary expansion in the country in question is greater (less) than the worldwide average. Furthermore, the only solution to such international disturbances are policies which facilitate the equalization of actual and desired money balances.

The futility of tariff and nontariff barriers to trade which attempt to alter balance-of-payments flows or exchange rate movements becomes readily apparent when one views them within the framework presented above. Suppose, for example, that an import tariff is imposed with the aim of reducing a balance-of-payments deficit in the money account. According to the MBOP, international reserve flows will assure that the balance-of-payments deficit disappears in the long run whether the tariff is imposed or not. That is, even if the tariff were not imposed, the excess money balances, and therefore the deficit, would disappear as a result of the outflow of international reserves. However, if the tariff is imposed, relative prices will be artificially altered from the levels consistent with the most efficient allocation of resources and maximum gains from trade. Furthermore, the situation is no better if the tariff is imposed in retaliation against restrictive trade practices on the part of other nations. In this case, all that the tariff accomplishes is to further distort relative prices and further reduce the welfare of all nations.

Another advantage of the MBOP is that it enables one to evaluate clearly the relative desirability of different exchange rate regimes in terms of their promotion of autonomy of domestic monetary policy and domestic as well as worldwide price stability. Under a system of freely floating exchange rates, a country retains dominant control over its money growth, incurs the full consequences of its domestic monetary policy, and is not subject to the effects of inflationary or deflationary monetary policies undertaken in other countries. Under a system of fixed exchange rates in a world in which there are no reserve currency countries, a country loses control of its rate of money growth, has the domestic impact of its monetary policy mitigated, and is subject to the effects of monetary policies pursued by other countries. Under a system of fixed exchange rates in a world in which there is at least one reserve currency country, we have the potential for the worst of both of the above systems. While the impact of expansionary (contractionary) monetary policies in the reserve currency country is imposed on the rest of the world, there may be no mitigation of their domestic impact. As a result, the entire world is prone toward large changes in its money supply which are initiated by actions taken in the reserve currency country. This conclusion appears to be consistent with the inflationary experiences of the Western world which began in the late 1960s.

Finally, if the balance of payments is viewed within the MBOP framework, the pitfalls of placing emphasis on any particular BOP subaccount are obvious. A deficit (surplus) in any one account need not have any effect on domestic aggregate economic activity if its impact on money balances is offset by a surplus (deficit) in another account.

This point is especially significant in view of the large merchandise trade deficits that many oil-consuming countries have been experiencing. The analysis presented in this article indicates that the impact of these deficits on money balances, and therefore on aggregate economic activity in the deficit countries, will be substantially reduced as a result of large inflows of capital from OPEC members. Of course, this does not mean that oil-consuming countries are no worse off now than they were prior to the fourfold increase in oil prices. The MBOP merely states that the impact on GNP will be mitigated through subsequent inflows of capital. The distribution of a given GNP between the residents of oil-consuming and oil-producing countries, however, is altered in favor of the oil producers.

A "Monetarist" Analysis of the Generation and Transmission of World Inflation: 1958-71

Michael Parkin

30

A widely accepted definition of inflation is that it "is a process of continuously rising prices, or equivalently, of a continuously falling value of money" (David Laidler and Michael Parkin, p. 741). An important observation suggested by this definition is that, in a world with *one* money, or equivalently with many monies linked to a single monetary standard via fixed exchange rates, there is *one* rate of inflation. Of course, index numbers may be computed for subaggregates of goods and services, some of which refer to particular geographical areas—countries—but rates of change in these indices do not measure inflation. Rather they measure a mixture of inflation and relative price changes. This observation has important implications for the analysis and explanation of inflation during the last two decades, for the period from the middle 1950s to 1971 was characterized by a single monetary standard[1] and hence only one inflation rate has to be explained. This paper attempts to explain that inflation rate. It contains no new theoretical ideas and no new empirical results. Rather it encapsulates in a short space the key results which have emerged from the by now large volume of work on the explanation of inflation in the fixed exchange

Reprinted from the *American Economic Review*, February 1977, pp. 164–171, by permission of the American Economic Association and the author.

[1]There were only six changes in exchange rates among the major currencies between 1956 and 1976; the revaluations of the Deutsch-mark in 1961 and 1969 and the Dutch guilder in 1961, and the devaluations of the French franc in 1958 and 1969 and of sterling in 1967.

rate world and attempts to identify the major questions which head the agenda of future research.

World Average Inflation in the Fixed Exchange Rate World: 1958-71

In a world[2] with one monetary standard and one rate of inflation the explanation of inflation must be sought at the level of the world economy rather than at the national level. To study inflation at the world aggregate level is to follow a tradition begun by Jean Bodin and David Hume and recently popularized by Robert A. Mundell and Harry G. Johnson (1972).[3] However, it in no way forces onto the analysis a monocausal "monetarist" explanation of inflation as presented in those earlier world aggregate analyses. On the contrary, it provides the simplest possible environment, that of a closed economy, for developing an entirely eclectic framework within which to discriminate among competing hypotheses on the causes of inflation.

Such a framework was developed in Malcolm R. Gray and Michael Parkin. The framework combines three interacting propositions which are capable of embracing all views on the generation of inflation. First, the rate of inflation is influenced by inflation expectations, excess demand and a variety of cost-push factors (including direct wage and price controls); secondly, inflation expectations respond to the history of inflation and to expectations of the movements of the exogenous variables which are believed to cause inflation; thirdly, excess demand is determined by the money supply, fiscal policy, and the behavior of the actual and expected price level. This eclectic view specializes to a variety of extreme positions by assuming some of the potential interlinkages to be either weak or absent. Two such extremes are worth singling out: "cost-push" and "monetarist."

The "cost-push" extreme denies the connection between excess demand and the rate of inflation but accepts the other propositions. It also adds a fourth proposition, namely that the money supply is endogenous and passively responds to movements in prices and aggregate excess demand. Thus, on this extreme view, inflation is caused by cost-push factors while a passive monetary policy ensures that real output does not decline (or not often) so that the push factors come through in both the inflation rate and the monetary expansion rate. Further, on this view, the way to

---

[2]The "world" here is the aggregate of countries which (ignoring the minor exceptions noted above) maintained a fixed exchange rate with the U.S. dollar and full convertibility. The "world" as used in much of the empirical work to be reported below is the "Group of Ten," i.e., Belgium, Canada, France, Germany, Italy, Japan, The Netherlands, Sweden, United Kingdom, and United States.

[3]Recent contributions which have also taken a world aggregate view are: Johnson (1975), Arthur B. Laffer and David I. Meiselman, Laidler and A. R. Nobay, Parkin and George Zis, eds. (1976 a,b), Edward S. Shaw, Alexander K. Swoboda (1975b), Ronald L. Tiegen, and H. Joannes Witteveen. For an excellent doctrinal history on the approach see Jacob Frenkel.

control inflation is to attack it at its supposed source with direct controls on wages and prices, preferably in an internationally synchronous fashion.

The "monetarist"[4] extreme view emphasizes the role of excess demand and inflation expectations (the latter with a coefficient of unity) as the sole proximate determinants of systematic movements in the rate of inflation with push factors affecting (at most) the detailed timing of random (zero mean) movements in its rate. Inflation expectations, however formed, will, in a steady state, line up with the actual rate of inflation. Finally, excess demand depends only on the behavior of the money stock, fiscal policy being unimportant, and further, aggregate excess demand is homogeneous of degree zero in the money stock and actual and expected prices. The policy implication of this view is that control of the money supply is both necessary and sufficient for the control of inflation and that the abandonment of money supply control in favor of aiming for a target real output level, other than zero excess demand, will lead to explosive price level and money supply behavior.

Empirical work on the world aggregate (Group of Ten—G-10) economy enables a start to be made in discriminating between these two extremes (and amongst the many intermediate eclectic positions embodied in the three general propositions) stated above. On price setting and expectations formation at the G-10 level, Nigel Duck et al. estimated equations of the standard form:

$$\Delta p = \alpha x_{-\tau} + \delta \Delta p^e + u \tag{1}$$

where p is the price level (in natural logarithms), x is proportionate excess demand (measured as the deviation from trend of the logarithm of real output), τ denotes a time lag, e denotes expectation, Δ is the first difference operator, u is an error term, and α and δ are positive parameters.

If the estimated value of α in equation (1) is not significantly different from zero and if there are large systematic errors in prediction (large variance and temporal dependence in u), then there is a presumption in favor of the "cost-push" extreme. If, alternatively, α is significantly nonzero, δ is not significantly different from unity and u does not display systematic autocorrelation, then the "monetarist" extreme is not rejected. Using a Box-Jenkins ARIMA procedure to estimate the forecasting scheme to generate Δp^e, Equation 4 below, Duck et al. report the following results using quarterly data, 1956–71 for G-10 (*t*-statistics in parentheses):[5]

$$\Delta p = 0.500 + 0.204 x_{-1} + 0.814 \ \Delta p^e \tag{2}$$
$$[1.23] \quad [3.58] \qquad [6.88]$$
$$\overline{R}^2 = 0.533 \ D.W. = 2.144$$

---

[4]I do not want to devote any space to defending this definition of "monetarist." For an extensive discussion of this and related issues, see Jerome L. Stein.

[5]For full details of data sources and methods, and estimation procedures, see Duck et al. (1976). The results reported here are not the best fitting but the simplest reported by Duck et al. A more complex expectations scheme than that embodied in Equation 4 gave even better results in the price equation.

$$\Delta p = -0.100 + 0.184x_{-1} + \Delta p^e \qquad (3)$$
$$[0.72] \quad [3.31]$$
$$\overline{R}^2 = 0.513 \ D.W. = 2.188$$
$$F = 2.465$$

$$\Delta p^e = 0.309 \ \Delta p_{-1} + 0.691 \ \Delta p_1^e \qquad (4)$$
$$[3.22] \qquad [7.19]$$
$$\overline{R}^2 = 0.378$$

Equation 3 imposes the restriction that the coefficient on Δp^e is unity and the reported F is that associated with the test of the hypothesis that the restriction is true. That restriction cannot be rejected at the 5 percent level, nor can the hypothesis of no first order autocorrelation; nor further can the hypothesis that the coefficient on x_{-1} is nonzero. Taking all these tests together, it is clear that Equations 2–4 imply the rejection of one aspect of the "cost-push" extreme view and to the nonrejection of the "monetarist" extreme view.

On the determination of excess demand, two things need to be established, the properties of the world demand for money function and the determinants of the world money stock. If there exists a stable world aggregate demand function for real balances, then one further aspect of the "monetarist" extreme position cannot be rejected. If, further, it can be shown that the direction of causation runs from money to prices and not vice versa, then the "cost-push" view has to be rejected as failing every test which may confront it while the "monetarist" position stands, pending the specification and performance of yet more searching tests.

Gray et al. (1976) estimated demand for money functions for G-10 of the following form:

$$(m^* - p) = k + \beta y + \gamma r \qquad (5)$$

$$\Delta(m - p) = \theta[(m^* - p) - (m_{-1} - p_{-1})] + u \qquad (6)$$

where m is the natural logarithm of the nominal money stock, r is the rate of interest, an * denotes desired, and the following sign restrictions apply to the parameters; $\beta > 0, 0 \geq \theta \geq 1, \gamma \leq 0$. Gray et al. report the following estimates of the parameters in 5–6 on quarterly G-10 data[6] for 1957–71 (ratios of asymptotic standard errors to parameters in parentheses)

$$k = 2.20 \qquad \beta = 0.53 \qquad \theta = 0.42$$
$$[13.92] \qquad [25.24] \qquad [5.45]$$

$$\text{with} \quad R^2 = 0.986.$$

[6]For full details of data sources and methods, and estimation procedures, see Gray et al. The m variable is narrow, M1, money; income is real GNP aggregated over G-10 with quarterly data based on linear interpolation of annual data and the interest rate is that on Eurodollars.

These parameters were estimated by imposing $\gamma = 0$ and a parameter of first order autocorrelation $\varrho = 0$. Freely estimating these parameters changes the estimated values of k, β and θ only slightly and the hypothesis that γ and ϱ take on the extreme values imposed cannot be rejected at the 95 percent level. Further, a permanent income formulation was rejected in favor of that reported above. However, it is worth noting that permanent income and partial adjustment can only be discriminated between on the basis of error structures and so the above results might alternately be interpreted as representing a permanent income demand for money function. Thus, the hypothesis that there exists a stable world demand function for real balances which is interest inelastic cannot be rejected by the data for this period.[7] These results imply that one further aspect of the monetarist position cannot be rejected and that the world aggregate effect of national fiscal policies is primarily on real interest rates and not on output and prices.

The last remaining matter which needs attention before the "cost-push" extreme can be completely disposed of concerns the direction of causation. It remains a possibility that inflation is caused by some (exogenous to the model) cost-push factors with money passively responding to inflation. If that is the case, Equation 2 or 3 has to be interpreted as determining excess demand in a manner analogous to that suggested by Irving Fisher, and, given that level of demand and exogenously given rate of inflation, the demand for money function determines the money stock. This reverse causation story immediately runs into a difficulty given the time lags involved in 2 and 3. It is excess demand lagged one quarter which is best correlated with the difference between actual and expected inflation. Thus, for the reverse causation story to make sense it would have to be argued that excess demand during the current quarter is caused by a discrepancy between actual and expected inflation which is not revealed until the next quarter. The timing makes life difficult for those who embrace the Fisher aggregate supply interpretation of the relation between excess demand and unanticipated inflation. It is also probably enough to discredit the reverse causation cost-push view. If it is not, there is yet a further body of evidence which goes against it. Hans Genberg and Alexander Swoboda (1975), using the test suggested by Christopher A. Sims show that "changes in the world money stock have, on the average preceded changes in both world income and the world price level during the last decade and a half."[8]

If the above results are brought together, they constitute a simple, yet complete model of the determination of the rate of inflation and the level of real output. The basic structure, repeated here for convenience is:

$$\Delta p = \alpha x_{-1} + \Delta p^e \tag{7}$$

$$\Delta p^e = \lambda \Delta p_{-1} + (1 - \lambda) \, \Delta p^e_{-1} \tag{8}$$

---

[7]Splitting the data period between the (overlapping) first and last 40 observations reveals considerable structural stability although, for the last 40 observations, the interest rate does become significantly nonzero; its coefficient estimate is $-.034$ with an asymptotic standard error of 0.016.

[8]Genberg and Swoboda (1975, p. 21).

$$\Delta(m-p) = \theta[(k+\beta y) - (m_{-1} - p_{-1})] \tag{9}$$

$$y = y^* + x \tag{10}$$

where all the variables are as already defined and where y^* is the natural logarithm of "full employment" real output.[9] Solving these equations for Δp and x gives the following.[10]

$$\Delta p = \left(2 - \frac{\alpha}{\theta\beta}\right)\Delta p_{-1} - \left[1 - \frac{\alpha}{\theta\beta}(2 - \lambda - \theta)\right]\Delta p_{-2} \tag{11}$$

$$- \frac{\alpha}{\theta\beta}(1-\lambda)(1-\theta)\Delta p_{-3} + \frac{\alpha}{\theta\beta}\Delta m_{-1} - \frac{\alpha}{\theta\beta}(2-\lambda-\theta)\Delta m_{-2}$$

$$+ \frac{\alpha}{\theta\beta}(1-\lambda)(1-\theta)\Delta m_{-3}$$

$$x = \left(2 - \frac{\alpha}{\theta\beta}\right)x_{-1} - \left[1 - \frac{\alpha}{\theta\beta}(2-\lambda-\theta)\right]x_{-2} - \frac{\alpha}{\theta\beta}(1-\lambda) \tag{12}$$

$$(1-\theta)x_{-3} + \frac{1}{\theta\beta}\Delta m - \left(\frac{2-\theta}{\theta\beta}\right)\Delta m_{-1} + \left(\frac{1-\theta}{\theta\beta}\right)\Delta m_{-2}$$

Given the particular values of α, β, λ, θ reported above, these two third-order difference equations generate a stable cyclical approach to the steady states (ignoring Δy^*) of $x^* = 0$ and $\Delta p^* = \Delta m$ with heavily damped cycles the period of which is twenty-four quarters. However, for a variety of reasons,[11] the equations are not suitable for a direct simulation test and probably would not track the history of p and x in a very close manner if dynamic simulation were performed. Nevertheless, the structural equations estimated do make it impossible to reject the basic "monetarist" explanation of world average inflation and do provide a set of simple reduced-form equations for prices and output which qualitatively have properties which the world clearly displays. Full employment ($x = 0$) and proportionality of inflation to money supply growth ($\Delta p = \Delta m$) are only steady state properties of the model advanced and any change in the rate of monetary expansion will be accompanied first by a change in the level of real economic activity and subsequently by a change in the inflation rate.

The discussion so far has treated the money supply as given and not enquired into the process whereby it is generated. Addressing this matter, Parkin et al. (1975)

[9]Models with similar structures and properties to this have been suggested by Laidler (1973) and John Vanderkamp.

[10]Equations 11 and 12 are different from those reported in Parkin (1976). The equations here are correct and those in my earlier paper contained an error in the specification of the demand for money function which led to an error in the difference equations.

[11]The key reasons for this are that y in the reported demand for money function was based on annual national income accounts with quarterly data obtained by linear interpolation while x in the price equation was based on deviations from trend in a quarterly G-10 industrial production index. These inconsistencies are being adjusted in work currently underway.

developed a simple model of the world money supply and, based on quarterly G-10 data from 1961 to 1971 concluded that there existed a stable, interest inelastic relation between the world money stock and the world monetary base, the latter defined as the sum of national monetary bases, with a secular increase in the broad money multiplier which they attributed to a gradual adjustment process in working off excess reserves. They also suggested that, up to 1968, the growth in domestic credit had been the main source of base growth but that after 1968, the growth of international liquidity began to dominate. However, they suggested that the relation between international reserves and total world base money was weak and therefore not exploitable for purposes of world monetary control.

More recent work makes it necessary to reevaluate and modify some of these conclusions. First, Swoboda (1975a) and Genberg and Swoboda (1976) show that there is an asymmetry in the effects of United States base and "rest of world" base on the world money supply arising from the fraction of reserves which the rest of the world holds as deposits with U.S. commercial banks and U.S. treasury bills as opposed to deposits with the Federal Reserve Banks. This makes U.S. base a "super-high-powered" money and predicts a larger multiplier effect of U.S. base on the world money stock than the bases of other countries. Empirical work performed by these authors confirms their proposition. Secondly, the connection between international liquidity and the world money supply has recently been thoroughly investigated by H. Robert Heller. He shows that there is a well determined distributed lag relation between these two variables with changes in liquidity clearly preceding changes in the world money supply.

The tentative conclusion which emerges from these studies is that the growth in the world money supply has been dominated by, though not completely determined by, the growth of international liquidity and that the growth of U.S. base money has been a key contributor to that liquidity and world money supply growth.

National Price Levels and the
International Transmission Process

There are two basic hypotheses concerning the international transmission of inflation under fixed exchange rates both of which have been attributed to Hume. One is that the law of one price has no respect for national boundaries, hence, any discrepancies between prices of similar goods in different countries will quickly be arbitraged away ensuring equality of prices and of rates of price change across countries. It is recognized that measured rates of inflation do differ but suggested that such differences are attributable to trend changes in relative prices arising from different underlying productivity growth rates. Given a national rate of inflation arising from arbitrage, payments balances will ensure that the exogenous world money supply is distributed (endogenous) to each country to validate its price level behavior. There is an important variant of this hypothesis of the international transmission mechanism which separates traded from nontraded goods and has international arbitrage equalizing traded goods prices only with competitive labor and domestic goods markets bringing the inflation rates of wages and nontraded goods prices into alignment with (but not in general to equality with) the world rate of inflation. (See especially G. Edgren, K. O. Flaxen and G. E. Ohdner, and Parkin 1972, 1974).

The second mechanism is one which has a rise in the world inflation rate leading to a fall in the relative domestic price level which generates excess demand and a balance of payments surplus. The excess demand and the money supply growth induced by the balance of payments surplus generate a process of rising domestic prices which continues until equilibrium has been restored. A variety of alternative *domestic* transmission mechanisms are compatible with this international transmission mechanism including those of the Keynesian-Phillips curve and the mechanical quantity theory. (See William H. Branson.)

The two international transmission mechanisms of inflation are clearly not mutually exclusive and a more general formulation would combine them. The simplest way of doing this is to adapt the standard expectations-augmented excess-demand model of price determination to the open fixed exchange rate economy. This has been done in a series of papers by Rodney Cross and Laidler, Laidler (1976), Franco Spinelli, Andrew Horseman, and Parkin et al. (1976). These studies postulate that domestic prices respond to domestic demand and to the expected rate of inflation where the latter variable is dependent not only on the history of domestic but also of world inflation. If the pure arbitrage story is a good approximation to the world then domestic excess demand will be unimportant in determining domestic price change, and world inflation will be the only influence on inflation expectations. If the other transmission mechanism is the only relevant one then domestic excess demand and inflation expectations based only on domestic considerations will dominate and world inflation will have no important separate influence on the domestic inflation rate.

The broad consensus of the empirical work performed and reported in the studies cited above is that neither extreme is an adequate simplification and that there are elements of both in the generation of national price level movements, at least as far as quarterly and annual averages are concerned. Over longer time averages, the arbitrage process seems much stronger (see Genberg, 1976) and no studies are available which suggest that foreign prices can be ignored when explaining price movements in open economies.

Those studies which have permitted expectations of world inflation as well as of domestic inflation to have a direct effect on domestic inflation have an important implication for inferences concerning the existence or otherwise of a long-run tradeoff between inflation and unemployment at the national level. The dominant finding of the studies just cited is that no long-run tradeoff exists. Parkin and Graham Smith show that earlier studies which did display a long-run tradeoff can be reconciled with those that do not by analyzing the consequences for parameter estimates of the omitted world inflation variable.

A further matter on which these studies shed some light concerns the specific foreign prices which have the main direct impact on domestic prices. Three broad possibilities have been suggested. Early postwar studies emphasized the role of import prices; the "Scandinavian" approach emphasizes export prices while the arbitrage approach suggests a broad index of all foreign prices. Studies can be found which show all to be important and the only direct attempt to compare some of the alternatives, by Laidler (1976), suggests that a broader index is better than a narrower one.

All the studies referred to above deal only with the proximate determinants of prices. Laidler (1975) has incorporated a price setting mechanism of the above type into a complete macro model and shown that, while there is no ambiguity that a rise in the world inflation rate raises domestic inflation, there *is* an ambiguity about its impact effect on domestic output which could fall if the impact on the price level exceeds that on the money stock. Spinelli has applied the Laidler model to the Italian economy and found it to have a high degree of explanatory power and to completely outperform an alternative "cost-push" explanation for that country. The alternative "cost-push" explanation of inflation at the level of the individual country has further been investigated by Peter D. Jonson for Australia and George Zis for the Group of Ten and again shown to be easily rejected.

Concluding Remarks

The preceding summary account of theoretical and empirical work on the generation and transmission of inflation in a fixed exchange rate world does not itself require a summary. It is worthwhile, however, to try to highlight the outstanding issues which need further attention. First, a fully consistent structural model of world average inflation capable of providing a close dynamic tracing of world output and price level movements remains to be built. Secondly, the precise effects on the world money supply of domestic credit creation in the United States and in the smaller countries need to be further clarified. Thirdly, the details of the international and domestic transmission mechanisms need further speculation. A key to the advancement of knowledge in these last areas will be the explicit *comparison* of competing hypotheses, all too little of which has been undertaken to date.

BIBLIOGRAPHY

BODIN, JEAN. "Response aux paradoxes de Malestroit touchant l'Encherissement de toutes Choses et le Moyen d'y remedier." English translation in Arthur E. Monroe, ed. *Early Economic Thought.* Cambridge, Mass., 1924.

BRANSON, WILLIAM H. "Monetarist and Keynesian Models of the Transmission of Inflation." *American Economic Review Proceedings* 65 (May 1975), pp. 115–19.

CLAASSEN, EMIL, and PASCAL SALIN. *Recent Issues in International Monetary Economics.* Amsterdam, 1976.

CROSS, RODNEY, and DAVID LAIDLER. "Inflation, Excess Demand and Expectations in Fixed Exchange Rate Open Economies: Some Preliminary Empirical Results." In M. Parkin and G. Zis, eds. *Inflation in the World Economy,* pp. 221–54. 1976a.

DUCK, NIGEL, MICHAEL PARKIN, DAVID ROSE, AND GEORGE ZIS. "The Determination of the Rate of Change of Wages and Prices in the Fixed Exchange Rate World Economy, 1956–1971." In Parkin and Zis, eds., pp. 113–42. 1976a.

EDGREN, G., K. O. FLAXEN, and G. E. OHDNER. "Wages Growth and the Distribution of Income." *Swedish Journal of Economics* 71 (1969), pp. 133–60.

FISHER, IRVING. *The Purchasing Power of Money.* New York, 1911 and 1963.

FRENKEL, JACOB A. "Adjustment Mechanisms and the Monetary Approach to the Balance of Payments." In E. Claassen and P. Salin. 1976.

GENBERG, HANS, and ALEXANDER K. SWOBODA. "Causes and Origins of the Current Worldwide Inflation." Ford Foundation International Monetary Research Project. Graduate Institute of International Studies. Discussion Paper. Geneva, November 1975.

———— and ————. "Worldwide Inflation under the Dollar Standard." Graduate Institute of International Studies. Mimeograph. Geneva, 1976.

————. "A Note on Inflation Rates under Fixed Exchange Rates." In Parkin and Zis, eds., pp. 183–88. 1976a.

GRAY, MALCOLM R., and MICHAEL PARKIN. "Discrimination between Alternative Explanations of Inflation." In Michele Fratianni and Karel Taverneir, eds. Proceedings of Conference on "Money, Banking and Credit in Open Economies." Catholic University of Louvain, 1973.

————, R. WARD, and GEORGE ZIS. "The World Demand for Money Function: Some Preliminary Results." In Parkin and Zis, eds., pp. 151–77. 1976a.

HELLER, H. ROBERT. "International Reserves and World Wide Inflation." *I.M.F. Staff Paper* 23 (March 1976), pp. 61–87.

HORSEMAN, ANDREW. "The Relation between Wage Inflation and Unemployment in an Open Economy." In M. Parkin and G. Zis, eds., *Inflation in Open Economies,* pp. 175–200. 1976b.

HUME, DAVID. "Of Money," and "Of the Balance of Trade." In *Essays, Moral, Political and Literary,* pp. 289–302, 316–33. 1741; Oxford, 1963.

JOHNSON, HARRY G. "Inflation and the Monetarist Controversy." *Professor Dr. F. de Vries Lectures.* Amsterdam, 1972.

————. "World Inflation and the International Monetary System." *The Three Banks Review,* no. 107 (September 1975), pp. 3–22.

JONSON, PETER D. "World Influences on the Australian Rate of Inflation." In Parkin and Zis. eds., pp. 237–58. 1976b.

LAFFER, A. B., and D. I. MEISELMAN. *The Phenomenon of Worldwide Inflation.* American Enterprise Institute for Public Policy Research. Washington, 1975.

LAIDLER, DAVID. "The Influence of Money on Real Income and Inflation: A Simple Model with Some Empirical Tests for the United States, 1953–1972." *Manchester School* 41 (December 1973), pp. 367–95.

————. *Essays on Money and Inflation.* Chap. 9, "Price and Output Fluctuations in an Open Economy," pp. 183–94. Manchester, 1975.

————. "Alternative Explanations and Policies towards Inflation: Tests on Data Drawn from Six Countries." Forthcoming in K. Brunner and A. H. Meltzer, eds. Carnegie-Rochester Conference Series on Public Policy, 1976.

———— and MICHAEL PARKIN. "Inflation: A Survey," *Economic Journal* 85 (December 1975), pp. 741–809.

————, and A. R. NOBAY. "Some Current Issues Concerning the International Aspects of Inflation." In Claassen and Salin. 1976.

MUNDELL, R. *Monetary Theory: Inflation, Interest and Growth in the World Economy.* Goodyear, 1971.

PARKIN, MICHAEL. Inflation, the Balance of Payments, Domestic Credit Expansion and Exchange Rate Adjustments.'' In Robert Z. Aliber, ed. Proceedings of the Conference on National Monetary Policies and the International Financial System. Racine, 1972.

————. "World Inflation, International Relative Prices and Monetary Equilibrium under Fixed Exchange Rates." Paper presented at the Conference on the Political Economy of Monetary Reform. Racine, 1974. Forthcoming in the Proceedings of that conference.

————. "International Liquidity and World Inflation in the 1960s." In Parkin and Zis, eds., pp. 48–63. 1976b.

————, IAN RICHARDS, and GEORGE ZIS. "The Determination and Control of the World Money Supply under Fixed Exchange Rates, 1961–1971." *The Manchester School* 43 (September 1975), pp. 293–316. Reprinted in Parkin and Zis, eds., pp. 24–47. 1976b.

————, and GRAHAM W. SMITH. "Inflationary Expectations and the Long-run Trade-off between Inflation and Unemployment in Open Economies." In Parkin and Zis, eds., pp. 280–90. 1976b.

————, M. T. SUMNER, and R. WARD. "The Effects of Excess Demand, Generalized Expectations and Wage-Price Controls on Wage Inflation in the U.K." In K. Brunner and A. H. Meltzer, *Proceedings of the Conference on Wage-Price Controls.* Rochester, 1973; Amsterdam, 1966.

————, and GEORGE ZIS, eds. *Inflation in the World Economy,* Manchester and Toronto, 1976b.

————, and ————, eds. *Inflation in Open Economies.* Manchester and Toronto, 1976b.

SHAW, EDWARD S. "International Money and International Inflation: 1958–1973," Federal Reserve Bank of San Francisco. *Business Review,* Spring 1975, pp. 5–17.

SIMS, CHRISTOPHER S. "Money Finance and Causality." *American Economic Review* 62 (1972), pp. 540–52.

SPINELLI, FRANCO. "The Determinants of Price and Wage Inflation: The Case of Italy." In Parkin and Zis, eds., pp. 201–36. 1976b.

STEIN, JEROME L. ed. *Monetarism.* Amsterdam, 1976.

SWOBODA, ALEXANDER K. "Gold, Dollars, Euro-dollars and the World Money Stock." Ford Foundation International Monetary Research Project, Graduate Institute of International Studies. Discussion Paper. Geneva, November. 1975a.

————. "Monetary Approaches to the Transmission and Generation of Worldwide Inflation." Ford Foundation International Monetary Research Project, Graduate Institute of International Studies. Discussion Paper. Geneva, March 1975b.

TEIGEN, R. L. "Interpreting Recent World Inflation." *American Economic Review Proceedings* 65 (May 1975), pp. 129–32.

VANDERKAMP, JOHN. "Inflation: A Simple Friedman Theory with a Phillips Twist." *Journal of Monetary Economics* (March 1975), pp. 117–22.

WITTEVEEN, H. JOHANNES. "Inflation and the International Monetary Situation." *American Economic Review Proceedings* 65 (May 1975), pp. 108–14.

ZIS, GEORGE. "Inflation: An International Monetary Problem or a National Social Phenomenon." In Parkin and Zis, eds., pp. 1–23. 1976b.

The Political Economy of Monetary Policymaking

Underlying most of the controversy between Monetarists and Keynesians is disagreement regarding whether government fiscal and monetary policies are necessary to stabilize an inherently unstable private sector or are themselves destabilizing. For example, in Section I, articles by Smith, Hines, and Minsky suggest that the private sector of the economy is not stable and requires a steadying counter-cyclical monetary and fiscal policy by the government. In contrast, in Section II the selection by Carlson and Spencer indicates that government fiscal activities might completely "crowd out" private expenditures, thereby having no impact on real aggregate demand. In Section III, articles by Humphrey and Carlson imply that government stabilization actions could not induce greater production and employment unless they were "policy surprises." In contrast, the essay by Modigliani in the same section contends that many of the major perturbations to the economy in the 1970s were not "policy surprises" but rather were "supply shocks" that should have been counteracted by active stabilization policy.

Where do we draw the line for policy activism? Between supposedly necessary response to "supply shocks" envisioned by Modigliani and presumably less useful manipulation of policy instruments to compensate for random variations in aggregate demand (considered, for example, in the article by Cacy in Section VIII)? Or between the latter and those largely destabilizing gyrations in monetary aggregates that are directed at smoothing variations in nominal interest rates (discussed in the essays by Davis, Pierce, and Lombra and Torto in Section VIII)?

The opening article of this section, by David Cobham, argues that monetary policy actions have become extremely sensitive to all sorts of actual and potential perceived "shocks" to the economy. Cobham emphasizes that the perception of and sensitivity to these shocks is fundamentally a political issue. Cobham uses this nexus to reconcile cost-push ("shock") and demand-pull (policy-induced) theories of inflation.

The second essay in this section, by Assar Lindbeck, indicates that there can be little progress made in understanding the macroeconomy until the political influences on policymaker actions are more accurately and rigorously modeled. How sensitive is the voting public to the state of the economy and the distribution of income? How compelled are incumbent politicians to cater to these sensitivities in the short run? (Will politicians risk excessive growth in monetary aggregates—and ultimately greater inflation—in the long run in order to temporarily reduce interest rates and unemployment in the short run?) Finally, how easily can incumbent politicians manipulate the central bank to produce monetary stimulation? The third essay, by Karl Brunner, speaks to several of these issues and leaves the reader with the impression that a proper understanding of the milieu in which economic policy is made demands training in history and the various social sciences as well as economics.

The Politics of the Economics of Inflation

David Cobham

31

Most work on inflation by academic economists has been addressed specifically to the economic "causes, consequences and cures" of inflation, and most economists have attempted, according to the precepts of "positive economics," to keep their own political opinions out of their economic analyses. In the nonacademic world, on the other hand, economic theories are often judged by the political viewpoint which is assumed to underlie them. Thus monetarism, for example, is widely regarded as being more conservative than Keynesianism and monetarist economics is rejected by many people on that basis. The question therefore arises, to what extent are the various economic theories of inflation related to particular political viewpoints?

One way of attempting to answer this question would be to go through large numbers of papers and articles by various economists, trying to pick out quotations indicating their political attitudes. This would be awkward, tedious and ultimately unsatisfactory because the evidence would in many cases necessarily be tendentious and any conclusions would therefore be open to all sorts of challenges.

Another way of approaching the issue would be to examine the economic views of various political figures or of those economists who have clear and stated political positions. Thus one would fairly classify Enoch Powell, Sir Keith Joseph and Milton Friedman as right of center, and conclude on that basis that monetarism was right-

Reprinted from *Lloyds Bank Review*, No. 128 (April 1978), pp. 19–32, by permission of the publisher and author.

wing. But it is not difficult to find a monetarist theory of inflation put forward by people who on any criterion must be considered to be on the left.[1] And similarly we shall find leftists putting forward what amounts to something very like a wage-push theory of inflation, yet no one would argue that Lord Barber or the Treasury were left-wing.

We have thus ruled out both detailed scrutiny of the writings of economists for indications of their politics and observation of the views on inflation of leading political figures, as ways of identifying the political character of the theories. The only other alternative is to examine each theory in order to see whether the economic mechanism of inflation logically implies a particular political position. This is the procedure followed in this article, which discusses the cost-push, monetarist and "international liquidity" theories of inflation, distinguishing between "crude" and "sophisticated" versions of the first two. Reference is made to writers supporting the various theories, but the emphasis is on the logical implications rather than the actual use to which the theories have been put. No attempt is made to distinguish between the theories on the grounds of empirical or theoretical validity: the emphasis is entirely on their political implications.

The Crude Versions

We can start with a "crude" version of the cost-push theory. According to this, prices are determined by the cost of inputs, and inflation is caused by increases in the costs of inputs. The most common political manifestation of this view is the argument that "monopolistic" trade unions cause inflation by pushing up wages through their "excessive" power in the area of collective bargaining. Clearly the politics of this argument is right-wing, since it sees organized workers as disrupting the (desirable) status quo of capitalism by using their "excessive" power in an irresponsible way which creates inflation. But the economic mechanism of this view can also be associated with a strongly left-wing position: in the editorials and letter columns of the *Morning Star,* for example, one can sometimes find a crude "profits-push" idea of inflation which is in many ways the mirror image of the "wage-push" idea put forward in many other newspapers.[2] If monopolistic companies can put up prices to restore profit margins after a wage increase, i.e., if demand is simply ignored, then they must also be able to put up prices to increase profits. Given a few simple assumptions about the reactions of workers to profit rises and the reactions of firms to pay rises, the two opposing positions would be hard to disentangle empirically.

The crude version of the monetarist theory is simply that increases in the money

---

[1]See, for example, the Marxist economists John Eaton, *Political Economy* (London: Lawrence and Wishart, 1949), p. 216; and Ernest Mandel, *Marxist Economic Theory* (London: Merlin Press, 1968), pp. 265–266.

[2]The "profits-push" view is spelt out in more detail in Emile Burns, *Inflation* (London: Lawrence and Wishart, 1967).

supply cause increases in prices. Just as the crude version of the cost-push theory ignores demand entirely and regards the actions of the "pushing" element as irresponsible and completely unnecessary in the sense that they could and should have chosen to act otherwise, so the crude version of monetarism ignores the possibility of money supply changes being reflected in movements of interest rates or real income and regards the behavior of the originators of the money supply increase as similarly irresponsible and unnecessary. The most common political context of this view is again a right-wing one: for electoral purposes governments spend too much, especially on social services and security, and therefore make the money supply grow too fast, so that inflation is the product of a combination of financial irresponsibility, political opportunism and (where governments are consciously using a disguised "inflation tax" in place of other, politically more sensitive, taxes) deliberate dishonesty. However, here again it is possible to use the economic mechanism in a different political context: electoral opportunism and financial irresponsibility can be viewed from the right as alternatives to the sound financial orthodoxy and political responsibility required to preserve and strengthen the capitalist system by creating a climate of security and confidence; but they can also be regarded from the left as alternatives to the fundamental changes in the structure of the economy and society which are necessary to create a better standard of living and quality of life for all (i.e., the introduction of socialism). And it has even been suggested on the left that inflation is a deliberate device to cut real wages:

> Keynes set himself to devise his alternative strategy for saving capitalism, elaborated in his *General Theory of Employment, Interest and Money* in 1936, to replace the method of direct wage cuts, which provoked resistance and revolt, by the method of 'a change in the quantity of money' such as would ensure 'a gradual and automatic lowering of real wages as a result of rising prices.'[3]

Sophisticated Cost-Push

The sophisticated version of the cost-push theory differs from the crude version in two main ways: first, it deals with the question of demand and the growth of the money supply by putting forward some mechanism by which the cost-push inflationary pressures themselves generate the required increase in the money supply; and, secondly, it attempts to make a serious analysis of the motivations of the "pushers" instead of resorting to name-calling as the crude version does.

It is argued that the money supply grows "automatically" as a result of government attempts to stabilize interest rates or employment at a time of cost-push inflation; as a result of unanticipated increases in the public sector borrowing requirement (due to cost-push inflation) financed by increased borrowing from the banking system rather than from the private sector; or as a result of government attempts to soften or "defuse" (temporarily at least) the "social tensions" which

[3]Editorial by R. Palme Dutt in *Labour Monthly,* August 1972.

would be produced by high unemployment, low profits and/or low business confidence. The sophisticated version of cost-push thus provides a logically consistent answer to the standard monetarist criticism that cost-push ignores demand, and this also enables it to get away from the pure mark-up theory of prices which is basic to the crude version of cost-push. A consequence of this is that the theory becomes more difficult to test since its predictions become much less precise.

The second area in which the sophisticated cost-push view differs from the crude is the attempt in the former to make a serious analysis of the reasons why the "pushers" push. It is useful here to consider specific examples. Lord Kahn, in his article in the January 1976 issue of this *Review,* puts forward the concept of "leapfrogging" as an explanation of the upward pressure on wages: different groups of workers continually compete with one another to improve their relative position. However, he does not discuss why leapfrogging occurs, except for comments on "the men who run" the TUC and CBI ("sadly lacking in intelligence") and trade union and unofficial labour leaders ("astonishing stupidity," "complete failure to take a long-sighted view") of a kind which, in terms of our distinction between crude and sophisticated versions of cost-push, makes his article fit more comfortably into the former category.

Sir John Hicks, in his article in this *Review* in October 1975, proposes a concept of "Real Wage Resistance":

> The wage-earner's test for fair wages is not simply a matter of comparison with other people's earnings; it is also a matter of comparison with his own experience, his own experience in the past. It is this which makes him resist a reduction in his money wage; but it also makes him resist a reduction in the purchasing power of his wage, and even a reduction in the growth of that purchasing power to which he has become accustomed. Thus there is a backlash of prices on wages—a Real Wage Resistance, it may be called. . . .

Sir John argues that this Real Wage Resistance will operate as a reaction to demand inflation, and that it may also be

> an independent cause of inflation: a cost inflation which is not a mere sequel to demand inflation but arises on its own. This . . . can happen, in a national economy, when the cause of the cost inflation comes in from outside.

Thus his general view of the last few years' inflation in the U.K. (the article was published in October 1975) is that the initiating cause was higher import prices and the inflation was magnified and continued by the refusal of workers to accept the resulting cut in their real wages. (This view of import-push, in which the rise in import prices is taken as given from outside, is also supported by Lord Kahn.)

Phelps Brown has produced a rather more sophisticated analysis of organized workers' behavior[4] in which emphasis is placed on "a change in the attitude of the

---

[4] "A Non-Monetarist View of the Pay Explosion," *The Three Banks Review,* March 1975.

individual employee.'' This change in the late 1960s is likened to another change of attitude said to have occurred in the period preceding the First World War, which did not however result in a "social upheaval" because of the impact of the war (replacing antagonism against the dominant social groups with antagonism against foreigners), because of the traumatic failure of the Triple Alliance and later of the General Strike, and because of the deep depression of the 1920s (in Britain at least) and 1930s. Subsequently, according to Phelps Brown, the influence of such factors was strongly reduced, in particular by the 1960s it was not within most workers' experience "that they need be restrained in pressing their claims by fear of losing their jobs. They had a new capacity for self-assertion.'' And this basic change in outlook (not just in the U.K.), combined with the "spark" of May 1968 in France, is seen as the cause of the pay explosion in the U.K. and elsewhere.

As a final example of this view we can take the OECD report of 1972.[5] This argues that there has been a "rising concern with the 'quality of life' " resulting in increased expenditure on housing, communal and leisure facilities, health and education. At the same time,

> . . . Governments seek to provide income maintenance, alleviate poverty, and carry through many other programmes designed to ensure a fair sharing of the fruits of material progress . . . of course, these things have to be paid for . . . these increasingly ambitious programmes to improve the quality of life have to be reconciled with the more directly material and market-oriented needs of individual consumers. . . . In the context of this report it is important to note that inflation is not only a symptom of unresolved tensions within the economy with highly undesirable economic, social and political consequences; it is also the mechanism by which efforts to alter the distribution of income or expenditure which are not accepted by those concerned are partially frustrated.[6]

Thus the four examples we have discussed try, some harder than others, to analyse the reasons for the "push,'' as well as locating its source. Lord Kahn and Sir John Hicks emphasize the effects of higher import prices (though these are taken as externally determined) and make some suggestions about the psychology of workers. Phelps Brown tries to analyse the development of class "antagonism" among workers over the last eighty years. The OECD stresses categories of expenditure other than private consumption in which there have been important increases and relates the increases to some changes in social attitudes and concerns. All four view the problem essentially as one of the breakdown in some way of "social order''—in Phelps Brown's words "a dissolution of consensus, a calling in question of once accepted norms and customary relativities, a debate and a struggle about shares in the national product,'' which have culminated in "an upsurge of forces that the established machinery cannot contain.'' And all four might be regarded, from the left at least, as right-wing in so far as they do not consider the relationship between inflation and the essential characteristics of the capitalist system, and do not envisage any fundamental transformation of that system.

---

[5]*Expenditure Trends in OECD Countries 1960–80,* July 1972.
[6]Op. cit., pp. 11–12.

It is of course perfectly possible to diagnose inflation as the result of a breakdown of social order, from a left-wing point of view. The difference is essentially in the attitude taken to that breakdown. For, from a left-wing point of view, the breakdown may be the inevitable product of a capitalist system in a particular stage of development. It may even be desirable, as a prelude to a social upheaval which would result in the introduction of some sort of socialism (it is however only a rather crude "leftism" which sees socialism arising out of chaos, and most leftists would repudiate the idea). But in any case this breakdown is not to the left the unfortunate, harmful or unnatural development which it is to the right.

One left-wing analysis which can be classed as sophisticated cost-push is that of Pat Devine[7] (who is certainly not a crude leftist in the sense just used). His diagnosis of inflation is close to that of the OECD (which he quotes) and that of Phelps Brown (which was written rather later but in common with which Devine stresses the effect on workers' attitudes of prolonged near-full employment in the 1950s and 1960s).[8] On the question of demand and the growth of the money supply he is much more explicit than Lord Kahn or Sir John Hicks:

> The expansion of the money supply is essentially a symptom, rather than a cause, of inflation. It is either the *result* of the state seeking to make expenditures that socio-political pressures make necessary and that these same pressures prevent from being financed by taxation or by borrowing from the private sector; or it is the *result* of the state being obliged to accommodate pressures elsewhere in the economy for fear of the socio-political consequences that would follow if it did not.

For his political analysis it is perhaps worth quoting his conclusion:

> This paper has attempted to situate the phenomenon of persistent inflation in the characteristics of modern capitalism. It has been argued that chronic inflation is a necessary feature of a social reality in which workers are impelled to struggle to realize their rising aspirations, cannot be prevented from struggling and the system cannot, necessarily cannot, meet those aspirations. Within this context it is unscientific to attempt to attribute 'blame' or 'responsibility' for inflation to different classes—workers (unions), capitalists (monopolists, multi-national firms, money lenders, speculators), landowners— or to the state. Inflation is a product of the capitalist *system* in its present stage of state monopoly capitalism.

International Liquidity

Before discussing the sophisticated version of the monetarist theory, it is convenient to take a brief look at the international liquidity theory of inflation and the

---

[7]"Inflation and Marxist Theory," *Marxism Today*, March 1974. Devine does not use the term "cost-push" to describe his theory which in the left-wing literature has come to be known as the "conflict" theory of inflation. For a brief survey of left-wing theories by another "conflict" theorist see James Harvey, "Theories of Inflation," *Marxism Today*, January 1977.

[8]He also draws on D. Jackson, H. Turner and F. Wilkinson, *Do Trades Unions Cause Inflation?* (Cambridge University Press, 1972).

monetary approach to the balance of payments with which it is associated. This approach differs from conventional monetarism in recognizing the interdependence of countries in a world of fixed exchange rates; in particular it is argued that countries' money supplies are linked through their balances of payments, and it is assumed that goods and capital markets are internationally integrated so that domestic prices and interest rates cannot diverge significantly from world levels. This assumption means that the ability of the domestic demand for money to adjust to the domestic supply of money is limited, and instead the balance of payments is seen as a mechanism by which surplus domestic money can be disposed of, or new money acquired. The policy variable is therefore domestic credit expansion (the potential increase in the money supply from domestic sources) rather than the money supply itself which, at least with fixed exchange rates, is "endogenous," i.e., determined by the demand.

On this theoretical basis the international liquidity theory of inflation sees the acceleration of inflation rates throughout the world from the late 1960s as the result of "excessive" increases in the world money supply caused by the U.S. government's decision to finance its domestic social programmes and the escalation of the Vietnam war by borrowing from the banks ("printing money"). This decision produced inflation and balance-of-payments deficits for the U.S., and therefore a double pressure on the price levels of other countries—direct influence from the dominating position in world markets of the (inflating) U.S., and indirect influence from increasing national money supplies as a result of balance-of-payments surpluses corresponding to the U.S. deficits.

The main proponents of this view (e.g., Harry Johnson)[9] have been politically conservative and have implicitly criticized U.S. policy as financially irresponsible. But this view actually fits quite easily into a left-wing analysis of rivalry between the major capitalist countries in which U.S. policy, objectively at least, represented a way of compelling the other countries to share with the U.S., through their balance-of-payments surpluses, the cost of the imperialist war in Vietnam, but evoked such opposition from countries like France that it led not merely to world inflation but also in the end to the collapse of the U.S.-dominated international monetary system worked out at Bretton Woods.

The international liquidity theory is a theory of world inflation under fixed exchange rates, with particular relevance to the acceleration of world inflation rates in the late 1960s and early 1970s. There are important differences between the "international monetarists" who use the theoretical framework of the monetary approach to the balance of payments and the more conventional monetarists who do not, but these differences are less important in analysis of a period such as the last few years when exchange rates were not fixed, and they are also relatively technical, in the sense that they do not greatly affect the political content of the views on inflation held by each kind of monetarist. For the purpose of this article it is not

---

[9]"Inflation: A 'Monetarist' View," in *Further Essays in Monetary Economics,* (London: Allen & Unwin, 1972); also *Inflation and the Monetarist Controversy* (North Holland, Amsterdam, 1972).

therefore useful to differentiate further between the two groups and we can proceed directly to discuss their common views under a single heading.

Sophisticated Monetarism

The crude monetarist view, in the distinction made in this article, ignores the impact of monetary growth on real income and interest rates and has a rather cavalier and philistine attitude to the determinants of monetary policy. The sophisticated version does not have a well-formulated theory of the division of the impact of monetary growth between real income, prices and interest rates, but this division is at least recognized as a key problem and some attempt is made to provide a plausible micro-economic foundation for the division, centered on the concepts of capacity constraints and price expectations.[10] The rate of inflation is held to be determined by excess demand and price expectations, where the latter term for the "international monetarists" at least depends partly on world inflation and the movement of the exchange rate.

Whereas the crude monetarist view attributes excessive monetary growth to governmental irresponsibility the sophisticated view starts in effect from the assumption that governments are neither stupid nor irresponsible, but (for the U.K. in particular) have not properly understood the importance of monetary growth and have therefore, in pursuit of other objectives, allowed monetary growth to be excessive. The question of the causes of inflation then requires an answer to the question of what other objectives were being followed. It is convenient to approach this question by analysing logically what objectives could have led to excessive monetary growth, referring to the views of specific economists only incidentally for purposes of illustration, and to start with the following identity:

> change in money supply for closed economy
> or domestic credit expansion for open economy
> ≡ public sector borrowing requirement (PSBR)
> − sales of public sector debt to private sector
> + bank lending to private sector.[11]

It follows from this identity that excessive monetary growth must be caused by an excessive PSBR, inadequate sales of debt to the private sector or excessive bank lending to the private sector; or by some combination of the three.

An excessive PSBR could be caused by the government yielding to political pressure of some kind to increase public expenditure without increasing taxation; or by inefficient methods of controlling public expenditure (such as the U.K. practice

---

[10]See for example Milton Friedman, "A Theoretical Framework for Monetary Analysis," *Journal of Political Economy,* 1970; also David Laidler, "Information, Money and the Macroeconomics of Inflation," *Swedish Journal of Economics,* January 1974.

[11]This is of course a simplification, but not one which is likely to be misleading for present purposes.

before 1976 of planning and controlling public expenditure in real terms only). Sales of debt to the private sector could be too low because the methods of selling government securities were technically inefficient; or because the government was trying to keep interest rates low either to stimulate industrial investment or under political pressure from owner-occupiers paying mortgages.

Bank lending to the private sector could be too high because the controls on bank lending were ineffective; or because the government wanted finance to be available for investment or for private consumption. And over-all monetary growth could be too high because the government was trying to minimize unemployment without realizing the inflationary impact of its policies.

It is possible to group these possible reasons in three categories: (1) technical factors (inefficiency in expenditure control, debt sales or control over bank advances); (2) the pursuit of short-run political popularity of a kind which could be described as electoral opportunism (some kinds of excessive public spending, maintenance of low interest rates for the benefit of owner-occupiers); and (3) sincere and responsible (but misguided) attempts to preserve and strengthen the system politically, socially or economically (the attempt to minimize the social tension resulting from mass unemployment by reducing unemployment or by some kinds of public expenditure, or the attempt to stimulate economic growth by keeping interest rates low to encourage investment).

In general, the reasons for excessive monetary growth grouped in category (2) are those stressed by the crude version of monetarism, while sophisticated monetarists tend to emphasize factors from groups (1) and (3). Parkin, in his article in the July 1975 issue of this *Review,* for example, gives a rather broad set of reasons which in terms of the distinction made here lie somewhere between crude and sophisticated:

> In general, then, it seems that we can explain the behaviour of monetary growth in terms of our attempts, both through the public sector and privately, to consume too much. The government attempts to spend more than it is prepared to tax from us and at the same time is not prepared to see interest rates move to the levels that would dissuade us from consuming and encourage us instead to buy public sector debt in sufficiently large quantities to cover the government's borrowing requirement.

A recent paper by Laidler[12] on the other hand deals in detail with the determinants of monetary policy in the U.K. from the 1971–72 reflation to the end of 1975, and stresses in particular the entirely cost-push theory of inflation on which the Conservative government's policy was based; the hope that expansion would fulfil "the very expectations of rising incomes the frustration of which, in conditions of slow growth, was supposed to be the main cause of inflation"; and technical problems in the control of public expenditure. His analysis is clearly a sophisticated one.

As they are reported here, it is not obvious that either of these papers is right-wing, nor is it obvious that any of the reaons in categories (1) and (3) above could

---

[12]"Inflation in Britain: A Monetarist Perspective," *American Economic Review,* September 1976.

not be accepted by a leftist—in particular a belief in the technical inefficiency of the Treasury and the Bank of England has long been a strand in left-wing economic thought, and the emphasis on growth fits neatly into a left-wing analysis of the inefficiency and "bankruptcy" of British capitalism, in which the growth rate is so low that the government has to try anything to raise it, but the economy still does not respond. So why is it that monetarism is so commonly thought of as right-wing?

The beginnings of an answer are provided, curiously enough, by a recent criticism of Milton Friedman made by Samuel Brittan, himself a monetarist journalist who could hardly be described as left-wing. In an "open letter" to Friedman in the *Financial Times* (December 2, 1976) Brittan criticized him for not distinguishing between "Friedmanite economics and the personal opinions of Professor Milton Friedman," on the grounds that

> Your eminence as an economist does not deprive you of your right to express your views as a citizen on wider topics—still less on those grey areas which are halfway between academic analysis and personal opinion. But there is a danger that your strong expression of what is purely speculative or personal may discredit the more securely established parts of your analysis.

In other words Friedman's economics do not logically imply his politics: monetarists do not have to

> denounce the whole welfare state . . . or . . . suggest that the developments of the last 70 years in Britain and Chile alike have been predominantly in the wrong direction.

But it can be taken a lot further than this. Just as Friedman's economics can be separated to some extent from his politics, so the monetarist theory of inflation can be separated from and does not logically require acceptance of other theories which are elements in the thinking of a large number of economists whose views on inflation can be classified as monetarist. Some of the latter may for example use marginal productivity theory to determine real wages, and this theory, in so far as it is interpreted as providing a justification for profits and a repudiation of any concept of exploitation of labour by capital, is normally thought of as right-wing. Some monetarists use the Walrasian equations of general equilibrium in their models to determine the real growth rate, and these equations are also generally considered as right-wing because they depict an automatically adjusting capitalist system free of class struggle and exploitation. But it is perfectly possible to accept the monetarist theory of inflation without accepting marginal productivity theory or Walrasian general equilibrium theory. In fact it is possible to have a "balance of power"/bargaining approach to the determination of wages together with a monetarist view of price determination.[13] Similarly, neither assumptions about the ability of a capitalist economy always to return to a full-employment equilibrium

---

[13]Since Phelps Brown's article cited above is actually about the *pay* explosion not the price explosion, it is possible to agree with most of what he says while maintaining a monetarist view of price inflation.

nor assumptions about the structure of financial incentives and the "taxable capacity" of a community are germane to the (fundamentally *macroeconomic*) monetarist theory of inflation.

More closely associated with monetarist thinking on inflation is a view of the economy as adjusting to disturbances with lags which are not known and may well be variable and unpredictable so that the economy is basically difficult to control. This view is again not necessary to the monetarist theory of inflation: the latter requires *some* transmission mechanism between monetary growth and the level of aggregate demand, but this could equally well be a quite predictable interest-sensitivity of at least some expenditure. However, even if the monetarist theory of inflation required such a view, the political complexion of monetarism would still not be obvious. The unpredictability of the economy suggests a presumption against an active "fine-tuning" policy of demand management. It is obvious how such a bias against active state intervention in the economy is consistent with a laissez-faire right-wing position. But it is also consistent with a traditional left-wing view of the capitalist economy as prone to uncontrollable cycles and crises, for as argued above the monetarist theory of inflation does not require the neo-classical assumption about the self-equilibrating capacity of a capitalist economy. Yet if monetarism implies less state intervention, surely it is right-wing? This brings us up against a problem which has so far in this paper been avoided, namely the question of the definition of "left" and "right." It is a problem over which there is considerable disagreement, which cannot for reasons of space be discussed here. Instead we will consider some alternative definitions and use them to summarize our main conclusions. But first it is worth reviewing the distinction made in this paper between crude and sophisticated versions of cost-push and monetarism.

Conclusions

In each case the distinction rests on two points, one economic and one political: crude cost-push is distinguished by its neglect of demand and its stigmatization of the "pushers" as acting in an irresponsible and unnecessary way (in the sense that they could and should have chosen to act otherwise); while crude monetarism is distinguished by its neglect of the income and interest-rate effects of monetary expansion and its stigmatization of the government's actions as irresponsible and unnecessary. And in each case the two points go together: it is only by neglecting demand, i.e. by neglecting the response of the government, that crude cost-push is able to identify trade unionists as the sole cause of inflation; and crude monetarism can similarly identify government irresponsibility only by excluding with its initial assumptions the possibility that the government might have any "responsible" objectives behind its monetary expansion, such as reducing unemployment or promoting growth. The point of the distinction then is to show that gross over-simplifications of economic and political reality are necessary to produce a theory of inflation which puts all the blame unequivocally on one particular social group (or the government) and ignores the complex interaction of the various groups (and the government) which make up a social totality. The left/right political implications of the crude versions have been adequately discussed above. Here we can merely note that appropriate variations in the economic mechanism (who are the pushers?) or the attitude to government (financial irresponsibility instead of what?) enable different political implications to be derived, and pass on to the sophisticated versions and the problem of the definition of "left" and "right."

If left and right are defined as anti- and pro-capitalist then the economic mechanisms of inflation discussed in the sophisticated versions are politically neutral: you can be a left-wing monetarist or anti-monetarist, or a right-wing monetarist or anti-monetarist. But left and right are sometimes defined in terms of for and against more "state intervention" in the economy. If "state intervention" refers to the size of the public sector, then again the mechanisms of inflation are politically neutral: monetary growth may be related to the PSBR but it does not depend on the level of public expenditure itself or on the share of the nationalized industries in total output. If however "state intervention" refers to intervention in the workings of the "free" market by fine tuning and direct price and income controls, then monetarism turns out to be politically right-wing, and cost-push left-wing. But this is a definition which makes Paul Samuelson, Edward Heath and the Bank of England, and even Richard Nixon in his time, into leftists. The point is that the two meanings of "state intervention" do not go together. There is no necessary relationship between the desired size of the public sector and the desired degree of demand-management and direct controls: it is, for example, quite possible to favour "fine-tuning" and denationalization at the same time. It therefore seems sensible to reject altogether this definition of left and right; in which case the general conclusion stands, that the economic mechanisms of inflation are politically neutral: it is not your monetarism or your anti-monetarism, but what you do with it, that is determined by your politics.

Stabilization Policy in Open Economies with Endogenous Politicians

Assar Lindbeck

32

The Political System: Endogenous Politicians

. . . It is obvious that macroeconomic fluctuations today are so intimately connected with government policies that realistic explanations and forecasts of macroeconomic fluctuations require that government behavior be analyzed as an integral part of the fluctuations. For instance, it seems that the differences between various short-term economic forecasts today depend less on divergent views on the functioning of the private sector than on different assumptions about the future economic policy. An important aspect of such assumptions is various hypotheses as to how governments most likely will react to future economic events. This means that it is useful to treat the government as an *endogenous* rather than an exogenous variable in the macroeconomic system.

Political Behavior Functions

Granting the need to "endogenize" politicians, it is obvious that this can be achieved in several alternative ways. One approach to the positive theory of political behavior is to assume that politicians are well informed and idealistic "guardians of the general good" (as defined, perhaps, by the ideology of the government). This

Reprinted, with deletions, from *American Economic Review,* Vol. 66, No. 2 (May 1976), pp. 10–19, by permission of the publisher and author.

would mean that the *normative* behavior functions derived from the welfare theory of economic policy—as developed by Tinbergen, James E. Meade and others—would be interpreted also as *positive* behavior functions of politicians.

An alternative approach to the theory of political behavior is to take the opposite position and assume, like Anthony Downs, that politicians are concerned with their own welfare, obtained by seizing and staying in power, rather than with the welfare of society as a whole. More specifically, a politician in a democracy is then, to quote Downs, regarded as "an entrepreneur selling policies for votes instead of products for money" (Downs, p. 137). Analytically, behavior functions for politicians could then be derived by replacing an "idealistic" preference function of politicians à la Tinbergen-Meade with a vote-getting function, which is maximized subject to the constraints defined by the trade-off possibilities between the various vote-creating variables.

A more "eclectic," and I think more realistic, approach would be to combine the idealistic and the popularity approaches, with the relative weights between the idealistic variables and the popularity variable changing systematically over time during the course of an election period—the popularity variable gaining weight relative to the idealistic variables when an election day is approached, which would mean that the Downs theory would be approached when the election comes closer. In an explicitly intertemporal model we could, with some exaggeration, say that as the time to the election approaches zero, the discount rate for the future economic variables goes to infinity. Every government wants, of course, to believe that this type of behavior coincides with what is "the general good for society as a whole" *in the long run.*

On the basis of this eclectic approach to the theory of economic policy behavior, three sets of relations have to be specified: (1) the properties of the asserted target-preference function of the government, i.e., a specification of both the idealistic and the popularity variables in the function, and their relative weights at different points of time; (2) a specification of how the popularity variable is influenced; and finally (3) a specification of the economic constraints within which the maximization of the target-preference function is supposed to take place, in particular a description of how the government can influence the economy. (For approaches along these lines, see for instance Frey-Lau; Lindbeck 1973).

Endogenous Stabilization Policy

When *stabilization policy* is discussed, it is probably important to include in the target-preference function at least four "idealistic" variables, each one characterized by falling marginal utility, or rising marginal disutility: real disposable income of households, unemployment, inflation, and the current account of the balance of payments (or the stock of reserves)—and most likely also the rate of change of these variables. When choosing an appropriate popularity variable in the preference function, several alternatives are possible. An expression for party sympathies among the electorate is perhaps a reasonable variable, operationally defined for instance as "sympathy" answers to Gallup polls.

It is likely that the popularity variable is influenced by approximately the same variables as we have chosen to treat as idealistic variables in the target-preference function, though possibly with different weights and different timing. In particular, I will make two assumptions which make a preference function that includes both idealistic variables and a popularity variable differ substantially from one which includes only the idealistic variables: (1) *Recent* events are assumed to be considerably more important for the popularity of the government than events long ago—an assumption about a "short memory" of voters. (2) The electorate is assumed to have very imperfect knowledge about the *future* effects of policy actions, such as effects that emerge after the next election.

That voters are interested in their real income and possibly its rate of change is, of course, consistent with conventional micro theory of household behavior. Moreover, a number of empirical studies indicate that governments tend to gain popularity in periods of prosperity and rising real income and lose it in periods of depression and falling (or only slowly rising) real income (Kramer; Åkerman).[1] Considering the important role, in the political discussion after the Second World War, of inflation, unemployment, and the current account of the balance of payments (or possibly the level of exchange reserves), and their rates of change, we should also expect these variables to be important for the popularity of a government. In fact, several empirical studies suggest that this is the case (Lepper; Nordhaus).

On the basis of these assumptions, we would expect two characteristic features of government behavior over the cycle.

First, due to the assumption of increasing marginal disutility of inflation, unemployment, and current account deficits, we would expect shifting emphasis on the various macroeconomic policy targets as these variables happen to change themselves due to exogenous disturbances—even without consideration of the popularity variable and also without having to assume any shift in the target-preference function. Inflation, current account (or balance-of-payments) deficits, and unemployment will succeed each other as "the Enemy Number One of the Country," thus generating a stop-go policy cycle in response to factual events.

Secondly, as soon as we also take account of the popularity variable in the target-preference function, we would expect that the closer we are to an election, the more inclined the government is to take expansionary actions. This conclusion follows already from the introduction of real disposable income, and/or its rate of change, in the popularity function, because of the ease and speed by which governments can "buy" popularity, and hence votes, simply by raising temporarily real disposable incomes of households *directly*—by way of tax cuts and increases in transfers and

---

[1]There is an identification problem here, however, in countries where the government can choose election time: elections may be held in periods of rising real disposable income, rather than the other way around. Or both may have been deliberately influenced by the government.

public consumption. The inference that expansionary tax and expenditure measures undertaken to boost disposable incomes of households tend to be large and frequent immediately before elections is, in fact, quite well confirmed by empirical data. For instance, Edward Tufte found in a multi-country study that disposable income usually has tended to go up immediately before elections—in fact in 21 out of 26 democracies studied (Tufte). In many cases, these increases were brought about by fiscal policy measures with a direct impact on real disposable income.

The other macroeconomic variables—inflation, unemployment and the current account—are much more difficult to manipulate by the government. However, let us assume that the government thinks, quite realistically, that it can expand output, at least for a while, by increasing excess demand for commodities and labor, and that the rate of inflation goes up *significantly* only after a time lag. In other words, it is assumed that an expansion of aggregate demand, to begin with, generates a movement up along a given short-term Phillips curve and that an upward shift of the curve will only occur later, if at all. These considerations further strengthen the conclusion that expansionary policy actions should be expected immediately before elections in order to reach a point as close as possible to the origin in a three-dimensional diagram with inflation, unemployment and the current account deficit on the three axes.

The model also predicts that the government will usually cut back aggregate demand after the election in order to bring down the rate of inflation, to squeeze out inflationary expectations and hence to shift down the short-term Phillips curve, as well as to reduce the deficits in the current account, well in time before the next election, so that new expansionary actions can be undertaken again before that election without immediately running into high inflation and a large current account deficit. The experiences of recent years have shown how high the economic and social costs are during this deflationary phase of the policy cycle.

This type of behavior would *contribute to,* though not necessarily generate, "clockwise loops" in a conventional price-Phillips-curve diagram, with the timing, in calendar time, of the loops influenced by the attempts of the authorities to reach positions on these loops as close as possible to the origin during the months immediately before election. Tendencies to such loops can, in fact, be noticed in several countries during the last decade (Grossman; Lindbeck 1975; Nordhaus).

Thus, when the responsibility for macroeconomic stability is relegated to the politicians, it is unavoidable that the interpretation and the implementation of this responsibility become strongly colored by the specific features of the political system, in particular by short-term vote-getting considerations, and that the business cycle therefore becomes a mixture of economic and political forces interacting with each other.

Of course, it is possible to reach more specific conclusions about the timing of these loops if the model is specified in more detail. For instance, it is not only conceivable but likely that the general public is more concerned with the *rate of change* than with the *level* of unemployment, at least as long as the level is not higher than has usually been the case during the postwar period. The reason is that a moderate level of unemployment only hits a small fraction of the population, whereas *increasing* unemployment creates lower job security for a considerable fraction of the population. There is, in fact, some empirical evidence for this in the sense that election outcomes seem to be more sensitive to the *change* than to the *level* of unemployment (Lepper).

If this is a correct hypothesis, and if it is also understood by the politicians, we would expect that the government is satisfied just to have passed "the lower turning point" of the inflation-unemployment loop shortly before an election, in order to reach, before the election, a situation with *falling* unemployment and still relatively modest inflation. On the basis of this theory, it is natural that the governments in the United States and West Germany waited so long to take expansionary actions in the 1974–75 stagflation period in view of the fact that the next election in both countries will not occur until the fall of 1976.

Many open economies also show a macroeconomic development pattern where a rapid increase in unit labor costs results for a while in squeezed profits and lagging investment and employment in the tradable sector, as well as a reallocation of resources to the nontradable sector, largely in fact to the public sector. After a while, a devaluation, or possibly a slowing down of wage inflation by way of a more restrictive economic policy, restores profits and investment incentives in the tradable sector, possibly followed by a new phase of falling profits, etc. Thereby a second type of political-economic cycle is superposed upon the short-term business cycle: a profit-investment-devaluation-demand management cycle, usually with a longer periodicity than the ordinary business cycle. We find such a cycle in several countries, such as the United Kingdom, Denmark, Finland, as well as in many LDCs.

Implications of Endogenous Policy

In reality we would expect that the control by the authorities of the business cycle is very imperfect, judged from the point of view of both the idealistic and the popularity variables. The earlier mentioned loops in inflation-unemployment space would therefore be expected to be rather irregular. There are several reasons for this: (1) the high frequency of exogenous shocks that continuously hit the economy, for instance from international sources; (2) the limited understanding among politicians and their advisers of the functioning of the very complex macroeconomic system; (3) the "imperfections" in the political-administrative system, including the celebrated "policy lags"—recognition lags, decision lags, and effect lags; and (4) the delicate balancing of the interests and opinions of various organizations which challenge the authority of the national government and often succeed in modifying both the actions of governments and the effects of such action.

All this put obvious limits on the possibilities of a successful fine tuning of the mixed economic and political business cycle.

In the context of this model—with a complicated interaction between markets and policies—it is not downward flexibility of the price and wage *level* that is important for the employment level, but rather the flexibility downwards in the *rate of change* in wages and prices. Moreover, it is not mainly the *automatic* effects of price and wage changes on private behavior, such as on demand for commodities and labor—

via real wages, interest rates and real balances—that is important, but the effects of such flexibility on *government behavior.*

More specifically, the more sensitive downwards the rate of price change is to reductions in aggregate demand, the shorter are the periods of unemployment that are necessary. In other words, the lengths of the "stop" periods in the go-stop cycles would be expected to be inversely related to the degree of downward flexibility of the rate of inflation. Hence, it is crucial for economic stability that institutional changes are brought about which make the rate of wage and price increases *more sensitive downward* in reductions in capacity utilization—as well as, of course, *less sensitive upward* to increased capacity utilization. Thus, the lag between quantity and price changes is both a prerequisite for the contemporary "political business cycle" and a reason for the duration of the stagflation periods.

Unfortunately, it is not very clear how such policies and institutional reforms could be brought about. In the case of commodity markets, increased competition, including international competition, and public studies on price setting behavior are often mentioned as potentially useful reforms (though such reforms may increase price flexibility *upward* as well, at very high levels of capacity utilization). Personally I would not object to the breaking up of some large corporations into somewhat smaller units. In the case of the labor market, increased competition, by way of a drastically reduced role of labor unions for wage formation, is hardly a feasible strategy in most countries—in view of the political role of labor unions. However, an increased understanding in society that aggressive wage policies and rigidity of relative wages in fact create and prolong unemployment periods could certainly help. It is perhaps too much to hope that governments would be able to limit inflationary wage increases by *announcing* before wage bargaining that aggregate demand in money terms will only be allowed to increase by a certain limited amount—though the West German government seems to have done just about that on some occasions, with considerable success.

It is very unfortunate that we economists are so empty-handed on this strategic issue in stabilization policy concerning institutional reforms that make the rate of price increase less sensitive upward and more sensitive downward to variations in capacity utilization.

Endogenous Targets and Instruments

A changing relative emphasis over time of the various target variables has been analyzed here as movements along a given preference function, with a given set of policy instruments, rather than as shifts in this function. A more general approach would also include as endogenous elements in the analysis (1) shifts in the evaluation of the target variables and (2) the development of new policy tools.[2]

---

[2]Changes in the tradeoff possibilities can, of course, also have fundamental consequences for such "shifts of emphasis." For instance, governments have often reacted to increased frictional or structural unemployment (with large elements of "voluntary unemployment") by further increasing aggregate demand—also when the frictional or structural changes are in fact caused by the government itself, for instance via more liberal rules for unemployment benefits.

One hypothesis along the first line would be that "policy successes" for a certain target variable create a tendency among politicians to raise the level of aspiration for this specific policy target. An obvious example is the increasingly ambitious formulations of the "full employment" target in many countries during the 1950s and 1960s when employment policy was very successful. Politicians started to argue that a low general level of employment was not enough, and also that "remaining pockets" of unemployment for specific regions, branches, and types of labor should be removed, thus making the unemployment target more and more differentiated.

Moreover, from the mid-1960s the tolerance for inflation increased in most countries along with the failures to achieve price stability; a rate of inflation characteristic of the peaks of previous booms became more and more regarded as minimum achievable "low points." Similarly, the failures in full employment policy during the international recession of 1974–75 seemed to have lowered dramatically the ambitions of full employment policies; levels that only recently were regarded as "politically impossible" were after a while regarded as levels to strive for, when the observed rates were much higher.

Thus, adjustments in the political aspiration level seem to work in both directions—raising aspirations as a response to success, and reducing aspirations as a response to failures—rather similar to the "psychological" analysis of household behavior by "the Katona school," and the analysis of "satisfying behavior" of firms by "the Carnegie school."

Moreover, both the successes and the failures of stabilization policy seem to stimulate a search for new policy tools. For instance, the early successes of broad full employment policies, and therewith connected increasingly ambitious full employment targets, made politicians develop new policy tools designed to deal with the new more ambitious targets, such as selective subsidies and retraining programs to remove pockets of unemployment in specific regions and branches of industry, and for specific groups of employees such as married women, minority groups, the handicapped, etc. Similarly, the striking policy failures in many countries with respect to price stability and balance-of-payments equilibrium in the early 1970s generated a search for a whole new set of policy tools or the restoration of tools which had not been used for a long time—such as price and wage controls, new types of selective taxes and subsidies, and various tools designed to create barriers between domestic and foreign asset markets.

The general conclusion would be that whereas success and failure with a policy target seem to change the level of aspiration up *or* down in response to successes and failures, respectively, both successes and failures seem to generate a search for new policy tools. The result is a gradual proliferation of new policy tools.[3]

These observations provide additional examples of the importance of endogenizing the behavior of politicians. . . .

---

[3]These generalizations probably have exceptions. After a period of particularly large policy failures, it is conceivable that the policy ambitions are lowered so much that fewer policy tools than earlier are necessary.

Concluding Remarks

In view of the experiences of economic policy so far, a *pessimist* or a *cynic* may even be tempted to say that the most severe difficulties of economic policy are imbedded in the political rather than in the economic system and that the main obstacle for a successful stabilization policy is, in fact, the government itself. Consequently, the best thing to do would be to avoid discretionary policies altogether rather than trying to make the interventions more sophisticated. He (she) can, of course, support this position by the reasonable assertion that the really dramatic macroeconomic disturbances during the last decade, and perhaps earlier as well, have been the result of government policies, rather than of instabilities in private behavior. In particular, it is difficult to avoid the empirical generalization that inflationary policies followed by restrictive, unemployment-creating actions have been a dominant macroeconomic feature. . . .

However, the main message of the lecture has probably been that as we have two interacting systems, the political and the economic, we cannot control one with the other, but we must try to redesign them *both* to improve the stability of each. Most of my suggestions here for such redesigns have referred to the "intersection" of the two systems, as reflected by the policy instruments. . . .

It is even more difficult to suggest changes in the *political system* that would improve macroeconomic stability and in particular make politicians follow what perhaps should be the Eleventh Commandment: "Thou shalt not *start* inflating!" However, features that may be singled out for consideration of reform are:

1. the length of the election period, and the authority of the government to decide the time of election;[4]

2. the choice between one-party government (or small coalitions) and broad coalitions for the purpose of limiting the "misuse" of short-term stabilization policy as an element in party-political competition;

3. experiments with "depoliticization" of some policy agencies, such as the central bank;

4. a more liberal use of discretionary powers of the cabinet without previous consent of parliament;

5. a more critical attitude by economists, and citizens in general, to attempts by governments to buy votes by way of nonsustainable expansions;

6. a new assignment of policy instruments and responsibilities between local, national, and international authorities.

The last point is perhaps the most important one. In particular, it is rather clear that the internationalization of the economic system during the post-World War II period has, in principle, considerably reduced the comparative advantage of the

---

[4]For instance, a theoretical possibility would be to let the exact time of elections be determined by a random process.

national government, relative to international coordination and to supernational organizations, in the field of stabilization policy. A good example is the need to control the supply of international credit, money, and liquidity. Another example is provided by the 1974–75 recession, when all countries seemed to hope for an export-led expansion, generated by expansionary policies in *other* countries!

To summarize, a solution of the problem of macroeconomic stability probably requires not only new and more elaborate policy instruments, as discussed above, but also some redesigning of both the economic and the political system—though, of course, without risking the two basic pillars of Western pluralism: the market system and political democracy. The present "crisis" in the Western economies is not, I think, mainly a "crisis in economics," though we economists have no doubt overestimated the stability of macroeconometric behavior functions. The main problem is not that we are unable to understand analytically what is happening, but rather that the institutional changes and the discretionary policies that are necessary for macroeconomic stability seem to be politically difficult to implement.

BIBLIOGRAPHY

ÅKERMAN, J. "Political Economic Cycles." *Kyklos* 1 (1947), pp. 107–17.

AUKRUST, O. "Inflation in the Open Economy." The Central Bureau of Statistics of Norway, 1974. Mimeo.

CALMFORS, L. and E. LUNDBERG. Inflation och arbetslöshet. Stockholm, 1974.

DOWNS, A. "An Economic Theory of Political Action in a Democracy." *Journal of Political Economy* 65 (April 1957), pp. 135–50.

EDGREN, G., K. O. FAXEN, and C. E. ODHNER. *Wage Formation and the Economy*. London, 1973.

FREY, B., and L. J. LAU. "Towards a Mathematical Model of Government Behaviour." *Zeitschrift für Nationalökonomie* 28 (December 1968), pp. 355–80.

GROSSMAN, H. I. "The Cyclical Pattern of Unemployment and Wage Inflation." *Economica* 41 (November 1974), pp. 403–13.

KOURI, P. J. K. "The Exchange Rate and the Balance of Payments in the Short Run and in the Long Run: A Monetary Approach." *Scandinavian Journal of Economics* 78, No. 2 (1976).

KRAMER, G. H. "Short-Term Fluctuations in U.S. Voting Behavior, 1896–1964." *American Political Science Review* 65 (March 1971), pp. 131–43.

LEPPER, S. J. "Voting Behavior and Aggregate Policy Targets." *Public Choice* 18 (Summer 1974), pp. 67–81.

LINDBECK, A. *A Study in Monetary Analysis*. Stockholm, 1963.

———. "Endogenous Politicians and the Theory of Economic Policy." Seminar paper no. 35. Institute for International Economic Studies, University of Stockholm, 1973.

———. "Is Stabilization Policy Possible? Time-lags and Conflicts of Goals." In W. L. Smith and J. M. Culbertson, eds. *Public Finance and Stabilization Policy,* pp. 269–300. Amsterdam, 1974. (Also Reprint No. 34, Institute for International Economic Studies, University of Stockholm.)

————. "Business Cycles, Politics and International Economic Dependence." *Skandinaviska Enskilda Banken Quarterly Review,* No. 2 (1975), pp. 53–68. (Also Reprint No. 39, Institute for International Economic Studies, University of Stockholm.)

NORDHAUS, W. D. "The Political Business Cycle." *Review of Economic Studies* 42 (April 1975), pp. 169–90.

REHN, G. "Some Thoughts on Employment Policy in the OECD Area during 1975 and Later Years." 1975. Mimeo.

TUFTE, E. R. "The Political Manipulation of the Economy: Influence of the Electoral Cycle on Macroeconomic Performance and Policy." Department of Politics, Princeton University, Sept. 1974. Mimeo.

Commentary on Monetary Economics

Karl Brunner

33

For many years you have been regarded as one of the leading advocates of a strict 'monetary' approach to economic policy. Together with Professor Meltzer you have played a leading part in bringing the monetarist approach to a wider public, both through the Shadow Open Market Committee in the United States and in the past two years in Europe through the Shadow European Economic Policy Committee (SEEPC). How much progress has been made in persuading public opinion of the merits of monetarism?

Economic policy covers a wide range of measures and the proper role of monetary policy should be clearly recognised. Public opinion occasionally interprets "monetarism" as a view attributing to money and monetary policy an all-embracing power. This involves a serious misconception. Monetarist analysis essentially emphasises two aspects of the range of policy problems: the relation between monetary growth and the basic rate of inflation, and the relation between monetary acceleration (or unanticipated monetary growth) and temporary changes in output and employment. The first relation determines monetarist propositions about anti-inflationary policies. The second relation determines, on the other hand, proposals bearing on a stable and predictable course of monetary policy. Monetarist analysis implies moreover that monetary manipulation cannot raise the trend of real growth.

Reprinted from *The Banker,* July 1978, by permission of the author and publisher.

Neither is monetary expansion a useful device under current circumstances to raise investment expenditures. The falling trend of real growth and investment expenditures is probably dominated by the persistent erosion of the "rules of the game" required for a well-functioning market economy. The pervasive uncertainty about economic policy and the gradual attrition of property rights lower real growth and raise the normal level of unemployment. This trend is reinforced by many governmental measures which affect relative wages and prices.

It often seems as if public opinion is largely on the side of the monetarists now while public policy continues to be inflationary. How do you explain this?

I doubt that a major portion of "public opinion" fully accepts the monetarist perspective in matters bearing on monetary policy and monetary events. The English establishment, including the media, cling, with a few exceptions, to the ancient Keynesian story. But let us consider the position of the bureaucracies and officials involved in the formulation and execution of monetary policy. They will find no reason to change their accustomed conceptions and procedures in the absence of serious costs or dangers to their position. The bureaucracies and policy institutions have a strong incentive to persist with their established pattern. The consequence of their misjudgments are usually borne by others. Changes in the conceptions governing an established institution usually require a major crisis, which encourages probing questions and a wide-ranging public debate, combined with a change in the management of the bureaucracy.

How would you sum up the present state of the debate?

Indeed, the discussion continues, It continues in scholarly journals and in the arena of public debate. But it is important to understand that the nature of the discussion has gradually shifted over the years. Substantial propositions originally advanced by monetarist analysis have been incorporated into professional thinking in the United States. Keynesian analysis still thrives on the other hand, even in archaic forms, in Germany and England. The meshing of ideas occurring between centres of active research has, however, unavoidably shifted the focus of the relevant issues over the past years. Three problems have, in my judgment, emerged from recent debates with a force requiring future attention by scholars. These problems are:

1. the possibility and usefulness of an activist approach to policy based on optimal control techniques;
2. the relative stability of the private and government sector;
3. the relevant perspective bearing on the behaviour of the government sector.

A neo-Keynesian position asserts the potential of optimal control techniques and an activist approach to policy-making. The Keynesian tradition also asserts the need for a stabilising government sector to contain or offset the inherent instability of the private sector. Lastly, this tradition reflects a conception of government expressed by the "public interest" or "goodwill" theory of government behaviour. This theory assumes that bureaucracies and politicians in general attempt to maximise social welfare. The alternative position rejects this neo-Keynesian perspective. It emphasises, in particular, that optimal control techniques and activism are likely to create instabilities in the economic process. It also stresses the basic stability of the private sector confronting a de-stabilising public sector. This destabilisation is linked to an analysis centered on the *entrepreneurial* behaviour of bureaucracies and politicians. This analysis rejects the "public interest" theory of government frequently used in discussions of stabilisation policy.

Why does it seem to have so strong a grip on policymakers? Or to put the question in other terms: Why do governments inflate when there are no benefits to be derived from such action?

Is it really so? We need to look more carefully. The apparent intractability of inflation cannot be explained in terms of the linkages and interactions of the economic process. A radical and sustained reduction of monetary growth below a critical benchmark level determined by a country's institutional environment would effectively remove over time any inflation. The relevant question should thus be addressed to central banks, treasuries and beyond to the nature of the political process shaping the behaviour of these institutions.

Three major channels have unleased over the past 12 years in various countries excessive rates of monetary growth. One channel works *via* large and persistent government deficits and corresponding pressures on the central bank to finance the deficit. Italy offers a classic example in this respect. Major groups, including the bureaucracy, find it advantageous to expand the budget. This behaviour is motivated by the wealth transfers produced with the expansion of the budget.

Another channel functions *via* large and increasing loans made directly or indirectly by central banks to commercial banks. Such loan expansion accelerates the monetary base and ultimately raises monetary growth rates. There emerges under the circumstances an apparently uncontrollable monetary growth. But this uncontrollability essentially results from the central bank's unwillingness, or political inability, to adjust the interest rate charged on central bank accommodation to the realities of the market place. France and Belgium offer some useful illustration in this context. The crucial link in the inflationary process under the circumstances is the political liability burdening the central bank's interest rate policies. And these liabilities reflect again implicit wealth transfers motivating the political constraints.

Lastly, determined efforts to maintain an undervalued exchange rate produce extensive interventions on the foreign exchange markets. These interventions are converted *via* an acceleration of the monetary base into "uncontrollable" rates of monetary growth. Maintenance of an undervalued exchange rate involves an abdication of monetary control. Domestic monetary growth is necessarily tied in this case to the inflationary policies of the leading nations. This policy reflects usually, the evident interests of major export industries. Involves again an implicit transfer of wealth, and it is this which lies behind the political pattern we observe.

So what are the fundamental mistakes made by those with whom you disagree?

Let us take the OECD as an illustrative example. The OECD vigorously preaches activist financial expansionism as a solution to the major problems of unemployment and low growth. It is caught in old conceptions and its bureaucracy seems unable to open a meaningful discussion of newer scientific developments. The measured rates of unemployment and sagging investment expenditures that have been recorded in recent years do not reflect a "deficient aggregate demand problem" of the nature experienced in the 1930s. The role of supply factors and the effect of institutions and policies on incentives to work and to invest, are basic factors not sufficiently recognised in traditional "Keynesian" conceptions of the world.

Do you think that price stability is the only economic objective a government should have?

Hardly. It is an important objective, but the government's essential function should be to provide a stable and predictable framework for the rules of the social game. This will never satisfy the social activist however. But I urge you to consider that social activism tends to produce institutions which lower our living standards and, ultimately, *via* a persistent growth of government, endanger our freedom.

Is it a fundamental assumption of your position that the real economy is inherently self-stabilising?

Yes. The Keynesian tradition proceeded on the view that the market system is inherently unstable or prone to settle, whenever left alone, around activity levels substantially below "potential output." This perspective, supplemented with the "public interest theory" of government, explains the activist approach to "stabilisation policy." We contend on the other hand that the market system is a shock-absorbing and self-regulating system with built-in stabilising properties. We also contend that the problem can be approached beyond metaphysics and ideology as an issue to be assessed by proper procedures of empirical examination.

A soft version of monetarism would allow the authorities to use fiscal policy in a discretionary manner, to offset swings in the business cycle, whilst insisting that they finance any budget deficits in a non-inflationary way. You, however, believe in balanced budgets. Why?

This kind of "soft monetarism" offers no adequate solution. It encourages actually the bad patterns inherited from the past. It implicitly assumes that the "government" attends to the public interest and can be relied upon to adjust the budget according to "the needs of stabilisation policies." This seems to be somewhat naive in our judgment. The political process increasingly produces a persistent deficit and larger budgets in the absence of well understood and widely accepted constitutional rules confining the government's fiscal operation. Moreover, a persistent deficit lowers the likelihood of proper monetary control.

It is often said that monetarists are good at laying down the ground-rules for some ultimate state where a monetary rule can be applied, but not at describing how we get there from the present. Is there force in this criticism?

None whatsoever. The assertion depends essentially on a tacit constraint imposed on monetarist proposals designed to move the economy towards a non-inflationary growth path. Our opposition claims that no anti-inflationary policies be admitted which lower temporarily employment and output. Such a condition rules out any meaningful anti-inflationary campaign. This is not because we desire lower employment and output. We desire to stabilise the economy around a stable price level and this requires, at this stage, a persistent reduction of monetary growth. This reduction, unfortunately, may produce a temporary decline of employment and output. The likelihood of this result increases with the length, magnitude and variability of the inflationary episode. But the fact remains that there is no other way to control inflation. I should also mention that the Shadow Open Market Committee in the United States and the Shadow European Economic Committee have repeatedly stated the policies required for the transition period.

A new term has recently crept into the discussion of economic policy, after "crowding out." This is "the wedge." Could you explain what this is?

"The wedge" refers to the widening gap between the cost to the employer of employing a unit of labour and the net wage received by the employee. This wedge affects various aspects of unemployment inaccessible to manipulation by aggregate demand. It is remarkable how frequently governments, as recently in England and Sweden, cope with labour market or budget problems with measures which increase the size of the wedge and thus intensify labour market problems. An increase in the wedge lowers employment and lengthens the average duration of unemployment.

Another common criticism of monetarism is that it sacrifices all other objectives of policy to that of achieving price stability. For instance, to attain price stability interest rates might have to go to such a level as to damage investment. How do you answer that criticism?

The issue is simply this: the social cost of persistent inflation exceeds, in our judgment, the social cost of a once-and-for-all return to a stable price level. Persistent inflation does not proceed in the pleasing fashion of a smooth and fully anticipated path involving fully-adjusted institutions and behaviour. It is an erratic process with large uncertainties generating large variations in real growth and a comparatively high level of normal unemployment. The road leading out of inflation is costly and unpleasant indeed, but the alternative is much worse. And as to interest rates, even politicians learn on occasion that the best way to lower interest rates *permanently* is to lower the rate of inflation. Of course, the reversal of the inflationary trend induces *temporary* increases in rates of interest. But acceptance of permanent inflation, in order to prevent a temporary rise in interest rates, is a typical example of the policies responsible for the contemporary mess.

Why have no central banks adopted a fixed monetary rule?

What are a central bank's incentives to do so? The traditional procedures serve in general the established bureaucracies much better. They offer more opportunities for evasive rhetoric. In particular, they permit banks to claim credit for good conditions and allow useful disclaimers of responsibility for bad developments (e.g., inflation). It is still remarkable to observe, however, that some central banks are approaching a policy of monetary control which need not involve a fixed rule of rigidly constant growth.

Having monetary targets seems in some ways to make it more difficult for a central bank to control the money stock. For instance, when monetary growth overshoots the target, institutions stop buying government debt because they anticipate higher interest rates and this in turn boosts such monetary expansion. What is your answer?

This involves two aspects. One bears on the institutions governing the quality of monetary control. Many central banks (France, Belgium, Germany, England and others) proceed under arrangements which substantially lower the likelihood of pursuing effective monetary control. Inappropriate institutions may effectively obstruct any rational monetary management. Central banks frequently disregard this issue and fail to recognise the importance of developing monetary arrangements which raise the degree of monetary control. Control will never be perfect and the question about speculation induced by deviations from the desired growth path continues to attract attention. But such deviations hardly affect securities with longer maturities. Given a credible policy of monetary control, investors will know that short-run errors in monetary growth will approximately wash out over time. Any short-run overshooting of monetary targets will not produce a decline in bond prices under such circumstances. It is even doubtful that very short-term rates would be seriously destabilised. Interest rates seem much more prone to fluctuate in response to policies geared to stabilise interest rates.

Given international mobility of capital, an attempt by a single country to control money by raising interest rates may, it is argued, result simply in an inflow of capital which will swell the money supply further. Do not small open economies have to accept the international inflation rate?

Most definitely not. Switzerland has not accepted the prevailing international rate of inflation. A regume of floating exchange rates offers each country an opportunity to determine the monetary base to the last cent in accordance with its wishes. This implies approximate control of monetary growth, irrespective of capital flows induced by relative interest rates or relative movements of exchange rates and interest rates.

Do we have to accept that exchange rates are bound to be volatile?

The volatility of exchange rates simply reflects the uncertainty about the course of financial policy in various countries. Substantial revisions in the markets' evaluation of future policies are immediately impounded into the current exchange rate. A stable and reliable course of financial policies reduces the fluctuations in exchange rates. No degree of intervention can be a substitute for proper financial policies. Intervention undermines monetary control (Germany and Switzerland) and affects exchange rates beyond the shortest horizon only in cases where markets revise (in response to persistent intervention) their expectations of the course of monetary policy.

Nevertheless central banks seem to be intervening on a larger and larger scale in the markets. Why is this?

Whether the magnitude of intervention increases remains to be seen. To some extent interventions are an instrument for controlling the monetary base without operating on domestic credit markets or manipulating advances to banks. But the major force behind the massive intervention is probably concern about the short-run effects on export industries.

Monetarist analysis has recently been applied to many areas beyond its original and continuing concern with monetary policy—for instance, to the economics of bureaucracies.

The connection between monetarist analysis and the emerging work on non-market institutions and the political process is the systematic use of proper *economic* analysis in both fields of research. There is no monetarist analysis of bureaucracy but there is indeed an analysis of bureaucracy. The motivation of this work lies in the increasing range and importance of the phenomenon.

Is this new economic approach going to put the sociologists out of business?

Hardly. More likely is the expanding application and use by sociologists of the analytic framework developed over many decades in economics. This development is visible in political science and also in psychology.

Monetarism has the reputation of being a hard, even heartless doctrine. How would you answer such a charge?

What is more heartless than irresponsible and foolish advice, or false promises? The hard problems do not change under a deceitful rhetoric. We have experienced rising and erratic inflation, increasing "unemployment" and lower rates of real growth as a result of "warm-hearted" policies. It is time to penetrate beyond this cloud of verbalism. We cannot expect to cope effectively with difficult problems under an essentially immoral commitment to refuse a hard and honest examination of the nature of the issues.

SILKS

Dick Francis has written forty-one novels, a volume of short stories (*Field of Thirteen*), his autobiography (*The Sport of Queens*) and the biography of Lester Piggott. He is rightly acclaimed as one of the greatest thriller writers in the world.

He has received many awards, amongst them the prestigious Crime Writers' Association's Cartier Diamond Dagger for his outstanding contribution to the genre. The Mystery Writers of America have given him three Edgar Allan Poe awards for the best novel of the year, and in 1996 made him a Grand Master for a lifetime's achievement. He was awarded a CBE in the Queen's Birthday Honours List in 2000.

Felix Francis is the younger of Dick's two sons. Having spent seventeen years teaching A-level Physics, he took on the role of managing his father's affairs in 1991. Over the last forty years, Felix has assisted with the research of many of the Dick Francis novels, not least *Twice Shy*, which drew on Felix's experiences both as a Physics teacher and as a marksman, *Shattered* and *Under Orders*. With the publication of *Dead Heat* Felix took on a more significant role in the writing – *Silks* is the second of this father-and-son collaboration.

SILKS

DICK FRANCIS
and
FELIX FRANCIS

MICHAEL JOSEPH
an imprint of
PENGUIN BOOKS

MICHAEL JOSEPH

Published by the Penguin Group

Penguin Books Ltd, 80 Strand, London WC2R ORL, England

Penguin Group (USA) Inc., 375 Hudson Street, New York, New York 10014, USA

Penguin Group (Canada), 90 Eglinton Avenue East, Suite 700, Toronto, Ontario, Canada M4P 2Y3
(a division of Pearson Penguin Canada Inc.)

Penguin Ireland, 25 St Stephen's Green, Dublin 2, Ireland (a division of Penguin Books Ltd)

Penguin Group (Australia), 250 Camberwell Road, Camberwell, Victoria 3124, Australia
(a division of Pearson Australia Group Pty Ltd)

Penguin Books India Pvt Ltd, 11 Community Centre, Panchsheel Park, New Delhi – 110 017, India

Penguin Group (NZ), 67 Apollo Drive, Rosedale, North Shore 0632, New Zealand
(a division of Pearson New Zealand Ltd)

Penguin Books (South Africa) (Pty) Ltd, 24 Sturdee Avenue,
Rosebank, Johannesburg 2196, South Africa

Penguin Books Ltd, Registered Offices: 80 Strand, London WC2R ORL, England

www.penguin.com

First published 2008

1

Set in 11.5/16 pt PostScript Adobe Sabon
Typeset by Rowland Phototypesetting Ltd, Bury St Edmunds, Suffolk
Printed in Great Britain by Clays Ltd, St Ives plc

A CIP catalogue record for this book is available from the British Library

HARDBACK ISBN: 978–0–718–15457–8
OM PAPERBACK ISBN: 978–0–718–15471–4

www.greenpenguin.co.uk

Our thanks to

Miles Bennett, barrister
Guy Ladenburg, barrister
David Whitehouse QC

PROLOGUE

March 2008

'Guilty.'

I watched the foreman of the jury as he gave the verdicts. He was wearing a light-coloured tweed jacket over a blue and white striped shirt. At the start of the trial he had also regularly sported a sober striped tie but perhaps, as time had dragged on, the ultra-casual dress of the other eleven had eventually made him feel uncomfortably formal and his shirt was now open at the neck. Unlike most of them, he was grey haired and upright in his stance. Maybe that was why he had been selected as their foreman. I imagined that he was a retired schoolmaster, well used to taking charge and keeping discipline in a classroom full of unruly youth.

'Guilty,' he said again rather nervously, but with a strong deep voice. He kept his eyes firmly on the robed and bewigged judge sitting slightly above him to his left. Not once did he look at the young man in the dock, who also sat slightly above him, but to his right. We were in number 3 court at the Old Bailey, which was one of the older, Victorian-built courtrooms of the Central Criminal Court, designed at a time when the process of the law was intended to be intimidating to the wrongdoer and a deterrent to others. However, for all its formality, the courtroom was small, no larger than a reasonably sized drawing room. The judge, sitting up high behind his long bench, dominated the space and all the other participants, defendant, counsel and jury were so close together that they would have been able to lean forward and touch one another, provided, of course, they had wanted to.

In all, the schoolmasterly foreman repeated the same word eight times before sitting back down with, I sensed, a small sigh of relief that the ordeal was finally over.

The jury had found the young man guilty on all eight counts, four of them for assault occasioning actual bodily harm, three of inflicting grievous bodily harm, and one of attempted murder.

I wasn't really surprised. I was also certain that the young man was guilty, and I was his defence counsel.

Why, I asked myself, had I wasted my most favourite days of the whole year sitting in the Old Bailey trying to save such an undeserving character from a lengthy stretch in the slammer?

Well, for the money, I supposed. But I would much rather have been at Cheltenham for the racing festival. Especially as, this afternoon, I had been expecting to ride my own twelve-year-old bay gelding in the Foxhunter Chase, also known as the Gold Cup for amateur riders.

British justice has, for the past five hundred years, held that a man is innocent until proven guilty. The courtesies of courtroom etiquette are maintained with the accused being referred to simply as the defendant. He is not required to prove his innocence, rather just to defend himself against allegations, allegations that have to be proven beyond a reasonable doubt. The defendant is addressed using the title Mister, Doctor or Sir, or My Lord, or even Reverend or, dare I say, Right Reverend or

Your Grace, as is appropriate. However, once the jury has pronounced his guilt, the defendant instantly becomes 'the offender' and loses the right to such niceties. The mood changes from one of polite discovery and laying bare of the pertinent facts, to one of punishment and retribution for misdeeds now proven.

Almost before the foreman settled again in his seat, the prosecution counsel rose to inform the court of the previous convictions of the offender. And previous there were. Four times before he had been convicted of violent offences including two of malicious wounding. On two occasions the young man had been detained for periods in a young-offenders' institution.

I watched the members of the jury as they absorbed the information. They had spent nearly a week in deliberations before delivering their verdicts. Now some of them were visibly shocked to discover the true character of the smartly dressed twenty-three-year-old young man in the dock who looked as if butter wouldn't melt in his mouth.

I again wondered what I was doing here. Why, I asked myself for the umpteenth time, had I taken on such a hopeless case? I knew the answer. Because I had been urged to do so by a friend of a friend of the young man's parents. They had all pleaded with me to take him on, promising that he was innocent and that the charges were the result of mistaken identity. And, of course, because they were paying me handsomely.

However, I had soon discovered that the only thing mistaken in this case was the unshakeable belief of his parents that their little angel couldn't possibly have done such a nasty thing as to attack a family with a baseball bat. The only motive for the attack was that the father of the family had complained to the police about the young man using the road outside their house as a drag-racing strip each night until two or three in the morning.

The more I had learned about my client the more I had realized my error in accepting the brief. So clear was it to me that he was guilty as charged that I thought the trial would be over nice and quickly and I would be able to go to Cheltenham races with a light heart and a heavy wallet. That the jury had inexplicably taken so long to reach a conclusion of the bleeding obvious was just one of those things.

I had thought about bunking off to the races, claiming sickness, but the judge was a racing man and he had only the previous evening commiserated with me that I would be unable to ride in the Foxhunters. To have feigned sickness and then ridden in the race would likely have put me up before him on contempt charges, and then I could kiss goodbye any aspirations I might have of promotion to QC, a Queen's Counsel – a silk.

'There will always be next year,' the judge had said with an irritating smile.

But one didn't just enter a horse in the Foxhunters, one had to qualify by winning other races, and this was the first time I had managed to do so in ten years of trying. Next year both horse and rider would be another year older and neither of us was in the first flush of youth. There might never be another chance for us together.

I looked at my watch. The race was due off in half an hour. My horse would still run, of course, but there would be another jockey on board and I hated the thought of it. I had played out the race so often in my head and now someone else would be taking my place. I should be in the Cheltenham changing room right now, pulling on the lightweight racing breeches and the brightly coloured silks, not sat here in pinstripe suit, gown and wig, far from the cheering crowd, in depression rather than anticipation.

'Mr Mason,' repeated the judge, bringing me back from my daydreaming. 'I asked you if the defence wishes to say anything before sentence.'

'No, Your Honour,' I said, half standing and then returning to my seat. As far as I could see there were no mitigating circumstances that I wanted to bring to the court's attention. I couldn't claim the young man was the product of a deprived or broken background, nor could I try to excuse his behaviour by reference to some past abuse. In fact quite the reverse was true. His parents were loving both of him and of each other, and he had been educated at one of the country's leading private schools, or at least he had until he was seventeen, when he had been expelled for bullying the younger boys and then threatening the headmaster with a broken bottle while being reprimanded for it.

'The prisoner will stand,' announced the court clerk.

The young man rose to his feet slowly, almost smugly. I stood up too.

'Julian Trent,' the judge addressed him, 'you have been found guilty by this court of perpetrating a violent and unprovoked attack on an innocent family including a charge of attempted murder. You have shown little or no remorse for your actions and I consider you a danger to society. You have previous convictions for violence and you seem unable or unwilling to learn the errors of your ways. I am conscious of my duty to protect the public. Therefore, you will go to prison for eight years. Take him down.'

Julian Trent simply shrugged his shoulders and was ushered down the stairs from the dock to the cells beneath by two burly prison officers. Mrs Trent in the public gallery burst into tears and was comforted by her ever-present husband. I wondered if a week of listening to the damning evidence in the case had made any changes to their rosy opinion of their little boy.

I had quietly hoped that the judge would lock young Julian up for life and throw away the key. I knew that in spite of the eight-year prison sentence it would be, in fact, only half of that before he was back on the streets, arrogantly using his baseball bat to threaten and beat some other poor soul who crossed his path.

Little did I realize at the time that it would be a good deal sooner than four years, and that it would be me on the receiving end.

PART I

Murder, Arrest and Remand

November 2008

CHAPTER 1

'Hi, Perry. How're you doing?'

'Fine, thanks,' I replied, waving a hand. My name isn't actually Perry, it's Geoffrey, but I have long since given up expecting the other jockeys in the changing room to use it. When one is a lawyer, a barrister even, with the surname Mason, one has to expect it. It's like being a White in the forces: invariably the nickname Chalky is added.

I was secretly quite pleased that I was addressed at all by the professionals with whom I occasionally shared a moment's contact. They were together, day in and day out, going about their daily work at the many racecourses around the country, while I averaged only a dozen or so rides a year, almost always on my own horse. An 'amateur rider', as I was officially defined, was tolerated, just, as long as he knew his place, which was next to the door of the changing room where it was always coldest and where clothes and towels were regularly trampled when the jockeys were called to the paddock by an official.

A few of the older changing rooms still had wood-burning stoves in a corner to provide comfort when it was wet and freezing outside. Woe betide some eager young amateur rider who took a seat near the heat, however early he might have arrived at the racecourse. Such comforts had to be earned and were the privilege of the senior jocks.

'Any juicy cases, Perry?' asked a voice from up the far end.

I looked up. Steve Mitchell was one of the elite, constantly vying over the past few seasons with two others for the steeple-chase champion jockey's crown. He was currently the reigning champion, having won more races in the previous year than any other, and he was lying third in the present campaign.

'Just the usual,' I said. 'Kidnap, rape and murder.'

'Don't know how you do it,' he said, pulling a white roll-neck sweater over his head.

'It's a job,' I said. 'And it's safer than yours.'

'Yeah, suppose so. But some guy's life depends on you.' He pulled on his breeches.

'They don't hang murderers any more, you know,' I said. More's the pity, I thought, for some of them.

'No,' said Steve. 'But if you mess up, someone might go to jail for years.'

'They may go to jail because they deserve to, no matter what I do,' I said.

'Does that make you a failure?' he said, buttoning up his blue and white hooped jacket.

'Ha,' I laughed. 'When I win I take some of the credit. When I lose I say that justice takes its course.'

'Not me,' he laughed back, throwing his arms open wide. 'When I win I take all the credit, and when I lose I blame the horse.'

'Or the trainer,' piped in another.

Everyone laughed. Changing-room banter was the antidote to danger. Five or six times a day, every day, these guys put their lives on the line, riding more than half a ton of horse over five-foot fences at thirty miles an hour with no seat belt, no air-bag, and precious little protection.

'Unless you stopped it.' The voice had a distinctive Scottish accent. The laughter died instantly. Scot Barlow was, it was safe to say, not the most popular regular in the jockeys' room. That comment from anyone else would have been the cause for renewed mirth but from Scot Barlow it had menace.

Like Steve Mitchell, Barlow was one of the big three and he currently led the title race by the odd winner or two. But the reason Scot Barlow was not the most popular of colleagues was not because he was successful, but because he had a reputation, rightly or wrongly, of bleating to the authorities about his fellow jockeys if they transgressed the rules. As Reno Clemens, the third of the big three, had once said to me by way of a warning, 'Barlow is a snitch, so keep your betting slips out of his reach.'

Professional jockeys were not allowed to bet on horses. It expressly said so in the terms of their riding licences. Some of them did, of course, and it was reliably reported to me that Scot Barlow had been known to go through his fellow jockeys' pockets to find the illicit betting slips to give to the stewards. Whether he had or not, I didn't know, it was hearsay evidence only and might be inadmissible in court, but the others believed it absolutely.

Somewhat strangely, as an amateur rider, I was allowed to bet, and I did so regularly, but usually only on myself to win. Always the optimist.

We were in the jockeys' changing room at Sandown Park racecourse, in Surrey, and I was riding in the fifth race, a three-mile chase reserved for amateur riders. It was a rare treat for me to be part of a big-race Saturday. Races for amateurs were rare these days, especially at the weekends, and I usually had to confine myself to such races as my weight had inexorably risen to what was considered natural for someone nearing his thirty-sixth birthday and standing five foot ten and a half in his socks. I tried my best to keep it down and regularly starved myself through the winter months to ride at the amateur riders' days in the spring. At least the races reserved for the likes of me tended to have higher weights than those in which I would compete with the pros. There was no chance of me seeing ten stone again and the lowest riding weight I could now seriously consider was eleven stone seven, as it included not only my expanding body, but also my clothes, my riding boots and my saddle.

The jockeys were called for the third race, the main event of the afternoon, and there was the usual lack of a mad rush for the door. Jockeys are generally very superstitious and many of them like to be the last one to leave the changing room for luck, while others simply don't want to spend any time making small talk in the parade ring with the owner and trainer of the horse they are riding. Some even hang around polishing and re-polishing their already clean goggles until the get-mounted bell has already been rung and the officials are having palpitations trying to get them out. I had grabbed all my stuff from off the floor and I now held it close to my chest to protect it until even the last of the tardy bunch had exited, then I put my tweed jacket over my silks and went out to watch the contest on the weighing-room televisions.

The blue and white hooped colours flashed past the post to win by a head in a tight finish. Steve Mitchell had closed the gap on Barlow and Clemens with one more win.

I went back into the jockeys' inner sanctum to begin my

mental preparation for the fifth race. I had discovered that I increasingly needed to get myself into the right frame of mind. If I wasn't properly prepared, the whole thing would seemingly pass me by, and be over before I was even ready for it to start. As I knew that my racing days were numbered, I didn't want to waste any of them.

I sat on the bench that ran all round the room, and went through again in my head where I wanted to be as the tapes went up, where I would be as we approached the first fence and where I hoped to be as we approached the last. Of course, in my mind's eye we would win the race and my apprehension would turn to joy. And that wouldn't be all that unexpected. My bay gelding and I would start as favourite. His win in the Foxhunters at the Cheltenham Festival in March would make sure of that.

Steve Mitchell came waltzing back into the changing room with a grin on his face wider than the eight-lane highway down the road.

'What about that then, Perry?' he said, slapping me on the back, bringing me out of my trance. 'Bloody marvellous. And I beat that bastard Barlow. You should have seen his face. Furious, he was.' He laughed expansively. 'Serves him bloody well right.'

'What for?' I asked innocently.

He stood still for a moment and looked at me inquisitively. 'For being a bastard,' he said, and turned away towards his peg.

'And is he?' I asked his back.

He turned round to face me. 'Is he what?'

'A bastard.'

There was a pause.

'You're a funny bloke, Perry,' he said, irritated. 'What bloody difference does it make whether he's a real bastard or not.'

I was beginning to wish I hadn't got into this conversation. Being a barrister didn't always help one to make friends.

'Well done anyway,' I said to him, but the moment had passed and he just waved a dismissive hand and turned his back on me once again.

'Jockeys!' An official put his head round the changing-room door and called the group of nineteen of us amateurs to the parade ring.

My heart rate rose a notch. It always did. Adrenalin pumped through my veins and I positively jumped up and dived through the doorway. No superstitious last one out of the changing room for me, I wanted to savour every moment. It felt like my feet were hardly touching the ground.

I adored this feeling. This is why I loved to ride in races. This was my fix, my drug. It was arguably less safe than sniffing cocaine and certainly more expensive, but it was a need in me, a compulsion, an addiction. Thoughts of heavy falls, of mortal danger, of broken bones and bruised bodies were banished simply by the thrill and the anticipation of the coming race. Such was the feeling on every occasion, undiminished by time and familiarity. I often told myself that I would hang up my saddle for good only when that emotion ceased to accompany the official's call for 'jockeys'.

I made it to the parade ring without floating away altogether and stood excited on the tightly mowed grass with my trainer, Paul Newington.

When I acquired my first horse some fifteen years ago, Paul had been thought of as the 'bright young up-and-coming trainer' in the sport. Now he was considered to be the man who never quite fulfilled his potential. He was originally from Yorkshire but had moved south in his late twenties, headhunted to take over from one of the grand old men of racing who had been forced into retirement by illness. Far from being up-and-coming, he was now in danger of becoming down-and-going, struggling to fill his expansive training establishment in Great Milton, just to the east of Oxford.

But I liked him, and my own experience of his skills had been nothing but positive. Over the years he had bought for me a succession of sound hunter-chasers that had carried me, for the most part, safely over hundreds of miles and thousands of fences. Mostly they had been steady rather than spectacular, but that had been my brief to him when buying. I wanted to be in one piece more than I wanted to win.

'I think you should beat this lot,' Paul said, loosely waving a hand at the other groups in the parade ring. 'Fairly jumping out of his skin, he is.'

I didn't like being expected to win. Even when defending in court I was generally pessimistic about my clients' chances. That way, winning was unexpected and joyful while losing wasn't too much of a disappointment.

'Hope so,' I replied. My apprehension grew as an official rang the bell and called for the jockeys to get mounted.

Paul gave me a leg-up onto my current pride and joy. Sandeman was the best horse I had ever owned by a long way. Paul had bought him for me as an eight-year-old with a mixed history of fairly moderate results in hurdle races. Paul had reckoned that Sandeman was too big a horse to run over hurdles and that he would be much better as a chaser and he had been right. The horse had quickly learned the skill of jumping the bigger obstacles and was soon shooting up the handicap. So far we had won eight races together and he had won five others without me in the saddle, including that victory in the Foxhunter Chase at Cheltenham.

This was his first run since the summer layoff. He would be thirteen on the first of January and, consequently, he was close to the twilight of his career. Paul and I had planned that he would race just twice before the Cheltenham Festival, before what we hoped would be a repeat victory in the Foxhunters.

I had first been introduced to steeplechase racing by my uncle Bill when I was twelve. Uncle Bill was my mother's younger brother and he was still in his early twenties when he had been delegated to take me out for the day and keep me out of mischief. I had been staying with him and his parents, my grandparents, while my own mother and father were away together on holiday in South America.

I had clambered eagerly into the passenger seat of his beloved open-topped MG Midget and we had set out for the south coast and the planned day at Worthing in West Sussex.

Unbeknown to me, or to his somewhat austere parents, Uncle Bill had no intention of spending the day dragging his young nephew across Worthing's steep pebble beach or along its elegant Victorian pier so I could be entertained by the amusement arcades. Instead he drove us about fifteen miles further to the west to Fontwell Park racecourse, and my abiding passion for jump racing was born.

At almost every British racecourse it is possible for the spectators to stand next to a fence, to experience the thrill of being so close up as half-ton horses soar over and through the tightly bound birch, to hear the horses' hooves thumping the turf, to feel the earth tremble, and to sense the excitement of being part of the race. But at Fontwell the steeplechase course is a figure of eight and one can run between the jumps that are near to the cross-over point and be close to the action twice on each circuit, six times in all during a three-mile chase.

Uncle Bill and I spent much of the afternoon running across the grass from fence to fence, and by the end of the day I knew for certain that I wanted to be one of those brave young men in their bright coloured silks fearlessly kicking and urging his mount into the air at thirty miles an hour with hope in his heart, trusting that the spindly legs of the Thoroughbred racehorse beneath him would save them both from crashing to the ground on the other side.

Such was my conviction that I could think of nothing else for weeks and I begged my uncle to take me with him to the races whenever I could get away from more mundane things like school and studying.

I enrolled at a local riding stables and soon mastered the art, not of dressage as they would have preferred, but of riding at speed over jumps. My teacher tried in vain to get me to sit upright in the saddle with my heels down. However, I was determined to stand in the stirrups crouching over the animal's withers just as I had seen the jockeys do.

By the time I was seventeen and learning to drive a car, I could navigate my way around the country not by the positions of the major cities but by the locations of the racecourses. Maybe I couldn't find my way to Birmingham, or to Manchester or to Leeds, but I knew unerringly the quickest route from Cheltenham to Bangor-on-Dee, or from Market Rasen to Aintree.

Sadly, by then I had come to terms with the fact that I was never going to earn my living from race riding. For a start, despite my best efforts in refusing my school dinners, I had grown too tall and was already showing signs of becoming too heavy to be a professional jockey. Coupled with that was an apparent gift for academic success, and the fact that my future career in the law had been planned out to the nth degree by my father. He had decided that I would follow him to his old college at London University, then, like him, to the College of Law in Guildford and, finally, into the same firm of high-street solicitors that he himself had joined some thirty years previously. I would spend my life, like his, conveyancing property from seller to buyer, drawing up last wills and testaments, and untying the knots of failed marriages in south-west London suburbia. The promised boredom of it all had filled me with horror.

I had been twenty-one and in my third year of a Bachelor of Laws degree at UCL when my darling mother had finally lost her long battle against leukaemia. Her death wasn't a surprise to me, in fact she had lived far longer than any of the family had expected, but, perhaps for the first time, it brought home to me the fallibility and transitory nature of the human state. She died on her forty-ninth birthday. There had been no cutting of cake with blown-out candles, no singing of 'Happy Birthday to You'. Just despair and tears. Lots and lots of tears.

The experience made me resolve to do what I really wanted and not what everyone else expected of me. Life, I suddenly decided, was too short to waste.

I had duly completed my degree, as it had somehow seemed a mistake to give it all up at such a late stage, but I had absolutely no intention of becoming a solicitor like my father. I had written to the College of Law to withdraw my application for the Legal Practice Course, the next step on the solicitors' ladder, and, much to my remaining parent's horror and anger, had arranged instead to go to Lambourn as unpaid assistant and amateur jockey with a mid-ranking racehorse trainer.

'But how will you afford to live?' my father had demanded in exasperation.

'I will use the legacy that Mum left me,' I'd replied.

'But . . ,' he had blustered. 'That was meant to be for the down payment on a house.'

'She didn't say so in her will,' I had said rather tactlessly, sending my father into a tirade about how the young these days had no sense of responsibility. This was not an uncommon rant in our household, and I was well used to ignoring it.

So I had graduated in June and gone to Lambourn in July, and had used my mother's legacy not only to pay my living expenses but also to acquire a seven-year-old bay gelding that I could ride in races, having correctly supposed that I was unlikely to get any rides on anyone else's horses.

I didn't tell my father.

August had mostly been spent getting fit. Each morning I would ride my horse in the stable string to the gallops on the hills above the village and then, each afternoon, I would run the same route on foot. By mid September both horse and jockey were showing signs of being ready for the racecourse.

Quite by chance, or was it fate, my first ride in a proper race had been at Fontwell in early October that year. The whole experience had seemed to pass me by in a blur with everything happening at once. Such was my naivety and nervousness that I nearly forgot to weigh out, had been unprepared and badly left at the start, had struggled for a full circuit to get back to the other runners before fading badly due to my own lack of stamina towards the end. We had finished eleventh out of thirteen, and one of the two I had beaten only because he had fallen in front of me at the last. It had not been an auspicious beginning. However the trainer had seemed relatively satisfied.

'At least you didn't fall off,' he had said on our way home in his car.

I had taken it as a compliment.

My horse and I had raced together five more times that year and on each occasion we had fared slightly better than the time before, finishing a close second in an amateur riders' steeple-chase at Towcester races the week before Christmas.

By the following March I had ridden over fences a total of nine times and I had also had my first racing fall, at Stratford. However, it had been my ego that had been more bruised than my body. My horse and I had been well in front with just one fence left to negotiate when the excitement of the moment had become too much for me and I had made a complete hash of it, asking my mount for a mighty leap while he had decided to put in an extra stride. The result was that we had ploughed through the top of the fence, ending up in a crumpled heap on the ground watching ruefully as the others had sailed past us to the finish.

In spite of this disaster, and even though I had not yet ridden a winner, I still loved the excitement of the actual races, but I had begun to be rather bored by the time between them. I was missing the intellectual stimulation that I had so enjoyed during my time at university. And my mother's legacy had started to show major signs of exhaustion. It was time to put my fantasy back in its box and earn myself a living. But as what? I remained steadfast in my aversion to being a solicitor, but what else could I do with my law degree?

Not all lawyers are solicitors, I remembered one of my tutors saying during my first weeks at university. *There are barristers as well*.

To someone who was expecting, and expected, to become a general practice high-street solicitor, the world of the barrister was mysterious and unknown. My choice of optional study topics in my degree had concentrated on those areas I could mostly expect to encounter: conveyancing, family, employment and contract law. I had tended to avoid advocacy, criminal law and jurisprudence as much as possible.

I had researched the differences between barristers and solicitors in the local library in Hungerford and had learned that barristers were advocates, standing up and arguing, while solicitors generally did the legal paperwork in the background. Barristers tended to spar verbally across courtrooms with other barristers, while solicitors drew up contracts and litigation alone in quiet offices.

All of a sudden the prospect of becoming a stand-up-and-argue barrister had excited me hugely and I had eagerly applied for a return to legal matters.

So here I was some fourteen years later, well established in the world of horsehair wigs, silk gowns and courtroom protocol, but still trying to master this racing lark.

'Jockeys! Walk in.' The starter's call brought me back to the matter in hand. How careless, I thought, to be daydreaming at such a time. Concentrate! I told myself sharply.

The nineteen of us walked up slowly in a straggly line, the starter pushed the lever, the tape flew up and we were off. Not that it was easy to tell as no one seemed keen to make the running. The pack slowly went from walk to trot, and then to canter as the race began in almost sedentary style.

The three-mile start at Sandown is on the side of the course just after the bend at the end of the home straight, so the horses have to complete almost two full circuits jumping a total of twenty-two fences. The first, which comes up very soon after the start, looks fairly innocuous but has caught out many an amateur and professional rider in its time. The landing side is some way below the take-off point and the drop tends to pitch horses forward onto their noses. The slow initial pace of this race, however, gave even the most inexperienced jockey, riding the world's worst jumper, time to haul on the reins to keep the animal's head up. So all nineteen runners were still standing as the pace picked up and we turned right-handed into the back straight to face the most famous seven-fence combination in steeplechasing. Two plain fences and an open-ditch fairly close together, then a slight gap to the water-jump, then the famous Railway fences – three plain fences very close together, closer than any others in British racing. It is always said that if you jump the first one well then all will be fine, but make a hash of the first and then horse and rider will be lucky to get to the far end intact.

Three miles is a long way, especially in November mud after a wet autumn, and none of us was making the mistake of going too fast too early. Consequently all nineteen runners were still standing and fairly closely bunched as we swung out of the back straight and round the long curve to the Pond fence and then up in front of the watching crowds for the first time.

The thing that struck me most when I started riding in races was the apparent isolation in which the participants find themselves. There may be thousands and thousands of eager gamblers in the grandstands, each shouting on their choices, but, for all the jockeys can tell, the stands may as well be empty and deserted. The sound of horses' hooves striking the turf, the same sound that had so excited me as a boy that first day at Fontwell Park, was the main noise that filled the senses. And obviously, unlike for the stationary spectator for whom it comes and goes, the noise travels along with the horses. There are other sounds too: the slap of the reins or whip, the clicking together of hooves, the shouts of the jockeys and the clatter of hoof or horseflesh on birch and wood as the animals brush through the top few inches of each fence. All of these together make the race a noisy place to be, and they exclude any utterances from outside this bubble. No word of encouragement can penetrate, not a single phrase of commentary can enter. Quite often, afterwards, the jockeys are the least informed about the triumphs and disasters of others. If it occurs behind them, they will have no idea that, say, the red-hot favourite has fallen, or a loose horse has caused mayhem in the pack. Unlike Formula 1 there are no team radios or pit-boards to inform and enlighten.

The pace quickened again noticeably as we turned away from the stands and went downhill past our starting point. The race was suddenly on in earnest.

Sandeman and I had been keeping to the shortest way round, hugging the inside rail, following the leading trio by a couple of lengths or so. Now, the horse immediately ahead of me began to tire slightly and I was concerned that I would be forced to slow with him as, with others alongside me, I had nowhere to go.

'Give me some damn room,' I shouted at the jockey ahead, more in hope than expectation. Amazingly, he pulled slightly away from the rail and I sailed up on his inside.

'Thanks,' I called to him as I drew alongside him on his right. A fresh faced, big eyed young amateur grimaced back at me. That was the difference, I thought, between how I was when I started and how I was now. These days I would never give a rival room even if he shouted at me all day. Racing was all about winning and one didn't win very often by being too courteous to the opposition. Not that I would purposefully baulk someone by cutting across them, although I had often been so treated by several of my colleagues. Some jockeys could be sweetness and light in the changing room both before and after the race, but vicious and ruthless in between. It was their job. Amateurs, in particular, should expect no favours from professionals.

Two horses fell at the next fence, the one with the drop. Both animals pitched forward on landing, going down on their knees and sending their riders sprawling onto the grass. One of the jockeys was the young man who had given me room up his inside. Phew, I thought, that was close. Thank goodness he hadn't fallen right in front of me. Being 'brought down' by tripping over another already prostrate horse was one of the worst ways of losing.

The remaining seventeen of us were becoming well spread out as we turned into the back straight for the second and last time. Sandeman was still going well beneath me and I kicked on hard into the first of the seven fences. He positively flew across the birch and gained at least a length on the two still in front.

'Come on, boy,' I shouted at him.

The tempo had now really quickened to a full-out gallop and I could hear some of those behind having problems keeping up.

'Pick up your effing feet,' shouted one jockey at his horse as it dropped its back legs into the water.

'Tell your sodding horse to jump straight,' shouted another as he was almost put through the wings of the first of the Railway fences.

We swung into the final long sweeping turn with just four

having a realistic chance. I was still on the inside next to the white plastic rail and so the others had to go further to get round me. Kick, push, kick, push, my hands and heels were working overtime as we straightened for the Pond fence. Sandeman was just in front and another great leap from him took the others briefly out of sight behind me.

'Come on, boy,' I shouted at him again, this time with diminished breath. 'Come on.'

We were tiring but so were the others. Three miles in bottomless going is a huge test of stamina. But who would tire the most? Me, I feared. My fatigued legs would no longer provide the necessary kicks to Sandeman's belly and I could barely summon up the energy to give him a slap of encouragement with my whip.

We still had our nose just in front as we took off at the second last but Sandeman hit the top of the fence and landed almost stationary on all four feet at once. Bugger. Two other horses came past us as if we were going backwards and I thought all was lost. But Sandeman had other ideas and set off in pursuit. By the last fence we were back alongside the others and the three of us jumped it line abreast.

Even though the three horses landed over the last together, both the others made it to the winning post ahead of us, their jockeys riding determined finishes while I was so tired that hanging on was about as much as I could do. We finished third, which was more to do with my lack of stamina rather than Sandeman's. I had clearly been spending too much of my time sitting on my backside in courtrooms and it showed. Three miles through the undulating Sandown mud had been just a bit too far. My pre-race apprehension hadn't turned to joy, more to exhaustion.

I slithered off Sandeman's back in the unsaddling enclosure and nearly sat down on the grass, so jelly-like were my legs.

'Are you all right?' Paul, the trainer, asked concerned.

'Fine,' I said, trying to undo the girths. 'Just a little out of puff.'

'I need to get you up on the gallops too,' he said. 'No good having a fit horse if the damn jockey sits there like a sack of potatoes.' It was a harsh assessment but probably fair. Paul had invested heavily on Sandeman to win in more ways than one. He gently brushed me aside, undid the buckle with ease and passed me the saddle.

'Sorry,' I mumbled. It was a good job I was paying the training fees.

Somehow I made it to the scales to be weighed in, and then back into the jockeys' changing room, where I sat down heavily on the bench and wondered if it was time to call it a day. Time to give up this race-riding malarkey before I did myself a proper injury. To date I had been very lucky, with only a few bumps and bruises plus one broken collarbone in fourteen years of racing. But, I thought, if I were to continue for another year I would have to become fitter than this or I might come to some serious harm. I leaned back wearily against the cream-painted wall and closed my eyes.

Only when the valets began to pack up the equipment into their large wicker baskets did I realize that the last race had already been run and I was almost alone in the changing room, and still I was not changed.

I stood up slowly and peeled off my lightweight riding strip, picked up my towel and went into the showers.

26

Scot Barlow was half sitting, half lying on the tiled floor, leaning up against the wall with a stream of water falling from the shower head onto his legs. He had a small trickle of blood coming from his right nostril and his eyes were puffy and closed.

'Are you all right?' I asked going over to him and touching his shoulder.

His eyes opened a little and he looked up at me but with no warmth in his expression.

'Sod off,' he said.

Charming, I thought. 'Just trying to help,' I said.

'Bloody amateurs,' he replied. 'Take away our livelihoods, you do.'

I ignored him and washed my hair.

'Do you hear me?' he shouted in full Scottish lilt. 'I said people like you take away my livelihood. I should be paid to let the likes of you ride races.'

I thought of trying to tell him that I had ridden in a race reserved only for amateurs and he wouldn't have been allowed to ride in it anyway. But it would probably have been a waste of time and he clearly wasn't in the mood for serious debate. I went on ignoring him and finished my shower, the warmth helping to return some strength to my aching muscles. Barlow continued to sit where he was. The bleeding from his nose had gradually stopped and the blood was washed away by the water.

I went back into the main changing room, dressed and packed up my stuff. The professional jockeys all used the valets to look after their equipment. Each night their riding clothes were washed and dried, their riding boots polished and their saddles soaped ready for the next day's racing. For me, who rode only about once a fortnight and often more infrequently than that, the services of a valet were unnecessary and counter-productive.

I stuffed my dirty things in a bag ready to take home to the washer-drier in the corner of my kitchen.

I was soon ready to go and there was still no sign of Scot Barlow. Everyone else had gone home so I went and again looked into the showers. He was still sitting there, in the same place as before.

'Do you need any help?' I asked. I assumed he must have had a fall during the afternoon and that his face was sore from using it on the ground as a brake.

'Sod off,' he said again. 'I don't need your help. You're as bad as he is.'

'Bad as who is?' I asked.

'Your bloody friend,' he said.

'What friend?' I asked him.

'Steve bloody Mitchell, of course,' he said. 'Who else do you think did this?' He held a hand up to his face.

'What?' I said, astounded. 'Steve Mitchell did this to you? But why?'

'You'd better ask him that,' he said. 'And not the first time, either.'

'You should tell someone,' I said, but I could see that he couldn't. Not with his reputation.

'Don't be daft,' he said. 'Now you piss off home like a good little amateur. And keep your bloody mouth shut.' He turned away from me and wiped a hand over his face.

I wondered what I should do. Should I tell the few officials left in the weighing room that he was there so they didn't lock him in? Should I go and fetch one of the ambulance staff? Or should I go and find a policeman to report an assault?

In the end I did nothing, except collect my gear and go home.

CHAPTER 2

'I don't fucking believe it,' someone said loudly in the clerks' room as I walked in on Monday morning.

Such language in chambers was rare, and rarer still was such language from Sir James Horley QC, the Head of Chambers, and therefore nominally my boss. Sir James was standing in front of the clerks' desks reading from a piece of paper.

'What don't you . . . believe?' I asked him, deciding at the last moment not to repeat his profanity.

'This,' he said, waving the paper towards me.

I walked over and took the paper. It was a printout of an e-mail. It was headed CASE COLLAPSES AGAINST JULIAN TRENT.

Oh fuck indeed, I thought. I didn't believe it either.

'You defended him the first time round,' Sir James said. It was a statement rather than a question.

'Yes,' I said. I remembered it all too well. 'Open-and-shut case. Guilty as sin. How he got a retrial on appeal I'll never know.'

'That damn solicitor,' said Sir James. 'And now he's got off completely.' He took back the piece of paper and reread the short passage on it. 'Case dismissed for lack of evidence, it says here.'

More like for lack of witnesses prepared to give their evidence, I thought. They were afraid of getting beaten up.

I had taken a special interest in the appeal against Julian Trent's conviction in spite of no longer acting for the little thug. That damn solicitor, as Sir James had called him, was one of the Crown Prosecution team who had admitted cajoling members of the original trial jury to produce a guilty verdict. Three members of the jury had been to the police to report the incident, and all three had subsequently given evidence at the appeal hearing stating that they had been approached independently by the same solicitor. Why he'd done it, I couldn't understand, as the evidence in the case had been overwhelming. But the Appeal Court judges had had little choice but to order a retrial.

The episode had cost the solicitor his job, his reputation and, ultimately, his professional qualification to practise. There had been a minor scandal in the corridors of the Law Society. But at least the appeal judges had had the good sense to keep young Julian remanded in jail pending the new proceedings.

Now, it seemed, he would be walking free, his conviction and lengthy prison sentence being mere distant memories.

I recalled the last thing he had said to me in the cells under the Old Bailey courtroom last March. It was not a happy memory. It was customary for defence counsel to visit their client after the verdict, win or lose, but this had not been a normal visit.

'I'll get even with you, you spineless bastard,' he'd shouted at me with venom as I had entered the cell.

I presumed he thought that his conviction was my fault because I had refused to threaten the witnesses with violence as he had wanted me to do.

'You'd better watch your back,' he'd gone on menacingly. 'One day soon I'll creep up on you and you'll never see it coming.'

The hairs on the back of my neck now rose up and I instinctively turned round as if to find him right here in chambers. At the time of his conviction I had been exceedingly thankful to leave him in the custody of the prison officers and I deeply wished he still was. Over the years I had been threatened by some others of my less affable clients, but there was something about Julian Trent that frightened me badly, very badly indeed.

'Are you all right?' Sir James was looking at me with his head slightly inclined.

'Fine,' I said with a slightly croaky voice. I cleared my throat. 'Perfectly fine, thank you, Sir James.'

'You look like you've seen a ghost,' he said.

Perhaps I had. Was it me? Would I be a ghost when Julian Trent came a-calling?

I shook my head. 'Just remembering the original trial,' I said.

'The whole thing is fishy if you ask me,' he said in his rather pompous manner.

'And is anyone asking you?' I said.

'What do you mean?' said Sir James.

'You seem well acquainted with the case, and the result is clearly important to you.' Sir James had never sworn before in my hearing. 'I didn't realize that anyone from these chambers was acting.'

'They aren't,' he said.

Sir James Horley QC, as Head of Chambers, had his finger on all that was going on within these walls. He knew about every case in which barristers from 'his' chambers were acting, whether on the prosecution side or the defence. He had a reputation for it. But equally, he knew nothing, nor cared little, about cases where 'his' team were not involved. At least, that was the impression he usually wanted to give.

'So why the interest in this case?' I asked.

'Do I need a reason?' he asked, somewhat defensively.

'No,' I said. 'You don't need a reason, but my question remains, why the interest?'

'Don't you cross-examine me,' he retorted.

Sir James had a bit of a reputation amongst the junior barristers for enjoying throwing his superior status around. The position of Head of Chambers was not quite what it might appear. It was mostly an honorary title often held by the most senior member, the QC of longest standing rather than necessarily the most eminent. All of the forty-five or so barristers in these chambers were self-employed. The main purpose of us coming together in chambers was to allow us to pool those services we all needed, the clerks, the offices, the library, meeting rooms and so on. Each of us remained responsible for acquiring our own work from our own clients, although the clerks were important in the allocation of a new client to someone with the appropriate expertise. But one thing our Head of Chambers certainly did not do was to share out the work amongst his juniors. Sir James had never been known to share anything if he could keep it all to himself.

'It doesn't matter,' I said as a way of finishing the discussion on the matter. He would tell me if he wanted to, or not if that was his choice. My questioning would not sway the matter one way or another. Sir James was like the most unhelpful court-room witness who has his own agenda about what evidence he will give and the direction of counsel's questioning will make no difference. Perhaps it takes an obdurate man to break down another of similar character, which was why Sir James Horley was one of the greatest advocates in the land.

'I was advising the judge in the case,' he said. So he did want to tell me after all. He was now showing off, I thought ungraciously.

'Oh,' I said noncommittally. I, too, could play his little game. I turned away to collect some letters from the pigeonhole behind me marked MR G. MASON. It was one of an array of wooden boxes each about twelve inches square lining one wall of the clerks' room. There were ten such spaces in each of six horizontal rows, open to the front, with each having a neatly printed label in a brass surround at the top showing the owner's name. They were not, of course, arranged in alphabetical order, which would have made finding someone else's box nice and easy; they were arranged in order of seniority, with Sir James's pigeonhole at the top right nearest the door. Consequently, our clutch of QCs had their boxes at eye-level while the juniors were below, even if the 'junior' had been called to the Bar long before the most recent QC and was easily old enough to be his father. Those juniors most recently called and those doing pupillage had almost to prostrate themselves on the floor to see what had been deposited in the deeper recesses of their boxes. I assumed that the whole plan was aimed at ensuring that the juniors did not forget their place. No doubt, if and when I myself made it to the lofty heights of being a QC, I would think that the system was ideal. Becoming a Queen's Counsel implied real status and was meant to be reserved for only the very best of the profession. Every barrister wanted to be a QC, but only ten per cent or so actually made it.

'The case hung on the question of intimidation,' Sir James said to my back, continuing our conversation.

It didn't surprise me. Julian Trent had intimidated me. I lifted a pile of papers from my box and turned back.

'The judge in the case and I were at law school together,' he went on. 'Known each other for forty years.' He gazed up as if remembering his lost youth. 'Anyway,' he said, looking back down at me, 'the problem with the new trial was that the prosecution witnesses now either refused to give evidence at all or said something completely opposite to what they had said before. It was clear that they had been intimidated.'

Intimidation in the legal system was rife and a major obstacle to criminal justice. We all had to deal with it on a day-to-day basis.

I stood patiently and waited through a silence as Sir James appeared to decide if he would continue or not. Having decided in the affirmative, he went on. 'So the judge wanted some advice as to whether the initial statements from witnesses taken by the police at the time of the incident could be read out in court as evidence without the prosecution calling the individuals concerned.'

I knew that Sir James had been a recorder for many years and that meant he sat as a Crown Court judge for up to thirty days per year. It was the first step to becoming a full-time judge and most senior practising QCs were or had been recorders. It was not uncommon for sitting judges to seek advice from them, and vice versa.

'And what advice did you give him?' I asked him.

'Her, actually,' he said. 'Dorothy McGee. I advised her that such evidence could be admissible provided the witness was called, even if the witness was now declared as being hostile to

34

the Crown's case. However, it seemed that all the witnesses in the case had changed their tune, including the victim of the beating and his family, who now claimed that the event didn't happen in the first place and that the injuries were due to him falling down some stairs. Do they really think we are stupid or something?' He was getting quite cross. 'I advised her to press on with the case. I told her that it is essential to justice that such intimidation cannot be seen to succeed and I was sure the jury would agree and convict.'

'Trent probably intimidated the jury as well,' I said. I wondered if he had intimidated the three jurors who had come forward at the appeal.

'We'll never know,' he said. 'This note says the case has collapsed so it probably never went to the jury. I suspect that in the face of no witnesses to the event, except those denying that it ever occurred, the CPS, or maybe it was Dorothy, they just gave up. What an absolute disgrace.' He suddenly turned on his heel and walked away, back towards his room down the hall. My audience was over.

'Morning, Mr Mason,' said the Chief Clerk suddenly, making me jump. He had been sitting impassive and silent at his desk during my exchange with Sir James and I had not noticed him behind the computer monitors.

'Morning, Arthur,' I replied, moving to see him more clearly. He was a smallish man but only in stature, not in personality. I presumed he was now in his late fifties or early sixties as he often claimed to have worked in these chambers for more than forty years. He had already been a well-established Chief Clerk when I had first arrived twelve years before and he didn't seem to have changed one bit in the interim, apart from the appearance of a little grey in a full head of thick black curly hair.

'Bit late this morning, sir?' He phrased it as a question but it was meant more as a statement.

I glanced up at the clock on the wall above his head. Half past eleven. I had to agree that it was not a particularly prompt start to the working week.

'I've been busy elsewhere,' I said to him. Busy in bed, asleep.

'Are you misleading the court?' he asked accusingly, but with a smile. Misleading the court was the most heinous of crimes for a barrister.

The Chief Clerk was supposed to work for the members of chambers but somehow no one had ever told Arthur that. He clearly presumed that the reverse was true. If a junior or pupil misdemeanoured in some way, either through their bad behaviour or their poor work, then it was usually the Chief Clerk rather than the Head of Chambers who dealt out the admonishment. Each member of chambers paid a proportion of their fees to provide for the services we enjoyed and to pay for the team of clerks who were our secretariat, our minders and our chaperones. It was rumoured that in some chambers, with many high-earning barristers, the Chief Clerk was earning more than any of the masters he served. Arthur may have been nominally subservient to me but, as a junior who had aspirations of becoming a silk, I would be a fool to cross him.

'Sorry, Arthur,' I said, trying to look as apologetic as possible. 'Any messages for me?'

'Only those already in your box,' he said, nodding towards the papers in my hand. Fortunately for me his telephone rang at this point and I scampered for the safety of my desk while he answered it. Why, I mused, did I always feel like a naughty schoolboy when in Arthur's company. Maybe it was because he instinctively knew when I was not where I should be at any given time, usually because I was on a racecourse somewhere having more fun.

Perhaps my nervousness was the result of a guilty conscience. On more than one occasion during my early years I had been forced to sit and listen to Arthur deliver a warning about my conduct, no doubt passed down from my more senior colleagues. Even though each of us was self-employed, the level of our billing was relevant to the smooth running of chambers and no one would be carried as a passenger if their fees were below par. Fortunately for me, in spite of taking days away to ride in races, my fee base was strong and none of my colleagues could ever accuse me of not pulling my weight, which had been eleven stone three, stripped, at Sandown Park races on the previous Saturday.

I sat at my desk and looked out of the window at the Gray's Inn Gardens, an oasis of calm in the centre of the great bustling metropolis of London. The lines of plane trees, which in summer gave shade to the hundreds of office workers who came to eat their lunchtime sandwiches, were now bare of their leaves and stood forlornly pointing skywards.

They reflected my mood. If our legal system couldn't lock away dangerous brutes like Julian Trent because they frightened people away from telling the truth, then we were all in trouble.

Al Capone in 1920s Chicago was untouchable by the police. No witnesses to his many crimes of murder or assault would ever give evidence against him. It would have been a death sentence to have done so. Capone was so bold as to make public appearances for the media and was something of a celebrity around town, so sure was he that no one would bear witness against him. In the end the evidence that convicted him was a crude accounting ledger, allegedly in his own handwriting, showing his vast unlawful income, which had been discovered in a desk during a routine police raid on an illicit liquor warehouse. United States law made it clear that even illegal earnings were subject to federal income tax, so he was found guilty, not of murder and mayhem but of tax evasion. Capone's middle name was Gabriel but he was certainly no angel. The jury for his trial was changed on the day of the proceedings to frustrate attempts to bribe or threaten the original panel, and still he was convicted on only five of twenty-two charges. But it was enough. A brave judge threw out the plea bargain and sentenced America's Public Enemy No. 1 to eleven years in jail. Justice had triumphed over intimidation.

As Sir James Horley had said, it was an absolute disgrace it hadn't done so in the Trent case.

I leaned back in my chair and yawned. Contrary to what Arthur might think, the reason I had arrived late was not that I was lazy, but because at five in the morning I had been still reading the case notes for a trial in which I was currently leading for the prosecution. The court was not sitting on this particular Monday and I could have spent the whole day in bed if I had been so inclined, but I needed to use the library.

The case was against a pair of brothers who had been accused of conspiracy. Such cases were always difficult to prosecute. When does dreaming about robbing a bank become conspiracy to do so? The brothers were accused of conspiring to defraud an insurance company through a loophole in their motoring policy. The brothers had claimed in court, and under oath, that they were only seeing if the scheme was possible in order that they could then tell the company so its security could be tightened, and that they had no intention of carrying through their plans and keeping the illegal payment.

This might have been perfectly believable, except that the brothers had twice before been convicted together of fraud and were suspected of many more. The question I had been spending so long researching, and for which I needed the chambers' detailed index of trial records, was whether these facts could or could not be used in court. English law relies heavily on precedent to determine whether something can occur. If it has been allowed before then, by definition, it can be again. If it hasn't happened in the past then it might be cause for appeal right up to the House of Lords for a ruling. The trial judge would make the decision, but counsel had to provide arguments first. In this instance, as the prosecutor, I needed to find similar circumstances from the past that would strengthen my case to have the brothers' previous convictions revealed to the jury to show pattern of behaviour as evidence of their guilt.

Not all the work of a barrister is as exciting as that depicted in TV trial dramas.

Consequently, I spent the rest of the day with my nose in leather-bound volumes of trial records and then in front of my computer screen searching on the internet. At least, for the most part, my search was fairly restricted. Prior to 2004 evidence of previous convictions was excluded from trials completely except in very special circumstances.

The fact that someone has committed a crime before is not, in itself, evidence that they have done so again. In many cases, quite rightly, former misdeeds should not be used to sway a jury to produce another guilty verdict. Each case should be tried on the current facts rather than on those of previous incidents. Even the most prosecution minded of judges could often believe that allowing previous guilty verdicts to be disclosed to the jury might be prejudicial to a fair trial, and hence grounds for a successful appeal. There is little worse for a barrister's ego than to win a case for the prosecution in the Crown Court only for the verdict to be overturned on appeal. All those late nights of work, all those missed social engagements, all that effort and for what? For nothing.

Well, I suppose there was the fee, of course, but for me, as in racing, it was the winning that was far more important than the money.

By seven thirty I'd had enough of ploughing through past judgments, but at least, by then, I had produced an all too short but fairly comprehensive list of precedents to further my argument. I packed everything I needed into a box ready for the morning and slipped out into the night.

I lived in Barnes, south of the Thames in west London, where my wife, Angela, and I had bought half of an early Edwardian detached house in Ranelagh Avenue overlooking Barnes Common. Typical of its time, the house had been built with a lower ground floor with high-up windows where the servants had performed their duties cooking, washing, and generally looking after the family above, but it had since been modernized and converted into two homes. Angela and I had acquired the top half, the upper two floors with views over the treetops from the dormer windows of the bedrooms. Our neighbours below occupied the original ground floor of the property with its grand rooms, together with the old servants' area below.

Angela and I had loved it. It had been the first home that we had owned together and we had lavished more time and money than was prudent on decorating the place and getting everything ready for the birth of our first child, a son, due six months after we had moved in. That had been seven years ago.

As usual, I walked home across the common from Barnes station. It was almost completely dark, with just a few beams of light filtering through the leafless trees from distant street lights, but I knew every step of the route. I was about half way when I remembered Julian Trent and his baseball bat. Perhaps it wasn't such a good idea to walk alone across Barnes Common in the dark, but I had always felt more threatened when sticking to the roads with their meagre lighting. I stopped to listen for anyone behind me and I did turn round a few times to check, but I made it safely to my door without incident.

The house was lit up, but, as was normally the case, it was only the bottom half of the house that was bright. The upper floors were in darkness where I'd turned off the lights as I had left that morning.

I let myself in through my front door and went upstairs into the dark.

Angela wasn't there, but I knew she wouldn't be. Angela was dead.

I wondered if I would ever get used to coming home to an empty house. Perhaps I should have moved away long ago, but those first few months here had been the happiest of my life and, somehow, early on, I hadn't wanted to abandon the memories, they were all I had left.

Angela had died suddenly of a massive pulmonary embolism just four weeks before our baby was due. She had kissed me goodbye on that fateful Monday morning as happy as I had

41

ever known her. It had been the first day of her maternity leave and she had still been in her dressing gown and slippers as I had left for work. All her life she had longed to have a child and now she was so close to fulfilling her dream. I had tried to call her several times during the day without any success but I had thought nothing was amiss until I had arrived home to find the place in darkness. Angela had always hated the dark, and she would have left lights on in the house even if she had gone out.

I had found her lying on the sitting-room floor, slightly curled as if she were asleep. But she had been so cold, and had obviously been dead for hours. Our son was dead too, inside her.

There had been no warning and no pre-existing condition. Regular checks at the clinic had revealed no hypertension, no pre-eclampsia. She had gone from healthy and happy to dead in the space of a few moments. So sad, the doctors had said, but it was the most common cause of sudden death during pregnancy. They also told me it would have been very quick and that she was likely unaware, losing consciousness almost instantaneously. Surprisingly, it was something of a comfort to know that she hadn't suffered, that she hadn't seen the void coming.

Everyone had been so kind. Friends had rallied round to make the necessary arrangements, my father had come to stay so I wouldn't be alone, and even the judge in the trial I had been prosecuting had adjourned the proceedings until after Angela's funeral. I could remember feeling like I was living in a time warp. There had been so much rushing around going on by others, while I had sat still and alone in my grief while the hours and days had dragged by.

Gradually, over the next few months, my life had sorted itself out. I had gone back to work and my father had returned home. Friends had come round less often with ready-cooked meals, and they had stopped speaking in hushed tones. Invitations began again to arrive, and people began to say things to each other like, 'He's still young enough to find somebody else.'

Now it was seven years later and I had not found somebody else. I didn't really want to because I was still in love with Angela. Not that I was foolish enough to think that she would come back from the dead or anything odd like that. I just wasn't ready to find anybody else. Not yet. Maybe not ever.

I turned on the lights in the kitchen and looked in the fridge for something to eat. I was hungry, having missed my lunch, so I decided on salmon with penne pasta and pesto sauce. Since Angela died I had become quite a dab hand at cooking for one.

I had just sat down to eat in front of the television news when the phone rang. Typical, I thought, damn thing always goes at the wrong moment. Reluctantly I put my tray to one side, leaned over and picked up the receiver.

'Hello,' I said.

'Perry?' said a voice.

'Yes,' I replied slowly. After all, I'm not really Perry. I'm Geoffrey.

'Thank God you're there,' said the voice. 'This is Steve Mitchell.'

I thought back to our strange conversation in the Sandown jockeys' changing room two days before.

'How did you get my number?' I asked him.

'Oh,' he said, as if distracted. 'From Paul Newington. Look, Perry,' he went on in a rush, 'I'm in a bit of trouble and I badly need your help.'

43

'What bit of trouble?' I asked him.

'Well, actually it could be rather a lot of trouble,' he said. 'That bastard Scot Barlow has got himself murdered and the bloody police have arrested me for doing it.'

CHAPTER 3

'And did you?' I asked.

'Did I what?' Steve replied.

'Murder Scot Barlow?' I said.

'No,' he said. 'Of course I bloody didn't.'

'Have the police interviewed you?' I asked him.

'Not yet,' he said in a somewhat resigned tone. 'But I think they plan to. I asked to call my lawyer. So I called you.'

'I'm hardly your lawyer,' I said to him.

'Look, Perry,' he said, 'you're the only lawyer I know.' He was beginning to sound a little desperate.

'You need a solicitor not a barrister,' I said.

'Solicitors, barristers, what's the difference? You are a bloody lawyer, aren't you? Will you help me or not?'

'Calm down,' I said, trying to sound reassuring. 'Where are you exactly?'

'Newbury,' he said. 'Newbury police station.'

'How long have you been there?' I asked.

'About ten minutes, I think. They came to my house about an hour ago.'

I looked at my watch. It was ten past ten. Which solicitors

did I know in Newbury that could be roused at such an hour?
None.

'Steve,' I said. 'I can't act in this matter as at the moment you need a solicitor, not a barrister. I will see what I can do to get you a solicitor I know to come to Newbury but it won't be for a few hours at least.'

'Oh God,' he almost cried. 'Can't you come?'

'No,' I said. 'It would be like asking a brain surgeon to remove your teeth. Much better for you if you get a dentist.' I was sure that, as analogies go, and with more time, I could have done better. And not many solicitors I know would have been happy to be called a dentist, not least by some brain-surgeon barrister.

'When will this bloody solicitor arrive?' he asked, again sounding resigned.

'As soon as I can arrange it,' I said.

'The police have told me that, if I want, I can talk to the duty solicitor, whoever that is,' Steve said.

'Well, you can,' I replied. 'And for free, but I wouldn't if I were you.'

'Why not?' he asked.

'At this time of night he's likely to be a recently qualified young solicitor, or else one that can get no other work,' I said. 'You are facing a serious charge and I'd wait for someone with more experience if I were you.'

There was a long, quiet pause from the other end of the line.

'OK, I'll wait,' he said.

'Fine,' I replied. 'I'll get someone there as soon as possible.'

'Thanks,' he said.

'And Steve,' I said earnestly, 'listen to me. You don't have to answer any questions until he arrives. Do you understand?'

'Yes,' he said with a yawn in his voice.

'What time did you get up this morning?' I asked him.

'Usual time,' he said. 'Ten to six. I was riding out at seven.'

'Tell the police that you are tired and need to sleep. Tell them that you have been awake for nearly seventeen hours and you are entitled to have a rest before being interviewed.' Strictly, it may not have been true, but it was worth a try.

'Right,' he said.

'And when the solicitor does arrive, take his advice absolutely.'

'OK,' he said rather flatly. 'I will.'

Did he, I wondered, sound like a guilty man resigned to his fate?

I called a solicitor I knew in Oxford and asked him. 'Sorry, mate,' he replied in his Australian accent, he was too busy teaching some gorgeous young university student the joys of sleeping with an older man. I had learned from experience not to ask him if the gorgeous young student was male or female. However, he did rouse himself sufficiently to give me the name of a firm in Newbury that he could recommend, together with one of their partners' mobile phone number.

Sure, said the partner when I called, he would go. Steve Mitchell was quite famous in those parts, and representing a celebrity client accused of murder was every local solicitor's dream. To say nothing of the potential size of the fee.

I returned to my, now cold, pasta and thought again about last Saturday at Sandown. I went over in my mind everything that had been said, and particularly I recalled the strange encounter with the battered Scot Barlow in the showers.

It was not unknown for barristers to represent their friends and even members of their own families. Some senior QCs, it

47

was said, had such a wide circle of friends that they spent their whole lives defending them against criminal or civil proceedings. Personally, I tried to avoid getting myself into such a position. Friendships to me were too important to place in jeopardy by having to lay bare all one's secrets and emotions. The truth, the whole truth and nothing but the truth is rare even amongst the closest of chums, and a friend would far more resent being asked a question he didn't want to answer by me than if a complete stranger had done it. Victory in court may cause the friendship to founder anyway due to too much intimate knowledge, and if one lost the case then one lost the friend for sure.

So I usually invented some little ruse to avoid the situation. I would often say that so-and-so in my chambers was much better qualified or experienced to accept the brief, or that I was too busy with other cases and that so-and-so could devote more time to preparing the defence case. I always promised to keep abreast of the facts in the case, and sometimes I even managed to.

However, this time I didn't need to invent an excuse. I couldn't act for Steve Mitchell because I was privy to some material evidence and was far more likely to be called to testify for the prosecution than to be one of the defence counsel. But, I thought, there had been no other witness to the exchange between Barlow and me in the Sandown showers, and now Barlow was dead. To whom, I thought, should I volunteer the information? And when?

The murder of top jump jockey Scot Barlow was the number one item on the eight o'clock television news bulletin the following morning. A reporter, standing outside the property, claimed that Barlow had been found lying in a pool of blood in the kitchen of his home with a five-foot-long, two-pronged pitch-fork embedded in his chest. The reporter also stated that some-one was helping the police with their enquiries. He didn't say that the someone was Steve Mitchell, but he didn't say it wasn't.

My mobile phone rang as I was buttering a slice of toast.

'Hello,' I said, picking it up.

'Is that Geoffrey Mason?' asked a very quiet well-spoken male voice in a whisper.

'Yes,' I replied.

'Do as you are told,' said the voice, very quietly, but very distinctly.

'What did you say?' I asked, surprised.

'Do as you are told,' the voice repeated in the same manner.

'Who is this?' I demanded, but, in response, the caller simply hung up.

I looked at the phone in my hand as if it would tell me.

Do as I was told, the man had said. But he hadn't told me what I had to do, or when. It couldn't have been a wrong number; he had asked me my name. How very odd, I thought.

I checked through the list of received calls but, as I expected, the caller had withheld his number.

The phone in my hand rang again suddenly, making me jump and drop it onto the kitchen counter. I grabbed at it and pushed the button.

'Hello?' I said rather tentatively.

'Is that Geoffrey Mason?' asked a male voice, a different male voice.

'Yes,' I replied, cautiously. 'Who is this?'

'Bruce Lygon,' said the voice.

'Oh,' I said, relieved. Bruce Lygon was the solicitor from Newbury I had called the night before.

'Are you all right?' he asked.

'Fine,' I said. 'I thought you might be someone else.'

'Your friend seems to be in a bit of a hole here,' he said. 'The cops think there's not much doubt he did it. That's clear from their questions. We've been at it since six this morning. We're just having a short break while the detectives have a conference.'

'What's the evidence?' I asked him.

'They haven't revealed much as yet but I gather that the victim was stabbed with some sort of fork.'

'They reported that on the television,' I said.

'Did they indeed?' he said. 'Well, it appears that the fork belongs to Mr Mitchell.'

'Oh,' I said.

'Yeah, and that's not all,' he said. 'As well as Mr Barlow, there were some betting slips also impaled on the fork and they belonged to Mr Mitchell as well. They had his name on them.'

'Oh,' I said again.

'And,' he went on, 'there was a text message received yesterday afternoon on Barlow's mobile from Mitchell saying that he was going to, and I quote, "come round and sort you out properly you sneaking little bastard".'

'And what does Mitchell have to say?' I asked.

'Nothing,' said Bruce. 'But then again, I told him not to. He just sits there looking pale and scared.'

'But what has he said to you privately?' I asked.

'He mumbled something about being framed,' Bruce replied, but I could tell from his tone that he didn't believe it. 'Do you want me to stay here?'

'It's not my decision,' I said. 'Steve Mitchell is your client, not me. Ask him.'

'I have,' he said. 'He told me to call you and to do whatever you said.'

Bugger, I thought. I just could not get involved with this case. I knew too much about it for a start, and it looked like it was pretty much a foregone conclusion, and that was another good reason for not getting involved. Acquiring a reputation in chambers for having too many courtroom losses wouldn't help my potential QC credentials either.

'You had better stay then,' I said, 'but remind Mr Mitchell that it's you and not me who's acting for him, and I can't make those decisions. Have they charged him yet?'

'No,' he replied. 'More questioning first. And I know they are searching his place. They told him so. There will be more questions from that, I expect.'

Under English law, the police could only question a suspect prior to charging.

'When's their time up?' I asked him. The police had a maximum of thirty-six hours from when he first arrived at the police station before they either charged Steve, brought him before a magistrate to ask for more time, or released him.

'According to the record, he was arrested at eight fifty-three last night and arrived at the police station at nine fifty-seven,' he said. 'So far they haven't asked for more time and I think it's unlikely they will. I don't think they need his answers. Their body language says that they have enough to charge without them.'

'So you'll stay until he's charged?' I asked.

'Only if they charge him before six,' he said. 'After that I'm taking my wife out to dinner for her birthday, and I'd rather

51

face the Law Society than fail to do that.' There was laughter in his voice. Steve Mitchell might be facing the toughest contest of his sporting life, but it was still just a job to Bruce Lygon. 'But don't worry, there'll be someone here from my firm if I'm not.'

'Great,' I said. 'Please keep me informed, but I'm not actually representing him.' But, like everybody else, I was curious about murder, especially as I also knew the victim.

'I will if I can, but only if he says so.'

He was right, of course, client confidentiality and all that.

Steve Mitchell's arrest was the front-page story on the midday edition of the *Evening Standard*. I grabbed a copy as I dodged the rain outside Blackfriars Crown Court on my way to a local café for some lunch. 'TOP JOCK HELD FOR MURDER', shouted the banner headline alongside a library picture of a smiling Scot Barlow. The story gave little more detail than I already knew, but the report speculated that the murder had been in revenge for Barlow giving the racing authorities details of Mitchell's illegal gambling activities.

I turned on my mobile phone. There was one voicemail message but it wasn't from Bruce Lygon. It was from the quiet, well-spoken male whisperer. 'Remember,' he said menacingly, 'do exactly as you are told.'

I sat in the window of the café eating a cheese and pickle sandwich, trying to work out what on earth it was all about. No one had told me to do anything, so how could I do it? I would have dismissed it as mistaken identity except that the caller this morning had asked if I was Geoffrey Mason. And, indeed, I was. But were there two Geoffrey Masons? There must be, but there was only one with my phone number.

I decided to ignore that problem and concentrate on the matter currently in hand. The judge that morning had not been very helpful and he had not been greatly swayed by my arguments concerning the admissibility of prior convictions in the conspiracy-to-defraud trial of the brothers. It made the case more difficult to prosecute, but not impossible. After all, the brothers had admitted having done it. All we had to do was convince the jury they had done it for gain.

I called Bruce Lygon.

'Any news?' I asked him.

'No.' He sounded bored. 'They are apparently waiting for the results of some forensics. From his clothes and shoes, I think. And his car.'

'How is he?' I said.

'Pretty fed up,' he said. 'Keeps saying he should be riding at Huntingdon races. Asks when he can go home. I don't think he fully realizes the extent of the mess he's in.'

'So you think he will definitely be charged?' I asked.

'Oh yeah, no question. They haven't even bothered to question him for the past four hours. They're sure he did it. One of them said as much to him and asked whether he wanted to confess and save them all a lot of trouble.'

'What did he say?' I asked.

'Told them to get lost, or words to that effect.' I smiled. I could imagine the actual exchange. Steve didn't talk to anyone without at least a few bloodys sprinkled in.

'Well, for your sake, I hope they charge him by six,' I said, thinking of his wife's birthday dinner. 'Will it be you that goes with him to the magistrate's court in the morning?'

'Will I? Are you kidding?' he said. 'It's not every day I get a case that leads on the lunchtime news. Even the wife says to stay here all night if I have to. Don't let him out of your sight, she said, just in case he finds himself another solicitor.'

Maybe it was more than just a job to Bruce, after all. But if he thought representing a guilty but popular and celebrated client would bring him any respect he was much mistaken. Two years before I had been dramatically unsuccessful in defending a much-loved middle-aged comedy TV actress from a charge of deliberate shoplifting and the subsequent assault of the store detective. She had committed the crimes but it had been me who had been universally denounced in the press for failing to get her off. Everyone knows it was George Carmen QC, who, in the face of overwhelming evidence, secured an acquittal for Ken Dodd for tax evasion, but no one remembers the counsel who failed to keep Lester Piggott out of jail on the same charge. Such as it is in life, and such as it is in racing. Winning is all. Coming second is a disaster, even if it's by the slightest margin, the shortest of short heads.

The afternoon was little better than the morning had been. The judge in the case seemed determined to be as unhelpful as possible, continually interrupting my questioning as I tried to cross-examine one of the defendants. In true Perry Mason style I was trying to trap him in a lie but, every time I thought I was getting close, the judge stopped me and asked if my line of questioning was relevant. This gave the defendant time to recover and recoup. He simply smiled at me and went on telling the jury his lies. I knew they were lies, and he knew they were lies. But, from their facial expressions, I realized that the jury were believing them. It was very frustrating.

I was beginning to think that I was about to notch up another courtroom loss when the elder of the brothers carelessly stated in response to my questions that you couldn't believe what a previous witness for the prosecution had said because, he claimed, the witness was a convicted felon and a proven liar. On such things do trials turn. Because the defendant had called into question the character of a witness against him, we, the prosecution, were now entitled to call his character into question as well, and all his previous convictions were suddenly admissible into court. Hurrah. The poor defending barrister sat there with his head in his hands. He had done so well to keep the information from the jury through the judge's earlier ruling, only for his own client to mortally hole the defence below the water line. A sinking was now inevitable.

The judge adjourned proceedings for the day soon after four o'clock with the prosecution well on top. Perhaps I would actually win the case.

I took a taxi back to chambers with my box of papers and my laptop. It had been a miserably wet autumnal November day in London and the daylight had fully gone by the time I paid off the cabbie on Theobald's Road near the gated entrance to Raymond Buildings.

Julian Trent was waiting for me between two rows of parked cars. Whereas, the previous evening, I had been somewhat wary crossing Barnes Common, I hadn't really been seriously concerned that I would be attacked. I had dismissed Trent's post-trial threats as mere bravado, a lashing-out reaction to losing the case. And why would he want revenge from me when he had got off anyway? But here he was, with his trusted baseball bat, oozing menace and danger.

55

I didn't actually see him until I had walked beyond his hiding place because I was concentrating on hunching my body to keep my computer dry as I balanced it on the box of papers. My peripheral vision detected a movement to my right and I turned in time to glimpse his face just before he hit me. He was smiling.

The baseball bat caught me across the back of both legs about half way up my thighs. The blow caused my knees to buckle and I was sent sprawling to the ground, my box of papers spilling out in front of me. The suddenness of the strike left me gasping for breath. Far from leaping to my feet to defend myself, I lay face down, immobile on the wet tarmac. Strangely there was no pain. My legs felt numb and somehow detached from the rest of my body. I used my arms to roll myself over onto my back. I was determined that he wouldn't be able to knock my brains out without me seeing it coming.

He stood above me, swinging the bat from side to side. There was no one else about in the private road but he seemed not to care anyway. He was clearly enjoying himself.

'Hello, Mister Clever-Dick Lawyer,' he said with a curl to his upper lip. 'Not so clever now, are we?'

I didn't reply, not out of some feeling of defiance but because I couldn't think of anything to say.

He raised the bat to have another swing and I felt sure that my time was up. I put my arms up around my head to protect myself, closed my eyes and waited for the crunch. I wondered if I would die here with my head beaten to a pulp. I also wondered if Angela would be waiting for me on the other side. Maybe it wouldn't be so bad after all.

The bat landed with a sickening thud but not on my head, not even on my arms or hands. Trent hit my unprotected laptop computer with all his might and it obligingly disintegrated into several parts that scattered noisily across the road.

I opened my eyes and looked at him.

'Next time,' he said, 'I'll smash your head.'

Next time! Dear God, I didn't want there to be a next time.

He then stepped forward and trod hard on my genitals, putting all his weight on his right foot and crushing my manhood between his boot and the road. This time there was pain, a shooting, stabbing, excruciating pain. I moaned and rolled away sideways and he thankfully released the pressure.

'And next time,' he said, 'I'll cut your balls right off. Understand?'

I lay there silently looking at him.

'Do you fucking understand?' he repeated staring back at me.

I nodded ever so slightly.

'Good,' he said. 'Now you be a good little lawyer.'

Then he suddenly turned and walked away, leaving me lying in a puddle, curled up like a baby to lessen the ongoing agony between my legs. Could this really have happened in central London just yards from hundreds of respectable high-earning fellow professionals? This was the sort of thing that happened to some of my clients, not to me.

I was shaking and I didn't know whether it was from fear, from shock or from the cold. Tears had come quite easily to me over the past seven years since Angela had died and I cried now. I couldn't help it. It was mostly due to the relief of still being alive when I had been sure that I would die. It was the body's natural reaction to intense emotion, and I had been frightened more than at any time in my life.

Only a few minutes had elapsed in real time since I had stepped out of the taxi but my life had changed from one of discipline and order to one of chaos and fear. How easily I had been castrated of my courtroom authority. How fearful I had so quickly become of castration of another kind.

In my line of work one encountered fear and intimidation on an almost daily basis. How self-righteous and condescending I imagined I must have been to potential witnesses too fearful to give evidence. 'We will look after you,' I would say to them. 'We will protect you from the bullies,' I would promise, 'but you must do what is right.' Only now did I appreciate their predicament. I should have told Julian Trent to go to hell but, in fact, I would have licked his boots if he had so asked, and I hated myself for it.

Eventually the intensity of the pain in my groin diminished, only to be replaced by a dull ache from the backs of my thighs where the baseball bat had first caught me. The shaking also gradually abated and I was able to roll over onto my knees. It didn't seem to help much but at least I was looking at the world the right way up. My computer was well beyond repair and all my previously neatly ordered court papers were blowing along the road in the rain, hiding beneath parked cars and flying up into the branches of the leafless trees. My gown and wig, which had also been in the box, were soaking up the water from another puddle. But I didn't really care. It was as much as I could manage to stand approximately upright and stagger the few yards to the door of my chambers. And still nobody appeared.

I leaned up against the board with all the barristers' names painted on it and looked at the blue front door. I couldn't remember the code for the security lock. I had worked in these chambers for almost thirteen years and the code hadn't been changed once in all that time, but still I couldn't recall it now.

So I pushed the bell and was rewarded with Arthur's friendly voice from a small speaker.

'Yes,' he said. 'Who is it?'

'Geoffrey,' I croaked. 'Geoffrey Mason. Can you come and help?'

'Mr Mason?' Arthur asked back through the speaker. 'Are you all right?'

'No,' I said.

Almost immediately the door opened and Arthur, my rather tardy Good Samaritan, at last came to my rescue, half carrying me through the hallway into the clerks' room. He pulled up a desk chair and I gratefully sat down, but carefully so as not to further inflame the problems below.

I must have been quite a sight. I was soaked through and both the knees of my pinstripe suit were torn where I had landed on the rough tarmac. My once starched white shirt clung like a wet rag to my chest and my hair dripped rainwater down my forehead. It is surprising how quickly one becomes wet from lying in persistent rain.

'Goodness gracious,' said Arthur. 'What on earth happened to you?'

I hadn't expected Arthur to be a 'goodness gracious' sort of chap, but he did spend his working life in close proximity to barristers who acted like they lived in the eighteenth or nineteenth centuries, and some of it must have rubbed off.

'I was mugged,' I said.

'Where?' he asked.

'Outside,' I said. 'My stuff is still on the road.'

Arthur turned and rushed outside.

'Be careful,' I shouted after him, but I didn't really expect

Julian Trent still to be there. It was me he had been after, not my clerk.

Arthur returned with my gown in one hand and my wig in the other, both dripping onto the light green carpet. He had just a few of my sopping papers stuck under his arm, and I suspected that most of the others had flown with the wind.

'Is that your computer?' he asked, nodding his head towards the door.

'What's left of it,' I agreed.

'Funny,' he said. 'Muggers normally steal things, not break them. Is anything missing?'

'No, I don't think so,' I said patting myself down. I could feel both my wallet and my mobile in the soggy pockets of my jacket.

'I'm calling the police,' said Arthur, moving round the desk and lifting the phone. 'Do you need an ambulance?' he asked me.

'No,' I said. 'But a change of clothes would be good.'

Arthur spoke to the police, who promised to send someone round as soon as possible, though it might be some time.

While we waited I changed out of my sodden clothes into a track suit that Arthur found in one of my colleagues' rooms, and then I tried to make some sort of order from the saturated paperwork. After a second attempt, Arthur had recovered about half of what had been in the box and I spent some time laying the sheets out all over my room to dry. I couldn't reprint them as nearly all the files had only been on my computer.

I thought that calling the police would be a waste of time and so it turned out. Two uniformed constables arrived about forty minutes after the call and they took a statement from me while I sat in the clerks' room with Arthur hovering close by.

'Did you see the mugger?' one of them asked me.

'Not at first,' I said. 'He hit me from behind with a baseball bat.'

'How do you know it was a baseball bat?' he asked.

'I saw it later,' I said. 'I assumed it was what he hit me with.'

'Whereabouts did he hit you?'

'On the back of my legs,' I said.

They insisted that I show them. Embarrassed, I lowered the track-suit trousers to reveal two rapidly bruising red marks half way up the backs of my thighs. Arthur's eyes were almost out on stalks.

'Funny place to hit someone,' said the other policeman.

'It knocked me over,' I said.

'Yeah, it would,' he agreed. 'But most muggers would have hit you on the head. Did you get a look at his face?'

'Not really,' I said. 'It was dark.' Why, I thought, had I not told them that it had been Julian Trent who had attacked me? What was I doing? Did I not stand up for justice and right? Tell them, I told myself, tell them the truth.

'Would you know him again?' the policeman asked.

'I doubt it,' I heard myself say. *Next time, I'll smash your head*, Trent had said. *Next time, I'll cut your balls right off.* I had no wish for there to be a next time. 'It was all a bit of a blur,' I said. 'I was looking mostly at the bat.'

'But you were sure it was a man?' he asked.

'I think so,' I said.

'Black or white?' he asked.

'I couldn't say.' Even to my ears, it sounded pathetic. I hated myself, again.

They asked me if I wanted hospital treatment for my injuries but I declined. I'd had bruising worse than this due to an easy fall in a steeplechase, and I had ridden again in the very next

61

race. However, there was a big difference this time. Racing falls were accidents and, although the laws of chance might imply that they were inevitable, the injuries produced were not pre-meditated, or man made.

The two policemen clearly thought that I was not a helpful witness and I could sense from their attitude that they, too, thought that the process was a waste of time and that another mugging would go unsolved, just another statistic in the long list of unsolved street crimes in the capital.

'Well, at least you didn't have anything stolen,' said one, clearly bringing the interview to a close. He snapped shut his notebook. 'If you call the station later they'll give you a crime number. You'll need one for any insurance claim on your computer.'

'Oh,' I said. 'Thanks. Which station?'

'We're from Charing Cross,' said one.

'Right,' I said. 'I'll call there.'

'Good,' said the other, turning for the door.

And with that, they were gone, no doubt to interview some other victim, on another street.

'You weren't much help,' said Arthur, rather accusingly. 'Are you sure you didn't see who it was?'

'I'd have told them if I had,' I said quite sharply, but I wasn't sure he completely believed me. Arthur knew me too well, I thought, and I hated myself again for deceiving him more than anyone. But I really didn't want a 'next time', and I had been frightened, very frightened indeed, by my confrontation with young Mr Julian Trent. This time, I was alive and not badly damaged. And I intended to keep it that way.

*

I sat at my desk for a while trying to recover some of my confidence. 'Be a good little lawyer,' Trent had said. What had that meant? I wondered. If I really had been a good little lawyer I would have told the police exactly who had attacked me and where to find him. Even now, he would be under arrest and locked up. But for how long? He wouldn't get any jail time for hitting me once on the back of the legs and smashing my computer. I had no broken bones, not even a cut, no concussion or damaged organs, just a couple of tears in my trousers and a rain-spoilt barrister's wig. A fine, or maybe some community service, would be all he'd get. And then he'd be free to visit me again for 'next time'. No thanks. And was he anything to do with the 'do as you are told' whispered phone message? I couldn't imagine so, but why else would he attack me? Something very strange was going on.

Arthur knocked on my open door and came in, closing it behind him.

'Mr Mason, he said.

'Yes, Arthur,' I replied.

'May I say something?' he said.

'Of course, Arthur,' I replied, not actually wanting him to say anything just at the moment. But there would be no stopping him now, not if his mind was made up.

'I think it is most unlike you to be so vague as you were with those policemen,' he said, standing full-square in front of my paper-covered desk. 'Most unlike you indeed.' He paused briefly. I said nothing. 'You are the brightest and sharpest junior we have in these chambers and you miss nothing, nothing at all. Do I make myself clear?'

I was flattered by his comments and I was trying to think what to say back to him when he went on.

63

'Are you in any trouble?' he asked.

'No, of course not,' I said. 'What sort of trouble do you mean?'

'Any sort of trouble,' he said. 'Maybe some woman trouble?'

Did he think I'd been attacked by a jealous husband?

'No, Arthur, no trouble at all. I promise.'

'You could always come to me if you were,' he said. 'I like to think I look after my barristers.'

'Thank you, Arthur,' I said. 'I would most definitely tell you if I was in any sort of trouble.' I looked him straight in the eye and wondered if he knew I was lying.

He nodded, turned on his heel and walked to the door. As he opened it he turned round. 'Oh yes,' he said. 'This came for you earlier.' He walked back to the desk and handed me an A5-sized white envelope with my name printed on the front of it, with *By Hand* written on the top right-hand corner.

'Thank you,' I said, taking it. 'Do you know who delivered it?'

'No,' he said. 'It was pushed through the letter box in the front door.'

He waited but I made no move to open the envelope, and he eventually walked over to the door and went out.

I sat looking at the envelope for a few moments. I told myself that it was probably a note from a colleague in other chambers about some case or other. But, of course, it wasn't.

It contained two items. A single piece of white paper folded over and a photograph. It was another message and, this time, it left me in no doubt at all that the whispered telephone calls and Julian Trent's visit had both been connected.

Four lines of printed bold capitals ran across the centre of the paper:

BE A GOOD LITTLE LAWYER,
TAKE THE STEVE MITCHELL CASE – AND LOSE IT.
DO AS YOU ARE TOLD
NEXT TIME, SOMEONE WILL GET BADLY HURT.

The photograph was of my seventy-eight-year-old father standing outside his home in Northamptonshire.

CHAPTER 4

An Englishman's house is his castle, at least so they say. So I sat in my castle with the drawbridge pulled up and thought about what was happening to me.

I had decided against my usual walk through Gray's Inn to the bus stop in High Holborn, the ride on a number 521 to Waterloo and a crowded commuter train to Barnes, followed by the hike across the common. Instead, I had ordered a taxi that had come right to the front door of chambers to collect me, and had then delivered me safe and sound to Ranelagh Avenue, to my home, my castle.

Now I sat on a bar stool at my kitchen counter and looked again and again at the sheet of white paper. TAKE THE STEVE MITCHELL CASE – AND LOSE IT. From what I had heard from Bruce Lygon there wouldn't be much trouble in losing the case. All the evidence seemed to point that way. But why was someone so keen to be sure that it was lost? Was Steve correct when he said he'd been framed?

DO AS YOU ARE TOLD. Did that just mean that I must take the case and lose it, or were there other things as well that I would be told to do? And how was the attack by Julian Trent

66

connected? *Next time, I'll smash your head*, he'd said. *Next time, I'll cut your balls right off.* Maybe being beaten up had absolutely nothing to do with Trent's trial last March. Perhaps it was all to do with Steve Mitchell's trial in the future.

But why?

I had once had a client, a rather unsavoury individual, who had told me that the only thing better than getting away with doing a crime was to get someone else convicted for having done it. That way, he'd explained, the police aren't even looking any more.

'Don't you have any conscience about some poor soul doing jail time for something you did?' I had asked him.

'Don't be stupid,' he'd said. 'It makes me laugh. I don't care about anyone else.' There really was no such thing as honour amongst thieves.

Was that what was going on here? Stitch up Steve Mitchell for Scot Barlow's murder and, hey presto, the crime is solved but the real murderer is safe and well and living in clover.

I called my father.

'Hello,' he said in his usual rather formal tone. I could imagine him sitting in front of the television in his bungalow watching the early evening news.

'Hello, Dad,' I said.

'Ah, Geoff,' he said. 'How are things in the Smoke?'

'Fine, thanks. How are things with you?' It was a ritual. We spoke on the telephone about once a week and, every time, we exchanged these pleasantries. Sadly, these days we had little else to say to one another. We lived in different worlds. We had never been particularly close and he had moved to the village of Kings Sutton, near Banbury, from his native urban Surrey after my mother had died. I had thought that it had been a strange choice but perhaps, unlike me, he had needed to escape his memories.

'Much the same,' he said.

'Dad,' I said. 'I know this is a strange question, but what have you been wearing today?'

'Clothes,' he said, amused. 'Same as always. Why?'

'What clothes?' I asked.

'Why do you need to know?' he demanded suspiciously. We both knew that I was apt to criticize my father's rather ageing wardrobe, and he didn't like it.

'I just do,' I said. 'Please.'

'Fawn corduroy trousers and a yellow shirt under a green pullover,' he said.

'Does the pullover have any holes in it?' I asked.

'None of your business,' he said sharply.

'Does it have a hole in the left elbow?' I persisted.

'Only a small one,' he said defensively. 'It's perfectly all right to wear around the house. Now what is this all about?'

'Nothing,' I said lightly. 'Forget it. Forget I asked.'

'You're a strange boy,' he said. He often said it. I thought he was a strange father, but I kept that to myself.

'I'll call you on Sunday then,' I said to him. I often called on Sundays.

'Right. Bye for now then.' He put down the receiver at his end. He'd never liked talking on the phone and he was habitually eager to finish a conversation as soon as it had started. Today we had been briefer than usual.

I sat and stared at the photograph in my hand, the photograph that had accompanied the note in the white envelope. It showed my father outside the front door of his bungalow wearing fawn-coloured trousers, a yellow shirt and a green pullover with a small hole clearly visible on the left elbow, the yellow of the shirt beneath contrasting with the dark green of the wool. The photo had to have been taken today. For all his reluctance to buy new clothes, my father could never be accused of wearing dirty ones, and he always put on a clean shirt crisp from the local laundry every morning. I suppose he might have had more than one yellow shirt, but I doubted it.

But how, I thought, had they, whoever they were, managed to get a photograph of my father so quickly? Julian Trent had been released from custody only on Friday, and Scot Barlow murdered only yesterday. I wondered if the one had been dependent on the other.

Bruce Lygon still hadn't called me, so I didn't even know if Steve Mitchell had yet been charged with murder, but here I was, already being told to make sure he was convicted.

As if on cue, my telephone rang.

'Hello,' I said, picking it up.

'Geoffrey?' said a now familiar voice.

'Bruce,' I replied. 'What news?'

'I'm on my way to have dinner with my wife,' he said. 'They charged Mitchell with murder at six this evening and he'll be in court tomorrow at ten.'

'Which court?' I asked.

'Newbury magistrates,' he said. 'He's sure to be remanded. No provincial magistrate would ever give bail on a murder charge. I'll apply, of course, but it will have to go before a judge for there to be any chance, and I think it's most unlikely, considering the cause of death. Very nasty.'

'Yes,' I replied. 'I agree, but you never know when there is a bit of celebrity factor.' Under English law the granting of bail was a basic right for all accused and there had to be a good reason for refusing it. In this case the reason given might be that the ferociousness of the attack provided reasonable grounds to believe that the accused might do it again, or that, owing to the seriousness of the charge, he might abscond. Either way, I would bet my year's pay that Steve Mitchell would find himself locked up on remand the following day.

'Mr Mitchell is very insistent that you should defend him,' Bruce Lygon went on.

How ironic, I thought. Did Steve also want me to lose?

'I'm only a junior,' I said. 'Someone of Steve Mitchell's standing would expect a silk.'

'He seems determined that it should be you,' he replied.

But even if I had wanted to lead the defence, the trial judge would be likely to ask some telling questions about how I intended to strengthen the defence team, especially at the front. It would be a coded recommendation to get a QC to lead.

The best I might expect was to be appointed as a silk's junior in the case. As such I might be responsible for doing most of the work. But I would get little of the credit for obtaining an acquittal, while shouldering most of the blame if our client were convicted. Such was the life of a junior.

What was I even thinking about? I told myself. I could not act in this case. The law wouldn't let me.

Do as you are told.

Next time, I'll smash your head.

I'll cut your balls right off.

Someone will get badly hurt.

Oh hell. What do I do?

'Are you still there?' Bruce asked.

'Sorry,' I said. 'I was thinking.'

'I'll contact your clerk in due course, then, I've got the number,' he said.

'Fine,' I replied. Was I mad? 'But Bruce,' I went on. 'Will you call me tomorrow and tell me what happens. And where Mitchell is sent. I'd like to go and talk with him.'

'OK,' he said, slowly. 'I suppose that will be all right.' I could tell from his tone that he didn't like it.

What a cheek, I thought. It had been me that had given him his celebrity client and now he was becoming protective of his position.

'Look, Bruce,' I said. 'I'm not trying to steal your client, whom, you might recall, I gave you in the first place. But I need to speak to Steve Mitchell and may need to do so more than once. If he chooses, and I have no intention of convincing him otherwise, you can act for him throughout, including at trial. All I ask of you is that you engage a brief from my chambers, whether it be me or not. Is that fair?'

'Oh, absolutely,' he replied, backtracking a little. Perhaps he too had suddenly worked out that Steve Mitchell was my friend and would, on my say-so, drop Mr Bruce Lygon quicker than a red-hot coal. Bruce needed me, not vice versa.

'Good,' I said. 'Then you will call me?'

'You bet,' he said. 'Straight after the hearing.'

'Fine,' I said. 'Now go and enjoy your dinner. Say happy birthday to your wife.'

'I will,' he said. 'I will.'

As expected, Steve Mitchell was remanded in custody at the brief hearing at Newbury magistrates' court at ten the following morning. According to the report on the lunchtime news, he

71

had spoken only to confirm his name and address. No plea had been entered, and none asked for. The report concluded with the fact that Mitchell had been remanded to Bullingdon Prison, near Bicester, to appear again at Oxford Crown Court in seven days' time.

I was watching the TV in one of the conference rooms in chambers. My conspiracy-to-defraud trial had ended abruptly and unexpectedly when the court had resumed at ten thirty that morning. Accepting the inevitable, the brothers had changed their pleas to guilty in the hope and expectation of getting a lesser sentence. The judge, caught slightly unawares, and having promptly thanked and dismissed the jury, ordered reports on the two men and then adjourned the case for sixteen days. We would reassemble for sentencing two weeks on Friday at ten.

I was pleased. Any victory is good, but one where the defendants change their plea is particularly gratifying as it means that, even though I would never know if I had actually persuaded the jury of their guilt, the defendants themselves were convinced that I had. So, now believing they had no chance of acquittal, they had jumped before they were pushed. And best of all, it also meant that I had two clear weeks that I had expected to spend at Blackfriars Crown Court now available for other things. And that was rare. Trials tended to overrun, not finish early. It felt like the end of term at school.

Arthur had not been around when I had arrived back from court but he was in the clerks' room when I went through from the conference room and back to my desk.

'Arthur,' I said. 'You might expect a call from a Mr Bruce Lygon. He's a solicitor in Newbury. He's acting for Steve Mitchell.'

'The jockey?' Arthur asked.

'One and the same,' I said. 'Apparently Mr Mitchell wants me as his counsel.'

'I'm sure we can find him a silk,' said Arthur. He wasn't being discourteous, just realistic.

'That's what I told Mr Lygon,' I said.

Arthur nodded and made a note. 'I'll be ready when he calls.'

'Thanks,' I said, and went on through to my room.

I called Bruce Lygon. He had left a message after the magistrates' hearing but I needed him to do more.

'Bruce,' I said when he answered. 'I want to visit the crime scene. Can you fix it with the police?' The lawyers for the accused were entitled to have access to the scene but at the discretion of the police, and not prior to the collection of forensic evidence.

'With or without me?' he asked.

'As you like,' I said. 'But as soon as possible, please.'

'Does this mean you will act for him?' he asked.

'No, it doesn't,' I said. 'Not yet. It might help me make up my mind.'

'But only his representatives have access,' he said.

I knew. 'If you don't tell the police,' I said, 'then they will never know.'

'Right,' he said slowly. I felt that he was confused. He was not the only one.

'And can you arrange an interview for me with Mitchell at Bullingdon?'

'But you're not . . .' he tailed off. 'I suppose it might be possible,' he said finally.

'Good,' I said. 'Tomorrow would be great.'

'Right,' he said again. 'I'll get back to you then.'

73

Bruce had been a lucky choice. He was so keen to be representing his celebrity client that he seemed happy to overlook a few departures from proper procedure, to bend the rules just a little. I decided not to tell Arthur what was going on. He wouldn't have been the least bit flexible.

Steve Mitchell was very agitated when I met him at noon the following day at Bullingdon Prison. I currently didn't own a car as I found it an unnecessary expense, especially with the congestion charge and the ever-rising cost of parking in London. However, I probably spent at least half of what I saved on hiring cars from the Hertz office on Fulham Palace Road. This time they had provided me with a bronze-coloured Ford Mondeo that had easily swallowed up the fifty or so miles to Oxfordshire.

'God, Perry,' Steve said as he came into the stark prison interview room reserved for lawyers to meet with their clients. 'Get me out of this bloody place.'

'I'll try,' I said, not wishing to dash his hopes too quickly.

He marched round the room. 'I didn't bloody do it,' he said. 'I swear to you I never did it.'

'Just sit down,' I said. Reluctantly, he ceased his pacing and sat on a grey steel stool beside the grey steel table and I sat on a similar stool opposite him. These functional items, along with two more identical stools, were securely fastened with bolts to the bare grey concrete floor. The room was about eight foot square with sickly cream walls. The only light came from a large, energy-efficient fluorescent bulb surrounded by a wire cage in the centre of the white ceiling. Absolutely no expense had been wasted on comfort.

'I didn't do it,' he said again. 'I tell you, I'm being framed.'

As it happened, I believed him. In the past I'd had clients who had sworn blind that they were innocent and were being framed, and experience had taught me not to believe most of them. One client had once sworn to me on his mother's life that he was innocent of setting fire to his own house for the insurance money, only for the said mother to confess that she and her son had planned it together. When she gave evidence against him in court, he had shouted from the dock that he'd kill her. So much for her life.

However, in Steve's case I had other reasons for believing him.

'Who's framing you?' I asked him.

'I've got no bloody idea,' he said. 'That's for you to find out.'

'Who is Julian Trent?' I asked him calmly.

'Who?' he said.

'Julian Trent,' I repeated.

'Never heard of him,' Steve said. Not a flicker in his eyes, not a fraction of hesitation in his voice. Asking questions for a living, I believed I was a reasonable judge of when someone was lying. But I was not infallible. Over the years I had frequently believed people who were telling me lies, but it was not often that I discovered that someone I thought was lying was actually being truthful. Either Steve was being straight with me, or he was fairly good at lying.

'Who is he?' Steve asked.

'No one important,' I said. It was my turn to lie. 'I just wondered if you knew him.'

'Should I?' he asked.

'No reason you should,' I said. I decided to change the subject. 'So why do the police think you killed Scot Barlow?'

'Because they just do,' he answered unhelpfully.

'But they must have some evidence,' I said.

'It seems that it was my bloody pitchfork stuck into the little bastard.' I could imagine that Steve referring to Barlow as 'the little bastard' hadn't gone down too well with the police. 'And would I be so stupid to have killed the little bastard with my own pitchfork? At least I would have then taken the bloody thing home again.'

'What else do they have?' I asked him.

'Something about spots of his blood and some of his hairs being found in my car, and his blood being on my boots. It's all bloody nonsense. I was never in his house.'

'So where exactly were you when he was killed?' I asked him.

'I don't know,' he said. 'They haven't told me when he actually died. But they did ask me what I was doing between one and six on Monday afternoon. I told them I was riding at Ludlow races. But I wasn't. The meeting was abandoned due to the bloody course being waterlogged.'

That was really stupid, I thought. Lying wouldn't have exactly endeared him to the police, and it was so easy for them to check.

'So where were you?' I asked him again.

He seemed reluctant to tell me, so I sat and waited in silence.

'At home,' he said eventually.

'On your own?' I pressed him.

'Yes,' he said. 'I was alone reading all afternoon.'

Now he was lying. I was sure of it and I didn't like it.

'That's a shame,' I said. 'If someone was with you, they would be able to give you an alibi.'

He sat silently.

'Do you know what the word "alibi" means?' I asked him. He shook his head. 'It's Latin. It means "somewhere else". An

76

unshakeable alibi is proof of innocence.' I tried to lighten the atmosphere. 'And even you, Steve, couldn't be in two places at once. Are you sure you were alone all afternoon?'

'Absolutely,' he said, affronted. 'Are you saying I'm a liar?' He stood up and looked at me.

'No, of course not,' I said. But he was. 'I'm just trying to make sure you remembered correctly.'

I rather hoped he would sit down again but he paced round the room like a caged tiger.

'I'll tell you what I do remember,' he said to my back. 'I remember that I've never been in Scot Barlow's house. Not on Monday. Not ever. I didn't even know where the little bastard lived.'

'What about the text message?' I said. 'The one saying you were coming round to sort him out.'

'I didn't send any bloody text message,' he replied. 'And certainly not to him.'

Surely, I thought, the police must have the phone records.

He walked around in front of me and sat down again.

'It doesn't look too good, does it?' he said.

'No, Steve, it doesn't.' We sat there in silence for a few moments. 'Who would gain from Barlow's death?' I asked him.

'Reno Clemens must be laughing all the way to the winning post,' he said. 'With Barlow dead and me in here, he's got rid of both of us.'

I thought it unlikely that Clemens would go to the extent of murder and a frame-up to simply get rid of his racing rivals. But hadn't someone once tried to break the leg of a skating rival for that very reason?

'I didn't do it, you know.' He looked up at me. 'Not that I'm sorry he's dead.'

77

'What was there between you two?' I asked. 'Why did you hate him so much?' I thought that I wouldn't ask him about the incident in the showers at Sandown. Not yet. Much better, at the moment, if absolutely no one knew I had seen Barlow lying in the shower, and what he had said to me.

'I hated him because he was a sneaky little bastard,' Steve said.

'But just how was he sneaky?' I asked.

'He just was.'

'Look, Steve,' I said. 'If you want me to help you, you will have to tell me everything. Now why was he sneaky?'

'He would sneak to the stewards if anyone did anything wrong.'

'How do you know?' I asked. 'Did he ever sneak on you?'

'What, to the stewards?'

'Yes,' I said, imploring. 'To the stewards.'

'Well, no,' he said. 'Not on me to the stewards, but he was a bastard nevertheless.'

'But why?' I almost shouted at him, spreading my arms and hands open wide.

He stood up again and turned away from me. 'Because,' he said in a rush, 'he told my bloody wife I was having an affair.'

Ah, I thought. That would account for the hatred. Steve went on without turning round. 'Then she left me and took my kids away.'

Ah, again.

'How did Barlow know you were having an affair?' I asked.

'I was having it with his sister,' he said.

'Do the police know about this?'

'I bleeding well hope not,' he said, turning round. 'Now that would give me a bloody motive, wouldn't it?'

'When did all this happen?' I asked him.

'Years ago,' he said.

'Are you still having the affair with Barlow's sister?' I asked.

'Nah, it was just a fling,' he said. 'Finished right there and then, but Natalie, that's my wife, she wouldn't come home. Went and married some bloody Australian and they now live in Sydney. With my kids. I ask you, how am I meant to see them when they're half the world away? It's all that bastard Barlow's fault.'

I thought that a jury would not necessarily agree with his assessment.

'And what about the betting slips found on the prongs of the fork?' I said.

'Nothing to do with me,' Steve said.

'But they had your name on them,' I said.

'Yeah, and would I be so stupid as to leave them stuck on the bloody fork if I had planted it in Barlow's chest? Don't be bloody daft. It's obviously a sodding stitch-up. Surely you can see that?'

It did seem to me that the police must think Steve to be very stupid indeed if they were so certain he had done it based on that. Or perhaps they had forensic evidence that we didn't yet know about. We would discover in due course, during pre-trial disclosure but, for the time being, we could only guess. Either way, it would be worth pursuing the matter at trial.

'Were they, in fact, your betting slips?' I asked him. We both knew that gambling on horses was against the terms of his riding licence.

'They may have been,' he said. 'But then they wouldn't have had my name on them. I'm not that bloody stupid.' He laughed. 'Least of my worries now, I suppose.'

'Is it true that Barlow used to go through other jocks' pockets looking for betting slips?' I said.

'I don't know,' he said. 'I doubt it. It was probably me that started that rumour.' He grinned at me. 'I'd have said anything to get at him.'

In truth, it was Steve Mitchell, and not Scot Barlow, who had been the sneaky little bastard.

'I hope it wasn't that rumour that got him killed,' I said.

Steve looked at me. 'Bloody hell,' he said.

CHAPTER 5

On Thursday night I stayed with my trainer, Paul Newington, at Great Milton.

I had left Steve Mitchell feeling very sorry for himself at Bullingdon Prison.

'When can you get me out of here?' he'd asked me as we had shaken hands.

'I really don't know, Steve,' I'd said. 'It is most unlikely that you would get bail on a murder charge.'

'But I didn't do it,' he had repeated yet again.

'The police don't see it like that,' I'd said. 'And I'm afraid the court will take more notice of them than of you.'

'But you will try?' he had implored.

I had privately thought it would be a complete waste of my time.

'I'll get Bruce Lygon to make another application,' I'd told him.

'I want you to do it,' he had demanded.

But I knew it wasn't always a good idea for a barrister to appear at a bail hearing. It was seen as overkill. In some eyes, it tended to make the accused look guilty. Sometimes that very fact could swing the decision against the award. And anyway, bail in murder cases was as rare as hen's teeth.

'I don't really think it would make any difference,' I'd told him.

'So when can I expect to get out?' he had asked in near desperation.

'Steve,' I'd said. 'I think you had better prepare yourself for quite a lengthy stretch in here. The trial date will likely not be set for at least six months and it could be as long as a year away.'

'A year!' he'd exclaimed, going white. 'Oh my God. I'll go mad.'

'I'll see what I can do to get you out sooner, but I don't want to build your hopes up too much.'

I had looked at him standing there with drooping shoulders, appearing much shorter than his five foot six. He may have been an arrogant ego maniac who annoyed most of those he encountered, but there was no doubt that he was one of the best in his chosen tough and physically demanding profession. He was basically a harmless victim and I was sure he was no murderer. And he didn't deserve to have been thrust into this nightmare.

I had thought he was going to cry. Perhaps for the first time he had appreciated the real fix he was in and he was far from pleased about it.

I hadn't liked leaving Steve in that state. Over the years I'd left clients in prison on remand in states of emotion that varied from utter rage to complete collapse. It was never easy, but this was the first time I'd felt real anger in tandem with my client. Hold on a minute, I thought suddenly, he's not my client and, what's more, he couldn't be.

*

82

It was always an escape from my usual work to go to Paul Newington's place. He was so different from the people I dealt with on a day-to-day basis. For a start, I don't think I had ever seen him in a tie, and almost never in a jacket. When he was at home he habitually wore blue denim jeans with scuffed knees and frayed legs, and, on this occasion, he sported a black sweat-shirt with 'Motorhead' emblazoned across its chest in lightning-strike letters. Perhaps it would not have been my choice of garb when entertaining one of his owners.

But I think that was why I liked him so much. He used to say that the horses didn't care if he was in his dressing gown so why should their owners. I tactfully didn't point out to him that it wasn't the horses that were paying him for their board and lodging. It was one of the reasons why he had never quite broken into the big time. Rich owners want to be appreciated and, in their eyes, afforded due reverence by their trainers. And rich owners buy the best horses.

Paul's richest owners had continually been wooed away by other trainers more willing to bow and scrape to their whims. I had resisted two such approaches myself because I liked the relaxed atmosphere of his stable. It was in such contrast to the old-fashioned formality I was all too familiar with in the courts.

Paul and I walked round the stables as his staff were busy mucking out and giving their charges food and water for the night. Sandeman looked wonderful in his box with his shining golden tan coat and showing no apparent ill effects from his race at Sandown the previous Saturday.

I walked over and slapped his neck.

'Good boy,' I said to him calmly. 'Who's a good boy?'

He blew through his nostrils and shifted his bulk, turning his head to see if I had a titbit for him. I never came to Paul's without some apples in my pocket and today was no exception. Sandeman gratefully munched his way noisily through a Granny Smith, dripping saliva and apple bits into his bedding. It was a satisfactory encounter for us both and I took my leave of him with a slap on his neck which caused him to lift and lower his head as if he were agreeing with me.

'See you in the morning, my boy,' I called to him as I left his box. I often wondered if our equine partners had any notion of the depth of our devotion for them.

Laura, Paul's wife, cooked us supper and, as always, we sat round the bleached-pine kitchen table, eating her best macaroni cheese with onions. It wasn't long before the conversation turned to the hot topic in racing circles.

'So, do you think he did it?' said Paul between mouthfuls.

'Who? Steve Mitchell?' I said.

'Umm,' he said while ladling another spoonful of the pasta into his mouth.

'The evidence seems to suggest it,' I said.

'What is the world coming to?' Paul said. 'When I used to ride there was always greater camaraderie than there is nowadays.'

I thought that Paul was wearing rose-tinted spectacles in his memory of how things used to be. Rivalry amongst jockeys had always been alive and well, and certainly had been in the nineteenth century, in the time of the great Fred Archer, when causing your rival to miss his steam train to the next meeting was as legitimate a tactic as out-riding him in a close finish.

'Well, do *you* think he did it?' I asked Paul.

'I don't know, you're the lawyer,' he replied.

'He would have to have been incredibly stupid to have left all those clues,' I said. 'The murder weapon left sticking in the victim belonged to him. And he supposedly texted a message to Barlow that afternoon saying he was coming round to sort him out.'

'I thought Steve Mitchell had more sense,' said Paul, shaking his head. He had clearly convicted the accused before any defence witnesses had been called.

'I'm not so sure,' I said. 'There are many questions that need answering in this case.'

'But who else would have done it?' asked Paul. 'Everyone knew that Mitchell hated Barlow's guts. You could cut the atmosphere between them with a knife.'

'Reno Clemens has done well with both of them being out of the way,' I said.

'Oh come on,' Paul said. 'Reno might be a damn good jockey but he's hardly a murderer. He hasn't got the brains.'

'He may have others around him who have,' I said.

Paul waved a dismissive hand and refilled our wine glasses.

'Do you know anyone called Julian Trent?' I asked into the pause.

'No,' said Paul. Laura shook her head. 'Is he a jockey?'

'No,' I said. 'It's not important, I just wondered.'

'Who is he?' Paul asked.

'Just an ex-client of mine,' I said. 'His name has popped up in connection with Barlow a couple of times and I just wondered if you knew him. It doesn't matter.'

There were a few moments of silence as we concentrated on our food.

'Do you know why Barlow and Mitchell hated each other so much?' I asked.

'Wasn't it something to do with Barlow's sister?' Paul said. 'Mitchell had an affair with her or something.'

'Such a shame,' Laura interjected unexpectedly.

'What's a shame?' I asked her.

'About Scot Barlow's sister,' she said.

'What about his sister?' I said.

'Don't you know?' she said. She went on when my blank expression gave her the answer. 'She killed herself in June.'

'How?' I asked, wondering why Steve Mitchell hadn't bothered to mention this to me.

'At a party,' Laura said. 'Apparently she was depressed and injected herself with a huge dose of anaesthetic.'

'How did she get anaesthetic?' I asked.

'She was a vet,' said Paul. 'Specialized in horses.'

'Where?' I asked.

'Lambourn,' Paul replied. 'She worked in the equine hospital there and most of the local trainers used her practice. She was one of a team, of course.'

'You must remember,' said Laura. 'There was a huge fuss on the television and the papers were full of it.'

'I was away for the first half of June,' I said. 'I must have missed it.' I had been away advising a client up on a money-laundering charge in Gibraltar. The long arm of the English law still stretched far to our remaining colonies and dependencies. 'Whose party was it?' I asked.

'Simon Dacey's,' said Paul.

I again looked rather blank.

'He's a trainer,' said Paul. 'Trains on the flat only. Moved to Lambourn about five years ago from Middleham in Wensleydale.' That may account for why I didn't know of him. 'He threw the party after winning the Derby. You know, with Peninsula.'

Now, even I had heard of Peninsula. Hottest horseflesh property in the world. Horse of the Year as a two-year-old and, this season, winner of the Two Thousand Guineas at Newmarket in May, the Derby at Epsom in June, the Breeders Cup the previous month at Santa Anita Park in California, and now on his way to some lucrative earnings at stud.

'That must have gone down well with the guests,' I said rather flippantly.

'It certainly didn't,' said Laura seriously. 'We were there. We've known Simon since our Yorkshire days. Paul worked for him as an assistant when we first started. The party was huge. Massive marquee in the garden with live bands and everything. It was great fun. At least it was until someone found Millie Barlow.'

'Where was she found?' I asked.

'In the house,' said Paul. 'Upstairs, in one of the bedrooms.'

'Who found her?' I said.

'No idea,' said Paul. 'The police arrived and stopped the party about nine at night. It had been going since noon. Started off as Sunday lunch and just went on.'

'What did the police do?' I asked him.

'Took our names and addresses and sent us home,' he said. 'Most of us hadn't even been in the house. They asked for witnesses to tell them when they had last seen Millie Barlow, but we didn't even know what she looked like so we left as soon as we could.'

'And were they sure it was suicide?'

'That's what everyone thought,' he said.

'What was she depressed about?'

'You seem very interested all of a sudden,' said Paul.

'Just my suspicious mind,' I said with a laugh. 'One violent death in a family is unfortunate; two within five months may be more than coincidental.'

'Wow,' said Laura, perking up her interest. 'Are you saying that Millie was murdered?'

'No, of course not,' I said. 'I just wondered if the inquest had found that she had killed herself, and why.'

'I don't know,' she said. 'I don't even know if the inquest has been held.'

I hadn't heard about the case, or read about it, but I knew that the Coroner's Court system, like every other aspect of the law, was slow and tedious at times. It wasn't unusual for an inquest to be opened and adjourned for many months, even years. I made a mental note to look it up on the internet.

'So, how's my horse,' I said, changing the subject.

'Slow and fat,' said Paul, laughing, 'like his owner.'

I toasted our slowness and fatness with good red wine, and added a few more ounces with a second helping of macaroni.

I adored riding out on cold, crisp winter's mornings with my breath showing in the air and the frost white on the ground, glistening in the brightness of the sunlight. Sadly, this Friday was not one of those. Rain fell steadily, the plop, plop of the large drops clearly audible as they struck my helmet from high above.

Sandeman and I were number six in Paul's string of ten horses as we walked through Great Milton on the way to the training gallops beyond the village, the horses' metal shoes clicking on the hard roads. Both horses and riders were soaked even before we had left the stable yard with the dawn at seven thirty sharp, and now the water ran in rivulets down my neck inside my semi-waterproof jacket. But I didn't care and neither did Sande-man. I could feel his rippling muscles beneath me. He knew exactly why he had been roused from his stable in the rain, and exactly where we were going. We were both clearly excited in anticipation of the gallop we would soon share.

The wind tore at my jacket and the raindrops stung my face, but nothing could wipe the grin from my mouth as we tore up the gallop at nearly thirty miles an hour with me trying hard to stop Sandeman going any faster. He clearly had recovered fully from the three miles last Saturday and he seemed as eager as I to get back on a racecourse.

Paul sat on horseback at the top of the gallop, watching as we moved smoothly up towards him. I was attempting to com-ply with the letter of his instructions. A steady three-quarter-speed gallop, he had said, keeping up-sides with one of his other horses. He had implored me not to ride a finish, not to over-tire my horse. I was doing my best to do what he had asked, but Sandeman beneath me seemed determined to race, keen as always to put his nose in front of the other horse. I took another tight hold of the reins and steadied him. In spite of Paul's sometimes casual manner with his owners, he was still a great trainer of racehorses and very rarely did his horses fail on the racecourse due to over- or under-training at home. I had never questioned his judgement in that department.

I pulled Sandeman up into a trot and then a walk, laughing as I did so. What a magnificent way to blow the courtroom cobwebs out of my hair. I walked him round and round in circles while he cooled and the other horses completed their work up the gallop. Then the string wound its way down the hill and back through the village to Paul's stables.

Oxfordshire was coming to life and the road traffic had

increased significantly during the time we had been on the gallops. Now, streams of impatient commuters roared past us on their way to join the lines of cars on the nearby M40 making the long drag into London. How lucky I am, I thought, to have this escape from the hurly burly of city life and, as I always did, I resolved to try to do this more often. Life here, deep in rural England, seemed a million miles from baseball bats and smashed computers. Perhaps, I mused, I should stay right here and let it all go away.

My dreams of leaving life's troubles behind lasted only until we arrived back at Paul's yard. Laura came out of the house as I was sliding off Sandeman's back.

'A Mr Lygon called for you about ten minutes ago,' she said as I led Sandeman into his stable. She followed us in. 'He seemed very insistent that you should call him as soon as you got back.'

'Thanks,' I said, wondering how he knew where I was. I looked at my watch. It was ten to nine.

I removed the bridle and saddle from Sandeman and replaced them with his head-collar and a dry rug.

'Sorry, old boy,' I said to him. 'I'll be back to finish you in a while.'

I shut the stable door before the horse bolted and went inside, dripping water all over Laura's clean kitchen floor.

'Bruce,' I said when he answered. 'How did you know where I was?'

'Your clerk told me that you weren't due in court today, and you had told him you wouldn't be in chambers, so he said you were probably riding your nag.' I could almost hear Arthur saying it. 'After that it was easy. I looked up who trained your nag on the *Racing Post* website.'

90

If Bruce Lygon could find me so easily, then so could young Julian Trent, or, indeed, whoever was behind Julian Trent, the smooth whispering man on the telephone. I must learn to be more careful.

'Do you often frequent the *Racing Post* website?' I asked Bruce sarcastically.

'All the time,' he said eagerly. 'I love my racing.'

'Well, don't tell me if you ever won or lost money on Scot Barlow or Steve Mitchell,' I said. 'I don't want to know.' And neither should anyone else, I thought.

'Blimey,' he said. 'Never thought of that.'

'So how can I help you?' I asked him.

'It's me helping you, actually,' he replied. 'I've managed to get us a visit to the crime scene.'

'Well done,' I said. 'When?'

'Today,' he said. 'The police say we can go there at two this afternoon. But they say it will be an accompanied visit only.'

Fair enough, I thought. I was surprised they would let us in at all this soon.

'That's fine,' I said. 'Where is it?'

'Great Shefford,' he said. 'Small village between Lambourn and Newbury. Place called Honeysuckle Cottage.' It didn't sound like a site of bloody murder. 'Meet you there at two?'

'Is there a pub?' I asked him.

'Yes,' he said. 'I think so. There's one on the main road.'

'Shall we meet there at one o'clock?' I said. 'For some lunch?'

'Ah.' He thought. 'Yes I think that will be fine. But keep your phone on just in case'

'OK,' I said. 'See you later.'

'How will you know which one is me?' he asked.

'You'll have a rolled up copy of the *Racing Post* under your arm.' I laughed, and so did he.

The *Racing Post* wasn't needed. There were only three other people in the bar when I walked into the Swan Inn at one o'clock sharp and two of them were clearly a couple, heads close together and holding hands as if they were having a secret lovers' tryst far from home.

The third person was a man who looked to be in his mid to late forties and who was wearing a light grey suit with white shirt and blue striped tie. He looked at me briefly, then his gaze slid over my shoulder back to the door as if expecting somebody else.

'Bruce?' I asked him, walking up close.

'Yes?' he said as a question, returning his gaze briefly to my face before again looking over my shoulder.

'I'm Geoffrey,' I said. 'Geoffrey Mason.'

'Oh,' he said. He seemed reluctant to take his eyes off the door. 'I was expecting someone . . . , you know, a bit older.'

It was a reaction I was used to. I would be thirty-six in January but, it seemed, I appeared somewhat younger. This was not always an asset in court, where some judges often equated age with ability. On this occasion I imagined that Bruce was expecting me to be dressed similarly to him, in suit and tie, while, in fact, I was in jeans and a brown suede bomber jacket over an open-necked check shirt. Maybe it was because I was still trying to tell myself that I couldn't actually represent Steve Mitchell that I had decided against my sober dark suit when I had changed out of my sopping wet riding clothes at Paul's.

'Older and wiser?' I said, adding to Bruce's discomfort.

He laughed. A nervous little laugh. He, too, was not quite what I had expected. Ironically, he was slightly older than I had thought from listening to him on the telephone, and he was less confident than I would have liked.

'What are you drinking?' I asked him.

'I'm fine,' he said pointing at a partially drained pint mug on the bar. 'My round.'

'Diet Coke then, please,' I said.

We also ordered some food and took our drinks over to a table in the corner, where we could talk without the barman listening to every word.

'Did you see Mitchell yesterday?' asked Bruce.

'Yes,' I said without elaborating.

'What did he say?' asked Bruce eagerly.

'Not much,' I replied. 'Says he's being framed.'

'I know that,' said Bruce. 'But do you believe him?'

I didn't answer. 'Did you know Scot Barlow had a sister?' I asked him.

'No,' he said. 'Should I?'

'Seems she killed herself last June,' I said. He didn't look any the wiser. 'During a big party in Lambourn.'

'What? Not that girl vet?' he said.

'One and the same,' I said. 'Millie Barlow.'

'Blimey,' he said. 'That was big news in these parts.'

'Why?' I asked him.

'Speculation, I suppose,' he said. 'And all those celebrities at that party being held by the police.'

'What sort of speculation?'

'Drugs,' he said. 'Lots of cocaine sniffing, apparently. Always the way with celebs. It was initially thought the vet had died of

93

an overdose of it, but it turned out to be horse anaesthetic and it seems she did it on purpose.'

'Do you know or are you guessing?' I asked.

'It's what everyone says,' he replied. 'Seems she left a note or something.'

'Seems a strange place to do it,' I said.

'Suicides do strange things,' he said. 'There was that one near here who drove his car onto the railway line and waited for it to get hit by a train. Stupid sod killed six more with him and injured hundreds of others. Why didn't he just shut himself into his garage and quietly leave the engine running?'

'Yeah, but ruining a party seems a bit . . .' I tailed off.

'Perhaps she had a grudge against the party giver, and she was extracting revenge. I once had a client whose ex-wife killed herself right outside the registry office as he was getting remarried inside.'

'How?' I asked.

'Walked out under a lorry. Just like that. The poor driver had no chance.'

'Bet that went down well with the wedding guests,' I said.

'I actually think my client was delighted,' he said, grinning. 'Saved him a fortune in alimony.' We both laughed.

I was growing to like Bruce, and his confidence was growing too.

'So tell me, what are we looking for at Barlow's place?' he said, changing the subject.

'I'm not sure,' I said. 'I always try to visit scenes of crime if I'm acting in a case. It helps me when it comes to questions in court. Also, it often gives some insight into the victim.'

'So are you now acting in this case?' he asked me.

'Temporarily,' I said, smiling at him. But was I acting for the prosecution or the defence?

We finished our lunch and Bruce drove us the few hundred yards to Church Street, leaving my hired Mondeo in the pub car park. Honeysuckle Cottage was a beautiful old stone building set back from the road amongst a copse of tall horse-chestnut trees, their branches now bare of the leaves that lay deep and uncollected on the driveway. I couldn't actually see or smell any of the honeysuckle after which the cottage had been named, but it was hardly the right season.

The place was surrounded on all sides by grand houses with large gardens, mostly invisible behind tall evergreen hedges or high stone walls. Not much chance here, I thought, of a nosey neighbour witnessing the comings and goings at the Barlow residence.

There were already two cars parked in front of a modern ugly concrete-block garage that had been built alongside the cottage with no respect for its surroundings. The driver's door of one of the cars opened and a young man got out as we pulled up behind him.

'Mr Lygon?' he asked, approaching.

'That's me,' said Bruce, advancing and holding out his hand.

'Detective Constable Hillier,' said the young man, shaking it.

'And this is Geoffrey Mason,' said Bruce, indicating me. 'Barrister in the case.'

DC Hillier looked me up and down and he, too, clearly thought I was under-dressed for the occasion. We shook hands, nevertheless.

'This will have to be a quick visit, I'm afraid. I can give you no more than half an hour,' said the policeman. 'And we are not alone.'

'Who else?' I asked.

'Barlow's parents,' he said. 'Took a coach down from Glasgow. They're inside at the moment.' He nodded towards the house.

Oh bugger, I thought, this could be a more emotional encounter than I had expected.

And so it turned out.

DC Hillier introduced us to Mr and Mrs Barlow in the hallway of the cottage.

'They are lawyers in the case,' he said. Mr Barlow looked at us in disgust, he clearly didn't like lawyers. 'They are acting for Mr Mitchell,' the policeman went on, rather unnecessarily, I thought.

Mr Barlow's demeanour changed from disgust to pure hatred, as if it were we who had killed his son.

'May you all burn in Hell for eternity,' he said with venom. He had a broad Scottish accent and the word 'burn' sounded like it could be spelt as 'berrrrn'. Bruce seemed rather taken aback by this outburst.

'We're only doing our job,' he said, defending himself.

'But why?' Mr Barlow said. 'Why are ye givin' that man any assistance? He is sent from the Devil, that one.'

'Now, now, dear,' said Mrs Barlow laying a hand on her husband's arm. 'Remember what the doctor said. Do not stress yourself.'

Barlow relaxed a fraction. He was a big tall man with heavy jowls and bushy eyebrows and he was wearing an ill-fitting dark suit with no tie. Mrs Barlow, in contrast, had a slight frame, was a good eight inches shorter than her husband and had a head of tightly curled grey hair. She wore an inappropriately cheerful flowery dress that appeared to be at least two sizes too big for her, and which hung on her like a sack.

'Aye, woman,' he said, irritated. He flicked his wife's hand from his sleeve. 'But he is still an evil one, that Mitchell.'

'He hasn't actually been convicted yet,' I said. It was a mistake. His doctor wouldn't have thanked me.

'I tell you,' Mr Barlow almost shouted, jabbing his right index finger towards me. 'That man is guilty and he shall have to answer to our Lord. And it's not just Hamish that he killed, but both of our bairns.'

'Who's Hamish?' I said. Another mistake.

'Hamish, man,' bellowed Barlow in a full rage. 'My son.'

Bruce Lygon grabbed my arm and spoke quickly into my ear. 'Scot Barlow's real name was Hamish.' I felt a fool. How could I have not known? On the racecourse, Barlow was always referred to as Scot, but, I now realized, that must have been only because he was one.

'But what did you mean about Mitchell killing both your children?' I asked him, recovering my position a little.

'He killed our Millie,' said Mrs Barlow quickly in a quiet, mellow tone that hung in the air.

'I thought she killed herself,' I said as gently as possible.

'Aye, but that man was still responsible,' said Mr Barlow.

'How so?' I said pressing the point.

'He was fornicating with my daughter,' said Mr Barlow, his voice rising in both tone and volume. I considered it a strange turn of phrase. And, surely, I thought, it takes two to fornicate, like to tango.

'How does that make him responsible for her death?' I asked.

97

'Because,' said Mrs Barlow in her gentle tone, 'he dumped her for someone else on the day she died.'

I wondered again why Steve Mitchell hadn't thought it was important enough to tell me that. And what was more, if what the Barlows said was true, then he had lied to me more than I thought, and I still didn't like being lied to by my clients. I didn't like it one little bit.

CHAPTER 6

Mr and Mrs Barlow hovered around us as Bruce and I made an inspection of the rest of their son's house. Everywhere we went they followed and watched. Everything I picked up to look at they took back from me and replaced exactly as it had been.

The police forensic team had previously moved through the house covering every shiny surface with a fine silvery powder, fingerprint powder, hoping, no doubt, to display some of Steve Mitchell's dabs. In due course, at pre-trial disclosure, we would find out how successful they had been.

According to the television reports Scot, or Hamish, had been found lying on his kitchen floor in a pool of blood with the pitchfork stuck in his chest. If there actually had been a pool of blood, someone must have since cleaned it up. However, the floor and the cupboard doors were covered with numerous little yellow labels with numbers written on them, which, I knew from experience, were to show positions where blood spots had been discovered. Unlike on some old American TV murder stories, there was no convenient white outline drawn on the floor to show the position where the body had been found.

Lying face down on the kitchen table was a broken photo

frame, its glass badly cracked but still held in place by the silver surround. But there was no photograph in the frame and the back of it was hanging off. As with everything else, it was covered with the slimy fingerprint powder.

'I wonder what was in here,' I said to Bruce, holding up the frame to show him.

'It was a picture of our Millie,' said Mrs Barlow from the doorway.

'Do you have it?' I asked her.

'No,' she said. 'He must have taken it.'

The emphasis she placed on the word 'he' left me in no doubt that she meant Steve Mitchell. But why would he take it? I wondered if the police had found the photograph at Mitchell's house, but, surely, even the most stupid of murderers wouldn't take such a clue home with them from the scene of the crime, although I knew some did, like keeping a souvenir, or a trophy.

'Was it a portrait picture?' I asked her.

'No,' she said. 'It was taken when she was at work in the equine hospital. It showed her with a horse. It used to be hers but Hamish had it when . . .' She couldn't finish. Tears began to well up in her eyes.

'I'm so sorry, Mrs Barlow,' I said. I knew only too well the despair that grief can engender.

'Thank you,' she said, dabbing her face with a white handkerchief that she had deftly removed from the sleeve of her dress. I imagined that she must have shed many a tear over her dead children.

'But it must have been a fairly significant photograph to have been in a silver frame,' I said. 'Do you remember which horse Millie was with?' I looked at Mrs Barlow.

'I'm afraid I don't,' she said. 'We lost touch with them both really, when they moved to England.' She made it sound like England was half-way round the world from Glasgow. 'But I recall seeing the picture in her room after she died. Hamish said he wanted it. To remember her by.'

'Where did she live?' I asked.

'What? When she wasn't living with that man?' she said with unexpected anger. She quickly composed herself. 'She had a flat at the equine hospital. She shared it with another vet.'

'Do you know who?'

'I'm sorry, I can't remember her name,' she replied.

'But you are sure it was a female vet?'

'Oh, I think so,' she said. 'At least I always thought it was a woman. She wouldn't have shared a flat with a man. Not my Millie.' But her Millie had shared a bed with Steve Mitchell.

DC Hillier had listened to most of the exchanges between the Barlows and me but he seemed unconcerned and disinterested. He had been too busy looking at his watch.

'Have you seen all you want?' he asked. 'I've got to go now and I need to lock up.'

Bruce held the Barlows at bay in the hallway while I had a quick peep at the bedrooms and bathrooms upstairs. There was nothing unusual or unexpected. There were no giveaway signs of a permanent female presence, like tampons in the medicine cabinet or a lady's smalls in the airing cupboard. Overall there was not much to see. Hamish Barlow had been a tidy man with a wardrobe of smart designer clothes and two cupboards on his landing full of racing-related memorabilia like piles of race cards, bundled copies of the *Racing Post* and numerous horse-related magazines and books. But there were no skeletons with them for me to find. And no other photo frames, with or without photos. Nothing at all that seemed to me to be in any way abnormal.

The policeman ushered us all out of the house, and then he padlocked the clasp on the front door and invited us all to leave the premises. I would have liked to have had a little longer to look around the garden and the garage. Maybe next time. Oh God, I thought. Next time.

A cold sweat broke out briefly on my forehead and I felt foolish in spinning through 360 degrees just to ensure that Julian Trent was not creeping up behind me. He wasn't. Of course, he wasn't. Calm down, I told myself, and my heartbeat slowly returned to normal.

'Do you have a telephone number where my solicitor could contact you?' I asked the Barlows as they were getting into their car.

Mr Barlow, who had been mostly quiet after his earlier out-burst, suddenly turned to me and said, 'Why would he want to contact us?'

'In case he has any more questions for you,' I said.

'I don't want to answer any more of your questions,' he said.

'Look,' I said. 'I know you don't want to help me, but I am as interested as you are in finding out who killed your son.'

'Mitchell killed him,' said Mr Barlow emphatically.

'How can you be so sure?' I asked him.

'Because Hamish used to say that, one day, Mitchell would kill him as sure as he killed his sister. And now he has. I hope he rots in hell.'

There wasn't much answer to that. I stood and watched them drive away. There were other ways of finding their telephone number if I needed it.

'Mr Barlow seems a bit too keen on hell and damnation, if

you ask me,' said Bruce as he reversed his car back onto the road.

'He's a good Scottish Presbyterian, I expect,' I said.

'Bit too dour for my liking,' said Bruce. 'And I wouldn't want to cross him in a dark alley.'

'He's all talk,' I said. 'He's far too God fearing to actually break the law. That's God's law, of course. Ten Commandments and all that. All Presbyterians love their Bible.'

'Not really my scene,' said Bruce.

'No,' I said. 'Nor mine either.' Except that English law owed much to the principles of the Ten Commandments, especially that one about bearing false witness against one's neighbour. Who, I wondered, was bearing false witness against Steve Mitchell?

Bruce dropped me back at the Swan Inn to collect my rental car, before making his apologies and rushing off for a meeting with another client. Meanwhile I decided, as I was almost there, to go and revive some memories by driving around Lambourn, and also to take the opportunity to see Steve Mitchell's place, at least from the outside.

It had been nearly fifteen years since I had lived in Lambourn and I had only been back there a couple of times in the interim, but nothing much had changed, except that there were now many more houses on the outskirts of the village and some of the shops had different names. The place felt the same. Just being here rekindled that feeling of excitement that had gripped me as a twenty-one-year-old starting an adventure, chasing a dream.

I stopped the car on the road opposite the end of the driveway belonging to the trainer for whom I had worked as an unpaid assistant all those years ago. Nicholas Osbourne still trained at the same establishment and I was tempted to drive up to his yard but, in truth, and for reasons I couldn't really understand, our relationship had not been great since my departure. It was why, one day, I had suddenly transferred my horses from him to Paul Newington, and that hadn't helped Nick's feelings either. So I now moved on and went in search of Steve Mitchell's house.

He lived in a modern red-brick detached monstrosity on the edge of the village set back from the Wantage Road. Behind the house was a small stable yard of half a dozen boxes with a small feed store and tack room. It wasn't yet big enough to be a full commercial racehorse training concern but there was plenty of room for expansion on the grassy field behind. I imagined that Steve had built the place himself with a view to turning to training after retiring from the saddle.

Everywhere was quiet and deserted so I wandered around the empty yard and looked into the six stable boxes. Two of them showed evidence of recent equine habitation with brown peat horse bedding still down on the concrete floor and water in the troughs in the corners. Two of the others had an assortment of contents ranging from some wooden garden furniture put away for the winter and an old push-along mower in one, to an old disconnected central-heating boiler and a stack of large cardboard boxes in the other, the latter obviously still unpacked from some past house move.

The last two stables in the line were empty, as was the tack room, save for a couple of horse rugs bundled in a corner. The feed store contained a small stack of hay and several bags of horse nuts, together with four bales of the brown horse bedding, one of them broken open and half used. Leaning up against the far end wall of the store were two long-handled, double-pronged pitchforks, identical, I imagined, to the one found embedded in Scot Barlow's chest on Monday afternoon.

The house was not so conveniently open as the stable block so I walked round the outside, looking in turn into each of the plentiful ground-floor windows. The daylight was beginning to fade fast before I had made my way completely round the house and I might have missed something, but there was absolutely nothing I could see to help me either way. So dark had it become by the time I had finished that several of the security lights were switched on by their movement sensors as I made my way back to the Hertz Mondeo and drove away.

I looked at the car clock. It told me that it was almost five o'clock. Five o'clock on a Friday afternoon. The start of the weekend. Funny, I thought, I hadn't liked weekends much since Angela had died. Occasionally I went racing and, more occasionally, I actually rode in a race, but overall I found the break from chambers life rather lonely.

I drove back into the centre of Lambourn, to the equine hospital on Upper Lambourn Road, and explained to the receptionist through a sliding glass panel that I was looking for someone who had shared a room with Millie Barlow before last June.

'Sorry,' she said in a high-pitched squeak, 'I'm new here. You'll have to ask one of the vets.'

'OK,' I said looking round the bare vestibule. 'Where are they?'

'We've got a bit of an emergency at the moment,' she went on in her squeak. 'They're all in the operating theatre.'

'How long are they going to be?' I asked.

'Oh, I don't really know,' she squeaked. 'They have been in there for quite some time already. But you're welcome to wait.' I looked about me again, there were no chairs. 'Oh,' she said again with realization. 'You can wait in the waiting room if you like. Through there.' She pointed at a wooden door opposite.

'Thank you,' I said. 'Please will you let the vets know that I am here.'

'Yes, OK,' she said. 'As soon as I can.'

I didn't have much confidence that she would remember.

I went through the door into the waiting room. It reminded me of going to the dentist. A dozen pink upholstered armchairs with pale wooden legs and arms were arranged around the walls with a few occasional tables between some of them. There was another door at the far end with a half-full wire magazine rack standing beside it, and the hard floor was covered with a thin blue carpet. It was functional rather than comfortable.

A man sat on one of the chairs on the right-hand side and he looked up as I entered. We nodded at each other in informal greeting and he went back to reading some of the papers he had spread out around him. I sat down opposite him and glanced through a copy of *Country Life* that someone had left on a chair.

Ten minutes or so passed. I went back out to the receptionist, who assured me that the vets were still operating but shouldn't be much longer. I was sure she actually had no notion how long they would be but, nevertheless, I went back into the waiting room and sat down.

I had looked at all the estate agents' adverts in the *Country Life* and was beginning to read the book reviews when someone came through the far door. It was a woman wearing green scrub tunic and trousers with short green wellington boots. A vet, I surmised, fresh from the operating theatre. But it wasn't me she was after. The other man stood up as she entered.

'How's it going?' he said eagerly.

'Fine,' she replied. 'I think we have managed to save most of the muscle mass in the shoulder. It shouldn't greatly impair him after proper healing.'

The man let out a sigh of relief. 'Mr Radcliffe will be relieved to hear it.' He didn't sound to me like he was the only one.

'I have to get back in there now,' said the vet. 'To finish off. We will keep him here overnight and see how he's doing in the morning.'

'Fine,' said the man. 'Thank you. I'll call you around nine.'

'OK,' she said. The man knelt down and began to collect together some of the papers he had been working on. The vet turned to me and raised her eyebrows as a question. 'Are you being looked after?' she said.

'No, not really,' I said. 'I was hoping to talk to someone who knew one of the vets that used to work here.'

'Which vet?' she asked.

'Millie Barlow,' I said.

The reaction from the man was dramatic. 'Right little bitch,' he said almost under his breath, but quite audibly in the quiet of the waiting room.

'I beg your pardon?' I said to him.

'I said that she was a right little bitch,' he repeated standing up and looking at me. 'And she was.'

'Look, I'm sorry,' the vet said to me. 'I have to go and close up the wound on the horse we have been operating on. If you'd like to wait, I'll talk to you when I'm finished.'

'I'll wait,' I said, and she disappeared through the door.

The man had almost collected his stuff.

'Why was she a right little bitch?' I asked him.

'Who wants to know?' he said.

'Sorry,' I said. 'I'm Geoffrey Mason, I'm a barrister.'

'I know you,' he said. 'You have horses with Paul Newington.'

'I do indeed,' I said. 'But you now have the advantage over me.' I looked at him quizzically.

'Simon Dacey,' he said holding out his hand.

Ah, I thought, no wonder he thinks Millie Barlow was a little bitch, she had ruined his party by killing herself in one of his bedrooms.

'Do you have a problem?' I asked him, nodding towards the door through which the vet had disappeared.

'One of my yearlings got loose,' he said. 'Gashed himself on a parked car. Always happens to one of the good ones.'

'Will he be all right?' I asked.

'I sincerely hope so,' he said. 'He cost almost half a million at the sales last month.'

'But he must be insured,' I said.

'Just for transport home and thirty days,' he said. 'Can you believe it? That ran out last Monday.'

'But surely,' I said, 'aren't all racehorses insured?' I knew mine was.

'Mr Radcliffe, that's the owner, he says that the premiums are too high. He has about a dozen with me and he says he would rather spend the money he saves on another horse. He maintains that's the best insurance.'

I knew that my insurance premium on Sandeman was quite high, more than a tenth of his value. But that was relatively small as he'd been gelded and there were no stud prospects. For a potential stallion with a good bloodline the premium would be enormous. But, even so, it was quite a risk.

'Doesn't he insure any of them?' I asked.

'Not normally, but I know he insured Peninsula against being infertile or being injured so he couldn't perform at stud.'

Oh, I thought, Mr Radcliffe owned Peninsula. He wouldn't be short of a bob or two.

'So tell me why Millie Barlow was a right little bitch,' I said, bringing the subject back to what really interested me.

'She ruined my party,' he said.

'That's a bit ungracious,' I said. 'The poor girl was so troubled that she killed herself. She probably didn't ruin your party on purpose.'

'But she did ruin it, nevertheless,' he said. 'Why didn't she go and do it somewhere else? That party for winning the Derby was the best day of my life until she spoiled it. How would you like it? Some of my guests were royalty. What chance do you think I have of them coming again? I'll tell you. None. The damn police even ended up questioning a Crown Prince about his visa. I ask you.'

I could see his point of view.

'Do you know why she killed herself?' I asked him.

'No idea,' he said. 'I hardly knew her.'

'Did you know she was having an affair with Steve Mitchell?' I asked.

'God, yes,' he said. 'Everybody knew that. Worst kept secret in Lambourn. Look, I really have to go now. Evening stables are already well under way.'

'OK,' I said. 'Thanks. Can I call you again if I need any more answers?'

'Why?' he asked.

'I'm representing Steve Mitchell,' I said, handing him one of my cards.

'Oh, are you?' He smiled, looking at it. 'Seems you may have your work cut out there.'

'Why does everyone think he did it?' I asked him.

'Because everyone in Lambourn would have heard them arguing at one time or another. They have been heard standing in the street shouting at each other. And word is that either of them would have thought nothing of putting the other through the wings.' Putting someone through the wings of a fence by squeezing them for room was one of the worst crimes one jump jockey could do to another. Even though the wings were nowadays made of bendable plastic, it was still one of the most dangerous of falls, and one of the most likely to cause serious injury.

'And no one much cares for either of them,' he went on. 'Barlow was slightly weird, and Steve Mitchell is arrogant.'

'But do you really think he's a murderer?' I asked.

'I don't know,' he said. 'I have to say I was surprised when I heard he'd been arrested. But people do funny things when they're angry. They lose control.'

How right he was. I'd once helped prosecute a psychopath who's family had sworn that he wouldn't normally have even said boo to a goose, but in a rage he had literally torn his wife limb from limb, with nothing more than his bare hands and a potato peeler.

'So can I call you if I need to ask you anything else?' I asked.

'I suppose so,' he said. 'But I can't think I would know anything that everybody else wouldn't know. I didn't have much to do with either of them. I don't have jumpers in my yard.'

'Sometimes even the smallest thing is important in a defence,' I replied.

'Do you really think he's innocent?' he asked me.

'That's not relevant,' I said. 'My job is to cast doubt on the prosecution's case. I don't have to prove his innocence, just create a reasonable doubt in the jury's mind about his guilt.'

'But surely,' he said, 'if you believe he's guilty then you're not doing the public any service by getting him off.'

'It is the prosecution's job to ensure that the jury have no reasonable doubt, not mine.'

He shook his head. 'It's a funny old system,' he said.

'I agree,' I said. 'But it has worked pretty well for hundreds of years.'

The jury system had its origins in Roman times, when huge juries would vote on the guilt or innocence of the accused. The right to be judged by a jury of one's peers was established under law in England as far back as the thirteenth century, although there were semblances of it even before then. Under English law there is a right to trial by jury for all but very minor offences, as there is enshrined in the United States Constitution. But that is not the case around the world, not even across Europe. There is no such thing as a jury trial in modern Germany, for example, where a judge or panel of judges decide alone on guilt or innocence.

'I really must go,' said Simon Dacey, collecting the last of his things.

'Fine,' I said. 'Nice to have met you. Good luck with the yearling.'

'Thanks.'

We didn't shake hands because his were full of papers, so we nodded again as we had done when I had arrived and he departed, me holding the door open for him on his way out.

I sat down again on a red armchair. The clock on the wall read 6.15.

What was I doing? I asked myself. I had now told far too many people that I was the barrister acting for the defence in Steve Mitchell's case, but I knew that I shouldn't act. I couldn't act. I was a potential witness in the case, but only I was aware of that. No one, apart from Scot Barlow and I, knew of our little exchange at Sandown. Or did they? Had Barlow told someone that he had been seen by a 'bloody amateur' in the showers? I doubted it. So what should I do?

All my training told me to go and make the incident known to the police, or at least to the prosecution. All my instincts as a barrister were to walk away from this case and never look back for fear of being turned to a pillar of salt like Lot's wife. Maybe I should just let justice take its course and have nothing to do with it.

But what was justice? I had been emphatically told by some-one to take the case and then to lose it. Was that justice? If I walked away would someone else be frightened into ensuring that Steve Mitchell was convicted? Did the very fact that some-one was so keen to see him sent down for the murder prove that he didn't do it? Then where would justice be if I walked away? But even if I could successfully defend him, where would that then leave me? 'Next time, I'll smash your head,' Trent had said. 'Next time, I'll cut your balls right off.' If I walked away and Mitchell was convicted with someone else in the defence chair, would Trent and whoever was behind him still come after me? And that prospect brought a cold sweat to my brow and a tremor to my fingers.

112

'Angela, my darling,' I said quietly into the empty waiting room. 'Tell me what to do?'

She didn't reply. Once again, I longed for her presence and her wisdom. She had always instinctively known what was right. We had discussed everything, sometimes to the point of exhaustion. She had trained as a psychologist and even the most mundane of family conversations between us could turn readily into a deeper analysis of meaning. I remember one year casually asking her whether we would be going to my father's house or staying with her parents for Christmas. Several hours later we had delved into the inner feelings we each had for our parents, and more particularly our feelings for our parents-in-law. In the end we had remained at home for the festivities, and we had laughed about it. How I now missed laughing with her.

Without warning my eyes began to fill with tears. I couldn't help it.

The lady vet in the green scrubs chose this moment to re-appear. I quickly wiped my eyes on my sleeve and hoped she hadn't noticed.

'Now how can I help you?' she asked wearily.

'Busy day?' It was more of a statement than a question.

'You bet,' she said, smiling. 'But I think we saved Mr Radcliffe his money.'

'Bad?' I said.

'Not life threatening,' she said. 'But it could have stopped him racing if we hadn't been careful. We had to rejoin some tendons and sew back some muscle tissue. He's young. He should heal as good as new. Stupid horse gashed its shoulder on a car wing mirror after breaking free.'

'Yes,' I said. 'Simon Dacey told me.'

She raised her eyebrows in slight surprise.

'And who are you exactly?' she asked.

'Geoffrey Mason,' I said, pulling out another card from my pocket and handing it over.

'Not selling, are you?' she asked, glancing briefly at the card.

'No,' I laughed. 'I'm after some information.'

'Why?' she said. 'What information?'

'I'm a barrister and I'm representing Steve Mitchell.' There I go again, I thought.

'Arrogant little shit,' she said, somewhat surprisingly.

'Is he?' I said. 'Why?'

'Thinks he's God's gift to women,' she said. 'Expects every female round here to drop their knickers on demand.'

'And do they?' I asked.

She looked at me and smiled. 'Remind me never to be in the witness box when you're asking the questions.'

'I'll try.' I smiled back. 'But at least tell me your name so I can be sure.'

'Eleanor Clarke,' she said, reaching out a hand, which I shook. 'I thought you said you wanted to ask about Millie Barlow.'

'I do,' I said. 'Did you know her?'

'Certainly did,' said Eleanor. 'She lived in the house here with three others of us.'

'House?' I asked.

'Yes, there's a house out the back where some of the staff who work here live. I live there and Millie lived there until . . . ,' she tailed off and looked down.

'Until she killed herself?' I asked, finishing her sentence.

'Yes,' she said, looking back at my face. 'That's right, until she killed herself. But she didn't sleep there every night.'

114

'Because she was with Steve Mitchell?' I said it as a question.

'Yes,' she replied rather hesitantly.

'Was she sleeping with anyone else?' I asked.

'God, you're sharp,' she said. 'But I'm afraid our Millie would sleep with anyone who asked nicely.'

'Any man, you mean,' I said.

'No,' she replied. 'Millie wasn't really that choosy. But she was a sweet girl. We all missed her after . . .'

'Why do you think she did it?' I asked.

'I don't know,' she said. 'Lots of people said afterwards that she had been depressed but I didn't think so. She was always so happy. She always had a plan to get rich quick.'

'Was she selling sex?' I asked.

'No,' she said with some emphasis. 'I don't think so. I mean, perhaps I exaggerated a bit. She didn't sleep with everyone. She had her favourites. And she would say no occasionally, especially to some of the married ones. She wasn't all bad.'

'But she was living with Steve Mitchell?' I asked.

'Not really,' Eleanor said. 'She lived in the house here but she did spend nights away with Mitchell, yes. Him more than any other, I'd say. But they were hardly living together.' I wondered if Mrs Barlow would be pleased or not. I wondered how strict Millie's upbringing had been. Maybe as soon as she was free of her father's control she went a little mad, sampling life's pleasures in excess.

'How did she get the anaesthetic?' I asked.

'Well, we have it here, of course, but it's funny.' She paused.

'What's funny?' I encouraged.

'The toxicology report on Millie indicated that she had injected herself with thiopental.'

I looked at her quizzically. 'Why is that funny?' I asked.

'We don't use thiopental in the hospital. We use ketamine, usually mixed with either xylazine or detomidine.' I raised a questioning eyebrow. 'They're sedatives,' she explained, leaving me none the wiser. 'Both types will cause unconsciousness, but thiopental is a barbiturate anaesthetic and ketamine is a hydrochloride salt.'

'Isn't it a bit odd that she used a different drug than you use at the hospital?' I asked.

'Well,' she said, 'a vet can get medicines from any drug supplier just by filling in a form. And anaesthetics are used by vets all the time.'

'But it does mean she didn't kill herself on the spur of the moment,' I said. 'Not if she had to order the stuff especially rather than just take some from here.'

'She may have already had it,' Eleanor said. 'I have a few things in my bag that didn't come from the hospital drug store. And barbiturate anaesthetics are used a lot. Thiopental is what's used every day in most vets' practices to put dogs and cats to sleep.'

'Where does the hospital get its drugs?' I asked her.

'We have a specialist veterinary pharmacist in Reading,' she said. 'We have a delivery almost every day during the week.'

'She must have ordered it separately from them,' I said.

'No,' she replied quickly. 'They had to check their records for the police and there was nothing.'

'How odd,' I said.

'Even if she had wanted to, she would have had trouble using any of the hospital stuff anyway,' said Eleanor. 'We have a very tight system of control. Anything like anaesthetic has to be signed out of the hospital drug store by two vets. Look, I've got

116

to go. We aren't normally open after six and there's someone waiting to lock up.'

'How about the horse you operated on?' I said.

'He's in the stables at the back now for the night. He has a monitor on him and CCTV to the duty vet's room. Otherwise we're closed, except, of course, for emergencies.'

'But I would really like to ask you some more questions about Millie,' I said imploringly.

'Let me get changed first,' she said. 'I fancy a drink. Are you buying?'

'How about supper?' I said.

'Don't push your luck, Mr . . .' She looked again at my card. 'Geoffrey Mason.'

'No. Sorry,' I mumbled. 'I didn't mean it like that.'

'Oh, thanks,' she said sarcastically. 'Just when I thought I was being asked out on a date, he says he didn't mean it.' She laughed. 'Story of my life.'

We went in separate cars to the Queen's Arms in East Garston, a village a few miles away.

'Let's not go to a pub in Lambourn,' Eleanor had said. 'Too many listening ears and wagging tongues.'

I was there well ahead of her. I ordered myself a diet Coke and perched on a bar stool, thinking about what questions I needed to ask and wondering why I thought that Millie Barlow's death could have anything to do with that of her brother.

I just didn't like coincidences, although they could never be used as evidence on their own. After all, coincidences do happen. Like all the ones involving the assassinated presidents Abraham

Lincoln and John F. Kennedy. Lincoln had a secretary called Kennedy, and Kennedy had a secretary called Lincoln, and both were succeeded by a Vice-President Johnson. But I still didn't like them.

I did not immediately recognize Eleanor Clarke when she walked into the dimly lit bar. She had changed out of her functional green scrubs and rubber boots and was now wearing a white rib-pattern roll-neck sweater over blue jeans. However, the main reason I didn't know her at first was because her blonde hair was no longer tied in a ponytail but hung down close to each side of her face. My first instinct was that the change of hairstyle was a mistake as it hid her beautiful arched cheekbones and somewhat reduced the sparkle from her stunning blue eyes.

I was suddenly quite shocked by these thoughts. I had hardly given a woman's face a second glance since the day I had first met and fallen instantly in love with Angela, and I had certainly not thought of beautiful cheekbones or stunning blue eyes on anyone else.

'There you are,' said Eleanor, coming over and sitting on the bar stool next to mine.

'What are you drinking?' I asked her.

'G and T, please.'

I ordered and we sat in silence as the barman poured the tonic over the gin.

'Lovely,' she said, taking a large gulp. 'It's been a long day.'

'I'd better order you another,' I said.

'I'm driving,' she said. 'I'll just have the one.'

'You could stay for dinner,' I said.

'I thought you didn't really mean it.' She looked at me with the sparkly blue eyes. They smiled at me.

'I meant that,' I said. 'I just didn't mean . . .' I was getting lost for words. 'You know, anything else.'

'Like what?' she said all seriously, but now with laughter in her eyes.

'Were you a barrister in a past life?' I said. 'I feel that I'm being questioned in court.'

'Answer the question,' she demanded with a stare.

'I just didn't want you to think I was propositioning you or anything.'

'And were you?' she asked.

'No, of course not,' I said.

'Oh thanks. Am I that unattractive?'

'No. I didn't mean that.'

'We seem to be going round in circles here, Mister Barrister Man,' she said. 'So what did you mean?'

'I thought it was going to be me asking you the questions,' I said. 'Not the other way round.'

'OK,' she said. 'I'm ready. Ask away.'

'Well,' I said. 'Firstly, will you stay to dinner?'

'Yes,' she replied without hesitation.

'Good,' I said.

'Are you married?' she asked suddenly.

'Why?'

'I just wondered,' she said.

I didn't immediately respond.

'Well, are you?' she persisted.

'Why do you want to know?' I asked again.

'Need to know where I stand,' she said.

'But I'm not propositioning you, so why does it matter?' I said.

'You might change your mind,' she said. 'And I can't be

bothered to invest any emotion unless I know where I stand. So, are you married?'

'Are you?' I asked her back.

'Only to my job,' she said. She waited a moment in silence. 'Well?'

'I was,' I said slowly.

'Divorced?' she said.

'Widowed.'

'Oh.' She was embarrassed. 'I'm sorry. I shouldn't have asked.'

'It was a long time ago,' I said. But it felt like only yesterday.

She sat silently as if waiting for me to go on. I didn't.

'Still painful?' she asked.

I nodded.

'Sorry,' she said again. Some of the sparkle had gone out of her eyes.

We sat in silence for a while.

'What do you want to know about Millie?' she asked eventually.

'Let's go and eat,' I said.

We opted for a table in the bar rather than in the restaurant. No tablecloth, less formal, but the same menu.

I chose a fillet steak while Eleanor decided on the pan-fried sea bream.

'Would you like a glass of wine?' I asked her.

'I'm still driving,' she said.

'You could leave your car here,' I said. 'I'm sure the pub won't mind if you leave it in their car park. I could drop you back at the hospital and you could collect it in the morning.'

'How about you?' she said. 'What are you drinking?'

'I'm on diet Coke but I'll have a small glass of red with my dinner,' I said. 'I do have to drive. Back to London tonight.' I had rented the car for only two days.

'Couldn't you stay down here and go in the morning?' she said.

'Are you propositioning me now?' I asked.

She blushed. 'I didn't mean that.'

Pity, I thought, again surprising myself.

I could always have called Hertz to keep the car for another day, but somehow I felt that I was betraying my Angela even to contemplate spending the night away from home, especially in order to have a lengthy dinner with another woman. I told myself not to be such a fool, but I felt it nevertheless.

'How well did you know Millie?' I asked, changing the subject and saving us both some embarrassment.

'Pretty well,' she said. 'We worked together at the hospital for three years and lived in the house together for most of that time.'

'Do you know why she killed herself?' I asked.

'No idea,' she said. 'She seemed pretty happy to me.'

'Did she have money worries?' I asked.

'No,' Eleanor replied emphatically. 'In fact she always seemed rather well off. She bought a brand-new red Mazda sports car the year before she died and she always had lots of nice clothes. I think her father still sent her an allowance, even though we all earn pretty good money at the hospital.'

I thought back to my earlier encounter with the Barlow parents in their ill-fitting clothes. Did they seem the sort of people who could afford to send their high-earning daughter an allowance?

'Was she pregnant?' I said. It was only a wild thought.

'I think it highly unlikely,' said Eleanor. 'She used to boast that she had a good supply of the morning-after pill just in case she forgot to take her other pills. She was medically trained, remember.'

'And medics have a higher suicide rate than almost every other profession,' I said.

'Do they?' She seemed surprised.

'Yes,' I said. 'I had to research the rates last year for a case where a doctor was accused of assisting a suicide.'

'I suppose medics have the knowledge of how to take their own lives,' she said.

'Painlessly, you mean,' I said.

'Absolutely. Just like putting an old dog to sleep,' she said. 'They also have easy access to the necessary drugs.'

'Did Millie get on with her brother?' I asked.

'Well enough, I think,' she said. 'But I don't think he was too happy with her reputation.'

'Reputation?' I asked.

'For being the easiest ride in the village.'

'No,' I said. 'Not really a reputation to cherish.' Especially not in Lambourn, where riding was its lifeblood. 'How many casual lovers would you say she had?'

'At least half a dozen on the go at once,' she said. 'I think you could safely say that she wasn't particularly discreet. Suffice to say she liked jockeys.'

'Was Reno Clemens one of them?' I asked.

'Probably,' she said. 'I didn't actually keep a list, but he was often around her. I sometimes saw them together in the pub.'

'But you didn't see him in her room?' I said.

'We have a sort of unwritten rule in the house,' she said. 'Long-term relationships are OK, but no casual partners to stay over. Needless to say, Millie broke it all the time. It was the only thing we argued about. But no, I can't say I ever saw Reno there.'

'How about Steve Mitchell?' I asked. 'Did he stay over?'

'No never,' she said. 'Millie was always too keen to go to his place. She was always telling us about his hot tub.' She lifted her eyebrows in disapproval.

'Why exactly do you dislike Mitchell?' I asked her.

'Is it that obvious?'

'Yes,' I said.

'When I first came to Lambourn about ten years ago he was just starting as a jockey and we went out for a while. I thought he was serious but he wasn't. He was two-timing me with some stable hand and, when the silly bitch got pregnant, he dumped me and married her.' She paused. 'I suppose she did me a favour really.'

'How long did his marriage last?' I asked.

'About six years. They had two children and Steve became very successful. They built the Kremlin together.'

'The Kremlin?' I asked.

'That's what everyone calls that red-brick eyesore he now rattles around in on his own. When Natalie, his ex-wife, finally saw some sense and left him, he came back to my door and wanted to carry on as if nothing had happened. I told him to piss off and Steve didn't like that. He likes to get his own way. I actually think he then made such a fuss over Millie to get back at me.'

So Steve's affair with Millie Barlow hadn't just been a fling as he had claimed, but had continued long after his wife had found out and left him. Mr and Mrs Barlow senior had been right, and Mitchell had indeed lied to me about it.

'Didn't Steve mind that she had other partners as well as him?' I asked.

123

'Mind? Are you kidding? According to Millie, Steve loved a threesome, or even more.'

'Do you think she was telling the truth?' I said.

'You may have a point there. Millie was a good vet, very good in fact, but she was known to exaggerate things a tad.'

'Do you remember a photo of her and a horse in a silver frame?' I asked.

She nodded. 'Her prized possession.'

'Why?' I asked.

'It was a picture of her with a new-born foal,' she said.

'But why was it so special?'

'It was the first foal she had ever delivered on her own, just after she arrived in Lambourn,' she said. 'Bit of an emergency in the middle of the night. She was the only vet on duty. But she did OK, apparently. I was away.'

I was disappointed. I thought it would be more interesting than that.

'Why are you interested in the photo?' she asked me.

'Because someone took it from Scot Barlow's house,' I said.

'What, when he was murdered?'

'That I don't know,' I said. 'But it is missing now.'

'Perhaps it was for the silver frame,' she said.

'No. Whoever took the photo left the frame. That's how I know the photo's gone.'

'Well, I can tell you that it was of Millie and a foal that was lying in the straw, with the mare and a stud groom behind.'

'Do you know who the stud groom was?' I asked. 'Or who took the photo?'

'No idea,' she said. 'But I know which foal it was. That's why it was Millie's prize possession.'

'Go on,' I encouraged her as she paused.

'Peninsula,' Eleanor said with a flourish.

Was that the reason why Millie Barlow was at Simon Dacey's party? Or was that just a coincidence? But, I didn't like coincidences.

PART II

Disclosure

March 2009

CHAPTER 7

By the time of the Steeplechase Festival at Cheltenham in March, Steve Mitchell had been in prison for four months and his name had all but been erased from the racing pages of the newspapers as well as from the considerations of the punters. With both Mitchell and Barlow out of the running, Reno Clemens had built up a commanding lead in the battle to be this year's champion jockey and much was expected of him at the festival. Most of his mounts would start as favourite.

Bruce Lygon had done his best at Oxford Crown Court in November to get Steve Mitchell bail but, unsurprisingly, the judge had listened to him with courtesy and then had promptly declined his application. I had sat beside Bruce in court but I hadn't really helped him much. I don't think it would have made much difference if I had. Letting murder suspects out on bail was never going to endear a judge to the general public and a few recent high-profile cases where the suspects had murdered again while out on bail had put paid to even the slimmest of chances.

I hadn't actually planned to attend the bail hearing but I had received another little reminder from God-knows-who two days before it was due to take place. It had been another slim white envelope delivered as before to my chambers by hand. It had been found on the mat inside the front door and no one had seen who had left it there. Again, in the envelope there had been a single sheet of folded white paper and a photograph. Thankfully the message hadn't been backed up this time by a personal visit from Julian Trent. However, the memory of his previous visit had remained vivid enough in my consciousness for the sweat to break out on my forehead as I had held the envelope tightly in my hands.

As before, there had been four lines of black print across the centre of the paper.

GOOD LITTLE LAWYER
I WILL BE WATCHING YOU IN OXFORD ON WEDNESDAY
DON'T GET MITCHELL BAIL
REMEMBER, LOSE THE CASE OR SOMEONE GETS HURT

The photograph had been of my dead wife Angela. In fact, to be accurate, it had been a photograph of a photograph of Angela in a silver frame. Around the sides I could see a few of the other things on the surface on which the frame had stood. I had known those items. The photograph of Angela was the one of her smiling that I had placed on her dressing table in our bedroom soon after she died. I said 'good morning, my darling' to that photograph every day. Someone had been into my house to take that shot. It made me very angry, but I was also more than a little afraid. Just who were these people?

I sat at my desk in chambers twiddling my thumbs and thinking. It was Monday morning and I was having a few easy days.

In order to prevent a repeat of last year, when I had been stuck in court instead of jumping my way round Cheltenham on Sandeman's back in the Foxhunter Chase, I had instructed Arthur to schedule absolutely nothing for the whole week.

I had recently finished acting for a large high-street supermarket in an out-of-date food case, which my client had won. Such relatively low-key cases were the bread and butter of many junior barristers, and highly sought after. In the big, high-profile criminal cases, the lead for the defence was almost invariably taken by a silk, a Queen's Counsel. However, many companies, especially large well-known firms, often preferred to engage a junior in cases where they were dealing with the 'little people', mostly their staff or their suppliers, or with simple breaks in hygiene regulations. To turn up at a magistrates court with a QC in tow seemed to imply they were guilty, quite apart from the excessive fees of a silk. Many a junior has made a fine reputation and an excellent living from the work. Some juniors, indeed, declined the chance to be promoted to QC for fear of losing their fee-base altogether.

Personally, I enjoyed the criminal Crown Court work far more, but I earned most of my money either in the magistrates' courts or at the disciplinary hearings of professional institutions.

But not this week. I was determined not to miss out again on a ride in the Foxhunters. Sandeman had qualified partly by virtue of winning the race last year and Paul had assured me at the end of January that the horse was fitter this time, implying that failure to win again this year would not be Sandeman's fault. It had been a direct warning to me not to be the weak link in the partnership, an explicit instruction to get myself fit.

For weeks now I had been running every day, mostly at lunchtime, which had the added advantage of avoiding the temptation to eat with fellow counsel either in the Hall at Gray's Inn, or at one of the many hostelries situated close to our chambers.

In addition, in mid February I had been skiing for a long weekend in Meribel in France and had pushed my aching legs time and again down the mountains. I loved to ski but, on this occasion, it had been ski boot-camp. I had risen early each morning in the chalet I'd shared with four other complete strangers whose sole passion in life was the snow. We had spent the whole day on the slopes, catching the very last lift of the day to the highest point and arriving back at the chalet exhausted, just as the daylight faded. Then I would spend hours in the sauna, sweating off the pounds, before a high-protein dinner and an early bed.

By the second week in March I was toned like I hadn't been since my time in Lambourn fifteen years before. Bring on Julian Trent, I said to myself. I was at my best fighting weight and relished the chance.

Arthur came into my room. In spite of an excellent internal telephone system, Arthur was of the old school and liked to talk face to face when making arrangements. 'Sir James would like to have a conference about the Mitchell case,' he said. 'I have scheduled it for nine thirty tomorrow. Is that all right with you?'

'I asked you not to schedule anything at all for this week,' I said to him.

'But you're not going to the races until Thursday,' he said. 'You will still be able to watch the Champion Hurdle tomorrow afternoon. The conference won't last all day.'

I looked at him. How did Arthur know I wasn't planning to go to Cheltenham until Thursday? It would be no good asking him. He would reply in the same way as he always did. 'It's my job to know everything about my barristers,' he would say. I wondered for the umpteenth time if he knew more about my little problem than he was letting on.

'Nine thirty tomorrow will be fine,' I said.

He smiled. 'I thought it might,' he said. 'I'll tell Sir James.'

Sir James Horley, QC, was now the lead in Steve Mitchell's defence. When Bruce Lygon had finally called Arthur to engage counsel for the case, Sir James had jumped at it. He could never be accused of not being eager to take on a prominent celebrity client, even if, as in this case, the 'celebrity' status of the client was somewhat dubious and the evidence was stacked up against him. Sir James loved the limelight. He adored the television cameras waiting each day outside court so that they could show him on the six o'clock news replying 'no comment' to each of the journalists' questions.

My heart had dropped when Arthur told me that Sir James would lead and I would be acting as his junior. Sir James has a reputation of doing very little, or nothing, in preparation for a trial while still expecting everything to be in order and complete on day one. He also had a reputation, richly deserved, for publicly blaming his junior whenever anything went wrong, whether or not they had anything to do with it. He seemed to expect his juniors to have powers of clairvoyance over the facts, yet be unable to stand up in court to question a witness, something he reserved solely for himself.

Needless to say, I still had not yet told anyone of my encounter with the murder victim in the showers at Sandown, even though I had been sorely tempted to do so in order to disqualify myself from acting alongside Sir James. But it had been so long since I should have said something that I couldn't really do so now without placing myself in a very compromising position. I would be damned if I did, and damned if I didn't, but, in the latter case, only if anyone else knew about it from Barlow. Was I prepared to take that risk? Perhaps I should simply plead insanity, excuse myself from the case altogether and commit myself to a mental hospital until it was all over. By then Steve Mitchell would have been tried, convicted and sentenced to life imprisonment for a crime for which I didn't believe he was responsible. I would then be safe from Julian Trent and life could go back to normal. That is, until the next time someone wanted to manipulate the outcome of a trial, and young Mr Trent and his baseball bat were sent to pass the message.

The news that I was no longer acting as the sole barrister in the case had spread far and wide to ears I didn't know, but ears of those who most definitely had an interest in the outcome.

Within only a few hours of the appointment of Sir James Horley as defence QC being posted on the courts' website, I had received a call on my mobile.

'I told you to take the Mitchell case,' the quiet well-spoken whisperer had said. 'Why are you not listed as the defence barrister?'

I had tried to explain that a QC would always have to lead in such a high-profile case and I wasn't one. I had told him that I would be assisting.

'You are to ensure Mitchell loses,' he had said.

'Why?' I had asked him.

'Just do it,' he had said, and then he'd hung up.

As before, and as expected, he had withheld his number.

Why, indeed, did they, whoever 'they' were, want Mitchell to lose? Was it solely to have someone else convicted of their crime or was there something else? Was it anything to do with Mitchell himself? Had Mitchell in fact done the crime and they were just making sure he got his just deserts? But how would they know he was definitely guilty unless they were there with him at the time?

No, I still believed that Steve was being set up. All the disclosed prosecution evidence put together would be very convincing to a jury, although any single part of it on its own could be described as circumstantial. No one questioned that the pitchfork, the murder weapon, had belonged to Steve Mitchell, but, as I had seen myself, his pitchforks had not been kept locked away and anyone could have taken one of them from the open feed store to stick into Barlow's chest. Blood and hairs from the victim had been found on a pair of Mitchell's wellington boots as well as in his car, but the boots had been kept in the same feed store as the pitchfork, and Mitchell swore that he had left his car unlocked on his driveway, as he always did, on the day of the murder. The Defence Case Statement stated that Mr Mitchell was being framed for the crime that someone else, unknown, had committed. And that the crime in question had been premeditated and planned meticulously so as to appear to have been perpetrated by our client.

The prosecution had been unable to establish definitively that Mitchell had indeed sent the text message to Barlow threatening to 'come round and sort you out properly you sneaking little bastard'. In spite of the message being signed with Mitchell's name, it could only be determined by the police that it had been sent by a free texting service accessible from any computer, by anyone, anywhere in the world.

The betting receipts, however, did indeed belong to Steve Mitchell and he had been stupid enough to have his own name on them. They were, in fact, debit-card receipts from a book-maker rather than actual betting slips. Steve denied that they were his but even I knew he wasn't telling the truth. I had explained to him that the time for lying about betting was now over, he had more serious allegations to deal with, but he was so used to denying that he gambled that it came naturally to him to continue to do so.

Add the mass of physical evidence, the well-known and well-documented antagonism between the victim and the accused, the lack of any semblance of an alibi and the defence's seeming inability to demonstrate who or why anyone would want to frame him, and I could imagine a jury returning a unanimous guilty verdict so quickly that they would hardly have to retire from the courtroom.

I had explained to Steve, during another trip to talk with him in prison, that if he had an alibi he must declare it prior to the trial. To suddenly produce one in court would not assist his case. The jury would be invited by the prosecution to draw whatever inferences they wished from the fact that no previous mention had been made of an alibi. However, he had remained adamant that he had been on his own at home reading all afternoon on that Monday.

'Steve,' I had implored. 'I am afraid I don't believe you. If you were with someone, perhaps someone you shouldn't have been with, you must tell me now. At the trial or afterwards will be too late.'

'I tell you I was on my own,' he had said. 'That's the truth. What do you want me to do? Lie?'

I had thought that it would be counter-productive to say that I knew he had lied to me before, about the ending of his affair with Millie Barlow.

'Don't you realize the mess you are in?' I'd shouted at him while banging on the grey metal table with my fist. 'You're facing a long stretch in prison for this. It's not some game in the park, you know.'

'I can't,' he had said finally.

'Yes, you can,' I'd screamed at him. 'No one would expect you to keep quiet if it meant you would be convicted of a murder you didn't do.'

'It's not that simple,' he had said, looking down at the table.

'Is she married?' I had asked, guessing the reason.

'Yes,' he'd said emphatically. 'And I don't even think I was with her when that bastard Barlow got himself killed. It was only a last-minute lunchtime bonk, arranged when the racing at Ludlow was called off. I'm certainly not embroiling her in this mess when it wouldn't even give me an alibi for the right time.'

The prosecution case was that Barlow had died sometime between two and four in the afternoon. His body had been discovered around six by a policeman responding to an anonymous call to Newbury police station's front desk about an intruder at Honeysuckle Cottage. As the caller had used the local landline and not the emergency 999 service there had been no record of the telephone number or any recording of the conversation.

This fact was one of the few plus points for our side because, as I had pointed out in our Defence Case Statement, Mitchell was hardly likely to call the police if he had, in fact, murdered Barlow, and the prosecution case was that he had acted alone in the killing. It was a minor point in the face of the wealth of prosecution evidence, but one I planned to exploit to the full at the trial.

'The fact that you were not alone all of the time from one o'clock until six might help to plant some doubt in the minds of the jury,' I had told him. 'And, at the moment, we need all the help we can get.'

'She was gone by two thirty at the latest,' he'd said. 'So what difference would it make? Barlow's bloody house is only ten minutes' drive from mine. I could easily have been there well before three anyway so it's not a bloody alibi.' He'd paused. 'No. I won't get her involved.'

'Tell me who it was,' I had said to him. 'Then I can ask her if she would be prepared to give a statement to the police.'

'No,' he had said. And he had been silent on the matter ever since.

I had also asked him about Millie Barlow and why he hadn't told me about her death at our first meeting.

'I didn't think that it was that important,' he'd said.

'Of course it was important,' I had shouted at him. 'You tell me absolutely everything and I'll decide whether it's important or not.'

He had looked at me with big eyes, like a scolded puppy. 'I'm in a bit of the shit here, aren't I?'

'Yes,' I'd said. 'Big shit.'

'I didn't do it, you know,' he'd said mournfully.

'Were you drunk that afternoon?' I'd asked him. 'Or high?'

'Nothing like that,' he'd replied quite sharply. 'We'd had a bit of red wine, I suppose, but not more than a bottle. That's why I stayed in after. Because I didn't want to get done for drunken driving.'

Shame, I'd thought, being banged up for a bit of driving under the influence would have provided a cast-iron alibi for Barlow's murder.

'So did Barlow blame you for his sister's suicide?' I had asked him.

'All the bloody time,' he'd replied. 'Kept going on and on about it. Called me a bloody murderer. I told him to shut up or I'd bloody murder him.' Steve had suddenly stopped and he had looked up at my face. 'But I didn't, I promise you I didn't.' He had then buried his head in his hands and begun to sob.

'It's all right, Steve,' I'd said, trying to reassure him. 'I know you didn't do it.'

He had looked back at my face. 'How do you know? How can you be sure?'

'I just am,' I'd said.

'Convince the bloody jury then.'

Maybe that is what I should do, I thought, sitting here at my desk. Perhaps I should tell the jury that I had been threatened to make sure I lost in court. That was it. I must tell Sir James that I had been approached and intimidated. Then I could become a witness instead of a barrister in the case and I could tell the jury all about baseball bats and Julian Trent. But would that be enough to help Steve? Probably not. The judge might not even allow testimony concerning intimidation of one of the lawyers to be admitted. It was hardly significant evidence in the case, irrespective of what I might think. It might just be relevant if the defence could use it as support for our belief that Steve was being framed. But in the face of the prosecution case, would the jury believe it?

And where would that leave me, I wondered. Did I just sit and wait to have my head smashed in and my balls cut off? And how about my elderly father in his holey green jumper? What danger would I be putting him in?

It seemed to me that the only solution to my multiple dilemmas was to discover who was intimidating me and then show that they were the true murderers of Scot Barlow, and to do it quickly, before any 'next time'.

Simple, I thought. But where do I start?

Julian Trent. He must be the key.

The following morning, I didn't tell Sir James Horley QC anything about intimidation, or anything about an encounter in the Sandown showers. He and I sat on one side of the table in the small conference room in the lower ground floor of chambers. Bruce Lygon sat opposite us. For two hours we had been once again going through every aspect of the prosecution case. We had received their secondary disclosure, but there was nothing new to help us.

The prosecution was required to disclose to the defence anything that they, or the police, had discovered which would assist us based on our Defence Case Statement. The response had been short but to the point. Their letter simply stated that they had no information other than that already disclosed in their primary disclosure and Statement of Case. We hadn't really expected anything.

'Are you sure that Mitchell shouldn't plead guilty?' said Sir James. 'The case against him is very strong.' I wondered, ungraciously, if Sir James liked the idea of a guilty plea to save him a courtroom loss. Maybe he was having second thoughts about taking this case.

'He says he didn't do it,' I said. 'He's adamant that he will not plead guilty to something he didn't do.'

'How about a plea based on a lesser charge?' said Bruce. 'Or on diminished responsibility, or temporary insanity.'

Insanity was right, I thought. They were clutching at straws.

'Our defence is that our client didn't do it and is being framed, so we shall have no guilty pleas to anything, OK?' I said firmly.

'Then we had better find out who's framing him,' said Sir James. 'Otherwise we shall have egg on our faces. Trial date is set for the second week in May at Oxford. That's eight weeks from now. I suggest we meet again in two weeks to see if we are any further on.' He stood up and tied the papers together with ribbon and bows, as if they were Christmas presents. The ribbon was pink. Pink for defence. Prosecution briefs were tied up in white ribbon.

Papers so tied could not be looked at by any member of chambers except those acting for the appropriate side in that case. It was not unusual for different counsel within chambers to be acting for both sides in the same trial. I had once been prosecuting an armed robbery case while a colleague who normally shared the same room as me was acting for the defendant. We had temporarily been separated to opposite ends of the building, but we still needed to be very careful not to discuss aspects of the trial in the other's hearing. Arthur had even installed segregated photocopiers so that a document carelessly left in one machine would not fall into the other camp's hands.

I went back to my room and looked at the desk of that colleague. As always, it was almost impossible to see the wood from which it had been constructed. The tough old English oak was doing its duty supporting stack upon stack of papers and box files. I was the tidiest of the three of us who shared this space, and even my area could look like a war zone at times. Stuff that couldn't fit on our desks was stacked in boxes on the floor or in the full-length bookshelves down the side of the room, opposite the windows. But nothing was ever lost. At least that's what we told everyone and it was almost the truth, although maybe not the whole truth.

There had been a large white envelope in my box in the clerks' room and I sat at my desk and looked at it. This envelope, however, had been expected and contained no sinister threatening note, and no photograph. I had ordered a full transcript of the Julian Trent appeal hearing from last November and now I eagerly scanned its close-typed pages looking for a certain name.

Josef Hughes of 845 Finchley Road, Golders Green, north London, was the rogue solicitor who had forced the appeal in the first place. It was his supposed intervention with the jury that had got Trent off. If, as I suspected, he had been coerced into giving his evidence to the Court of Appeal, then he might be prepared to help me find out how and why Julian Trent was connected to Scot Barlow's murder. I went to Golders Green first thing on Wednesday morning.

Josef Hughes went white and his knees buckled as soon as I mentioned Julian Trent. I thought he was going to pass out completely in the doorway of his bed-sit, one of half a dozen or so bed-sits crammed into the large 1930s-built semi-detached house at 845 Finchley Road.

He might have collapsed right down to the floor if I hadn't

held him by his left elbow and helped him through the door and into the room. He sat down heavily on the side of the double bed that took up most of the available floor space. We were not alone. A young woman, not much more than a child, sat on an upright wooden chair nursing a young baby. She didn't move as I helped Josef over to the bed but sat silently staring at me with big brown, frightened eyes.

I looked around. Apart from the green blanket-covered bed and the chair there was a small square table under the window, another upright chair that matched the first, and a tiny kitchenette in the corner, half hidden by a thin curtain that was badly in need of a wash.

I went over to the kitchen sink to fetch Josef a glass of water. There were no glasses visible but there was a moderately clean though badly chipped coffee mug upturned on the drainer. I splashed some water into it and held it out to him.

He looked up at me in real horror, but he took the mug and drank some of the water. The colour in his face improved fractionally.

'It's all right,' I said in as comforting manner as I could muster. 'I haven't been sent here by Julian Trent.'

At the sound of the name, the young woman gave out a slight moan and I was suddenly afraid that she too was about to pass out. I stepped towards her as if to catch her baby but she pulled the child away from me and curled her body round it as protection.

What on earth had Julian Trent done to these people to make them so afraid?

I looked around the room again. Everything was very basic, with threadbare carpets, paper-thin curtains and bare cream-painted walls that were overdue a redecoration. A plastic tubular travel cot was folded and leaned up against the wall behind the door with three blue baby romper suits hanging on it to dry.

'We used to have the big flat on the top floor,' said the girl, watching me look. 'With our own bathroom. Then Joe lost his job and we had to move down here. Now, we share a bathroom on the landing with three other rooms.'

'How old is the baby?' I asked her.

'Eight months on Friday,' she said. I thought she was close to tears.

'What's his name?' I asked her, smiling.

'Rory,' she said.

'That's nice,' I said, smiling at her again. 'And what's your name?'

'Bridget,' she said.

We sat there in silence for a while, Josef and me on the bed, with Bridget holding Rory on the upright chair.

'What do you want?' Josef said eventually.

'Tell me what happened,' I said quietly.

Josef shivered next to me.

'It was a man,' said Bridget. 'He came here, to our flat upstairs.'

'No,' said Josef suddenly and forcefully.

'Yes,' said Bridget back to him. 'We need to tell someone.'

'No, Bee,' he said again firmly. 'We mustn't.'

'We must,' she pleaded. 'We must. I can't go on living like this.' She started to cry.

'I promise you,' I said, 'I'm here to try and help you.' And to help myself.

'He broke my arm,' said Bridget quietly. 'I was six months pregnant with Rory and he came into our flat, hit me in the face and punched me in my stomach. Then he broke my arm by slamming it in the door.'

'Who did?' I asked her. Surely, I thought, Julian Trent had been in prison.

'Julian Trent's father.'

Chapter 8

In the end, between them, they told me everything. It was a horror show.

The man who had said he was Julian Trent's father had arrived wearing a smart suit and tie one evening soon after Josef had arrived home from his work at the Crown Prosecution Service. Josef had qualified as a solicitor only the year before and the CPS was his first job and he had loved it. He and Bridget had married while he was at the College of Law and they had moved into their first family home together in preparation for the birth of their first child. Everything was fine and they had been blissfully happy together. That is, until the shadow of Julian Trent had been cast over their lives.

At first the man had been nice and had even offered Josef some money to get some information for him.

'What information?' I asked him.

'Stuff that was already in the public domain,' he said.

'What sort of stuff?' I asked again.

'Names and addresses of jurors,' he said.

'In the Julian Trent trial?' I asked, but I already knew what the answer would be.

He nodded. 'It was the first trial I had worked on at the Old Bailey. And the jurors' names are in the transcript,' he said in his defence. 'Their names had been read out in open court.' He was trying to justify his actions. The jurors' names may have been in the public domain, but their addresses wouldn't have been.

'And we really needed the money,' said Bridget. 'What with the baby coming, there were things we had to buy.'

'And it wasn't against the law,' said Josef, almost in despair.

'But you knew it was wrong,' I said to him. It may or may not have been against the letter of the law, I wasn't sure, but it was definitely against the Law Society rules, and would quite likely have been in contempt of court.

He nodded again.

'So when did he come back?' I asked them.

'The following day,' Josef said. 'He was meant to be bringing the money for the information I had ready for him.'

'But he hit Bridget instead?' I said.

He nodded again, and now tears welled up in his eyes. 'I couldn't believe it. He just walked straight into the flat and hit her. He knocked her down, then he dragged her over to the door and broke her arm while she was lying on the floor. It was horrible.' The tears began to flow and he swallowed hard. 'I felt so helpless to stop it.'

Bridget placed a hand on his arm. His tears flowed faster. 'It all happened so fast,' he wailed. It was obviously his inability to protect his wife that hurt him most.

'Then what happened?' I said.

'He demanded the information,' Josef said.

'Did you give it to him?' I asked.

'I asked him for the money,' he said. 'But he said to give him the stuff immediately or he'd break Bridget's other arm.' He sobbed again.

'What happened next?' I asked when his sobs had diminished a little.

'I had to get an ambulance,' he said. 'We were so afraid we would lose the baby. Bridget was in hospital for nearly a week.'

I had really meant what happened next with the man.

'Did you call the police?' I asked him.

'The hospital did. They seemed to think that I had done it,' he said. 'The police didn't believe me when I said it was another man.'

'Did you tell them who he was?' I asked. 'Or what he wanted?'

'No.' He cried again. 'He said he would come back and make Bridget lose the baby if we told anyone.' He looked at me and I wondered if he was now thinking that telling me had been a mistake. 'The man said that if we told anyone, he would make sure we would never be able to have any children ever.'

I was certain that Josef had believed it. *Next time I'll smash your head, next time I'll cut your balls right off.* I believed it, too.

'But the man came back?' I asked him.

'Not in person,' he said. 'He sent me a letter at work the month after the trial was over.'

'Saying what?' I asked, but I suspected I already knew that, too.

'He told me to go to Julian Trent's lawyer and tell him that I had talked to some of the jury to try and ensure that Julian Trent was convicted,' he said in a rush. 'But I hadn't, I swear it.' But he had sworn at the appeal hearing that he had. I had read the transcript.

'Did the letter say which jurors you had to say you had approached?' I asked him.

148

'Yes,' he said. 'Three of them.'

I knew their names too. They were also in the transcript.

'What was the name of the lawyer?' I asked. I had been Julian Trent's defence lawyer at the trial.

'Some solicitor in Weybridge,' he said. 'I can't remember the name of the firm. Funny, though, I felt sure he was somehow expecting me when I arrived. He knew exactly what I was going to say.'

'Please try and remember who it was,' I said to him. The solicitor who had engaged me to act for Trent at his first trial had been from a central London firm, not one in Weybridge.

'I can't,' he said. 'I had it on the letter, but the lawyer took that. I know it was in Weybridge High Street, above some shops. I could probably find it again. I was all in a bit of a daze.'

'Was there anything else with the letter?' I asked.

'There was a photograph.' He gulped. 'It showed Bridget and me coming out of her ante-natal class at the local hospital. Someone had drawn an arrow on it with a red marker pen. The arrow was sticking into her stomach.'

Altogether I spent more than an hour with Josef and Bridget Hughes. Their lives had been totally destroyed by the visit of the friendly, well-dressed man offering money for information. He must have known they were young and vulnerable. He had drawn them into his scheme and tossed their futures away without a second thought. Josef had been stripped of the professional qualifications that he had worked so hard to obtain and had avoided a criminal prosecution only by a whisker.

But it was what he had done to their confidence that was worse. Bridget was now almost too timid to step out of her door. They were prisoners in a bed-sit, a bed-sit they could now hardly afford to live in with Josef having to do casual work stacking supermarket shelves at night. He would come home in the mornings with out-of-date food as part of his wages.

'Please help us,' Josef had pleaded as he came downstairs to the main door of the property. 'I only keep going for Bee and Rory.'

'How can I contact you?' I asked him.

'There's a pay phone here.' He pointed at it just inside the front door and I took down the number. I also gave him one of my cards.

'Call me if you need anything,' I said.

He nodded slightly, but I doubted that he would. His life may have been in tatters but he had kept his pride.

We shook hands inside the hallway and Josef peered cautiously round the door as he opened it to the street. I pressed some banknotes into his hand. He looked at the money and started as if to refuse it.

'Buy some food for the baby,' I said.

He looked up at my face. 'Thank you,' he mumbled, fighting back the tears. Things were so bad that he couldn't refuse the cash, even though he clearly hated not doing so.

Next I went to see one of the three jurors from the original trial who had testified at the appeal and who lived in Hendon, close to Golders Green in north London.

George Barnett tried to slam the door in my face as soon as he saw who it was. He obviously recognized me from the trial, as I did him. He was the schoolmasterly white-haired gentleman who had been the jury foreman, but he seemed a shadow of his former self. Gone were the upright posture and the air of self-assurance. In their place there was an old-age stoop, and fear. Lots of fear.

'Go away,' he shouted through the crack in the door that my foot was preventing from closing. 'I did what you asked. Now leave me alone.'

'Mr Barnett,' I called to him round the door. 'I've come here to try and help you.'

'That's what he told me,' he said.

'I have not been sent by Mr Trent,' I said back to him.

There was a muffled 'Oh God' from inside and he pushed harder on the door so that the wood bent. 'Go away,' he shouted again.

'Mr Barnett,' I called again, not moving my foot out of the door. 'I was also beaten up by Julian Trent. I want to find out why. I need your help.'

'Please go away,' he said again, but this time he sounded tired.

'All right,' I said. 'I am going to move my foot now.' I lifted it and he slammed the door shut.

'Mr Barnett,' I called through the door. 'Do you want to spend the rest of your life in fear, or do you want to help me stop these people?'

'Go away,' he said again, pleading.

I pushed one of my business cards through his letter box. 'Call me if you change your mind,' I said. 'I promise I'm on your side.'

He hadn't actually told me anything useful but he had at least confirmed what I had suspected. Julian Trent, together with his friends and relations, had left a trail of broken lives wherever they went, attacking and then intimidating good people into doing what they wouldn't normally contemplate, perverting the course of justice for their own ends and to hell with the consequences for everyone else, including me.

But I had no intention of living in fear for the rest of my life.

It was time to take a stand.

On Thursday, I left my troubles behind and went to Cheltenham for the races.

The Foxhunter Chase, my ambition, was the following afternoon, directly after the Gold Cup. Thursday was World Hurdle day, the long-distance hurdle race for the best 'stayers' in the country.

Today I was having a day off as a guest of a Lambourn horse-transport company that had hired a private box. I had acted for them the previous year when I had successfully defended a charge of careless driving against one of their drivers, and they were honouring their promise to give me a day at Cheltenham as a bonus.

The private box was on the top level of the huge grandstand that would later hold tens of thousands of cheering race fans, shouting home the winners at the greatest jump-race festival in the world. This was the meeting that all owners, trainers and jockeys worked towards for the preceding twelve months. The Grand National may be the most famous English steeplechase, known around the world, but the Cheltenham Festival is where most would love to win, especially one of the two major blue-riband events, the Gold Cup and the Champion Hurdle.

The festival excitement can be almost cut with a knife as the crowds stream through the turnstiles, eager to find themselves a pie and a pint before the serious business of choosing their fancies and placing their bets in good time to bag a vantage point on the grandstand steps.

Fortunately, for me, my vantage point was assured on the viewing balcony of the private box, so I had time to absorb the atmosphere, to walk amongst the tented village of shops and galleries, and to stroll through the Racing Hall of Fame on my way to level 5.

'Ah, Geoffrey.' Edward Cartwright, the transport-company owner extended a large plump hand as he came to meet me at the door. I shook it warmly. 'Welcome to Cheltenham,' he said. 'Let's hope for a great day.' His gaze slid past me as another guest appeared behind me, his attention moving in turn to the new arrival.

The box was about four metres square and the centre was taken up with a large rectangular cloth-covered table set for lunch. I quickly scanned the places. There would be twelve of us in all, about half of whom had so far arrived. I gratefully accepted a glass of champagne that was offered by a small dark-haired waitress and then went out to join some of the other guests that I could see on the balcony outside.

'Hello,' said one of them. 'Remember me?'

'Of course,' I said, shaking his hand. I had last seen him at the equine hospital in November. 'How's the yearling?'

'Two-year-old now,' Simon Dacey said. 'Almost ready for the racecourse. No apparent ill effects, but you never know. He may have been faster still without the muscle damage.'

I looked at the other three people on the balcony.

'Oh, sorry,' said Simon. 'Can I introduce you to my wife, Francesca?' I shook the offered petite hand. Francesca Dacey was blonde, tall, slim and wearing a yellow suit that touched her in all the right places. We smiled at each other. Simon waved towards the other two, a middle-aged couple, he in a pinstripe suit and she in an elegant long brown open jacket over a cream top and brown slacks. 'And Roger and Deborah Radcliffe.' Ah, I realized, they were the Peninsula connections.

'Congratulations last June,' I said. 'With the Derby.'

'Thank you,' said Deborah Radcliffe. 'Greatest day of our lives.'

I could imagine. I was hoping that the following day would prove to be mine. To win at Cheltenham was a dream, to have done so at Epsom in the Derby must be anyone's lifetime ambition. But I could remember Simon Dacey saying when we met in the equine hospital that his party had been the best day of his life – until, that was, Millie Barlow had decided to kill herself in the middle of it.

'I'm so sorry,' said Simon Dacey. 'I remember you have horses with Paul Newington, but I'm afraid I have forgotten your name.'

'Geoffrey Mason,' I said.

'Ah yes, Geoffrey Mason.' The introductions were completed and hands shaken. 'Lawyer, I think you said?'

'Yes, that's right,' I replied. 'But I'm here as an amateur jockey.' I smiled. 'I have a ride in the Foxhunters tomorrow.'

'Best of luck,' said Deborah Radcliffe, rather dismissively. 'We don't have any jumpers.' She said it in a way that gave the impression that she believed jumpers weren't real race-horses and were more of a hobby than proper racing, not like the flat. More fool her, I thought. I had always believed the reverse.

Roger Radcliffe, who obviously agreed with her, took the opportunity to move back inside the box to replenish his champagne. Why, I wondered, did they bother to come if they weren't excited by the racing? But it was not my problem. I was in seventh heaven and my only concern was having too much to eat and drink today and having to put up overweight in the race tomorrow.

Francesca Dacey and Deborah Radcliffe moved to the far end of the balcony for, I imagined, some girly talk. It left Simon and me standing alone. There was an awkward silence for a few moments as we both drank from our champagne glasses.

'Didn't you say you were acting for Steve Mitchell?' Simon Dacey finally asked, almost with relief.

'That's right,' I said, relaxing. 'I'm one of his barristers.'

'When's the trial?' he asked.

'Second week in May.'

'Has Mitchell been inside all this time?' he said.

'Certainly has,' I said. The defence had applied twice for bail without success. Two chances were all you had.

'Can you get him off?' he asked.

'One doesn't get people off,' I said sarcastically. 'It is my job to help the jury determine if he is guilty or not. I hope to provide them with sufficient doubt.'

'Beyond a reasonable doubt,' he said as if quoting.

'Exactly.'

'But there is always some doubt, isn't there?' he said. 'Unless you have it on film.'

'There's some doubt even then,' I said. 'Gone are the days of a hard negative to work from. Don't let anyone ever tell you that a digital camera never lies. They do, and often. No, my job is to persuade the jury that any doubt they may have is at least reasonable.'

'How genteel.' He laughed.

Genteel is not how I would describe the Julian Trent baseball-bat approach to persuasion.

'Have you ever heard of anyone called Julian Trent?' I asked him.

'No,' he said. 'Should I?'

'I just wondered,' I said. He hadn't appeared to be lying. If he was, he was good at it.

'Is he in racing?' he asked.

'No, I don't think so,' I said. 'I asked just on the off chance.'

'It's funny,' he said. 'Our industry, racing that is, it's very insular. Everyone in it knows everyone else but we really don't know anyone not connected, anyone from outside.'

I knew what he meant. The law could be like that too. It was one of the reasons I had chosen to continue taking my pleasure from a sport so far removed from the formality and deathly slow pace of the courts.

The small dark-haired waitress popped her head out of the door and informed us that lunch was about to be served, so would we please take our seats.

The remaining guests had arrived while I had been out on the balcony and I found myself sitting on the long side of the table between Francesca Dacey and Joanna, wife of Nicholas Osbourne, the trainer I had gone to in Lambourn all those years ago. Nicholas and I had nodded cordially to each other as we had sat down. Sadly, there had been no warmth in our greeting. Too many years of animosity, I thought, and I couldn't even remember why.

Joanna, meanwhile, couldn't have been friendlier and even

squeezed my knee beneath the table cloth as I sat down. She had always flirted with me. I suddenly wondered if that was why Nick had become so antagonistic towards me. I looked across the table at him. He was fuming, so I winked at him and laughed. He didn't seem at all certain how to react.

'Nick,' I said loudly. 'Will you please tell your wife to stop flirting with me, I'm a married man.'

He seemed unsure how to reply.

'But . . .' he tailed off.

'My wife might be dead,' I said, with a smile that I didn't feel. 'But I'm still in love with her.'

He seemed to relax a little. 'Joanna, my darling,' he said. 'Leave the poor boy alone.' And he smiled back at me with the first genuine sign of friendship for fifteen years.

'Silly old fool,' Joanna said quietly to me. 'He gets so jealous. I'd have left him years ago if I was ever going to.'

I squeezed her knee back. Nicholas would have had a fit.

'So tell me what you're up to,' she said as we ate the starter of steamed asparagus with Hollandaise sauce.

'I'm representing Steve Mitchell,' I said.

Francesca Dacey, on my other side, jumped a little in her seat. The chairs were so close together round the table that I felt it clearly.

'How exciting,' said Joanna with relish. 'Is he guilty?'

'That's for the jury to decide,' I said.

'Don't be so boring,' Joanna said, grabbing my knee again beneath the table. 'Tell me. Did he do it?'

'What do you think?' I asked her. Francesca was trying not to show that she was listening.

'He must have,' she said. 'Otherwise why have they kept him in prison for so long?'

'But he hasn't been tried yet,' I said.

'Yeah, but it stands to reason,' she said. 'They wouldn't have arrested him if he didn't do it. And everyone knows that Barlow and Mitchell hated each other's guts.'

'That doesn't make him a murderer,' I said. 'In fact, if everyone knew that he hated Barlow so much then he was the obvious person to frame for his murder.'

'That's a bit far-fetched though, isn't it?' she said. 'Doesn't everyone who's guilty say they were framed?'

'A few must be telling the truth,' I said.

Our empty starter plates were removed and were replaced with the main course of chicken breast in a mustard sauce. Francesca Dacey had the vegetarian option of penne pasta with pesto.

Joanna Osbourne turned to talk to the man on her left, another Lambourn trainer whose reputation I knew rather better than the man himself. I, meanwhile, turned to Francesca on my right. She was giving a good impression of a health inspector, so keen was she to keep her eyes firmly fixed on her food.

'So how long have you known Steve Mitchell?' I asked her quietly.

'I don't,' she said. But both of us knew she was lying.

'Were you with him the day Scot Barlow died?' I asked her, so quietly that no one else would have been able to hear.

'No,' she replied in the same manner. 'I don't know what you mean.' But we both did.

'Were you really gone from Steve's house by two thirty?' I said, keeping my eyes firmly on my chicken.

'Oh God,' she said under her breath. I thought for a moment that she was going to get up and leave, but she took a couple of deep breaths and went on studying her pasta. 'Yes,' she said. 'Absolutely. I had to be home by two thirty to meet the plumber. He came to fix the dishwasher.'

So, just as Steve had told me, getting her involved wouldn't actually give him an alibi for Barlow's murder.

'Steve didn't tell me,' I said to her, turning towards her ear so that others wouldn't hear. 'He refused to say who it was he was with.'

I wasn't sure whether she was pleased or not.

'Please.' She gulped. 'Please don't tell my husband,' she pleaded in a whisper.

'No,' I said. 'No need to.'

She half coughed, half sobbed and then suddenly stood up.

'Sorry,' she croaked to our host. 'Something went down the wrong way.' She rushed out, holding a white linen napkin to her face. One of the other ladies followed her out. Simon Dacey watched in obvious embarrassment.

Cheltenham during the Festival is like no other day at the races anywhere in the world. After lunch I wandered around absorbing the atmosphere. I walked down to the Guinness Village, now an institution at the track and the transient home to thousands of Irish whose annual pilgrimage to Gloucestershire does much to make this event so unique. Irish folk bands and English rock bands vied for favour in the huge marquee behind a scaffold-built temporary grandstand, entertaining the crowd prior to the main attraction of the afternoon, the racing itself.

I leaned on the white plastic rail next to the horse walk to watch a quartet of happy punters from across the Irish Sea.

They all wore outrageous green and black huge leprechaun hats and they had linked arms in a line like a scene from *Zorba the Greek*. They were trying to perform an Irish jig and I laughed out loud as they came a cropper and sat down heavily on a grassy bank. All were in good humour, aided and abetted by a continuous flow of the black stuff, the Guinness.

'Hello, stranger,' said a familiar voice behind me. I smiled broadly and turned round.

'Hello, Eleanor,' I said, and I gave her a kiss on the cheek. 'How lovely to see you. Are you here for work or pleasure?'

'Both really,' she said. 'Busman's holiday for me today. I am technically on call but that means I can do pretty much what I want. I just have to carry this bleep.' She produced a small rectangular black item from her cavernous handbag.

'Fancy a drink?' I asked.

'Yes, but not here,' she said indicating the Guinness bar.

'No,' I agreed.

We went in search of one of the bars under the grandstand but they were all packed with a scrum ten deep to get served.

'Come on,' I said. 'Let's go up to the boxes.'

I was sure that Edward Cartwright, my host, wouldn't mind me bringing Eleanor into his box and so it turned out. In fact, he rather monopolized her and left me wishing we had stayed in the crush downstairs.

I had seen Eleanor twice since the previous November. The first time had been in London just a week later, when I had asked her to a black-tie dinner in the Hall at Gray's Inn. It hadn't been a particularly successful evening. I should have opted for a table for two in a candle-lit Italian restaurant rather than the long refectory tables and benches in Hall.

The seating plan had us sitting opposite each other rather

than side by side as I had hoped and conversation between us had been difficult, not only due to the noise of three hundred people eating and talking at once, but also because the centre of the table was full of flowers, silver candelabras, and a detritus of wine glasses, condiments and place-cards.

We had hardly spoken a word to each other the whole evening and I think she had been bored by the speeches, which had contained too many 'in' jokes for the lawyers. At the end of the dinner she had jumped straight back into a cab and rushed off to Paddington for the last train home.

Why I had asked her to that dinner, I could not imagine. If I had wanted a romantic evening à deux, I couldn't have chosen anything less appropriate. Maybe, that was the trouble. Maybe I hadn't actually wanted a romantic evening à deux in the first place. It was silly to admit, but perhaps I was scared to embark on a new amorous adventure. It also made me feel guilty. Guilty that I was somehow deserting Angela.

The second time we had met had been even more of a disaster. We had both been guests at a Christmas ball thrown by a big racing sponsor in the grandstand at Newbury racecourse. I had been there in a party put together by Paul and Laura Newington, and Eleanor had been in another group, one of the many from Lambourn. I had been so delighted to see her again and had immediately asked her to dance. But she had been with someone else and he'd been determined that I wouldn't get a look-in with 'his' girl. I had felt wretched all evening. It was not just that I had lost out to another, it was that, maybe, I had suddenly realized that the time was now right and I had missed my chance. The bus had come along willingly and had opened its doors to pick me up, but I had declined the offer and now it had driven off, leaving me standing alone at the bus-stop. I now worried that it might have been the last bus, and that I would remain waiting at the stop for ever.

'Penny for your thoughts,' Eleanor said, coming up behind me again. I had been leaning on the balcony rail aimlessly watching the massed crowds below and I hadn't noticed her escape the clutches of Edward and come outside to join me.

'You,' I said, turning and looking into her blue eyes.

She blushed, the crimson colouring spreading up from her neck and over her face.

'Did you know,' I said, 'that if you are naked you blush all over your body.'

'Bastard,' she said. She turned away and laughed.

'What are you doing tonight?' I asked her.

'I'm not coming to another of your awful dining-in nights, that's for sure.'

We laughed together.

'I have to admit that it was a bit of a disaster,' I agreed. 'But I'm sure the next one will be better.'

'Forget it,' she said. 'I had always thought lawyers were boring, and now I know they are.'

'You just haven't met the right lawyers,' I said.

She paused and smiled at me. 'Oh yes I have,' she said.

Wow, I thought. The bus had made a round trip. Now do I get on?

CHAPTER 9

Sadly, I didn't spend the evening with Eleanor, nor the night.

In fact, I spent very little time with her at all. Her bleep went off as we were still on the balcony and she rushed off to find a quiet spot to make a call, returning only briefly to tell me that she had to go back to Lambourn. There was an emergency at the hospital, something about a prize stallion and a twisted gut.

'Will you be here tomorrow?' I shouted after her rather forlornly as she rushed away.

'Hope so,' she called back. 'Call me on the mobile in the morning.'

Suddenly she was gone. I was surprised at how disappointed I felt. Was I really ready after seven and a half years? Don't rush things, I told myself.

I spent much of the rest of the afternoon drifting between the box upstairs and the parade ring. I had intended to use the time to familiarize myself with the surroundings, the sounds and the smells of the Festival in mental preparation for the race the following day. Instead, I spent most of the time thinking about Eleanor, and about Angela. They were quite different but in many ways they were the same. Eleanor was blonde with blue eyes whereas Angela had been dark with brown, but they both had a similar sense of humour, and a love for life and fun.

'Which one do you fancy?'

I looked at the man standing next to me who had spoken. I didn't know him.

'I beg your pardon?' I said.

'Which one do you fancy?' he said again, nodding at the horses. We were leaning up against the rail of the parade ring where the horses for the next race were walking round and round.

'Oh,' I said in sudden understanding. 'Sorry, I don't even know what's running.'

He lost interest in me instantly, and went on studying the horseflesh on parade in front of him prior, no doubt, to making an investment with the bookies.

I went back upstairs to the box, telling myself to snap out of this daydreaming and pay attention to the racing.

'How's he doing?' Francesca Dacey whispered in my ear as she stood behind me to watch the race on the balcony.

'Fed up,' I said, turning slightly. 'But otherwise OK.'

'Say hi to him for me if you get the chance,' she whispered again before moving away to her left and talking to another of the guests.

The World Hurdle, the big race of the day, was a three-mile hurdle race for horses with stamina for the long distance, especially the uphill finish in the March mud. And stamina they had. Four horses crossed the last obstacle in line abreast and each was driven hard for the line, the crowd cheering them on with fervour, the result to be determined only by the race judge and his photographs.

There was a buzz in the crowd after the horses swept past the winning post, such had been the exhilarating effect of the closest of finishes; the adrenalin still rushed round our veins, our breathing was still just a tad faster than normal. Such moments were what brought the crowds back time and again to Cheltenham. The best horses, ridden by the best jockeys, stretching to reach the line first. Winning was everything.

'First, number seven,' said the announcer to a huge cheer from some and a groan of misery from others. Reno Clemens on horse number seven stood bolt upright in his stirrups and punched the air, saluting the crowd, who roared back their appreciation. How I longed for it to be me doing just that the following afternoon.

Most of the guests rushed off to watch the winner come back to the unsaddling enclosure, where he would receive a fresh wave of cheering and applause. I, however, decided to stay put. I had done my share of aimlessly wandering the racecourse wishing that Eleanor had been with me to share it.

The lunch table had been pushed up against one wall and was now heaving under large trays of sandwiches and cakes ready for tea. I looked longingly at a cream-filled chocolate éclair and opted instead for the smallest cucumber sandwich I could find.

'I hear you are a lawyer,' said a female voice on my right.

I turned to find Deborah Radcliffe standing next to me. Why did I think she didn't like lawyers? Maybe it was the way she looked down her nose at me. Lots of people didn't like lawyers, that is until they got themselves into trouble. Then their lawyer became their best friend, maybe their only friend.

'That's right,' I said, smiling at her. 'I'm a barrister.'

'Do you wear a wig?' she asked.

'Only in court,' I said. 'Lots of my work is not done in courts. I represent people at professional disciplinary hearings and the like.'

'Oh,' she said, as if bored. 'And do you represent jockeys at enquiries?'

'I have done,' I said. 'But not very often.'

She seemed to lose interest completely.

'How is Peninsula?' I asked her.

'Fine, as far as I know,' she said. 'He's now at Rushmore Stud in Ireland. In his first season.'

Retired at age three to spend the rest of his life treated like royalty, passing his days eating, sleeping and covering mares. Horse paradise.

'But he wasn't born himself at Rushmore?' I said.

'Oh no,' she replied. 'We bred him at home.'

'Where's home?' I asked her.

'Near Uffington,' she said. 'In south Oxfordshire.'

'Where the White Horse is,' I said. The Uffington White Horse was a highly stylized Bronze Age horse figure carved into the chalk of the Downs a few miles north of Lambourn.

'Exactly,' she replied, suddenly showing more interest in me. 'I can almost see White Horse Hill from my kitchen window.'

'I've never actually seen the horse,' I said. 'Except in photos.'

'It's not that easy to see unless you get up in the air,' she said. 'We are forever getting tourists who ask us where it is. They seem disappointed when you show them the hill. The horse is almost on the top of it and you can't even see it properly if you walk up to it. Goodness knows how they made it in the first place.'

'Perhaps it was the fact that they couldn't see it properly that made it such a weird-looking horse,' I said.

'Good point,' she said.

'Do you remember Millie Barlow being there when Peninsula was born?' I asked.

'Who?' she said.

'Millie Barlow,' I repeated. 'She was the vet who was present.'

'Not really,' she said. 'We have foals being born all the time. We have a sort of maternity hospital for horses. They come to us to deliver, especially if they are to then be covered by a local stallion.'

'But I would have thought you would remember Peninsula,' I said.

'Why?' she said. 'We didn't know at the time that he would turn out so good. He had good breeding but it was not exceptional. We were just lucky.'

It made sense. After all, the world knows that William Shakespeare died on 23 April 1616, but it is not known for sure exactly where and on which day he was born, although it is often assumed, for neatness, to be the same day of the year as his death. All that is actually recorded is that he was baptized on 26 April 1564.

'Why do you ask about this vet?' Deborah asked me.

'It's just that she killed herself last June and I wondered if you remembered her at Peninsula's birth,' I said.

'Not that vet who killed herself during the party?' she said.

I nodded.

'I remember her doing that, of course,' she said. 'But I didn't know it was the same vet who had been there to foal Peninsula.'

'So you didn't see a photo of her with Peninsula after the birth?' I asked.

'No,' she said emphatically. 'Why? Should I have done?'

'It seems to have gone missing,' I said.

'Sorry,' she said, losing interest again. 'I can't help you.'

A large group of the other guests suddenly returned to the box for their tea and I decided to go back outside onto the balcony rather than be continuously beguiled by the chocolate cream éclairs.

I woke early the following morning with butterflies rather than éclairs hovering in my stomach. I was used to that feeling. It happened almost every time I had a ride in a race but this time it was something special. The Foxhunter Chase at Cheltenham is known as the amateur riders' Gold Cup. It is run over the same course and distance as its big brother, although, while the Gold Cup had the highest prize money at the Festival, the Foxhunter Chase had the lowest. But it wasn't the prize money that mattered. For me as a jockey, winning the Foxhunters would be like winning the Gold Cup, the Grand National and the Derby all rolled into one.

I spent some of the morning on the phone, chasing some information for the Mitchell case that we had requested several weeks before. As a matter of course we had received copies of Scot Barlow's bank statements with the rest of the prosecution disclosure, but I had also asked for those of his sister, Millie. The bank had kicked up a bit of a fuss about confidentiality and I had needed to go back to court and argue in front of a judge as to why they were needed.

It had now been two weeks since the hearing. I had referred to our Defence Case Statement in so far as we believed that Mitchell had been framed and that therefore, in our opinion, some unknown third party had been involved in the crime. Thus Barlow's bank statements had been needed to determine if any unusual or relevant transactions had occurred between him and an unknown third party. I further pointed out that Millie Barlow, sister of the victim and lover of the accused, had, according to her friends, seemed quite well off prior to her suicide the previous June. More well off than might have been expected from her salary alone. I had argued that she might have been receiving an allowance from her brother, a successful sportsman who, at the time, had been earning near the top of his profession. Millie Barlow's bank statements were needed therefore to cross reference with his, so as to be able to eliminate transactions on his statements made by him to her during her lifetime.

I was not altogether sure if the judge had believed me, or even if he had understood my argument, but he could see no reason why the bank statements of a suicide, whether or not she was the sister of a murder victim, should still have been covered by the bank's confidentiality policy, and he made an order for the bank to produce them. He clearly rated suicides lower than criminals.

However, the bank was being very slow in complying with the order. Arthur had finally found me a telephone number that didn't connect to an overseas call centre, so I rang Bruce Lygon and asked him to telephone the bank and tell them that, unless the statements were on my desk by Monday morning, we would have no option but to go back to the judge and argue that the bank was in contempt. I also told Bruce to ensure that he dropped into his conversation that the punishment for criminal contempt of court was a two-year term of imprisonment and/ or an unlimited fine.

Bruce called me back within five minutes. He was laughing. He had clearly laid on thick the bit about a prison sentence and the bank's commercial director had promised him absolutely that the statements would be couriered to our chambers this very day. I congratulated him.

Next I called Eleanor.

'Hello,' she said, sounding sleepy.

'Late night?' I asked.

'More like early morning,' she said. 'I was in theatre until nearly four.'

My heart sank. I had so hoped she would be there to see me ride.

'Are you coming today?' I asked without any real hope.

'Probably not,' she said. 'Believe it or not, but I'm still technically on call if there's another emergency. I must get some sleep sometime.'

'Yes,' I said. 'I suppose so.'

'I'll try and be there if I can,' she said. 'What time is the race?'

'Four,' I said.

'If I don't make it, I'll make sure I watch it on the telly,' she said. 'Call me after. OK?'

'Yes,' I said. 'OK.'

'From the winner's circle,' she said.

'I hope so,' I replied with more of a smile in my voice.

'I must dash,' she said. 'Good luck.'

'Thanks,' I said, but the line was already dead.

I surprised myself by the degree of my disappointment. Angela had always hated watching me ride. She used to say that she couldn't eat beforehand and that her stomach was twisted into knots by the fear that I would be injured. I had almost stopped riding altogether towards the end of her life as I could

170

see how much she hated it. After she died I had slowly returned to the saddle, using early mornings on Paul Newington's gallops as a sort of therapy for the agony and the loneliness. It had been a natural progression to return to riding in races as well.

Now I wished so much that Eleanor would be there this afternoon. But perhaps she would hate it too, and maybe, I thought with hope, for the same reason.

I arrived at the racecourse early to miss the traffic. I had stayed the night in a small hotel on Cleeve Hill overlooking the track. It was where I should have been a year ago and the couple who owned and ran the place had been very happy to have pocketed my non-refundable 100 per cent deposit and then re-let the room when I couldn't make it. To their credit, they had eagerly accepted my booking for this year, perhaps in the hope of again making a sizable profit. There was not a hotel room within fifty miles of Cheltenham that wasn't filled and pre-purchased at least twelve months in advance for these four days.

I parked my rented car in the jockeys' car park, made my way into the racecourse enclosures, through to the weighing room and then on into the inner sanctum, the jockeys' changing room. I slung my bag of kit on a peg and walked out onto the weighing-room terrace, feeling completely at home amongst the crowd of trainers, journalists and other jockeys. This was where I loved to be, not in some musty courtroom where the pace of the action was so slow as to be painful.

A racing correspondent from one of the national dailies came up to me.

'Hi, Perry,' he said. 'How's that client of yours?'

'Which client?' I asked. 'And the name's Geoffrey.'

He laughed. I knew that he knew my real name as well as I did.

'OK, Geoffrey,' he said with sarcasm. 'How's your client, Steve Mitchell?'

'Fine,' I said. 'As far as I'm aware. But you probably know better than me.'

'Is he guilty?' he asked.

'I couldn't possibly comment on a case that's still before the courts,' I said. 'I would be in contempt.'

'I know that,' he said. 'But, off the record?'

'Wait for the trial,' I said. 'Then the jury will decide.'

'Won't take 'em long if what I hear is true?' he said with a laugh.

'And what have you heard?' I asked him.

'That Mitchell stuck him one because Barlow accused him of killing his sister.'

'And who exactly told you that?' I asked him.

'That's the word in the press room,' he said. 'Everyone's saying it.'

'And is that what you think?' I asked him.

'Yeah,' he said uncertainly. 'Suppose so.'

We stood together in awkward silence for a moment before he turned away with a slight wave of a hand and went off in search of someone else.

I stood and drank in the atmosphere. Even the weather was joining in the enthusiasm. The sun peeped out from behind a fluffy white cumulus cloud to warm the hearts and souls of seventy thousand racegoers. This was Cheltenham on Gold Cup day and there was nothing quite like it.

'Hi, Geoff.' It was Nick Osbourne, with a smile.

'Hello, Nick.' We shook hands warmly. The truce from the

previous day was still holding. 'Any runners today?' I knew he didn't have one in the Gold Cup or the Foxhunters but, apart from those races, I had no idea what was running.

'One in the novice hurdle,' he said. 'Not much chance really.'

'Good luck anyway,' I said.

'Good luck to you too,' he replied. 'On Sandeman.'

'Thanks.'

We stood in easy companionship for a while discussing our chances and, as always on this day, coming back to who we thought would win the big one.

By the time of the first race at two o'clock my guts were twisted tighter than those of Eleanor's equine patient, and the nerves were beginning to get to me. I sat on the bench around the changing room and made myself calm down. I even managed to force down a cheese and pickle sandwich and a cup of tea that had thoughtfully been provided for the jockeys in the weighing room.

I was not alone in feeling nervous. Even for the top professionals, chances on good horses at Cheltenham were few and far between. For the jockeys of the three or four top-rated horses in the Gold Cup this was a day that could define their careers. Gold Cup winners, both horses and jockeys, were remembered and revered.

I spent much of the afternoon sitting in the changing room alone with my thoughts, mentally running the race over and over in my head, deciding where I wanted to be and when, whether to be on the inside to take the shortest route or to run further wide and give myself more room. Sandeman was fit and so was I. There would be no repeat of Sandown the previous November when it had been my fault we hadn't won. On this day the horse and jockey would both have the stamina to come up the Cheltenham hill after three and a quarter miles.

I stood on the scales in my riding clothes holding my saddle, together with the felt pad that goes under it, the number cloth and the weightcloth, a devious contraption that sits beneath the saddle with lead sheets in pockets to add weight. The digital read-out settled on twelve stone, the required mark, and the clerk of the scales ticked me off on his list. As a rule jockeys don't like carrying extra lead as it sits as dead weight on the horse's back, but I was secretly quite pleased that I had eight pounds of it in my weightcloth, especially as I was using a heavier saddle than many of the other amateurs waiting for their turn on the scales. All that running and skiing had done the trick and I was lighter than I had been for quite a while. I was now well under eleven stone in my birthday suit, so carrying twelve was easy.

I had never really had much trouble doing the weight on Sandeman as he had always been fairly highly rated and, even in handicaps, he had always been near to top weight. Some jockeys, however, had an ongoing struggle every day to keep their weight down, a problem that to me seemed to be getting worse as the average size of the population grew while the racing weights stayed the same.

You could always tell when someone was in trouble doing the weight. There were little games they would play with the clerk of the scales, who was probably wise to every one. They would leave their cap on their helmet and place it on the table. The rule stated that the cap should be weighed even if the helmet wasn't. Others would weigh-out using paper-thin boots, known by jockeys as cheating boots, which they would then change for their regular riding boots when safely back in the changing room. It had also been known for jockeys to weigh-out with a much lighter saddle than they actually intended using, or indeed, if things were desperate, with no saddle at all. Over-weight was frowned upon by the stewards, and by owners and trainers alike, and could make the difference between keeping or losing the ride on that horse in the future.

Having successfully cleared the scales, I handed my saddle and the rest of the tack to Paul Newington, who was standing by waiting to receive it.

'See you in the parade ring,' he said, and turned on his heel.

I could tell that he was nervous as well and I watched his back as he hurried away to get Sandeman ready in the saddling boxes.

I went into the changing room to get a jacket to put over my silks and then back out onto the weighing-room terrace to watch the Gold Cup on the big screen set up near the paddock. The favourite won easily with Reno Clemens in the saddle. They had jumped clear of the chasing pack over the last two fences in the straight and stormed up the hill to win by eight lengths. They received a hero's welcome from the huge crowd. But Steve Mitchell in his prison cell wouldn't like it, I thought. He should have been riding that winner. He had ridden the horse all the way through its career only to miss out on its crowning glory.

With the Gold Cup over, now it was my turn. The Foxhunter Chase was less than half an hour away and the butterflies in my stomach had turned into full size eagles. I went back into the changing room and made all my last-minute adjustments once again, making sure I was wearing my back protector and that it was correctly fitted, checking that my silks were on properly with rubber bands around the wrists to stop the wind rushing up the sleeves, tying and retying the cords on my cap to get them right, to ensure it didn't fly off my helmet during the race.

I went once again to the loo and nervously paced around. It was like waiting outside the exam room before my law finals at university, or being in a dentist's waiting room before an extraction.

Finally, the call was made for the jockeys to go out to the parade ring. As always, I felt the burst of adrenalin course through my body but, this time, I wasn't so sure I was enjoying it. The expectation was too great. Riding last year's winner and this year's favourite, as well as carrying so many punters' hopes, was taking much of the fun out of it.

Paul and Laura stood on the grass in the paddock and both seemed to hop from foot to foot with nervousness.

'Good luck,' said Laura breathlessly, giving me a kiss on the cheek.

'Look,' I said. 'Let's just enjoy it. Eh?' They both looked at me as if I were mad. 'Win or lose, it's been a great day out.'

I smiled at them. They didn't smile back. Oh no, I thought, they've had a big bet on us to win. I could read it in their faces. Oh, woe is me. Just another load of pressure I could have done without.

Paul gave me a leg-up onto Sandeman's back and he slapped a hand on his neck. 'Go get 'em, cowboy,' he said nervously in a mock American accent, looking up at me.

'Do my best, pardner,' I said back to him in the same manner.

We circled around the ring a couple of times as the horses sorted themselves out and then we were led out towards the course by two huntsmen in scarlet jackets.

Sandeman beneath me was eager to get going and he didn't

like being crammed in on all sides by the massive crowd five deep against the horse-walk rail.

'Good luck, Geoffrey,' called a voice to my left.

I looked down from my vantage point atop a seventeen-hand horse and there was Eleanor, waving madly. She had made it after all. How wonderful.

'Thanks,' I shouted at her inadequately above the bustle of the crowd.

I turned to take one last look at her before Sandeman and I went out onto the course. She was smiling broadly, still waving, but something else caught my eye. Standing just behind her and a little to her right was someone else I recognized.

It was Julian Trent, and he was smiling at me too.

Oh shit. I tried to stop and turn round, to go back and warn her, but the stable lad just thought that Sandeman was playing up a little so he took a tighter hold of the reins and pulled us forward.

I turned right round in the saddle and tried to shout to Eleanor but she didn't hear me. What should I do? I wanted to jump off, to run back, to protect her. But Sandeman and I were now out of the horse walk and on the course, walking up in front of the expectant crowd. Surely, I told myself, Eleanor would be safe amongst all those people. Perhaps Trent had not seen the exchange between us and he would think of her as just another eager spectator.

The horses were to be led up in front of the grandstand and then we would turn and canter back past the horse walk and on to the start of the race at the far end of the finishing straight.

So distracted was I that I almost fell off when the stable lad turned Sandeman and let him go with a reminding slap on his rump. Instinct made me gather the reins tight in my hands and set off in a gentle canter to the start while I searched the thousands of faces in the crowd, desperate for a glimpse of Eleanor, or of Trent, but unable to spot either.

I felt sick.

All my pre-race planning of where I wanted to be at the start went out the window as my mind was elsewhere. When the tapes flew up Sandeman was caught flat-footed owing to my negligence and I instantly gave the rest of the field ten lengths' start. I could imagine Paul swearing on the trainers' stand and wishing that he had convinced me to let last year's jockey ride again. And he wouldn't be the only one, I thought. This was a televised race and I had been napping at the start. In any other circumstances it would have been unforgivable, but somehow I didn't care. I was more concerned about Eleanor's safety.

Sandeman set off in pursuit of the others and made a magnificent leap at the first with me hardly participating at all. Come on, I said to myself, Eleanor will be fine, concentrate on the matter in hand.

I eased Sandeman back from his headlong gallop to a steadier pace. There was plenty of time to get back to the pack. This was a three-and-a-quarter-mile chase with twenty-two jumps, twice round the Cheltenham course. I settled him down and we steadily closed the gap until, although still last, there was no air between us and the rest. Fortunately the first circuit was not being run too fast as everyone realized there was a long way to go in fairly heavy ground.

At the top of the hill for the first time, I pulled Sandeman slightly wider and we overtook eight other horses easily in the run down to the point where we had started. As we began the second circuit we were in the middle of the pack, lying about tenth, but with those ahead tightly bunched.

By the time we reached the water jump half-way down the back straight the race was really on in earnest. Sandeman flattened his back and sailed over the water like a hurdler. We passed three horses in mid-air and landed running fast. But two other horses had got away at the front of the pack and a three-length gap had opened up behind them.

I kicked Sandeman hard in the ribs.

'Come on boy,' I shouted in his ear. 'Now is the time.'

It was as if he changed gear. We were eating up the ground and two great leaps at the open ditches found us lying third, turning sharp left and starting down the hill for the last time.

I was exhilarated. I wasn't tired and Sandeman didn't feel a bit tired beneath me. I looked ahead. The two horses in front seemed also to be going well and they were about four lengths away, running side by side.

I gave Sandeman a little bit of a breather for a few paces, sitting easily on his back rather than pushing hard at his neck. There were two fences down the hill and I took a measured look at the first one. I adjusted Sandeman's stride and asked him for a big leap. He responded immediately and flew through the top of the fence, gaining half the distance on his rivals ahead. So full of energy had he been that for the first time I thought I might win.

I now kicked him and asked for his final effort. Sandeman had always been a horse with great stamina but without an amazing sprint finish. We needed to be ahead at the last with the momentum to carry us up the hill to the finish in front.

'Come on boy,' I shouted again in his ear. 'Now, now, now.'

Both the horses in front wavered slightly as they approached the fence and I knew, I suddenly knew, that we were going to win.

I gave a slight pull on the reins, setting Sandeman right for another great leap. I was watching the ground, looking at our take-off point, and only peripherally did I see one of the horses ahead hit the top of the fence hard. I pulled Sandeman slightly wider, but it was the wrong way. The horse in front over-balanced badly on landing, rolled sharply to its right and onto the ground, straight into our path. Sandeman and I were in mid-air before I realized that we had nowhere to land. My horse did his best to avoid the carnage but without any real hope of success.

Sandeman tripped over the bulk of prostrate horseflesh in front of him and somersaulted through the air. My last memory of the day was of the green grass rushing up to meet me, just before the blackness came.

PART III

Trial and Punishment

May 2009

CHAPTER 10

I sat at my desk in chambers reading through the paperwork for an upcoming disciplinary hearing at which I would be representing one of a group of senior doctors who had been accused of professional misconduct over the untimely death of a patient in their hospital.

The phone on my desk rang. It was Arthur.

'Mr Mason,' he said 'There's someone here to see you. He's in the clerks' room.'

'Who is it?' I asked.

'He won't say,' said Arthur, clearly disapproving. 'He just insists on talking to you, and only you.'

How odd, I thought.

'Shall I bring him along?' Arthur asked.

'Yes please,' I said. 'But will you stay here until I ask you to leave?'

'All right,' he said. 'But why?'

'Just in case I need a witness,' I said. But I hoped I wouldn't. Surely Julian Trent wouldn't show up and demand to see me in my room.

I put the phone down. It was a general rule hereabouts that

members of chambers met with clients and visitors only in one of the conference rooms on the lower ground floor but, since I had returned to work after Cheltenham, Arthur had been kind enough to grant me special dispensation to meet people in my room. Climbing up and down even just a few stairs on crutches wasn't easy, particularly as the stairs in question were narrow and turning.

There was a brief knock on the door and Arthur entered, followed by a nervous looking man with white hair wearing the same light coloured tweed jacket and blue and white striped shirt that I had seen before in court number 3 at the Old Bailey. However, his shirt had then been open at the collar whereas now a neat red and gold tie completed his ensemble. It was the schoolmasterly foreman of the jury whom I had last glimpsed when I'd had my foot in his front door in Hendon.

'Hello, Mr Barnett,' I said to him. 'Come on in. Thank you, Arthur, that will be all.'

Arthur looked at me with a questioning expression and I smiled back at him. Eventually, he turned on his heel and left me alone with my visitor. I stood up clumsily and held out my hand. George Barnett approached cautiously and briefly shook it.

'Please sit down,' I said to him, indicating the chair in front of my desk.

'Did Trent do that?' he asked, pointing at the cast that stretched from my left foot to my upper thigh.

'No,' I replied. 'I had a fall.'

'I had one of those last June,' he said. 'In my bathroom. Cracked my pelvis.'

'Mine was from a horse,' I said. 'In a race.'

'Oh,' he said.

'Smashed my knee,' I said.

'Oh,' he said again.

I didn't bother telling him about the cracked vertebrae, the broken ribs and the collapsed lung. Or the concussion that, seven weeks later, still plagued me with headaches.

We sat for a moment in silence while he looked around at the mass of papers and boxes that filled almost every available inch of space in my room.

'Mr Barnett,' I said, bringing his attention back to my face. 'How can I help you?'

'I thought it was me who needed to help you,' he said.

'Yes, indeed,' I said, slightly surprised. 'Yes, please. Would you like some coffee or tea?'

'Tea would be lovely,' he said. 'Milk and one sugar.'

I lifted the phone on my desk and asked one of the junior clerks if he would be kind enough to fix it.

'Now, Mr Barnett,' I said. 'Tell me everything.'

He was reluctant at first but he relaxed when the tea arrived, and the whole sorry story was spilled out.

'I was initially pleased when I received the summons for jury service,' he said. 'I had been retired for about four years and I thought it would be interesting, you know, stimulating for the mind.'

'What had you retired from?' I asked him.

'I was in the Civil Service,' he said. I had been wrong about him having been a schoolmaster. 'I was a permanent under-secretary in the Lord Chancellor's Department, but it's called something else now, Constitutional Affairs or something. They change everything, this government.' It didn't sound like he approved.

'Had you done jury service before?' I asked.

'No,' he said. 'I was called once, years ago, but I was exempt through my work in the administration of justice. But they've changed the law on that now too. Even judges and the police now have to serve on juries if they are summoned.'

I knew. Lawyers used to be excluded too, but not any more.

'So tell me what happened,' I encouraged.

He looked around him as if about to tell a big secret that he didn't want anyone else to overhear. 'I turned up at the Old Bailey as I had been asked to and there were a whole load of us. We sat around for ages in the jury area. Then we were given a talk about being a juror and it was all rather exciting. We were made to feel important, if you know what I mean.'

I nodded. I suspected that, as a permanent under-secretary, he had indeed been quite important in the Civil Service but retirement had brought a return to anonymity. Like the head-masters of the great British public schools who may have princes and lords hanging on their every word while they are in post, only to be turned out to fairly low-paid pasture and obscurity on the day they depart. George Barnett would have enjoyed once again being made to feel important, as we all would.

'In the end,' he said. 'I spent the whole of the first day sitting in the jury collection area reading the newspapers. When I was told I could go home, I was rather disappointed. But the following day I was selected for a trial. I remember being so excited by the prospect.' He paused. 'That was a mistake.' He smiled ruefully at me.

'The Trent trial?' I said.

He nodded. 'It was all right for a while,' he said. 'Then during the first weekend a man came to see me at home.' He paused again. 'He said he was from the jury service so I let him in.'

'Did he give a name?' I asked him.

'Not at first,' he said. 'But then he said he was Julian Trent's father, but I don't think he actually was.'

'Why not?' I said.

'I called him Mr Trent a couple of times and I didn't think he realized I was talking to him.'

'What did he say?'

'Well, when he gave me that name I immediately told him to leave,' he said. 'I knew that we shouldn't talk to anyone about the case, especially not to the defendant's family. But he wouldn't go away. Instead, he offered me money to vote not guilty.'

I sat quietly, waiting for him to continue.

'I told him to go to hell,' he said. 'But . . .' He tailed off, clearly distressed by the memory. I waited some more.

'But he just sat there on a chair in my living room and looked around him. He said that I had a nice place and it would be a shame if I lost it all, or if my wife was injured in an accident.' He stopped again. 'I asked him what he meant. He just smiled and said to work it out.'

'So did you vote not guilty?' I asked.

'My wife has Parkinson's disease,' he said. 'And a bad heart.' I assumed that meant yes, he had. 'I knew that you only need ten of the twelve people on the jury to vote guilty in England to convict, so my vote wouldn't really matter.' I suppose he was trying to justify himself, and to excuse his behaviour. But he must surely have realized that the man would approach other jurors too.

'So what happened in the jury room?' I asked him. It was against the law for him to tell me and I could quite likely get disbarred for even just asking him, but what difference did one more misdemeanour matter, I thought. I could have been disbarred for lots of things I had done, or not done, recently.

187

'There was a terrific row,' he said. 'Nine of them said straight away that they thought he was guilty as hell. There were three of us who didn't.' He stopped and looked up at the ceiling. 'I think now that the man must have been to see all three of us. None of us could give any reason for saying he was not guilty. We just did. The others thought we were mad. One or two of them got really angry as the time dragged on and on.'

I remembered. I'd been really angry as well.

'But you did return a guilty verdict in the end,' I said.

'I know,' he said. 'And it was me who had to say it in court as they had made me foreman right at the start. It was terrible.'

I remembered back a year, to the nervousness with which he had delivered the verdicts.

'Who cracked?' I said, trying to make light of the situation.

'One of the other two,' he said. 'A woman. She did nothing for days and days but cry. It was enough to send anyone mad.'

I could imagine the emotions in that room. It had taken more than six days for one of the three to change their vote to guilty.

'I was so relieved,' he said. 'I had often so nearly changed my vote, but every morning the man had called me and reminded me that my wife would have an accident if I didn't stay firm. I just couldn't believe that it went on for so long.'

Neither could I. I had fully expected the judge to declare a mistrial because the jury couldn't make a decision. But he hadn't. He had kept calling the jury back into court to ask them to try again to reach a verdict on which at least ten of them agreed. We would never know for how much longer he would have persevered.

'So what happened afterwards?' I asked him.

'Nothing for ages, at least a month,' he said. 'Then the man turned up at my door and pushed me over when I tried to shut him out. He simply walked into the house and kicked me.' It was clearly painful for him simply to describe it. 'It was awful,' he went on. 'He kicked me twice in the stomach. I could hardly breathe. Then he went over to Molly, that's my wife, and just tipped her out of her wheelchair onto the floor. I ask you, who could do such a thing.' His eyes filled with tears but he choked them back. 'Then he put his foot on her oxygen tube. It was absolutely horrid.'

I could see that it was.

'And he told you,' I said, 'to go to the police and say that you had been approached by a solicitor who had asked you to make sure you found Trent guilty?' It was a question but, as all barristers know, one should never ask a question to which you don't already know the answer.

He nodded and looked down into his lap.

'It was dreadful, lying like that in the court,' he said. 'The appeal judges kept asking me if I was telling the truth or was I saying it because I had been told to do so by someone else. I was sure they knew I was lying. I felt so ashamed.' He said the last part in little more than a whisper. 'That's why I'm here,' he said more strongly. 'When you came to my house I was afraid of you. I've been afraid of nearly everyone for the past year. I've hardly been out of the house since the trial. I've been looking at your business card for weeks and been trying to pluck up the courage to come here.'

'I'm so glad you did,' I said. He smiled a little. 'And how is your wife?'

'They took her into a nursing home yesterday, poor thing. The Parkinson's is beginning to affect her mind and it's becoming too much for me to manage on my own. She's so confused.

That's another reason I'm here today,' he said. 'She's safe now. The security at the nursing home is pretty good, mostly to stop the patients wandering off. Now I only have to worry about myself.'

'And what would you like me to do about what you have told me?' I asked.

'What do you mean?' he said, looking nervous again.

'Do you want to go to the police?' I asked him.

'No,' he said quite firmly. He paused. 'I don't think so.'

'Are you still frightened of this man?' I asked.

'Damn right I am,' he said. 'But you can't live your life being too frightened to step out of your own house.'

Bridget Hughes was, I thought.

'So what do we do?' I said.

'I don't know,' he said. 'Perhaps I shouldn't have come here. I'm sorry. I think I should go now.' He stood up.

'Mr Barnett,' I said to him. 'I won't tell anyone what you have told me, I promise. But if I try to stop this man and put him behind bars where he belongs, will you help me?'

'How?' he asked.

'I don't know yet,' I said. I didn't even know who the enemy was. 'Would you recognize the man again?'

'I certainly would,' he said. 'I'll never forget him.'

'Tell me what he looked like,' I said.

Mr Barnett did his best but he often contradicted himself. He said he was big but then he also said he was shorter than me. He described him as muscular but also as fat. He was a little confused himself, I thought. In the end I had very little idea about the man who said he was Julian Trent's father other than he was white, middle aged and fairly average in every way. Much the same as Josef Hughes had said and not very helpful.

Short of getting a police artist or a photofit expert, it was the best he could do.

He departed back to his home in north London, again looking nervously from side to side. I was left to ponder whether I was any further on in finding out how, and why, Julian Trent had his fingers into the Scot Barlow murder.

Steve Mitchell's trial was now less than a week away and we still had almost nothing to use in his defence except to claim that he definitely didn't murder Scot Barlow, that someone else did – someone who was making it appear that our client was responsible. A classic frame-up, in fact, that no one else could see, not least because Steve Mitchell was not the most likable of characters and people didn't seem to care enough whether he was convicted or not. But I cared. I cared for the sake of justice, and I also cared for the sake of my personal survival. But were the two compatible?

I could foresee that the trial was unlikely to fill the two weeks that had been allocated for it on the Oxford Crown Court calendar unless we came up with something a bit more substantial, and quickly.

After a sandwich lunch at my desk, I took a taxi to University College Hospital to see an orthopaedic surgeon, with my left leg resting straight across the back seat. Seven whole weeks had now passed since I had woken up in Cheltenham General Hospital with a pile-driver of a headache that had made my skull feel as if it were bursting. With a return to consciousness had also come the discovery that I had to remain flat on my back, my left leg in traction, with a myriad of tubes running from an impressive collection of clear plastic bags above my left shoulder to an intravenous needle contraption in my forearm.

'You are lucky to be alive,' a smiling nurse had cheerfully informed me. 'You've been in a coma for three days.'

My head had hurt so much that I had rather wished that I had remained so for another three.

'What happened?' I had croaked at her from inside a clear plastic mask that had sat over my nose and mouth and which, I'd assumed, was to deliver oxygen to the patient.

'You fell off your horse.'

I had suddenly remembered everything – everything, that is, up to the point of the fall.

'I didn't fall off,' I had croaked back at her. 'The horse fell.' An important distinction for every jockey, although the nurse hadn't seemed to appreciate the difference.

'How is my horse?' I had asked her.

She had looked at me in amazement. 'I have no idea,' she had said. 'I'm only concerned with you.'

Over the next few hours my headache had finally succumbed to increasing doses of intravenous morphine and the roaring fire in my throat had been extinguished by countless sips of iced water via a green sponge on a stick.

Sometime after it was dark, a doctor had arrived to check on my now-conscious form and he had informed me of the full catalogue of injuries that I had sustained, first by hitting the ground at thirty miles and hour and then having more than half a ton of horse land on top of me.

My back was broken, he had said, with three vertebrae cracked right through but, fortunately for me, my spinal cord was intact, thanks probably to the back protector that I had been wearing under my silks. Four of my ribs had been cracked and one of those had punctured a lung that had subsequently partially collapsed. My head had made hard contact with something or other and my brain had been badly bruised, so much so that a neurosurgeon had been called to operate to reduce the pressure inside my skull by fitting a valve above my right ear that would drain away the excess fluid. My left knee had been broken, the doctor had explained, and he himself had operated to fix it as best he could, but only time would tell how successful he had been.

'So will I live?' I had asked him flippantly.

'It was a bit touch and go for a while,' he had replied seriously. 'But I think you will. There was no real damage to your main internal organs other than a little bruising to the left kidney, and a small tear in your left lung that will heal itself. Yes, I think you'll be fine in time, especially now you are conscious and there doesn't appear to be any major damage to your brain either.'

'And will I ride again?' I'd asked him more seriously.

'More difficult to say,' he'd replied. 'Again, time will tell. I suspect it will depend on how mad you are. I personally think that all you jump jockeys have a screw loose. The same ones come in here year after year to be patched up and plastered.' He shook his head. 'They're completely bonkers.'

'How about my horse?' I had asked him.

'I don't know,' he'd said. 'But surely it wasn't your own horse you were riding?'

'Yes it was,' I'd said. I had tried explaining about being an amateur jockey and the Foxhunter Chase but he hadn't really been interested, and he had no idea whether Sandeman had been injured or not, or even if he was alive. It had only been when Paul and Laura Newington had come to see me later that evening that I had heard the full story of the disaster.

They had been watching the race from the stands and they were just getting excited about the prospect of another famous win when Sandeman and I had so spectacularly disappeared in a flurry of legs, and then we had both lain prostrate and unmoving on the turf.

Paul, it seemed, had run the half-mile from the grandstands, down the course, to where we had both been hidden from the sight of the thousands of spectators behind hastily erected green canvas screens. Sandeman, it appeared, had been badly winded and had also damaged his back. He had taken a full fifteen minutes to get gingerly to his feet and only Paul's personal intervention had prevented the racecourse vet from putting him down there and then. Fortunately for me, no questions had been asked about whether or not to shoot the jockey. Paul told me that I had been lying on the turf being attended to by the paramedics and the racecourse doctor for nearly an hour before being lifted ever so carefully into an ambulance and driven away at a snail's pace. The following race had been required to bypass the fence and was nearly abandoned altogether.

'There was someone else down there as well,' he had said. I had thought he must have meant Julian Trent but I'd been wrong. 'A girl. Ran all the way down the course in high-heeled shoes. Nice looker. Called herself Eleanor. Do you know her?'

I'd nodded to him.

'She seemed a bit cut up about you,' he'd said, almost surprised. 'I thought she must have the wrong guy but she was certain it was you. She said she had met me before at that do at Newbury in December but I don't remember.'

'What happened to her?' I'd asked him.

'I think she went in the ambulance with you but I don't know. I was so busy trying to get Sandeman sorted out.'

'How is he?' I'd asked him.

'Not great,' he'd said. 'He was taken straight to the equine hospital in Lambourn. They are treating him for a badly strained back and severe bruising.'

I'd laughed at him. 'Eleanor is a vet at that hospital.'

'What a coincidence,' he'd said laughing back.

But I didn't like coincidences.

'I think that cast can come off your leg,' said the orthopaedic surgeon. 'The X-rays show the knee mending well and there's no reason why it needs to be immobilized any longer. How long is it now?'

'Seven and a half weeks,' I said.

'Mmm,' he pondered. 'Should be fine, but you will need to keep using the crutches and just put a little weight on it for a while. Build up the weight over the next few weeks.'

'What about my back?' I asked him.

'The scans show that the bones are mending slowly but you still need to keep that straightjacket on for another six weeks at least.'

He was referring to the hard white plastic shell that I wore to prevent me bending my back. The damned thing reached from just below my neck almost to my groin in the front and from my shoulder blades to the top of my buttocks behind. It was very uncomfortable and made sitting at a desk near impossible, but wearing it had at least allowed me to walk around. Without it I would probably still be lying flat on my back.

'Six weeks?' I said in exasperation.

'You broke the T10, T11 and T12 vertebrae right through and you don't want to finish now what your fall started,' he said. 'You are a very lucky man. With that injury you could have so easily been paralysed, or dead.'

I would just have to put up with the discomfort, and the ignominy of having to ask my downstairs neighbour to come and help me get out of the wretched thing at night and back into it in the morning. The shell was actually made in two halves that had been heat moulded to fit my torso exactly, the two parts being held together round my upper body by half a dozen Velcro-covered nylon straps that needed to be fed through metal loops and pulled tight. I even had to shower in the damn thing.

The surgeon inspected the device before I gratefully hid it again from sight beneath my shirt.

'It's damned uncomfortable, you know,' I said to him. 'It makes me itch all the time.'

'Better than being paralysed,' he replied.

And there was no answer to that.

'How's the head?' he asked. It wasn't technically his department.

'Getting better slowly,' I said. 'I saw the neurologist last week and he is happy with my progress, but I still have some headaches.'

'Do you still have the valve implant?' he asked.

'No,' I said putting my hand up to my right ear. 'He took it out four weeks ago now.'

'No problems?' he asked.

'A little dizziness at first,' I said. 'But that went after a couple of days. No, I feel fine, just a few headaches and they are getting more infrequent and less troublesome.'

'Good,' he said looking down and making some notes.

'When can I start riding again?' I asked him.

He stopped writing and looked up. 'Are you serious?'

'Absolutely,' I said.

He put his pen down and looked at me with his head inclined to the side. 'Well, I suppose from my point of view, all your bones will heal and they'll be as good as new in a few months, but I would be worried about your head. The brain can only take so many knocks like that.'

I had to admit that it had been quite a bang. I had seen what was left of my racing helmet and it was cracked right through from front to back. Without it, I would have certainly died.

'But I don't intend to ever land on my head again,' I said.

'No one intended there to be a second world war after the first one. But there was.'

'That's a bit different,' I said.

'OK,' he conceded. 'But you should never try to predict the future.'

I knew that well enough. Especially in the law.

When I returned to chambers later that afternoon I felt I was walking on air, albeit with only one leg. In spite of the fibreglass and polyurethane material being much lighter than the old-fashioned white plaster of Paris, the full-length cast had still been very heavy and annoyingly restrictive. Without it, I felt at least partially released from the cage in which I had been existing.

The surgeon had told me that I would need lots of physio-therapy to get the knee back to full movement, and I still had to walk using the crutches, but it was such a joy to once again scratch an itch in my thigh, or to rub away an ache in my kneecap.

Arthur looked up at me from his desk as I hopped my way through the clerks' room. 'On the mend, I see,' he said.

'Slowly,' I agreed. 'I still have to wear this body armour for another six weeks.' I tapped the hard shell beneath my shirt.

'Still need the recliner then?' he said, smiling.

He referred to the new chair I had acquired from a friend that sat behind my desk. It allowed me to lean right back and reduce the pressure that the shell made on my groin.

'I might just keep it anyway,' I said to him with a laugh. He had found me asleep in the chair two or three times when I had first returned to chambers about three weeks previously.

'There's another one of those hand-delivered envelopes in your box,' Arthur said, immediately wiping the smile from my face. 'It came while you were out.'

'Right,' I said. 'Thanks.'

Arthur looked me in the eye and I thought for a moment that he was going to ask me straight out what was in the envelope, but he didn't, instead returning his attention to something on his desk.

I went over to the boxes and looked into mine. I had been temporarily promoted to the top row as I was unable to bend down to my usual level, and there, on its own, was a slim A5-sized white envelope, just as before.

I was sure that Arthur was watching me so I picked it up casually and stuffed it into my trouser pocket before negotiating the corridor on my crutches to the safety and privacy of my room. Thankfully, the two others junior barristers who also shared this space with me were both away in Manchester acting for a big local football club that was up to its neck in a tax-evasion scandal involving half a dozen of their most highly paid players.

I sat in my recliner chair and carefully opened the envelope. As before there was a single sheet of folded paper, and a photograph. On the sheet of paper there were just two short lines, again in black capital letters.

**JUST REMEMBER, LOSE THE CASE
MITCHELL GETS CONVICTED**

The photograph showed Eleanor in her blue scrub tunic and trousers walking along the gravel path between the house she lived in and the equine hospital in Lambourn.

CHAPTER 11

Why was it, I wondered, that I felt like I was being dangled on a string by an unknown hand, being made to dance a jig by some puppet-master hidden from the light. My house, my job, my father and even my friends were somehow under his spell. Sometimes I even began to wonder if my fall at Cheltenham had been his doing, but I knew that was ridiculous.

I sat at my desk and turned the photo of Eleanor over and over in my hands. Even if Julian Trent had seen her call and wave to me at Cheltenham, how did he know where she worked or how to get her photograph?

Photograph, photograph. Why did I keep thinking about the photograph taken from Scot Barlow's house the day he was murdered? Why not steal the frame as well? If someone had wanted to keep that picture then, surely, wouldn't they have taken the frame with it? Not, I supposed, if it had been highly individual and easily recognizable. But it hadn't. It had been a simple silver frame available in any high-street jeweller or department store.

So had the photograph been taken simply to destroy it? Was the image in fact a clue to whoever had been the murderer?

I was pondering these questions when my phone rang.

I picked it up with some trepidation but there was a familiar voice at the other end, one I was beginning to hope might become more familiar still.

'What did the doctor say?' Eleanor asked immediately.

'He told me I can go on living,' I replied with a smile.

'Good,' she said. 'So he must have told you that you were quite well enough to take me out to dinner tonight?'

'He said that it was completely out of the question,' I replied. 'He insisted that I should eat in at my place, alone. Matter of life or death.'

'Well, you'll just have to die then,' she said laughing. 'Because you, sunshine, are taking me out to Maximillian's tonight whether you like it or not.'

I liked it.

'How's the conference?' I asked her. She was attending a two-day international equine-medicine symposium at the London Veterinary School.

'Boring,' she said. 'Look, I must dash. They're about to start a lecture about the caecum and its role in colic.'

'Sounds like fun,' I said.

'Anything but,' she said. 'See you at the restaurant at seven thirty.' She disconnected before I had time to say goodbye.

I think she had applied to attend the symposium only so that she could spend a night in a London hotel, and spend the evening with me.

I had seen her four or five times since my fall at Cheltenham.

'Typical,' she had said when she first came to see me in hospital after I had woken up.

'What's typical?' I'd replied.

'I sit here beside him trying to wake him up for nearly three whole days and nights and then, when I have to go to work, hey presto, he opens his eyes.'

I had smiled at her. 'You didn't have to do that,' I'd said.

'I didn't have to,' she'd said. 'But I wanted to.'

That was nice, I'd thought.

She had been back to see me a couple more times during the week that they had insisted on keeping me in Cheltenham hospital, and then she had helped me on the day I went back home to Ranelagh Avenue, SW13.

Strangely, for the first two weeks after hospital I had been permitted only to lie flat on my back or to stand upright. Sitting, other than for a few minutes at a time, had been banned by the doctors. It had made life very complicated as it was impossible to travel anywhere by car. An ambulance had been needed to take me home on a stretcher, yet I was able to climb the stairs to my house, albeit on one leg and a pair of crutches, with Eleanor standing behind me so I didn't topple over backwards and do myself more mischief.

She had stayed that first night I was home, sleeping in the room that, seven and a half years before, Angela and I had so gleefully decorated with teddy bears' picnic wallpaper as a nursery for our unborn son, and which I hadn't yet bothered to change. I realized that, since my father had gone home soon after Angela's funeral, Eleanor was the first person other than me to have slept in my home. It wasn't that I was particularly averse to having guests, it was just that I hadn't yet got round to actually asking anyone to stay. I kept thinking that there was plenty of time, and the last seven years had seemingly passed in a flash.

But I think Eleanor had felt uneasy sleeping at my place, as uneasy as I had at her being there. She had stayed only one night in Barnes before returning to Lambourn, and she hadn't been back, although we had twice met elsewhere, on neutral territory, as it were, and we had spoken often on the telephone.

I liked her. I liked her a lot. But I still wasn't sure if I was yet ready for a serious relationship. I had become used to my solitary existence. I had grown accustomed to looking after myself and not having to worry about getting home from work at a reasonable time. Maybe I was set in my ways, and not very sure that I was prepared to change them.

However, I was greatly looking forward to seeing her again for dinner, and I had a spring in my one-footed step as I finally left chambers at seven o'clock and went in search of a taxi.

Julian Trent was standing next to the gate onto Theobald's Road, leaning on the brick-built gatepost, and I saw him immediately when I walked out of chambers. He was making no attempt at concealment as he had done before, the previous November, when he had hidden between the parked cars before stepping out to hit me with his baseball bat.

I realized there was no point in me trying to run away. The best speed I could manage on one leg and two crutches would have hardly outrun a two-year-old toddler let alone a fit and healthy young man of twenty-four. I turned towards him and he watched me as I carefully and slowly covered the sixty or so yards between us. He stood up straight and stopped leaning on the brickwork as I approached. I hoped he couldn't actually see my heart beating fast inside my chest.

He took a few steps forward and I was beginning to regret that I hadn't simply gone back inside my chambers as soon as I had seen him. However, I did gratefully note that he wasn't accompanied today by his sidekick, the baseball bat, but it might, I thought, have been lurking somewhere nearby.

He seemed about to say something to me but I beat him to it. 'What the hell do you want?' I shouted at him.

He seemed a little taken aback and looked around to see if anyone else had heard me. Theobald's Road was a busy place at seven o'clock on a sunny May evening and a continuous stream of pedestrians flowed past the gated entrance. A few heads had turned as I'd shouted but no one had actually stopped.

'Didn't you hear me?' I shouted again. 'I asked you what the hell do you want.'

He was definitely unnerved by a reaction he hadn't been expecting.

'Did you get the message?' he said.

'Do you mean this?' I shouted at him pulling the envelope and the paper out of my trouser pocket and ripping them both into several pieces. By this time he was standing less than ten feet from me. I threw the bits of paper into the air and they fluttered to the ground at his feet. 'Now sod off,' I shouted at him.

'Stop shouting,' he said.

'Why should I?' I shouted even louder, the sound of my voice echoing back to me from the buildings all around us. 'What are you afraid of?'

'Shut up,' he said, hissing at me.

I stood my ground and raised one of the crutches as a potential weapon. 'I'll shut up,' I shouted at the top of my voice, 'when you go away and leave me in peace.'

He clenched and unclenched his right fist. Perhaps he was regretting not bringing his baseball bat with him after all.

'Do as you're told,' he said menacingly, again almost under his breath, as if being extra quiet might compensate for my extra noisiness.

'Why?' I shouted again at full volume. 'Who wants me to? Who are you working for, you little creep? Get out of my life, do you hear? And stay out.'

One or two heads out on Theobald's Road were turned our way and one man stopped and stared at us. Julian Trent seemed to be losing his nerve.

'You'll regret this,' he said quietly through gritted teeth. 'You'll bloody regret this.'

And with that, he was gone, dodging out through the gateway, past the staring pedestrian, and off down Theobald's Road towards Clerkenwell. I stood there for a moment breathing deeply and wondered if I had made a big mistake. Perhaps, as Trent had said, I would regret it. But simply rolling over was not an option. I would not be dictated to, and my father and Eleanor would, like me, have to take their chances. To succumb to these threats in this case would simply invite more threats in the future. Both Josef Hughes and George Barnett had complied with the first demands and, in each case, the menace had returned for more.

I was aware that over the past few months I had become fairly ambivalent about the outcome of the Steve Mitchell trial. If he was convicted, then I would have nothing to fear from Julian Trent, or whoever was behind him. If he was acquitted then I could hold my head up for justice.

Now, suddenly, the result became incredibly important to me. If Mitchell was innocent, and I was sure that he must be, then I had to find a way to show it. And to do that, I had to find out who actually had committed the murder, and soon.

As things stood, I was pretty sure that he would be convicted simply because there was no credible indication to show that he didn't do it and the circumstantial evidence would be enough to sway the jury. True, there was none of Mitchell's DNA at the scene, but Barlow's blood and DNA had been found on Mitchell's boots and in his car, and that alone was very damning. If I were the prosecutor in the case, I would be highly confident of a guilty verdict. Even Sir James Horley QC, who was meant to be leading for the defence, seemed sure of the defendant's guilt and had even suggested to me that I go and see Mitchell in prison and encourage him to plead guilty. I had the distinct impression that, just this time, Sir James was going to be happy to let me conduct the case throughout. I suspected that he would find a good reason not to go to Oxford on the first day, and then he would use that as the excuse for not going at all. And that would suit me just fine.

But, short of resorting to the Trent method of intimidating the jury into returning a 'not guilty' verdict, I still couldn't see what I could do to get Mitchell off the charge.

What exactly was Julian Trent's connection with racing, and with a murdered jockey? Was the man who had been to see both Josef Hughes and George Barnett actually Julian Trent's father or was it somebody else? It was time to find out.

Eleanor was at the restaurant in Berkeley Square before me. She was seated on a stool at the bar facing away from me. I could see her back. I had been looking forward to this evening all day, so why did I now have cold feet? Why, all of a sudden, did I experience the urge to run away? Why did I feel so afraid? I had just faced up to Julian Trent, so why should I have any fears of Eleanor?

She turned round on the stool, saw me at the door, smiled and waved. I waved back. What, I asked myself, was I really afraid of here? It was a question I couldn't even begin to answer.

Over dinner, Eleanor and I discussed everything except ourselves, and specifically our relationship. I asked her about the equine symposium and she seemed to be surprised at how useful it was being.

'I've learned a lot,' she said over our starters. 'Some of the new treatments have potential for us in Lambourn, especially in the treatment of ligaments and tendons. There are some wonderful things being done with artificial replacements. Some horses that in the past would have been retired due to tendon trouble will soon be able to continue racing.'

'Bionic horses,' I said flippantly. 'The six-million-dollar horse.'

'No. Much much more than that,' she said, laughing. 'Peninsula was syndicated to stud for ten times that.'

'Wow,' I said. 'And to think he was foaled by a first-time vet.'

'Quite a responsibility,' she agreed. 'But, of course, they didn't know then how good he'd turn out to be.'

'I wish I had a copy of that photograph,' I said.

'The one of Millie with Peninsula as a foal?' Eleanor said.

'Yes,' I said. 'It was taken from Scot Barlow's house the day he was murdered.'

'You really think it's important?' she asked.

'I don't know,' I said. 'But the murderer must have thought it was important enough to remove from its frame and take away with him.'

'How do you know it was the murderer who took it?' she asked.

'I don't for sure,' I said. 'But whoever did take it also took care to wipe the frame clean. There were no fingerprints on it.'

'I remember that photograph so well,' Eleanor said. 'Millie showed it to everyone. She kept it on the mantelpiece in her room and she was always polishing the frame.'

'Describe it,' I said.

'It was just a photo,' she said. 'Millie was kneeling on the straw with the foal's head in her lap. The mare was standing behind them but you couldn't really see her properly. You could only see her hind quarters.'

'Wasn't there someone else in it as well?' I asked.

'There was the stud groom standing behind Millie. I think he was cleaning the mare after foaling, you know.'

I couldn't see how it was so important.

'And you don't know who took the picture?' I asked her.

'No idea,' she said.

'Wasn't Peninsula foaled at the Radcliffe place?' I said.

'They have lots of foals born there,' Eleanor said. 'They've made quite a business out of it. But we have less to do with them than we used to.'

'Why?' I asked.

'They've got so big that they now have a resident vet. They don't use the hospital practice any more unless one of their horses needs surgery.'

Our main courses arrived and we ate in silence for a few minutes.

'Tell me what the doctor told you,' Eleanor said between mouthfuls of sea bass.

'I've got to wear this damned body shell for another six weeks at least,' I said, 'and it's very uncomfortable.'

The restaurant had kindly given us a booth table and I was able to sit half sideways and lean back against the wall whenever it began to hurt too much.

'But at least that cast is off your leg,' she said.

'Thank goodness,' I said. I had been trying to bend my knee ever since the hospital circular saw had sliced through the last inch of the cast and set my leg free. So far I had only managed about twenty to thirty degrees, but that was a huge improvement over dead straight.

Main course finally gave way to coffee, with a Baileys on the rocks for her and a glass of port for me.

'I asked the surgeon when I could ride again,' I said, watching her face carefully to spot any reaction.

'And?'

'He said that my bones would be fully healed and as good as new in about three months, but he wasn't so sure about my brain.'

'What about your brain?' she asked.

'He said it couldn't take too many bangs like that.'

'Seems all right to me,' she said, smiling at me broadly with her mouth slightly open and all her perfect top teeth showing. The sparkle in her lovely blue eyes was there again, the same sparkle I had noticed at the equine hospital at our first meeting.

I sat opposite her and smiled back. But then suddenly I looked away, almost in embarrassment.

'Tell me about her,' she said.

'About who?' I asked. But I knew who she meant before she replied.

'Angela.'

'There's not much to tell really,' I said, trying to deflect her direct approach. 'Why do you want to know?'

She sat silently for a while, looking up at the ceiling as if making a decision. The jury was out deliberating.

Finally, she looked down again at my face and answered softly, 'I need to know what I'm up against.'

I looked down at the table and cupped my mouth and nose in my hands. I breathed out heavily once or twice, feeling the hot air on my skin. Eleanor just sat quietly, leaning forward slightly, with an expectant expression on her face.

'We met while I was doing the Bar Vocational Course, that's the course you study to become a barrister,' I said. 'Angela was a second-year student at King's reading clinical psychology. We were both guests at the same party and we just clicked. Right there and then.

'We got married six months after that first meeting, in spite of her parents' disapproval. They wanted her to wait until after she had finished her degree but we were so keen to marry straight away. There was a huge row and they never really forgave us. Silly really, but it seemed to matter so much to us back then. Now her mother blames me for her death.'

Eleanor reached forward across the table and took my hand.

'We were so blissfully happy together for five years. She wanted to have a baby as soon as we were married but I talked her into waiting until she had qualified, but then we discovered that having a child was not as straightforward as we thought. We tried for ages without success, but a scan then showed that her tubes were blocked so we had to try for *in vitro*, you know, test-tube baby and all that. And that worked absolutely straight away. It was brilliant. And we were both so pleased that she was carrying a boy.'

I stopped. Tears welled in my eyes for Angela and our unborn son.

'She was eight months pregnant when she died.' I had to stop again and take a few deep breaths. Eleanor went on holding my hand and saying nothing.

'It was a pulmonary embolism,' I said. 'I found her lying on the floor. The doctors said it would have been very sudden.' I sighed loudly. 'That was more than seven years ago now. Sometimes it seems like yesterday.' I let go of Eleanor's hand and held the cotton table napkin up to my face. It was as much as I could do not to sob.

We sat there together in silence for what felt like ages until a waiter came over and asked us if we wanted some more coffee.

'Thanks,' I said, back in control. He poured the hot black liquid into our cups and then left us alone again.

'So,' said Eleanor with a sigh. 'Not much chance for me then.'

We laughed, a short embarrassed laugh.

'Give me some more time,' I said. But I'd had seven years. How much longer did I need?

'How much more time?' she said.

'I don't know,' I said in exasperation.

'But I need to,' she said in all seriousness. She stared at my face. 'I like you, Mister Barrister. I like you a lot. But I do need some response if I'm going to invest my time and my emotions. I'm thirty-three years old and, as they say, my body clock is ticking. I want . . .' She tailed off and dropped her eyes.

'What?' I said.

'You . . . I think,' she said, suddenly looking back up at my face. 'And a house and kids and . . . family life.' She paused and I waited patiently. 'When I started out as a vet, with all the years of training, I only cared about my job and my career. I loved it, and I still do. But now I find I need more than just that. I realize that I want what my parents had,' she said. 'Love, home and family.' She paused again for a moment and took my hand again in hers. 'And I think I want it with you.'

CHAPTER 12

Eleanor went back to her hotel near Tower Bridge for the night and I took a taxi home to Barnes. It wasn't that we took a conscious decision to go in diametrically opposite directions, it was just sensible logistically. The equine symposium would start again for her at nine in the morning while, at the same time, I was due to be collected from my home by a car from a private hire company and taken to Bullingdon Prison to see my client. However, I now spent the whole journey home from the restaurant, along the Cromwell Road, past the V&A and Natural History museums, under the dark sloping walls of the London Ark and across Hammersmith Bridge, wondering whether I should ask the taxi driver to turn round and take me back to Eleanor at the Tower.

Then, quite suddenly and before I had made up my mind, we were outside my home at Ranelagh Avenue in Barnes. I clambered unsteadily out of the cab and paid off the driver, who gunned his engine and noisily departed, no doubt back to the West End to find another late-night passenger in need of a ride home.

I stood for a moment on my crutches and looked at the old

Edwardian property with its two side-by-side front doors and I speculated about what it was that had kept me here these past seven years. Perhaps I really had been foolish enough to think that life would have somehow returned to the blissful time with Angela. Maybe I had been living too long with my head in the sand and now was the time to make a fresh start with someone different. But how could I dispel the feeling that doing so would somehow be disloyal to Angela's memory?

A car turned slowly into the far end of the avenue and all of a sudden I felt very vulnerable, standing alone on the poorly lit pavement at nearly midnight with no one else about, no one this time to come running to my rescue if I shouted. Even my downstairs neighbour's lights were out. And Julian Trent, or whoever had been into my house to take that photograph, knew exactly where I lived.

I hurried as best I could up the half a dozen outside steps to the front doors and fumbled with my keys and the crutches. The car's headlights moved little by little down the road towards me and then swept on past, round the bend and out of sight.

I breathed a huge sigh of relief, found the right key, and let myself in. I leaned up against the closed front door and found that I was trembling. I slid the bolt across behind me and carefully negotiated the stairs.

Why did I exist like this? I had asked myself that question umpteen times over the past weeks as I had struggled with the six steps up from the street to my front door and then the thirteen steps up from there to my sitting room. I had often not bothered with the twelve more to my bedroom, sleeping, instead, stretched out on the sofa. I had no garden, no terrace, no deck, not even a balcony. Just a view of Barnes

Common, and even that was obscured in the summer months from all but the topmost bedroom windows by the leaves on the trees.

I had stayed here for the memories but maybe it was time now to make more memories elsewhere. Time to shake off this half-life existence. Time to live my life again to the full.

Steve Mitchell was a shell of his former self. As a jockey, he was well used to existing on meagre rations, and prison food was not exactly appealing to the discerning palate. But it was not the lack of food that had made the greatest difference to Steve, it was the lack of his daily diet of riding up to six races with the muscle toning and stamina which comes from regular exercise as a professional sportsman. He looked pale, thin and unfit, because he was, but he seemed to be coping fairly well mentally, considering the circumstances. Steeplechase jockeys had to be strong in mind as well as in body, to cope with the inevitable injuries that came with the job.

'What news?' he said, sitting down opposite me at the grey table in the grey interview room.

'Not much, I'm afraid,' I said.

He looked at the crutches lying on the floor beside me. This was the first visit I had been able to make to see him since my fall at Cheltenham.

'Sandeman?' he asked.

'Yes,' I said.

'Read about it in the paper,' he said. 'Knees are a bugger.'

'Yes,' I agreed.

'Also read about that bastard Clemens winning the Gold Cup on my bloody horse,' he said. The 'bastard' tag, I noticed, had

215

now been moved from Scot Barlow to Reno Clemens. 'It's bloody unfair.'

Yes, it was, but, as my mother had told me as a child, life is unfair.

'But you did meet with Sir James Horley?' I said it as a question. 'When I couldn't make it last time.'

'Bit of a cold fish, if you ask me,' said Steve. 'Didn't like him much. He kept talking to me as if I'd done it. Even asked me to examine my conscience. I told him to bloody sod off, I can tell you.'

I knew. I had heard about it at length from Sir James on his return from Bullingdon to Gray's Inn. As a rule Sir James didn't much care for visiting his clients on remand, and this time had been no exception. He preferred that to be a job for his junior, but I had been rather incapacitated and he'd had no alternative but to go himself. The interview had clearly not gone well. Mitchell may not have liked his lead counsel very much but that was nothing compared to the utter disdain in which Sir James now held his client. Not for the first time I thought that Sir James would be rather pleased to lose this case.

'Can't you act without that silly old buffer?' he said.

'He is a very experienced Queen's Counsel,' I replied.

'I don't care if he's the Queen herself in drag,' he said, 'I would much rather have you defending me in court.'

'Steve,' I said seriously. 'I'm not altogether sure it would make much difference who defended you in court at the moment.' I paused while my underlying meaning sank in.

'I didn't do it,' he said finally. 'I tell you. I didn't bloody do it. Why will no one believe me?'

'I believe you,' I said. 'But we need something to make the jury believe you, and there's nothing. The evidence is quite compelling. There's the blood in your car and on your boots, and the fact that the pitchfork was also yours doesn't help. And everyone knows you hated Barlow. Those betting receipts and your lack of any sort of alibi are going to hold considerable sway with the jury.'

'There must be something you can do,' he said rather forlornly.

'I haven't given up hope yet,' I said, trying to sound more optimistic than I felt. 'The evidence is either circumstantial or can be explained away. When the prosecution finish presenting their case, I will make a submission to the judge that you have no case to answer. But I think it's unlikely that he or she will agree and, with nothing new turning up, I fear that things may not go well.'

'So what's the down side?' he said.

'In what way?' I said.

'How long if I get convicted?'

'How long a sentence?' I asked.

'No,' he said, irritated. 'How long until I get an appeal? Until something comes up to show I didn't do it.'

'There's no guarantee you would get an appeal,' I said. 'It would have to be either because there is a question of law, say a ruling or the summing up by the trial judge was considered questionable or biased, or if new evidence has appeared in the case. Either way it would be quite some time. Appeals against short sentences are heard more quickly than those for longer ones. It's not much good waiting two years for an appeal against a three-year sentence, you'd already be out. But life . . .'

'Life?' Steve said loudly, interrupting me.

'Murder carries a life sentence,' I said. 'Mandatory. But life doesn't actually mean life in most cases.'

'Oh God,' he said resting his forehead on his hand. 'I'll go bloody mad if I have to stay in here much longer.'

The private hire silver Mercedes was waiting for me outside the prison and it pulled up to the main gate when I appeared. Bob, the driver, stepped out to hold the door for me as I clambered awkwardly into the back seat. Then he carefully placed the crutches in the boot. I could get quite used to this, I thought.

'Back to London, sir?' Bob asked.

'Not yet,' I said, and I gave him directions to our next stop.

Sandeman was eating from his manger when I went in to see him. He looked casually in my direction, blew hard down his nostrils and then went back to concentrating on his oats. I hobbled over to him and slapped him down his neck with the palm of my hand while feeding him an apple from my pocket.

'Hello, old boy,' I said to him as I fondled his ears and rubbed his neck. He put his head down against me and pushed me playfully.

'Whoa,' I said amused. 'Careful, my old boy, I'm not yet able to play.' I slapped him again a couple of times and left him in peace.

'He's doing well,' said Paul Newington at the door, from where he'd watched the exchange. 'We've started walking him around the village every morning, and he has even trotted a bit round the paddock on a lunge. Still too early to put any weight on that back, of course, but he doesn't seem to be in any pain.'

'Good,' I said. 'He looks well.'

'Plenty of time for Kit to brush his coat.' Kit was the stable lad that 'did' for Sandeman.

'Will he ever be able to race again?' I asked Paul. I had asked him that several times before on the telephone and he'd always been rather noncommittal in his answer.

'I suspect he could,' he said. 'But he's thirteen now and he would quite likely not be fit enough to run before he becomes fourteen.' All horses in the northern hemisphere became a year older on 1 January, irrespective of the actual day on which they were born. In the south the date was, for some reason I had never worked out, not 1 July as one would expect, but a month later on 1 August.

'Are you saying he'd be too old?' I asked.

'Racehorses can race at that age,' he said. 'I looked it up on the internet. The oldest ever winner was eighteen, but that was over two hundred years ago.'

We stood there leaning on the lower half of the stable door, looking at my dear old horse.

'I'm not saying he couldn't get back to fitness,' Paul went on. 'I'm just not sure it would be cost effective, or even if it's fair on the old boy.'

'You think it's time to retire him?' I was miserable. Retiring Sandeman from the racecourse would be tantamount to retiring myself from race riding. I knew that I was too old to start again with a new horse.

'I do,' he said bluntly. 'And I do realize that it would quite likely mean that you wouldn't have a horse with me again.'

'But what would we do with him?' I asked forlornly.

'Now don't take this the wrong way,' he said, 'but I am in need of a new hack. And that's not, I promise, the reason I think you should retire Sandeman.'

'I know that,' I said. 'But what about old Debenture?'

Debenture had been Paul's hack for almost as long as I could remember and Paul rode him up to the gallops every morning to watch his horses work.

'He's too old now,' said Paul. 'It's time to put him out to grass. Every time I've got on him recently I've feared he's about to collapse under me.'

'So you'd replace him with Sandeman?' I asked.

'I would like to, if Sandeman recovers sufficiently,' he said. 'And I think he probably will, if his progress so far is anything to go by.'

'Well, I suppose that would be fine by me,' I said. 'But can he go on living in this stable?'

'Geoffrey, you are far too sentimental,' he said, laughing. 'No way. He'll have to live in the dog kennel.' He laughed loudly, mostly at my expense. 'Of course he can stay here and Kit will continue to look after him.'

'Can I still ride him?' I asked.

'Geoffrey,' he said laying a hand on my shoulder. 'You don't want to ride him as a hack. I would simply walk him through the village at the head of the string and then I'd sit on him as I watched the other horses, before he walked back here. If you really want to ride out, you can ride one of the others.'

'Do you mean that?' I asked, surprised.

'Of course I do,' he said. 'And I won't even make you pay training fees for the privilege. Come any time you like, as long as you stay reasonably fit, and light. I won't let you if you go over twelve stone.'

'I have absolutely no intention of doing that,' I said.

'That's what all those fat ex-jockeys said.' He laughed.

Sandeman finished his lunch and came over to the stable door for another apple from my pocket. I rubbed his ears and massaged his neck. If only he could talk, I thought yet again, he could tell me what he wanted.

'Well, old boy,' I said to him. 'Seems like you and I have run our last race. Welcome to old age.'

'We'll look after him,' said Paul, stroking Sandeman's nose.

I didn't doubt it, but somehow this felt like a defining moment in my life. Gone, abruptly and unexpectedly, were the days of excitement and adrenalin that I had coveted for so long. My racing days had been what I had lived for. When one was past, I spent my time working but with half an eye on the calendar to show me when I was next due to weigh out and hear the familiar call for 'jockeys'. But suddenly, this minute, I was no longer an injured jockey on the road to recovery and my next ride. I had become, here and now, an ex-jockey, and I was very aware of having lost something. There was an emptiness in me as if a part of my soul had been surgically excised.

'Are you OK?' said Paul, as if he, too, was aware of the significance of the moment.

'Fine,' I said to him with a smile. But I wasn't really fine. Inside I was hurting.

'You'll just have to get a new hobby,' Paul said.

But riding races had never felt like a hobby to me. It had been what I had lived for, especially these past seven years. It really was time to get a new life, and now I didn't have any choice in the matter.

I stayed for a leisurely lunch with Paul and Laura and then Bob drove me further west to Uffington and the Radcliffe Foaling Centre. I had called ahead and spoken to the manager, Larry

Clayton, who seemed bored with his job and quite keen to show a visitor around the place.

The tyres of the Mercedes crunched over the gravel as we drove slowly up the driveway and pulled up in front of a new looking red-brick single-storey building to the side of the main house. 'Visitors Report Here' ordered a smartly painted notice stuck into the grass verge. So I did.

'It's very quiet at this time of the year,' said Larry Clayton as we sat in his office. 'Most of the mares and foals are gone by now.'

'Where to?' I asked.

'Back to their owners for the summer, most of them,' he said. 'Some have gone to Ireland. A few of the mares have gone back into training. I don't really know.' And it sounded like he didn't really care.

'So when's your busy time?' I asked.

'January to April,' he said. 'That's when most of them are born. Absolutely crazy here in February and March. Foals dropping every five minutes.'

'How many?' I asked.

'Too many,' he said with a wry smile. 'About a hundred, and they want to double that next year.'

'Is that more than in the past?' I said.

'Dunno,' he said putting his feet up on his desk. 'My first year here. But I think it must be. The Radcliffes built more foaling boxes last summer, and these offices. I think it was pretty small fry before then.'

I looked at his feet on the desk. He was wearing badly scuffed cowboy boots under tight blue jeans with a check-pattern open-necked shirt. I wondered if the Radcliffes knew that their manager was so casual with their guests. I had picked up some of their marketing material stacked upright in a rack in the reception area on my way in. It was a well produced large glossy brochure with plenty of impressive facts and figures about the equine care provided for the expectant mothers, and a smiling picture on the front of Roger and Deborah Radcliffe standing together next to some mares and foals in a paddock.

'Are they at home?' I asked Larry, indicating the picture. 'I didn't get an answer on their home phone when I called them yesterday.'

'Nope,' he said. 'They are in Kentucky for the sales and the Derby. Not back until next week.'

'Can I have a look round?' I asked.

'Sure,' he said, lifting both his feet together off the desk. 'Not much to see.'

We walked around the new complex of foaling boxes and other stalls, each angle covered by a closed-circuit television camera.

'How many staff do you have?' I asked.

'About a dozen in the high season but only a couple now,' he said. 'We have an onsite delivery team who are on constant standby when we're foaling. But they've gone now. We only have a few horses here at the moment and they mostly belong to the Radcliffes. Two of them are mares that dropped in early March and their foals will be fully weaned by the end of July, ready for the sales.'

We walked past the rows of deserted stables and looked into the new foaling boxes. They had hard concrete floors devoid of the soft cushion of straw that would be laid down for the arrival of a new foal, possibly a new superstar like Peninsula.

'Where was Peninsula foaled?' I asked.

'No idea,' he said. 'Here somewhere. But lots has changed.'

'Do you know if the stud groom still works here?' I asked. 'The one who helped with Peninsula.'

'No idea,' he said again. 'Do you know who it was? Stud grooms come and go round here like wet Sundays.'

'Have you ever heard of anyone called Julian Trent?' I asked him.

'Nope,' he said. 'Should I?'

I decided that it really hadn't been a very helpful excursion. In fact, the whole day had been rather disappointing so far from start to finish. I could only hope that it would get better.

Bob dropped me back at Ranelagh Avenue around quarter to eight and, in spite of the bright spring evening light, I asked him to wait while I made it up the steps to the front door and then safely inside it.

But he had driven away before I realized that there was something very wrong. I was about half-way up the stairs when I first heard the sound of running water where there shouldn't have been.

It was running through the light fitting in the ceiling of my sitting room onto the floor below. It wasn't just a trickle, more of a torrent. And that wasn't the only problem. My home had been well and truly trashed.

I made my way as quickly as possible up to the top floor to turn off the water only to discover that doing so was not going to be that easy. The washbasin in the second bathroom had been torn completely away from its fittings and the water was jetting out of a hole in the wall left by a broken pipe. The stream was adding to the inch depth that already existed on the bathroom floor and which was spreading across the landing and down the top few steps like a waterfall.

Where, I wondered, was the stop cock?

I carefully descended the wet stairs again and used the telephone to call my downstairs neighbours to ask for help. There was no answer. There wouldn't be. It was Wednesday and they were always out late on Wednesdays, organizing a badminton evening class at the school where they both taught. I had become quite acquainted with their routine since I had needed to call on their assistance over the past six weeks. They would have stayed on at the school after lessons and would usually be back by nine, unless they stopped for some dinner on the way home, in which case it would be ten or even half past. By then, I thought, their lower floor, set as it was below ground level, might be more akin to an indoor swimming pool than a kitchen.

I sat on the torn arm of my sofa and looked about me. Everything that could have been broken had been. My brand-new expensive large flat-screen plasma television would show no pictures ever again. Angela's collection of Royal Worcester figurines was no more, and the kitchen floor was littered deep with broken crockery and glass.

I looked at the phone in my hand. At least that was working, so I used it to dial 999 and I asked the emergency operator for the police.

They promised to try and send someone as soon as possible but it didn't sound to me like it was an urgent case in their eyes. No one was hurt or imminently dying, they said, so I would have to wait. So I thumbed through a sopping copy of Yellow Pages to find an emergency plumbing service and promised them a big bonus to get here as soon as humanly possible. I was still speaking to them when the ceiling around the light fitting, which had been bulging alarmingly, decided to give up the struggle and collapsed with a crash. A huge mass of water suddenly fell into the centre of my sitting room and spread out towards my open-plan kitchen area like a mini tidal wave. I lifted my feet as it passed me by. The plumbing company promised that someone was already on the way.

I hobbled around my house inspecting the damage. There was almost nothing left that was usable. Everything had been broken or sliced through with what must have been a box cutter or a Stanley knife. My leather sofa would surely be unrepairable with so many cuts through the hide, all of which showed white from the stuffing beneath. A mirror that had hung this morning on my sitting-room wall now lay smashed amongst the remains of a glass-and-brass coffee table, and an original oil painting of a coastal landscape by a successful artist friend was impaled over the back of a dining chair.

Upstairs in my bedroom the mattress had also received the box-cutter treatment and so had most of the clothes hanging in my wardrobe. This had been a prolonged and determined assault on my belongings of which almost nothing had survived. Worst of all was that the perpetrator, and I had little doubt as to who was responsible, had smashed the glass and twisted to destruction the silver frame that had stood on the dressing table, and had then torn the photograph of Angela into dozens of tiny pieces.

I stood there looking at these confetti remains and felt not grief for my dead wife, but raging anger that her image had been so violated.

The telephone rang. How was it, I wondered, that he hadn't broken that too?

I found out. 'I told you that you'd regret it,' Julian Trent said down the wire, his voice full of menace.

'Fuck off, you little creep,' I said and I slammed down the receiver.

The phone rang again almost immediately and I snatched it up.

'I said to fuck off,' I shouted into the mouthpiece.

There was a pause. 'Geoffrey, is that you?' Eleanor sounded hesitant.

'Oh God. I'm so sorry,' I said. 'I thought you were someone else.'

'I should hope so,' she said with slight admonishment. 'I called because I have some good news for you.'

I could do with some.

'I've found a copy of the photo of Millie with the foal.'

CHAPTER 13

It took the emergency plumbers forty-five minutes to arrive at
Ranelagh Avenue, by which time not only had the ceiling in my
sitting room collapsed but also two ceilings below. I know
because I heard about it at full volume from my neighbours
when they arrived home at five past nine. It was a shame, I
thought, that they had decided not to eat out. They wouldn't
be able to produce much of a dinner in the flood. Only when
they came upstairs and saw the state of my place did they
understand that it hadn't been a simple thing like leaving a tap
running or overflowing a bath.

The police showed up at least an hour after the plumbers had
successfully capped off the broken pipe and departed. Two
uniformed officers arrived in a patrol car and wandered through
the mess, shaking their heads and denigrating the youth of today
under their breath.

'Do you have any idea who may have done this?' they asked me.

I shook my head. Somehow not actually speaking seemed to
reduce the lie. Why didn't I just tell them that I knew exactly
who had done it. It had been Julian Trent and I could probably
find his address, or, at least, that of his parents.

But I also knew that Julian Trent was far from stupid, and that he would not have been careless enough to have left any fingerprints or other incriminating evidence in my house, and that he would have half of London lined up to swear that he was nowhere near Barnes at any time during this day. If he could get himself off an attempted murder rap, I had no doubts that he would easily escape a charge of malicious damage to property. To have told the police the truth would simply have given him an additional reason to come back for another dose of destruction – of me, of my father, or, as I feared most, of Eleanor.

The police spent some time going all round my house both outside and in.

'Whoever did this probably got in through that window,' one of the policemen said, pointing at the now-broken glass in my utility room. 'He must have climbed the drainpipe.'

I had changed the locks and bolstered my security on the front door after the time I'd had an unwanted guest with his camera. I now wished I had put in an alarm as well.

'Is there anything missing?' asked one of the policemen finally.

'I have no idea,' I said. 'It doesn't seem so. It's just all broken or slashed.'

'Mmm,' said the policeman. 'Mindless vandalism. Happens all the time, sadly. You should be grateful that the whole place isn't also smeared with shit.'

'Oh thanks,' I said rather sarcastically. But Julian Trent wouldn't have done that for fear of leaving some speck of his own DNA along with it. 'So what happens now?' I asked them.

'If nothing's been stolen then CID won't really be interested,' he sounded bored himself. 'If you call Richmond police station in the morning they will give you a crime number. You'll need that for your insurers.'

That's why I had called them in the first place.

And with that, they left. No photos, no tests, no search for fingerprints, nothing. As they said, no one was hurt and nothing had been stolen, and the insurance would deal with the rest. End of their problem. They had no hope or expectation of ever catching the person responsible, and, to be fair, I hadn't exactly been very helpful with their inquiries.

I sat on a chrome kitchen stool and surveyed my ruined castle.

Surprisingly the electrical system seemed to have suffered no ill effects from the cascade of water through the sitting-room light fitting. I had quite expected there to be a blue flash followed by darkness when I chanced turning on the switch, but instead I was rewarded with two bulbs coming on brightly. The remaining bulbs, those in the wall brackets, had received the baseball bat treatment. At least, I assumed that Trent had been accompanied by his weapon of choice. The damage to some of the fittings was too much to have been the result of only a kick or a punch. Even the marble worktops in the kitchen were now cracked right through. Young Julian clearly had considerable prowess in the swing of his bat.

Eleanor arrived at just before ten. She had been so distressed to hear me on the telephone describing the shambles that was now my home that she had driven up from Lambourn as soon as she could. She had only been back there an hour, having caught the train from London to Newbury at the end of the veterinary symposium.

I hobbled down the stairs to the front door to let her in and we stood in the hallway and hugged. I kissed her briefly with closed lips. It was a start.

She was absolutely horrified at the damage and I was pleased that she cared. For me, over the past couple of hours since I had first discovered it, I had grown somehow accustomed to the mess, anaesthetized by its familiarity. Seen through a fresh pair of eyes, the true scale of the devastation was indeed shocking.

It wasn't that I didn't care about my stuff – I cared a lot. It was just that the loss of everything fitted in quite well with the feeling I had of moving on, of starting again. Perhaps it might even make things easier.

'Have you called the police?' she asked.

'They've just left,' I said. 'They didn't hold out much hope of catching whoever did this.'

'But Geoffrey,' she said seriously. 'This isn't some random attack by an opportunistic vandal. This was targeted directly at you personally.' She paused and fingered a tear in my sofa. 'You must have some idea who did this.'

I said nothing. It was answer enough.

'Tell me,' she said.

We sat amid the wreckage of my home for two hours while I told her what I knew about Julian Trent and his apparent connection with the murder of Scot Barlow. I told her how I shouldn't be acting in this case and how I had withheld information from the police and from my colleagues. I told her about Josef Hughes and George Barnett. And I told her about seeing Trent standing behind her at Cheltenham races before the Fox-hunter Chase. I showed her the photograph I had received in the white envelope showing her walking down the path near the hospital in Lambourn. I had kept it in the pocket of the jacket I'd been wearing, and it had consequently survived the demolition.

She held the photograph in slightly shaking hands and went quite pale.

I dug around in the kitchen and finally found a pair of unbroken plastic mugs and a bottle of mineral water from the fridge.

'I'd rather have some wine,' Eleanor said.

My designer chrome wine rack, along with its dozen bottles of expensive claret that a client had given me as a gift for getting him off a drink-driving charge of which he had really been guilty, lay smashed and mangled, a red stain spreading inexorably across the mushroom-coloured rug that lay in my hallway.

I went back to the fridge and discovered an unbroken bottle of champagne nestling in a door rack. So we sat on my ruined sofa next to the damp ceiling plaster and amongst the other carnage, and drank vintage Veuve Clicquot out of plastic mugs. How romantic was that?

'But why didn't you tell me about this photo sooner?' she asked accusingly. 'I might have been in danger.'

'I don't believe you are in real danger as long as Trent, or whoever is behind him, still thinks I will do as they say. It's the threat of danger that's their hold.'

'So what are you going to do about it?' Eleanor asked. 'How can you defeat this Trent man? Surely you have to go to the police and tell them.'

'I don't know,' I said inadequately.

'Darling,' she said, using the term for the first time, and raising my eyebrows. 'You absolutely have to go to the authorities and explain everything to them. Let them deal with the little horror.'

'It really isn't that simple,' I said to her. 'In an ideal world, then yes, that would be the best route, but we don't live in an ideal world. For a start, doing that might cost me my career.'

'Surely not,' she said.

'Oh yes,' I said. 'I have been very economical with the truth in a business where it is the truth, the whole truth and nothing but. In fact I have told outright lies to the police, and the law is pretty unforgiving of lies. I may have even been guilty of holding the court in contempt. I have certainly misled the court and that is the most heinous of crimes for a barrister. That alone is enough to get disbarred.'

'But you have a good reason,' she said.

'Yes, indeed I have,' I said. 'I was scared. And I still am. When I saw Trent outside my chambers yesterday I was so scared I nearly wet myself. But all that will have little bearing for the court. I know. I have dealt with intimidation in some form or other almost every week of my working life and, until recently, I was like every other lawyer who would tell their client not to be such a wimp and to tell the truth no matter what the consequences. The courts are not very forgiving of those who fail to tell the truth, even if they are frightened out of their wits. I've seen witnesses sent to prison for the night because they refuse to tell the judge something they know but are too afraid to say. People don't understand until it happens to them. And it's happening to me now. Look around you. Do you think I wanted this to happen?'

I was almost in tears. And they were tears of frustration.

'So what are you going to do?' she asked finally.

'I am going to defeat him by getting Steve Mitchell acquitted,'

I said. 'The only problem is that I'm not quite sure how I'm going to manage it.'

'But then what?' she said. 'He won't just go away.'

'I'll cross that bridge when I get to it,' I said with a laugh. But it wasn't really a laughing matter.

'But won't that get you even deeper into trouble?' she said.

'Maybe,' I said. 'But at least if Mitchell gets convicted he would then have grounds for an appeal. And I'm sure he didn't murder anyone.'

'Does the picture of Millie help?' she asked.

'It might,' I said. 'Where is it?'

'Here,' she said, pulling out a digital camera from her hand-bag. 'It's not that good. That photo frame was in the back-ground of some pictures I took in Millie's room when we had a drinks party there for her birthday. I thought about it during a boring lecture this morning after what you said last night. I checked when I got home and there it was.' She smiled in triumph.

She turned on the camera and scrolled through the pictures until she arrived at one of three girls standing with glasses in their hands in front of a mantelpiece. And there between the heads of two of them could be clearly seen the frame and the missing photo. Eleanor zoomed in on the image.

'Amazing things, these cameras,' she said. 'Over eight million pixels, whatever that means.'

It meant that she could zoom right in and fill the whole screen with the picture of Millie Barlow with Peninsula's head in her lap with the mare standing behind with the stud groom. At such a magnification it was a little blurred but it was just as Eleanor had described it.

'Well?' she said as I studied the image.

'I don't know,' I said. 'It surely has to be important, otherwise why was it stolen from Barlow's house? But I just can't see why. It must be something to do with the stud groom, but I don't recognize him. You can see his face quite clearly in spite of the blurring, but I'm certain I've never seen him before. It's not Julian Trent, that's for sure.' Somehow I had suspected that it might have been.

Eleanor spent her second night in my house and, this time, she didn't sleep in the room with the teddy bears' picnic wallpaper. She slept alone in my bed, or what was left of it, while I dozed fully clothed on the torn-up sofa downstairs with my crutches close to hand. Neither of us felt that it had been the right circumstance to make any further moves towards each other and I was still worried that, with a broken window in the utility room, my castle was far from secure.

I woke early with the daylight, and what it revealed was no better than it had been the night before.

Julian Trent had been vindictive in his approach to the destruction and had even cut up my passport. It wasn't that I couldn't replace what he had destroyed, but he had made my life so much more complicated and annoying. Where did one start to get rid of all this mess?

I looked in the drawers of my desk for my insurance policy. Clearly not all the wine was soaking into the rug. Trent had saved a couple of bottles to pour into my paperwork, which was now red and still dripping.

Eleanor padded down the stairs wearing my dressing gown.

'Careful,' I said, looking at her bare feet. 'There's broken glass all over the floor.'

She stopped on the bottom stair and looked around. 'Must have been quite a party,' she said with a smile.

'The best,' I said, smiling back.

She retreated back to my bedroom and soon reappeared, dressed and with her shoes on. I was a little disappointed at the transformation from my dressing gown.

'I'd better be going,' she said, more serious now. 'It's well gone six and I need to be at work at eight. Will you be all right?'

'I'll be fine,' I said. 'I have a car picking me up at eight.'

'You'd better have this,' she said, handing me her camera.

'Right,' I said. 'Thanks. I may use it to take some shots of this lot for the insurance company.'

'Good idea,' she said, standing still in the middle of the hallway.

It was as if she didn't really want to go.

'What are you doing tonight?' I asked.

'I'm on call,' she said miserably. 'I have to stay in Lambourn.'

'Then can I come down there and return your camera to you this evening?' I asked.

'Oh, yes please,' she said with a wide grin.

'Right, I will. Now get going or you'll be late for your patients.'

She skipped down the stairs, and I waved at her from the kitchen window as she drove away, her right arm gesticulating wildly out of the driver's window until she disappeared round the corner at the top of the road.

I used the rest of the free memory in Eleanor's camera to take shots of every aspect of Julian Trent's handiwork, right down to the way he had poured all the contents from the packets in my kitchen cupboards into the sink, which was now blocked. I didn't know what good the photos would be but it took up the time while I waited for the car.

I found a clean shirt lurking in the tumble drier that young Mr Trent had missed with his knife and, even though there was no water in the bathrooms with which to shower or wash, I had managed to shave with an unbroken electric razor and I felt quite respectable as I hobbled down the steps and into Bob's waiting Mercedes at eight o'clock sharp.

I had brought my mobile phone and the Yellow Pages into the car and, while Bob drove, I set to work finding someone to fix the utility-room window.

'Don't worry about the mess,' I said to the first glazier I called, who finally agreed to do the job for a fat fee. 'Just go through the kitchen to the utility room and fix the window.'

'How shall I get in?' he asked. 'Is there someone there?'

'I left the front door open,' I said. After all, there wasn't much left to steal. 'The keys are on the stairs. Lock the door when you are finished and put the keys back through the letter box. I've got another set.'

'Fine,' he said. 'Will do.'

Next I called my insurance company and asked them to send me a claim form. They might want to come and have a look, they said. Be my guest, I replied, and I fixed for them to come on the following afternoon at five o'clock. They could get a key from my downstairs neighbours, who would be back from their school by then.

Bob took me first to chambers, where he went in to collect my mail while I half sat and half lay on the back seat of the car. Bob reappeared with a bundle of papers which he passed in to me through the window. And he also had Arthur in tow.

'Mr Mason,' said Arthur through the window, formal as always.

'Morning, Arthur,' I said. 'What's the problem?'

'Sir James is very keen to see you,' he said. I bet I knew why. 'He needs to speak to you about Monday.' Monday was the first day of Steve Mitchell's trial in Oxford.

'What about Monday?' I said. I, too, could play this little game.

'He thinks it may be impossible for him to attend on Monday as the case he is on at the moment is overrunning.'

What a surprise, I thought. I bet it's overrunning because Sir James keeps asking for delays.

'Tell Sir James that I will be fine on my own on Monday,' I said. 'Ask him to call me over the weekend on my mobile if he wants me to request an adjournment for a day.' I wouldn't hold my breath for the call, I thought.

'Right,' said Arthur. 'I will.'

Both he and I were plainly aware of what was going on, but protocol and good manners had won the day. So I refrained from asking Arthur to also inform Sir James that he was a stupid old codger and a fraud, and it was well past the time he should have hung up his silk gown and wig for good.

Next, Bob drove me just round the corner to Euston Road, to the offices of the General Medical Council, where I spent most of the day sitting around waiting and very little time standing on my right foot, leaning on my crutches, arguing my client's case against a charge of professional misconduct in front of the GMC Fitness to Practise Panel. Each of the three accused doctors had a different barrister and the GMC had a whole team of them. It made for a very crowded hearing and also a very slow one. By the time we had all finished our representations and each of the witnesses had been examined and cross-examined, there was no time left in the day for any judgments and the proceedings were adjourned until the following morning, which was a real pain for me as I wanted to be in Lambourn.

I tut-tutted to my client and told him, most unprofessionally, that it would mean much greater expense, another day's fees. He almost fell over himself to ask the chairman of the panel if I would be required on the following day. He seemed greatly relieved when the chairman informed him that it was up to the accused to decide if and when they had professional representation, and not the members of the GMC. I was consequently rapidly released by my client. My fellow barristers looked at me with incredulity and annoyance. Two days' fees may have been better for them than just one but, there again, they hadn't planned to go and see Eleanor tonight.

I called Arthur on my mobile and asked him to arrange for all my boxes, papers, files, gown, wig, and so on for the Mitchell trial, to be sent direct to my hotel in Oxford, where I would be spending the weekend in preparation for Monday. No problem, he said. Sending boxes of papers by courier all over the country for court hearings was normal practice.

Bob was waiting for me in the Mercedes outside the GMC offices.

'Back to Barnes?' he asked.

'No, Bob,' I said. 'Could you take me to Lambourn?'

'Be delighted to,' he said with a big smile. Bob was being paid by the mile. 'Round trip or one way?' he asked.

'One way for tonight, I think,' I said. 'I need to make a call or two. And, Bob, can we find a photo shop that's still open, one where you can stop outside to drop me off?'

He found one in Victoria Street and I spent about half an hour at a self-service digital photo machine printing out the pictures I had taken that morning with Eleanor's camera. I also printed out ten six-by-four-inch copies of the blown-up image of the Millie and foal picture. They weren't perfect, and looked

239

a little more blurred than on the camera, but they would have to do.

Eleanor was delighted when I called her to say I was still coming to Lambourn, but she seemed a little hesitant when I told her that I had nowhere yet to stay.

'Oh,' she said. 'I suppose . . .'

'I'll find a pub or a hotel,' I said, interrupting her.

'Oh, right,' she said, sounding relieved. 'It's just we have the house rule . . .' she tailed off.

'It's all right,' I said. 'I hadn't expected to stay with you anyway.'

From the house-rule point of view, I was clearly still seen as a casual rather than a long-term relationship. And I suppose that was fair, I thought. Eleanor and I had hardly kissed, so staying the night with her would have been a huge step.

I phoned ahead to the Queen's Arms Hotel in East Garston, the pub where Eleanor and I had met for our first drink and meal back in the previous November.

'Yes,' they said. 'We have rooms available for tonight. For how many people?'

'For one,' I said. 'But I would like a double-bedded room please.' Well, you never knew.

Bob took me straight to the hotel, where the receptionist was surprised that I had no luggage, not even a wash bag. It was too complicated to explain, so I didn't. She kindly allocated me a room on the ground floor in a modern extension alongside the eighteenth-century inn, and I went and lay down on the bed to rest my aching back and to wait for Eleanor to arrive to look after me.

*

We had dinner at the same table as before but, on this occasion, our evening was interrupted by an emergency call on her pager.

'I just don't believe it,' said Eleanor, disconnecting from her mobile phone. 'No one who's been on call this week has been needed and now this.' She took another mouthful of her fish. 'I'll try and come back.' She stood up.

'Do you want me to save your dinner?' I said.

'No, I'll be longer than that,' she said. 'I'll call you.'

She rushed off to her car and left me sitting alone. I was disappointed. And, for the first time, I realized that I didn't feel guilty about being out with someone other than Angela.

I finished my dinner alone, drank my wine alone and, in time, went along the corridor to my bed, alone.

Eleanor did call eventually, at five to midnight.

'I'm so sorry,' she said. 'A two-year-old with a bad haemorrhage in its lung. Still a bit touch and go. I'll have to stay here. Also it's a bit late for dessert and coffee.' She laughed nervously at her own little joke.

'I'm in bed anyway,' I said. 'It's fine. I'll call you in the morning.'

'Right.' Did she sound relieved? Or was it my imagination? 'Goodnight.'

'Night,' I replied, and disconnected.

Life and love were very complicated, I reflected, as I drifted off to sleep.

CHAPTER 14

On Friday morning I went shopping in Newbury. A taxi picked me up from the hotel and I spent a couple of hours buying myself, maybe not a complete new wardrobe, but enough to see me through the next few weeks at Oxford Crown Court.

The hotel receptionist raised a questioning eyebrow when I arrived back at the Queen's Arms with two suitcases of luggage that I hadn't had the previous night.

'Lost by the airline,' I said to her, and she nodded knowingly.

She carried the cases to my room as I struggled along behind her with the damn crutches.

'Are you staying tonight, then?' she asked.

'I'm not sure yet,' I said. 'Someone told me at breakfast that late check-out would be OK.' For a fee, of course.

'Oh yes, that's fine,' she said. 'The room is free tonight if you want it.' I presumed she didn't mean free as in money, but free as in unoccupied.

'Thank you,' I said. 'I'll let you know.' And I closed the door.

I eased myself out of the white plastic shell and chanced standing in the shower without it, letting a stream of cool water wash away the grime and bring relief to my itching body. I washed my hair with new shampoo, brushed my teeth with a new toothbrush, and shaved my chin with a new razor. I then reluctantly put myself back in the plastic straightjacket before dressing in crisp clean new shirt and trousers. I suddenly felt so much better. Almost a new man, in fact.

The taxi returned after lunch and took me to Uffington, back to the Radcliffes' place. I had called Larry Clayton to say I was coming and he was sitting in his office when I arrived about two thirty, the same scuffed cowboy boots resting on his desk. It had been only two days since I had been here, but somehow it seemed longer.

'How can I help?' he said, not getting up.

I handed him a copy of the Millie and foal photo.

'Do you recognize anyone in this picture?' I asked him.

He studied it quite closely. 'Nope,' he said finally.

'The foal is Peninsula,' I said.

He looked again at the picture.

'Sorry,' he said. 'Still can't help you.'

'When did you say you arrived here?' I asked him.

'Last September,' he said.

'Where were you before?' I said.

'Up in Cheshire,' he said. 'I managed a meat-packing plant in Runcorn.'

'Bit different from this,' I said. 'How did you get this job?'

'I applied,' he said. 'Why, what's your problem?' He lifted his feet off the desk and sat upright in his chair.

'Sorry,' I said. 'No problem. Just seems funny to move from meat packing to foals.'

'Perhaps they wanted me for my man-management skills,' he said, clearly annoyed with my questions.

'Is there anyone working here now who was here when Peninsula was born?' I asked, trying to change direction.

'Doubt it,' he said unhelpfully, leaning back and replacing his feet on the desk. It was his way of telling me that my time was up.

'Well, keep the photo anyway,' I said. 'If anyone recognizes the man will you ask them to give me a call.' I handed him one of my business cards but I suspected that he would put it in the waste bin beside his desk as soon as I was through the door, together with the photo.

'When did you say the Radcliffes will be back?' I asked him from the doorway.

'The Kentucky Derby is at Louisville tomorrow,' he said, leaning further back in his chair. 'They'll be back sometime after that.' He seemed determined not to be too helpful.

'Right,' I said. 'Would you ask them to look at the picture as well, please?'

'Maybe,' he said.

The taxi had waited for me and I asked the driver to take me back to the Queen's Arms. That had all been a waste of time, I thought.

I called Eleanor and asked her if I should stay for a second night or go on to Oxford. Arthur had booked my hotel from the Friday, and I had already called to check that all my boxes had arrived there safely.

'I'm on call again,' she said.

'Is everything all right?' I asked her. She seemed strangely reticent for someone who had previously been so forthcoming, almost eager.

'Fine,' she said. 'I'm just very busy at the moment.'

Was it something I had said, I wondered.

'But would you like to have dinner together?' I asked. 'You may not be paged tonight.' There was a pause from the other end of the line. 'But we can leave it if you like,' I went on quickly. Was I being too pushy?

'Geoffrey,' she said seriously. 'I'd love to have dinner with you, but . . .'

'Yes?' I said.

'I'll have to come back here afterwards.'

'That's fine,' I said, upbeat. 'Why don't we have dinner at the Fox and Hounds in Uffington, and then I'll get a taxi to take me on to Oxford while you go back to Lambourn.'

'Great,' she said, sounding a little relieved.

'Are you sure everything's all right?' I asked her again.

'Yes,' she said. 'I promise. Everything is fine.'

We disconnected and I was left wondering whether men could ever fully understand women.

We had arranged to meet at the Fox and Hounds at eight. I had noticed the pub on both my trips to the Radcliffe place. It was a yellow plastered building set close to the road in Uffington High Street and I arrived early at ten past seven in a taxi with my two suitcases.

'I'm sorry,' said the publican as I struggled in through the door with both cases and my crutches. 'We don't have any accommodation, we're only a pub.'

I explained to him that another taxi was picking me up later and he kindly allowed me to store my bags in his office in the interim.

'Now,' he said as I half sat myself on one of the Windsor-style bar stools. 'What can I get you?'

'Glass of red, please,' I said. 'Merlot, if you have it.'

He poured a generous measure and set the glass down on the wooden bar top.

'I called and booked for dinner,' I said.

'Mr Mason?' he said. I nodded. 'For two? At eight?'

'Yes,' I said. 'I'm early.' I looked around the bar. I was so early that, even on a Friday evening, I was his only customer. 'Quiet tonight,' I said to him.

'It'll be much busier later,' he said. 'All my regulars will be in soon.'

I rather hoped that Larry Clayton would not be amongst them.

I pulled a copy of the Millie and foal photograph from my jacket and placed it on the bar. 'Do you recognize either of the people in this picture?' I said, pushing it towards him.

He had a good look. 'I don't know the woman,' he said. 'But I think the man is Jack Rensburg.'

'Does he live round here?' I said. I could hardly control my excitement. I had thought the pub might be a long shot and hadn't expected to get an answer so quickly.

'He used to,' the publican replied. 'He worked at the stables on the Woolstone road. He's been gone for two or three years, at least.'

'How well did you know him?' I asked.

'Is he in trouble?' he said.

'No, nothing like that,' I assured him with a laugh.

'He used to talk a lot about cricket,' he said. 'He's South African. He played for the village team here and they come into the pub after matches in the summer. He was always going on about how much better the South Africans were than the English team. But it was just banter. He's a nice enough chap.'

'Do you know why he left?' I asked.

'No idea,' he said. 'I think he went away on holiday and never came back.'

'And you don't know when exactly?' I asked him.

He thought for a moment but shook his head. 'Sorry.'

Some more customers arrived and he went off to serve them.

So, I thought, the stud groom was called Jack Rensburg and he was a South African who liked cricket and he had left Uffington at least two or three years ago, possibly to go on a holiday from which he had not returned. Young men the world over, especially those living away from their homeland, went on holidays all the time from which they didn't return. The nomadic life of the young expatriate male should not be a surprise to anyone. Perhaps he met a girl, or simply went home and stayed there.

Eleanor arrived promptly at eight and I was still half standing, half sitting on the bar stool enjoying a second glass of Merlot.

She came over, gave me a peck on the cheek and sat on the stool next to me and ordered a glass of white. Where, I thought, had the kiss on the lips gone?

'Had a good day?' she asked rather gloomily, tasting her wine.

'Yes, actually, I have. I've bought up most of the menswear in Newbury, washed, shaved and preened my body, and,' I said with a flourish, 'I've discovered the name of the man in the picture.'

'Wow,' she said, mocking. 'You have been a busy boy.' She smiled and it felt like the sun had come out.

'That's better,' I said, smiling back. 'And what have you been up to?'

'I've spent most of the day monitoring the two-year-old from last night. And discussing his future with the owner.' She raised her eyes to the heavens. 'He would have much rather I put the animal down than save its life.'

'How come?' I said.

'Seems it's insured against being dead, but not against being a hopeless racehorse.'

'And is it a hopeless racehorse?' I asked.

'It might be after yesterday,' she said. 'Might not be able to race at all. Much more profitable to him dead.'

'Is bleeding in the lungs common in horses?' I asked.

'Fairly,' she said. 'But mostly EIPH. This one was a static bleed.'

'EIPH?' I said.

'Sorry,' she replied, smiling. 'Exercise-induced pulmonary haemorrhage.'

I began to wish I'd never asked.

'Lots of horses bleed slightly into their lungs during stressful exercise but that usually clears up quickly and spontaneously without too much damage and without any blood showing externally. Horses' lungs are big and efficient but they need to be. A racehorse needs masses of oxygen delivered to its muscles to run fast. You just have to see how hard they blow after the finish.' She paused, but only for breath herself. 'During the race their action helps their breathing. As they stretch out their hind quarters, they draw air in, and then that's blown out again by their legs coming forward in the stride. It makes Thoroughbreds very efficient gallopers when both their hind legs move together, pumping air in and out of their lungs like pistons. But it also means that the air fairly rushes in and out at hurricane speeds and that sometimes damages the lining, which, by definition, has to be flimsy and fragile to let the oxygen pass into the bloodstream in the first place.'

I sat there listening to her, understanding every word and

loving it. Not since Angela had died had I enjoyed the experience of a bright, educated and enthusiastic female companion describing to me something complicated because it interested her, and not just because I had asked her to do so as part of my job.

'So, is a static bleed worse?' I asked her.

'Not necessarily,' she said. 'But it might make EIPH more likely. And horses that regularly show blood on their nostrils after racing are discouraged from running again and, in some countries, they're not allowed to. The horses are usually referred to as having burst a blood vessel, or having had a nosebleed.'

I had heard both the terms used often on the racecourse.

'It's not really a blood vessel as such,' she said. 'And the blood comes not from the nose but from the alveoli in the lungs. In America they all use a drug called Lasix to help prevent it, but that's against the Rules of Racing here.'

I didn't really want to stop her but the publican came over and asked us if we were ready to eat, so we moved to a table in the corner of the bar.

'Tell me about the man in the picture,' Eleanor said as we sat down.

'Not really much to tell,' I said. 'His name is Jack Rensburg, and he's a South African who used to work for the Radcliffes but has now gone away.'

'Where to?' she said.

'I haven't found that out yet,' I said.

'Is he coming back?' she said.

'I don't know that either, but I doubt it. He's been gone for two years or more.'

'Bit of a dead end, then?' she said.

'Yeah,' I agreed. 'But I'll set Arthur onto it on Monday. He loves a challenge.'

'Arthur?' she asked.

'Chief Clerk at my chambers,' I said. 'Knows everything, walks on water, that sort of thing.'

'Useful,' she said, smiling broadly, but the smile faded.

'Horse walks into a bar –' I said.

'What?' said Eleanor, interrupting.

'Horse walks into a bar,' I repeated. 'Barman says, "Why the long face?"'

She laughed. 'The old ones are always the best.'

'So, why the long face?' I said to her again.

She stopped laughing. 'It's nothing,' she said. 'I'm just being silly.'

'If it's nothing,' I said. 'Tell me.'

'No,' she said in mock seriousness. 'It's private.'

'Have I done something wrong?' I said.

'No, of course not,' she said. 'It's nothing. Forget it.'

'I can't,' I said. 'For the first time in more than seven years I don't feel guilty at being out with another woman and, suddenly, there's something wrong. And I'm worried it's because of what I've said or done.'

'Geoffrey,' she said laying a hand on my arm. 'It's nothing like that.' She laughed, throwing her head back.

'Well what is it, then?' I asked determinedly.

She leaned forward close to me. 'Wrong time of the month,' she said. 'I was so afraid you would ask me to sleep with you, and I don't want to, not like this.'

'Oh,' I said, embarrassed. 'I'm so sorry.'

'It's not a disease you know,' she said with a laugh, the sparkle back in her eyes. 'It'll be gone by Monday, or Tuesday.'

'Oh,' I said again. 'Monday or Tuesday,' I repeated rather vaguely.

'And I'm not on call on either night,' she giggled.

I didn't know whether to feel embarrassed, excited or just plain foolish.

The publican came over to our table to save me from further blushes. There was another man behind him. 'There's a chap here who used to play cricket with Jack,' he said. 'He may be able to help you.'

'Thank you very much,' I said.

The man pulled up a chair and sat down at the table.

'Pete Ritch,' the man said by way of introduction. 'Hear you're looking for Jack Rensburg.'

'Yes,' I said. 'I'm Geoffrey Mason and this is Eleanor.' He nodded at her.

'What do you want him for?' he asked.

'I'm a lawyer and I'd like to talk to him,' I said.

'Is he in trouble?' he said.

He was the second person who thought he might have been in trouble.

'No. No trouble,' I said. 'I just need to talk to him.'

'Is it some inheritance thing?' he asked. 'Has some aunt left him a pile?'

'Something like that,' I said.

'Well, I'm sorry, then, 'cause I don't rightly know where he is no more.'

'When did you last see him?' I asked.

'Years ago now,' he said. 'He went on holiday and just never came back.'

'Do you know where he went?'

'Somewhere exotic it was,' said Pete. I thought that anywhere out of Oxfordshire might seem exotic to him. 'Far East or something.'

'Can you think exactly when that was?'

'It was during the last England tour to South Africa,' he said with some certainty. 'Him and me had a wager on the result and he never came back to pay me when England won. I remember that.'

'Cricket tour?' I asked.

'Yeah,' he said. 'Dead keen on his cricket was Jack. His name was actually spelt with a "ques" at the end, like that famous South African cricketer Jacques Kallis. He was proud of that. But we all just called him Jack.'

'Do you know anything else about him?' I asked. 'Does he have any family here, or did he own a house or a car?'

'No idea,' he said. 'I only knew him from in here, and at the cricket club. He could bowl a bit. Spinners, mostly.'

'Thank you so much, Pete,' I said to him. 'You've been most helpful.'

He made no move to stand up or to leave our table.

'Sorry,' I said, understanding. 'Can I buy you a drink?'

'That would be handsome,' he said.

I waved at the publican, who came over.

'Would you please give Pete here a drink on me,' I said. 'And one for yourself as well.'

They went off together to the bar and, subsequently, Pete waved a full pint in my direction. I nodded at him and smiled. Eleanor was trying very hard not to completely collapse in a fit of giggles.

'Stop it,' I said to her under my breath while trying hard not to join in. 'For goodness' sake, stop it.' But she didn't, or she couldn't.

*

My taxi arrived at ten fifteen sharp, as I had ordered, and it whisked me off to Oxford, leaving Eleanor waving to me from the pub car park. The evening had flown by and I wasn't at all ready to go when the driver arrived. But he couldn't wait. He had other trips booked after mine.

'Now or never,' he'd said.

I was tempted to say never, but I would just have to wait until Monday, or Tuesday.

Eleanor and I kissed each other goodnight firmly, with open mouths. It was a revelation to me after such a long time. Something stirred inside me and I so reluctantly struggled into the back seat of the taxi to be borne away from her to the City of Dreaming Spires. I, meanwhile, was dreaming of the future, and especially of Monday, or Tuesday.

CHAPTER 15

I spent an hour early on Saturday connected to the internet, dealing with my e-mails, paying bills and generally managing my bank account. I also looked up when England had last played cricket on tour in South Africa. The rest of the morning was spent going through, yet again, the boxes of papers for the case. By now I knew many of them off by heart but one or two of them were new since I had last been through them.

At last, after several more threatening requests, the bank had finally produced Millie Barlow's bank statements and I spent quite a while examining these. They did indeed show that Millie had a regular payment into her account over and above her salary from the equine hospital veterinary practice. And Scot's statements showed that the money didn't come from him, or at least it didn't come from his bank account.

The amounts weren't that big, just a few hundred every month, and, from the statements that had been sent by the bank, I was able to tell they had been paid to her for at least a year and a half before she died. But I didn't have any information for before that.

I thought back to when I had met her parents at Scot Barlow's house. Were they likely to have been sending their daughter money? One never knew. Their ill-fitting clothes, their cheap coach travel and their simple ways didn't necessarily mean they had no spare cash. It might just mean they were careful with their money, and there was no crime in that.

Scot, meanwhile, had been doing very well indeed, thank you very much. Almost all his deposits were from Weatherbys, the racing administrators, who paid all the riding fees and win bonuses to owners, trainers and jockeys. There had been a few other minor deposits but nothing that amounted to much. Scot had been at the top of his profession and earning accordingly, but the statements indicated that there was nothing unusual in any of his transactions, at least nothing that I had been able to spot.

I met with Bruce Lygon on Saturday afternoon and we fairly gloomily went through the prosecution case once again. At first glance the evidence seemed overwhelming but, the more I looked at it, the more I began to believe that we had a chance to argue that Mitchell had no case to answer. Everything was circumstantial. There was no proof anywhere in their case that our client had ever been to Honeysuckle Cottage, let alone killed its owner.

'But the evidence does show,' Bruce said, 'that whoever killed Barlow used Mitchell's pitchfork as the murder weapon, was wearing Mitchell's boots as he did it, probably drove Mitchell's car from the scene, and,' he emphasized, 'also had access to Mitchell's debit card slips.'

'But that doesn't mean it was definitely Mitchell who did it,' I said.

'What would you think if you were on the jury?' he said. 'Especially when you add in the fact that Mitchell hated Barlow.

Everyone knew it, and Mitchell had often been heard to threaten to kill Barlow in exactly the manner in which he died.'

'That's why we have to argue that there's no case to answer,' I said. 'If it goes to the jury we are in deep trouble.'

On Sunday, I went by train to have lunch with my father in his bungalow in the village of Kings Sutton. He came down to the village station to collect me in his old Morris Minor. He had always loved this old car and there was nothing he adored more than tinkering for hours with the old engine beneath the bulbous bonnet.

'She's still going well, then?' I said to him as the car made easy work of the hill up from the station.

'Never better,' he said. 'The odometer has just been round the clock again.'

I leaned over and saw that it read just twenty-two miles.

'How many times is that?' I asked.

'Can't remember,' he said. 'Three or four at least.'

This car had been the greatest delight of his life and he had been married to it for far longer, and much more passionately, than he had been to my mother.

It had been the first car I had ever driven. I am sure that the Health and Safety Executive would not have approved of the practice, but I could remember the joy of sitting on my father's lap and steering at an age when my feet wouldn't reach the pedals. Thinking back, it was a surprise that I hadn't wanted to become a racing driver rather than a jockey.

My father's stone-built bungalow sat in a cul-de-sac at the edge of the village with six other similar bungalows, all of them subtly different in design or orientation. He had four bedrooms

256

in a house that looked smaller, but he had converted the smallest bedroom into an office with bookshelves full of law books and Morris Minor manuals.

Just as he had been an infrequent visitor to Barnes since Angela died, I had only been here to Kings Sutton to see him about half a dozen times in the previous three years. My father and I had never been really affectionate towards each other, even when I had been a small child. I suppose we loved each other in the way that parents and children must, and I think I would probably miss him after his days, that is if Julian Trent didn't see me off first. But closeness and a cosy loving relationship between us was something that neither of us had wanted for a very long time, if ever.

However, that Sunday, I had a lovely time with him, sitting at his dining-room table eating a roast beef lunch with Yorkshire puddings and four different vegetables that he had cooked for us.

'I'm very impressed,' I said, laying down my knife and fork. 'I never realized you could cook so well.'

'You should come more often,' he said in response, smiling.

Over lunch we hadn't discussed the Mitchell case, or any other case. I think, in the end, he had been pleased that I had become a barrister, but there had been so many things said between us in those early years, things we probably both would now regret having said, that the whole question of my job and career had never been mentioned again.

'Would you do me a favour?' I asked him as we moved with our coffees into his sitting room.

'Depends what it is,' he said.

'Would you contemplate going away for a couple of weeks?' I said.

'What on earth for?' he said.

How could I explain to him that it might be for his own protection? How could I say that it was so he couldn't be used as a lever to make me do something I didn't want to?

'I'd like to give you a holiday,' I said.

'But why?' he said. 'And where would I go?'

'Wherever you like,' I said.

'But I don't want to go anywhere,' he said. 'If you really want to give me something then give me the money to have my windows and guttering painted.'

'It might be safer for you to go away,' I said.

'Safer?' he said. 'How would it be safer?'

I explained to him just a little about how some people were trying to influence the outcome of a trial by getting me to do things I didn't want to do.

'You ought to go and tell the police,' he said.

'I know,' I replied. 'I will. But for the time being it might be best if the people concerned didn't know where you were.'

'Don't be ridiculous, boy,' he said, putting on his most authoritative voice. 'Why on earth would anyone care where I live?'

I took a photograph out of my pocket and passed it to him. It was the one of him standing outside his front door wearing the green jumper with the hole in the elbow.

He studied it carefully and looked up at my face.

'Are you saying that someone else took this?' he said.

I nodded at him. 'Last November,' I said. 'Do you remember me calling you about that hole in your jumper?'

'Vaguely,' he said, still staring at the picture.

'Well,' I said, 'I just don't want these people coming here to trouble you again, that's all.' I was trying to play down the matter and make light of it so as not to frighten him unnecessarily.

'But why would they want to?' he persisted.

'Because,' I said with a forced laugh, 'I have no intention of doing what they want me to do.'

Steve Mitchell's trial started at ten thirty sharp on Monday morning in court number 1 at Oxford Crown Court with a red-robed High Court judge parachuted in from London for the purpose. This was a murder trial with a celebrity, albeit a minor one, in the dock and nothing was to go wrong.

As expected, I had received no call over the weekend from Sir James Horley QC asking me to request an adjournment and had, in fact, been advised by Arthur in an e-mail that Sir James was now doubtful of making it to Oxford at any time before Thursday at the earliest. I thought that he was in danger of being severely reprimanded by the trial judge, but, as they were probably old golfing chums, that wouldn't have amounted to much.

The first hour of any trial is taken up mostly with court procedures. The jury members have to be selected and sworn in, the judge needs to become acquainted with counsel, the clerk of the court has to be happy that the right defendant is in the right court, and so on. Boxes of papers are sorted and everything has to be just right before the judge calls on the prosecution to start proceedings proper by outlining the case for the Crown.

Without exception, all criminal proceedings in the English Crown courts are prosecuted in the name of the reigning monarch. The court papers in this case were headed by *R. v. Mitchell*, meaning in this case Regina, the Queen, versus Steve Mitchell.

Criminal cases under English law are adversarial. There are

two sides, the prosecution acting for the Crown and the defence acting for the defendant. The two sides argue against each other with the judge sitting like an independent and neutral referee in the middle. The judge is solely responsible for ensuring that the law, and its procedures, are correctly followed. The jury, having heard all the arguments and also having listened to the answers given by the witnesses called by both prosecution and defence, then decide amongst themselves, in secret, what are the facts in the case before pronouncing on the guilt, or otherwise, of the defendant. If the verdict is guilty, then the judge determines the sentence, in theory following guidelines as laid down by the Sentencing Advisory Panel.

The system has operated in this way for hundreds of years and the spread of English-style administration around the world in the sixteenth, seventeenth and eighteenth centuries carried this legal system with it. Consequently it remains the practice in much of the world, including in the United States and in most of the old British Commonwealth.

However, in most of continental Europe the courts follow a different pattern known as the inquisitorial system where the judge, or a panel of judges, investigate the facts in the case, question the witnesses, determine the verdict and then pass sentence, all without the use of a jury. Exponents claim that it may be more precise in finding out the truth, but there is no real evidence to say that one system is more accurate than the other in reaching the correct conclusion.

Number 1 court at Oxford was set out for the adversarial system, as was every other Crown Court in the land, and both the prosecution and the defence teams were laying claim to their space. In our case, the defence consisted solely of Bruce Lygon, his secretary and me. I had asked him to bring his secretary to court so that we didn't, as a line-up, appear too thin on the ground. To be fair, we also had Nikki Payne at our disposal. Nikki was an eager young solicitor's clerk from Bruce's firm, but she wasn't in court at the start of the trial because she was busy in London trying to discover the answers to some questions I had set her the previous evening.

The prosecution, meanwhile, had seven players in situ. A top QC from London was leading, with a local barrister as his junior. These two sat in the front row, to our right, and also slightly to the right of the judge's bench as we looked at it. Two CPS solicitors sat behind them, with two other legal assistants in the row behind that, plus a cross between a secretary and a gofer in row four. If they were trying to impress and intimidate the defence by weight of numbers, it seemed to be succeeding.

'They look very well organized,' Bruce said to me quietly.

'So do we,' I replied. 'So appearances can be deceiving.'

Members of the public and the press were admitted, taking their respective places on the right-hand side of the court. The press were represented in force, both front-page and back-page reporters of the national dailies filling all of the green upholstered seats in the press box. This trial was going to be big news, and the thirty or so seats reserved for the public were mostly full as well.

Mr and Mrs Barlow, Scot's parents, were both seated in the front row of this public area, which, in Oxford, was not an elevated gallery as at the Old Bailey, but on the floor of the courtroom alongside the press.

Next, Steve Mitchell was brought into court from the cells by a prison officer in uniform. Both the prison officer and Steve sat in the glass-fronted dock at the back of the court, behind the barristers' benches. I turned round and gave Steve an encouraging smile. He looked pale and very nervous but was dressed, as I had suggested, in the blazer, white shirt and tie that I had bought for him in Newbury the previous Saturday. Courts are formal places and most of the trial participants were in legal dress or lounge suits. Only juries and the public galleries were casual, and seemingly more so each year.

'All rise,' announced the clerk. Everyone stood and the judge entered the court from his chambers behind. He bowed. We bowed back. And then everyone sat down again. The court was now in session.

The court clerk stood up. 'The defendant will rise,' she said. Steve stood up.

'Are you Stephen Miles Mitchell?' said the clerk.

'Yes, I am,' Steve replied in a strong voice that was partly muffled by the glass front of the dock that ran right to the ceiling of the court.

'You may sit down,' said the clerk, so he did.

'Are you leading for the defence, Mr Mason?' the judge asked loudly, making me jump.

I struggled to my feet. 'Yes, My Lord,' I said.

'Do you not think that your team needs strengthening some-what?' he asked.

It was his coded way of asking whether I thought that a QC might be more appropriate, as he clearly did.

'My Lord,' I replied. 'Sir James Horley is nominally leading for the defence in this case but is unable to be here today due to another case in which he is acting having run over time.'

'You have not asked for an adjournment,' he said, somewhat accusingly.

'No, My Lord,' I said. 'Sir James and I have made the preparations for the case, and my client is content for the case to proceed today with me acting for him.' I couldn't exactly tell the judge that my client had been ecstatic that Sir James was not here when I'd told him earlier in the cells beneath the court.

'I need to make it clear to you, and to your client, that this will not be grounds for an appeal if the case goes against you.'

'I understand that, My Lord,' I said. 'And so does my client.'

Steve Mitchell nodded his agreement to the judge from the dock.

'Very well,' said the judge. 'I have, in fact, spoken to Sir James this morning when he called me to present his apologies.'

Then why, I thought, did you ask me in the first place, you silly old fart?

The prosecution team were all looking at me and smiling, confidence oozing out of their every pore. I simply smiled back.

'The defendant will rise,' the clerk said again.

Steve stood up in the dock.

'You are charged,' the clerk said to him, 'that on the seventeenth of November 2008, you did murder Hamish Jamie Barlow, also known as Scot Barlow. Do you understand the indictment?'

'Yes,' Steve replied.

'How do you plead?' the clerk asked him.

'Not guilty,' Steve said strongly.

Next came the selection and swearing in of the jury.

Everyone watched as a mixed bag of individuals entered the court and sat on more green-covered seats on the other side. There were eighteen of them in total, drawn randomly from the electoral roll and summoned to attend the court, whether they wanted to or not. Unlike in the United States neither the defence nor the prosecution had any prior knowledge of who they were or where they lived. We were not allowed to ask them any questions and, since 1989, the defence has not been able to object to a juror simply because they didn't like the cut of his coat. Objections to jurors now had to be based on firm grounds and, even then, the judge was most likely to dismiss the objection.

Twelve of the eighteen had their names drawn from a box by the court clerk and each one, in turn, took their places in the jury box to my left and were sworn in, on oath, promising to try the case according to the evidence.

The six people, four women and two men, who had not been selected looked decidedly disappointed as they were excused by the judge back to the jury rooms upstairs, maybe to get luckier in one of the other courts.

And now we were ready to begin in earnest.

The court clerk stood up and read out the indictment to the jury. 'That on the seventeenth of November 2008, Stephen Miles Mitchell did murder Hamish Jamie Barlow, known as Scot Barlow, contrary to common law.'

'Ladies and gentlemen of the jury,' the prosecution QC was on his feet almost before the clerk had sat down. 'You will hear, in this case, of a bitter feud in the world of horse racing that was so acrimonious that it led to the gruesome killing of one jockey at the hands of another. A story of rivalry and revenge that goes far beyond the accepted limits that exist in any competitive sport.' He paused briefly to draw breath, and also to find a sheet of paper that he picked up from the desk and consulted, not that he probably needed to. It was simply for show. 'Members of the jury, you will hear how the defendant did premeditatively murder the victim by driving a metal-pronged pitchfork deep into his chest, deep into his heart, and how the defendant now claims that he is innocent of the charge and is being framed by person or persons unknown. But the evidence presented to you will convince you, beyond a reasonable doubt, that the defendant is, in fact, culpable of the murder, and that his claims of being framed are meaningless and unfounded, nothing more than the last refuge of a guilty soul.' He replaced the paper onto the desk.

He was good, I thought. Too damned good. He was also far too melodramatic for my taste but it was working. I could see some of the jury members glancing at the dock with distaste.

In all, it took him more than an hour to fully outline, in considerable detail, the case for the prosecution by which time every one of the jury members was eyeing Steve with contempt. As was always the way with the English legal system, the prosecution had first go in the jury persuasion stakes. The defence would have their turn, in time. I just hoped that something would turn up by then that I could use to help me.

The judge adjourned proceedings for lunch. The slow pace of trials, especially murder trials, was becoming clear to both the jury and the defendant. The rest of us knew already.

I went straight down to the cells to see Steve.

'My God,' he said. 'Did you see the way the jury was looking at me? They all think I'm guilty. I've got no bloody chance. I wanted so much to call that lawyer a bloody liar.'

'Calm down, Steve,' I said. 'It's always like that at the beginning of a trial. We'll get our turn later.' I didn't add that it might get worse when they started calling their witnesses. 'Have some lunch. I'll see you in court when we resume, and try to keep calm. Remember what I said to you earlier – don't say anything, ever. It will not look good to the jury, and it will antagonize the judge. Just bite your lip and keep quiet. You will get your turn. Do you understand?'

He nodded. 'It's bloody difficult, though.'

'I know,' I said. 'But it's very important. I'll see you later.'

I went up in the lift and made some calls on my mobile.

There was no reply from Nikki's phone, so I tried Arthur.

'How's it going?' he asked.

'Same as always at the start of a trial,' I said.

'That bad, huh?' he said.

'Worse. Have you heard from Nikki Payne?' I asked him.

'Who?' he said.

'Nikki Payne,' I said again. 'Solicitor's clerk from Bruce Lygon's firm. She said she would pass a message to me through you.'

'Ah yes,' he said. 'Hold on.' I could hear him rustling papers. 'Apparently she's got something from the embassy and she's chasing the lead. Does that make sense?'

'Yes,' I said. 'Good. And thank you for my hotel. Very amusing.'

'Thought you'd feel at home,' he said, laughing.

Arthur had made reservations for me in Oxford at a hotel conveniently placed just a few hundred yards from the court building. And the reason he amusingly thought that I would feel at home was because the hotel had been created by converting the old Oxford Prison, which had housed a different clientele as recently as 1996. My room was in what had been 'A' wing of the prison, with galleried landings and rows of old cell doorways. It had all been tastefully converted but it still looked just like the interior of an old Victorian prison, except, of course, for the carpets. The hotel had obligingly left one cell as it had been in the prison days so the hotel guests could see how miserably the other half had once lived. I was amused to notice that porridge was on the breakfast menu.

'Tell Nikki to call me later if she calls you again,' I said to him. 'I want to hear how she's doing.'

'Right,' he said. 'I will. Anything else you need?'

'A cast-iron alibi for the defendant would be nice.'

'See what I can do,' he said, laughing, and hung up. Arthur would have to really work a miracle, I thought, to get Mr Mitchell out of this hole.

The afternoon proved to be as frustrating as the morning had been, with the investigating police officer in the witness box for the whole two and a half hours. Only once did the judge briefly adjourn things for a few minutes for us all to stretch our legs and visit the lavatories, and to give me some relief from the damn body shell cutting into my groin. How I wished I could have had my recliner chair from my room in chambers, instead of the upright seats of the court.

The policeman, having consulted his notebooks, went through the whole affair in chronological order, from the moment that the police had first arrived at Barlow's house to discover the body until they had arrested Steve Mitchell at eight fifty-three that evening. He also went on to describe the investigation after the arrest, including the interviewing of the suspect and the forensic tests that the police had performed on Mitchell's boots and car together with his understanding of the results, but, as he said, he was no expert on DNA testing.

We were assured by the prosecution that they would be calling their DNA expert witness in due course, together with a member of the police forensic team that had carried out the tests.

'Inspector,' said the prosecution QC. 'What model of car did the defendant own at the time of the murder?'

'An Audi A4,' he said. 'Silver.'

'Yes,' went on the QC, 'and in the course of your enquiries did you determine if this car was fitted with a security alarm and immobilizer system?'

'Yes,' he said. 'It was.'

'And was the system found to be functioning correctly when the car was examined after the defendant's arrest?'

'Yes,' he said again. 'It was.'

'So would it be accurate to say that the car could only be unlocked and then driven if the correct key had been used for the purpose?'

'That is my understanding, yes,' said the inspector.

'Did you find any keys for the vehicle?' the QC asked him.

'Yes,' he said. 'There were two such keys found in Mr Mitchell's premises when he was arrested. One was on the defendant, in his trouser pocket on a ring with other keys, and the other one,' he consulted his notebook, 'was in the top drawer of Mr Mitchell's desk in his study.'

'And did you approach an Audi dealer and ask them about keys for their cars?'

'Yes,' he said again. 'They informed me that it was normal for two keys to be issued with a new car and also that replacement or additional keys are only provided after strict security checks.'

'And had any additional keys been requested for Mr Mitchell's car?'

'No,' he said. 'They had not.'

'One last thing, Inspector,' the QC said with a flourish.

'Was Mr Mitchell's car locked when you went to his home to arrest him?'

'Yes,' he said. 'It was.'

'Your witness,' the prosecution QC said, turning to me.

I looked at the clock on the courtroom wall. It read twenty past four.

'Would you like to start your cross-examination in the morning, Mr Mason?' asked the judge expectantly.

'If it pleases My Lord,' I said, 'I would like to ask a few questions now.'

The judge looked at the clock.

'Ten minutes, then,' he said.

'Thank you, My Lord.' I turned to the witness and consulted my papers. 'Inspector McNeile, can you please tell the court how it was that the police first became aware that Mr Barlow had been murdered?'

He had left that bit out of his evidence.

'I can't remember how I first heard of it,' he said.

'I asked, Inspector, not how you personally found out, but how the police force in general was informed.'

'I believe it was a call to the police station reporting an intruder at Mr Barlow's residence,' he said.

'Who was this call from?' I asked him.

'I'm sorry, I don't have that information.'

'But surely, Inspector, all emergency calls to the police are logged with the time they are made, and who they are from?'

'That is the usual practice, yes,' he said.

'So how is it that you have no record of who it was that called the police to tell you that an intruder had been seen at Barlow's house?'

He looked slightly uncomfortable. 'The call was taken by the telephone on the desk of a civilian worker in the front office of the police station.'

'Was that not unusual?' I said.

'Yes,' he replied.

'And was the number of that telephone widely available to the public?' I asked him.

'Not that I'm aware of,' he said.

'Do you not think it is strange that the call was taken on a telephone where the number was not widely known, a telephone where no log was taken of incoming calls, and a telephone on which no recording equipment was attached so that the caller and his number would be unknown?'

'Mr Mason,' the judge interjected. 'That's three questions in one.'

'I'm sorry, My Lord,' I said. 'Inspector McNeile, would you agree with me that, until the police arrived at Mr Barlow's house to discover his body, it is likely that the only person or persons who knew that Mr Barlow was dead would be those responsible for his murder?'

'I suppose so, yes,' he said.

'Inspector, how many years in total have you been a detective?' I asked him.

'Fifteen,' he said.

'And how often in those fifteen years,' I said to him, 'have you been telephoned anonymously, on an unrecorded line, to report an intruder in a property so that the police would turn up there and discover a murder victim surrounded by a mass of incriminating evidence?'

'That's enough, Mr Mason,' said the judge.

'My Lord,' I said respectfully, and sat down. It had been a minor victory only, in a day of unremitting bad news.

'Court adjourned until ten o'clock tomorrow morning,' said the judge.

'All rise.'

Eleanor didn't come to Oxford on Monday night. In one way I was relieved, in another, disappointed. When I arrived back at the hotel from court I lay down on the bed, my head aching slightly from all the concentration. This slight headache soon developed into a full-on head-banger.

It was the first such headache I had suffered for some time and I had begun to forget the ferocity of the pain behind my eyes. During the first three weeks immediately after the fall at Cheltenham, I had suffered these on most days and I knew that relaxing horizontally on a bed for a couple of hours was the best and only remedy. A couple of paracetamol tablets took the edge off it, but I had carelessly left my stronger codeine pills at home. They were somewhere in the shambles that had once been my bathroom.

At some point I drifted off to sleep because I was awakened by the phone ringing beside the bed.

'Yes?' I said into it, struggling to sit up because of the shell.

'Mr Mason?' a female voice said.

'Yes,' I replied.

'This is Nikki Payne here,' she said. 'I've been to the Home Office and the South African embassy as you asked and neither of them had any record of a Jacques Rensburg. But they did of someone called Jacques van Rensburg. In fact there are three of them who live in England. Apparently van Rensburg is quite a common name in South Africa.'

It would be.

'Two of the South African Jacques van Rensburgs living here are at university, here on student visas. One is at Durham and the other is a post-graduate at Cambridge and both have been here for the past two years.'

I suppose it was possible that the Jacques we wanted had given up working with horses for a life of academia, but somehow I doubted it.

'What about the third one?' I asked.

'His visa has expired, but it seems he's still here although his right to work has expired too. But, apparently, that's not unusual. That's all I have for the moment.'

'Well done,' I said to her.

'I'm not done yet,' she said. 'A nice chap at the embassy is searching for the third Jacques back in South Africa just in case he went home without telling the Home Office. There aren't any proper records kept when people leave the UK, only when they arrive.'

It was true, I thought. No one from the immigration department checks your passport on the way out, only on the way in. The airlines only check their passengers' passports to ensure they have the same names as on their boarding passes.

'But you did show them the photo?' I asked her.

'Of course I did,' she said. 'My friend at the embassy is trying to get me a copy of this Jacques van Rensburg's passport snap sent from the South African Department of Home Affairs in Pretoria so I can see if it is actually him.'

'Good,' I said. 'Call me tomorrow if you get anywhere.'

She hung up and I rested my head back onto the pillow. My headache was only slightly better, so I lay there for a while longer, reclosed my eyes and drifted back off to sleep.

The phone on the bedside cabinet rang once more, waking me again. Damn it, I thought, can't a man have any peace?

'Hello,' I said, irritated.

'Just make sure you lose the case,' said a whispering voice.

I was suddenly wide awake.

'Who are you?' I demanded loudly down the line.

'Never mind who,' said the whisperer. 'Just do it.'

The line went dead.

CHAPTER 16

Detective Inspector McNeile was back in the witness box on Tuesday morning for further cross-examination.

'I remind you that you are still under oath,' the judge said to him.

'Yes, My Lord,' he replied.

I levered myself to my feet, pulling on the lectern on the bench in front of me.

'Inspector McNeile,' I said. 'Yesterday afternoon you told us how the police came to find out about the murder of Mr Barlow from a phone call to a non-recorded, non-emergency number, is that right?'

'Yes,' he replied. There was no harm, I thought, in reminding the jury.

'Yes, thank you,' I said. 'Now I believe that the police also discovered that Mr Barlow had received a text message on his mobile telephone on the day of his death. Is that correct?'

'Yes,' he said again.

'And did this text message say, and I quote.' I picked up a sheet of paper myself and read from it. '"I'm going to come round and sort you out properly you sneaking little bastard"?'

I paused for effect. 'And then the message was signed off with Mr Mitchell's name?'

'I haven't got access to the actual text,' he said, turning to the judge as if for assistance.

'No,' I said. 'But does that sound about right to you?'

'Yes,' he said. 'I believe it said something like that.'

'Thank you,' I said, putting down the paper. 'And were the police able to establish that this text message had indeed been sent to Mr Barlow by Mr Mitchell?'

'No,' he said softly.

'Sorry, Inspector,' I said. 'Could you please speak up, so the jury can hear you?'

'No,' he repeated more strongly.

'And were the police able to establish who was, in fact, responsible for sending that text message to Mr Barlow?' I asked.

'No,' he said. 'We were not.'

'Am I correct in saying that you discovered that the message had been sent anonymously by a free text messaging service available to anyone with access to any computer and the internet anywhere in the world?'

'Yes,' he said. 'That is correct.'

'And is it correct that you were unable to establish which computer had been used to send the message?'

'That is correct,' he replied.

'So, in addition to an anonymous, unrecorded telephone call to the police directing them to a murder scene to discover incriminating evidence against the defendant.' I glanced at the judge who was looking back at me intently. 'There was also an anonymous text message sent to Mr Barlow's telephone that was made to appear as if it had come from the defendant?'

'I didn't say that it hadn't come from the defendant,' said the inspector. 'I only said that we were unable to establish that it had.'

'Are you claiming now that, in fact, it did come from the defendant?' I asked him with mock astonishment.

'We don't know who it was from,' he said, digging himself further into a hole.

'Thank you,' I said to him. 'No further questions.'

I sat down feeling rather pleased with myself. Bruce Lygon patted me gently on the shoulder. 'Well done,' he whispered.

I turned round to thank him and caught sight of young Julian Trent sitting right next to Mr and Mrs Barlow in the seats reserved for the public. He was watching me. I went quite cold. Damn it, I thought, how much of that cross-examination had he been listening to?

The next witness for the prosecution had been called and there was a lull in proceedings as the court usher went outside the courtroom trying to find the right person. Julian Trent watched me watching him and he clearly decided it was time to leave. He stood up and pushed past the usher as he made his way to the exit. For a moment I thought about going after him, but good sense prevailed so I stayed put. I could hardly chase him on crutches and I am sure the judge wouldn't have taken kindly to me leaving the court in the light of the continued, but unsurprising, absence of Sir James Horley QC.

My cross-examination of Detective Inspector McNeile proved to be the high point of the day for the defence. The three further witnesses called by the prosecution gave us little respite from the damning evidence that implied that the murder had been carried out by the man in the dock.

A specialist DNA witness was followed by a police forensic science expert. Both explained to the jury, in monotonous detail, the method of extracting DNA from blood and hair, and then went on to show beyond any doubt that drops of blood and two hairs from Scot Barlow had been found in the driver's footwell of Steve Mitchell's car and also that more of Barlow's blood and four more of his hairs had been found adhering to the underside of both of Steve Mitchell's wellington boots, subsequently discovered at the Mitchell premises.

They further were able to show that fresh bloody footprints at the scene matched both of Mr Mitchell's wellingtons.

I did manage to extract a small victory for our side by getting the forensic expert to concede that none of Mr Mitchell's DNA had been discovered in Barlow's residence, on the murder weapon, or on the deceased's body. Furthermore, I also got them both to agree that, even though Barlow's DNA had been found on Mr Mitchell's boots and in his car, this did not prove that Mr Mitchell had been wearing his boots at the time, nor driving his car at any point during that afternoon.

In re-examination by the prosecution, however, the first expert did state that traces of Mr Mitchell's DNA had been found inside his own boots, as you might have expected, but that no other person's DNA had also been found there. It didn't exactly further our argument that someone else must have been wearing Mitchell's wellies at the time of the murder, but it didn't destroy it completely either. I managed partly to salvage the situation by getting the second expert to agree that someone could wear a pair of rubber boots without leaving any DNA trace in them, especially someone who was keen not to do so.

The final witness of the day was the pathologist who had done the post-mortem examination of Scot Barlow's body, and his evidence wasn't for the squeamish. The two curved metal prongs of the pitchfork had not, as I had imagined, passed through the rib cage and then into the heart, but had been thrust upwards underneath the ribs, through the diaphragm, one of them entering the heart from below. The five-feet-long double-pronged murder weapon was produced as an exhibit. It looked huge and menacing in the stillness of the courtroom with its ten-inch-long thin, curved, and very sharp metal prongs glinting in the light. The pathologist was invited by the prosecution counsel to demonstrate, on the floor of the court, the upward thrusting action that would have been needed to cause the injuries sustained by Barlow's body. It was a moment of high drama and I noticed some members of the jury shuddering with revulsion. The pathologist explained that a single strike had been sufficient to cause death within just a few minutes with only moderate bleeding from the two wounds, and also a little from the victim's mouth.

The bleeding had not been so moderate, I thought, that both of Mitchell's wellington boots hadn't been able to walk in it.

The pathologist conceded that considerable force would have been needed to cause the fatal injury but, as he said, probably less than that needed to go through the rib cage, where there would have been the risk of one of the fork's prongs hitting and bouncing off a rib. The prosecution counsel then established without difficulty that a fit man of thirty-three, especially one who was a professional sportsman, would have easily had the strength required to deliver the fatal blow, even if he did only stand five foot six inches tall in his socks.

'Had the murder weapon been withdrawn from the victim after death?' I asked him in cross-examination.

'No,' he said. 'When I was first called to the scene, I found the pitchfork still stuck very firmly into Mr Barlow – so firmly, in fact, that it proved impossible to remove at the scene. And I later determined that the puncture wounds to his abdomen, his diaphragm and his heart were all consistent with the weapon having been inserted into the body just once.'

'So anything found on the prongs of the fork between Mr Barlow's body and the fork handle would have had to have been there prior to the fatal blow being struck?'

'Indeed,' he said.

'And was there anything on the prongs?' I prompted him.

'Yes,' he said. 'There were some pieces of paper.'

'Debit card receipts, I believe?' I said.

'I'm not aware of what they were, just that they were present,' he said. 'They were taken away by the police during the post-mortem examination at the Royal Berkshire Hospital in Reading, when the murder weapon was finally removed from the body.'

I could only imagine the trouble someone must have had in transporting Barlow's dead body the twenty-six miles from his kitchen floor to the Royal Berkshire Hospital mortuary with a five-foot-long pitchfork firmly embedded in its chest.

The judge adjourned early for the day at four o'clock.

Eleanor didn't come to Oxford on Tuesday night either. There was a message from her on my mobile after the adjournment explaining that one of her colleagues was ill and she had to stay in Lambourn to cover for her. Again, strangely, I was somewhat relieved.

Perhaps it was the expectation, her expectation, that worried me most. It had been a long time since I had slept with anyone, and then it had been Angela, with whom I had been familiar, relaxed and comfortable. Suddenly the prospect of someone new between my sheets filled me with apprehension and worry. Stop being stupid, I said to myself, but the nagging fear of failure and rejection still persisted.

There were, in fact, two messages on my phone.

The other one was from the whisperer.

'Lose the case,' he whispered. 'Or else.'

The message had been left at twelve noon that day. No doubt shortly after Julian Trent had reported back to him on the court proceedings and my determined efforts to undermine the police inspector. How long would it take the whisperer to work out, I wondered, that I became more and more determined to win every time he told me to lose?

I hadn't been outside the court at lunchtime for fear of running into young Mr Trent. Now, at the end of the day, I waited in the courthouse lobby until I saw my taxi pull up close to the doors before I emerged. Most of my boxes remained in the court secure storage overnight but I had one with me in order to prepare for the following day's witnesses.

I clambered into the taxi with my box and crutches and made it safely, unmolested, back to my hotel.

The reception staff thought me a little crazy when I insisted that under no circumstances were they to give my room number to anyone, not even, I said, if they tell you they're my father. And, also, they were not to put any calls through to my room without asking the caller for their name, and telling me that first.

I also asked them how many rooms were free in the hotel for the night.

'Twelve,' one of the female staff said.

'Then could I please change rooms from last night?' I asked.

'Didn't you like your room, sir?' she said.

'It was fine,' I said. 'I would just like to have another one tonight.'

'I will have to check with my manager,' she said. 'The old room would then need to be cleaned and the staff have left for the day.'

'Could it not be left until tomorrow?' I said.

'But then, sir, we couldn't let it tonight, could we?' She was being rather condescending, I thought.

I decided not to mention that, with twelve rooms still unreserved at five o'clock in the afternoon, it was unlikely that they would all be needed.

She went out the back to consult and returned to tell me that it would be fine to move but I would need to pay a late check-out fee on the first room.

'Right, then,' I said to her. 'Can you please arrange a taxi to take me to the Randolph?'

She rapidly disappeared out the back again. A man in a suit, presumably the manager, came out from his office.

'Mr Mason,' he said. 'I'm sorry about the confusion. Of course you may change rooms if you wish. There will be no extra charge.'

'Fine,' I said. 'Would you please send a porter up for my things?'

'Which room would you like to have?' he said.

'One at the Randolph,' I replied.

'Now Mr Mason,' he said with a smile. 'I am sure we can come to an arrangement.'

We did. I secured a twenty per cent discount on the room rate, backdated to last Friday, together with a complimentary bottle of red wine to be sent up to my new room. It really was useful, sometimes, to be trained in advocacy.

In truth, I didn't really want to move hotels at all. I knew the Randolph, and I liked it, but the converted modern interior of this place made it much easier for me to cope with the crutches even if the room doors were rather narrow as they had been the cell doors of the old prison.

Having settled in to my new room, I lay on the bed with a glass of wine and started reading through the papers for the next day.

The phone rang. I answered it.

'Mr Mason? This is the hotel operator. I have a Miss Clarke on the phone for you. Will you accept the call?

Miss Clarke? Who was Miss Clarke?

Suddenly I remembered. 'Oh yes, thank you,' I said to the operator.

'What's all that about?' Eleanor asked when she was put through.

'Just my way of screening unwanted calls,' I said cheerfully.

'And have you had any?' she asked me seriously.

'One or two,' I said.

'From Julian Trent?' she said.

'From whoever is behind him,' I said.

'You take care,' she ordered.

'You take care too,' I said. 'Remember, he knows where you live. Don't go anywhere on your own. Not even across to the hospital from your house.'

'Surely I'm safe enough here?' she said.

'Trent attacked me within five yards of the front door of my chambers,' I said. 'Please don't assume anything when it comes to this man. He's very dangerous.'

'Stop it. You're frightening me,' she said.

'Good,' I said. 'Be frightened. Be very frightened. I am.'

'OK, OK,' she said. 'You've made your point.'

'Are you sure you can't come over here?' I said. 'I would be much happier if you were here with me.'

'Now, now, Mister Barrister Man, don't be too eager.' She laughed.

'I really meant for your security,' I said seriously.

'You really do mean it, don't you?' she said.

'Yes. I do. You have no idea how frightening these people are until it's too late. Remember what they did to my house.'

There was a long pause at the other end of the line.

'How are we ever going to be free of them?' she said.

'I'm working on it,' I said. But I didn't know how either.

Detective Constable Hillier, the young policeman I had first met at Barlow's house with Bruce Lygon, was the next witness for the prosecution when the court reconvened at ten thirty on Wednesday morning.

I had kept my eyes open for Julian Trent as I had arrived at the court building but there had been no sign of him. Somewhat perversely, I had rather hoped that he would be there, as it meant he wouldn't have been elsewhere delivering mayhem to my loved ones or their property. Now, I simply worried.

DC Hillier proved to be a model witness for the Crown, stating clearly and persuasively to the jury how the murder weapon was found to be identical to two other pitchforks found at Mitchell's property and how further investigations had discovered a receipt from a Newbury supplier showing that Mitchell had purchased three of the forks the previous year.

He went on to describe how he had ascertained that the debit card receipts, found impaled on the prongs of the fork between Mr Barlow's body and the fork handle, were from a Maestro debit card issued by Lloyds Bank in the name of Mr Stephen Mitchell. Furthermore, the said debit card receipts were from payments made by Mr Mitchell to a licensed bookmaker based in Hungerford.

'Detective Constable Hillier,' I said, starting my cross-examination. 'Do you not think it is strange that a murderer would leave incriminating debit card receipts with his name on them at the scene of the crime?'

'No, not particularly,' he said nonchalantly. 'Many criminals do strange things.'

'But did you not suspect that the receipts had been left on the fork by someone who simply wanted the police to believe that Mr Mitchell had been responsible for the crime?'

'Not really,' he said. 'Perhaps Mitchell put them on the fork to goad Barlow and he hadn't really intended leaving them behind. Maybe he just panicked, or perhaps he couldn't get the murder weapon out of the body to remove them, or indeed to take the fork back home with him.'

'This is conjecture,' interrupted the judge. 'The witness will confine himself to the facts he knows, rather than those he can merely speculate about.'

'Sorry, Your Honour,' said DC Hillier. But the damage had already been done.

I thought of further pointing out that the murderer could surely have ripped the receipts away from the fork without removing it from Barlow's body if, of course, he'd actually wanted to, but this whole line of questioning clearly wasn't helping our case so I let it go.

The next witness was the Hungerford bookmaker who confirmed that the receipts had been issued by the card machine at his premises.

'And are you aware,' the prosecuting counsel said to him, 'that betting on horse racing by a professional jockey is against the Rules of Racing?'

'Yes,' he said. 'I am aware of that.'

'But you took the bets anyway?' the QC asked.

'Yes,' said the bookmaker. 'It was not against either the terms of my permit or the licence of my premises.'

'Was it a regular arrangement with Mr Mitchell?'

'Fairly regular,' the bookmaker replied.

I started to rise but the judge beat me to it.

'Is the regularity of any significance?' he asked the prosecutor.

'Perhaps not, My Lord,' said the QC.

The bookmaker was dismissed. I could have asked him if he regularly took bets from other jockeys but that also wouldn't have been significant, and would probably have antagonized him and the jury unnecessarily, so I didn't. I had no reason to think that he had taken bets from Scot Barlow, so I didn't ask him that either. As for how Steve Mitchell's debit card receipts had found their way onto the pitchfork was anyone's guess. Steve still, unbelievably, refused to comment on the matter, but he wasn't here being tried for gambling in contravention of the Rules of Racing, he was being tried for murder.

'You have one new message,' said my voicemail when I turned my phone on at lunchtime. It was from Nikki Payne.

'Mr Mason,' her disembodied voice said in some excitement. 'I've found your Jacques van Rensburg, or at least I've found out who he is. Call me back when you get this message.'

I called her immediately.

'He was the third one,' she said in a rush. 'They sent his passport photo over from South Africa and there was no mistake.'

'So he's still somewhere here with an expired visa?' I asked.

'Well, no,' she said. 'Not exactly.' She then went on to give me some very interesting information about Mr Jacques van Rensburg, information that explained why the photograph of Millie and the foal had been important. So important that someone had taken it from Scot Barlow's house. Maybe so important, indeed, that Barlow had been murdered to get it.

CHAPTER 17

The afternoon sitting of the court was taken up almost exclusively by witnesses called by the prosecution to testify about the well-known antagonism, even hatred, that had existed between the defendant and the victim for some time.

Any hopes that we, the defence, had of keeping quiet about Barlow's sister Millie were dispelled by the very first on the list, Charles Pickering, a racehorse trainer from Lambourn.

'Mr Pickering,' said the prosecution QC, 'how well did you know Mr Barlow?'

'Very well indeed,' he replied. 'I knew him like my own son. Scot had ridden for me as number one jockey ever since he came down south from Scotland eight years ago. He lived as a member of my family for a while when he first started out.'

'And how well do you know the defendant, Mr Mitchell?'

'Reasonably well,' he said. 'He's ridden my horses a few times, when Scot was unavailable or injured. And I know him by reputation. He's a top steeplechase jockey.'

'Yes, Mr Pickering,' said the QC. 'But please tell us only what you know personally rather than what you assume from a reputation.'

Charles Pickering nodded.

'Now, Mr Pickering,' the QC went on. 'Did you ever hear Mr Mitchell and Mr Barlow arguing?'

'All the time,' he said. 'Like cat and dog, they were.'

'So there was no love lost between them?'

'I should say not,' replied Pickering with a smile.

'Do you know what they argued about?'

'Scot's sister, mostly,' said Charles Pickering, firing another shot into the defence case.

'Scot Barlow's sister?' the QC said for effect, turning towards the jury.

'Yes,' Pickering said. 'Scot accused Mitchell of as good as killing his sister. Mitchell used to tell him to shut up or he'd kill him too.'

'Were those his exact words?'

'Absolutely,' he said. 'It was the same argument every time. Scot's sister had killed herself about a year ago and he believed that Mitchell's treatment of her had driven her to it.'

'Were Barlow and Mitchell on reasonable terms before Barlow's sister killed herself?' the QC asked, while knowing quite well what the answer would be.

'Oh, no,' said Pickering. 'They've hated each other for years. Scot didn't like Mitchell seeing his sister at all, right from the start.'

'And when was the start?' the QC asked.

'About three or four years ago, when Barlow's sister came down from Scotland to live in Lambourn.'

'Thank you, Mr Pickering,' said the QC. 'Your witness.' He smiled at me.

'No questions, My Lord,' I said. And Charles Pickering was allowed to depart.

There was nothing I could ask him which would undo the

damage he had already done to our case, and I didn't want to inadvertently lead him to reveal more damning details such as Barlow's disclosure of the affair to Mitchell's wife. Now that really would have provided a motive for murder.

However, my hopes of keeping that a secret only lasted as long as it took for the next witness to be sworn in.

'Mr Clemens,' said the QC. 'I believe you are a steeplechase jockey, is that correct?'

'Yes, sir. That's correct,' said Reno Clemens in his Irish accent.

'Are you a successful jockey?' the QC asked.

'I am, sir,' Reno said. 'I am leading the jockeys' table at the moment.'

'So that means you have ridden more winners than anyone else so far this year?'

'This season, yes, sir,' he said.

'So you know the defendant well?'

'Yes, sir.' He glanced briefly at Steve in the dock before returning his eyes to the prosecuting counsel.

'And you knew Mr Barlow well?'

'Yes, sir. I did.'

'Did you ever hear Mr Mitchell and Mr Barlow arguing?' the QC asked.

'Were they ever not?' said Reno. 'Sometimes they would even argue all the way round during a race. The rest of us got fed up listening to them.'

'And what did they argue about?' asked the QC.

'Anything and everything,' said Reno. 'But mostly about Barlow's sister and Mitchell having had an affair with her.'

'And was Mitchell married at the time of the affair?' asked the QC.

Oh no, I thought, here we go.

'He was at the beginning,' said Reno. 'But not at the end.'

'Do you know if Mitchell's wife was aware of his affair with Scot Barlow's sister?' the QC asked almost smugly.

'She was after Barlow told her,' Reno said.

'Is that something you know, Mr Clemens, or just something you have heard from others?'

'I heard it from Mitchell himself,' Reno said. 'He would often shout at Barlow in the jocks' changing room and accuse him of being a Judas for snitching to his wife.'

'You bloody lying bastard,' Steve Mitchell stood up and shouted at him from the dock, hammering on the glass partition with his fists.

The judge had his gavel banging down almost before the echo in the courtroom had died away.

'Silence,' he ordered. 'Silence in court. Mr Mitchell,' he pointed the gavel at the dock, 'another outburst like that and I will have you taken down to the cells. Do you understand?'

'Yes, My Lord,' said Steve sheepishly. 'I'm sorry.'

Steve sat down again. But more damage had been done to our side.

The prosecution QC had remained standing throughout, and now he had a slight smirk on his face.

'Now, Mr Clemens,' he said, greatly enjoying himself. 'Let me get this straight. Are you telling the court that you had often heard the defendant shouting at Mr Barlow that he, Barlow, had been a Judas for telling Mitchell's wife that Mitchell was having an affair with Barlow's sister?'

'Yes, sir,' said Reno Clemens very distinctly. 'I am.'

A motive for Barlow's murder had just been clearly established by the prosecution.

*

Two more prosecution witnesses completed the day's proceedings. Both of these gave testimony to reinforce that already given by Charles Pickering and Reno Clemens.

The first was another jockey, Sandy Webster, who did little more than confirm that Mitchell and Barlow argued a lot. When asked what they had argued about he couldn't really say because 'he didn't bother to listen to them ranting on all the time'.

I imagined the prosecution was regretting having called him because he was so nervous that his voice was continuously quivering, and he was hardly giving them the answers they wanted. In my experience, witnesses who were over nervous tended to be discounted by juries, who were inclined to think they were lying.

The second witness was Fred Pleat, a former employee of Mitchell, who had worked as a groom at Mitchell's home soon after the stables were built and when horses were housed there at livery.

'Now, Mr Pleat,' said the prosecution QC in his smarmy manner. 'Were you present at Mr Mitchell's property the day three new pitchforks were delivered?'

'Yes, I was,' he replied.

'And can you recall the actions of Mr Mitchell when he saw that they had been delivered?'

'Yes,' he said again. 'Steve, that's Mr Mitchell, picked one of them up and thrust it forward and said something about sticking that bastard Scot Barlow with it.'

There was a moment of silence in the court.

'Thank you, Mr Pleat,' said the QC. 'Your witness.'

I rose to my foot.

'Mr Pleat,' I said to him. 'Were you frightened by this action you say Mr Mitchell performed?'

'No,' he said.

'Why not?' I asked him.

'I figured Steve was only joking, like,' he said. 'He was laughing. We were both laughing.'

'Thank you, Mr Pleat,' I said. 'No more questions.'

Fred Pleat left the court and, as a bonus to our side, he gave Steve a slight wave as he passed the dock. I hoped the jury had been watching.

'My Lord, that concludes the case for the prosecution,' said their QC.

The judge looked at the clock on the courtroom wall that showed ten past four, then he turned towards the jury.

'Ladies and gentlemen of the jury,' he said. 'You are free to go now until tomorrow morning at ten o'clock. May I remind you not to discuss the case amongst yourselves, nor with anybody else, not even your families. You will get your chance to deliberate in due course.'

The jury was then ushered out of court.

'Mr Mason,' the judge said when the jury door had been closed. I had earlier informed the judge that I wished to make a submission at the conclusion of the prosecution's case, and members of the jury were never present in court during legal argument.

'Yes, My Lord,' I said, struggling upright. 'Thank you.' I collected together some papers in front of me. 'My Lord, the defence wishes to make a submission to the court that the defendant has no case to answer. The prosecution have presented nothing more than circumstantial evidence. There is nothing to show that my client was ever in Mr Barlow's house, let alone being there at the time of the murder.'

I took my time going over each of the witnesses' evidence in some detail.

'In conclusion,' I said. 'The forensic evidence may be able to place my client's pitchfork and wellington boots at the scene, but this does not prove that my client was there with them at the time. The prosecution may also be able to show that hair and blood from the victim were found in my client's car, but they were not able to demonstrate that the car had ever been at Mr Barlow's residence, nor that it had been locked throughout the afternoon and early evening on the day of the murder, while it sat on Mr Mitchell's driveway.

'While the defence readily accepts that our client and Mr Barlow held an ongoing and deep-seated antagonism towards each other, this is not evidence of murder. If it were, then half the nation would be so tainted. The defence further accepts that our client does not have an alibi for the time of the murder, but failure to have an alibi is not evidence of guilt. It is our contention that the prosecution has failed to present prima facie evidence of Mr Mitchell's guilt. My Lord, we submit that you should direct the jury to return a not guilty verdict because there is no case for Mr Mitchell to answer.'

I sat down.

'Thank you, Mr Mason,' said the judge. 'I will consider your submission overnight and make a ruling in the morning. Court adjourned until ten o'clock tomorrow.'

'All rise.'

Eleanor finally did come to Oxford on Wednesday night. She was waiting for me in the dimly lit hotel lobby when I returned from court. I hadn't expected her to be so early, and I was worried that there might be a message for me giving yet another good reason why she couldn't make it tonight either. So I was caught unawares as I struggled with both my box of papers and the crutches. She came up behind me and took the box just before it dropped to the floor.

'Oh, thank you,' I said, thinking it had been one of the hotel staff.

Eleanor peeped at me round the side of the box.

'Hello,' I said with a grin from ear to ear. 'How absolutely wonderful. You can catch my boxes any day you like.'

'I thought I'd surprise you,' she said. 'I've been here more than an hour.'

'Blimey,' I said. 'If I'd known that I would have been here more than an hour ago.'

'Why weren't you?' she said in mock annoyance.

'I was busy telling my client what a complete fool he'd been,' I said.

'Why?' she said.

'He shouted at one of the witnesses,' I said. 'What an idiot!'

I had indeed spent the last hour giving Steve a roasting in the holding cells beneath the court.

'I'm sorry,' Steve had whined at me. 'I couldn't help it. I was so mad. That bloody Clemens has been riding all my horses. He'd be delighted if I got convicted. Be laughing all the way to the bloody winner's circle.'

'But you still mustn't do it,' I had urged him again. 'It is the very worst thing you could have done and now the judge has to make a decision about whether we carry on with the trial or if he lets you go, and he will not have been impressed by your actions. You showed him your temper. He might just think that your temper has something to do with the murder.'

'I'm sorry,' he had said again.

'And,' I had said, rubbing salt into his wound, 'Clemens wasn't even lying when you shouted at him. You have often said that Barlow was a Judas. I've heard you myself in the changing rooms.'

Steve had sat on the bare wooden chair in the cell looking very shamefaced. For a change, he'd seemed quite pleased when the prison officer had unlocked the cell door to say that the transport was ready and he had to go. Perhaps I had been a little hard on him but, if the trial were to continue, I needed him to remain sitting calmly and silently in the dock, no matter what the provocation.

Eleanor now leaned forward and gave me a brief kiss on the lips.

'Do you want to go for a drink?' I asked her. 'It's nearly six.'

'No,' she said emphatically. 'I want to go to bed.'

In the end we did both.

I ordered a bottle of champagne and two glasses from the bar to take up to my room.

'I've never made love in a prison before,' said Eleanor excitedly as we came out of the lift onto one of the galleried landings of 'A' wing. 'In fact, I've never even been in a prison before.'

'They're not usually like this,' I said. 'For a start, they always smell dreadful. A mixture of disinfectant and stale BO. Never enough showers.'

'Ugh,' she said.

All my apprehension about this encounter came flooding back with a vengeance and I was shaking like a leaf by the time we had negotiated the long gallery to my room, so much so that I couldn't even get the cork out of the champagne bottle.

'Here,' said Eleanor taking it from my trembling hands. 'Let me do that.' She poured the golden bubbling liquid into the two tall flutes. 'My, we are a nervous boy,' she said as I took the glass with a tremor.

'I'm sorry,' I said.

'Don't be,' she said. 'I'm pretty nervous, too.'

I sat on the edge of the bed, kicked off my shoes and lay down, putting my feet up on the bedcovers. I tapped the hard plastic shell beneath my shirt.

'This damn thing doesn't help either,' I said.

'Let me look after you,' she said, coming over and lying down beside me.

And she did.

All my apprehension drifted away to nothing and all my fears were unfounded. Maybe it really was like riding a bicycle, I thought. Once you had learned the knack you never forgot it.

Eleanor helped ease my itchy body out of the plastic straightjacket and also out of my clothes. I lay naked on the bed as she washed and cooled me using damp towels from the bathroom, and then she herself stripped off and climbed in beside me, between the sheets.

Making love with a broken back is, by necessity, a gentle and tender process. But we discovered it could also be a sensual and passionate one.

Afterwards, we lay entwined together for a while, drifting in and out of light sleep. I would have been so happy to stay like that all night but I needed to do some reading, ready for the morning.

I rolled over gently to look at the digital clock on the bedside cabinet. Seven forty-five. I tried to ease myself up, although it was against my back surgeon's rules. Eleanor stirred as I tried to remove my arm from beneath her waist.

'Hello,' she said, smiling up at me. 'Going somewhere already?'

'Yup,' I said, smiling back. 'Got to get back to my wife.'

She suddenly looked alarmed, but relaxed when she saw I was joking.

'You kidder,' she said, snuggling into my chest.

'But I really do need to get back to my work,' I said. 'I have to be prepared for tomorrow. And, what's more, I'm hungry.'

'I'm hungry for you,' Eleanor said back to me, seductively fluttering her eyelashes.

'Later, dear. Later,' I said. 'Man cannot live by sex alone.'

'But we could try,' she said. Then she sighed and rolled off my arm, releasing me.

She helped me back into my plastic corset and then into a towelling robe.

'Let's have some room service,' I said. 'Then I can work and eat.'

Eleanor called down for the food while I set about looking through the papers that I would need in the event that the judge did not rule in our favour over the defence submission. To be honest, I didn't really expect him to. Even though much of it was circumstantial, there was probably enough evidence to convict, and certainly enough to leave the question to the jury.

If it was in the balance, the judge might simply allow the trial to continue because the decision was then taken out of his hands and passed to the jury. And Steve Mitchell's conduct during the afternoon had almost certainly not endeared him to the judge – not that that should be a consideration, but it probably would be.

Since the Criminal Justice Act 2003 had come into force, the prosecution had the right to appeal rulings by judges over whether there was a case to answer, and, in my experience, judges had since become less inclined to so rule for fear of having their decision overturned on appeal.

All in all, I wasn't too hopeful, and so I still had to do my homework.

However, over our room-service dinner, eaten in our bathrobes, I told Eleanor about the news I had heard from Nikki at lunchtime.

'What are you going to do about it?' she asked.

I explained to her about the defence submission I had made to the court at the end of the prosecution case.

'If the judge doesn't rule in our favour in the morning,' I said, 'and I don't think he will, I intend calling a couple of witnesses to explore what Nikki found out.'

'Can you call anyone you like as a witness?' she asked.

'Yes and no,' I said.

'Explain,' she said.

'I can call whoever I like as long as their evidence is relevant to the case,' I said. 'But if I'm going to call the defendant as a witness, I have to call him first. I couldn't call someone else first and then go back to Steve. But I don't think I'll be calling him anyway in this case. He's a bit too volatile. And our defence is that he's being framed, so all he could say is that he didn't do it, and he knew nothing about it, and I can say that to the jury anyway.'

I paused to take a mouthful of my dinner.

'I did think about calling character witnesses but I'm not sure that would be a good idea. Steve's character is hardly as pure as the driven snow.'

'You can say that again,' she said. And she should know.

'I asked my solicitor, Bruce Lygon, to contact both my new witnesses this afternoon,' I said. 'I am still waiting to hear what he says but I fully expect that at least one of them won't want to come to court.'

'But what happens then?' Eleanor asked.

'In the end, they don't get any choice in the matter,' I said. 'I can apply to the court for a witness summons which is then served on the potential witnesses and then they have to be there. If they don't turn up, the judge can issue a warrant for their arrest.'

'But surely that doesn't mean they also have to answer your questions.'

'No,' I agreed. 'But if they don't, they have to give a reason not to answer, and the only reason here would be that in doing so they might incriminate themselves. And that should, at least, do some good as it ought to put some doubt into the minds of the jury as to Steve's guilt.' I took another mouthful. 'But what I really need is time. Time to get the witnesses I need to court, but mostly time for more investigating.'

'And what will you do if the judge doesn't give you time?' she asked.

'Probably lose the case,' I said.

At least Julian Trent would then be pleased.

CHAPTER 18

As I had expected, on the Thursday morning at two minutes past ten, and prior to the arrival of the jury in the courtroom, the trial judge rejected the defence submission that there was no case to answer.

'If it then please My Lord,' I said, standing up. 'The defence would like to submit a list of witnesses we wish to be summonsed.'

'And how many witnesses are there on this list, Mr Mason?' the judge asked rather sternly.

'Initially I have two names, My Lord,' I said, picking up a sheet of paper. 'But there may be more, depending on the evidence of these witnesses.'

I passed the paper to the court usher who delivered it to the judge. He looked down at its brief contents.

'Why have these names not been previously submitted to the court, so that summonses might have been issued to them in good time?' he asked me.

'My Lord,' I said. 'Information came to our knowledge only yesterday which indicates that these witnesses are essential to our case.'

'And how is that?' he asked.

'Our case, My Lord,' I said, 'as detailed in the Defence Case Statement, previously submitted to the court, is that the defendant is innocent of the charges and that he is being framed for a crime he did not commit. In the light of fresh information, the defence now wishes to further this argument by calling these witnesses.

'My Lord,' I continued. 'Mr Mitchell's solicitor made an attempt to contact these potential witnesses during yesterday afternoon and evening. One of them indicated verbally to the solicitor that they had no wish, or intention, of attending court to assist the defence in this matter. Consequently, I would like to apply to the court for a witness summons.'

'How about the other?' asked the judge.

'As yet we have been unable to contact the second one, My Lord,' I said. 'But I have every reason to expect the same outcome.'

'Mr Mason,' said the judge. 'Have you shown your list to the prosecution?'

'I have, My Lord,' I said. 'I gave a copy to my learned friend just prior to the court sitting this morning.'

The judge invited the prosecution to respond to the request.

'My Lord,' said the smarmy prosecution QC. 'The prosecution has no objection to the summonsing of these witnesses if it is likely to aid justice. However, the defence has had ample time to prepare for this case and further procrastination should not be tolerated.'

Or in other words, I thought, we don't object but, oh yes, we do after all. Anything to sound reasonable, while not actually being so.

The judge, God bless him, chose to hear only the first part of the QC's statement.

'Very well,' he said. 'As the prosecution have no objection, I will allow a witness summons to be issued for each name. But be warned, Mr Mason, I will take a firm line if I consider that the defence is in any way wasting the court's time. Do I make myself clear?'

'Absolutely, My Lord,' I said.

'Will these witnesses be ready to be examined by this afternoon?' asked the judge.

'My lord,' said the prosecution QC rising rapidly to his feet. 'The prosecution requests more time to consider the names of these witnesses and to prepare for cross-examination.'

It was exactly as I had hoped, because I was not in any position to call my witnesses. Not yet, anyway.

'Would you be ready by tomorrow?' asked the judge.

'We would prefer Monday, My Lord,' said the smarmy QC.

'Any objection, Mr Mason?' asked the judge.

'No, My Lord,' I said, trying hard to keep a grin off my face. 'No objection.'

'Very well,' said the judge. He was probably already looking forward to an extra day on the golf course. 'Court is adjourned until ten o'clock on Monday morning.'

Excellent, I thought. Just what I had wanted, and just what I needed.

I ordered a taxi to take all my papers back to the hotel. I had previously been to the court office to get the witness summonses issued for Monday, and Bruce Lygon had departed eagerly to try and personally deliver them into the correct hands.

As I waited inside the court building lobby, I called Nikki.

'I now have the documentation,' she said excitedly. 'It all came through this morning.'

'Great,' I said. 'Now I have something else for you to do.'

'Fire away,' she said.

'I need you to go to Newbury to ask some more questions,' I said.

'No problem,' she replied.

I explained to her exactly what information I wanted her to find out, and where to get it.

'Right,' she said. 'Call you later.'

She hung up as my taxi arrived.

The taxi took me to the hotel and then waited as the porter carried all the boxes up to my room and I packed a few clothes into one of my new suitcases. Then the taxi took me and my suitcase to Oxford station, where we caught a fast train to London.

'What are you doing here?' asked Arthur as I walked into chambers soon after noon.

'The case has been adjourned until Monday,' I said. 'Perhaps Sir James will be ready to take over from me by then.'

'Er,' said Arthur, floundering. 'I believe that his case is still running on.'

'Arthur,' I said sarcastically. 'I pay you to lie *for* me, not *to* me.'

'Sir James pays me more than you do,' he said with a smile.

'Just so long as we know where we stand,' I said.

I had no intention of telling Sir James Horley anything about my new witnesses. The last thing I wanted was for him to now feel that the case wasn't such a lost cause after all, and for him to step back in and hog all the limelight. No way was I going to let that happen.

I went through to my room and set about looking a few things up in my case files and then I telephoned Bob, the driver from the car comapny. I urgently needed some transportation.

'I'll be there in about half an hour,' he said.

'Fine,' I said. 'I have some more calls to make anyway.'

One of them was to my father on the new mobile phone I had bought him.

'Having a nice time?' I asked him.

'I suppose so,' he said, rather reluctantly. 'But everyone else here is so old.' Just like him, I thought, rather unkindly.

I had sent him to the seaside, to stay in the Victoria Hotel in Sidmouth, Devon, where he could walk along the beach each day and get plenty of healthy fresh air, and where, I hoped, Julian Trent wouldn't think of looking for him.

Next I called Weatherbys, the company that administered British horse racing, the company that had paid Scot Barlow his riding fees as detailed on his bank statements. I needed some different information from them this time and they were most helpful in giving me the answers.

I also called Eleanor and left a message on her mobile phone.

She had left the Oxford hotel early in the morning to get back to work in Lambourn, but not so early that we hadn't had time for a repeat of the previous evening's lovemaking.

She called me back on my mobile as Bob drove me away from chambers.

'I got my time from the judge,' I said to her. 'And the witness summonses, too.'

'Well done you,' she replied.

'I'm in London,' I said. 'The judge adjourned until Monday morning. I've already been to my chambers, and I'm now on my way to Barnes to face the mess. And I'll probably stay there tonight.'

'I won't plan to go to Oxford, then,' she said, laughing.

'No,' I said. 'I won't be back there until Sunday night.'

'Sunday night!' she said. 'Don't I get to see you before then?'

'You could always come to London,' I said.

'I'm on call again,' she said.

'Isn't anyone else ever on call?' I asked.

'It's only for tonight,' she said. 'I could come tomorrow.'

'I have plans for during the day tomorrow,' I said. 'And then I thought I'd come down to you for the night, if that's OK.'

'Great by me,' she said.

The state of my home was worse than I had remembered. The stuff from the fridge that Trent had poured all over the kitchen had started to smell badly. It had been a warm May week with plenty of sunshine having streamed through the large windows into the airless space. The whole place reeked of rotting food.

I was sorry for my downstairs neighbours for having to live beneath it all for the past week, and I hoped for their sake that smells rose upwards like hot air.

I opened all the windows and let some fresh air in, which was a major improvement. Next I found an industrial cleaning company in the Yellow Pages and promised them a huge bonus if they would come round instantly to do an emergency clear-up job. No problem, they said, for a price, a very high price.

While I waited for them I used a whole can of air freshener that I found, undisturbed, beneath the kitchen sink. The lavender scent did its best to camouflage the stink of decomposing fish and rancid milk, but it was fighting a losing battle.

A team of four arrived from the cleaning company. They didn't seem to be fazed one bit by the mess that, to my eyes, was still appalling.

'Had a teenager's party?' one of them asked in all seriousness.

'No,' I said. 'It was malicious vandalism.'

'Same thing,' he said, laughing. 'Now, is there anything you want to keep from this lot?' He waved a hand around.

'Don't throw out anything that looks unbroken,' I said. 'And keep all the paperwork, whatever condition it's in.'

'Right,' he said. He gave directions to his team and they set to work.

I was amazed at how quickly things began to improve. Two of them set to work with mops, cloths and brooms, while the other two removed the torn and broken furniture and stacked it on the back of their vehicle outside.

Within just a few hours the place was unrecognizable from the disgusting state that I had returned to. Most of the furniture was out, and the carpets and rugs had been pulled up. The kitchen had been transformed from a major health hazard into gleaming chrome and a sparkling floor. Maybe they couldn't mend the cracks in the marble worktops, but they did almost everything else.

'Right, then,' said the team leader finally. 'That wasn't too bad. No rats or anything. And no human remains.'

'Human remains?' I said, surprised.

'Nasty stuff,' he said. 'All too often these jobs involve cleaning places where old people have died and no one notices until the smell gets so bad.'

I shivered. 'What a job,' I said.

'Pays well,' he said.

'Ah, yes,' I said. 'Didn't find my chequebook did you?'

'All your paperwork's over there,' he said, pointing at a couple of large cardboard boxes sitting alone on the floor. Amazingly, my chequebook had survived, and was only slightly stained by the red wine.

I wrote him out a cheque for the agreed exorbitant amount and then they departed, taking with them most of my worldly goods to be delivered to the council dump.

I wandered aimlessly around my house, examining what remained. There was remarkably little. The cleaners had put cardboard boxes in each of the rooms, into which they had placed anything left unbroken. In my bedroom, the box merely contained a few trinkets and some old perfume bottles that had stood on Angela's dressing table. Other than the fitted wardrobe, the dressing table was the only piece of furniture remaining in the room, and that was only because I couldn't bear to see it go. I had asked the men to return it to the bedroom when I had caught sight of them loading it onto their truck.

Angela had sat for hours in front of its now-broken triple mirror every morning, drying her hair and fixing her make-up. She had loved its simplicity and, I discovered, it was too much of a wrench to see it taken away, in spite of the broken mirror on top and the snapped-off leg below.

My bed had gone, Julian Trent's knife having cut not only the mattress to ribbons, but the divan base beneath as well. In the sitting room everything had been swept away to the tip. Only a couple of dining chairs and the chrome kitchen stool had survived intact, although I had also kept back the antique dining-room table in the hope that a French polisher could do something about the myriad of Stanley-knife grooves that had been cut into its polished surface. I had also saved my desk from the dump to see if a furniture restorer could do anything about the green embossed panel that had once been inlaid into its surface but which now was twisted and cut through, the sliced edges of the leather curled upwards like waves in a rough sea.

The trip back to Barnes had been necessary and worthwhile. Not only had I managed to bring some semblance of order to my remaining belongings, but my hatred and contempt for Julian Trent had been rekindled. There was fire in my belly and I aimed to consume him with it.

I decided not to spend the night at Ranelagh Avenue as there was nothing left for me to sleep on, other than the floor, and I didn't fancy that. At about six o'clock I ordered a taxi and booked myself into the West London Novotel, overlooking Hammersmith flyover.

I lay on the bed in the room for a while idly watching the continuous stream of aircraft on their approach into London's Heathrow airport. One every minute or so, non-stop, like a conveyor belt, each aluminium tube in turn full of people with lives to lead, places to go, each of them with families and friends, wives and husbands, lovers and admirers.

I thought about other eyes that might also have been watching the same aircraft. Some of my past clients, plus a few that I had prosecuted, were housed at Her Majesty's expense in Wormwood Scrubs Prison, just up the road from the hotel.

At least I was able, if I wished, to join the throng in the air, coming or going on holiday to anywhere in the world I liked. Depriving someone of their liberty by sending them to prison may rob them of their self-respect, but, mostly, it deprives them of choice. The choice to go where and when they please, and the choice to do what they want when they get there. To lose that is the price one pays for wrongdoing, and for getting caught.

As I watched those aircraft, and their apparent freedom from the bounds of earth, I resolved once more to release Steve Mitchell from the threat of a lifetime spent watching the world pass him by through the bars of a prison window.

Bob collected me in the silver Mercedes at eight-thirty on Friday morning, and we set off northwards from Hammersmith to Golders Green.

Josef Hughes was waiting for us when we arrived at 845 Finchley Road. I hadn't been very confident that he would be there, firstly because I'd had to leave a message for him with someone else in the house using the payphone in the hallway, and secondly because I had real doubts that he would be prepared to help me. But, thankfully, my fears were unfounded as he came quickly across the pavement and climbed into the back seat of the car.

'Morning, Josef,' I said to him, turning round as best I could and smiling.

He continued to peer all around him, sweeping his eyes and head from side to side. It was the frightened look that I had come to know so well.

'Morning,' he said to me only after we had driven away. He turned to glance a few more times through the rear window and then finally settled into his seat.

'This is Bob,' I said, pointing at our driver. 'Bob is most definitely on our side.' Bob looked at me somewhat strangely but I ignored him.

'Where to now?' Bob asked me.

'Hendon,' I said.

We picked up George Barnett from outside the Hendon bus station as he had requested. He didn't want me going near his home, he'd said, in case anyone was watching. He, too, looked all around him as he climbed into the car.

I introduced him to Bob, and also to Josef.

'Where now?' asked Bob. I purposely hadn't told any of them where we were going.

'Weybridge,' I said to him.

Josef visibly tensed. He didn't like it, and the closer we came to Weybridge the more agitated he became.

'Josef,' I said calmly. 'All I want is for you to point out where you were told to go and tell the solicitor about approaching the members of the jury in the first Trent trial. We will just drive past. I don't expect you to go back in there yourself.'

He mumbled something about wishing he hadn't come. The long finger of fear extended by Julian Trent and his allies was difficult to ignore. I knew, I'd been trying to do so now for weeks.

As we went slowly along the High Street Josef sank lower and lower in the seat until he was almost kneeling on the floor of the car.

'There,' he said breathlessly, pointing above a Chinese take-away. COULSTON AND BLACK, SOLICITORS AT LAW was painted onto the glass across three of the windows on the first floor.

Bob stopped the car in a side street and then he helped me out with the crutches. I closed the door and asked Bob to try and ensure that neither of his remaining passengers lost their nerve and ran off while I was away. I also asked him to get Josef out of the car in precisely three minutes and walk him to the corner and stay there until I waved from the window. Then I walked back to the High Street and slowly climbed the stairs to the offices of Coulston and Black, Solicitors at Law.

A middle-aged woman in a grey skirt and tight maroon jumper was seated at a cream-painted desk in the small reception office.

'Can I help you?' she said, looking up as I opened the door.

'Is Mr Coulston or Mr Black in, please?' I asked her.

'I'm afraid they're both dead,' she said with a smile.

'Dead?' I said.

'For many years now,' she said, still smiling. This was obviously a regular turn of hers, but one that clearly still amused her. 'Mr Hamilton is the only solicitor we now have in the firm. I am his secretary. Would you like to see him?'

'Yes please,' I said. 'I would.'

'Accident, was it?' she said, indicating towards the crutches. 'Personal injury case is it?'

'Something like that,' I replied.

'What name shall I say?' she asked, standing up and moving as if to go through the door behind her.

'Trent,' I said boldly. 'Julian Trent.'

The effect on her was startling. She went into near collapse and lunged at the door, which opened wide and sent her sprawling onto the floor inside the other room. There I could see a smartly dressed man sitting behind a rather nicer desk than he provided for his secretary.

'Patrick,' the woman managed to say. 'This man says he's Julian Trent.'

There was a tightening around the eyes but Patrick Hamilton was more in control.

'It's all right, Audrey,' said Mr Hamilton. 'This isn't Julian

Trent. Julian Trent is only in his early twenties.' He looked from Audrey up to my face 'Who are you?' he said. 'And what do you want from me?'

'Tell me what you know about Julian Trent,' I said to him, walking across to his desk and sitting down on the chair in front of it.

'Why should I?' he said.

'Because otherwise,' I said, 'I might go straight to the Law Society and report you for aiding and abetting a known offender. I might tell them about your role in getting Julian Trent off an attempted murder conviction.'

'You can't,' he said. 'You don't have the evidence.'

'Ah,' I said. 'There you might be wrong. I assume you've heard of Josef Hughes?'

He went a little pale. I stood up and went to the window. Bob and Josef were both standing on the corner opposite.

'Would you like me to ask him to come up and identify you?' I said to Hamilton.

He stood up and looked out of the window. Then he sat down again, heavily, into his chair. I waved at Bob.

'Now, Mr Hamilton,' I said. 'What do you know of Julian Trent?'

In all, I spent forty-five minutes in Patrick Hamilton's office listening to another sorry tale of petty greed gone wrong. As before, the chance of a quick buck had been the carrot dangled in front of his nose. Just a small thing had been asked for, to start with. Just to collect a statement from someone who would deliver it with no questions asked and to notarize it as a sworn affidavit. Then had come the further demands to attend at the High Court and, if necessary, commit perjury in order to convince the appeal judges as to the truth of the statement. There was no risk, he'd been told by his persuasive visitor. Josef Hughes would never tell anyone, the visitor had guaranteed it. Fortunately for him, he hadn't needed to testify, so technically he was in the clear. That was, until the next time.

I showed him the pictures of my house.

'This is what happens to those who stand up and fight,' I said. 'Unless we all do it together.'

I showed him another photo and he seemed to visibly shrink before my eyes. I didn't need to ask him if the photo was of the visitor. I could tell it was.

I stood up to go.

'Just one last question,' I said. 'Why you?'

I didn't really expect an answer, but what he said was very revealing.

'I've been the Trent family solicitor for years,' he said. 'Drawn up their wills and done the conveyancing of their properties. Michael and Barbara Trent have now moved to Walton-on-Thames, but they lived in Weybridge for years.'

'But your visitor wasn't Julian Trent's father?' I said to him.

'No, it was his godfather.'

CHAPTER 19

I took Josef Hughes and George Barnett to lunch at the Runnymede Hotel, in the restaurant there overlooking the Thames. Nikki Payne, the solicitor's clerk from Bruce's firm, came to join us. I had chosen the venue with care. I wanted somewhere peaceful and quiet, somewhere stress free and calming. I wanted somewhere to tell Josef and George what I had discovered and what I needed them to do to help me.

The four of us sat at a table in the window, with Nikki next to me and Josef and George opposite us. For a while we made small talk and chatted about the weather as we watched the pleasure boats moving up and down through the lock, and we laughed at a duck and her brood waddling in a line along the river bank. Everyone relaxed a little, and a glass of cool Chablis further eased their anxieties.

Finally, after we had eaten lunch from the buffet, we sat over our coffee while I told them about the murder of Scot Barlow. I told them how Steve Mitchell had been arrested for it, and how he was currently on trial at Oxford Crown Court.

'I've seen reports in the papers,' George said, nodding.

'Doesn't seem to be much doubt he did it, if you believe what you read there.'

'Never believe anything you read in the papers,' I said seriously. 'I have no doubt whatsoever that Steve Mitchell is innocent, and he is being framed.'

Both Josef and George looked at me with that same expression of incredulity that people have when a politician says that he really cares about drug addicts, or illegal immigrants.

'It's true,' I said. 'And I believe he's being framed by this man.' I placed a copy of the photograph I had shown to Patrick Hamilton on the table in front of them.

The effect was immediate. Both Josef and George shied away from the image as if it could somehow jump up and hit them. Josef began to take fast, shallow breaths, and I feared he was in danger of passing out, while George just sat there grinding his teeth together, never once taking his eyes off the man in the picture.

'It's all right, guys,' I said, trying to lighten the moment. 'He isn't here. And he doesn't know we're here, or even that I know either of you.'

Neither of them was much mollified by my assurances. They went on looking scared and uncertain.

'With your help,' I said. 'I can put this man behind bars where he can't get at you.'

'Julian Trent was behind bars,' said Josef quickly. 'But . . .' He tailed off, perhaps not wanting to say that it had been he who had helped get him out. 'Who says he can't still get at us from there? Where's the guarantee?'

'I agree with Josef,' said George with a furrowed brow. 'Julian Trent would simply repay the favour and get him out, and then where would we be?'

I felt that I was losing them.

'Let me first explain to you what I want to do,' I said. 'And then you can decide if you'll help. But, I'll tell you, I'm going to try and get this man, whether you help me or not. And it will be easier with your backing.'

Between us, Nikki and I told them everything we had discovered.

'But why do you need us?' said Josef. 'Why don't you just take all this to the police and let them deal with it?'

'I could,' I said. 'But, for a start, in this sort of case the police would take ages to do their investigating and, in the meantime, Steve Mitchell would be convicted of murder. And, as you both well know, it is easier to get someone acquitted at the first trial than to have to wait for an appeal.'

'So what do you intend to do?' asked George.

I told them.

I had to trust them all, including Nikki, not to tell anyone of my plans. So I didn't tell them quite everything. I did think about showing them the other photos, the ones of the wreckage of my house, which were still in my jacket pocket. Then Josef and George would understand that I was in the same position as they were. But it would also mean telling Nikki the inconvenient truth that I was being intimidated to influence the outcome of a trial, and that might put her under an obligation to tell the court, or, at least, to tell Bruce, who was her immediate superior. I didn't want to have to ask her to keep more confidences than I already had, and certainly not to do so when it would be so blatantly against the law.

When I had finished, the three of them sat silently for quite a while, as if digesting what I had said.

Eventually it was George who broke the spell.

'Do you really think it will work?' he said.

'It's worth a try,' I said. 'And I think it might if you two play your part.'

'I don't know,' said Josef, all his unease returning in full measure. 'I've got to think of Bridget and Rory.'

'Well, I'm game,' said George, smiling. 'If only to see his face.'

'Good,' I said, standing up. 'Come on. Let's go. There's something I want to show you.'

Bob drove us the half a mile or so to the far end of Runnymede Meadow and then waited in the car while the rest of us went for a walk. It was a bright sunny spring day but there was still a chill in the air, so the open space was largely deserted as we made our way briskly across the few hundred yards of grass to a small round classical-temple-style structure set on a plinth at the base of Cooper's Hill, on the south side of the meadow.

It had been no accident that we had come to lunch at Runnymede. This was where King John had been forced to sign the Magna Carta, the Great Charter of 15 June 1215. The Magna Carta remained the basis of much of our common law, including the right to be tried by a panel of one's peers, the right to trial by jury.

The Magna Carta Memorial had been built in 1957 and paid for by voluntary donations from more than nine thousand lawyers, members of the American Bar Association, in recognition of the importance of the ancient document in shaping laws in their country, and throughout Western civilization. The memorial itself is of strikingly simple design with eight slim pillars supporting an unfussy, flattish, two-step dome about fifteen feet or so in diameter. Under the dome, in the centre of the memorial, stands a seven-foot-high pillar of English granite with the inscription: TO COMMEMORATE MAGNA CARTA, SYMBOL OF FREEDOM UNDER LAW.

Every lawyer, myself included, knew that most of the clauses were now either obsolete, or had been repealed or replaced by new legislation. However, four crucial clauses of the original charter were still valid in English courts, nearly eight hundred years after they were first sealed into law, at this place, by King John. One such clause concerns the freedom of the Church from royal interference, another with the ancient liberties and free customs of the City of London and elsewhere, while the remaining two clauses were about the freedom of the individual. As translated from the original Latin, with the 'we' meaning 'the Crown', these two ran:

> No *freeman shall be seized, or imprisoned, or dispossessed, or outlawed, or in any way destroyed; nor will we condemn him, nor will we commit him to prison, excepting by the legal judgement of his peers, or by the laws of the land.*

and

> To *none will we sell, to none will we deny, to none will we delay right or justice.*

These clauses provided for freedoms that most of us took for granted. Only when the likes of Julian Trent or his godfather came along, acting above and beyond the law, did we understand what it meant to have our rights and justice denied, to be destroyed and dispossessed without proper process of the laws of the land.

I had spent the time we had been walking telling the others about the great meeting that had taken place so long ago on this very spot between King John and the English barons, and how the king had been forced to sign away his autocratic powers. And how, in return, the barons, together with the king, had agreed to be governed by the rule of law, and to provide basic freedoms to their subjects.

Now, I leaned against the granite pillar and its succinct inscription.

'So will you help me?' I said to Josef. 'Will you help me get justice and allow us freedom under law?'

'Yes,' he said, looking me straight in the eye. 'I will.'

Bob took Josef and George back to their respective homes in north London, while Nikki drove me to the railway station at Slough.

'Mr Mason?' Nikki said on the way.

'Yes?' I replied.

'Is what you're doing entirely legal?' she asked.

I sat silently for a moment. 'I'm not sure,' I said. 'In England, I know that it's not against the law *not* to tell the police about a crime, provided that you didn't stand idly by and let it happen, when informing the police might have prevented it. Other than where stolen goods are involved, and also for some terrorism offences, members of the public are not under any legal obligation to report something that other people have done just because they know it was unlawful.' She sat silently concentrating on her driving, and probably trying to make some sense of what I had said. 'Does any of that help?' I said.

'Yes,' she said. 'That's fine.'

'Is there a problem?' I asked her.

'No,' she said uncertainly. 'I don't think so. I just don't want to get into any sort of trouble.'

'You won't,' I said. 'I promise.' It was me, not her, who might get into trouble for not having told the court about the intimidation.

She dropped me at the station and gave me a small wave as she drove off. I wondered if she might go and talk to Bruce after all. I looked at my watch. It was quarter past four on Friday afternoon and the case would resume at ten on Monday morning. Even if she called Bruce now, would it stop me on Monday? Maybe. I would just have to take my chances. I had needed to tell Nikki my plans. I still wanted more help from her.

As I waited on the platform at Slough my phone rang in my pocket.

'Hello,' I said.

'What does it take to get you to do as you're told?' said the whispering voice.

'More than you could ever know,' I said, and hung up.

What he probably didn't realize was how frightened I had been at what he might do. In fact, I still was.

I called Eleanor.

'Are you free from now on for the night?' I asked.

'All weekend,' she said happily.

'Good,' I said. 'Please will you pack a bag now. Put everything from your room that you absolutely couldn't bear to lose in your car and go to Newbury station and wait for me there.'

'Geoffrey,' she sounded worried. 'You're frightening me again.'

'Eleanor, please,' I said. 'Do it now and quickly. Get away from the hospital and the house and then call me.' I was thinking fast. 'Are you in your room or in the hospital?'

'In my room,' she said.

320

'Is there anyone else with you?'

'No. But there are still a few in the hospital.'

'Call them,' I said. 'Get as many as you can to come over to the house and be with you while you pack. Ask someone to get your car to the door and then go. Do it. Go now.'

'Right,' she said. 'I'm on my way.' The urgency of my voice had clearly cut through her reservations.

'And make sure you're not followed,' I said. 'Go round roundabouts twice and stop often to see if anyone stops behind you.'

'Right,' she said again.

'I'll be at Newbury in forty-five minutes,' I said. 'Try and keep on the move until then and don't take lonely lanes. Main roads only.'

'OK,' she said. 'I get the message.'

Good girl, I thought.

I sat restlessly on the train until Eleanor called to say she was safely away from Lambourn and she was now on the M4, travelling eastwards between junctions fourteen and thirteen.

'Is anyone following you?' I asked her.

'Not that I can see,' she said.

'Good,' I said. 'I'll see you at Newbury station.'

'Right,' she said. 'There are two exits at Newbury. Come out of the station on the same side as the platform you get off the train. I'll be there.'

She pulled up outside the red-brick station building as I struggled through the narrow doorway with my suitcase and the crutches. I tossed the suitcase onto the back seat of her car and climbed into the passenger seat. Eleanor leaned over and gave me a kiss.

'Where to?' she said, driving away.

'Oxford,' I said.

One of the good things about having a room in an ex-prison was that it was just as difficult to break into as it had once been to break out of. My room at the hotel was as safe a place as I could think of to spend the weekend, especially as the cell-door locks were now controlled by the person on the inside.

I made Eleanor drive twice round the roundabout where the A34 crosses the M4 but, if there was someone tailing us, I couldn't see them.

'Do you really think that someone would have come to Lambourn looking for me?' asked Eleanor.

'Yes,' I said. 'I do. I think these people will stop at nothing. It's no longer about Steve Mitchell any more, it's to do with them not getting convicted for the murder of Scot Barlow. Once you've killed one person, it's much easier to kill again.'

I'd once been assured by one cold-bloodied client, following his well-deserved conviction for a string of murders, that, after the first couple, it had been as easy as stepping on a spider.

For the rest of the journey Eleanor spent almost as much time looking in the rear-view mirror as she did watching the road in front, but we made it to the hotel safely without hitting any-thing, and also without seeing anyone tailing us.

As we pulled up at the hotel entrance, Eleanor's phone rang.

'Hello,' she said, pushing the button. She listened for a few moments. 'Suzie, hold on a minute.' She put her hand over the microphone and turned to me. 'It's Suzie, one of the other vets at the hospital. Seems a young man has turned up there asking for me, says he's my younger brother.'

'And is he?' I asked her.

'I'm an only child,' she said.

'Does the young man know that Suzie is making this call?' I asked.

Eleanor spoke into the phone, asked the question and listened for a moment.

'No,' she said. 'The young man has talked his way up into my room and is waiting there. Suzie is downstairs.'

'Let me talk to her,' I said.

Eleanor spoke again into the phone and then handed it to me. I tossed my own phone at Eleanor. 'Call the police,' I said to her. 'Tell them there's an intruder in the house there with a girl on her own.' That should bring them coming with the sirens blazing.

'Suzie,' I said into Eleanor's phone. 'This is Geoffrey Mason, I'm a friend of Eleanor's.'

'I know,' she said, laughing. 'She's talked of nothing else for weeks.'

'Are you there on your own?' I asked her, cutting off her laughter.

'Yes,' she said. 'Except for him upstairs. The others have gone down the pub, but I didn't feel up to it.'

'Suzie, this is a serious situation,' I said. 'I don't want to alarm you too much, but the young man is not Eleanor's younger brother. She doesn't have any brothers. And I fear he could be dangerous.'

There was silence from the other end of the line.

I went on. 'Eleanor is talking to the police now.'

'Oh God!' she said shakily.

'Suzie,' I said urgently, not wanting her to go into a complete panic. 'As he's asked for Eleanor, go and tell him that she's gone to stay with her boyfriend in London. He might then go away.'

323

'I'm not going up there again,' she said with real fear in her voice.

'All right,' I said calmly. 'If you can leave the house without him seeing you, then go straight away. Go round to the pub, and stay there with the others.'

'OK,' she said rapidly. 'I'm going now.'

'Good. But go quickly and quietly,' I said. 'Are you talking on a mobile phone?'

'Yes,' she said.

'Then keep talking to me as you leave the house. Do it now.'

I could hear her breathing and also the squeak of a door being opened, and then it slammed shut.

'Bugger,' she said to the world in general.

'Quietly,' I hissed into the phone, but I don't think she heard me.

There was the sound of her feet crunching on the gravel as she ran down the path.

'Oh my God,' she screamed. 'He's coming after me.'

'Run,' I said.

I didn't need to say it. I could hear Suzie running. Then the running stopped and I heard a car door slam.

'I'm in my car,' she said breathlessly. 'But I haven't got the damn keys.' She was crying. 'Help me,' she shouted down the phone. 'Oh my God,' she said, her voice again in rising panic. 'He's walking down the path.'

'Can you lock the doors?' I said to her.

'Yes,' she said. I heard the central locking go click.

'Good,' I said. 'Does the horn work?'

I could hear her bashing at the button but there was no noise.

'It won't work,' she cried, still bashing. It obviously needed the key in the ignition.

324

'Where's Eleanor Clarke?' I could hear Julian Trent shouting, his voice muffled by the car doors and windows.

'Go away,' screamed Suzie. 'Leave me alone.'

It was like listening to a radio drama – all sound and no pictures. The noise of Trent banging on the windows of the car was plainly audible and I could clearly visualize the scene in my mind's eye.

'Go away,' Suzie screamed at him again. 'I've called the police.'

'Where's Eleanor?' Trent shouted again.

'With her boyfriend,' shouted Suzie back at him. 'In London.'

Well done her, I thought. It went quiet, save for the sound of Suzie's rapid shallow breathing.

'Suzie?' I asked. 'What's happening?'

'He's run off,' she said. 'He's disappeared round the corner of the hospital. Do you really think he's gone?'

'I don't know,' I said. 'But stay in the car. We've called the police. They are on their way. Stay in the car until they come.' I hoped that Trent hadn't disappeared round the corner of the hospital simply to get his trusty baseball bat, so he could smash his way into Suzie's car.

'Who the hell was it?' she asked me.

'I don't know,' I lied. 'But he definitely wasn't Eleanor's brother. I think he may have been someone on the lookout for women.'

'Oh my God,' she said again, but without the urgency of before. 'He might have raped me.'

'Suzie,' I said as calmly as possible. 'Be happy he didn't. You're fine. Describe him to the police and they will look after you. Ask them to get the others back from the pub to stay with you.'

'But I don't think I want to stay here,' she said.

'OK, OK,' I said. 'You can do whatever you please.'

By now she had calmed down a lot. Vets were obviously made of stern stuff.

'The police are here.' She sounded so relieved.

'Good,' I said. 'Give Eleanor a call later, after you've spoken to them.'

'OK,' she said. 'I will.' She sounded quite normal, almost as if she was now rather enjoying the situation. It must be due to the release of tension, I thought.

I hung up and passed the phone back to Eleanor.

'Why didn't you tell her that it was Julian Trent?' she said, almost accusingly.

'We don't absolutely know for certain that it was him, even if we are pretty sure that it was. The police are bound to be in touch with us soon because it was my phone you used to call them, so they'll have the number, and you must have had to give them your name.'

She nodded.

'If we want, we can give them Trent's name then as a possible suspect,' I said. 'But I certainly will not be telling them that I think he went there intending to threaten you so that I would purposely lose the Mitchell case.'

'No,' she said with conviction. 'Nor will I.'

Good girl, I thought, again.

Next, I called my father.

'Hello,' he said.

'Hi, Dad,' I said to him. 'How are things in sunny Devon?'

'Boring,' he said. 'When can I go home?'

'Soon,' I said. 'I'll let you know when. But please stay there for a bit longer.'

'Why?' he said. 'Why do I have to stay here?'

I hadn't explained everything to him about Julian Trent. Perhaps I should have, but I hadn't wanted to worry him. These days he tended to live in a more gentle world of pottering about in his garden and playing bridge with his neighbours. Baseball-bat wielding maniacs were not his typical concerns.

'I'll tell you everything next week,' I said. 'In the meantime, can't you go off on a drive somewhere? Go and visit Dartmoor or something.'

'I've been there before,' he said unhelpfully. 'Why would I want to go again?'

I gave up. 'Just stay in Sidmouth for a few more days,' I said sharply.

'Don't you tell me what to do,' he said with irritation.

'Please, Dad,' I said more gently.

'You're a strange boy,' he said. It was his usual answer for everything.

'Maybe,' I said. 'But please, Dad, stay there. It's important. Please just do as I ask.'

'All right,' he said reluctantly. 'At least you're paying.'

Indeed I was, and the Victoria Hotel in Sidmouth wasn't cheap. I'd had to give them my credit-card details over the phone, and send them a signed fax guaranteeing the full amount.

With the knowledge that Julian Trent had been in Lambourn only fifteen minutes previously, Eleanor and I felt quite relaxed as we made our way into the hotel with the stuff from her car, which was then taken away to the hotel car park.

I closed and locked the room/cell door with us securely on the inside, and felt safe for the first time in hours. Then I called down to the front desk and ordered a bottle of red wine and some glasses. Eleanor and I may need to be locked up in a prison cell for the weekend, but it didn't mean we couldn't have a few of life's little pleasures to while away the time.

When the room-service waiter delivered the wine, we ordered some food as well. I then asked the receptionist to ensure that I wasn't disturbed and that no calls were put through. 'Certainly sir,' she said.

'So tell me,' said Eleanor finally. 'Why do you suddenly think that I am now in danger from Julian Trent when I wasn't before?'

'Because since the witness summonses were delivered, he now knows for sure that I won't do what he wants. I think he would try to use you as a lever rather than as just an implied threat.'

'And it seems you are right,' she said. 'So now what?'

I glanced around our prison-secure room. It had been created out of three old cells knocked together, complete with the high-up barred windows that had been intended to give the prisoners only light rather than a view. Thankfully, a modern bathroom had been added during the conversion so 'slopping out' was no longer required.

'Eleanor,' I said, turning to look at her face. 'No one, not even you, has really understood what sort of people we are dealing with here, although I think you might now be beginning to. We are not living here in some television drama where the blood is fake and the characters mostly behave in a fairly decent manner. This is a story of blackmail and murder, where seriously nasty people would as easily kill you as they would a fly.' She stared at me with wide eyes. 'But I don't intend to let them do either.'

'But how?' she said.

I told her. Some of it she knew, and some she didn't. I spoke for more than an hour with her listening intently to what I said.

Only after I stopped did she ask me the big question. 'Why don't you just take all this to the police?' she said.

'Because I want my day in court,' I said. And I didn't want to have to admit that I had been intimidated for so long without saying anything. I valued my career.

I told her what I proposed to do on Monday morning when the trial resumed.

'Just as long as we are both still alive on Monday morning,' she said.

Now, for a change, she was frightening me.

CHAPTER 20

'All rise,' called the court clerk.

The judge entered from his chambers, bowed slightly towards us and took his seat behind the bench. Everyone else then sat down. The court was now in session.

'Mr Mason,' said the judge.

'Yes, My Lord,' I said, rising.

'Still no sign of Sir James Horley?' he asked with raised eyebrows.

'No, My Lord,' I said.

'And you, and your client, are happy to continue with the case for the defence with you acting alone?' he said.

'Yes, My Lord,' I said. Steve nodded at the judge from the dock.

'I don't need to remind you of what I said about that not being grounds for an appeal,' said the judge.

'I understand, My Lord,' I said.

He nodded, as if to himself, and consulted a sheet of paper on the bench in front of him.

'Are your witnesses present?' he asked.

'As far as I am aware, My Lord,' I replied. I hadn't actually been outside into the waiting area to check, but Bruce Lygon seemed happy they were ready.

In fact, I hadn't been outside at all since last Friday.

At ten thirty on Friday evening the telephone in the hotel room had rung. 'I thought I said no calls,' I had complained to the hotel operator when I'd answered it.

'Yes, Mr Mason, we are very sorry to disturb you,' she had said. 'But we have your nephew on the telephone, and he's frantic to get in touch with you. I'm very sorry, but he tells me your elderly father has had a fall and that he's been taken to hospital.'

'Did you confirm to my nephew that I was here?' I'd asked her.

'Of course,' she'd said. 'Shall I put him through?'

'Thank you,' I'd said. There had been a click or two, but no one had been on the line. Trent had already gained the information he had wanted. Thereafter Eleanor and I had not left the room for the whole weekend, not even for an exercise period in the old prison yard, although we had made up for it with plenty of exercise in bed. We had ordered room service for every meal and had instructed the staff to ensure that they were completely alone when it was delivered. They had probably thought we were totally mad, but they had been too polite to say so, to us at least.

I had called Bruce to discuss the question of how to get safely to court on Monday morning. Without telling him exactly why I was concerned, I explained to him that I really didn't want to run into either of my two witnesses before they were called and I needed some secure transport from the hotel to the court buildings. He had come up with the ingenious idea of getting one of the private security companies to collect me in a prison transfer van. It transpired that Bruce was a friend of the managing director, and he had thought the idea was a great hoot and had been happy to oblige, for a fee of course.

So, at nine o'clock on Monday morning, Eleanor and I had moved as quickly as my crutches would allow along the hanging gallery of 'A' wing, down in the lift and out through the hotel lobby. We had gone from the front door of the hotel, across six feet of paving, straight into the waiting white box-like vehicle with its high dark-tinted square windows, while Bruce had stood by on guard. Some of the hotel staff had watched this piece of theatre with wide eyes. I was sure that they must believe we were either escaped lunatics or convicts, or both.

Needless to say, Julian Trent had been nowhere to be seen, but it was better to be safe than dead.

Our prison van had then delivered us right into the court complex through the security gates round the back, just as it would have done if we had been defendants on remand. We had emerged into court number 1 along the cell corridor beneath, and then via the steps up to the dock. Eleanor, who had called the equine hospital to say she wasn't coming in to work, now sat right behind me in court, next to Bruce.

'Very well,' said the judge. He nodded at the court usher, who went to fetch the jury. As we waited for them, I looked around the courtroom with its grand paintings of past High Sheriffs of Oxfordshire. On the wall above the judge there was the royal crest with its motto, HONI SOIT QUI MAL Y PENSE, written around the central crest. *Evil to him who evil thinks* was a translation from Old French, the medieval language of the Norman and Plantagenet kings of England. How about 'Evil to him that evil does', I thought. That would be much more appropriate in this place.

The press box was busy but not quite so full as it had been at the start of the trial the week before. Public interest had waned a little as well, and only about half of the thirty or so of the public seats were occupied, with Mr and Mrs Barlow senior sitting together in the front row, as ever.

The five men and seven women of the jury filed into the court and took their seats to my left in the jury box. They all looked quite normal. Mothers and fathers, brothers and sisters, professional people and manual workers, all of them thrown together into a panel by simple chance. There was nothing unusual or extraordinary about any one of them, but collectively they had to perform the extraordinary task of determining the facts, and deciding if the defendant was guilty or not. They'd had no training for the task, and they had no instruction manual to follow. Our whole legal system was reliant on such groups of people, who had never met one another prior to the trial, doing the 'right' thing and together making exceptional decisions on questions far beyond their regular daily experiences. It was one of the greatest strengths of our system, but also, on occasion, one of its major weaknesses, especially in some fraud trials where the evidence was complex and intricate, often beyond the understanding of the common man.

I looked at the members of this jury one by one, and hoped they had been well rested by four days away from the court. They might need to be alert and on the ball to follow what would happen here today, and to understand its significance.

'Mr Mason,' said the judge, looking down at me from the bench.

It was now time.

'Thank you, My Lord,' I said, rising. 'The defence calls . . .' Suddenly my mouth was dry and my tongue felt enormous.

333

I took a sip from my glass of water. 'The defence calls Mr Roger Radcliffe.'

Roger Radcliffe was shown into court by the usher, who directed him to the witness box. He was asked to give his full name. 'Roger Kimble Radcliffe,' he said confidently. He was then given a New Testament to hold in his left hand and asked to read out loud from a card. 'I swear by almighty God that the evidence I shall give shall be the truth, the whole truth, and nothing but the truth.'

One could but hope, I thought.

I stood up but, before I had a chance to say anything, Radcliffe turned to the judge.

'Your Honour,' he said. 'I have no idea why I have been asked to come here today. I knew Scot Barlow only by reputation. I have never spoken to him and he has never ridden any of my horses. Your honour, I'm a very busy man running my own company and I resent having to waste my time coming to court.'

He stood bolt upright in the witness box looking at the judge with an air of someone who had been greatly inconvenienced for no good reason. His body language was clearly asking the judge to allow him to get back to his business.

'Mr Radcliffe,' the judge replied. 'The defence have every right to call whomsoever they wish, provided that their evidence is relevant to the trial. As yet, I cannot tell if that is the case here because I haven't yet heard any of the questions that Mr Mason wishes to ask. But rest assured,' he went on, 'if I consider that your presence is a waste of your time, or of the court's time, then I shall say so. But that decision shall be mine, not yours. Do you understand?'

'Yes, Your Honour,' Radcliffe said.

'Mr Mason,' invited the judge.

'Thank you, My Lord,' I said.

I had been thinking of nothing else all weekend except how to conduct this examination of my witness and now, when I had to start, I felt completely at sea. I had intended opening by asking him how well he knew Scot Barlow, but that point seemed to have been covered already.

I took another sip of water. The silence in the courtroom was almost tangible and every eye was on me, waiting for me to begin.

'Mr Radcliffe,' I said. 'Could you please tell the jury what it is your company does?'

It was not what he had expected and he seemed to relax a little, the stress-lines around his eyes loosened a fraction and his furrowed brow flattened slightly.

'My main business,' he said, 'is the running of the Radcliffe Foaling Centre.'

'And could you please explain to the jury what that involves?' I asked him.

Roger Radcliffe looked imploringly at the bench.

'Is this relevant?' the judge asked me, getting the message.

'Yes, My Lord,' I said. 'I will show the relevance as my examination proceeds.'

'Very well,' said the judge. He turned to the witness box. 'Please answer the question, Mr Radcliffe.'

Roger Radcliffe blew down his nose with irritation. 'It involves exactly what the name implies.'

I waited in silence.

He finally continued without further prompting. 'We have about two hundred mares come to us each year. The foals are delivered in special conditions with proper veterinary care on

335

hand and a team of specially trained grooms. The whole set-up has proved very popular with owners of mares as they feel more comfortable with the care their animals receive.'

Two hundred was about double the number of mares that Larry Clayton had claimed ten days previously while he had been resting his cowboy boots on his desk, but I was hardly going to accuse Roger Radcliffe of perjury over a minor exaggeration of the size of his business.

'And how long has your business been in operation?' I asked him.

'About seven or eight years,' he said. 'But it has become much bigger recently, and it continues to expand.'

'And are there specific reasons for that expansion?' I asked.

'We are doing well,' he said. 'And over the last twelve months I have been able to inject a substantial investment into the business.'

'Would that investment have been possible due to the success of your horse Peninsula?' I asked.

'Yes,' he said. 'Exactly so.'

'Mr Radcliffe,' I said. 'Some members of the jury may not be familiar with horse racing so perhaps you could tell them about Peninsula.'

I glanced at the judge. He was looking at me intently and raised his eyebrows so that they seemed to disappear under the horsehair of his wig.

'Technically, Peninsula is no longer my horse,' said Roger Radcliffe. 'He was syndicated for stud at the end of last year and is now part owned by a number of individuals or organizations. I have retained only two shares in him out of sixty.'

'But you did own him throughout his racing career?' I asked.

'Yes, I did.' He smiled at the memory. 'And I bred him.

I owned his mare and he was foaled at my place. I decided to keep him rather than sending him to the sales, and now I am so glad I did.'

'So he was a success on the racecourse?' I asked.

'Yes, indeed he was,' said Radcliffe. 'He was both the Champion two-year-old and he was named Horse of the Year in 2007. But that was nothing compared with last year.' Radcliffe was enjoying himself now and was totally relaxed. 'He won the Two Thousand Guineas at Newmarket in May, the Derby at Epsom in June and the Breeders' Cup Classic in California last October. It was quite a year.' He smiled at the jury and many of them smiled back at him.

Nikki came into the courtroom and sat down next to Eleanor.

'All set,' she said quietly to my back.

I turned around and leaned down to her.

'Good,' I said quietly. 'Keep watch from the door, I'll give you the signal. Go back out now.'

She stood up, bowed slightly to the bench, and departed.

'Mr Mason,' said the judge. 'I am sure the jury and I have enjoyed our little lesson in Thoroughbred racing, but could you please show us the relevance of your questions, or else I shall release Mr Radcliffe back to his busy business schedule.'

'Yes, My Lord,' I said rather sheepishly.

Roger Radcliffe continued to stand ramrod stiff in the witness box. He was enjoying my discomfort. Now, I thought, it was time to rub that smirk off his face.

'Mr Radcliffe,' I said to him. 'We have heard already that you hardly knew the victim of this murder, but how well do you know the defendant, Mr Mitchell?'

'About the same as Barlow,' he said. 'Mitchell has been champion jockey over the jumps. I personally don't have jump horses but I know him by reputation. We may have met a few times at events. I really can't remember.'

'And how about Miss Millie Barlow, Scot Barlow's sister. Did you know her?'

I noticed a very slight tightening of the skin around his eyes. He was getting a little worried.

'I don't believe I did,' he said calmly.

It was his first lie.

'Are you sure?' I asked him.

'Quite sure,' he said.

'She was an equine veterinary surgeon,' I said. 'Sadly, she died last June. Does that jog your memory?'

'I know that a vet died during a party last year,' he said. 'Was that her?'

'Yes,' I said. 'It was. An inquest jury in January concluded that she had taken her own life by injecting herself with a substantial dose of the barbiturate anaesthetic thiopental.'

'Very sad,' he said, rather condescendingly. 'But I can't see the relevance.'

'Mr Radcliffe,' I said, ignoring his comment. 'Were you having an affair with Millie Barlow?'

'No I was not,' he almost shouted. 'How dare you suggest such a thing?'

He glanced across at his wife, Deborah. She had come into the court with him when he had been called, and she was now sitting in the public seats behind Mr and Mrs Barlow. I turned to look at her but I couldn't see the expression on her face.

'Mr Radcliffe, did you attend the party where Millie Barlow died?'

'Yes,' he said. 'As a matter of fact, I did.'

'And can you recall if there was a reason for the party?'

'Yes, there was,' he said. 'It was a party given jointly by me and Simon Dacey, at Simon's house, to celebrate Peninsula winning the Derby.'

'Simon Dacey being the trainer of the horse?' I said.

'Yes,' Radcliffe replied.

'Can you recall why Millie Barlow was also a guest at this party?' I asked him.

'Mr Mason,' said the judge. 'Are these questions really relevant to the case before this court?'

'My Lord,' I said. 'The prosecution has previously made it clear that the relationship that existed between the defendant and Miss Barlow was a major cause of the antagonism between the defendant and the victim, and hence, they claim, it ultimately provided the motive for murder. It is my intention to explore this relationship further by reference to Miss Barlow's untimely death last June.'

'Very well,' he said. 'You may continue.'

'Thank you, My Lord.' I turned back to the witness box. 'Now, Mr Radcliffe,' I said. 'I was asking you if you knew why Millie Barlow was invited to the party.'

'I have no idea,' he said. 'I told you I didn't know her.'

'Then why,' I said, picking up a piece of paper from the table, 'did you purchase a brand-new sports car and give it to her as a gift?'

He was initially flustered, but he recovered fast. 'I have no idea what you are talking about.'

'I'm talking about a bright red Mazda MX-5 Roadster purchased in September 2007 from the Mazda dealership in Newbury,' I referred to the piece of paper in front of me that Nikki had obtained from the dealership the previous Friday, 'at a cost of fifteen thousand, seven hundred and fifty pounds.'

He stood silently in the witness box staring at me.

'Come now, Mr Radcliffe,' I said. 'Are you telling the court that you did not know the person to whom you gave a brand-new car worth more than fifteen thousand pounds?'

'I still have no idea what you are talking about,' he said. 'I've never been to any Mazda dealer.'

'Mr Radcliffe,' I said. 'Last Friday my solicitor's clerk visited the dealership and they told her they remembered this car being bought. They remembered because it was paid for, in full, with a banker's draft, which is most unusual. The draft did not have the name of the purchaser on it. However, the sales representative remembered the purchaser, and he was able to positively identify you from this photograph.'

I held up the large glossy brochure that I had taken from the foaling centre on my first visit there, the brochure with the photograph on the front of a smiling Roger and Deborah Radcliffe standing in a paddock with some mares and foals. The same brochure I had showed first to Patrick Hamilton in his office, and then to Josef Hughes and George Barnett at Runnymede the previous Friday.

'I can call the Mazda sales representative as a witness if you want me to.' I paused. He said nothing. 'Now, Mr Radcliffe, please can you tell the jury why you gave a brand-new car worth over fifteen thousand pounds to Miss Millie Barlow in September 2007?'

'It's none of your business,' said Radcliffe defiantly.

'Mr Radcliffe,' the judge intervened. 'You will answer the question, unless, that is, you wish to claim that, in doing so, you might incriminate yourself. And if that is the case, then, one can assume, the question may be of interest to the police.'

Radcliffe stood silent for a moment and then he smiled. 'It

was a gift to her for doing a fine job when Peninsula was foaled. She was the attending vet. I didn't want to say so, or to give my name when I purchased the car as I didn't want there to be a tax implication for her. I didn't want the Inland Revenue to consider it as a payment for services and require her to pay income tax on its value, or require me to pay the National Insurance contributions.'

He stood relaxed in the witness box smiling at the jury. 'I am sorry I tried to avoid a little tax,' he said with a laugh. 'We all try it occasionally, don't we? I will pay the back tax right away.'

He had done well, I thought. Quick thinking, in the circumstances.

'Was it not payment to her because she was blackmailing you?' I asked him.

The smile disappeared from his face. 'Blackmail?' he said.

'Yes, Mr Radcliffe, blackmail.'

'That's nonsense,' he said with an air of confidence.

I turned and waved at Nikki, who was watching me through the glass panel in the courtroom door.

She entered the court followed by two other people.

All three of them bowed slightly to the bench and then came and sat behind Eleanor and Bruce.

I watched the colour drain out of Roger Radcliffe's face as he stared at the newcomers. He gripped the sides of the witness box as if to prevent himself falling over.

Both Josef Hughes and George Barnett sat quite still and stared back at him.

'Mr Radcliffe,' I said calmly. 'Do you know someone called Julian Trent?'

Roger Radcliffe was more than flustered this time. He was in

341

a panic. I could tell from the way the skin had tightened over his face and there was a slight tic in the corner of his left eye. He stood quite still in the witness box. But I was sure that, behind those steely eyes, his brain was moving fast.

'Julian Trent is your godson, isn't he?' I asked him.

'Yes,' he said quietly.

'I'm sorry, Mr Radcliffe,' I said. 'Would you please speak up. The jury can't hear you if you whisper.'

The irony of the comment was not lost on him. He positively glared at me.

I noticed that the press box had filled considerably since the start of the day. Word had clearly been passed outside that something was afoot and more reporters had been dispatched to the court. The public seats had also noticeably filled, and two court security officers now stood either side of the door. Detective Inspector McNeile, his evidence completed, was sat in a row of seats positioned in front of the press box, and he too was taking a keen interest in the proceedings.

I poured myself more water from the carafe on my table, and then slowly drank some of it.

'Now, Mr Radcliffe,' I said finally. 'Can we return to the question of blackmail?'

'I don't know what you mean,' he said, but the confidence had gone out of his performance.

'We have heard that you bought a new car and then gave it to Millie Barlow,' I said. 'Is that correct?'

'Yes,' he said quietly.

'Speak up,' said the judge.

'Yes,' Radcliffe repeated louder.

'I repeat my question,' I said. 'Was that car given by you to Millie Barlow as a payment for blackmail?'

'No. That's utter rubbish,' he said.

I collected some more papers together in my hands.

'These are bank statements,' I said. 'Millie Barlow's bank statements. They show that she received regular payments into her account over and above her salary from the equine hospital. Can you explain these payments?'

'Of course not,' Radcliffe said.

'Were these also blackmail payments, Mr Radcliffe, and did they come from your bank account?'

'No,' he said. But he didn't convince me, and some of the jury looked sceptical as well.

'Mr Radcliffe,' I said, changing direction. 'Do you ever have need for anaesthetics at your equine maternity unit?'

'No,' he said firmly. 'Why should we?'

'Perhaps for a Caesarean birth if a foal cannot be born naturally?' I asked.

'No,' he said, suddenly back on surer ground. 'The mare would be transferred to one of the local equine hospitals and anaesthetized there.'

'And what would happen if a foal was born grossly deformed, or blind?'

'That is very rare,' he said.

'But it must have happened at least once or twice in your experience.'

'A few times, yes,' he said.

'And would the foal be immediately put down?'

He could see where I was going, and he didn't like it.

'I suppose so,' he said.

'And isn't a very large dose of a barbiturate anaesthetic used for that purpose, a barbiturate anaesthetic like thiopental for example?' I asked.

343

'I wouldn't know,' he said.

'Mr Radcliffe,' I said, changing tack again. 'Do you know of someone called Jacques van Rensburg?

'I don't think so,' he said. But he started to sweat.

'You may have known of him simply as Jack Rensburg,' I said. 'He used to work for you as a groom.'

'We have lots of grooms during the foaling season,' he said. 'And they come and go regularly. I tend to use their first names only. We've had quite a few Jacks.'

'Perhaps I can help you,' I said. 'I have a photograph of him.'

I took a stack of the Millie and foal pictures out of one of my boxes and passed them to the court usher, who passed one to the judge, one to the prosecution, six to the jury and, finally, one to Radcliffe in the witness box.

Some of the colour had returned to his face but now it drained away again and he swayed back and forth. Unfortunately both the judge and the jury had been looking at the photograph and had missed it.

'Members of the jury,' I said, 'you will see that the photo-graph is of a new-born foal. The woman in the picture is Millie Barlow, the veterinary surgeon who had been present at the birth, and the man standing behind her, who you can clearly see in spite of the slightly blurred image, is Jacques van Rensburg, a South African citizen. Isn't that right, Mr Radcliffe?'

'If you say so,' he said.

'I do. And the foal is Peninsula, the horse that went on to be such a champion,' I said. 'Isn't that right?'

'It might be,' he said. 'Or it could be another foal. I can't tell. Many foals look alike.'

'Of course,' I said. 'But I assure you that the foal in this picture is Peninsula. He was the very first foal that Millie Barlow had delivered on her own. She was so proud of that horse and her part in its life that she kept a copy of that picture in a silver frame. It was her most prized possession. Isn't that right, Mr Radcliffe?'

'I have no idea,' he said.

'After his sister's death, Scot Barlow asked for the picture in the silver frame to keep in his home as a lasting reminder of her. But the photo was removed from its frame and taken away from Scot Barlow's house on the night he was killed. Why do you think that was?'

'I have no idea,' he said again.

'I put it to you, Mr Radcliffe, that the picture was removed because it was being used by Scot Barlow to blackmail you in the same way that his sister had done previously. Isn't that right?'

'No,' he said. 'That's nonsense. I don't know what you're talking about. Why would anyone blackmail me?'

'Does Jacques van Rensburg still work for you?' I asked him.

'No,' he said. 'I don't believe he does.'

'No,' I said. 'He couldn't, could he? Because he's dead. Isn't that right, Mr Radcliffe?'

'I have no idea,' he said yet again.

'Oh yes, I think you do,' I said. 'Jacques van Rensburg went on holiday to Thailand, didn't he?'

'If you say so,' Radcliffe replied.

'Not if I say so, Mr Radcliffe,' I said, taking yet another sheet of paper from my stack and holding it up. 'The South African Department of Home Affairs in Pretoria says so. He went to Thailand on holiday and he never came back, isn't that right?'

Roger Radcliffe stood silently in the witness box.

'Do you know why he didn't come back, Mr Radcliffe?' I asked.

Again he was silent.

'He didn't come back because, as the South African government records show, he was drowned on Phuket beach by the Great Asian Tsunami. Isn't that right?'

Radcliffe still said nothing.

'And, Mr Radcliffe, do you know when the Great Asian Tsunami disaster occurred?'

Radcliffe shook his head and looked down.

'It is sometimes known as the Boxing Day Tsunami, is it not, Mr Radcliffe?' I said. 'Because it took place on December the twenty-sixth. Isn't that right?'

He made no move to answer.

I continued. 'Which means that, as Jacques van Rensburg was drowned in Thailand by the Great Asian Tsunami on the twenty-sixth of December 2004, this picture had to have been taken before Christmas that year. Which also means, does it not, Mr Radcliffe, that, even though the record of the birth submitted by you to Weatherbys shows otherwise, Peninsula had to have been foaled prior to the first of January 2005 and was therefore, in fact, officially a four-year-old horse when he won the Two Thousand Guineas and the Derby last year and not a three-year-old as demanded by the Rules of Racing?'

For what seemed like an age, the silence in the court was broken only by the sound of fast-moving pencils on notebooks in the press box, and by a slight sob from Deborah Radcliffe in the public seats.

The judge looked intently at Roger Radcliffe, who was standing silently in the witness box with his head down, his previous ramrod appearance now nothing but a distant memory.

'Well?' said the judge to him. 'The witness will please answer the question. Was Peninsula a four-year-old horse when he ran in the Derby?'

Radcliffe lifted his head a fraction. 'I refuse to answer on the grounds that I might incriminate myself.'

It was as close to a confession as we were likely to get.

But I hadn't finished with him yet.

'Mr Radcliffe,' I said. 'Did you murder Millie Barlow?'

His head came up sharply and he looked at me. 'No,' he said, but without much conviction.

I pressed on. 'Did you murder Millie Barlow because she made further blackmail demands on you after Peninsula had won the Derby?'

'No,' he said again.

'And did you then murder Scot Barlow when he took over the blackmail demands from his dead sister?'

'No,' he said once more.

'Or was it your godson, Julian Trent, who actually carried out that second murder, on your instructions, after you had used intimidation of these innocent people in order to secure his release from prison for that very purpose?' I waved my right hand towards Josef Hughes and George Barnett behind me.

Radcliffe's demeanour finally broke completely.

'You bastard,' he shouted at me. 'You fucking bastard. I'll kill you too.'

He tried to leave the witness box, but he had made just two

steps towards me before he was surrounded by court security guards, and the police.

The judge banged his gavel and silence was briefly restored.

'The defence rests, My Lord,' I said, and sat down.

Perry Mason himself would have been proud of me.

CHAPTER 21

The judge adjourned the case for lunch while Roger Radcliffe was arrested by Inspector McNeile. Radcliffe was cautioned and made aware that he had the right to remain silent, but that advice was obviously a bit late. The man I had come to know as 'the whisperer' was finally led away, still spouting obscenities in my direction.

The smarmy prosecution QC came across and firmly shook my hand. 'Well done,' he said with obvious warmth. 'We don't often get to see the likes of that in an English court.'

'Thank you,' I said. 'I intend to make another "no case" application and request an acquittal.'

'Up to the judge, old boy,' he said, 'I'll seek instruction from the CPS, but I don't think there will be any objection from our side. This jury would never convict Mitchell after hearing that lot.' He laughed. 'Best fun I've had in years. I don't even mind losing this one.'

Eleanor, behind me, rubbed my shoulders.

'You were brilliant,' she said. 'Absolutely brilliant.'

I turned and smiled at her. Josef Hughes and George Barnett sat behind her, beaming away as if smiles could go out of fashion.

'You two can have your self-respect back,' I said. 'Without you here I think he might have bluffed his way out.'

If it was possible, they smiled even wider, and then shook me and each other by the hand. I thought it unlikely that the Law Society would give Josef back his right to practise, but he was still a young man and he was bright. I was confident that, without the fear that had consumed them over the past fifteen months, he and Bridget and baby Rory would now be fine.

'How about a coffee?' I said to them.

As we made our way out of court I bumped into Scot Barlow's parents. Mr Barlow senior was a big man and he stood full-square in front of me, blocking my path to the door. He was also considerably taller than I, and now he stood quite still and silent, looking down at me. I wondered if he was pleased or not. He had just discovered the truth about who had killed his children and why, but he had also discovered that they had both been blackmailers. Perhaps he might have preferred it if Steve Mitchell had been convicted of the murder of his son. That would have brought finality. Now he would have to endure another trial, and some unpleasant revelations.

He went on staring at me while I stood waiting in front of him, staring back. Eventually he nodded just once, and then turned aside to let me pass.

Eleanor, Josef, George, Bruce, Nikki and I sat at one of the tables in the small self-service cafeteria area in the main court corridor, drinking vending-machine coffee from thin brown plastic cups, toasting our success.

'But why was it so important?' asked Bruce.

'Why was what so important?' I said.

'About the horse's age,' he said. 'So what if the horse was a year older than it was supposed to be when it ran in the Derby?

I know that it was cheating and all that, but was it really worth murdering someone over? It was only a race.'

'Bruce,' I said. 'It may have been "only a race", but horse racing is very big business indeed. That horse, Peninsula, was sold to stud for sixty million US dollars. And mainly because it won that race.'

His eyebrows rose a notch or two.

'But it was because he won it as a three-year-old running against other three-year-olds that he was worth all that money. Three is young for a horse, but only horses of that age are allowed to run in the "classic" races held in England, and also the Triple Crown races in America.'

'I never realized,' said Bruce.

'Peninsula was syndicated into sixty shares,' I said. 'That means that he was sold in sixty different parts. Radcliffe says that he kept two for himself, so there are fifty-eight other shareholders who each paid Radcliffe a million dollars for their share. I suspect that most of those will soon be wanting their money back. I'd like to bet there are now going to be a whole bunch of law suits. It will all get very nasty.'

'But why didn't Radcliffe just register the horse with the right age and run him the year before?' Josef asked.

'Most racehorse foals are born between the first of February and the end of April, certainly by the middle of May,' I said. 'The gestation period for a horse is eleven months and mares need to be mated with the stallion at the right time so that the foals arrive on cue. The trick is to get the foals born as soon as possible after the turn of the year so that they are as old as possible, without them actually being officially a year older. In Peninsula's case, either someone messed up with the date of his mare's covering or, more likely, he was simply born a couple of weeks prematurely when he was due to be a very early foal anyway. Radcliffe must have decided to keep his birth secret until January. If he had registered it correctly in December then Peninsula would have been officially a yearling when he was biologically less than a month old. Then he would have been at a great disadvantage against the other horses born nearly a whole year before him but classified as being the same age. He would most likely still have been a good horse, but not a great one. Not sixty million dollars great. To say nothing of the prize money that Radcliffe will now have to give back for all of those races. The Epsom Derby alone was worth over seven hundred thousand pounds to the winner, and the Breeders' Cup Classic had a total purse of more than five million dollars.' I had looked them both up on the internet. It was going to be a real mess.

'But Millie knew the truth because she'd been there when Peninsula was foaled,' said Eleanor.

'Exactly,' I said. 'Radcliffe had probably paid her off. But maybe she was greedy, and that cost her her life. It was our good fortune that you were able to find an image of that picture of Millie and Peninsula as a foal.' I smiled at her. 'But the silly thing is that, if Radcliffe hadn't taken that photo from the silver frame in Scot Barlow's house, I would never have realized that it was important. He'd have literally got away with murder, and the racing fraud. I suppose, to Radcliffe, it must have shone bright as a lighthouse, advertising his guilt, but no one else would have thought so, certainly not this long after the event.'

'But how did you know about Millie's car?' Eleanor said.

'I became suspicious when I couldn't find any regular pay-ments to any car-finance companies on Millie's bank state-ments,' I said. 'And there was no one-off large payment around the date you told me she had bought it. And Scot's statements didn't show that he had bought it for her, so I sent Nikki to the dealer in Newbury to ask some questions.'

Nikki smiled. 'But you were a bit naughty telling Radcliffe that they definitely recognized him from the photo,' she said. 'They only said that it might have been him, but they weren't at all sure.'

I looked at their shocked faces and laughed. 'It was a bit of a risk, I know. But I was pretty sure by then that I was right, and Radcliffe couldn't take the chance of me calling the Mazda chap.'

'How about Julian Trent?' asked George. 'What will happen to him?'

'I hope the police will now be looking for him in connection with Barlow's murder,' I said. 'In the meantime, I intend to keep well clear of him.'

'So do we all,' said George seriously. He was clearly worried and still frightened by the prospect of coming face to face with young Mr Trent. And with good reason.

'What about the second witness?' Bruce asked, indicating towards a man sitting alone reading a newspaper at one of the other tables. 'Aren't you going to call him?'

'No,' I replied. 'I always intended calling only one of them, but last Thursday when we got the witness summonses, I didn't know which of them it would be. I only found out on Friday when I showed the picture of Radcliffe to Josef and George and saw their reaction.'

I'd had a second picture in my pocket on Friday. A picture of my second witness, cut out from the *Racing Post*, but it hadn't been needed.

Now I stood up and walked over to him on my crutches.

'Hello,' I said. 'Thank you so much for coming. But I'm afraid I don't think I'll be needing you any more.'

353

Simon Dacey turned in his chair and faced me. 'This has all been a waste of time, then,' he said with slight irritation. He folded his newspaper and stood up.

'Yes,' I said. 'I'm sorry.'

'What's been going on in there?' he asked, nodding his head towards the door of number 1 court. 'There seems to have been lots of excitement.'

'You could call it that, I suppose,' I said. 'Roger Radcliffe seems to be in a spot of bother.'

There was a slightly awkward moment of silence while he waited for me to explain further, but I didn't. The trial was not yet technically over, and he was still, in theory, a potential witness.

'No doubt I'll find out why in due course,' Dacey said with a little more irritation.

Indeed he would, I thought. For a start, he would also be losing his win percentage from all those Peninsula race victories. He might even lose his training licence, but I rather hoped not. I suspected that he knew nothing about the fraud, or the murders, just as he knew nothing about his wife's affair with Steve Mitchell.

Francesca Dacey's affair had been a bit of a red herring in my thinking. At one point I had wondered if Mitchell had been framed by her husband simply to get him out of the way. But the truth was that Steve had been nothing more than a convenient fall guy.

Radcliffe had clearly been determined that Mitchell should be convicted so as to close the police file on the case, to ensure that no further investigations were made, investigations that might uncover the blackmail, and the true reason for Barlow's murder. Radcliffe's whispering intervention with me, the belt

354

and braces of his frame-up plot, had ultimately led to his downfall. Without it, I was quite certain, Steve Mitchell would, even now, be starting a life sentence behind bars, and I would have been one of the prosecution witnesses, describing in detail my encounter with Scot Barlow in the showers at Sandown Park racecourse.

Ironically, the very attempt to pervert the cause of justice had ultimately been responsible for justice being done.

When the court resumed at two o'clock, I hardly had to make my submission. The judge immediately asked the prosecution for the Crown's position and their QC indicated that he had been instructed not to oppose the application. The judge then instructed the jury to return a not-guilty verdict and Steve Mitchell was allowed to walk free from the dock.

The story had travelled fast and there was a mass of reporters and television cameras outside the court building when Bruce and I emerged with Steve Mitchell at about three o'clock, into a wall of flash photography. Sir James Horley QC, I thought while smiling at the cameras, would be absolutely livid when he watched the evening news. He had missed out completely on the number one story of the day.

As we were engulfed by the sea of reporters, Eleanor shouted that she would go and fetch her car. There would be no chance of finding a taxi with all this lot about.

'Be careful,' I shouted back at her, thinking of Julian Trent, but she was gone.

Steve and Bruce answered questions until they were nearly hoarse from having to talk loudly over the traffic noise and the general hubbub, and even I was cajoled by some of the reporters into a rash comment or two. I was careful not to say things that would find me in hot water for giving out privileged or sensitive information, things that might be pertinent to the future trial. However, Steve Mitchell had no such qualms. He eagerly laid into the now-ruined reputation of Roger Radcliffe, and also managed to include some pretty derogatory remarks about his old adversary, Scot Barlow, as if it had somehow been all Barlow's fault that Radcliffe had framed him. I thought that it was a good job that, under English law, the dead couldn't sue for slander.

Finally, with deadlines approaching and their copy to file, the reporters began to drift away and eventually to leave us in peace.

'Bloody marvellous, Perry,' Steve said to me while pumping my hand up and down. 'Almost as good as winning the National. Thank you so much.'

I decided not to mention my fee – not just yet, anyway.

Bruce and Steve departed together on foot, while I stepped back inside the court building to wait for Eleanor and the car.

I decided to call my father.

'Hello, Dad,' I said when he answered. 'How are things?'

'It's good to be home,' he said.

Alarm bells suddenly started ringing in my head.

'What do you mean, it's good to be home?' I said.

'Got back here about ten minutes ago,' he said. 'I left the hotel as soon as I got your message.'

'But I didn't give anyone a message,' I said.

'Yes you did,' he said with certainty. 'On this phone. One of those damned text things. Hold on. I could hear him pushing the buttons. Here it is. "Hi Dad, Everything fine. Please go home as quickly as possible. Love Geoffrey".'

'What time did you get it?' I asked him.

'About half past ten this morning,' he said. 'My old Morris is quite slow on the motorway these days.'

Radcliffe had already been in the witness box at half past ten. The message had to have been sent by Julian Trent.

'I thought I told you not to tell anyone where you were.'

'I didn't,' he said, sounding pained. 'No one knew where I was other than you, but I still don't see why it was so important.'

'But who else knew the number of that phone?' I asked.

'Oh, I called and gave it to Beryl and Tony on Saturday,' he said. 'They're my neighbours. Just in case anything happened to the house.'

I could just imagine Julian Trent turning up to find the place deserted and asking the neighbours, in his most charming manner, if they knew where Mr Mason had gone. He probably told them he was Mr Mason's grandson, come to surprise him. Of course they would have given him the phone number.

'Dad,' I said quite urgently. 'Please go back out and get in the car and drive anywhere, but get away from your house. Or go next door to Beryl and Tony's. Just please get away from the house.'

'What on earth for?' he said, annoyed. 'I've only just got back.'

'Dad, please just do it, and do it right now.'

'Oh, all right,' he said. 'I'll just make my cup of tea. I've put the kettle on.'

'Please, Dad,' I said more urgently. 'Leave the tea. Go now.'

'All right,' he said, his annoyance showing again. 'You're a strange boy.'

'Dad, take the phone with you. I'll call you back in a few minutes.'

Eleanor pulled up in the car outside the court buildings, and I hobbled out to her as quickly as I could.

'Drive,' I said urgently as I struggled in. 'Straight on.'

'I can't,' she said pointing at the sign. 'Buses and taxis only.'

'Ignore it,' I said. 'I think Julian Trent is somewhere around my father's bungalow.'

She looked at me, then back to the road. 'But surely your dad is still in Devon.'

'I wish,' I said. 'He's gone home. Trent sent him a text message this morning as if it had come from me, telling him to go back home as soon as possible.'

'Oh my God,' she said, putting her foot down on the accelerator.

'I'm calling the police,' I said.

I dialled 999 and the emergency operator answered almost immediately.

'Which service?' she said.

'Police,' I replied.

Eleanor dodged a few shiny metal bollards and then drove straight down Cornmarket Street, which was usually reserved for pedestrians, but it was the best short cut through the city. A few people looked at us rather strangely, and some shouted, but no one actually stopped us and we were soon racing down St Giles and away from the city centre northwards.

I heard the police come on the line and the telephone operator gave them my phone number. 'Yes,' said a policeman finally. 'How can we help?'

I tried to explain that my father was alone in his house and that he was in danger from a potential intruder. I should have lied to them but, stupidly, I told them the truth.

'So there isn't actually an intruder in the house at the moment?' the policeman said.

'No,' I replied. 'But I think that he might be outside, watching and waiting.'

'And why is that, sir?' he said.

What could I say? 'I just do,' I said unconvincingly.

'We can't send police cars as an emergency all over the country just because people think they may be troubled at some time in the future. Now can we, sir?'

'Look,' I said. 'I am a barrister and I have been acting at the Crown Court in Oxford and I'm telling you that I have very good reason to believe that my father may be in great danger. I am on my way to his house right now, but I will be at least another twenty minutes getting there. Will you please send a patrol car immediately?'

'I'll do what I can, sir,' he said. 'I'll record the incident as a priority, but it will take some time to get a car to that part of Northamptonshire.' It was his way of saying that the police wouldn't actually be there for quite a long while. 'Perhaps you could give us another call when you arrive, sir.'

'Hopeless,' I said to Eleanor, hanging up. 'Mind the speed camera!'

She slammed on the brakes and we crawled past the yellow box at exactly thirty miles an hour. Then we were off again, considerably faster.

I dialled my father's mobile number again.

'Are you out of the house?' I said when he answered.

'Nearly,' he said.

'What have you been doing?' I asked him in exasperation. It had been at least ten minutes since I had first called him. I wondered if everyone's parents became so cantankerous and obstinate as they neared their eightieth birthdays.

'I've been looking for the little present I bought Beryl and Tony in Sidmouth,' he said. 'I know it's in my suitcase somewhere.'

'Dad, please,' I almost shouted at him. 'Just get yourself out of the house right now. Get the present for them later.'

'Ah,' he said triumphantly. 'I've found it.'

'Good,' I said. 'Now get out of the house and stay out.'

'Hold on a minute,' he said. 'There's someone at the door.'

'Don't answer it,' I shouted urgently into the phone, but he obviously didn't hear me.

I hoped that it might have been Beryl and Tony coming round from next door to welcome him home, but, of course, it wasn't. The phone was still connected in his hand and I could faintly hear the exchange taking place on my father's front doorstep.

'What do you want?' I heard my father say rather bossily. There was something that I didn't catch from his visitor, and then I could hear my father again, his voice now full of concern. 'No,' he said. 'I don't want any. Please go away.'

Suddenly there was a crash and the phone line went dead.

I quickly called the house landline number, but it simply rang and rang until, eventually, someone picked it up. But it went dead again before I had a chance to say anything. I tried it again, but this time there was nothing but the engaged tone.

'Oh my God,' I said. 'I think Julian Trent has just arrived, and my father is still there.'

Eleanor floored the accelerator as we swept onto the A34 dual carriageway north. Fortunately, the rush hour had yet to get into full swing and we hurtled up to the motorway junction and onto the M40 at breakneck speed.

I tried my father's landline once more, but it was still engaged.

360

'Call the police again,' said Eleanor.

This time I was connected to a different policeman and he now recorded the incident as an emergency. He promised to dispatch a patrol car immediately.

'How long will it take?' I said.

'About twenty minutes,' he said. 'At best. Maybe longer.'

'Twenty minutes!' I said incredulously. 'Can't you get someone there sooner than that?'

'Kings Sutton is right on the edge of the county,' he said. 'The patrol car has to come from Towcester.'

'How about Banbury?' I said. 'That's got to be closer.'

'Banbury is Thames Valley,' he said. 'Kings Sutton is Northamptonshire Constabulary.'

'I don't believe it,' I said. 'Just get someone there as soon as you can.'

Throughout the call, Eleanor had been driving like a woman possessed, overtaking a lorry around the outside of a roundabout when turning right, and then causing a group of mothers and toddlers crossing the road to leap for their lives. But we made it safely to Kings Sutton in record time and she pulled up where I told her, round the corner and just out of sight of my father's bungalow.

'Wait here,' I said, climbing out of the car and struggling with the crutches.

'Why don't you wait for the police?' she said. She came round the car and took my hand. 'Please will you wait?'

It had only been about seven or eight minutes since I had last spoken to them. And they wouldn't be here for ages yet.

'Eleanor, my darling, my father's in there on his own with Julian Trent,' I said. 'Would you wait?'

'I'll come with you, then,' she said.

361

'No,' I said. 'You must wait here and speak to the police when they arrive. Show them which is the right house.'

Eleanor grabbed me and hugged me hard. 'Be careful, my Barrister Man,' she said. 'I love you.'

'I love you more,' I said, but then I pushed her away. I had things to do.

I made my way gingerly through an herbaceous border and along the side of the bungalow to my father's front door. It was standing wide open. I peeped inside but could see nothing unusual, save for the mobile phone, which lay on the floor with its back off, the battery lying close by. I reckoned my father must have dropped it as Trent had forced his way in.

I stepped through the doorway into the hall, rather wishing that the crutches didn't make so much of a clink when I put them down on the hard wood-block floor. But I needn't have worried about the noise. As I moved across the hallway I could clearly hear Julian Trent and his baseball bat systematically doing to my father's home what he had previously done to mine. He was down the far end of the corridor causing mayhem in the bedrooms.

I looked into the sitting room. My father lay face down on the carpet, with blood oozing from his head. I quickly went over to him and bent down, using one end of the light blue sofa for support. He was not in great shape, not at all. I turned him over slightly and saw that he had been struck severely at least once across his face, and also that there was a nasty wound behind his right ear. I couldn't really tell if he was breathing or not, and I tried unsuccessfully to find a pulse in his neck. However, the cuts on his head were still bleeding slightly, which gave me some hope. I checked that his mouth and airway were open by tilting his head back a bit and laying him more on his side.

Where were those damn police? I thought.

The noise of destruction in the bedrooms suddenly ceased and I could hear Trent's footsteps coming back along the corridor. I struggled up and hid behind the open sitting-room door. Perhaps he would go past me. Perhaps he would go away.

My father groaned.

In truth, it was not much more than a sigh, but Trent heard it and he stopped in the doorway.

I looked down at my father on the floor and realized with horror that I'd left one of my crutches lying right next to him on the carpet.

It was too late to retrieve it now.

Trent came into the sitting room. I pressed myself back tight against the wall behind the door and sensed rather than saw him, but there was no doubt he was there. I could see the end of the baseball bat as he held it out in front of him. From where he stood, he would be clearly able to see my father, and the crutch.

'OK,' he said loudly into the silence, making me jump. 'I know you're here. Show yourself.'

Oh shit, I thought. I was hardly in any shape to fight a twelve-year-old cripple, let alone someone twice that age who was very fit and healthy, and who was holding a baseball bat to boot. I stayed exactly where I was.

The door was pulled away from me, exposing my hiding place. And there he was, in blue denim jeans and a short-sleeved dark green polo shirt, swinging his baseball bat back and forth. And, once again, he was smiling.

'Time to complete some unfinished business,' he said with relish.

'It won't do you any good,' I said defiantly. 'Your godfather was arrested in court this morning and the police are on their way here to arrest you.'

He hardly seemed to care. I glanced out of the window. Where were those wretched police?

'I'd better make it quick, then,' he said nonchalantly. 'That's a shame. I was planning to take my time and enjoy killing you.'

'No handy pitchfork for you to use this time,' I said.

'No,' he said, still smiling. 'That is a pity, but this will do instead.'

He swung the baseball bat at my head so fast that he almost caught me unawares.

At the last moment I ducked down and the wooden bat thumped into the wall, right where my head had been only a fraction of a second before. I dived away from him, hopping madly on one leg. I would just have to put the other foot down, I thought, and hope my knee would carry my weight. I tried it as I made my way across the room and without too much of a problem. But I was too slow, and Trent had time to turn and swing the bat again, landing a glancing blow on my left biceps, just above the elbow. It wasn't a direct hit but it was enough to cause my arm to go completely dead, numb and useless.

I leaned up against the wall by the window, breathing heavily. Two months of inactivity since the races at Cheltenham had left me hopelessly unfit. This battle was going to be over much too soon for my liking.

The feeling and movement in my left arm began to return slightly, but I feared it was too little, too late. Trent advanced towards me, grinning broadly, and he raised the bat for another strike. I stood stock still and stared at him. If he was going to kill me he would have to do it with me watching him. I wasn't going to cower down and let him hit me over the back of the head, as he had clearly done to my father.

I dived down to my left at the last instant and the bat thumped again into the wall above my right shoulder. I grabbed it with my good right hand, and also with my nearly useless left. I clung on to the bat for dear life. I gripped it so tight that my fingers felt as if they were digging into the wood.

With both hands up above my shoulders, my body was completely unprotected by my arms. Trent took his right hand off the bat and punched me as hard as he could in the stomach.

It was a fatal error on his part.

While, to him, my abdomen may have appeared to be defenceless, he clearly didn't know, or perhaps he had forgotten, about the hard plastic body shell that I still wore out of sight beneath my starched white shirt.

He screamed. A long, loud, agonizing scream.

It must have been like punching a brick wall. The bones in his hand would have cracked and splintered from the impact.

He dropped the baseball bat from his other hand and went down on his knees in obvious agony, clutching at his right wrist.

But I wasn't going to let him get off that easily.

I picked up the bat and hit him with it, audibly breaking his jaw and sending him sprawling on to the floor, seemingly unconscious.

I sat down on the arm of the sofa and looked out of the window. There was still no sign of the boys in blue, but now I wasn't so worried, I was even a little bit pleased.

I leaned down to the telephone, picked up the dangling handset and used it to call for an ambulance. Then I went across to my father. He was definitely alive, but only just. His breathing was perceptible but shallow, and I still couldn't find a pulse in his neck but there was a faint one in his wrist. I moved him properly into the recovery position and he obligingly groaned again. I stroked his blood-matted hair. I may have been a strange boy, and he was definitely a strange and stubborn father, but I still loved him.

Julian Trent moaned a little, so I went back and sat on the arm of the sofa and looked down at him lying on the carpet in front of me, the young man who had brought so much misery to so many innocent people.

He began to stir, pulling his knees up under him so he was kneeling on the floor facing away from me. He cradled his right hand in his left, and his head was bowed down in front. As I watched him, his head came up a fraction and he tried to slowly reach out with his left hand towards the baseball bat that I had put down on the sofa beside him.

Would he ever give up? I asked myself.

I leaned down quickly and picked up the bat before he could reach it. Instead, he used his left hand to push down on the blue upholstery, as if he were about to try and stand.

No, I suddenly realized. He would never give up, not ever.

Eleanor and I might make our life together but there would always be three of us in the relationship, the spectre of Julian Trent hovering nearby in the darkness, forever waiting for the chance to settle the score in his favour. Even if he was convicted of Scot Barlow's murder, and past form gave no guarantee of that, I was under no illusion that a lengthy term of imprisonment would reform or rehabilitate him. He would simply spend the time planning the completion of what he thought of as his 'unfinished business'.

Just like Josef Hughes and George Barnett, we would never be free of the fear. Not for as long as Julian Trent was alive.

In common law, self-defence is called an 'absolute defence', that is, it doesn't just mitigate a crime, it means that no crime exists in the first place. But in order for a justification of self-defence to succeed, certain conditions needed to apply. I knew this because I had recently defended someone accused of causing grievous bodily harm to a would-be mugger.

The conditions were a two-stage test, one of which was subjective and the other objective. First, did the accused genuinely believe that force was necessary to protect himself? And, secondly, if he did have that belief, then was the degree of force reasonable to meet the threat as he saw it?

The degree of force used was always the key. The law demanded that the force used should not have been excessive or, if it had been, then the perpetrator was making an honest, even if over zealous, attempt to uphold the law rather than taking the law into his own hands for the purposes of revenge or retribution.

In a landmark case in 1971 Lord Morris, the Lord of Appeal, stated, 'If there has been an attack so that self-defence is reasonably necessary, it will be recognized that a person defending himself cannot weigh to a nicety the exact measure of his defensive action. If the jury thought that, in a moment of unexpected anguish, the person attacked had only done what he honestly and instinctively thought was necessary, that would be the most potent evidence that only reasonable defensive action had been taken.'

I glanced briefly out of the window. There was still no sign of the police, nor of the arrival of an ambulance.

Julian Trent drew his left leg forward beneath him and slowly began to rise.

It had to be now or never.

I stood up, lifted my arms high over my head and hit him again, bringing the bat down hard and catching him at the base of the skull where the neck joins the head. I hit him with the very end of the bat in order to gain maximum leverage. There was a terrible crunching noise and he went flat down again onto the carpet, and lay still.

I wasn't certain whether it had been a lethal blow or not, but it would have to be enough. I felt sick.

All the frustration and fear of the past six months had gone into that strike, together with the anger at losing my possessions, the rage I had for him having torn to shreds the photograph of my Angela, the resentment I bore for having to dance to his tune for so long, and the fury at what he had done to my father.

I sat down again calmly on the arm of the sofa.

It was finally over. I had done only what I honestly and instinctively thought had been necessary to meet the threat as I saw it, and I would have to take my chances in court.

I glanced out of the window once more.

At long last, I could see two policemen coming down the driveway.

But now I needed help of a different kind.

I picked up the telephone and called Arthur.